J.R. Clark Hall

With a Supplement by
Herbert D. Meritt

A CONCISE
ANGLO-SAXON DICTIONARY
FOURTH EDITION

Published by University of Toronto Press
Toronto   Buffalo   London
in association with the Medieval Academy of America

Originally published 1894
Fourth edition © 1960
Cambridge University Press
Reprinted by permission of Cambridge University Press
Printed in Canada
ISBN 0-8020-6548-1
Reprinted 1984, 1988, 1991, 1993, 1996, 2000, 2002, 2004, 2006, 2007, 2008

Canadian Cataloguing in Publication Data

Hall, J. R. Clark (John Richard Clark), 1855–
    A concise Anglo-Saxon dictionary

    (Medieval Academy reprints for teaching; 14)
    4th ed., with a supplement by Herbert D. Meritt.
    Reprint. Originally published: Cambridge
    [Cambridgeshire]: Cambridge University Press, 1960.
    Includes bibliographical references.
    ISBN 0-8020-6548-1

    1. English language – Old English, ca. 450-1100 –
    Dictionaries – English.   I. Meritt, Herbert Dean,
    1904–   .   II. Medieval Academy of America.
    III. Title.   IV. Series.

    PE279.H34 1984   429′.321   C84-007675-4

PREFACE TO THE SECOND EDITION

The first edition of this dictionary having been exhausted, it has been extensively revised, and certain new features and alterations have been introduced into it.

1. The principle of arranging all words according to their actual spelling has been to a considerable extent abandoned. It was admittedly an unscientific one, and opened the door to a good many errors and inconsistencies. The head form in this edition may be either a normalised form or one which actually occurs.

2. Words beginning with *ge-* have been distributed among the letters of the alphabet which follow that prefix, and the sign + has been employed instead of *ge-* in order to make the break in alphabetical continuity as little apparent to the eye as possible. The sign ± has been used where a word occurs both with and without the prefix.

3. References to Cook's translation of Sievers' *Anglo-Saxon Grammar*, and to the Grammatical Introduction to Sweet's *Reader* have been taken out, as Wright's or Wyatt's *Old English Grammar* will have taken their place with most English students.

4. A new feature which, it is hoped, will prove widely useful, is the introduction of references to all, or nearly all, the headings in the *New English Dictionary* under which quotations from Anglo-Saxon texts are to be found. A vast mass of valuable information as to the etymology, meaning and occurrence of Old English words is contained in that Dictionary, but is to a very large extent overlooked because it is to be found under the head of words which are now obsolete, so that unless one happens to know what was the last form which they had in Middle English, one does not know how to get at it. This information will be made readily available by the references in the present work, which will form a practically complete index to the Anglo-Saxon material in the larger dictionary and will at the same time put the student on the track of interesting Middle English examples of the use of Old English words. Besides directing the reader (by means of quotation marks) to the heading in the *New English Dictionary* where the relevant matter may be found, an indication has been given of the texts from which quotations are made therein, when these do not exceed four or five.

5. There have been many valuable contributions to Anglo-Saxon lexicography (by Napier, Swaen, Schlutter, Förster, Wülfing and

others) since the first edition of this Dictionary appeared, and these have been made use of, but (as before) unglossaried matter has not been systematically searched for words not hitherto recorded in Anglo-Saxon Dictionaries.

6. The number of references to passages has been very largely increased. All words occurring only in poetical texts have been marked. If they occur more than once they bear the sign †, if only once, a reference to the passage is generally given. If not they are marked ‡. As regards prose texts, the rule has been only to give references to particular passages in the case of rare words,—more especially ἅπαξ λεγόμενα. The references to AO, CP and Æ which were given in the earlier edition have been retained, as a useful indication that the word occurs in Early West Saxon or Late West Saxon prose, as the case may be.

7. By various devices it has been found possible, while much increasing the amount of matter in the book, to add very slightly to the number of pages, and at the same time to reduce the number of columns on a page from three to two. Most of these devices are more or less mechanical, but one method of saving space may be mentioned. Certain compound words, descriptive of places, which, as far as I know, occur only in charters and which may often be more correctly regarded as proper nouns, have not been separately inserted. Their meaning can however always be ascertained by referring to their components, and where the abbreviation Mdf is inserted the reader will understand that examples of words so compounded, or of the components, or of both, will be found in Birch's *Cartularium Saxonicum*, or in Earle's *Land Charters*, and that references to those examples are given in Middendorff's *Altenglisches Flurnamenbuch*.

8. In the List of Abbreviations, etc. at the commencement of the book, editions of texts which are furnished with a glossary have been specially indicated.

J. R. C. H.

January 1916

PREFACE TO THE THIRD EDITION

In this new edition account has been taken of the important publications concerned with Anglo-Saxon lexicography which have appeared within the last sixteen years, and notably of the final instalments of '*Bosworth-Toller*' (BT) and the *New English Dictionary* (NED). A considerable number of words from twelfth-century texts, which have not been recorded in BT, has been inserted in the Dictionary, as there seemed to the writer that there was no sufficient ground for their exclusion.

Generally speaking, the preface to the Second Edition still holds good, except that a few words now marked † do not occur exclusively in poetical texts but appear very rarely elsewhere, e.g. in glosses. References to lines have been given in the case of all poetical words which occur only once, the sign ‡ being thus rendered unnecessary; and as regards prose words, references to page and line have usually been limited to those occurring once, or very rarely, or to passages which are not noted in other dictionaries.

In the same preface it was stated that references to the texts from which quotations have been made in the NED have only been given as a rule when the numbers did not exceed four or five. As regards the cases in which the quotations contained in the NED are more numerous, this has been indicated in the present edition by the NED word being printed in small capitals, an asterisk being added where inflectional or other forms are specially illustrated in that Dictionary by examples.

For the rest, the number of references has again been materially increased, an indication having often been given of one or two texts in which the more common words are to be found. It may be added that a few words have been given on the authority of BT, NED or Sweet alone when I have not been able to trace their source, or to verify the references given in those dictionaries.

J. R. C. H.

EASTBOURNE

April 1931

LIST OF SIGNS AND ABBREVIATIONS
WITH THEIR EXPLANATION

Note 1. Where references are in *italic type*, quotations from the texts indicated will be found in the *New English Dictionary*, under the head of the English word which is distinguished in the article by quotation marks (see Preface). When the quotations in the NED have been too numerous to allow of reference to them in this Dictionary, the Modern English word has been put in SMALL CAPITALS; and an asterisk is affixed to it when examples of inflectional or other forms of an Anglo-Saxon word are given in the NED. In references to special passages volumes have been marked off from pages by an inverted full stop, and lines or verses have been shown, *where they follow other numerals*, by small superior figures. Occasionally where lines have not been numbered in a quoted text, the mark ' has been inserted to show that the quotation is in the lower part of a page. References to page and line have, as a rule, been restricted to words only occurring once.

Note 2. In the following list the number (1) after an edition of a text indicates that the edition is supplied with a complete referenced glossary or word-index, (2) that it has a complete glossary, but without references, and (3) that it has a partial glossary or word-index.

Note 3. Some of the abbreviations given below are used in combination, *e.g.* MtLR = the Lindisfarne and Rushworth MSS of St Matthew; BJPs = the Bosworth and the Junius Psalters; asf. = accusative singular feminine; EK = Early Kentish.

Note 4. If any meanings of adverbs are given, they are *additional* to those which may be inferred from the corresponding adjective.

Note 5. In settling the spelling and alphabetical order of words preference has been given to EWS forms in ie or īe whenever they occur. Where other spellings (i, y; ī, ȳ) have been adopted ' = ie' or ' = īe' has been added in the case of the more important forms.

' ' Quotation marks are used to enclose the English words which should be looked up in the NED in order to find etymological information as to, and examples of the use of, the Anglo-Saxon words to which the articles in this Dictionary relate, see Note 1 above. If they enclose Latin words, they indicate the lemmata of Anglo-Saxon words in glosses or glossaries etc., or the Latin equivalent of such words in the Latin texts from which they are translated. The Latin is especially so given when ·the Ags. word seems to be a blindly mechanical and literal equivalent.

* is prefixed to hypothetical forms. Normalised forms of Ags. words which actually exist are not usually so marked. See also Note 1.

' See Note 1 above.

+ = ge-.

± indicates that the Ags. word to which it is prefixed is found both with and without the prefix ge-.

† = occurs only or mainly in poetical texts. (For references to those texts v. GK.)

a. = accusative.

A = Anglian, or, if followed by numerals, Anglia, Zeitschrift für Englische Philologie, Halle, 1877 etc. AB = Anglia Beiblatt.

AA = Alexander's Letter, in Three English Prose Texts, ed. S. Rypins (EETS), 1924 (1).

Æ = Ælfric. (References followed by numerals in parentheses relate to certain Homilies attributed to Ælfric in HL.) References to books in Ælfric's version of the Heptateuch, in Grein's *Ælfric de vetere et novo Testamento* (Bibl. der Ags. Prosa, vol. 1), or in S. J. Crawford's Heptateuch (EETS), 1929, are given under the abbreviations of their titles (GEN etc.). Words peculiar to Crawford's text are marked C. See also ÆT.

ÆGR = Ælfric's Grammatik und Glossar, ed. J. Zupitza, Berlin, 1880.

ÆH = Ælfric's Homilies, ed. B. Thorpe, London, 1844–6. (Quoted by vol., page and line.)

ÆL = Ælfric's Metrical Lives of Saints, ed. W. W. Skeat (EETS), 1881–1900 (3).

ÆP = Ælfric's Hirtenbriefe (Pastoral Letters), ed. B. Fehr, Hamburg, 1914 (Bibl. der Ags. Prosa, vol. 9).

ÆT = the prefatory matter in Ælfric's Heptateuch (see Æ). Quoted from Crawford by line only up to p. 75, and after that by page and line.

AF = Anglistische Forschungen, ed. J. Hoops, Heidelberg.

ALM = the poem on Alms, in GR.

AN = the poem of Andreas, in GR; or ed. G. P. Krapp, Boston, U.S.A., 1905 (1).

ANDR = the prose legend of St Andrew, in BR.

ANS = Herrig's Archiv für das Studium der neueren Sprachen, Brunswick, 1846 etc.

ANT = Analecta Anglo-saxonica by B. Thorpe, London, 1846 (2).

anv. = anomalous verb.

AO = Alfred's translation of Orosius, ed. H. Sweet (EETS), 1883. (v. also Wfg.)

AP = the poem of the Fate of the Apostles, in GR; or included with Andreas in Krapp's edition (v. AN).

APs = the Arundel Psalter, ed. G. Oess (AF vol. 30), Heidelberg, 1910.

APT = Anglo-Saxon version of Apollonius of Tyre, ed. B. Thorpe, London, 1834.

AS = King Alfred's version of Augustine's Soliloquies, ed. Endter, Hamburg, 1922, or H. L. Hargrove (Yale Studies in Old English), Boston, U.S.A., 1912 (1). References are to Endter. See also SHR.

Az = the poem of Azarias, in GR.

B = the poem of Beowulf, in GR; also ed. A. J. Wyatt and R. W. Chambers, Cambridge, 1914 (1); or ed. W. J. Sedgefield, Manchester, 1912 (1); or F. Klaeber (Klb.), Boston, U.S.A., 1922 (1).

BAS = The Admonition of St Basil, ed. H. W. Norman, London, 1849.

BB = Bonner Beiträge zur Anglistik, ed. M. Trautmann.

BC = Cartularium Saxonicum, ed. W. de Gray Birch, London, 1883 etc., 3 vols.

Bd = Bede.

BDS = Beiträge zur Geschichte der deutschen Sprache, ed. E. Sievers, Leipzig, 1874 etc.

BF = Byrhtferth's Manual, ed. S. J. Crawford (EETS), 1929. Also in A vol. 8, from which the quotations in NED are made.

BH = the Anglo-Saxon version of Bede's Ecclesiastical History, 2 vols., ed. T. Miller (EETS), 1891–6. (Reference is usually made to the pages in vol. 1 as regards the various readings recorded in vol. 2—not to the pages in the latter vol.) Sch = ed. J. Schipper, Hamburg, 1899.

BK = Texte und Untersuchungen zur AE Literatur, etc., by R. Brotanek, Halle, 1913.

BL = The Blickling Homilies, ed. R. Morris (EETS), 1874–80 (1).

BLPs = Blickling Glosses to the Psalms, at the end of BL.

Bo = King Alfred's translation of Boethius, with the Metres of Boethius, ed. W. J. Sedgefield, Oxford, 1899 (1).

BPs = die AE Glossen im Bosworth-Psalter, ed. U. Lindelöf (Mémoires de la Soc. néo-philologique à Helsingfors, tom. 5), 1909 (3).

BR = An Anglo-Saxon Reader, ed. J. W. Bright, New York, or London, 1923 (1).

BR = the poem of Brunanburh, in GR or †CHR.

BT = An Anglo-Saxon Dictionary, by J. Bosworth and T. N. Toller, Oxford, 1882–98; BTs = the Supplement, 1908–21; BTac = Additions and Corrections at the end of the Supplement.

BTK = C. G. Bouterwek, de officiis horarum, in pref. to Caedmon's Biblische Dichtungen, Gütersloh, 1854 (pp. 194–222).

ByH = 12th Century Homilies in MS Bodley 343, ed. A. O. Belfour (EETS vol. 137), 1909.

CAS = Legends of St Andrew and St Veronica, in Cambridge Antiq. Society's Publications, 1851.

CC = The Crawford Charters, ed. A. S. Napier and W. H. Stevenson (Anecdota Oxoniensia), Oxford, 1895.

CHR = Two of the Saxon Chronicles Parallel, ed. J. Earle and C. Plummer, Oxford, 1892 (1). The poetical passages are marked †CHR.

CHRD = the Rule of Chrodegang, ed. A. S. Napier (EETS), 1916.

CM = the tract 'de Consuetudine Mona-
chorum,' in Anglia, vol. 13, pp. 365–
454.

Coll. Monast., v. WW.

Cos = Altwestsächsische Grammatik,
by P. J. Cosijn, Haag, 1888.

cp. = compare.

CP = King Alfred's trans. of Gregory's
Pastoral Care, ed. H. Sweet (EETS),
London, 1871.

Cp = the Corpus Glossary, in OET, or in
WW (cols. 1–54) or (if the numbers
are followed by a letter) in A Latin-
Anglo-Saxon Glossary, ed. J. H.
Hessels, Cambridge, 1890 (1).

CPs = Der Cambridge-Psalter, ed. K.
Wildhagen, Bibl. der Ags. Prosa, vol.
7, Hamburg, 1910. (CHy = Cambridge Hymns in the same vol.) (3).

CR = the poem of Crist, in GR.

CRA = the poem of Men's Crafts, in GR.

CREAT = the poem of the Creation, in
GR.

Ct = Charters, wills and other like documents, as contained in BC, CC, EC,
KC, TC and WC.

d. = dative. dp. = dat. pl. ds. = dat.
singular; etc.

DA = the poem of Daniel, in GR; or ed.
T. W. Hunt (Exodus and Daniel),
Boston, 1885.

DD = the poem 'Be Dōmes Dæge' ('de
die judicii'), ed. J. R. Lumby
(EETS), London, 1876 (1); or in GR
(vol. 2, pp. 250–272).

DEOR = the poem of Deor's Complaint,
in GR and KL.

DEUT = Deuteronomy (see Æ).

DHy = the Durham Hymnarium, ed.
J. Stevenson (Surtees Society, vol.
23), London, 1851. (GL by H. W.
Chapman, Yale Studies, No. 24,
Boston, 1905.)

DOM = the poem 'Be Dōmes Dæge'
from the Exeter Book, in GR (vol.
3, pp. 171–4).

DR = the Durham Ritual, ed. J.
Stevenson (Surtees Society), London,
1840, as re-edited by Uno Lindelöf.
1927. Lines of Anglo-Saxon only
counted. [GL by Lindelöf, Bonn,
1901 (BB vol. 9).]

E = Early.

EC = Land Charters and other Saxonic
Documents, ed. John Earle, Oxford,
1888 (3).

EETS = Early English Text Society's
Publications.

EHR = English Historical Review.

EK = Early Kentish.

EL = the poem of Elene, in GR; or ed.
Kent, Boston, 1889.

Ep = the Epinal Gloss., in OET.

EPs = Eadwine's Canterbury Psalter,
ed. F. Harsley (EETS), London, 1889.
Late text. (EHy = Hymns in the
same vol.)

Erf = the Erfurt Gloss., in OET.

ES = Englische Studien, Heilbronn and
Leipzig, 1876 etc.

Ettm. = L. Ettmüller, Lexicon Anglo-
saxonicum, 1851.

EWS = Early West Saxon.

Ex = the poem of Exodus, in GR or in
Hunt's edition (v. DA). If followed
by two kinds of numerals = Exodus
in Ælfric de vetere et novo Testamento
in the Bibl. der Ags. Prosa, vol. 1,
Cassel, 1872, or in Crawford's
Heptateuch (ExC).

exc. = except.

f. = feminine. fp. = fem. plural.

FAp = the poem 'Fata Apostolorum,'
in GR.

FBO = Das Benediktiner Offizium, ed.
E. Feiler (AF vol. 4), Heidelberg,
1901.

FIN = the poem of Finnsburg, in GR,
and most editions of Beowulf.

FM = The Furnivall Miscellany, Oxford, 1901.

FT = the poem 'A Father's Teachings,'
in GR.

FTP = Falk-Torp, Wortschatz der
Germ. Spracheinheit, Göttingen,
1909.

g. = genitive. gs. = gen. singular. gp. =
gen. pl.; etc.

G = the Anglo-Saxon Gospels, ed. W. W.
Skeat, Cambridge, 1871–87, or by
Bosworth (B) or Kemble (K). See
also LG, NG, RG, WG. (GL to WG
by M. A. Harris, Yale Studies, vol. 6,
Boston, 1899.)

GBG = The meaning of certain terms in
Ags. Charters, by G. B. Grundy,
English Association Essays and
Studies, vol. 8, 1922.

GD = Die Dialoge Gregors den Grossen,
ed. Hans Hecht (Bibl. der Ags. Prosa,
vol. 5), Cassel, 1900–7.

GEN = the poem of Genesis, in GR. If
followed by two kinds of numerals =
Genesis in Ælfric de vetere et novo
Testamento, in the Bibl. der Ags.
Prosa, vol. 1, Cassel, 1872, or in
Crawford's Heptateuch (GENC).

Ger. = German.

GF = Legends of St Swithhun etc., ed. J. Earle, London, 1861 (Gloucester Fragments).

GK = Grein's Sprachschatz der Ags. Dichter, revised by Köhler and Holthausen, Heidelberg, 1912. (A complete referenced glossary to GR.)

GL = Glossary. Used also as a comprehensive sign for all or any of the extant Anglo-Saxon glosses or glossaries: Cp, Ep, Erf, GPH, HGL, KGL, Ln, OEG, WW etc.

GN = The Gnomic Verses, in GR. GNE = those in the Exeter Book and GNC those in the Cotton MS. Separate edition also by B. C. Williams, New York, 1914 (1).

GPH = Prudentius Glosses, in Germania, Vierteljahrsschrift für deutsche Altertumskunde, vol. 11 (ns).

GR = Bibliothek der Angelsächs. Poesie, ed. C. W. M. Grein and revised by R. P. Wülker, Cassel, 1883–98.

GU = the poem of St Guthlac, in GR.

GUTH = the (prose) Life of St Guthlac, ed. C. W. Goodwin, London, 1848 (pp. 8–98), or (pp. 100–176) ed. P. Gonser (AF vol. 27), Heidelberg, 1909.

HELL = the poem of Hell, in GR.

HEPT = Heptateuchus, etc., Anglo-Saxonice, ed. E. Thwaites, Oxford, 1698. See also Æ.

HEX = The Hexameron of St Basil, ed. H. W. Norman, London, 1849, or ed. S. J. Crawford (HEXC), Bibl. der Ags. Prosa, vol. 10, 1921.

HGL = Glosses in (Haupt's) Zeitschrift für deutsches Altertum, vol. 9 (1853).

HL = Homilien und Heiligendleben, ed. B. Assmann, Bibl. der Ags. Prosa, vol. 3, Cassel, 1889. v. also Æ and SHR (3).

HR = Legends of the Holy Rood, ed. R. Morris (EETS), 1871.

HU = the poem 'The Husband's Message,' in GR.

HY = the collection of 'Hymns' at the end of most of the Ags. versions of the Psalms. v. the various Psalters (PS). [The numbering of verses etc. usually follows that in Wildhagen's Cambridge Psalter (CPS).] †HY = the 'Hymnen und Gebete,' in GR.

i. = instrumental (case).

IF = Indogermanische Sprachforschungen, 1891 etc.

IM = 'Indicia Monasterialia,' ed. F. Kluge, in Techmer's Internationale Zeitschrift für allgemeine Sprach-

wissenschaft, vol. 2, Leipzig, 1885, pp. 118–129.

intr. = intransitive.

JAW = Eigentümlichkeiten des Anglischen Wortschatzes, by R. Jordan (AF vol. 17), Heidelberg, 1906.

JGPh = Journal of (English and) Germanic Philology, Urbana, 1897 etc.

Jn = the Gospel of St John. v. G and NG (JnL = Lindisfarne MS; JnR = Rushworth MS, v. LG, RG).

Jos = Joshua (see Æ).

JPs = der Junius-Psalter, ed. E. Brenner (AF vol. 23), Heidelberg, 1909 (JHy = the Hymns in the same vol.).

JUD = the poem of Judith, in GR, or ed. A. S. Cook, Boston, 1889 (1); or if followed by two kinds of numerals = Judges, in Crawford's Heptateuch.

JUL = the poem of Juliana, in GR.

K = Kentish.

KC = Codex Diplomaticus Aevi Saxonici, ed. J. M. Kemble, 6 vols., London, 1839–48. (3) at end of vol. 3.

KGL = Kentish Glosses to the Proverbs of Solomon (= WW 55–88, or, if quoted by number, in KL).

KL = Angelsächsisches Lesebuch, by F. Kluge, 3rd edition, Halle, 1902 (2).

KLED = F. Kluge's Etymologisches Wörterbuch, or J. F. Davis' translation, London, 1891.

KPS = Psalm 50 (Kentish), in GR, KL or SwtR.

L. = Latin.

LCD = Leechdoms, Wortcunning and Starcraft of the Anglo-Saxons, ed. O. Cockayne, London, 3 vols., Rolls Series, 1864–6 (vol. 2, and pp. 1–80 of vol. 3 are referred to by the folio of the MS, so that the references may also be available for G. Leonhardi's edition of that part of the LCD, in the Bibl. der Ags. Prosa, vol. 6) (3).

LEAS = the poem 'Be manna lease,' in GR.

LEV = Leviticus, in Æ.

LF = An OE Ritual text, ed. B. Fehr, and Keltisches Wortgut im Eng. by M. Förster, in F. Liebermann's Festgabe, Halle, 1921.

LG = the Lindisfarne Gospels, in Skeat's ed. of the Anglo-Saxon Gospels (v. G). (Glossary by A. S. Cook, Halle, 1894.) LRG = Lindisfarne and Rushworth Gospels. v. RG.

Lieb. = F. Liebermann (v. LL).

Lk = the Gospel of St Luke. v. G and

NG (LkL = Lindisfarne MS; LkR = Rushworth MS; v. LG, RG).

LL = the Anglo-Saxon Laws, as contained in Liebermann, Schmid, Thorpe or Wilkins. If followed by numerals not in parentheses, or only partially in parentheses, the reference is to 'Die Gesetze der Angelsachsen,' by F. Liebermann, 3 vols., Halle, 1903–16 (1); if by numerals *entirely* in parentheses, to vol. 2 of 'Ancient Laws and Institutes,' by B. Thorpe, 2 vols., London, 1840 (3).

Ln = the Leiden Glossary, ed. J. H. Hessels, Cambridge, 1906 (1).

Lor = the Lorica Hymn, in Kleinere angelsächsische Denkmäler, by G. Leonhardi (Bibl. der Ags. Prosa, vol. 6), Hamburg, 1905.

LPs = Der Lambeth-Psalter, ed. U. Lindelöf, Acta Soc. Sc. Fennicae, vol. 35, Helsingfors, 1909 (1). (LHy = the Hymns in the same vol.)

LV = Leofric's Vision, ed. A. S. Napier, in the Transactions of the Philological Society for 1907–10, pp. 180–188.

LWS = Late West Saxon.

M = Mercian.

m. = masculine. ms., mp., etc. = masc. sing., masc. plur., etc.

Ma = the poem of the Battle of Maldon, in Gr, also in Br, Kl or Sweet's Anglo-Saxon Reader, Oxford.

Mdf = Altenglisches Flurnamenbuch, by H. Middendorff, Halle, 1902. [See Preface.]

Men = the Menologium, at the end of Chr, or in Hickes' Thesaurus, vol. 1

Met = the Metres of Boethius; v. Bo.

MFB = Max Förster's contribution to A. Brandl's Festschrift (Anglica II, pp. 8–69 in Palaestra 148), Leipzig, 1925. (Quoted by line; v. also RWH.)

MFH = Vercelli-Homilies, etc., in the Festschrift für L. Morsbach (Studien zur Eng. Philologie, vol. 50), Halle, 1913, ed. Max Förster, pp. 20–179; v. also VH.

MH = An Old English Martyrology, ed. G. Herzfeld (EETS), London, 1900. See also Shr.

Mk = the Gospel of St Mark; v. G and NG. (MkL = Lindisfarne MS; MkR = Rushworth MS of St Mark; v. LG, RG.)

MLA = Publications of the Modern Language Association of America, Baltimore.

MLN = Modern Language Notes, Baltimore, 1886 etc.

MLR = Modern Language Review, Cambridge, 1905 etc.

Mod = the poem 'Bi Manna Mōd,' in Gr.

MP = Modern Philology, Chicago.

Mt = the Gospel of St Matthew; v. G and NG. (MtL = Lindisfarne MS; MtR = Rushworth MS of St Matthew; v. LG, RG.)

n. = nominative, *or* neuter, *or* note. (np., nap., etc. = nom. plural, nom. and acc. plur., etc.)

N = Northumbrian.

Nar = Narratiunculae, ed. O. Cockayne, London, 1861.

NC = Contributions to Old English Lexicography by A. Napier, in the Philological Society's Transactions for 1903–1906, London (mostly late texts).

NED = the New English Dictionary, ed. Sir J. A. H. Murray and others, Oxford, 1888–1915. (See Prefaces, and Note 1.)

neg. = negative.

NG = the Northumbrian Gospels, contained in Skeat's edition (v. G, LG, RG).

Nic = the Gospel of Nicodemus, in MLA 13·456–541, MP 1·579–604 and RWH 77–88 (referred to by pages in those texts).

NP = Neophilologus, Groningen, 1915 etc.

NR = The Legend of the Cross (Roodtree), ed. A. S. Napier (EETS), London, 1894.

Num = Numbers (see Æ).

obl. = oblique.

occly. = occasionally.

OEG = Old English Glosses, ed. A. Napier (Anecdota Oxoniensia), Oxford, 1900 (1).

OEH = vol. 1 of Morris, Old English Homilies (pp. 296–304 only) (EETS), 1867.

OET = The Oldest English Texts, ed. H. Sweet (EETS), 1885 (1).

OF. = Old French.

OHG. = Old High German.

ON. = Old Norse.

OP = Oratio Poetica, in DD (Lumby).

OS. = Old Saxon.

p. = page, *or* plural.

Pa = the poem of the Panther, in Gr.

Part = the poem of the Partridge, in Gr.

PH = the poem of the Phoenix, in GR or BR.

pl. = plural.

PPs = the Paris Psalter, ed. B. Thorpe, London, 1835. The prose portion (Psalms 1–50) also ed. Bright and Ramsay, Belles Lettres Series, Boston, 1907, and the remainder (verse portion) in GR.

PR = Proverbs, at end of SOL (Kemble), pp. 258–268.

Ps = any one or more of the Anglo-Saxon Psalters. [NB. In the numbering of the Psalms, the Authorised Version is usually one ahead of the MSS.] v. A, B, C, E, J, L, R, S and VPs; also Hy. PsC = Psalm 100 in GR.

PST = Philological Society's Transactions (v. also LV and NC).

QF = Mone, Quellen u. Forschungen zur Geschichte der teutschen Lit. u. Sprache, Aachen und Leipzig, 1830.

RB = der Benedictinregel, ed. A. Schröer, Bibl. der Ags. Prosa, vol. 2, Cassel, 1885–8 (3).

RBL = the Anglo-Saxon and Latin Rule of St Benet (Interlinear Glosses), ed. H. Logeman (EETS), London, 1888.

RD = The Riddles of the Exeter Book, in GR, or ed. F. Tupper Junr., Boston, 1910 (1).

RG = the Rushworth Gospels, in Skeat's ed. of the Anglo-Saxon Gospels (v. G). Mt (all), Mk 1–2¹⁵ and Jn 18¹⁻³ are in a Mercian dialect, and are usually known as R¹; the rest (R²) is in a Northumbrian dialect (v. also LG). Glossary to R¹ by Ernst Schulte, Bonn, 1904; to R² by U. Lindelöf, Helsingfors, 1897.

RIM = The Rhyming Poem, in GR.

ROOD = the poem 'Dream of the Rood,' in GR.

RPs = der Regius-Psalter, ed. F. Roeder (Studien in Eng. Philologie, vol. 18), Halle, 1904. (RHy = the Hymns in the same vol.)

RSL = Transactions of the Royal Society of Literature, London.

RUIN = the poem of the Ruin, in GR.

RUN = the Rune-poem, in GR.

RWH = Homilies in MS Vesp. D. XIV (12th cent.), ed. R. D. N. Warner (EETS vol. 152), 1917. (pp. 77–88 = NIC, and pp. 134–139 = MFB.)

s. = strong; also = singular. sv. = strong verb. swv. = strong-weak verb.

SAT = the poem 'Christ and Satan,' in GR.

sb. = substantive.

Sc = Defensor's Liber Scintillarum, ed. E. Rhodes (EETS), London, 1889 (3). Lines of Ags. only counted.

SCR = Screadunga, by C. G. Bouterwek, Elberfeld, 1858.

SEAF = the poem of the Seafarer, in GR.

SF = Streitberg Festgabe, Leipzig, 1924.

SHR = the Shrine by O. Cockayne, London, 1864–70 [pp. 29–33 and 46–156 = MH; pp. 35–44 = HL pp. 199–207; pp. 163–204 = AS].

SHy = Surtees Hymnarium = DHy.

SkED = An Etymological English Dictionary by W.W. Skeat, Oxford, 1910.

SOL = the poem Solomon and Saturn, in GR (if followed by page and line, or marked SOLK, the reference is to the prose version, ed. J. M. Kemble). Ags. proverbs (PR) are included at pp. 258–268.

SOUL = the poem of the Soul, in GR.

SPs = Psalterium Davidis Latino-Saxonicum, ed. J. Spelman, London, 1640. No Hymns. (Stowe MS, but includes marginal readings from APs, CPs and EPs.)

S²Ps = Psalter Glosses in Salisbury Cathedral Library MS 150 (noted in CPs).

STC = Life of St Christopher, in 3 OE Prose Texts (v. AA).

Swt. = The Student's Dictionary of Anglo-Saxon by H. Sweet, Oxford, 1897.

SwtR = Sweet's Anglo-Saxon Reader, Oxford, 1922.

TC = Diplomatarium Ævi Saxonici, ed. B. Thorpe, London, 1865 (3).

tr. = transitive.

TF = The Capitula of Theodulf, at the end of CHRD.

usu. = usual, usually.

v. = vide, or very.

VH = an art. in A vol. 54 pp. 9–24 on the Homilies in the Vercelli Book; v. also MFH.

v.l. = varia lectio.

VPs = the Vespasian Psalter, in OET (1). [VHy = Hymns at the end of the Psalter.] Glossary also by Conrad Grimm (AF vol. 18), Heidelberg, 1906.

V²Ps = Psalter-Glosses in Cotton Vitellius E 18 (noted in CPs).

W = (I) Wulfstan's Homilies, ed. A. Napier, Berlin, 1883. Glossary by

L. H. Dodd, New York, 1908. (II) West Saxon.

WA = the poem of the Wanderer, in GR.

WAL = the poem of Waldhere, in GR.

WC = D. Whitelock, Anglo-Saxon Wills, Cambridge, 1930.

WE = Wonders of the East, in 3 OE Prose Texts (v. AA).

Wfg = die Syntax in den Werken Alfreds, by J. E. Wülfing, Bonn, 1894–1901 (copious material, and indexes to words in AO, BH, Bo, CP, AS, PPs, etc.).

WG = West Saxon Gospels (v. G).

WH = the poem of the Whale, in GR.

WID = the poem of Widsith, in GR, or ed. R. W. Chambers, Cambridge, 1912.

WIF = the poem of 'the Wife's Complaint,' in GR.

WNL = Wanley's Catalogue, in vol. 2 of G. Hickes' Thesaurus Antiquae Literaturae Septentrionalis, Oxford, 1705.

WS = West Saxon.

Wt = An Old English Grammar by J. and E. M. Wright, 2nd edition, Oxford, 1914.

WW = Old English Vocabularies, ed. by T. Wright and R. P. Wülker, London, 1884. Cols. 1–54 = Cp; 55–88 = KGL; pp. 89–103 = *Colloq. Monast.* in NED.

Wy = the poem 'Be manna wyrdum,' in GR.

WYN = Wynfrith's Letter, in MLR vol. 18.

ZDA = Zeitschrift für deutsches Altertum, Leipzig and Berlin, 1853 etc.

ZDPh = Zeitschrift für deutsche Philologie, Halle, 1869 etc.

A CONCISE
ANGLO-SAXON DICTIONARY

A

ā I. (āwa, ō) adv. *always, ever, at all, continuously, for ever,* Æ,AO,CP. ā on ēcnisse; ā butan ende *world without end: at any time: in any degree.* [*ON.* ei, ey] **II.** f.=ǣ

ā- (unemphatic verbal prefix); **I.** orig.= *forth, away,* but as a rule only intensitive in meaning. **II.**=on- **III.** ym(b)- **IV.**= ā(I.) in pronouns and participles, and gives a sense of indefiniteness. **V.**=ǣ-

āā (Bᴛ)=ā

āǣlan=onǣlan; **āǣðan**=āīeðan; **āb**= ōweb

ābacan[6] *to bake,* ÆH 2·268[9]

ābǣdan *to compel, restrain, ward off: exact, take toll: force out, extract.*

ābǣligan=ābylgan

ābǣran *to disclose, bring to light,* DD 41.

ābǣre (W 274[24])=ǣbǣre

ābǣrnan=onbǣrnan; **abal** (Gᴇɴ 500)=afol

ābannan[7] *to summon, convoke, command: announce, proclaim.* ā. ūt *call out, assemble,* Chr. ['*abanne*']

ābarian *to lay bare, disclose,* Jos,RBL: *strip,* CM.

abbad=abbod

abbod (a, u) m. '*abbot*,' BH,Chr; Æ. [*L.* abbatem]

abboddōm m. *abbatial jurisdiction,* BH.

abbodesse f. *abbess,* Cʜʀ.

abbodhād m. *abbatial rank, dignity,* LL.

abbodlēast f. *lack of an abbot,* BC 1·155'.

abbodrīce n. *abbey, abbacy, office or jurisdiction of an abbot* (used even of a convent of nuns).

abbot, abbud=abbod

ābēatan[7] *to beat, strike, break to pieces, make to fall,* Cr. ['*abeat*']

ābēcēdē f. *ABC, alphabet,* Bꜰ 180, 194.

ābedecian (eðe-) *to get by asking,* Bo,Cʜʀᴅ.

abedisse=abbodesse; **ābēgan**=ābȳgan

ābelgan[3] *to make angry, irritate, offend,* Sol; Æ,AO,CP: *hurt, distress: be angry with.* ['*abelgen*']

ābeligan=ābylgan

ābēodan[2] *to order, proclaim, bid, command, direct: summon, call out: announce, relate, declare, present, offer,* AO; Æ. hǣl ā. *to wish one good luck, greet, bid farewell to.* ['*abede*']

ābēoflan=ābifian; **ābēogan**=ābūgan

ābeornan[3] *to take fire,* PPs 105[16].

ābēowan (WW 217[46])=ābȳwan

āberan[4] *to bear, carry,* Mt: *endure, suffer,* Bo; Æ,CP: *bear (a child),* Æ: *take away, remove: reveal:* (refl.) *restrain oneself: do without,* NC 268. ['*abear*']

ā-berd, -bered *crafty, cunning,* Lᴄᴅ,Sᴄ.

āberendlīc *bearable,* LL.

ābernan (N)=ābeornan

āberstan[3] *to burst out, break out,* Æ,CP: *break away, escape.* ūt ā. *break out.*

ābeðecian=ābedecian; **ābicgan**=ābycgan

ābīdan[1] *to '* abide,' *wait, remain, delay, remain behind,* Chr; AO: *survive: wait for, await,* Æ: *expect,* Mt 11[3].

ābiddan[5] *to ask for, request, require, demand, pray, pray to, pray for,* Æ: *get by asking, obtain,* Æ,AO,CP: *call out (an army).*

ābies f. *silver fir-tree,* AA 12[8]. [*L.*]

ābifian (eo) *to tremble, quake, shake.*

ābīlgð, ābilhð=ǣbylgð; **ābiran**=āberan

ābirgan (y) *to taste, eat,* Bꜰ.

ābir(g)ing f. *taste* (Bᴛs).

ābisgian (y, -seg-) *to busy, occupy, employ,* CP: *be busy with, engage in, undertake: take up, fill,* GD.

ābisgung (y) f. *occupation: trouble,* CP.

ābītan[1] *to bite in pieces, tear to pieces, devour, gnaw,* Æ,AO: *taste, partake of, consume.* [=on-b.]

ābit(e)rian *to turn bitter,* CP 341[24]: *embitter.*

āblācian *to become pale, grow faint: become tarnished,* CP 135[2].

āblǣcan *to bleach, whiten,* BJPs 50[9].

āblǣcnes f. *pallor, gloom,* Lᴄᴅ 1·294 n 6.

āblǣcung f. *pallor,* HGʟ 518.

āblǣst *inspired, furious: blowing fiercely* (of flame), SᴛC 69[5].

āblāwan[1] *to blow, blow away, breathe upon* Æ: *puff up, swell,* Lᴄᴅ 93b. ['*ablow*']

āblāw-nes, -ung f. *inflation,* Lᴄᴅ.

āblegned *ulcerated,* Lᴄᴅ.

āblendan *to blind, put out the eyes of,* Æ, CP: *dazzle, deceive, delude,* Æ. ['*ablend*']

āblered *bare, uncovered, bald,* ES 8·62. [blere]

āblīcan[1] *to shine, glitter,* Ps.

āblicgan=āblycgan; **āblignes**=ǣbylgnes

āblindan *to make blind,* Bʟ 151[4].

āblindian *to become blind,* Lᴄᴅ,MH.

āblinnan[3] *to cease, leave off, desist,* Æ,AO, CP

āblinnednes (A5·465) = āblinnendnes
āblinnendlīce *indefatigably*, HGL429³².
āblinnendnes f. *cessation*, ÆL23b⁹⁸.
āblisian (Æ) = āblysian
āblissian *to make glad, please*, GD335n.
āblongen = ābolgen, pp. of ābelgan.
āblycgan (i) *to grow pale*, Æ : *make afraid*.
āblynnan = āblinnan
āblysian *to blush*, Ps.
āblysung f. *blushing, shame*, RB133¹¹.
ābodian *to announce, proclaim*, LkR12³.
ābolgennes f. *irritation*, WW230¹⁹. [ābel-
gan]
āborgian *to be surety for*, LL : (w. æt)
borrow.
āborian = ābarian
ābracian *to engrave, emboss*, GL.
ābrǣdan I. *to spread out, dilate* : *stretch
out*, Æ. II. *bake*, LCD44a.
ābraslian *to crash, crackle*, GD236¹².
[brastlian]
ābrēac pret. 3 sg. of ābrūcan.
ābrēat pret. 3 sg. of ābrēotan.
ābrecan⁴ (tr.) *to break, break to pieces, break
down, conquer, capture, violate, destroy*,
Æ,AO,CP : (intr.) *break out, away, forth*,
Æ,AO,CP.
ābrēdan = ābregdan
ābredwian *to lay low, kill*, B2619.
ābrēgan *to alarm, terrify*, BH,GD.
ābregdan³ *to move quickly, draw, unsheath,
wrench, pull out*, Mt : *withdraw, take
away, draw back, free from*, Æ,AO. ūp
ā. *to draw up, raise, lift up*, Æ. : *start up,
awake*. ['*abraid*']
ābrēotan² *to destroy, kill* : *fail, deteriorate*.
ābrēotnes f. *extermination*, OET182.
ābrēoðan² (intr.) *to fail, decay, deteriorate,
perish, be destroyed*, Ma ; Æ. ābroðen (pp.)
degenerate, reprobate, ÆGr. (tr. and wk.)
destroy. [v. '*brethe*']
ābrerd- = onbryrd-
ābroðennes f. *baseness, cowardice*, W.
ābrūcan³ *to eat*, A11·1¹⁷.
ābryrd- = onbryrd-
ābrȳtan *to destroy*, CPs36⁹.
ābūfan (= on-) adv. *above*, CHR1090E.
ābūgan² (= on-) *to bow, incline, bend, submit, do reverence*, B,Chr; Æ : *swerve, turn
(to or from), deviate*, CP : *withdraw,
retire* : *be bent or turned, turn oneself*.
['*abow*']
ābunden *unimpeded*, WW.
ābūrod *not inhabited*, TC162'.
ābūtan (e³, o³) I. prep. acc. *on, 'about,'
around, on the outside, round about*, Chr.
II. adv. '*about,' nearly*, Chr. [= onbūtan]
ābycgan *to buy, pay for, requite* : *redeem* :
perform, execute.

ābyffan *to mutter*, WW447²⁴.
ābȳgan (ē, ē² ; = īe²) *to bend, deflect* : *subdue,
bring low* : *convert*.
ābȳgendlíc v. un-ā
ābyl(i)gan (æ², e²) *to irritate, provoke*,
MtR,W.
ābyrg- = ābirg- ; ābysg- = ābisg-
ābȳwan (ēo) *to rub off, polish, cleanse, purify*.
ac I. conj. *but* : *but also, moreover, nevertheless, however* : *because, for* (?). ac gif *unless,
except*, BL151'. [*Goth.* ak] II. interrog.
particle *why, wherefore, whether* : in direct
questions = L. *nonne, numquid*.
āc f. gds. and np. ǣc '*oak*,' Æ,Ct,Lcd ;Mdf :
ship of oak, RUN77 : (w. nap. ācas) name
of the rune for a. [*OHG.* eih]
ācǣgan = acīegan
ācǣglod *studded with pegs?* (BTs), AA31².
ācǣnn- = ācenn- ; ācǣrran = ācirran
ācalan⁶ *to become frost-bitten*, LCD2b.
acan⁶ *to ' ache,' suffer pain*, Æ.
acas, acase f. (NG) = æcs
ācbēam m. *oak-tree*. accent m. *accent*. [*L.*]
ācbearo m. *oak-grove*, KC5·232'.
accutian? = ācunnian
āccynn n. *a kind of oak*, WW430⁶.
ācdrenc m. *oak drink, drink made from
acorns?* WW.
ace = ece
ācealdian *to become cold*, CP. ['*acold*']
ācēapian *to buy off, buy out*, Ct,LL.
ācēlan *to cool off, still, quiet*, Met. ['*akele*']
ācelma = ǣcelma ; ācen = ǣcen
ācennan *to bring forth, produce, renew*,
Æ,Bo,RG : *attribute to*. [' *akenne(d)*']
ācennedlíc '*genuinus*,' *native*, CHRD,RPs.
ācennednes (WG ; Æ), -cennes (NG ;
AO,CP) f. *birth*. [' *akenn(ed)nes*']
ācennend m. *parent*, DR197¹¹.
ācennicge f. *mother*, DR.
ācenning f. *birth*, BK16.
ācēocian (tr.) *to choke* : (intr.) *burn out*.
ācēocung f. *rumination*, WW179².
āceorfan³ *to cut off, hew down*, AO,CP.
onweg ā. *to cut away*. of ā. *to cut off*,
AO.
ācēosan² *to choose*, AO,CP.
acer = æcer ; ācerr- = ācirr-
ācīgan (= īe) *to call, summon*.
ācirran (æ, e, y ; = īe) (tr.) *to turn, turn
away or aside* : (intr.) *turn oneself, go,
return*.
-ācirrednes v. onweg-ā.
ācl = ācol ; āclǣc = āglǣc
āclǣnsian *to cleanse, purify*, Æ.
āclēaf n. *oak leaf*, LCD.
āclēofan² *to cleave*, EC351¹⁰.
ācleopian *to call out*, WW378⁵.
+āclian† *to frighten, excite*. [ācol]

āclungen *contracted*, WW239³⁷. [clingan]
ācmelu n. *acorn meal*, LCD.
ācmistel f. *mistletoe*, LCD. ācn-=ēacn-
ācnāwan¹ *to know, recognise, understand.*
ācnyssan *to drive out, expel*, SPs35¹³.
ācofrian *to recover*, Lcd. ['*acover*']
ācol† *affrighted, dismayed.*
ācōlian *to grow cold*, CP.
ācolitus m. *acolyte*, LL. [*L.*]
ācolmōd† *fearful minded, timid*
+ācolmōdian *to alarm, sadden*, WW209¹⁶.
ācordian *to make terms, reconcile*, CHR 1120.
ācorenlic *eligible, worthy of choice*, CP409³⁶.
ācostnian *to try, test, prove*, CM,WW.
ācræftan *to think out, devise*, AO46²⁹.
ācrammian *to cram*, WW236¹⁰.
ācrēopian *to creep, crawl*, ExC16²⁰.
ācrimman³ (y) *to cram, stuff*, WW.
ācrind f. *oak-bark*, LCD.
ācrummen pp. of ācrimman.
acs=æx; ācs-=āsc-; acse=asce
ācstybb m. *oak-stump*, KC (v. MLR17).
āctān m. *oak-twig*, LCD.
āctrēo n. *oak-tree*, WIF28, 36.
ācucian (Æ)=ācwician
ācul=ācol; ācum, ācuma (Æ)=ācumba
ācuman⁴ *to come, come forth (from)*, Æ :
bear, bring : endure, withstand, Æ : *get to
or from, reach*, Gen. ['*acome*']
ācum-ba m., -be fn. '*oakum*,' *hards, tow*,
Lcd,OEG,WW : *ashes of oakum : parings,
clippings.* [cemban]
ācumendlic *tolerable*, Æ : *possible.*
ācumendlicnes f. *possibility*, OEG3393.
ācunnan (NG)=oncunnan
ācunnian *to try, test, prove : experience*, CP.
ācunnung f. *experience, trial*, GD.
ācusan *to accuse*, MtL12¹⁰. [*L.*]
ācwacian *to tremble*, GD,PPs.
ācwæncan=ācwencan
ācweccan (tr.) *to move, swing, shake, vibrate,
Ma*; Æ : (intr.) *quiver*, Æ. ['*aquetch*']
ācwelan⁴ *to die, perish*, Æ,AO,CP.
ācwellan *to kill, destroy*, JnL; Æ,AO,CP.
['*aquell*']
ācwellednes (eæ²) f. *slaughter*, EPs43²².
ācwencan (æ²) *to quench, extinguish, Mt*;
AO. ['*aquench*']
ācweorna m. *squirrel*, Gl. ['*aquerne*']
ācweorran³ *to guzzle, gorge*, EPs77⁶⁵.
ācwern=ācweorna
ācwerren=ācworren pp. of ācweorran.
ācweðan⁵ *to say, speak out, declare, utter,
express, answer, Gen : reject, banish*, GEN
304. ['*aqueath*']
ācwician (tr.) *to quicken, vivify, Ps* : (intr.)
revive, BH. ['*aquick*']
acwīnan¹ *to dwindle away, disappear, go
out* (of fire), BH,LPs.

ācwincan³ *to vanish, be extinguished or
eclipsed*, Æ.
ācworren pp. of ācweorran.
ā-cwucian, -cwycian=ācwician
ācwudu m. *an oak wood*, KC6·218'.
ācwylman (=ie) *to kill, slay.*
ācwylmian (=ie) *to be tormented*, W220⁵.
ācwyncan=ācwincan
ācynned=ācenned pp. of ācennan.
ācyrr-=ācirr-
ācȳðan *to show, proclaim, reveal, announce,
confirm, prove.*
ād mn. *heap, funeral pile, pyre*, AO : *fire,
flame.* [*OHG.* eit]
ādǣlan *to divide, separate*, BL,BO.
ādēadian *to fail, decay, mortify, become
torpid or callous*, Æ.
ādēafian *to become deaf*, WW179²⁵.
ādēafung f. *deafening, making deaf*, Lcd.
[v. '*adeave*']
ādel I.=ādl. II.=ādela
ādela m. *mud, dirt, filthy place*, Æ. ['*addle*']
ādelfan³ *to delve, dig, excavate*, Æ,AO,CP.
ādeliht *filthy*, WW.
ādelsēað m. *sewer, sink*, Æ.
ādēman *to judge, try, deprive of or exclude
from by a legal decision : try; afflict.*
ādeorcian *to become dull, obscure, tarnished,
CP : grow dark*, W.
āderian *to hurt*, GD219¹⁹.
adesa m., adese f. '*adze*,' *hatchet*, BH,W.
ādexe=āðexe
ād-faru f. ds. -fære *way or path to the funeral
pile*, B3010.
ādfini n. *limit? ash-heap of a beacon?*
EC354⁵.
ādfȳr n. *sacrificial fire*, Ex398.
+ādgian=+ēadgian
ādīdan (GENC7²², 9¹¹)=ādȳdan
-ādihtian v. fore-ā.
ā-dīlegian, -dīl(i)gian (ȳ) *to destroy, blot out,
annihilate, devastate*, CP.
ādimmian *to become dim or dull, to darken,
obscure, Bo* : CP. [v. '*dim*']
ādl fn., ādle f. *disease, infirmity, sickness*,
AO,CP.
ādlēg m. *flame of the funeral pile*, PH222.
±ādlian *to be diseased or ill, languish*, Æ :
cause disease, DR : *become ill*, ANS
120·297.
ādlig *sick, diseased*, Æ.
ādliga m. *sick person.* ādliht=ādeliht
ādloma m. *one crippled by fire*, GU884.
[lama?]
ādlsēoc *in bad health : sick of a contagious
disease?* ES39·322.
ādl-ðracu f. gs. -ðræce *force of disease*,
GU935.
ādlung f. *illness*, ÆH1·122³¹.

ádlwērig *weary from illness*, Gu981.

ádōn (for conj. v. dōn) *to take away, send away* : *cast out, expel, destroy* : (w. preps. tō, on, fram, etc.) *put, place, take, remove, set free*, AO,CP.

adosa = adesa; ádrǣdan = ondrǣdan

ádrǣfan (ē) *to drive away, shut out, expel, NED*; AO,CP. [' *adrefe* ']

ádrēnct = ádrenced pp. of ádrencan.

ádragan⁶ *to draw (sword)*, HL15³⁵⁶.

ádrēfan = ádrǣfan

adreminte f. *feverfew* (BT).

ádrencan *to submerge, immerse, drown*, Ps; AO. [' *adrench* ']

ádrēogan² *to act, do, practise*, Æ : *bear, suffer, endure, An*; CP : *pass time, live*, Æ. [' *adree* ']

ádrēogendlic ' *agendus*,' ' *gerendus*,' DHy, RBL.

ádrēohan = ádrēogan

ádrēopan² *to drip, drop*, An.

ádrēosan² *to fall to pieces, decline, vanish, fail*.

ádrīfan¹ (īe) *to drive, drive away, drive out, pursue, follow up, LL*; Æ,AO,CP : *stake out (a ford)* : *chase (metal)*, Æ. [' *adrive* ']

ádrīgan = ádrÿgan

ádrincan³ *be drowned, extinguished, BH*; AO. [' *adrink* ']

ádrūgian, ádrūwian (Æ,Mt) *to dry up*. [' *adroughe* ']

ádrÿgan (ī) *to dry up* : *dry, wipe dry*, CP.

ádrysnan *to extinguish, repress*, NG.

adsa = adesa; adulsēaŏ = adelsēaŏ

ádumbian *to become dumb, keep silence, Mk*; Æ. [v. ' *dumb* ' vb.]

a-dūn, -dūna, -dūne adv. *down, downward*, Æ. [= ofdūne]

adūne(ā)stīgan *to descend*, CPs.

adūnfeallan *to fall down*, EPs144¹⁴.

adūnweard adv. *downwards, ChrL*. [' *a- downward* ']

ádūstrigan = andūstrian

ádwǣscan (ē) *to put out, quench, extinguish, blot out, destroy*, AO : *suppress*, Æ,CP.

á-dwelian *to wander, stray*, Æ,LL.

ádwellan, pret. 3 sg. -dwealde *to seduce, lead astray* : *hinder*, Æ.

ádwēscan = ádwǣscan

ádwīnan¹ *to dwindle or waste away*, Bf74¹¹

ádÿdan (ī; = īe) *to destroy, mortify, kill*, Æ. [' *adeaden* ']

ádÿfan (= īe) *to overpower with sound*, Sol152¹³.

ádylf = ádealf pret. of ádelfan.

ádÿlgian, ádÿlegian = ádīlegian

ádymman = ádimmian

ádysgian *to make foolish*, W185¹².

ǣ- accented verbal prefix, = (1) *without*; (2) ā-.

ǣ I. f. also ǣw f. (and m. or n.? in NG) *law (divine or human), custom, covenant*, AO, CP; WG,NG. butan ǣ *outlaw* : (esp. in pl.) *rite, ceremony* : *faith, religion*, unrihte ǣ *false religion*. Crīstes ǣ *gospel* : *scriptures, revelation* : *marriage*, Æ : *(lawful) wife*. For some comps. v. ǣw-. [' *ǣ* '] II. = ēa I. III. interj. *oh! alas!*

ǣa I. = ēa I. II. gp. of ǣ; ǣal- = eal-

ǣalā interj. = ēalā; ǣar = ēar-

āeargian *to become remiss*, AO212²⁰.

ǣbǣre (ā¹, ē¹) *manifest, notorious, public, open, evident, clear, LL*. [' *eber* ']

áebbian *to ebb away, recede*, Chr.

ǣbbung (= ebb-) f. ' *ebbing*.' sǣ æ. *gulf, bay*, WW154.

ǣbebod n. *injunction of the law, command*, PPs118¹⁰².

ǣbēc fp. *books of the law*, WW439¹⁵.

ǣbēre = ǣbǣre; ǣbesn = ǣfesn

ǣbilg-, -bili(g)- = ǣbylg-; ǣblǣc- = āblǣc-

ǣblǣce *lustreless, pale, pallid*, Æ.

ǣbod m. *business*, WW114³⁶ : *statute*, WW114³⁵.

ǣboda m. *messenger, preacher*, Gu909

ǣbrǣce, -breca = ǣwbrǣce, -breca

ǣbrecŏ f. *sacrilege*, LPs.

ǣbrucol *sacrilegious*, GPH402.

ǣbs f? *fir-tree*, Æ. [L. abies]

ǣbylg n. = ǣbylgŏ

ǣbylga m. *anger*, LPs77⁴⁹.

±ǣbyl-gan, -i(g)an *to exasperate, offend*, Æ.

ǣbylgnes (ā¹) f. *anger, offence*, Æ.

ǣbylgŏ, -bylgŏu (ā¹) f. *anger*, AO.

ǣbylig- = ǣbylg-; ǣ-bylŏ, -bylygŏ = ǣbylgŏ

ǣc I. f. = āc; II. (N) = ēac

ǣcambe f. = ācumbe

ǣcan = īecan; ǣccyrn = æcern

ǣce, ǣce = ece, ēce; ǣced = eced

ǣcēlan = ācēlan

æcelma m. *chilblain*, OEG,WW.

ǣcelmehte (ēcil-) *having chilblains*, OEG 1523.

ǣcen I. *a wood of oaks*. II. *oaken*, WW 270¹⁴. III. = ēacen pp. of ēacan.

ǣcer ńap. æcras m. *field, cultivated land, Mt*; AO,CP; Mdf : *a certain quantity of land, strip of plough-land* (GBG), ' *acre*,' Æ; v. LL2·267 : *crop*.

ǣcerceorl m. *rustic, ploughman, armer*, Chrd,WW.

ǣceren = æcern

ǣcerhege m. *hedge of a field*, KC3·33².

ǣcermǣlum *by acres*, KC6·98⁵.

ǣcermann m. *farmer*, WW. [' *acreman* ']

ǣcern (ī²) n. *nut, mast of trees*, Æ : ' *acorn*,' WW.

ǣcernspranca m. *oak sapling?* ÆGr69¹⁵.

æcersǣd n. *seed enough for an acre?* CHR 1124.

æcertēoðung f. *tithe of the produce of the soil,* W 310²⁴.

æcertȳning f. *fencing,* EC 377⁹.

æcerweorc n. *field-work,* GPH 391.

æces = æx

æcest, æceð pres. 2 and 3 sg. of acan.

æcilma = æcelma; æcirn = æcern

æclǣca = āglǣca; æclēaw = æglēaw

æcnōsle *degenerate, not noble,* WW.

+æcnōsliende *degenerating,* WW 218¹².

æcræft† m. *knowledge of law or ordinances, religion.*

æcræftig *learned in the law,* DA; as sb. = *lawyer, scribe, Pharisee,* MtL.

æcras v. æcer; æcren = æcern

æcs f. *'axe,' pickaxe, hatchet,* CP; *Mt* (æx).

æcst, æceð pres. 2 and 3 sg. of acan.

æcumba = ācumba; æcur = æcer

æcyrf m. *(wood-)choppings,* BH 224¹⁵.

æd (NG) = æt; æd- = ed-

ædderseax (WW) = ædreseax

æddre, ædr = ædre

ædre I. f. *artery, vein, pulse, nerve, sinew,* AO : pl. *veins, B : kidneys, Ps* 73²¹ : *runlet of water, fountain, spring, stream.* ['eddre']
II. adv. *at once, directly, instantly, quickly :* (†) *fully, entirely.* [OS. ādro]

ædreseax (daer) n. *lancet,* WW 410¹⁰.

ædrīfan = ādrīfan; ædwist = edwist

æfæst = æfest; æfǣst = æwfæst

æfdæll -dell (NG) = ofdæle

æfdȳne m. *declivity,* GL.

æfelle *without skin, peeled,* WW 190³¹.

æfen = efen

æfen (ē) nm. *'even,' evening, eventide, B, MkL,Gu* (ēfn), *RB : eve,* CHR. *tō æfenes till evening.*

æfencollatio *the 'collatio' read before compline,* CHRD 60³⁵.

æfendrēam m. *even-song,* RB.

æfengebed n. *evening service,* WW 129³⁴.

æfengereord n. *evening meal, supper* (often used in pl. of one meal).

æfengereordian *to sup, give supper to,* CM 1030.

æfengereordung f. *supper,* NC 269.

æfengeweorc n. *evening work,* LCD 70b.

æfengl(e)fl n. *evening repast, supper,* AO,CP.

æfen-glōm (*Gu*), -glōma (BF) m., -glōmung (omm-, BH) f. *gloaming, twilight.* [v. 'even']

æfengrom *fierce at eve,* B 2074.

æfenian = æfnian

æfenlāc n. *evening sacrifice, evening prayer,* PPs 140³.

æfenlǣcan *to grow towards evening,* Lk 24²⁹.

æfenlēoht n. *evening light,* B 403. [v. 'even']

æfenlēoð† n. *evening song.*

æfenlic *of the evening;* adv. -līce.

æfenlof n. *lauds (service),* CM 1035.

æfenmete m. *supper, MtR;* WW. [v. 'even']

æfenoffrung f. *evening sacrifice,* CHRD 30²³.

æfenrǣding f. *reading (during the evening meal at a monastery), 'collatio,'* CM.

æfenrepsung f. *nightfall,* Æ.

æfen-rest, -ræst† f. *evening rest,* B.

æfensang m. *'evensong,'* Æ,RB.

æfensceop m. *evening singer, bard,* RD 9⁵. [scop]

æfenscīma m. *evening splendour,* GEN 2448.

æfensprǣc f. *evening talk,* B 759.

æfensteorra m. *the evening star, Hesperus, Bo; Æ.* ['evenstar']

æfen-tīd (*Mk*) f., -tima (*GD*) m. *eventide,* Æ. [v. 'even']

æfenðēnung f. *evening service,* TF : *evening repast, supper,* RBL.

æfenðēowdōm m. *evening service or office,* WW 129³⁴.

æfenung = æfnung; æfer = æfre

æferðe f. *name of a plant,* LCD.

æfes- = efes-

æfesa? m., æfese (m.) f. = æfesn

æfesian *to shear,* ÆGR 157¹⁶.

æfesn, æfesen f. *relish, dainty, special pasturage, pannage; the charge for special pasturage,* LL.

æfesne? = æpsen?

æfest mf. *envy, hatred, malice, spite,* CP; *El,Ps : zeal, rivalry,* CHRD. ['evest']

æfest = æwfæst

æfestful *full of envy,* APT.

±æfest-ian, -igian *to be or become envious.*

æfestig *envious,* CP : *zealous,* CP.

æfestlīce = ofstlīce

æfgælō f. *superstition,* OEG.

æfgerēfa (-groefa) *'exactor,'* LkL 12⁵⁸.

æfgrynde n. *abyss,* PPs 35⁶.

æfhynde = ofhende

æfian (-an?) *to be in a miserable condition,* CR 1357 (or æfnan? Gollancz).

æfisc (EC 291) = efesc

æflāst m. *a wandering from the way?* Ex 473.

±æfnan (e) *to carry out, do, perform, fulfil : cause : endure, suffer :* (+) *hold, sustain.*

æfne = efne

±æfnian *to grow towards evening,* Æ.

æfnung f. *'evening,' sunset,* Æ.

æfre adv. *'ever,' at any time, Sat,Mt : always, constantly, perpetually, Æ,Cr,RB, Sat; CP : henceforth :* ne æ.; æ. ne (=næfre) *never;* æ. tō aldre *for ever.* æ. ælc, *W,Chr.* æ. ænig *any at all,* KC.

æfreda m. *what is taken or separated from,* OEG (Napier). [æf; *hreda (hreddan)] : *tow, oakum* (BTs).

ǣfremmende *pious, religious,* Jul 648.

æfse I. = efes; II. = æbs

æfsecgan *to confute,* ES 42¹⁶³

æfst = æfest

æfsweorc n. *pasturage,* WW 410¹⁹ (= *æfesweorc).

æft = eft

æftan adv. *from behind, behind, in the rear,* Br. ['aft']

æftanweard adj. *behind, in the rear, following,* RD 63⁵.

æftemest adj. *last, hindmost,* Æ,AO.

æfter I. prep. (w. d., i. and—chiefly N.—a.) (local and temporal) '*after', along, behind,* B,Chr,G : *through, throughout, during* : (causal) *following, in consequence of, according to, for the purpose of,* Æ : (object) *after, about, in pursuit of, for,* B. II. adv. *after, then, afterwards, thereafter : thereupon, later, back* (= *in return*). æ. ðon, ðæm, ðisum; æ. ðæm (ðon, ðan) ðe; *afterwards, thereafter.*

æftera = æfterra

æfterǣ f. *the book Deuteronomy,* ÆT 333 (æftre-).

æfterboren adj. '*afterborn,' posthumous,* ÆGr.

æftercnēoreso *posterity,* DR 61⁹.

æftercweðan⁵ *to speak after, repeat : renounce, abjure,* Chr 1094. æftercweðendra lof *praise from posterity.*

æftercyning m. *later king,* BH 140b²⁴.

æfterealu n. *small beer,* WW 129⁴.

æfterfili-, æfterfilig- = æfterfylg-

æfterfolgere m. *follower,* AO 142²³.

æfter-folgian, -fylgan (AO) *to follow after, succeed, pursue.*

æfterfylgednes f. *sequel,* ÆL 23b³⁶⁵.

æfterfylgend m. *follower, successor,* AO. adv. -lice *in succession.*

æfterfylgendnes f. *succession,* DHy 11⁴.

æfterfylgung (eft-, e³) f. *pursuit,* KGl 371.

æfterfylg- = æfterfylg-

æfter-genga, -gengea m. *follower, successor : descendant,* Æ.

æftergengel m. *successor,* KC 5·30.

æftergengnes f. *succession,* Æ : *posterity : inferiority.*

æftergyld n. *further payment,* LL.

æfterhǣða m. *autumn drought,* AO 102⁷.

æfterhyrigan *to imitate,* BH.

æfterlēan n. *reward, recompense, restitution, retribution,* Gen 76.

æfterlic *second,* WW 505¹⁹.

æfterra (comp.) *second, following, next, latter, lower,* CP.

æfter-rāp (Æ) -rǣpe m. *crupper.*

æfterrōwan⁷ *to row after,* ES 41³²⁵.

æfterryne m. '*occursus,'* CPs 18⁷.

æftersang m. (*after-song*), *matins,* CM.

æftersingallic (= -sanglic) *of matins,* CM 476.

æftersingend m. *succentor,* WW 129²³.

æftersōna *soon, afterwards, again,* NG.

æftersprǣc f. *after-claim,* LL 398,7.

æftersprecan⁵ *to claim,* LL 226,9⁴.

æfterspyrian *to track out, search, inquire into, examine,* CP.

æfterweard adj. *after, following, further, behind, in the rear, later,* Æ. .on æfterweard-an, -um *at the end.*

æfterweardnes f. *posterity,* WW 464¹⁸.

æfterwriten *written afterwards,* Lcd 69b.

æfter-yld, -yldo f. †*advanced age, old age : after age, later time,* BH. [ield(o)]

æfteweard = æfterweard

æftewearde adv. *behind,* Æ(Ex 33²³).

æftra = æfterra

æftresta superl. *last.*

æftum adv. *after,* MtR 24²¹.

æftyr = æfter

æfðanc, æfðanca (o, u) m. *insult, offence : grudge, displeasure, anger.*

æf-weard (CP), -ward (BH) *absent.*

æfweardnes f. *absence,* Bo,GD.

æfwela f. *decrease of wealth,* Lcd 3·170¹³.

æfwendla (WW 223¹) = æfwyrdla.

æfwyrdelsa (e²) m. *injury, damage, loss.*

æfwyrdla, m. *injury, damage, loss : fine for injury or loss.*

æfwyrð(u)? f. *degradation, disgrace,* RBL.

ǣfyllende *fulfilling the law, pious,* Cr 704.

ǣfyn = æfen

ǣfyrmða fp. *sweepings, rubbish,* ÆGr. [feormian]

ǣg n. (nap. ǣgru) '*egg,'* Ct,G,Lcd,Lk,Met.

ǣg = īeg; ǣgan = āgan

ǣge = ege; ǣgen = āgen

ǣgera (K) dp. of ǣg.

ǣgerfelma f. *egg-skin,* Lcd 20b.

ǣgergelu n. *yolk of egg,* Gl. [ǣg, geolu]

ǣgesetnes f. *law-giving, the* (*Old*) *Testament,* Bf 136⁵.

ǣgflota m. *seafarer, sailor,* An 258. [īeg]

ǣggemang n. *egg-mixture,* WW.

ǣg-hwā mf., -hwæt n. pron. *each one, every one, everything, who or whatever.* ǣghwæt neut. *anything.*

ǣghwǣr *everywhere, in every direction,* Mk; Æ : *in every case, in every respect : anywhere.* ['aywhere']

ǣghwǣs (gs. of ǣghwā) *altogether, in every way, entirely, wholly, throughout, in general.*

ǣghwæt v. ǣghwā.

æghwæðer (ægðer, āðer). **I.** pron. adv. *every one, 'either,' both, AO,KC,Mt* (gð) : *each, An.* **II.** conj. æghwæðer (ge)...ge; ægðer...and *both...and*; *as well...as.*

æg-hwanan, -hwanon(e), -hwannon, -hwa-num *from all parts, everywhere, on every side, in every way.*

æg-hwār, -hwēr = æghwǣr

æghwelc = æghwilc

æghweðer = æghwæðer

æghwider *on every side, in all directions* : *in any direction, anywhere.*

æghwilc adj. *each, every, whosoever, whatso-ever, all, every one, Bo,Met* : *any.* æ. ānra *each.* æ̆. ōðer *each other, Ma.* æghwilces *in every way.* [v. *'each'*]

æg-hwonan, -hwonon (CP), -hwonene = æghwanan

æghwyder=æghwider; æghwylc=æghwilc

ægift f. (m? n?) *restitution, repayment.*

ægilde (y²) adv. *receiving no 'wergild' as compensation, LL.*

ægilt = ægylt; æglǣc=āglǣc

æglēaw *learned in the law, An,Lk.*

æglēca = āglǣca

æglīm m. *white of egg, WW* 164¹². [līm]

ægmang (WW 4²⁹) = æggemang

ægmore f. *root of the eye, socket? Lcd* 3·98⁵. [ēage]

ægnan sb. pl. *awns, sweepings, chaff, Gl.* [v. egenu]

ægnes = āgnes, v. āgen; ægnian = āgnian

ægru v. æg; ægsa = egesa

ægscill (y) f. *eggshell, Lcd.*

ægðer = æghwæðer

ægweard f. *watch on the shore, B* 241. [īeg]

ægwern = æghwǣr

ægwyrt f *dandelion, Lcd* 158b.

ægylde = ægilde

ægylt (i²) m. *sin, offence, WW.* [æw, gylt]

ægȳpe (=īe²?) *without skill or cunning* (BTs),PPs 106¹⁰. [gēap]

æhher (MkR 4²⁸) = ēar

æhīw n. *pallor, OEG* 4897.

æhīwe *pallid* : *deformed, OEG* 2⁴⁹⁸.

æhīwnes f. *pallor, Lcd* 1·294³.

æhlȳp m. *breach of the peace, assault, LL.* [cp. æthlȳp]

æht=eaht

æht **I.** f. (rare in sg.) *possessions, goods, lands, wealth, cattle, Mk; AO* : *serf* : *ownership, control.* [āgan : 'aught' sb.] **II.** = ōht

āēhtan *to persecute, LkL* 21¹².

æhtboren *born in bondage, RB* 138²⁰.

æhte = āhte pret. sg. of āgan.

æhteland n. *territory, BH* 358¹⁴.

æhtemann m. *farmer, Æ* : *serf, LL.*

æhteswān m. *swineherd who was a chattel on an estate, LL* 449,7.

æhtgesteald n. *possession, Jul* 115.

æhtgestrēon n. *possessions, Ph* 506.

æhtgeweald† mn. *power, control.*

æhtian = eahtian

+æhtle f. *esteem, B* 369.

æhtowe (LkR 2²¹) = eahta

æhtspēd f. *wealth, riches, LPs* 103²⁴.

æhtspēdig *rich, Bl,Jul.*

æhtwela† m. *wealth, riches.*

æhtwelig *wealthy, rich, Jul* 18.

æ̆-hwænne, -hwǣr, -hwār = āhwænne, āh-wǣr

æhwyrfan = āhwierfan

æhx = æcs; æig = æg

æl- prefix = **I.** eal(l)-; **II.** el(e)-

æl m. *piercer, 'awl,' Æ.*

æl m. *'eel,' Lcd,WW*; Mdf.

ælā = ēalā

ælǣdend m. *legislator, SPs* 9²¹.

ælǣrend m. *teacher of (God's) law, EL* 506.

ælǣte **I.** n. *desert place.* **II.** *desert, W* 47²¹ : *empty, ERHy* 9⁵³. **III.** f. *divorced woman, LL.*

ælǣten **I.** = ālǣten pp. of ālǣtan. **II.** = ælǣte II.

ælagol *law-giving, GPH* 397³⁶³.

±ǣlan *to kindle, light, set on fire, burn, Æ,CP.*

ælārēow (-lārua) m. *teacher of the law, Pharisee, NG.*

ælātēow m. *legislator, CJPs* 9²¹.

ælað = ealað; ælbeorht = eallbeorht

ælbitu (Gl) = ilfetu

ælc, elc, ealc, ylc (VPs); v. 'EACH*.' **I.** (pron. subst.) *any, all, every, each (one), Æ,AO,CP.* ælc...ōðrum *the one...the other.* **II.** (adj. pron.) *each, Lcd* : *any, CP.*

ælceald *altogether cold, very cold, Met* 24¹⁹.

ælcor, ælcra = elcor, elcra

ælcræftig *almighty, all-powerful, Met* 20³⁸.

ælcuht (AO), ælcwuht n. *everything.*

æld = æled; æld- = ield-

ældewuta (NG) = ealdwita

ælecung = ōleccung

æled† m. gs. ældes *fire, firebrand.* æ̆. weccan *to kindle a fire, Wн* 21. [*ON.* eldr]

æledfȳr n. *flame of fire, Ph* 366?

æledlēoma m. *fire-brand, B* 3125.

ælednes = ālǣtnes

ælegrǣdig *greedy, ÆL* 18²¹³. [eall-]

ælegrēne = eallgrēne

ælelendisc = elelendisc

ælemidde f. *exact middle, Æ.*

ælenge **I.** *lengthy, tedious, vexatious, C.P.* ['elenge'] **II.** (i²) *weariness, Met* 151⁶.

ælengnes f. *tediousness, Sc,WW.*

ælepe? '*origanum*,' *wild marjoram*, WW 299¹⁹. [ælene? BTs]

ælepūte f. '*eel-pout*,' *burbot*, *WW*.

æleð pres. 3 sg. of alan; æleð, ǣlð = æled MLR17).

ælewealdend = eallwealdend

ælf mf. (pl. ielfe, ylfe) '*elf*,' *sprite, fairy, goblin, incubus, B,Lcd*.

ælfādl f. *nightmare*, Lcd 123b.

ælfæle = ealfelo

æl-faru, -fær f. *whole army, host*, Ex66.

ælfcynn n. *elfin race*, Lcd 123a.

ælfen (e¹) f. *nymph, spirit*, WW352¹⁰.

ælfer = ælfaru

ǣl-fisc, -fix m. *eel*, TC242¹¹.

ælfitu = ilfetu

æl-fremed, -fremd, (el-) *strange, foreign,* Æ : (+) *estranged*, LPs57⁴ : (w. fram) *free, separated from*, Æ.

ælfremedung f. '*alienatio*,' RHy5¹⁴.

ælf-scīene (ī²ȳ²)† *bright as an elf or fairy, beautiful, radiant*.

ælfsiden f. *elvish influence, nightmare,* Lcd 120b.

ælfsogoða m. *hiccough (thought to have been caused by elves)*, Lcd 124b.

ælfðeodlīce = elðeodiglīce

ælfðone f. *nightshade*, Lcd 123b.

ælfylce (=el-) n. *strange land*, El 36 : *oreign band, enemy*, B2371

ǣlhyd f. *eel receptacle? eel-skin?* (BTs), LL455,17

ǣlic *of the law, legal, lawful*, Æ. adv. -līce.

ǣlīf (ā) n. *eternal life*, MFH 150.

ælīfn f. *sustenance*, GL? (v. ES42·166)

ǣling f. *burning*, Æ : *ardour*, Met.

ǣling- = æleng-; æll- = æl-, eal(l)-, el(l)-

ælmes = ælmesse

ælmesæcer m. *ground of which the yield was given as alms, first-fruits*, A11·3⁶⁹.

ælmesbæð n. *gratuitous bath*, W171².

ælmesdǣd f. *almsdeed*, Æ.

ælmesdōnd *alms-giver*, Chrd 93²⁸.

ælmesfeoh n. *alms* : *Peter's pence, Rome-scot, LL*. ['*almsfee*']

ælmesfull *charitable*, Chr,LL.

ælmesgedāl n. *distribution of alms*, LL,W.

ælmesgeorn *charitable*, Æ.

ælmesgifa (y³) m. *giver of alms*, W72⁴.

ælmesgifu f. *alms, charity*, W159²⁰.

ælmeshand *almsgiving, charitableness,* Chrd 12¹⁹.

ælmeshlāf (e¹) m. *dole of bread*, TC474'.

ælmeslāc *giving of alms*, NC269.

ælmeslēoht n. *a light in church provided at the expense of a pious layman*, LL (288¹).

ælmeslic *charitable* : *depending on alms, poor*. -līce; adv. *charitably*, OET (Ct).

ælmeslond (a¹) m. *land granted in frankalmoigne*, (BT)

ælmesmann m. '*almsman*,' *bedesman, beggar, Lcd*; Æ.

ælmespening m. *alms-penny*, KC (v. MLR17).

ælmesriht n. *right of receiving alms*, W.

ælmesse f. '*alms*,' *almsgiving, Da,Mt*; Æ, CP. [*L*. eleēmosyna]

ælmessylen (e³) f. *almsgiving*, GD,LL.

ælmestlīce = ælmeslīce

ælmesweorc n. *almsdeed*, Bl 25¹⁷.

ælmidde = ælemidde; ælmiehtig = ælmihtig

ælmihtig (ea², e²) adj. '*almighty*,' *Ps,TC*; AO,CP : m. *the Almighty, B*.

ælmihtignes f. *omnipotence*, AS59¹⁹.

ælmyrca m. *one entirely black, Ethiopian,* An432.

ælmysse = ælmesse

ǣlnet n. *eel net*, BH304¹¹.

ǣlpig (Chr 1085) = ānlīpig

ælren adj. *of an alder tree*, KC3·316'. ['*aldern*']

ælreord = elreord

ælsyndrig *separately*, LkR2⁸.

æltǣwe (ēo, ō) *complete, entire, perfect, healthy, sound, true,* Æ,AO,CP : *noted, Æ*. [*Goth*. tēwa] -līce adv.

ælðeod, (ælðīed) = elðeod

æl-walda, -wealda = ealwealda

ælwiht† m. *strange creature, monster* [=*elwiht] : (in pl.) = eallwihta.

æmbern = embren

ǣmelle *insipid*, WW429³⁰.

ǣmelnes f. *slackness, sloth,* Æ : *weariness, disgust*, WW.

ǣmen, ǣmenne (AO) *uninhabited, desolate, desert*.

ǣmend = ǣmynd

ǣmenne *solitude*, AS4¹ (v. Wfg3).

ǣmerge f. *embers, ashes, dust, Lcd*; Æ. ['*ember*']

ǣmet- = ǣmett-

ǣmetbed n. *ant-hill*, Lcd 121b.

ǣmethwīl (ā¹) f. *leisure*, Æ.

ǣmethyll m. *ant-hill*, CP191²⁵.

ǣmetian = ǣmtian

ǣmetta m. *leisure, rest*, CP. [mōt]

ǣmette f. '*emmet*,' *ant*, WW; Æ.

ǣmettig (CP), -m(e)tig (Æ) '*empty*,' *vacant,* Æ,Bl : *unoccupied, without employment,* Æ : *un-married*, CP.

ǣmettigian = ǣmtian

æmn- = emn-, efen-

ǣmōd (ā) *dismayed, disheartened*, Æ,AO.

ǣmt- = ǣmett-

±ǣmtian *to* '*empty*,' Æ : *to be at leisure, have time for*, Æ,CP.

ǣmtignes f. *emptiness*, GD35¹⁷.

ǣmuða m. '*cæcum intestinum*,' WW160¹¹.

ǣmynd (e²) f. *jealousy*, Lcd 1·384'.

ǣmyrce *excellent*, WW 393³⁸.
ǣmyrie = ǣmerge; ǣmytte = ǣmette
ǣn = ān; +ǣn- = +en-
+ǣnan (ē)? *to unite oneself to, join with*,
AS 39⁶.
ǣnbrece = unbrece; ǣnd- = end-
ǣne (āne) *once, at some time, Æ,B : at any
time : at once.* [' *ene* ']
ǣned = ened
ǣnes adv. *once*, GD,LL
ǣnetre = ānwintre
ǣnett, ǣnetnes = ānet; ǣnga = ānga
ǣngancundes *in a unique way?* (BTs),
Lcd 162b.
ǣnge, ǣngel = enge, engel
Ænglisc = Englisc; ǣnid = ened
ǣnig adj. pron. and sb. '*any*,' *any one,
Mk,Jn.* ǣnige ðinga *somehow, anyhow.*
adv. *only*, Ps,Rd (v. BTac). [ān]
ǣnigge = āneage
ǣnigmon *any one, some one*, NG.
ǣniht = āwuht; ǣninga = ānunga
ǣnlānan = onlǣnan; ǣnlefan = endlufon
ǣnlēp- = ānlep-
ǣnlic *one,* '*only,*' *singular, solitary, Ps :
unique, glorious, noble, splendid, excellent,
Bo; Æ,AO.* adv. *-lice, WW.*
ǣnlīpig (Æ) = ānlīpig
ǣnne (AO,CP) v. ān.
ǣnote *useless*, LL 254,3³⁴.
ǣnrǣdnis = ānrǣdnes; ǣnyge = āneage
ǣnytte = ānet; ǣpl = ǣppel
ǣpled = ǣppled
ǣppel m. (nap. ǣpplas, rarely ap(p)la,
ǣppla) *any kind of fruit, fruit in general :
'apple,' CP,Gen : apple of the eye, ball,
anything round, Bo,CP,Sol.*
ǣppelbǣre *fruit-bearing*, Gen 1¹¹,HexC 198.
ǣppelbearu m. *orchard*, PPs 78².
ǣppelberende *apple-bearing*, DR 98¹⁶.
ǣppelcynn n. *kind of apple*, Lcd 67a.
ǣppelcyrnel n. *apple-pip*, WW 440²³.
ǣppelfæt n. *apple-vessel*, ZDA 31·15⁴⁰¹.
ǣppelfealu *apple-yellow, bay*, B 2165.
ǣppelhūs n. *fruit storehouse*, WW.
ǣppelscealu f. *apple-core*, WW 371¹.
ǣppelscrēada np. *apple-parings*, WW 118¹.
ǣppeltrēow n. '*apple-tree,*' *WW.*
ǣppeltūn m. *fruit garden, orchard*, Æ,CP.
ǣppelðorn m. *crab-apple tree*, BC 3·93'.
ǣppelwīn n. *cider*, WW 430⁹.
ǣppled† *shaped like an apple, round, embossed, El,Jul.* [' *appled* ']
ǣppul- = apul-; ǣps = ǣsp, ǣbs.
ǣpsen *shameless?* OEG 7³⁰¹ and n.
ǣpsenes f. *shame, disgrace*, Sc 174⁹.
ǣr I. adv. comp. ǣror; sup. ǣrost, ǣr(e)st
'ERE,' *before that, soon, formerly, beforehand, previously, already, lately, till;*

(comp.) *sooner, earlier*; (sup.) *just now,
first of all : early, prematurely.* on ǣr;
ǣr ðissum *previously, formerly, beforehand,
CP.* tō ǣr *too soon.* ǣr oððe ǣfter *sooner
or later.* hwonne ǣr *how soon? when?*
hwēne ǣr *just before.* on ealne ǣrne
mergen *very early in the morning.* ne ǣr
ne siððan *neither sooner nor later.* ǣr and
sið *at all times.* II. conj. '*ere*,' *before that,
until, Æ,AO,CP.* ǣr ðam (ðe) *before.*
III. prep. (w.d.) *before.* IV. adj. only in
comp. and sup. (ǣrra, ǣrest) q.v. V.
f. = ǣr f. VI. n. = ǣr n. VII. = ēar II.
ǣr- = *early, former* (v MP 28·157)
ǣra I. m. *scraper, strigil*, Gl. II. = ǣrra
ǣrǣt m. *too early eating*, W.
ǣrbe- = yrfe-, ierfe-
ǣrbeðoht *premeditated*, LL 428¹².
ǣrboren *earlier born, first-born* (or ? two
words), Gen 973.
ǣrc = earc; ǣrce = arce
ǣrcwide m. *prophecy?* Mod 4.
ǣrdǣd f. *former deed*, Lk,W.
ǣrdæg m. (nap. ǣrdagas) *early morn,
dawn :* in pl. *former days, past times*, AO.
ǣrdēað m. *premature death*, Ex 539.
ǣrdian = eardian
ǣrdon = ǣrndon? from ǣrnan (Gr),Ma 191.
ǣrdung = eardung
ǣre I. = ȳre. II. in comp. = -*oared.*
ǣrēafe (= ǣ²) *detected*, TC 230¹⁶.
ǣreldo '*anteritus,*' WW 347¹².
ǣren I. *made of brass, brazen, Æ,AO,CP :
tinkling?* [ǣr; cp. Ger. ehern] II. *oar-
propelled*, GD 347.
ǣrendbōc f. *message, letter*, Da,WW 511²⁵.
ǣrenddraca (AO,CP) = ǣrendraca
ǣrende n. '*errand,*' *message, BH,Gu;* AO :
mission, An,Chr : answer, news, tidings,Æ.
ǣrendfæst *bound on an errand*, ÆL 26²²¹.
ǣrendgāst m. *angel*, Gen 2296.
ǣrendgewrit n. *written message, letter, Æ,
CP.*
±ǣrendian *to go on an errand, carry a
message, send word to, CP : intercede, Æ :
seek for, obtain*, BH 2·132⁵ : (+) *speed,
succeed*, W 238⁹. [' *ernde* ']
ǣrendraca m. *messenger, apostle, ambassador, angel, Æ,CP.* AO : *representative, substitute, proxy*, BH 276¹⁹.
ǣrendscip n. *skiff, small boat*, WW 287²⁸.
ǣrendsecg m. *messenger*, Gen 658.
ǣrendsprǣc f. *message*, Rd 61¹⁵.
ǣrendung f. *errand : errand-going : intercession, RB.* [' *ernding* ']
ǣrend-wraca (AO), -wreca (CP) = ǣrendraca
ǣrendwrit = ǣrendgewrit
ǣrenscip = ǣrendscip; ǣrer = ǣror

ǣrest I. adv. and superl. adj. *first, at first, before all,* Æ,CP. ðā, ðonne, siððan ǣ. *as soon as.* ǣ. ðinga *first of all.* **II.** = ǣrist

ǣrfæder m. *forefather,* B 2622.

ǣrfæst = ārfæst; **ǣrfe** = ierfe, yrfe

ǣrgedōn *done before,* CP.

ǣrgefremed *before committed,* LL (434¹⁴).

ǣrgelēred *previously instructed,* MtL 14⁸.

ǣrgenemned, -gesæd = ǣrnemned

ǣrgestrēon† n. *ancient treasure.*

ǣrgeweorc† n. *work of olden times.*

ǣrgewinn n. *former strife or trouble, old warfare,* Cross 19.

ǣrgewyrht† n. *former work, deed of old.*

ǣrglæd *bright in armour,* Ex 293.

ǣrgōd† *good from old times,* B.

ǣrhwīlum† *erewhile, formerly.*

ǣrian = erian; **ǣrig** (OET) = earh

ǣriht† n. *code of law or faith,* EL.

ǣring f. *day-break, early morn,* Jul,MkL.

ǣrisc = ēarisc

ǣrist I. (ē) mfn. *rising, VPs : resurrection, awakening, CP,Jn.* ['*arist*'] **II.** = ǣrest

ǣrlēof? 'gratus' OEG 56²⁹⁶.

ǣrlēst = ārlēast

ǣrlic (ā) adj.; -līce adv. '*early,*' Jn.

ǣrlyft f. *early morning air,* WW 415¹³.

ǣrm = earm

ǣrmorgen (a¹, a², e²) m. *dawn, day-break.*

ǣrmorgenlic *of early morning,* DR.

ǣrn (ea) n. *dwelling, house, building, store, closet* (v. G.BG).

ǣrn = ǣren

ǣrnan (strictly causative) *to 'run,' ride, gallop, BH : (+) to ride, run to, reach, gain by running or riding, AO.*

ǣrndian = ǣrendian

ǣrne-mergen, -merigen (Æ) = ǣrmorgen

ǣrnemergenlic *matutinal,* CM 277.

ǣrnemned (æ²) *aforementioned,* LL.

ǣrneweg m. *road for riding on, race-course,* BH 398³⁰; Bo 112²³. [iernan]

ǣrnian = carnian

ǣrning f. '*running,*' *riding, racing, Bo,GD : flow of blood,* MtL 9²⁰ (iorn-).

ǣrnð = ernð

ǣrnðegen (rend-) m. *house-officer,* GL.

ǣrnung = earnung; **ǣron** = ǣrran

ǣror I. adv. *earlier, before, beforehand, formerly,* B,Rood; Æ,AO : *rather.* **II.** prep. (w. d.) *before.* ['*ever*']

ǣrost = ǣrest

ǣrra m. ǣrre fn. adj. *earlier, former, preceding, Bo,El;* CP. on ǣrran dæg *the day before yesterday.* ['*ere,*' '*ever*']

ǣrror = ǣror; **ǣrs** = ears

ǣrsceaft f. *ancient building,* Ruin 16.

ǣrschen, ǣrshen = erschen; **ǣrst** = ǣrest

ǣrstæf = ārstæf

ǣr-ðam, -ðon, -ðamðe v. ǣr; **ǣrð-** = yrð-

ǣrwacol *early awake,* Æ.

+**ǣrwe** *depraved, wicked,* EPs 100⁴.

ǣrwela m. *ancient wealth,* B 2747.

ǣrworuld f. *ancient world,* Cr 937.

ǣrynd = ǣrend; **ǣryr** = ǣror

ǣryst I. = ǣrist. **II.** = ǣrest

ǣs n. *food, meat, carrion : bait.* [OHG. ās]

ǣsc I. m. nap. ascas '*ash*'-*tree, Gl,KC;* Mdf: *name of the rune for* æ : (†) *spear, lance,* B : *ship,* Æ. **II.** = æcs

ǣscǣre *unshorn, untrimmed,* LL. [scieran]

ǣscan *to demand (legally),* LL 177'.

ǣscapo (WW 273³⁵) = ǣsceapa

ǣscbedd n. *an ash-plot,* KC 5·126'.

ǣscberend† m. *spear-bearer, soldier.*

ǣsce = asce

ǣsce f. *asking, inquiry, search, LL : claim (to insurance money for theft of cattle),* LL 175². ['*ask*' sb.]

ǣsceap (ē¹) n. *remnant, patch,* LkL,WW.

ǣsceda fp. *refuse,* WW 148³³.

ǣscegeswāp n. *cinders, ashes,* TC 318'.

ǣscen I. fm. *vessel of ash-wood, bucket, pail, bottle, cup.* **II.** adj. *made of ash-wood, ashen,* Lcd.

ǣscfealu *ashy-hued,* WW 204²³.

ǣscgrǣg *ashy gray,* WW 204²⁴.

ǣschere m. *naval force,* Ma 69.

ǣscholt† n. *spear of ash-wood, spear-shaft, lance* (v. also Mdf).

ǣscian = āscian

ǣscmann m. *ship-man, sailor, pirate,* Chr, WW. [æsc]

ǣscplega m. *play of spears, battle,* Jud 217.

ǣscrind f. *bark of the ash-tree,* Lcd.

ǣscrōf† *brave in battle.*

ǣscsteall? (æts-) m. *place of battle,* Wald 1²¹.

ǣscstede m. *place of battle,* Mod 17; Mdf.

ǣscstederōd f. *cross marking a battlefield?* (BTs), KC 3·135'.

ǣscstybb m. *stump of an ash-tree,* BC.

ǣsctir m. *glory in war,* Gen 2069.

ǣscōracu f. *battle,* Gen 2153.

ǣscōrot-e, -u f. *a plant, ferula? vervain?* Lcd.

ǣscwert = ǣscwyrt

ǣscwiga† m. *(spear-)warrior.*

ǣscwyrt f. *verbena, vervain.*

ǣsellend (y²) m. *lawgiver,* Ps.

ǣsil = hæsel

ǣslītend m. *law-breaker,* LPs.

ǣsmæl *smallness of the eye,* Lcd.

ǣsmogu np. *slough (of snake)* Lcd 88a. [āsmūgan]

ǣsne- = esne-; **ǣsp** = æspe I.

ǣspe I. f. *aspen-tree, white poplar, Gl;* Mdf. ['*asp*¹'] **II.** = æbs

ǣsphangra m. *aspen wood,* KC.

æspreng, æspring(e) = æspryng

æsprind (ps) f. *aspen bark*, Lcd. ['*asp*']

æspringnes = āsprungenes

æspryng nf. *spring, fountain*, CP. [ēa] : *departure*, CREAT 77.

æst I. = ǣrest. II. = ēst

āstǣnan = āstǣnan; **æstan** = ēastan

æstel m. *some thin kind of board?* CP 9, ÆGR 31⁹, WW 327¹ (v. BTac and NED s.v. '*astel*')

æsul = esol

æswāpa sbpl. *sweepings, rubbish*, OEG.

æswic I. m. *offence, stumbling-block, infamy, seduction, deceit.* II. adj. *apostate*, GD 304²⁸.

æswica m. *offender, deceiver, hypocrite, traitor*, GD.

æswice m. *violation of God's laws* (or? *adultery*), W 164³.

±**æswician** *to offend, deceive*, Æ : *apostatize*, WW 342¹² : *desert*, Æ.

æswicnes f. *stumbling-block*, LPs 105³⁶ : *reproach*, 122⁴.

æswicung f. *offence, stumbling-block*, Æ : *deceit*, Æ : *sedition*, WW 116²⁶.

æswind *idle, slothful*, WW 422¹³. [swīð]

æsyllend = æsellend

æt I. prep. (w. d. and, more rarely, a) (local) '*AT*,' *near, by, in, on, upon, with, before, next to, as far as, up to, into, toward*, Chr : (temporal) *at, at the time of, near, in, on, to, until* : (causal) *at, to, through* : (source) *from* : (instrumental) *by.* æt fēawum wordum *in few words*, BH : *in respect to, as to.* II. adv. *at, to, near.* æt nehstan, æt siðestan *finally.* æt- in composition=*at, to, from.*

æt I. (ē) mfn. *eatables, food, meat, flesh*, Æ, Gu; AO. æt and wǣt *food and drink*, Æ : *the act of feeding, eating*, PPs; MkL. ['*eat*' sb.] II. pret. 3 sg. of etan.

æt-=oð-; **ǣt-**=āte-; **-ǣta** v. self-ǣta.

ætǣwian=ætīewan

āetan⁵ *to eat, devour*, AS 18², 38².

ætbēon anv. *to be present*, DHy.

ætberan⁴ *to carry to, bring, produce, show*, Da : *carry off*, B. ['*atbear*']

ætberstan³ *to break out, or away, escape from*, Æ. ['*atburst*']

ætbrēdan=ætbregdan

ætbrēdendlic *ablative*, ÆGR 23⁷.

æt-bregdan, -brēdan³ *to take away, carry off, deprive of, snatch away, draw off, withdraw*, Mt; Æ : *release, rescue, enlarge* : *prevent*, ÆL 31¹²⁶. ['*atbraid*']

ætclifian *to adhere*, BJPs 101⁶.

ætclīðan *to adhere*, OET 181.

ætdēman *to refuse, give judgment against*, EC 202¹⁹.

ætdōn anv. *to take away, deprive*, LL (246¹⁰).

ǣte=āte

ætēaca (eth-) m. *addition*, OEG 53¹⁸.

ætēacnes (BH)=ætȳcnes

ætealdod *too old*, Æ (2¹⁵⁹).

ætēaw-=ætīew-, ætȳw-

ætēcan=ætȳcan; **ætegār**=ætgār

æteglan *to harm*, PPs 88¹⁹.

ætēode pret. 3 sg. of *ætgān.

æteorian=āteorian

ætēow-=ætīew-, ætȳw-, oðīew-

ætercyn=ātorcyn

ǣtere (ē¹) m. '*eater*,' *glutton*, KGl; NG.

ǣtern I. (NG) *viper.* II.=ǣtren

ætēw-=ætīew-, ætȳw-

ætfæstan (=oð-) *to inflict on, afflict with* : *fasten to, drive into, impart to*, CP 115¹⁹ : *commit, entrust* : *marry to.*

ætfæstnian *to fasten? entrust?* AS 22¹⁰.

ætfaran⁶ *to escape*, SHR 14²³.

ætfeallan⁷ *to fall, fall out* : *fall away, fail, be reduced*, LL; Æ : *happen.* ['*atfall*']

ætfele m. *adhesion*, PPs 72²³.

ætfeng m. *attaching, distraint* v. LL 2·279.

ætfeohtan² *to grope about*, WY 18

ætfēolan³ (T²) *to stick to* : *adhere, apply oneself to, continue in*, CP.

ætfeorrian *to take from*, Sc 160⁷ : *remove oneself from*, CHRD 93³.

ætferian *to carry away, bear off*, CHRD, LL.

ætfīlan=ætfēolan

ætflēon² *to flee away, escape by flight*, Æ. ['*atflee*']

ætflōwan⁷ *to flow together, accumulate*, SPs 61¹⁰.

ætfōn⁷ *to seize upon, lay claim to*, LL. ['*atfong*']

ætforan I. prep. w. d. *before, in the presence of, in front of, close by*, JnL; Æ. ['*atfore*'] II. adv. *beforehand* (time).

ætfyligan, -fylgan *to adhere, cling to*, GD.

æt-gædere (AO), -gæddre (CP), -gædre, -gæderum adv. *together, united, at the same time.* [gadrian]

æt-gǣre n., -gār m. *spear, dart, javelin*, GL.

ætgangan⁷ *to go to, approach*, Az 183. ['*atgo*']

ætgeddre, -gedre=ætgædere

ætgenumen *taken away*, WW 529³⁹.

ætgiefa† (eo, i) m. *food-giver, feeder.*

ætgifan⁵ *to render, give*, B 2878.

ætglīdan¹ *to slip away, disappear*, OEG 7¹³².

ætgrǣpe *seizing.* æ. weorðan *seize*, B 1268.

æthabban *to retain*, Æ.

æthealdan⁷ *to keep back*, Sc 109¹⁸.

æthebban⁶ *to take away, take out, hold back*, Æ : *exalt oneself*, CP 113¹³.

æthindan prep. w. d. *behind, after, Chr*; Æ. ['athinden']

æthlēapan[7] *to run away, flee, escape*, W 162[5].

æthlӯp m. *assault*, LL. [cp. æhlӯp]

æthrīnan[1] *to touch, move, Mt*; Æ. ['atrine']

æthrine m. *touch*, LCD.

æthwā *each, every one*, LL,PA.

æthwāre *somewhat*, HGL 421[37].

æt-hwega, -hwæga, -hweg(u) adv. *somewhat, tolerably, a little : how.*

æthweorfan[3] *to return, go back*, B 2299.

æthwōn adv. *almost, nearly.*

æthȳd *'eviscerata,' deprived of its sinews*, MtL, WW 392' (v. A 47·34).

ætiernan[3] *to run away*, Æ. ['atrin']

ætīewan (oð-; ē, ēa, ēo, ī, ӯ) pret. sg. -īe(w)de, (tr.) *to show, reveal, display, disclose, manifest, Mt*; CP : (intr.) *show oneself, become visible, appear, Mt.* ['atew'] For compounds see ætӯw-.

æting (ē) f. *eating*, Sc 170[5] : *pasture?* Mdf.

ætinge (=y[2]) *speechless*, OEG 46[45].

ætis pres. 3 sg. of ætwesan, ætbēon.

ætīw-=ætīew-, ætӯw-

ætlǣdan (=oð-) *to drive away*, Æ. ['atlead']

ætlic (ē) adj. *eatable*, WW,LkL.

ætliogan[5] *to lie idle*, ÆGr 2[22]. ['atlie']

ætlimpan[3] *to fall away, escape, be lost*, Æ.

ætlūtian *to lurk, hide*, Æ. ['atlutien']

ætnēhstan (ӯ) adv. *at last.*

ætnes f. *edibility*, WW 226[11].

ætniman[4] *to take away, deprive of*, Ex 414.

ætol=etol

æton pret. pl. of etan.

ætor, ættorcynn=ātor, ātorcynn

ætran=ætrian

ætreccan w. d. and a. *to declare forfeit, deprive of*, LCD.

ætren *poisoned, poisonous, MtL* (-ern). ['attern']

ætrenmōd *of venomous spirit, malignant* (or? two words), GNE 163.

ætrennes f. *poisonous nature*, LCD 55a.

±ætrian *to poison, AO : become poisonous.* ['atter']

ætrig *poisonous*, Lcd; Æ. ['attery']

ætrihte (y) I. adj. *right at, near, present, close at hand.* II. adv. *almost, nearly, immediately.*

ætsacan[6] *to deny, Lk*; Æ : *renounce, Mk.* ['atsake']

ætsamne (æ, e, o) adv. *united, together, at once*, AO.

ætscēotan[2] *to escape, disappear*, MFH 150.

ætsittan[5] *to sit by, remain, stay, Chr.* ['atsit']

ætslāpan[7] *to sleep beside*, LCD 83a.

ætslīdan[1] *to slip, glide, fall*, Æ.

ætsomne (Æ)=ætsamne

ætspornan[3] (u) *to strike against, stumble, go wrong*, CP : *rebel* (æt).

ætspornung f. *offence, stumbling-block, misfortune*, CM 230.

ætspringan[3] *to rush forth, spurt out*, B 1121. ['atspring']

ætspringnes, -sprung(en)nes f. *failing*, Ps 118[53].

ætspurnan=ætspornan

ætspyrning=ætspornung

ætst=itst pres. 2 sg. of etan.

ætst-=oðst-

ætstæl m. *aid, assistance* (GK);=ætsteall (BT), GU 150.

ætstæppan[6] *to step up to*, B 745.

ætstandan[6] *to stand still, stand at, near, in or by, Æ : remain, stand up : check, resist, Æ : cease, Lk*; Æ. ['atstand']

ætstandend m. *bystander, attendant*, Æ.

ætstandende *standing by*, GD 284[21].

ætsteall m. *assistance, meeting with hostile intent* (GK) : *station, camp station* (BT), or ? æscsteall (Sedgef.), WALD 1[21].

ætstentan=ætstyntan

ætstillan *to still*, LCD 25b.

ætstrengan *to withhold wrongfully*, LL 206'.

ætstyntan *to blunt, dull, weaken*, GL,HY.

ætswerian[6] *to deny on oath*, LL.

ætswīgan *to keep silence*, GD 217[18].

ætswimman[3] *to escape by swimming, swim out*, CHR 918.

āettan (āyttan) *to eat up*, LPs 79[14].

ætter, ættor=ātor; ættr-=ætr-

ætōringan[3] *to take away from, deprive of*, AN,GD.

ætwegan[5] *to bear away, carry off*, B 1198.

ætwela *abundance of food, feast*, SOUL 123.

ætwenian *to wean from*, LL 368'.

ætwesan anv. *to be present*, BF,BH 276[20].

ætwesende *at hand, imminent*, WW.

ætwindan[3] *to escape*, Æ. ['atwind']

ætwist I.† f. *presence.* II.=edwist

ætwītan[6] *to reproach (with), censure, taunt*, B,Met,Ps; CP. ['atwite']

ætwrencan *to seize by fraud*, PR 34.

ætȳcan *to add to, increase*, BH. [iecan]

ætȳcnes f. *increase*, BH.

ætȳnan=ontȳnan; ætynge=ætinge

ætys=ætis pres. 3 sg. of ætwesan.

æt-ȳwan, -ȳwian=ætīewan

ætȳwednes f. *showing, appearance, manifestation, revelation*, GD.

ætȳwigendlic *demonstrative*, ÆGR.

ætȳwnes f. *showing, manifestation, revelation : apparition*, Æ : *Epiphany.*

ætȳwung f. *manifestation, Epiphany*, CM 531.

āðan I. (±) *to make oath, swear.* +āðed *under oath*, LL 210,6. [āð] II.=īeðan

æðel=æðele; æðel=ēðel
æðelboren *of noble birth, distinguished, Æ* :
free-born, Æ : inborn, natural.
æðelborennes f. *nobility of birth or nature,*
Æ : inborn nature, OEG 4518.
æðelcund *of noble birth,* GD.
æðelcundnes f. *nobleness,* Bo 46¹³.
æðelcyning m. *noble king (Christ), Æ.*
æðelduguð f. *noble retinue,* CR 1012.
æðele *noble, aristocratic, excellent, famous,*
glorious, Ex,Gen; Æ,AO,CP : splendid, fine,
costly, valuable :_ lusty, young : pleasant,
sweet-smelling, Gen : (+) *natural, con-*
genial, suitable. ['*athel'*]
æðel-ferðingwyrt, -fyrdingwyrt f. *stitch-*
wort (plant), LCD.
+æðelian† *to make noble or renowned, Hy.*
['*i-athele'*]
æðelic=æðellic; æðelic=ēaðelic
æðeling m. *man of royal blood, nobleman,*
chief, prince, Chr; AO (v. LL 2·274) :
†*king, Christ, God, Cr :* †*man, hero, saint;*
in pl. *men, people, Gen.* ['*atheling'*]
æðelinghād n. *princely state,* LCD 3·438⁵.
æðellic *noble, excellent.* adv. -līce.
æðelnes f. *nobility, excellence,* BL,MH.
æðelo=æðelu
æðelstenc m. *sweet smell,* PH 195.
æðeltungol† n. *noble star.*
æðelu fn. *nobility, family, descent, origin,*
B; CP : *nature : noble qualities, genius,*
talents, pre-eminence, Bo : produce, growth.
['*athel'*]
ǣð-=ēð-
ǣðm (ē) m. *air, breath, breathing, B;* CP :
vapour, Sat. : blast, Æ. ['*ethem'*]
ǣðmian *to fume, exhale, emit a smell,* GL,
MH.
ǣðre=ǣdre
ǣðreclic *terrible,* RPs 95⁴.
ǣðret-=ǣðryt-
ǣðrot n. *disgust, weariness,* GL,RB.
[āðrēotan]
ǣðryt I. *troublesome, wearisome, disgust-*
ing. II. n. *weariness, disgust, tediousness,*
Æ.
ǣðryte=ǣðryt I.
ǣðrytnes f. *tedium,* v. OEG 4582.
±ǣðryttan *to weary, Æ,*RWH 123⁸
ǣðða (Bd, Death-song)=oððe
ǣw I.=ǣ. II.=ǣwe
ǣwǣde *without clothes,* WW 230⁸⁸.
ǣwan *to despise, scorn,* KPs 129.
ǣwbrǣce *despising the law, Æ : adulterous,*
LL.
ǣwbreca (i, y) m. *adulterer,* LL. ['*eau-*
bruche²']
ǣwbryce m. *adultery, Æ; LL.* ['*eau-*
bruche¹']

ǣw-da, -damann m. *witness, compurgator,*
LL.
ǣwe I. fn. *married woman, Æ : married*
people. II. *lawful : married : born of the*
same marriage.
ǣwelm=ǣwielm
ǣwenbrōðor m. *brother by the same mar-*
riage, WW 413²⁹.
ǣwēne *doubtful, uncertain,* DEUT 28⁶⁶.
ǣwerd adj.? *religious,* or sb.? *regular priest,*
ANS 128·298. [cp. ǣweweard]
ǣwerd-=ǣfwyrd-, ǣwierd-
ǣweweard m. *priest,* BL 161'.
ǣwfæst *upright, pious, devout, religious,*
*Æ,*CP : *married, Æ.*
ǣwfæsten n. *legal or public fast,* A 11·102.
ǣwfæstlic *lawful : religious,* CP (ǣf-). adv.
-līce.
ǣwfæstnes f. *religion, piety,* Æ,BH.
ǣwicnes f. *eternity,* RPs 102¹⁷ (v. p.303).
ǣwielm (e, i, y), -wielme m. *source, fount,*
spring, beginning, AO,CP. [=ēawielm]
+ǣwierdlian (e²) *to injure,* BH 202b²⁰.
ǣwintre=ānwintre; ǣwis-=ǣwisc-
ǣwisc I. nf. *offence, shame, disgrace, dis-*
honour, AO. [*Goth.* aiwisks] II. *dis-*
graced, shameless, indecent.
ǣwisc-=ēawisc-
ǣwiscberende *shameful,* WW 264⁴².
ǣwisce=ǣwisc I.
ǣwisc-ferinend (GL), -firina (NG) m.
shameless sinner, publican.
ǣwisclic *disgraceful, infamous,* OEG.
ǣwiscmōd† *ashamed, abashed, cowed.*
ǣwiscnes (ēa-) f. *shameless conduct : open-*
ness, WW : *reverence,* CP 34²⁶.
ǣwita m. *counsellor,* EL 455.
ǣwlic *legal, lawful.* adv. -līce.
±ǣwnian *to marry, Æ.*
ǣwnung f. *wedlock,* OEG.
ǣwul *basket with a narrow neck for catching*
fish, WW 181¹¹. [?=cawl, BTs]
ǣwumboren *lawfully born,* LL 76'.
ǣwung=ǣwnung; ǣwunge=ēawunge
ǣwyll m. *stream,* BC 1·542.
ǣ-wylm, -wylme=ǣwielm
ǣwyrdla=ǣfwyrdla
ǣwyrp m. *what is cast away,* RB : *an*
abortion, LL. [āweorpan]
ǣwysc-=ǣwisc-; æx=æcs, eax; æxe=
asce
æxfaru f. '*apparatus,*' *naval expedition?*
(=æsc-? v. ES 37·184), GL.
æxian=ascian; æxl=eaxl; æxs=æcs
āfǣdan=āfēdan
āfǣgan *to depict, figure,* BH 58²⁵. [fāg]
āfǣgrian (æ) *to ornament, adorn,* BH 38b²⁷.
ā-fǣlan, -fǣllan=āfyllan II.
āfǣman *to foam out,* PPs 118¹³¹.

áfǣran _to frighten_, _PPs,Mk,Chr_; AO,CP. ['_afear_,' '_afeared_']

áfæst=ǣwfæst

áfæstan I. _to fast_, LL,W. II. _to let out on hire_, MkR 12[1].

áfæstlá interj. _certainly! assuredly!_ Æ.

áfæstnian (e) _to fix upon_, _fasten_, _make firm_, _confirm_, AO : _enter_, _inscribe_, Æ : _build_.

áfǣttian _to fatten_, _anoint_, APs 22[5]; LPs 140[5].

áfandelic=áfandodlic

áfandian _to try_, _test_, _prove_, _tempt_, _Lk,Lcd_; Æ,CP : _find out_, _experience_, Æ. áfandod (and áfanden?) _approved_, _excellent_, Æ. ['_afond_']

áfand-igendlic, -odlic _proved_, _approved_, _laudable_. adv. -odlíce.

áfandung f. _trial_, _experience_, Æ,GD,WW.

áfangennes f. _reception_, _assumption_, EHy 15[35].

áfara=eafora

áfaran _to go out_, _depart_, _march_, _travel_, _Da_; Æ,AO. ['_afare_']

áfeallan[7] _to fall down_, _fall in battle_, _Lk_; CP : _fall off_, _decay_. ['_afalle_']

áfeallan=áfyllan

áfédan _to feed_, _nourish_, _bring up_, _maintain_, _support_, Æ; AO : _bring forth_, _produce_. ['_afede_']

áfégan _to join_, DR (oe).

áfehtan (DR)=áfeohtan

áfellan=áfyllan; **áfelle**=ǣfelle

áfeohtan[3] _to fight_, _fight against_; _attack_, AO : _tear out_, _destroy_.

áfeormian _to cleanse_, _purge_, _purify_, Æ,LCD.

áfeormung f. _scouring_, _cleansing_, _purging_, CM,LCD,SC.

á-feorran, -feorrian (CP)=áfierran

áfeorsian _to remove_, _do away_, _expel_, _dispel_, Æ : _go away_.

áfer=eafor; **áfer**=áfor; **áféran**=áfǣran

áfercian _to support_, CHRD 90[11].

áferian _to provide horses for team work_ (_as service for a lord_), v. LL 445, 446 and 3·247.

á-ferian (GL), -ferran=áfierran

áferscan _to become fresh_, Bo 86[20].

áfersian=áfeorsian

áfestnian (WW 49[8])=áfæstnian

áfetigan=hafetian

áfierran (eo, i, y) _to remove_, _withdraw_, _depart_ : _estrange from_, _take away_, _expel_, _drive away_, CP. [feorr]

áfierrednes (y) f. _removal_, NC 270.

áfigen _fried_, GL.

áfilgan=áfylgan

áfindan[3] (=on-) _to find_, _find out_, _discover_, _detect_, _Jn_; Æ : _experience_, _feel_, Æ. ['_afind_']

áfir-=áfierr-, áfeor-, áfyr-

áflǣgen pp. of áfléan.

áflǣman=áflíeman

áfléan[6] _to strip off_, _flay_, GD.

áflégan (DR)=áflíegan; **áfléman**=áflíeman

áfléon[2], -fléogan _to fly_, _flee away_, _Gu_ : _fly from_, _escape_. ['_aflee_']

áfléotan[2] _to skim_, LCD.

áflían=áflíegan

+**áflian**? _to get_, _obtain_? OEG 7[118] (v. BTac).

áflíegan (í, é, ý) _to put to flight_, _expel_, Æ. ['_afley_']

áflíegung (í) f. _driving away_, LCD 1·338[12].

áflíeman (ý) _to put to flight_, _expel_, _scatter_, _disperse_, _rout_, _Chr_; CP : _banish_. ['_afleme_']

áflíg-=áflíeg-

-**áflíung** v. mete-á.

áflote '_afloat_,' KC 4·24[1]. [=on flote]

áflówan[7] _to flow_, _flow away or from_, _pass away_, AO,CP.

áflýg-, áflýh-=áflíeg-

áflygennes f. _attack_ (BTs), LCD 1·336[7].

áflýman=áflíeman; **áfógian**=áwógian

áfol n. _power_, _might_, LL (304 n 1).

áfón (=on-) _to receive_, _take in_, _take_, _Mk_, _Ps_ : _lay hold of_, _seize_, _MtR_,_Jul_ : _hold up_, _support_. ['_afong_']

áfondian=áfandian

áfor _bitter_, _acid_, _sour_, _sharp_ : _dire_, _fierce_, _severe_, _harsh_, _impetuous_. [OHG. eipar]

áfora=eafora

áforhtian _to be frightened_, _take fright_, _wonder at_, Æ.

á-fréfran, -fréfrian _to comfort_, _console_, _make glad_, CP. [frófor]

áfrem-dan, -dian _to alienate_, Æ : _become alienated_.

áfremðan (VPs)=áfremdan

áfremðung f. _alienation_, VHy 6[28].

áfréon _to deliver_, _free_, DR,LkR.

áfréoðan[2] _to froth_, LCD 45 b.

afslóg=ofslóg; **after**=æfter

áfúlian _to become foul_, _putrefy_, _rot_, _be corrupt_, _defiled_.

áfulic _perverse_, MtL. ['_awkly_']

áfulliend m. _fuller_, MkR 9[3].

áfunde rare wk. pret. 3 sg. of áfindan.

áfundennes f. _invention_, _device_, _discovery_, Æ.

áfýlan _to foul_, _stain_, _defile_, _corrupt_, CP; Æ. ['_afile_']

áfylgan (i[2]) _to pursue_, GEN 14[15].

áfyllan I. (w. g. or d.) _to fill_, _fill up_, _replenish_, _satisfy_, Æ; AO : _complete_, _fulfil_. ['_afill_'] II. (y;=ie) _to cause to fall_, _fell_, _beat down_, _overturn_, _subvert_, _demolish_, _abolish_, _Lk_; Æ : _slay_, _kill_. ['_afelle_']

áfyndan=áfindan; **áfyr-**=áfierr-, áfeor-

áfýran _to emasculate_. áfýred (CP), áfýrd pp. as sb. _eunuch_.

áfyrhtan _to frighten_, _terrify_, Æ,AO.

amel m. *sacred vessel*, WW 348. [*L.*]

āmelcan³ *to milk*, LCD.

āmeldian *to let out, make known, betray*, Æ,AO.

āmeltan³ v. āmolten.

ameos *bishop-weed*, LCD 71b. [*Gk.*]

amerian=hamorian

āmerian *to test, examine : purify, refine*, LCD.

āmerran=āmierran

āmetan⁵ *to measure, estimate : mete out, assign, grant, bestow*, Æ.

āmētan *to paint, depict*, CP : *adorn*, Æ.

āmetendlīc *compendious, measurable, limited*, LPs 38⁶. adv. -līce.

āmethwīl=æmethwīl

āmetsian *to provision*, CHR 1006 E.

āmiddan=onmiddan

āmiddian *to be foolish*, RHy 6⁶.

āmīdlian *to bridle*, ByH 56²⁷, WW 226³⁸.

āmierran (e, i, y) *to hinder, obstruct, prevent, delay*, CP : *mar, injure, disturb, scatter, consume, waste, spoil, destroy*, Lk, Bo; AO,CP : *lose*. ['amar']

āmigdal m. *almond*, LCD. [*Gk.*]

āmōd=æmōd

āmolcen pp. of āmelcan.

āmolsnian *to decay, weaken*, W 147²⁹.

āmolten *molten*, ÆL 5²³⁴.

amore=omer

am-pelle (o², u²) f. *flask, vessel*, Æ. [*L.*]

ampre I. '*varix,' tumour, swelling*, Gl. ['amper'] II. f. *dock, sorrel*, LCD.

āmundian *to protect, defend*, Æ.

āmyltan (tr.) *to melt*, Æ.

āmyrdrian (LL 348,56A)=āmyrðrian

āmyrgan *to delight, cheer*, SOL 240.

āmyrian=āmerian

āmyrran=(1) āmierran; (2) (LL 348,56G,B) āmyrðran

ā-myrðran, -myrðrian *to murder, kill*, LL; CHR 1049 c. ['amurder']

an I. adv. and prep.=on. II. pres. 1 sg. of unnan.

an- in composition represents (1) and-; (2) un-; (3) in-; (4) on-.

ān I. adj. strong mfn. (asm. ānne, ænne) 'ONE*,' Æ,Chr. in plur. *each, every one, all*. ān and (æfter) ān *one by one*. ānes hwæt *some single thing, a part* : a, an : *alone, sole, only*; in this sense it is used also in the weak form (sē āna; hē āna, AO,CP) and with a pl. : *lonely?* AN 258 : *singular, unique : single, each, every one, all* (gp. ānra) : *any*. II. adv. (also wk. āna) *alone, only*. on ān *continually, continuously, ever, in one, once for all, immediately*. ðæt ān *only that*. ān and ān *one by one*, Æ.

ana=heonu; āna v. ān.

ānad, ānæd†
einöde]

ānægled nai

anæl-=onæl

anæðelian=

ananbeam m

anawyrm m.

anbærnes=o

anbestingan⁸

anbid (=on-
AO,CP : *in*

±an-bidian (
w. g. *wait f*

anbīdstōw (o

±anbidung n
lay, OEG 3:

anbiht=amb

anbiscopod=

ānboren† ptc

anbringelle=

anbrōce (EL

anbrucol (=o

anbryrd-=on

anbūend m. *

anbūgan (AO

anbyhtscealc

anbȳme *mad*
WW 181³³.

+anbyrdan (
oppose, LL.

anbyrdnes f.

anbyrignes (=

ān-cenned (æ

ancer=ancor

an-clēow n.,

ancnāwan=o

ancor m. '*a*
Gk.]

an-cor, -cora
['anchor']

ancorbend (o

ancorlic *like*

ancorlīf n. *so*

ancorstōw f. *

ancorstreng (

ancra=ancor

āncra (a¹?)
WW; Æ. [

ancsum=ang

ancuman⁴ *to*

āncummum o

ancyn adj. *or*

āhryran (=īe) *to cause to fall*

āhrysian=āhrisian

ahse=asce; āhsian=āscian

aht, āht=eaht, āwiht; ahta=

āhte, āhton pret. 3 sg. and p

āhtes (=g. of āht) *of any acco*

āhtlīce *stoutly, manfully*, CHR

āhwā pron.. *any one*, LL.

āhwænan *to vex, grieve, affl* ['awhene']

āhwænne adv. *when, whene time, any time*, RB : *at all ti*

āhwǣr (ā, ē) *anywhere*, Bo,L. *time, ever, in any way*. ['ow*

āhwǣrgen=āhwergen

āhwǣt n. *anything*, CM 371.

āhwæðer (āwðer, āðer, āðor) *one, something; any one : anyt* and conj. *either*, AO,CP. a *either...or*, AO. ['OUTHER']

āhwanon=āhwonan; āhwǣr=

āhwelfan=āhwylfan

āhwēnan=āwēnan

āhweorfan³ (tr.) *to turn, turn a* (intr.) *turn aside, turn away*, ['awherf']

āhwēr=āhwǣr; āhwerfan=āh

āhwergen (æ²) *anywhere : in a*

āhwettan *to whet, excite, kindl out to, provide : reject.*

āhwider *in any direction, from a*

āhwierfan *to turn away, turn* CP.

āhwilc=æghwilc; āhwistlian v

āhwītian *to whiten*, BJPs 50⁹.

āhwonan *from any source, an* Bo.

āhwonne=āhwænne; āhwyder=

āhwylfan (e;=ie) *to cover ove subvert*, Æ : *roll to*, RWH 78¹ *up, loosen.*

āhwyrfan=āhwierfan

āhycgan† *to think out, devise.*

āhȳdan *to hide, conceal*, GD,W.

āhyldan=āhildan

āhyldendlīc *enclitic*, ÆGR 265¹.

āhyltan *to trip up*, PPs 139⁵.

āhȳran (ē) *to hire*, G.

āhyrd-=āhierd-

āhyrsian=āhrisian

āhyrstan (e²;=ie) *to roast, fry* BPs 101⁴.

āhyspan *to reproach*, LPs 101⁹.

āhȳðan (īe, ȳ) *to plunder, destr* EL,VPs. [hūð]

āīdan (ȳ)? '*eliminare*' (v. OEG

ā-īdlian, -īdlan, -īdelian *to be or m frustrate, empty, annul*, Æ,CP *be free from : deprive (of).* [īde

āfȳrida=āfȳred; āfyrran=āfierran

āfyrsian=āfeorsian

āfyrðan (i) *to remove*, LCD 1·294².

āfȳsan (intr.) *to hasten : inspire with longing*, BL : (tr.) *urge, impel, excite : drive, drive away*. [fūs]

āga m. *proprietor, owner*, GD 230¹¹.

āgǣlan *to hinder, keep back, preoccupy, detain, hold back, retard, delay*, AO : *neglect*, CP : *profane.*

āgǣlwan (e) *to terrify, astonish*, AO.

āgalan⁶ *to sound forth, sing, chant*, B,W.

āgald=āgeald pret. 3 sg. of āgieldan.

āgālian *to become slack*, CP 65¹⁸.

āgan I. (conj. Wt 546) *to own, possess, have, obtain*, An,Bo,Mt; AO,CP : *have control over, take charge of : give, give up, deliver, restore : have to pay, 'owe*,' Mt,Lk : have to do*, ANS 123·417. ā. ūt *find out, discover.* II. pret. 3 sg. of āginnan (onginnan). āgān (conj. v. gān) *to go, go by, pass (of time)*, Mk: *pass into possession (of inherited property)*, TC 486' : *occur, befall*, Æ : *come forth, grow*, Ps : *approach : lose strength.* of ā. *go away.* ['ago']

āgangan=āgān

āge f. *possessions, property*, SAT,BH 196¹⁸. [*ON.* eiga]

agēan=ongēan; āgehwǣr=æghwǣr

āgeldan I. †*to punish.* II.=āgieldan

āgelwan=āgǣlwan; āgēman=āgȳman

±āgen I. '*own,' proper, peculiar*, Æ,BH,G, Met,Sat; AO,CP,CHR : *proper* (gram.), ÆGR. ā. cyre *freewill*. āgnes ðonces *voluntarily, spontaneously.* II. n. *property*, LL : *own country.* III. pp. of āgan.

āgēn=ongēan

āgēnbewendan *to return*, G.

āgēncuman⁴ *to return*, Lk 8⁴⁰.

āgend m. *owner, possessor, master, lord*, LL. se ā. *the Lord*, B,Ex.

āgendfrēa I. m. *lord, owner.* II. f. *mistress?* GEN 2237.

āgendfrēo=āgendfrēa

āgendlīce *properly, as one's own : imperiously*, CP 145⁵ : *correctly*, v. MLR 17·165.

āgen-friga, -frige=āgendfrēa

āgēngehweorfan³ *to return*, Lk 2⁴³

āgēnhwyrfan (y;=ie) *to return*, Mk 6³¹

āgēniernan³ *to run against, meet*, Mk.

āgēnlædan *to lead back*, WW 91⁹.

āgēnlic *own : owed, due*, DR.

āgennama m. *proper name*, ÆGR 25¹⁶.

āgennes f. *property*, Æ.

āgēnsendan *to send back*, Lk.

āgenslaga m. *slayer of oneself, suicide*, Æ.

āgēnstandan⁶ *to press, urge*, Lk.

āgenung=āgnung

āgēode=āēode pret. 3 sg. of āgān.

āgeolwian *to become yellow*, LCD,W.

āgēomrian *to mourn, grieve*, GD.

āgeornan (=ie) *to desire, be eager for*, GD 205¹⁹.

āgēotan² *to pour out, pour forth, shed*, An, MtL; CP : *melt, found* (of images) : *destroy : deprive (of)*, JUD 32. ['ageten']

āgētan=āgītan

āgiefan⁵ (eo, i, y) *to give, impart, deliver, give up, yield, relinquish*, Mt : *restore, return, repay, pay*, AO. eft ā. *give back, return.* ['agive']

āgieldan³ (e, i, y) *to pay, repay, compensate, yield, restore, reward*, AO : *offer oneself, offer up* (as a sacrifice) : *perform* (an office), Æ : *allow : to punish?* PH 408.

āgīemelēasian (i, y) *to neglect, despise*, CP. āgīemelēasod *neglectful, careless*, NC 337.

āgīeta=āgīta; āgīfan (AO,CP)=āgiefan

āgīfan *to bestow, grant*, DR 124¹⁹

āgift=ægift; āgildan (CP)=āgieldan

āgilde=ægilde

āgiltan=āgyltan

āgīemelēasian (C)=āgīemelēasian

āgimmed *set with precious stones*, Æ.

āginnan=onginnan

āgīta m. *prodigal, spendthrift*, CP.

āgītan (y²) *to find, find out*, RB,W.

āgītan (ē;=īe) *to waste, destroy*, Chr. ['aget']

āglāchād m. *state of misery*, RD 54⁵.

āg-lǣc, -lāc† n. *trouble, distress, oppression, misery, grief.*

āglǣca† (ē) m. *wretch, monster, demon, fierce enemy.*

āglǣccræft (āc-) m. *evil art*, AN 1364.

āglǣcwīf n. *female monster*, B 1259.

āglǣdan? *to cause to slip.* v. AB 19·163.

āglēca=āglǣca

āglīdan¹ *to glide, slip, stumble*, LCD,WW.

agn-=angn-

āgnere m. *owner*, ÆGR 110¹⁹.

āgnes=āgenes gmn. of āgen adj.

āgnett n. *interest, usury*, LkL 19²³ (or ? āgnettung, v. ES 42·163).

āgnettan *to appropriate*, GL.

±āgnian *to 'own,'* MtL,Rd : *claim : appropriate, usurp*, Bo; CP : *make over (to)*, Æ : *dedicate, adopt*, CP : *enslave*, Ex.

āgnīdan¹ *to rub off*, WW 386¹⁶.

āgniden I. f. *rubbing*, GL? (v. A 31·533). II. *used, threadbare*, WW 220²⁴.

āgniend (āh) m. *owner, possessor*, GEN 14²².

±āgniendlīc *possessive, genitive* (case), ÆGR.

+āgnod *own*, CP 262²³.

āgnung f. *owning, ownership, possession : claim, declaration or proof of ownership :* (+) *acquisition*, KC 2·304⁵.

āgotenes f. *effusion, shedding*, Æ,LCD.

ágrafan⁶ *to carve,* ...
  grave, inscribe, ...
ágrafenlic *sculptu*...
ágrápian *to grasp* ...
ágrétan (oe) *to a*...
agrimonia '*agrim*...
ágrísan¹ (ý) *to qu*...
ágrówen *overgrow*...
ágrymetian *to rag*...
ágrýndan *to desce*...
ágrýsan=ágrísan
agu f. *magpie,* W...
Agus-tus, -tes (A...
ágyf-, ágyld-=ági...
ágylpan³ (=ie) *to* ...
ágyltan *to offend,* ...
  ['*aguilt*']
ágyltend m. *debto*...
ágylting f. *guilt, o*...
ágyltnes f. *guilt,* N...
ágýman (é;=íe) *t*...
ágýmeléasian=ági...
ágýmmed=ágimm...
ágytan=ágitan
ah (AO,CP)=ac (...
áh pres. 3 sg. of á...
áhabban *to restr*...
  (*fram*), BH : *su*...
áhaccian *to pick o*...
áhæbban=áhebba...
áhældan=áhildan...
áhafennes f. *rising*...
áhalsian *to implor*...
áhangian *to hang,* ...
áhátan *to name,* M...
áhátian *to become* ...
áhealdan⁷ (=on-) ...
áhealtian *to limp,* ...
áheardian *to be or b*...
  inured, CP : *end*...
áheardung f. *harde*...
áhéawan⁷ *to cut o*...
  cut wood into pla...
áhebban⁶ (occl. wh...
  áhefed) (often w....
  raise, exalt, erec...
  remove : support, ...
áhebbian=áebbian...
áhefegian (CP), -...
  heavy, oppress : b...
áheld (VPs)=áhild...
áhellian? *to cove*...
  OEG 5410.
áhelpan³ *to help, s*...
áhénan *to humble* ...
  [híenan; héan]
áheolorian *to weigh*...
áhéran=áhýran
áherian *to praise,* ...

álétan=álætan; **áléðran**=álýðran
alewe, al(u)we f. '*aloe*,' Jn,Lcd.
áléwed ptc. *feeble, weak, ill,* RB51¹⁶. [léf]
alexandre f. *horse-parsley,* Lcd. ['*alexanders*']
alfæle (AN770)=ealfelo
álfæt n. *cooking vessel, cauldron,* LL. [ælan]
álgeweorc n. *fire-making, tinder,* GL.
algian=ealgian; **alh**=ealh
álibban *to live, pass one's life,* AO.
áliccan⁵ *to be subdued, fail, cease, yield, perish,* AO.
áliefan (é, í, ý) *to allow, give leave to, grant,* AO,CP : *hand over, yield up.*
áliefedlic *lawful, permissible.* adv. -líce (Æ,CP).
áliesan (é, í, ý) *to loosen, let loose, free, redeem, release, absolve,* Mt; AO,CP. ['*alese*']
álies-ednes (*Mt*), -(e)nes (*Cr,MtLR*) (é, ý) f. *redemption, ransom : remission (of sins),* ERHy9⁷⁷. ['*alese(d)ness*']
áliesend (é, í, ý) m. *liberator, deliverer, Redeemer,* CP.
áliesendlic (ý) *loosing, liberating,* BH.
áliesendnes=áliesednes
áliesing, -liesnes=áliesednes
álíf=ælíf
álífan=áliefan; **álíflan**=álibban
álíh (DR) imperat. sg. of áléon.
álíhtan I. *to lighten, relieve, alleviate, take off, take away,* CP,LL : '*alight*,' ÆGr. II. *to light up,* Æ,Met (=onlihtan).
álimpan³† *to occur, happen.*
álinnan=álynnan; **álísend**=áliesend
álíðian (eo) *to detach, separate,* Gen : *set free.* ['*alithe*']
all (strictly Anglian, but found in AO,CP) =eal, eall
almes-=ælmes-; **aln-**=ealn-
alo-=ealu-
áloccian *to entice,* AO.
alor, al(e)r m. '*alder*,' Gl,KC,Lcd; Mdf.
alorbedd (ælr-) *alder bed,* KC5·153'.
alordrenc m. *drink made of alder sap?* Lcd40a.
alorholt nm. *alder-wood,* WW.
alorrind m. *alder-bark,* Lcd12b.
aloð=ealu; **alr**=alor; **alswá**=ealswá
alter, altar(e), altre m. '*altar*,' G; CP. [L.]
álúcan² *to pluck up, pull out, separate, take away,* GD.
álútan² (=onl-) *to bend, incline, bend or bow down,* Æ. áloten pp. *submissive.*
aluwe, alwe=alewe; **alwald-**=eal(l)weald-
álýbban=álibban; **álýfan** (Æ)=áliefan
álýfed I.=áliefed pp. of áliefan. II.=áléfed pp. of áléfian; **álýfed-**=áliefed-
álýht-=onlíht-; **ályhtan**=álíhtan

---

and (e) conj. '*AND*' : *but : or,* LL2·13. gelíce and...*like as if*...AO.
and-=an-, on-, ond- (*opposition, negation*; Ger. ent-); and occasionally a-.
anda m. *grudge, enmity, envy, anger, vexation,* Mt; Æ : *zeal,* Æ,CP : *injury, mischief : fear, horror,* NG. ['*ande*,' '*onde*']
andæge† *for one day, lasting a day.*
andæt-=andet-
ándaga m. *appointed day,* Æ.
±ándagian *to fix a day for appearance : adjourn,* EC163'.
andb-=anb-, onb-
andbícnian *to make signs to,* WW378³ (andbét-).
andbita m. *feast (of unleavened bread),* WW.
andcléow=ancléow
andcweðan '*contradicere, frustrari*,' HGl 491.
andcwiss f. *answer,* Gu992.
andcýðnes f. *evidence,* BH158⁵.
andd-=and-, ond-; **ande**=ende
andéages (æ) *eye to eye, openly?* B1935.
andéaw *arrogant, ostentatious,* Sc.
andefn, -efen f. *measure, quantity, amount,* AO : *capacity, nature,* CP.
andel-bær, -bære *reversed,* OEG.
andergilde *in repayment, in compensation,* Pr41.
andet-=andett-
andetla m. *declaration, confession,* LL18,22.
±andetnes (ond- CP) f. *confession,* Æ : *thanksgiving, praise.*
andetta (o¹, æ²) m. *one who confesses,* Bl, LL. a. béon *to acknowledge.*
±andettan *to confess, acknowledge,* Æ,CP : *give thanks or praise : promise, vow.* [and, hátan]
andettere m. *one who confesses,* Æ,CHRD.
andettian=andettan
andettung m. *confession, profession,* CP.
andfang n. *acceptance,* WW.
andfangol '*susceptor*,' LPs45¹².
ándfealdlíce=ánfealdlíce
andfeax *bald,* W46¹.
andfeng (on-) m. *seizing, receiving, taking,* Æ,RB : *defence : defender : attack, assault : revenue, means,* Lk14²⁸,Bk10 : *illegal occupation (of land).*
andfenga m. *receiver, defender, undertaker,* Ps.
andfenge I. (anf-, onf-) *acceptable, agreeable, approved, fit, suitable,* Æ,CP : *that can receive : taken.* II. m. *undertaker, helper,* PPs.
andfengend m. *helper, defender,* PPs : *receiver.* gafoles a. *tax collector.*
andfengnes f. *acceptance, receiving : receptacle : acceptableness,* W253³¹.

---

andfengstów f. *receptacle,* CHRD109³.
andfex=andfeax; **andgelóman**=andlóman
andget=andgit
andgete *plain, manifest,* CR1243. [andgiete]
andgit (ond-; e, i, y) n., andgiete f. *understanding, intellect,* Mt; Æ,CP : *knowledge, perception,* CP : *sense, meaning,* Æ,CP : *one of the five senses : plan, purpose.* ['*angit*']
andgietful (e,i,y) *intelligent, sensible,* RB,W.
andgietfullic (i,y) *intelligible, clear,* ÆGr4¹¹. adv. -líce, CP.
andgietléas (i) *foolish, senseless,* Æ.
andgietléast (i,y) f. *want of understanding,* Æ.
andgietlic (i) *intelligible, clear,* AS5¹⁶. adv. -líce, WW.
andgiettácen n. *sensible token, sign,* GEN 1539.
andgit=andgiet
andgitol *intelligent, sensible,* RB,WW.
andhéafod n. *heading, unploughed headland of a field,* EC.
andhetan, andhettan=andettan
andhweorfan³ *to move against, blow against,* B548. [or ? onhweorfan]
andian *to be envious or jealous,* Æ.
andiendlíce *enviously,* TF108¹⁸.
andig *envious, jealous,* OEG.
andláman=andlóman
andlang (o¹, o²) I. adj. *entire, continuous, extended.* andlangne dæg, niht *all day (night) long,* An,Gu. ['*along*'] II. prep. w. g. '*along*,' *by the side of,* Æ,Chr,KC; AO.
andlangcempa (anl-) *soldier fighting in line,* WW450¹⁸.
andlanges adv. prep. *along,* Ct.
andlata (CR1436)=andwlita
andléan† n. *retribution, retaliation.*
and-leofen (ie, i, y) f., -leofa m. *nourishment, food : money, wages.* [libban]
andlícnes=onlícnes
andliefen (AO,CP), andlifen=andleofen
andlóman (á², u²) m. pl. *utensils, implements, vessels,* GL.
andlong=andlang; **andlyfen**=andleofen
andmitta=anmitta; **andrædlíce**=undrædlíce
Andréasmæsse f. *St Andrew's day* (30 Nov.), ÆGr43¹¹. [v. '*mass*']
andrecefæt? n. *wine or oil press,* WW 123³⁷.
andribb n. '*pectusculum*,' *breast,* ExC29²⁶,²⁷
andriesne=ondrysne
an-drysen-, -drysn-=ondrys(e)n-
andsaca†‡ m. *adversary : denier, apostate.*
andsacian *to dispute, deny,* CP.
andsæc m. *denial, oath of purgation,* El,LL : *refusal : strife, resistance.* ['*andsech*']

andsǣte adj. *hateful, odious, repugnant,*
ÆGr : *hostile.* ['*andsete*']
andslyht† (=ie) m. *blow,* B (hond-).
andspurnan³ (y) *to stumble against,* NG.
andspurnes (y) f. *offence,* MtR.
āndstreces=ānstreces
and-sumnes, -sundnes (=on-) f. *purity,*
chastity, virginity. v. OEG 1696.
±andswarian *to '* answer,' *Lk*; Æ,CP.
andswaru f. '*answer*,' *reply,* B,*Jn*; CP.
and-swerian (VPs), -sworian=andswarian
andsȳn=ansīen
andtimber (y²)=ontimber
andŏr-=onŏr-
andung f. *jealousy,* LPs 77⁵⁸.
andūstrian *to deny (with oaths),* MtR 26⁷⁴.
andūstrung f. '*abominatio,*' MtR 24¹⁵.
andwǣscan=ādwǣscan
andward-=andweard-
andweal-=onweal-
±andweard *present, actual, existing,* Æ,CP :
opposite to.
±andweardian *to present, bring before one.*
(+andweardian also=andwyrdian.)
andweardlic *present, actual.* adv. -līce.
andweardnes f. *presence,* CP : *present time,*
BH : *dispensation,* W 243²⁵.
andwendednes=onwendednes
andweorc n. *matter, substance, material,* CP :
cause.
andwerd=and-weard, -wyrd
andwīg m. *resistance,* GU 147.
andwille=ānwille
andwirdan=andwyrdan
andwīs *expert, skilful,* JUL 244.
andwīsnes f. *experience,* WW 20⁵.
andwist f. *support,* AN 1542.
andwlata=andwlita
+andwlatod *shameless,* OEG 8³⁶⁵.
andwlita (a, eo) m. *face, forehead, counte-*
nance, form, B,*MtR*; AO,CP. ['*anleth*']
andwlite n.=andwlita
andwliteful '*vultuosus*,' GPH 393.
andwrāð *hostile, enraged,* PA 17.
andwreðian (?=āwr-) *to support,* CHRD 62²⁹.
and-wurd, -wyrd=andweard
±and-wyrdan, -wyrdian (e, i) *to answer,*
Æ,*AO,Mt*; CP. ['*andwurde*']
andwyrde n. *answer,* AO.
andwyrding f. *conspiracy,* WW 373¹¹.
andyde pret. of andōn (ondōn).
andytt-=andett-
āne=(1) ǣne, (2) heonu
ān-ēage, -ē(a)gede (*ÆL*) '*one-eyed,*' *blind*
of one eye.
ānecge adj. *having one edge,* WW 142³⁷.
+āned v.+ānian.
ānēge, ānēgede=ānēage
ānēhst=ānīhst

ānemnan *to announce, declare, Gu.* ['*aname*']
ānerian *to deliver, rescue,* LPs 24¹⁵; EPs 49²².
ānes=ǣnés; ānescian=āhnescian
ānett mn., ānetnes f. *solitude, seclusion,* CP.
anf-=onf-
ān-feald, -fald, -fealdlic *single, unmixed,*
unique, superior, CP : *simple, modest,*
honest, sincere, Mt; CP : *fixed, invariable* :
singular (gram.), *ÆGr.* ā. gerecednes *or*
sprǣc *prose.* ['*afald*'] adv. -līce.
ānfealdnes f. *unity, concord,* AO : *simplicity,*
CP.
anfealt f. *anvil,* OEG 11⁶⁷ and n. [cp. anfilte]
anfeng=andfeng
ānfēte *one-footed,* RD 59¹.
an-filt (*Æ*), -filte (*Gl*), n. '*anvil.*'
anfindan=onfindan
ānfloga m. *lonely flier,* SEAF 62.
anfōn (AO)=onfōn
anforht *fearful,* CROSS 117.
ānforlǣtan⁷ *to let go, lose, relinquish, aban-*
don, surrender, CP : *omit, neglect.*
ānforlǣtnes f. *loss, desertion,* BL 85' :
intermission.
anforngean *in front of,* RWH 45¹².
anga (o) m. *stimulus, sting, goad,* CP.
ānga† (ǣ, ē) *sole, only* : *solitary.*
angbrēost n. *tightness of the chest, asthma,*
LCD.
ange=enge
angeald pret. 3 sg. of angildan.
angēan=ongēan
angel I. m. '*angle,*' *hook, fish-hook, Bo,*
MtL (ongul). II. m.=engel
Angel n. *Anglen, a district in Schleswig,*
from which the Angles came, AO.
Angelcynn n. *the English people* : *England,*
AO.
āngeld=āngilde
Angelfolc n. *the English people,* BH 472¹⁷.
angelic *like, similar,* Bo 44¹⁸.
angeltwicce fm. *a certain worm used as bait,*
earthworm? Lcd,*WW.* ['*angletwitch*']
Angelðeod f. *the English people* : *England.*
Angelwitan (o²) mp. *English councillors,*
LL 236 G 2.
āngenga I. *solitary, isolated,* Æ. II. m.
solitary goer, isolated one, B.
angerǣd=ungerād
āngetrum n. *illustrious company,* Ex 334.
angeweald=onweald
±anglan *to be in anguish,* RPs 60³; 142⁴.
anglen=anginn; angil=angel I.
angildan=ongieldan
āngilde (e, y) I. n. *single payment or rate of*
compensation for damage, LL : *the fixed price*
at which cattle and other goods were received
as currency, LL. ['*angild*'] II. adj. *to be*
compensated for. III. adv. *simply, only,* LL.

ângildes=ângilde III.
anginn n. *beginning, Æ*; AO,CP : *intention, design, enterprise, undertaking,* CP : *action, onset, attack* : *rising (of sun)* : *tip (of finger),* Bᴀ154⁶. [*' angin'*]
anginnan (AO)=onginnan
angitan=ongietan; **angitful**=andgietful
Angle mp. *the Angles or English* (v. Angel).
angmôd *sad, sorrowful,* Æ,RB.
angmôdnes f. *sadness, sorrow,* W188⁶.
angnægl m. *corn,* '*agnail,*' Lcd30b.
angnere (on-) m. *corner of the eye,* WW 423³⁴.
angnes f. *anxiety, trouble, pain, fear,* Lᴄᴅ, Ps.
angol-=angel-
angrisla (y) m. *terror,* Bʟ203⁷.
angrislic (y²) *grisly, terrible.* adv. -(en)lice.
ang-set, -seta m. *eruption, pustule, carbuncle,* WW.
angsum *narrow, hard, difficult.* adv. -sume.
±angsumian *to vex, afflict,* Æ.
angsumlic *troublesome, painful,* RB5¹⁹. adv. -lice, Æ.
angsumnes f. *pain,* Æ : *sorrow, trouble* : *difficulty, perplexity.*
ângum=ænigum dat. of ænig.
ângyld, ângylde=ângilde
angyn, angytan=anginn, ongietan
anh-=onh-
ânhaga (o²)† m. *solitary being, recluse.*
anhende (=on-) *on hand, requiring attention,* AO88²⁴.
ânhende *one-handed, lame, weak,* Æ.
ânhîwe '*uniformis,*' OEG1046.
anhoga m. *care, anxiety,* Gᴜ970.
ânhoga=ânhaga
ânhorn, ânhorna m. *unicorn,* Ps.
ânhrædlîce=ânrædlîce
ânhundwintre *a hundred years old,* Gᴇɴ 47⁹.
ânhýdig† *resolute, firm, constant, stubborn, brave.*
ânhyrne I. m. *unicorn.* **II.**=ânhyrned
ânhyrn-ed, -e(n)de *having one horn,* Ps.
+ânian *to unite,* BH214⁹. [*' one'* vb.]
ânîdan (ê, ŷ;=îe) *to restrain, repel* : *force.* ût a. *expel, drive out.* [nîed]
ânig=ænig; **ân-îge,** -îgge=ânêage
anîhst (=îe) *last, in the last place,* Wɪᴅ 126.
ânîman⁴ (y) *to take,* GD : *take away or from, deprive of, Mt*; CP. [*' anim'*]
âninga=ânunga
ânîôrian *to cast down,* Cʜʀ675ᴇ.
anl-=andl-, onl-; **anlǣc**=anlêc
±ânlǣcan *to unite,* ÆL : *collect,* ÆL.
ânlaga *acting alone,* WW491²³.
anlang-=andlang-; **ânlâp-** (NG)=ânlîp-

anlêc (on-) m. *respect, regard, Æ.*
ânlegere *consorting with one man,* WW 171¹⁵.
ân-lêp-=ânlî(e)p-
ânlic '*only,*' *unique, Lk* : *solitary, Ps* : *catholic* : *beautiful.* [cp. ænlic]
+anlician=+onl-
ân-lîepig, -lîpig (Cʜʀ), lîpe (CP), -lîpie (æn-; ê, ŷ) **I.** adj. *single, separate, solitary, private, individual, special,* PPs,BH, MtR. [*' anlepi,*' '*onlepy'*] **II.** adv. *alone, only, severally.*
ânlîpnes (on-, ê², ŷ²) f. *loneliness,* BH128²³.
ânlîpum (ê²) *singly,* MtR26²².
ânlŷp-=ânlî(e)p-
+anmêdan *to encourage,* AO. [môd]
ânmêde n. *unanimity, concord,* PPs54¹³.
anmêdla m. *pomp, glory* : *pride, presumption, arrogance* : *courage.* [môd]
anmitta m. *weight, balance, scales,* Gʟ. [and, mitta]
ânmôd *of one mind, unanimous, El*; Æ : *steadfast, resolute, eager, bold, brave, fierce, proud,* CP. [*' anmod'*] adv. -lice.
ânmôdnes f. *unity, unanimity,* CP: *steadfastness, resolution,* Lᴄᴅ3·170²².
ann pres. 3 sg. of unnan.
anna=heonu; **ânne** (AO,CP) v. ân.
ânnes f. *oneness, unity, BH*; Æ : *agreement, covenant, Chr* : *solitude, Gu.* [*' annesse'*]
ânnihte adv. *one day old,* Lᴄᴅ.
anoða=anda
ânpæð† m. *narrow path.*
anpolle f. (Æ)=ampella; **anr-**=onr-
ânrǣd *of one mind, unanimous* : *constant, firm, persevering, resolute, Æ.* [*' anred'*]
ânrǣdlic *constant, resolute* : *undoubting,* Bʟ13¹³. adv. -lice *unanimously* : *resolutely, persistently, constantly, earnestly,* Æ : *definitely, decidedly.*
ânrǣdnes f. *unanimity, agreement* : *constancy, firmness, diligence, AO*; Æ. [*' anrednesse'*]
ânreces (Cʜʀ1010ᴄᴅᴇ)=ânstreces
ânrêd-=ânrǣd-; **anribb**=andribb; **ans-**= ands-, ons-, uns-
an-scêatan (Cp), -scêotan (Erf)=onscêotan
ânseld n. *lonely dwelling, hermitage,* Gᴜ 1214.
ânsetl n. *hermitage,* RB135⁹.
ânsetla m. *anchorite, hermit,* GD,RB.
ansîen I. (on-; ê, î, ŷ) fn. *countenance, face,* CP,G : *form, figure, presence* : *view, aspect, sight, thing seen,* AO : *surface.* [*' onsene'*] **II.†** f. *lack, want.*
ansîene (on-, ŷ²)† *visible.*
anspel n. *conjecture,* WW382⁵.
anspilde *salutary,* Lᴄᴅ11b.
ânsprǣce *speaking as one,* PPs40⁷.

ānstandende ptc. *standing alone*, RB9[7]. as sb. *hermit*, Æ.

ānstapa m. *lonely wanderer*, PA15.

ānstelede *one-stalked, having one stem*, LCD.

ānstīg f. *narrow path? path up a hill?* (GBG) KC.

ānstonde=ānstandende

ānstræc (ǣ?) *resolute, determined*, CP.

ānstreces (ē?) *at one stretch, continuously, continually*, CHR894A.

ansund *sound, whole, entire, perfect, healthy*, Æ (on-) : *solid*, BF80[26].

an-sundnes, -sumnes f. *soundness, wholeness, integrity*.

ānswēge *harmonious, accordant*, WW129[44].

ansȳn=ansīen; ant-=and-, ont-, unt-

Antecrist m. *Antichrist*. [*L.*]

antefn m. *antiphon, 'anthem,'* BH; Æ.

antefnere (CM), antemnere (ÆP154[6]) m. *book of antiphons*.

āntīd (and-?) f. *similar time?* (*i.e.* the corresponding time of a following day) *appropriate time?* (Klb.) B219.

antifon=antefn

antre f. *radish*, LCD.

ānum *alone, solely*, Æ.

anunder=onunder

anung f. *zeal*, NG.

ānunga (i[2]) *at once, forthwith : quickly, shortly : entirely, altogether, throughout, by all means, uninterruptedly*, B : *necessarily, certainly*.

anw-=andw-, onw-, unw-

anwedd n. *security, pledge*, TC201[16].

ānwīg n. *single combat, duel*, Æ,AO.

ānwīglīce *in single combat*, WW512[21].

ānwiht=āwiht

ānwille I. adj. *wilful, obstinate*, CP, WW; Æ. ['*onwill*'] II. adv. *wilfully, obstinately*.

ānwillīce *obstinately*, CP.

ānwilnes f. *self-will, obstinacy, persistence*, CP. mid ānwilnesse *wantonly, wilfully*.

ānwintre adj. *one year old, yearling*, Ex12[5].

ānwīte n. *single fine*, LL64,31[1].

anwlōh (DAN585)=onwealg?

ānwuht=āwiht

ānwunung f. *solitary abode*, RB134[12].

ānwylnes=ānwilnes

+anwyrdan *to conspire*, WW209[42].

+anwyrde *known, acknowledged, confessed*.

anxsum-=angsum-

ānȳdan=ānīdan; anȳhst=anīhst

ānyman=āniman; anȳwan=onȳwan

apa m. '*ape,*' Gl,Lcd.

āpǣcan *to seduce, lead astray*, LL.

āparian *to discover, apprehend*, G,EC164[17].

apelder-=apuldor-

āpinsian *to weigh, estimate, ponder, recount*, CP. [*L.* pensare]

āpinsung f. *weighing*, OEG1757.

apl=appel

āplantian *to plant*, ÆH.

āplatod *beaten into (metal) plates*, OEG. [v. '*plate*']

āpluccian *to pluck, gather*, ÆGR170[14],BF 198[21].

apostata m. *apostate*, LL (322[14]).

apostol (CHR), apostel m. *messenger*, JnL : '*apostle,*' MtR : *disciple*, ÆH1[520]. [*L.* from Gk.]

apostolhād† m. *apostleship*.

apostolic *apostolic*, BH; Æ. ['*apostly*']

appel, apple=æppel

Aprelis m. *April*, BF,MEN56.

āpriccan *to prick*, W146[21].

Aprilis (BF84)=Aprelis

aprotane f. *southernwood, wormwood*, LCD 22a. [*L.* abrotonum; from Gk.]

apulder, apuldor fm. *apple-tree*, LCD,WW.

apuldorrind f. *bark of apple-tree*, LCD.

apuldortūn (e[3]) m. *apple-orchard*, WW.

apuldre, apuldur=apulder

āpullian *to pull*, LCD1·362[10].

āpundrian? *to measure out, requite?* (GK) : *estimate?* (BTac), EL580.

āpyffan *to exhale, breathe out*, GL.

āpyndrian *to weigh*, HGL512[78] (āwynd-?).

āpȳtan *to put out (eyes)*, NC338.

ār m. I.† *messenger, servant, herald, apostle, angel*. [Got. airus] II. f. '*oar,*' Chr,Gn. III. f. *honour, worth, dignity, glory, respect, reverence*, BH,Gen,JnLR,Ph; AO, CP : *grace, favour, prosperity, benefit, help*, B : *mercy, pity, An* : *landed property, possessions, revenue*, Æ,AO : *ecclesiastical living, benefice* : *ownership*, LL : *privilege*, LL,76,42[2]. ['*are,*' '*ore*'] IV. n. '*ore,*' *brass, copper*, Æ,BH,CP,G,PS; AO. V. (NG)=ǣr

āracsian=ārasian

ārǣcan wv. *to reach, get at*, Chr : *hold forth, reach out*, Æ : *get (a thing for a person)*, ÆGr. ['*areach*']

ārǣd I. (ē) m. *welfare*, LL184n. II. *prepared, resolute, determined*, WA5; GNE 192?

arǣda (Bo46[22])=aroda? v. arod.

ārǣdan[1] (but usu. wk.) *to appoint, prepare* : *arrange, settle, decide*, BH : *guess, prophesy, interpret, utter*, Lk,Bo,Da,CP : *read, read out, read to (any one)*, CP. ['*aread*']

ārǣdnes (ē[2]) f. *condition, stipulation*, BH.

ārǣfan *to set free, unwrap*, WW.

ārǣfn-an, -ian *to carry out, accomplish* : *endure, suffer*, Æ,AO : *keep in mind, ponder*, Æ. [æfnan]

ārǣfniendlic *endurable, possible*, WW.

ārǣman *to raise, elevate (oneself)*, Æ : (†) *rise, stand up*.

āræpsan (*-ræf-) *to intercept*, GL.
ārǣran *to lift up, raise, set up, create, establish, An,Chr,Jn* : *build, erect, Jn* : *rear (swine)*, LL449 : *spread, disseminate* : *disturb, upset*. ūp ā. *bring up, raise up, exalt, CP*. ['*arear*']
ārǣrend m. *one who arouses*, DHy18¹⁵.
ārǣrnes f. *raising, elevation*, AO.
ārǣsan *to rush*, ÆH140¹³.
ārāflan *to unravel, disentangle*, CP.
ārāsian *to lay open, search out, test, detect, discover* : *reprove, correct*, CP : *suspect*, BHo256²⁹. ārāsod *skilled*, Bf94¹.
ārblæd n. *oar-blade*, Æ.
arblast m. *cross-bow*, CHR1079D. [*O.Fr.* arbaleste]
arc mf. (also earc, earce) *ark, coffer, chest, box*, Æ. [*L.* arca]
arce I. (æ, e) m. *archiepiscopal pallium*, CHR. II. f. (Bf192³³)=arc
arcebiscop (æ¹, e¹, y³, e⁴, eo⁴) m. '*archbishop*,' CP,Chr,KC.
arcebiscopdōm m. *post of archbishop*, CHR 616.
arcebiscophād (eo) m. *post of archbishop*, BH49²³.
arcebiscoprīce n. '*archbishopric*,' *post of archbishop, Chr*.
arcebiscopstōl m. *archiepiscopal see*, CHR.
arcediacon m. '*archdeacon*,' WW.
arcehād (e) m. *post of archbishop*, ÆH.
arcerīce n. *archbishopric*, CHR1051.
arcestōl (æ¹) m. *archiepiscopal see*, CHR.
ārcræftig *respected, honourable*, DA551.
ārdǣde *merciful*, BL131².
ārdagas mp. *festival days*, WW206³¹.
ardlic=arodlic; āre f.=ār III.
āréaflan *to separate, divide*, Ex290.
āreccan *to spread out, put forth, stretch out: lift up, erect, build up* : *say, relate, declare, speak out, explain, expound, translate, CP,G* : *astonish* : *adorn? deck?* RIM10. ['*arecche*']
ārēceléasian *to be negligent, neglect*, A9·102⁶⁸, VH,WYN66.
ared=arod
ārēd=ārǣd
āreddan=āhreddan
āredian *to make ready, devise, provide, arrange, carry out*, CP : *find, find one's way, reach* : *find out, understand*. [rǣde]
ārēfnan=ārǣfnan
ārendan *to tear off*, LCD101a.
ārengan *to make proud, exalt*, A11·117³²? (? arencan, BTs).
ārēodian *to redden, blush: put to shame*, RPs69⁴.
ārēosan=āhrēosan; ārēran=ārǣran
ārētan *to cheer, gladden*, Æ. [rot]

arewe=arwe
ārfæst *respected, honest, pious, virtuous*, Æ, CP : *merciful, gracious, compassionate*, Æ : *respectful*.
ārfæstlic *pious*, DR,RWH94¹⁴. adv. -līce.
ārfæstnes f. *virtue, honour, grace, goodness, piety* : *pity, mercy*, Æ;
ārfæt nap. -fatu, n. *brazen vessel*, Æ.
ārfest=ārfæst
ārful *respected, venerable* : *favourable, kind, merciful* : *respectful*. adv. -līce *graciously*, Æ.
arg (NG)=earg; argang=earsgang
ārgeblond=ēargebland
argentille f. *argentilla (plant)*, GL. [L.]
ārgēotere m. *brass-founder*, AO54²⁰.
ārgesweorf n. *brass filings*, LCD30b.
ārgeweorc n. *brass-work*, WW398²⁴.
ārgifa m. *giver of benefits*, CRAFT11.
arhlice=earglice
ārhwæt *eager for glory*, †CHR937A.
±ārian *to honour, respect*, Æ,CP : *endow* : *regard, care for, favour, be merciful to, spare, pardon*, Æ; CP. ['*are*']
ārīdan¹ *to ride*, AO118³³.
āriddan=āhreddan
āri(g)end mf. *benefactor, benefactress*, LCD, W257⁴.
āriht '*aright*,' *properly*, LL.
ārīman *to number, count, enumerate*, CP; AO : *relate*. ['*arime*']
ārinnan³ *to run out, pass away*, SOL479.
ārīsan I. (sv¹) *to* '*ARISE*,' *get up*, Æ,CP : *rise* : *spring from, originate* : *spring up, ascend*. II.=+rīsan I.
ārist=ǣrist
ārlēas *dishonourable, base, impious, wicked*, Æ,CP : *cruel*, JUL4. [*Ger.* ehrlos] adv. -līce Æ.
ārlēasnes f. *wickedness*, BH,Bo.
ārlēast f. *disgraceful deed*, MET.
ārlic I. *honourable* : *fitting, agreeable, proper*, AO : *delicious*. II.=ǣrlic
ārlīce adv. I. *honourably, becomingly, graciously, kindly, pleasantly, mercifully*, CP. II. (RG)=ǣrlice
ārloc n. '*oarlock*,' *rowlock*, WW288⁶.
arm=earm
armelu '*harmala*,' *wild rue*, Lcd.
ārmorgen=ǣrmorgen
arn pret. 3 sg. of iernan. arn-=earn-
arod (wk. aroda) *quick, bold, ready*, CP.
ārod pp. of ārian.
arodlic *quick*. adv. -līce *quickly: vigorously*, Æ,CP.
arodnes f. *spirit, boldness*, CP41¹⁷.
arodscipe m. *energy, dexterity*, CP.
ārōm? *copperas*, LCD (v. MLR17·165).
aron (NG) used as pres. pl. of wesan.

ārsāpe f. *verdigris*, Lcd 3·14[31]. [sāpe]
ārscamu f. *shame, modesty*, PPs 68[19].
ārsmið m. *coppersmith*, WW 99[3].
ārstæf† m. (often in pl.) *support, assistance, kindness, benefit, grace.*
art, arð (NG)=eart, pres. 2 sg. of wesan.
ārðegn m. *servant*, BH 378[11].
ārðing n. *a thing of value*, LkR 21[1].
arud=arod
ārung f. *honour, respect, reverence*, AO : *pardon.*
ārunnen=āurnen, pp. of ārinnan.
arwe (rew-, ruw-) f. '*arrow*,' *An,Chr.*
ārwela v. ēarwela
ār-weorð, -weorðe *honourable, venerable, revering, pious*, CP. adv. -weorðe.
ārweorðful (u[2]) *honourable*, Æ.
±ārweorðian (u[2], y[2]) *to honour, reverence, worship, extol.*
ārweorðlic *venerable, honourable.* adv. -līce *reverentially, solemnly, kindly*, Æ. ['*ar-worthly*']
ārweorðnes f. *reverence, honour*, CP.
ārweorðung (y[2]) f. *honour*, Ps.
ārwesa *respected*, RB 115[20].
+ārwierðan? (y[2]) *to honour*, LkL 6[34] (BTs).
ārwierðe=ārweorð
ārwlöðe f. *oar-thong, rowlock*, Æ.
arwunga, arwunge (A)=earwunga
ārwurð, -wyrð=ārweorð
āryd-dan, -dran, -tran *to strip, plunder*, GL.
āryderian *to blush, be ashamed*, BRPs 69[4].
ārypan *to tear off, strip*, Rd 76[7].
āryð v. ēaryð.
āsadian *to satiate, surfeit*, MFH 150.
āsæcgan=āsecgan; āsægdnes=onsægednes
āsælan† *to bind, fetter, ensnare.*
āsændan=āsendan
asal, asald (NG)=esol
āsānian *to droop, flag*, Gu 1148, LV 57.
āsāwan[7] *to sow, sow with*, Æ.
asca (NG) m.=asce; āscacan=āsceacan
āscādan=āscēadan
āscæcan=āsceacan
āscæfen pp. of āsceafan.
āscǣre=æscǣre; āscafan=āsceafan
āscamelic *shameful*, HGL 500.
āscamian (ea) *to feel shame*, Ps,Cr. ['*ashame(d)*']
ascas nap. of æsc.
ascbacen (ax-) *baked on ashes*, GD 86[30].
asce (æ, cs, x) f. (*burnt*) '*ash*,' Lcd : *dust (of the ground)*, MtL.
āsceacan[6] (a) *to shake off, remove*, Mt : *depart, flee, desert, forsake*, Æ : *shake, brandish*, Ph. ['*ashake*']
āscēadan[7] (ā) *to separate, hold aloof or asunder, exclude*, CP: *make clear, cleanse, purify.*
āsceafan (a) *to shave off*, Lcd.

āscealian *to peel off*, WW 398[10].
āsceaman *to be ashamed*, WW 229[20].
āscearpan=āscirpan
āscellan=āscillan, āscilian
āscēofan=āscūfan; āsceon-=onscun-
āsceortian=ascortian
āscēotan[2] *to shoot, shoot out*, Æ,AO : *drop out, fall*, Æ : *lance* (surgery), ÆL 20[63] : *eviscerate*, OEG 46[47].
āsceppan=āscieppan; āscer-=āscir-
āscian (ācs-, āhs-, āx-) *to* '*ask*,' *inquire, seek for, demand*, CP : *call, summon* : *examine, observe* : (+) *learn by inquiry, discover, hear of*, Chr : (†) *announce.*
āsciendlic (āx-) *interrogative*, ÆGr 260[14].
āscieppan[6] *to make, create*, Ex : *appoint, determine, assign*, AO. ['*ashape*']
āscihtan (=y[2]) *to drive away*, RPs 87[19].
āscildan (=ie) *to protect*, DR.
āscilian *to separate, divide*, v. OEG 1367n.; FM 100.
āscīmian *to shine*, Lcd 86b.
āscīnan[1] *to flash or shine forth, beam, radiate, be clear*, GD.
āsciran (e, y;=ie) *to cut off, cut away*, Æ.
āscirian (y;=ie) *to cut off, separate, divide, remove*, Æ : *set free, deprive of* : *arrange, destine.*
āscirigendlic (y[2]) *disjunctive*, ÆGr 259[14].
āscirpan (e, ea, y;=ie) *to sharpen, make acute*, CP.
āscortian (eo) *to become short, fail*, Æ : *pass away, elapse.*
āscrēadian *to prune, lop*, ÆH 2·74[12].
āscrencan *to displace, trip up, cause to stumble*, CP. ['*aschrench*']
āscrepan[5] *to scrape, clear away*, GL,Lcd.
āscrūtnian (ūdn) *to investigate, examine*, Bf.
āscūfan[2] *to drive out, remove, expel, banish*, Æ : *push (away), give up (to).*
ascun-=onscun-
±āscung f. '*asking*,' *questioning, inquiring, question*, Bo,Met; Æ,CP.
āscyhhan *to scare away, reject*, RPs 50[13].
āscylfan *to destroy*, GPH 393[49].
āscylian, āscyllan=āscilian
āscyndan *to separate, part (from)* : *drive away (from)*, Æ : *take away*, RHy 12[12].
āscyr-=āscir-
āscȳran *to make clear*, Æ. [scīr]
āsealcan (Gen 2167)=āseolcan
āsēarian *to wither, dry up*, Lcd; CP. ['*asear*']
āsēcan *to seek out, select* : *search out, examine, explore* : *seek for, require, ask*, PPs : *search through, penetrate.* ['*aseek*']
āsecgan I. *to say out, express, tell, narrate, explain, announce*, AO. II.=onsecgan
āsecgendlic *utterable*, Æ.
āsēdan (oe) *to satiate*, WW 45[8]. [sæd]

āsegendnes f. *an offering*, AA 36¹⁷.
āsellan *to give up, hand over, deliver* : *expel, banish*.
āsencan *to sink, immerse*, OEG 829.
āsendan *to send away, send forth, send, give up, Mt*; Æ. ['*asend*']
āsengan (JUL 313)=āsecgan
āseolcan³ *to become slack, remiss, relaxed, weak*, Æ,CP.
āsēon I. sv⁵ *to look upon, behold*, HL 16²⁵⁵. II. sv¹ *to strain*, LCD.
āseonod *relaxed*, WW 228²⁵: [seonu]
āseōðan² *to seethe, boil*, CP : *refine, purify* : *examine*.
āsēowan *to sew*, Cp 421 P (io).
āsetnes f. *institute, law*, LL.
asettan=onsettan
āsettan *to set, put, place* : *store up*, Lk 12¹⁹ (MLR 17) : *fix, establish, appoint, set up or in, erect, build, plant, AO,Mt*; Æ : *apply*, PPs 68²⁸ : *transport oneself over, cross (the sea, etc.)* : *take away*, LL 11,12. sīð *or* sīðas ā. *to perform a journey, travel.* ['*aset*']
āsēðan *to affirm, confirm*, Æ. [sōð]
āsīcan I. sv¹ *to sigh*, Sc. II. (=ȳ) *to wean*, CPs 130².
āsiftan *to sift*, LCD 13b.
āsīgan¹ *to sink, sink down, decline, fall down, Chr*; CP. ['*asye*']
āsincan³ *to sink down, fall to pieces*, Æ.
āsingan³ *to sing out, sing, deliver (a speech), compose (verse)*, BH.
āsittan⁵ *to dwell together, settle, El* : *apprehend, fear* : *run aground.* ūt a. *starve out.* ['*asit*']
āslacian *to become slack, decline, diminish*, Æ,CP : *grow tired* : *make slack, loosen, relax, dissolve*.
āslacigendlic *remissive*, ÆGR 228⁵.
āslæccan *to slacken, loosen*, WW.
āslæcian=āslacian
āslǣpan⁷ (ā) *to slumber, dream* : *be paralysed*, LCD : *be benumbed*, MFH 91⁶.
āslǣwan *to blunt, make dull*, OEG 18b⁶⁵.
āslāpan=āslǣpan
āslāwian *to become sluggish, be torpid*, CP. [slāw]
āslēan⁶ *to strike, beat, cut*, Æ : *erect* : *make way* : *paralyse.* of ā. *strike off, behead, Mt*; AO. ['*aslay*']
āslēpen=āslēopen pret. opt. 3 pl. of āslūpan.
āslīdan¹ *to slide, slip, fall, Ps*; Æ,CP. ['*aslide*']
āslīding f. *slipping*, GPH 388⁶².
āslītan¹ (ȳ) *to slit, cleave, cut off, destroy*, CP.
āslūpan² *to slip off, escape, disappear (of), Gen.* ['*aslip*']
āslȳtan=āslītan

āsmēagan *to consider, examine, investigate, devise, elicit, treat of, think*, Æ : *look for, demand*.
āsmēagung f. *scrutiny, consideration*, APT 3¹⁶.
āsmēan=āsmēagan
±āsmir-ian, -wan *to smear, anoint*, LEV 2⁴.
āsmīðian *to do smith's work, fashion, forge, fabricate*, Æ,WW.
āsmorian *to smother, strangle*, AO,CP.
āsmorung f. *choking, suffocation*, LCD 18a.
āsmūgan=āsmēagan
āsnǣsan (ā²) *to spit, impale, stab*, LL 68,36. ['*asnese*']
asnīðan¹ *to cut off*, LCD.
āsoden (WW 20⁴⁴) pp. of āsēoðan.
āsogen pp. of āsūgan.
āsolcen (pp. of āseolcan) *sluggish, idle, indifferent, dissolute*, Æ.
āsolcennes f. *sleepiness, sloth, laziness*, W; Æ. ['*aswolkeness*']
āsolian *to become dirty*, A 2·374.
āspanan⁶ *to allure, seduce, persuade, urge, insinuate*, AO.
āspannan⁷ *to unbind, unclasp*, GD 214²⁴.
āsparian *to preserve*, GD 159²⁴.
āspeaft (JnL 9⁶)=āspeoft
āspēdan *to survive, escape*, AN 1628.
āspelian *to be substitute for, represent, take the place of*, LL,RB. ā. of *be exempt from*, CHRD.
āspendan *to spend, expend, distribute, squander, consume, AO*; Æ. ['*aspend*']
āspeoft pret. 3 sg. *spit out*, JnR 9⁶. [v. speoft]
āsperian=āspyrian
aspide m. *asp, adder, serpent, Ps*; Æ. ['*aspide*']
āspillan *to destroy*, JnL 12¹⁰.
āspinnan³ *to spin*, WW.
āspirian=āspyrian
āspīwan¹ (ȳ) *to spew up, vomit*, Æ,CP.
āsplǣtan? *to split.* v. ES 49·156.
āspornan *to cast down*, EPs 145⁷. [spurnan]
āsprēadan *to stretch out, extend*, EPs 35¹¹.
āsprecan *to speak out, speak*, PPs.
āsprengan *to cause to spring, fling out*, ÆL 8²¹³.
āsprettan=āspryttan
āsprindlad *ripped up*, LCD 80b.
āspringan³ (y) *to spring up or forth, break forth, spread*, Æ; AO : *arise, originate, be born*, Æ : *dwindle, diminish, fail, cease.* āsprungen *dead.* ['*aspring*']
āspringung f. *failing*, VPs 141⁴.
āspritan=āspryttan
āsproten pp. of āsprūtan.
ā-sprungennes, -sprungnes f. *failing, exhaustion, death* : *eclipse*.

āsprūtan² (=ēo) to sprout forth, PPs 140⁹.
āspryngan=āspringan
āspryttan¹ (e, i) to sprout out, bring forth, Æ.
āspylian to wash oneself, Bo 115⁷.
āspyrgend m. investigator, VHy 13²⁵.
āspyrging f. 'adinventio,' WW 513¹⁵.
āspyrian (e, i) to track, trace out, investigate, study, explore, discover, BF,SolK.
āspȳwan=āspīwan
assa m. he-ass, Æ,Mt,Jn; CP. ['ass']
assen f. she-ass, WW 108²⁶.
assmyre f. she-ass, Gen 32¹⁵.
āst f. kiln, WW 185³⁰; A 9·265. ['oast']
āstǣgan to go up, embark, MkR 6³².
āstǣlan to lay to one's charge, LL (264¹⁵).
āstǣnan¹ to adorn with precious stones, W.
āstæppan to imprint (a footstep), NC 344¹ (v. MLR 17).
āstærfan (MtR)=āstyrfan
āstandan⁶ to stand up, stand forth, rise up, arise, B; Æ : continue, endure, Lk; CP. ['astand']
āstandennes f. perseverance, ÆL 23b²⁷² : existence, subsistence.
āstēapan=āstȳpan
āstellan I. to set forth, set, put, afford, supply, display, appoint, AO,CP : set up, establish, confirm, institute, ordain, undertake, start, AO; Æ : undergo, Æ. II. to fly off, rush.
āstemnian to found, build, BH 4¹⁷.
āstemped engraved, stamped, WW 203²⁷.
āstencan to scatter, GD 42³³.
āstēop-=āstȳp-
āsteorfan³ to die, MH 62²⁷.
āstēp-=āstȳp-; āster-=āstyr-
asterion 'asterion,' pellitory, Lcd 1·164.
āstīfian to become stiff, Æ.
āstīfician=āstȳfecian
āstīgan¹ to proceed, go, Æ : (usu. w. ūp, niðer, etc.) rise, mount, ascend, descend, Jn; Æ,CP : be puffed up, AO 264⁸. ['astye']
āstīgend m. rider, ARHy 4¹.
āstīgian to ascend, mount, MkL,WW 93²¹.
āstīgnes (ǣ¹) f. ascent, EPs 103⁴.
āstihtan to determine on, decree, Chr 998.
āstihting (OEG)=ātyhting
āstillian to still, quiet, RWH 75³⁰.
āstingan³ to bore out, pierce out, Chr : stab.
āstintan=āstyntan; āstirian=āstyrian
āstīðian to become hard, dry up, wither : grow up? become powerful? TC 203²⁰.
āstondnes=āstandennes
āstrǣlian to cast forth, hurl, RPs 75⁹.
āstreccan to stretch out, stretch forth, extend, lay low, Æ : prostrate oneself, bow down, CP. ['astretch']
āstregdan to sprinkle, GD,LL.
āstregdnes? f. sprinkling, DR.
āstrenged (made strong), malleable, WW.

āstrīenan† (ēo, ȳ) to beget.
āstrogden pp. of āstregdan.
āstrowenes f. length, HGL 443.
āstrȳnan=āstrīenan
āstundian to take upon oneself, Æ.
āstȳfecian to suppress, eradicate, CP.
āstyllan=āstellan
āstyltan to be astonished, LkLR.
āstyntan (i) to blunt, repress, restrain, stop, overcome, Gl. ['astint']
āstȳpan (ē, ēa, ēo) to deprive, bereave, GD. āstȳpte orphans. [stēop]
āstȳp(ed)nes (ē², ēo²) f. privation, bereavement, GD,WW.
āstȳran to guide, control, AS 9¹³.
āstyrfan (æ, e;=ie) to kill, destroy, Cr,Mt. ['asterve']
āstyrian to stir up, excite, move, move forward, raise, JnMk; Æ : be roused, become angry, Æ. āstyred weorðan be or become anxious, Æ. ['astir']
-āstyriendlic v. un-ā.
āstyrigend m. a stirrer-up, GPH 393⁷⁸.
āstyrred starry, Sc.
āstyrung f. motion, Lcd.
ā-sūcan², -sūgan to suck, suck out, drain : consume, WW 501³³ (ōsogen).
ā-sundran, -sundron=onsundran
āsundrian=āsyndrian
āsūrian to be or become sour, Lcd,WW.
āswǣman to roam, wander about : pine, grieve, Æ : be ashamed, LPs 24²⁰.
āswǣrn-=āswarn-
āswǣtan to burst out in perspiration, MH 20¹².
āswāmian to die away, Gen 376 : cease.
āswāpan⁷ (but pp. āswōpen) to sweep away, remove, clean, CP.
āswārcan to languish, LPs 38¹².
āswārcnian to confound, BSPs 70²⁴.
āswārnian to be confounded, Ps.
āswārnung f. shame, confusion, LPs 43¹⁶.
āswaðian to investigate, OEG 5¹¹.
āsweartian to turn livid, become ashy or black, CP.
āswebban† to lull, soothe, set at rest : put to death, destroy, Jud. ['asweve']
āswefecian to extirpate, WW.
āswellan³ to swell, CP.
āsweltan³ to die, Chr.
āswencan to afflict, DR.
āswengan to swing off, shake off, cast forth. ā. on cast upon, RPs 21¹¹.
āsweorcan³ to droop, Jos 2¹¹.
āsweorfan³ to file off, polish, GPH.
āswēpa=ǣswǣpa
āswerian⁶ to swear, PPs 131¹¹.
āswic-=ǣswic-
āswīcan¹ to desert, abandon, betray, deceive, Mt : offend, irritate, provoke. ['aswike']

āswīfan[1] *to wander, stray*, WW.
āswind=āswind
āswindan[3] *to become weak, shrink, fade away, perish, decay, dissolve*, Bo; Æ,CP. ['*aswind*']
āswingan[3] *to scourge*, DR42⁶.
āswōgan[7] *to cover over, choke*, CP411¹⁷.
āsworettan *to sigh, grieve*, GD.
āswornian (NC271)=āswarnian
āswundennes f. *idleness*, BH160²⁵.
āsynderlic *remote*, OEG2514.
±āsynd-ran, -rian (u²) *to separate, divide, disjoin, sever, Soul*; Æ,CP : *distinguish, except*. ['*asunder*']
āsyndrung f. *division*, WW.
at=æt; **ātēfran** (CP467¹⁹)=ātīefran
ātǣsan *to wear out, injure, strike, smite*, Æ : *wound*, CP296¹⁸.
atāwian=ætīewan
āte (ǣ) f. '*oats*,' *Lcd* : *wild oats, tares, Gl,WW*.
āteallan=ātellan; **ātēfran**=ātīefran
ategār=ætgār; **atel**=atol
ātellan *to reckon up, count, Bo*; AO. ā. wið *balance against* : *tell, enumerate*, CP : *explain, interpret*. ['*atell*']
ātemian *to tame, subdue, render quiet*, CP.
ātendan *to set on fire, kindle, inflame, Chr* : *trouble, perplex*, BF94⁹. ['*atend*']
ātending f. *incentive*, Sc221¹⁷.
āteon² *to draw up, out, off or from, remove, pull out, lead out, draw, B,BH*; AO,CP. ūp ā. *draw up, move away* : *protract*, Æ : *move, journey, roam* : *deal with, dispose of, apply, use, Mt*; Æ,CP. ['*atee*']
āteorian *to fail, become exhausted, weary, cease, Ps*; Æ : *be defective*, ÆGR. ['*atire*']
āteorl(g)endlic *transitory, perishable*, Æ : *failing* : *defective*, ÆGR.
āteorodnes f. *cessation, exhaustion*, Æ(3⁴⁹⁵); BPs118⁵³.
āteorung f. *failing, weariness*, Æ.
āteowan=ōðīewan; **āter**=ātor
āteran⁴ *to tear away*, CP359²⁰.
āteriendlic=āteoriendlic
āterima (ētr-) *oat-bran*, LCD3·292'.
ātertānum dp. *with poisoned twigs or poison-stripes?* (or ? -tēarum *with poison-drops*) B1460.
āteshwōn adv. *at all*, CM987. [āwiht]
athēd (GL)=æthȳd
ātīdrian *to grow weak*, GD59²⁶ (ydd).
ātīefran (ǣ, ē, ī, ȳ) *to draw, depict*, CP.
atiewan=ōðīewan; **ātiht-**=ātyht-
ātillan *to touch, reach*, GENC11⁴.
ātimbr-an, -ian *to erect, build*, AO,CP.
ātimplian *to provide with spikes*, NC271.
ātīwan=ōðīewan
ātland *oat-land*, EC208'.

ātlēag m. *oat-field*, EC448⁹.
atol I. (e², u²) *dire, terrible, ugly, deformed, repulsive, unchaste*, B. ['*atel*'] II.† n. *horror, evil*.
+atolhīwian *to disfigure, make hideous*, WW220³¹.
atolian *to disfigure*, WW220²⁶.
atolic, atollic *dire, terrible, deformed, repulsive*, Æ. adv. -līce.
ātor, āt(to)r, (ǣ) n. *poison, venom, Lcd*; AO, CP : *gall, Gl*. ['*atter*']
ātorbǣre *poisonous*, ÆH1·72²².
ātorberende *poisonous, venomous*, LCD,W.
ātorcoppe (ǣ) f. *spider, Lcd*; LPs38¹² (-loppe). ['*attercop*']
ātorcrǣft (āttor-) m. *art of poisoning*, W.
ātorcyn (ǣ) n. *poison*, SOL219.
ātordrinca m. *poisonous draught*, MH.
ātorgeblǣd n. *swelling caused by poison*, LCD162b.
ātorlāðe f. *plant used as antidote to poison, betonica? Lcd,WW*. ['*atterlothe*']
ātorlic *poison-like, bitter, WW*. ['*atterlich*']
ātorsceaða† m. *poisonous enemy*.
ātorspere n. *poisoned spear*, RD18⁹.
ātorðigen (ātt-) f. *taking of poison*, LCD1·4⁵.
ātr=ātor; **ātr-**=ādr-
ātrahtnian *to treat, discuss*, BF72,142.
ātredan⁵ *to extract, extort*, LL.
ātreddan *to search out, examine*, PPs.
ātrendlian *to roll*, MET5¹⁷. [v. '*trendle*']
ātres gs. of ātor.
atrum n. *ink*, A13·28¹⁵. [L. atramentum]
ātter, āttor=ātor
attrum=atrum
atul=atol; **ātur**=ātor
ātwēonian *to cause doubt*, BF182⁸.
ātyddrian=ātīdrian
ātȳdran *to beget, create*, EL1279. [tūdor]
ātȳfran=ātīefran
ātyhtan (i) *to entice, allure, incite* : *be attentive* : *produce*, RD51³ : *stretch, extend, turn*.
ātyhting (i) f. *intention, aim* : *instigation*, OEG2³⁰⁴.
ātymbran=ātimbran
ātȳnan I. *to shut off, exclude*, PPs,WW. [tūn] II.=ontȳnan
ātyndan=ātendan; **ātȳrian**=ātēorian
atȳwan=ōðīewan
āð m. '*oath*,' (*judicial*) *swearing, B,Chr,Mt*; AO : *fine for an unsuccessful oath*, KC (v. BTac).
āð-=ōð-
aðamans m. *adamant*, CP271². [L.]
āðbryce m. *perjury*, W164⁷.
āðecgan *to take food, consume?* LCD57a : *oppress?* RD1²,⁷(Tupper).
āðegehāt=āðgehāt
āðegen *distended* (*with food*), WW.

āðencan *to think out, devise, contrive, invent,*
AO : *intend,* B.
āðenenes f. *extension,* VHy 7⁴⁸.
ā-ðennan, -ðenian *to stretch out, extend,
draw out, expand,* AO : *apply (the mind),*
CP : *prostrate.*
āðenung f. *stretching out, distension,* LCD
71b : '*stratum,*' ALRPs 131³.
āðeodan=āðīedan
āðēostrian (ē, īe, ī) *to become dark, obscured,
eclipsed,* Bo; CP,VPs. ['*athester*']
āðer=āhwæðer
āðerscan *to thresh out,* ÆL 31¹²¹⁷.
āðēstrian=aðēostrian; āðēwan=āðȳwan
āðexe f. *lizard,* Cp 1182.
āðfultum m. *confirmation (confirmers) of an
oath,* LL.
āðgehāt (āðe-) n. *promise on oath, oath,* WW.
āðiddan (=y) *to thrust, push,* OEG 50³.
āðiedan (ēo, ȳ) *to separate,* CP.
āðierran *to clean,* CP.
āðiestrian (CP)=āðēostrian
āðindan³ *to swell, puff up, inflate, increase,*
CP : *melt, pass away.* (cp. ðindan)
āðindung f. *swelling,* LCD 93a.
ā-ðīstrian, -ðīsðrigan (CP)=āðēostrian
āðl (BH,VPs)=ādl
āðloga m. *perjurer,* CR 165.
āðol=ādl
āðolian *to hold out, endure, suffer,* Æ.
āðolware mp. *citizens,* GNE 201.
āðor=āhwæðer
āðracian *to dread : frighten.* [=onðracian]
āðrǣstan *to twist out, wrest out,* GL.
āðrāwan⁷ *to curl, twist, twine,* Æ.
āðrēatian *to dissuade from,* CP 293¹⁰ : *chide,
rebuke,* GENC 37¹⁰.
āðrēotan² (pers. and impers.) *to tire of,
weary, be tiresome to, displease, disgust,*
Æ,AO,CP.
āðrescan=aðerscan
āðrīetan (ȳ) *to weary,* Æ,AO.
āðringan³ *to crowd or press out : rush forth,
break out.* ūt ā. *emboss.*
āðrīostrian (MtR 24²⁹)=āðēostrian
āðrīstian *to be bold, presume,* GD 70³⁰.
āðrotennes f. *wearisomeness,* WW 409²².
āðrotsum *irksome,* WW 510¹².
āðrōwian *to suffer,* LCD 68b.
āðroxen pp. of āðerscan.
āðrunten (pp. of *āðrintan) *swollen,* RD 38².
(or? āðrūten)
āðrūten? (pp. of *āðrūtan) *swollen,* LCD.
āðryccan *to press, oppress,* DR.
āðrȳn *to rob? drive out?* GL (ES 43·331)
ā-ðrysemian, -ðrysman (*AO*) *to suffocate,
smother.* ['*athrysm*']
āðrytnes (æ¹,e²) f. *weariness,* DHy. [ðrēotan]
āðstæf m. *oath,* CPs 104⁹.

āðswara m?=āðswaru
āðswaring=āðswerung
āðswaru f. *oath-swearing, oath,* Æ.
āðswerian? *to vow with an oath,* WW 387⁹.
āðswerung f. *oath-swearing,* CHR,RSPs
104⁹.
āðswyrd (æ¹, eo²) n. *oath-swearing,* EJVPs
104⁹; B2064.
āðum m. *son-in-law,* Æ; AO : *brother-in-
law.* ['*odam*']
āðumswerian mp. *son-in-law and father-in-
law,* B84.
āðundennes f. *swelling, tumour,* LCD : *contumacy,* WW 87¹⁷.
āðwǣnan *to diminish, soften,* LCD.
āðwēan⁶ *to wash, wash off, cleanse, baptize,
anoint,* Æ,CP.
āðwedd n. *promise on oath,* WW 115¹⁶.
āðweran⁴ *to stir up, churn,* LCD.
āðwīnan *to vanish,* NC 338.
āðwītan¹ *to disappoint,* SPs 131¹¹.
āðwyrðe *worthy of credit.* v. LL 2·376.
āðȳan=āðȳwan
āðȳdan=āðīedan
āðȳlgian *to bear up,* ARSPs.
āðȳn=āðȳwan
āðȳnnian (i) *to make thin, reduce,* DHy 8¹⁰.
āðȳstrian (Æ)=āðēostrian
āðȳtan I. *to sound, blow (a horn),* DD
109. II. *to expel,* WW 19¹².
āðȳwan (ē) *to drive away,* AO : *press out or
into, squeeze out.*
āuht=āwiht; āuðer=āhwæðer
āw=ǣ; āwa=ā
āwacan⁶ (on-) *to awake,* Æ : *arise, originate,
spring forth, be born.* ['*awake(n)*']
āwacian *to awake,* Æ.
āwācian *to grow weak, decline, fall, belittle,*
Æ,CP : *fall away, lapse, desist from, abstain,* Æ : *mollify, appease,* MFH 142⁶.
āwacnian=āwæcnian; āwǣc-=āwec-
āwǣcan *to weaken,* BHB 250⁶.
āwǣc-nian, -nan (on-; a, e) *to awaken,
revive,* Æ : *arise, originate, spring from,*
AO. ['*awake(n)*']
āwǣgan *to deceive : destroy, annul, make
nugatory,* Æ.
āwǣlan *to harass, afflict,* NG.
āwǣled pp. of āwilwan.
āwǣltan=āwyltan
āwǣmmian=āwemman
āwǣnd-=āwend-, onwend-
āwǣnian=āwenian
āwǣrd pp. of āwierdan.
āwǣrged=āwierged
āwǣrlan *to avoid,* DR 39¹³.
āwǣscan=āwascan; āwǣstan=āwēstan
āwandian *to fear, hesitate,* ÆGR 162².
āwanian *to diminish, lessen,* DR,KC.

āwannian *to become livid or black and blue,* GD 20³² (v. NC 332).

āwansian *to diminish,* KC 4·243⁶.

āwār=āhwǣr

āwārnian *to be confounded,* APs. (=āswarnian)

āwascan⁶ (æ) *to wash, bathe, immerse,* Lcd.

āweallan⁷ *to well up, flow out, break forth, issue, swarm,* CP : *be hot, burn.*

āweardian *to guard, defend,* AO 202²⁴ (v.l.).

āweaxan⁶ *to grow, grow up, arise, come forth,* CP.

āweb=ōweb; āwec-=āwæc-

āweccan *to awake, rouse, incite, excite, Mk, Lk;* Æ,CP : *raise up, beget.* ['awecche']

āwecenes (æ) f. *incitement,* GD 199⁷.

āwecgan *to undermine, shake, move,* Æ.

āwēdan *to be or become mad, rage, AO;* Æ. ['awede'; wōd]

āwefan⁵ *to weave, weave together,* Æ.

āweg (=on-) '*away,' forth, out, Chr,Mt;* CP.

āwegan⁵ *to lift up, carry away, Ex :* weigh, weigh out, Æ : *estimate, consider : distinguish.* ['aweigh']

āwegāworpnes f. *abortion,* LL (154').

āwegcuman⁴ *to escape,* AO 102¹⁰.

āwegēade *went away, JnL* 4⁵⁰ [v. 'away'; ēode]

āwegflēon² *to fly or flee away,* OEG 2169.

āweggān *to go away,* BH 326¹⁰.

āweggewītan¹ *to depart,* AO 74²⁶.

āweggewītenes f. *departure, Æ : aberration (of mind),* JPs 115¹¹.

āwegweard *coming to a close,* RWH 133³⁷.

āwehtnes f. *arousing,* BH 422²⁰.

awel (o², u²) m. *hook, fork,* Gl.

āwellan=āwillan

āwemman (æ²) *to disfigure, corrupt,* Bf,HL.

āwemmendnes f. *corruption,* LPs 15¹⁰.

āwēnan *to consider,* RBL 4¹² (āhw-).

āwendan (=on-) *to avert, turn aside, remove, upset, Ps : change, exchange, alter, pervert, Æ;* CP : *translate,* Æ,CP : *turn from, go, depart, Ps;* AO : *return : subdue.* ['awend']

āwended-=āwendend-

āwendendlic *that can be changed, changeable,* Æ.

āwendendlicnes f. *mutability,* Æ.

āwende(n)dnes f. *change, alteration,* Æ.

āwendennes f. *change,* OEG 191.

āwending f. *subversion, change,* ES 39·322, Sc 188⁴.

āwenian *to disaccustom, wean,* BH,Ps.

āwēodian *to root out, extirpate,* LL,W.

āweorpan³ *to throw, throw away, cast down, cast out, cast aside, degrade, depose, Mt;* Æ, AO,CP. āworpen *divorced, rejected, destroyed, apostate.* of, ūt ā. *to throw out.* ['awarp']

āweorpnes=āworpennes

āweorðan³ *to pass away, vanish, become worthless, Mt* : (NG)=+weorðan. ['aworth']

āweosung f. 'subsistentia,' WW 516⁴.

āwer=āhwǣr

āwerdan=āwierdan

āwerde (æ²) m. *worthless fellow,* WW 111²⁹.

āwerg-=āwierg-, āweri-, āwyrig-

āwerian I. *to defend, AO :* hinder, restrain, Chr : *protect, cover, surround, enclose :* ward off from oneself, spurn from oneself. II. *to wear, wear out (clothes),* RB.

āwerpan=āweorpan

āwescnes (VPs)=æwiscnes

āwēstan *to lay waste, destroy, AO;* Æ. ['awest']

āwēst(ed)nes f. *desolation, destruction,* Lcd.

āwēstend m. *devastator,* W 200¹⁹.

āwexen=āweaxen pp. of āweaxan.

+āwian=+īewan

āwīdlian *to profane, defile,* LL,OEG.

āwierdan (e, y) *to spoil, injure, hurt, corrupt, seduce, destroy, kill,* CP.

āwierding (y) f. *corruption, blemish,* HGL 421⁵⁷.

āwierdnes (y) f. *hurt, harm, destruction,* Æ : defilement.

āwierg-an, -ian (æ, e, i, y) I. *to curse, damn, denounce, outlaw,* Æ,Mt,CP,VPs. sē āwier(ge)da *fiend, devil.* ['awarie'] II. (i, y) *to strangle, suffocate, AO;* Æ. ['aworry']. For compounds see āwyrg-.

āwiht I. n. '*aught,' anything, something, Ps.* II. adv. *at all, by any means.* tō āhte *at all.* III. *good, of value,* Æ.

āwildian *to become wild,* Æ,LL.

āwillan (e, y;=ie) *to bring into commotion, boil,* Æ.

āwille (WW)=ānwille II.

awil-wan, -wian (æ;=ie) *to roll (tr.).*

āwindan³ *to wind, bend, plait : slip from, withdraw, escape,* CP : *become relaxed? cramped?* (BTac), W 148³.

āwindwian (y) *to winnow, blow away, disperse,* Ps.

āwinnan³ *to labour, strive, JnL : gain, overcome, endure, Da.* ['awin']

āwirgan=āwiergan

āwirgnes=āwyrgednes; āwisc-=æwisc-

āwisnian *to become dry, wither,* LkL.

āwistlian *to hiss,* W 147³¹. [hwistlian]

āwītegian *to prophesy,* VH 9.

āwlacian *to be or become lukewarm,* Lcd,RB.

āwlǣtan *to befoul, make loathsome, defile,* Æ.

āwlancian *to exult, to be proud,* OEG 1159.

āwlencan *to make proud, enrich,* DR 59¹.

āwlyspian *to 'lisp,' MLN* 4·279 (NC 338).

āwo=ā (āwa)

āwofflan *to become proud, insolent* : *rave, be delirious, insane,* Æ.

āwōgian *to woo,* Æ.

āwōh (*crookedly*), *wrongfully, unjustly,* LL. [=on wōh]

āwol=āwel; **āwolflgan**=āwoffian

āwonian (DR)=āwanian; **āwor**=āfor

āwordennes f. *degeneration,* WW 87²¹.

āworpednes (EPs 21⁷)=āworpennes

āworpenlic *worthy of condemnation,* CP. adv. -līce *vilely.*

āworp(en)nes f. *rejection, what is cast away* : *exposure (of children)* : *a casting out,* BH 482¹¹.

āwrǣnan *to make wanton,* Lᴄᴅ 54b.

āwrǣnsian, *to wax wanton,* A 30·128.

āwrǣstan *to wrest from, extort,* WW 397³⁷.

āwrecan⁵ *to thrust out, drive away* : *strike, pierce* : *utter, sing, relate, recite* : *punish, avenge,* Chr,LL. ['awreak']

āwreccan *to arouse, awake,,* Æ.

āwregennes=onwrigenes

āwrēon¹,² (=on-) *to disclose, discover, reveal* : *cover,* NG.

āwreðian *to support, uphold,* CP.

āwrīdian *to originate, spring from,* A 11·2.

āwrigenes=onwrigennes

āwringan³ *to wring, squeeze out,* Æ : *express,* Bғ 100¹⁰.

āwrītan *to write, write down, describe, compose, CP*; Æ,AO,Cʜʀ : *mark, inscribe, draw, carve, copy,* Æ. ['awrite']

āwrīðan¹ I. *to turn, wind, bind up, bind, wreathe.* II.=onwrīðan

āwrygenes=onwrigenes

āwðer, āwðor=āhwæðer

āwuht=āwiht; **āwul**=āwel

āwuldrian *to glorify,* DR,JnL.

āwundrian *to wonder, wonder at, admire,* G,GD.

āwunian *to remain, continue,* BH.

āwunigende ptc. *continual,* Bʟ 109².

āwurt-wallan, -warian=āwyrtwalian

āwurðan=āweorðan; **āwyht**=āwiht

āwylian (Æ)=āwilwian

āwyllan=āwillan; **āwylm**=ǣwielm

āwyltan (æ;=ie) *to roll, roll away,* Æ : *harass,* DR.

āwyndwian=āwindwian

āwyrcan *to do,* Bo 149¹⁶,LL.

āwyrd- (Æ)=āwierd-; **āwyrdla**=æfwyrdla

āwyrg-=āwierg-, āwyrig-

āwyrgedlic (Nɪᴄ 490²⁰) *detestable, shameful, abominable.*

āwyrgednes (o³) f. *wickedness,* Æ : *curse, cursing.* [wearg]

āwyrgendlic (CAS 34²²)=āwyrgedlic

āwyrigende *accursed,* ÆL 18³²⁴.

āwyrigung f. *a curse,* ÆL 15¹¹⁵.

āwyrn (Mᴇɴ 101)=āhwergen

āwyrpan (=ie) *to recover (from illness),* ÆL 20⁶⁵ (v.l.), A 41·109⁸⁵.

āwyrtlian=āwyrtwalian

āwyrttrumian *to root out,* MFH 161

āwyrtwalian *to root out,* CP.

āwyrðung f. *stain, aspersion,* HGʟ 421.

ax-=asc-, ox-; **āx-**=āsc-; **axe**=æcs

āȳdan (OEG 8¹⁰⁸)=āīdan; **āȳdlian**=āīdlian

āyldan *to delay,* GD 21²². [ieldan]

āyppan '*experiri*' (*aperire ?*) DR 70⁵.

āyrnan=āiernan

āȳtan *to drive out,* OEG 4080. [ūt]

āyttan=āettan

B

bā nafn. and am. of bēgen *both.*

bac- v. bæc.

bacan⁶ *to 'bake,'* Æ.

bacas nap. of bæc II.

bacca m. *ridge,* BC (bacce f. Mdf).

bacu nap. of bæc I.

bād I. f. *forced contribution, impost, pledge,* LL : *expectation.* [bīdan] II. (±) pret. 3 sg. of bīdan.

-bādere v. nied-b.

bādian *to take a pledge or fine,* LL.

bæ-=ba-, be-, bea-

bæc I. n. '*back,*' Bo,MtL,Ps; CP. on b. *backwards, behind,* '*aback.*' on b. settan, lǣtan *to neglect.* ofer b. *backwards, back.* under b. *behind, backwards, back.* ofer b. būgan *to turn back, flee.* clǣne b. habban *to be straightforward, honest,* LL 128,5. II. mfn. *beck, brook, KC.* [v. ES 29·411,GBG and '*bache*']

+bæc n. *bakemeats,* Gᴇɴ 40¹⁷ : *baking,* ÆGʀ 176.

bæcbord n. *left side of a ship, larboard,* AO.

bæce I. *back parts,* WW 160¹⁰. II.=bæc II.

bæce=bēce

bæcen-=bēacen-

bæcere I. m. '*baker,*' WW. II.=bæzere

bæcering m. *gridiron,* WW.

bæcern n. *bakery, bakehouse,* Æ.

bæcestre fm. *baker,* Æ. ['baxter']

bæceð, bæcð, pres. 3 sg. of bacan.

bæcistre=bæcestre

bæcling(e), bæclinga (on) adv. *backwards, behind, JnR: back to back,* RWH 86²⁷. on b. gewend *having one's back turned,* Æ. ['backlings']

bæcslitol adj. *backbiting,* W 72¹⁶.

bæcðearm m. *rectum* ; pl. *bowels, entrails,* Æ.

+bæou np. *back parts,* LPs.

bæd I. pret. 3 sg. of biddan. II.=bed

bædan *to defile*, EPs 78[1].
bǽdan *to urge on, impel*, CP : *solicit, require* : *afflict, oppress*.
bædd=bedd
bæddæg=bæðdæg
bæddel m. *effeminate person, hermaphrodite*, WW. [v. '*bad*']
bæddryda=bedrida
bǽdend m. *inciter*, WW.
bǽdewēg n. *drinking vessel*, Gu,BH 370[30]. [wǽge]
bǽdling m. *effeminate person*, WW. ['*badling*']
bǽdon pret. pl. of biddan.
bædryda=bedrida; bædzere=bæzere
bæfta, bæftan (*Mt*; Æ)=beæftan
bæftansittende *idle*, ÆGR 52[2].
-bæftlan (ea[1], a[2]) v. hand-b.
bǽg=bēag; bǽgen=bēgen; bǽh=bēag
bǽl n. *fire, flame, B* : *funeral pyre, bonfire, B.* ['*bale*']
bǽlblys, -blyse, -blǽse† f. '*blaze*' *of a fire, funeral blaze, Gu.*
bǽlc I.† m. *pride, arrogance.* II. m. *covering, cloud?* Ex 73.
bǽlcan *to cry out*, MOD 28.
+bǽlcan *to root up*, CPs 79[14].
bǽldan=bieldan
bǽldo (CP), bǽldu=bieldo
bǽlegsa m. *terror of fire*, Ex 121.
bǽlfýr n. '*bale-fire*,' *funeral or sacrificial fire, B.*
bǽlg, bǽlig (NG)=belg
bǽlstede m. *place of a funeral pile*, B 3097.
bǽl-ōracu f. (ds. -ōrǽce) *violence of fire*, PH 270.
bǽlwudu m. *wood for a funeral pile*, B 3112.
bǽlwylm m. *flames of a funeral fire*, JUL 336.
bǽm=bām (v. bēgen); bǽnd=bend
+bǽne n. *bones*, GD 86[11]n.
bǽnen *made of bone*, Æ,LCD.
bǽr I. gsmn. bares '*bare*,' *uncovered, Bo* : *naked, unclothed, Gen.* II. pret. 3 sg. of beran.
bǽr I. f. '*bier*,' *El*; Æ : *handbarrow, litter, bed, BH, JnR.* [beran] II. *a pasture*, KC. III.=bār (AB 14·233).
+bǽran *to behave, conduct oneself, CP* : *fare*, B 2824 : '*exultare*,' PPs. ['*i-bere*']
bǽrbǽre *barbarous*, EPs 113[1].
bǽrdisc m. *tray*, WW. [beran]
bǽre=bere pres. 1 sing. of beran.
bǽre-=bere-
-bǽre suffix (from beran); forms derivatives from substantives, as in cwealm-bǽre. [*Ger.* -bar]
bǽre=bǽr
+bǽre n. *manner, behaviour, El* : *gesture, cry* : *action.* ['*i-bere*'; beran]

bǽrfōt *barefoot*, LL,W.
bǽrhtm (A)=bearhtm
bǽrlic I. adj. *of barley*, KC 6·79[10]. II. *open, clear, public.* adv. -līce.
bǽrmann m. *bearer, porter, Æ.* ['*berman*']
bǽrn=bereǽrn
±bǽrnan (e) *to cause to burn, kindle, burn, consume, Sol*; AO,VPs. [v. '*burn*']
bǽrnelāc (e) n. *burnt-offering*, PPs.
bǽrnes=bǽrnnes
+bǽrnes f. *bearing, manner*, WW 529[13].
bǽrnett (y[2]) n. *burning, burn, cautery, Æ* : *arson, LL.*
bǽrning f. *burning* : *burnt offering*, BPs 50[18].
bǽrnīsen n. *branding-iron*, OEG 7[113].
bǽrnnes, bǽrnes f. *burning*, BH.
bǽro=bearu; bǽron pret. pl. of beran.
bǽrs m. *a fish, perch*, GL. [*Ger.* barsch]
+bǽrscipe (LkL)=+bēorscipe
bǽrst pret. 3 sg. of berstan.
bǽrstl-=brastl-
bǽrsynnig (eo[2]) m. *notorious sinner, publican*, NG.
+bǽru v. +bǽre and BTs; bǽrwe=bearwe
bǽst m? n? *inner bark of trees*, '*bast*,' *Æ, OET.*
bǽsten *made of bast*, JUD 15[13].
bǽstere=bǽzere
bǽtan I. *to bait, hunt, worry, Æ.* [v. '*bait*'] II. *to beat against the wind?* (BT) : *make fast?* (Sedgef.=III), Bo 144[31]. III.(±) *to furnish with a bit or bridle, saddle, curb.*
+bǽte(l) n. *bit, bridle*, pl. *trappings*, BH.
bǽtera, bǽttra=betera
bǽting (ē) f. *beating (against the wind?)* (BTs), *cable* (Sedgef.), Bo 144[31].
bǽð n. nap. baðu '*bath*,' *action of bathing, Lcd* : *laver, AO,Bl* : *liquid in which one bathes, medicinal spring, BH, Jul, KC.* ganotes b. *gannet's bath (i.e. the sea), B.*
bǽð(c)ere=bǽzere
Bǽðdæg m. *Epiphany (day of Christ's baptism)* DR 2[1].
bǽðern n. *bath-house*, NC 272.
bǽðfæt n. *bathing-tub*, LL 455,17.
bǽðhūs n. *bathing-place, Æ.*
bǽðian=baðian
bǽðsealf f. *bathing-salve*, LCD.
bǽðstede m., bǽðstōw f. *bathing-place*, WW.
bǽðweg† m. *sea*, AN,EX.
bǽzere m. *baptizer, baptist*, G. [*L.* baptista]
bal-=beal-
balc, balca m. *bank, ridge, Bo, WW.* ['*balk*']
ballīce (NG)=bealdlīce
bal-sam, -samum n. '*balsam*,' *balm, Lcd, WW.*
balsmēðe f. *bergamot*, LCD 3·90'.

balsminte f. *spear-mint, water-mint,* WW 136[6].

bal-zam n., -zame f., -zamum (AA) n.= balsam

bām dmfn. of bēgen.

+ban=+bann

bān n. '*bone,*' *tusk, Æ,Gl,Jn;* AO,CP : *the bone of a limb.*

+bān *bones,* GD 86[11].

bana (o) m. *killer, slayer, murderer, B,Chr* : *the devil* : f. *murderess,* A 10·155. ['*bane*']

bānbeorge f. *leg-armour, greaves,* WW.

bānbryce m. *fracture of a bone,* LCD.

bāncofa† m. *the bodily frame.*

ban-coða m., -coðu f. *baneful disease.*

band pret. 3 sg. of bindan.

bānece *in pain in the thigh,* LCD.

bān-fæt† n. nap. -fatu *body, corpse.*

bānfāg *adorned with bonework* (deer antlers?), B 781.

bangār (o) m. *murdering spear,* B 2031.

bāngeberg n.=bānbeorge

bāngebrec n. *fracture of a bone,* AN 1439.

bānhelm m. *helmet, shield?* FIN 30 (v. also bārhelm).

bānhring† m. *vertebra, joint.*

bānhūs† n. *body, chest, breast.* bānhūses weard *the mind,* Ex 523.

bānlēas *boneless,* RD 46[3].

bānloca† m. *joint, limb.*

+bann n. *proclamation, summons, command,* Æ,CP : *indiction (cycle of* 15 *years).*

±bannan[7] *to summon, command, proclaim.* b. ūt *call out,* CHR.

bannend m. *summoner,* GL.

+banngēar (o[1], -ē[2]) n. *indiction, year of the indiction,* Ct.

bannuc m. *a bit, small piece, ZDA* ; OEG. [v. LF 123 and '*bannock*']

bānrift (y) n. *leggings, leg-armour, greaves,* GL,WW (-rist).

bānsealf f. *salve for pain in the bones,* LCD 138b.

bānsele m. (*bone-house*), *body,* DOM 102.

bānwærc m. *pain in the bones,* WW 200[12].

banweorc n. *homicide, manslaughter,* LL 244'.

bānwyrt f. *violet? small knapweed?* LCD.

bār (ǣ) m. '*boar,*' *ÆGr.*

bara, bare wk. forms of bær adj.

barda m. *beaked ship,* WW 289[12].

bārhelm m. *helmet with the image of a boar?* FIN 30 (v. also bānhelm).

barian *to lay bare, uncover* : *depopulate,* W 310[5]. [bær I.]

barice=barricge; barm=bearm

barn I. pret. 3 sg. of biernan. II.=bearn

barricge '*braugina,*' '*baruina,*' WW.

bārspere n. *boar-spear,* BF,GL.

bārsprēot m. *boar-spear* (Swt).

barstlung=brastlung

barð m. *barque,* '*dromo,*' WW 181[29].

barða=barda

baru napn. of bær adj.

basilisca (ea[1]) m. *basilisk,* EPPs 90[13].

basing m. *cloak,* Æ.

±bāsnian *to await, expect,* AN,GEN.

bāsnung f. *expectation,* DR.

bastard m. *bastard,* CHR 1066 D. [*OFr.*]

basu (e, ea, eo) gsmn. baswes *purple, scarlet, crimson.* baswa stān *topaz.*

basuhǣwen *purple,* WW 430[7].

+baswian *to stain red,* ES 33·177.

bāt I. fm. '*boat,*' *ship, vessel, Chr.* II. pret. 3 sg. of bītan.

batian *to heal* : *grow better* : *improve in health,* CP 173[20].

bātswegen m. *boatman,* EC 254[5].

batt *bat, cudgel, club,* OEG 18b18.

bātwā=būtū

bātweard m. *ship's watchman,* B 1900.

bað=bæð

±baðian *to wash, lave,* '*bathe*' (tr. and intr.), *give baths* (*to others*), Lcd; Æ,AO.

baðu v. bæð.

be- prefix. 1. specializes the meaning of a tr. vb. (as in behōn, besettan). 2. makes an intr. vb. transitive (beswīcan, beðenc-an). 3. is privative (bedǣlan, beliðan). 4. does not alter the meaning (becuman).

be prep. w. d. and instr. (of place) '*BY,*' *near, in, on, upon, with, along, at, to* : (of time) *in, about, by, before, while, during* : *for, because of, in consideration of, by, by means of, through, in conformity with or imitation of, in comparison with, Æ,AO* : *about, concerning, in reference to* : *on penalty of.* be āwihte *in any respect.* be sumum dǣle *partly.* be ānfealdum *single.* be twīfealdum *twofold.* be eallum *altogether.* be fullan *in full, fully, perfectly* : *in excess.* be ðām mǣstan *at the most.* be ðām (ðān) ðe *because, as, according as, how.* be norðan, sūðan *to the north, south of...,* AO. be æftan=beæftan

±bēacen (ē) n. '*beacon,*' *sign, token, phenomenon, portent, apparition, JnL* : *standard, banner, B* : *audible signal,* CHRD 32[26].

bēacenfýr n. *beacon fire, lighthouse,* OET 180[7] (ǣ).

bēacenstān m. *stone on which to light a beacon fire,* WW.

bēacn- v. also bīcn-.

+bēacnian *to make signs, indicate,* B,Bo.

+bēacnung f. '*categoria,*' WW 382[32].

bead=bed

bēad I. pret. 3 sg. of bēodan. II. (NG)=bēod

beado=beadu; beadowig=bǣdewēg

beadu† f. gds. beaduwe, beadowe *war, battle, fighting, strife.*

beaducāf *bold in battle,* Rd 1¹¹.

beaducræft m. *skill in war,* An 219.

beaducræftig† *warlike.*

beaducwealm m. *violent death,* An 1704.

beadufolm f. *battle-hand,* B 990.

beadugrīma m. *war-mask, helmet,* B 2257.

beaduhrægl n. *coat of mail,* B 552.

beadulāc† n. *war-play, battle.*

beadulēoma m. *(battle-light), sword,* B 1523.

beadumægen n. *battle-strength, force,* Ex 329.

beadumēce m. *battle-sword,* B 1454.

beadurǣs m. *rush of battle,* Ma 111.

beadurinc† m. *warrior, soldier.*

beadurōf† *strong in battle, renowned in war.*

beadurūn f. *secret of a quarrel,* B 501.

beaduscearp *keen in battle (sword),* B 2704.

beaduscrūd n. *coat of mail,* B 453; 2660?

beadusearo n. *war equipment,* Ex 572.

beaduserce f. *coat of mail,* B 2755.

beaduðrēat m. *war-band, army,* El 31.

beaduwǣpen† n. *weapon of war,* Rd.

beaduwang† m. *battlefield,* An 413.

beaduweorc† n. *warlike operation.*

beaduwrǣd (o²) m. *fighting troop,* Lcd 125b.

beæftan I. adv. *after, hereafter, afterwards, behind,* AO; CP (bi-). ['baft'] II. prep. w. d. *after, behind,* Chr,Mt. ['baft']

beǣwnian *to join in marriage, marry,* Chr 1052 d. [ǣw]

beaftan *to strike (the hands) together? lament? MtL* 11¹⁷. ['beft']

bēag I. (ǣ, ē) m. *ring (as ornament or as money), coil, bracelet, collar, crown, garland,* Æ,WW; CP. ['bee'; būgan] II. pret. 3 sg. of būgan.

bēag-gifa, -gyfa† m. *ring-giver, lord, king, generous chief.*

bēaggifu (bēah-)† f. *ring-giving.*

bēaghord (h)† n. *ring-hoard,* B.

bēaghroden† *diademed, adorned with rings or armlets.*

bēaghyrne (h) f. *corner of the eye,* WW 156⁴¹.

±bēagian (ē) *to crown,* Ps.

bēag-sel n., -sele† m. *hall in which rings are distributed.*

bēagðegu (h) f. *receiving of rings,* B 2176.

bēagwīse n. *round shape,* GD 343¹⁵.

bēagwrīða (h) m. *armlet,* B 2018.

bēah I.=bēag. II. pret. 3 sg. of būgan.

beāh-=bēag-

beāhsian *to ask advice,* Bl 199´; 205´.

bealanīð=bealunīð

bealcan, bealcettan *to 'belch,' utter, bring up, splutter out, give forth, emit,* Mod,Ps; Æ : *come forth.*

beald (a) *'bold,' brave, confident, strong,* Ps; AO,CP : *presumptuous, impudent,* CP.

bealde adv. *boldly, courageously, confidently : without hesitation, immediately.*

bealdian *to be bold,* B 2177. ['bold']

bealdlīce (a¹) *'boldly,'* Jul.

bealdnes (a) f. *boldness,* MH 6²⁵.

bealdor† m. *lord, master, hero.*

bealdwyrde *bold of speech,* Æ.

beale-=bealu-

bealg, bealh pret. 3 sg. of belgan.

beallucas mp. 'testiculi,' WW. ['ballock']

bealo, bealo-=bealu, bealu-

bealu I.† gs. b(e)al(u)wes n. 'bale,' *harm, injury, destruction, ruin, evil, mischief,* Chr,Ps,Sat : *wickedness, malice : a noxious thing,* Æ. II. adj. *baleful, deadly, dangerous, wicked, evil.*

bealubend m. *pernicious bond,* W 178².

bealubenn f. *mortal wound,* Ex 238.

bealublonden *pernicious,* GnE 198.

bealuclomm mf. *oppressive bond,* Hell 65.

bealucræft m. *magic art,* Met 26⁷⁵.

bealucwealm m. *violent death,* B 2265.

bealudǣd† f. *evil deed, sin.*

bealuful 'baleful,' *dire, wicked, cruel,* Cr.

bealufūs *prone to sin,* Rim 50.

bealu-hycgende, -hȳdig *meditating mischief,* B.

bealuinwit n. *deceit, treachery,* PPs 54²⁴.

bealulēas† *harmless, innocent,* Chr,Gn. ['baleless']

bealunīð† m. *malice, wickedness.*

bealurāp m. *oppressive fetter,* Cr 365.

bealusearu n. *wicked machination,* Jul 473.

bealuslīð† m. *hurt, adversity : death.*

bealusorg f. *dire sorrow,* Ph 409.

bealuspell n. *baleful message,* Ex 510.

bealuðonc m. *evil thought,* Jul 469.

bealuwes, bealwes v. bealu.

bēam I. m. *tree,* KC,Rd : *'beam,' rafter, piece of wood,* Chr,Mt; CP,Mdf : *cross, gallows,* Cr : (†) *ship,* Rd : *column, pillar : sunbeam,* Chr,Ps : *metal girder,* AO. II. (NG)=bȳme

bēamere (Mt)=bȳmere

bēamsceadu† f. *shade of a tree.*

bēamtelg m. *ink or dye from wood,* Rd 27⁹.

bēamweg m. *road made with logs,* BC 1·417´.

bēamwer m. *wooden weir?* BC 2·242´.

bēan (ie) f. 'bean,' *pea, legume,* Lcd; Mdf.

bēan-belgas (LkL), -coddas (Lk) mp. *bean-pods, husks or cods.* [v. 'belly,' 'cod']

bēanbroð v. bēonbroð.

bēancynn n. *a kind of bean,* WW 205³.

bēanen adj. *of beans,* Lcd 1·282⁹.

bēanlēag f. *land where beans grow,* KC 5·265. [v. 'bean']

bēanmelu n. *bean-meal*, Lcd 31b.

bēansǣd n. *bean-seed*.

bēansc(e)alu f. *bean-pod*, OEG 608.

bēanset n. *bean-plot*, KC 1·315′.

bēar (NG)=bēor

bearce (æ) f. *barking*, Gl.

beard m. *'beard,'* VPs; Æ.

+bearded *having a beard*, GD 279¹⁴.

beardlēas *beardless, youthful,* ÆGr,Gl.

bearg I. (e) m. *'barrow' pig, hog*, Mt,Rd. II. pret. 3 sg. of beorgan.

bearh=bearg I and II; **bearht**=beorht

bearhtm I. (br-, e, eo, y) m. *brightness, flash : twinkling (of an eye), instant.* adv. bearhtme *instantly.* II.=breahtm

bearhtmhwæt *swift as the twinkling of an eye, momentary*, Az 107 (br-).

bearhtmhwīl f. *moment, twinkling of an eye, point of time*, GD.

bearm I. (a) m. *lap, bosom, breast*, Lk : *middle, inside* : (†) *possession.* II. *emotion, excitement?* PPs 118. III.=beorma

bearm-clāð, -hrægl n. *apron*, WW 127². [v. *'cloth'*]

bearmtēag *yeast-box*, LL 455,17.

bearn I. (a, eo) n. *child, son, descendant, offspring, issue*, B,Mt,TC ; AO,CP. lēoda b. *children of men.* mid bearne *pregnant*, LL. [*'bairn'*] II.=barn pret. 3 sg. of biernan. III. pret. 3 sg. of beiernan. IV.=bereærn

bearnan (N)=biernan

bearncennicge *mother*, DR.

bearn-ēaca (Æ,CP), -ēacen (CP), -ēacnod, -ēacnigende (Æ) *pregnant.*

bearnende (NG)=biernende ptc. of biernan.

bearngebyrda fp. *child-bearing*, B 946.

bearngestrēon n. *procreation of children.* Rd 21³⁷.

bearnlēas *childless*, Æ.

bearnlēast (ē²) f. *childlessness*, Bo 24¹⁰.

bearnlufe *affection (for a child), adoption*, BH 454¹¹.

bearn-myrðra m., -myrðre f. *murderer or murderess of a child*, W.

bearntēam m. *offspring, posterity*, AO : *procreation of children*, HL. [*'bairnteam'*]

bearo=bearu

bears=bærs; **bēarscipe**=bēorscipe

±bearu gs. bearwes m. *grove, wood*, BH ; CP; Mdf. [berwe]

bearug=bearg

bearunǣs m. *woody shore*, Rd 58⁵.

bearwe (æ) f. *basket, wheelbarrow*, LL 455,15.

bearwes v. bearu; **beasu**=basu I.

+bēat n. *scourging*, Æ,H 1·406⁸.

±bēatan⁷ pret. bēot and (rarely) beoft (ES 38·28) *to 'beat,' pound, strike, thrust, dash*, Bo,Bl,Ps : *hurt, injure*, Da 265 : *tramp, tread*, B.

bēatere m. *beater, boxer*, Æ.

bēaw m. *gad-fly*, WW.

bebaðian *to bathe, wash* (tr. intr. and refl.), Ph. [*'bebathe'*]

bebēodan² *to offer, commit, entrust*, CP : *bid, enjoin, instruct, command, require*, Æ,Lk ; AO,CP : *announce, proclaim.* [*'bibede'*]

bebēodend m. *commander, master*, CP.

bebēodendlic *imperative*, ÆGr.

bebeorgan³ *to be on one's guard, defend, protect*, B. [*'bibergh'*]

beber (WW 11¹⁴)=befer

beberan⁴ *to carry to, supply with*, LL 4,18.

bebindan³ *to bind about, bind fast*, Æ.

be-birgan, -birigan=bebyrgan

bebītan (bi-) *to bite*, Cp 251m.

beblāwan *to blow upon*, Lcd,LPs.

bebod n. *command, injunction, order, decree*, Mt ; Æ,AO,CP. ðā bebodu *the (ten) commandments.*

beboddæg m. *appointed day*, A 11·102⁶⁷.

bebodian wv.=bebēodan

bebodrǣden f. *command, authority*, LPs 118¹¹⁰.

bebrǣdan *to spread, cover*, MH 44¹⁹.

bebrecan⁴ *to break to pieces*, Sol 295.

bebregdan³ *to pretend*, LkL 20²⁰.

bebrūcan² *to practise*, Æ : *consume (food)*, GD.

bebūgan² *to flow round, surround, enclose* : *turn from, shun, avoid*, El : *reach, extend.* [*'bibugh'*]

bebycgan *to sell*, LRG,MH.

bebycgung f. *selling*, WW.

bebyrdan *to fringe, border*, WW 375⁴¹.

be-byrgan (AO) -byrian I. *to raise a mound to, bury, inter*, Æ. [*'bebury'*] II.=bebeorgan

be-byrgednes, -byrig(ed)nes f. *burial, burying.*

bebyrgung f. *burial*, ÆL,GD.

bebyrig-=bebyrg-

bebyrwan (?=-bȳwan, BTs) *to rub over*, GD 318³.

bec=bæc; **bēc** v. bōc.

becæflan *to ornament*, WW 137²².

+bēcan *to make over in writing, grant by charter*, EC 202′.

becarcian *to be anxious (about)*, MFB 99.

becc=bæc II.

becca m. *pick, mattock*, WW ; Æ. [*'beck'*; v. also IF 24 and LF 140]

beccen m. *buyer*, WW (KGl) 75³⁶. [=bycgend]

bece m.=bæc II.

bēce (oe) f. *'beech' (tree)*, Gl. (v. also bōc.)

becēapian¹ *to sell*, Æ : *buy*, Æ.

becefed=becæfed, pp. of becæfian.
bēcen I. '*beechen,*' *made of beechwood*, Lcd, WW. II. (NG)=bēacen
beceorfan³ *to cut, cut off, separate*, Æ. hēafde b. *to behead.*
beceorian *to murmur at, complain of*, Chr, RB.
becēowan² *to gnaw in pieces*, Soul 111.
becēpan I. *to take notice of*, LPs. II.= becȳpan
beceð pres. 3 sg. of bacan.
becīdan *to complain of*, ÆH 2·470⁶.
becierran (e, y) *to turn, turn round, pass by, avoid*, Met; CP : *wind, twist : pervert*, Chr : *give up, betray.* ['*bicharre*']
beclǣman *to plaster over, poultice*, Lcd.
beclǣnsian *to cleanse*, SPs 18¹⁴.
beclemman *to bind, enclose*, Sol 71.
beclencan *to hold fast*, LPs 104¹⁸.
beclēsung=beclȳsung
beclingan³ *enclose, bind*, El 696.
beclippan (CP)=beclyppan
beclīsung=beclȳsung
beclypian (eo;=i) *to accuse, challenge, sue at law*, LL. ['*beclepe*']
beclyppan *to clasp, embrace*, Mk : *encompass, hold*, Ps; Æ. ['*beclip*']
beclypping f. *embrace*, OEG.
beclȳsan *to close, shut up, enclose, confine, imprison*, Lk; Æ. [clūse; '*beclose*']
beclȳsung f. *enclosure, cell*, OEG 1522 : *period, syllogism*, OEG.
bēcn=bēac(e)n; bēcn-=bi(e)cn-
becnāwan⁷ *to know*, RB 38¹⁷.
becnedan⁵ *to knead up*, Lcd 93a.
bēcnydlic=bīcnendlic
becnyttan *to knit, tie, bind*, Æ,CP.
becol-a? m., -e? f. *spectre*, WW 530³³.
bēc-rǣde, -rǣding, -trēow=bōc-rǣding, -trēow
becrēopan² *to creep into, crawl*, AO : *be hidden*, Æ.
becst pres. 2 sg. of bacan.
becuman⁴ *to come, approach, arrive, enter, meet with, fall in with*, AO,B; Æ,CP : *happen, befall*, Æ,Bo : (impers.) *befit*, MkL 14³¹. ['*become*']
bēcun (NG)=bēacen
becwelan⁴ *to die*, LL 400,1.
becweðan⁵ *to say : speak to, address, exhort*, A,Ps : *admonish, blame* : '*bequeath*,' *leave by will*, KC; Æ.
becweðere m. *interpreter, translator*, EHy 16 (proem.).
becwyddod *bespoken, deposited*, WW 115³⁹.
becwylman? *to torment* (BTs).
becyme m. *event, result*, BH 372¹⁹.
becȳpan (ē;=īe) *to sell*, G,RB.
becyrran=becierran

±bed I. n. *prayer, supplication*, Æ,CP : *religious ordinance, service*, Æ. II.=bedd. III.=bæd pret. 3 sg. of biddan.
bedǣlan *to deprive, strip, bereave of, rob*, Æ : *release, free from.* ['*bedeal*']
bēdan=bēodan; +bēdan=+bǣdan
bedbǣr (ē) f. *portable bed*, NG.
+bedbigen f. *payment for prayers*, LL 258,51. [bycgan]
bedbolster m. *bolster, pillow*, WW 124²⁰. ['*bedbolster*']
bedbūr n. *bed-chamber*, HGl 481.
±bedcleofa (e, i, y) m. *bed-chamber*, Ps : *lair.*
bed-cofa m., -cofe f. *bed-chamber*, Gl,HL.
bedd n. '*bed*,' *couch, resting-place*, Jn,KC; CP : *garden-bed, plot*, Lcd; Mdf.
+bedda mf. *bedfellow, consort, wife, husband*, B; Æ. ['*i-bedde*']
±beddagas mpl. *Rogation days*, ÆH.
beddclāð m. *bed-covering*; pl. *bed-clothes*, HL.
beddclyfa=bedcleofa
+bedde (KC 3·50³)=+bedda
beddgemāna m. *cohabitation*, CP 99²⁵.
beddian *to make a '*bed*,' WW : *provide one with a bed*, LL.
bedding f. '*bedding*,' *bed-covering*, LPs, WW; Æ : *bed.*
bedd-rēaf, -reda=bed-rēaf, -reda
beddrest† f. *bed*, WW 154¹.
beddstōw f. *bed*, BH 410¹².
-bede v. ēað-b.
be-dēaglian (-dēahl) *to conceal*, Gu,KGl.
bedecian *to beg*, Æ,CP.
bedēglian=bediglian; bedēlan=bedǣlan
bedelfan³ *to dig round*, Lk : *bury*, Rood; AO. ['*bedelve*']
bedelfung f. *digging round*, WW 149¹¹.
beden pp. of biddan.
be-dēpan (VPs), -deppan=bedīpan, -dyppan
bedfelt mn. *bed-covering*, RB 91¹⁶.
bedgerid n. *food in an ant's nest*, Lcd 118a.
+bedgiht f. *evening*, WW 117⁸.
±bedhūs n. *chapel, oratory*, Æ.
+bedian *to pray, worship*, BH 408²⁹.
bedician *to surround with a dyke, embank, fortify*, Chr 1016e.
bedidrian=bedydrian
be-diglian (-dīhl-; ē, ēo, īo;=īe) *to conceal, hide, obscure, keep secret*, Æ : *be concealed, lie hid.*
bedigling f. *secret place*, RPs 80⁸.
beding=bedding
bedīolian (K)=bediglian
bedīpan (ē, ȳ) *to dip, immerse : anoint*, CPs 140⁵.
+bedmann m. *worshipper, priest*, Bo,LL.
bedol=bedul
bedon *to shut*, PPs 147². ['*bedo*']

±bedrǣden f. *prayer, intercession*, Æ.
bedragan v. pp. bedrŏg.
bedrēaf n. *bed-clothes, bedding*, Ct,RB.
bedreda (i, y) m. (and adj.) *bedridden (man)*, Æ. ['*bedrid*']
bedrēf=bedrēaf
bedrēosan² *to overcome, deceive?* GEN 528, 823 : *deprive of, bereave, despoil*.
bedrest=beddrest; bedrida=bedreda
bedrīfan¹ *to drive, beat, strike, assail*, AO : *follow up, pursue : surround, cover*.
bedrincan³ *to drink up, absorb*, LCD.
bedrīp n. *compulsory service rendered to a landowner at harvest time*, LL. [v. '*bedrip*']
bedrŏg *beguiled*, GEN 602.
bedrūgian *to dry up*, LCD 1·336⁴.
bedryda=bedreda
bedrȳpan *to moisten*, GPH 391¹⁸.
+bedscipe† m. *cohabitation, wedlock*, GEN.
+bedsealm m. *precatory psalm*, LCD 51a, 138a.
+bedstŏw f. *place of prayer, oratory*, BH, BL.
bedstrēaw n. *straw for bedding*, ÆL 31⁵⁷².
bedtīd f. *bed-time*, WW 176².
+bedtīd *time of prayer*, MH 126¹⁸.
bed-ŏegn, -ŏēn m. *chamber-servant, chamberlain*, WW.
bedu f. *asking, prayer*, CP. [*Goth.* bida]
bedūfan² *immerse, submerge, drown*, Æ. ['*bedove*']
bedul *suppliant*, WW 180¹².
bedwāhrift n. *bed-curtain*, Ct.
bedydrian *to conceal from*, Æ : *deceive*, Æ. ['*bedidder*']
bedȳfan *to immerse*, GD 73²⁴; CPs 68¹⁶.
bedȳglan=bedīglian; bedȳpan=bedīpan
be-dyppan (e), *to dip, immerse*, Æ,Mt. ['*bedip*']
bedyrnan *to conceal*, Æ. [dierne]
beēastan *to the east of*, Chr; AO. ['*beeast*']
beēastannorŏan *to the north-east of*, AO.
beebblan *to leave aground by the ebb tide, strand*, CHR 897A.
beefesian *to cut off the hair*, ÆL 33⁸⁴.
beegŏan *to harrow*, BYH 74¹¹.
beerf-=beyrf-; befǣdman=befǣŏman
befǣlon pret. 3 pl. of befēolan.
befǣstan *to fasten, fix, ground, establish, make safe, put in safe keeping*, Æ,CP : *apply, utilize : commend, entrust to*, Æ, CP.
befǣstnian (ea) *to fix*, Æ : *pledge, betroth*.
befǣttian *to fatten, anoint*, LPs 140⁵.
befǣŏ-man, -mian *to encircle*, Æ.
befaran⁶ *to go, go round or among, traverse, encompass, surround*, AO : *come upon, surprise, catch*, LL 230,13¹.

befealdan⁷ *to fold, roll up, envelop, clasp, surround, involve, cover*, Æ; CP : *attach*. ['*befold*']
befealdian (intr.) *to roll up*, MFH 117¹¹.
befealh pret. of befēolan
befeallan I. (sv⁷) *to fall*, CP,Mt; Æ : *deprive of, bereave of : fall to, be assigned to :* '*befall*,' ÆGR. II.=befyllan
befeastnian (NG)=befǣstan
befēgan *to join*, ÆL 23⁴²⁵.
befelgan=befyllan; befellan=befyllan
befelŏrǣd (HGL 489)=hefeldŏrǣd
befeohtan³ *to take by fighting*, Rd 4³². ['*befight*']
befēolan³ *to put away, bury : deliver, grant, consign, entrust to*, Ps : *betake oneself to, apply oneself, devote oneself to, persist, persevere*, CP : *importune : put up with, be pleased with*. ['*bifele*']
befēon *to deprive of property*, OEG 3157.
befer (eo¹, y¹, o²) m. '*beaver*,' ÆGr; Mdf.
befēran *to surround*, Æ : *come upon, overtake, pass by : go about : fall among*, NG.
beficIan *to deceive*, LL (320').
befīlan, befilgan=befȳlan, befyllan
beflod (HGL 480) pp. of befēon.
beflēan⁶ *to peel, skin, flay*, WW. beflagen flǣsc *entrails*. ['*beflay*']
beflēogan² *to fly upon*, BH. ['*befly*']
beflēon² (w. a.) *to flee from, flee, escape, avoid*, Ps; CP. ['*beflee*']
beflōwan⁷ *to flow round, over*, Wif. ['*beflow*']
befōn⁷ *to surround, clasp, include, envelop, encase, clothe*, Bl; Æ,AO,CP : *comprehend, seize, attach (at law), lay hold of, catch, ensnare*, Gen : *contain, receive, conceive : explain*, CP. wordum b. *tell, relate*. on b. *have to do with, engage in*. ['*befong*']
befor=befer
beforan I. prep. a. (w. d.) (local) '*before*,' *in front of, in the presence of*, Æ,Bl,G; CP : (temporal) *before, prior to, sooner than*, G. β. (w. a.) *before*, G. II. adv. (local) *before, in front*, B : (temporal) *before, formerly, in former times, earlier, sooner : at hand, openly*, An.
beforhtian *to dread*, Æ 23b⁵²⁵.
befōtian *to cut off one's feet*, Æ 25¹¹⁷.
befrēogan *to free, liberate*, Ps.
be-frīnan, -frignan³ *to question, ask, learn*, Æ.
befrīnung f. *inquiry*, OEG 2309.
befrȳnan=befrīnan; beftan=beæftan
befullan *entirely, completely, perfectly*, CP 5²⁰.
befȳlan (ī) *to befoul, defile*, Lcd; Æ. ['*befile*']
befylgan *to follow after, pursue, persevere with*, LCD.

befyllan I. *to fell, lay low, strike down,* GEN : *take by killing, bereave,* GEN. [feallan] **II.** *to fill up,* BH 64⁵n (Schipper). [full]
bēg=bēag
bēga gmfn. of bēgen.
begalan⁶ *to sing incantations over, enchant,* Lcd ; Æ. ['bigale']
begān *to go over, traverse,* Æ : *get to, come by, fall into* : *go to, visit, care for, cultivate,* Lcd ; AO : *inhabit, occupy,* Æ,BH,Lcd : *surround, beset, overrun,* Chr,Job : *practise, do, engage in, perform, attend to, be diligent about,* Æ,CP : *honour, serve, worship* : *profess.* on borh b. *pledge oneself,* CP. ūtan b. *besiege,* Chr. ['bego']
bēgan=bīegan, bēagian
begang (i¹, o²) mn. *way, course, circuit, extent* : *district, region* : *business, undertaking, practice, exercise, service, reverence, worship* : *cultivation,* GD. [=bīgeng]
beganga=bīgenga ; **begangan**=begān
be-gangnes, -geongnes (DR), -gannes (WW), f. 'calendæ,' *celebration.*
begangol (bigeong-) m.? *cultivator,* LkR : *worship,* DR.
begbēam m. *bramble, thorn-bush,* G,WW.
bēge=bēgen ; **bēgea**=bēga
bēgean=bīegan
begēat I. m. *attainment,* Æ : *acquisitions, property,* Æ. **II.** pret. 3 sg. of begēotan.
begeg-=begeng- ; **begēm-**=begīm-
begēmen (KGL)=begīmen
bēgen nm. (but where one thing is m. and the other f. or n., the nom. is bā, bū), nf. bā, nn. bū ; gmfn. bēg(e)a, bēgra ; dmfn. bǣm, bām ; am. bū ; af. bā ; an. bū *both,* El,G,Lcd. v. also būtū. ['bo']
begenga m. *cultivator,* MtR.
bege(n)gnes (i¹) f. *application, study,* GD, WW.
begēomerian *to lament,* W 75¹⁵.
begeondan (AO,CP), begeonde, -geonan prep. w. a. d. ; and adv. 'beyond,' *on the other side,* Æ,Chr,Jn.
begeong-=begang- ; **begeotan**=begietan
begēotan² *to pour over or upon, anoint, infuse, flood* (with), *sprinkle, cover with fluid,* Chr ; Æ. ['bigeten']
beger n. *berry,* GL.
beget=begeat pret. 3 sg. of begietan.
begeten pp. of (1) begēotan, (2) begietan.
bēgian=bēagian
begiellan³ (i¹, e²) *to scream, screech,* Seaf 24. [v. 'yell']
begietan⁵ (e, i, y) *to get, find, acquire, attain, receive, take, seize,* AO,CP : *happen* : *beget.*
begietend (e) m. *one who gets,* WW 214³⁵.
begīman (ȳ ; =īe) *to look after, take care of* : *do service, attend* : *take heed, observe.*

begīmen f. *attention, observation,* GL,Lcd.
begīmend (ȳ) m. *guide, ruler,* Sc.
begīming (ȳ) f. *invention, device* : *observance* : *care, regard,* OEG.
begīnan¹ *to open the mouth wide, swallow,* GD,RD.
beginnan³ *to* 'begin,' Æ ; AO,CP : *attempt, undertake,* Æ : *attack,* AO.
begir=beger ; **begirdan**=begyrdan
begitan (AO,CP)=begietan
begleddian *to befoul, pollute,* Æ : *stain, dye,* Æ.
beglīdan¹ *to leave, desert,* PPs 56¹.
begnagan⁶ *to gnaw,* MH 118¹⁰.
begneorð? *attentive,* BH 370² (?=*becneord, BT).
begnīdan¹ *to rub thoroughly,* Lcd 50a.
begnornian *to mourn for,* B 3179.
begong=begang
bēgra gmfn. of bēgen.
begrǣtan=begrētan
begrafan⁶ *to bury,* El 835. ['begrave']
begrētan *to lament,* PPs 77⁶³.
begrindan³† *to grind, polish, sharpen,* RD 27⁶ : *deprive of, rob,* GEN 1521.
begrīpan¹ *to grip, seize* : *chide,* Ps. ['begripe']
begriwen ptc. *steeped in,* Æ.
begroren *overwhelmed,* SAT 52.
begrornian=begnornian
begrynian *to ensnare, entrap,* WW 92¹⁰. [grīn]
begyldan *to adorn with gold,* CVPs 44¹⁰.
begylpan (=ie) *to boast, exult,* B 2007?
begȳm-=begīm-
begyrdan *to gird, clothe,* Ps ; Æ : *surround, fortify,* BH ; CP. ['begird']
begytan=begietan ; **bēh**=bēag, bēah
behabban *to include, hold, surround, comprehend, contain,* AO,CP : *detain, withhold.*
behādian *to unfrock* (a priest), LL.
behæfednes f. *restraint, temperance,* WW 504¹⁰.
behæpsian *to fasten a door,* ÆL 31²¹⁴.
behǣs f. *vow,* CHR 1093. [v. 'behest']
behǣttian *to scalp,* Æ : *make bald,* OEG.
behaldan=behealdan
behamelian *to mutilate,* ÆL 25¹²⁷, MH 216²⁴.
behammen 'clavatus,' (of shoe) *patched* (BT), *studded with nails* (Napier), GD 37¹³.
behāt n. *promise, vow,* Lk ; Æ : *threat,* LCD. ['behote']
behātan⁷ (often w. d. pers.) *to promise, vow, pledge oneself,* Æ ; CP : *threaten.* ['behight*']
behātland n. *promised land,* GD 204¹².
behāwian *to see clearly, take care, consider,* Mt. ['bihowe']

beheaſdian *to 'behead,' Mt*; Æ,AO.
behēaſdung f. *beheading,* Æ.
behēaſodlic *capital* (*punishment*), OEG 4042.
behealdan[7] *to hold, have, occupy, possess,* Gen : *guard, preserve,* CP : *contain, belong,* KC : *keep, observe, consider,* Bl,Ps; AO, CP : '*behold,' look at, gaze on, observe, see,* Æ,CP : *signify,* Æ : *avail, effect* : *take care, beware, be cautious,* CP : *restrain* : *act, behave.*
behealdend m. *beholder, spectator,* BH 26[23].
behealdennes f. *observance,* DR : *continence,* DR.
behealdnes f. *regard, observation,* Æ.
behēawan[7] *to cut, chip, chop, beat,* CP : *cut off from, deprive of.*
behēdan (KGL)=behȳdan
be-hēſe, -hēf(e)lic *suitable, proper, necessary,* G; Æ. ['*biheve*']
behēſnes f. *convenience, utility,* GL.
behēſō(u) f. *want, need,* RWH 134,136
behegian *to hedge round,* MLR 17·166.
behelan[4] *to cover over, hide,* AA,BH,BL.
beheldan=behealdan
behelian *to cover over, conceal, bury,* CP.
behelmian *to cover over,* SOL 104.
behēoſian *to lament,* LPs,Sc.
be-heonan, -heonon prep. (w. d.) and adv. *on this side of, close by.*
be-hēot, -hēt pret. 3 sg. of behātan.
behicgan=behycgan; behīdan=behȳdan
behīdiglīce=behȳdiglīce
behienan (CHR)=beheonan
behildan *to depart,* EPs 138[19].
behindan I. prep. (w. d., a.), adv. '*behind,' after,* Chr,Leas,LG,Met; CP.
be-hinon, -hionan=beheoṇan
behīring=behȳrung
behīwian *to dissimulate,* RBL 16[7].
behlæmman=behlemman
behlǣnant *to surround.*
behlēapan[7] *to leap upon, settle on, fix upon, devote oneself to,* CP.
behlehhan=behlyhhan
behlemmant *to dash together.*
behlēotan *to assign by lot,* MLR 17·166.
behlīdan[1] *to close, cover over,* Æ,AO.
behliden=beliden pp. of belīðan.
behlīgan[1] *to accuse,* RWH 4[1].
behlyhhan[6] (e;=ie)† *to deride, exult over,* Gu. ['*bilaugh*']
behlȳðan *to rob, deprive of,* RD 15[10].
behōſ n. *behoof, profit* : *need,* OEG 27[84].
behōſian (abs. and w. g.) *to have need of, require, want,* BH,Lcd; Æ,CP : (impers.) *it behoves, concerns, belongs, is needful or necessary,* MtL,Jn. ['*behove*']
behōſlic *necessary,* MkL. ['*behovely*']

behogadnes f. *practice,* WW 427[87].
behogian *to care for,* RB. ['*bihogien*']
behogod *careful, prudent,* DR. adv. -līce.
behōn[7] *to hang round,* CP. ['*behung*']
behorsian *to deprive of horses,* CHR.
behrēosan[2] *to fall*: *cover, shelter.* pp. behroren *divested of.*
behrēowsian *to rue, repent of, make amends,* Æ : *compassionate,* Æ. ['*bireusy*']
behrēowsung f. *repentance, penitence,* Æ. ['*bireusing*']
behrēowsungtīd f. *time of repentance, Septuagesima,* Æ.
behrīman *to cover with hoar-frost,* WIF 48.
behringan *to surround,* CP.
behrōpan[7] *to plague, importune,* Lk 18[5].
behrūmian *to besmirch,* WW.
behrūmig *sooty,* MH 52[27].
bēhð f. *witness, sign,* JUD 174.
behwearf I. (eo) pret. 3 sg. of behweorfan. II. (EPs)=behwearft
behwearft m. *exchange,* LPs 43[13].
behweolfan (A)=behwylfan
behweorfan[3] *to turn, change, spread about* : *see to, arrange, prepare, treat,* Æ : *bury,* Æ.
behwerfan=behwirfan
behwirfan (e, y;=ie) *to turn, change, convert,* CP : *exchange* : *prepare, instruct, exercise.*
behwon *whence,* BH.
behwylfan (eo;=ie) *to cover, vault over,* Ex,MFH.
behwyrfan (Æ)=behwirfan
behycgan *to consider, bear in mind* : *confide, trust* (on).
behȳdan (ī) *to conceal, shelter,* Mt; Æ. ['*behide*']
behȳd(ed)nes f. *concealment,* LL : *secret place,* LPs.
behȳdig *careful, watchful, anxious,* Æ. adv. -hȳdiglīce, -hȳdelīce.
behȳdignes f. *solicitude, care, anxiety.* v. MP 1·393. [hygdig]
behygd-=behȳd-
behyhtan *to trust,* W 48[8].
behyldan *to flay, skin,* AO.
behylian *to cover, veil,* ÆL 33[237].
behȳpan (ē;=ie) *to surround,* BH 188[14]. [hȳpe]
behȳpian *to heap up,* OEG 3322.
behȳran *to let on hire,* WW.
behȳrung f. *letting, loan,* WW.
behȳðelīce *sumptuously,* WW 513[6].
beiernan[3] (i, y) *to run up to, over, or into* : *incur* : *occur to.*
beigbēam=begbēam; beinnan=binnan
beinsiglian *to seal up,* RHy 6[34].
beirnan=beiernan
beiundane=begeondan; bel-=behl-

belācan⁷ to enclose, RD 61⁷.
belādian to excuse, clear, Æ,AO,CP.
belādiendlic apologetic, that can be excused, OEG.
belādigend m. apologist, WW 332².
belādung f. apology, excuse, WW.
belǣdan to lead astray, RB. ['belead']
belǣfan to leave, spare : be left, remain, survive, Ps; Æ. ['beleave']
belǣndan=belandian
belǣðan to make hateful, pervert, W 47⁷.
be-lǣwa (Æ), -lǣwend m. betrayer.
belǣwan to betray, Æ.
belǣwung f. betrayal, treachery, Æ.
belāf pret. of belīfan.
belandian to deprive of lands, CHR 1091.
belcedswēora adj. having an inflated neck, RD 79¹. [bælc]
belcentan, belcettan=bealcettan
beld, beldo=bieldo
+beldan I. to cover, bind (a book)? JnL p 188³. II.=+bieldan
belē- (NG)=belǣ-
belēan⁶ to censure, reprove : charge with : dissuade, forbid, prevent, CP.
belecgan to cover, invest, surround, afflict, An; AO : attribute to, charge with, accuse. ['belay']
belēfan=belȳfan; belendan (CHR 1096)= belandian
belene (eo¹, o²) f. henbane, GL,LCD.
belēogan² to deceive by lying, GD : (impers.) be mistaken. ['belie']
belēoran to pass by, pass over, MkL,VPs.
beleorendlic past. DR.
belēosan²† to be deprived of, lose.
belēweda (LL 438⁵)=belǣwend
belewit=bilewit
belflȳs n. bell-wether's fleece, LL 451,14.
belg (æ, i, y) m. bag, Mt,WW : purse, leathern bottle, pair of bellows, pod, husk. ['belly']
+belg m. anger : arrogance, RB 69²⁰.
±belgan³ (intr., refl.) to be or become angry, Æ,AO,CP : offend, provoke.
belgnes f. injustice, MtL 20¹³ (bælig-).
+belh=+belg
belhring m. bell-ringing, RB 67²⁰.
belhūs=bellhūs
belibban=belīfian
belicgan⁵ to lie round, surround, Gen : hedge in, encompass, Æ; AO. ['belie']
belīfan¹ (ȳ) to remain over, be left, Æ. pp. belifen dead, AO. ['belive']
belīfend m. survivor, OEG.
belīfian to deprive of life, Æ; belig=belg
belīman to glue together, Sc 96¹⁹.
belimp n. event, occurrence, affair. of belimpe by chance.

±belimpan³ to concern, regard, belong to, conduce to, Bo; CP : happen, befall, B; Æ : become : (impers.) befit. ['belimp']
belis(t)nian to castrate, Æ. belis(t)nod pp. as sbm. eunuch. wæs b. 'stupratur,' HGL 507.
belīðan¹† to deprive of. pp. beliden departed, dead, AN 1087.
bell=belle
bellan³ to bellow, bark, grunt, roar, Rd. ['bell']
belle f. 'bell,' KC; Æ,CP.
bellhūs n. 'bell-house,' belfry, LL,WW.
belltācen n. indication (sounding of the hour) by a bell, HL 11⁶⁵.
belltīd f. a canonical hour marked by the ringing of a bell. (cp. belltācen)
belōcian to behold, RPs 44⁵.
belone=belene
belt m. 'belt,' girdle, WW.
belūcan² to lock, shut up, close, Bl,CP,Mt; AO : surround, enclose, embody, VPs : stop, impede, block up, choke, Æ : preserve, protect : shut out, exclude, Æ : sum up, define, RWH 137⁴. ['belouke']
belune=belene
belūtian to lie hid, GD 293¹⁵.
belȳfan (ē;=īe) to believe, Æ. pp. belȳfed having belief.
belympan=belimpan
belyrtan (N) to deceive, MtL 2¹⁶. ['belirt']
belytegian to allure, seduce, AO 112²⁶. [lytig]
bemǣnan to 'bemoan,' bewail, lament, Æ.
bemancian to maim, LCD 3·214²⁰.
bēmare=bȳmere; bēme=bīeme
bemeldian to disclose, reveal, denounce (BTs).
bēmere=bȳmere
bemetan⁵ to account, consider, AO. ['bemete']
bemīðan¹ to hide, conceal, CP : lie hid.
bemurc(n)ian, to murmur at, AO 48¹⁷.
bemurnan³ (also wk.) to mourn, bewail, deplore, be sorry for : care for, take heed for.
bemūtian to exchange for, GU 42. [L. mutare]
bemyldian to bury, WW. [molde]
ben=benn
bēn I. f. (±) prayer, request, Lk; AO, CP : compulsory service, LL 447 (v. 2·418, Fron.). ['bene'] II. pret. 3 sg. of bannan.
bēna m., bēne f. suitor, petitioner, AO.
benacian to lay bare, Hy. [nacod]
benǣman (ē) to take away, deprive of, rob of, Æ,AO. [niman]

benc f. '*bench*,' B.
bencian *to make benches*, LL455,13.
bencsittend† m. *one who sits on a bench.*
bencswēg m. *bench-rejoicing, sound of revelry*, B1161.
bencðel† n. *bench-board, wainscotted space where benches stand*, B. [v. '*theal*']
bend mfn. (+b. MtL) *bond, chain, fetter*, BH,Bl,Mt,Ps; CP : *band, ribbon, ornament, chaplet, crown*, WW. ['*bend*']
bēndagas mpl. *days of prayer, Rogation days*, BF166¹⁴.
±bendan *to bend* (*a bow*), Ps : *bind, fetter*, Chr. ['*bend*']
bendfeorm=bēnfeorm
-bene v. ēað-b.
beneah (pret. pres. vb.) pl. benugon, pret. benohte *to have at one's disposal, possess, enjoy : require.*
beneced=benacod pp. of benacian.
benēman=benǣman
benemnan *to name : stipulate, settle, declare, asseverate.*
benēotan²† *to deprive of, rob.*
beneoðan (i, y) prep. w. d. '*beneath*,' *under, below*, Æ,Bo,KC,LL.
bēnfeorm f. *food during* (*or after*) *compulsory labour for the lord?* LL452' and 3·252.
bengeat n. *wound-gash*, B1121.
benīdan (ē) *to compel*, A11·110.
beniman⁴ *to take, assume, obtain*, AO : *take away from, deprive of, bereave, rob*, BH, Gen,Met; AO,CP : *contain : catch, apprehend.* ['*benim*']
beniming f. *deprival*, WW (bi-).
beniðan=beneoðan
bēnlic (oe) *that may be entreated*, DR. adv. -līce *beseechingly*, DR.
benn† n. *wound, mortal injury.* [bana]
+benn n. *edict*, WW398³⁷. [=+bann]
bēnn pret. 3 sg. of bannan.
benne f. *reed-grass*, BC (Mdf).
±bennian† *to wound*, RD.
benohte v. beneah.
benorðan *in the north, northwards* (*of*), Chr1087; AO. ['*benorth*']
benoten pp. of benēotan.
benotian *to use, consume*, Chr. ['*benote*']
bēnrīp n. *compulsory service rendered to a landowner at harvest time*, LL448. [cp. bedrīp]
±bēnsian *to pray, supplicate*, BH.
benst pres. 2 sg. of bannan.
bēntīd f. *prayer time, Rogation days*, MEN 75.
bēntīgðe, bēntīð(ig)e *granting requests, gracious*, LPs : *obtaining requests, successful*, CHR.
benð pres. 3 sg. of bannan.

benugon v. beneah.
bēnyrð f. *ploughing required from a tenant* LL448,5².
benyðan=beneoðan
bēo I. f. nap. bēon; dp. bēo(u)m '*bee*,' Lcd Ps,WW; Æ. II. pres. 1 sg. of bēon.
bēobrēad n. *honey with the comb*, Lk,Me₁ VPs; Æ. ['*bee-bread*']
bēoce=bēce
bēoceorl m. *bee-master, bee-keeper*, Ll 448,5.
bēocere m. *bee-keeper*, LL. [MHG. bīkar]
+beod=+bed
bēod m. *table*, Mt : *bowl, dish.* ['*beod*']
bēodærn n. *refectory, dining-room*, Æ (-ern). on bēoderne *at table.*
beodan=bidon pret. pl. of bīdan.
±bēodan² *to command, decree, summon*, Chr; Æ,AO,CP. b. ūt *call out* (*an army*), *banish : declare, inform, announce, proclaim*, Gu,LL : *threaten : offer, proffer, give, grant, surrender*, Æ,Gen; AO : (refl.) *show oneself, behave : exact, collect.* ['*bid*,' '*i-bede*']
bēodbolle f. *table-bowl*, GL.
bēodclāð m. *table-cloth, carpet*, ÆGR 34⁸.
bēoddern=bēodærn
bēoddian *to do joiner's work*, LL455, 13.
bēodend m. *preceptor*, CM967.
bēodendlīc=bebēodendlic
bēodern (Æ)=bēodærn
bēodfæt n. *table-vessel, cup*, WW204²⁵.
bēodfers n. *grace at meal-time*, GD,RB.
bēodgæst m. *table-companion*, AN1090.
bēodgenēat† m. *table-companion*, B.
bēodgereord n. *feast*, NC,GEN1518.
bēod(h)rægl n. *table-cloth*, WW126³³.
bēodlāfa fp. *table-leavings*, BL53¹³,VH9.
bēodland n. *land from which the table of monasteries, etc., was supplied, glebe-land*, Ct.
bēodrēaf n. *table-cloth*, TC530'.
bēod-scēat n., -scȳte m. *table-napkin, towel*, WW449²².
bēodwyst f. *a table with food on it*, LPs22⁵. [wist]
beofer (o²)=befer; beofian=bifian
beoft redupl. pret. of bēatan; beoftadon is from a later wk. *beoftian (ANS141·176).
beofung=bifung
bēogang m. *swarm of bees*, WW.
+bēogol (ū, ȳ) *submissive, obedient : forgiving*, Æ. [būgan]
bēohāta m. *chief? prince?* Ex253. [bēot-?]
beolone=belene
bēom I. dp. of bēo I. II.=bēam. III.= bēo pres. 1 sg. of bēon.

bēomōder f. *queen-bee*, OEG.

bēon I. anv. [conj. in full (WS and A) Wt 548] *to* 'BE*,' *exist, become, happen.* b. ymbe *to have to do with.* b. of *to be gone.* (v. also eom, wesan.) **II.** nap. of bēo I.

bēona gp. of bēo I.

bēonbrēad=bēobrēad

bēonbroð n. *mead?* (or? bēanbroð, ES 38·302).

bēonnon pret. pl. of bannan.

bēor n. *strong drink,* '*beer*,' *mead, Lk,WW* (v. A 27·495 and FTP 276).

+bēor m. *pot-companion, guest,* Æ.

beora=bearu; **±beoran**=beran

bēorbyden f. *beer-barrel,* LL 455,17.

beorc I. (e, i, y) f. '*birch,*' *Gl,Lcd;* Mdf : *name of the rune for* b. **II.** (±) n. *barking,* ÆGR,LCD.

beorcan³ (tr.) *to* '*bark,*' *ÆGr,CP* : (intr.) *bark at, Lcd.*

beorce=beorc

beorcholt (y) *birch wood,* WW 138,361.

beorcragu (e¹) f. *lichen from a birch-tree,* LCD 99b.

beorcrind (e¹) f. *birch-bark,* LCD 119b.

beord (BH 392²⁷)=bord

bēordrǣst(e) f. *dregs of beer,* LCD.

beorg m. *mountain, hill, AO,Lk;* Mdf : *mound,* '*barrow,*' *burial place, Æ,Lcd.*

+beorg n. *protection, defence, refuge, W.* ['*bergh*']

beorgælfen f. *oread* (Swt).

±beorgan I. sv³ (w. d.) *to save, deliver, preserve, guard, defend, fortify, spare, An, Ps;* AO,CP : (w. refl. d.) *beware of, avoid, guard against.* ['*bergh*'] **II.**=birgan

beorg-hliðᵗ (u) n. nap. -hleoðu *mountain-height, mountain-slope.*

+beorglic *fitting, profitable,* LL,W : *safe, prudent,* Æ.

beorgseðel n. *mountain dwelling,* GU 73. [setl]

beorgstede m. *mound,* PH 284 (rh).

±beorh (1)=beorg; (2) imperat. of beorgan.

beorhlēode (WW 178⁴¹)=burglēode

+beorhnes f. *refuge,* CPs 30³.

+beorhstōw f. *place of refuge,* PPs31⁸.

beorht (e, y) **I.** 'BRIGHT,' *shining, brilliant, light, clear* : *clear-sounding, loud* : *excellent, distinguished, remarkable, beautiful, magnificent, noble, glorious* : *pure, sublime, holy, divine.* **II.** n. *brightness, gleam, light* : *sight.* ēagan b. *twinkling of an eye.*

beorhtan=bierhtan

beorhtblōwende *bright-blooming,* LCD 1·404⁹.

beorhte *brightly, brilliantly, splendidly, B, Met* : *clearly, lucidly, distinctly,* CP.

beorhthwīl (RWH 41¹⁸)=bearhtmhwīl

beorhtian (e) *to glisten, shine, BH,Ps* : *to sound clearly, B* : *to make bright, VPs.* ['*bright*']

+beorhtian=+beorhtnian

beorhtlic *brilliant, clear, shining, splendid.* adv. -līce, *Mk;* Æ. ['*brightly*']

beorhtm=bearhtm

beorhtnan *to grow bright,* OEG 534.

±beorhtnes (æ) f. '*brightness,*' *clearness, splendour, beauty, JnL,Lk;* CP : *lightning,* LPs 109³.

±beorhtnian (e) *to glorify,* NG.

beorhtrodor m. *shining heavens,* EX 94.

beorhtte (=*beorgihte) pl. *mountainous,* AO 10²⁵.

beorhtu=bierhtu

beorhtword (y¹) *clear-voiced,* SAT 238.

bēorhyrde m. *cellarer, butler,* CRA 75.

beorm-=bearm-

beorma m. '*barm,*' *yeast, leaven, Mt.*

+beormad *leavened,* MtR 13³³. ['*barm*']

beorn I.ᵗ m. *man* : *noble, hero, chief, prince, warrior, B,Ma* : *rich man,* RUN 12. ['*berne*'] **II.**=barn pret. 3 sg. of biernan. **III.**=bearn

beornan (VPs)=biernan

beorncyning m. *lord of heroes,* B 2148.

beorne=byrne

Beornice mp. *Bernicians, inhabitants of part of Northumbria,* BH.

beorning (=ie) f. *incense,* LkL 1¹¹.

beornðrēat m. *troop of men,* PA 50.

beornwiga m. †*warrior, hero.*

bēorscealc *reveller, feaster,* B 1240. [v. A 46·233]

±bēorscipe m. *feast, banquet, revel,* Æ,CP.

bēorseleᵗ m. *beer-hall, banqueting hall.*

bēorsetl n. *ale-bench,* JUL 687.

beorswinig (NG)=bærsynnig

bēorðeguᵗ f. *beer-drinking.*

-beorðling (ie) v. hyse-b.

±beorðor (e, o, u, y) n. *child-bearing, childbirth* : *what is born, foetus, offspring.*

beorðorcwelm m. *abortion,* WW 348²³.

beorðor-ōīnen, -ōīnenu (broðor-) f. *midwife,* GEN 38²⁸.

beoruh=beorg; **beosmrian**=bismerian

bēost m. *beestings, the first milk of a cow after calving, WW* : *swelling (of the ground)?* v. Mdf. ['*beest*']

beosu=basu

±bēot I. n. *boastful speech, boast, threat, Æ, Gen.* on b. *boastfully* : *promise, vow,* AO : *command* : *peril, danger,* DA 265. [=behāt; '*beot*,' '*i-beot*'] **II.** pret. 3 sg. of bēatan.

±bēotian I. *to threaten, Jul* : *boast, vow, promise,* AO. ['*beoten*'] **II.**=bōtian

±bēotlic *arrogant, exulting, boastful, threatening,* Æ. adv. -līce.

bēotmæcg m. *leader*, DA 265.

bēoton pret. pl. of bēatan.

bēotung f. *threatening*, BH,LCD.

bēotword† n. *boast*, B : *threat*, JUL.

bēoðēof m. *bee-thief*, LL 54,9².

bēoum dp. of bēo.

bēow n. *barley*, GL.

bēowan=bȳwan

bēowyrt f. *bee-wort, sweet flag*, LCD.

bepǣcan *to deceive, seduce*, Mt; Æ. ['*bi-peche*']

bepǣcend m. *deceiver*, Æ.

bepǣcestre f. *whore*, ÆGR 175⁹.

bepǣcung f. *deception*, OEG.

beprīwan (ē) *to wink*, BO,W.

bēr (NG)=bǣr

bera m. '*bear*,' Æ.

beræccan=bereccan

berǣdan *to deprive, take by treachery, rob* : *betray*, Æ : *deliberate on* : *get the better of.*

berǣsan *to rush upon or into*, Æ,CP.

±beran⁴ (eo) *to* '*bear*,' *carry, bring, take away, carry out, extend, AO,B*; Æ,CP : *bring forth, produce, Bl,Mt,Gen*; Æ : *be situated by birth, LL* : *wear, AO* : *endure, support, sustain, LL,Mt*; CP. (with ūp) *set forth, open* (*a case*), CHR 1052 E. berende *fruitful.* +boren *born.* [v. also '*i-bere*']

berascin n. *bear-skin*, EC 250¹⁷.

+berbed '*vermiculatus*,' *barbed*, DR 4³.

ber-bēne, -bīne f. *verbena*, LCD.

berc-=beorc, berec-

+berd-, +bēre=+byrd-, +bǣre

bere m. *barley*, Æ,JnLR. ['*bear*']

bereærn n. '*barn*,' Lk. [bere, ærn]

berēafere m. *despoiler*, OEG 46³⁶.

berēaflan *to* '*bereave*,' *deprive of, take away, seize, rob, despoil*, BO ; Æ,AO.

berēafigend m. *despoiler, robber*, APT,GL.

berebrytta m. *barn-keeper*, LL 451,17.

berēcan *to cause to smoke, smoke* (tr.), LCD 1·106¹⁶.

bereccan *to relate* : *excuse or justify oneself*, CP.

berecorn n. *barley-corn*, GL,LL.

berecroft m. *barley-field*, KC 3·260¹ (berc-).

+bered *crushed, kneaded*, WW : *harassed, oppressed*, NG.

berēflan (KGL)=berēafian

bereflōr m. *barn-floor, threshing-floor*, LkL. [v. '*bear*']

beregafol n. *rent paid in barley*, LL 116,59¹. [cp. gafolbǣre]

beregræs n. *barley-grass, fodder*, WW 148²⁶.

berehalm n. *barley-haulm, straw*, LCD 157a.

bereland (ber-) *barley-land*, KC 3·367⁹.

beren I. *of barley*, Æ. II.=biren. III.=bereærn

berend m. *bearer, carrier*, GL.

berendan *to peel, take off husk*, LCD.

berende *fruitful*, BH. [beran]

berendlīce *with fecundity*, DR 32⁸.

berendnes f. *fertility*, DR 108¹¹.

berenhulu f. *barley-husk*, SC 95¹⁹.

berēnian *to bring about*, EX 147 : *ornament, mount* (*with silver*), KC 6·101'.

berēocan² *to fumigate*, LL (164⁵).

berēofan²† *to bereave, deprive, rob of.*

berēotan² *to bewail*, HELL 6.

berēowsian=behrēowsian

-berere v. wæter-b.

berern (NG)=bereærn

beresǣd n. *barley*, BH 366²⁷.

beretūn m. *barley-enclosure, threshing-floor, barn*, MtL; Æ. ['*barton*']

berewǣstm m. *barley-crop*, LCD 1·402⁸.

berewīc f. *barley-yard, demesne farm, TC.* ['*berewick*']

berg=(1) bearg, (2) beorg

berg-=beri-, birg-, byrg-

berh=bearh pret. 3 sg. of beorgan.

berht, berht-=beorht, beorht-, bierht-

berhtm-=breahtm-

berian I. *to make* '*bare*,' *clear*, B 1239. [bær] II.=byrgan II.

+berian=+byrian

bericge=barricge

berīdan¹ *to ride round, surround, besiege, LL* : *overtake, seize, occupy*, CHR. ['*beride*']

berie f. '*berry*,' Lcd : *grape*, Æ : *vine*, WE 63²⁰.

berig I. n. *berry*, RPs 77⁴⁷. II.=byrig, ds. of burg.

berigdrenc m. *drink made of mulberries*, WW 114²².

berige=berie; berigea=byrga

berind(r)an *to strip off bark, peel*, LCD.

beringan=behringan

berinnan³ *to run upon, run over, wet, bedew*, CR 1176. ['*berun*']

berīsan¹ *to be fitting*, BYH 78¹³.

berland, bern=bereland, bereærn

bern-=bærn-, biern-

bernan (VPs; v. AB 40·343)=bærnan

bernhus n. *barn*, GD 68²². [=beren-]

berōfon (pret. pl. of *berafan or *berebban) *despoiled*, GEN 2078.

berōwan⁷ *to row round*, CHR 897A.

berst=byrst

+berst n. *bursting*, LCD,W 186⁷.

±berstan³ (intr.; tr. at RD 2⁸) *to break*, '*burst*,' *fail, fall, B,Lcd,LL,Ma*; Æ,AO : *break away from, escape* : *break to pieces, crash, resound.*

berthwīl=bearhtmhwīl; bertūn=beretūn

berð-=beorð-, byrð-

+bēru=+bǣru, +bǣre

berūmod=behrūmod pp. of behrūmian.

berunnen pp. of berinnan.

berwe ds. of bearu.

berwinde f. *'bearbind,' navel-wort,* WW 300[19].

berȳfan *to deprive,* Mod 63. [rēaf]

berȳpan (=īe) *despoil of, strip, spoil, rob,* Æ.

besǣgan *to sink,* GPH 388[85].

besǣncan=besencan

besǣtian *to lay wait for,* AO 146[11].

besārgian *to lament, bewail, be sorry for, pity,* Æ. [sārig]

besārgung f. *compassion,* Æ.

besāwan[7] *to sow,* Æ.

bescēad (bi-) n. *distinction,* G.

bescēadan[7] *to separate, discriminate : scatter, sprinkle over,* Lcd 20b.

bescead(uw)ian, *to overshadow,* Sol; RWH 138[5], RPs 139[8]. [*'beshade'*]

besceafan[6] *to scrape thoroughly,* Lcd 143b.

bescēan pret. 3 sg. of bescīnan.

besceatwyrpan *'despondi,'* v. OEG 4555; 2[846]; ES 42·170.

bescēawere m. *observer,* DHy 24[15].

bescēawian *to look round upon, survey, contemplate, consider, watch,* Æ,AO : *look to, care for.* bescēawod *thoughtful, prudent,* Lcd 3·436[11].

bescēawiendlic *contemplative,* OEG 991.

bescēawodnes f. *vision, sight,* EPs 9[12].

bescēawung f. *contemplation,* GD,GL.

besceddan=besceadan

bescencan *to give to drink,* Gu 596.

bescēofan=bescūfan

besceoren (WW 217[24])=bescoren pp. of bescieran.

bescēotan[2] *to shoot into, plunge into, implant : happen, occur,* AO.

be-sceran, -scerwan=bescieran

bescerian=bescierian

bescieran[4] *to shear, shave, cut hair, give the tonsure,* Æ,AO. [*'beshear'*]

besclerednes (y[2]) f. *deprivation,* WW 351[13].

bescierian *to separate from, deprive of,* Chr : *defraud.*

bescīnan[1] *to shine upon, light up, illuminate,* Rd; Æ. [*'beshine'*]

bescir-an, -ian=bescier-an, -ian

bescītan[1] *to befoul,* WW 507[28].

bescrēadian *to scrape off, clean off,* ES 42·171.

bescrepan[5] *to scrape,* Lcd 101a.

bescrȳdan *to clothe,* RWH 136[32].

bescūfan[2] *to shove, impel, thrust down, hurl, throw,* Æ,AO : *force,* Æ.

bescȳlan (=īe) *to look askance,* Bo 121[30]. [sceol]

bescyldian *to shield, defend,* Wyn.

bescyr-=bescier-

besēcan *to beseech, beg urgently,* MFH 151.

besecgan *to announce, introduce : defend, excuse oneself :* (w. on) *accuse,* Æ.

besellan=besylian

besellan *to surround, cover (over) : hand over,* RPs 105[41].

besema=besma

besencan *to cause to sink, submerge, immerse, drown,* Bl,Mt; AO,CP : *plunge into (fire),* GD 317. [*'besench'*]

besendan *to send,* Æ.

besengan *to singe, burn,* AO.

besēon I. sv[5] (tr., intr. and refl.) *to see, look, look round, behold,* Æ,Mk,Ps; AO : *observe : look after, go to see, visit : provide for.* b. tō *look upon, have regard to,* CP. [*'besee'*] II. sv[1] *to suffuse,* Cr 1088.

besēoðan *to boil down,* Lcd.

besēowian (ī, ȳ) *to sew together, sew up,* Ep, WW. [*'besew'*]

be-serian, -serwan=besierwan

besettan *to put, place, set near, appoint,* Æ : *own, keep, occupy :* '*beset,' cover, surround with, adorn,* B; Æ,CP : *besiege, invest, An : institute, set going.*

besibb *related,* RWH 139[4]. (as sb.).

besīdian *to regulate the size of anything,* RB 89[18]. [sīd]

besierwan *to ensnare, surprise, deceive, defraud, oppress,* AO. [searu]

besīgan (on) *to rush,* v. OEG 4126.

besilfran *to silver,* VPs 67[14].

besincan[3] (intr.) *to sink,* AO. [*'besink'*]

besingan[3] *to sing of, bewail : sing charms, enchant,* Æ.

besirwan (AO,CP)=besierwan

besittan[5] *to sit round, surround, beset, besiege,* Chr; AO : *hold council : occupy, possess.* [*'besit'*]

besīwian=besēowian

beslǣpan[7] *to sleep,* LL (284[8]).

beslēan[6] *to strike, beat, cut off, take away, deprive by violence,* Æ.

beslēpan *to slip on, cover, put on, clothe,* Bo,Ps.

beslītan[1]† *to slit, tear,* Soul.

besma m. *'besom,' broom, rod,* AO,Mt.

besmēagan *to consider about,* ÆL 23b[633].

+besmed *bellied* (of sails), WW 515[9]. [bōsm]

bēsming f. *curve, curvature,* WW. [bōsm]

besmirwan (y[2];=ie[2]) *to 'besmear,'* WW.

besmītan[1] *to soil, defile, pollute, dishonour,* Bl; Æ,CP. [*'besmit'*]

besmītenes f. *soil, stain, defilement, degradation, dirtiness,* Æ.

besmittian *to defile,* RB,MP 1·613.

besmiðian *to work (in metal), forge, surround with forged work,* B,EETS 46·17.

besmocian *to smoke, envelop with incense,* ANS 84·3.

besmyred=besmirwed pp. of besmirwan.

besnǣdan† to cut, mutilate, DA.

besnīwian to cover with snow, WW. ['be-snow']

be-snyðian, -snyððan† to rob, deprive of.

besolcen stupefied, dull, inactive, slow, CP.

besorg dear, beloved, Æ.

besorgian to regret : be anxious about, dread, shrink from, Æ.

besorh=besorg

bespǣtan to spit upon, ÆH 2·248',RWH 137²⁴.

bespanan⁶ to lead astray, entice, incite, urge, persuade, AO.

besparrian to bar, shut, GL.

bespirian=bespyrigan

besprecan⁵ to speak about : speak against, accuse of, Ps : claim at law, LL : complain, AO. ['bespeak']

besprengan to besprinkle, Lcd : bespatter, CHRD 64³⁶. ['bespreng']

bespyrigan to track, trace, LL.

besta, beste wk. forms of superl. adj. betst.

bestǣlan (ē) to lay a charge against, convict.

bestæppan⁶ to tread upon, step, go, enter, Æ.

bestandan⁶ to stand round or about, beset, surround, Æ : attend to, Æ : beset, harass, Jn. ['bestand']

bestealcian to move stealthily, steal, 'stalk,' ÆL 32⁴⁰. [stealc]

bestefnod ptc. having a fringe, WW 375⁴¹.

bestelan⁴ to move stealthily, steal away, steal upon, AO,LL; Æ,CP : (†) deprive. ['besteal']

bestēlan=bestǣlan; bestēman=bestȳman

bestēpan (=īe) to deprive of (children), GD 76¹⁸.

bestingan³ to thrust in, push, Æ.

bestrēdan to bestrew, cover, BHB 154²⁷.

bestrēowian to 'bestrew,' besprinkle, Job.

bestreðan (y²) to bestrew, cover over, RD.

bestrīcan¹ to make a stroke, Lcd 186b. [strīca]

bestrīdan¹ to 'bestride', mount, Æ.

bestrīpan to strip, plunder, Chr. ['bestrip']

bestrūdan⁷ to spoil, plunder, rob, GEN, WW 424³³.

bestrȳpan=bestrīpan

bestryððan=bestreððan

bestuddian to be careful for, trouble about, RWH 134¹⁰.

bestȳman† (ē;=īe) to bedew, wet, flood. [stēam]

bestyrian to heap up, BH. ['bestir']

bestyrman to agitate, Bo 9¹¹.

besu=basu

besūpan² to sup up, swallow, Lcd 113b.

besūtian to besmirch, GPH 403²⁶.

besūðan in the south, southwards (of).

beswǣlan to burn, singe, scorch, B; Æ. [v. 'sweal']

beswǣpan=beswāpan

beswǣtan to sweat, toil, Sc 111¹⁴.

beswāpan⁷ to clothe, cover over, veil, protect, BH; CP : persuade, BH. ['beswape']

beswelgan to swallow up, EPs 106²⁷ ; 123³.

beswemman to make to bathe, Bo 115⁸.

beswencan to afflict, CPs 68¹⁸.

besweðian (bi-) to swathe, wrap up, wind round, CR, JnL.

beswic n. treachery, deceit, AO,CP : snare.

beswica (bi-) m. deceiver, BL.

beswīcan¹ to deceive, seduce, betray, circum-vent, frustrate, Bl,Mt; AO,CP: to overcome, supplant, AO. ['beswike']

beswicend m. deceiver, seducer, GL.

beswicenes f. deception, MH : surrender, GL.

beswicfalle f. trap, WW 17¹.

beswician to escape, be free from, BH.

beswicol deceitful, CP 238¹⁶. (bi-)

beswicung f. deception, WW.

beswincan³ to toil, exert oneself, make with toil, Jn : till, plough, Æ. beswuncen exhausted, tired out. ['beswink']

beswingan³ to flog, scourge, beat, strike, Æ; CP. ['beswinge']

beswyllan to drench, flood, ROOD 23. [swilian]

besyftan to sprinkle, ÆL 23¹⁵⁵. [siftan]

besylfran=besilfran

besylian to sully, defile, stain, Æ.

besyr-ewian, -i(a)n=besierwan

bet adv. better, Bo. ['bet']

-bēta v. dǣd-b.

betācnian to betoken, designate, RWH 136²⁰.

betǣcan (w. d.) to make over, give up to impart, deliver, entrust, commend to, Lk, Mt,WW; AO,CP : betroth : appoint (for), set apart as, dedicate : show, point out, Lk : give orders, RB 130⁴ : pursue, hunt, WW 92²⁸. ['beteach']

±bētan to amend, repair, restore, cure, CP : make good, make amends, reform, remedy, compensate, atone, pay 'bōt' for an offence, Æ,CP,Lcd,Mt; AO : attend to (fire or light), AO. ðurst b. quench thirst. [bōt; 'beet' vb.]

betast=betst

betboren of higher birth, LL.

bēte f. 'beet,' beetroot, Lcd. [L. beta]

-bēte v. twi-b.; bētel=(1) bīetl; (2) bītol

beteldan³† to cover, hem in, surround : over-load, oppress.

betellan to speak about, answer, defend one-self (against a charge), exculpate oneself, Chr; Æ. ['betell']

bētend m. restorer, RUIN 28.

+bētendnes f. amendment, OEG 58⁶.

betēon[1],[2] *to cover, surround, enclose, AO*; Æ, CP : *dispose of, bestow, bequeath : impeach, accuse.* ['*betee*']

betera '*better*,' *AO,Bl,Bo,Mk.* w. g. *better in respect of....*

-bētere v. dǣd-b.

±beterian *to* '*better*,' *improve, CP* : *trim (lamp)*, GD.

±beterung f. *improvement,* Æ.

betest=betst; betīenan (WW 383[17])=betȳnan

betihtlian *to accuse,* LL.

betillan=betyllan

betimbran *to construct, build, B.* ['*betimber*']

betīnan=betȳnan; bēting=bǣting

bētl=bīetl

betlic† *grand, excellent.*

bētnes f. *reparation, atonement,* LL (264[16]).

betoce=betonice

betogenes f. *accusation,* LL.

betolden pp. of beteldan.

betonice f. '*betony*,' *Lcd.*

betost=betst; betr-=beter-

betrǣppan=betreppan

betredan[5] *to tread upon, cover,* CPs 138[10].

betrendan *to roll,* ES 37·180.

betreppan *to entrap, catch, Chr.* ['*betrap*']

be-trymman, -trymian *to enclose, surround, besiege.*

betst I. superl. adj. '*best*,' *first, AO,B,Chr, Cr*; CP. as sb. *people of position, Chr,WW.* II. adv. *in the best manner, most, Bo.*

betstboren *best-born, eldest,* Æ.

bett=bet

be-tuh, -tuoxn (CP), -tux=betwux

betuldon pret. pl. of beteldan.

+bētung f. *repair, maintenance,* LL.

betwēnan=betwēonan

betweoh, betweohs *(Æ)*=betwux

betwēonan, betwēonum I. prep. w. g. d. a. *between, among, amid, in the midst, B,Bl, G,Ps.* II. adv. '*between*,' *BH* : *in the meantime, meanwhile* : *in turn, by turns,* CM (-twȳn-).

betweox *(LL),* betweoxn, betwih(s) *(RG)*=betwux

betwīn-=betwēon-

betwīnforlētnes f. *intermission,* DR.

betwux *(Æ,AO,CP),* betwuht, betwix, betwux(t), betwisc prep. w. d. a. *between, among, amongst, amidst : during.* b. ðisum *meanwhile.* b. ðǣm ðe *whilst.* ['BETWIXT']

betwuxālegednes f. *interjection,* ÆGR 278[2].

betwuxāworpennes f. *interjection,* ÆGR 10[20].

betwuxblinnes (twih) f. *intermission,* DR 12[3].

betwuxīæc (yx) *internal,* OEG 3861.

betwuxgangende (twih) *separating,* VPs 28[7].

betwuxgesett (eoh, ih, yh) *interposed,* Bᴘ 66[22], BH 288[23].

betwuxlicgan[5] (twih) *to lie between,* BH 72[10].

betwuxsendan *to send between,* CM 104.

betwuxt, -twyh, -twyx(t)=betwux

betȳhtlian=betīhtlian

betyllan *to allure, decoy,* BH 358[4].

betȳnan (ī, īe) *to hedge in, enclose, shut, bury,* AO,CP : *shut out : end,* BH. [tūn]

betȳnung f. *conclusion,* OEG 3210.

betyran *to pitch, stain a dark colour,* Lcᴅ. [teoru]

betyrnan *to turn round : prostrate oneself,* RB.

beð I.=bið pres. 3 sg. of bēon. II.=bæð

beðæncan=beðencan

beðan=beðian

beðearfan *to need,* RWH 6[36].

beðearfende *needy, indigent,* KGʟ 708.

beðearflic *profitable,* ÆL 23b[242].

beðearfod *needy,* ES 8·474[50].

beðeccan *to cover, protect, cover over, conceal.*

beðen=beðung

beðencan *to consider, remember, take thought for, take care of, care for, Gu* : (refl.) *reflect,* '*bethink*' *oneself, Lk*; Æ : *trust, confide in, entrust to,* AO.

be-ðenian, -ðennan *to cover, stretch on or upon, spread over,* Rᴅ.

beðēodan *to be joined (to),* RB 134[20].

beðerscan *to winnow, thresh,* PPs 43[7].

beðettan *to bathe, foment,* Lcᴅ 3·90[15] (A 30·397).

±beðian *to heat, warm, foment, Lcd*; Æ : *cherish.* ['*beath*']

beðrāwan[7] *to twist,* GPH 391[16].

beðridian (y) *to circumvent, overcome, force,* AO.

beðringan[3]† *to encircle, encompass : beset, oppress, burden.*

beðryccan *to press down,* CR 1446.

beðrydian, beðryððan=beðridian

beðrȳn *to press,* NC 273.

beððan=beðian

beðuncan (Rᴅ 49[7])=beðencan

beðung f. *bathing, bath, fomentation, cataplasm, Lcd*; Æ,CP. ['*beathing*'; bæð]

be-ðurfan swv. pres., 3 sg. -ðearf, pl. -ðurfon, pret. -ðorfte. (w. g. or a.) *to need, have need of, want,* Æ,CP.

beðwēan[6] *to moisten, wet,* LPs 6[7].

beðwyrian *to deprave,* WW 386[7]. [ðweorh]

beðȳn *to thrust,* AO 158[6].

beufan=bufan; beūtan=būtan

bewacian *to watch, guard,* Æ.

bewadan[6] *to emerge,* Rᴅ 88[24].

bewǣfan *to enfold, wrap round, cover over, clothe,* Æ,CP.

bewǣgan *to deceive, frustrate,* BVPs.

bewǣgnan *to offer, proffer*, B1193.
bewǣlan *to oppress, afflict*, AN 1363.
bewǣpnian *to disarm*, Æ.
bewǣrlan *to pass by* : *be free from*, DR.
bewarenian *to guard against, be on one's guard*, CP.
bewarian *to keep watch, guard, preserve, ward off*, CP.
bewarnian=bewarenian
bewāwan[7] *to blow upon*, WA 76. (biwāune= biwāwene)
bewealcan *to involve*, CHRD 74[33].
beweallan[7] *to boil away*, LCD.
bewealwian *to wallow*, Bo 115[9].
beweardian *to guard, protect* : *observe closely*.
beweaxan[7] *to grow over, cover over, surround*, Æ.
beweddendlic *relating to marriage*, OEG 1122.
beweddian *to betroth, marry*, Æ : *give security*. ['*bewed*']
beweddung f. *betrothal*, LL442Ha.
bewefan[5] *to cover over*, LCD 3·146[4].
bewegan[5] *to cover*, Bo,WY.
bewēled (oe[2], ȳ[2]) *poisoned, polluted*, GD, JPs,WW; ES38·344. [wŏl]
bewellan (=ie) *to knead, mix together*, GD, WW.
bewendan *to turn, turn round, Mk*; (refl.) *Mt*9[22] : *turn one's attention, convert*, Æ. ['*bewend*']
bewenian† *to entertain, take care of, attend upon*, B.
beweorcan=bewyrcan
beweorpan[3] *to cast, cast down, plunge, throw*, Æ,AO : *beat*, Æ : *surround*.
beweorðian *to adorn*, DD 118.
beweotian=bewitian
bewēpan[7] *to weep over, mourn, bewail*, Æ. pp. bewōpen *tearful, weeping*, AO 92[30]. ['*beweep*']
bewēpendlic *lamentable*, GL,HL12[66].
bewēpnian=bewǣpnian
beworenes f. *prohibition*, BH 86[13].
bewerian *to guard, protect, defend*, Æ,AO : *check, prevent, forbid*, Æ.
bewerigend m. *protector, keeper*, Æ.
bewerung f. *defence, fortification*, CM,Sc.
bewestan prep. w. d. or adv. *to the west of, Chr*; AO. ['*bewest*']
bewīcian *to encamp*, CHR 894w.
bewindan[3] *to wind round, clasp, entwine, envelop, encircle, surround, B,Mt*; AO,CP : *brandish* (*a sword*) : *turn, wind, revolve*. hēafe b. *bewail*. ['*bewind*']
bewindla (bi-) m. *hedge, border*, BC(Mdf).
bewitan swv., pres. 3 sg. -wāt, pret. 3 sg. -wiste *to keep, care for, watch over, superintend, administer, lead, guide*, Æ,AO.

bewitian (eo) *to observe, attend to, care for, administer* : *perform*.
bewlātian *to look at, behold*, LPs 32[14].
bewlītan[1] *to look round*, GEN 2925.
bewōpen pp. of bewēpan.
bewrecan[5]† *to drive* : *drive away, banish* : *drive round, beat round*.
bewrencan *to deceive*, PR 34.
bewrēon[1,2] *to cover, hide, cover over, enwrap, protect, clothe, Sol,Met*; CP. ['*bewry*']
bewreðian *to sustain, support*, RD 81[21].
bewrigennes f. *a covering*, WYN 10[13].
bewrītan[1] *to record?* CREAT 19 : *score round*, LCD 1·244.
bewrīðan[1]† *to bind, wind about, surround*, CR.
bewrixl(i)an *to change* : *exchange, sell*, PPs.
bewuna adj. indecl. *accustomed, wont*, AO.
bewyddian=beweddian; bewȳled=bewēled
bewyllan (=ie) *to boil away*, LCD.
bewylwian (=ie) *to roll down, roll together*, Sc,WW.
bewȳpð=bewēpð pres. 3 sg. of bewēpan.
bewyrcan *to work, construct, surround with, enclose, cover, B*; Æ,AO : *work in, insert, adorn, Lcd*. ['*bework*']
bewyrpan=beweorpan
beyrfeweardian *to disinherit*, A13·321.
beyrnan=beiernan; bezera=bæzere
bi, bī (1)=be (prep.); (2) f.=bēo
bi- v. also be-; bīad=bēod
biblioðēce f. biblioðeoco (AO), bibliðēca m. *library* : *bible*, Æ. ['*bibliotheca*' (*L.*)]
bībrēad=bēobrēad
bicce, bice f. '*bitch*,' *Lcd,WW*.
biccen=byccen
bicgan (Æ)=bycgan; bicge=bicce
±bīcn-an, -ian=bīecnan
+bīcnend (ē), ±bīcni(g)end m. '*index*,' *indicator, discloser*, Sc : *forefinger*, GL.
bīcnendlic, +bīcni(g)endlic *allegorical* : (gram.) *indicative*, ÆGR 124[14].
bīcnol *indicating, indicative*, GPH 398[193].
+bīcnung (ēa, ē) f. *beckoning, nodding* : *token, symbol, figure*, Æ : *figurative speech*.
bīcwide m. *byword, proverb, fable, tale*, Æ. ['*bequeath*']
bīd n. *lingering, hesitation, delay, halt, Rd*. ['*bide*']
±bīdan[1] (intr.) *to stay, continue, live, remain, delay, AO,G,Ps* : (tr. usu. w. g.) *wait for, await, expect, B,Bl,Mt*; AO,CP : *endure, experience, find* : *attain, obtain* : *own*. ['*bide*']
biddan[5] *to ask, entreat, pray, beseech, A,AO, Bl,G* : *order, command, require*, AO,CP. b. and bēodan, hālsian *to beg and pray*. ['*bid*']

+**biddan**⁵ (often refl.) *to beg, ask, pray, Bl,
Mt*; Æ,CP : *worship*, Æ,AO. ['*i-bid*']
biddend *petitioner*, Sc 32³.
biddere m. *petitioner*, GD,WW.
bidenfæt=bydenfæt
biderīp=bedrīp
bideð (CP) pres. 3 sg. of biddan.
bīdfæst† *firm, forced to stand out.*
bīding f. *abiding place, abode*, Gu 180.
bīdsteall† m. *halt, stand.*
bīe=bēo pres. 1 sg. of bēon.
bīecn=bēacen
bīecn-an, -ian (ē, ī, ȳ) *to make a sign,
'beckon,' wink, nod, Lk*; CP : *signify :
summon.* [bēacen] For comps. see bīcn-.
bīegan (ē, ī, ȳ) *to bend, turn, turn back, incline, Bo,Mk : depress, abase, humiliate :
subject : persuade, convert.* ['*bey*,' būgan]
±**bīeldan** (æ, e, i, y) *to encourage, excite,
impel, exhort, confirm, CP,Ma*; Æ,AO.
['*bield*'; beald]
bīeld-o, -u (y) f. *boldness, courage, arrogance,
confidence, BH*; CP. ['*bield*']
bīelg=belg; **bīelw-**=bilew-
bīeme (ē, ī, ȳ) f. *trumpet, CP,Mt,WW :
tablet, billet.* ['*beme*']
bīen=bēan; **bīencoddas**=bēancoddas
+**bīerde**=+byrde
+**bīerhtan** (e, y) *to brighten, be or make
bright, illuminate, enlighten, CP : make
clear : celebrate.* [beorht]
bīerhtu (e, eo, i, y) f. *brightness, effulgence,
brilliance, CP.* [beorht]
bīerm=bearm
bīernan³ (ea, eo, i, y) tr. and intr. *to 'burn,'
be on fire, give light, Æ,Lk,Ex,Sol,VPs.*
bīersteð, bierst pres. 3 sg. of berstan.
bīerð pres. 3 sg. of beran.
bīesen=bisen; **bīesgian**=bisgian
bīeter-=biter-
bīetl (ē, ī, ȳ) m. '*beetle,' mallet, hammer,
CP,Jud.*
bīetr-=biter-
bīeð=bēoð pres. pl. of bēon.
bīfēran *to feed*, Guth 126⁸⁸.
bifian *to tremble, be moved, shake, quake,
Bo,Ps*; Æ. ['*bive*']
bifigendlic (byfg-) *terrible*, Chrd 93²⁷.
bifung (y) f. *trembling, shaking*, ÆH.
-**bifung** (eo¹) v. eorð-b.
bifylce n. *neighbouring people*, BH 196¹.
[folc]
big=be; **big-**=be-, bī-, bycg-; **bīg**=bēag
bīgan=bīegan; **bīge**=byge
+**bīgednes** f. *inflection, declension, case,*
Ægr.
bīgegnes=begegnes
bīgels m. *arch, vault*, Æ : *curvature*, OEG
2228.

+**bīgendlic** *inflectional*, Ægr 91⁸.
+**bīgendnes**=+bīgednes
bīgeng f. *practice, exercise, observance, worship, Ægr : cultivation, Æ.* ['*bigeng*']
bīgenga m. *inhabitant : cultivator, Æ : worshipper, Æ : benefactor.*
bīgenge n. *practice, worship*, Sc,SPs.
bīgengere m. *worker*, WW : *worshipper*, KC.
bīgengestre f. *handmaiden, attendant, worshipper*, GL.
bīgengnes=begengnes
+**bīgeð**=+bygeð pres. 3 sg. of +bycgan.
bīging (=īe) f. *bending*, WW 216⁸⁸.
bīgleaf- (eo, i)=bīleof-
bīgnes f. *power of bending, bending, winding,*
BH,GD. [bīegan]
+**bīgnes** f. '*confrequentatio*,' EPs 117²⁷.
+**bīgð**=+bigeð
bīgyrdel m. *girdle, belt, purse, Æ,Mt :
treasury.* ['*bygirdle*']
bīgytan=begietan
bihianda (MtL 5²⁷)=behindan
bīhst=bȳhst pres. 2 sg. of būgan.
+**bīhð** (Gu 346)=+byht
bil=bill; **bilcettan**=bealcettan
bildan=bieldan
bile m. '*bill,' beak, trunk (of an elephant),*
WW : *prow.*
bīle=bȳle; **bīlefa**=bīleofa
bīlehwīt=bilewit
bīleofa (i²) m., **bīleofen** f. *support, sustenance, food, nourishment, Æ,WW : money,
pay.* ['*bylive*'; libban]
bīleofian *to support, feed upon*, Guth 34⁷.
bilewet=bilewit
bilewit *innocent, pure, simple, sincere, honest,
BH,Mt*; Æ,CP : *calm, gentle, merciful,
gracious : plausible.* ['*bilewhit*']. adv.
-līce.
bilewitnes f. *mildness, simplicity, innocence,
purity*, Æ,CP.
bilgesleht=billgesliht
bilgst, bilhst pres. 2 sg. of belgan.
bilgð pres. 3 sg. of belgan.
bilherge=billere
bilibb-, bilif-=bīleof-; **bilig**=belg
biliw-=bilew-
bill n. '*bill,' chopper, battle-axe, falchion,
sword, B,WW.*
billere m. '*bibulta*' (*plant*), WW.
billgesliht n. *sword-clash, battle*, †Chr 937.
billhete m. *murderous hate, strife*, An 78.
+**bilod** *having a bill or beak*, HexC 256.
[bile]
bil-swæð n. (nap. -swaðu) *sword track,
wound*, Ex 329.
bilw-=bilew-; **bīlyht**=bȳliht
bīma (m.?), bīme=bīeme; **bin**=binn
bīnama m. *pronoun*, Bf 94¹⁵.

+**bind** n. *binding, fetter* : *costiveness* : *a bind* (measure), TC328′ (v. BTs).

±**bindan** sv³ *to tie, 'bind,' fetter, fasten, restrain,* Æ,*Bl,G,WW*; AO,CP : *adorn.*

binde f. *head-band?* KC6·133. ['*bind*']

bind-ele, -elle f. *binding*, LL : *bandage*, LCD.

bindere m. '*binder*,' Rd28⁶.

binding f. *binding*, OEG324b.

binn f. '*bin*,' *basket, crib, manger, Bl, LkL,WW.* (*Keltic*, LF124).

binna (*LG*)=binnan

binnan I. prep. (w. d. a.) *within, in, inside of, into, Jn.* II. adv. *inside, within, less than, during, whilst, LG.* ['*bin*']

binne=(1) binn; (2) binnan (RG)

bint pres. 3 sg. of bindan.

bio-=beo-, bi-; **biosmrung**=bismerung

birce=beorc, beorce; **bird** (*LkLR*)=bridd

+**bird**=+byrd; **birele**=byrele

biren f. *she-bear*, OET(Ct).

birg=byrg

+**birg** n. *taste*, DR116⁸.

+**birgan** (e, eo, y) *to taste, eat*, BH,NG.

birging (y) f. *taste*, LCD.

birgnes (eo, y) f. *taste*, BH,WW.

birgŏ, birhŏ pres. 3 sg. of beorgan.

birht-=bierht-

birig, birig-=byrig, byrg-

birihte (y) prep. w. d. *near, beside*, AN 850.

birhto=bierhtu; **birle**=byrele

+**birman** (y;=ie) *to ferment, leaven*, LCD 37a. [beorma]

birnan (*Æ*)=biernan

birst, birsteŏ pres. 3 sg. of berstan.

birst pres. 2 sg., bir(e)ŏ pres. 3 sg. of beran.

biryhte=birihte

bisæc n? m? *wallet*, MtR10¹⁰. [*LL.* bi-saccium]

bisæc *contested, disputed*, LL.

bisǣc f. *visit*, Gu188.

bisceop (e², o², u²) m. '*bishop*,' CP : *high-priest, chief priest (Jewish), heathen priest*, AO,MkL.

bisceopcynn (o²) n. *episcopal (high-priestly) stock*, ÆP116¹².

bisceopdōm m. *episcopate, bishopric, Chr* : *excommunication*. ['*bishopdom*']

bisceopealder m. *high-priest*, HL.

bisceopfolgoŏ m. *episcopate*, GD65⁸¹.

bisceopgegyrelan mpl. *episcopal robes*, BH90².

bisceophād m. '*bishophood*,' *office of bishop, ordination as bishop, episcopate, bishopric, Ps* ; CP.

bisceophādung f. *episcopal ordination*, ÆL 31²⁸⁶.

bisceophām m. *bishop's estate*, EC365¹⁷.

bisceophēafodlīn (o²) n. *head ornament worn by bishops*, WW152²³.

bisceophīred (o) m. *clergy subject to a bishop*, MH,WW.

bisceopian *to confirm*, LL. ['*bishop*']

bisceopland (o) n. *episcopal or diocesan land*, LL173¹⁰.

bisceoplic '*bishoply*,' *episcopal*, BH.

bisceoprīce n. '*bishopric*,' *diocese, province of a bishop*, BH : *episcopal demesne or property*, WC·16⁸.

bisceoprocc (o²) m. *bishop's rochet, dalmatic*, LCD3·202′.

bisceoprōd f. *bishop's cross*, KC4·275¹¹.

bisceopscīr, -scȳr f. *diocese* : *episcopate*, BH.

bisceop-seld, -setl, -seŏl n. *bishop's seat or see, bishopric*, BH,CHR.

bisceopseonoŏ m. *synod of bishops*, A11·8¹.

bisceopstōl m. *episcopal see, bishopric, KC*; CP : *bishop's palace*, GD. ['*bishopstool*']

bisceopsunu m. *godson at a 'bishoping' or confirmation*, CHR,LL.

bisceopŏēnung f. *office of a bishop*, BH.

bisceopung f. *confirmation*, Æ,CHRD.

bisceopweorod (o²) n. *bishop's company*, BH309¹¹ (Schipper).

bisceopwīte n. *fine payable to a bishop?* (BTs), *forced entertaining of a bishop?* (Lieb : v. LL2·667).

bisceopwyrt f. *bishop's-wort, betony, vervain, marshmallow*, LCD,WW.

bisceopwyrtil (o²) *vervain*, WW134⁴¹.

biscep=bisceop

bi-sceran, -scerian (i², y²)=be-scieran, -scierian

biscop, bisc(u)p=bisceop

bisegu=bisgu

bisen, bisene (ie, y) fn. *example, pattern, model, JnLR*; Æ,AO,CP : *similitude, parable, parallel* : *rule, command, precept*. ['*bysen*']

bisene (y) *blind*, MtL; NC274; JAW22. ['*bisson*'?]

±**bisenian** (ie, y) *to give, set an example, instruct by example*, Bo; Æ : *follow an example or pattern*, CP : *express figuratively*. ['*bysen*' vb.]

bisenung (y) f. *example, pattern*, Æ.

bises m. *the extra day intercalated in leap year*, MEN32. [*L.* bissextus]

±**bisgian** *to occupy, employ*, Æ,Bo; CP : *trouble, afflict*, Lcd,Met. ['*busy*']

bisgu, bisigu f. *occupation, labour*, Bo; Æ, CP : *affliction, trouble*. ['*busy*']

bisgung f. *business, occupation, care*, CP.

bisig (y) '*busy*,' *occupied, diligent*, Ma,Sol.

bisignes f. '*business*,' MtL (Cont. p. xx).

bismær-=bismer-; **bisme**=besma

bismer (y) nmf. *disgrace, scandal, shame, mockery, insult, reproach, scorn, AO,Bl*; CP : *filthiness, defilement,* Æ. tō bismere *ignominiously, shamefully* : *blasphemy* : *infamous deed, AO.* ['*bismer*']

bismerful (y) *infamous, shameful, ignominious,* Æ.

bismergléow (y) n. *shameful lust,* Æ236²⁴¹.

±**bismerian** (y) *to mock, revile, illtreat, blaspheme, Mk*; Æ,AO. ['*bismer*' vb.]

bismeriend m. *mocker,* KGL298.

bismerléas (y) *blameless,* CR1326.

bismerléoð n. *scurrilous song,* GL.

bismerlic *shameful, ignominious, contemptuous, AO* : *ridiculous, frivolous.* adv. -līce.

bismernes f. *pollution* : *insult* : *contemptibleness.*

bismer-spr ǣc, -spǣc f. *blasphemy,* G.

±**bismerung** (y) *mockery, scorn* : *blasphemy* : *infamy, disrepute,* AO.

bismerword (æ²) n. *reproach, insult,* LL10¹¹.

bismor, bism(o)r-=bismer, bismer-

bisn-=bisen-

+**bisnere** f. *imitator,* DR45⁷.

bispell (big-) n. *example, proverb,* Æ : *parable, fable, allegory, story, MtL*; CP. ['*byspel*']

bispellbōc (big-) f. *book of Proverbs,* ÆT496.

bissextus, gen. -te *the intercalary day of leap year* : *leap year.* [*L.*]

bist pres. 2 sg. of bēon.

bist=bīdst pres. 2 sg. of bīdan.

biswæc (e²) *tripping up, treachery,* RPs40¹⁰.

biswic=beswic

bit pres. 3 sg. of biddan.

bit pres. 3 sg. of (1) bīdan; (2) bītan.

bita m. I. '*bit,*' *morsel, piece, Jn*; Æ. II. *biter, wild beast.*

±**bītan**¹ *to* '*bite,*' *tear, B,Rd*; Æ : *cut, wound* : (+) *dash down,* MkL9¹⁸.

bite m. '*bite,*' *sting, AO,Lcd* : *sword-cut, Ap,B* : *cancer.*

bitela m. '*beetle,*' *Gl.*

biter '*bitter,*' *sharp, cutting, Gu*; Æ : *stinging,* PPs117¹² : *exasperated, angry, embittered* : *painful, disastrous, virulent, cruel, B,Bl.* adv. -līce, *Mt.*

bitere=bitre

±**biterian** *to be or become bitter, CP* : *make bitter.* ['*bitter*' vb.]

biternes f. '*bitterness,*' *grief,* Æ,Bl; CP.

biterwyrde *bitter in speech,* Æ.

biterwyrtdrenc m. *drink of bitter herbs,* WW114¹⁸.

bitl=bīetl

bitmǣlum *piecemeal, bit by bit,* ÆGR239¹⁰.

bitol n. *bridle,* SPs31⁹.

bitor=biter

bitre *bitterly, sharply, painfully, severely* : *very.*

bitres, bittres gsmn. of biter.

bitst pres. 2 sg. of biddan.

bitst pres. 2 sg. of bīdan and bītan.

bitt I. pres. 3 sg. of (1) biddan; (2) beodan. II.=bytt

bitt pres. 3 sg. of bītan.

+**bitt** n. *biting, gnashing,* ÆH.

bitter=biter

bittor, bittre=biter, bitre; **bitula**=bitela

bið pres. 3 sg. of bēon.

biwāune v. bewāwan.

biwist fm. *sustenance, food, provision, necessaries,* Æ,Bo. ['*bewiste*']

biword (u) n. *proverb, household word* : *adverb,* BF94²⁰.

biwyrde n. '*byword,*' *proverb, WW.*

bixen=byxen

blāc I. (ǣ) *bright, shining, glittering, flashing, Rd* : *pale, pallid, wan,* AO,CP. ['*bleak,*' but v. FTP286] II. pret. 3 sg. of blīcan.

blac=blæc

blāchlēor† *with pale cheeks.*

blācian *to turn pale,* Æ.

blācung f. *a turning pale, pallor,* Æ.

bladesian *to flame, blaze, be hot* : *emit an odour,* OEG554.

bladesnung (at-) f. *odour,* WW405¹.

bladesung (æ¹) f. *shining, lightning,* EPs 76¹⁹.

blæc (a) I. '*black,*' *dark,* Æ,B,BH,KC. II. n. *ink, LL,WW.* ['*bleck*']

blæc=blāc

blǣcan *to bleach, whiten* : (+) *disfigure,* CPs 79¹⁴. [blāc]

blæcce f. *black matter,* OEG652.

blǣce n.? *irritation of the skin, leprosy,* LCD.

blǣcern n. *lamp, candle, light,* CP.

blǣcernleoht (ā) n. *lantern-light,* LV59.

blæcfexede *black-haired,* ÆH1·456¹⁶. [feax]

blæcgymm m. *jet,* BH26¹⁶.

blæchorn (e) n. *ink-horn,* ANS119·125,IM 128¹³.

blǣco f. *pallor, WW*; LCD. ['*bleach*']

blǣcpytt m. *bleaching-pit?* EC383'.

blǣcða *leprosy,* WW53²⁸.

blǣcðrustfel n. *leprosy,* Cp103B (? two words).

blæd n. (nap. bladu) '*blade,*' *WW* : *leaf, Gen.*

blǣd (ē) I. m. *blowing, blast, BH* : *inspiration, Ph* : *breath, spirit,* Æ : *life, mind* : *glory, dignity, splendour* : *prosperity, riches, success.* ['*blead*'; blāwan] II.=blēd I.

blǣdāgende *renowned,* B1013.

+**blǣdan** *to puff up, inflate,* APs34²¹

blǣdbylig m. *bellows,* WW241³³.

blǣddæg† m. *day of prosperity.*

blædderwǣrc m. *pain in the bladder*, LCD.
blǣddre=blǣdre
±**blǣdfæst**† *glorious, prosperous.*
+**blǣdfæstnes** f. *success*, ÆL 23b⁴⁹².
blǣdgifa† m. *giver of prosperity*, AN.
blǣdhorn m. *trumpet*, Æ.
blǣdnes f. *blossom, fruit*, BF 86². [blēd]
blǣdre (ē) f. *blister, pimple*, Æ,*Lcd*; AO : '*bladder*,' *Gl*,*Lcd*. [blāwan]
blǣdwela m. *abundant riches*, CR 1392.
blǣge f. *gudgeon, bleak*, WW. ['*blay*']
blǣgettan (a) *to cry*, GD 278¹².
blǣhǣwen *light blue*, LEV 8⁷.
blæs=blæst
blǣsbelg (OET 28)=blǣstbelg
blǣse (a) f. *firebrand, torch, lamp*, Æ,*Jn*. ['*blaze*']
blǣsere m. *incendiary*, LL.
blǣshorn m. *trumpet*, LL 194,8.
blǣst m. *blowing*, '*blast*' (*of wind*), *breeze, Ex : flame.*
blǣstan *to blow, belch forth.*
blǣstbelg m. *bellows*, GL.
blǣstm m? *flame, blaze*, MFH 90⁷.
blǣtan *to '*bleat*,' ÆGr,Rd.*
blǣtesung=bladesung; **blǣts-**=blēts-
blǣwen (WW 163²⁹)=blǣhǣwen
blǣwest, blǣwst pres. 2 sg., blǣw(e)ð pres. 3 sg. of blāwan.
blagettan=blǣgettan
blan pret. 3 sg. of blinnan.
blanca† m. (*white?*) *horse*, B. ['*blonk*']
±**bland**† n. *blending, mixture, confusion.*
±**blandan**⁷ *to blend, mix, mingle, Rd : trouble, disturb, corrupt.* ['*bland*']
blandenfeax† *grizzly-haired, grey-haired, old.* [blandan]
blann pret. 3 sg. of blinnan.
blase, blasere=blǣse, blǣsere
blāstbelg=blǣstbelg; **blaster**=plaster
blāt† *livid, pale, wan, ghastly : low, hoarse* (*sound*)? *or pale?* (BTs), AN 1279. [cp. blēat] adv. blāte *lividly, pallidly*, MET.
blates(n)ung=blades(n)ung
blātian *to be livid, pale*, GEN 981 (GK).
±**blāwan**⁷ (ō) (tr. or intr.) *to '*blow*,' breathe*, Mt,*Lk*,*Jn*; Æ : *be blown, sound* : *inflate* : (+) *kindle, inflame*, WW 208¹⁴ : (+) *spit*, MkLR 7³³.
blāwend m. *inspirer*, ÆH 2·478⁸.
blāwende *blowing hard* (wind), ANS 120²⁹⁶.
blāwere m. '*blower*,' CP.
blāwung f. '*blowing*,' blast, Æ : *inflation.*
bleac=blǣc
blēat *miserable?* Gu 963. ['*blete*']. adv. blēate, B 2824.
blēað *gentle, shy, cowardly, timid, Rd : slothful, inactive, effeminate*, AO. ['*blethe*']
blec=blǣc; **blēc-**=blǣc-

bled. blēd-=blǣd, blēt-
blēd I. (ǣ) f. *shoot, branch, flower, blossom, leaf, foliage, fruit*, Mt,*Lcd*; CP : *harvest, crops.* ['*blede*'; blōwan] **II.**=blǣd I.
blēdan *to '*bleed*,' let blood*, Sol.
blēdhwæt *growing quickly? profusely?* RD 2⁹.
blēdre=blǣdre
bledu f. *dish, bowl, goblet*, ÆL.
blegen, blegne f. '*blain*,' *boil, blister, ulcer*, Lcd.
+**blegenod** *blistered*, Lcd 1b, 18b. [v. '*blain*']
blencan *to deceive, cheat*, Mod. ['*blench*']
blēnd (e) pret. 3 sg. of blandan.
blendan I. *to blind, deprive of sight*, Bo,*Chr* : *deceive.* ['*blend*'] **II.** *to mix*, WW 425³⁸.
blendian (CHR 1086)=blendan I.
blendnes f. *blindness*, DR 385.
blent pres. 3 sg. of (1) blendan, (2) blandan.
±**blēo** n. gs. blēos, ds. blēo, gp. blēo(na), dip. blēom, blēo(w)um *colour*, Æ,*Bo*,*Met*; CP : *appearance, form*, Sol. ['*blee*']
blēobord n. *coloured board, chess-board*, WY 71.
blēobrygd n? *combination of colours, scintillation*, PH 292. [bregdan]
blēocræft m. *art of embroidery*, WW 354⁹.
+**blēod** *beautiful*, CR 909 : *variegated*, KGL (īo).
bleodu=bledu
blēofāg *variegated*, GL.
bleoh=blēo
blēomete m. *dainty food*, GD 99¹⁸.
blēona gp. of blēo.
blēorēad *purple*, WW.
blēostǣning f. *tesselated pavement*, WW 444¹⁰.
blēot pret. 3 sg. of blōtan.
blēoum dip. of blēo.
blēow pret. 3 sg. of (1) blāwan, (2) blōwan.
blēowum dip. of blēo.
blere, blerig *bald*, WW.
blese=blǣse
blētan=blǣtan
±**blē**(later e)**tsian** *to consecrate, ordain*, Mt, *JnL*(oe) : '*bless*,' *give thanks, adore, extol*, Da,*Lk*,*Ps*: *sign with the cross*, Æ: *pronounce or make happy*, Æ,*G*,*Gen*. [blōd; v. NED]
blētsingbōc f. *blessing-book, benedictional*, EC 250'.
blētsingsealm m. *the Benedicite*, RB 36¹⁸.
blētst pres. 2 sg. of blōtan.
blētsung f. *consecration*, Chr : '*blessing*,' *benediction*, Chr; Æ : *favour* (*of God*), Bl,*VPs.*
blēw=blēow pret. 3 sg. of blāwan.
blēwð pres. 3 sg. of blōwan.
blĭcan¹ *to glitter, shine, gleam, sparkle, dazzle*, Sol 235 : *appear*, SOL 144. ['*blik*']

bliccettan *to glitter, quiver*, GL.
bliccettung f. *glittering, shining*, VPs.
blice m. *exposure*, LL 5,34.
-blicgan=-blycgan
blician *to shine*, A 2·357,OEG 1499.
blicð pres. 3 sg. of blican.
blids=bliss
blin imperat. of blinnan.
blind '*blind*,' *Mk,Mt*; Æ,CP : *dark, obscure, opaque, DD*; Æ : *internal, not showing outwardly* : *unintelligent, Mt* : *not stinging*, WW 322²⁹. adv. -lice *blindly, rashly*, AO.
blindboren *born blind*, JnL 9³².
blindenetele *archangelica* (*plant*), WW 136, 544.
+blindfellian *to blind, blindfold*, HL 8²⁷⁶.
-blindian v. of-b.
blindnes f. *blindness*, Æ.
blinn n? *cessation*, BH,EL.
±blinnan³ *to cease, leave off, rest from, Mt*; CP : *lose, forfeit, An : be vacant* (bishopric). ['*blin*'; be, linnan]
blinnes f. *cessation, intermission*, LL (156⁵).
blis (CP)=bliss; **blisa**=blysa
bliscan=blyscan
blisgere m. *incendiary*, LL. [blysige]
bliss f. '*bliss*,' *merriment, happiness, Bl,Ps*; CP : *kindness, friendship, grace, favour, Met* : *cause of happiness, Ps.* [blīðe]
±blissian (intr.) *to be glad, rejoice, exult, CP,Lk*; Æ : (tr.) *make happy, gladden, endow*, †Hy : *applaud*, ANS 109·306. ['*bliss*']
blissig *joyful*, RPs 112⁹.
blissigendlic *exulting*, ÆH 1·354¹¹.
blissung f. *exultation*, EPs 64¹³.
blīð=blīðe
±blīðe I. '*blithe*,' *joyous, cheerful, pleasant, Bl,Cr*; Æ,AO,CP : *gracious, well-disposed, friendly, kind, El* : *agreeable, willing* : *quiet, peaceful, gentle, Ps.* II. adv. *Ps.*
blīðelic *gentle, pleasant, glad, well-wishing.* adv. -lice *Lk*; AO. ['*blithely*']
blīðemōd *glad, cheerful* : *well-wishing, friendly*, BH.
blīðeheort *happy, joyful*, AN : *kind, merciful*, GEN.
+blīðian *to make glad*, RPs 91⁴.
blīðnes f. *joy, gladness, pleasure, Lcd*; AO. ['*blitheness*']
blīðs=bliss
bliwum=blēo(w)um, dp. of blēo.
blod=bold
blōd n. '*blood*,' *Æ,Chr,G,Lcd*; AO,CP : *vein*.
blōd-=blōt-
blōd-dolg, -dolh n. *bleeding wound*, LCD.
blōddrync m. *bloodshed*, AO 162³.
blōdegesa m. *bloody horror*, Ex 477.

+blōdegian=blōdgian
blōden *bloody*, WW 217³⁵ ?
blōdfāg† *blood-stained, bloody*.
blōdgemang n. *a blood-mixture*, WW 220⁷.
blōdgemenged *blood-stained*, W 182¹¹.
blōdgēot=blōdgȳte
blōdgēotend m. *shedder of blood*, LPs 50¹⁶.
blōdgēotende *bloody*, LPs 5⁸.
±blōdgian *to be bloodthirsty*, WW 215⁴³ : *make* '*bloody*,' B.
blōdgyte m. *bloodshed*, AO.
blōdhrǣcung f. *spitting of blood*, WW 113⁶.
blōdhrēow *sanguinary, cruel*, Ps.
blōdig '*bloody*,' *WW*; AO.
blōdigtōð *bloody-toothed*, B 2083.
blōd-lǣs, -lǣswu f. *blood-letting, bleeding, Lcd.* ['*bloodles*']
blōdlǣstīd f. *time for blood-letting*, LCD 55a.
blōdlǣte f. *blood-letting, bleeding*, LCD 6a.
blōdlǣtere m. '*blood-letter*,' *WW*.
blōdlēas *bloodless*, ÆGR 56¹⁴.
blōdrēad *blood-red*, LCD.
blōdrēow=blōdhrēow
blōdryne m. *issue of blood, bloody flux* : *bursting of a blood-vessel*, AO 288²⁷.
blōdscēawung f. *supply of blood?* LCD 83a.
blōdseax (æ, e) n. *lancet*, GL.
blōdseten *something to stop bleeding*, LCD.
blōdsihte f. *flowing of blood*, LCD 64a.
blōdōlgen f. *tasting of blood*, LL.
blōdwīte n. *blood-offering*, LPs 15⁴ (*i.e. penalty for bloodshed?* v. LL 2·25 and 318) : *right to exact such a penalty*, KC 4·216⁵. ['*bloodwite*']
blōdyrnende *having an issue of blood*, BH 78¹⁶ B.
bloedsung (DR 123³)=bletsung
blōma m. *lump of metal, mass*, WW. ['*bloom*']
blon pret. 3 sg. of blinnan.
blonca=blanca; **blond-**=bland-
blonn pret. 3 sg. of blinnan.
blōsa, blōsma=blōstma
blōstbǣre=blōstmbǣre
blōstm (Æ), blōstma mf. '*blossom*,' *flower, fruit, Bl,Lcd.*
blōstmbǣre (Æ), -bǣrende *flower-bearing.*
blōstmfrēols m. *floral festival*, OEG 4720.
blōstmian *to* '*blossom*,' *bloom*, BH.
blōstmig (sm-) *flowery*, WW 256³.
±blōt n. *sacrifice*, AO. [blōd]
blōt-=blōd-
blōtan⁷ (and ? wv) *to sacrifice, kill for sacrifice*, AO,CP.
blōtere m. *sacrificer*, GPH 398⁹⁹.
blōtmōnað m. *month of sacrifice* (8 Oct.– 8 Nov.), *November*.
blōtorc m. *sacrificial vessel*, GPH 397.

+blōtsian *to bless*, Percy Soc. vol. 88 p. iii.
blōtspīung f. *spitting of blood*, WW 113⁷.
blōtung f. *sacrifice*, AO 102¹⁶.
±blōwan I. sv⁷ *to 'blow,' flower, flourish, blossom*, Lcd. II.=blāwan
blōwendlic *blooming*, WW 240²⁸.
blunnen pp., blunnon pret. pl. of blinnan.
-blycgan v. ā-b.; blys, blyss=bliss
blysa m. *firebrand, torch*, Æ.
blyscan '*rutilare*,' HGL 434⁷⁵ (v. OEG 1196 and '*blush*').
blyse f.=blysa; blysere=blæsere
blysian *to burn, blaze*, PPs 17⁸.
blysige=blyse; blyssian (Æ)=blissian
blȳðe, blȳðelīce=blīðe, blīðelīce
bō=bā, nafn. of bēgen.
bōc I. fn. ds. and nap. bēc '*beech'-tree*, WW; Mdf: *beech-nut*, CHRD 15¹⁰: '*book,' writing, Bible, Bl,CP,Jn*; Æ,AO : *deed, charter, conveyance, Mk,TC*. Crīstes b. *gospel*. II. pret. 3 sg. of bacan.
bōcæceras mpl. *freehold lands*, KC.
bōcblæc (e) n. *ink*, W 225¹.
bōcce=bēce
bōc-cest, -cist(e) f. *book-chest*, APT,RBL.
bōccræft m. *learning, science, Bo*. ['*bookcraft*']
bōccræftig *book-learned*, BF 192⁸, JUL 16.
bōcere m. *scholar, scribe, writer*, Æ.
bōcfell n. *parchment, vellum*, LL. ['*bookfell*']
bōcfōdder n. *bookcase*, WW 194¹³.
bōcgesamnung f. *library*, WW 203¹⁵.
bōcgestrēon n. *library*, BH.
bōchaga m. *beech-hedge*, BC 1·515.
bōchord n. *library*, WW. ['*bookhoard*']
bōchūs n. *library*, WW 185³⁵.
±bōclan *to grant by charter : supply with books*.
bōclæden (e²) n. *literary Latin, learned language, Chr*. ['*bocleden*']
bōcland n. *land held by written title*, LL; Æ,AO. v. LL 2·323. ['*bookland*']
bōclār f. '*book-lore,' learning*, LL.
bōcleden=bōclæden
bōclic *of or belonging to a book*, Æ : *scientific*, BF 60⁸ : *biblical, scriptural*. b. stæf '*ars liberalis*,' HGL 503.
bōcon pret. pl. of bacan.
bōcrædere m. *reader of books*, WW 439²⁵.
bōcrǣding f. *reading of books*, WW.
bōcrēad *red colour used in illuminating manuscripts, vermilion*, WW.
bōcrēde f. *reading of books*, A 10·143¹⁰¹.
bōcriht n. *right given by will or charter*, LL 444(1).
bōcstæf m. nap. -stafas *letter, character, El*. ['*bocstaff*'; *Ger*. buchstabe]
bōcstigel f. *beech-wood stile*, BC 1·515.

bōc-tǣcung, -talu f. *teaching or narrative, written in books*, LL.
bōctrēow n. *beech-tree*, ÆGR,WW.
bōcung f. *conveyance by charter or deed*, KC 5·257¹².
bōcweorc n. *study of books*, LL (314¹⁸).
bōcwudu m. *beech-wood*, RD 41¹⁰⁶.
±bod (+exc. N) n. *command, message, precept, Bo,Hy*; Æ : *preaching*. ['*bode,' 'i-bod*']
boda m. *messenger, herald, apostle, angel*, Æ,CP : *prophet*. ['*bode*']
bodan=botm
bode pret. of bōgan.
bodeg=bodig
boden pp. of bēodan.
bodere m. *teacher*, NG.
±bodian *to tell, proclaim, announce*, †Hy; AO,CP : *preach, Mt*; Æ,CP : *foretell, El : boast*. ['*bode*']
bodiend m. *proclaimer, teacher, preacher*, GL,HL.
bodig n. '*body,' trunk, frame, bodily presence*, Æ,BH,Gl,Lcd; CP : *main part*, LCD.
bodigendlic *to be celebrated*, ÆL 7²³².
bodlāc n. *decree, ordinance*, CHR 1129.
±bodscipe† m. *command, message*, GEN.
bodung f. *message, recital, preaching*, Æ : *interpretation : assertiveness*, RB 136²².
bodungdæg m. *Annunciation Day*, ÆH 1·200²⁵.
bōg m. *arm, shoulder*, Æ; CP : '*bough,' twig, branch, Mt*; CP : *offspring*. [bōgan]
boga m. '*bow*' (weapon), *Gn*; Æ : *arch, arched place, vault, B : rainbow*, Æ,Lcd : *folded parchment*. [cp. *Ger*. bogen]
bōga=bōg
bōgan *to boast*, RB.
boganet=bogenett
bogefōdder m. *quiver*, WW 143¹⁹.
bogen I. *name of a plant*, LCD. II. pp. of būgan.
bogenett n. *wicker basket with a narrow neck for catching fish*, WW.
bogetung f. *curve*, WW 355¹⁵.
bōgh=bōg
bōgian I. ±(intr.) *to dwell*, Æ : (tr.) *to inhabit*. II.=bōgan
bogiht *full of bends*, MtL 7¹⁴.
bōgincel n. *small bough*, OEG.
bōgung (bōung) f. *boastfulness, arrogance, display*, Æ.
bōh=bōg
bohscyld m. *curved shield?* (WC 172n), EC 226'.
bohte pret. 3 sg. of bycgan.
bōhtimber n. *building-wood*. [v. AS 1³ and ES 42·172]
bōian=bōgan

bol? m. *bole, trunk*, LCD 143a.

bolca m. *gangway of a ship*, AN,B,GL.

bold (=botl) n. *house, dwelling-place, mansion, hall, castle, B : temple.* ['*bold*']

boldāgend† m. *homestead-owner.*

boldgestrēon (botl)† *household goods*, GEN.

boldgetæl *collection of houses* : (*political*) *district, county, province*, GD.

boldgetimbru npl. *houses*, SOL 412.

boldweard (botl-) m. *housekeeper, steward*, ÆGR,WW.

boldwela† (botl-) m. *wealth : splendid dwelling, paradise, heaven : village*, GEN 1799.

bolgen pp. of belgan.

bolgenmōd† *enraged.*

bolla m., **bolle** f. '*bowl,' cup, pot, beaker, measure*, ÆL,Jn,Lcd.

bolster mn. '*bolster,' cushion, B*; CP.

+bolstrian *to support with pillows, prop up*, BF 74[16].

bolt m. '*bolt' : cross-bow for throwing bolts or arrows*, WW.

bolttimber n. *building timber, beams.* [v. AS l[3] and ES 42·172]

bōn I. f. *ornament*, CHR 1063 D. II.=bōgan

bon-, bond-=ban-, band-

bōnda m. *householder*, LL : *freeman, plebeian : husband.* ['*bond*']

bōndeland n. *land held by a* bōnda, CHR 777 E. [ON. bōndi]

bōne=bēn

+bōnian *to ornament*, TC. [bōn]

bonn=bann

bor *borer, gimlet*, GL : *lancet, scalpel, graving tool*, GL. [borian]

bora m. *ruler*, SAT 500. [? rǣdbora]

borcen pret. 3 sg. of beorcan.

borcian *to bark*, RD 84[6].

bord n. '*board,' plank, Æ : table, Ps : side of a ship, Gen : ship, El,Gn : shield, El.* innan, ūtan bordes *at home, abroad, CP.*

borda m. *embroidery, ornament*, GL.

bordclāð m. *table-cloth*, OEG 56[22].

bordgelāc n. *weapon, dart*, CR 769.

bordhæbbende *shield-bearing*, B 2895.

bordhaga m. *cover of shields*, EL 652.

bordhrēoða (ē)† m. *shield-ornament : phalanx.*

bordrand m. *shield*, B 2559.

bordrima (e[2]) m. *rim, edge*, Ln.

bordriðig *a stream running in a channel made of planks?* (BTs),EC 450[11].

bordstæð n. *sea-shore*, AN 442.

bordðaca m. *shield-covering, testudo*, GL : *board for roofing*, WW.

bordweall m. *wall of shields, phalanx : buckler, shield : side of ship*, RD 34[6].

bordwudu m. *shield*, B 1243

boren (B,Chr,Cp) pp. of beran. ['*y-born*']

borettan *to brandish*, GL.

borg m. *pledge, security, bail, debt, obligation, LL* (v. 2·331; 641); CP : *bondsman : debtor.* ['*borrow*' sb.]

borgbryce m. *breach of surety*, LL. ['*borrowbreach*']

borgen pp. of beorgan.

borggelda m. *borrower : lender*, CPs 108[11].

borgian *to* '*borrow,' Mt,Ps : lend : be surety for*, OEG 3812.

borgiend m. *lender, usurer*, SPs 108[10].

borg-sorg (burg-) f. *trouble on account of lending or security*, RIM 63.

borgsteall *a steep path up a hill?* BC,KC (v. BTac and Mdf).

borgwedd n. *pledge*, WW 279[16].

borh=borg

borhfæst *fast bound*, HL 203[254].

±borhfæstan *to bind by pledge or surety*, CHR.

borhhand fm. *security, surety* (person), Æ.

borhlēas *without a pledge, without security*, LL 230,5.

borian *to bore, perforate*, GL.

borlīce *very, extremely, fitly, excellently*, BF.

born=barn pret. 3 sg. of biernan.

+borsnung=+brosnung

borsten pp. of berstan.

borðor=beorðor

bōsig m? n? *stall, crib*, LkLR. ['*boosy*']

bōsm (CP), **bōsum** m. '*bosom,' breast, womb, Æ : surface, An : ship's hold*, GEN.

bōsmig *sinuous*, OEG 8[2].

bōt f. *help, relief, advantage, remedy, An,Da, Lcd*; AO : *compensation for an injury or wrong, LL* (v. 2·336) : (*peace*) *offering, recompense, amends, atonement, reformation, penance, repentance, B,Bl*; CP. tō bōte *to '*boot,' besides, moreover.*

bōtan=bētan

bōtettan *to improve, repair*, W.

bōtian *to get better*, BH,LCD.

±botl (Æ,CP)=bold

bōtlēas *unpardonable, not to be atoned for by* bōt, LL,W.

botm m. '*bottom,' ground, foundation, B, Sat,WW : abyss*, GEN.

bōtwyrðe *pardonable, that can be atoned for by* bōt, LL,W. [cp. bōtlēas]

bōð=bōgeð pres. 3 sg. of bōgan.

bōðen mn? *rosemary : darnel*, Æ : *thyme*, GPH 390.

bōung=bōgung

box mn. *box-tree*, KC,WW : '*box,' case, M., WW.* [L.]

boxtrēow n. *box-tree*, ÆGR 20[19].

braccas mp. *breeches*, LCD 3·198'. [L.]

bracce (Mdf)=bræc I.

brachwīl f. *moment*, BF 118[24].

-bracian v. ā-b.

brād I. comp. brādra, brǣdra '*broad*,' *flat*, *open, extended, spacious, wide*, Bl,Gen, Chr,Ps; Æ,AO,CP : *ample, copious*, B,El. **II.** n. *breadth*, LV,Rim.

brādæx f. *broad axe*, Gl.

brādbrim† n. *wide sea*.

brāde† *far and wide, broadly, widely*, W.

brādelēac n. *leek*, Gl.

brādhand f. *palm of the hand*, WW 264³⁴.

brādian *to extend, reach*, AO 234¹⁰ : (+) VPs 47³.

brādlāstæx f. *broad axe*, Gl.

brādlinga *flatly, with the hand open*, IM.

brādnes sf. *breadth, greatness, extent, surface*, Æ : *liberality*.

brādpanne=brǣdepanne

brǣc I. *a strip of untilled land?* (BT),KC. **II.**=pret. 3 sg. of brecan. **III.** (+) (e) n. *noise, sound*, CP.

brēc I. (±) n. *catarrh, cough*. **II.** f. *breaking, destruction*, ÆL 5²⁹². **III.**=brēc nap. of brōc I.

bræcce *breeches*, Cp 1788. [*L.*]

brǣccoðu f. *falling sickness, epilepsy*, WW 112²⁷.

brǣcdrenc (ē) *cough medicine*, WW 351⁸⁸.

+**brǣceo**=brǣc I.

brǣclian *to crackle, make a noise*, GD 236¹².

brǣcon pret. pl. of brecan.

±**brǣcsēoc** *epileptic, lunatic*, BH,Lcd.

brǣd I. f. *breadth, width*, AO. [brād] **II.** f. *flesh*, Ph 240. [*OHG.* brāt] **III.** m. *trick, fraud, deceit, craft*, LL,MtL. [=*brǣgd; '*braid*'] **IV.** pret. 3 sg. of brēdan, bregdan. **V.** pres. 3 sg. and pp. of brǣdan.

brǣd-=brǣgd- (bregd-)

±**brǣdan** (e) **I.** *to make broad, extend, spread, stretch out*, BH; AO : *be extended, rise, grow*. ['*brede*'; brād] **II.** *to roast, toast, bake, broil, cook*, WW. ['*brede*']

brǣde m. *roast meat*, WW. ['*brede*']

-**brǣdels** v. ofer-b.

brǣdepanne f. *frying-pan* (v. WW 363n3).

brǣding I. f. *extension*, Bo 46⁶ : *bedding, bed?* DR. **II.** f. *roast meat*, OEG 3760.

brǣdingpanne=brǣdepanne

brǣdīsen (ē) n. *chisel*, Gl,WW.

brǣdra v. brād.

brǣd-u, -o f. *breadth, width, extent*, Ps. ['*brede*']

+**brǣgd**=brǣd III; **brǣgdan**=bregdan

brǣgdboga m. *deceitful bow*, Cr 765.

brǣgden (e) **I.** (±) *deceitful, crafty*, AO. adv. -līce. [bregdan] **II.** *fraud*, LL.

brǣgdwīs *crafty*, Gu 58. [bregd]

brǣgen (a, e) n. '*brain*,' Lcd,Ps; Æ,CP.

brǣgenpanne f. *brain-pan, skull*, OEG 2815.

brǣgensēoc *brain-sick, mad*, OEG.

brǣgn=brǣgen

brǣgnloca (hrǣgn-) m. *brain-house, head*, Rd 72²¹.

brǣgpanne=brǣgenpanne

brǣhtm (A)=breahtm

brǣmbel, brǣmel=brēmel

brēme (NG)=brēme; **brǣr**=brēr

brǣs n. '*brass*,' *bronze*, WW.

brǣsen '*brazen*,' *of brass*, LPs; Æ.

brǣsian *to do work in brass, make of brass*, ÆGr 215¹⁷. ['*braze*']

brǣsne=bresne

brǣð m. *odour, scent, stink, exhalation, vapour*, AO,WW. ['*breath*']

brǣw (ēa) m. *eye-brow, eye-lid*, BH,Lcd,Ps, WW; CP. ['*bree*']

bragen=brǣgen

brahton=brohton pret. pl. of bringan.

brand (ō) m. *fire, flame*, B; Æ : '*brand*,' *torch*, JnL,Da; Æ : *sword, weapon*, B,TC.

brandhāt† *burning hot, ardent*.

brandhord (o¹) n? *treasure exciting ardent desires* (BT); *care, anxiety* (GK), Rim 46.

brand-īren, -īsen n. *fire-dog, trivet, grate*, WW. ['*brandise*']

brandōm (o¹) m. '*rubigo*,' WW 44¹⁴.

brandrād (o², e²) f. *fire-dog, trivet*, WW. ['*brandreth*']

brandrida m. *fire-grate*, WW 266²⁶.

brandstæfn (o¹) *high-prowed?* An 504. [=brant-?]

brang pret. 3 sg. of bringan.

brant† (o) *deep, steep, high*, An,El. ['*brant*']

brasian=brǣsian

+**brastl** (-sl) n. *crackling* (*of flames*), DD,W.

brastlian (-sl) *to roar, rustle, crackle*, Æ. ['*brastle*']

brastlung f. *crackling, rustling, crashing*, Æ.

bratt m. *cloak*, MtL 5⁴⁰. ['*bratt*'; v. LF 125]

brēac pret. 3 sg. of brūcan.

brēad n. *bit, crumb, morsel* : '*bread*,' JnL.

+**breadian** (e) *to regenerate, restore*, Ph 372, 592.

brēag=brēw

breahtm I. (bearhtm; æ, e, eo, y) m. *cry, noise, revelry*. **II.**=bearhtm

breahtmian (earht) *to creak, resound*, Gl.

breahtmung f. '*convolatus*,' WW 376³.

breahtumhwæt=bearhtmhwæt

breard=brerd; **brēat-**=brēot-

brēað *brittle*, Lcd 1·260⁷.

brēaw=brǣw

brēawern n. *brew-house*, WW 145²⁹.

+**brec**=+brǣc III.

brēc v. brōc; ±**brēc**=±brǣc

±brecan I. sv⁴ to 'break,' shatter, burst, tear, B,Bl,G,Ps : curtail, injure, violate, destroy, oppress, B,Chr,Da,KC; AO,CP :· break into, rush into, storm, capture (city), Ma, Chr; CP : press, force : break or crash through, burst forth, spring out, An,Ph : subdue, tame, CP. II. to roar? CR951.

brĕchrægl n. breeches, PPs108²⁸.

brecmǣlum=brytmǣlum

±brecnes f. breach, EPs.

-brecŏ v. ǣ-, eodor-b.

brecŏa m. broken condition. mōdes b. sorrow of heart, B171.

brecung f. 'breaking,' LkR.

bred n. surface : board, plank, CP : tablet, Æ. ['bred']

brēd=(1) brȳd, (2) brād, (3) brǣd III.

brēdan I. to produce, or cherish, a brood, Æ. ['breed'] II. (±)=bregdan. III. (±)=brǣdan I. and II.

breden (i, y) of boards, wooden, Æ,CHR.

brēdende deceitful, cunning, AO. [bregdan]

brēdettan=brogdettan

+bredian=breadian

brēdi(ng)panne=brǣdepanne

brēdīsern=brǣdīsen

bredweall m. wall of boards, palisade, ES 20·148.

+brēfan to write down shortly, BF72²⁰. [cp. Ger. brief]

brēg (VPs)=brǣw; brega (Æ)=brego

brēgan to alarm, frighten, terrify, Lk; Æ, CP. ['bree'; brōga]

bregd=brǣd III.

+bregd I. n. quick movement, change, Ph57. [v. 'braid'] II.=brǣd III.

bregdan³ (brēd-) to move quickly, pull, shake, swing, throw (wrestling), draw (sword), drag, B,Ma : bend, weave, 'braid,' knit, join together, ÆGr : change colour, vary, be transformed, Ex,Sol,Gu : bind, knot : (intr.) move, be pulled : flash, Æ. up b. bring up (a charge) : (+) scheme, feign, pretend : (+) draw breath, breathe.

bregden=brægden

+bregdnes (ē?) f. quick movement? sudden terror? MFH133¹⁷ (v. BTac).

+bregdstafas mp. learned arts, SOL2.

bregen=brægen

brēgendlic terrible, RPs46³.

brēgh=brǣw

brēgnes f. fear, terror, EPs87¹⁷.

bregot (eo) m. ruler, chief, king, lord. b. engla, mancynnes God.

bregorīce n. kingdom, GEN1633.

bregorōf majestic, mighty, B1925.

bregostōlt m. ruler's seat, throne : rule, dominion.

bregoweardt m. ruler, prince, lord, GEN.

bregu=brego

breht-=breaht-, beorht-, bierht-

brehtnian=bearhtmian

brēman I. (±) to honour, extol : respect, fulfil, CHRD18³⁵ : celebrate, CHRD114¹⁷. [brēme] II. (oe) to rage, NG.

brēmbel (Æ), brēμnber=brēmel

brēμe (oe, ȳ) I. adj. famous, glorious, noble, PPs; AO. ['breme'] II. adv. An.

brēmel (ǣ) m. brier, 'bramble,' blackberry bush, Æ,Lcd; Mdf. [brōm]

brēmelæppel m. blackberry, Lcd. [v. 'apple']

brēmelberie f. blackberry, Lcd. ['brambleberry']

brēmelbrǣr (ǣ¹) m. bramble-brier, WW 269³⁸.

brēmellēaf n. bramble-leaf, LCD.

brēmelrind f. bramble-bark, LCD.

brēmelŏyrne f. bramble-bush, Æ.

brēmen=brēme I.

brēmendlic noted, OEG.

brēmer=brēmel

brēmlas nap. of brēmel.

bremman to rage, roar, JnL, WW. [Ger. brummen]

bremung f. roaring, WW242³⁹.

brencŏ pres. 3 sg. of brengan.

brene=bryne

breneŏ=berneŏ (pres. 3 sg. of bernan) (RUN43)

±brengan to bring, AO,CP : produce, NG.

brengnes f. oblation : (+) food, support, MkL12⁴⁴.

brenting m. ship, B2807. [brant]

breo-, brēo-=bre-, brē-

brēod (NG)=brēad

breodian to cry out, MOD28.

breodwian to strike down, trample? GU258, LCD32¹¹.

breoht-=bearht-, beorht-

brēosa (īo) m. gadfly, WW. ['breeze']

brēost nmf. (usu. in pl.) 'breast,' bosom, B, G,Lcd; AO,CP : stomach, womb : mind, thought, disposition, Gen; CP : 'ubertas,' CPs35⁹.

brēostbān n. 'breast-bone,' WW158.

brēostbeorg=brēostgebeorh

brēostbyden (e²) f. breast, GL.

brēostcearut f. heart-care, anxiety.

brēostcofat m. heart, affections.

brēostgebeorh m. bulwark, WW466¹⁴.

brēostgehygdt, -hȳdt fn. thought.

brēostgeŏancet m. mind, thought.

brēostgewǣdut np. corslet, B.

brēostgyrd f. sceptre? OEG3303; 2¹⁸⁸.

brēosthordt n. thought, mind.

brēostlīn n. stomacher, WW407².

brēostlocat m. mind, soul.

brēostnet† n. *coat of mail.*

brēostnyrwet n. *tightness of chest,* LCD 189b.

brēostrocc m. *chest-clothing,* WW 151³⁹.

brēostsefa† m. *mind, heart.*

brēosttoga m. *chieftain,* SOL 184.

brēostðing n. *region of the heart,* LCD 3·146¹⁸.

brēostwærc m. *pain in the chest,* LCD.

brēostweall m. *breastwork, rampart,* WW 490¹³.

brēostweorðung f. *breast-ornament,* B 2504.

brēostwylm (e²) m. *breast-fountain, teat,* SPs 21⁸ : *emotion, sorrow,* B.

Breot-=Bryt-

brēotan²† *to break in pieces, hew down, demolish, destroy, kill.*

Breotas=Brittas

Breoten, Breoton=Bryten

breoton=bryten; brēoton pret. pl. of brēatan.

brēoðan² *to decay, waste away,* LCD 63a, RPs 4¹⁶.

±brēowan² *to 'brew,'* AO.

brēowlāc n. *brewing,* ÆL 17¹⁰³.

brēr (ǣ) f. *'brier,' bramble,* Lcd,WW.

brerd (ea, eo, y) m. *brim, margin, border, surface,* Jn,WW : *shore, bank,* Æ. ['*brerd*']

brerdful *brim-full,* ÆL 6²⁸². ['*brerdful*']

brērhlǣw m. *brier-hillock,* EC 450⁹.

brērðyrne f. *brier-bush,* KC 6·221¹³.

brēsan=brȳsan; bresen=bræsen

bresne (æ)† *mighty, strong.*

Bret=Bryt; bret-, brēt-=bryt-, brȳt-

brēt pres. 3 sg. of brēdan, bregdan.

brēð=bræð; brēðel=briðel

brēðer ds. of brōðor.

brēw (KGL)=brǣw

bric-, brīc-=bryc-, brȳc-

briceð pres. 3 sg.; bricst pres. 2 sg. of brecan.

brid=bridd; brīd=brȳd

bridd m. *young 'bird,' chicken,* Gl,Lk; Æ, CP,Mdf.

bridel, bridels (ȳ) m. *'bridle,' rein, curb, restraint,* Run; Æ,CP.

bridelshring m. *bridle-ring,* EL 1194.

bridelðwangas mp. *reins,* WW 97¹⁰.

briden=breden

brīd-gift, -gifu=brȳd-gift, -gifu

±brīdlian *to 'bridle,' curb,* Bo; CP.

briengan=bringan

brig=brycg; brīg=brīw

brigd n. *change or play of colours,* PA 26. [bregdan]

brigdils (GL)=brīdels

briht-=beorht-, bierht-

brim† n. *surf, flood, wave, sea, ocean, water,* B : *sea-edge, shore.* ['*brim*']

brimceald† *ocean-cold,* PH.

brimclif n. *cliff by the sea,* B 222.

brimfaroð n. *sea-shore* (BT), DA 322 (or ? 2 words).

brimflōd m. *flood, sea,* Az,WW.

brimfugol m. *sea-bird, gull,* WA 47.

brimglest m. *sailor,* RD 4²⁵.

brimhengest† m. *(sea-horse), ship.*

brimhlæst f. *sea-produce, (fish),* GEN 200.

brimlād† f. *flood-way, sea-way.*

brimliðend† m. *seafarer,* B : *pirate,* MA.

brimmann† m. *sailor, pirate,* MA.

brimrād† f. *(sea-road), sea,* AN.

brimsa? *gadfly?* (v. Ln 49⁸² and NC 354).

brimstæð n. *sea-shore,* AN 496.

brimstrēam† m. *current, sea : rapid, river.*

brimðyssa† m. *ship.*

brimwīsa m. *sea-king, captain,* B 2930.

brimwudu† m. *(sea-wood), ship.*

brimwylf f. *(she-)wolf of the sea or lake,* B 1507.

brimwylm m. *ocean surge, sea-wave,* B 1494.

bring m. *offering,* CPs 50²⁰.

bringādl f. *epilepsy?* (or? hringādl v. MLR 19·201).

±bringan³ (e, ie, y) (and wv) *to 'bring,' lead, bring forth, carry, adduce, produce, present, offer,* B,Gen,Jn,Met ; AO,CP.

-bringelle v. on-b.; brīosa=brēosa

brīst, britst pres. 2 sg., brit pres. 3 sg. of bregdan.

Brit-, brit-=Bryt-, bryt-

briðel (e) *fragile, weak,* LCD 1·384¹⁴ (BTac).

brīw m. *pottage, porridge,* ÆGr,Lcd. ['*bree*']

±brīwan *to prepare food, cook, make pottage : make a poultice,* LCD 25a.

brīwðicce *as thick as pottage,* LCD 190a.

broc I. (±) n. *affliction, misery, care, toil, adversity,* Bl,Bo,TC; Æ,AO,CP : *disease, sickness,* Æ : *fragment,* G : *breach.* ['*broke*'; brecan] II. n. *use, benefit.* III. *a kind of locust?* WW 460. ['*brock*'] IV.=brocc

brōc I. f. pl. brēc *breeches,* RB,WW : *the breech?* Lcd (ES 38·345). II. m. *'brook,' torrent,* Bo,WW ; Mdf.

brocc m. *badger,* Lcd. ['*brock*']

broccen *of badger's skin,* WW 152¹.

brocchol n. *badger's hole,* EC 239¹².

broccian *to tremble,* GD 156.

brocen pp. of (1) brecan, (2) brūcan.

brocenlic *fragile,* ByH 130²⁹.

±brocian *to crush, hurt, afflict, molest,* Æ, AO,CP : *blame.* [broc]

broclic *full of hardship,* W 248¹.

brōcminte f. *brookmint, horsemint,* LCD, WW.

brōcrið *a tributary stream,* KC 5·194'.

brōcsēoc=brǣcsēoc

brocung f. *affliction, sickness,* ÆH1·472[7].
brod *shoot, sprout,* LHy6[3].
brōd f. *'brood,' Æ : foetus : breeding, hatching,* WW380[44].
broddetan=brogdettan
broddian=brōdian
brōden pp. of brēdan.
brōdenmǣl† n. *damascened sword.*
brōder=brōðor; **brōdet-**=brogdet-
brōdian *to glitter, shine,* OEG.
brōdig adj. *broody,* BF78[16].
brōga m. *terror, dread, danger,* CP : *prodigy.*
brogden (*El*) pp. of bregdan. ['*browden*']
brogdenmǣl=brōdenmǣl
brogdettan *to shake, brandish : tremble, quake : glitter,* HGL435?
brogdettung f. *trembling, shaking : figment, pretence,* CPs102[14].
±brogne *bough, bush, branch,* DR (v. ES 38·340 and JAW).
broht '*viscellum,*' WW54[1]. (?=broð '*juscellum,*' MLR19·201)
brōht pp., brōhton pret. pl. of bringan.
brōhōrēa m. *dire calamity,* GEN1813. [brōga]
brōm m. '*broom,*' *brushwood,* Lcd; Mdf.
brōmfæsten n. *enclosure of broom,* WW414[7].
brōmig *broomy,* BL207[27]? (BTs and ac).
bron-=bran-; **brond**=brand, brant
brord m. *prick, point : blade* (e.g., *of grass or corn*) : *herbage,* BH366[26].
±brosnian *to crumble, decay, fall to pieces, rot, wither, be corrupted,* AO,CP.
brosniendlic (Æ), +brosnodlic (BL,W) *corruptible, perishable, transitory.*
±brosnung f. *decay, corruption, ruin,* Æ.
+brot n. *fragment,* G. [breotan]
Broten=Bryten
broten pp. of brēotan.
brotettan *to burst forth, shoot, sprout?* HGL435, OEG1218n (or?=brogdettan, BTs)
brōtetung=brogdettung
broð n. '*broth,*' WW. [brēowan]
brōðar, brōðer=brōðor
brōðhund (WW329[38]; 548[19])=roðhund?
brōðor m. ds. brēðer '*brother*,*' Chr,Mt,Lk. nap. (±) brōðor, brōðru, *Gen,Jn* : *fellowman, Ps : co-religionist, Mt : monk.*
brōðorbana m. *fratricide* (*person*), GEN1526.
brōðorcwealm m. *fratricide* (*act*), GEN1030.
brōðordohter f. *niece,* WW173[30].
brōðorgyld n. *vengeance for brothers?* Ex199.
brōðorlēas *brotherless,* RD85[16].
brōðorlic '*brotherly,*' ÆGr.
brōðorlīcnes f. *brotherliness,* BH.
brōðorlufu (-e[2]) *love,* DR.
brōðorrǣden f. *fellowship, brotherhood,* Æ : *membership of a brotherhood.* ['*brotherred*']

brōðorscipe m. *brotherliness, love, MtL* : (+) *brotherhood, fraternity,* AO. ['*brothership*']
brōðorsibb f. *kinship of brothers : brotherly love.*
brōðorslaga m. *brother-slayer,* Æ.
brōðorslege m. *fratricide* (*act*), CP.
brōðorsunu m. *brother's son, nephew,* CHR.
brōðorsybb=brōðorsibb
broðor-ōinen, -ōineùn=beorðorōinen
brōðorwīf n. *brother's wife, sister-in-law,* BH.
brōðorwyrt (e[2]) f. '*pulegium,*' *penny-royal,* WW300[24].
+brōð-ru, -ra mp. *brothers, brethren, Mt.* ['*i-brotheren*']
brōður=brōðor
+browen pp. of brēowan.
brū f. nap. brū(w)a, gp. brūna '*brow,*' *eyebrow, eye-lid, eye-lash,* Rd,WW.
±brūcan[2] *to* '*brook,*' *use, enjoy, possess, partake of, spend, B,Wa.* *brocen cyrtel a coat which has been worn,* Æ : *eat, Æ,JnL* : *execute an office,* CP : *cohabit with.*
brūcendlīce *serviceably,* OEG53[1].
brūcung f. *function, occupation,* BC1·154[13].
brūdon, brugdon pret. pl. of brēdan, bregdan.
brūn '*brown,*' *dark, dusky, Ex,Met : having metallic lustre, shining* (v. NED).
brūna gp. of brū.
brūn-basu, -be(o)su *brownish-purple,* OEG.
brūnecg† *with gleaming blade.*
brūneða m. *itch, erysipelas,* Lcd18a.
brūnewyrt=brūnwyrt
brūnfāg *burnished? brown-hued?* B2615.
brungen pp., brungon pret. pl. of bringan.
brūnian *to become brown,* Lcd106b.
brunna=burna
brūnwann *dusky,* AN1308.
brūnwyrt f. '*brownwort,*' *water-betony, woodbetony,* Lcd.
bruðon pret. pl. of brēoðan.
brūwa nap. of brū.
±bryce (i) **I.** m. '*breach*' ('*bruche*'), *fracture, breaking, infringement, Gu,LL;* Æ : *fragment,* OEG. [brecan] **II.** *fragile, brittle, worthless, fleeting, Bl.* ['*bryche*'] **III.** n. *use, enjoyment, service, exercise, advantage, gain, profit, fruit,* Æ,CP.
brȳce *useful, profitable,* PPs. ['*briche*']
-brycel v. hūs-b.
bryceð pres. 3 sg. of brecan.
brycg f. '*bridge,*' Æ; AO,Mdf.
brycgbōt (i) f. *repairing of bridges,* LL.
brycggeweorc (i[1]) n. *work of building or repairing bridges,* Ct,LL.
brycgian *to* '*bridge,*' *make a causeway, pave,* An.
brycgweard (i[1]) m. *keeper or defender of a bridge,* Ma85. ['*bridgeward*']

brycgwyrcende '*pontifex*'! DR194'.

±**brȳc-ian**, -sian *to use, enjoy*, DR : *profit, benefit*.

brycŏ pres. 3 sg. of brecan.

brȳcŏ pres. 3 sg. of brūcan.

brȳd I. (ē, i) f. '*bride*,' *betrothed or newly-married woman, wife, consort, G,WW* ; Æ, CP. brȳdes wǣde *wedding garment* : (†) (*young*) *woman*. II.=brygd

bryd-, brȳd-=bred-, brīd-

brȳdbedd n. *bridal bed*, Æ.

brȳdblētsung (ī) f. *marriage blessing*, LL 72,38[1].

brȳdboda m. *paranymph, bridesman*, OEG 18b[71].

brȳdbūr (BL) n., brȳdcofa (HGL) m. *bride-chamber, bed-chamber*.

+**bryddan** *to frighten, terrify*, SOL16.

-brȳde v. un-b.

brȳdeala, brȳdealo(ŏ) n. *bride-ale, marriage-feast, Chr*. ['*bridal*']

brȳdelic=brȳdlic

brȳdgifta fpl. *betrothal, espousals*, APT.

brȳdgifu (ī) f. *dowry*, ÆGR57[14] : (pl.) *espousals*, WW171[5].

brȳdguma (Æ,CP), brȳdiguma (Æ) m. '*bridegroom*,' *Jn* : *suitor*.

brȳdhlōp n. *ceremony on conducting a bride to her new home, bridal, wedding, Chr,MtL*. ['*bridelope*']

brȳdhūs n. *bride-chamber*, APs18[6].

+**brȳdian** *to marry*, MH.

brȳdlāc n. *bridal, wedded condition*, Æ : (pl.) *marriage ceremony*, LL ; Æ. ['*bridelock*']

brȳdlēoŏ n. *epithalamium*, OEG.

brȳdlic *bridal*. b. gewrit *Song of Solomon*, WW388[20]. ['*bridely*']

brȳdloca m. *bride-chamber*, BL.

brȳdlōp=brȳdhlōp

brȳdlufe f. *love of a bride*, JUL114.

brȳdniht f. *wedding-night*, MH14[26].

brȳdrǣst f. *bridal bed*, GD.

brȳdrēaf n. *wedding garment*, MtL22[11].

brȳdsang m. *epithalamium*, WW.

brȳdsceamol? *bridal bed*, DR110[1] (BTs).

brȳdŏing np. *nuptials*, Bl. ['*brydthing*']

brygc=brycg

brygd I. (bryd) m. *drawing out, unsheathing, brandishing*, LL356,2. II.=brǣd III.

bryht=beorht ; bryhtan=bierhtan

±**bryidan** *to seize property improperly held by another*, LL. [=*brigdan? BTs]

brym, brymm m. *surf, sea*, AB35·240.

brȳm-=brēm-

bryne m. *burning, conflagration, BH* : *fire, flame, heat, MtL* ; AO : *inflammation, burn, scald, Lcd* : *torch* : *fervour, passion*. ['*brune*'; beornan]

brȳne f. '*brine*,' *WW* ; Æ.

bryneādl f. *fever*, WW238[26].

brynebrōga m. *fire-terror*, Az161.

brynegield† (i[3]) m. *burnt-offering*, GEN.

brynehāt *burning hot*, DOM51.

brynelēoma m. *fire-gleam, flame*, B2313.

brynenes f. *hard, fiery trial*, HGL469.

brynetēar m. *hot tear*, CR152.

bryne-wylm, -welm† m. *wave of fire, flame, burning heat*.

bryngan=bringan

brynig *fiery, burning*, DD211.

brynstān m. *brimstone*, RWH143[31].

bryrd=brerd

bryrdan *to urge on, incite, encourage*, MET 13[3]. [brord]

bryrdnes f. *incitement, instigation*, BH.

±**brȳs-an**, -ian (ē ; =īe) *to* '*bruise*,' *crush, pound, BH,DD* : *season*, SC20[20].

+**brȳsednes** f. *bruising, crushing*, WW211[22].

brȳsewyrt f .*daisy, soap-wort*, Lcd1·374. ['*bruisewort*']

brystmian=brytsnian

brȳt pres. 3 sg. of brēotan.

Bryt (e, i) m. *Briton* : *Breton*.

bryta=brytta

±**brȳtan** *to crush, pound* : (+) *break up, destroy*.

-brytednes v. for-b.

Bryten (e, eo, i, o) f. *Britain*.

bryten (eo) *spacious, roomy*, SAT687.

brytencyning m. *powerful king*, WY75.

brytengrūnd m. *broad earth*, CR357.

Brytenlond n. *Britain* : *Wales*.

brytenrīce (eo) n. I. *spacious kingdom*, Az 107. II. *kingdom of Britain*.

Brytenw(e)alda m. *wielder of Britain, Bretwalda, chief king*, CHR,KC.

brytenwongas mp. *spacious plains, the world*, CR380.

brȳtest pres. 2 sg. of brēotan.

brytian=bryttian

brȳting (ē) f. *breaking* (*of bread*), LkL24[35].

Bryt-land, -lond=Brytenlond

brytmǣlum *piecemeal*, OEG1553n.

brytnere m. *steward*, CP459[11].

±**brytnian** (i) *to divide, distribute, dispense, administer, B* ; CP. ['*britten*']

brytnung f. *distribution*, WW222[43].

brȳtofta pl. *espousals*,WW171[5]. [brȳd, ŏoft]

Bryton=Bryten

±**brytsen** f. *fragment*, FM,G.

brytsnian *to parcel out, distribute*, OEG 2195 : (+) *enjoy, possess*, ES8·473[33].

brȳtst pres. 2 sg. of brēotan.

Brytt- v. also Bryt-.

brytta† (e) m. *dispenser, giver, author, governor, prince, lord*. sinces b. *treasure-giver, lord*. [brēotan]

+**bryttan**=+brȳtan

Bryttas mp. *Britons, BH* : *Bretons*, CHR.

±bryttlan (i) *to divide, dispense, distribute,*
CP : *rule over, possess, enjoy the use of.*
Bryttlsc (e) '*British,' Chr.*
Bryttwealas, Brytwalas mp. *Britons of
Wales,* CHR.
Brytwylisc *British, Welsh,* CHR.
brȳðen f. *brewing, drink, Gu,Lcd.* ['*bru-
then*'; broð]
brȳwlāc (Æ)=brēowlāc
bū I. n. nap. bȳ *dwelling.* [*Ger.* bau]
II. v. bā, bēgen.
±būan anv. (intr.) *to stay, dwell, live,* AO :
lie (of land), WE66[16] : (tr.) *inhabit,
occupy : cultivate.* [*Ger.* bauen]
būc, bucc m. *belly, stomach, Æ : pitcher, Æ :
beaver (of helmet)?* ['*bouk*']
bucca m. '*buck,' he-goat, male deer, Æ,Lcd,
WW;* CP.
budda m. *beetle,* WW543[10].
būde 3 sg., būdon pl. pret. of būan.
budon pret. pl. of bēodan.
būend m. *dweller, inhabitant,* G,LPs.
bufan I. prep. (w. d.) *over, 'above,' Æ,Chr;*
AO : (w. a.) *on, upon, above,* AO. II. adv.
above, overhead, before, Æ.
bufan-cweden, -nemd, -sprecen *above-mentioned,* GD.
bufon=bufan; būg-=bū-
±būgan I. (sv²) *to 'bow,' bow down, turn,
bend, stoop, sink, Æ,AO,Rood : submit, give
way, Æ,B,Chr : depart, flee, retire, Æ,AO :
join, go over to, Æ : convert, Æ.* II.=būan
būgol v. bēogol
būh imperative of būgan.
būian=būan; būl=būla I.
bula m. *bull, steer,* EC449[22].
būl(a) m. *bracelet, necklace, brooch* [bȳl]
bulberende *wearing an ornament,* WW
195[37]; OEG8[319].
bulentse f. *a plant,* LCD44b.
bulgon pret. pl. of belgan.
bulluc m. *male calf, 'bullock,' Sc.*
bulot, bulut *ragged robin, cuckoo-flower,*
LCD.
būn=būan
bund f? *bundle,* MtL13[30].
būnda=bōnda
bunden (*B*) pp., bundon pret. pl. of bindan.
['*y-bound*']
bundenheord *with bounden tresses,* B3151.
+bundennes f. *obligation,* LPs.
bundensteīna adj. (*ship*) *with an ornamented
prow,* B1911.
bune I.† f. *cup, beaker, drinking vessel.* II.
reed, cane? WW198[12]. ['*bun*']
+būnes f. *dwelling,* NC292.
būr n. '*bower,' apartment, chamber, Gen,
WW : storehouse, cottage, dwelling, B,KC;*
Æ. ⌈būan]

±būr (usu.+; but būr at LL92,6³) m. *free-
holder of the lowest class, peasant, farmer.*
['*gebur*']
būrbyrde (æ²) *of peasant birth,* Ct.
būrcniht n. *chamberlain, eunuch,* HL.
būrcot n. *bed-chamber,* CP.
burg (burh) f. (gds. and nap. byrig) *a
dwelling or dwellings within a fortified
enclosure, fort, castle, Chr,WW;* CP :
'*borough,' walled town, AO,Mt;* Æ. [v.
GBG and Mdf]
burg- v. also burh- and beorg-.
burgāgend m. *city-owner,* EL1175.
burgat=burggeat
burgbryce m. *breaking into a (fortified)
dwelling,* LL : *penalty for that offence,*
LL.
burgen=byrgen
būrgerihta np. *peasant's rights or dues,*
LL446,4.
būrgeteld† n. *pavilion, tent,* JUD.
burgfæsten n. *fortress,* GEN1680.
burgfolc n. *townspeople,* B2220.
burggeat n. *castle gate, city gate.*
burghege m. *fence of a 'burg,'* Ct.
burg-hlið† n. nap. -hleoðu *fortress-height*
(or?=beorg-hlið).
burglagu f. *civil law,* GPH388.
burg-lēod, -lēoda m. *citizen,* AO.
burgloca† m. *fortified enclosure, walled town.*
burglond n. *native city,* CR51.
burgon pret. pl. of beorgan.
burgrǣced n. *fortress,* RUIN22.
burgrūn f. *sorceress;* pl. *fates, furies,* GL.
burg-sæl† n. nap. -salu *city-hall, house.*
burgsǣta (ē²) m. *town-dweller, citizen,* WW.
burgscipe m. *borough,* WW497[19].
burgsele m. *castle-hall, house,* RIM30.
burgsittende† mpl. *city-dwellers.*
burgsorg=borgsorg
burgsteall m. *citadel? city?* WW205[36]. (or?
borg-)
burgstede† m. *city, castle.*
burgstrǣt *town road,* BC3·15[11].
burgtūn m. *city, Wif*31. ['*borough-town*']
burgðelu f. *castle floor, Fin*30 (burh-). [v.
'*theal*']
burg-waran, -waru fp., -ware (AO,CP),
-waras mp. *inhabitants of a 'burg,'
burghers, citizens.*
burgweall m. *city-wall, Æ.*
burgweg m. *road, street, Æ.*
burgwīgend m. *warrior,* EL34.
burh=burg
burhbiscop m. *bishop of a city,* HR15[16].
burhbōt f. *liability for repair of the walls of a
town or fortress,* LL.
burhealdor m. *burgomaster, mayor, Æ.*
burhgeard m. *castle yard,* EC328'.

burhgemet n. *measure used in a town*, LL 477,6.

burhgemōt n. *town's meeting*, LL.

burhgerēfa m. *chief magistrate of a town, provost, mayor*, WW. ['*borough-reeve*']

burhgerihta np. *town due*, TC 432, 433.

burhgeðingō f. *town council (as judicial body)*, LL 228,1².

burhmann m. *citizen*, WW. ['*borough-man*']

burhrǣdden f. *citizenship*, WW 441¹⁰.

burhrest f. *chamber-couch*, IM 125⁸⁶. [?= *bürrest, ES 38·347]

burhriht n. *town right, town law*, LL 477,6.

burh-rūn, -rūne f. *fury, sorceress,*WW 245¹⁶.

±**burhscipe** m. *township, civil district*, Gl, LL. ['*boroughship*']

burhscīr f. *city limits, city, township*, Æ.

burhsprǣc f. *courtly speech*, GL.

burhstaðol m. *foundation of the wall of a* '*burg*,' LCD 1·328'.

burhðegn m. *living in a* '*burg*'; or?= bürðegn

burhwarumann m. *burgess*, BH 40³¹.

burhwealda m. *burgess*, BH 40³¹B.

burhweard† m. *city defender*.

burhwela m. *treasure of a city*, B 3100.

burhwelle f. *spring in a* '*burg*'? KC 3·394'.

burhwerod n. *townsfolk*, KC,WW.

burhwita m. *town councillor*, CC.

būrland n. *land occupied by peasants*, EC 384', (+) BC 201¹⁴.

burn f., **burna** (CP) m., **burne** f. *brook, stream*, Jn (v. GBG and Mdf) : *spring or well water*, Cp,WW. ['*burn*']

burnon pret. pl. of biernan.

burnsele m. *bath-house*, RUIN 22.

burnstōw f? *bathing-place*, KC.

bürrēaf n. *tapestry (for a* bür), TC 530'.

būrscipe=burhscipe

burse f. *bag, pouch*, LCD.

burston pret. pl. of berstan.

būr-ðegn, -ðēn m. *page, chamberlain*, CC,MA.

burðre f. *birth, issue*, BL 105²⁰.

buruh=burg

būst pres. 2 sg. of būan.

būt m. *a vessel*, LL 455' (?=būc; BTs).

būta=(1) būtan, (2) būtū

būtan (o²) I. prep. w. d. and (rarely) a. *out of, outside of, off, round about*, Æ : *except, without, all but, but only*, Chr : *besides, in addition to : in spite of.* II. conj. (w. ind.) *except, except that, but, only.* b. ðæt *except* : (w. subj.) *unless, save that* : (w. subst.) *except, but, besides, if only, provided that*, AO. III. adv. *without, outside*, Chr. ['BOUT,' 'BUT']

būte=(1) būtan, (2) būtū

butere f. '*butter*,' Lcd; Æ : *milk for butter-making*, LCD (v. A 52·186). [L.]

buter-flēoge, -flēge f. '*butterfly*,' WW.

butergeōwēor n. *butter-curd, butter*, WW 98³.

+**buterian** *to butter*, LCD 121a.

buter-ic, -uc=butruc

buterstoppa m. *butter-vessel*, WW 280²⁵.

būton=būtan; **butre**=butere

butruc m. *(leather) bottle*, Æ.

butsecarl m. *boatman, mariner*, Chr. ['*buscarl*']

buttorflēoge=buterflēoge

buttuc m. *end, small piece of land*, KC 4·19'.

būtū (būtwu, būta, būte) *both* (neuter). v. also begen.

butueoh (CHR) v. betwux.

būtun=būtan; **buturuc**=butruc

būtwū=būtū; **būwan**=būan

bȳ=bū; **bȳan** (N)=būan

byccen (i) *of a goat, goat's*, CHRD 48²⁶.

bȳcera m.=bēocere

±**bycgan** (i) *to* '*buy*,' *pay for, acquire*, Mt, Jn : *redeem, ransom* : *procure, get done* : *sell*, LL.

bycgend v. beccen; **bȳcn-**=bēacn-, bīecn-

byd-, **bȳd-**=bed-, bid-, bīd-

bydel m. '*beadle*,' *apparitor, warrant officer*, Lk; Æ : *herald, forerunner*, Æ : *preacher*, Æ. [bēodan]

bydelæcer m. *land of a* '*bydel*,' KC 6·152'.

byden f. *measure, bushel : bucket, barrel, vat, tub*. [*Low L.* butina; *Ger.* bütte]

bydenbotm m. *bottom of a vessel*, WW 123⁴.

bydenfæt n. *bushel, barrel*, BL.

bȳdla m. *worshipper*, NG.

bȳencg (DR)=bȳing; **bȳend**=būend

byf-=bif-, beof-

-byffan v. ā-b.

byg-, **bȳg-**=big-, bē-, bī, bīg-

bȳgan=bīegan

byge (ȳ?; i) m. *curve, bend, corner, angle, cone (of a helmet)*, AO,CP : *traffic, commerce*, LL 128,5.

bȳgel. bȳgle=bēogol

bygen f. *purchase*, LL (328¹¹).

bygendlic *easily bent, flexible*, BH.

bȳgeð pres. 3 sg. of bycgan.

bȳgeð pres. 3 sg. of būan.

+**bygu** f. *a bend*, KC. [=byge]

byht m. I. (±) *bend, angle, corner, Ct : bay, bight.*' [būgan] II.† n? *dwelling.* [būan]

+**byhte**=byht I. +**byhð**=byht II.

bȳhð pres. 3 sg. of būgan.

bȳing=bū I.

bȳl m? **bȳle** f? '*boil*,' *carbuncle*, WW.

bylcettan=bealcettan

±**byld**=bieldo

bylda m. *builder? householder?* CRA 75. [bold]

byldan I. *to build, construct*, KC. II.= bieldan

byldu, byldo=bieldo; **bȳle**=bȳl

·**byledbrēost** (=bylged-?) *puff-breasted*, RD 81[1].

bylewit=bilewit; **bylg**=belg

bylgan *to 'bellow*,' MH.

+**bylgan** *to anger, provoke*, GD.

bylgð pres. 3 sg. of belgan.

bylig=belg, bylg

bȳliht (īly-) *ulcerous*, LCD 63b.

bylwet, byl(y)wit=bilewit

bȳme (ÆE)=bīeme

bȳmere (WW), bȳmesangere (ē, ēa; =īe) m. *trumpeter*, Æ. ['*bemer*']

bȳmian (=īe) *to blow the trumpet, Ps,WW* : *trumpet forth*, BF172[28]. ['*beme*']

bynd=bind

byndele, byndelle=bindele

bȳne *cultivated, inhabited, occupied*, AO. [būan]

+**bȳran** *to colonize*, WW210[14].

byrc, byrce=beorc, beorce

byrcð pres. 3 sg. of beorcan.

byrd I. (i) f. *birth* (pl. w. sg. meaning), APT11[20]. II. f. *burden*, GD215[1].

+**byrd** I. fn.; +byrdo, -u f. *birth*, Cr : *descent, parentage, race*, BH : *offspring*, BL : *nature, quality, rank*, Æ,AO : *fate*. ['*birde*'; beran] II. *burdened*, MtR11[48]. III.=+byrded

+**byrdan** *to beard, fringe, embroider*, GL.

-**byrdan** v. an-b-, +ed-b.

+**byrdboda** m. *herald of a birth*, OP17.

+**byrddæg** m. *birthday*, Mt14[6].

byrde *of high rank, well-born, noble, rich*, AO.

+**byrde** I. *innate, natural*, BO,EL. II.= +byrd I.

+**byrdelīce** *energetically, zealously*, CP160[19].

byrden=byrðen

byrdicge f. *embroideress*, WW262[18].

byrdinenu=byrððinenu

byrding f. *embroidering*, WW294[10].

-**byrding** v. hyse-b.

byrdistre *embroiderer* (v. ANS123·418).

+**byrdlic** *harmonious*, AS5[13].

byrdling *tortoise*, OEG23[21].

-**byrdling** v. in-, frum-b.

byrdscype m. *child-bearing*, CR182.

+**byrd-tīd** (G) f., -tīma (W) m. *time of birth*.

+**byrdu**=+byrd I.

+**byrdwiglere** m. *birth-diviner, astrologer*, WW108[14].

+**byrdwītega** m. *astrologer*, WW189[1].

byre I.† m. (nap. byras, byre) *child, son, descendant* : *young man, youth*. [beran] II. m. *mound*. III. (±) m. *time, opportunity*, Æ : *occurrence*, AS62? IV. m. *strong wind, storm*, GPH400.

bȳre n. *stall, shed, hut*, Gl. ['*byre*']

+**byredlic** *suitable, fitting, convenient, congenial*, DR. adv. -līce.

byrele (i) mf. *cup-bearer, butler, steward, B*, Gen. ['*birle*']

byrelian *to give to drink, serve with drink*, Gu. ['*birle*' vb.]

+**byrelic**=+byredlic

byren I. (and byrene) f. *she-bear*, MH,WW. [bera] II.=beren

-**bȳren** v. nēahge-b.

byres f. *borer, graving tool, awl, chisel*, GL. [borian]

byreð I.=bierð pres. 3 sg. of beran. II.= pres. 3 sg. of byrian I.

byrg gds. and nap. of burg.

byrg- v. also byrig-, birg-.

+**byrg**, bēon on gebyrge (w. d.) *to help, protect*. [beorgan]

byrga m. *security, surety, bail, one who gives bail*, GL. [Ger. bürge]

±**byrgan** I. (i) *to raise a mound, hide, 'bury*,' *inter*, Hy; AO. II.=birgan. III.=beorgan

+**byrgednes** f. *burial*, BH (Sch.) 546[3].

byrgels (e, i) m. *tomb*, Æ,Ct. ['*buriels*']

byrgelslēoð (e[1]) n. *epitaph*, HGL427.

byrgelssang m. *dirge*, OEG : *epitaph*, HGL 427.

byrgen (i, u) f. *burying-place, grave, sepulchre*, El,Mt; Æ,AO,CP : *burial*. ['*burian*'; beorgan]

+**byrgen** I. f. *caul? grave?* (BTs), LCD 185a. II. '*tinipa*,' WW277[2].

byrgend m. *grave-digger*, PPs78[3].

byrgenlēoð n. *epitaph*, BH94[12].

byrgensang m. *dirge*, OEG.

byrgenstōw f. *burying-place*, W.

byrgere m. *corpse-bearer*, WW. ['*burier*']

byrgian=byrgan

byrging I. f. *burial*, A11·173. II.=birging

byrglēoð n. *dirge, epitaph*, GL.

byrht, byrht-=beorht, beorht-, bierht-

byrhtm=breahtm

±**byrian** I. (impers.) *to happen, pertain to, belong to, befit*, Æ,Chr,Mk,MtR; AO,CP. ['*bir*'; '*i-bure*'] II.=byrgan

byric=beorc

byrig=burg, and gds. of burg.

byrig-=byrg-, burh-

byrigberge f. *mulberry*, LCD 86a.

byrignes I. f. *burial*, BH : *grave*, BYH 124. ['*buriness*'] II.=birgnes

-**bȳrild** v. nēah-geb.; **byris**=byres

byrisang (i) m. *dirge*, HGL488[57].

byrl-=byrel-

byrla m. *trunk (of body)*, LCD 58b.

+**byrman** (i; =ie) *to ferment, leaven* : *swell up, be proud*. [beorma]

+**byrmed** n. *leavened bread*, Ex12[15],[19].

byrnan (ÆE)=biernan

byrne I. f. *corslet,* WW; CP. [*'burne'*]
II.=burne, burn. **III.**=bryne
byrnete f. *barnacle,* NC275.
byrn-ham, -hamaǂ m. *corslet.*
+**byrnod** *corsleted,* ÆGr256[16]. [*'i-burned'*]
byrnsweord n. *flaming sword,* BL109[34].
byrnwigaǂ m. *corsleted warrior,* AA.
byrn-wīgend, -wīggendǂ m. *corsleted warrior.*
byrs, byrse=byres
byrst I. (e) m. *loss, calamity, injury, damage, defect,* Æ. [berstan] **II.** n. *(land-)slip,* KC3·52[9] (v. also KC5·112[19] and Mdf).
III. f. *'bristle,'* Ep,Lcd,WW; Æ. [*'birse,'* *'brust'*] **IV.** pres. 3 sg. of berstan. **V.** pres. 2 sg. of beran.
+**byrst** *furnished with bristles,* OEG23[3].
byrstende *'rugiens'?* DR122[7].
byrstful *disastrous,* CHR1116.
byrstig *broken, rugged,* OEG,RWH141[38]. [berstan]
+**byrtīd**=+byrdtīd
byrð pres. 3 sg. of beran.
byrðen f. *'burden,' load, weight,* Bl,G,WW; Æ,CP : *charge, duty.*
+**byrðen** f. *what is born, a child,* W251D[14].
byrðenmǣlum *a heap at a time,* ÆH 1·526'.
byrðenmǣte (ē[3]) *burdensome,* KGL1011
byrðenstān m. *millstone,* MtL18[6].
byrðenstrang *strong at carrying burdens,* ÆH1·208[13].
byrðere=byrðre
byrðestre (e) f. *female carrier,* HGL498[18].
byrðling (e) m. *carrier,* OEG4922.
byrðor=beorðor
byrðre I. m. *bearer, supporter,* ÆH. [beran]
II. f. *child-bearer, mother,* W251[13].
+**byrðtīd**=+byrdtīd
byrðōīnenu f. *midwife,* GPH392.
bysceop=bisceop; **byseg-**=bysg-
bysen=bisen; **bysig-,** bysg-=bisg-
bysmer, bysmor=bismer; bysmr-=bismr-
bysn=bisen
byst=bist pres. 2 sg. of bēon.
bȳsting (=īe) f. *'beestings,'* WW129[2]. [bēost]
byt I.=bit pres. 3 sg. of biddan. **II.**=bytt
bȳt pres. 3 sg. of (1) bēodan, (2) bēatan.
bȳtel, bȳtl=bīetl; **byter**=biter
bytlaǂ=bylda
bytlan, ±bytlian *to build, erect,* Æ,CP. [botl]
+**bytlu** np. *building, dwelling,* Æ.
±**bytlung** f. *building,* Æ.
bytme fǂ *keel : head of a dale,* Ct.
bytming f. *hold, keel of ship,* ÆH1·536.
bytne=bytme
bȳtst pres. 2 sg. of bēatan and bēodan.

bytt I. f. *bottle, flagon,* Mt,WW; Æ : *cask.* [*'bit'*] **II.** *small piece of land,* KC3·85[11]. **III.** pres. 3 sg. of biddan.
bytte=bytt I.
byttehlīd n. *butt-lid,* WW213[23].
byttfylling f. *filling of casks,* LL178,8[1].
byð=bið pres. 3 sg. of bēon.
bȳð pres. 3 sg. of būan.
byðme=bytme
bȳwan (ēo;=īe) *to rub, brighten, furbish up, adorn,* B,WW.
byxen (i) *made of boxwood,* WW. [box]

C

cæb-, cǣc-=cæf-, cēac-
cæcepol *taxgatherer,* WW111[9]. (hæce-)
cæderbēam=cederbēam; **cæf** = ceaf
cæfertūn=cafortūn
cæfester (cæb-) n. *halter,* GL. [*L.* capistrum]
-**cæflan** v. be-, ofer-, ymb-c.
cæfing f. *hair-ornament,* GL.
cæfl m. *halter, muzzle,* WW.
cǣg, cǣge f., cǣga m. *'key'* (lit. and fig.), Ex,G,LL,MH,Rd : *solution, explanation,* CP.
cǣgbora m. *key-bearer, jailor,* GL,MH.
cǣghiorde m. *keeper of keys, steward,* WW.
cǣgloca m. *locked depository,* LL362,76[1].
-**cǣglod** v. ā-c.
cæh-=ceah-; **cæl-**=cel-, ceal-, ciel
cælð pres. 3 sg. of calan.
cæm-; cæn-=cem-; cen-, cyn-
cæpehūs=cīepehūs
cæppe f. *'cap,'* WW : *cope, hood.* [*Lat.*]
cæpse f. *box,* NC276. [*L.* capsa]
cær-=car-, cear-, cer-, cier-
cærse (e) f. *'cress,' water-cress,* Lcd; Mdf.
cærsiht *full of cress,* KC3·121[18].
cærte=carte
cǣs=cēas pret. 3 sg. of cēosan.
cǣse=cȳse; **cæstel**=castel
cæster (NG)=ceaster
cāf *quick, active, prompt,* Æ : *strenuous, strong : bold, brave.* adv. cāfe, El. [*'cofe'*]
cāflic *bold.* adv. -līce *promptly, vigorously : boldly,* ÆL. [*'cofly'*]
caflwyrt=cawlwyrt
cāfnes f. *energy,* ÆH2·282[4].
cafortūn (æ, ea[1], e[2]) m. *vestibule, court, courtyard,* Æ : *hall, residence,* Æ.
cāfscipe m. *alacrity, boldness,* RB,W.
+**cafstrian** *to bridle, curb,* CP218[22]. [cæfester]
cahhetan=ceahhetan; **cāl**=cawl, cawel
calan[6] *to grow cool or cold,* BH,Bo.

calc I. m. *shoe, sandal*, Mk6⁹. [*L.*] II.= cealc

calcatrippe=coltetræppe

calcrond *shod (of horses)*, GNE143.

cald (A)=ceald

cālend m. *the beginning of a month*, AO : *month*, Men : (†) *span of life*. ['*calends*']

cālendcwide m. *tale of days*, SOL479.

calf (A)=cealf

calfur (VPs) nap. of cealf.

calic m. '*chalice*,' *Lcd,Lk,Mt,Ps*. [*L.*]

-calla (ZDA10·345) v. hilde-c.

calu (cal(e)w- in obl. cases) '*callow*,' *bare, bald, Rd,Pr*.

calwer (*Gl*)=cealer

calwer-clim, -clympe *curds?* WW.

cāma m. *muzzle, collar, bit*, PPs31¹¹. [*L.*]

camb (o) m. '*comb*,' *crest, Ep,WW* : *honey-comb*, LPs.

cambiht *combed, crested*, WW.

cambol=cumbol

camel m. '*camel*,' *Mt,Mk*.

cammoc (u²) nm? '*cammock*,' *rest-harrow*, *Lcd,WW*.

±camp (o) I. mn. *combat, battle, struggle, warfare, B,Rd*. ['*camp*'] II. *field, plain?* EC183². [*L. campus*]

campdōm m. *military service, warfare*, Æ.

campealdor m. *commander*, OEG4433.

campgefēra m. *fellow-soldier*, GL.

camphād m. *warfare*, BH.

±camplan (o) *to strive, fight, Gu*; Æ. ['*camp*']

camplic *military*, Æ,CHRD.

camprǣden f. *war, warfare*, AN4.

campstede† m. *battlefield*.

campung f. *fighting, warfare*, BL,GL.

campwǣpen (o¹) n. *weapon*, RD21⁹.

campweorod (e², ea², e³) n. *army, host*, BH.

campwīg (o¹) n. *battle, combat*. JUD333

campwīsa m. *director of public games*, HGL 405.

campwudu m. *shield?* EL51.

can pres. 1 and 3 sg. of cunnan.

cān m. *germ, sprout?* PPs79¹⁰. [*OS. cīnan*]

±canc n. *jeering, scorn, derision*, GL.

canceler m. *chancellor*, CHR1093. [*Low L.* cancellarium]

cancer m. *cancer*, Æ. [*L.*]

cancerādl f. *cancer*, LCD41a.

cancerwund f. *cancerous wound*, LCD.

cancet(t)an, *to cry out, mock, deride*, GL, LL.

cancetung f. *boisterous laughter*, WW382³⁶.

cancor=cancer

candel (o¹, o²) fn. *lamp, lantern*, '*candle*,' *Gl*; Æ. [*L.* candela]

candelbora m. *acolyte* (Swt).

candelbryd (?=bred; BTs) *flat candlestick*, IM120.

candellēoht n. '*candle-light*,' *RB*.

Candelmæsse f. '*Candlemas*,' *the feast of the Purification, Chr*.

Candelmæsseæfen n. *Candlemas eve*, LL.

Candelmæssedæg m. *Candlemas day*, NC 276.

candelsnȳtels m. *candle-snuffers*, WW126²⁸. [v. '*snitels*']

candelstæf m. *candlestick, Mt,WW*. ['*candlestaff*']

candelsticca m. '*candlestick*,' EC250'.

candeltrēow n. *candelabrum*, MtR5¹⁵.

candeltwist m. *pair of snuffers*, GL.

candelwēoce f. '*candle-wick*,' *torch*, WW.

candelwyrt f. *candlewort*, WW137⁹.

cann I. f. *cognizance, averment, asseveration, clearance*, LL. II. (±) pres. 3 sg. of cunnan.

canne f. '*can*,' *cup*, WW.

cannon sbp. *reed, cane*, AA30¹⁹. [*L.* canna]

canon m. *canon, rule*. canones bēc *canonical books*. [*L.* canon]

canonbōc *a book of canons*, LL(316¹⁴).

canonic I. m. *canon*, LL. II. *canonical*, Æ.

canoniclic (e³) *canonical* (BT).

cans=canst pres. 2 sg. of cunnan.

cantel m? n? *buttress, support*, BF142²³.

cantelcāp m. *cope*, CHR1070E.

cantercæppe f. *cope* (*vestment*), Ct.

cantere m. *singer*, CM904.

canterstæf m. *chanter's staff*, EC250¹⁵.

cantic (Æ), canticsang (CPs), m. *canticle, song*. [*L.*]

-cāp v. cantel-c.

capellan m. *chaplain*, EC,CHR (late). [*L.*]

capian *to look*. ūp c. *to look up, lie on its back (of the moon)*, LCD3·266²³. capiende '*supinus*,' GPH393a.

capitel=capitol

capitelhūs n. *chapter-house*, IM122⁴.

capit-ol, -ul, -ula m. *chapter (cathedral or monastic)* : *chapter (division of a book), lesson, LL* : *anthem*. ['*chapitle*']

capitolmæsse f. *early mass, first mass*, WW 101¹⁶.

+capitulod *divided into chapters*, LL(204²).

cappa=cæppe

capun m. '*capon*,' WW. [*L.* capōnem]

carbunculus m. *carbuncle*, CP. [*L.*]

carc-ern (AO,CP), -ærn n. *prison, jail*. [*L.* carcer]

carcernŏystru f. *prison darkness*, LL.

carcernweard m. *jailor*, MH24¹⁵,¹⁹.

-carcian v. be-c.

cārclife=gārclife; care-=car-

carful (ea) *anxious, sad, Gu,Soul* : '*careful*,' *attentive, painstaking, Ps,WW* : *troublesome*. adv. -līce, LL.

carfulnes f. *care, anxiety* : '*carefulness*,' Æ, Lcd.

cargealdor (ea¹) n. *sorrowful song*, JUL618.
cargēst (ea¹) m. *sad spirit, devil*, GU365.
carian *to ' care' for, be anxious, grieve*, B,Cr;
Æ.
caricum dp. of sb. *with dried figs*, ÆL23b⁶⁶¹.
[L. carica]
carig (ea, e)† *sorrowful, anxious*, Cr,Soul :
grievous, DD. ['chary']
carl m. *man*, LCD. [ON. karl]
carlēas *'careless,' free from care*, Ex,RB.
carlēasnes, carlēast f. *freedom from care,
security*, WW. ['carelessness']
carlfugol (ea¹, e⁸) m. *male bird, cock*, RWH
148⁴.
carlīce (ea) *wretchedly*, PPs85⁶.
carlmann m. *male, man*, CHR1086.
carr m. *stone, rock*, NG. [Keltic]
carseld (ea) n. *home of care*, SEAF5.
carslō̆ (ea) *painful journey*, B2396.
carsorg f. *sad anxiety*, GEN1114.
carte (æ) f. *paper for writing on*, Æ : *document, deed : letter*, RWH87³⁴. [L. charta]
caru (ea) f. *' care,' concern, anxiety, sorrow*,
B,Lk,Ps; AO.
carwylm (æ², e²)† m. *welling sorrow.*
casebill n. *club*, GPH394 (v. A31·66).
cāserdom m. *imperial sway*, DR,LL.
Cāsere (Cāser, JnL) m. *Cæsar, emperor*,
Bo; Æ,AO. ['Kaser']
cāsering f. *coin with Cæsar's head on it,
drachma, didrachma*, NG.
cāserlic *imperial*, WW427⁴⁰.
cāsern f. *empress*, AO266¹⁴.
cassuc m. *hassock, sedge*, LCD.
cassuclēaf np. *hassock or sedge leaves*, LCD
170a.
castel I. m. *' castle,' fort*, Chr : *walled enclosure?* Ct (v. GBG). II. n. *town, village*,
Mt,Mk,Lk.
castelmann m. *townsman*, CHR.
castelweall (æ¹) m. *city wall, rampart*,
RWH134²⁷.
castelweorc n. *castle-building*, CHR1137.
castenere m. *cabinet, chest*, TC531⁷.
casul m. *over-garment, 'birrus,' cloak*, WW
196³⁹. ['casule']
cāsus m. *(grammatical) case*, ÆGR.
catt m., catte f. *' cat,' Gl*; Mdf.
caul [S6N1]=cawl I. and II.
caulic *a medicine*, LCD102b.
cawellēaf n. *cabbage-leaf*, LCD166b.
cawelsǣd n. *cabbage-seed*, LCD187a.
cawelstela m. *cabbage-stalk*, LCD3·102⁷.
cawelstoc (cāl-) m. *cabbage-stalk*, LCD1·378⁸.
cawelwurm m. *caterpillar*, WW121²⁹. [v.
'cawel']
cawl I. (e, ea, eo) m. *basket*, AO,Gl. ['cawl']
II. (ā?) m. *' cole' ('caul,' 'cawel'), kale,
cabbage*, Lcd.

cēac sm. *basin, pitcher, jug*, Æ,CP : *kettle,
cauldron (for hot-water ordeal)*, LL24;
104; 116.
cēacādl (ēo) f. *jaw-ache*, LCD109a,113a.
cēacbān n. *' cheek-bone,' jaw*, WW.
cēacbora m. *yoke for buckets*, GL.
cēace (ē, ei, ēo) f. *' cheek,' jaw, jawbone*, G,
Lcd,VPs,WW.
ceacga m. *broom, furze*, BC,KC.
ceacl=ceafl
ceaf (e) n., nap. ceafu *'chaff,'* Æ,Mt,Lk,
WW; CP.
ceaf-=caf-, ceaf-, cief-
ceaffinc m. *chaffinch*, ANS76·206.
ceafl m. *jaw, cheek, jaw-bone, cheek-bone,
Æ,Whale.* ['jowl']
ceaflādl (cealf-) f. *disease of the jaws*, LCD90b.
ceafor (e) m. *cock-' chafer,' beetle*, Ps,WW;
Æ.
ceahhe f. *daw*, KC3·48'.
ceahhetan *to laugh loudly*, BH428¹.
ceahhetung f. *laughter, jesting*, Æ.
cealc (a) m. *' chalk,' lime, plaster*, AO; Mdf :
chalkstone, pebble, Ep,WW.
+cealcian (æ) *to whiten*, MtL23²⁷.
cealcpyt m. *chalk-pit*, KC5·346. [v. 'chalk']
cealcsēað m. *chalk-pit*, KC.
cealcstān m. *limestone, chalk*, GL,LCD.
ceald (a) I. adj. *' cold' ('cheald'), cool*, A,
Mt,Jn; AO,CP. adv. cealde. II. n. *coldness, cold.*
cealdheort (a) *cruel*, AN138.
cealdian *to become cold*, Rim. ['cold']
cealdnes f. *coldness, cold*, ÆL23b¹⁷⁵.
cealer m. *' galmaria,' pressed curds, jelly of
curds or whey*, Gl. ['calver']
cealerbrīw m. *pottage of curds*, LCD.
cealf I. (æ, e) nm. (nap. cealfru) *' calf,'* Æ,
G,Gl. II.=ceafl
+cealfe *great with calf*, GENC33¹³.
cealfādl=ceaflādl
cealfian *to calve*, Æ.
cealfloca m. *calf-pen*, KC1·312⁶.
cealfre=cealre, cealer
cealfwyrt (a) *' eruca,'* WW136¹⁷.
ceallian *to ' call,' shout*, Ma91. [ON. kalla]
cealre=cealer and das. of cealer.
cēap (ē, ȳ) m. *cattle*, CP : *purchase, sale,
traffic, bargain, gain*, B; CP : *payment,
value, price*, LL : *goods, possessions,
property*, Chr; AO : *market*, Æ. dēop c.
high price. būtan cēape *gratis.* ['cheap']
cēapcniht m. *bought servant, slave*, GL.
cēapdæg m. *market-day*, WW.
cēapēadig? *rich, wealthy*, GNE108.
cēapealeðel n. *alehouse*, LL(410¹⁸)? (v.
BTs).
cēapgyld n. *purchase money, market price :
compensation*, v. LL2·338.

±cēapian *to bargain, trade, Mt* : *buy, Jn,Cr*;
AO : *endeavour to bribe*, DA 739. ['*cheap*']
cēapland *purchased land*, TC 580¹³.
cēapman m. '*chapman*,' *trader, BH,LL.*
cēapsceamul m. *seat of custom or toll, treasury,* G.
cēapscip n. *trading vessel*, AO 116⁴.
cēapsetl (ē¹) n. *toll-booth,* G.
cēapstōw f. *market-place, market,* CP.
cēapstrǣt (ē, ȳ) f. *market-place,* ÆGR.
cēapung f. *traffic, trade, LL.* ['*cheaping*']
cēapunggemōt n. *market*, WW 450¹.
cear=car
cearcetung f. *gnashing, grinding*, W 200¹⁸.
cearcian *to creak, gnash,* Æ. ['*chark*']
cearde=cierde pret. 3 sg. of cierran.
+cearfan (NG)=+ceorfan
cearm m. *noise*, W 186¹⁸.
cear-rige, -ruce *a vehicle?* GL.
ceart I. *wild common land,* KC. II.=cræt
cearwund *badly wounded?* LL 6,63 and 3·12
(or ? scearw- BTs).
cēas I.=cēast. II. pret. 3 sg. of cēosan.
-cēasega v. wæl-c.
cēaslunger *contentious,* CHRD 19¹².
cēast (ǣ, ē) f. *strife, quarrelling, contention,*
WW : *reproof.*
ceastel=castel
ceaster (æ, e) f. *castle, fort, town,* CP :
†*heaven, hell.*
ceasterǣsc m. *black hellebore,* LCD.
ceasterbūend m. *citizen,* B768.
ceastergewar-=ceasterwar-
ceasterherpað *high road?* (BTs),KC 5·217¹.
ceasterhlid n. *city gate,* CR 314.
ceasterhof n. *house in a city,* AN 1239.
ceaster-lēod f. np. -lēode *citizens,* NC 276.
ceasternisc (æ) *urban, municipal,* TC 244¹³.
ceaster-sǣtan, -sǣte mp. *citizens,* TC.
±ceaster-waran mp., -ware, -waru f.
burghers, citizens.
ceasterweall (e¹) m. *city wall,* MH 150⁹.
ceasterwīc f. *village,* BL 69³⁵.
ceasterwyrt f. *black hellebore,* LCD.
cēastful *contentious,* Sc 105⁵.
ceastre=ceaster
cēaw pret. 3 sg. of cēowan.
ceawl (MtL)=cawl I.
cēce (VPs)=cēace
cēcel (coecil) *a little cake, Ep.* ['*kechel*']
cecil '*suffocacium*,' WW 49²⁸.
cecin '*tabetum*,' *a board,* WW 279¹.
cēde (VPs)=cīegde pret. 3 sg. of cīegan.
cedelc f. *the herb mercury, Lcd,WW.* ['*ked-lock*']
ceder nmf. *cedar,* BLPs. [*L.* cedrus]
ceder-bēam mn., -trēow (ȳ) n. *cedar-tree,*
Ps.
cedor-=ceder-

cēdrisc *of cedar,* DR 65¹⁵.
cef (Æ)=ceaf; cef-=ceaf-, cif-
cēgan (VHy), cēgian=cīegan
cehhettung=ceahhetung
ceīce (MtLR); ceig- (N)=cēace; cīg-
ceir *cry, clamour,* DR.
cel=cawl
cēlan (æ) *to cool, become cold, be cold, MH,*
VPs (oe) : (+) *quench* (*thirst*), *refresh.*
['*keel*']
celc (1) (VPs)=calic. (2)=cealc
celde f. *copious spring?* KC 3·429¹³.
celdre=ceoldre; cele=(1) ceole; (2) ciele
celen-dre f., -der n. '*coliander*,' *coriander,*
Lcd.
cele-ðonie, -ðenie, cileðonie f. *celandine,*
swallow-wort, LCD.
celf (A)=cealf; celic=calic
+celfe (GEN 33¹³)=+cealfe
cēling f. *cooling,* Æ : *cool place,* Æ.
celis '*peditis*,' *foot-covering,* A 37·45.
celiwearte=cielewearte
cell m. (*monastic*) *cell,* CHR 1129.
cellender n., cellendre f.=celendre
cellod (ē?)† part. *round? hollow? embossed?*
beaked? FIN 29 (or ? celced=cealced); MA
283.
celmertmonn m. *hireling,* NG (v. ES
42·172).
±cēlnes f. *coolness, cool air, breeze,* CP.
[*cōl*]
celod v. cellod.
celras=ceallras, nap. of cealer.
±cemban (æ) *to comb,* Æ. ['*kemb*']
cemes f. *shirt,* GD. [*L.* camisia]
cempa (æ) m. *warrior, champion, Gl,Ma*;
Æ,AO,CP. [camp; '*kemp*']
cempestre f. *female warrior,* OEG.
cēn† m. *pine-torch, pine* : *name of the rune*
for c. [*Ger.* kien]
cendlic=cynlic
cēne *bold, brave, fierce, CP,Ex,Lcd,Ma,Ps*;
Æ,AO : *powerful, Ps* : *learned, clever, Met*
10⁵¹. ['*keen*'] *also adv.*
cenep m. *moustache,* CHR : *bit* (*of a bridle*),
WW 486¹⁶. [*ON.* kanpr]
cenlic=cynlic
cēnlīce *boldly,* Æ. ['*keenly*']
±cennan *to conceive, bring forth,* Æ : *beget,*
create, produce, Mt,VPs; CP : *nominate,*
choose out, Æ : *assign, attribute, give* :
declare, show oneself, clear oneself, make
a declaration in court (v. LL 2·32; 279,
'*cennan*,' 'Anefang'), *B,LL,Ps.* ['*ken*']
cennend m. *parent,* BL.
cennendlic *genital,* GD.
cennes f. *produce, what is produced,* EHy
6²² : *childbirth* : *birthday.*
+cennes f. *summons,* BH 436¹⁵ (cæne-).

cennestre f. *mother*, Æ.
cenning f. *procreation*, CP : *parturition, birth*, Æ : *declaration in court* (v. cennan).
cenningstān (y¹) m. *testing-stone*, LL192,4.
cenningstow f. *birthplace*, Æ.
cenningtīd f. *time of bringing forth*, Æ.
cennystre=cennestre
Cent, Centescīr f. *Kent*. [*L.* Cantia]
centaur m. *centaur*, WW.
centaurie f. *centaury* (plant), LCD.
Centingas mp. *Kentish men*, CHR.
Centisc *Kentish*, CHR.
Cent-land, -lond (AO) n. *Kent*.
Centrīce n. *kingdom of Kent*.
centur m. *centurion*, G.
Centware mp. *inhabitants of Kent*, CHR.
cēnðu f. *boldness*, B2696.
cēo f. *chough, jay, jackdaw*, ÆGR.
cēoce (*WW*)=cēace; -cēocian v. ā-c.
ceod? ceode? *bag, pouch*, CP,LL.
ceodor-=ceder-; ceofl, ceol (NG)=cawl I.
cēol m. *ship*, AN,B,CHR.
ceolas mp. *cold winds, cold*, Az103. [ciele?]
ceolbor-=cilfor-
ceoldre I. f. *milk-pail*, WW33¹⁷. II.=cealre
ceole (e) f. *throat : gorge, chasm : beak of ship*, GL. [*Ger.* kehle]
ceolor m. *throat*, GL : *channel*, Ct.
cēol-ðel n., -ðelu? f. *deck of a ship*, Hu8.
ceolwærc m. *pain in the throat*, LCD113a.
ceorcing f. *complaining*, GPH398.
±ceorfan³ *to cut, cut down, slay*, Mk,Æ; LkL : '*carve*,' *cut out, engrave : tear*.
ceorfæx f. *axe*, AO160¹⁵.
ceorfingīsen n. *branding iron*, Sc43².
ceorfsæx n. *surgeon's knife, scalpel*, Æ.
±ceorian *to murmur, complain*, Æ,AO.
ceorig *querulous, complaining*, OEG.
ceorl m. '*churl*,' *layman, peasant, husband-man*, CP : *freeman of the lowest class*, LL; AO,CP : *man : husband*, Jn,WW; CP : †*hero, noble man*.
ceorlǣs (=ceorllēas) *unmarried* (of women), LL360,73B.
ceorlboren *low-born, not noble*, LL.
ceorlfolc n. *common people*, ÆGR.
±ceorlian *to marry* (of the woman), LL,Mt; Æ. ['*churl*']
ceorlic=ceorllic
ceorlisc (ie) *of a* '*ceorl*,' '*churlish*,' *common, rustic*, LL,WW. adv. -lisce.
ceorllic *common, belonging to the people generally*. adv. -līce *commonly, vulgarly, popularly*.
ceorlman m. *freeman*, LL73; 463.
ceorlstrang *strong as a man*, WW108¹⁸.
ceorm=cirm
ceorran I. (sv³) *to creak*, LCD160a. II. (+) =cierran

ceorung f. *murmuring*, Æ.
±cēosan² *to* '*choose*' ('*i-cheose*,' '*y-core*'), *seek out, select*, AO; Æ : *decide, test : accept, approve*, B,Gen.
ceosel (i, y) m. *gravel, sand, shingle*, Ep,Mt; Æ. ['*chesil*']
ceoselbǣre *gravelly, shingly*, A13·32.
ceoselstān m. *sand-stone, gravel*, WW.
ceoslen (OEG7¹⁶¹), ceoslig (4⁴⁰) *gravelly*.
ceosol I. m? n? *gullet, maw*, GL. II.=ceosel
±cēowan² *to* '*chew*,' *gnaw*, Æ,Soul : *eat, consume*, Æ.
ceowl (NG)=cawl
cēowung (ī, ȳ) f. '*chewing*,' WW.
cēp=cēap; cēp-, cēpe-=cēap-, cȳp-
cēpan I. *to seize*, Æ : *seek after, desire*, Æ : *await*, Æ : *receive*, RBL : '*keep*,' *guard, observe, attend, watch, look out for, take heed*, Æ,Chr,Lcd,Ps : *take*, Æ : *avail oneself of, betake oneself to, take to, bear : meditate : regulate by*. II.=cȳpan
cēpnian *to await eagerly*, NC276.
cer=cierr
ceren I. (æ, y) n? *new wine, sweet wine*, GL, LCD. [*L.* carenum] II.=cyrn
cer-felle, -fille f. '*chervil*,' Lcd,WW. [*L.* cerefolium]
cerge=carig; cerlic=cirlic
cerm=cirm; cerr=cierr
cers-=cærs-; cert-=cyrt-
certare *charioteer*, ÆL18²⁹⁵.
ceruphin *cherubim*, EL750.
ces-=ceos-; cēs-=cīs-, cȳs-
cēs=cēas pret. 3 sg. of cēosan.
Cēsar (AO)=Cāsere
cester=ceaster; cestian=cystian
cēte=cȳte; cetel, cetil=citel
cēðan=cȳðan; cewl (NG)=cāwl
chor, chora m. *dance, choir* (*singers*), CP : *church-choir* (*place*). [*L.* chorus]
chorglēo n. *dance*, LPs.
cian sbpl. *gills*, GL. [*Ger.* kieme]
cicel=cycel
cicen (y) n. '*chicken*,' Mt,WW.
cicene (Æ)=cycene
cicropisc *cyclopean?* WW217¹³.
+cīd n. *strife, altercation*, CP,DR,GD : *reproof*, RB.
±cīdan (w. d. or wið) *contend, quarrel*, Æ, WW : *complain*, Æ : '*chide*,' *blame*, Mk; Æ,CP.
cīdde (1) pret. 3 sg. of cīdan. (2)=cȳðde pret. 3 sg. of cȳðan.
cīdere m. *a chider*, CHRD41³⁰.
cīdung (ȳ) f. *chiding, rebuke*, AO,EPs.
ciefes=cifes
±cīegan (ē, ī, ȳ) (tr.) *to call, name*, Æ : *call upon, invoke, summon, convene*, CP : (intr.) *call out*. For comps. v. cīg-.

ciele (e, i, y) m. *coolness, cold,* '*chill,*' *frost,* Bl,CP,VPs; AO. [ceald]
cielegicel† (y¹) m. *icicle.*
cielewearte (e¹, y¹) f. *goose-skin,* WW.
cielf=cealf
cielle (i, y) f. *fire-pan, lamp,* BH,GD. [*OHG.* kella]
cīepa (e, i, y) m. *merchant, trader,* Æ,CHRD.
cīepe=cīpe
cīepehūs (ǣ¹) n. *storehouse,* WW 186¹¹.
cīepemann (CP), cīepmann (LL) m. *merchant.*
cīepeðing (ē, ȳ) np. *merchandise,* BH,GL.
cīeping (ē, ī, ȳ) f. *marketing, trading,* CP : *market-place, market* : *merchandise* : *market dues,* WW 145²⁸.
cīeplic (ȳ) *for sale, vendible,* Sc 98¹⁷.
cierice=cirice; cierlisc=ceorlisc
cierm=cirm
cierr (e, i, y) m. *turn, change, time, occasion,* Æ,CP,Lk,Lcd : *affair, business.* æt sumum cierre *at some time, once.* ['*chare*']
±cierran (eo, i, y) (tr. and intr.) *turn, change,* Ps,Sat : (intr.) *turn oneself, go, come, proceed, turn back, return,* Mt; Æ : *regard* : *translate* : *persuade, convert, be converted, agree to,* CP : *submit,* CHR,W : *make to submit, reduce.* ['*chare,*' '*i-cherre*']
+cierrednes (y) *conversion,* Æ : *entrance, admission,* RB.
±cierring (e, y) f. *turning,* LPs 9⁴ : *conversion,* NC 341.
cīest, cīesð pres. 3 sg. of cēosan.
cifes (ie, e, y) f. *concubine, harlot,* AO. [*Ger.* kebse]
cifesboren adj. *bastard,* OEG 5042.
cifesdōm m. *fornication,* OEG 5042.
cifesgemāna m. *fornication,* LL (Wilk.) 84¹.
cifeshād (y) m. *fornication,* WW.
cīgan=cīegan
+cīgednes f. *calling, summons* : *name* (cīed-), OEG 1503.
+cīgendlic *calling, vocative,* ÆGR 23².
cīgere (ei) *one who calls,* DR 194¹.
+cīgnes f. *calling, invocation, entreaty* : *name,* A 10·143⁷⁹.
±cīgung f. *calling, invocation,* GD 289, NC 292.
cild (y) (nap. cild, cild-ra, -ru; gp. -ra) n. '*child*,' *infant,* Ct,G,Lcd,WW; Æ,AO, CP : *a youth of gentle birth,* KC.
Cildamæssedæg m. *Childermas, Innocents' Day* (Dec. 28).
cildatrog=cildtrog
cildclāðas mp. *swaddling-clothes,* Gl. [v. '*cloth*']
cildcradol m. *cradle,* Æ.
cildfaru f. *carrying of children,* GEN 45¹ᵇ.

cildfēdende *nursing,* MtR 24¹⁹.
cild-fōstre, -fēstre f. *nurse,* LL. [v. '*foster*']
cildgeogoð f. *childhood,* ÆL 30³²⁰.
cildgeong *youthful, infant,* LCD,RB.
cildhād m. '*childhood,*' MkL.
cildhama m. *womb,* GL : *after-birth,* WW.
cildisc '*childish,*' Gen.
cildiugoð=cildgeogoð
cildlic *childish, young, BH;* Æ. ['*childly*']
cildru v. cild.
cildsung f. *childishness,* LL (314').
cildtrog (cilt-, cilda-) m. *cradle,* GL.
cile (AO)=ciele
cilforlamb (eo¹) n. *ewe-lamb,* Æ,WW. ['*chilverlamb*']
cilic m. *sack-cloth of hair,* NG. [*L.* cilicium]
cille=cielle, cyll; cim-=cym-
cimbal(a) m. '*cymbal,*' Lcd,VPs. [*L.*]
cimbalglīwere m. *cymbal-player,* GD 61²⁰.
cimbing f. *commissure, joining,* WW 15⁵; 206¹². [v. '*chime*']
cimblren n. *edge-iron?* (*joining-iron, clamp?* BTs), LL 455,15.
cimbstān m. *base, pedestal,* Sc 226². [v. '*chimb*']
cin=(1) cinn; (2) cynn, n.; cin-=cyn
cīnan¹ *to gape, yawn, crack,* GL,LCD. ['*chine*']
cinbān n. *chin-bone, jaw-bone,* Æ.
cinberg f. *defence of the chin or cheek, cheek-guard,* EX 175. [beorg]
cincung f. *boisterous laughter,* WW 171³⁹.
cind=cynd
cine I. f. *sheet of parchment* (*folded*), '*diploma,*' Æ. II. f. *chink, fissure, depth, cavern,* Æ,Bo,WW. ['*chine*']
cine-=cyn(e)-
cineht (io) *chinky, cracked,* WW 43³⁷.
cing, cining=cyning
cinn (1) n. '*chin,*' WW. (2)=cynn n.
cinnan *to gape, yawn?* RIM 52.
cintōð m. *front tooth, grinder,* GL.
cinu=cine II.
cio-=ceo-; cīo=cēo
cip=cipp; cīp-=cēap-, cīep, cȳp-
cīpe (ie) f. *onion,* GL,LCD. [*L.* cepa]
cīpelēac n. *leek,* WW 380²⁹.
cipersealf (y) f. *henna-ointment,* WW 205¹¹. [*L.* cypros]
cipp (y) m. *log, trunk,* WW : *coulter, plough-share,* WW : *weaver's beam,* LL 455,15¹.
cir=cierr; circ-=ciric-
circian *to roar,* LCD 1·390¹¹ (v. A 31·56).
circolwyrde m. *computer, mathematician,* BF 66⁹.
circul m. *circle* : *cycle, zodiac,* LCD. [*L.* circulum]
circulādl f. *the shingles,* LCD.
cirebald (AN 171)=cynebeald?

ciricǣw nf. *marriage to the church* (as when one takes orders), LL.

ciricbelle f. *'church-bell,'* Lcd.

ciricbōc f. *'church-book,' manual of the church services,* W.

ciricbōt f. *repair of churches,* LL.

ciric-brǣc f., -bryce m. *sacrilege,* Æ.

ciric-dor n., -duru *church-door,* LL.

cirice (ie, y) f. *'church*,' religious community,* Æ,BH,CP,G,LL,OET : *church (building),* temple, *AO,Bl,Chr,Ct*; CP : *congregation (non-Christian),* Ps.

ciricend m. *an ecclesiastic,* MtLp8[10].

ciricfriŏ mn. *right of sanctuary : penalty for breach of the right.* v. LL2·537.

ciricfultum m. *support from the church,* LL.

ciricgang (y) m. *going to church,* LL473,7 : *churching, purification (of the B.V.M.),* CM484.

ciricgemāna (y) m. *church-membership,* W103[23].

ciricgeorn *zealous in church-going,* LL,W.

ciricgeriht (y) n. *church-due,* LL(328[1]).

ciricgriŏ (y) n. *church-peace, right of sanctuary,* LL : *penalty for breach of the right,* LL263,3; v. 2·537. [*'church-grith'*]

cirichād m. *an order of the church,* LL.

cirichālgung f. *consecration of a church,* Chr.

cirichata m. *church-tormentor, persecutor,* W.

ciricland (y) n. *land of the church,* GD.

ciriclic (circ-) *ecclesiastical, BH,Chr,Wnl.* [*'churchly'*]

ciricmǣrsung (y) f. *dedication of a church,* W277[10].

ciricmangung f. *simony,* LL.

ciricmitta m. *church measure (of ale),* TC144'.

ciricnēod f. *requirements of the church,* LL.

ciricnytt f. *church service,* Cra91.

ciricragu f. *church-lichen or moss,* Lcd51b.

ciricrēn (y[1]) n. *sacrilege,* LL254k. [rān]

ciricsang m. *hymn : church-singing,* BH.

ciricsangere m. *church-singer,* BII466[17].

ciricsceat m. *'church-scot,' church-due at Martinmas, BH,W.*

ciricsceatweorc n. *work connected with the grain given as church-scot,* KC.

ciricsōcn (y[1]) f. *church-privilege, sanctuary,* LL : *territory of a church : attendance at church.* [*'churchsoken'*]

cirictīd (y[1]) f. *service-time,* LL(314[20]).

cirictūn m. *churchyard,* LL(250[7]).

ciricŏēn m. *minister of a church,* LL.

ciricŏēnung (y) f. *church-duty or service,* LL.

ciricŏing n. *object belonging to a church,* LL381,27.

ciricŏingere m. *priest,* WW155[29] (yrc).

ciricwæcce f. *vigil,* LL.

ciricwǣd f. *vestment,* LL258,51.

ciricwāg m. *wall of a church,* LL.

ciricwaru f. *congregation,* LL400'; 2·539.

ciricweard (e[2], y[2]) m. *church-keeper, warden, sexton, Æ.* [*'churchward'*]

cirisbēam m. *cherry-tree,* Gl. [L. cerasum]

cirlic I. (e, y) *charlock,* Lcd. II.=ciriclic

cirlisc=ceorlisc

cirm (e, eo, y;=ie) m. *cry, shout, outcry, uproar, Gl,MtR.* [*'chirm'*]

cirman (e, y;=ie) *to cry, cry out, call, shriek, Gu,Jud.* [*'chirm'*]

cirnel (Gl)=cyrnel

cirps (y) *curly,* Æ. [*'crisp'*]

±**cirpsian** (y) *to crisp, curl,* Chrd,Gl.

cirr=cierr

cīs (=ie) *fastidious,* Lcd,Chrd23[9]. [cēosan]

cīse=cȳse

cisel, cisil=ceosel

ciseræppel m. *dried fig,* WW367[2]. [=ciris-?, *cherry* (BTs)]

ciser-bēam, cisir-=cirisbēam

cīsnes f. *fastidiousness,* Lcd65a,RB63[12].

cist (e, y) I. f. *'chest,' casket, Gl,JnR : coffin, BH,Lk : rush basket, WW : horn (as receptacle?),* WW. II.=cyst I.

cīst pres. 3 sg. of cēosan.

ciste=cist I.

cistel I. *'cistella'?* Ct (v. GBG). II.=cystel

cistenbēam m. *chestnut-tree,* Gl. [L. castanea]

cīstmēlum *earnestly,* OEG4[32]. [cēast]

citel (e, y) m. *'kettle,' cauldron, Ep,Lcd.*

citelflōde (y[1]) f. *bubbling spring,* BC2·371[9].

citelhrūm (e[1]) m. *kettle-soot,* Lcd50a.

citelian *to tickle* (Ettm., Leo).

citelung f. *tickling,* WW278[6]. [*'kittling'*]

citelwylle (y[1]) *bubbling spring,* BC2·270[4].

citere, citre (y) f. *cithara,* CJVPs.

ciŏ m. *seed, germ, shoot,* Æ : *mote,* CP. [*'chithe'*]

ciŏfæst *well-rooted,* ÆH1·304'.

cīwung=cēowung; **clā**=clēa, clāwu

clābre (Gl)=clōfre; **olac**=clæc-, cleac-

clacu f. *injury,* W86[10] (v. FTp55).

+**clāded** (MkL5[15]) pp. of +claŏian.

cladersticca m. *rattle-stick,* Gl.

clæclēas *harmless,* WW419[1] : *uninjured.* [clacu]

clædur (ea) *rattle,* Gl. [clader]

clæferwyrt f. *clover,* Lcd.

clǣfre f. *'clover,' trefoil, Lcd,WW*; Mdf.

clǣg m. *'clay,' WW.*

clǣig *'clayey,'* Ct.

±**clǣman** *to smear, caulk, plaster, anoint, Æ,Lcd.* [*'cleam'*]

clǣming f. *blotting, smearing,* ÆGr256[4].

clǣmman (e) *to press,* GD.

clæmnes f. *torture,* BH290[2].

clǣne (ā, ē) I. 'clean,' CP,Ct,LL : pure, chaste, innocent, Æ,Bl : unencumbered, unfettered : hallowed : clear, open, El,Lcd,Ps. on clǣnum felda in the open field (of battle), CP227²⁵ : honourable, true : acute, sagacious, intellectual. II. adv. clean, clearly, fully, purely, entirely, Æ,Ct; AO, CP.

clǣngeorn yearning after purity, celibate : cleanly, CHRD 19¹⁹,²⁰.

clǣnheort pure in heart, Æ.

clǣnlic ('cleanly'), pure, Bo,Met : excellent. adv. -līce (Bf)=clǣne II.

clǣnnes f. (moral) 'cleanness,' purity, chastity, BH; Æ,CP.

clǣnsere (e) m. priest, CP139¹⁵; W72⁶.

±clǣnsian (āsn-) to 'cleanse' ('yclense'), purify, chasten, Æ,CP : clear out, purge, Lcd : (w. a. and g.) justify, clear oneself, LL.

clǣnsnian=clǣnsian

±clǣnsung f. 'cleansing,' purifying, chastening, castigation, expiation, Mk; Æ : purity, chastity.

clǣnsungdæg m. day for purging, LCD 1·330⁸.

clǣnsungdrenc (sn) m. purgative, MH72²⁷.

clæppan (a¹) to clap, beat, throb, LCD 3·88⁵.

clæppettan to palpitate, LCD,WW.

clæppetung f. clapping : pulsation, pulse, Æ.

clǣsn-=clǣns-; clǣð=clāð

clǣweða=cleweða

clāf pret. 3 sg. of clīfan.

clāfre (GL)=clæfre

clām I. m. paste, mortar, mud, clay, Æ,Lcd : poultice. ['cloam'] II.=clēam dp. of clēa.

clamb pret. 3 sg. of climban.

clamm m. band, bond, fetter, chain, An,Bl, Rd : grip, grasp. ['clam']

clān-=clǣn-

clang pret. 3 sg. of clingan.

clap-=clæp-

+clāsnian (JVPs)=clǣnsian

clātacrop=clāte

clāte f. bur, burdock, clivers, Gl,Lcd. ['clote']

clatrung f. clattering, noise, WW377²⁷.

clāð m. 'cloth,' Mt : 'clothes,' covering, sail, Bo,Cp,Ps,Chr,Jn,Lcd; AO,CP. under Crīstes clāðum in baptismal garments, CHR688E.

clāðflyhte m. patch, MtR9¹⁶.

+clāðian (clēðan) to 'clothe,' LG.

clāðwēoce f. wick of cloth, GPH391.

clauster=clūstor

clāwan⁷ to claw, ÆGR,WW.

clāwian to scratch, 'claw,' ÆGr170¹¹n.

clawu (ā?) f. nap. clawe 'claw,' Æ,Gl,Ph : hoof, Æ : hook : (pl.) pincers? Æ.

clāwung f. griping pain, LCD.

clea-=clǣ-, cleo-

clēa=clawu

cleac f. stepping-stone, KC4·36. [Keltic]

cleacian to hurry, ÆL23⁴⁹³.

clēaf pret. 3 sg. of clēofan.

clēm-, clēn-=clǣm-, clǣn-

-clencan v. be-c.

clengan to adhere, RD29⁸.

cleo-; clēo-=cli-; clīe-, clū-

clēo=clēa, clawu

cleofa (ea, i, y) m. cave, den, BH : cell, chamber, cellar, Æ,Ps. ['cleve']

clēofan² to 'cleave,' split, separate, A,Bo,Ct.

cleofian=clifian; cleofu=nap. of clif

clēofung f. 'cleaving,' WW.

clēone=clēowene, ds. of clēowen, clīewen.

cleop-=clip-

clep-=clæp-, clip-; clerc=cleric

cler-ic (-ec, -oc; clerus, PPs67¹³) m. 'clerk' in holy orders, WW : clerk in minor orders, LL : educated person, Chr. [L. clericus]

clerichād m. condition of a (secular) clerk, clerical order, priesthood, CHR,RB.

cleweða (æ¹) m. itch, CP71¹⁹. [clāwan]

clib-=clif-

clibbor clinging, MEN245. [clifian]

+clibs (e; cleps; clæsp, y) clamour, CP.

clid-ren, -rin f. clatter, Ep,Erf928.

cliepian=clipian

clīewen, cliewen? (ēo, īo, ī, ȳ) n. sphere, ball, skein, Æ,CP,Ph,WW : ball of thread or yarn, KC : mass, group. ['clew']

clif n. (nap. cleofu, clifu) 'cliff,' rock, promontory, steep slope, An,B,Ct; Æ,CP.

clifa=cleofa; clifæhtig=clifihtig

clīfan¹ to 'cleave*,' adhere, Æ,CP.

clife f. 'clivers' ('cleavers'), burdock, Lcd, WW.

clifeht=clifiht

clifer m. nap. clifras claw, GPH; Æ. ['cliver']

cliferfēte cloven-footed, ÆL25⁷⁹.

clif-hlēp, -hlȳp m. a cliff-leap, plunge to ruin? (BTs),GL.

+clifian (eo, y) to adhere, Æ,CP.

clifig, clif-iht, -ihtig steep, GL.

clifr- v. clifer.

clifrian to scarify, scratch, Æ,CHRD.

clifrung f. clawing, talon, GPH398.

clifstān m. rock, WW371²³.

cliftwyrt f. cliff-wort, water-wort, foxglove, WW134³ and N.

+cliht pp. of +*cliccan, clyccan.

-clīm v. calwer-c.

climban³ (y) to 'climb,' Sol.

climpre=clympre

clincig rough, DHy104¹⁸.

clingan³ to stick together, An : shrink, wither, pine, Æ,Sol. ['cling'] clipian (e, eo, y) (tr. and intr.) *to speak, cry out, call,* DR,Chr,Mt,Jn,Ps; CP : (±) *summon, invoke,* Æ : (w. d.) *cry to, implore.* ['*clepe,*' '*yclept*']

clipigendlic (y) *vocalic,* ÆGR5 : *vocative* (gram.), ÆGR23.

clipol *sounding, vocal,* BF94[29] : *vocalic, vowel,* BF100[16].

clipung (e, eo, y) f. *cry, crying, clamour,* MtR : (±) *prayer,* Ps : *call, claim,* CHR 1129. ðā clypunga *kalends.* ['*cleping*']

clipur m. *bell-clapper,* WNL 109b[16,20].

cliroc=cleric; +clistre=+clystre

clite f. *coltsfoot,* LCD 146a.

cliða (eo, y) m. *poultice,* Æ,LCD.

-cliðan v. æt-c.

cliðe f. *burdock,* GL. [v. '*clithe,*' '*clithers*']

cliðwyrt f. '*rubea minor,*' '*clivers,*' Lcd 173b.

clīwe, clīwen=clīewen

cloccettan *to palpitate,* LCD 82b.

cloccian *to cluck, make a noise,* BF78[17].

clodhamer m. *fieldfare,* WW 287[17].

clof-=cluf-

+clofa m. *counterpart (of a document),* CC 80. [clēofan]

clofe f. *buckle,* GL.

clofen pp. of clēofan.

clomm I. m.=clamm. II. pret. 3 sg. of climban.

clop m? *rock?* v. Mdf.

clott *lump, mass,* HGl 488. ['*clot*']

clucge f. *bell,* BH 340[6].

clūd m. *mass of stone, rock,* Æ,AO : *hill,* ES 38·13. ['*cloud*']

clūdig *rocky, hilly,* AO. ['*cloudy*']

clufeht(e) (i[2]) *bulbous,* Lcd. [v. '*cloved*']

clufon pret. pl. of clēofan.

clufðung, clufðunge f. *crowfoot : a vegetable poison.* v. OEG 896.

clufu f. *clove (of garlic, etc.), bulb, tuber,* LCD. [clēofan]

clufwyrt f. '*batrachion,*' *buttercup,* Lcd. ['*clovewort*']

clugge=clucge

clumben pp. of climban.

clum(m)ian *to murmur, mumble, mutter,* W.

clungen pp. of clingan.

clūs, clūse f. *bar, bolt : enclosure : cell, prison.* [L. clausum]

cluster=clyster; clūster=clūstor

clūstor n. *lock, bar, barrier : enclosure, cloister, cell, prison.* [L. claustrum]

clūstorcleofa m. *prison-cell,* AN 1023.

clūstorloc n. *prison,* GL.

clūt m. '*clout,*' *patch, cloth,* Ep : *piece of metal, plate,* Æ.

+clūtod '*clouted,*' *patched,* Æ.

±clyccan *to clutch, clench,* IM,Sc. ['*clitch*']

clyf=clif; clyf-=clif-, cleof-

+clyft adj. *cleft,* GPH 393. [clēofan]

clymmian *to climb, ascend,* SOL 414.

-clympe v. calwer-c.

clympre m. *lump of metal,* LCD,RD,WW. ['*clumper*']

clyne n. *lump of metal,* GL.

clynian I. *to roll up, enfold,* GPH. II.= clynnan

clynnan (intr.) *to resound, ring,* EL 51 : (tr.) *knock,* NG.

clyp-=clip-

clypnes f. *embrace,* BH 238[3].

clypp m., clypping f. *embracing,* GD.

±clyppan *to embrace, clasp,* Æ,LG : *surround, enclose,* VPs : *grip,* Gen : *prize, honour, cherish,* CP. ['*clip*']

-clysan v. be-c. [clūse]; +clysp=+clibs

clyster, +clystre n. '*cluster,*' *bunch, branch,* Æ,Cp,WW.

clȳsung f. *enclosure, apartment,* Æ : *closing, period, conclusion of a sentence, clause.*

clyða=cliða; clȳwen=clīewen

cnæht (NG)=cniht

cnæpling m. *youth,* Æ. [cnapa]

cnæpp (e) m. *top, summit,* Æ,Lk : *fibula, button,* WW. ['*knap*']

+cnǣwe (w. g.) *conscious of, acknowledging,* Æ : *known, notorious, manifest,* Æ.

cnǣwð pres. 3 sg. of cnāwan.

cnafa, cnapa m. *child, youth,* Æ,Sc : *servant,* Æ,Mt,Ps. ['*knape,*' '*knave*']

±cnāwan[7] (usu. +) *to '*know*' ('*y-know*'), perceive,* Æ,B,Bl,Jul,OEG : *acknowledge : declare :* (+) *ascertain.*

+cnāwe=+cnǣwe

cnāwelǣcing f. *acknowledgement,* KC 4·193[12].

cnāwlǣc (ē[2]) *acknowledgement,* CHR 963 (ES 42·176).

+cnāwnes f. *acknowledgement,* EC 265[2].

cnēa gp. of cnēo(w).

cnearr m. *small ship, galley (of the ships of the Northmen),* †CHR. [ON. knorr]

±cnēatian *to argue, dispute,* GL.

cnēatung f. *inquisition, investigation,* OEG : *dispute, debate,* Sc.

cnedan[5] *to '*knead*',' Lcd,LkL.*

cneht (VPs)=cniht; cnēo=cnēow

cnēodan, cneoht=cnōdan, cniht

+cneord *eager, zealous, diligent,* Æ,BH.

±cneordlǣcan *to be diligent, study,* Æ.

cneordlic *diligent, earnest, zealous,* Æ. adv. -lice.

±cneordnes f. *zeal, diligence, study,* GL.

cnēordnes (Æ)=+cnēorenes

+cnēor-(e)nes, -ednes f. *generation, race,* GL.

cnēores=cnēoriss

cnēorift n? *napkin* (BTs), *kneehose?* (Kluge), GL.

cnēorisbōc f. *Genesis*, WW 414²⁹.

cnēorisn (BL), cneor(n)is(s) f. *generation, posterity, family, tribe, nation, race*.

cneorōlǣcan=cneordlǣcan

cnēow I. (cnēo) n. 'KNEE,' *AO* : *step in a pedigree, generation, LL*; Æ. **II.** pret. 3 sg. of cnāwan.

cnēowbīgung f. *kneeling, genuflection*, CM.

cnēow-ede, -ade *having big knees*, WW.

cnēowgebed n. *prayer on one's knees*, Æ.

cnēowholen m. '*knee-holly*,' *butcher's broom*, Lcd.

cnēowian I. (±) *to kneel*, Æ 2¹⁵⁴. ['*knee*'] **II.** *to know carnally*, ÆL 12⁷.

cnēowlian *to* '*kneel*,' *LL*.

cnēowmǣg m. (nap. -mǣgas, -māgas) *kinsman, relation, ancestor*.

cnēowrīm† n. *progeny, family*, GEN.

cnēowsibb f. *generation, race* (BDS 8·527).

cnēowung f. *kneeling, genuflection*, CM.

cnēowwǣrc m. *pain in the knees*, LCD.

cnēowwyrst f. *knee-joint*, WW.

cnepp=cnæpp; **cnēw**=cnēow

cnīdan¹ *to beat*, MtR 21³⁵.

cnieht=cniht

cnīf m. '*knife*,' *WW*.

cniht (e, eo, ie, y) m. *boy, youth, AO,Bl,LL* : *servant, attendant, retainer, disciple, warrior, Chr,Mt,Met* : *boyhood, ÆGr* : *junior member of a guild* (BTac),Ct. ['*knight*']

cnihtcild (eo¹) n. *male child, boy*, BH 284³⁰, MH 12⁹.

cnihtgebeorðor n. *child-birth, child-bearing*, BL 3¹².

cnihtgeong *youthful*, EL 640.

cnihthād m. *puberty, youth, boyhood*, Æ, Bo; AO : (*male*) *virginity*. ['*knighthood*']

cnihtiugoð f. *youth*, BF 12³.

cnihtlēas *without an attendant*, ÆL 23³⁹⁵.

cnihtlic *boyish, childish*, Guth. ['*knightly*']

cnihtōēawas mp. *boyish ways*, GD 111⁹.

cnihtwesende† *when a boy, as a youth*, B.

cnihtwīse f. *boyishness*, GUTH 12¹³.

cnissan=cnyssan

cnītian *to dispute*, Sc 51¹².

cnittan=cnyttan; **cnocian**=cnucian

±cnōdan (ēo) *to attribute to, assign to, load with*, CP.

cnoll m. '*knoll*,' *Ps*; Mdf : *summit*, Æ, Bo.

cnop '*ballationes*,' *knob*, WW 8²⁸; 357³².

-cnoppa v. wull-c.

+cnos n. *collision*, WW 376². [cnyssan]

cnōsl n. *stock, progeny, kin, family* : *native country*.

cnossian *to strike, hit upon*, SEAF 8.

cnotmǣlum '*strictim*,' A 13·35²⁰¹.

cnotta m. '*knot*,' *fastening*, Æ : *knotty point, puzzle*, Æ.

±cnucian (o) *to* '*knock*' (*door*), *Æ,G* : *beat, pound, IM,Lcd*.

cnūlan, cnūwian *to pound*, LCD.

+cnyc n. *bond*, DR 59,66.

±cnyccan pret. 3 sg. cnycte, cnyhte *to tie*.

+cnycled *bent, crooked*, WW 458³³.

cnyht=cniht; **cnyhte** v. cnyccan.

cnyll m. *sound or signal of a bell*, RB,WW. ['*knell*']

±cnyllan *to toll a bell*, RB : *strike, knock*, LkR,MtL; LV 28. ['*knell*']

cnyllsian (LkL)=cnyllan; **cnyrd-**=cneord-

±cnyssan *to press, toss, strike, hew to pieces, dash, crash* (*together*), *beat*, Æ,AO,CP : *overcome, overwhelm, oppress*, CP.

cnyssung f. *striking, stroke*, ÆGR.

±cnyttan *to fasten, tie, bind*, '*knit*' ('*i-knit*,' *Mt,WW*), *Æ,Lcd*; CP : *add, append*, BF 32³⁰. [cnotta]

cnyttels m. *string, sinew*, OEG 2935.

coc=cocc

cōc m. '*cook*,' *Æ,Ps*; CP. [*L.* coquus]

cocc m. *cock, male bird*,*Æ,CP,Lcd,Mt*; Mdf.

coccel m. '*cockle*,' *darnel, tares*, *Bf,Mt*.

cocer (o², u²) m. *quiver, case, sheath*, Æ : *spear*, Ps.

cōcerpanne f. *cooking-pan, frying-pan*, PRPs.

+cōcnian (cōca-) *to season food*, WW 504¹².

cōcnung f. *seasoning*, LCD,WW.

cocor=cocer

cōcormete m. *seasoned food*, WW 281⁶.

+cōcsian *to cook, roast*, RPs 101⁴.

cōcunung=cōcnung; **cocur** (Æ)=cocer

codd m. '*cod*,' *husk*, Lcd : *bag*, Mt : *scrotum*.

coddæppel m. *quince*, WW 411¹⁵.

codic (coydic) '*lapsana*,' *charlock?* A 37·47.

cofa m. *closet, chamber* : *ark* : *cave, den*. ['*cove*']

cofgodas mp. *household gods*, GL.

cofincel n. *little chamber*, WW.

-cofrian v. ā-c.

cohhetan *to make a noise, cough?* JUD 270.

col n. (nap. colu, cola) '*coal*,' *live coal*, Æ,CP,Lcd,VPs.

cōl I. '*cool*,' *cold*, B,Bo,Lcd : *tranquil, calm*. **II.** pret. 3 sg. of calan.

cōlcwyld f. '*frigida pestis*,' *ague?* WW 243¹¹.

-cole v. ōden-, wīn-c.

cōlian *to* '*cool*,' *grow cold, be cold*, An,Gu,Lcd.

coliandre f. *coriander*, LCD.

coll-, cōll-=col-, cōl-; **-colla** v. morgen-c.

collecta f. *collect*, ÆP,CM.

+collenferhtan *to make empty*, LPs 136⁷.

collen-ferhð, -fyrhð, -ferð† *proud, elated, bold*. [*cwellan* (*to swell*)?]

collon-croh, -crog m. *water-lily, nymphæa*, LCD,WW.

colmāse f. '*coal-mouse*,' *tit-mouse*, *WW*.
cōlnes f. '*coolness*,' *Ps*.
colpytt m. (*char-*)*coal pit*, Ct.
colsweart *coal-black*, NC277.
colt m. '*colt*,' *Æ*.
coltetræppe f. *a plant*, '*caltrop*,' *WW*.
coltgræg f? *colt's-foot*, WW136¹⁸.
coltræppe=coltetræppe
col-ōrǣd, -ōrēd m. *plumb-line*, GL.
columne f. *column*, AA6.
cōm pret. 3 sg. of cuman.
coman (AO70²⁴)=cuman
comb, combol=camb, cumbol
comēta m. *comet*, †CHR975. [*L.*]
commuc=cammoc
communia *psalm sung at Eucharist*, ÆP
  168¹⁶.
cōmon pret. pl. of cuman.
comp=camp
con (v. '*con**')=can pres. 1, 3 sg. of cunnan.
condel=candel
conn=cann pres. 1, 3 sg. of cunnan.
consolde f. *comfrey*, LCD125b. [*L.*]
const=canst pres. 2 sg. of cunnan.
consul m. *consul*, AO. [*L.*]
coorte f. *cohort*, AO240, 242. [*L.*]
cop=copp
cōp m? '*ependytes*,' *cope, vestment*, GL.
+cōp *proper, fitting*, CP.
copel *unsteady, rocking?* (BTs),BC3·624.
cōpenere m. *lover*, CP405¹⁴.
coper, copor n. '*copper*,' *Lcd,WW*. [*L.*
  cuprum]
coplan *to plunder, steal*, WW379¹⁷.
+cōplic *proper, fitting*, GD. adv. -līce, Bo.
copp I. m. *top, summit*, HGl. ['*cop*'] II. m.
  cup, NG. ['*cop*']
-coppe v. ātor-c.
copped *polled, lopped, pollard*, Ct. ['*copped*']
cops (*WW*)=cosp
+cor n. *decision*, OET436¹⁵,¹⁶. [cēosan]
corcīō m. *increase? choice growth?* LCD
  3·212⁹ (v. A31·56).
+corded *having a cord?* WW187.
cordewānere m. '*cordwainer*,' *shoemaker*,
  EC257'. [*OFr.*]
±coren (pp. of cēosan) *chosen, elect, choice,
  fit, Æ : precious, dear*.
corenbēg m. *crown*, A11·172. [*L. corona*]
+corenlic *elegant*, WW393³⁷. adv. -līce,
  WW396²⁶.
±corennes f. *choice, election* : (+) *goodness*.
±corenscipe m. *election, excellence*, DR.
corfen pp. of ceorfan.
corflian *to mince*, IM,LCD. [ceorfan]
corn n. '*CORN*,' *grain*, *Chr,CP*; *Æ,AO* :
  seed, berry, *CP,Jn,Lcd*; *Æ* : *a corn-like
  pimple, corn*, LCD.
cornæsceda fp. *chaff*, WW118¹.

cornappla np. *pomegranates*, OEG.
corn-bǣre (*Æ*), -berende *corn-bearing*.
corngebrot n. *corn dropped in carrying t̥
  barn*, LL451,17.
corngesǣlig *rich in corn*, LCD3·188¹¹.
corngesceot n. *payment in corn*, Ct.
cornhūs n. *granary*, WW185²⁸
cornhwicce (æ², y²) f. *corn-bin*, Æ.
cornlād f. *leading of corn*, LL453,21⁴.
cornsǣd n. *a grain of corn*, GD253¹.
corntēoðung f. *tithe of corn*, W.
corntrēow n. *cornel-tree*, WW.
corntrog m. *corn-bin*, WW107¹.
cornuc, cornuch (WW25)=cranoc
cornwurma m. *scarlet dye*, GL.
corōna m. *crown*, NC277. [*L.*]
+corōnian *to crown*, PPs5¹³.
corsnǣd f. *piece of consecrated bread which
  an accused person swallowed as a test of
  innocence*, LL.
corðort, corðert fn. *troop, band, multitude,
  throng, retinue* : *pomp*.
corwurma=cornwurma; cos=coss
cosp m. *fetter, bond*, Bo. ['*cops*']
+cospende, +cosped *fettered*, LPs.
coss m. '*kiss*,' *embrace*, *Æ,Lk,WW*.
cossetung f. *kissing*, NG.
cossian *to* '*kiss*,' *ÆGr,BH,G*.
cost I. m. *option, choice, possibility* : *manner,
  way*, DR : *condition*. ðæs costes ðe on
  condition that. ['*cost*'; v. NC341] II. (±)
  †*tried, chosen, excellent*. [cēosan] III. m?
  costmary, tansy, Lcd. ['*cost*']
costere I. m? *spade, shovel*, WW106¹⁸.
  II. m. *tempter*, Æ.
±costian (w. g. or a., also intr.) *to
  tempt, try, prove, examine*, AO,CP. [*Ger.*
  kosten]
costigend m. *tempter*, BL.
costn-=cost-
+costnes f. *proving, temptation, trial*, BH
  218¹⁰.
costnungstōw f. *place of temptation*, DEUT
  6¹⁶.
±costung, costnung f. *temptation, testing,
  trial, tribulation*, Mt; Æ,CP. ['*costnung*']
cot (AO) n. (nap. cotu) ; cote (*LL?*) f. '*cot*,'
  cottage, bed-chamber, den, *AO,Lk,Mt*; Mdf.
  [v. also '*cote*']
cotlīf n. *hamlet, village, manor*, Chr :
  dwelling. ['*cotlif*']
cotsetla (cote-) m. *cottager*, LL. ['*cotsetla*']
cotstōw f. *site of cottages*, KC.
cott=cot
cottuc, cotuc m. *mallow*, GL.
coða m., coðe f.=coðu
coðig *diseased*, CHRD62⁸.
coðlīce *ill, miserably*, MET25³⁶.
cōðon (AO)=cūðon pret. pl. of cunnan.

coðu f. *disease, sickness, Æ,Chr,Lcd.*
['*cothe*']
+**cow** n. *thing to be chewed, food,* NC292.
cowen pp. of cēowan.
crā n? *croaking,* WW208[10].
crabba m. '*crab,*' WW : *Cancer (sign of the zodiac),* Lcd.
cracelung? '*crepacula,*' OEG56[249].
crācettan (ǣ) *to croak,* GD119[25]. [crā]
crācetung (ǣ) f. *croaking,* GUTH48[4].
cracian *to resound,* '*crack,*' Ps.
cradol, cradel m. '*cradle,*' *cot,* WW.
cradolcild n. *child in the cradle, infant,* W158[14].
crǣ=crāwe
crǣcet-=crācet-
crǣf-=craf-
crǣft m. *physical strength, might, courage, A,AO,Sol : science, skill, art, ability, talent, virtue, excellence, Bo; Æ,CP : trade, handicraft, calling, BH,CP,RB; Æ : work or product of art, Hex : trick, fraud, deceit, BL : machine, instrument.* in pl. *great numbers, hosts?* DA393 (v. MP26·434). ['*craft*']
crǣfta=crǣftiga
±**crǣftan** *to exercise a craft, build : bring about, contrive, Æ.*
crǣftelīce=crǣftlīce
+**crǣftgian** *to strengthen, render powerful,* AO.
crǣftglēaw *skilful, wise,* †CHR975.
crǣf-t(i)ca, -t(e)ga=crǣftiga
crǣftig *strong, powerful, AO : skilful, cunning, ingenious, Bl : learned, instructive,* BF132[8] : *knowing a craft, scientific,* RB. ['*crafty*']
crǣftiga m. *craftsman, artificer, workman, Æ,CP : architect,* BH.
crǣftiglīce *skilfully,* WW.
crǣftlēas *artless, unskilful,* RBL52[1].
crǣftlic *artificial,* BF112[25] : *skilful.* adv. -līce.
crǣftsprǣc f. *scientific language,* ÆGR18[15].
crǣftwyrc n. *skilled workmanship,* Sc109[5].
crǣt n. nap. cr(e)atu *cart, waggon, chariot, Æ.*
crǣtehors n. *cart-horse,* WW108[24].
crǣtwǣn m. *chariot,* AO.
crǣtwīsa m. *charioteer,* ÆL18[295].
crǣwð pres. 3 sg. of crāwan.
craflan (æ) *to* '*crave,*' *ask, implore, demand, Chr,LL : summon,* Lcd.
crafing (æ) f. *claim, demand,* TC645[4].
±**crammian** *to* '*cram,*' *stuff,* ÆGr.
crammingpohha m. '*viscarium,*' CHRD68[9].
crampul m. *crane-pool,* Ct(Swt). [=cran, pōl]
cran m. '*crane,*' WW.
crancstæf m. *weaving implement, crank,* LL455,15 and 3·254.

crang pret. 3 sg. of cringan.
cranic m. *record, chronicle, Æ.* [L.]
cranicwrītere m. *chronicler,* OEG7[24].
cranoc m. '*crane,*' WW (corn-).
crat (WW140[31])=crǣt; **cratu** v. crǣt.
crāwa m., crāwe f. '*crow,*' *raven, Gl,Ps.*
±**crāwan**[7] *to* '*crow,*' *Mt;* CP.
crāwan-lēac (crāw-) n. *crow-garlic,* WW.
crēac-=crēc-
crēad pret. 3 sg. of crūdan.
creaft-=crǣft-
crēap pret. 3 sg. of crēopan.
crēas *fine, elegant,* NC277 : *dainty,* BDS 48·460.
crēaslic *dainty, rich.* v. NC277.
crēasnes f. *elegance : presumption, elation,* OEG1108.
creat=crǣt
Crēcas (ēa, v. AB40·342) mp. *the* '*Greeks,*' *AO,BH.*
Crēce=Crēcas
Crēcisc *Grecian, Greek,* AO.
crēda m. *creed, belief, confession of faith, Æ.* [*L.* credo]
credic? *a bowl,* OEG29[3].
creft (AS)=crǣft
crencestre f. *female weaver, spinster,* KC 6·131'. [cranc]
±**crēopan** (occly. refl.) *to creep, crawl, Æ, Bo;* AO,CP.
creopel=crypel
crēopere m. *cripple,* ÆL,GF. ['*creeper*']
crēopung f. '*creeping,*' Gl.
crēow pret. 3 sg. of crāwan.
crepel=crypel
cressa m. (GL), cresse f.=cærse
cribb (y) f. '*crib,*' *stall, Cr*1426 : *couch,* CHRD31[3].
cricc=crycc
crīde pret. 3 sg. of crīgan.
crīgan? *to bubble up.* v. OEG7[101].
±**crimman**[3] *to cram, put in, insert,* LCD, WW.
crinc '*cothurnus,*' ZDA33·250[3].
crincan=cringan
cring (gr-) *downfall, slaughter,* EL115.
±**cringan**[3]† *to yield, fall (in battle), die.*
cringwracu (gr-) f. *torment,* JUL265.
cripel=crypel; **crippan**=cryppan
crīpð pres. 3 sg. of crēopan.
crisma m. *chrism, holy oil,* LL : *chrisome-cloth,* BH : *anointing,* CHR.
crismal m? n? *chrismale,* W36[17].
crismhālgung f. *consecration of the chrism,* WNL121b'.
crismlīsing (ȳ[2]) f. *chrism-loosing, loosing of the chrismale, confirmation,* CHR.
crisp (BH)=cirps ['*crisp*']
Crīst m. *Anointed One, Christ, Æ,CP.*

cristalla m. *crystal*, Æ.
cristallisc *of crystal*, AA7⁶.
cristelmǣl=cristesmǣl
cristelmǣlbēam m. *tree surmounted by a cross? upright shaft of a cross?* EC385'.
cristen '*Christian*,' *AO,BH*; Æ. ða cristnan=*the English as opposed to the Danes*, CHR894.
cristen m., crist(e)na m. '*Christian*,' *Ao*.
cristendōm m. '*Christendom*,' *the church, Christianity, AO,Jud*; Æ.
cristenlic *Christian*, DR91'.
cristenmann m. *a Christian*, MH170²⁵.
cristennes f. *Christianity : Christian baptism*, LL412,1; 413,13a.
Cristes-mǣl (CHR), -mēl mn. (*Christ's mark*), *the cross*. wyrcan C. *to make the sign of the cross*.
Cristesmæsse f. *Christmas*, CHR1021D.
cristlic *Christian*, LL (Thorpe) 1·318¹¹n4.
cristna=cristen
cristnere m. *one who performs the rite of* cristnung, MH92¹.
cristnes=cristennes
±cristnian *to anoint with chrism (as a catechumen)*, '*christen*,' *baptize*, *BH*.
cristnung f. *christening, anointing with chrism or holy oil*, W33¹⁶.
crið=crigeð (v. crigan)?
crocc f., crocca m. '*crock*,' *pot, vessel*, *Lcd*.
crocchwer? m. *earthen pot*, OEG4672.
croced=croged
+crōcod *crooked, bent*, NC292.
crocsceard n. *potsherd*, Æ.
crocwyrhta m. *potter*, ÆGR.
+crod v. hlōð-gec.; lind-gec.
croden pp. of crūdan.
croft m. '*croft*,' *small field*, *KC*; GL.
crog, croh m. *saffron*, *Lcd*. [v. '*crocus*']
crōg m. *crock, pitcher, vessel*, *Gl*. ['*croh*']
crōgcynn n. *kind of vessel, wine-jar*, WW 210³⁹.
+crōged (ōc) *saffron-hued*, OEG5204n.
crōh I. m. *shoot, twig, tendril*. II. (*WW*431') =crōg ['*croh*']
crohha=crocca; croma=cruma
crompeht '*placenta*,' *a flat cake, crumpet*, WW241³⁴(A40·352); A37·48.
crong=crang pret. 3 sg. of cringan.
crop=cropp
cropen pp. of crēopan.
crop-lēac, -lēc n. *garlic* LCD,WW.
cropp, croppa m. *cluster, bunch : sprout, flower, berry, ear of corn*, *Ep,LkL,WW* : '*crop*' (*of a bird*), Æ : *kidney : pebble*.
croppiht *clustered*, LCD38b.
crūc m. *cross*, *Lcd*; LV74. ['*crouch*']
crūce f. *pot, pitcher*, *Gl*. ['*crouke*']
crucethūs n. *torture-chamber*, CHR1137.

crūdan²† *to press, hasten, drive*.
cruft m? crufte f. *crypt*, GL. [*L.*]
cruma (o) m. '*crumb*,' *fragment*, *Mt,WW*.
crumb, crump *crooked, bent, stooping*, *Gl*. ['*crump*']
crumen (crumm-) pp. of crimman.
cruncon pret. pl. of crincan.
crundel mn. *ravine, chalk-pit, quarry*, Ct (v. GBG and Mdf).
crungen pp. of cringan.
crupon pret. pl. of crēopan.
crūse f? *cruse*, A37·50.
crūs(e)ne f. *fur coat*, GL. [cp. *Ger*. kürschner]
crybb=cribb
crycc (i) f. '*crutch*,' *staff*, *BH*; Æ.
cryccen *made of clay*, GPH398.
crydeð pres. 3 sg. of crūdan.
crymbing f. *curvature, bend, inclination*, WW382². [crumb]
+crymian, +crymman (tr.) *to crumble*, LCD3·290²⁸.
+crympan *to curl*, WW378²⁶.
crypel I. (eo) m. '*cripple*,' *LkL*. II. (o²) *crippled*, HL179³²². III. (e, i) m. *narrow passage, burrow, drain*, OEG; v. Mdf.
crypelgeat n. *small opening in a wall or fence?* BC2·399¹.
crypelnes f. *paralysis*, Lk.
crypeð, crypð pres. 3 sg. of crēopan.
±cryppan *to crook (finger), close (hand), bend*, IM.
cryps=cirps; crysm-=crism-
crȳt=crydeð pres. 3 sg. of crūdan.
cū f. gs. cū(e), cȳ, cūs; ds. cȳ; nap. cȳ, cȳe; gp. cū(n)a, cȳna; dp. cūm; '*cow*,' *Æ,G, VPs*; Mdf.
cūbutere f. *butter*, LCD. [cū]
cūbȳre m. *cow-byre, cow-shed*, Ct.
cuc=cwic
cūcealf (æ) n. *calf*, *Erf, LL*. ['*cowcalf*']
cuceler, cuce(le)re=cucler(e)
cucelere '*capo*,' WW380²⁵.
cucler, cuculer, cuclere m. *spoon, spoonful*, LCD. [cp. *L*. cochlear]
cuclermǣl n. *spoonful*, LCD.
cucu (Æ,AO,CP) v. cwic.
cucurbite f. *gourd*, LCD92a. [*L*.]
cudele f. *cuttlefish*, WW181⁷.
cudu (Æ)=cwudu
cūeage f. *eye of a cow*, LL116Bn.
cueðan=cweðan
cufel f. '*cowl*,' *hood*, *BC* (at NED2 p. ix).
cūfel=cȳfl
cufle, cuffie=cufel
cugle, cug(e)le, cuhle f. *cap*, '*cowl*,' *hood, head-covering*, *RB, WW* (v. '*cowl*').
cūhorn m. *cow's horn*, LL116.
cūhyrde m. '*cowherd*,' LL.

cūle=cugle

culfer, cul(e)fre f. '*culver*,' *pigeon, dove, Gen,VPs,WW*.

culmille f. *small centaury*, LCD 22a.

culpan as. of *culpa? m. or *culpe? f. *fault, sin*, CR 177.

culpian *to humble oneself, cringe*, Bo 71²⁴.

culter m. '*coulter*,' WW : *dagger, knife*, WW. [*L*. culter]

culufre=culfre; **cūm** v. cū.

cuma mf. *stranger, guest*, Æ,AO,CP. cumena hūs, inn, wīcung *inn, guest-chamber*.

cuman⁴ *to* 'COME*,' *approach, get to, attain*, Æ,AO,CP. c. ūp *land, be born* : (±) *go, depart*, Æ,AO : *come to oneself, recover* : *become* : *happen* (also c. forð) : *put* : (+) *come together, arrive, assemble*, Æ : (†) w. inf. of verbs of motion, forming a sort of periphrastic conjugation for such verbs. cōm gangan *he came*. cōm swimman *he swam, etc.*

cumb I. m. *valley*, BC; Mdf. ['*coomb*'] **II.** m. *liquid measure*, BC. ['*coomb*']

cumbelgehnād (BR 49)=cumbolgehnāst

cumbl=(1) cumbol; (2) cumul

cumbol† n. *sign, standard, banner*.

cumbolgebrec (KPs 11), -gehnāst, BR 49 (*v.l.*), n. *crash of banners, battle*.

cumbolhaga m. *compact rank, phalanx*, JUL 395.

cumbolhete m. *warlike hate*, JUL 637.

cumbolwīga† m. *warrior*, JUD.

cumbor, cumbul=cumbol

cumen pp. of cuman.

cumendre f. *godmother, sponsor*. [=cumedre, *cumædre. v. A 37·52]

cūmeoluc f. *cow's milk*, LCD 15a.

Cumere? -eras? np. *Cumbrians*, ÆL 21⁴⁵¹.

cumfeorm f. *entertainment for travellers*, Ct. [cuma, feorm]

cū-micge (LCD 137a) f. -migoða (LCD 37a) m. *cow's urine*.

cuml=cumbl

cumlīðe *hospitable*, Æ,W. [cuma]

cumlīðian *to be a guest*, RBL 11¹.

cumlīðnes f. *hospitality*, Æ : *sojourn as guest*, RB.

cummāse f. *a kind of bird*, '*parra*,' WW 260¹⁹.

cumpæder m. *godfather*, CHR 894A. [*L*. compater]

cumul, cuml n. *swelling*, LCD.

cūna v. cū; **cund**=cynd

-cund adjectival suffix denoting derivation, origin or likeness. (-kind) as in deofol-cund, god-cund.

cuneglæsse f. *hound's-tongue*, LCD 41b. [*L*. cynoglossum]

cunel(l)e, cunille f. *wild thyme*. [Ger. quendel]

cuning=cyning

±cunnan pres. 1 and 3 sg. can(n), pl. cunnon; pret. cūðe, pp. cūð swv. *to be or become acquainted with, be thoroughly conversant with, know*, AO,B,Lcd,Mt; CP : *know how to, have power to, be able to, can*, Æ,CP : *express* (*thanks*), Chr 1092 : *have carnal knowledge*, CR 198. ['*can**,' '*con**']

cunnere m. *tempter*, NG.

±cunnian (w. g. or a.) *to search into, try, test, seek for, explore, investigate*, B,Bo,Cr, Sol; Æ,CP : *experience* : *have experience of, to make trial of* : *know*. ['*cun*']

cunnung f. *knowledge* : *trial, probation, experience* : *contact, carnal knowledge*, DR 110¹ (A 45·187).

cuopel f? *small boat*, MtL. ['*coble*']

cuppe f. '*cup*,' Lcd,WW; Æ.

curfon pret. pl. of ceorfan.

curmealle (e, i) f. *centaury*, LCD.

curnstān=cweornstān

curon pret. pl. of cēosan.

curs m. *imprecatory prayer, malediction*, '*curse*,' Ct,LL,Sc. [v. MP 24·215]

cursian I. *to* '*curse*,' Ps. **II.** *to plait?* MkR 15¹⁷.

cursumbor *incense*, MtL 2¹¹.

cursung f. '*cursing*,' *damnation*, LkL : *place of torment*, MtL.

cūs v. cū.

cūsc *chaste, modest, virtuous*, GEN 618. [*Ger*. keusch]

cūscote (eo, u) f. '*cushat*' *dove, wood-pigeon*, Gl.

cūself f. *cow's fat, suet*, GPH 392. [sealf]

cū-sloppe, -slyppe f. '*cowslip*,' Lcd,WW.

cūsnes=cīsnes

cūtægl m. *tail of a cow*, LL 169,59B.

±cūð *known, plain, manifest, certain*, Rd; Æ,AO,CP : *well known, usual, Da,Ps* : *noted, excellent, famous, Ex* : *intimate, familiar, friendly, related*. ['*couth*']

cūða m. *acquaintance, relative*, CP.

cūðe I. *clearly, plainly*, Ps. ['*couth*'] **II.** pret. 3 sg. of cunnan.

cūðelic=cūðlic

±cūðian *to become known, take knowledge of, regard*, JVPs 143³.

cūðice=cūðlīce

±cūðlæcan *to make known* : *make friends with*, ÆL.

cūðlic *known, certain, evident*. adv. -līce *clearly, evidently, certainly, openly*, BH, Jul; Æ,CP : *familiarly, kindly, affably*, An,BH; Æ : *therefore, to be sure, hence*. ['*couthly*']

cūðnes f. *acquaintance, knowledge*, HL.

cŭðnoma m. *surname*, NG.
cŭðon pret. pl. of cunnan.
cūwearm *warm from the cow (milk)*, LCD
126a.
cuwon pret. pl. of cēowan.
cwacian *to 'quake,' tremble, chatter (of
teeth)*, Æ,AO,Cr,LkL,VPs.
cwacung f. *'quaking,' trembling*, Æ,VPs;
AO.
cwæc-=cwac-
cwǣdon pret. pl. of cweðan.
cwæl pret. 3 sg., cwǣlon pret. pl., of
cwelan.
cwæl-=cwal-, cwiel-, cwil-
cwǣman=cwēman; cwǣn=cwēn
cwærtern=cweartern
cwǣð pret. 3 sg. of cweðan.
cwal-=cweal-
cwalstōw (LL556,10²)=cwealmstōw
cwalu f. *killing, murder, violent death, destruction*, Æ,CP. [cwelan]
cwānlan† (tr. and intr.) *to lament, bewail,
deplore, mourn*. [*Goth.* kwainon]
cwānig *sad, sorrowful*, EL377.
cwānung f. *lamentation*, NC279.
cwartern=cweartern
cwatern *the number four at dice*, GL. [*L.*]
cwēad n. *dung, dirt, filth*, LCD. [*Ger.* kot]
cweaht pp. of cweccan.
cweald pp. of cwellan.
cwealm (e) mn. *death, murder, slaughter :
torment, pain : plague, pestilence*, ÆH;
AO. ['*qualm*'; cwelan]
+cwealmbǣran (e, y) *to torture*, LPs.
cwealmbǣre *deadly, murderous, blood-
thirsty*, Æ.
cwealmbǣrnes (e) f. *mortality, destruction,
ruin*, Æ.
cwealmbealu n. *death*, B1940.
cwealmberendlic (ȳ¹) *pestilent, deadly*,
NC279.
cwealmcuma m. *death-bringer*, B792.
cwealmdrēor m. *blood shed in death*, GEN985.
+cwealmful (ȳ¹) *pernicious*, HGL428.
cwealmlic *deadly*, WYN281b (MLR17·166).
cwealmnes f. *pain, torment*, BH40³³.
cwealmstede m. *death-place*, GL.
cwealmstōw f. *place of execution*, Æ,Cp.
[v. '*qualm*']
cwealmðrēa m. *deadly terror*, GEN2507.
cwearn=cweornstān
cweartern (a, æ, e) n. *prison*, Æ.
cwearternlic *of a prison*, GPH400.
cwearte(r)nweard? *jailor*, GPH399.
±cweccan *to shake, swing, move, vibrate*,
Mt,VPs; Æ : *shake off, give up*, CHRD99³⁴.
['*quetch*'; cwacian]
cweccung f. *moving, shaking, wagging*, LPs
43¹⁵.

cwecesand m. *quicksand*, WW357⁶.
+cwed n. *declaration*, WW423²².
cweddian=cwiddian; cwedel=cwedol
cweden pp. of cweðan.
+cwedfæsten f. *appointed fast*, A11·99; ES
43·162.
cwedol *talkative, eloquent*, LCD.
+cwedrǣden (i, y) f. *agreement*, AO : *conspiracy*.
+cwedrǣdnes (y) f. *agreement, covenant*,
NC292.
+cwedstōw f. *appointed place, place of
meeting*, GD183⁷.
cwehte pret. sg. of cweccan.
cwelan⁴ *to die*, Lcd; Æ,CP. ['*quele*']
cweldeht *corrupted, mortified*, LCD47b.
[=*cwildeht]
cwelderǣde (æ¹)? *evening rider? bat*, SHR
29⁸. [*ON.* kveld]
±cwellan *to kill, murder, execute*, Æ, CP;
AO. ['*quell*']
cwellend m. *killer, slayer*, GPH400.
cwellere m. *murderer, executioner*, BH,Mk;
Æ. ['*queller*']
cwelm=cwealm (but v. MFH106), cwielm
cwelmere ·velre=cwellere
±cwēmə d.) *to gratify, please, satisfy,
propit.* E,AO,CP,Sol : *comply with, be
obedient to, serve.* ['*queme*,' '*i-queme*']
±cwēme *pleasant, agreeable, acceptable*, NG,
WG. ['*i-queme*']
cwēme-, cwēmed=cwēm
±cwēming f. *pleasing, satisfaction, com-
plaisance*, CP.
±cwēmlic *pleasing, satisfying, suitable.*
adv. -līce *graciously, kindly, humbly,
satisfactorily.*
±cwēmnes f. *pleasure, satisfaction, mitigation.*
+cwēmsum *pleasing*, OEG5000.
cwēn (ǣ) f. *woman*, Sc; Æ : *wife, consort*,
AO,Gen : '*queen,' empress, royal princess*,
Æ,AO,Chr,VPs : *Virgin Mary*, Bl,Cr.
[*Goth.* kwēns]
-cwencan v. ā-c.
cwene f. *woman*, Rd,W : *female serf*, '*quean,*'
prostitute, AO. [*Goth.* kwinō]
cwenfugol *hen-bird*, RWH148⁵.
cwēnhirde m. *eunuch*, MtL19¹².
cwēnlic *queenly*, B1940.
cweodu=cwudu
cweorn f. '*quern,' hand-mill, mill*, Æ,MtL;
CP.
cweornbill '*lapidaria,' a stone chisel for
dressing querns* (BT),WW438¹⁸.
cweornburna m. *mill-stream*, Ct.
cweorne=cweorn
cweornstān m. *mill-stone*, MtL. ['*quern-
stone*']

cweorntēð mp. *molars, grinders*, GL.

-cweorra v. mete-c.; -cweorran v. ā-c.

cweorð *name of the rune for* cw(q).

cwern̶(NG)=cweorn; cwertern=cweartern

±cweðan⁵ *to say, speak, name, call, proclaim, summon, declare*, BH,Bl,VPs; Æ, AO,CP : (+) *order, give orders : propose*, AO 68¹⁶ : ±c. (tō) *agree, settle, resolve, Chr* : (+) *consider, regard*, ÆL 1¹¹⁷. c. *on hwone assign to one*. cwyst ðū lā *sayest thou? 'numquid.'* cweðe gē *think you?* ['*quethe*']

cwic [cuc, cucu (this last form is archaic, and has an occasional asm. cucone, cucune)] 'QUICK,' *living, alive, CP*; AO : as sb. *living thing*, PPs 103²⁴.

cwicǽht f. *live-stock*, LL 60,18¹.

cwicbēam m. *aspen, juniper*, Gl,Lcd. ['*quick-beam*']

cwicbēamen *of aspen*, LCD 3·14²⁵.

cwicbēamrind f. *aspen bark*, LCD.

cwiccliende *moving rapidly? tottering?* OEG 2234.

cwice fm. '*couch*' ('*quitch*')-*grass*, Gl,Lcd.

cwicfȳr n. *sulphur*, LkR 17²⁹.

cwichege *a quick hedge*, KC 3·380¹¹.

cwichrērende *living and moving*, CREAT 5.

±cwician *to quicken, create*, JnL : *come to life, come to one's self*, Æ,Lcd. ['*quick*']

cwiclāc n. *a living sacrifice*, NG.

cwiclic *living, vital*, DR. adv. -līce *vigorously, keenly*, Ps. ['*quickly*']

cwiclīfigende† *living*.

cwicrind=cwicbēamrind

cwicseolfor n. '*quicksilver*,' Lcd; WW.

cwicsūsl nf. *hell-torment, punishment, torture*, Æ.

cwicsūslen *purgatorial*, ApT 26.

cwictrēow n. *aspen*, WW.

cwicu=cwic

+cwicung f. *restoration to life*, GD 218¹⁷.

cwicwelle *living (of water)*, JnR.

cwid-=cwed-, cwud-

cwidbōc f. *Book of Proverbs*, CP : *book of homilies*, MFH 136,152.

cwiddian (e, y) *to talk, speak, say, discuss, report : make a claim against*, LL 400,3¹.

cwiddung (y) f. *speech, saying, report*, Æ.

cwide (y) m. +cwide n. *speech, saying, word, sentence, phrase, proverb, argument, proposal, discourse, homily*, Bo; Æ,CP : *opinion : testament, will, enactment, agreement, decree, decision, judgment, TC*; Æ. ['*quide*'; cweðan]

cwidegiedd (i) n. *speech, song*, WA 55.

cwideléas (y) *speechless*, Æ : *intestate*, EC 212¹⁷.

±cwielman (æ, e, i, y) *to torment, afflict, mortify, destroy, kill*, Bl,VPs; AO,CP. ['*quelm*'] For compounds v. cwylm-.

cwiferlīce *zealously*, RB 122². ['*quiverly*']

cwild (y;=ie) mfn. *destruction, death, pestilence, murrain*. [cwelan] For compounds v. also cwyld-.

cwildbǽre (æ, y) *deadly, dangerous, pestiferous*, Sc : *stormy*. adv. -bǽrlīce.

cwildberendlic (y) *deadly*, NC 279.

cwild(e)flōd nm. *deluge*, CJVPs 28¹⁰, 31⁶.

±cwildful (y) *deadly*, OEG.

cwildrōf *deadly, savage*, Ex 166.

cwildseten (u, y) f. *first hours of night*, GL.

cwildtīd (u) m. *evening*, WW 211⁴². [ON. kveld]

cwilman=cwielman

cwilð pres. 3 sg. of cwelan.

-cwīnan v. ā-c.; -cwincan v. ā-c.

cwine=cwene

+cwis *conspiracy*, OEG 4955.

-cwisse v. un-c.

cwist pres. 2 sg. of cweðan.

cwið I. (also cwiða) m. *belly, womb*, LCD. [Goth. kwiðus] II. pres. 3 sg. of cweðan.

cwīðan *to bewail : accuse*, LL.

cwiðe=cwide

cwiðenlic *natural*, WW 412³⁰.

cwīðnes f. *complaint, lament*, GD.

cwiðst pres. 2 sg. of cweðan.

cwīðung (qu-) f. *complaint*, WW 488³⁷.

cwolen pp. of cwelan.

-cwolstan v. for-c.

cwōm pret. 3 sg. of cuman.

cwuc, cwucu=cwic

cwudu (eo, i) n. *what is chewed, cud*, Æ : *resin of trees*. hwīt c. *chewing gum, mastic*.

cwyc=cwic; cwyd-=cwed-, cwid-, cwidd-

cwydele f. *pustule, tumour, boil*, WW 112, 161.

cwyl-=cwild-; cwyld=cwild

cwylla m. *well, spring*, KC 2·265³⁰. [Ger. quelle]

cwylm=cwealm; cwylman=cwielman

cwylmend m. *tormentor, destroyer*, GD.

+cwylmful *pernicious*, HGl 428.

cwylmian (intr.) *to suffer* : (tr.) *torment, kill, crucify*, Æ. [cwealm]

cwylming f. *suffering, tribulation*, Æ : (metaph.) *cross : death*.

cwylttīd (WW 117⁸)=cwildtīd

cwylð pres. 3 sg. of cwelan.

cwyne=cwene; cwyrn=cweorn

±cwȳsan *to squeeze, dash against, bruise*, Æ.

cwyst pres. 2 sg. of cweðan.

cwyð pres. 3 sg. of cweðan.

cwȳðan, cwyðe=cwīðan, cwide

cȳ v. cū.

cycel (i) m. *small cake*, Lcd 159b. ['*kichel*']

cycen=cicen, cycene

cycene f. '*kitchen*,' Æ,WW. [L. coquina]

cycenðēnung f. *service in the kitchen*, NC 279.

cycgel m. '*cudgel*,' *BDS,CP.*

+**cȳd(d)** (*Chr,HR*)=+cȳðed pp. of +cȳðan. ['*ykid*']

cȳdung=cīdung

cȳe I. v. cū. **II.**=cēo

cȳf f. *tub, vat, cask, bushel*, Æ. ['*keeve*']

cyfes=cifes

cȳfl m. *tub, bucket*, BC.

cȳgan, cȳgling=cīegan, cȳðling

+**cygd**=+cīd; +**cȳgednes**=+cīgednes

cylcan '*ructare*,' OEG 20².

cyld=(1) cild; (2) ceald

cyle=ciele

cylen f. '*kiln*,' *oven*, *Cp,WW*. [*L.* culina]

cyleðenie=celeðonie; **cylew**=cylu

cylin=cylen

cyll f. *skin, leather bottle, flagon, vessel, censer*, Æ,AO,CP. [*L.* culeus]

cylle I. m.=cyll. **II.**=cielle

cyllfylling f. *act of filling a bottle*, GD 250²⁷.

cyln=cylen

cylu *spotted, speckled*, WW 163²⁹.

cym imperat. of cuman.

cymbala=cimbala

cyme (i) m. *coming, arrival, advent, approach*, *Bo,MtR*; AO,CP : *event* : *result*, BH 372B¹⁹. ['*come*']

cȳme (ī) *comely, lovely, glorious*, PPs.

cymed n. *germander*, LCD.

cymen I. mn. '*cumin*,' *CP,Mt*. [*L.*] **II.** pp. of cuman. **III.** (and cymin)=cinimin

cȳmlīc† '*comely*,' *lovely, splendid*, Ps. adv. -līce, *B.*

cȳmnes f. *fastidiousness, daintiness*, GL.

cymst pres. 2 sg., cym(e)ð 3 sg. of cuman.

cyn=(1) cynn; (2) cinn

cȳna gp. of cū.

cyncan ạṣ. of sb. *small bundle, bunch?* (BTs),LCD 2·58²².

±**cynd** (usu.+) nf. *origin, generation, birth* : *race, species*, *Bl,Bo,El* : *place by nature* : *nature*,'*kind*' ('*i-cunde*'), *property, quality* : *character*, *Bo* : *offspring* : *gender*, *Ph* : '*genitalia*,' *Æ.*

+**cyndbōc** f. *Book of Genesis*, ÆT 77⁴⁶.

+**cynde** *natural, native, innate*, *B,Bo,Gen, WW*; Æ,AO,CP : *proper, fitting, Met : lawful, rightful*, *Chr,Met.* ['*kind*,' '*i-cunde*']

±**cyndelic** '*kindly*,' *natural, innate*, *Bl,Bo, Lcd* : *generative, of generation*, LL 7,64 : *proper, suitable*, *Bo* : *lawful*, BH. adv. -līce, *Bo.*

+**cyndlim** n. *womb*, Lk : pl. '*genitalia*.'

+**cyndnes** f. *nation* : *produce, increase*, RHy 6²².

+**cynd-o**, -u f.=cynd

cyne=cine II.; **cȳne**=cēne

cynebænd m. *diadem*, NC 279.

cynebeald† *royally bold, very brave*, B.

cynebearn (a³) n. *royal child, Christ*, CHR, LCD.

cyneboren *royally born*, Æ.

cynebōt f. *king's compensation*, LL 462',463'.

cynebotl n. *palace*, Æ,WW.

cynecynn n. *royal race, pedigree or family*, Æ,AO.

cynedōm (cyning-, *Da*) m. *royal dignity, kingly rule, government*, *Chr,Gl*; AO : *royal ordinance or law* : '*kingdom*' ('*kindom*'), *royal possessions.*

cyneg=cyning

cyne-geard, -gerd=cynegyrd

cynegewǣdu np. *royal robes*, BH 32²⁵.

cynegierela (e³) m. *royal robe*, MET 25²³.

cynegild n. *king's compensation*, LL 462.

cynegōd† *noble, well-born, excellent.*

cynegold† n. *regal gold, crown.*

cyne-gyrd, -ge(a)rd f. *sceptre*, Æ,GL.

cynehād m. *kingly state or dignity*, CP.

cynehām m. *royal manor*, EC.

cyne-helm, -healm m. *diadem, royal crown*, Æ : *royal power.*

±**cynehelmian** *to crown*, MFB,Sc.

cynehlāford m. *liege lord, king*, Æ.

cynehof n. *king's palace*, GPH 391.

cynelic I. *kingly, royal*, CP : *public.* adv. -līce. **II.**=cynlic

cynelicnes f. *kingliness*, BH 194³⁴.

cynemann m. *royal personage*, NG.

cynerēaf n. *royal robe*, VH 10.

cyneren=cynren

cynerīce (cyning-) n. *rule, sovereignty*, Chr, *Ct*; CP : *region, nation*, AO. ['*kinrick*,' '*kingrick*']

cyneriht n. *royal prerogative*, EC 202¹⁸.

cynerōf† *noble, renowned.*

cynescipe m. *royalty, majesty, kingly power*, Æ.

cynesetl (æ³) n. *throne, capital city*, Æ,AO.

cynestōl m. *throne, royal dwelling, city*, Æ, AO,CP.

cynestrǣt f. *public road*, WW 71⁶.

cyneðrymlic *very glorious*, NC 279.

cyneðrymm† m. *royal glory, majesty, power* : *kingly host*, DA 706.

cynewāðen *of royal purple*, TC 538¹⁰. [?=cynewǣden]

cynewīse f. *state, commonwealth*, BH.

cynewiðõe f. *royal diadem*, GL.

cyneword n. *fitting word*, RD 44¹⁶. [cynn]

cynewyrðe (u) *noble, kingly*, BF 74¹², MFH 157.

cyng, cynig=cyning

cyning m. '*king*,' *ruler*, *Bo,Bl,Chr,Ct*; Æ, AO,CP : *God, Christ*, *Bl,Ct* : (†) *Satan.*

cyning-=cyne-

cyningǣðe *man entitled to take oath as a king's thane*, LL112,54BH.

cyningeswyrt f. *marjoram*, WW301[17].

cyningfeorm f. *king's sustenance, provision for the king's household*, KC2·111'.

cyninggenīola m. *great feud*, EL610.

cyninggereordu np. *royal banquet*, WW 411[28].

cynlic I. *fitting, proper, convenient, becoming, sufficient.* adv. -līce. II.=cynelic

cynn I. (i) n. *kind, sort, rank, quality : family, generation, offspring, pedigree, 'kin,' race, people*, Æ,CP,Chr : *gender, sex,* Æ : *propriety, etiquette.* II. adj. *becoming, proper, suitable*, CP.

+cynn=+cynd; **cynn-**=cenn-, cyn-

cynnig *noble, of good family*, OEG.

cynnreccenes f. *genealogy*, NG.

cynren (y²), cynrēd (EPs) n. *kindred, family, generation, posterity, stock*, CP : *kind, species.*

cynresu *a generation*, Mt (pref.).

cȳo, cyp=cēo, cipp; **cȳp-**=cīep-

cȳpa m. I. (also cȳpe) f. *vessel, basket, Lk, OEG.* ['kipe'] II. (ē, ī) m. *chapman, trader, merchant*, Æ.

±cȳpan (ī;=īe) *to traffic, buy, sell, barter.* [Ger. kaufen]

+cȳpe adj. *for sale*, ÆH.

cȳpe-=cēap-, cīepe-

cȳpedæg m. *market day*, OEG.

cȳpend m. *one who sells, merchant*, Mt.

cypera m. *spawning salmon*, MET19[12] : 'esox,' pike? A38·516.

cyperen (Æ)=cypren; **cypp**=cipp

cypersealf (i) f. *henna-ointment*, WW205[11] [L. cyperos]

cypren *made of copper, copper*, AO. [copor]

cypresse f. *cypress*, LCD3·118'. [L.]

cypsan=cyspan; **cyr-**=cer-, cier-, cir-

cyre m. *choice, free-will*, Æ. ['cure']

cyreāð m. *oath sworn by an accused man and by other chosen persons.* v. LL2·293.

cyrelīf n. *state of dependence on a lord whom a person has chosen? : person in such a state* (v. BTs and NC279).

cyren=(1) ceren, (2) cyrn

cyrf m. *cutting, cutting off*, Æ : *what is cut off.* ['kerf']

cyrfæt=cyrfet

cyrfel m. *little stake, peg*, WW126[18].

cyrfet m. *gourd*, LCD. [Ger. kürbis]

cyrfþ pres. 3 sg. of ceorfan.

ðyric-=ciric-

cyrige v. wæl-c.

cyrin, cyrn (e) f. 'churn,' WW.

cyrnel (i) mn. (nap. cyrnlu) *seed,* 'kernel,' *pip*, Æ,Lcd : (*enlarged*) *gland, swelling*, Lcd. [corn]

+cyrnod, +cyrnlod *granulated, rough*, OEG.

cyrps=cirps

cyrriol *the Kyrie Eleison*, BF126[3].

cyrs-=cærs-, cris-

cyrstrēow n. *cherry-tree*, WW 138. [ciris; L.]

+cyrtan *to shorten*, GPH400.

cyrtel m. (*man's*) *tunic, coat*, Æ,AO : (*woman's*) *gown*, Ct. ['kirtle']

cyrten I. *fair, comely*, Æ : *intelligent.* adv. -līce (and cyrtelīce) *elegantly, neatly, fairly, well, exactly.* II. *ornament?* WW216[7].

cyrtenes (e¹) f. *elegance, beauty*, OEG.

±cyrtenlǣcan (e¹) *to beautify, make elegant*, Æ : (+) *make sweet*, OEG.

cyrð pres. 3 sg. of cyrran.

cys-=cyse-, ceos-

cȳse (ǣ, ē;=īe) m. 'cheese,' WW.

cȳsefæt n. *cheese vat*, WW379[27] (v. LL 3·255).

cȳsehwǣg n. *whey*, LCD119b.

cȳsfæt (LL455,17)=cȳsefæt

cȳsgerunn n. *curd-like mass*, WW98[3] (v. A51·158).

cysirbēam=cirisbēam

cȳslybb n. *rennet*, Cp,Lcd. ['cheeselip']

±cyspan *to fetter, bind*, Æ. [cosp]

±cyssan *to 'kiss,'* Æ,BH,Mt. [coss]

cȳssticce n. *piece of cheese*, CHRD15.

cyst I. fm. *free-will, choice, election* : (w. gp.) *the best of anything, the choicest*, Æ : *picked host : moral excellence, virtue, goodness*, CP, Æ : *generosity, munificence*, CP. [cēosan] II.=cist I.

cȳst pres. 3 sg. of cēosan.

cystan *to spend, lay out, get the value of*, CHR1124.

cystbēam=cistenbēam

cystel, cysten (=cist-) f. *chestnut-tree*, LCD, WW.

cystelīce=cystiglīce

cystian (e) *to put in a coffin*, W. [cist]

cystig *charitable, liberal, generous*, CP; Æ : *virtuous, good.* ['custi'] adv. -līce.

cystignes, cystines f. *liberality, bounty, goodness*, Æ : *abundance.*

cystlēas *worthless, bad*, GEN1004.

cystlic=cystig; **cystnes**=cystignes

cȳsð=cīesð pres. 3 sg. of cēosan.

cȳswucu f. *the last week in which cheese was allowed to be eaten before Lent*, Mt(B)5[43]n.

cȳswyrhte f. (*female*) *cheese-maker*, LL 451,16.

cȳta m. 'kite,' *bittern*, Cp.

cȳte (ē) f. *cottage, hut, cabin*, Æ : *cell, cubicle*, Æ.

cytel=citel; **cytere**=citere

cytwer m. *weir for catching fish*, KC3·450.

cȳð=(1) cȳðð, (2) cīð

±**cȳðan** to proclaim, utter, make known, show forth, tell, relate, Cp,Cr,HR,Jn; CP : prove, show, testify, confess, Mt,VPs : become known : exercise, perform, practise, B : (+) confirm, LL : (+) make celebrated. wundor c. perform a miracle. ['kithe*'; 'y-kid']

+**cȳðednes** f. testimony, LPs 121⁴.

cȳðere m. witness, martyr, Æ.

cȳðig known : (+) knowing, aware of, DR.

cȳðing f. statement, narration, GD 86¹⁴.

±**cȳðlǣcan** to become known, GL.

cȳðling=cȳðing

±**cȳðnes** f. testimony : testament (often of Old and New Test.), Æ : knowledge, acquaintance.

cȳðð, cȳððu f. kinship, relationship : 'kith,' kinsfolk, fellow-countrymen, neighbours, Lk : acquaintance, friendship : (±) native land, home, Bo; AO,CP : knowledge, familiarity, Æ,BH.

cywes-=cyfes-

cȳwð pres. 3 sg. of cēowan.

cȳwung=cēowung

D

dā f. 'doe' (female deer), ÆGr; WW 320³⁵.

dǣd I. (ē) f. (nap. dǣda, dǣde) 'deed,' action, transaction, event, Æ,B,Bl,VPs. II.=dēad

dǣdbana m. murderer, LL 266,23.

dǣdbēta m. a penitent, Æ.

dǣdbētan to atone for, make amends, be penitent, repent, Æ. [dǣdbōt]

dǣdbētere m. a penitent, CHRD 80²⁴.

dǣdbōt f. amends, atonement, repentance, penitence, Mt; AO. ['deedbote']

dǣdbōtlihting f. mitigation of penance, LL (288').

dǣdbōtnes f. penitence, Sc 41⁴.

dǣdcēne bold in deed, B 1645.

dǣdfrom energetic, PPs 109⁸.

dǣdfruma† m. doer of deeds (good or bad), worker.

dǣdhata m. ravager, B 275.

dǣdhwæt† energetic, bold.

dǣdlata m. sluggard, OET 152⁸.

dǣdlēan n. recompense, Ex 263.

dǣdlic active, ÆGr.

dǣdon=dydon pret. pl. of dōn.

dǣdrōf† bold in deeds, valiant.

dǣdscua (CR 257)=dēaðscūa?

dǣdweorc n. mighty work, Ex 575.

dæf-=daf-

±**dæftan** to put in order, arrange, Æ,CP.

+**dæfte** mild, gentle, meek, Mt. ['daft']

+**dæftelīce**, +dæftlīce fitly, in season, in moderation, gently, CP.

+**dæftu** f. gentleness, GD 202¹².

dæg m. gs. dæges; nap. dagas 'day*,' lifetime, Æ,Mt,Mk; AO,CP : Last Day, Bl : name of the rune for d. andlangne d. all day long. dæges, or on d. by day. tō d., tō dæge to-day. d. ǣr the day before. sume dæge one day. ofer midne d. afternoon. on his dæge in his time. dæges and nihtes by day and by night. lange on d. far on, late in the day. emnihtes d. equinox. ealle dagas always, Mt.

dægcandel (o²)† f. sun.

dægcūð open, clear as the day, DD 40.

dǣge f. (female) bread maker, WW 277². ['dey']

dæge-=dæg-

dægehwelc daily, DR 90'.

dægenlic of this day, A 17·121.

dæges adv. v. dæg.

dæges-ēage, -ēge n. 'daisy,' Lcd,WW.

+**dægeð** pres. 3 sg. dares? braves? W 220²⁸.

dægfæsten n. a day's fast, Lcd,LL.

dægfeorm f. day's provision, EC 226².

dæghlūttre adv. clearly, as day, Gu 665.

dæghryne=dægryne

dæghwām (ā²) adv. daily, Gu,Lcd.

dæghwāmlic (ā²) of day, daily, Æ. adv. -līce, Æ,AO.

dæghwīl f. (pl.) days, lifetime, B 2726.

dæghwonlīce=dæghwāmlīce

dæglang (o²) lasting a day, Sol 501.

dæglanges adv. during a day, Æ.

dæglic=dæghwāmlic

dægmǣl nm. horologe, dial, Bf,Lcd.

dægmǣlspilu f. gnomon of a dial, WW 126³¹.

dægmǣlscēawere m. astrologer, WW.

dægmete m. breakfast, dinner, WW 267¹³.

dægol=dīegol

dæg-rēd (or? dægred) (Æ,CP), -rǣd n. daybreak, dawn, Lk. ['dayred']

dægrēdlēoma m. light of dawn, NC 280.

dægrēdlic belonging to morning, early, WW.

dægrēdoffrung f. morning sacrifice, ExC 29⁴¹.

dægrēdsang m. matins, RB,CM.

dægrēdwōma† m. dawn.

dægrīm† n. number of days.

dægrima m. dawn, daybreak, morning, Æ. ['dayrim']

dægryne daily, of a day, WW 224²⁹.

dægsang m. daily service, W 290²².

dægsceald m? (shield by day?) sun, Ex 79.

dægsteorra m. 'daystar,' morning star, Æ, Lcd.

dægswǣsendo np. a day's food, LL (220 n3).

dægtīd f. day-time, time, period. on dægtīdum at times, Rd.

dægtīma m. *day-time, day*, LPs 120⁶.

dægðerlic *of the day, of to-day, daily, present*, Æ.

dægðern f. *interval of a day*, LCD.

dægðerne adj. *for use by day, every-day*, CM.

dægwæccan fp. *day-watches*, WW 110²⁴.

dægweard m. *day-watchman*, WW 110²⁵.

dægweorc n. *work of a day, fixed or stated service, Ex : day-time.* ['*daywork*']

dægweorðung f. *feast-day*, EL 1234.

dægwilla *wished for day*, GEN 2776.

dægwine n? *day's pay*, GL.

dægwist f. *food, meal*, Æ,RB.

dægwōma (EX,GU)=dægrēdwōma

dæl I. nap. dalu n. '*dale,*' *valley, gorge, abyss, AO : hole pit*, Gl (v.GBG). II. pret. 3 sg. of delan.

dæl (ā) m. (p. dæl-as, -e) *portion, part, share, lot, Cp,Bl,Bo,G,VPs*; AO,CP : *division, separation, Æ : quantity, amount, Lcd : region, district*, AO : *part of speech, word*, ÆGR. d. wintra *a good number of years.* be dæle *in part, partly.* be healfum dæle *by half.* be ænigum dæle *at all, to any extent.* be ðæm dæle *to that extent.* cyðan be dæle *to make a partial or 'ex parte' statement.* sume dæle, be sumum dæle *partly.* ['*deal*']

±dælan *to divide, part, separate, share, Da*; Æ,CP : *bestow, distribute, dispense, spend, hand over to, An,Mk : take part in, share with, Gen : be divided : diffuse : utter.* †hilde, earfoðe dælan *to fight, contend, Ma.* ['*deal*']

+dæledlīce *separately*, WW 487¹⁹.

dælend m. *divider*, Lk 12⁴.

dælere m. *divider, distributor, WW : agent, negotiator, Æ : almsgiver, Æ.* ['*dealer*']

dæling f. *dividing, sharing*, HGL 423.

+dælland=+dālland

dællēas *deficient, unskilled, WW : destitute of, without*, W.

dælmælum adv. *by parts or pieces*, ÆGR, LCD.

dæl-neom-, -nym-=dælnim-

dælnes f. *breaking (of bread)*, LkL p11¹¹.

dælnimend m. *sharer, participator, VPs*; Æ : *participle*, ÆGR. [v. '*deal*']

dælnimendnes f. *participation*, BJPs 121³.

dælnimung f. *participation, portion, share*, Ps,RBL.

dælnumelnes=dælnimendnes

dæm-, dæn-=dēm-, den-; dæp=dēop

dære v. daru; dærēd (S²Ps 62⁷)=dægrēd; dærne=dierne

dærst, dærste, dræst (e¹) f. *leaven*, NG,DR : (pl.) *dregs, refuse*, Lcd,Ps. ['*drast*']

+dærsted *leavened, fermented*, NG.

dæð, dæwig=dēað, dēawig

+dafen I. n. *what is fitting*, GD 84⁶. II. *becoming, suitable, fit, proper.*

+dafenian (often impers.) *to beseem, befit, be right*, Æ.

+dafenlic *fit, becoming, proper, suitable, right.* adv. -līce.

±dafenlicnes f. *fit time, opportunity*, Æ.

+daflic=+dafenlic; dafn-=dafen-

+dafniendlic=+dafenlic

dāg m? (dāh) '*dough,*' *Lcd : mass of metal.*

dagas, dages v. dæg.

dagian *to dawn, be day*, BH; Æ. ['*daw*']

dagung f. *daybreak, dawn, BH.* on dagunge *at daybreak.* ['*dawing*']

dāh, dāl=dāg, dæl

+dāl n. *division, separation, sharing, giving out, CP : distinction, difference : destruction : share, lot*, GD 311¹¹.

+dālan (VH 10)=+dælan

dalc m. *bracelet, brooch*, GL.

dalf (NG)=dealf pret. 3 sg. of delfan.

dalisc (? for *dedalisc) '*dedaleus,*' WW 221³.

+dālland n. *land under joint ownership, common land divided into strips.* v. LL 2·443.

dālmæd f. *meadow-land held in common and apportioned between the holders*, KC 3·260³.

dalmatice? f. *dalmatic* (vestment), GD 329²⁴.

dalu v. dæl; darað, dareð=daroð

darian *to lurk, be hidden*, ÆL 23³²².

daroð† m. *dart, spear, javelin.* daroða lāf *those left by spears, survivors of a battle.*

daroðhæbbende *spear-bearing*, JUL 68.

daroðlācende† (eð) mp. *spear-warriors.*

daroðsceaft (deoreð-) m. *javelin-shaft*, GEN 1984.

daru f. gds. dære *injury, hurt, damage, calamity*, Æ.

datārum m. (indecl.) *date*, BF 46.

dað '*bloma,*' *mass of metal*, WW 141³⁶.

Davīdlic (DHy).

Davītic adj. *of David*, LCD 3·428¹⁷.

dēacon=dīacon

dēad (±) '*dead,*' *Æ,B,Mt*; AO,CP : *torpid, dull : still, standing (of water).* d. blōd *congealed blood.*

dēad-=dēað-

dēadboren *still-born*, LCD 1·206⁶.

±dēadian *to die*, JnL. ['*dead*']

dēadlic *subject to death, mortal, perishable, Æ : causing death, 'deadly,' fatal, AO : about to die.* adv. -līce.

dēadrægel n. *shroud*, WW 37⁶. [hrægl]

dēadspring m. *ulcer*, LCD.

dēadwylle *barren*, AO 26¹⁶.

dēaf I. '*deaf,*' *Mt,Jul*; VPs : *empty, barren*, CP 411²⁰. II. pret. 3 sg. of dūfan.

-dēaflan v. ā-d.; dēaflic=dēfelic
dēafu f. deafness, LCD.
deag=dæg
dēag I. hue, tinge, Æ,WW : 'dye,' WW.
II. pres. 3 sg. of dugan.
dēagel=dī(e)gol
dēaggede gouty, WW161³¹. [dēaw]
±dēagian to 'dye,' OEG.
dēagol=dīegol
dēagung f. 'dyeing,' colouring, Æ.
dēagwyrmede gouty, WW161³¹. [dēaw]
dēah=dēag I. and II.
dēahl, deal=dīegol, deall
dealf pret. 3 sg. of delfan.
deall† proud, exulting, bold, renowned.
dēap-=dēop-
dear pres. 3 sg. of *durran.
dearc, dearcð=deorc, daroð
dearf I. pret. 3 sg. of deorfan. II. bold,
NG.
dearflic bold, presumptuous, NG.
dearfscipe m. boldness, presumption, NG.
dearn-unga, -unge (e², i²) secretly, privately,
insidiously, Æ,AO,CP.
dearoð=daroð
dearr pres. 3 sg. of *durran.
dearste (VPs)=dærste
dēað (ēo) m. 'death,' dying, An,Bo,G; CP :
cause of death, Bl : in pl. 'manes,' ghosts.
dēað-=dēad- (v. ES39·324).
dēaðbǣre deadly, CP.
dēaðbǣrlic (dēad-) deadly, Mk16¹⁸.
dēaðbǣrnes (ē²) f. deadliness, destructive-
ness, LkL,OEG.
dēaðbēacnigende boding death, DD,W.
dēaðbēam m. death-bringing tree, GEN638.
dēaðbedd† n. bed of death, grave, B.
['death-bed']
dēaðberende fatal, deadly, CP.
dēaðcwalu† f. deadly throe, agony, EL: death
by violence, B.
dēaðcwealm m. death by violence, B1670.
dēaðcwylmende killed, LPs78¹¹.
dēaðdæg† m. 'death-day,' OET; VH.
dēaðdenu† f. valley of death.
dēaðdrepe m. death-blow, Ex495.
dēaðfǣge doomed to death, B850.
dēaðfiren f. deadly sin, CR1207.
dēaðgedāl n. separation of body and soul by
death, GU936.
dēaðgodas mp. infernal deities, WW447¹⁹.
+dēaðian to kill, DR48⁷.
dēaðlēg m. deadly flame, GR983.
dēaðlic 'deathly,' mortal, Bl : deadly : dead.
dēaðlicnes f. mortal state : deadliness,
liability to death, BL.
dēaðmægen n. deadly band, GU867.
dēaðrǣced (=e²) n. sepulchre, PH48.
dēaðrǣs m. sudden death, AN997.

dēaðrēaf n. clothing taken from the dead,
spoils, WW397²².
dēaðrēow murderous, fierce, AN1316.
dēað-scūa, -scufa m. death-shadow, spirit of
death, devil.
dēaðscyld f. crime worthy of death, LL130'.
dēaðscyldig (LL), dēadsynnig (NG) condemned to death.
dēaðsele† m. death-hall, hell.
dēaðslege m. death-stroke, RD6¹⁴.
dēaðspere n. deadly spear, RD4⁵³.
dēaðstede m. place of death, Ex589.
dēaðsynnignes f. guiltiness of death, DR
42'.
dēaððēnung f. exequies, last offices to the
dead, funeral, NC,WW.
dēaðwang m. plain of death, AN1005.
dēaðwēge n. deadly cup, GU964. [wǣge]
dēaðwērig dead, B2125.
dēaðwīc n. dwelling of death, B1275.
dēaðwyrd f. fate, death, WW408²³.
dēaw mn. 'dew,' Æ,Cp,VPs.
+dēaw dewy, bedewed, LCD10a,35a.
dēawdrīas m. fall of dew? DA277. [drēosan]
dēawig (ǣ, ē) 'dewy,' Ex : moist, Lcd.
dēawigendlic? dewy, HGL408.
dēawigfeðera† dewy-feathered.
dēawung f. dew, EHy7⁶⁴.
dēawwyrm m. 'dew-worm,' ring-worm,
tetter, Lcd.
decan m. one who has charge of ten monks,
RB125n.
±dēcan to smear, plaster, Æ, Lcd. ['deche']
decanhād m. office of a 'decan,' RBL54³.
decanon=decan
December m. g. -bris December, MEN.
declīnian to decline, ÆGR88,100.
declīnigendlic subject to inflection, ÆGR88.
declīnung f. declension, BF94¹⁶.
dēd I. (A)=dǣd. II.=dēad
dēde (KGL)=dyde pret. 3 sg. of dōn.
+dēfe (doefe once, in NG) befitting, suitable,
proper : meek, gentle, kindly, good. also
adv.
+dēf-elic, -edlic fit, becoming, proper. adv.
-līce, BH.
defen-=dafen-; dēflic=dēfelic
+dēfnes f. mildness, gentleness, LPs89¹⁰.
+deftlīce=+dæftlīce; deg=dæg
dēg (NG)=dēag pres. 3 sg. of dugan.
dēg-=dēag-, dīeg-, dīg-; degn=ðegn
dehter ds. of dohtor.
dehtnung (KGL)=dihtnung; del=dæl
dela nap. of delu.
dēlan=dǣlan
+delf n. digging, excavation, Æ,AO : what is
dug, trench, quarry, canal, Mdf.
delfan³ to 'delve,' dig, dig out, burrow, Æ,
Bo,G,VPs; AO : bury.

delfere m. *digger*, Bo 140[13].
delfin *dolphin*, WW 293[13]. [*L.*]
delfisen n. *spade*, WW.
delfung f. *digging*, WW 149[10].
+**delgian**=+telgian
dell nm. *dell, hollow, dale*, BH; Mdf.
delu f. *teat, nipple*, CP 405[1]. [*OHG.* tili]
dem=demm
dēma m. *judge, ruler*, Æ,CP.
±**dēman** *to judge, determine, decide, decree, sentence, condemn, BH,Cra,El,G,VPs*; CP : *assign* : '*deem*' ('*i-deme*'), *consider, think, estimate, compute*, Æ,BH,Cp : (†) *praise, glorify* : (†) *tell, declare, FAp.*
dēmedlic *that may be judged*, GD 336[20].
dēmend† m. *judge, arbiter.*
dēmere m. *judge, MtL* (oe). ['*deemer*']
demm m. *damage, injury, loss, misfortune*, AO,CP.
-**demman** v. for-d.
dēmon *demon, devil*, DR.
den=denn, denu; **dēn**=dōn pp. of dōn.
Denalagu, f. *the* '*Dane law*,' *law for the part of England occupied by the Danes, LL.*
den-bær f., -berende n. *swine-pasture*, Mdf.
dene=denu
Dene mp. *the* '*Danes*,' *Chr*; AO.
deneland (æ) *valley*, LPs 59[8].
Denemearc (æ[1], a[3], e[3]), Denemearce f. *Denmark.*
dengan (ncg) *to beat, strike*, CHRD 60[30].
denge=dyncge
Denisc '*Danish*,' *Chr.* wk. nap. ðā Deniscan *the Danes.*
denn n. '*den*,' *lair, cave, B,WW*; Æ : *swine-pasture.* v. Mdf.
dennian *to stream?* BR 12 (v. ANS 118·385).
denstōw f. *place of pasture*, BC 3·144[21]
denu f. **I.** *valley, dale*, Æ,Lk,VPs; Mdf. ['*dean*'] **II.** (MFH 108)=denn
dēof=dēaf pret. 3 sg. of dūfan.
dēofel-, dēofl-=dēofol-
deofenian=dafenian
dēofol mn. gs. dēofles, nap. dēoflu, dēofol *a* '*devil*,' *demon, false god, B,Cr,G,VPs*; AO : *the devil, Cp,G,Jul,Sol,VHy*; Æ: *diabolical person, JnLR.* [*L.* diabolus]
dēofolcræft m. *witchcraft*, AO,BH.
dēofolcund *fiendish*, JUD 61.
dēofolcynn n. *species of devil*, RWH 105[21].
dēofoldǣd f. *fiendish deed*, DA 18.
dēofol-gield (AO,CP), -gild, -geld (AO,VHy), -gyld (Æ) n. *devil-worship, idolatry* : *idol, image of the devil*, Æ.
dēofolgielda (y[3]) m. *devil-worshipper, idolater*, ÆH 1·70'.
dēofolgieldhūs n. *idol-temple*, AO 284[9].
dēofolgītsung (dīwl-) f. *unrighteous mammon*, LkL 16[11].

dēofollic *devilish, diabolical, of the devil*, Æ. ['*devilly*'] adv. -līce.
dēofolscīn n. *evil spirit, demon, Sc.* ['*devil-shine*']
dēofolscīpe m. *idolatry*, NC 286.
dēofolsēoc *possessed by devils, lunatic*, Æ.
dēofolsēocnes f. *demoniacal possession*, G.
dēofolwītga m. *wizard, magician*, DA 128.
dēoful=dēofol
dēog pret. 3 sg. of dēagan (MLR 24·62).
dēohl, dēogol=dīegol
±**dēon** *to suck*, LG (JAW 19).
dēop **I.** '*DEEP*,' *profound* : *awful, mysterious*, CP : (†) *heinous* : *serious, solemn, earnest.* d. cēap *high price, great price.* **II.** n. *deepness, depth, abyss, Ex,Mt* : *the* '*deep*,' *sea, Lk.*
dēope adv. *deeply, thoroughly, entirely, earnestly, solemnly, Ps.* ['*deep*']
dēophycgende† dēophȳdig† *deeply meditating, pensive.*
±**dēoplan** (ēa) *to get deep*, DR 81[24],LCD 125b.
dēoplic *deep, profound, thorough, fundamental*, Æ,CP : *grievous.* adv. -līce '*deeply*,' *Bo,WW* : *ingeniously*, BF 64, 70.
dēopnes f. *depth, abyss, LPs,Nic* : *profundity, mystery, Hy*; Æ : *subtlety, cunning*, W. ['*deepness*']
dēopþancol *contemplative, very thoughtful*, BF 164[28]; W 248[7]. adv. -līce.
dēor **I.** n. *animal, beast* (usu. *wild*), Lk,Met, WW; Æ,CP : '*deer*,' *reindeer*, AO. **II.** *brave, bold, An,Sal,Seaf,Sol* : *ferocious, B* : *grievous, severe, violent, Da,Sol.* ['*dear*'] **III.**=dēore
±**dēoran** (ȳ)† *to hold dear, glorify, endear.*
dēorboren *of noble birth*, LL 104,34[1].
deorc '*dark*,' *obscure, gloomy, B,Ps* : *sad, cheerless, Wa* : *sinister, wicked, Lk,Sat.* adv. deorce.
deorcegrǣg *dark grey*, WW.
deorcful *dark, gloomy, Sc.* ['*darkful*']
deorclan *to grow dim*, LPs.
deorclīce '*darkly*,' *horribly, foully*, GPH 391[22].
deorcnes f. '*darkness*,' *Sc* 228[8].
deorcung f. *gloaming, twilight, WW*; Æ. [y. '*dark*' vb.]
dēorcynn n. *race of animals*, Bo.
dēore **I.** '*dear*,' *beloved, G,Jul* : *precious, costly, valuable, AO,Bo* : *noble, excellent, Ps,Rd.* **II.** adv. *dearly, at great cost, Met, WW.* **III.** adv. *fiercely, cruelly.* [dēor II.]
dēoren *of a wild animal*, GL.
deoreōsceaft=daroðsceaft
±**deorf** n. *labour*, WW 91 : *difficulty, hardship, trouble, danger*, Æ. ['*derf*']

dēorfald m. *enclosure for wild beasts*, WW 201³⁴.

±deorfan³ *to exert oneself, labour*, Æ : *be in peril, perish, be wrecked*, AO. ['*derve*']

dēorfellen *made of hides*, WW 328¹⁸.

+deorflēas *free from trouble*, GL.

+deorfnes f. *trouble, tribulation*, LPs 45².

dēorfrið n. *preservation of game*, Chr 1086. [v. '*frith*']

+deorfsum (y¹) *troublesome, grievous*, CHR 1103; 1005.

dēorgēat n. *gate for animals*, Ct.

dēorhege m. *deer-fence*, LL.

deorian (CHR)=derian

dēorlic *brave, renowned*, B585.

dēorlīce '*dearly,*' *preciously, richly*, El : *sincerely, acceptably*, AS4¹⁹ (or ? dēoplīce).

dēorling (ī, ȳ) m. '*darling,*' *favourite, minion*, Æ,Bo,CP : *household god.*

dēormōd† *courageous, bold.*

dēornett n. *hunting-net*, WW 183¹².

deornunga=dearnunga

deorsterlīce=dyrstiglīce

dēortūn m. *park*, GL.

dēor-wierðe (CP), -wurðe (Æ), -wyrðe *precious, dear, costly*, Bl,Bo. ['*dearworth*']

dēorwyrðlic (eo², u²) *precious, valuable.* adv. -lice *splendidly*, Æ : *as a thing of value*, Æ.

dēorwyrðnes (u²) f. *treasure*, Bo : *honour, veneration*, RWH139¹⁸ ['*dearworthness*']

dēoð (NG)=dēað; dēpan=dȳpan

dēpe=dēop; deppan=dyppan; dēr=dēor

Dēra, Dēre mp. *Deirans, inhabitants of Deira.*

+derednes f. *injury*, LCD 1·322¹.

derian (w. d.) *to damage, injure, hurt*, Bo, Chr ; Æ,AO,CP. ['*dere*']

deriendlic *mischievous, noxious, hurtful*, Æ.

dērling (NG)=dēorling

derne=dierne

dernunga (NG)=dearnunga

derodine m. *scarlet dye*, CP 83²⁵.

derste (VPs)=dærste

derung f. *injury*, GD.

desig=dysig; dēst v. dōn.

dēð I. 3 p. sg. pres. of dōn. II. '*manipulus,*' *sheaf?* EPs 125⁶.

+dēðan (=īe) *to kill*, NG : *mortify*, DR.

dēðing f. *putting to death*, DR 72¹³.

deððan? *to suck*, LkR 11²⁷.

dēwig=dēawig

dīacon (ǣ) m. '*deacon,*' *minister, Levite*, Æ,BH,Jn. [L. diaconus]

dīacongegyrela m. *deacon's robe*, BH 90².

dīaconhād m. *office of a deacon*, ÆH.

dīaconrocc m. *dalmatic*, CM 723.

dīaconðēnung f. *office of a deacon*, BH 272¹⁷.

dīan (A)=dēon

dīc mf. '*dike,*' *trench, ditch, moat*, AO,BH, Chr,Ct; Æ; Mdf : *an earthwork with a trench.*

+dīcan=+dīcian

dīcere m. *digger*, WW 149¹⁶. ['*diker*']

±dīcian *to make a dike or bank*, BH. ['*dike*']

dīcsceard n. *breach of a dike*, LL 455,13. [v. '*shard*']

dīcung f. *construction of a dike*, WW. ['*diking*']

dīcwalu f. *bank of a ditch?* KC5·334'.

dide, didon=dyde, dydon (v. dōn).

diegan *to die*, NR 38.

dīegel=dīegol

±dīeglan, -lian *to hide, cover, conceal, hide oneself*, CP.

dīegle=dīegol

dīegol (ǣ, ē, ēa, ēo, ī, ȳ) I. adj. *secret, hidden, obscure, unknown, deep*, B,DD. ['*dighel*'] II. n. *concealment, obscurity, secrecy, mystery* : *hidden place, grave.*

dīegolful (ē¹) *mysterious*, RD 80¹⁴.

±dīegollīce (ē, ēa, ēo, ī, ȳ) *secretly*, AO,CP : *softly (of the voice)*, ÆP 28.

dīegolnes f. (ē, ī, īo, ȳ) *privacy, secrecy, solitude*, CP : *secret, secret thought, mystery*, Æ,AO,CP : *hiding-place, recess*, Æ.

dielf=dealf pret. 3 sg. of delfan.

dielgian=dīlegian

diend m. *suckling*, NG. [dēon]

dīere (ȳ) '*dear,*' *beloved*, Lk : *precious, costly*, AO : *noble, excellent.*

±diernan (e, y) *to keep secret, hide, restrain, repress*, Æ,AO : *hide oneself.* ['*dern*']

dierne (æ, e, y) I. *hidden, secret, obscure, remote*, B,El,Lk,Ps; CP : *deceitful, evil, magical*, B,CP,Gen. ['*dern*'] For comps. v. dyrne-. II. (y) n. *secret*, GnE. ['*dern*']

dīerra comp. of dīere, dēore.

dīgan=dēagian

+dīgan (ē, ȳ;=īe) *to endure, survive, overcome* : *escape* : *profit*, LCD.

dīgel=dīegol (wk. dīgla, dīgle).

dīgl-, dīhl-=dīegl-, dīegol-

digner=dīnor

dīgol, dīgul=dīegol

dihnian=dihtian

diht n. *arrangement, disposal, deliberation, purpose*, Æ : *administration, office* : *direction, command, prescription*, Æ : *conduct*, Æ : (+) *piece of writing, composition, literary work.*

±dihtan, dihtian *to arrange, dispose, appoint, direct, dictate, impose*, Æ,G : *compose, write*, Æ : *make, do.* ['*dight*']

dihtere m. *informant, expositor*, WW : *steward*, Æ (=dihtnere) : *one who dictates*, Guth. ['*dighter*']

dihtfæstendæg m. *appointed fast*, Swt (? for riht-).

dihtig=dyhtig

dihtnere m. *manager, steward*, ÆH 2·344[5].

dihtnian=dihtian

±**diht-nung**, -ung f. *ordering, disposition*.

dile m. *'dill,' anise, Gl,Mt,Lcd*; CP.

±**dīlegian** *to destroy, blot out, CP* : *perish*, LL. [*'dilghe'*]

dīlemengan v. for-d.

dilfō pres. 3 sg. of delfan.

dīlgian (CP)=dīlegian

dīlignes f. *annihilation, destruction*, GL.

dill, dim=dile, dimm

dimhīw *of dark colour*, DD 106.

dim-hof n., -hofe f. *place of concealment*, Æ.

dimhūs n. *prison*, OEG.

dimlic (y) *dim, obscure, secret, hidden*, Æ.

dimm *'dim,' dark, gloomy, obscure, Bo,Gen, Sat* : *blurred, faint, MH* : *wicked* : *wretched, grievous*.

dimmian *to be or become dim*, LCD.

dimnes (y) f. *'dimness,' darkness, obscurity, gloom, Lcd,VPs*; Æ : *evil* : *obscuration, moral obliquity*, LL 476,14 : *a dark place*.

dimscūa m. *darkness, sin?* AN 141.

dincge=dyncge; **dīner**=dīnor

ding I. v. dung I. II.=dung II.

dinglung f. *manuring, WW* 104[8]. [v. *'dung'*]

dīnig? (A 8·450)=dung

dīnor m. *a piece of money*, ÆGR. [*L*.denarius]

dīo-=dēo-; **dīowl-** (NG)=dēofol-

dippan=dyppan

dirige *dirge, 'vigilia,'* CM 433,444.

dīrling (CP)=dēorling

dirn-=diern-, dyrn-; **dis-**=dys-

disc m. *'dish,' plate, bowl, Gl,Mt.*

discberend m. *dish-bearer, seneschal*, WW.

discipul m. *'disciple,' scholar, BH,MtL.*

discipula *female disciple*, BH 236[34].

discipulhād m. *'disciplehood,' BH* 362.

disc-ðegn, -ðēn m. *dish-servant, waiter, seneschal, steward*, Æ.

disg, disig=dysig

dism (ðism) m. *'vapor,' 'fumus,'* ES 41·324.

disma m., disme f. *musk*, OEG 46[6] (A 30·123) : *'cassia,'* Ps 44[9] (y).

distæf m. *'distaff,' WW*; Æ.

dīō-=dēō-

dīwl-=dēofol; **dob-**=dof-, dop-

dix (LL 455)=disc

dōc m. *bastard son*, WW.

docce f. *'dock,' sorrel, Lcd.*

docga m. *'dog,' GPH.*

dōcincel n. *bastard*, GL.

dōefe v. +dēfe.

doeg, doema (NG)=dæg, dēma

dōere m. *doer, worker*, DR 198[6].

doeð-=dēað-

dofen pp. of dūfan.

dofian (dobian) *to be doting*, GL.

dofung f. *stupidity, frenzy, madness*, GL (?+at OEG 418).

dōger=dōgor; **dogga**=docga

dogian *to endure?* RD 1[9].

dōgor mn. (ds. dōgor(e)) *day*, AO,CP.

dōgor-gerīm, -rīm† n. *series of days, time, allotted time of life*.

dōh=dāg; **dohtar**, dohter=dohtor

dohte pret. 3 sg. of dugan.

dohtig *competent, good, valiant, 'doughty,' Chr.* [dugan]

dohtor f. gs. dohtor, ds. dohtor, dehter, .nap. ±doh-tor, -tra, -tru *'daughter,' Mt*; Æ,AO,CP : *female descendant, Jn.*

dohtorsunu m. *daughter's son, grandson*, CHR 982 c.

dohx=dox

dol I. adj. *foolish, silly, Seaf*; CP : *presumptuous*. [v. *'dull'*] II. n. *folly*, CP.

dolc=dalc; **dolcswaðu**=dolgswaðu

dolfen pp. of delfan.

dolg (dolh) nm. *wound, scar, cut, sore* : *boil, tumour*, Æ.

dolgbenn f. *wound*, AN 1399.

dolgbōt f. *fine or compensation for wounding*, LL 62,23[2].

±**dolgian** *to wound*, RD.

dolgilp m. *idle boasting*, B 509.

dolgrūne f. *pellitory*, LCD 25a.

dolgsealf f. *poultice for a wound*, LCD.

dolgslege† m. *wounding blow*, AN.

dolgswæð n., dolgswaðu f. *scar*, Æ.

dolh=dolg

dolhdrenc m. *drink for a wound, antidote*, LCD.

dolhsmeltas mp. *linen bandages*, WW 107[33].

dolhwund *wounded*, JUD 107.

dol-lic *audacious, rash, foolhardy, foolish*. adv. -līce, CP : *bewildered*, BF 144[1].

dolmanus=dulmunus

dolsceaða m. *fell destroyer*, B 479.

dolscipe m. *folly, error*, CP 387[34].

dolsmeltas=dolhsmeltas

dolspræc f. *silly talk*, CP 385[6].

dolwillen I. *rash, bold*, JUL 451. II. n. *rashness, madness*, JUL 202.

dolwīte n. *pain of a wound?* (BTs), *punishment of the wicked, pains of hell?* (Tupper), RD 27[17].

dōm m. *'doom,' judgment, ordeal, sentence, BH,JnL*; Æ,CP : *decree, law, ordinance, custom, Æ,VPs* : *justice, equity, Mt,VPs* : *opinion, advice* : *choice, option, free-will* : *condition* : *authority, supremacy, majesty, power, might, Jn*; AO : *reputation, dignity, glory, honour, splendour*, AO : *court, tribunal, assembly* : *meaning, interpretation*.

-**dōm** masc. abstract suffix=*state, condition, power, etc.*, as in frēodōm.
dōmærn n. *judgment-hall, tribunal*, Æ.
dōmbōc f. *code of laws, statute-book, manual of justice*, Æ,LL. ['*doombook*']
dōmdæg m. '*doomsday,*' *judgment-day*, Mt.
dōmēadig† *mighty, renowned.*
dōmere m. *judge, Bo,LL*; CP. ['*doomer*']
dōmern (Æ)=dōmærn
dōmfæst† *just, renowned, mighty.*
dōmfæstnes f. *righteous judgment*, LPs 100¹.
dōmgeorn† *ambitious : righteous.*
dōmhūs n. *law-court, tribunal*, GL.
dōmhwæt adj. *eager for renown? strenuous in judgment?* CR 428.
dōmian† *to glorify, magnify*, DA.
dōmisc adj. *of the day of judgment*, SOL 148'.
dōmlēas† *inglorious, powerless.*
dōmlic *famous, glorious, praiseworthy : judicial*, Æ : *canonical*, CM 268. adv. -līce.
domne mf. *lord*, CHR : *nun, abbess.* [*L.*]
dōmsetl n. *judgment-seat, tribunal*, Æ.
dōmsettend m. *jurisconsult*, WW 429⁶.
dōmstōw f. *tribunal*, W 148³¹.
dōmweorðung† f. *honour, glory.*
±**dōn** anv. pres. ptc. dō(e)nde, pres. 2 sing. dēst, 3 dēð, pret. sg. dyde, pl. dydon (æ,i), pp. dōn *to* '*DO**' ('*i-do*'), *make, act, perform : cause* (often followed by the inf. with a passive sense—as in hig dydon rīcu settan *they caused kingdoms to be founded*, i.e. *they founded kingdoms*—or by ðæt) : *add* (to) : *put, place, take* (*from, to or away*) : *give, bestow, confer : consider, esteem : observe, keep*: to avoid repetition of another verb, Æ : (+) *arrive at*, CHR : (+) *halt, encamp, cast anchor*, CHR : (+) *reduce*, CHR. d. tō hīerran hāde *promote, advance to a higher position.* d. tō nāhte *annul, make of none effect.* d. tō witanne *cause to know.* betre, furðor, d. *prefer.* +d. forð *manifest, show forth.* d. ūp *put ashore.* +d. ūp *exhume.*
dōnlic *active*, RBL.
dop-ened, -ænid f. *diver, water-fowl, moorhen, coot*, GL.
dopfugel m. *water-fowl, moorhen*, GL.
-**doppa** v. dūfe-d.; -**doppe** v. fugol-d.
doppettan *to plunge in, immerse*, Æ.
dor n. (nap. doru, dor) *door, gate : pass, Lcd, Ps.* [v. '*door*']
dora m. *humble-bee, Ep,Lcd,WW*; Æ. ['*dor*']
dorfen pp. of deorfan.
dorste (Æ,AO,CP) pret. 3 sg. of *durran.
dorweard m. *doorkeeper*, DR,MkRL.
dott m. *head of a boil*, Lcd. ['*dot*']
-**dōung** v. on-d.
dox *dark-haired, dusky, A ,WW.* ['*dusk*']

doxian *to turn dark, VH* (v. ES 43·330). ['*dusk*']
draca m. *dragon, sea-monster, B,MH,Ps : serpent, Pa,Ps : the devil : standard representing a dragon or serpent*, GPH 392. ['*drake*']
drā-centse, -cente, -conze f. *dragon-wort*, LCD. [*L.* dracontea]
dræce (N)=draca
drædan⁷ *to dread, fear*, Sc 67¹.
dræf=drāf; **dræf-**=drēf-
±**dræfan** *to drive, drive out*, CHR.
dræfend I. m. *hunter*, CRA 38. II.=drēfend
+**dræg**† n. *concourse, assembly : tumult.*
dræge f. *drag-net*, WW. [drāgan]
drægeð pres. 3 sg. of dragan.
drægnett n. *drag-net, WW.* ['*draynet*']
dræhð, drægð pres. 3 sg. of dragan.
dræn, drænc=drān, drinc
dræp pret. 3 sg. of drepan.
dræst=dærst
dræstig *full of dregs, rubbishy, WW.* [dærste; '*drasty*']
dræt pres. 3 sg. of drædan.
drāf I. f. *action of driving, Bl : expulsion, LL : '*drove,*' herd, Chr*; Æ : *company, band, W*; Æ : *road along which cattle are driven, KC 5·217⁶.* [drīfan] II. pret. 3 sg. of drīfan.
dragan⁶ *to drag, '*draw*,*' JnL,CP : go : protract*, CHRD 57⁷.
drāgense=drācentse
drān (æ) f. '*drone,*' WW; Æ.
dranc pret. 3 sg. of drincan.
drapa=dropa; **drēa**=drȳ
drēag, drēah pret. 3 sg. of drēogan.
+**drēag**=+dræg
drēahnian (ē) *to* '*drain,*' *strain out*, Lcd,Mt.
dreaht pp. of dreccan.
drēam m. *joy, gladness, delight, ecstasy, mirth, rejoicing, Ct,Chr,Sat*; AO : *melody, music, song, singing*, Æ. ['*dream*']
drēamcræft m. *art of music*, Bo 38⁷,MH 212³⁰.
drēamere m. *musician*, Bo 38⁷.
drēam-hæbbende (GEN 81), -healdende (B 1227) *happy, joyful.*
drēamlēas† *joyless, sad.*
drēamlic *joyous, musical*, GL.
drēamnes f. *singing*, LPs 136³.
drēap pret. 3 sg. of drēopan.
drēap- (VPs)=drēop-
drēariend *inrushing tide?* WW 225¹².
drēarung=drēorung
drēas pret. 3 sg. of drēosan.
±**dreccan** *to vex, irritate, trouble, torment, oppress, afflict*, Æ,Gen,OET. ['*dretch*']
±**drec(c)ednes** (Æ), dreccung (Sc) f. *tribulation, affliction.* ['*dretching*']

drēd=drǣd pret. 3 sg. of drǣdan.

±**drēfan** to stir up, excite, disturb, trouble, vex, afflict, B,Jn; Æ,CP. [drōf; 'dreve']

+**drēfedlic** oppressive, AO 38¹⁴.

±**drēfednes** (ǣ) f. tribulation, trouble, distress, scandal, disorder.

±**drēfend** (ǣ) m. disturber, LPs,RB.

drefilan to 'drivel,' WW.

+**drēfnes** f. confusion : tempest, OEG.

drēfre m. disturber, RB 121¹². [drōf]

drēfung f. disturbance, WW 109².

drēge, drēgan=drȳge, drȳgan

drēhnian (Mt)=drēahnian

dreht pp. of dreccan.

+**drehtnes** f. contrition, BH 424¹³.

drēm-=drȳm-

drenc m. 'drink,' drinking, draught, Æ,Lcd, WW; CP : drowning. ['drench,' 'drunk']

drencan to give to drink, to ply with drink, make drunk, Ps; CP : soak, saturate : submerge, drown, Æ. ['drench']

drenccuppe f. drinking-cup, WW 329¹⁹.

drence-=drenc-, drinc-, drync-

drencflōd† m. flood, deluge.

drenchorn m. drinking-horn, Ct. ['drench']

drenchūs n. drinking-house, WW 186²⁵.

dreng m. youth, warrior, Ma 149. ['dreng'; ON.]

drēocræft (Bl)=drȳcræft

dreofon=drifon pret. pl. of drīfan.

+**drēog** I. n. a dressing for keeping (shoes) in good condition, Æ : usefulness? gravity? RB 123⁶. tō +d. gān to ease oneself, RB 32²². II. fit, sober, serious : tame, gentle (horse), GD 78¹².

±**drēogan²** to lead a (certain) life, do, work, perform, fulfil, take part in, conduct, Gu,Ps; AO. wīde d. wander : be busy, employed : experience, suffer, endure, sustain, tolerate, Ex; CP : to enjoy. ['dree,' 'i-dree']

+**drēoglǣcan** to put in order, regulate, arrange, attend to, Æ.

+**drēoglīce** (h) discreetly, carefully : meekly, modestly, humbly.

drēoh=drēog

±**drēopan²** to drop, drip, PPs. ['dreep']

drēopian (ēa) to drop, drip, trickle, Ps.

drēopung (ēa) f. dropping, VV²Ps.

drēor† m. blood. [drēosan]

dreord pret. 3 sg. of drǣdan.

drēorfāh bespattered with gore, B 485.

drēorgian=drēorigian

drēorig adj. †bloody, blood-stained, B : cruel, grievous, Gu : sad, sorrowful, Æ : headlong? ['dreary'] adv. -līce sorrowfully, Æ. ['drearily']

drēorigferð sorrowful, Cr 1109.

drēorighlēor sad of countenance, WA 83.

drēorigian to be 'dreary,' sad, Ruin; Æ.

drēorigmōd sad in mind, Gen 2804. ['dreary-mood']

drēorignes f. sadness, sorrow, GD; Æ. ['dreariness']

drēorilic, drēorlic=drēorig

drēorsele m. dreary hall, Wif 50.

drēorung† (ēa) f. falling, distilling, dropping. [drēosan]

±**drēosan²** to fall, perish : become weak, fail.

drēosendlic perishable, ByH 130⁸.

drep=ðrep?

+**drep** m. stroke, blow, An 1446.

±**drepan⁵** to strike, kill, overcome, B. ['drepe']

drepe† (y) m. stroke, blow, violent death.

+**drettan** to consume, PPs 70¹².

drī-=drȳ-

±**drif** f. fever, MkR 1³¹; ANS 84·324.

+**drif** I. n. a drive, a tract through which something moves rapidly (BTs), SolK 186. II. what is driven, stubble, EPs 82¹⁴.

±**drīfan¹** to 'drive*,' force, hunt, follow up, pursue, Æ,AO,CP : drive away, expel, BH, Gen,Met,Mk,Ps : practise, carry on, RB ; Æ : rush against, impel, drive forwards or backwards, Cr,KC : undergo.

drīg(i)ð, **drīhð** pres. 3 sg. of drēogan.

+**drīhð** f. sobriety, gravity, LL (314,318).

drīm=drēam

±**drinc** (y) 'drink,' beverage, Bo,Chr,G : draught, Cp,Mt : drinking, carousal. [v. also 'drunk']

drinc- v. also drync-, drenc-.

drinca (m.), drince (f.)=drinc

+**drinca** m. cup-bearer, RWH 39².

±**drincan¹** to drink, Æ,Lk ; AO,CP : be entertained, LL 3,3 : to swallow up, engulf, Æ. pp. druncen refreshed, elate (with drink), drunk.

drincere m. 'drinker,' drunkard, MtL.

drīorig=drēorig

drisne (y) f. 'capillamenta'? v. A 41·108.

+**drītan¹** 'cacare,' Lcd 1·364⁹. ['drite']

drīting f. 'egestio' (sc. ventris), WW ; A 8·449. [v. 'drite']

±**drōf** dirty, muddy, swampy, turbid, troubled, Lcd. ['drof'; drēfan]

drōfe grievously, severely, Lcd 3·286¹¹.

+**drōfednes**=+drēfednes

drōfig troubled, Bas 44¹⁶.

drōflic troublesome, tormenting, Dom 19.

drōg pret. 3 sg. of dragan.

droge f? excrement, Lcd 118b.

drogen pp. of drēogan.

drōgon pret. pl. of dragan.

drōh pret. 3 sg. of dragan.

drohnian=drohtnian

droht I. m? n? condition of life. II. (ō?) pull, draught, WW 486²⁷.

drohtað m. *mode of living, conduct* : *environment, society* : *condition, employment.*

drohtian (CP), drohtnian (Æ) *to conduct oneself, behave, associate with, lead a life, live, continue.* [drēogan]

droht-(n)oð, -nung=droht-að, -ung

±**drohtnung** f. *condition, way of life, reputation, conduct,* Æ,CP.

dronc=dranc pret. 3 sg. of drincan.

dropa m. *a 'drop,' Az,Lcd,Lk,VPs*; AO, CP : *gout? Lcd* : *humour, choler.*

+**dropa** m. *a kind of date,* OEG 474.

dropen I. pp. of drēopan. **II.** (B 2891)= drepen pp. of drepan.

drop-fāg, -fāh **I.** *spotted, speckled,* LCD. **II.** *starling,* GL.

dropian *to 'drop,' drip, trickle, Ps.*

dropmǣlum *drop by drop,* Æ. [*'dropmeal'*]

droppetan, -ian *to drop, drip, distil,* Ps.

droppetung, drop(p)ung (*Ps*) f. *'dropping,' dripping, falling,* Æ.

droren pp. of drēosan.

+**drorenlic** *perishable,* NC 293.

drōs, drōsna (*Æ*) m., drōsne (VPs) f. *sediment, lees, dregs, dirt, ear-wax, WW.* [drēosan; *'dros,' 'drosen'*]

drūgað=drūgoð

±**drūgian** *to dry up, wither,* LRG,Ps. [drȳge]

drugon pret. pl. of drēogan.

drūgoð f., drūgoða m. *'drought,' dryness, WW* : *dry ground, desert, LPs.* [drȳge]

drūgung=drūgoð

druh m. *dust?* SOUL 17.

druncen I. n. *drunkenness, LG,LL.* [*'drunken'*] **II.** pp. of drincan. **III.** adj. *'drunken,' drunk, Sc*; AO.

druncenes=druncennes

druncengeorn *drunken,* HL,RB.

druncenhād m. *drunkenness,* CHR 1070.

druncenig *drunken,* LkL 12^{45}.

druncenlǣwe *'inebrians,'* CPs 22^{5}.

druncennes f. *'drunkenness,' AO,Lk*; Æ.

druncenscipe m. *drunkenness,* HL $12n^{34}$.

druncenwillen *drunken,* CP 401^{29}.

druncmennen n. *drunken maidservant?* RD 13^{1}.

±**druncnian** *to be drunk,* Æ : *get drunk* : *furnish with drink,* EPs 22^{5} : *sink, drown, MtL.* [*'drunken'*]

druncning f. *drinking,* LPs 22^{5}.

druncon pret. pl. of drincan.

drupian=dropian

drupon pret. pl. of drēopan.

drūpung f. *drooping, torpor, dejection,* WYN 59.

druron pret. pl. of drēosan.

drūsian† *to droop, become sluggish, stagnant, turbid.* [drēosan]

drūt f. *beloved one,* DD 291.

drūw-=drūg-

drȳ (ē, ī) m. *magician, sorcerer,* Æ,AO : *sorcery.* [*Kelt.* drūi]

+**drycned** *dried up, emaciated,* AO 102^{10}.

drȳcræft (ēo) m. *witchcraft, magic, sorcery,* Æ,AO : *magician's apparatus,* ÆH $2{\cdot}418^{8}$.

drȳcræftig *skilled in magic,* Bo 116^{3},Ex 7^{11}.

drȳcræftiga m. *sorcerer,* GD 27^{15}.

drȳecge=drȳicge

drȳfan=(1) drīfan; (2) drēfan

±**drȳgan** (ī) *to 'dry,' dry up, rub dry, Bo,Jn*; CP.

drȳge (ī) *'dry,' A,Bo,Mt* : *parched, withered, Lk.* on drȳgum *on dry land.* tō drȳgum *to the dregs.*

drȳgnes (ī) f. *dryness,* Ps.

drȳgscēod *dry-shod,* W 293^{17}.

drȳhst pres. 2 sg. of drēogan.

dryht (i) **I.**† f. (±) *multitude, army, company, body of retainers, nation, people, Ex* : pl. *men.* [*'dright'*; drēogan] **II.** (+) f. *fortune, fate,* OEG.

+**dryhta** m. *fellow-soldier* (BT).

dryhtbealo=dryhtenbealu

dryhtbearn n. *princely youth,* B 2035.

dryhtcwēn f. *noble queen,* WID 98.

dryhtdōm m. *noble judgment,* VPs 9^{17}.

dryht-ealdorman (CHRD), -ealdor (WW) m. *'paranymphus,' bridesman.*

dryhten (i) m. *ruler, king, lord, prince,* Æ,B : *the Lord, God, Christ,* CP. [*'drightin'*]

dryhtenbēag (drihtin-) m. *payment (to a lord) for killing a freeman,* LL 3,6.

dryhtenbealu† n. *great misfortune.*

dryhtendōm m. *lordship, majesty,* AN 1001.

dryhtenhold (i) *loyal,* GEN 2282.

dryhtenlic *lordly* : *divine, of the Lord,* Æ. adv. -līce.

dryhtenweard m. *lord, king,* DA 535.

dryhtfolc† n. *people, troop, Ex.* [*'drightfolk'*]

dryhtgesīð m. *retainer, warrior,* FIN 44.

dryhtgestrēon n. *princely treasure,* RD 18^{3}.

dryhtguma m. †*warrior, retainer, follower, man* : *bridesman.*

dryhtin-=dryhten-

dryhtlēoð n. *national song, hymn,* EL 342.

dryhtlic (i) *lordly, noble, B,Gen.* d. gebed *the Lord's Prayer.* [*'drightlike'*] adv. -līce.

dryhtmann m. *bridesman,* GL.

dryhtmāðm m. *princely treasure,* B 2483.

dryhtnē m. *warrior's corpse,* Ex 163.

dryhtscipe† m. *lordship, rulership, dignity* : *virtue, valour, heroic deeds.*

dryhtsele† m. *princely hall,* B.

dryhtsibb† f. *peace, high alliance,* B.

dryhtwēmend, -wēmere (i) m. *bridesman,* OEG 1774.

dryhtweras† mp. *men, chieftains,* GEN.

dryhtwuniende *living among the people,* CRA 7.

dryhtwurŏ (i) *divine,* ÆL.

dryhtwurŏa (i) m. *theologian,* ÆL.

dr̄yhŏ pres. 3 sg. of drēogan.

dr̄yicge f. *witch,* MH 28³ (-egge), NC 282.

dr̄ylic *magic, magical,* NAR 50¹³.

dr̄yman (ē;=īe) *to sing aloud, rejoice,* LPs. ['*dream*']

dr̄ymann m. *sorcerer, magician,* Æ.

±**dr̄yme** (ē), +dr̄ymed *melodious, harmonious, cheerful,* Æ,GL.

drync m. *drink, potion, draught, drinking,* Cp; AO,CP. ['*drunk*'] (v. also drinc.)

drync- v. also drenc-, drinc-.

dryncehorn (i) *drinking-horn,* TC 555⁶.

dryncelēan (i) n. *scot-ale, the ale given by a seller to a buyer on concluding a bargain* (BT). v. LL 2·56.

dryncfæt n. *drinking vessel,* AA 7⁶.

dryncgemett (i) n. *a measure of drink,* CHRD 15²⁴.

+**dryncnes** f. *immersion, baptism,* ÆL 23b, 723.

dryncwīrig *drunk,* WW 437²¹. [wērig]

±**dr̄ypan** (=īe) *to let drop, cause to fall in drops,* Æ,AO : *moisten,* Æ. ['*dripe*']

drype=drepe

dryppan? *to drip* (v. NED '*drip,*' BTs and FTP 214).

dryre† m. *ceasing, decline : fall, deposit.* [drēosan]

dryslic *terrible,* WW 191²⁸.

drysmian† *to become obscure, gloomy.*

±**drysnan** *to extinguish,* NG. [drosn]

+**drysnian** *to vanish, disappear,* LkL 24³¹.

dubbian *to '* dub,' *strike, knight* (by *striking with a sword*), Chr 1085 E.

dūce f. '*duck,*' Ct.

±**dūfan²** *to duck,* '*dive,*' Rd; Æ : (+) *sink, be drowned,* AO,CP.

dūfedoppa m. *pelican,* LPs. ['*divedap*']

dugan pres. 1, 3 dēag, dēah, pl. dugon, pret. dohte swv. (usu. impers.) *to avail, be worth, be capable of, competent, or good for anything,* Chr,MtL : *thrive, be strong : be good, virtuous, kind,* B,Fa,Sat. ['*dow*']

dug-að, -eð, -oð=duguð

duguð fm. *body of noble retainers, people, men, nobles, the nobility,* An,Ex; AO : *host, multitude, army : the heavenly host : strength, power : excellence, worth,* Hy; Æ, AO : *magnificence, valour, glory, majesty : assistance, gift : benefit, profit, wealth, prosperity, salvation,* Cr : *what is fit or seemly, decorum.* ['*douth*']

duguðgifu (a², e²) f. *munificence,* GL.

duguðlic *authoritative, chief, noble,* OEG. adv. -līce.

duguðmiht f. *supreme power,* LCD.

duguðnǣmere m. '*municeps,*' OEG 7¹².

duhte=dohte (v. dugan).

dulfon pret. pl. of delfan.

dulhrune=dolgrune

dulmunus? m. *a kind of warship,* AO 46,80.

dumb '*dumb,*' *silent,* An,Mt; Æ,CP.

-dumbian v. ā-d.

dumbnes f. *dumbness,* NC 282.

dun=dunn

dūn fm. nap. dūna, dūne '*down,*' *moor, height, hill, mountain,* Bl,Chr,Mt; Æ; Mdf. of dūne *down, downwards.*

dūn-ælf, -elf, -ylf f. *mountain elf,* BF,GL.

dūne *down, downwards,* LkL 4³¹. [dūn]

dūnelfen f. *mountain elf,* WW 189⁹.

dūnestīgende *descending,* VPs 87⁵.

dunfealu *dun-coloured,* WW.

dung I. f. ds. dyng, ding *prison,* AN 1272. II. f. '*dung,*' WW.

dungrǣg *dark, dusky,* WW 246⁴. [dunn]

dunh-=dimh-

dūnhunig n. *downland honey,* LCD 132a.

duniendlic (dunond-) *falling down, tottering,* LPs 108¹⁰ (BTs).

dūnland n. *downland, open country,* ÆT, LCD.

dūnlendisc *mountainous,* ÆGR 11¹⁵.

dūnlic *of a mountain, mountain-dwelling,* WW 376⁶.

dunn '*dun,*' *dingy brown, dark-coloured,* Ct,WW.

dunnian *to obscure, darken,* Bo. ['*dun*']

dunondlic v. duniendlic.

Dūnsǣte mp. *inhabitants of the mountains of Wales,* LL.

dūn-scræf† n. nap. -scrafu *hill-cave.*

dure=duru

durfon pret. pl. of deorfan.

durhere (durere) m. *folding door,* GL.

durran* (+in NG) swv. pres. 1, 3 sg. dear(r), 2 dearst, pl. durron, subj. durre, dyrre, pret. sg. dorste (u, y), pl. dorston *to '* dare*,*' *venture, presume,* Æ,AO,BH,Bo,Met.

durstodl n. *door-post,* WW.

duru (dure) f. gs. dura, ds. and nap. dura, duru '*door,*' *gate, wicket,* B,Bl,G,VPs; CP, CHR.

duruhaldend (e²) *doorkeeper,* JnL 18¹⁷.

durustod (WW)=durstodl

duruðegn m. *doorkeeper,* AN 1092.

duruðīnen f. *female doorkeeper,* Jn 18¹⁶,¹⁷.

duruweard m. *doorkeeper,* Æ,JnL (durweard). ['*doorward*']

dūst (u) n. '*dust,*' Æ,Lcd,MH,Mt; AO,CP.

dūstdrenc m. *drink made from the pulverized seeds of herbs,* LCD 114a.

dūstig *dusty*, OEG 15; 3⁹.

dūstscēawung f. (*viewing of dust*), *visit to a grave*, Bʟ 113²⁹.

dūstswerm m. *dust-like swarm*, OEG 23⁵².

dūsõ=dūst

dūõhamor (ȳ¹, o², e³) m. *papyrus, sedge*, WW 135³⁵, 492⁴⁰.

dwæl-=dwel-; +dwǣrian=+ðwǣrian

±dwǣs I. *dull, foolish, stupid.* II. m. *clumsy impostor*, ÆL 23⁶⁹⁶.

±dwǣscan *to put out, extinguish, destroy*, GD,Lᴄᴅ.

dwǣsian *to become stupid*, Æ (6¹⁴⁶).

dwǣslic *foolish*, W. adv. -līce, LL.

+dwǣsmann m. *fool*, ÆL 17¹⁰¹.

dwǣsnes f. *stupidity, foolishness*, Æ.

dwal-=dwol-

dwān pret. 3 sg. of dwīnan.

dwealde pret. 3 sg. of dwellan.

dwel-=dwol-

±dwelian *to go astray : lead astray, deceive*, Æ.

dwellan pret. sg. dwealde, pp. dweald *to lead astray, hinder, prevent, deceive*, Æ,Bo, Rd : *to be led astray, wander, err*, Æ,Mt. ['*dwele*,' '*dwell*']

dwelsian *to wander*, LPs 118¹¹⁰.

+dweola (BH), +dweolsa=+dwola

dweoligan=dwellan

dweorg (e, i) m. '*dwarf*,' Gl. [Ger. zwerg]

dweorge-dwosle, -d(w)os(t)le f. *pennyroyal, flea-bane*, Gʟ,Lᴄᴅ.

dweorh=dweorg

±dwild (y;=ie) n. *wandering*, Bғ 172⁸ : *error, heresy*, Chr. ['*dwild*']

+dwildæfterfolgung (dwel-) f. *heresy*, A 8·450; 13·318.

+dwildlic (y) *deceptive?* W 196²⁰.

+dwildman m. *heretic*, Cʜʀᴅ,NC.

-dwilman v. for-d.

±dwimor (e²) n. *phantom, ghost, illusion, error*, Æ.

+dwimorlic *illusory, unreal.* adv. -līce, Æ.

dwīnan¹ *to waste away, languish, disappear*, Lᴄᴅ,WW. ['*dwine*']

+dwol *heretical*, GD.

±dwola m. *error, heresy*, BH,MtLR : *madman, deceiver, heretic*, Æ,Bʟ : '*nenia*,' MtL p 8⁹. ['*dwale*,' '*dwele*']

+dwolbiscop m. *heretical bishop*, Gᴅ.

±dwolcræft m. *occult art, magic*, Aɴ,Bʟ.

dwolema=dwolma

+dwolen† *perverse, wrong, erroneous*, Gʟ.

+dwolenlic *foolish*, Cʜʀᴅ 115⁵.

+dwolfær n. *a going astray*, RHy 6³⁶.

+dwolgod m. *false god, idol, image*, W 106³⁰.

+dwolhring m. *erroneous cycle*, BH 470²¹.

±dwolian *to be led astray, err, wander*, BH; CP. ['*dwele*']

dwollic *foolish* : *erroneous, heretical*, Æ. adv. (±) -līce.

±dwolma m. *chaos*, WW 378¹⁶.

±dwolman m. *one who is in error, heretic*, Æ,AO,CP.

+dwolmist m. *mist of error*, Bo,Mᴇᴛ.

dwolscipe m. *error*, Bғ 130¹⁸.

+dwolsprǣc f. *heretical talk*, ÆL 23³⁶⁹.

+dwolsum *misleading, erroneous*, ÆT 80¹.

dwolõing n. *imposture, idol : sorcery*, Lᴄᴅ.

dwolung f. *foolishness, insanity*, WW 390³¹.

dwomer=dwimor

dworgedwostle=dweorgedwosle

dwyld=dwild

dwy-mer, -mor=dwimor

dwyrgedwysle=dweorgedwosle

dybbian *to pay attention to*, OEG 645.

dȳdan (=īe) *to kill*, LL 132,1. [dēad]

dyde pret. 3 sg., dydon pret. pl. of dōn.

dyder-=dydr-

dydrian *to deceive, delude*, Bo 100⁵.

dydrin m? *yolk*, Lᴄᴅ. [Ger. dotter]

dydrung f. *delusion, illusion*, Æ.

±dȳfan (=ī) *to dip, immerse*, BH,RD. ['*dive*']

dȳfing f. *immersion*, W 36⁹.

dȳfst pres. 2 sg. of dūfan.

dȳgel-, dȳgl-, dȳhl-=dīegol-, dīeg(o)l-

dyht, dyhtan=diht, dihtan

dyhtig (o) '*doughty*,' *strong*, B,Chr,Gen. [dugan]

dyl-=dil-; +dȳlegian=+dīlegian

dylmengon (=dilemengum? dat. of sb.) *dissimulation*, Cʜʀᴅ 45¹⁰.[cp. fordilemengan]

dylsta m. *festering matter, filth, mucus*, Lᴄᴅ.

dylstiht *mucous*, Lᴄᴅ 26a.

dym-, dyn-=dim-, din-; ±dyn=dyne

dyncge f. *dung, manure, litter : manured land, fallow land*, OEG. [dung]

±dyne m. '*din*,' *noise*, Sat,Sol.

+dyngan (AO), dyngian (WW) *to* '*dung*.'

dynian *to make a* '*din*,' *sound, resound*, B; Æ.

dȳnige f. *a plant*, Lᴄᴅ 113b. [dūn]

dynn, dynnan=dyne, dynian

dynt m. '*dint*,' *blow, stroke, bruise, stripe*, CP,JnL : *thud*, Bo 117³⁰.

dȳp=dēop

dȳpan (ē;=īe) I. (±) *to dip : baptize*, MtR : (+) *anoint*, EPs 140⁵. ['*depe*'] II. *to make greater*, LL 388¹. ['*deep*']

dȳpe=dēop

dyple *double*, Bғ 186¹⁵.

dyppan (e, i) *to* '*dip*,' *immerse*, Lᴄᴅ,Mk : *baptize*, MtR.

dȳr=dēor; dyre ds. of duru.

dȳre adj.=dīere

+dyre n. *door-post, door*, Æ.

±**dyrfan** (=ie) *to afflict, injure : imperil, endanger*. v. ES39·342. [deorfan]
dyrfing (=ie) f. *affliction*, GPH395.
dyrfð pres. 3 sg. of deorfan.
dyrn-=diern-, dern-
dyrneforlegen *adulterous*, LL(144′).
dyrneforlegernes f. *fornication*, BH280³.
dyrne(ge)legerscipe (e¹) m. *adultery, fornication*, JnLR8³.
dyrnegeligre I. (ie, e) n. *adultery*, AO,CP. II. m. *fornicator*, DR107¹.
dyrneleger (e¹) *adulterous*, NG.
dyrnelegere (e¹) I. *licentiously*, NG. II. (RWH78⁴)=dyrnegeligre I.
dyrngewrit n. *apocryphal book*, WW347³³.
dyrnhǣmende (i) *fornicating, adulterous*, WW383⁴⁰.
dyrnlic *secret*, LL. adv. -līce, LCD3·424′.
dyrnlicgan⁵ *to fornicate*, CPs108³⁹.
dyrnmaga m. *president at mysteries*, GPH 397.
dyrnunga=dearnunga; **dyrodine**=derodine
dȳrra=dīerra; **dyrre** v. *durran.
+**dȳrsian** *to praise, glorify, hold dear, prize*, JUD300. [diēre]
+**dyrst** f. *tribulation*, HELL108.
dyrste=dorste pret. 3 sg. of *durran.
+**dyrstelīce**=dyrstiglīce
±**dyrstig** *venturesome, presumptuous, daring, bold*, CP. adv. -līce. [*durran]
+**dyrstigian** *to dare, presume*, BH468¹⁹.
±**dyrstignes** f. *boldness, insolence, daring, presumption, arrogance, rashness*, Æ,CP.
dyrstingpanne=hyrstingpanne
±**dyrstlǣcan** *to presume, dare*, Æ.
dyrstlǣcung f. *courage, boldness*, GD71¹⁹.
+**dyrstlic**=+dyrstig
±**dyrstnes**=dyrstignes
dyru ds., dyrum dp. of duru.
dȳr-wurðe, -wyrðe=dēorwierðe
dys-=dis-; **dyseg**=dysig, dysg-
dyselic (Æ)=dyslic
±**dysgian** *to act foolishly, make mistakes*, Bo; Æ : *blaspheme*, G. ['dizzy']
dysgung f. *folly, madness*, LCD53b.
dysian=dysgian
dysig (e, i) I. *foolish, ignorant, stupid*, Bl, Mt,VHy; Æ,CP. ['dizzy'] II. n. *foolishness, error*, AO,CP. III. m. *fool*, VPs91⁶.
dysigan=dysgian
dysigcræftig? (i¹, ea³) *skilled in foolish arts*, ANS128·300 (BTac).
dysigdōm m. *folly, ignorance*, CM,Sc.
dysiglic *foolish*, VH10. adv. -līce, ·VH10.
dysignes f. *folly, madness, blasphemy*, BH, Mk; Æ,AO : *foolish practice*, NC300²⁵. ['dizziness']
dysigu=dysig II.
dyslic *foolish, stupid*, Æ,CP. adv. -līce.

dȳstig *dusty*, WW517²³. [dūst]
dyttan *to shut to, close, stop*, Lk,PPs. ['dit']
dȳð f. *fuel, tinder*, OEG2⁴³; cp. 1655n.
dȳð-homar, -homer=dūðhamor

E

ē ds. of ēa.
ēa I. f. (usu. indecl. in sg., but with occl. gs. ēas; ds. īe, ē, ǣ, ēæ; nap. ēa, ēan; gp. ēa; dp. ēa(u)m, ēan) *water, stream, river*, Æ, Chr,Ps; AO. ['ea'; 'æ'] II. interj. v. ēalā.
ēac I. adv. *also, and, likewise, moreover*, B, Ep,Mt; AO,CP. ge...ge ēac *both...and also*. nē...nē ēac...*neither...nor even*.... ēac swā, ēac swilce *also, likewise, moreover, as if.* ēac gelīce *likewise.* ēac hwæðre *however, nevertheless.* ēac ðon *besides.* ['eke'] II. prep. w. d. *together with, in addition to, besides.*
ēaca m. *addition, increase, reinforcement, advantage, profit, usury, excess*, Chr,Sol; Æ,AO,CP. tō ēacan (w. d.) *in addition to, besides, moreover*, Bo. ['eke']
ēacan *to increase*, Bo,LL.
ēacen *increased, augmented : richly endowed, strong, great, vast, vigorous : pregnant.*
ēacencræftig *huge*, B2280.
ēacerse f. *water-cress*, Lcd35b. [ēa; v. 'cress']
ēacian *to increase*, CP163,231.
±**ēacnian** *to add, increase, be enlarged : become pregnant, conceive, bring forth*, Æ,CP.
ēacniendlic adj. *to be increased*, OEG1078.
±**ēacnung** f. *increase*, GL : *conception, bringing forth*, Æ.
ēad† n. *riches, prosperity, good fortune, happiness.*
ead-=ed-; **ēad-**=eað-
·**ēaden†** (pp. of *ēadan) *granted (by Fate*, [ēad]
eadesa=adesa
ēadfruma† m. *giver of prosperity.*
ēadga wk. form of ēadig.
ēadgian=ēadigan
ēadgiefa† m. *giver of prosperity.*
ēadgiefu† f. *gift of prosperity.*
ēadhrēðig† *happy, blessed, triumphant.*
ēadig *wealthy, prosperous*, Cr : *fortunate, happy, blessed, perfect*, Gu,VPs; Æ,CP. ['eadi']
±**ēadigan** *to count fortunate, call blessed*, HL : *enrich, make happy.*
ēadiglic *prosperous, rich, happy, blessed.* adv. -līce, B. ['eadily']
ēadignes f. *happiness, prosperity*, Æ.

eadlēan=edlēan

ēadlufu f. *blessed love*, Jul 104.

ēadmēd, ēadmōd=ēaðmōd

ēadmētto=ēaðmēttu

ēadnes f. *inner peace, ease, joy, prosperity,
Run : gentleness.* ['*eadness*'; ēað]

ēadocce f. *water-lily*, WW 116¹⁶. ['*edocke*']

eador=(1) geador, (2) eodor

ēadorgeard m. *enclosure of veins, body?*(GK),
An 1183 (or ?ealdor-).

eaduse (A 10·143⁹⁰)=adesa

ēadwela† m. *prosperity, riches, happiness.*

ēæ v. ēa, eæ-=ea-; eafera=eafora

ēafisc† m. *river-fish.*

eafor I. mn? *the obligation due from a tenant
to the king to convey goods and messengers?*
KC (v. IF 48·262). II. (afer) *draught-horse,*
v. LL 498f and 2·57. III.=eofor

eafora† m. *posterity, son, child; successor,
heir.* [cp. Goth. afar]

eafoð† n. *power, strength, might,* B.

eafra=eafora; eaftra=æfterra

ēagbrǣw m. *eyelid,* Lcd 1·352. ['*eyebree*']

ēagduru f. *window,* MH.

ēage (ē) n. '*eye*,' G,Lcd,RB,VPs; AO,CP :
aperture, hole, Lk.

ēagēce m. *eye-ache,* Lcd.

ēagflēah m. *albugo, a white spot in the eye,*
WW.

ēaggebyrd f. *nature of the eye,* Ph 301.

ēaggemearc (ēah-) n. *limit of view, horizon,*
DD 148.

ēaghring (ēah-, ēh-) m. *eye-socket, pupil,*
Æ.

ēaghðyrl=ēagðyrel

ēaghyll m. *eyebrow?* WW 415²².

ēaghyrne (hēah-) m. *corner of the eye,* WW
156⁴¹.

ēagmist (ēah-) m. *dimness of the eyes,* Lcd
11a.

ēagor=ēgor; eagospind=hagospind

ēagsealf f. '*eye-salve,*' WW.

ēagsēoung f. *eye-disease, cataract,* WW
414¹².

ēagsȳne *visible to the eye,* An. adv. -sȳnes,
Æ.

ēagðyrel n. *eye-hole, window,* BH. ['*eye-
thurl*']

ēag-wærc (y²), -wræc m. *pain of the eyes,*
Lcd.

ēagwund f. *wound in the eye,* LL 20,47.

ēagwyrt f. *eye-wort, eye-bright,* Lcd 117a.

ēah-=ēag-, ēa-

eaht (a, æ, e) f. *assembly, council.* e. besittan
*to hold a council : esteem, estimation, esti-
mated value.*

ēaht=ǣht

eahta (a, æ, e) '*eight*,' B,Chr,Men; CP.

eahtafeald *eightfold,* Æ.

eahtahyrnede *eight-cornered,* ÆH 2·496'.

eahtan† I. *to persecute, pursue.* II. *to
estimate, appreciate.*

eahtanihte *eight days' old (moon),* Lcd
3·178¹⁴.

eahtatēoða '*eighteenth,*' AO.

eahta-tīene, -tȳne '*eighteen,*' Lk (eht-).

eahtatig *eighty,* AO.

eahtatȳnewintre *eighteen years old,* ÆL
33³⁶

eahtawintre *of eight years old,* Æ.

eahtend m. *persecutor,* PPs 118¹⁵⁰.

-eahtendlic v. unge-e.

eahtēoða=(1) eahtatēoða, (2) eahtoða

eahtere (e¹, æ¹) m. *appraiser, censor,* Lcd.

eahteða (AO)=eahtoða

±eahtian (æ, e) *to estimate, esteem,* CP : *consult about, consider, deliberate : watch over,*
Æ : *speak of with praise.* [Ger. achten]

ēahtnes=ēhtnes

eahtoða '*eighth*,' Men; Chr.

eahtung f. *estimation, valuation,* CP :
(+) *deliberation, counsel,* PPs.

eal=eall, æl (LL); eala=ealu

ēalā interj. *alas! oh! lo!* Æ,AO,CP. [ēa II.]

ēalād f. *watery way,* An 441.

ēaland n. *island,* Chr : *maritime land, sea-
board,* B 2334.

ealað v. ealu.

ealbeorht=eallbeorht; ēalc=ǣlc

eald (a) comp. ieldra, yldra; sup. ieldest,
yldest '*old**,' *aged, ancient, antique,
primeval,* Æ,CP; AO : '*elder,' experienced,
tried : honoured, eminent, great.* ða
ieldstan men *the chief men.*

ealda m. *old man,* RHy 6²⁵ : *chief, elder : the
Devil,* Leas. ['*old*']

ealdbacen *stale,* ÆP 31⁷.

eald-cȳðð (AO), -cȳððu f. *old home, former
dwelling-place : old acquaintance,* Æ.

ealddagas (æa¹) mp. *former times,* AO.

ealddōm m. *age,* AO 76².

ealde=ielde

ealdefæder m. *grandfather,* Chr.

ealdemōdor f. *grandmother;* Ct.

ealder=ealdor

ealdfæder m. *forefather,* Æ,B. ['*eldfather*']

ealdfēond (ī)† m. *old foe, hereditary foe, the
devil.*

ealdgecynd† n. *original nature,* Met.

ealdgefā m. *ancient foe,* AO 118³⁴.

ealdgefēra m. *old comrade,* AO 152²⁴.

ealdgemǣre *ancient boundary,* BC 3·546'.

ealdgenēat m. *old comrade,* Ma 310.

ealdgenīðla† m. *old foe, Satan.*

ealdgeriht (a¹) n. *ancient right,* TC 70²².

ealdgesegen f. *ancient tradition,* B 869.

ealdgesīð† m. *old comrade.*

ealdgestrēon n. *ancient treasure,* AO.

ealdgeweorc† n. *old-standing work, the world*, MET.

ealdgewinn n. *old-time conflict*, B 1781.

ealdgewinna m. *old enemy*, B 1776.

ealdgewyrht† n. *former deeds : deserts of former deeds?* B 2657.

ealdhettende mp. *old foes*, JUD 321.

ealdhláford m. *hereditary lord*, AO,CP.

ealdhríðer? n. *an old ox*, LL.

±ealdian (a) *to grow old, Jn,VPs*; Æ. ['*eld*,' '*old*']

ealdland n. *land which has been long untilled?* (BTs), *ancestral property?* (Earle), EC 327¹⁴.

ealdlandrǣden f. *established law of landed property*, LL 448,4⁶ (or ? two words, BT).

ealdlic *old, venerable*, Æ.

ealdnes f. *old age*, Æ. ['*eldness*,' '*oldness*']

ealdor (a¹, e²) I. m. *elder, parent, BH,Gen.* pl. *ancestors : civil or religious authority, chief, leader, master, lord, prince, king, G;* Æ : *source : primitive*, ÆGR. [eald; '*alder*'] II. n. (f?) (†) *life, vital part :* (†) *age, old age : eternity.* on ealdre tō ealdre *for ever, always.* āwa tō ealdre, tō wīdan ealdre *for ever and ever.* [*Ger.* alter]

ealdorapostol (a) m. *chief apostle*, NC,BH 314⁷.

ealdorbana (a¹) m. *life-destroyer*, GEN 1033.

ealdorbealu† n. *life-bale, death.*

ealdorbiscop m. *archbishop*, Æ : *high-priest*, Æ.

ealdor-bold, -botl n. *palace, mansion*, BH.

ealdorburg f. *metropolis*, BH,GL.

ealdorcearu (a¹) f. *great sorrow*, B 906.

ealdordæg† m. *day of life*, B.

ealdordēma† (a¹) m. *chief judge, prince*, GEN.

ealdordēofol m. *chief of the devils*, NC 282.

ealdordōm (a¹) m. *power, lordship, rule, dominion, authority, magistracy, PPs*; Æ, AO,CP : *superiority, preeminence : beginning?* JUL 190. ['*alderdom*']

ealdordōmlic *preeminent*, EPs 50¹⁴ (cp. ealdorlic).

ealdordōmlicnes f. *authority, control*, RBL 68¹².

ealdordōmscipe? m. *office of alderman*, CHR 983 c.

ealdorduguð† f. *nobility, flower of the chiefs.*

ealdorfrēa (a¹) m. *lord, chief*, DA 46.

ealdorgeard m. *enclosure of life, body*, AN 1183? (or? ēador-).

ealdorgedāl† n. *death.*

ealdorgesceaft f. *state of life*, RD 40²³.

ealdorgewinna† m. *deadly enemy.*

ealdorlang *life-long, eternal*, †CHR 937 A.

ealdorlēas I. *lifeless, dead*, B 15. II. *deprived of parents, orphaned : without a chief.*

ealdorlegu† f. *destiny : death*, GU.

ealdorlic '*principalis*,' *chief, princely, excellent : authentic.* adv. -līce.

ealdorlicnes f. *authority*; CP.

ealdormann (o³) [v. LL 2·359] m. '*alderman*,' *ruler, prince, chief, nobleman of the highest rank, high civil or religious officer, chief officer of a shire, Chr*; Æ,AO,CP : as trans. of foreign titles, *JnL,Mt.*

ealdorneru† f. *life's preservation, safety, refuge*, GEN.

ealdorsācerd m. *high-priest*, AN,G.

ealdorscipe m. *seniority, headship, supremacy, sovereignty*, Æ.

ealdorstōl m. *throne*, RIM 23.

ealdorðegn m. *chief attendant, retainer, distinguished courtier, chieftain : chief apostle*, MFH,VH.

ealdorwisa (a¹) m. *chief*, GEN 1237.

ealdoð (ald-aht, -ot) *vessel*, GL.

ealdriht n. *old right*, LL 11,12.

Eald-Seaxe, -Seaxan mp. *Old-Saxons, Continental Saxons*, AO.

ealdspell n. *old saying, old story*, Bo.

ealdsprǣc f. *proverb, by-word*, PPs 43¹⁵.

ealdung f. *process of growing old, age*, Æ,AO.

ealdur=ealdor

ealdwerig (=-wearg) *accursed from old times*, EX 50.

ealdwīf n. *old woman*, GEN 18¹³.

ealdwita m. *venerable man, priest, sage*: BH,LL.

ealdwrītere m. *writer on ancient history*, OEG 5449.

ēales v. ealh.

ealfara m. *pack-horse*, AA 13⁷ and n.

ealfela† *very much.*

ealfelo *baleful, dire*, AN 771 (ælfæle), RD 24⁹.

ealgearo† *all ready, prepared.*

±ealgian *to protect, defend*, Æ.

ealgodwebb n. '*holosericus*,' *all-silk cloth*, WW 395¹⁵.

ealgodwebben *all-silk*, WW 501².

ealh† (a) m., gs. ēales *temple.*

ealhstede† m. *temple*, DA.

ealifer f. *liver-wort?* Lcd. ['*eileber*'?]

ēallðend m. *seafaring man*, AN 251.

eall I. adj. (has no weak form) '*ALL*,' *every, entire, whole, universal, Æ,Chr.* pl. *all men*, Æ. II. adv. *fully, wholly, entirely, quite, Cr,GD,Gen.* e. swā *quite as, just as.* e. swā micle swā *as much as.* mid ealle, mid eallum *altogether, entirely*, CP. ealra swīðost *especially, most of all.* ealne weg (also contr. ealneg) *always.* ofer e. (neut.) *everywhere, into all parts.* III. n. *all, everything*, Æ.

ealla=gealla

eallbeorht† (æl-) all-bright, resplendent, Sat. [v. 'all']

eallcræftig† (æl-) all-powerful.

eallencten m. season of Lent, RB66[5].

eallenga=eallunga

ealles, ealle adv. (g. of eall) entirely, wholly, fully, quite. e. for swīðe altogether, utterly.

eallgelēaflic universally believed, catholic, BH (Sch) 648[3].

eallgōd all-good, ÆT65.

eallgrēne all-green, green, An : young, fresh, RV²Ps 127[3]. [v. 'all']

eallgylden (æl-) all-golden, B,CP 169[21].

eallhālgung f. consecration, A41·106.

eallhālig 'all-holy,' Met; PPs131[8].

eallhwīt entirely of white, C†.

eallic universal, catholic, GD.

eallinga=eallunga

ealliren entirely of iron, B2338.

eallīsig all-icy, very cold, Bo,MET.

eallmægen† n. utmost effort, MET.

eallmæst (al-, æl-) adv. nearly all, 'almost,' for the most part, Æ,Chr.

eallmiht f. omnipotence, PPs 135[12].

eallmihtig=ælmihtig

eallnacod entirely naked, GEN 871.

eallneg=ealneg

eallnīwe quite new, Æ. [v. 'all']

eallnunge=eallunga

ealloffrung f. holocaust, WW 130[12] (eal-).

eallreord=elreord

eallrihte adv. just, exactly, RB 131[13].

eallseolcen entirely made of silk, GL.

eallswā just as, even as, 'as,' as if, so as, likewise, Æ,Mt.

eallswilc just such, Æ,CHR.

ealltela adv. quite well, GEN 1905.

eallunga adv. altogether, entirely, utterly, quite, indeed, Æ,Bo,Mt; CP. ['allinge']

eallwealda† I. all-ruling, almighty. II. m. God, the Almighty.

eallwealdend (alw-) m. ruler of all, Hu; ÆL. ['all-wielding']

eallwealdende (alw-) 'all-wielding,' all-ruling, Æ.

eallwihta† (æl-) fp. all creatures, W.

eallwriten adj. holograph, WW 463[28].

eallwundor n. marvel, Ex578.

ealm-=eallm-; ealmihtig=ælmihtig

ealneg (AO,CP), ealneweg, ealnuweg, ealnig, ealning(a) always, quite, perpetually.

ealnunga=eallunga; ealo=ealu

ealoffrung f. holocaust, WW 130[12].

ēalond=ēaland; ealoð (AO) v. ealu.

ealsealf f.' ambrosia,' an aromatic plant (BT).

ealswā=eallswā; ealtēawe=æltēawe

ealu (ealo) m? n? gds. ealoð (AO), ealað; gp. ealeða 'ale,' beer, Æ,Lcd. [v. A27·495]

ealubenc† f. 'ale-bench,' B.

ealuclyfa m. beer-cellar, OEG 4[42].

ealufæt n. ale-vat, LCD 53b.

ealugafol n. tax or tribute paid in ale, LL 448.

ealugāl drunk with ale, GEN 2408.

ealugālnes f. drunkenness, MFH 94[1].

ealugeweorc (o²) n. brewing, AO 222[7].

ealuhūs (a²) n. alehouse, LL 228,1[2].

ealumalt (alo-) n. malt for brewing, LCD 157a.

ealuscerwen f. (ale-deprival), deprival of joy, distress, mortal panic? B770.

ealuscop m. singer in alehouses, LL.

ealusele m. alehouse, AB34·10.

ealuwæge† n. ale-flagon, ale-can, B. [v. 'ale']

ealuwosa (o²) m. ale-tippler, WY49.

ealw-=eallw-; eam (VPs)=eom (v. wesan).

ēam I. m. uncle (usu. maternal; paternal uncle=fædera), Æ,B; AO. ['eme'] II. dp. of ēa.

+ēane yeaning, GEN 33[13].

±ēanian to bring forth young (usu. lambs), LPs 77[71]. ['ean']

ēaōfer m. river-bank, MET 19[22].

eapel, eapl=æppel; eappul-=æppel-

ear 'occa,' harrow? OEG 2359 (v. A36·72).

ēar I. n. 'ear' (of corn), Cp,Mt; AO. II. (ǣ)† m. wave, sea, ocean. III.† m. earth : name of the rune for ēa. IV.=ǣr. V.=ēare

ēar- v. ār-

ēaracu f. river bed, KC5·122[15].

earan-=earon; earb-=earf-

ēarblæd (ē¹) n. stalk, blade (of corn), straw.

earc, earce (a, æ, e) f. chest, coffer, Rd : 'ark,' Mt,Ps; CP. [L.]

ēarclænsend m. little finger, WW 265[1].

earcnanstān=eorcnanstān

ēarcoðu f. 'parotis,' a tumour near the ears, WW 113[31].

eard m. native place, country, region, dwelling-place, estate, cultivated ground, B,Ps; Æ,AO,CP : earth, land : condition, fate, †Hy. ['erd']

eardbegenga m. inhabitant, LPs.

eardbegengnes f. habitation, RLPs.

eardeswrǣcca (LPs 118[19])=eardwrecca

eardfæst settled, abiding, AO.

eardgeard† m. place of habitation, world.

eardgyfu f. gift from one's homeland, PPs 71[10].

±eardian tr. and intr. to inhabit, dwell, abide, live, AO,B,G; Æ,CP. ['erde']

eardiend m. dweller, GD.

eardiendlic habitable, BH 366[10].

eardland n. native land, PPs 134[12].

eardlufe f. dear home? B693.

eardrīce n. habitation, GU 825.

eardstapa m. *wanderer*, WA 6.

eardstede m. *habitation*, PH 195.

±eardung f. *living* : *abode, tabernacle, Ps.* ['*erding*']

eardungburg f. *city of habitation*, Ex 1¹¹.

eardunghūs n. *tabernacle, habitation*, GD.

eardungstōw f. *tabernacle, habitation, Mt*; CP. ['*erdingstow*']

eardweall m. *land-rampart, bulwark*, B 1224?

eardwīc† n. *dwelling.*

eardwrecca m. *exile*, LL 51n5.

eardwunung f. *dwelling in one's own country*, W 120¹³.

ēare n. '*ear,*' *Mt,Rd,VPs*; Æ,CP.

ēarede *having a handle*, WW 122⁸⁹.

ēarefinger m. *little finger, ÆGr*; WW. ['*earfinger*']

ēarelipprica=ēarliprica

earendel (eo) m. *dayspring, dawn, ray of light*, Bl,Cr.

earfað-=earfoð-

earfe, earbe f? *tare*, Lcd. [*L.* ervum]

earfed-=(1) earfoð-; (2) yrfe-

earfeð=earfoð

ēarfinger=ēarefinger; earfod-=earfoð-

earfoðcierre (að-) *hard to convert*, MH 112²⁰.

earfoðcynn n. *depraved race*, PPs 77¹⁰.

earfoðdǣde *difficult*, CP 147¹².

earfoðdæg m. *day of tribulation*, PPs 76².

earfoðe I. n. *hardship, labour, trouble, difficulty, suffering, torment, torture*, AO,CP. [*Ger.* arbeit] II. adj. *hard, difficult, troublesome, Æ,Bo.* ['*arveth*'] III. adv. *with difficulty.*

earfoðfēre *difficult to pass through*, AS 44²⁵.

earfoðfynde *hard to find*, ÆL 23⁸². [cp. ēaðfynde]

earfoðhāwe *difficult to be seen*, Met.

earfoðhwīl f. *hard time*, Seaf 3.

earfoðhylde *dissatisfied*, ÆH 1·400¹.

±earfoðian *to trouble*, Ps.

earfoðlǣre *hard to teach*, GD 110¹⁹ : *undisciplined*, Chrd 18⁶.

earfoðlǣte *hard to discharge*, WW 113²⁰.

earfoðlic *difficult, full of hardship, Æ.* ['*arvethlich*'] adv. -līce *with difficulty, painfully, reluctantly, hardly, scarcely, Mt.* ['*arvethliche*']

earfoðlicnes (Æ)=earfoðnes

earfoðmæcg† m. *sufferer.*

earfoðnes f. *difficulty, hardship, trouble, affliction, pain, misfortune, Æ.* ['*arvethness*']

earfoðrecce *hard to relate*, W 22¹⁴.

earfoðrihte *hard to correct, incorrigible*, Chrd 42¹.

earfoðrīme *hard to enumerate*, Bo 1⁷.

earfoðsǣlig *unhappy, unfortunate*, Cra 8.

earfoðsīð† m. *troublesome journey* : *misfortune.*

earfoðtǣcne *difficult to be shown*, Met 20¹⁴⁷.

earfoððrāg f. *sorrowful time*, B 283.

earfoðwylde *hard to subdue*, Lcd 3·436¹².

earg (earh) *slothful, sluggish, Gn : cowardly, BH; AO : craven, vile, wretched, useless, MtL.* ['*argh*'] adv. earge.

eargēat=earngēat

ēargebland† (ār-) n. *wave-blend, surge.*

ēargespeca m. *whisperer, privy councillor*, WW 351². [=-spreca]

±eargian (i, y) *to shun, fear, turn coward, Æ : terrify.*

earglic *slothful, shameful, bad, Æ.* adv. -līce. *timidly, fearfully? Gen* 20⁴ : *basely*, Chr 1086. ['*arghly*']

eargnes (arog-) f. *licentiousness*, MkR 8³⁸.

ēargrund m. *bottom of the sea*, Az 40.

eargscipe m. *idleness, cowardice* : *profligacy.*

earh I. f. '*arrow,*' *An,LL.* =earg

earhfaru f.† *flight, or shooting, of arrows.*

ēarhring m. '*ear-ring,*' Æ; WW.

ēarisc (ǣ, ēo) f. *rush, reed, flag*, Gl,Lcd. [ēa]

ēarlð m. *water-stream*, Guth 20⁵.

ēarlæppa m. *external ear*, WW 157. ['*earlap*']

ēarliprica m. *flap of the ear, external ear*, NG.

ēarlocc m. *lock of hair over the ear*, WW 152³⁰.

earm (a) I. m. '*arm*' (of the body, sea, etc.), *AO,LkL : foreleg, Æ : power, Jn.* II. *poor, wretched, pitiful, destitute, miserable, Chr, Mk; Æ,CP.* ['*arm*']

earm-bēag, -bēah m. *bracelet*, B,Gl.

earmcearig† *full of sorrows.*

earme adv. *miserably, badly*, Gen.

earmella m. *sleeve*, RB 136²³.

earmful *wretched, miserable*, Lcd 3·440' : *poor in spirit, humble*, VH 10.

earmgegirela m. *bracelet*, WW 386¹³.

earmheort *humble, poor in spirit*, CP 209² : *tender-hearted, merciful.*

earmhrēad f. *arm-ornament*, B 1194.

earmian *to pity, commiserate*, Chr,HL.

earming m. *poor wretch, Æ.* ['*arming*']

earmlic *miserable, pitiable, mean, Met.* adv. -līce, BH. ['*armlich(e)*']

earmscanca m. *arm-bone*, LL 82,55.

earmsceapen *unfortunate, miserable.*

earmslīfe f. *sleeve*, RBL 93⁹.

earmstoc n. *sleeve*, IM 128¹¹⁰.

earmstrang *strong of arm, muscular*, WW 158⁷.

earmswīð *strong of arm, muscular*, WW 435³³.

earmðu f. *misery, poverty, Bo.* ['*armthe*']

earn I. m. *eagle, El,Mt; Æ.* ['*erne*'] II.= ærn. III.=arn (v. iernan).

earnan (VPs)=ǣrnan

earncynn n. *eagle tribe*, Lev 11[13].

earn-gēap (v. AB 19·164), -gēat, -gēot f. *vulture*, Gl.

±**earnian** (a) (w. g. a.) *to 'earn,' merit, win*, Ct : *labour for*, Bo,Gu.

earningland n. *land earned or made freehold* (=bōcland; BT), Ct.

earnung f. *merit, reward, consideration, pay*, Æ : *labour*, Bo 52[20].

earo=gearo

earon (VPs)=sindon pres. 3 pl. of eom (v. wesan).

ēaron=gēarum dp. of gēar.

earp *dark, dusky*, RD 4[42]. [*ON.* jarpr]

earpa=hearpa

ēarplætt m. *box or blow on the ear*, ÆH 2·248'.

±**ēarplætt(ig)an** *to box the ears, buffet*, ÆH, RWH 137[25].

ēar-prēon, -ring m. *ear-ring*, Æ.

earre (N)=ierre

ears (æ) m. *fundament, buttocks*, WW. ['*arse*']

ēarscripel (ēo[1], y[2]) m. *little finger*, Gl.

ēarsealf f. *ear-salve*, Lcd.

earsendu np. *buttocks*, WW.

earsgang (ars-) m. *privy*, Lcd,OEG : *excrement*, Lcd : '*anus*' (BT).

ēarslege m. *a blow that strikes off an ear*, LL 20,46.

earsling *backwards*, Ps. ['*arselings*']

earslȳra? m? *buttocks, breech*, Æ. [līra]

earsode '*tergosus*,' WW. ['*arsed*']

ēarspinl f. *ear-ring*, KGl 960.

earsðerl n. '*anus*,' WW 160[1].

eart 2 sg. of eom pres. of wesan.

earð I.=eorð, yrð. II.=eart

ēarðan=ǣr ðam (v. ǣr II.).

earðe (N)=eorðe

ēarðyrel n. '*fistula, arteria*,' *ear-passage?* (BT),WW 238[29]. [or=ears-ðyrel, -ðerl?]

earu=gearu; **earun** (VPs)=earon

ēarwærc n. *ear-ache*, Lcd 14b.

ēarwela (ā[1]) m. *watery realm*, An 855.

earwian (APs 22[5])=gearwian

ēarwicga (ēo) m. '*earwig*,' Lcd,WW.

earwunga *gratuitously* : *without a cause*, PPs.

ēarȳð (ā[1]) f. *wave of the sea*, An 535.

ēas v. ēa.

ēase '*caucale*' (*caucalia?*), *lipped vessel, beaker*, WW 202[1] (v. IF 48·266).

ēaspring=ǣspryng

ēast I. adj. comp. ēast(er)ra, sup. ēastmest, ēastemest *east, easterly*. II. adv. *eastwards, in an easterly direction, in or from the east*, BH,Gen,Met. ['*east*']

ēastæð (e[2]) n. *river-bank, sea-shore*, Ma 63.

ēastan, ēastane *from the east, easterly*, AO. ['*east*']

ēastannorðan *from the north-east*, WW.

ēastannorðanwind m. *north-east wind*, WW 364[5].

ēastansūðan *from the south-east*, WW 3[4].

ēastansūðanwind m. *south-east wind*, WW 144[3].

ēastanwind (e[2]) m. '*east wind*,' WW 143[36].

ēastcyning m. *eastern king*, AO 148[35].

ēastdǣl m. *eastern quarter, the East*, Æ,AO.

ēaste f. *the East*, OEG 1894.

ēastemest (AO) v. ēast.

ēastende m. '*east-end*,' *east quarter*, Chr; AO,LV.

ēastene=ēastane

Eastengle mpl. *the East-Anglians* : *East Anglia*.

Easterǣfen m. *Easter-eve*, BH,Chr.

Easterdæg m. *Easter-day, Easter Sunday, day of the Passover*, Æ. on ðōran Easter-dæge *on Easter Monday*, Chr 1053c.

Easterfæsten n. *Easter-fast, Lent*, BH,Chr.

Easterfeorm f. *feast of Easter*, LL 450,452'.

Easterfrēolsdæg m. *the feast day of the Passover*, Jn 13[1].

Eastergewuna m. *Easter custom*, ÆL 23b[643].

Easterlic *belonging to Easter, Paschal*, Lk. ['*Easterly*']

Eastermōnað m. *Easter-month, April*, Men, MH.

Easterne *east, 'eastern,' oriental*, Æ,Gen, WW.

Easterniht f. *Easter-eve*, Hell 15; MP 1·611'.

ēasterra v. ēast.

Eastersunnandæg (tor) m. *Easter Sunday*, W 222[21].

Eastersymbel (tro) n. *Passover*, Jn 19[42] (mg).

Eastertīd f. *Easter-tide, Paschal season*, Æ.

Easterðēnung f. *Passover*, Mt 26[19]. [v. '*theine*']

Easterwucu f. *Easter-week*, Guth. [v. '*week*']

ēasteð=ēastæð

ēasteweard (e[2]) *east, eastward*, Mt.

ēastfolc n. *eastern nation*, WW 396[30].

ēastgārsecg m. *eastern ocean*, AO 132[29].

ēastgemǣre n. *eastern confines*, AO 132[29].

ēasthealf f. *east side*, Chr 894A.

ēastland n. *eastern land, the East*, Æ : *Esthonia*, AO. ['*Eastland*']

ēastlang *to the east, eastwards, extending east*, Chr 893A.

ēastlēode mpl. *Orientals*, BH 254[33].

ēastmest v. ēast.

ēastnorð *north-easterly*, AO 16.

ēastnorðerne *north-east*, ApT 11[2].

ēastnorðwind m. *north-east wind*, GL.
ēastor-=ēaster-
ēastportic n. *eastern porch*, ÆH 2·578[12].
ēastra v. ēast.
Ēastre (usu. in pl. Ēastron, -an; gs. -es in N) f. '*Easter*,' *BH,WW* : *Passover*, *Bl*, *Mk* : *spring*.
ēastrēam m. *stream, river*, DA 385.
+ēastrian *to elapse (during Easter)*, W 208[24].
ēastrīce n. *eastern kingdom, eastern country, empire* : *the East*, Æ,AO : *East Anglia*.
ēastrihte (y²) *due east, eastwards*, AO 17[14].
ēastrihtes (ēst-) *due east*, KC 3·449'.
Ēastro, Ēastru, np.=Ēastre; Ēastro-=Ēaster-
ēastrodor m. *eastern sky*, PPs 102[12].
Ēastron dp. of Ēaster.
ēastsǣ f. *east sea*, BH.
East-Seaxan, -Seaxe mpl. *East-Saxons, people of Essex* : *Essex*.
ēaststǣð n. *east bank of a stream*, Ct.
ēastsūð *south-eastwards*, AO. be ēastsūðan *to the south-east*.
ēastsūðdǣl m. *south-east part*, BH 264[22].
ēastsūðlang *from east to south*, AO 22[17].
ēastðēod f. *an eastern people*, AA 4[17].
ēast-weard, -werd *east*, '*eastward*,' *Ct,Mt*.
ēastweardes *eastwards*, ÆL.
ēastweg† m. *path in or from the east*.
eata (N)=eta imperat. of etan.
eatan=etan; eatol=atol
ēað (ē, ȳ)=(1) ēaðe, (2) īeð
ēað-bede, -bēne *easy to be entreated*, Ps.
ēaðbe-gēate, -gēte *easy to get*, LCD.
ēaðbylgnes f. *irritability*, NC 288.
ēaðbylige (y¹, e²) *easily irritated*, VH 10, W 253[11].
ēaðcnǣwe *easy to recognise*, ÆGR 147[8].
ēaðdǣde (ȳ) *easy to do*, LCD,W.
ēaðe (ē, ēo) I. *easy*,'*B* : *smooth, agreeable, kindly* : *easily moved*. II. adv. *easily, lightly, soon*, *Met*; AO,CP : *willingly, readily, An*. ē. mæg *perhaps, lest*. ['*eath*'] III. n. *an easy thing*, W 185¹.
ēaðelic (ǣ) *easy, possible, Mt* : *insignificant, scanty, slight, BH*; Æ. ['*eathly*'] adv. -līce (*Lk*).
ēaðelicnes (ēð-) f. *easiness*, WW 400[39].
ēaðfēre *easy for travelling over*, WW 146[29].
ēaðfynde (ē, ȳ)† *easy to find*.
ēaðgeorn (ēð-) *easily pleased*, WW 218[16].
ēaðgesȳne (e¹, y¹, ē³)† *easily seen, visible, Cr.* [v. '*eathe*']
ēað-gēte, -gēate *easy to obtain, prepared, ready, Æ*. [v. '*eathe*']
ēaðhrēðig=ēadhrēðig
ēaðhylde *contented, satisfied*, RB.
ēað-lǣce (ā²), -lǣcne *easy to cure*, LCD.

ēaðlǣre (ēad-) *capable of being taught, instructed*, Jn 6[45] : *easily taught*, CHRD 96[13].
±ēað-mēdan, -mēttan, -mēdian *to humble, humble oneself, prostrate oneself, adore* : *lower*.
ēaðmēde=(1) ēaðmōd, (2) ēaðmēdu
ēaðmēdlīce (ēad-) *humbly*, CHR 1070.
ēaðmēdu, -mēdo (CHR) f. *gentleness, humility*, Ps : *obedience, submission, reverence* : *good-will, kindness, affability*. ['*edmede*']
ēaðmēdum *humbly, kindly*, AN.
ēaðmelte=ēaðmylte
ēað-mēttu, -mētto np. *humility, weakness, impotency*, AO.
ēað-mōd (CP), -mēde *humble-minded, gentle, obedient, Mt,Ps* : *benevolent, friendly, affectionate, gracious*. ['*edmede*']
ēaðmōdheort *humble-minded*, Az 152.
±ēaðmōdian *to humble or submit oneself, obey* : (+) *condescend* : (+) *adore, worship*.
ēaðmōdig=ēaðmōd
ēaðmōdlic *humble, respectful*, CP. adv. *humbly, meekly*, CP : *kindly*.
ēaðmōdnes (ēad-) f. *humility, meekness, Bo*; AO : *kindness, condescension*. ['*edmodness*']
ēaðmylte *easily digested*, LCD.
ēaðnes f. *easiness, lightness, facility, ease* : *gentleness*.
ēaðrǣde (ēð-) *easy to guess*, ES 36·326.
ēaðwylte (ēð-) *easily turned*, OEG 1151.
ēaum dp. of ēa.
ēaw=(1) ēa; (2) ēow V.; (3) ǣ(w)
ēawan=īewan
ēawdnes f. '*ostensio*,' *disclosure*, LL 412,3.
ēawenga (AO)=ēawunga
ēawesc-=ēawisc-; ēawfæst=ǣwfæst
ēawian=īewan
ēawisc- v. also ǣwisc- (but see SF 395).
ēawiscllc *manifest, open*, DR. adv. -līce, BH.
ēawlā=ēalā; ēawu=ēowu
ēawunga (CP,Æ), ēawunge (LG) adv. *openly, plainly, publicly*. [īewan]
ēawyrt f. *river-wort, burdock*, LCD.
eax (æ) I. f. *axis, axle, axle-tree, Bo,Gl*. ['*ax*'] II.=æcs
eaxelgespann n. *place where the two beams of a cross intersect*, ROOD 9.
eaxl, eaxel (æ) f. *shoulder*, Æ.
eaxlclāð m. *scapular*, LEV 8[7].
eaxle=eaxl
eaxlgestealla† m. *shoulder-companion, comrade, counsellor* : *competitor?* HGL(BTs).
eb-=ef-, eof-; ēb-=ǣb-
ebba (æ) m. '*ebb*,' *low tide*, Ma.
±ebbian *to* '*ebb*,' Gen.
ebind (Ln 33[6])=+bind

ebol- (N)=yfel-
Ebrēīsc (e, i) *Hebrew, Bf,Jn.* ['*Hebreish*']
ēc=ēac
ēca wk. m. form of ēce adj.
ēcambe=ācumbe; ēcan=īecan
ēccelic=ēcelic
ece (æ) m. '*ache,' pain, BH,Lcd*; Æ. [acan]
ēce *perpetual, eternal, everlasting, Ct,VPs*;
Æ,CP : *durable,* ÆP 126²⁶. adv. *eternally,*
ever, evermore. ['*eche*']
eced (æ) mn. *acid, vinegar,* Æ. [*L.* acētum]
eced-drenc (LCD), -drinca (VH) m. *acid*
drink, vinegar.
ecedfæt n. *vinegar-vessel,* GL.
ecedwīn (æ) n. *wine mingled with myrrh,*
MkL 15²³.
ēcelic *eternal, everlasting.* adv. -līce, *VPs.*
['*echliche*']
ēcen=ēacen; ecer=æcer
ēcere gfs. of ēce adj.
ecg f. '*edge,' point, B,Lk*; Æ,CP; Mdf : (†)
weapon, sword, battle-axe, B.
±ecgan *to sharpen : harrow, Cp.* ['*edge*']
ecgbana† (o²) m. *slayer with the sword,* B.
ecgheard *hard of edge,* AN 1183.
ecghete† m. *sword-hatred, war.*
ecghwæs? *keen-edged,* B 1459,2778 (Trautmann).
ecglāst mf. *sword's edge,* SOL 150¹⁹,²¹.
ecgplega m. *battle,* JUD 246.
ecgōracu f. *hot contest,* B 596.
ecgung f. *harrowing,* WW 104¹².
ecgwæl n. *sword-slaughter,* GEN 2089.
ēcilm- (M)=æcelm-
eclinga (=ecgl-) *on the edge,* IM.
eclypsis n. *eclipse,* AA 42¹³. [*L.*]
ēcnes f. *eternity, VPs.* ā on ēcnesse *for ever*
and ever. ['*echeness*']
ēcre dfs. of ēce.
ēcsōð, ēcsōðlīce (NG) *verily.*
ed- prefix, denotes *repetition, turning.*
ēd-=ēað-
+edbyrdan *to regenerate,* SOUL 100.
edcēlnes f. *refreshment,* VPs 65¹¹ (oe).
+edcennan *to regenerate, create,* ÆH.
edcenning f. *regeneration,* ÆH.
+edcīegan (ē²) *to recall,* LPs 101²⁵.
edcierr (e, i, y) m. *return,* CP.
+edcucoda (ea¹) m. *man restored to life,* Æ.
edcwic *regenerate, restored to life,* CM 499.
±edcwician (cwyc-, cuc-) *to re-quicken,*
revive, Æ.
edcwide (eð-) m. *relation, narrative,* WW
43.
edcynn-=edcenn-; edcyrr=edcierr
ēde=ēowde; eder=eodor; edesc=edisc
+edfrēolsian *to re-grant by charter,* EC 197n.
edgeong† *becoming or being young again.*
edgift f. *restitution,* TC 202'.

edgrōwung f. *growing again,* WW 149²¹:
edgung=edgeong
edgyldan² (=ie) *to remunerate,* Sc 162¹¹.
edgyldend m. *remunerator,* Sc 127¹⁷.
+edhīwian *to re-shape, conform, reform,*
Sc 58.
edhwierfan (æ) *to return, retrace one's steps,*
RHy,RPs.
edhwyrft† m. *change, going back (to a former*
state of things), reverse.
+edhyrtan *to refresh, recruit,* GPH 390.
edisc (e²) m. *enclosed pasture, park, Ct,Gl,*
Ps; Mdf. [v. '*eddish*']
edischenn (e²) f. *quail, VPs;* ExC 16¹³. [v.
'*eddish*']
ediscweard m. *park-keeper, gardener,* GL.
ediung=edgeong
±edlæcan *to repeat, renew,* ÆL.
edlæcung f. *repetition,* LL (416').
edlæht pp. of edlæcan.
edlæs-=edles-
+edlæstan *to repeat,* ANS 84·6.
edlēan n. *reward, retribution, recompense,*
requital, Bo; Æ,CP. ['*edlen*']
+edlēanend m. *rewarder,* OET 420²⁸.
±edlēanian (ēæ) *to reward, recompense,* Ps.
edlēaniend m. *rewarder,* GD.
±edlēanung f. *recompense, remuneration,*
retribution, GL.
edlēc-=edlæc-
±edlesende *relative, reciprocal,* ÆGR.
edlesendlic *relative, reciprocal.* adv. -līce, Æ.
edlesung (æ², y²) f. *relation, relating,* ÆGR.
edmæle (ē) n. *religious festival,* WW 45⁹.
edmēltid f. *festival time,* TC 158²⁰.
ēdmōd=ēaðmōd; ednēow-=edniw-
edniwan adv. *anew, again,* OEG.
edniwe I. *renewed, new,* Æ. II. adv. *anew,*
again, Æ.
±edniwian (ēo) *to renew, restore, reform,* Æ.
edniwigend m. *restorer,* A 11·115⁹.
edniwinga (ēo², u³) *anew, again,* AA 26³.
+edniwung f. *renewal, reparation, renova-*
tion, Æ,CP.
ēdo (NG)=ēowde; edor=eodor
ēdr-=ædr-; edrec=edroc
edreccan *to chew, ruminate,* WW 533³⁸.
[=eodorcan]
edric=edroc; edrine=edryne
edring f. *refuge?* (GK),SOUL 107. [or? ieðr-]
edroc m. *gullet,* GL : *rumination,* GL.
edryne m. *return, meeting,* ERPs 18⁷.
edsceaft f. *new creation, regeneration : new*
creature, Bo.
edsihð (etsith) f. *looking again, respect,*
WW 43³³.
+edstalian *to restore,* CM 366¹⁵.
±edstaðelian *to re-establish, restore,* Æ.
±edstaðeligend m. *restorer,* Æ.

±**edstaðelung** f. *re-establishment, renewal*, Æ.

edstaðol-=edstaðel-

edðingung f. *reconciliation*, WW 172[40].

+**edðrāwen** *twisted back*, OEG 1062.

ēdulfstæf=ēðelstæf

ed-walle, -welle=edwielle

edwendan *to return*, RPs 77[39].

ed-wend(en)† f. *change, reversal, end*, B.

edwīd=edwīt

edwielle (a, e, i) f. *eddy, vortex, whirlpool*, GL.

edwihte? *something, anything*, GEN 1954.

edwille=edwielle

ed-winde, -wind f. '*vortex,*' *whirlpool*, GL.

edwist f. *being, substance*, Æ : *sustenance, food.*

+**edwistlan** *to feed, support*, LPs 22[2] : *make to share?* 140[4].

edwistlic *existing, substantive*, ÆGR 201[8].

edwīt n. *reproach, shame, disgrace, scorn, abuse, Ps*; AO,CP. ['*edwit*']

edwītan[1] *to reproach, VPs.* ['*edwite*']

edwītful *disgraceful*, GL. adv. -līce.

edwītlan=edwītan

edwītlīf n. *life of dishonour*, B 2891.

edwītscipe m. *disgrace, shame*, WALD 1[14].

edwītsprǣc† f. *scorn*, AN,PPs.

edwītspreca m. *scoffer*, GU 418.

edwītstæf† m. *reproach, disgrace*, PPs.

edwylm m. *whirlpool of fire*, WHALE 73.

±**edwyrpan** (=ie) *to amend, recover, revive*.

edwyrping f. *recovery*, ÆH 2·26[29].

+**edyppol** adj. *that is to be reviewed*, GPH 396.

efe-=efen-

efen (æfen, efn, emn) I. adj. '*even,*' *equal, like, level*, AO : *just, true*, Æ : *calm, harmonious, equable*, CP. on efen v. onemn. II. adv. *evenly*, Æ,Ps : *equally*, Bo : *exactly, just as*, B,Cr : *quite, fully*, CP,Gen : *namely*, Gu,Met.

efen- often=L. con-

ēfen n.=æfen

efenæðele (emn-) *equally noble*, Bo.

efenāmetan=efenmetan

efenapostol (efn(e)-) m. *fellow-apostle*, DR.

efenbehēfe (efn-) *equally useful or needful*, MET 12[7].

efenbeorht† *equally bright*, MET.

efenbisceop (-cop) m. *co-bishop*, BH 112[27].

efenblissian *to rejoice equally*, BH,GD.

efenblīðe *rejoicing with another*, MH 28[8].

efenboren *of equal birth*, LL (256 n 5).

efenbrād *as broad as long*, ES 8·477.

efenbyrde *of equal birth*, ÆL 33[3].

efenceasterwaran mp. *fellow-citizens*, BH 62[20]; GD 205[1].

efencempa m. *fellow-soldier*, Æ.

efencrīsten (em-) *fellow-Christian*, LL. ['*even-Christian*']

efencuman[4] *to come together, agree*, BH.

efendȳre *equally dear*, LL.

efenēadig *equally blessed*, †Hy 8[21].

efeneald *contemporary, coeval*, Æ,Wid. ['*evenold*']

efeneardigende *dwelling together*, CR 237.

efenēce† (efn-) *co-eternal*, CR. adv. B.

efenedwistlic *consubstantial*, ÆH.

efenēhð f. *neighbourhood? neighbouring district?* CHR 894A (v. BTs).

efenesne (efne-) m. *fellow-servant*, DR,MtL.

efenetan *to eat as much as*, RD 41[63].

efenēðe *just as easy*, MET 20[167] (efn-).

efenfela (eo[3]) num. adj. *just so many, as many*, AO (em-).

efenfrē-fran, -frian '*consolari,*' EPs 125[1].

efengedǣlan (efn-) *to share alike*, Ex 95.

efengefēon[5] *to rejoice together, sympathise*, BH.

efengelic *like, co-equal*, G.

efengelīca m. *equal, fellow*, W.

efengemæcca (efn-) m. *companion, fellow, consort*, CP.

efengemyndig *commemorative*, BL 101[1].

efengespittan '*conspuere,*' MkL 14[65].

efengōd (emn-) *equally good*, Bo.

efenhāda m. *an equal in rank, co-bishop*, GD 43[22].

ēfenhālig *equally holy*, BL 45[18].

efenhēafda m. *fellow, comrade*, NC 283.

efenhēafdling m. *mate, fellow*, GUTH 14[3].

efenhēah *equally high*, SOL 85'.

efenhēap m. *band of comrades*, WW 375[20].

efenhemman? *to fetter*, EPs 145[7].

efenheort(e)? -nes? *harmony*, DR (æfne-).

efenherenes f. *praising together*, CPs 32[1].

efenherian *to praise together*, VPs 116[1].

efen-hlēoðor (PH 621) n., -hlēoðrung (WW 213[37]) f. *harmony, union of sounds or voices.*

efenhlēoðrian *to sing together*, NC 283.

efenhlȳte (ē[3]) *equal in rank*, BH.

efen-hlytta, -hlēta m. *sharer, partner*, ÆH.

efenlēðe (ē) *just as easy*, MET 20[167].

±**efenlǣcan** *to be like : make like, match, imitate*, Æ. ['*evenleche*']

efenlǣcend m. *imitator*, ÆH.

efenlǣcere m. *imitator*, OEG 1957.

+**efenlǣcestre** f. *female imitator*, Sc 71[11].

±**efenlǣcung** f. *copying, imitation*, Æ.

efenlang (em-) *equally long : prep. (w. d.)* -lange *along.*

efenlāste f. *the herb mercury*, Lcd. ['*even-lesten*']

efenlēof (em-) *equally dear*, AO.

efenleornere m. *fellow-disciple*, OEG 56[264].

±**efenlic** *even, equal, comparable to, of like age, Cr.* ['*evenly*'] adv.-lice *equally, evenly, alike* : *patiently.*
efenlica (efn-) m. *equal,* MET 20¹⁹. ·
+**efenlician** *to make equal, liken,* BH 372³¹ : *adjust* : (±) *conform to,* AV²Ps 25³.
efenlicnes f. *evenness, equality,* CP,Ps. (ēm-). ['*evenliness*']
efenling (efn-) m. *consort, fellow,* EPs 44⁸. ['*evenling*']
efenmǣre (efn-) *equally famous,* MET 10³².
efenmæssepreost m. *fellow-priest,* GD 283³.
efenmedome (efn-) *equally worthy,* MH 134⁹.
efenmetan⁵ *to assemble together,* EPs 61⁹ : *compare,* VPs 48²¹.
efenmicel *equally great* : *just as much as,* LCD.
efenmid adj. *middle,* PPs 73¹².
efenmihtig *equally mighty,* W 16⁷.
efenmodlice *with equanimity,* OEG 2978.
efenneah adv. *equally near,* Bo,MET.
efenneahtlic *equinoctial,* A 52·190.
efennehð=efenehð
efennes f. *equity, justice, Ps* : *comparison.* [v. '*even*']
efen-niht f., -nihte? n. *equinox* (23 Sep.).
efenreðe (emn-) *equally fierce,* AO 68⁶.
efenrice *equally powerful,* BH 416⁹.
efensacerd m. *fellow-priest,* A 11·7⁴.
efensare (emn-) *equally bitterly,* CP 413²⁹.
efensargian *to sorrow with, commiserate,* Æ.
efensargung f. *sympathy,* GD 180⁸.
efensarig adj. (w. d.) *equally sorry* (*with*), AO : *compassionate,* GD.
efenscearp *equally sharp,* PPs 63³.
efenscolere (emn-) m. *fellow-pupil,* AO 132¹.
efenscyldig *equally guilty,* LL 364,76².
efensorgian (efn-) *to be sorry for,* GD 345¹⁸.
efenspediglic *consubstantial,* BH 312.
efenspræc (efne-) *confabulation,* LkL p11¹¹.
efenstalian *to prepare, make ready, execute,* WW 208²⁶. [=*efenstaðelian]
efensung=efesung
efenswiðe (efn-) *just as much,* CP.
efenteam (efne-) m. *conspiracy,* JnL 9²².
efenðegn (efne-) m. *fellow-servant,* NG.
efenðenung f. *supper* (BT).
efen-ðeow, -ðeowa m. *fellow-servant,* Æ,CP. -ðeowen f. *fellow-servant* (*female*), HL 18²⁵⁶.
efenðrowian *to compassionate, sympathise,* CP (efn-), Æ (em-).
efenðrowung f. *compassion,* Sc 147,148.
efenðwære *agreeing,* CM 32.
efenunwemme *equally inviolate,* LL 250,14.
efenwæge f. *counterpoise,* GL.
efenweaxan *to grow together,* LCD.
efenwel *as well,* LL (324¹). e. and *equally as well as,* AS 61¹¹ (æmn-).

efenweorð *of equal rank* : *very worthy equivalent.*
efenwerod n. *band of comrades,* WW 381¹⁶.
efenwesende *contemporaneous, co-existent,* CR 350.
efenwiht n. *equal, fellow, associate,* CHR,W.
efenwritan (emn-) '*conscribere,*' EPs 149⁹.
efenwyrcend (æ) m. *cooperator,* BH 464²⁵.
efenwyrhta (em-) m. *fellow-worker,* Æ.
efenwyrðe=efenweorð
efenyrfeweard m. *co-heir,* WW; BH. [v '*even*']
efeostlice (CHR 1114 E)=ofostlice
efer, eferfearn=eofor, eoforfearn; **efer** v. yfre.
efern (N)=æfen
efes, efesc f. '*eaves*' (*of a house*), LPs *brim, brink, edge, border* (*of a forest*), *side,* Chr.
efesdrypa=yfesdrype
±**efesian** *to clip, shear, cut,* ÆGr. ['*evese*']
efest (VPs)=æfest, ofost
±**efestan** *to hasten, hurry,* Æ. [=ofestan]
efestlice *hurriedly,* NG.
efestung f. *hastening,* GD,VPs.
efesung f. *shearing, shaving, tonsure, Cp,* WW. ['*eavesing*']
efeta (WW) m., efete (Æ) f. '*eft,*' *newt, lizard,* Æ.
efgælð (OEG 8¹⁶⁸)=æfgælð; **efn**=efen
±**efnan** I. *to make even, level, Rd* 28⁸ : *liken, compare, MtL.* ['*even*'] II.=æfnan
efne I. adv. '*even,*' *evenly, Bo,Ps* : *quite, fully, CP,Gen* : *equally, exactly, indeed, precisely, just, only, simply, merely, B,Cr* : *alike, likewise* : *just now* : *namely, Gu,Met.* e. swā *even so, even as, just as if, when.* e. swā ðeah *even though.* e. tō *next to.* II. (æ ,eo) interj. *behold! truly! indeed!* Æ. [efen] III. f? *alum,* WW. IV.? (æ) n. *material,* DR 116'.
efne-=efen-
efnenū interj. *behold now,* CLPs 7¹⁵.
efnes *quite, exactly,* DD,W.
±**efnettan** (emn-) *to equal, emulate* : *make even, adjust* : (+) *compare.*
efnian=efnan I.
efning m. *partner,* BHCA 194⁴.
efod (RPs 49⁹)=eowd
efol-=eoful-; **efor**=eofor; **efre**=æfre
efsian=efesian
efst-=efest-
eft adv. *again, anew, a second time,* Æ,VPs ; CP : *then, thereupon, afterwards, hereafter, thereafter, Chr;* Æ : *back,* CHR : *likewise, moreover, Mt.* ['*eft*']
eftacenned *born again,* DR.
eftacenn(edn)**es** f. *regeneration,* DR,MtR.
eftærist (ē) *resurrection,* NG.

eftārīsan[1] *to rise again*, VPs.
eftbētung f. *making whole*, NG.
eftboren *born again*, JnLR3[5].
eftbōt f. *restoration to health*, NG.
eftcerran=eftcyrran
eftcneoreso *regeneration*, DR108'.
eftcuman[4] *to come back*, BH,Bo.
eftcyme† m. *return*.
eftcymeð pres. 3 sg. of eftcuman.
eftcynnes (=cen-) f. *regeneration*, NG.
eftcyrran (=ie) *to turn back, return*, Æ.
eftdrægend (? -ðræcend) 'recalcitrans' LkLp3[6].
eftedwītan[6] *to reprove*, MtL21[42].
efter=æfter
eftern? *evening*, LkL24[29].
eftflōwan[7] *to flow back*, HGL418; 462.
eftflōwung f. *redundance*, HGL418[45].
eftforgifnes f. 'remissio,' 'reconciliatio,' NG,DR.
+**eftgadrian** *to repeat*, GD277[1].
eftgeafung f. *remuneration*, DR59[1].
eftgecīgan *to recall*, BH250[21].
eftgecyrran=eftcyrran
eftgemyndgian *to remember*, DR.
eftgemyndig *remembering*, NG,DR.
eftgian *to repeat*, CP421[10,11] : (+) *restore, strengthen*.
efthweorfan[8] *to turn back, return*, BH.
efthwyrfan (i[2]) *to return*, EPs108[14], V[2]Hy 6[15] : *recur*, ÆL23B[613].
eftlēan n. *recompense*, CR1100.
eftlēaniend m. *rewarder*, DR89'.
eftlīsing (ē) f. *redemption*, NG.
eftlōcung f. 'respectus,' *regard*, DR86'.
eftmyndig *remembering*, NG.
eftnīwung f. *restoration*, DR.
eftonfōnd? *receiver*, MtLp16[8].
eftryne m. 'occursus,' *return*, VPs18[7].
eftscēogian *to put one's shoes on again*, CM687.
eftsel(e)nes f. *requital*, NG,DR.
eftsittan[5] 'residere,' ÆGR157[5].
eftsīð† m. *journey back, return*, B.
eftsīðgende *turning back, retreating*, WW 491[19].
eftsōna *a second time*, Mk : *repeatedly : soon after, again, likewise*, Mt. ['eftsoon']
eftspellung f. *recapitulation*, WW491[24].
efttöselenes=eftselenes
eftðingung f. *reconciliation*, DR88[5].
eftwyrd f. *judgment day, resurrection day?* (or? adj. *future*, GK),Ex539.
eftyrn=eftryne
efulsung=yfelsung; **ēg**=īeg
ēg-=æg-, ēag-, īeg-; **eg** v. eg-lā-eg.
-ēgan v. on-ē.
egcgung (WW104[12])=ecgung
egde (OET,Ep)=egðe

ege (æ) m. 'awe,' *fear, terror, dread*, Chr,Ps, MtL; Æ,AO,CP : *overawing influence*, Æ : *cause of fear*, VPs.
egean (WW459[15])=ecgan
egeful 'awful,' *inspiring or feeling awe*, Æ,Bo. adv. -līce.
egelāf? f. *survivors of a battle*, Ex370 (or ? ēgorlāf, GK).
egelēas *fearless*, CP. ['aweless'] adv. -līce, CP.
egelēasnes f. *boldness*, BL85'.
egelic *terrible*, SPs75[7].
egenu f. *chaff, husk*, WW412[3].
egesa m. *awe, fear, horror, peril : monstrous thing, monster : horrible deed*, W281[4]. [ege]
egesful=egeful
egesfullic *terrible*, BH. adv. -līce.
egesfulnes f. *fearfulness, fear*, JPs,LL.
egesgrīma m. *terror-mask, ghost*, GL,MH 54[1].
±**egesian**[1] *to frighten*, AO,CP : *threaten*, OEG2481.
egesig (eisig) *terrible*, SAT36.
egeslic *awful, dreadful, terrible, threatening*, CP. adv. -līce *sternly*, GD59[20].
egesung f. *threatening, terror*, CHRD,RBL.
egeswīn n. *a kind of fish*. v. NC284.
egeðe=egðe
egeðgetigu npl. *harrowing implements*, LL 455,17.
egewylm m. *terrible wave*, PPs106[24].
+**eggian** *to egg on, incite*, MkL15[11].
ēghw-=æghw-
egide I.=ecgede pret. 3 sg. of ecgan. II.=egðe
egile=egle
Egipte (y) mp. *Egyptians*, ÆT.
Egiptisc (y) *Egyptian*, ÆT.
egis-=eges-; **egiðe**=egðe
egl fn? *mote, beard, awn, ear (of barley)*, Lk : *claw, talon*. ['ail']
eg-lā-eg 'euge!' BRPs69[4].
±**eglan** tr. (*Jud,Lcd*) and impers. (*Chr,LL*) *to trouble, plague, molest, afflict*, Æ,CP. ['ail']
egle I. *hideous, loathsome, troublesome, grievous, painful*, RD. ['ail'] II.=egl
eglian=eglan
ēgnes f. *fear*, EPs88[41].
egnwirht 'merx,' EPs126[3] (=gēnwyrht? BT; āgenwyrht? ES38·1).
ēgo (NG)=ēage
ēgor n? *flood, high tide*, WW386[29]; 474[4].
ēgorhere† m. *flood, deluge*, GEN.
ēgorstrēam† (ēa), m. *sea, ocean*.
egs-=eges-; **ēgs-**=ēges-, īegs-
+**egðan** *to harrow*, BF30[17].
egðe f. *harrow, rake*, GL.

egðere m. *harrower*, GL.
egðwirf n. *a young ass used for harrowing?*
(BTac),BC3·367'.
Egypt-=Egipt-
eh=eoh; ēh-=ēag-, īeg-, īg-
eher (NG)=ēar; ehhēoloðe=hēahhēoloðe
ehsl=eaxl; eht=æht, eaht
ēht? (æ) f. *pursuit*, B2957? [=ōht]
ehta=eahta
±ēhtan *to attack, persecute, pursue, harass*,
Æ,AO,CP : (+) *acquire, purchase*, Æ.
[ōht]
ehtefeald=eahtafeald
ēhtend m. *pursuer, persecutor*, AO.
ēhtere m. *persecutor*, Æ,CP.
ēhtian=ēhtan
ēhtnes f. *persecution*, Æ,AO,CP.
ēhtre=ēhtere
ēhtung f. *persecution*, AO274¹⁰.
ehtuwe (RD37⁴)=eahta
ēig=īeg; eige=ege; eis-=eges-
el-, ele- (prefix) *foreign, strange*.
ēl=(1) īl, (2) ǣl; elan=eglan
elboga (Æ)=elnboga
ēlc (NG)=ǣlc; elch=eolh
elcian *to put off, delay*, Æ.
elciend m. *procrastinator*, ÆL12¹⁶⁶.
elcor adv. *else, elsewhere, otherwise, except*,
besides, BH. ['*elchur*']
elcora, elcra, elcran (æ¹) adv. *else, otherwise*.
elcung f. *delay*, Æ.
elcur=elcor; eld=ield; eldor=ealdor
ele mn. *oil*, Lcd,Mt; Æ,AO,CP. ['*ele*'; L.]
ele-=el-
elebacen *cooked in oil*, ÆT.
elebēam m. *olive-tree*, Æ : *elder? privet?*
elm-tree? (GBG),EC379'.
elebēamen *of the olive-tree*, WW128⁷.
elebēamstybb m. *stump of an elder*, EC190'.
elebearu m. *olive-grove*, NG.
eleberge f. *olive*, GD,Ps.
eleboga (WW)=elnboga
elebytt f. *oil-vessel, chrismatory*, WW432²⁵.
electre=elehtre
eledrōsna pl. *dregs of oil*, Lcd1·310'.
elefæt n. *oil-vessel, ampulla*, WW. ['*elvat*']
elegrēofa m. *oil-vessel?* OEG (v. BTs).
elehorn m. *oil-flask*, WW434⁷.
elehtre f. *lupine*, Lcd. [L. electrum]
elelēaf n. *olive-leaf?* Lcd102b.
elelēast f. *lack of oil*, GD44²¹.
elelendisc *strange, foreign*, GL,Ps. as sb.
stranger, exile. [ellende]
elene=eolone; elesdrōsna=eledrōsna
eleself f. *oil-salve, nard*, HGL405.
eleseocche f. *oil-strainer*, WW154¹².
elestybb=ellenstybb
eletredde f. *oil-press*, GD.
eletrēow n. *olive*, GD, Ps.

eletrēowen *of olive-trees*, Swt.
eletwig n. *oleaster*, WW460²⁸.
ēleð m. *allodium, freehold*, Gu38. [=ēðel]
elewana m. *lack of oil*, GD44⁹.
elfen=ælfen
elfetu=ilfetu; elfremed=ælfremed
elh=eolh
elhygd f. *distraction, ecstasy*, GD,Lcd.
ell m. *the letter* l, ÆGR200.
ell-=el-
ellærn (Cp), ellarn=ellen II. and III.
elland† n. *foreign country*, B. ['*eilland*']
elle I. (pl. of *el) *the others*, MtR22⁶. [v
elra] II.=ealle. III.=ellen II.
ellefne (An)=endleofan
ellen I. nm. (always n. in †) *zeal, strength,
courage*, B,Bo,Gu : *strife, contention*, WW
424¹². on e. *boldly*. ['*elne*'] II. n. '*elder*'-
tree, Gl,Lcd; Mdf. III. adj. *of elder-wood*,
Lcd.
ellenahse f. *elder ash*, Lcd121b. [=asce]
ellencræft m. *might, power*, PPs98⁵.
ellendǣd† f. *heroic deed*.
ellende I. adj. *foreign, strange, exiled*. II. n.
foreign parts.
ellenga=eallunga
ellengǣst m. *powerful demon*, B86.
ellengrāfa m. *elder-grove*, BC2·469²⁷.
ellenheard† *mighty, brave, bold*.
ellenhete m. *jealousy*, A11·98²⁶.
ellenlǣca m. *champion, combatant*, WW.
ellenlēaf n. *elder-leaf*, Lcd122a.
ellenlēas *wanting in courage*, Jul. ['*ellen-
laes*']
ellenlic *brave*, Æ. adv. -līce.
ellenmǣrðu† f. *fame of courage*, B.
ellenrind f. *elder-bark*, Lcd.
ellenrōf† *courageous, powerful*, Æ.
ellenseoc *mortally wounded*, B2787.
ellensprǣc f. *strong speech*, Gu1128.
ellen-stubb, -stybb m. *elder-stump*, Ct.
ellentān m. *elder-twig*, Lcd116b.
ellentrēow n. *elder-tree*, KC3·379¹⁵.
ellenðrīste *heroically bold*, Jud133.
ellenweorc† n. *heroic deed: good work*, VH
11.
ellenwōd I. f. *zeal*, PPs68⁹. II. *furious*,
Jul140 : *zealous, earnest*, OEG364.
ellenwōdian *to emulate*, CPs,WW.
ellenwōdnes f. *zeal*, BH,EPs.
ellenwyrt f. *elderwort, dwarf-elder*, Lcd,WW.
ellenwyrttruma m. *root of elder*, Lcd101a.
elleoht n. *elision of the letter* l, OEG5471.
ellern=ellen II.
elles adv. *in another manner, otherwise*, Mt;
Æ,CP : '*else*,' *besides*, Bl,Seaf; Æ,CP :
elsewhere, OEG2²⁵². e. hwǣr, hwergen,
hwider *elsewhere*. e. hwæt *anything else,
otherwise*.

ellicor (CHRD 80²²)=elcor
ellnung=elnung
ellor† *elsewhere, elsewhither, to some other place*. e. londes *in another land*.
ellorfūs† *ready to depart*.
ellorgāst† (æ) m. *alien spirit*, B.
ellorsīð m. *death*, B 2451.
ellreord, ellreordig=elreord
ellðēod=elðēod
elm m. '*elm*,' elm-*tree*, Lcd. [*L*. ulmus]
elm-=ælm-; elmboga=elnboga
elmrind f. elm-*bark*, LCD.
eln f. *fore-arm*, '*ell*' (a foot and a half to two feet), *Mt,WW*; Æ,AO,CP.
elnboga m. '*elbow*,' *WW*(ele-); CP.
elne, elnes ds. and gs. of ellen.
elngemet n. ell-*measure*, GEN 1309.
±elnian *to emulate, be zealous* : *strengthen, comfort oneself* : *gain strength*, LCD.
elnung f. *comfort, consolation*, ÆL 23⁵²⁵ : *emulation, zeal*, Æ.
elone=eolone; elotr, eloðr (GL)=elehtre
elpan- (VPs), elpen-=elpend-
elpend (y¹) m. *elephant*, AO.
elpendbǣnen (elpan-, ylpen-) *of ivory*, Ps 40⁹.
elpendbān n. *ivory*, AA 6¹⁸,GL.
elpendtōð m. *ivory*, WW 397²⁷.
elpent=elpend
elra comp. adj. *other*, B 753. [*el; *Goth.* aljis]
el-reord (BH), -reordig (AA) *of strange speech, barbarous*.
elreordignes f. *barbarism*, GL(Swt).
-els masc. suffix for inanimate things, as in rēcels, wǣfels.
eltst (Æ)=ieldest superl. of eald.
elðēod f. *strange people, foreign nation*, (in pl.) *foreigners, enemies* : (pl.) *all people, all nations*, CR 1084, 1337 : *exile*, AO.
elðēod(g)ian *to live abroad, wander as a pilgrim* : (+) *make strange, disturb*, Sc 106¹⁹.
elðēodgung=elðēodung
elðēodig (æ¹) *foreign, strange, barbarous, hostile*, Bo,*Met* (æl-); AO,CP : *exiled*. wk. form mp. el-ðēodian, -ðēodigan *strangers, foreigners, pilgrims, proselytes*. [' altheodi']
elðēodige (īo) *abroad*, LkR 15¹³.
elðēodiglic (æ¹) *foreign, strange, born abroad*. adv. -līce.
elðēodignes (æ¹) f. *foreign travel or residence, pilgrimage, exile*, AO,CP,CHR.
elðēodisc *foreign, strange*, Mt 27⁷.
elðēodung f. *residence or travel abroad*, BH 332¹⁸.
elðīld-, elðīed-, elðīod-=elðēod-
eluhtre=elehtre; elwiht=ælwiht
em m? *the letter* m.

em-=ef(e)n-, emn-, ym-, ymb-, ymbe-
ēm-=ǣm-
emb, embe=ymb, ymbe
embeht (NG)=ambiht
embehtian=ambihtan; emblht=ambiht
embren (æ¹, i²) n. *bucket, pail*, GL. [*Ger.* eimer]
emdenes, emdemes=endemes
emel=ymel; emer=omer
emleoht n. *elision of* m *before vowels in scanning verse*, OEG 5473.
emn, emne=ef(e)n, efne
emnet n. *plain*, AO 186²². [efen]
emtwā (on) *into two equal parts, in half*, Æ.
-en suffix I. *diminutive* (neut.) as in mægden (from mægð). II. *to form feminines* (a) *with mutation* (gyden, *from* god). (b) *without mutation* (ðēowen *from* ðēow). III. *adjectival, with mutation, denoting material*.
ēn-=ān-, ǣn-; end conj.=and
+endadung f. *finishing*, DR 105¹⁴.
ende m. '*end*,' *conclusion*, Ct,*Met*,Mt,Ps : *boundary, border, limit*, Ps; Æ,AO,CP : *quarter, direction* : *part, portion, division*, Chr; AO : *district, region*, AO : *species, kind, class* : *death*. æt (ðǣm) e. *finally*.
ende-berd-, -bird-, -bred-=endebyrd-
endebyrd f. *order*, MET 13⁴.
±endebyrdan *to arrange, ordain, dispose*, Æ.
endebyrdend m. *one who orders or arranges*, OEG.
endebyrdes† *in an orderly manner, regularly, properly*, MET.
endebyrdian=endebyrdan
endebyrdlic *ordinal*, ÆGR 282¹⁴. adv. (±) -lice *in an orderly manner, in order, in succession*, Æ,CP.
endebyrdnes f. *order, succession, series, arrangement, method, rule*, Æ,CP : *grade, degree, rank, condition*, Æ,CP.
endedæg† m. *last day, day of death*.
endedēað m. *death as the end of life*, CR 1653?
endedōgor† mn. *last day, death-day*.
endefæstend m. *finisher*, DR 27¹⁵.
endefurh f. end-*furrow*, KC 3·384¹⁶.
endelāf f. *last remnant, last*, B 2813.
endelēan† n. *final retribution*.
ende-lēas, -lēaslic (Æ) '*endless*,' *boundless, eternal*, Bo. adv. -lice, Æ.
endelēasnes f. *infinity, eternity*, ÆGR 116¹⁰.
endelīf n. *life's end, death*, EL 585.
endemann m. *man of the world's* (*supposed*) *final age*, Æ.
endemes (Æ,CP), endemest adv. *equally, likewise, at the same time, together, unanimously* : *fully, entirely* : *in procession*.
endemest (ænde-) *last*, MFH 157.

endemestnes? f. *extremity*, RBL33[15] (?= endenēhstnes, BTs).
ende-nēhst, -nēxt (ī, ȳ) *extreme, final, last*, Æ.
enderīm m. *number*, SAT 12.
endesǣta m. *border-watchman*, B241.
endespǣc f. *epilogue*, CM1166.
endestæft m. *end, conclusion*.
endetīma m. *end of life, last hour*, LL.
endeðrǣst (ænde-) f. *end, destruction*, GD 337[9].
±endian *to 'end,' finish*, G; Æ : *abolish, destroy*, Ps; AO,CP : *to come to an end, die*, Gu; AO. [v. also 'yend']
end-lefte (AA16',31'), -lifta=endlyfta
endleofan (e², i², u², y²; o³) num. *'eleven,'* Æ,BH.
endlifangilde *entitled to eleven-fold compensation*, LL3,1; 470,7.
endlyfenfeald *eleven-fold*, ByH36[14].
end-lyfta, -leofta, -leofeða *'eleventh,'* Bl,Mt.
endlyfte *in the eleventh place, eleventhly*, LL182,11.
+endodlic *finite*, Bo44[21].
±endung f. *'ending,' end*, Mt; CP : (+) *death*. ['yend']
endwerc n. *pain in the buttocks*, LCD174a. [wærc]
ened (æ¹, i²) mf. *drake, duck*, Gl. ['ende']
enelēac=ynnelēac
ēnetere=ānwintre; ēnga=ānga
enge I. (a, æ) *narrow, close, straitened, constrained* : *vexed, troubled, anxious* : *oppressive, severe, painful, cruel*. II. (a, o) adv. *sadly, anxiously*.
+enged *troubled, anxious*, WW357[7].
engel (æ) m. *'angel,' messenger*, Mt; Æ,CP. [L. angelus]
Engel=Angel
engelcund *angelic*, Gu72.
engelcynn† n. *race or order of angels*.
engellic *angelic, of angels*, ÆH.
engetrēow=hengetrēow
Englaland n. *country of the Angles, 'England,'* BH.
Englan, Engle mp. *the Angles* (as opposed to the Saxons) : *the English generally*. [Angel]
engellic=engellic
Englisc *'English,'* Ct,LL; CP. on E. *in (the) English (language)*, ÆGr,BH,Mt.
Engliscman m. *'Englishman,'* LL.
engu† f. *narrowness, confinement*.
enid=ened; ēnig=ænig; ēnitre=ānwintre
enlefan=endlufon; ēnlīpig=ānlīpig
enne-lēac, -lēc=ynnelēac; eno=heonu
ent m. *giant*, Æ,AO (v. AB40·21ff).
entcynn n. *race of giants*, NUM13[34].
entisc *of a giant*, B2979.

entse=yndse
enu=heonu
ēnwintre=ānwintre
eobor, eobot=eofor, eofot; ēoc=gēoc
ēode (B,G,Gl) I. pret. 3 sg. of gān. ['yode'] II.=ēowde
eodor† m. *hedge, boundary* : *limit, region, zone* : *enclosure, fold, dwelling, house* : *prince, lord*.
eodor-brecō f., -brice m. *breach of an enclosure, house-breaking*, LL.
eodorcan *to chew, ruminate*, BH346². [=edrocian]
eodorgong (eder-) m. *begging?* (GK) : *robbery?* (Liebermann), CR1676. (v. also BTac.)
eodorwīr m. *wire fence*, RD18².
eodur=eodor; eofel=yfel
eofer=eofor; eofera=eafora
eofermodig=ofermodig
eofet=eofot; eofne=efne
eofole f? *danewort, endive?* LCD.
eofon=heofon
eofor (e¹, ea¹, e²) m. *boar, wild boar*, Lcd,Ps : *boar-image on a helmet*. ['ever']
eofora=eafora
eoforcumbol n. *boar-image on a helmet? boar-shaped ensign?* EL76; 259.
eoforfearn (e¹) n. *a kind of fern, polypody*, Lcd,WW. ['everfern']
eoforhēafodsegn (ea¹) n. *banner with a boar's head design?* B2152 (? two words, Klb. p. 196).
eoforlīc m. *boar-image (on a helmet)*, B303.
eoforspere (u²) n. *boar-spear*, OEG7[56].
eoforsprēot n. *boar-spear*, GL.
eoforswīn n. *boar*, LCD98b.
eoforðring m. (*boar-throng*), *the constellation Orion*, Cp1464 (ebur-).
eoforðrote f. *carline thistle*, LCD.
±eofot n. *crime, sin, guilt*, LL.
eofoð=eafoð; eoful- (A)=yfel-
eofur (VPs)=eofor; eofut (NG)=eofot
ēogor=ēgor; eogoð=geoguð
eoh† nm., gs. ēos *war-horse, charger* : *name of the rune for e*. [Goth. aihwa]
ēoh† [=īw] m. *'yew'-tree*, WW : *name of the rune for ēo*.
eola, eolc=eolh; eoldran=ieldran
eolene=eolone
ēoles gs. of eolh.
eolet n. *voyage?* (Cosijn), B224.
eolh m. [g. ēoles] *elk*, GL : *name of a rune*, RUN15. [OHG. elho]
eolh-sand (-sang, HGL431) n. *amber*, GL.
eolhsecg (eolhx-, eolx-, ilug-) m. *'papyrus,' reed, sedge*, GL.
eolhstede (AN)=ealhstede
eolone f. *elecampane*, GL,LCD.

eoloð=ealað (v. ealu).

eolxsecg=eolhsecg

ᴊeom I. v. wesan. II.=heom, him dp. of
hē, hēo, hit.

eond=geond

eonde?=ende (but v. JAW31).

eonu=heonu

eor-; ēor-=ear-, ier-; ēar-
eorcnanstān (AA), eorc(l)anstān† m. precious stone. [Goth. -airkns]

ēored (o²) nf. troop, band, legion, company :
chariot? AA13⁵. [eoh, rād]

ēoredcist (o², ie³, e³, y³)† f. troop, company.

ēoredgeatwe fpl. military apparel, B2866.

ēoredgerīd n. troop of horsemen, WW229¹.

ēoredhēap m. troop, host, DD113.

ēoredmæcg m. horseman, RD23³.

ēoredmann m. trooper, horseman, BH,WW.

ēoredmenigu f. legion, GD73,74.

ēoredōrēat m. troop, host, RD4⁴⁹.

ēored-weorod, -wered n. band, company,
GD71⁶.

eorl m. brave man, warrior, leader, chief, B,
Cr,Gen,Rd : man : 'earl,' nobleman (origly.
a Danish title=the native 'ealdorman'),
Ct,LL,Ma.

eorlcund noble, LL.

eorldōm m. earldom, rank of an earl, CHR.

eorlgebyrd† f. noble birth, MET.

eorlgestrēon† n. treasure, wealth.

eorlgewǣde n. armour, B1442.

eorlic (1)=ierlic; (2) eorllic

eorlisc of noble rank, LL173.

eorllic chivalrous, manly, B,WW416³³.

eorlmægen† n. band of noble warriors.

eorlriht n. earl's right, LL458,5.

eorlscipe† m. manliness, courage.

eorlweorod n. host of noble warriors, B2893.

eormencynn (y¹)† n. mankind.

eormengrund n. wide world, B859.

eormenlāf f. huge legacy, B2234.

eormenstrȳnd f. race, generation, SOL329.

eormenðēod (y¹) f. mighty people, MEN139.

eorn-=georn-

eornes f. anger, BL123⁸; HL.

eornest=eornost

eornost f. earnestness, zeal, Æ,CP : seriousness, W : battle. on eornost(e) in earnest,
earnestly, truly. ['earnest']

eornoste (e²) I. 'earnest,' zealous, serious,
Æ. II. adv. courageously : fiercely.

eornostlīce I. adv. 'earnestly,' strictly, truly,
in truth, indeed, Mt,LL. II. conj. therefore, but.

eornust=eornost; ēorod=ēored

eorp=earp; eorre (AA37¹⁶)=ierre

eorð=eorðe, heorð

eorð-æppel m. nap. -æppla 'earth-apple,'
cucumber, Æ : 'mandragora,' WW.

eorðærn† (e²) n. earth-house, grave, WW.

eorðbeofung (i²) f. earthquake, AO.

eorðberge f. strawberry, WW242⁶. [berie]

eorðbīgenga m. earth-dweller, BH268³¹.

eorðbīgennes f. agriculture, WW144²¹.

eorðbrycg f. bridge of poles covered with
earth, BC3·223²¹.

eorð-būend†, -būg(ig)end m. earth-dweller,
man, Æ.

eorðburh=eorðbyrig

eorðbyfung=eorðbeofung

eorðbyrgen f. grave, NC284.

eorðbyrig f. earthwork, mound, embankment,
road, Ct,GL.

eorðcafer m. cockchafer, WW122¹⁶. [cea-
for]

eorð-cenned, -cend earth-born, Ps.

eorðcræft m. geometry, OEG3119.

eorðcry(p)pel m. paralytic, palsied man,
NG.

eorðcund, eorðcundlic (CP) earthly, mortal.

eorðcyning m. earthly king, king of the
country.

eorðcynn n. human race, Ex370.

eorðdenu f. valley, NC284.

eorðdraca m. dragon that lives in the earth,
B. [v. 'earth']

eorðdyne m. earthquake, Chr1060. ['earth-
din']

eorðe f. ground, soil, Æ,B,LkL; AO,CP :
'earth,' mould, Gu : world, Æ,B,Mt :
country, land, district, Jn.

eorðen adj. of or in the earth, OEG3312?

eorðern=eorðærn

eorðfæst 'earthfast,' firm in the earth, Æ.

eorðfæt n. earthly vessel, body, SOUL8.

eorðg(e)alla m. earth-gall, lesser centaury,
Lcd; GL. [v. 'earth']

eorðge-byrst, -berst n. landslip, Ct.

eorðgemǣre n. boundary of the earth, PPs
21²⁵.

eorðgemet n. geometry, GL.

eorðgesceaft f. earthly creature, MET20¹⁹⁴.

eorðgræf n. hole in the earth, RD59⁹.

eorðgrāp f. earth's embrace, RUIN6.

eorðhele m. a covering of the ground, Ex16¹⁴.

eorðhrērnes f. earthquake, BL,NG.

eorðhūs n. cave-dwelling, den, ÆL.

eorðīfig (ea¹, ȳ²) n. ground-ivy, Lcd, WW:
'terebinthus,' DR68'. [v. 'earth']

eorðlic 'earthly,' worldly, Bl,Mt; Æ. adv.
-līce.

eorðling=yrðling

eorðmægen n. earthly power, RIM69.

eorð-mata [-maða?] m. 'vermis,' worm, GL.

eorðmistel m. basil (plant), Lcd33a.

eorðnafela (a³, o³) m. asparagus, Lcd.

eorðnutu f. 'earth-nut,' pig-nut, Ct. [hnutu]

eorðreced n. cave-dwelling, B2719.

eorðrest f. *bed laid on the ground*, WW 362[11].
eorðrīce n. *earthly kingdom*, CP : *earth*, Lcd.
eorðrima m. *a plant*, Lcd 120a.
eorðscræf n. ds. -scrafe *cave-dwelling, cavern*, CP : *sepulchre*.
eorðsele† m. *cave-dwelling*.
eorðslihtes *close to the ground*, Num 22[4].
eorðstede m. *earth*, PPs 73[7].
eorðstirung=eorðstyrung
eorð-styren (GD), -styrennes (NG), -styrung (Æ) f. *earthquake*.
eorðtilia m. '*earth-tiller*,' *husbandman, farmer*, Æ(Gen); W 305[31]. [=yrðtilia]
eorðtilð f. '*earth-tilth*,' *agriculture*, WW.
eorðtūdor n. *human race*, PPs 117[22].
eorðtyrewe f. *earth-tar, bitumen*, AO 74[17].
eorðu (N)=eorðe
eorðwæstm f. *fruit of the earth*, BH,LL.
eorð-waran (CP), -ware mpl., -waru fpl. *earth-dwellers*, AO. ['*earthware*']
eorðweall m. *earth-wall, mound*, B,BH.
eorðweard m. *region of earth*, B 2334.
eorðweg† m. *earth*, El,Ps.
eorðwela m. *wealth : fertility*, AO.
eorðweorc n. *work on the land*, Ex 1[14].
eorðwerod n. *inhabitants of earth*, W 25[21]; 203[5].
eorð-westm, -ȳfig=eorð-wæstm, -īfig
ēorwicga=ēarwicga
ēos gs. of eoh.
eosel, eosol=esol
eosen=iesen
ēost-=ēast-; eosul=esol
eotan (VPs)=etan; Eotas=Eotenas
eoten† m. *giant, monster, enemy*. [v. '*eten*']
Eotenas mpl. *Jutes*, B.
eotend=etend
eotenisc *gigantic*, B. ['*etenish*']
Eotolware mp. *Italians*, BH 108[11].
ēoton=ǣton pret. pl. of etan.
eotonisc=eotenisc
eotonweard f. *watch against monsters?* B 668.
ēoðe (N)=ēaðe
ēow I. dat. of gē pers. pron. *to you*, 'you:'
II. interj. *wo! alas!* III.=gīw. IV.=īw. V. m. *sheep*.
ēowā=ēow II.; ēowan=īewan
ēowberge=īwberge; ēowcig=ēowocig
ēowd f. *sheepfold*, Æ : *flock, herd*, Æ.
ēowde fn. *flock (of sheep), herd*, An,Ps. ['*eowde*']
ēowdescēap n. *sheep of the flock*, PPs 64[14].
ēowe I. gs. of ēowu. II.=ēowu
ēowed, ēowede=ēowd, ēowde
ēowende (dat.) '*testiculis*,' LL 64,25[1].
ēower I. gp. of gē pers. pron. (2nd pers.). II. possess. pron. your, *yours*.

ēowerlendisc *of your land*, '*vestras*,' ÆGr 94[1].
ēowestre (ē[1], ēa[1], i[2]) mf. *sheepfold*, GD.
ēowian=īewan
ēowic acc. pl. of ðū (v. gē).
ēowistre=ēowestre
ēowocig '*yolky*,' *greasy with yolk, as unwashed wool*, Lcd 16a (v. NED).
ēowod, ēowode=ēowd, ēowde
ēowohumele f. *female hop-plant*, Lcd.
ēowomeoluc f. *ewe's milk*, Lcd 70a.
ēowu f. '*ewe*,' Æ,KC,LL.
ēowunga=ēawunga
epactas sbp. *epacts*, Lcd.
epistol, epistola m. *letter*, AA.
epl, eppel=æppel; eppan=yppan
er-=ær-, ear-, ier-, yr-
ēr=(1) ǣr, (2) ȳr, (3) ēar I.
erce=arce; ercna(n)stān (NG)=eorcnanstān
eretic *heretic*, BH 312[19]. [L.]
erian, erigean *to plough*, Æ,Bo,Lk; CP. ['*ear*']
erinaces pl. *hedgehogs*, PPs 103[17].
eringland n. *arable land*, KC 6·200[7].
erlung f. *ploughing*, WW 104[6].
ernð (æ) f. *crop of corn*, BHc 44[23].
ersc m? *stubble-field*, EC 282'; 290'.
erscgrāfa *a copse near a stubble-field?* KC 374'.
erschen f. *quail*, Æ,WW.
ēsa v. ōs.
ēsceap=æsceap; esl=eaxl
esne m. *labourer, slave, servant, retainer : youth, man*, CP. [Goth. asneis]
esnecund *of a labourer*, WW 212[44].
esnemon (æ[1]) m. *hireling*, JnR 10[13].
esnewyrhta m. *mercenary, hireling*, GD,LL.
esnlīce *like a man, manfully*, Æ,CP.
esol mf. *ass*, CP. [L. asellus]
esole f. *she-ass*, Bl.
ess m. *name of the letter* s, ÆGr.
essian *to waste away*, RPs 118[139].
ēst mf. *favour, grace, bounty, kindness, love*, An,B : *pleasure*, Lk : *harmony, consent* : (usu. in pl.) *delicacies*, WW; Æ. ['*este*']
ēstan (w. d.) *to live luxuriously*, W 190[17].
ēstan=ēastan
ēste *gracious, liberal*, B,Gen. ['*este*']
ēstelic *kind, gracious*, EPs 68[17] : *devout*, DR : *delicate, dainty (of food)*, MFH 157. adv. -līce, CP : *courteously*, An 292 : *luxuriously*, WW. [v. '*este*']
ēstful *gracious, devoted, devout*, Æ : *fond of luxuries*, WW 218[18],[19]. ['*estful*'] adv. -līce.
ēstfulnes f. *devotion, zeal*, CP : *daintiness*, WW : *luxury, lechery*. [v. '*este*']
ēstgeorn *delicate, fond of luxuries*, WW 218[18].

ēstig *gracious, liberal*, Pa 16.
ēstines f. *benignity*, EPs 64¹².
ēstlic=ēstelic
ēstmete m. *dainty (food), delicacy, luxury,* ÆGr. [v. '*este*']
-estre=f. agent, as in wītegestre, *prophetess.*
ēstum† *freely, willingly, gladly.*
esul=esol
esulcweorn f. *mill-stone turned by an ass,* CP 31¹⁷.
ēswic=æswic
et I.=æt prep. II. pres. 3 sg. of etan.
et-=æt-, ed-; ēt (NG)=æt
±etan⁵ (ea, eo) *to 'eat,'* Æ,AO,Jn : *devour, consume, Jn*; CP : (tr.) *feed* : (reflex.) *provision oneself* : (+) *eat together.* [v. also '*yeten*']
etelond n. *pasture land*, KC 2·95¹⁴.
etemest=ytemest; eten=eoten
etend I. m. *eater, glutton.* II. *voracious, gluttonous*, WW 396,523 (eot-).
etenlǣs f. *pasture*, LL 452,20.
eting f. *eating*, Sc 170⁵.
etol (ettul) *voracious*, ÆGr 69⁷,WW 226¹.
etolnes (ettul-) f. *greediness, gluttony*, Sc 55⁶.
etonisc (B)=eotenisc; etsomne=ætsamne
etst=itst pres. 2 sg. of etan.
ettan *to graze, pasture land*, AO 18²⁵.
ettul=etol
ēð I. comp. adv. *more easily.* II.=ȳð
eð-=æð-, ed-
ēð-=ǣð-, ēað-, īeð-
eðcwide (GL)=edcwide
ēðel (oe, N) mn. gs. ēðles *country, native land, ancestral home, Lk,Met*; CP : *name of the rune for* œ. †hwǣles ē. *the sea,* Chr 975A. [' *ethel*']
ēðelboda m. *land's apostle, native preacher,* Gu 976.
ēðelcyning m. *king of the land*, Cr 997.
ēðeldrēam m. *domestic joy*, Gen 1607.
ēðeleard m. *native dwelling*, Gen 1945.
ēðelfæsten n. *fortress*, Rd 72²².
ēðelland† n. *fatherland, country.*
ēðellēas† *homeless, exiled.*
ēðelmearc† f. *boundary of one's country, territory*, Gen.
ēðelrīce† n. *native country.*
ēðelriht† n. *hereditary right.*
ēðel-seld†, -setl† n. *settlement*, Gen.
ēðelstæf (ul, yl) m. *heir, successor*, Gen 2223.
ēðelstaðol m. *settlement*, Gen 94.
ēðelstōl† m. *hereditary seat, habitation* : *royal city, chief city.*
ēðelstōw† f. *dwelling-place*, Gen.
ēðelturf† f. (ds. -tyrf) *fatherland.*
ēðelðrymm m. *glory of one's own land*, Gen 1634.

ēðelweard† m. *lord of the realm, man.*
ēðelwynn† f. *joy of ownership*, B.
ēðgung f. *breath, breathing, inspiration* : *hard breathing*, RB 68³.
±ēðian *to breathe*, GD : *smell.* ['*ethe*']
ēðmian=ǣðmian
ēðr (N)=ǣdr, ǣdre; ēðr-=īeðr-
eðða (MtR)=oððe
ēðung I. f. *laying waste, destroying*, GL. [ēðe, īðan] II.=ēðgung
ēðwilte *easily turned*, OEG 1151.
ēuwā interj. *woe!* GL.
evangelista m. *evangelist*, VH 11.
ēw-=ǣw-, ēaw-, ēow-, īew-; ēwe=ēowu
ex, exe f. *brain*, Lcd (v. A 30·129).
ex-=eax; exen v. oxa.
exlistealla (HGL 405)=eaxlgestealla
exorcista m. *exorcist*, ÆL 31¹⁴¹.

fā v. fāh I.
faca gp. of fæc.
fācen n. nap. fācnu *deceit, fraud, treachery, sin, evil, crime*, Mt,LL; Æ,AO : *blemish, fault (in an object)*, LL 114,56; 398,9. ['*faken*']
fācendǣd f. *sin, crime*, PPs 118⁵³.
fācen-ful, -fullic *deceitful, crafty.* adv. -līce.
fācengecwis f. *conspiracy*, WW.
fācenlēas *guileless*, VH 11 : *pure*, NG.
fācenlic *deceitful*, RB 95¹², ¹⁵. adv. -līce, Æ. ['*fakenliche*']
fācensearu† n. *treachery.*
fācenstafas mp. *treachery, deceit*, B 1018.
fācentacn n. *deceitful token*, Cr 1566.
facg m. *plaice? loach?* WW 180³².
fācian *to try to obtain, get*, AO 152⁷ : *get to, reach*, BC 2·305′.
fācn=fācen; fācne=fæcne
fācnesful=fācenful
facum dp. of fæc.
±fadian *to arrange, dispose, guide*, LL; Æ. ['*fade*'? v. IF 48·257]
fadiend m. *manager*, OEG 56³⁰⁸.
±fadung f. *arrangement, order, disposition, dispensation, rule*, Æ : *interpretation, version*, Bf 238¹⁶.
fadur (A)=fæder
fæc (e) n. *space of time, while, division, interval, Lk*; Æ,CP : *period of five years, lustrum*, WW 431¹⁶. ['*fec*']
fǣcan *to wish to go*, LL 128b².
fæccan=feccan
fæcele (e¹) f. *torch*, WW. [Ger. fackel]
fǣcenlic=fācenlīce
fǣcful *broad, spacious*, Sc 185¹⁵.
fæcile (GL)=fæcele

fæcne I. *deceitful, treacherous, Ps* : *vile, worthless.* II. adv. *deceitfully, maliciously, disgracefully* : (†) *exceedingly.* ['*faken*']

fæcnig *crafty,* RPs 72[18].

+**fæd** I. *orderly, well-conducted,* LL : *calm, composed,* W 51[24]. II. n? *discretion,* LL (244[15]). [fadian]

fæd-=fēd-

fæder (e[1]) m. usu. indecl. in sg. '*father,*' *Æ, VPs*; AO,CP : *male ancestor, LkL,Mt* : *the Father, God, Jn,Mt,VPs* : (in pl.) *parents, Æ.* eald f. *grandfather.* ðridda, fēower-ða f. etc. *great-grandfather, great-great-grandfather, etc.*

fædera (e[1]) m. *paternal uncle,* AO. [cp. *Ger.* vetter]

+**fædera** m. *male sponsor, godfather, Æ.* [*Ger.* gevatter]

fæderæðelo† npl. *patrimony* : *paternal kinship.*

+**fædere** f. *female sponsor, godmother,* LL.

fæderen *paternal,* ÆT,Sc.

+**fæderen** *born of the same father,* AO 114[14].

fæderenbrōðor m. *brother* (*from the same father*), PPs 68[8].

fæd(e)rencnōsl n. *father's kin,* LL 54,9.

fæderencynn n. *father's kin,* CHR.

fæderenfeoh=fæderfeoh

fæderenhealf f. *father's side,* CHR 887A.

fæderenmǣg m. *paternal kinsman,* CHR 887E.

fæderenmǣgð f. *paternal kindred,* LL 392,3.

fæderēðel m. *fatherland,* AO.

fæderfeoh n. *dowry paid by the father of the bride,* LL.

fædergeard m. *father's dwelling,* GEN 1053.

fædergestrēon n. *patrimony,* GL.

fæderhīwisc n? '*paterfamilias,*' NG.

fæderingmǣg=fæderenmǣg

fæderland n. *paternal land, inheritance,* CHR 1101.

fæderlēas *fatherless,* W.

fæderlic '*fatherly,*' *paternal, ancestral, El.* adv. -līce.

fædern-=fæderen-

fæderslaga m. *parricide,* WW.

fæderswica m. *traitor to one's father,* ÆL 19[224].

+**fædlic** *fit, suitable, proper.* adv. -līce *orderly, quietly* : *craftily?* CPs 82[4]. [fadian]

fædm=fæðm; **fædr-**=fæder-

+**fædred** (AO)=+fæderen

fæfne (LkR 1[29])=fæmne

+**fæge** *popular with, acceptable to,* B 915. [*OHG.* gifag]

fægan *to paint,* GL.

fæge '*fey,*' *doomed* (*to death*), *fated, destined, An,B,Ma* : *dead* : *unhappy, accursed, Cr* : *feeble, cowardly, Gu.*

±**fægen** (w. g.) '*fain,*' *glad, joyful, rejoicing, B,Bo*; AO,CP.

fægenian=fægnian

fægennes f. *joy,* NC 285.

fæger I. '*fair,*' *lovely, beautiful, B,Bo,Gen*; AO,CP : *pleasant, agreeable, Ex* : *attractive, Gen*; Æ. II. n. *beauty, Bo* : *beautiful object.*

fæger-=fægr-

fægerlīce *splendidly,* LkL 16[19].

fægernes f. '*fairness,*' *beauty, LPs,Sc*; Æ.

fægerwyrde *smooth-speaking,* FT 12.

fægn=fægen

fægnes (LPs 44[15])=fāgnes

+**fægnian** (a) (w. g. etc.) *to rejoice, be glad, exult, Bo,Met* : *fawn, Æ* : *applaud.* ['*fain*']

±**fægnung** f. *rejoicing, Æ,* ELSPs.

+**fǣgon** pret. pl. of +fēon.

fægre (e) *fairly, elegantly, beautifully, Æ, Gen* : *pleasantly, softly, gently, kindly, Gen,Men* : *well, justly* : *early,* LkR 24[1]. ['*fair*']

±**fægrian** *to become beautiful, Seaf* : *adorn, decorate.* ['*fair*']

fǣgð? f. *imminent death,* AN 284(GK).

fǣhan=fāgan; **fǣht**=feoht

fǣhð f. *hostility, enmity, violence, revenge, vendetta,* AO. [fāh; cp. *Ger.* fehde]

fǣhðbōt f. *payment for engaging in a feud,* LL 266,25; 286,5[2d].

fǣhðe, fǣhðo, fǣhðu=fǣhð

fæl-=feal-, fel-, fiel-, fyl-

fǣlǣcan=fālǣcan

fǣle† I. *faithful, trusty, good, Ps* : *dear, beloved.* ['*fele*'] II. adv. *truly, well, pleasantly.*

±**tǣlsian** *to cleanse, purify* : *expiate,* WW : (+) *pass through.*

fǣman *to* '*foam,*' *MkL.* [fām]

fǣmhādlic=fǣmnhādlic; **fǣmig**=fāmig

fǣmnanhād=fǣmnhād

fǣmne (ē) f. *maid, virgin, bride, Æ* : (+) *woman* : *virago.*

fǣmne(n)dlic=fǣmnhādlic

fǣmnhād m. *virginity, maidenhood,* AO.

fǣmnhādesmon m. *virgin,* RB 136[24].

fǣmnhādlic (OEG), fǣmn(en)lic *maidenly, virginal.*

fǣn=fen

fǣr n. nap. faru (±) *way, journey, passage, expedition, Bf,Ex,Lk.* mannes f. *highway,* ÆL 25[441] : *movement,* MET 31[4] : *proceedings, life, Æ* : *movable possessions, means of subsistence,* HL : *ark, ship.* ['*fare*']

fǣr (ē) I. m. *calamity, sudden danger, peril, B,Ex* : *sudden attack* : *terrible sight,* BL 199[24]. ['*fear*'] II.=fēfer. III.=fæger

fær-=fer-, fear-, feor-, fier-, for-

fǣr- prefix=(1) *sudden, fearful*; (2) fēr-

fǣrǣrning f. *quick riding,* GD 14[24].

fǣran (ē) *to frighten, Æ*; CP: *raven*, MtL 7¹⁵. ['*fear*']

fǣrbēn-a, -u m. *peasant, small-holder?* (Lieb.), LL 383,50 : '*epibata*,' Erf 1112.

fǣrbifongen *beset by dangers*, B 2009.

fǣrblǣd (ē¹) m. *sudden blast (of wind)*, JUL 649.

fǣrbryne m. *scorching heat*, Ex 72.

fǣrclamm (ē) m. *sudden seizure*, Ex 119.

fǣrcoðu f. *apoplexy*, LCD.

fǣrcwealm m. *sudden pestilence*, LL,W.

fǣrcyle m. *intense cold*, GEN 43.

fǣrdēað m. *sudden death*, MH,WW 351¹⁹.

fǣrdryre m. *sudden fall*, CRA 48.

fǣredlic (Æ)=fǣrlic; **fǣreht**=fǣrriht

fǣreld (a¹) nm. *way, journey, track, passage, expedition*, Æ,AO,CP : *retinue, company*, AO : *course of life, conduct*, Æ : *movement, progress, power of locomotion*, Æ : *vehicle*, OEG : *the Passover*, Æ.

fǣreldfrēols m. *Passover-feast*, JOS 5¹⁰.

fǣrelt (AO,CP)=fǣreld

fǣrennes=fǣrnes

fǣreð pres. 3 sg. of faran.

fǣrfyll (on) *headlong*, WW 426⁸.

fǣrgripe† m. *sudden grip*, B.

fǣrgryre† m. *awful horror*.

fǣrhaga m. *hedge of terrors*, GU 933.

fǣring (ē) f. I.† *journey, wandering*. II. *accusation*, WW 27⁸. III. *ecstasy*, WW 398¹⁶.

fǣringa (ē) *suddenly, unexpectedly, quickly, forthwith, by chance*, Lk; Æ,CP. ['*feringe*']

fǣrlic *sudden, unexpected, AO,WW*; Æ,CP, *rapid.* adv. -līce, Lk. ['*ferly*']

fǣrnes f. *passage, traffic*, BH,MtR.

fǣrnīð m. *hostile attack*, B 476.

fǣrrǣs m. *sudden rush*, LkL 8³³.

fǣrrǣsende (ē¹) *rushing headlong*, DR 125¹⁶.

fǣrriht n. *passage-money*, ÆL 23b³⁵².

fǣrsceatt m. *passage-money, fare*, ANDR.

fǣrsceaða m. *enemy*, MA 142.

fǣrscyte m. *sudden shot*, CR 766.

fǣrsearo n. *sudden artifice*, CR 770.

fǣrsēað m. *deep pit*, WW 193⁶.

fǣrslide m. *sudden fall*, PPs 114⁸.

fǣrspell† n. *dreadful tidings*.

fǣrspryng m. *sudden eruption*, LCD 134a.

fǣrst pres. 2 sg. of faran.

fǣrsteorfa m. *murrain*, LCD 177a.

fǣrstice m. *sudden stitch (pain)*, LCD 3·52¹¹.

fǣrstylt m? *amazement*, LkL 5²⁶.

fǣrswīge (ē) f. *amazement*, MkL 5⁴².

fǣrswile m. *sudden swelling*, LCD 27b.

fǣrð I.=ferð. II.=pres. 3 sg. of faran.

fǣrunga, fǣrunge (Æ)=fǣringa

fǣruntrymnes f. *sudden sickness*, LCD 107b.

fǣrweg m. *cart road*, Ct.

fǣrwundor n. *terrible wonder*, Ex 279.

fǣs (a, ea) n. *fringe, border*, MtL. ['*fas*']

fǣsceaftnes=fēasceaftnes

fǣsl† n? *seed, offspring, progeny*, GEN.

fǣsnian=fæstnian

fǣst I. '*fast*,' *fixed, firm, secure*, Bo,Lcd; CP : *constant, steadfast*, BH : *stiff, heavy, dense*, Lcd : *obstinate, bound, costive*, Lcd; Æ : *enclosed, closed, watertight*, CP : *strong, fortified*, BH; Æ,AO:*reputable? standard?* (BTs), AO 286⁴. II. (GU 192)=fæsten

±**fæstan** I. *to fasten, make firm, ratify, establish*, LkL : *entrust, commit.* ['*fast*'] II. *to '*fast*'* ('*i-fast*'), *abstain from food*, Bf, Bl,Lcd; CP : *atone for (by fasting)*, DA 592.

fæste (e) '*fast*,' *firmly, securely*, BH,Bo; Æ : *straitly, strictly* : *heavily (sleep)* : *speedily*.

fæsten n. I. *fastness, stronghold, fortress*, AO,CP : *cloister*, Æ : *enclosure, prison* : *fastener*. II. (±) *fast (abstinence from food)* Bl,LL,Mt,VPs; CP : *firmament, sky*. ['*fasten*']

fæstenbryce m. *breach of fast*, LL,W.

fæstendæg m. *fast-day*, Ct; RB,W. [v. '*fasten*']

fæstendīc m. *fort-ditch, moat*, KC 1·257'.

fæstengangol=fæstgangol

fæstengeat n. *castle-gate*, JUD 162.

fæstengeweorc n. *liability for repair of the defences of a town*, KC.

fæstenlic (ern) *quadragesimal, Lenten*, DR.

fæstentīd f. *fast*, LL. [v. '*fasten*']

fæstenwuce f. *week of fasting*, ÆL 23b¹¹¹.

fæstermōdor=fōstormōdor

fæstern n. *fast* : *Quadragesima*, LG. [=fæsten II.]

fæstern-=fæsten-

fæstgangol (o², e³) *steady, faithful*, CRA 80.

fæsthafol *retentive, tenacious*, Æ : *sparing, miserly*, CP.

fæsthafolnes f. *economy*, CP 453²⁸ : *stinginess*, DD.

fæstheald *firmly fixed*, ÆL 23⁴²³.

fæsthȳdig† *constant, steadfast*.

±**fæstian** (ea) *to commend, entrust, commit*, LkL.

fæsting f. *commendation, trust, guardianship*, GD 239¹⁵,LL 58,7 : *quartering (of the king's servants)*, KC 2·60'.

fæstingan=fæstnian

fæstingmann m. *a kind of retainer*, EC.

fæstland (o²) n. *land easily defended*, AA 25⁸.

fæstlic *firm, fixed, steadfast, resolute.* adv. -līce *certainly*, AS 32²¹ : (+) *fixedly, steadily, constantly*, Bo : *unceasingly*, Æ,Bl : *verily, but*, NG : *strictly*, CHRD. ['*fastly*']

fæstmōd *constant in mind*, AO 288¹⁷.

fæstnes f. *firmness, massiveness, stability,* Bo : '*fastness*,' *stronghold,* Æ : *firmament,* Æ.

fæstnian to '*fasten*,' *fix, secure, bind,* An, Ps : *confirm, ratify, conclude (peace),* Ct, Ma : *betroth* : *bestow upon, secure for,* VH 11.

±**fæstnung** f. *fastening, bond*: *strengthening, stability* : *security, safety* : *protection, shelter* : *confirmation, ratification, pledge, engagement* : *exhortation,* MkL p 25.

fæstrǣd *firm, constant, steadfast,* B,Bo; Æ, CP. ['*fastrede*']

fæstrǣdlic *constant, steadfast,* Bo 20²¹. adv. -līce.

fæstrǣdnes f. *constancy, fortitude,* Bo.

fæststeall *standing firmly,* PPs 121².

fæsŏ=fæst

fæt n. nap. fatu *vat, vessel, jar, cup,* Æ,B, JnL,WW; AO,CP : *casket,* El 1026 : *division,* Bꜰ 4²⁶. ['*fat*']

fǣt I.† n. *plate, beaten out metal (especially gold), gold ornament.* II.=fǣtt I.

±**fǣtan** to *cram, put (in), load,* CP : *adorn.*

fǣted I.† *ornamented with gold.* [pp. of fǣtan] II.=fǣtt

fǣtedhlēor *with cheek ornaments,* B 1026.

fǣtedsinc n. *beaten gold,* Aɴ 478.

fǣtels, fǣtel m. *vessel,* AO,Lcd; Æ : *pouch, bag, sack,* Æ,CP. ['*fetles*']

fǣtelsian to *put into a vessel,* Lcᴅ 1·328¹⁷.

fǣtelsod=fetelsod

fǣtfyllere (a¹, e²) m. *cupbearer,* GD,TC,WW.

fǣtgold n. *beaten gold,* B 1921.

fǣthengest m. *riding-horse,* Rᴅ 23¹⁴.

fǣtian=fetian

fǣtnes f. '*fatness*,' Ps; Æ,CP : *the richest part of anything,* Ps.

+**fǣtnian**=+fǣttian

fǣtt I. (ē) '*fat*,' *fatted,* Æ,AO,Lk,Ps,Rd. II. =fǣted

fǣttian (+) to *become fat,* Ps : (+) *anoint,* Ps : *fatten.* ['*fat*']

+**fǣttig** *fat, rich,* CPs 19⁴.

fǣŏe=fēŏe

fǣŏel *play-actor?* v. OEG 39².

fǣŏer=feŏer

fǣŏm (e) m. fǣ ŏme f. *outstretched or encircling arms, embrace, grasp,* An,Rd : *protection* : *interior, bosom, lap, breast, womb* : '*fathom*,' *cubit,* Æ,Cp,WW; Æ : *power,* B,Cr : *expanse, surface.*

fǣŏman, fǣŏmian to *surround, envelop, clasp, embrace,* An,B. ['*fathom*']

fǣŏmlic *embracing, enclosing, sinuous,* WW 486⁴.

-**fǣŏmnes** v. on-f.

fǣŏmrīm n. *fathom, cubit,* Pʜ 29.

fǣx=feax

fāg I. *variegated, spotted, dappled, stained, dyed,* B,Gl,Lcd : *shining, gleaming,* Ps. ['*faw*'] II.=fāh I.

fāg-=fāh-; **fāge** f. (WW 94)=facg

fagen, fagen-=fægen, fægn-

fāgettan to *change colour,* Lcᴅ 3·240²³. mid wordum f. *speak evasively.*

fāgetung f. *change (of colour),* ÆH 2·538'.

±**fāgian** to *change in colour, vary, be variegated,* RB 137⁸.

fāgnes f. *scab, ulcer, eruption,* Æ : *variety of colour, brilliancy,* HL,OEG.

fagnian=fægnian

fāgung f. *variety (esp. of colour),* DR,GD.

fāgwyrm m. *basilisk,* VPs 90¹³.

fāh I. nap. fā *hostile,* B : (±) *proscribed, outlawed, guilty, criminal,* B. ['*foe*'; fēogan] II. (±) m. '*foe*,' *enemy, party to a bloodfeud,* LL; Æ,AO. III.=fāg I.

fahame '*polentum*,' WW 40²⁸.

fāhmann m. '*foeman*,' *object of a bloodfeud,* LL 50,5.

fahnian=fægnian

fala I. (WW 52¹¹) ? d. of *fealh *tube? pipe? plank?* (BTs) (ES 38·337). II.=fela

fālǣcan to *be at enmity with, show hostility to,* LL 160,20⁷.

fal-d, -æd, -od, -ud m. '*fold*,' *stall, stable, cattle-pen,* Gl,Jn,LL.

fald- (N)=feald-

faldgang m. *going to the (sheep-)fold,* W 170²⁰ᴇ.

faldhrīŏer n. *stalled ox,* MFH 158.

faldian to *make a fold, hurdle off sheep,* LL 454,9. ['*fold*']

falew-=feal(e)w-

fall- (VPs; NG)=feall-; **falod**=fald

fals I. '*false*,' WW; LL,W 272⁴. II. n. *falsehood, fraud, counterfeit.* [L.]

falŏing *mass, load,* WW 33⁸.

falu=fealu; **falud**=fald

fām n. '*foam*,' BH,Ep; Æ : *sea,* Rd.

fāmbig=fāmig; **-fāmblāwende** v. lig-f.

fāmgian to *foam, boil,* Ex 481.

fāmig (ǣ) '*foamy*,' Rd.

fāmigbord *with foaming banks (of a stream),* Mᴇᴛ 26²⁶.

fāmigbōsm *with foamy bosom,* Ex 493.

fāmigheals† *foamy-necked.*

fana m. *banner, standard,* Met; OEG : *plant, iris?* Lcd. ['*fane*']

+**fāna** gp. of +fā.

fanbyrde *standard-bearing,* v. OEG 1744.

fand pret. 3 sg. of findan.

fandere m. *trier, tester,* Sc 206⁴.

±**fandian** (often w. g., but also d. and a), to *try, attempt, tempt, test, examine, explore, search out, experience, visit,* AO,B,Gen, Mk,Run; CP. ['*fand*,' '*fond*'; findan]

fandung f. *investigation, trial, temptation, test, proof, A,Gen*; Æ,CP. ['*fanding*']
fane (1) (NG, o¹)=fann. (2)=fanu
fang m. *plunder, booty, Chr* 1016. ['*fang*']
fangen pp. of fōn.
+**fangian** *to join, fasten,* Bo 96¹⁴.
fann f. winnowing, '*fan*,' *Cp,Lk,LL*. [*L*. vannus]
fannian *to* '*fan*,' *winnow, Sc* 186¹⁷.
fant (o) m. *fount,* '*font*,' *LL* : *baptismal water,* HL 15²⁹³.
fantbæð n. *baptismal water, laver of baptism,* ÆL,W.
fantblētsung f. *consecration of a font,* ÆP 188¹².
fantfæt n. *baptismal font,* ÆH 2·268'.
fanthālgung (o¹) f. *consecration of a font,* W 36².
fanthālig *holy from connection with the font,* LCD 140b.
fantwæter (o¹) n. '*font-water,*' *water used at baptism, laver of baptism, Lcd*; Æ.
fanu=fana
fāra gp. of fāh I.
+**fara** m. *travelling companion, comrade,* BH,RD.
±**faran**⁶ *to set forth, go, travel, wander, proceed, Bl,Chr,Gen,JnL* ; AO,CP :*be, happen, exist, act, Bo* : '*fare*' ('*i-fare*'), *get on, undergo, suffer, Æ* : (+) *die,* AO,CP : (+) *attack, overcome, capture, obtain,* AO.
faraŏ-=faroŏ-; **fareld**=færeld
fareŏ-=faroŏ-
Fariseisc *of or belonging to the Pharisees,* OEG,WG.
farm=feorm
farnian *to prosper,* DR 176¹³.
faroŏ† m. *shore : stream.*
faroŏhengest (ea¹) m. *sea-horse, ship,* EL 226.
faroŏlācende† *swimming, sailing.* as sb. *sailors.*
faroŏrīdende *sailing,* AN 440.
faroŏstrēt f. *path of the sea,* AN 311,900.
faru f. *way, going, journey, course, Æ* : *expedition, march* : *procession, retinue, companions* : *life, proceedings, adventures, Æ* : *movable possessions.*
fas-=fæs-; **fatian** (NG)=fetian
fatu v. fæt.
faŏe, faŏu f. *father's sister, paternal aunt, Æ.*
faŏusunu m. *father's sister's son,* CHR 1119.
faul m? *evil spirit,* LCD 43a.
fēa I. (±) m. *joy,* AO,CP. II. n.=feoh. III. (fēawa) adj. nap. fēawe, superl. fēawost, fēast '*few,*' *B,BH,Chr,Mt,VPs.* fēawum sīŏum *seldom.* adv. *even a little, at all.*
feadur (A)=fæder;±**fēagan**(NG,Ps)=±fēon
feah=feoh

±**feaht** I. pret. 3 sg. of feohtan. II.=feoht
feal-=fel-
+**feald** n. *region, abode?* WALD 2¹⁰.
±**fealdan**⁷ *to* '*fold,*' *wrap up, furl, entangle, Æ,Bo,Rd* : *roll about,* MkR 9²⁰.
fealdestōl=fyldstōl
feale, fealewes v. fealu.
fealewian=fealwian; **fealfor**=felofor
fealg pret. 3 sg. of fēolan.
fealga v. fealh.
fealgian *to fallow,* LL 454,9 (v. A 36·71).
fealh I. f. nap. fealga, *fallow land.* II. (e) f. '*felloe,*' *felly (of a wheel), Bo,WW.* III. pret. 3 sg. of fēolan. IV. v. fala.
+**fēalic** *joyous, pleasant.* adv. -līce, W 284¹⁶.
feall=fiell
feallan⁷ (±) *to* '*fall*' ('*i-falle,*' '*y-falle*'), *Bl, Ps* : *fall headlong, fail, decay, die, B,Ps;* AO,CP : *inflict* (*on*), *attack : flow,* AO 19¹⁸ : (+) *overthrow,* DR 115⁶ (æ).
fealle f. *snare, trap,* OEG 4979. ['*fall*']
feallen(d)**lic** *unstable, perishable, transient,* BL,W.
fealletan (a¹) *to fall down,* '*concīdere,*' (mistaken for *concīdere*), MkLR 5⁵.
-feallung v. feax-f.
+**fealnis** (æ) f. *ruin,* LkL 2³⁴.
fealo=(1) fealu; (2) fela
fēalōg w. g. *destitute,* GU 217.
fealohilte *yellow-hilted,* MA 166.
fealu I. (feale) adj. gsm. feal(e)wes, fealuwes '*fallow,*' *yellow, tawny, dun-coloured, grey, dusky, dark, B,Rd;* Æ. II. n. *fallow ground,* EC 179'.
fealu-=felo-
fealuwian=fealwian; **fealwes** v. fealu.
fealwian *to become* '*fallow,*' *fade, wither, Sol : grow yellow, ripen.*
fēanes f. '*fewness,*' *paucity,* BH,Ps. [= fēawnes]
+**fēanes** f. *joy,* GUTH 134,VH 12.
fear=fearr; **fēar**=fearh
fēara gen. of fēa.
fearh (æ, e) m. gs. fēares *little pig, hog, Ep, WW.* ['*farrow*']
fearhhama m. *hide of pig,* WW 161⁵ (IF 48·254).
fearhrȳŏer (e¹) n. *bull,* BL. [fearr]
+**fearhsugu** f. *sow in farrow,* WW.
fearlic *of a bull,* OEG 11¹⁸⁷
fēarlic=fǣrlic
fearm m. *freight, cargo,* GEN 1394.
fearn n. '*fern,*' *Bo,Cp;* Æ; Mdf.
fearnbed n. *fern-bed,* BC,WW.
fearnbracu f. *fern-brake,* KC 5·173¹⁸.
fearnedisc n. *fern-pasture,* BC 1·519².
fearnhege m. *hedge with ferns,* KC 3·54'.
fearnig *fern-covered,* Ct.
fearnlæs n. *fern-pasture,* KC 2·59¹⁹.

fearoð-=faroð-

fearr I. m. *beast of burden, ox, bull*, Æ,AO.
II.=feorr

feas (VPs)=fæs

fēasceaft† *destitute, miserable, helpless, poor*.

fēasceaftig *destitute, poor*, Seaf 26.

fēasceaftnes (ǣ¹) f. *poverty*, OEG 1171.

feast-=fæst-

featu (VPs)=fatu nap. of fæt.

fēaw-=fēa-; fēawa=fēa

fēawlic *few*, EPs 104¹².

fēawnes f. *fewness, paucity*, LPs 101²⁴.

feax (æ, e) n. *hair, head of hair, B,BH,Lcd*;
Æ,CP. ['*fax*']

feaxclāð n. *cap*, WW 411¹⁷.

+feaxe *furnished with hair*, BH 96¹¹.

feaxēacan m. pl. *forelocks*, WW 343³³.

feaxede *hairy, bushy* : *long-haired (of a
comet)*, Chr 892. ['*faxed*']

+feaxen (WE 61¹⁴?)=+feaxe

feaxfang n. *seizing or dragging by the hair*,
LL 5,33.

feaxfeallung f. *shedding of hair, mange*,
WW 113³⁰.

feaxhār *hoary, grey-haired*, Rd 73¹.

feaxnǣdel f. *crisping-pin*, WW 108².

feaxnes (æ, e) f. *head of hair*, WW.

feaxnett n. *hair-net*, WW.

+feaxod=+feaxe

feaxprēon m. *hair-pin*, WW 107³⁸.

feaxscēara (e¹) fp. *scissors for hair-cutting?
curling-tongs?* WW 241⁴¹.

feaxwund f. *wound under the hair*, LL 20,45.

feb-=fef-; fec=fæc

±feccan (æ) *to 'fetch,' bring, bring to, draw,
Æ,Mt : seek : gain, take.* [=fetian]

fecele=fæcele; fecgan=feccan

±fēdan *to 'feed,' nourish, sustain, foster,
bring up, Bl,Mt,Ps; Æ,CP : bear, bring
forth, produce.* pp. +fēd, OEG. [fōda]

fēdednes=fēdnes

fēdelfugol (oe¹) m. *fatted bird*, MtR 22⁴.

fēd-els, -esl m. *feeding, keep : fatted animal
(bird?), WW*; Cp. ['*feddle*']

fēdelswīn *fattened pig*, NC 343.

feder, federa=fæder, fædera

fēding f. '*feeding,' CP.*

fēdnes (ǣ) f. *nourishment*, BH 88⁶.

fedra=fædera

fēfer mn. gs. fēfres '*fever,' Lk,G*; CP.

fēferādl f. '*fever,' AO.*

fēfercyn n. *a kind of fever*, Lcd 5b.

fēferfūge f. *feverfew*, Lcd,Gl. [L. febrifugia]

fēferian *to be feverish, suffer from fever*,
Lcd.

fēferig (o²) *feverish*, Lcd 1·334'.

fēfersēoc *feverish*, WW 405³⁴.

fēfor, fēfur=fēfer

fēfr-=fēfer-

+fēg n. *joining, joint*, Æ : *composition :
diagram*, Bf 10⁸. [*Ger.* gefüge]

fēgan I. (±) *to join, unite, fix, adapt, Lcd,
Rd*; Æ,CP : *compose, confine.* ['*fay*'] II.
(WW 469⁸)=fǣgan?

+fēgednes f. *conjunction, connection : bond,
fetter*, DHy 5⁶ : *figure*, ÆGr 105²⁰.

fēger, fegere=fæger, fægre

±fēging f. *conjunction, composition*, ÆGr
10⁸.

+fēgnes f. *association, companionship : conjunction*, Bf 94²³.

feh=feoh

+feh=+feah pret. 3 sg. of +fēon.

feht *sheepskin with the fleece on it?* TC 119²¹;
v. ES 37·177.

+feht=+feoht; fehtan (N)=feohtan

fēhð pres. 3 sg. of fōn.

fel=fell; fēl=fēol

fela (ea, eo) I. sbn. and adj. (w. g., or in
agmt.: rarely inflected) *many, much*, Chr.
II. adv. *very much, many.* ['*fele*']

felaǣte '*mordax*,' QEG 23¹⁵.

felafǣcne *very treacherous*, GnE 148.

felafeald *manifold, many times over*, Ps.
['*felefold*']

felafealdnes (fele-) f. *multitude*, EPs 5¹¹.

felafrēcne *very fierce, bold*, Run 2.

felagēomor *very sad, sorrowful*, B 2950.

felageong *very young*, FT 53.

felageonge *much-travelled*, Creat 3. [gan-
gan]

felahrōr *full of exploits*, B 27.

felaīdelsprǣce *emptily chattering*, CP 174²⁵.

felalēof *very dear*, Wif 26.

felameahtig† *most mighty*.

felamōdig† *very bold*, B.

±fēlan I. (w. g.) *to touch, 'feel' ('y-fele'),
AO : perceive, Rd.* II. (VPs)=fēolan

felaspecol *talkative*, Lcd,Ps.

fela-specolnes, -sprecolnes f. *talkativeness*,
BH,Sc.

felasprǣc (eo) f. *much speaking, loquacity*,
MtR 6⁷.

felasprǣce *talkative*, CP 281¹⁴.

felasynnig *very guilty*, B 1379.

felawlonc *very stately*, Rd 13⁷.

felawyrde *talkative*, W 40¹⁸.

felawyrdnes f. *talkativeness*, GD 208⁴.

felcyrf m. *foreskin* (BT).

feld m. ds. felda, felde *open or cultivated
land, plain, Bf,Met,RBL; AO,CP; Mdf :
battlefield.* on clǣnum felda *in the open
field (of battle)*, CP 227²⁵. ['*field*']

feldælbin (WW 352¹⁰)=feldelfen

feldbēo f. *humble-bee*, WW.

feldbisceopwyrt f. *field-bishopwort*, ANS
84·325.

feldcirice f. *country church*, LL 264,5¹; 282,3².

felde=fylde pret. 3 sg. of fyllan.

feldefare? f. *fieldfare?* WW 287¹⁷ (-ware).

feldelfen f. *wood-nymph,* WW 189⁶. [v. '*elven*']

feldgangende† *roaming over the land,* Sol.

feldhriðer n. *field-ox,* NC 285 (cp. feldoxa).

feldhūs† n. *tent,* Ex.

feldlǣs (ē²) n. *pasture in open country,* KC.

feldland n. '*field-land,' meadow-land, plain,* Æ.

feldlic *rural,* ÆGr : *growing wild,* ÆH.

feldmædere f. *field-madder, rosemary,* Lcd; WW 300¹⁰. [v. '*field*']

feldminte f. *field-mint, wild mint,* WW.

feld-more, -meru f. *parsnip,* Lcd.

feldoxa f. *field-ox* (i.e. an ox out to grass, not a stalled ox), ÆH 2·576'.

feldrude f. *wild rue,* Lcd 3·325.

feldsæten f. *field,* LPs 77¹². [seten]

feldswamm m. *fungus, toadstool,* WW 404²⁶.

feldwēsten n. *desert,* Deut 1¹.

feldwōp m. *plantain,* Gl (?=*feldhoppe, ANS 119·435; FM 200) : *peewit?* (BTs).

feldwyrt f. *gentian,* Lcd.

+fēle *sensitive,* Lcd.

fele-=felo-

felefeald=felafeald

fēlelēas *insensible, dead,* Wy 40.

felg(e) f. '*felloe,' rim of a wheel,* Bo. [fēolan]

felge-role, -roðe '*polipodium,*' A 24·432 (v. MLN 23·186).

felh=fealh pret. 3 sg. of fēolan.

felhð (KGl)=fylgð pres. 3 sg. of fylgan.

feligean=fylgan

fell I. n. '*fell,' skin, hide,* B,*Jul,Lcd;* Æ,AO, CP : *garment of skin,* Chrd 64³³. [*L.* pellis]   **II.** m.=fiell

fell-=fyll-

fellen (i¹) *made of skins,* Æ.

fellerēad (ēo³; =*pællerēad? ES 43·31) *purple,* NG.

fellstycce n. *piece of skin,* Lcd 1·330⁵.

fēllun=fēollon pret. pl. of feallan.

-felma v. æger-f.; **felmen-**=fylmen-

±fēlnes f. *sensation, feeling,* Æ.

felo-=fela-

felofe(o)rð (eo¹, e², u², ea³) *stomach, maw* (*of an animal*), Lcd,Gl.

felofor (ea¹, eo¹, u², e³) m. *bittern,* Gl.

fēlon (A)=fulgon pret. pl. of fēolan.

+fēlsian=+fælsian

felst pres. 2 sg. of feallan.

felt m? n? '*felt,' WW.*

felt-ere, -erre *a plant,* Lcd.

feltūn m. *privy, dunghill,* CP. [=feld-]

feltūngrēp f. *dunghill,* NC 285.

feltwurma m. *wild marjoram,* Lcd.

feltwyrt f. *mullein* (*plant*), ÆGr, Lcd.

felð=fielð pres. 3 sg. of feallan; **fēlð**=fȳlð

felða (Cp 128 s) rare gp. of feld.

felu-=felo-; **fēm-,** fēmn- (VPs)=fæmn-

fen=fenn

fenampre (o²) f. *a marsh plant,* Lcd 38b.

fencerse f. *water-cress,* Lcd. [v. '*fen*']

fenester n? m? *window,* GD 220. [*L.*]

fenfearn n. *marsh-fern,* '*salvia,' water-fern,* WW 135⁴.

fenfisc m. *fen-fish,* Lcd 95b (n.).

fenfreoðo f. *fen-refuge,* B 851.

fenfugol m. *moor-fowl,* Lcd 95b?

±feng m. *grip, grasp, embrace* : *capture* : *prey, booty.* [fōn]

fēng pret. 3 sg. of fōn.

fengel† m. *lord, prince, king,* B.

fengelād n. *marsh-path, fen,* B 1359.

fengnes f. '*susceptio,'* CPs 82² (? for and-f.).

fengnett n. (*catching-*)*net,* PPs 140¹².

fengon pret. pl. of fōn.

fengtōð (æ) m. *canine tooth,* LL 81 n16.

fenhleoðu np. *fen-coverts,* B 820. [hlið]

fenhop n. *fen-hollow,* B 764.

fenix m. *the bird* '*phœnix,'* ÆGr,Ph : *date-palm.*

fenland n. *fen-land, marsh,* Æ,AO.

fenlic *marshy,* Æ,Guth. ['*fenlich*']

fenminte f. *water-mint,* Lcd 14b.

fenn nm. *mud, mire, dirt,* CP,WW : '*fen,' marsh, moor,* B,Bo; AO : *the fen country,* Chr 905.

fenn-=fen-

fennig I. *marshy,* WW : *muddy, dirty,* CP. ['*fenny*']   **II.**=fynig

fennðæc n. *covering of thatch from a fen,* OET (Bd²).

fenol=finul; **fenompre**=fenampre

fenȳce f. *snail?* OET,WW : *tortoise?* Rd 41⁷¹.

fēo=feoh; also ds. of feoh.

fēode pret. 3 sg. of fēogan.

+fēogan (fīa, N; fēon) *to hate, persecute,* LG. ['*ivee*']

feogað *hatred,* MtR.

fēogȳtsung (BH 130³⁴)=fēohgītsung

feoh n. gs. fēos, ds. fēo *cattle, herd,* LL,Sol; AO : *movable goods, property,* Bo,Ps; AO : *money, riches, treasure,* B,BH,Mt,OET; Æ,CP. wið licgendum fēo *for ready money,* ÆL 9⁵⁴ : *name of the rune for* f. ['*fee*']

feohbehāt n. *promise of money,* Chr 865 e.

feohbīgenga m. *cattle-keeper,* AA 28².

feohbōt f. *money compensation,* LL 46 n5; 258,51.

feohfang n. *offence of taking a bribe,* LL 318,15¹.

feohgafol n. *usury,* Chrd 76³².

feohgehāt n. *promise of money,* Chr 865 a.

feohgeorn *covetous, greedy,* LL,RWH.

feohgerêfa m. *steward*, LkLR 12⁴².

feohgesceot n. *payment of money*, Bκ 28, 29.

feohgesteald n. *possession of riches*, Jul 685.

feohgestrêon n. *treasure, possessions, riches*, Chrd,W.

feoh-gīdsere, -gīetsere (CP)=feohgītsere

feohgīfre *avaricious*, Wa 68.

feohgift† f. *bounty-giving, largess*.

feohgītsere m. *miser*, Bo,Met.

feohgītsung f. *avarice*, CP 1496.

feohgōd n. *property (in cattle)*, LL 60 n1.

feohgyrnes (=eo²) f. *greed*, LL 396,4.

feohhūs n. *treasure-house*, WW.

feohlænung f. *lending of money*, WW 115⁴⁵.

feohland n. *pasture*, PPs.

feohlēas *without money* : *not to be bought off, past compensation*, B 2441.

feohlēasnes f. *want of money*, Swt.

feohsceatt n. *money-payment*, Da 744.

feohspēda fp. *riches*, GD 273².

feohspilling f. *waste of money*, Chr 1096.

feohstrang *well off*, Gl.

±feoht (i, o, y) n. *action of fighting*, B,Ps : '*fight*,' *battle*, AO : *strife*, Mod.

±feohtan³ (e) *to fight, combat, strive*, Chr, Lk,Rd,LL; Æ,AO,CP.: (+) *gain by fighting, win.* on f. *attack, fight against*.

+feohtdæg m. *day of battle*, PPs 139⁷.

feohte f.=feoht

feohtehorn (y¹) m. *battle-horn*, PPs 74⁹.

feohtend m. *fighter*, OEG 3805.

feohtere m. *fighter*, ES 39³²⁶.

feohtgegyrela m. '*falarica*,' WW 399³⁰.

feohtlāc n. *fighting*, LL. ['*fightlac*']

feohtling (y¹) m. *fighter*, GD 110¹³; MP 1·610.

+feohtsumnes f. *joyfulness*, NC 292. [+fēon]

feohtwīte (i¹, y¹, ȳ²) n. *penalty for fighting*, LL.

feohwīte n. *fine for coining false money*, LL 319 col. 2.

fēol pret. 3 sg. of feallan.

fēol (ē, ī) f. '*file*,' Cp,Rd; ÆL.

feola=fela

fēolaga m. *partner*, '*fellow*,' Chr 1016 D. [ON. fēlagi]

fēolagscipe m. *fellowship*, TC.

±fēolan³ (ē) *to cleave, be joined to, adhere* : *enter, penetrate, pass into, through or over, betake oneself to*, Chr : *undergo* : *persevere in*. [Goth. filhan]

fēold pret. 3 sg. of fealdan.

feolde=folde

fēoldon pret. pl. of fealdan.

fēolheard *hard as a file? hard enough to resist the file? file-hardened?* Ma 108 (or ?=*felaheard).

fēolian *to file*, ÆL 32²⁰³.

fēoll pret. 3 sg., fēollon pret. pl. of feallan.

feologan *to become discoloured?* Lcd 125b.

feolu=fela; feolu-fer, -ferð, -for=felofor

feon=fenn

fēon I. (±, usu. +) sv⁵ w. in or g. *to be glad, rejoice, exult*, CP. II. (ēa) *to gain*, MtL 16²⁶. III.=fēogan

fēond (īe, ȳ) m. ds. fīend, fēonde, nap. fīend, fēond *adversary, foe, enemy*, B,Bf,Mt; AO,CP [f.=*female enemy*] : '*fiend*,' *devil*, Gu; CP : *the Devil*, Lcd,Hy. [pres. ptc. of fēogan]

fēondæt m. *eating things sacrificed to idols*, PPs 105²⁴.

fēondgrāp f. *grip of a foe*, B 636.

fēondgyld n. *idolatry, idol*, GD,PPs : *demoniacal possession?* MtL 4²⁴.

fēondlic *hateful, hostile, fiendish*, WW; Æ. adv. -līce, Jul. ['*fiendly*']

fēondrǣden f. *enmity*, Æ.

fēondrǣs m. *hostile attack*, Gen 900.

fēondsceaða† m. *enemy, robber*.

fēondscipe m. *hostility, hatred*, AO,CP.

fēondsēoc *devil-possessed, demoniac*, BH 184⁵.

fēondulf m. *public enemy, criminal, malefactor*, GPH 396. [fēond, wulf]

fēong=fēoung; feonn=fenn

feor=feorr; fēor=feorh, fēower

fēora gp. of feorh.

+fēora=+fēra

feorbūend *dwelling far off*, B 254.

feor-cumen, -cund=feorran-cumen, -cund

feorcȳðð f. *distant land*, B 1838.

feord, feord-=fierd, fierd-, fyrd-

fēores gs. of feorh; feorg=feorh

feorh (e) mn. gs. fēores, nap. feorh *life, principle of life, soul, spirit*, AO,CP. tō wīdan fēore *for eternity, for ever*. f. gesellan, āgiefan *to die* : *living being, person*.

feorhādl f. *fatal disease*, Æ.

feorhbana† m. *man-slayer*, Gl.

feorhbealu† n. *deadly evil, violent death*, B.

feorhbenn f. *deadly wound*, B 2740.

feorhberend† m. *living being*.

feorhbold n. *body*, Rood 73.

feorhbona=feorhbana

feorhbora m. *life-bearer*, Rd 92².

feorhcwalu† (e) f. *slaughter, death*, Gl.

feorhcwealm† m. *slaughter, death*, Gen.

feorhcynn† n. *race of mortals*, B.

feorhdagas mp. *days of life*, Gen 2358.

feorhdolg n. *deadly wound*, Cr 1455.

feorhēacen *living*, Gen 204.

feorhfægen *fain of life, glad to preserve one's life*, ÆL 23³⁰⁹.

feorhgebeorh n. *refuge*, Ex 369.

feorhgedāl† n. *death*.

feorhgener n. *preservation of life*, LL 204,7³.

feorhgenīōla† m. *mortal foe*, B.

feorhgiefa† m. *giver of life*.

feorhgiefu f. *gift of life*, RIM 6?

feorh-gōme? f. *means of subsistence*, or -gōma? m. *jaw*. CR 1547.

feorhhord† n. *breast, soul, spirit*.

feorhhūs n. *soul-house, body*, MA 297.

feorhhyrde m. *life's guardian, protector*, BH.

feorhlāst m. *step taken to preserve life, flight? step stained by one's life-blood?* (BTs), *track of vanishing life?* (Klb), B 846.

feorhlēan n. *revenge for bloodshed? gift for life saved?* (BTs), EX 150.

feorhlegu† f. *death*, B, EL.

feorhlic (fera-, ferh-) *vital*, HGL 453.

feorhlīf n. *life*, PPs 142².

feorhloca m. *breast*, GU 625.

feorhlyre m. *loss of life*, LL 466,3.

feorhneru f. *preservation of life, refuge, salvation : nourishment of life, food*.

feorhrǣd m. *salvation*, AN 1656.

feorhscyldig *guilty of death*, LL.

feorhsēoc *mortally wounded*, B 820.

feorhsweng m. *fatal blow*, B 2489.

feorhðearf f. *urgent need*, PPs 69¹.

feorhwund f. *deadly wound*, B 2385.

feorland (o²) n. *distant land*, PA 10.

feorlen=fyrlen

feorlic *far off, alien, strange*, RWH 137'.

feorm (a, æ, o, y) f. *food, provision, sustenance : entertainment, meal, feast, supper*, Æ, AO, CP : *goods, possessions : stores : rent in kind*, EC : *profit, benefit*, CP : *tilling*, LL 454,8.

feorma=forma

feormehām m. *farm*, CHR 1087.

feormend I. m. *entertainer*, WY 30. II. *cleanser, polisher, furbisher*, B 2256.

feormendlēas *wanting a burnisher*, B 2761.

feormere m. *purveyor*, KC 4·278²¹.

feormfultum m. *help in food*, LL 356,69¹.

±feormian I. *to entertain, receive as guest : cherish, support, sustain, feed : consume : benefit, profit :* (+) *harbour* (stolen goods), LL 108,4⁶. II. *to scour, cleanse, furbish*, Lk. ['farm']

feormung f. I. *harbouring*, LL. II. *furbishing, cleansing*, LL.

feornes f. *distance*, BH 72¹⁰.

feorr I. comp. fi(e)rra, fyrra; sup. fierresta '*far,*' *remote, distant*, Wif; CP. II. adv. comp. fierr, firr, fyr(r); sup. fi(e)rrest, fyrrest '*far,*' *far away, distant, remote*, BH, Cr, RBL, VPs; CP : *far back* (in time) : *further, besides, moreover*.

feorran I. adv. *from afar, from a remote time or place*, B, El, Gen : *far off, at a distance*, Bo; Æ, CP. ['ferren'] II. (æ, y) *to remove, avert, turn aside, withdraw*, B : *proscribe*. ['far']

feorrancumen *come from afar, strange*, LL.

feorrancund (B), feorrcund (LL) *come from afar, foreign born*.

feorrane, feorren(e)=feorran I.

feorrian (ea) *to keep apart*, Æ : (±) *depart*, NG.

feorrung f. *removal, departure*, GD 49¹⁶.

feorsian (y) *to go beyond : put far from, expel : depart, remove, separate*, Ps. ['ferse']

feorsibb *distantly related*, LL 346,51.

feorsn=fiersn

feor-stuðu, -studu (e¹) f. *support*, WW.

feorting f. '*pedatio,*' WW 162⁴².

feorð=ferhð

fēorða (ēa, N) '*fourth,*' Lk, MkL; AO, CP. fēorðe healf *three and a half*.

feorðandǣl *fourth part*, Æ.

feorðe *fourthly*, LL 158,15.

feorðēod *a far country*, WYN 186.

fēorð-ling, -ung m. *fourth part :* '*farthing,*' MkL, LkL; Æ. ['ferling']

fēorum dp. of feorh.

feorweg† m. *remote part*.

feorwit=fyrwit

fēos gs. of feoh.

feostnode (CHR 963 E)=fæstnode pret. 3 sg. of fæstnian.

feot-=fet-

fēoð pres. 3 sg. of fēogan.

fēoðer-, fēoðor-=fēower-, fiðer-

fēoung f. *hatred*, CP. [fēogan]

feow-, fēower- v. also fiðer-.

fēower, fēowere [indecl. before a sb. but when alone, usu. g. fēow(e)ra, d. fēowerum] '*four,*' Cr; Æ, AO, CP : *four times*.

fēowerdōgor mn. and adj. *four days*, JnR 11³⁹.

fēowerecg(ed)e *four-cornered, square*, LCD.

fēowerfeald *four-fold*, Lk 19⁸.

fēowerfealdlīce *quadruply*, BL.

fēowerfēte *four-footed*, AO; Æ. ['four-foot']

fēower-fōte (BH), -fōtede (HL) *four-footed*.

fēowergild n. *four-fold compensation*, LL 228'.

fēowerhwēolod (fȳr-) *four-wheeled*, RHy 4¹⁹ (v. ES 38·15).

fēowernihte *four days old*, BH 392¹².

fēowerscȳte *four-cornered, square*, AO. [scēat]

fēowertēme (fēoður-) *four-teamed*, VHy 6³⁴.

fēower-tēoða, -tēogða '*fourteenth,*' BH, MH; AO.

fēowertīene (ē³, ȳ³) '*fourteen,*' MtL; AO.

fēowertīeneniht (ȳ) *fortnight*, LL. [v. *'fourteen'*]

fēowertīenewintre (ȳ) *fourteen years old*, LL.

fēowertig *'forty*,' *MtL*; AO.

fēowertigfeald *forty-fold*, Æ,WW.

fēowertiggēare adj. *of forty years*, ÆL 3⁴⁶⁹.

fēowertiglic *quadragesimal*, BH.

fēowertigoða *'fortieth*,' *Æ* (-tēoða; in error).

fēowertȳne=fēowertīene

fēowerða (*Mt*)=fēorða

fēowerwintre *four years old*, ÆGR 287¹⁹.

fēowr-=fēower-, fēor-

fēowra v. fēower.

±fēowung f. *rejoicing, joy*, OEG 1118. [+fēon]

fēowur-=fēower-; **fer**=fær

fer-=fær-, fear-, fier-, feor-, for-, fyr-

fēr=(1) fær I.; (2) fēfer; **fēr-**=fǣr-, fȳr-

+fēra (fera in A only) m. *associate, comrade, fellow-disciple*, Æ,G,OET ; AO,CP : *wife : man, servant*, v. LL 2·427f. [*'fere*,' *'y-fere'*]

fēran *to go, come, depart, set out, march, travel*, B,JnL (oe); CP : *behave, act* : (+) *accomplish, attain, obtain* : (+) *fare, speed, undergo, suffer* : *bring*, MkR 1³². [*'fere'*]

fērbedd n. *portable bed, litter*, WW 154⁴.

fērblǣd=færblǣd

fercian (ē?) *to convey, bring, Chr : support*, ÆL 23⁵⁹⁷ : *stuff up (with lies)*, ÆL 23⁷¹³ : *proceed*, BF 68²⁹. [*'ferk, firk'*]

fercung f. *sustenance, provision, food*, Æ (9¹⁷²), CHRD.

ferdwyrt ? *a plant* (or ?=feld-), LCD 57b.

fēre *able to go, fit for (military) service*, CHR.

+fēre I. n. *company, community*. II. m. *companion*. III. *accessible*, PH 4. [faran]

+fēred *associated*, WW 216¹³.

ferele f. *rod*, GD. [*L.* ferula]

fērend† m. *sailor*, WH : *messenger*, JUL.

fērende *mobile*, GD.

feresceat m. *passage-money*, WW 34³.

feresōca? '*sibba*,' WW 277²³.

fereð pres. 3 sg. of (1) faran, (2) ferian.

fēreð pres. 3 sg. of fēran.

fergan=ferian

fergenberig (N)=firgenbeorg

ferht I. (=eo) *honest*, GL. II.=ferhð

ferhtlic (=eo) *just, honest*, PPs 95¹⁰.

ferhð I.† (ferð) mn. *mind, intellect, soul, spirit : life : person*, SEAF 26. **wīdan** f. *eternally, for ever*. II.=fyrhð

ferhðbana m. *murderer*, Ex 399.

ferhðcearig *of anxious mind*, GEN 2217.

ferhð-cleofa, -cofa† m. *breast*.

ferhðfrec *bold, brave*, B 1146.

ferhðfriðende (rð) *sustaining life*, RD 39³.

ferhðgenīðla m. *mortal enemy*, B 2881.

ferhðgewit (rð) n. *understanding*, CR 1184.

ferhðglēaw† *wise, prudent*.

ferhðgrim (rð)† *savage*, JUL,WA.

ferhðloca† m. *breast, body*.

ferhðlufu (y) f. *heartfelt love*, AN 83.

ferhðsefa† (i, y) m. *mind, thought*, EL.

ferhðwērig† *soul-weary, sad*.

±ferian *to carry, convey, bring, An,B,El; Æ* : (with refl. a.) *betake oneself to, be versed in : depart, go, Ma*. [*'ferry'*]

feri(g)end m. *leader, bringer*, SOL 80.

fering f. *vehicle*, GD.

+fērlǣcan (ē²) *to associate, unite*, Æ.

+fērlic *associated*. adv. -lice *sociably, together*; -līðlīce GD 313²⁴.

±fērnes f. *passage, transition, passing away*, BL 163¹² (v. BTs).

+fērrǣden (usu. +) f. *companionship, fellowship*, Æ,AO,CP : *friendship : society, fraternity, congregation*, Æ.

fers nm. *verse*, Æ : *sentence*, Æ. [*L.*]

fersc '*fresh*' (*not salt*), AO : *not salted*, KC.

-ferscan v. ā-f.

fersceta m. *freshet*, A 20·382.

±fērscipe m. *fraternity, community, retinue : order, clan : society, fellowship, companionship*, CP : *wedlock*, OEG 2544.

+fērscipian *to accompany*, DR.

fersian *to versify*, ÆGR 218³.

ferð=ferhð

ferðan=furðum

ferðe m. *skin, hide?* LCD 8b.

ferwett-=fyrwit-

fēsan, fēsian=fȳsan, fȳsian

fest=fæst; **fēst**=fȳst; **fēster-**=fōstor-

fēstermenn mp. *bondsmen*, BC,LL.

fēstrian=fōstrian

fet pres. 3 sg. of fetian.

fēt I. pres. 3 sg. of fēdan. II. ds. and nap. of fōt.

+fetan⁴ *to fall*, MtR 13⁷,⁸. (v. FTP 225).

fetel, fetels m. *belt, Bo,Met*. [*'fettle'*]

fetelhilt n. *belted or ringed sword-hilt*, B 1563.

fētels=fǣtels

±fetelsod *provided with a sheath?* BC 3·215².

feter=fetor

+feterian† *to fetter, bind*.

±fetian (æ) *to bring near, fetch, obtain*, AO, B,Gen,Sol : *bring on, induce*, Pr : *marry*. [*'fet*,' *'y-fet'*]

fetor (eo¹, e²) f. '*fetter*,' *shackle, Cp,MkL, Ps : check, restrain, Wa*.

fetorwrāsen f. *fetter, chain*, AN 1109.

+fetran, +fetrian=+feterian

fętt I. pres. 3 sg. of fēdan. II.=fǣtt

fęttan=fetian

fette pret. 3 sg. of fetian.

fēð=fēhð pres. 3 sg. of fōn.

fēða m. *foot-man, foot-soldier*, AO : *band of foot-soldiers, troop*, Æ.

fēðan *to go on foot?* Æ (116[449]).

fēðe n. *power of locomotion, walking, gait, pace,* Æ,AO.

fēðecempa† m. *foot-soldier,* B.

fēðegang m. *journey on foot,* GEN 2513.

fēðegeorn *anxious to go,* RD 32[9].

fēðegest† m. *guest coming on foot, traveller.*

fēðehere m. *infantry,* AO.

fēðehwearf m. *band of footmen,* GU 162.

fēðelāst† m. *step, track, course.*

fēðelēas† *footless, crippled.*

fēðemann m. *pedestrian,* LRG,WW 481[3] : *foot-soldier,* WW 399[27].

fēðemund f. *fore-paw,* RD 16[17].

feðer (æ) f. nap. feð(e)ra, feð(e)re *'feather,'* Lcd,Ph; pl. *wings,* Bo,Mt,OET; CP : *pen,* Lk; CP.

feðer-=fēower-, fiðer-; **feðeran**=fiðerian

feðerbǣre *having feathers, winged,* GPH 390.

feðerbedd n. *'feather-bed,'* WW 124[19].

feðerberend m. *feathered creature,* WW 465[20]. [v. *'feather'*]

feðercræft m. *embroidery,* WW 491[3].

feðergearwe fp. *feathers of the arrow,* B 3119.

feðergeweorc n. *feather-embroidery,* WW 459[27].

feðerhama m. *wings, plumage,* Cp,Gen. [*'featherham'*]

fēðespēdig *speedy of foot,* CRA 53.

fēðewīg† m. *battle on foot, affray.*

feōm=fæðm

feðorbyrste *split into four,* LCD 148a.

feðra, feðre v. feðer.

fēðre *loaded,* A2·373.

feðrian *to become fledged,* OEG 26[27].

+fēðrian *to load,* AS 1[10]. [fōðor]

feðriht *feathered,* MtL p 7[17].

fēðu (WW 110[29])=fēða

fēðung f. *walking, motion,* ÆH 2·134.

fex=feax

fiag- (N)=fēog-; **fibulae** (GL)=fifele

+fic n. *deceit,* EL,RB [v. *'fickle'*]

fic m. *fig, fig-tree,* MtR : (*fig-disease*), *venereal ulcer, hemorrhoids,* LCD. [*'fike'*; L. ficus]

ficādl f. *fig-disease* (v. fic), LCD.

ficæppel m. *fig,* Æ,GL.

ficbēam m. *fig-tree,* Æ,CP.

fician *to flatter,* AB 34·10.

ficlēaf n. *fig-leaf,* GEN 3[7].

ficol *'fickle,' cunning, tricky,* KGl; W.

fictrēow n. *fig-tree,* G.

ficung f. *fraud, trickery,* LL 242,24; 254, 28[2].

ficwyrm m. *intestinal worm,* LCD 122a.

ficwyrt f. *fig-wort,* WW 134[32].

fieftiene=fiftiene

fieht pres. 3 sg. of feohtan.

±**fiell** (æ, e, ea, y) mn. *fall, destruction,* AO, CP : *death, slaughter* : *precipice* : *case, inflection,* ÆGR 91[14]. [feallan] For comps. v. fyll-.

fielt pres. 3 sg. of fealdan.

fielð pres. 3 sg. of feallan.

fiend=fēond, also ds. of fēond.

+fiend (ȳ) mp. *foes, enemies,* Lk; AO. [*'i-feond'*]

fiendwic n. *enemy's camp,* LPs 77[28].

fier v. feorr II.; **fier-**=fēower-

fierd (æ, e, eo, y) f. *national levy or army, Chr* : *military expedition, campaign, Ma, PPs;* AO : *camp.* [*'ferd'*] For comps. v. fyrd-.

fieren-=firen-; **fierfēte**=fēowerfēte

-fierme (eo) v. or-f.

fierra, fierrest, fierresta v. feorr II.

fiersn (e, eo, y) f. *heel,* GEN,WW. [*Ger.* ferse]

fierst=first

fīf usu. indecl. before sb.; but when alone, has na. fīfe, g. fīfa, d. fīfum *'five,'* Bf,G, Gen.

fifalde f. *butterfly,* GL. [*Ger.* falter]

fīfbēc fp. *Pentateuch,* WW 470[8].

fīfe v. fīf.

fīfecgede *having five angles,* ÆGR 289[15].

fifel n. (*huge*) *sea-monster, giant,* WALD 2[10].

fifelcynn f. *race of sea-monsters,* B 104.

fifeldōr n. *door of sea-monsters, river Eider,* WID 43.

fīfele f. *buckle,* WW 403[7]. [*L.* 'fibula']

fifelstrēam m. *ocean, sea,* MET 26[26].

fifelwǣg m. *ocean, sea,* EL 237.

fiffalde=fifalde

fiffeald *'five-fold,'* ÆGr : *five each,* CM 840.

fiffētede *five-footed* (*verse*), OEG 130.

fiffingre f. *'potentilla,' 'primula,' cinquefoil, oxlip?* Lcd. [*'fivefinger'*]

fiffōre *five-storied,* Æ. [flōr]

fifgēar n. *period of five years, lustrum,* WW 431[16].

fifhund(red) num. *five hundred,* EL,GL.

fiflæppede *having five lobes,* LCD 59b.

fif-lēaf n., -lēafe f. *'potentilla,' cinquefoil,* Lcd. [*'fiveleaf'*]

fifmægen n. *magic power,* SOL 136. [fifel]

fifnihte *five days old,* ANS 129·22.

fifta *'fifth,'* Æ,Chr,Lcd; AO,CP.

fiftafæder v. fæder.

fifte *fifthly,* LL 158,16.

fiftig=fiftig; **fiftegða**=fiftēoða

fiftēne=fiftiene

fiftēogoða (i[2]) *'fiftieth,'* ÆGr; CP.

fīf-tēoða (ȳ[1]), tēða, -tegða *'fifteenth,'* BH, Lcd.

fíftíene (ȳ¹, ē², ȳ²) (often w. g.) 'fifteen,' B,Bf,Gu; AO.

fíftíenenihte fifteen days old, LCD 3·180.

fíftíenewintre (e²) fifteen years old, BL 213¹.

fíftig num. 'fifty,' ÆB : sb. a set of fifty, Mk.

Fíftigdæg m. Pentecost, MkL p 5¹⁰.

fífti(g)esman m. captain of fifty, Ex 18²¹, DEUT 1¹⁵.

fíftigeða, fíftigoða=fífteogoða

fíftigfeald 'fifty-fold,' containing fifty, Æ.

fíftigwintre fifty years old, Jn 8⁵⁷.

fíftȳne (Æ)=fíftíene

fífwintre five years old, ÆGR 287¹⁴.

-fígen v. ā-f.

+fígo ? np. a disease, 'cimosis' (? +fligo, v. BTac), LCD la, 14a.

fíhl, fihle m? cloth, rag, NG. [?=fliht]

fíht I. pres. 3 sg. of feohtan. II.=feht

fíht-=fyht-; **fíhtan**=fȳhtan

+fíhð pres. 3 sg. of +féon.

fíl (GL)=féol

+fílan=+fȳlan; **+fílce**=+fylce

fíld sb. curdled milk, LCD 53b (LF130).

fíldcumb m. milk-pail, LCD 122b.

fílde field-like, of the nature of a plain, AO 74¹².

+fílde n. field, plain, AO 12¹⁰. [feld]

fíleðe n. hay, PPs 36².

fílgð, filhð pres. 3 sg. of féolan.

fílí-=fylg-

fíllende ptc. rubbing, WW 407³⁶.

fílíðe=fíleðe

fílíðlēag m. meadow, Ct.

fíll=fyll

fílle f. thyme, LCD,OEG 56³⁸. [=cerfille?]

fíllen I.=fellen II. (?) f. a dropping, LCD 18a (fyln).

fílmen (y) n. 'film,' membrane, thin skin, Lcd; Æ : foreskin, Æ.

fílst-=fylst-

fílð pres. 3 sg. of feallan.

fín f. heap, pile. v. OEG 2456.

fín-=fyn-

fína m. woodpecker, WW 49².

fínc m. 'finch,' Ep,WW.

fínd=fíend

fíndan³ (but occl. wk. pret. funde) (±) to 'find' ('y-find,' 'y-found'), meet with, B, BH,Gen,Jul,LG,Met : discover, obtain by search or study, recover, Cr,MtL,Ps : provide : consider, devise, arrange, dispose, decide, AO,CP : show, inform. f. æt obtain from.

fíndend m. finder, GPH 391.

+fíndig (y) capable, ÆGR 69⁴.

fínding f. invention, initiative, CM 1082.

fínel=fínol

fínger m. 'finger,' Bf,MtL,VPs; Æ,CP.

fínger-æppla, -appla npl. finger-shaped fruits, dates, ÆL,OEG.

fíngerdocca? m? finger-muscle, GL.

fíngerlíc belonging to a finger or ring, WW 291²⁶.

fíngerlíð n. finger-joint, NC 343.

fíngermǽl n. finger's length, NR 22⁸.

fínn m. 'fin,' Æ.

fínol (e¹, u², y²) m. 'fennel,' Ep,WW. [L. foenuculum]

fínolsǽd n. fennel-seed, LCD 157a.

fínst=fíndest pres. 2 sg. of fíndan.

fínt pres. 3 sg. of fíndan.

fínta† m. tail : consequence, result.

fínu(g)l m., fínu(g)le f.=fínol

fío=féo; **fír**=fȳr

fíras† mp. men, human beings.

fírd=fíerd; **fírd-**=fíerd-, fyrd-

fíren f. transgression, sin, crime : outrage, violence : torment, suffering.

fírenbealu n. transgression, CR 1276.

fírencrǽft m. wickedness, JUL 14.

fírendǽd† f. wicked deed, crime.

fírenearfeðe n. sinful woe, GEN 709.

fírenfremmende sinful, CR 1118.

fírenful (y) sinful, wicked, Æ.

fírengeorn sinful, CR 1606.

fírenhicga (y¹, y²) m. adulterer, GPH 389.

fírenhicge (fyrn-) f. adulteress, OEG.

fírenhicgend (fyrn-) adulteress, harlot, OEG.

±fírenian (y) to sin : commit adultery : revile.

fírenleahter (y¹) m. great sin, ÆH 2·420¹⁶.

fírenlíc (y) wicked. adv. -líce vehemently, rashly, WALD 1²⁰ : sinfully.

fírenligerian to commit fornication, RSPs 105³⁹.

fírenlust m. lust, sinful desire, luxury, wantonness, AO,CP.

fírenlustful wanton, luxurious, A 12·502¹⁰.

fírenlustgeorn wanton, W 253⁵.

fírensynn f. great sin, JUL 347.

fírensynnig sinful, CR 1379.

fírentácnian (y) to commit misdeeds, RHy 6²¹.

fírenðearf (y) f. dire distress, B 14.

fírenðéof (i², ēa²) m. robber, DR.

fírenum excessively, very, intensely : malignantly. [dp. of fíren]

fírenweorc† n. evil deed, sin, CR.

fírenwyrcende† sinning, sinful, PPs.

fírenwyrhta (y)† m. evil-doer, PPs.

fírfoda=fȳrfoda

fírgenbēam (y) m. mountain tree, B 1414. [Goth. fairguni]

fírgenbeorg (fergenberig) mountain, RUNE-CASKET (v. FM 368).

fírgenbucca m. ibex, LCD.

firgendstrēam=firgenstrēam

firgen-gāt f. nap. -gǣt *ibex*, GL.

firgenholt n. *mountain-wood*, B 1393.

firgenstrēam† m. *mountain-stream, woodland-stream.*

firgin-=firgen-; **firh**=fyrh

firht=friht; **firhð**=ferhð

firigendstrēam=firgenstrēam

firinggāt=firgengāt; **firmdig**=frymdig

firmettan *to ask, beg*, AO 186[6].

firn-=firen-, fyrn-

firr, firra, firre, firrest v. feorr.

first I. (e, ie, y) mn. *period, space of time, time, respite, truce*, B,Chr; CP. ['*frist*']
II. (ie) f. *ceiling, (inner) roof*, WW : *ridgepole*. ['*first*'] III.=fyrst

firsthrōf n. *ceiling, ridge-pole*, OEG 2812.

first-mearc, -gemearc fm. *period of time, appointed time, interval, respite.*

firð-=fyrð-; **firwet**=fyrwit

fisc m. '*fish*,' VPs; Æ,AO,CP; Mdf.

fisc-að, -(n)oð m. *fishing*, AO : *fishpond* : *a catch of fish* : *fishing rights.* [v. NC 286]

fiscbrȳne m. *fish-brine*, WW 128[39]. [v.'*fish*']

fisccynn n. *fish tribe*, ÆT.

fiscdēah f. *fish-dye, purple*, OEG 5193.

fiscere m. '*fisher*,' *fisherman*, AO,Mt : *kingfisher* (*bird*).

fiscfell (NG)=fiscpōl

fiscflōdu? m. *fish-flood, sea*, OET 127[4].

fischūs n. *place where fish is sold*, WW 184[40].

fiscian *to* '*fish*,' Bo.

fisclacu f. *fishpond or stream*, BC 2·374[16].

fiscmere m. *fishpond*, WW 484[11].

fiscnað=fiscað

fiscnett n. *fishing-net*, MET 176[11].

fiscnoð, fiscoð=fiscað

fiscpōl m. *fishpond*, JnL,WW. ['*fishpool*']

fiscōrūt m. *small fish*, MtL 15[34].

fiscwelle m. *fishpond*, A 13·321.

fiscwer m. '*fish-weir*,' *fish-trap*, LL 454,9 : *fishing-ground*, Lk.

fiscwylle *full of fish*, BH. [weallan]

fisting f. '*fesiculatio*,' WW. ['*fisting*']

fitelfōta *white-footed* (BTs),WW 161[20].

fitersticca m. *tent-nail*, WW 187[5].

fitt I. f? *struggle, contest, fight*, Gen 2072. ['*fit*'] II. f. '*fit*,' *song, poem*, Bo; GL (FTP 226).

fiðele f. *fiddle* (BT).

fiðelere m. '*fiddler*,' WW 311[23].

fiðelestre f. *female fiddler*, WW 311[24].

fiðer-=fēower-, feðer-

fiðerbǣre *feathered*, OEG.

fiðercian *to flutter*, GD 100[19]. [fiðere]

fiðerdǣled *quadripartite, quartered*, OEG.

fiðere (y) n. nap. fið(e)ru, fiðera(s) *wing*, Æ,CP.

fiðerfeald *four-fold*, EHy 4[19].

fiðerflēdende (y[1]) *flowing in four streams*, GPH 390.

fiðerflōwende *flowing in four streams*, OEG 48[2].

fiðerfōtnieten (e[1]) m. *four-footed animal*, AA 23[20].

fiðerhama (y[1]) m. *wing-covering*, ÆL 34[74].

+fiðerhamod *covered with feathers*, ÆH 1·466[27].

fiðerhīwe '*quadriformis*,' OEG 177.

+fið(e)rian *to provide with feathers or wings*, Bo; PPs. ['*feather*']

fiðerlēas *without wings*, Wy 22.

fiðerrīca (y[1]) m. *tetrarch*, ÆH.

fiðerrīce (y[2]) n. *tetrarchy*, CHR 12c.

fiðerscēatas mp. *four quarters?* SOL 32.

fiðersleht m. *flapping of wings, joy?* OEG 4892.

fiðertēme (eo[1], u[2]) *with four horses abreast*, VHy 5[34]. [v. '*team*']

fiðertōdǣled=fiðerdǣled; **fiðoru** v. fiðere.

fixa, fixas, fixum=fisca, fiscas, fiscum, gp., nap. and dp. of fisc.

fixen=fyxen

fixian, fixoð, fixnoð=fiscian, fiscað

flā f. *arrow*, AO. ['*flo*';=flān]

flacg *cataplasm, plaster*, WW 380[28].

flacor† *flying (of arrows)*. [cp. *Ger.* flackern]

flæ-=flea-, fleo-

flǣ-=flēa-, flēo-, flīe-

flǣre f. *earlap*, WW 157[12].

flæsc (DD 51)=fleax

flǣsc (ē) n. '*flesh*,' Æ,Cp,Lk,VP; CP : *body* (*as opposed to soul*), B,Jn : *carnal nature*, Mt : *living creatures*, Lk,Ps.

flǣscǣt m. *animal food*, RB.

flǣscbana m. *murderer, executioner*, GD.

flǣscbesmitennes f. *defilement of the flesh*, Sc 69[11].

flǣsccofa m. *body*, LPs 118[120].

flǣsc(c)wellere m. *executioner*, WW 382[29].

flǣsccȳping f. *meat-market*, WW 145[26].

flǣsceht *fleshy*, LCD 83a.

flǣscen *of flesh, like flesh*, GPH; Æ. ['*fleshen*']

flǣscennes (BF 142[12])=flǣscnes

flǣscgebyrd f. *incarnation*, OEG 429.

flǣschama (o[2])† m. *body, carcase.*

+flǣschamod *incarnate*, Æ.

flǣschord n. *body*, SOUL 103.

flǣschūs n. '*flesh-house*,' *place where meat is sold*, WW.

flǣsclic '*fleshly*,' *corporeal, carnal*, Æ,BH, Bl,Bo.

flǣsclicnes f. *incarnate condition*, Æ. ['*fleshliness*']

flǣscmangere m. *butcher*, WW. ['*fleshmonger*']

flǣscmaðu f. *maggot*, WW 122[13].
flǣsc-mete m. nap. -mettas *flesh, animal food, LL*; Æ,CP. ['*fleshmeat*']
±**flǣscnes** f. *incarnation*, CHR.
+**flǣscod** *incarnate*, Æ.
flǣscsand *portion of meat*, CHRD 14'.
flǣscstrǣt f. *meat-market*, Æ.
flǣsctǣwere m. *torturer of the flesh, executioner*, WW 189[19].
flǣsctōð m. *one of the teeth*, WW 415[24].
flǣscðēnung f. *allowance of food*, CHRD 15[11].
flǣscwyrm m. *maggot*, Lcd. ['*fleshworm*']
flǣslic=flǣsclic
flǣðecomb m. *weaver's comb*, WW.
flǣx (MtR)=fleax
flagen pp. of flēan.
flāh I. n. *wickedness, treachery*, RIM 47.
II.† adj. *wily, deceitful, hostile*. [ON. flār]
flān mf. *barb, arrow, javelin, dart*, B,Ma; Æ,AO,CP. ['*flane*']
flānboga† m. *bow*, B.
flanc m. *flank*, OEG 50[35].
flāngeweorc† n. *shooting-gear, arrows*.
flānhred? *arrow-swift? arrow-equipped?* (*of death*), RIM 72.
flāniht (e) *relating to darts*, WW 425[34].
flānðracu† f. *onset, attack*.
flasce (x) f. '*flask*,' *bottle*, GD,WW.
flāt pres. 3 sg. of flītan.
flaxe=flasce
flaxfōte *web-footed*, HExC 251. [=flox-]
flēa I. mf. '*flea*,' Ep,Lcd. II. (LCD)=flēah n.
flēag pret. 3 sg. of flēogan.
flēah I. n. *albugo, a white spot in the eye*, CP 69. II. m.=flēa I. III. pret. 3 sg. of flēogan. IV. pret. 3 sg. of flēon.
flēam m. *flight*, B; Æ,AO. on f. gebrengan *to put to flight*. on f. weorðan *to flee*. ['*fleme*']
flēamdōm m. *flight*, NC 287.
flēamlāst m. *apostasy*, WW 500[3].
flēan[6] *to* '*flay*,' Cp.
±**fleard** n. *nonsense, vanity, folly, deception, fraud, superstition*, LL; OEG. ['*flerd*']
fleardere m. *trifler*, CHRD 20[12].
fleardian *to be foolish, err, go astray*, CHRD, LL.
flēat I. pret. 3 sg. of flēotan. II.=flēot
fleaðe, fleaðorwyrt f. *water-lily*, LCD.
flēawyrt f. *fleabane*, WW. ['*fleawort*']
fleax (æ, e) n. '*flax*,' *linen*, CP; Æ.
fleax- v. flex-.
flecta=fleohta; **fled**=flett
-flēdan v. ofer-f.
flēde adj. *in flood, full, overflowing*, AO. [flōd]
flēding f. *flowing*, ÆH 2·180[2].
flēg- (N)=flēog-
flēge *little ship*, JnL 6[22](oe).

flehta, flehtra=fleohta; **flēm-**=flīem-
flene=flyne; **flēo**=flēa
+**flenod** *describes some attribute of a cloak*, WW 187[14].
±**flēogan**[2] (intr., cp. flēon) *to* '*fly*,' B,El, Jud,Jul; Æ,CP : *flee, take to flight*, Ma.
flēoge (ē, ȳ) f. *any winged insect*, '*fly*,' Æ, MtL; CP.
flēogenda m. *bird*, CPs.
flēogende '*flying*,' *winged*, ÆGr 44[9].
flēogendlic *flying, winged*, ÆGR 55[2].·
flēogryft n. *fly-curtain*, WW 373[21].
flēohcynn m. *a kind of flies*, PPs 104[27].
flēohnet n. '*fly-net*,' *curtain*, Jud.
fleohta (flecta) m. *hurdle*, Cp 600. [Ger. flechte]
±**flēon**[2] *to fly from*, '*flee**,' *avoid, escape*, An, B,G,Met,VPs; AO,CP : *put to flight*, Æ : *fly* (intr.), Æ.
flēos (VPs)=flīes; **fleos-**=fles-
flēot (ēa) m. I. *water, sea, estuary, river*, AO. II. *raft, ship*, Hy. ['*fleet*']
flēotan[2] *to float, drift, flow, swim, sail*, Æ,B, CP : (tr.) *skim*, LCD. ['*fleet*']
flēote=flīete
flēotende *floating*, Gen 1447. ['*fleeting*']
flēotig *fleet, swift*, RD 52[4].
flēotwyrt f. *seaweed*, LCD 101a.
fleoðe (ea) f. *water-lily*, LCD.
flēow pret. 3 sg. of flōwan.
flēowð=flēwð pres. 3 sg. of flōwan.
-flēre v. ðri-, fīf-f.
flēring f. *story* (*of a building*), Æ. [flōr]
flēs=flīes; **flēsc**=flǣsc
fleswian (eo) *to whisper? pull a wry face?* BH 122[17] (JAW 30). [or ? flēswian *dissemble*, ES 44·470]
flet=flett; **flēt**, flēte=flīete
fletræst f. *couch*, B 1241.
fletsittend† m. *sitter in hall, courtier, guest*.
flett n. *floor, ground*, B,LL : *dwelling, hall, mansion*, B,LL. ['*flet*']
flettgefeoht n. *fighting in a house*, LL 18,39.
flettgesteald† n. *household goods*, GEN.
flettpǣð m. *floor of a house*, GEN 2729.
fletwerod n. *hall-troop, body-guard*, B 476.
fleðecamb=flǣðecomb
flēwsa m. *flowing, flux, issue* (*bodily disorder*), LCD. [flōwan]
flēwð pres. 3 sg. of flōwan.
flex=fleax
flexæcer (y[3]) m. *flax land*, KC 5·389[16].
flexgescot n. *contribution of flax*, W 171[27].
flexhamm m. *flax field*, KC 5·374'.
flexlīne f. *flax-winder, reel? flax line? thread?* LL 455,15.
flicce n. '*flitch*' *of bacon, ham*, Gl,KC.
flicorian (e[2]) *to move the wings, flutter*, Æ. ['*flicker*']

flīe=flēah I.

flīehð pres. 3 sg. of flēon.

flīema (ē, ī, ȳ) m. *fugitive, exile, outlaw*, Æ, *Gen*; AO. Godes f. *excommunicate person*, LL 352,66. ['*fleme*']

±flīeman (ǣ, ē, ȳ) *to put to flight, drive away, banish, Gen*; CP. ['*fleme*'; flēam]

flīeman-feorm, -feorming f. *offence of, or penalty for, sheltering fugitives from justice*, LL 102,30; 2·302.

+flīeme (ē) adj. *fugitive*, DR 147⁶.

flīeming (flȳmig) sb. *fugitive*, OEG 2965.

flīes (ē, ēo, ī, ȳ) n. '*fleece,' wool, fur, sealskin, LL,Ps.

flīet (WW 489³)=flēot; flīetan=flītan

flīete (ē, ēo, ȳ) f. I. *cream, curds*. II. *punt, boat, raft*, WW.

flīg=flēah I.; flīg-=flēog-, flȳg-

flīgel m? n? '*flail,*' *A* 9·264.

fliht=flyht; flīht-, flihte-=flyhte-

flīhð pres. 3 sg. of flēon.

flīma=flīema

flint m. '*flint,' rock*, Æ,*Cr,Ep,WW.

flinten *of flint*, W 252¹.

flintgrǣg *grey like flint*, RD 4¹⁹.

flīo=flēah I.; flīs=flīes

±flit (usu. +) n. *strife, Ps : dispute, contention : 'scandalum'*; tō +flītes *emulously*. ['*flite*']

±flītan¹ *to strive, quarrel, dispute, contend*, B,*BH*; Æ,CP. ['*flite*']

flītcræft m. *dialectics, logic*, OEG.

flītcræftlic *logical*, HGL 481.

flītere m. *disputer, chider, brawler, schismatic, Gl.* ['*fliter*']

±flīt-ful (OEG), -fullic (CHR) *contentious*.

+flītfulnes f. *litigiousness*, A 11·102⁸⁴.

±flītgeorn I. (±) m. *contentious person*, BF, LCD. II. (+) *contentious*, RB 130²⁰.

+flītglīw n. *mockery*, WW.

+flītlīce *emulously*, BH 406¹⁷.

±flītmǣlum *contentiously, emulously*, OEG, RBL.

-flītme? v. un-f.

flīusum (OET)=flēosum dp. of flēos.

flōc n. *flat fish, flounder*, WW.

flōcan *to clap, applaud*, RD 21³⁴.

flocc m. '*flock,' company, troop*, Æ,*Chr*.

floccmǣlum *in troops*, AO. ['*flockmeal*']

floccian *to spring forth*, GPH 399.

flocrād f. *invading band, troop*, CHR.

flōd mn. *mass of water,* '*flood,' wave*, Æ,*Gen, Chr,Mt,VPs*; AO,CP : *flow (of tide as opposed to ebb), tide, flux, current, stream*, AO : *the Flood, Deluge*, B,*Lk*; Æ.

flōdblāc *pale as water? pale through fear of drowning*, Ex 497.

flōde f. *channel, gutter*, GL : *flood?* (Earle), EC 120³¹.

flōdegsa m. *flood-terror*, Ex 446.

flōden *of a river*, WW 240.

flōdhamm m. *piece of land surrounded by water?* KC 1·289¹⁶.

flōdlic *of or belonging to a stream*, ÆGR 54⁹.

flōdweard f. *sea-wall*, Ex 493.

flōdweg† m. *watery way, sea.*

flōdwudu m. *ship*, CR 854.

flōdwylm† m. *flowing stream, raging billows*. [weallan]

flōdȳð f. *wave of the sea*, B 542.

+flog n. *infectious disease*, LCD 3·34⁹.

flogen I. pp. of flēon. II. pp. of flēogan.

flogettan *to fluctuate : flutter*, Sc,GD 100¹⁹.

flogoða m. *liquor*, GPH 402.

flōh f. *chip*, WW 416⁴.

flohtenfōte *web-footed*, LCD 33b.

flōr fm. ds. flōra, flōre '*floor,' pavement, ground*, B,*Bo,Lk*; Æ : *bottom (of a lake, etc.), Sat.*

flōrisc *flowery*, CM 44.

flōrstān m. *paving-stone, tessella*, WW 150²⁷.

flot n. *deep water, sea*. on flot(e) '*afloat,' Chr,Ma.*

flota m. (*floater), boat, ship, vessel : fleet, Chr : crew : sailor : (†) pirate.* ['*flote*']

+flota m. *floater (whale)*, WH 7.

floten pp. of flēotan.

floterian *to flutter, fly, flicker*, Æ : *float, be carried or tossed by waves*, Æ.

flothere m. *piratical fleet*, B 2915.

flotian *to 'float,' Chr.* [flēotan]

flotlic *nautical, naval*, WW 205²⁷.

flotmann m. *sailor, pirate*, ÆL,W.

flotorian=floterian

flotscip n. *ship, bark*, WW.

flotsmeru n. *floating grease, fat*, LL 453,4.

flotweg m. *ocean*, HU 41.

flōwan⁷ *to 'flow,' stream, issue*, Bf,*Sol,VPs*; AO,CP : *become liquid, melt, VPs : abound, PPs : (+) overflow*, AO.

flōw(ed)nes f. *flow, flux, overflow, torrent*, CP.

flōwende '*flowing,' Ma 65.*

flōwendlic *flowing*, LPs 147¹⁸.

flōwing f. '*flowing,' flux, MtL.*

flugl- (OET 26)=fugl-

flugol *fleet, swift : fleeting*, Sc.

flugon I. pret. pl. of flēogan. II. pret. pl. of flēon. III.=fulgon pret. pl. of fēolan.

flustrian *to plait, weave*, WW 485¹ (IF 48·254).

fluton pret. pl. of flēotan.

flycerian=flicorian

-flycge v. unfl-.

flycticlāð (GL)=flyhteclāð

flyge† (i) m. *flight.*

flȳge=flēoge

flygepīl n. *flying dart*, Mod 27. [v. '*pile*']

flygerēow *wild in flight*, Gu 321.

flygul=flugol

flȳhst pres. 2 sg. of flēon.

flyht (i) m. *flying*, '*flight*,' *Æ,OET.* on flyhte *on the wing*.

flyhte m. *patch*, MkLR 2²¹.

flyhteclāð (i) m. *patch, Cp.* [v. '*cloth*']

flyhthwæt† *swift of flight*, Ph.

flȳhð pres. 3 sg. of flēon.

flȳm-=flīem-

flyne (e) f. *batter*, Lcd.

flȳs (Æ)=flīes; **flyt**, flȳt-=flit, flīt-

flȳt pres. 3 sg. of flēotan.

flȳte=flēot(e), flīete

flȳtme f. *fleam (blood-letting instrument)*, Gl. [*L.* phlebotomum]

flyð=flyht

±**fnæd** n. nap. fnadu *fringe, border, hem*, Æ.

fnǣran, fnǣrettan *to breathe heavily, snort, fume.* v. NC 356.

fnæs I. n. dp. fnasum *fringe*, WW 425²⁷. II. pret. 3 sg. of fnesan.

fnǣst m. *blowing, blast, breath, Lcd: voice*, LF 56³. ['*fnast*']

fnǣstian *to breathe hard, Lcd.* [v. '*fnast*']

fnēosung f. *sneezing*, WW. [v. '*fnese*']

fnēsan⁵ *to pant, gasp*, GD : (+) *sneeze*, Lcd.

fnora m. *sneezing*, Æ,Gl.

fō pres. 1 sg. of fōn.

foca m. *cake (baked on the hearth)*, ÆL 18¹⁶⁴.

fōd-=fōdd-

fōda m. '*food*,' *nourishment*, *Æ,CD* : *fuel, Sc.*

fōdder (o², u²) I. n. gs. fōd(d)res '*fodder*,' *food, Æ,LL* : *darnel, tares*, MtL 13 (fōter). II. n. *case, sheath*, Gl,MH. III. *hatchet?* WW.

fōdderbrytta m. *distributor of food, herdsman*, WW 111³⁹.

fōddergifu (u²) *food*, PPs.

fōdderhec *rack for food or fodder*, LL 455,17.

fōddornoð m. *sustenance*, GD 193¹⁷.

fōddorðegu† f. *feeding, repast, food.*

fōddurwela m. *wealth of food, provisions*, Rd 33¹⁰.

fōdnoð m. *substance, food*, TC.

fōdrað (OET 180²⁰)?=fōdnoð

fōdrere m. *forager*, AO 156³⁵.

foe- (N)=fe-, fē-

+**fōg** I. n. *joining, joint.* II. n. *suitability*, Lcd 10b. III. *suitable*, Lcd 89b.

+**fōgstān** (fōh) m. *hewn stone*, CP 253¹⁹.

fōh imperat. of fōn.

foht=feoht

fohten pp. of feohtan.

fol (wk. adj.)=full

+**fol** adj. *with foal*, Gen 32¹⁵.

fol-=ful-

fola m. '*foal*,' *colt, Bl,MkL;* Æ.

folc n. '*folk*,' *people, nation, tribe, Æ,B, Chr;* AO,CP : *a collection or class of persons, laity, Bl,Bo* : *troop, army.*

folcāgende† *ruling.*

folcbealo n. *great tribulation*, Men 125.

folcbearn† n. *man*, Gen.

folccū (folcū) f. *people's cow*, PPs 67²⁷.

folccūð *noted : public*, BH.

folccwēn f. *queen of a nation*, B 641.

folccwide n. *popular saying*, NC 287.

folccyning† m. *king of a nation.*

folcdryht† f. *multitude of people.*

folcegetrum=folcgetrum

folcegsa m. *general terror*, PPs 88³³.

folcfrēa m. *lord of the people*, Gen 1852.

folcfrig *having full rights of citizenship*, LL 13,8; 344,45. [v. '*folk*']

folcgedrēfnes f. *tribulation*, NC 287.

folcgefeoht n. *pitched battle*, AO.

folcgemōt n. *meeting of the people of a town or district*, LL. ['*folkmoot*']

folcgerēfa m. *public officer*, WW.

folcgeriht=folcriht

folcgesīð† m. *prince, noble, chief, officer.*

folcgestealla† m. *companion in war*, Gen.

folcgestrēon n. *public treasure*, Gen 1981.

folcgetæl n. *number of fighting men*, Ex 229.

folcgetrum† n. *army, host*, Gen.

folcgewinn n. *fighting, war*, Met 1¹⁰.

folcherepað m. *highway*, KC.

folcisc *of the people, popular, secular, common*, LL.

folclǣsung=folclēasung

folclagu f. *law of the people, public law*, LL.

folcland n. *land held by freemen according to tribal rules of family inheritance*, LL (v. 2·403 and NED). ['*folkland*']

folclār f. *homily*, GD.

folclēasung f. *slander*, LL. [v. '*folk*']

folclic *public*, Æ : *common, popular, secular : populous*, OEG.

folcmægen† n. *public force, army, tribe.*

folcmǣgð† f. *tribe, nation*, Gen.

folcmǣlum=floccmǣlum

folcmǣre *celebrated*, Gen 1801.

folcmōt=folcgemōt

folcnēd f. *people's need*, PPs 77¹⁶.

folcrǣd† m. *public benefit.*

folcrǣden f. *decree of the people*, Cra 42.

folcriht I. n. *right of the people, common law*, LL. ['*folkright*'] II. adj. *according to common law*, LL 30¹³.

folcsæl n. *house*, Rd 2⁵.

folcscearu† f. *people, nation, province : people's land*, B 73 (Earle).

folcsceaða m. *villain*, An 1595.

folcscipe m. *nation, people*, Rd 33¹⁰.

folcslite n. *sedition*, WW 116²⁶.

folcsōð n. *simple truth?* ÆL 23⁶⁶.

folcstede† m. *dwelling-place*, B : *battlefield.* [v. *'folk'*]

folcstōw f. *country place*, BH160¹⁶.

folcswēot m? *troop, multitude*, Ex577.

folctalu f. *genealogy*, Ex379.

folctoga† m. *chieftain, commander.*

folctruma m. *host*, LPs.

folcū=folccū

folcweleg *populous*, WW476¹⁶.

folcwer† m. *man*, GEN.

folcwiga m. *warrior*, RD15²³.

folcwita m. *public councillor, senator*, CRA 77.

folcwōh n. *deception of the public*, ÆL 23²⁶¹.

foldærn† n. *earth-house, grave.*

foldāgend m. *earth-possessor, earth-dweller*, PH5. (MS folcāgend)

foldbold n. *house, castle*, B773.

foldbūend m. *earth-dweller, man, inhabitant of a country*, CP.

folde (eo) f. *earth, ground, soil, terra firma*, B,*Jud* : *land, country, region, Gen* : *world.* [*'fold'*]

foldgræf† n. *earth-grave.*

foldgrǣg *grey as the earth?* GNC31.

foldhrērende *walking on the earth*, PA5.

foldrǣst f. *rest in the earth*, CR1029.

foldwæstm m. *fruits of the earth*, PH654.

foldweg† m. *way, path, road* : *earth.*

foldwela m. *earthly riches*, RIM68.

foldwong† m. *plain, earth.*

folen, folgen pp. of fēolan.

folgað (AO)=folgoð

folgere m. *'follower,' attendant, disciple*, Bo, WW ; Æ,CP : *successor*, AO150²⁷ : *freeman who is not a householder.*

±folgian (often w. d.) *to 'follow,'* *Jn,Lk* : *accompany, Chr,Ps* : *follow after*, B : (+) *attain*, CP383²⁷ : *obey, serve, observe*, *El.* (v. also fylgan.)

folgoð m. *body of retainers, following, retinue* : *pursuit, employment, service, dignity, office, rule*, Æ,AO,CP : *jurisdiction, district* : *condition of life, destiny.*

folm†, folme f. folma m. *palm, hand.* [fēlan]

fon=fann; **fon-**=fan-

fōn⁷ (±) *to take, grasp, seize, catch*, B, BH,*Gen,Ma*; AO,CP : *capture, make prisoner, Chr* : *receive, accept, assume, undertake*, B,*Sol*; CP : *meet with, encounter.* f. on *take up, begin, resume, take to*, Æ,*Bo,Chr* : *attack*, CHR1085E. f. tō rīce *ascend the throne, Chr*; AO. f. tōgædre *join together, join issue, engage in battle.* him tōgēanes feng *clutched at him*, B. him on fultum feng *helped them*, JUD 300. hlyst +f. *listen.* [*'fang,' 'i-fang'*]

fond=fand pret. 3 sg. of findan.

fong-=fang-; **fonn**=fann; **font**=fant

fonu=fanu

for I. prep. (with d., inst. and a.) (local) *before, in the sight of, in or into the presence of, as far as*, IM119¹³ : (temporal) *during, before*, Æ : (causal) '*FOR*,' *on account of, for the sake of, through, because of, owing to, from, by reason of*, Æ : *as to* : *in order to* : *in place of, instead of, equivalent to, at the price of*, Æ : *in preference to*, Rood : *in spite of, Chr.* for worulde *as regards this world*, Æ. for Dryhtne *by God.* II. conj. *for, because.* for hwȳ, for hwām, for hwon *wherefore?* for ðām, for ðon, for ðȳ (*'forthen'*) *therefore*, BH : *because, since.* for ðām ðe (ðȳ), for ðȳ ðe *because, AO.* for ðȳ ðæt, for ðām ðæt *in order that.* III. adv. *too, very*, Æ. for ān *only.*

for- I. *denotes loss or destruction* (as in fordōn, forgiefan), *or is intensive or pejorative*, as in forbærnan, forrotian. It is not connected with the preposition 'for.' [*Ger.* ver-] II. occly.=fore-

fōr I. f. *going, course, journey, expedition*, BH; AO : *way, manner of life.* [*'fore'*] II. m. *pig, hog*, OEG. III. pret. 3 sg. of faran.

fora (N)=foran; **fora-**=fore-; **forad**=forod

foran I. prep. (w. d.) *before, opposite.* II. adv. *before, in front, forward*, Rd; Æ, AO,CP : *to the front*, Da. foran ongean *opposite.* fōran tō *opposite* : *beforehand.* [*'forne'*]

foranbodig n. *thorax, chest*, WW158⁴¹.

forandæg *early part of the day*, Æ(NC).

forane *opposite* : *beforehand.*

foranhēafod n. *forehead*, Æ.

foranlencten m. *early spring*, LCD96a.

foranniht f. *early part of the night, dusk, evening*, Æ.

forannihtsang m. *compline*, BTK194,218.

foraō=foreað

forbærnan *to cause to burn, burn up, consume by fire, be consumed*, Æ,*Chr*; AO. [*'forburn'*]

forbærnednes f. *burning*, LCD.

forbearan=forberan

forbearnan=forbærnan

forbed n. *portable bed, litter*, ZDA31.

forbēgan=forbīgan

forbelgan³ *to be enraged*, BL.

forbēn f. *prayer*, DHY138¹³.

forbēodan *to 'forbid,' prohibit, Chr,G*; Æ : *restrain*, Ps : *refuse*, Lk : *repeal, annul*, LL42,49.

forbēodendlic *dehortative, dissuasive*, ÆGR 225¹¹.

forbeornan³ (e, y) *to burn, be consumed by fire*, AO,B. [*'forburn'*]

forberan I. (sv⁴) *to ' forbear,' abstain from,
refrain,* CP : *suffer, endure, tolerate, humour,*
CP,B,BH,Mt : *restrain.* II.=foreberan

forberendlīce *tolerably,* Sc 137⁶.

forbernan=forbærnan

forberstan³ *to break, burst asunder, vanish,
fail,* LL : *let go by default,* EC 201'. ['*for-
burst*']

forbētan=forebētan

forbīgan (ē, ȳ) *to bend down, bow down,
depreciate, abase, humiliate, degrade.*

forbīgels m. *arch, arched roof,* WW 126³.

forbindan³ *to bind (up), muzzle,* CP 105⁷.
['*forbind*']

forbisen=forebysen

forbītan¹ *to bite through,* HL 18³⁹¹.

forblāwan⁷ *to blow,* AO : *blow out, inflate,*
Lcd. ['*forblow*']

forblindian *to blind,* MkR 6⁵².

forbōc f. *itinerary,* OEG 2023.

forbod n. *prohibition,* LL ; CP. ['*forbode*']

forboda=foreboda

forbrecan⁵ (æ²) *to break in pieces, bruise,
violate, crush, destroy,* Jn ; AO,CP. for-
brocen *broken down, decrepit.* ['*forbreak*']

for-brēdan³, -bregdan *to tear, pull, snatch
away* : *draw over, cover* : *change, transform,*
Bo. ['*forbraid*']

forbrītan *to break in pieces, crush, bruise.*

forbrȳt-ednes (ESPs), -ennes (V²Ps) f. *contrition.*

forbrytian, forbryttan=forbrītan

forbūgan² *to bend from, refrain from, avoid,
decline,* Æ,Ma ; CP : *flee from, escape,* CP :
hold down. ['*forbow*']

forbȳgan=forbīgan

for-byrd, fore- f. *abstention,* AO 30³⁵ : *long-
suffering,* CP 41¹⁷.

forbyrdian *to wait for,* EPs 32²⁰.

forbyrdig *forbearing,* NC 287.

forbyrnan (Æ)=forbeornan

force f. forca m. *'fork,'* Æ,WW.

forcēap *forestalling (in trade),* LL 234,2¹⁰.
[=*forecēap]

forcel m. *pitchfork,* NC 287.

forceorfan³ *to carve out, cut down, cut off,
cut through, divide,* Æ,Chr ; AO,CP. ['*for-
carve*']

forcēowan² *to bite off,* Bo 36²³.

forcierran (e², y²) *to turn aside, prevent,
avert, avoid,* CP : *turn oneself away, escape* :
pervert.

forcierrednes (e², y²) f. *perversity,* GD
119¹⁵ : *turning aside,* BPs 125¹.

forcierring (e, y) f. *turning aside,* CVPs 125¹.

forcilled *chilled,* LCD.

forcippian (y) *to cut off,* RHy 2¹². [v. '*chip*']

forclǣman *to stop up,* GL.

forclas pl. of forcel.

forclingan³ *to wither, shrink up,* CAS 36¹⁹,
Cp. ['*forcling*']

forclyccan *to stop, close (ears),* RPs 57⁵.

forclȳsan *to close up,* Lcd 3·92'.

forcnīdan=forgnīdan

forcostian *to tempt,* ByH 98³².

forcraflan *to require,* RBL 82⁵.

forcuman⁴ *to come before, prevent, surprise* :
harass, wear out, destroy : *reject,* LG : *overcome, conquer, obtain* : *surpass.*

forcunnian *to tempt, try,* G.

for-cūð (Æ) *bad, wicked, infamous, foul,
despicable, despised,* Æ,Bo ; AO,CP. adv.
-cūðe. ['*forcouth*']

forcūð-līc, -līce=for-cūð, -cūðe

forcweðan⁵ *to speak ill of, abuse, revile,* CP :
reprove : *refuse, reject,* CP : *boast, promise
great things,* GnE 49.

forcwolstan³? *to swallow,* Lcd 18a.

forcwȳsan *to shake violently,* SPs 109⁷.

forcyppian=forcippian

forcyrran (Æ)=forcierran

forcȳðan *to reprove, rebuke* : *refute?* Sol.

ford m. ds. forda *'ford,'* Æ,AO ; Mdf.

fordǣlan *to spend,* Lk(B) 8⁴³.

fordēad *dead,* MtL 28⁴.

fordelfan³ *to delve, dig up,* EC 120²⁸.

fordēman *to condemn, sentence, doom,* Mt ;
Æ : *prejudice,* EC 145' : *decide,* Sc 125⁵.
['*fordeem*']

fordēmedlic *to be condemned,* GD 208⁹.

fordēmednes f. *condemnation, proscription,*
BH 34⁵.

fordēmend m. *accuser,* JnL p5⁹.

fordēming f. *plunder, spoliation,* OEG 3149.

fordemman *to dam up, block up,* EPs 57⁵.

fordettan (KGl)=fordyttan

fordīcigan *to shut out by a ditch, block up,* CP.

fordilemengan *to gloss over,* CHRD 18⁹.

for-dīlgian, -dīlegian, -dīligian *to blot out,
destroy, abolish,* BH. ['*fordilghe*']

fordimmian *to obscure, darken,* Sc. ['*for-
dim*']

fordittan=fordyttan

fordōn anv. *to undo, bring to nought, ruin,
destroy,* BH,MtL ; Æ,AO : *abolish,* Chr :
kill, LL : *corrupt, seduce, defile.* pp. fordōn
corrupt, wicked, abandoned. ['*fordo*']

fordrǣfan *to drive, compel,* LL 24,62.

fordrencan (æ) *to make drunk, intoxicate,*
Æ. ['*fordrench*']

fordrīfan¹ *to drive, sweep away* : *drive on,
impel, compel,* AO : *drive away, expel,*
Chr ; Æ : *overtax.* ['*fordrive*']

fordrifnes f. *objection, opposition,* MkL
Pref 2¹⁵.

fordrincan³ *to make drunk, be drunk,* CP.

fordrūgian *to become dry, wither,* Met ;
ÆL ['*fordry*']

fordruncen pp. *drunk, CP.* [*'fordrunken'*]

fordruncnian (fore-) *to be made drunk,* LL.

fordrūwian=fordrūgian

forduttan (VPs)=fordyttan

fordwer m. *weir at a ford,* KC.

fordwilman *to confound,* Bo 14[5].

fordwīnan *to vanish, ÆL.* [*'fordwine'*]

fordyslic *very foolish,* Bo 42[10].

fordyttan (e, i, u) *to obstruct, block up, close, Cp,VPs;* Æ. [*'fordit'*]

fore I. prep. w. d. a. (local) *before, in the sight of, in presence of, B* : (causal) *because of, for the sake of, through, on account of, by reason of, from, BH* : (temporal) *before, Cr* : *for, instead of.* II. adv. *before, beforehand, formerly, once, Ps.* [*'fore'*]

fore-=for-

foreādihtian *to arrange, order beforehand,* CP 9[9].

forealdian *to grow old, decay, BH;* Æ,CP. [*'forold'*] .

foreāstreccan *to lay low, overthrow,* EPs 105[26].

foreāð m. *preliminary oath, LL* (v. 2·546). [*'foreoath'*]

for-ēaðe (Æ), -ēaðelīce *very easily.*

forebē(a)cen n. *sign, portent, prodigy, Æ.*

forebegān *to intercept,* CHR 1009 E.

foreberan *to prefer,* BH 294[7].

forebētan *to make legal amends (vicariously),* LL.

forebirig=forebyrig ds. of foreburh.

forebiscop m. *high-priest,* MtL 1[18](mg).

forebisegian *to preoccupy,* OEG 1236.

foreblǣsting (ē) f. *shoot, branch,* EPs 79[12].

fōrebōc (HGL 454)=fōrbōc

forebod n. *prophecy, preaching,* NG.

foreboda m. *forerunner, messenger, crier,* ANS 84[14].

forebodere m. *herald, crier,* DR 48,194.

forebodian *to announce, declare,* ASPs.

forebodung f. *prophecy,* NG.

forebrǣdan *to prolong,* EPs 119[5] : *overshadow,* MkL 9[7].

forebrēost n. *chest,* WW.

foreburh f. *outwork* : *outer court, vestibule,* Æ.

forebyrd=forbyrd

forebysen f. *example,* CHR(Thorpe) 67'.

foreceorfan[3] '*praecidere,'* ÆGR 172[4].

foreceorfend m. *front tooth,* WW 264[11].

forecēosan *to choose in preference,* BCJRPs 131[13],[14].

foreclipian (y) '*proclamare,'* BHy 3[4]; ANS 122·265.

forecnēo(w)ris(n) f. *progeny,* ERPs.

forecnyll m. *first ringing (of a bell),* RBL 82[11].

forecostigan *to profane,* EPs 88[32].

forecostung f. *profanation,* EPs 88[35].

forecuman[4] *to come before, prevent, BH* : *overcome? Ps* : *come out, come upon,* NG. [*'forecome'*]

forecweden *aforesaid,* GD 12,344.

forecweðan[5] *to preach, predict,* G,DR.

forecwide m. *prophecy* : *introduction, heading (of chapter),* NG.

forecyme m. *proceeding forth,* MtL p 4[3].

fore-cynren, -cynrēd n. *progeny,* RPs, WW.

forecȳðan *to make known (beforehand), tell forth,* EPs,TC : *prophesy,* GD 339[21].

fored=forod

foreduru f. -dyre, -dere n. *vestibule,* GL.

foredyrstig? *presumptuous,* LL 409,22.

forefæger *very fair,* ES 8·479[89].

fore-feng, -fong=forfang

forefēran *to go before,* BL,LkLR.

forefex (=ea[2]) n. *forelock,* OEG 5326 ; 2[453].

foreflēon *to flee,* MkL 14[52].

forefōn[7] *to prevent, anticipate,* CPs,DR.

foregān anv., foregangan[7] *to go before, precede, BH,VPs* : *go in front of, project* : *excel.* [*'forego'*]

forege-=for(e)-

foregearwung f. *preparation, parasceve,* G.

foregebiddan[5] *to intercede,* RB 62[8].

foregeblind *blinded,* MkL 6[53].

foregecēosan *to choose beforehand,* Æ.

foregegān=forgangan

foregehāt n. *vow,* ÆL 23b[543].

foregehātan *to promise* : *invite,* NG.

foregelēoran *to pass away,* LkL.

foregenga m. *forerunner* : *predecessor, ancestor, CP* : *attendant,* JUD 127.

foregengel (for-) m. *predecessor,* CHR 963 E.

foregescēaw-=forescēaw-

foregesecgan *to predestine,* MtL p 1[9].

foregesettan=foresettan

foregeswuteliende '*indagande,'* OEG 1504.

foregetēon[2] *to point out,* HGL 411.

foregeðingian=foreðingian

foregeðistrod *darkened,* MkL 6[52].

foregidd n. *proverb,* JnR 16[29].

foregielpan[3] *to boast greatly,* AO 4[18],BF 188[13].

foregīmnes (ē[3]) f. *observation,* LkL 17[20].

foregīsl m. *preliminary hostage,* CHR 878.

foreglēaw *foreseeing, provident, wise, prudent, Æ.* adv. -līce.

foregyrnan *to show before,* Sc 203[17].

forehālig *very holy,* ANS 84·3.

forehrādian *to hasten before,* CHRD 26[18].

forehūs n. *porch,* LV 33.

foreiernan (for-) *to run before, outrun,* JnL 20[4]. [*'forerun'*]

fore-iernend, -iernere m. *forerunner,* WW.

forelād-tēow, -twa m. *chief, leader*, LkLR 22²⁶.
forelǣdan *to lead forth*, MtL15¹⁴.
forelǣrend m. *teacher*, Bl149¹³.
forelār f. *preaching*, MtL p16⁵.
forelcian *to delay*, RWH142³⁴.
foreldan=forieldan
forelegnis=forlegis
forelēoran *to go before, pass by*, NG.
forelēornes (EPs100³)=forlēornes
forelocc m. '*forelock*,' OEG.
forelōcian '*prospicere*,' EPs101²⁰ : '*respicere*,' EPs101¹⁸.
foremǣre *illustrious, renowned, famous*, Æ.
foremǣrlic *eminent*, Bo75²⁴.
foremǣrnes f. *eminence, fame*, Bo.
foremanian *to forewarn*, BH412³⁰.
foremanig *very many*, MtL p18¹².
foremeahtig=foremihtig
foremearcod *before-mentioned*, CM378.
foremearcung (e²) f. *title, chapter*, NG.
foremihtig (ea) *most mighty*. adv. -lice.
foremunt m. *promontory*, WW464¹⁷.
forenama m. '*pronomen*,' RBL11¹³.
forene=forane
forenemnan *to mention beforehand*, VH12.
forenyme m. *taking before*, WW42⁷.
forerīm m. *prologue*, Mt(K) pref. 1¹.
forerynel m. *forerunner, herald, morning star*, Æ,CP.
foresacan⁶ *to forbid*, MtL3¹⁴.
foresǣd *aforesaid*, Æ. ['*foresaid*']
fore-sægdnes, -saga f. *preface*, NG.
foresǣndan=foresendan
forescēawere (for-) m. '*provisor*,' ES39·327.
forescēawian *to* '*foreshow*,' *foresee*, Æ : *preordain, decree, appoint*, Æ : *provide, furnish with*, Æ.
forescēawodlīce *with forethought, thoughtfully*, CM76.
forescēawung f. *contemplation, foresight, providence*, Sc; Æ. ['*foreshowing*']
forescēotan (Bo124¹¹)=forscēotan
forescieldnes f. *protection*, EPs120⁵.
forescynian *to shun*, NG.
forescyttels m. *bolt, bar*, Cr312.
forescȳwa m. *shadow*, DR13¹⁴.
forescȳwung f. *overshadowing*, DR28⁶.
foresēcan *to appeal (for justice)*, LL152,3 and nn.
foresecgan *to mention before*, Æ : *proclaim, preach* : *foretell*, BH. ['*foresay*']
foreseld n. *first seat*, MtL23⁶.
foresellan *to spend, advance (money)*, LL (or ? 2 words).
foresendan *to send before*, ÆGr; CM448. [v. '*fore*']
foresēon⁵ *to* '*foresee*,' Ps : *provide*, BH : *provide for*, BH.

foresēond m. *provider*, BH338¹⁰.
foresēones f. *cave, foresight, providence*, BH.
fore-setnes, -sete(d)nes f. *proposition, purpose*, BF2⁸ : *preposition*, ÆGr267¹⁵.
foresettan *to place before, shut in, VPs : propose : prefer : precede*. ['*foreset*']
foresingend m. *precentor*, WW129²¹.
foresittan⁵ *to preside over*, BH.
fore-smēagan, -smēan *to think beforehand*, G,Gl.
foresnotor *very wise*, B3163.
fore-spǣc, -speca=fore-sprǣc, -spreca.
fore-sprǣc (CP), -sprēc, -spǣc (WW) f. *advocacy, defence, excuse : agreement, arrangement : preamble, preface, prologue*, Æ,CP : *promise*. ['*forespeech*']
forespreca m. *intercessor, advocate, mediator : sponsor*, LL442,1.
foresprecan⁵ I. *to speak or answer for, be surety for, intercede for*, CP : *say before*. foresprecen *above-mentioned, aforesaid*, Bo. ['*forespoken*'] II.=forsprecan
forestæppan⁶ (e³) *to precede, go before, anticipate*, Æ : *excel : forestall, prevent*.
forestæppend m. *precursor*, Lk22²⁶.
forestæppung f. *anticipation*, BF172¹⁷.
forestandan⁶ *to preside, lead : excel*, WW 464¹⁵ : *prevail against*, MtL16¹⁸.
forestapul *going before*, GPH396.
foresteall (for-) m. *intervention, hindrance (of justice) : ambush, assault, offence of waylaying on the highway*, Æ,LL : *fine for such an offence : resistance, opposition*. ['*forestall*']
forestemman *to prevent, hinder*, NG.
forestēora m. *look-out man, pilot*, WW 464⁸.
foresteppan⁶=forestæppan
forestīgan¹ *to excel*, ÆGr154¹¹n.
forestige m. *vestibule*, OEG4688 and n.
forestihtian *to fore-ordain*, Æ.
forestihtung f. *predestination*, Æ.
foreswerian⁶ *to swear before*, Num11,14.
foretācn n. '*fore-token*,' *prognostic, prodigy, sign, wonder*, Bo; CP.
foretācnian *to foreshow*, BH216¹⁷.
foreteohhian *to fore-ordain*, WW219³¹.
foreteohhung f. *predestination*, Bo.
foretēon *to fore-ordain, frame beforehand, arrange*, BH,PPs.
foretēð mp. *front teeth*, WW. ['*foretooth*']
foretīge m. *forecourt, porch*, Mt11¹⁶.
foretrymman *to testify*, JnL13²¹.
foretȳned *shut in*, BH386².
foreðanc m. *forethought, providence, consideration, deliberation*, CP.
foreðancful *prudent*, AS14⁵.
foreðanclic *thoughtful, careful, prudent*, CP. adv. -līce.

foreðancol (u³) *prudent.* CP305².
foreðancolnes f. *prudence,* PPs48³.
foreðencan *to premeditate, consider, be mindful,* CP. ['*forethink*']
foreðēon *to surpass, excel,* RB131¹⁹.
foreðingere m. *intercessor, mediator,* Æ.
foreðinglan *to plead for, intercede, defend,* Bo,LL.
foreðingiend m. *intercessor,* WNL294³⁰,³².
fore-ðingrǣden (WNL), -ðingung (Æ) f. *intercession.*
foreðonc=foreðanc; **forewall**=foreweall
foreward=foreweard
forewarnian *to take warning beforehand :* *forewarn,* NC288.
foreweall m. *rampart, bulwark, Ex.* ['*forewall*']
foreweard (a², e²) I. fn. *condition, bargain, agreement, treaty, assurance, Chr.* ['*foreward*'] II. m. *outpost, scout.* III. adj. '*forward,*' *inclined to the front,* Æ : *fore, early, former,* BH; Æ. f. gēar *new year.* IV. adv. (-wearde at AS55¹⁴) *in front,* CP : *towards the future, Gen.* on f. *at the beginning,* BF174 : *above all,* ByH40⁵. fram foreweardum *once more,* RB.
foreweardnes (e³) f. *beginning,* BF198².
foreweorðan³ *to predestinate,* MkLp1¹⁶
fore-wesan anv. pret. 3 sg. -wæs *to be over, rule over,* BH.
forewīs *foreknowing,* HL18³⁶³.
forewitan swv. *to foreknow,* Bo. ['*forewıt*']
forewītegian *to prophesy,* ÆH.
forewītegung f. *prophecy,* ÆL,OEG.
forewitig *knowing,* LCD3·436 : *foreknowing,* Æ : *prophetic,* OEG.
forewitol *foreknowing,* CHR1067D.
forewittiendlic *prescient,* ØEG1502.
foreword n. *stipulation, condition,* KC, LL.
forewost=forwost.
forewrēgan=forwrēgan
forewriten *above or before-written,* CM.
forewrītennes f. *proscription, exile,* WW 466⁵.
forewyrcend m. *servant,* ÆL2¹⁵⁶.
forewyrd f. *agreement, condition,* GL.
±**forewyrdan** (æ³) *to agree,* KC3·274¹².
forfang (forefeng) n. *capture, (legal) seizure, recovery of cattle or other property,* LL : *reward for rescuing property, LL* (v. 388–391 and 2·279). ['*forfang*']
forfangfeoh n. *reward for rescuing cattle or other property,* LL390,3².
forfaran⁶ *to pass away, perish, Chr* : *lose* : *destroy, ruin, cause to perish, LL* : *intercept, obstruct.*
forfeallan *to overwhelm,* AA35⁴.
forfeng I. pret. 3 sg. of forfōn. II.=forfang

forfēran *to depart, die, Chr*; Æ. ['*forfere*']
forferian *to let die,* LL58,17.
forflēon² *to flee from, escape, avoid, evade,* Æ.
forflȳgan *to put to flight,* ZDA31·16⁴¹⁸.
forfōn⁷ *to seize : anticipate, forestall : surprise : prevent : forfeit.*
forfyllan *to stop up, obstruct,* WW463¹⁰.
forg-=foreg-
forgǣgan *to transgress, trespass, prevaricate,* Æ : *pass by, omit, neglect,* OEG,W.
forgǣgednes f. *transgression, trespass,* Æ.
forgǣgend m. *transgressor,* CHRD41³¹.
forgǣgung f. *fault, excess,* Sc115⁹.
forgǣlan *to avoid,* LkL.
for-gān, -gangan I. *to go or pass over, by or away,* Æ,MtL : '*forgo,*' *abstain from, neglect, lose,* Æ; CP,Æ. II.=foregān
forgeare *very certainly,* ÆL23⁵⁵⁶.
forgedōn=fordōn
forgeearnung f. *merit,* DHy132¹.
forgefenes=forgiefnes
forgēgan=forgǣgan
forgeldan=forgieldan
forgēm-=forgiem-
forgenge *hard to carry out?* (BTs), TC159².
forgeorne *very earnestly, very attentively,* BL.
forgeot-=forgit-, ofergit-
forget-=forgiet- pres. 3 sg. of forgietan.
forgief- v. also forgif-
forgiefan⁵ (i, y) *to give, grant, allow,* BH,Bl; CP : '*forgive,*' *overlook, Gen,Lk,Mt*; AO, CP : *give up, leave off,* CP : *give in marriage.*
forgiefen (e², ea², i²) *indulgent,* AO : *mild, tolerable,* NG.
for-giefnes (e, i, y) f. *pardon,* '*forgiveness,*' *remission, Bl*; CP : *indulgence, permission, BH* : *gift?* CR425.
forgieldan³ (e, i, y) *to pay for,* CP : *requite, reward, Bl*; AO,CP : *indemnify, make good : pay double (as penalty),* LL : *give : give up, forfeit,* VH12. ['*foryield*']
forgielpan³ *to boast in public, trumpet forth,* W234¹⁶.
forgīeman (ē, i, ȳ) *to neglect, pass by, transgress,* B. ['*foryeme*']
forgīemelēasian (ī, ȳ) *to neglect, abandon, give up, omit,* CP.
forgietan⁵ (i, y) w. a. or g. *to* '*forget,*' *Bf*; Bo,G,Ps; AO,CP. For comps. v. forgit-.
forgif- v. also forgief-.
forgifendlic (y²) *dative,* ÆGR22¹⁶.
forgifenlic *excusable, tolerable,* Mt. ['*forgivelich*']
forgifestre f. *female giver,* DHy49⁶.
forgifu f. '*gratia,*' DHy78⁷ (? 2 words).
forgifung f. *gift,* WW115¹².
forgildan=forgieldan
forgīm-=forgiem-

forgit-=forgiet-, ofergi(e)t-

forgitel (eo², ȳ², o³, u³) *forgetful, Æ.* ['*forgetel*']

forgitelnes (ȳ²) f. *forgetfulness, oblivion, LPs.* ['*forgetelness*']

forgiten pp. *forgetting, forgetful, Æ,Bl.*

forgiting f. *forgetfulness,* CM 1065.

forglendrian *to devour, swallow up,* W.

forgnagan⁶ *to eat up, Æ.* ['*forgnaw*']

forgnīdan¹ *to grind together, dash down, crush, break, LPs.* ['*forgnide*']

forgniden *contrite,* SPs 50¹⁸.

forgnidennes f. *tribulation,* APs 146³,LPs 13³.

forgnȳdan=forgnīdan

forgrindan³ I. *to grind down, ruin, destroy, consume.* II. (=ȳ²) *to send to the bottom, destroy,* A 11·2⁴⁰. [grund]

forgrindet n. *grinding, pounding,* Cp. 776c.

forgrīpan¹ *to seize, assail, attack, overwhelm.*

forgrīwan *to sink (in vice),* NC (BTs).

forgrōwen *grown up? overgrown? Rᴍ46.* [v. '*forgrow*']

forgumian (LL 474,2)=forgīman

forgyf-=forgief-, forgif-

forgyldan=forgieldan

forgyltan *to sin, be or become guilty,* W. *forgylt condemned, guilty.*

forgȳm-=forgīem-

forgyrd=forðgyrd

forgyrdan *to enclose, encircle,* Cʜʀ 189 n 4.

forgyt-=forgiet-, forgit-

for-habban, pret. 3 sg. -hæfde *to hold in, restrain, retain, keep back : draw back, refrain from, avoid, Æ.* forhæfed *continent, abstemious, celibate,* CP.

forhæbbend m. *abstinent, continent person,* OEG 1254.

forhǣfd=forhēafod

forhæf(e)(d)nes f. *temperance, continence, self-restraint, abstinence, BH; Æ,CP : parsimony,* OEG 3748. ['*forhevednes*']

forhæfendlīce *continently,* Cʜʀᴅ 42²⁹.

forhǣlan *to injure?* WW 464⁴.

forhǣtan *to overheat,* Lᴄᴅ 91b.

forhǣðed *burnt up,* WW 234¹.

forhātan⁷ *to renounce, forswear, Æ.* se forhātena *the devil,* Gᴇɴ 609. ['*forhight*']

forheafdnes (AS 23⁷)=forhæfednes

forhēafod n. '*forehead,*' *brow, skull, WW; Æ.* [=fore-]

forhealdan⁷ *to forsake, fall away from, rebel against, B : let go,* LL 360,11 : *defile, pollute,* Bʟ : *withhold,* LL 130,6¹ : *misuse, abuse,* Bo. ['*forhold*']

forhealdnes f. *unchastity,* NC 288.

forheard *very hard,* Mᴀ 156.

forheardian *to grow hard,* LVPs 89⁶.

forhēawan⁷ *to hew in pieces, cut down, kill, Ma.* ['*forhew*']

forhefednes=forhæfednes

forhegan (KGʟ)=forhogian

forhelan⁴ *to cover over, conceal, hide, protect, Æ,Bo; CP.* sacne f. *conceal a guilty man.* ['*forhele*']

forhelian *to hide,* OEG 5410n : *cover, clothe,* Cʜʀᴅ 108¹³.

forhergend m. *ravager,* Gʟ.

for-hergian, -herigean, -heregian *to plunder, harry, ravage, devastate, destroy,* AO,CP. [*Ger.* verheeren]

for-hergung, -her(g)iung f. *harassing, devastation,* AO 74³⁶.

forhicgan=forhycgan

forhīenan *to cast down, defeat, humiliate, outrage, oppress, waste,* AO. [*Ger.* verhöhnen]

forhigan=forhycgan

for-hoged-, -hogd-=forhogod-

forhogian *to neglect, disregard, despise, BH; Æ,CP.* ['*forhow*']

forhogiend m. *despiser,* Cʜʀᴅ,GD.

forhogi(g)endlic *contemptible,* Sc.

forhogod pp. of forhycgan.

forhogodlic *contemptuous,* Bʟ 77²³. adv. -līce.

forhogodnes f. *contempt,* BHʙ 342¹⁰.

forhogung f. *contempt,* BPs,CM.

forhohnes=forhogodnes

forhradian *to hasten,* CP : *prevent, anticipate, frustrate, Æ,CP.*

forhraðe *very speedily, quickly, soon, Æ.*

forhrēred *annulled,* WW.

forht *afraid, timid, cowardly,* AO,CP: *frightful, terrible.* adv. forhte *despairingly.*

forhtful *fainthearted, timorous,* WW 93⁹.

±forhtian (tr. and intr.) *to be afraid, surprised, fear, dread, Æ.*

forhtiendlic *timorous,* WW 442⁵ : *dreadful,* GD.

forhtige *humbly, submissively,* RB 70⁵.

forhtigend *timid,* W : *dreadful,* W.

forhtlic *fearful, afraid : dreadful.* adv. -līce.

forhtmōd *timorous, timid, Æ.*

forhtnes f. *fear, terror, Æ.*

forhtung f. *fear, ÆH.*

forhugian=forhogian

forhwæn, forhwan=forhwon

forhwega (æ²) *somewhere, somewhere about, Æ,AO.*

forhweorfan³ *to come to an end, be destroyed,* W 183⁴.

forhwerf-=forhwierf-

for-hwī, -hwig=forhwȳ

forhwierfan (e, i, y) *to change, transform : remove, transfer : pervert,* CP.

forhwierfedlic (y²) *perverse*, BL 31⁴.
forhwierfednes (y²) f. *perversity*, NC 288.
forhwon *wherefore, why, for what reason*, BH.
forhwȳ (ī²) *why, wherefore*, Ps. ['*forwhy*']
forhwyrf-=forhwierf-
forhycgan *to disdain, despise, reject*, CP.
forhȳdan *to hide*, Ps; CP. ['*forhide*']
forhygdelic *despised*, LPs 118¹⁴¹.
forhylman *to refuse obedience to*, AN 735.
forhȳnan=forhīenan
forhyrdan (i) *to harden*, EPPs 94⁸. [heard]
forieldan *to put off, delay*, CP.
foriernan=foreiernan
forierð (y) *a head-land* (v. heafodlond) *in the case of land with furrows at right angles to those of the adjacent land* (BTs), KC 5·153²¹.
forinlīce *thoroughly, exceedingly*, Bo 94⁶.
forinweardlīce *thoroughly, genuinely*, Bo 137¹⁵.
forlācan⁷† *to mislead, seduce, deceive, betray*.
forlǣdan *to mislead, seduce*, Æ,AO,CP : *bring out* (=forð-), Æ. [*Ger.* verleiten]
forlǣran *to teach wrongly, lead astray, seduce, pervert*, An,CP; Æ. ['*forlere*']
forlǣtan⁷ *to let go, relinquish, surrender, lose, leave, abandon, neglect*, An,Bl; Æ,CP : *remit, pardon, excuse* : *loose, release* : *let, permit, allow*, BH : *grant, give*. ūp, in f. *to direct upwards, within*. ān(n)e f.=ānforlǣtan. ['*forlet*']
for-lǣtennes (Æ), -lǣt(ed)nes f. *leaving, departure, absence* : *loss, perdition* : *intermission, cessation, end* : *remission* : *divorce*.
forlǣting f. *leaving, intermission*.
forlǣtu sbpl. *losses, sufferings*, VH 12.
forlǣðan *to loathe*, W 165³.
forlēan *to blame much*, A 12·517.
forlecgan *to cover up*, LCD 25a.
forlegen pp. of forlicgan.
forlegenes=forlegnes
forlegenlic *mean-looking, ugly* (Swt).
for-legis, -leges f. *prostitute, adulteress*, CP.
for-legis-, -legor-=forliger-
forlegnes f. *fornication*, BH,CP.
forlegnis f. *prostitute*, CP.
forlēogan² *to lie, perjure oneself, slander*, Æ.
forlēoran (EPs 143¹⁴)=forelēoran
forlēornes f. *transgression*, EPs 100³ (cp. ofer-l.).
forleornung f. *deception*, BL 183³⁴.
forleorte redupl. pret. sg. of forlǣtan.
forlēosan² *to lose, abandon, let go*, B; Æ,AO, CP : *destroy, ruin*, Gen. ['*forlese*']
forlēt-=forlǣt-
forlettan (fore-) *to prevent*, MkL 10¹⁴.

forlicgan⁵ *to commit adultery or fornication*, AO,LL; Æ,CP: *fail, lapse, be neglected*, LL 178,7: *screen* (*a thief*), LL 274,12. ['*forlie*'] pp. forlegen used as sb. *adulterer, fornicator*.
forlicgend m. *fornicator*, Sc,WW.
forliden I. *much-travelled*, CAS 9·11. II. pp. of forlīðan.
forlidennes=forliðennes
forligan=forlicgan
for-ligenes, -lignes=forlegnes
forliger I. n. *adultery, fornication, wantonness, immorality*, Æ. II. m. *whoremonger, adulterer*, Æ: f. *fornicatress, adulteress*. III. adj. *adulterous*.
forligerbed n. *bed of fornication*, ÆH.
forligere=forliger I.
forligeren adj. *fornicating*, OEG 8²³².
forligerhūs n. *house of ill fame*, OEG.
forligerlic *unchaste, impure*, OEG. adv. -līce.
forligerwīf (e², o³) n. *prostitute*, MH 140¹⁹.
forliges=forlegis
forliggang m. *adultery, fornication*, WW 499¹².
forligrian *to commit fornication*, ERSPs 72²⁶.
forlīr=forliger II.
forlīsgleng *harlot's dress*, OEG 8³⁶¹ (= forlegis-).
forlīðan¹ *to suffer shipwreck*, OEG.
forlīðennes f. *shipwreck*, OEG.
for-long, -longe adv. *long ago*, NG.
forlor m. *loss, destruction*, AO,CP. tō forlore gedōn *to destroy*, CP.
forlorenes f. *state of being forlorn, perdition, destruction*, VPs. ['*forlornness*']
for-lorian, -losian *to lose*, NG.
forlustlīce *very willingly*, Bo 51¹⁸.
forlytel *very little*, Bo.
form=feorm; **form-** (NG)=frum-
forma (eo) *first, earliest*, B,Bo,Mt; CP. ['*forme*'] on forman *at first*.
for-mǣl, -māl fn. *negotiation, agreement, treaty*, LL. [mǣl II.]
formǣr-=foremǣr-
formanig (æ², o², e³) *very many*, MA,RB.
formelle f. *bench*, ANS 84·9. [*L.* formella]
formeltan³ (y) *to melt away, dissolve, liquefy, burn up*, AO; Æ. ['*formelt*']
formengan *to associate*, CP 395⁴.
formesta=fyrmesta wk. superl. of forma.
formete m. *food for a journey*, Æ.
formicel (y²) *very great*, CP,LL.
formogod *corrupted*, ÆL 23³⁷⁵.
formolsnian *to rot away, crumble, decay*, Æ.
formolsnung f. *corruption*, OEG 1251.
formycel=formicel; **formyltan**=formeltan

formyrðrian *to murder*, LL,W.
forn I. f? m? *trout*, WW 180³⁹. II.=foran
fornǣman *to be worn out, afflicted (with grief)*, GD 245³.
forne=foran adv.; forne f.=forn
fornēah *very nearly, almost, about*, Æ,AO, CP.
for-nēan (Æ), -nēh, -nēon=fornēah
fornerwian (=ie²) *to check the growth or fecundity of*, LCD 3·164'.
Fornētes folm *a plant*, LCD (v. BTs).
fornēðan *to expose to danger, sacrifice*, AO 222¹.
forniman⁴ *to take away, deprive of, plunder waste, devastate, destroy, consume*, B,Lcd; Æ,AO : *annul* : *disfigure* : *overcome*. ['fornim']
fornȳdan (=īe) *to coerce, compel*, W 158¹⁰.
fornyman=forniman
fornytlice *very usefully*, GD 174²⁰.
forod (a², e²) *broken down, worn out, useless, void, abortive*, Æ,AO,CP.
foroft *very often*, Æ.
forpǣran *to turn away, lose, spoil, pervert, destroy*, Æ,CP.
forpyndan *to do away, remove*, CR 97.
fŏrracu f. *itinerary*, OEG 7¹²¹.
forradian=forhradian
forrǣda? m. *traitor, plotter*, MP 1·592.
forrǣdan *to plot against, betray*, W : *condemn* : *injure*. ['forrede']
forraðe (Æ)=forhraðe
forrepen *taken*, JnLp 5⁸. [hrepian]
forrīdan¹ *to intercept by riding before*, CHR 894A.
forridel m. *fore-rider, forerunner, messenger*, Æ. ['forridel']
forrotednes (a³, o³) f. *corrupt matter, rottenness*, Æ.
forrotian *to rot away, decay*, CP, WW : *putrefy*, Æ. ['forrot']
forrynel=forerynel
forsacan⁶ *to object to, reject, oppose, deny, refuse*, AO,Cp,LL : *give up, renounce*, AO, CP. ['forsake']
forsacennes f. *denial*, RWH 102¹⁰.
forsacung f. *denial*, RWH 144²⁵.
forsǣcan=forsēcan
forsǣtian *to lay wait for, beset, surround*, AO 146¹⁰.
forsǣtnian=forsetnian
forsǣwestre=forsewestre
forsawen=forsewen
forsc=frosc
forscād-=forscēad-
forscǣncednes (LPs 40¹⁰)=forscrencednes
forscamian *to make ashamed* (impers. w. a.), CP,Sc : *be ashamed*. ['forshame']
forscamung f. *modesty*, GPH 390.

forscapung f. *mishap, mischance*, AO 40,50.
forscēadan⁷ *to scatter, disperse*, CP : *damn, condemn?* GU 449 (GK).
forsceamian=forscamian
forsceap n. *evil deed?* GEN 898.
forscēaw-=forescēaw-
forscending f. *confusion*, LkR 21²⁵.
forsceorfan³ *to gnaw off, bite, eat up*, AO 226⁹.
forscēotan *to anticipate, forestall, prevent*, Bo.
forsceppan=forscieppan
forsceta *flood-gate*, BLPs 41⁸. [=forsscēta]
forscieppan⁶ *to change, transform*, Æ. ['forshape']
forscip n. 'foreship,' *prow*, WW. [=fore-]
forscired *the dead?* VH 12.
forscrencan (ǣ²) *to supplant, overcome, vanquish, cast down*, Æ : *dry up*, OEG 4926.
forscrencednes (scænc-) f. *supplanting, deceit*, LPs 40¹⁰.
forscrencend m. *supplanter*, ÆH 1·198'.
forscrīfan¹ *to decree*, GL : *proscribe, condemn, doom*, Æ : (†) *bewitch*.
forscrincan³ (intr.) *to shrink, dry up, wither away*, Æ,Mt. ['forshrink']
forscūtan² *to cast down (pride)*, EX 204.
forscyldig *wicked*, Æ (58¹⁷⁰).
forscyldigian *to condemn*. pp. *guilty*, Æ.
forscyppan=forscieppan
forscyrian *to separate*, MFH 159.
forscyttan *to exclude, prevent, obviate*, Æ. ['forshut']
forsēarian *to sear, dry up, wither*, Æ,CP.
forseawennes=forsewennes
forsēcan I. *to afflict, attack*. II.=foresēcan
forsecgan *to accuse falsely, slander, accuse*, Æ : *to speak about, discourse on*.
forsegen-=forsewen-
forsēgon=forsāwon pret. pl. of forsēon.
forsellan *to sell*, ÆP 202⁷ : *give up, lose*, LL.
forsencan *to reject*, CP 345¹³.
forsendan *to send away, banish, send to destruction*, AO.
forsēon⁵ *to overlook, neglect, scorn, despise, reject, renounce*, Bl; Æ,AO,CP : *refrain from*. ['forsee']
forsēones=forsēones
forsēoðan² *to wither, consume*, ÆH 1·84¹⁵.
forsērian (AS 10³?)=forsēarian
forsetnian (æ) *to beset*, ERPs 21¹⁷.
forsettan I. *to hedge in, obstruct*, BH : *oppress*. ['forset'] II.=foresettan
forsettednes=foresetnes
forsewen I. f. *contempt*, LPs 122⁴. II. pp. of forsēon.
forsewenlic *despicable, ignominious, wretched, of poor appearance*. adv. -līce, Æ.

forsewennes f. *contempt*, Æ,AO.

forsewestre (æ²) f. *female despiser*, OEG 4430.

forsingian=forsyngian

forsittan⁵ *to neglect, delay*, LL : *block, obstruct, besiege*, AO : *injure* : *absent oneself* (*from*). ['*forsit*']

forsīō=forðsīð

forsīōian *to perish*, B 1550.

for-slǽwan, -slāwian *to be slow, unwilling, delay, put off, Bo*; CP. ['*forslow*']

forslēan⁶ *to cut through, strike, break, kill, destroy*, AO.

forslegenlic *mean, ignominious*, MH 156²⁰.

forsliet m. *slaughter*, WW 28¹⁶. [slieht]

forslītan *to consume, devour*, PPs 77⁴⁶.

forsmorian *to smother, choke, stifle*, Æ.

forsorgian *to despond*, W 69¹⁶.

forsōð *indeed, verily, Bo*. ['*forsooth*']

forspǽc=foresprǽc

forspanan⁶ *to mislead, lead astray, seduce, entice*, Æ; CP. ['*forspan*']

forspaning f. *allurement*, OEG.

forspeca=forespreca

forspecan=forsprecan

forspēdian *to speed, prosper*, SPs (? forswefian).

forspendan *to spend, give out, squander, consume*, AO. ['*forspend*']

forspennen (OEG 612)=forspenning

forspennend m. *procurer*, ÆGR 36¹¹.

forspenn-ende, -endlic *seductive, voluptuous, defiling*, OEG.

forspennestre f. *procuress*, ÆGR 36¹².

forspenning f. *enticement, seduction, evil attraction*, ÆL.

forspild m. *destruction*, CP 294¹⁹.

forspildan *to waste, lose, disperse, bring to nothing, destroy, ruin, kill, CP*. ['*forspill*']

forspillan (*AO*)=forspildan

forspil(le)dnes f. *waste, destruction, perdition*, Æ.

forspillian *to wanton*, OEG.

forsprec-=foresprec-; forspyll-=forspill-

for-sprecan, -specan⁵ *to speak in vain : state amiss : deny : denounce : lose* (*a case*).

forspyrcan (=ie) *to dry up*, PPs 101³.

forst (frost) m. '*frost,*' Gl,Ph,Rd. [frēosan]

forstǽppan=forestæppan

forstal (*LL*)=foresteall

forstalian (refl.) *to steal away*, LL.

forstandan⁶ *to defend, help, protect*, LL : *withstand, prevent, hinder, resist, oppose*, Met : *benefit, avail*, CP : *understand, Bo*; CP : *signify, be equal to*, EC,LL. ['*forstand*']

forsteall=foresteall

forstelan⁴ *to steal away, steal, rob, deprive*, MtR,LL; Æ. ['*forsteal*']

forstig *frosty*, ÆL 23b⁵⁷⁵. [v. fyrstig]

forstīlc *glacial, frozen*, WW 175¹⁶.

forstoppian *to stop up, close*, LCD 15b.

forstrang *very strong*, RD 51⁴.

forstregdan³ *to destroy*, JPs 105²³.

forstrogdnes f. '*precipitatio,*' NC 289 (v. BTs).

forstyltan *to be amazed*, MkLR.

forstyntan *to blunt, break, crush*, WW 375⁶ : *check, impair*, WYN 132.

forsūcan² *to suck up*, OEG 3343.

forsūgan² *to suck in*, LCD.

for-sugian (Æ,AO), -suwian (Æ)=forswigian

forsuwung f. *silence*, OEG 2085.

forswǽlan *to burn, burn up, inflame, consume*, Æ. ['*forsweal*']

forswǽð (DHy 38¹⁶)=fōtswæð

forswāpan⁷† *to sweep away, drive off*.

forswarung f. *perjury*, CHRD 40³⁴.

forsweflan (-sweb-) *to prosper*, EPs 88²³ (forð-), 117²⁵.

forswelan⁴ *to burn, burn up*, PH 532.

forswelgan³ *to swallow up, devour, consume, absorb, B*; Æ,CP. ['*forswallow*']

forsweltan³ *to die, disappear, Bo*; WW. ['*forswelt*']

forsweogian=forswigian

forsweolgan=forswelgan

forsweorcan³ *to grow dark, obscure*, B,W.

forsweorfan³ *to polish, cleanse*, WW 227¹⁷ : *grind away, demolish*, WW 218²⁸.

forsweotole *very clearly*, AS 2¹⁷.

forswerian⁶ (refl. and intr.) *to swear falsely*, Æ,LL : *make useless by a spell*, B. ['*forswear*']

forswigian *to conceal by silence, suppress, pass over*, Æ,CP : *be silent*.

forswīð *very great*, CREAT 26.

forswīðan, forswīðian *to crush, press upon, overcome, repress*, CP.

forswīðe adv. *very much, utterly*, Bo.

forsworcenlic *dark, obscure*, DHy 24¹⁰.

forsworcennes f. *darkening, darkness*, Æ, W.

forsworen (pp. of forswerian) '*forsworn,*' *perjured*, Æ,Chr,WW.

forsworennes f. *perjury*, Æ. ['*forswornness*']

for-swugian (CP), -sygian=forswigian

forsyngian (i) *to sin greatly*, LL. ['*forsin*'] pp. as sb. forsyngod m. *sinner*.

fortācen=foretācn

fortendan *to burn away, sear*, AO 46¹⁴.

fortēon² *to mislead, seduce*, Cr : *draw over, cover, obscure*. ['*fortee*']

fortiht-=fortyht-

for-timbran, -timbrian *to close up, obstruct*, CVPs 62¹².

fortog n. *gripes*, LCD 109[6].
fortogen *pulled together*, WW 106[14].
fortogenes f. *griping, spasm*, LCD 89a.
fortogian *to contract*, LCD 3·120[8].
fortredan[5] *to tread down, trample on*, Æ; CP. ['fortread']
fortreddan *to tread down*, BH 44[23].
fortreding f. *treading down, crushing*, Sc 95[10].
fortrendan *to block (by rolling a stone)*, v. OEG 114.
fortrūgadnes, fortrūwednes=fortrūwodnes
fortrūwian *to be presumptuous, over-confident, rash*, CP.
fortrūwodnes f. *presumption*, CP.
fortrūwung f. *presumption*, Bo,CP.
fortrymman *to testify, confirm*, NG.
fortyhtan *to seduce*, EL 208.
fortyhtigend m. *polluter, defiler*, OEG 3337.
fortyllan *to seduce*, CR 270.
fortymbrian=fortimbrian
fortȳnan *to shut in, enclose, block up*, CP.
forð I. adv. 'FORTH,' *forwards, onwards, further*, Æ : *hence, thence : away*, Æ : *continually, still, continuously, henceforth, thenceforward, simultaneously*. f. mid ealle *forthwith*. and swā f. *and so forth*, ÆGr. swā f. swā *so far as*, LL. f. on *continually*. fram orde oð ende f. *from the beginning to the end*. f. ðæt *until*. II. prep. *during*, Bo.
forð- (N)=furð-
forðācīgan *to call forth*, BH 444[24].
forðādilgian *to bring to nothing, blot out*, MFH 160.
forðǣm, forðām, forðan (CP), forðon (AO, CP) I. conj. *for (the reason) that, owing to (the fact) that, for, because, on that account, therefore, seeing that*. for ðǣm ðe, etc. with same signification. II. adv. *for that cause, consequently, therefore*.
forðāgoten *poured forth*, ÆL 23b[798].
forðahting (=eaht-) f. *exhortation*, CM 447.
forðancful *very thankful*, ES 18·336; 43·162.
forðātēon[2] *to bring forth, produce*, Æ. pp. forðātogen.
forðāurnen ptc. *elapsed*, BH 280[21].
forðbǣre *productive*, GEN 132.
forðbecuman[4] *to come forth*, BH,PPs.
forðberan[4] *to bring forth, produce*, BH; Æ. ['forthbear']
forðbesēon[5] *to look forth*, LPs 101[20].
forðbi, forðbie prep. *by, past*, CP 197[13].
forðbigferende *passing by*, NC 343.
forðblǣstan *to blow forth, burst out*, WW 393[33],WYN 24.
forðblāwan *to blow or belch forth*, WW 397[10].
forðboren *of noble birth*, LL.

forð-brengan, -bringan *to bring forth, produce, Bl,Lk : bring to pass, accomplish : bring forward : adduce, quote*, Æ. ['forthbring']
forðbylding f. *emboldening, encouragement*, CHR 999 E.
forðclypian *to call forth*, Gal (Lye). ['forthclepe']
forðcuman[4] *to come forth, proceed, arrive at, succeed : come to pass, come true : be born*.
forðcyme m. *coming forth, birth*, Æ. ['forthcome']
forðcȳðan *to announce, declare*, CVPs 118[26].
forðdǣd f. *advantage*, Æ.
forðdōn *to put forth*, BH. ['forthdo']
forðeahtung (a[2]) f. *exhortation*, A 13·447.
forðearle *very much, greatly, strictly*, Æ.
forðearlīce *absolutely, entirely*, RB 11[19].
forðeccan *to shield, protect*, APs 18[6].
forðelgian (KGL)=forðyld(g)ian
forðencan I. (æ) *to mistrust, despise, despair*, Ps. pp. forðōht *despaired of*; as sb. *poor wretch*, Æ. ['forthink'] II.=foreðencan
forðēofian (īo) *to steal*, MkL 10[19].
forðēon I. *to crush, oppress*, ROOD 54. II.=foreðēon
forðēostrian (īe) *to darken*, LPs 104[28].
forðerscan[3] *to beat down*, GD 57[4].
forðfæder m. *forefather, ancestor*, Æ. ['forthfather']
forðfæderen *paternal*, CHRD 96[6].
forðfaran[6] *to depart, die*, Bo,Chr; Æ. ['forthfare']
±**forðfēran** *to depart, die*, Æ.
forðfērednes f. *death*, BHcs 290[29].
forðfēring f. *death*, Sc 65[8].
forðflōwan *to flow*, BH 418[21].
forðfolgian *to follow*, CM 1052.
forðfōr I. f. *departure, death*, BH. ['forthfore'] II. pret. 3 sg. of forðfaran.
forðforlǣtenes f. *licence*, Bo 12[2].
forðframian *to grow to maturity*, WW 465[10].
forðfromung f. *departure*, CVPs 104[38].
forðfyligan *to follow, fall out, happen*, CM 1109.
forðgān anv., pret. 3 sg. -ēode *to go forth, advance, proceed, pass by, go away, go on, precede, succeed*, Chr,Mk. ['forthgo']
forðgang m. *going forth, progress, advance, success : privy, drain : purging, evacuation*, ÆL 16[207].
forðgangan[7] *to go forth*, Ma. ['forthgang']
forðgecīgan *to call forth*, REPs 67[7] : *exhort*, BH 54[15].
forðgeclipian (y) *to call forth, provoke*, Sc, EPs.

forðgefaran=forðfaran
forðgeféran=forðféran
forðgegyrdu *ornaments of a* forðgyrd, WW 195[29].
forðgelǣstan=forðlǣstan
forðgelang *dependent*, LL (280[12]).
forðgeléoran *to pass away, die*, BH.
forðgeléorednes f. *departure, death*, GD 282[11].
forðgelócian (BPs 101[20])=forðlócian
forðgenge *increasing, thriving, effective, successful*, Æ,CP.
forðgeong=forðgang
forðgeorn *eager to advance*, MA 281.
forðgéotan[2] *to pour forth*, BH. ['*forthyete*']
forðgerîmed *in unbroken succession*, B 59.
forðgesceaft† f. *creature, created being or thing, world : future destiny*.
forðgestranglan '*confortare*,' LPs 68[5].
forðgesȳne *visible, conspicuous*, CRA 1.
forðgewítan[1] *to go forth, pass, proceed, go by : depart, die*. forðgewiten tíd, tíma *past tense*, ÆGR.
forðgewitenes f. *departure*, LPs 104[38].
forðgyrd m. *fore-girdle, martingale*, WW.
forðheald *bent forward, stooping : inclined, steep*, RB 5[20].
forðhealdan[7] *to hold to, follow out, keep up, observe*, Æ.
forðheold I.=forðheald. II. pret. 3 sg. of forðhealdan.
forðherge m. *van* (*of an army*), Ex 225.
forðhlífian *to be prominent*, BH 322[24].
forðhnîgan[1] *to fall down, fall forward*, VH 13.
forðhréosan *to rush forth*, Sc 101[13].
forðî=forðý
±**forðlan** *to put forth, contribute : further, advance : carry out, accomplish*, Chr. ['*forth*']
forðîg=forðý
forðîndan[3] *to swell up*, LCD 127a.
forðinglan *to arrange for a man's* wergild, LL (Wilk.) 39[34].
forðlǣdan *to lead forth, bring forth*, Sat; Æ. ['*forthlead*']
forðlǣdnes f. *bringing forth*, BH 76[15].
forðlǣstan *to persevere in, accomplish*, BH 352[14].
forðlǣtan[7] *to send forth, emit*, BL.
forðléoran *to proceed*, BH 312[27].
forðlic *forward, advanced*, CHR 1066 D: *thoroughly*, RWH 138[16]. adv. -líce.
forðlîfian=forðhlífian
forðlócian *to look forth*, BL.
forðlûtan *to lean forward, fall down*, VPs: *be prone* (*to*), CHRD 54[31].

forðmǣre *very glorious*, CREAT 69.
forðman m. *man of rank*, NC 289.
forðmest *foremost*, MtL. ['*forthmost*']
forðolian *to go without, lack*, WA 38.
forðon I. *forthwith*, MH. ['*forthon*'] II.= forðæm
forðoncol=foreðancol; **forðor**=furðor
forðrǣcan (tr.) *to protrude*, ÆL 25[135].
forðrǣsan *to rush forth, rise up : jut out, protrude*, RPs 72[7]. [rǣsan]
forðrǣstan (ê) *to crush, afflict, oppress*, VPs: *suppress, stifle : destroy*, CPs 104[16]. ['*forthrast*']
forðrǣst(ed)nes (ê) f. *tribulation*, VPs.
forðres-=forðrys-
forðriccednes=forðryccednes
forðriht adj. *direct, plain*, WW. ['*forthright*' adj.]
forðrihte adv. *straightway, at once : unmistakeably, plainly : straight on*, ZDA 9·406. ['*forthright*' adv.] -rihtes *without a break*, RBL 48[6].
forðringan *to rescue from, defend against*, B 1084 : *elbow out, displace*, RB 115[7].
forðroccetan *to belch forth*, APs 18[3].
forðryccan *to press, squeeze, crush, oppress, suppress*.
forðryccednes (i) f. *pressure, oppression*, G, Ps.
forðrycnes f. *extortion, oppression, tribulation*, LL; MFH 159 (fore-).
forðryne m. *onward course*, GEN 215.
for-ðrysman, -ðrysmian *to choke, suffocate, strangle : becloud*, WW 246[6]. [ðrosm]
forðscacan[6] *to pass away*, RPs 143[4].
forðscencan *to pour forth, give to drink*, WW 464[9].
forðscype m. *progress*, BHc 92[14].
forðsetennes f. '*propositio*,' MtR 12[4].
forðsîð m. *going forth, decease*, Chr; Æ,CP. ['*forthsithe*']
forðsnoter (tt)† *very wise*, EL.
forðspell n. *declaration*, MOD 47.
forðspôwnes f. *prosperity*, BH 106[25].
forð-stæppan, -steppan[6] *to issue forth, proceed, pass by*, ÆL,BF 184,198.
forðstæpping f. *advance*, DHy 80[14].
forðstefn m. *prow*, LCD 3·180[4].
forðswefian=forswefian
forðsyllan *to give out, pay out*, LL 175,3.
forðtége (KGL)=forðtíge
forðtéon[2] *to draw forth, bring forth*, GEN 1[12].
forðtíge (e[2], y[2]) m. *vestibule*, OEG 3828.
forððegn m. *chief noble*, ÆL 6[125].
forððéon *to profit*, GD 200[11].
forðum=furðum
forðung f. *furtherance*, LCD 3·198' (v. ANS 125·49).

forðweard (e²) I. *inclined forwards or to-wards* : *advanced, progressing, growing, ready* : *enduring, everlasting, continual* : *future.* adv. *continually,* PPs : *prospectively,* ÆGr : *from now on* : *forwards, onwards,* W 17⁸. ['*forthward*'] II. m. *look-out man, pilot,* GEN 1436.

forðweardes (e²) *forwards,* HL 16²⁰³.

forðweardnes f. *progress,* GD 117¹⁹.

forðweaxan *to break forth, burst forth, GD.* ['*forthwax*']

forðwegt m. *journey, departure.* in (on) forðwege *away.*

forðwerd=forðweard

forðwīf n. *matron,* WW 309⁴⁴.

forðwyrīt *tortured, mutilated,* v. OEG 5028.

forðȳ I. conj. *for that, because, therefore, Jn.* ['*forthy*'] II. adv. *for that, therefore, consequently.*

for-ðyldian, -ðyld(i)gian, -ðyl(de)gian *to bear, support, endure, wait patiently,* Æ.

forðylm-an, -ian *to shut in, enclose, envelop, obscure, cover over, overwhelm* : *choke, suffocate, consume.*

forðyppan *to make manifest,* CVPs.

forðyrnan³ *to run before, precede* : *continue,* Æ.

forðyrrian *to dry up,* LCD 82b.

forðysmed *obscured,* WW 246⁶.

forðȳðe=forðȳ; forud=forod

for-ūtan, -ūton adv.; prep. w. d. *except, without,* Chr 1122. ['*forout*']

forwærnan=forwiernan

forwærnian (WW 442¹⁸)=forweornian

forwana m. *abundance?* CP 465¹⁶.

forwandian *to hesitate, be reluctant,* CP : *be ashamed* : *reverence.*

forwandung f. *shame,* VPs 68²⁸.

forwarð=forwearð pret. 3 sg. of forweorðan.

forweallan *to boil away,* LCD 95a.

forweard I. (NG) *beginning, front* : *heading, title, chapter.* II. adv. *continually, always,* GEN 788. [?=forðweard; or foreweard, JGPh 12·257]

forweardmercung f. *heading,* JnL p 3¹.

forweaxan⁷ *to progress, grow too much, become overgrown, CP;* AO. ['*forwax*']

forweddod *pledged,* WW 115⁴⁴. [wedd]

forwegan⁵ *to kill,* MA 228.

forwel adv. *very, very well,* Æ.

forwened '*insolens,*' GL. [wenian]

forwēned '*suspectus,*' BDS 30·12¹⁰⁶. [wē-nan]

forwenednes f. '*insolentia,*' ANS 79·89.

forweoren=forworen

forweornan=forwiernan

forweornian *to dry up, wither, fade, grow old, rot, decay,* Æ.

forweorpan *to throw, cast out, cast down, drive off, reject, throw away, squander, B.* ['*forwerpe*']

forweorpnes f. *migration,* MtL 1¹⁷.

forweorðan³ (y) *to perish, pass away, vanish, Mt;* AO,CP,Æ : *deteriorate, sicken.* f. on mōde *be grieved.* ['*forworth*']

forweorðenes=forwordenes

forweorðfullic *excellent,* Bo 65¹⁵.

forweosnian=forwisnian

forwercan=forwyrcan; forwerd=foreweard

forwered=forwerod

forweren (WW 217¹⁵)=forworen

forwerennes (RPs 70¹⁸)=forwerodnes

forwerod *worn out, very old,* Æ. [werian]

forwerodnes (e³) f. *old age,* SPs 70¹⁹.

forwest=forewost

forwiernan (e, eo, i, y) *to hinder, prohibit, prevent, repel, refuse, repudiate, deny, withhold, oppose,* AO,B; CP. ['*forwarn*']

forwiernedlīce (e²) *continently,* W 284⁸.

forwiernednes (y²) f. *restraint, self-denial, continence,* BH 160¹⁰,MFH 118.

for-wird, -wirn-=for-wyrd, -wiern-

forwisnian (eo) *to dry up, decay, rot.*

forwitan=forewitan

forwitolnes f. *intelligence, diligence,* RBL 58¹⁰. [=fore-]

forwlencan *to fill with pride, puff up, CP.* ['*forwlench*']

forword I. n. *iota,* MtL 5¹⁸. II.=foreword

forwordenes f. *destruction, failure,* CHR 1105.

forwordenlic *perishable,* W 263¹³ : *perishing,* ByH 130²⁹.

forworen (pp. of *forweosan) *decrepit, decayed,* OEG 2109.

forwost (e²) m. *chief, captain,* NG.

forwracned *banished,* RB 82².

forwrecan⁵ *to drive forth, carry away* : *expel, banish.*

forwrēgan *to accuse, calumniate,* Chr. ['*forwray*']

forwrēon¹ *to cover over,* LkR 23⁴⁵.

forwrītan¹ *to cut in two,* B 2705.

forwrīðan¹ *to bind up,* LCD 122a.

forwundian *to wound,* Chr. ['*forwound*']

forwundorlic *very wonderful,* GD. adv. -līce.

forwurðan=forweorðan

forwynsumian *to enjoy thoroughly,* VH 13.

forwyrcan I. (e) *to do wrong, sin,* Æ,CP. forworht mann *criminal,* CP : *ruin, undo, destroy, Cr* ; Æ,AO,CP : *condemn, convict, curse* : *forfeit.* ['*forwork*'] II. *to barricade, obstruct, close up.*

forwyrd fn. *destruction, ruin, fall, death,* Æ,CP. [forweorðan]

forwyrdan *to destroy,* GD 201¹⁵.

forwyrdendlic *perishable,* Sc 43¹¹ (wyrð-).

forwyrht f. *misdeed*, LL : *ruin*, MFH 160.

forwyrhta m. *agent, deputy : evil-doer, male-factor, ruined person.* [fore-]

forwyrn- (Æ)=forwiern-

forwyrpnes f. *casting out*, LPs 21⁷.

foryld=foreald; foryldan=forieldan

foryldu f. *extreme old age*, RB 114¹¹.

foryrman *to reduce to poverty, bring low*, BH,W. [earm]

foryrð=forierð

fōster=fōstor

fōstor m. *sustenance, maintenance, food, nourishment, Lcd*; Æ. ['foster']

fōstorbearn n. *foster-child*, GL.

fōstorbrōðor m. '*foster-brother*,' WW.

fōstorcild (e²) n. *foster-child*, ÆL.

fōstorfæder m. '*foster-father*,' Cp,MH.

fōstorland (e²) n. *land granted for the support of the recipients*, TC. [v. '*fosterland*']

fōstorlēan n. *payment for maintenance*, LL 442,2; MEN 152.

fōstorling m. *foster-child, nursling, pupil*, WW. ['*fosterling*']

fōstormann (ē) m. *bondsman, security*, LL 668,18.

fōstormōdor f. '*foster-mother*,' MH.

fōstornōð m. *pasture, sustenance*, EPs 22².

fōstorsweostor f. *foster-sister* (BT).

fōstrað (e²) m. *food : manna*, JnL 6⁴⁹.

-fōstre v. cild-f.

fōstrian (ē) *to 'foster,' nourish, Sc*; MFB 205.

fōstring m. *foster-child, disciple*, NG.

fōstur=fōstor

fōt m. ds. fēt, fōte, nap. fēt, fōtas 'FOOT' (*as limb and as measure*),B,LL,NG: Æ,AO,CP.

fōtādl fn. *gout in the feet* : '*morbus regius*,' OEG (v. BTs).

fōtādlig *having gout in the feet*, ÆH 2·26¹⁹.

fōtbred n. *foot-board, stirrup*, WW 107⁶.

fōtclāð m. *joining, patch*, MtL 9¹⁶.

±fōtcopsian, +fōtcypsan *to fetter*, Pss.

fōt-cosp, -cops m. *foot-fetter*, VPs,WW ; Æ. [v. '*cops*']

fōtcoðu f. *gout in the feet*, OEG : '*morbus regius*' (v. fōtādl).

fōtece m. *gout in the feet*, LCD.

fōter=fōdder I.

fōtfeter f. *fetter of the feet*, WW 116⁸.

fōtgangende *going on foot*, OEG 5254.

fōtgemearc n. *space of a foot*, B 3043.

fōtgemet n. *foot-fetter*, EPs 104¹⁸.

fōtgewǣde fn? *covering for the feet*, RB 88¹⁴.

+fōtian *to hasten up*, MkL 15⁴⁴.

fōt-lāst (Æ), -lǣst mf. *footprint, spoor : foot*.

fōtlic *on foot*, ÆH 2·468²¹ : *pedestrian*, GPH 403.

fōtmǣl n. *foot-measure, foot*, WE 55¹.

fōtmǣlum adv. *step by step, by degrees*, CM 883.

fōtrāp m. *the loose part of the sheet by which a sail is trimmed to the wind*, '*propes*,' WW 167¹¹.

fōtsceamol (e², e³, u³) m. *footstool*, Æ.

fōtsceanca m. *foreleg*, Lcd 1·362'. [v. '*shank*']

fōtsetl n. *footstool*, CHR 1053 c.

fōtsīd *reaching to the feet*, NC 289.

fōtspor n. *footprints, spoor*, LCD.

fōtspure n. *foot-rest, foot-support*, CHR 1070 E.

fōtstān m. *base, pedestal*, WW 191³⁵.

fōtstapol m. *footstep*, LPs 17³⁷.

fōtswǣð n. (nap. -swaðu), fōtswaðu f. *footprint, footstep : foot*, Æ.

fōtswyle (i) m. *swelling of the foot*, LCD.

fōtðwēal n. *washing of the feet*, W,WW.

fōtwǣrc n. *pain in the foot, gout*, LCD 1·342¹⁰.

fōt-welm, -wylm, -wolma m. *instep*, Æ (v. I F 48·254).

fōð ind. pres. pl. of fōn.

fōð-or I. (-er, -ur) n. *load, cartload, Chr : food, fodder.* ['*fother*'] II. *covering, case, basket*, GL.

fōðorn m. *lancet?* LCD 19b (v. BTac).

fōwer=fēower

fox m. '*fox*,' Lk,VPs.

foxesclāte f. *burdock*, LCD 54a.

foxesclīfe f. *foxglove? greater burdock?* WW 135n1.

foxesfōt m. *fox-foot, xiphion*, LCD.

foxesglōfa m. *foxglove*, WW 296²⁵.

foxhol n. *fox-hole*, KC.

foxhyll m. *fox-hill*, SR 57'.

foxung f. *foxlike wile, craftiness*, ÆL 16¹⁶².

fra=fram; fraced, fraceð, fracod=fracoð

fracoð I. adj. *vile, bad, wicked, criminal, impious, filthy, abominable*, BH : *useless, worthless.* ['*fraked*'] II. n. *insult, contumely, disgrace : wickedness.*

fracoðdǣd (-od) f. *misdeed*, W 188¹⁵.

fracoðe adv. *shamefully*, PPs.

fracoðlic *base, ignominious, shameful, lewd*, Æ,CP. adv. -līce, CP.

fracoð(lic)nes f. *vileness, coarseness, obscenity*, Æ.

fracoðscipe (-od) *scandalous conduct*, RB 141⁵.

fracoðword n. *insulting word*, GD 152⁷.

fracud, fracuð=fracoð; frǣ-=frēa-

frǣc=frec; frǣc-=frēc- (v. ES 39·327 ff. as to these four forms).

frǣcūð (GL)=fracoð

fræfel n? and adj. *cunning*, GL.

fræfelian *to be cunning*, GL.

fræfellīce (e¹) *shamelessly*, AO : *carefully : astutely.*

fræfelnes f. *sharpness, shrewdness*, OEG.

+**frǣge** (ē) I.† n. *hearsay, report, knowledge.* mine +f. *as I have heard say.* II. adj. *well-known, celebrated, reputable,* CP: *notorious, disreputable.* [fricgan]

frægn I. pret. 3 sg. of frignan. II. fregen II.

frægning f. *questioning,* GD 323²³.

frǣm-=frem-

frǣng=frǣgn

±**frǣpgian** (NG) *to accuse,* MtL: *reverence,* LG.

frǣt I.† *perverse, proud, obstinate:* *shameful.* II. pret. 3 sg. of fretan.

frǣtegung (Æ)=frǣtwung

frǣtenes f. *ornament,* WW 524⁵.

frǣtew-=frǣtw-

frǣtgenga (ē¹) m. *apostasy,* GL.

frǣtig *perverse, proud,* Jul 284.

frǣtlæppa m. *dew-lap,* WW 179³.

frǣton pres. pl. of fretan.

frǣtwa, frǣtwe fp. *treasures, ornaments, trappings, armour* : m. *adorner,* Cr 556. [+tāwe]

frǣtwǣdnes=frǣtwednes

±**frǣtwan,** frǣt(te)wian *to ornament, adorn,* AO : *clothe, cover over,* CP 83¹⁰.

frǣtwednes (æ², o²) f. *adorning, decoration, ornament,* BH.

frǣtwian v. frǣtwan.

±**frǣtwung** f. *adorning, ornament,* Æ.

fragendlic=framigendlic

+**frāgian** *to learn by inquiry,* MtL 2¹⁶.

fram (o) I. prep. w. d. (instr.) (local) 'FROM,' *by,* Æ,Chr : (temporal) *from, since :* (agent) *by : as a result of :* (with verbs of saying and hearing) *of, about, concerning.* f. **gān** *to depart.* comps. v. fram-, from-. II. adv. *from, forth, out, away.* III. adj. (eo) *strenuous, active, bold, strong.* [*Ger.* fromm]

framācyrran=framcyrran (In this and the following words fram- may often be taken as a separate preposition).

framādōn anv. *to take from, do away, cut off, cut out,* Lcd,LPs.

framādrȳfan¹ *to drive away, expel,* WW 98¹⁹.

framāhyldan *to turn from,* Lcd 1·328¹⁰.

framānȳdan *to drive away,* Lcd 1·226¹³.

framāscæcan⁶ *to shake off,* GD,Sc.

framāstyrian *to remove,* RPs 65²⁰.

framātēon² *to draw away from,* Ps.

framāteran⁴ 'diripere,' ÆGr 168¹⁰.

framāwendan *to turn from or away,* Sc 169².

framāweorpan³ *to cast away,* ÆGr.

frambige m. *backsliding, apostasy, default,* KC,W.

frambringan³ *to take away,* Lcd.

framcyme (o) m. *issue, posterity,* Gen 1765.

framcynn† (o) n. *issue, posterity : origin.*

framcyrran (e) *to turn from, avert : take from.*

framdōn anv. *to put off, stop, interrupt,* Sc 131⁸.

frameald *very old,* KC 3·60¹⁷.

fram-fær, -færeld mn. *departure,* Æ.

framfaru (o) f. *excess,* DR 17⁸.

framfundung f. *departure,* BH.

framgewītan¹ *to apostatize,* Sc 83².

framian *to avail, benefit,* RB.

framierning (o¹, e²) f. *outflowing,* DR 8¹.

framigendlic *effective, beneficial,* Lcd.

framlād (o) f. *departure,* Gen 2098.

framlēce *turned from,* GPH 401.

framlic *strong, daring,* BH 30²⁸. adv. -lice *boldly, strongly, strenuously, quickly.*

framlōcian (o) *to look back,* CP 403⁶.

framnes (o) f. *vigour, excellence,* AA 10¹⁷.

framrinc (o) *chief, prince,* RHy 4¹.

framscipe (o) I. m. *exercise, action: progress, success,* BH 92¹⁴. II. m. *fraternity,* BH 160⁶.

framsīþ (o) m. *departure,* GD.

framslītnes (o) f. *desolation,* NG.

framswengan *to swing away, shake off,* WW 524³⁰.

framung=fremung

framweard (o) *about to depart, departing, doomed to die,* Bo,Seaf; CP : *with his back turned,* Lcd 126a. ['fromward']

framweardes (o) adv. *away from,* Lcd. ['fromwards']

framwesende *absent,* DR 178'.

frān pret. 3 sg. of frīnan.

franca m. *lance, javelin,* ÆL.

±**frāsian** *to ask, inquire, find out by inquiry : tempt, try.*

frāsung f. *questioning, temptation,* Gu 160, Mt p 19.

fratwian=frǣtwian

frēa† I. m. gs. frēan *ruler, lord, king, master: the Lord, Christ, God : husband.* [*Goth.* frauja] II. (VPs)=frēo·I.

frēa- intensitive prefix (=L. prae-).

frēabeorht *glorious,* Bl.

frēabeorhtian (ǣ) *to proclaim,* CPs 41⁹.

frēabodian *to proclaim, declare,* LPs 118¹⁷².

frēabregd? *mighty device,* MLR 22·3.

frēadrēman *to exult,* LPs.

frēadrihten† m. *lord and master.*

frēafætt (ǣ¹) *very fat,* WW 532²⁴.

frēaglēaw *very wise,* Dan 88.

frēahræd (ǣ¹, -hræð) *very quick,* GL.

frēamǣre (ǣ¹) *very celebrated,* Pa,WW.

frēamicel (ǣ¹) *preeminent,* WW 530¹³.

frēamiht *great strength,* RPs 42².

freamsum=fremsum

frēan=frēon

frēaofestlice (ǣ¹) *very quickly,* WW 530¹³.

frēareccere m. *prince,* LRPs 118¹⁶¹.

frēas pret. 3 sg. of frēosan.

frēasian=frāsian

frēatorht *very bright, radiant*, Gl.

frēaðanclan *to exult*, RPs52⁷.

frēawine† m. *lord and friend*, B.

frēawlitig *very beautiful*, NC290.

frēawrāsn f. *splendid chain*, B1451.

frēbran=frēfran

frec (æ, i) *greedy*, MtL; Æ : *eager, bold, daring*, Met : *dangerous* (v. ES39·327 ff.). ['*freck*']

freca† m. *warrior, hero*.

frēced-=frēcen-; **frēcelnes**=frēcennes

frēcelsod *exposed to danger*, WW465²⁵.

frēcendlic, frēcenlic (CP) *dangerous, mischievous, perilous, terrible*. adv. -līce, AO.

frēcennes f. *harm, danger*, CP.

frecful (æ) *greedy*, OEG2445.

frecian *to be greedy*, WW(BTs).

freclīce *greedily*, GD31¹.

frecmāse f. *titmouse*, WW.

frēcn-=frēcen-

frēcne (æ) **I.** *dangerous, perilous*, CP : *terrible* : *savage, wicked* : *daring, bold*. [v. ES39·328f.] **II.** n. *peril*. **III.** adv. *dangerously* : *fiercely, severely* : *boldly, audaciously*.

frecnes f. *greediness*, Gl.

±frecnian *to make bold*, DA184 : *endanger, imperil*, ÆL30·436.

frecwāsend m. *gluttony*, A6·100.

+frēdan *to feel, perceive*, Æ,Bo; CP. ['*frede*'; frōd]

+frēdendlic *perceptible*, ÆGr4⁶.

+frēdmǣlum *little by little*, OEG3245.

+frēdnes f. *feeling, perception*, Bo.

+frēdra *more acute*, CP123¹⁹.

frefelīce=fræfellīce

frēfer (Chrd), frēfernes (LkL) f. *consolation*.

frefllce=fræfellice

±frēfran *to cheer, console*, BH; CP. ['*frover*']

frēfrend (ie²) mf. *comforter, consoler* : *the Comforter* (Holy Ghost), Bl.

frēfrian (Jn; Æ)=frēfran

frēfriend=frēfrend

frēfrung f. *consolation*, Gen37³⁵, LPs93¹⁹.

+frēge=+frǣge

fregen, fregn **I.**=frægn pret. 3 sg. of frignan. **II.** n. *question*, An255.

fregensyllic *very strange*, WNL223a²⁴.

fregnan=frignan

fregnðearle *inquiringly*, ÆL23⁵⁶⁶.

fregnung f. *questioning*, MkL p4¹⁹.

freht=friht

frem=fram adj.

fremde *foreign, alien, strange*, JnL,LL; AO,CP : *unfriendly*, Sol (-ede) : *estranged from, devoid of, remote from*. ['*fremd*']

±fremdian *to estrange*, RB : *curse, anathematize, excommunicate*.

freme I.† *vigorous, flourishing*, B,Gen. ['*frim*'; fram] **II.**=fremu

fremede=fremde

fremedlǣcan *to alienate*, RPs57⁴.

fremedlīce *perfectly*, Sc129³.

±fremednes f. *fulfilment, effect*, Æ.

fremful *useful, profitable, beneficial*, Lcd : *well-disposed*, WE67³. ['*fremeful*'] adv. -līce *efficaciously*.

fremfullic=fremful

fremfulnes f. *utility, profit*, RB83¹⁶.

±fremian *to avail, benefit, do good*, Æ,Mt. ['*freme*']

fremigendlic *profitable*, Lcd,OEG.

fremlic (eo, o) *profitable*, BH30²⁸.

fremman *to further, advance, support*, An, B : *frame, make, do, accomplish, perfect, perpetrate, commit, afford*, B,Gen; CP. ['*freme*']

±fremming f. *purpose, effect, performance, progress*, Æ.

fremnes=fremednes

fremsum *beneficent, benign, kind, gracious*, Æ,CP. adv. -sume.

fremsumlic *benignant, kind*, GD280. adv. -līce, CP.

fremsumnes f. *benefit, benignity, kindness, liberality*.

fremð- (NG)=fremd-

+fremðian (MkL14⁷¹)=fremdian

fremðlic=frymðlic

fremu f. *advantage, gain, benefit*, Bo,Ep, Lcd; CP. ['*freme*']

fremung (eo, o) f. *advantage, profit, good*, LL.

frence f. *a coarse cloak*, WW212²⁶.

Frencisc 'French,' Chr.

frēnd=frēond

frendian (WW484³¹)=fremdian

freng=frægn pret. 3 sg. of frignan.

frēo I. nap. often frīge '*free*,' Bo,Ex,G; Æ, CP : (†) *glad, joyful* : (†) *noble, illustrious*, Gen. [frēo- v. also frīg-, friŏ-] **II.†** f. *woman, lady*. **III.** m.=frēa. **IV.** imperat. of frēogan. **V.** f? *freedom, immunity* (Swt).

frēobearn† n. *child of gentle birth*, WW.

frēoborh=friŏborh

frēobrōðor m. *own brother*, Ex338.

frēoburh f. *city*, B694.

frēod I.† f. *peace, friendship* : *good-will, affection*. **II.** pp. of frēogan. **III.**=frēot

frēode pret. 3 sg. of frēogan.

frēodohtor f. *freeborn daughter*, W193⁶.

frēodōm m. '*freedom*,' *state of free-will, charter, emancipation, deliverance*, Bf,Bo; AO,CP.

frēodryhten†=frēadrihten

frēodscipe (ES39·340)=frēondscipe?

±**frēogan** to '*free*' ('*y-free*'), *liberate, manumit*, Æ,*Chr*; AO : *love, embrace, caress, think of lovingly, honour*.

+**frēoge**=+**frǣge**; **frēoh**=frēo

+**frēogend** (ī) m. *liberator*, CPs.

frēolāc n. *free-will offering, oblation*, LPs 50²¹.

frēolǣta m. *freedman*, WW.

±**frēolic** *free, freeborn* : *glorious, stately, magnificent, noble*, B,*Rd* : *beautiful, charming*. ['*freely*'] adv. -līce '*freely*,' *readily*, Bo,*VPs* : *as a festival*, ÆP196¹².

frēols I. mn. *freedom, immunity, privilege* : *feast-day, festival*. [origl. frīheals] II. adj. *free, festive*.

frēolsǣfen m. *eve of a feast*, LL383,56.

frēolsbōc f. *charter of freedom*, Ct.

frēolsbryce (i) m. *breach of festival*, LL,W.

frēolsdæg m. *feast-day, festival-day*, Æ.

frēolsdōm=frēodōm

frēols-end, -iend m. *liberator*, EPs.

frēolsgefa m. *emancipator*, LL13,8.

frēolsgēr (=ēa²) n. *year of jubilee*, WW420³¹.

±**frēolsian** (ī, ȳ) *to deliver, liberate*, BL, EPs : *to keep a feast or holy day, celebrate*, Æ. ['*frels*']

frēolslic *festive, festival*, CM350. adv. *freely* : *solemnly*.

frēolsmann m. *freedman*, KC3·295⁶.

frēolsniht f. *eve of a festival*, NC290.

frēolsstōw f. *festival-place*, LL338,38.

frēolstīd f. *festival, feast-day*, Æ.

frēolsung f. *celebration of a feast*, LL.

freom=fram III.; **freom-**=fram-, frem-

frēomǣg† m. *free kinsman*, GEN.

frēomann m. '*free-man*,' *freeborn man*, Gen, LL.

frēonama m. *surname*, BH.

frēond m. ds. frīend, nap. frīend, frēond, frēondas '*friend*,' *relative*, B,*Chr,El,Gen*; AO,CP : *lover*.

frēondheald *amiable*, LCD3·192¹⁵.

frēondhealdlic *related, akin*, WW217²⁹.

frēondlār f. *friendly counsel*, B2377.

frēondlaðu f. *friendly invitation*, B1192.

frēondlēas '*friendless*,' *JnL* : *orphan*. f. mann *outlaw*, LL.

frēondlēast f. *want of friends*, LL336,35.

frēondlic '*friendly*,' *well-disposed, kindly*, BH; W. adv. -līce, CP.

frēondlīðe *kind to one's friends*, ES39·340.

frēondlufu f. *friendship, love*, GEN1834.

frēondmyne f. *amorous intention*, GEN1831.

frēondrǣden f. *friendship*, Bo; Æ : *conjugal love*. ['*friendrede*']

frēondscipe m. '*friendship*,' B,*Lcd*; AO, CP : *conjugal love*.

frēondspēd f. *abundance of friends*, GEN 2330.

frēondspēdig *rich in friends*, LL(286¹³).

frēone asm. of frēo adj.

frēonoma=frēonama

frēorig† *freezing, frozen, cold, chilly* : *blanched with fear, sad, mournful*. [frēosan]

frēorig-ferð, -mōd† *sad*, GU.

frēoriht n. *rights of freemen*, LL,W.

±**frēosan²** *to* '*freeze*,' Æ,*Bl,Gn*.

frēosceat m. *freehold property*, RB138²¹.

frēot m. *freedom*, LL. frēotes ðolian *to be reduced to slavery*.

frēotgifa m. *liberator*, WW.

frēot-gifu, -gift f. *emancipation*, WW.

frēotmann m. *freedman*, BK,TC,W.

freoð-=frið-; **-frēoðan** v. ā-f.

freoðo-, freoðu-=friðo-, friðu-

frēowīf (ī¹) n. *free-woman*, LL7,73.

frēowine=frēawine; **Fresan**=Frisan

Fresic (y) *in the Frisian manner, Frisian*, CHR. [Frisan]

±**fretan⁵** *to devour, eat, consume*, Æ,*B. Chr,LG*; CP : *break*, EX147. ['*fret*,' '*y-fret*']

fretgenga=frætgenga

frettan *to feed upon, consume*, CHR,PPs. [fretan]

frettol *greedy, gluttonous*, WW171³⁴.

fretw-=frætw-

freðo=frið0

frī=frēo I.; **frīa**=frēa

frīand (A)=frēond

frīborh (v. LL2·81)=friðborh

fric (NG)=frec

fricca, friccea m. *herald, crier*, CP (? v. ES 39·336).

fricgan⁵† *to ask, inquire into, investigate* : (+) *learn, find out by inquiry*.

frician *to dance*, Mt. ['*frike*']

friclan† w. g. *to seek, desire*.

friclo f. *appetite*, LCD73a.

frico f. '*usura*,' MtL25²⁷ (v. ES39·328f.).

fricolo (OP21)=friclo

frictrung (OET26)=frihtrung

frīdhengest v. friðhengest.

frīenan=frīnan, frignan

frīend v. frēond.

+**frīend** (ȳ) pl. *friends*, AO,*Lk*. ['*i-freond*']

frīg=frēo; **Frīgdæg**=Frīgedæg

frīge I.† fp. *love*. II. v. frēo.

frīgea m. *lord, master*, LL (=frēa).

Frīgeǣfen m. *Thursday evening*, Æ.

Frīgedæg m. '*Friday*,' LL,*Ma*; Æ.

frigenes=frignes

Frīgeniht f. *Thursday night*, LL,W305²⁴.

frigest, frigeð pres. 2, 3 sg. of fricgan.

±**frignan³**, frīnan² *ask, inquire*, B,BH,*Cp, Ps*; AO,CP : †*learn by inquiry*. ['*frayne*']

±**frignes** f. *interrogation, question*, BH.

frīgnes f. *freedom,* CHR 796.

frignung f. *question,* GD 137²⁹.

frīgst, frihst pres. 2 sg. of fricgan.

frīht (e, y) n. *divination,* DR,LL.

frīhtere m. *diviner, soothsayer,* NAR 37².

frihtrian *to divine,* KL.

frihtrung f. *soothsaying, divination,* WW.

frimdig=frymdig; **frīnan**=frignan

frīnd=frīend; **frīo**=frēo

frīs (ȳ) *crisped, curled,* GNE 96.

Frīsan (e) mp. *Frisians,* AO.

frisca=frysca

fristmearc (GL)=firstmearc

frit, friteð, fritt pres. 3 sg. of fretan.

frið (y) mn. *peace, tranquillity, security, refuge, AO,Chr,MtL;* CP, Æ. f. niman *to make peace : privilege of special protection, and penalty for the breach of it,* LL 10,5 : *restoration of rights (to an outlaw),* LL 316,13. ['*frith*']

frīð *stately, beautiful,* RD 10⁹.

frīða (eo) m. *protector,* PPs 70³.

friðāð m. *oath of peace,* CHR 1012 E.

friðbēna m. *suppliant, refugee,* LL.

friðborh m. *surety for peace,* LL.

friðbrǣc f. *breach of the peace,* LL.

friðburg f. *town with which there is peace, city of refuge,* LL 222,2¹.

friðcandel f. *the sun,* GEN 2539.

friðelēas=friðlēas

friðgeard m. *enclosed space, asylum, sanctuary,* LL : *court of peace (heaven),* CR.

friðgedāl n. *death,* GEN 1142. [ferhð?]

friðgegilda m. *member of a peace-guild,* LL 173 Pro.

friðgeorn *peaceable,* MtL 5⁹.

friðgewrit m. *peace agreement,* LL 144.

friðgild n. *peace-guild,* LL 181. [v. '*frith*']

friðgīsl m. *peace-hostage,* LL 378,9¹.

frīðhengest (frīd-) m. *stately horse? (ON.* frīðr), *or horse of peace?* (frið-h.), RD 23⁴.

frīðherpað m. *king's highway,* KC 5·214'.

friðhūs n. *sanctuary,* WW 186²³.

friðian (eo) *to give '*frið*' to, make peace with, be at peace with :* (±) *cherish, protect, guard, defend, keep, AO,Chr;* CP : *observe.* ['*frith*']

friðiend m. *helper, defender,* PPs,W 239⁷.

friðland n. *friendly territory,* CHR.

friðlēas *peaceless, outlawed,* LL 318.

friðlic *mild, lenient,* LL.

friðmāl n. *article of peace,* LL 220 Pro.

friðmann m. *man under special peace-protection,* LL 222.

friðo=friðu

friðobēacen (eo¹) n. *sign of peace,* GEN 1045.

friðoscealc (eo¹)† m. *angel,* GEN.

friðosibb f. *peace-bringer,* B 2017.

friðospēd (eo¹)† f. *abundant peace.*

friðotācn n. *sign of peace,* GEN 2369.

friðoðēawas (eo¹) mp. *peaceful state,* GEN 79.

friðowǣr (eo¹)† f. *treaty of peace.*

friðowang (eo¹) m. *peaceful plain,* B 2959.

friðowaru (eo¹)† f. *protection.*

friðo-webba (eo¹) m., -webbe† f. *peace-maker.*

friðscip n. *ship for defence,* LL 441 (? read fyrdscip).

friðsōcn f. *sanctuary, asylum,* LL.

friðsplott m. *peace-spot, asylum,* LL (248⁵).

friðstōl m. *sanctuary, asylum,refuge, LL,Ps.* ['*frithstool*']

friðstōw f. *refuge, sanctuary,* CP.

friðsum *pacific, peaceful :* (+) *safe, fortified.*

friðsumian *to make peaceful, reconcile,* NC 290.

friðu (eo) fm. *peace, safety, protection, AO, Chr,MtL : refuge, asylum.* [v. '*frith*']

friðu-=friðo-; **frocga**=frogga

frōd† *wise : old.* [ON. frōðr]

frōdian *to be wise,* RIM 32.

frōfer=frōfor; **frōferian**=frēfran

±**frōfor** fmn. (e², u²) gs. frōfre *consolation, joy, refuge, Æ;* CP : *compensation, help, benefit.* ['*frover*']

frōforbōc (e²) f. *book of consolation,* Bo 50⁶.

frōforgāst (frōfre-) m. *consoling spirit, Holy Ghost, Comforter, BH,Jn;* Æ. [v. '*frover*']

frōforlic (e²) *kind, helpful,* W. adv. -līce, W 295³.

frōfornes f. *consolation,* LkL 6²⁴ (oe).

frōforword n. *word of consolation,* GD 344²⁸.

frōfrian=frēfran

frogga m. '*frog,' Æ,WW.*

froht (NG)=forht

from=fram; **from-** also=frem-, frum-

froren pp. of frēosan.

frosc m. *frog, Æ* (frox); GL. ['*frosh*']

frost=forst

frōwe f. *woman,* DD 291. [Ger. frau]

frox (Æ)=frosc

frugnen pp., frugnon pret. pl. of frignan.

frum I. *primal, original, first.* II.=fram

fruma m. *beginning, origin, cause, B,Mt;* AO,CP : *creation,* CHR 33 : *originator, inventor, founder, creator : first-born,* CPs 135¹⁰ : (†) *prince, king, chief, ruler.* on fruman *at first.* wæstma fruman *first-fruits.* ['*frume*']

frumācennes f. *nativity,* JnLp 5¹⁹.

frumbearn† n. *first-born child.*

frumbyrd f. *birth,* TC 369⁹.

frumbyrdling n. *youth,* WW 171²³. ['*frumberdling*']

frumcenned *first-begotten,first-born, Æ,AO : original, primitive, ÆGR.*

frumcennende *primitive,* OEG 1775.

frumcnēow n. *primal generation,* Ex 371.

frumcyn† n. *ancestry, origin, descent, lineage* : *race, tribe.*

frumcynnend=frumcenned

frumcyrr m. *first time,* LL164,25².

frumdysig n. *first offence, beginning of sin,* Chrd 18¹⁶.

frum-gār†, -gāra† m. *leader, patriarch, chieftain, noble.* [cp. *L.* primi-pilus]

frumgesceap n. *creation of the world,* Cr840.

frumgeweorc n. *original construction,* A 11·174⁶.

frumgewrit n. *deed, document,* W252¹².

frumgifu f. *prerogative, privilege,* Gl.

frumgripa m. *firstling,* W113⁶.

frumgyld n. *first instalment,* LL190.

frumhēowung (=ī²) f. *original formation,* WW467²⁷.

frumhrægl n. *first garment* (sc. *of fig-leaves*), Gen943.

frumildo f. *early age,* WW341²². [ieldo]

frumlēoht n. *dawn,* AF4·56.

frumlic *original, primitive,* Gl. adv. -līce, Gl.

frumlida m. *chief sailor.* v. OEG32.

frumlyhtan *to dawn,* Bl207³⁵.

frummeoluc f. *'nectar' (new milk?* BTs), WW456¹⁸.

frummynetslæge m. *first coinage,* ÆL23⁴⁷⁹.

frumrǣd m. *primary ordinance,* LL246.

frumrǣden f. *space of time,* An147.

frumrinc=framrinc

frumripa m. *first-fruits,* LL40,38.

frumsceaft m. *first creation, origin, primeval condition, B,BH* : *creature* : *home.* ['*frumschaft*']

frumsceapen *first created, first,* Æ.

frumsceatt m. *first-fruits,* ELPs.

frumscepend m. *creator,* DR16¹⁰.

frumscyld f. *original sin,* Sol445.

frumsetnes f. *authority,* DR123⁸.

frumsetnung f. *foundation, creation,* JnR 17²⁴.

frumslǣp m. *first sleep,* Æ,AO.

frumspellung f. *first relation, original story,* OEG1153; 2³¹.

frumsprǣc f. *opening words,* ÆL23¹²⁰ : †*promise.*

frumstaðol m. *first state,* Rd61³.

frumstemn m. *prow,* WW288²¹.

frumstōl m. *first or principal seat, paternal home,* LL.

frumtalu f. *first statement in an action?* (Lieb), *of a witness?* (BT), LL385 and 3·226.

frumtid f. *beginning,* GD212⁵.

frumtyhtle f. *first accusation, first charge,* LL336,35. [tēon II.]

frumð=frymð

frumwæstm mf. *first-fruits,* Æ.

frumweorc n. *primeval work, creation,* An 805.

frumwifung f. *first marriage,* W304²⁷.

frumwylm (e²) m. *new-born zeal,* RB135⁵ : *first inflammation,* Lcd30b.

frumwyrhta m. *creator,* DR37⁴.

frunen pp., frun(n)on pret. pl. of frīnan.

frungon=frugnon pret. pl. of frignan.

fruron pret. pl. of frēosan.

frȳ=frēo; **fryccea**=fricca

fryht=friht

fryht- (N)=forht-, fyrht-

frylsian (Bo)=freolsian

frym-=frum-, fyrm-

frymdig (i) *curious, inquisitive,* Æ : *desirous.* f. bēon *to entreat.*

frymetling f. *young cow,* LL451,13.

frymð I. mf. *origin, beginning, foundation,* Bo; Æ,AO : *creature,* (in pl.) *created things,* El. ['*frumth*'] II.=fyrmð

frymð-lic, -elic *primeval, primitive, first* : *chief.* adv. -līce, OEG5211.

frymðu, frymðo (*MtL*)=frymð

frymðylde *of early age?* v. OEG2381.

frȳnd (Æ) nap. of frēond.

+frȳnd=+friend

frȳs=frīs

Frysan=Frisan

frysca I. (i) m. *kite, bittern,* Gl. II. '*pusio*'? Gl (v. A19·495).

frȳsð pres. 3 sg. of frēosan.

fryt pres. 3 sg. of fretan.

frȳð=frið; **frȳð-** also=fyrð-

fugel m. gs. fugles '*fowl*,' *bird, B,Mt*; CP.

fugelbona m. *fowler,* Cra80.

fugelcynn n. *bird-tribe,* Æ. ['*fowlkin*']

fugeldæg (u²) m. *day on which poultry might be eaten,* TC460²⁰.

fugeldoppe f? *water-fowl,* WW131²⁰.

fugelere (AO)=fuglere

fugeleswȳse f. *larkspur,* WW298²⁴.

fugelhwata m. *augur,* WW140⁵.

fugellim m. *bird-lime,* OEG3105.

fugelnett n. *bird-net,* WW277¹⁵.

fugelnoð, fugeloð *bird-catching, fowling,* Æ.

fugeltimber n. *young bird,* Ph236.

fugeltrēo n. *prop (of a snare for birds),* WW 349¹⁹.

fugelweohlere m. *augur,* WW108¹². [wiglere]

fugelwylle (o²) *swarming with birds,* BH 30¹⁰ [weallan]

fuglere m. '*fowler*,' AO.

fuglesbēan f. *vetch,* Gl.

fuglian *to catch birds,* ÆGr. ['*fowl*']

fuglung f. *bird-catching,* WW268,352.

fugol-, fugul-=fugel-; **fuhl-**=fugl-

fūht *damp, moist,* Lcd,Chrd64³⁶. [Ger. feucht]

fūhtian *to be moist*, NC 290.

fuhton pret. pl. of feohtan.

ful I. n. *beaker, cup*, Æ. **II.**=full

fūl I. '*foul,' unclean, impure, vile, corrupt, rotten*, Æ,*Bl,Cp,Cr,Gl*; CP : *guilty*, LL. f. bēam *black alder*, LCD 29b. **II.** n. *filth, foulness, impurity, crime, offence, El,OET*. ['*foul*']

fulbeorht *very bright, resplendent*, CP 87²³.

fulbrecan⁴ *to violate*, LL 280,2².

fulqon anv. *to complete, perform*, RB 70²¹ : *arrange*, ÆL 33¹⁴²⁵.

fūle adv. *foully*, Æ.

fulēode pret. 3 sg. of fullgān.

fūletrēo n. *black alder*, Cp 430 A.

fulfæstnian *to ratify fully*, CHR 675 E.

fulfaran⁶ *to travel*, LL 383,56.

fulfealdan⁷ '*explicare*,' ÆGR 138⁹.

fulgeare *quite well*, ÆL 3⁴⁵⁶. [gearwe]

fulgōd *very good*, ÆL 6¹²⁴.

fulgon pret. pl. of fēolan.

fulhār *entirely grey, very hoary*, WW 380¹³.

fulhealden *contented*, WW 211³⁰.

fulht-=fulwiht-

fūlian *to be or become* '*foul*,' *decay, rot*, AO, Ps,Sc.

full I. adj. (w. g.) '*FULL*,' *filled, complete, perfect, entire, utter*, Æ,AO,CP : *swelling, plump*, LCD. be fullan *fully, perfectly, completely*. **II.** adv. *very, fully, entirely, completely, thoroughly*, Bo,Chr,Met,Ps. f. nēah *almost, very nearly*. ['*full*' adv.] **III.**=ful

full- v. also ful-.

fulla I. m. *fulness*, ÆL 13¹⁰⁴. **II.** m. *assembly?* Ct (Swt).

fullæst (ā, ē; fylst) m. *help, support*, Ex, Met. ['*filst*']

±fullæstan (ē) w. d. *to help, support*, AO, Lk. ['*filst*']

fullæðele *very noble*, Bo 24⁷.

+fullan=+fyllan

fullberstan³ *to burst completely*, W 267¹⁸.

fullbētan *to make full amends*, ÆGR,RB.

fullblīðe *very glad*, JUD 16²³.

fullboren *fully born*, CP 367¹⁸ : *of noble birth*.

fullbryce m. *complete breach of the peace*, LL : *violation of the rights of a clerical offender*, LL.

fullclæne *very pure*, AS 30².

fullcuman⁴ *to attain*, RWH 136¹.

fullcūð *well-known, notorious, famous*, HL 201²¹¹.

-fulle v. sin-f.

fullendian *to complete*, BH. ['*fullend*']

fullere m. '*fuller*,' *bleacher, Mk*.

fullest=fullæst

fullflēon² *to take to flight, escape completely*, ÆGR 179¹⁶.

fullforðian *to fulfil*, NC 291, RWH 138²⁵.

fullfrem-ed, -edlic *perfect*, CP. adv. -līce *fully, perfectly, completely*, Bl. ['*fullfremed(ly)*']

fullfremednes f. *perfection*, BH; CP. ['*fullfremedness*']

±full-fremman, -fremian *to fulfil, perfect, practise, complete*, Bo; CP. ['*fullfreme*']

fullfyligan *to follow, obey*, W 95¹⁹ : *pursue*, EPs 7⁶.

fullfyllan *to* '*fulfil*,' ÆGr 153¹.

full-gān pret. 3 sg. -ēode anv., -gangan⁷ *to accomplish, fulfil, perform, carry out*, Æ : *follow, imitate, obey* : *help*, AO.

fullgearwian *to finish, complete*, GD 126² : *prepare fully*, CP.

fullgedrifen (w. g.) *full (of wild beasts)*, SOL 150²³.

fullgeorne *very eagerly*, CP 255²².

fullgewēpned *fully armed*, CHR 1083.

fullgrōwan⁷ *to grow to perfection*, CP 67²³.

fullhāl *thoroughly well*, GD 248¹.

fullhealden *contented*, WW 211³⁰.

±fullian I. *to complete, fill up, perfect*. **II.** (Jn)=fulwian

fullic *full : universal, catholic*, CHy 15. adv. -līce *entirely,* '*fully,' perfectly, completely*, Bf,BH; Æ.

fūllic *foul, unclean, objectionable, shameful, base*, LCD,W. adv. -līce.

fulligan=fulwian

fullmægen n. *great power*, W 186¹⁴.

fullmannod *fully peopled*, Bo 40¹⁷.

full-medeme *excellent, perfect*, GD. adv. -medomlīce, GD 320²¹, 331¹³.

fullnes f. *fulness*, DR 11¹³.

fūllnes=fūlnes

fulloc *final or definite agreement?* LL 385.

fulloft adv. *very often*, CP.

fullraðe adv. *very quickly*, AO.

fullricene *very quickly, immediately*, PPs 140².

fullrīpod *mature*, RB 139⁹.

fullslēan *to kill outright*, ÆP 138⁴.

fullsumnes f. *abundance*, EPs 48⁷.

fullðungen (ful-) *full-grown*, RB 133¹.

fullðungennes f. *full development*, MFH 160.

fulluht=fulwiht

fullunga adv. *fully*, N

fullwearm *fully warm*, CP 447⁵.

fullweaxan *to grow to maturity*, CP 383³⁰, ByH 6¹¹.

fullwelig *very rich*, Bo 24⁷.

fullwēpnod *fully armed*, CHR 1070 E.

fullwer m. *complete* 'wer,' *full atonement*, RD 24¹⁴?

fullwērig *very tired*, MFH 160.

fullwyrcan *to complete, fulfil*, ÆL.

fulnēah I. adj. *very near*. II. adv. *very nearly, almost*, CP.

fūlnes f. *foulness, filthy smell*, BH,GL.

fūlon rare pret. pl. of fēolan.

fūlstincende *foul-stinking*, GD,LCD.

fultēam (Erf.)=fultum

fultem- (CP), fultom-=fultum-

fultrūwian *to confide in*, Bo 60²³.

fultum (ēa) m. *help, support, protection, B, Gl*; Æ,AO,CP:*forces, army*, AO. ['*fultum*'] +**fultuma** m. *helper*, SPs 18¹⁶.

±**fultum-an**, -ian *to help, support, assist*, Æ,CP : (†) *be propitious to, overlook*.

±**fultum(i)end** m. *helper, fellow-worker*, Æ, CP.

fultumlēas *without help*, AO 56²¹.

fulwa m. *fuller*, MH 26²⁶.

fulwere m. *baptizer, baptist*, MH 14,102.

±**fulwian** *to baptize*, BH,Jn,MH; AO,CP. ['*full*']

fulwiht, fulluht (*Mt*) mfn. *baptism, Christianity*, *Mt*; AO,CP. ['*fullought*']

±**fulwiht-an**, -ian *to baptize*, CHR,NG.

fulwihtbæð n. *baptismal bath, font*, Æ (fulluht-).

fulwihtbēna m. *applicant for baptism*, WW 207¹⁶.

fulwihtele m. *baptismal oil*, LL(258¹⁵).

fulwihtere m. *baptizer* : *the Baptist*, Æ,G.

fulwihtfæder m. *baptismal father, godfather, baptizer*, BL 205¹⁷.

fulwihthād m. *baptismal order or vow*, BL 109²⁶.

fulwihtnama m. *baptismal name, Christian name*.

+**fulwihtnian** (fulhtn-) *to baptize*, NC 291.

fulwihtstōw f. *baptistry*, BL 140²⁰.

fulwihttīd f. *time of baptism*, MEN 11.

fulwihtðēaw m. *rite of baptism*, MET 1³³.

fulwihtðēnung (-uht) f. *baptismal service*, W 38⁹.

fulwihtwæter n. *laver of baptism*, NC 291.

fulwihtwere m. *baptist*, BL 161⁶.

fulwuht=fulwiht

funde wk. pret. 3 sg., funden pp. of findan.

-fundelnes, -fundennes v. on-f.

fundian I. (w. of, tō) *to tend to, wish for, strive after, go, set out, go forward, hasten*, Æ,B,Cr,Gen,Gu; CP : *spread?* LCD 125b. ['*found*'] II.=fandian

fundon pret. pl. of findan.

fundung f. *departure*, Chr 1106; ByH 12²⁰. ['*founding*']

funta? funte? *spring? brook?* KC (v. ES 54·102) or ?=finta (IF 48·255).

fūra v. furh.

furh f. gs. fūre, ds. fyrh, furh, gp. fūra '*furrow*,' *trench*, BC,Bo; Æ.

furhwudu m. *pine*, Cp 420 P.

±**fūrian** *to furrow*, OEG.

furlang n. *length of furrow*, '*furlong*,' BH, Lk : *land the breadth of a furrow*, KC.

furðan, furðon=furðum

furðor adv. (of place and time) '*further*,' *more distant, forwards, later*, Æ,Bf,Chr; CP : *more* : *superior*, CP 117². f. dōn *to promote*, CP.

furðorlucor (e²) cp. adv. *more perfectly*, MFB 133 and n 30.

furðra cp. adj. '*further*,' *greater, superior*, Jn.

furðum (-an, -on) adv. *even, exactly, quite, already, just as, at first*, Bl,Mt; AO,CP : *further, previously*. syððan f. *just as soon as*. ['*forthen*']

furðumlic *luxurious, indulging*, AO 50³⁰.

furður=furðor; **furuh**=furh

fūs *striving forward, eager for, ready for, inclined to, willing, prompt, B*; Æ : *expectant, brave, noble* : *ready to depart, dying*. ['*fous*']

fūslēoð† n. *death-song, dirge*.

fūslic *ready to start* : *excellent*. adv. -līce *readily, gladly*.

fūsnes f. *quickness*, EHy 6²⁵.

fustra (OEG 1428). ?=fȳrstān (BTs).

fȳf-=fif-; **fyhfang**=feohfang

fyht-=feoht-

fȳhtan (ī) *to moisten*, OEG. [fūht]

fyl=fiell, fyll

±**fȳlan** *to befoul, defile, pollute*, Æ.

+**fylce** n. *band of men, army, host*, CP. [folc]

±**fylcian** *to marshal troops*, CHR 1066 C,D. [folc]

fyld m. *fold, crease*, OEG.

fyld(e)stōl m. *folding-stool*, ZDA 31·10. ['*faldstool*']

fylen=fellen?

±**fylgan** w. d. or a. *to '*follow*,' pursue*, LG; Æ,CP:*persecute* : *follow out, observe, obey* : *obtain* : *attend to* : *practise*, Bl.

fylgend m. *follower, observer*, BH 472⁷.

fylgestre f. *female follower*, OEG 1228.

fylgian=fylgan

fylging f. I. *following*, DR. II. (æ) *fallow-land*. [fealh]

fylian, fyligan=fylgan

fyligendlic *that can or ought to be imitated*, CM 803.

fylignes f. *following, practice*, BH 160²³.

fyll=(1) fyllu; (2) fiell

±**fyllan** I. *to '*fill*,' fill up, replenish, satisfy*, An,Gen; Æ : *complete, fulfil*, Az. [full] II.±(æ, e;=ie) wv. *to cause to fall, strike down*, '*fell*' ('*y-fell*'), *cut down*, AO,Bl,Ps, Rd : *throw down, defeat, destroy, kill*, BH, Cr,Ps : *tumble* : *cause to stumble*, MtR. +**fylled** (wdg.) *bereft*.

fyllað m. *filling, filling up*, GEN 1513.

+**fyllednes** (i) f. *fulness, completion, fulfilment*, Æ.

fyllen (=i) f. *a dropping*, LCD 18a.

-**fyllen** (fylen) v. mōnað-f.

fyllend=fylgend

+**fyllendlic** *filling, expletive*, ÆGR 261[5] : *capable of completion*, WW 209[38].

fylleseoc (=ie) *epileptic*, LCD,WW 112[27].

fylleseocnes f. *epilepsy*, LCD 1·164[9].

fylleðflod m. *high tide*, GL.

fyllewærc (e[1];=ie) n. *epilepsy*, LCD 65a.

±**fylling** f. *filling*, GD : *completion*, LRSPs.

+**fyllingtīd** f. *compline*, WW 207[44]n.

±**fyllnes** f. *fulness, plenitude, satiety* : *supplement* : *completion, fulfilment.*

fyllo, fyllu f. *fulness (of food)*, '*fill*,' *feast, satiety, AO,B*; CP : *impregnation*.

fylmen=filmen

fylnes I. (±) f. *fall, stumbling-block, offence, ruin*, NG. **II.**=fyllnes

fylnes=fūlnes

fylst I. m. *help, aid, Mt*; Æ,AO. **II.** pres. 2 sg. of feallan. **III.** pres. 2 sg. of fyllan.

+**fylsta** m. *helper*, Æ.

±**fylstan** (w. d.) *to aid, support, help, protect*, Æ,AO. [=fullæstan]

±**fylstend** m. *helper*, Æ,BRPs.

fylt pres. 3 sg. of fealdan.

fylð I. pres. 3 sg. of fyllan. **II.** pres. 3 sg. of feallan.

fylð f. '*filth*,' *uncleanness, impurity, Mt,Sc, W*. [fūl]

fylwērig *faint to death*, B 963. [fiell]

fyn-=fin-; **fynd**=fēond; +**fynd**=+fiend

fyndele m. *invention, devising*, Sc. ['*findal*']

fyne m? n? *moisture, mould*, WW 183[19].

fynegian *to become mouldy*, LL. ['*finew*']

fynig (i) *mouldy, musty, Jos*. ['*fenny*']

fyniht *fenny, marshy*, LCD 92a.

fyr v. feorr.

fȳr (ī) n. '*fire*,' *Ex,G,VPs*; Æ,AO,CP : *a fire*, *Gen*.

fȳran I.=fēran. **II.** (±) *to cut a furrow*, OEG 2492n : *castrate*, LCD 3·184[19].

fȳras=fīras

fȳrbǣre *fire-bearing, fiery*, OEG.

fȳrbæð† n. *fire-bath, hell-fire*, CR.

fȳrbend m. *bar forged in the fire*, B 722.

fȳrbēta m. *fireman, stoker*, WW.

fȳrbryne m. *conflagration*, AO 252[20].

fyrclian (ȳ?) *to flash, flicker*, CHR 1106.

fȳrclomm m. *band forged in the fire*, SAT 39.

fȳrcrūce f. *crucible, kettle*, GL.

fȳrcynn n. *fire*, AO 252[20] c.

fyrd=fierd

fyrdcræft (i) m. *warring host*, NUM 22[4].

fyrdend *enrolled for military service*, ÆL 25[363].

fyrdesne m. *warrior*, BH 148[8].

fyrdfæreld n. fyrdfaru f. *going to war, military service*, LL. [v. '*ferd*']

fyrdfōr f. *military service*, KC.

fyrdgeatewe fp. *war-gear*, RUN 27.

fyrdgemaca m. *fellow-soldier*, Æ.

fyrdgestealla† m. *comrade in arms*.

fyrdgetrum† n. *band of warriors*, EX.

fyrdhama (o[2]) m. *corslet*, B 1504.

fyrdhrægl n. *corslet*, B 1527.

fyrdhwæt† *warlike, brave*.

fyrdian (e) *to go on an expedition*, CHR.

fyrding (e) f. *soldiering* : *army, expedition, militia*, LL ; Æ : *camp* : *fine for evading military service*, LL : *march, progression*, BF 46[28]. ['*ferding*']

fyrdlāf f. *remnant of an army*, ÆL 25[377].

fyrdlēas (ie) *without an army*, CHR 894 A.

fyrdlēoð† n. *war-song*, B.

fyrdlic *martial*, Æ.

fyrdmann m. *warrior*, BO 40[18].

fyrdnoð (e) m. *liability to military service*, BC 3·71[7].

fȳrdraca m. *fire-spewing dragon*, B 2689. ['*firedrake*']

fyrdrian *to serve in the army*, ÆL 28[11].

fyrdrinc† (e) m. *warrior, soldier*.

fyrdsceorp n. *armour*, RD 15[13].

fyrdscip n. *battle-ship*, LL.

fyrdsearu† n. *accoutrements*, B.

fyrdsōcn f. *military service*, Ct.

fyrdstemn m. *body of soldiers who serve for a fixed term, army-corps*, CHR 921.

fyrdstrǣt f. *military road*, KC.

fyrdtīber n. *military sacrifice?* (Swt), WW 418[22]; A 15·187.

fyrdtruma m. *martial band, army*, ÆH 1·442'.

fyrdung=fyrding

fyrdwǣn (i) m. *military carriage?* EC 250'.

fyrdweard f. *military watch*, LL 444,1.

fyrdwerod n. *host, army*, WW 399[30].

fyrdwīc n. *camp*, Æ.

fyrdwīsa m. *chieftain*, CRA 77.

fyrdwīse f. *military style*, AA 14[5].

fyrdwīte n. *fine for evading military service*, LL.

fyrdwyrðe *distinguished in war*, B 1316.

-**fyrede** v. twi-, ðri-f.

fyren=firen

fȳren *of fire, fiery, Bl,MH*; AO,CP : *on fire, burning, flaming*. ['*firen*']

fȳrenful *fiery*, LPs,W.

fyrengāt (WW 423[11])=firgengāt

fȳrentācen n. *fiery sign*, MFH 131[12].

fyrentācnian *to pollute with sin*. RHy 6[21].

fȳrenðecele f. *firebrand*, BH 476[15].

fyres=fyrs

fyrest=fyrst, fyrmest superl. adj.

fyrewyt=fyrwit

fȳrfeaxen *fiery-haired*, WW 425,519.

fȳrfōda (ī) m. *fuel, twigs for burning*, OEG 7⁸⁸.

fȳrgearwung f. *cooking*, WW 401⁹.

fȳrgebeorh *fire-screen*, LL 455,17.

fȳrgebrǣc n. *crackling of fire*, GEN 2560.

fyrgen=firgen

fȳrgnāst m. *spark of fire*, AN 1548. [*ON.* gneisti]

fyrh I. f. *fir*, KC 6·102'. II. v. furh.

fȳrhāt *hot as fire, burning, ardent*, EL. ['*firehot*']

fȳrheard *hardened by fire*, B 305.

±fyrht I. *afraid, timid.* [forht] II.=friht

±fyrht-an, -ian (fryht-, N) *to fear, tremble*, DR : *frighten, terrify*, BH. ['*fright*,' vb.]

fyrhtnes f. *fear*, AO,MtL.

±fyrhto, fyrhtu (fryht-, N) f. '*fright*,' *fear, dread, trembling*, Ps,VHy; Æ,AO,CP : *horrible sight*, NR 26⁶,⁹. [forht]

fyrhð=ferhð

±fyr(h)ð, fyrhðe nf. *wooded country*, Ct. ['*frith*']

fȳrhūs n. '*caminatum*,' *house or room with a fireplace in it?* WW; CHRD 45⁶. ['*firehouse*']

fȳrhwēolod v. fēowerhwēolod.

fyrian (B 378)=ferian

fȳrian I. *to supply with firing*, LL. ['*fire*' vb.] II. (±) *to cut a furrow.* [furh]

fyrlen I. (eo, e) *far off, distant, remote*, Æ. II. n. *distance*, Æ.

fȳrlēoht n. *gleam of fire*, B 1516. ['*firelight*']

fȳrlēoma m. *gleam of fire*, SAT 128.

fȳrlīce=fǣrlīce

fȳrloca m. *fiery prison*, SAT 58.

fyrm I. (=ie) *cleansing*, LL 454⁸. II.=feorm

fyrm-=frym-

fȳrmǣl m. *mark burnt in by fire*, AN 1136.

fyrmest (o) superl. of forma I. '*foremost*,' *first*, LCD; Æ,CP : *most prominent, chief, best*, El,Mt. II. adv. *first of all, in the first place, at first, most, especially, very well, best.*

fyrmð (=ie) f. I. *harbouring, entertainment*, LL. II. *cleansing, washing.*

fyrn I. (i) adj. *former, ancient*, Rd. II. adv. (±) *formerly, of old, long ago, once*, Gu; ÆL. ['*fern*']

fyrn-=firen-

±fyrndagas mp. *days of yore*, An; ÆL. [v. '*fern*'] frōd fyrndagum *old, aged.*

fyrngēarn. *former year(s)*, Gn,Ps : *preceding year*, LCD 3·228. ['*fernyear*']

fyrn-geflit† n. nap. -geflitu *former quarrel, old strife.*

fyrngeflita m. *old-standing enemy*, PA 34.

fyrngemynd n. *ancient history*, EL 327.

fyrngesceap n. *ancient decree*, PH 360.

fyrngesetu np. *former seat, habitation*, PH 263.

fyrngestrēon n. *ancient treasure*, SOL 32.

fyrngeweorc† n. *former, ancient work*, PH.

fyrngewinn n. *primeval struggle*, B 1689.

fyrngewrit† n. *old writings, scripture*, EL.

fyrngewyrht n. *former work, fate*, GU 944.

fyrngidd n. *ancient prophecy*, EL 542.

fyrnmann m. *man of old times*, B 2761.

+fyrnnes f. *antiquity*, CHRD 25,26.

fyrnsǣgen f. *old saying, ancient tradition*, AN 1491.

fyrnsceaða m. *old fiend, devil*, AN 1348.

fyrnstrēamas mp. *ocean*, WH 7.

fyrnsynn (JUL 347)=firensynn

fyrnweorc† n. *work of old, creation.*

fyrnwita (eo²)† m. *sage, counsellor.*

fȳr-panne, -ponne f. '*fire-pan*,' *brazier*, WW.

fyrr v. feorr.

fȳrrace (fērrece) f. *fire-rake*, WW 273⁶.

fyrran=feorran

fyrs I. m. '*furze*,' *gorse, bramble*, Bo,WW. II. n.=fers

fȳrscofl f. '*fire-shovel*,' WW 358¹⁶.

fyrsgāra m. *furzy corner*, KC 4·8'.

fyrsian=feorsian

fyrsīg (=īeg) f. *furzy island*, KC 5·300¹⁷.

fyrslēah m. *furzy lea*, KC 5·232'.

fȳrsmeortende v. smeortan; fyrsn=fiersn

fȳrspearca m. *fire-spark*, WW 100².

fyrspenn m. *a pen of furze*, EC 266'.

fyrst I. '*first*,' Chr,Ex : *foremost, principal, chief*, LL. II. adv. *in the first place, firstly, at first, originally*, Ct. III. (Æ)=first I. and II.

+fyrst n. *frost*, LL 454,11.

fyrst-=first-

fȳrstān m. '*firestone*,' *stone used for striking fire, flint*, WW.

fyrstig '*frosty*,' BH 216²⁷. [v. forstig]

fȳrsweart *black with smoke*, CR 984.

fȳrtang f. '*(fire-)tongs*,' LL 453,15. [v. '*fire*']

fȳrtorr m. *beacon, lighthouse*, WW.

fyrð=fyrhð; fȳrð-=fēorð-

fȳrðolle f. *furnace*, EPs 20⁹ : *stage on which martyrs were burned*, OEG.

±fyrðran (GL,AO), fyrðian (Bo; Æ) *to '*further*,' urge on, advance, promote, benefit.*

fyrðriend m. *promoter*, BC.

+fyrðring f. *removal*, CHRD 79¹⁵.

fyrðringnes f., fyrðrung (Lcd; W) f. *furtherance, promotion.* ['*furthering*']

fyrwit (e²) I. n. *curiosity, yearning*, Æ. II. adj. *curious, inquisitive.*

fyrwitful (æ¹, e²) *curious, anxious*, LkL 12²⁶.

fyrwitgeorn *curious, anxious, inquisitive.*

fyrwitgeornes (e², e³, y³) f. *curiosity*, BL 69²² : *fornication?* MFH 146¹¹.

fyrwitgeornlīce (e²) *studiously*, GD 174²⁸.
fyrwitnes f. *curiosity*, Æ.
fȳrwylm m. *wave of fire*, B 2672.
±fȳsan *to send forth, impel, stimulate : drive away, put to flight, banish* : (usu. reflex.) *hasten, prepare oneself*, An,Gen. ['*fuse*']
fȳsian (ē) *to drive away*, LL,W. ['*feeze*']
fȳst (ē) f. '*fist*,' Æ,Gl; CP.
fȳstgebēat n. *blow with the fist*, CP 315.
+fȳstlian *to strike with the fist*, Sc 7¹⁴.
fȳstslægen *struck with the fist*, WW 396³³.
fyðer-=fiðer-, fēower-
fyðera, fyðeras, fyð(e)ru, nap. of fiðere.
fyðerling=fēorðling
fyx=fisc
fyxe f. *she-fox, vixen*, KC 2·29'.
fyxen (i) adj. *of a fox*, Lcd.
fyxenhȳd (i) f. *she-fox's skin*, Lcd 1·342¹¹.

G

gā imperat. and pres. 1 sg. ind. of gān.
gab- (Gl)=gaf-
gabote (u²) f. *side-dish*, EGL. [*L*. gabata]
gād I.† n. *lack, want, need, desire*. [*Goth*. gaidw] II. f. '*goad*,' *point, arrow-head, spear-head*, Cp,Sol.
±gada m. *comrade, companion*, ÆL. [*Ger*. gatte]
+gadere *together*, ÆL 30³⁸⁵.
+gaderednes f. *gathering, abscess*, Lcd.
gaderian (Æ)=gadrian
±gaderscipe (æ) m. *matrimony*, OEG.
gadertang (æ, ea) *continuous, united*, KC.
gadertangnes (æ) f. *continuation*, Sc 52¹.
±gaderung (æ) f. *gathering together* : '*gathering*,' Bf,Lcd : *union, connection*, BH : *assembly*, Jn : *text*, Mtp 8¹⁷.
±gaderwist (o²) f. *companionship*, WW 174⁴⁵.
+gaderwyrhtan np. *assembled workmen*, ÆL 6·186.
gadinca m. *wether sheep*, WW.
gād-īren (LL 455,15), -īsen n. *goad*.
gador=geador; gador-=gader-, gadr-
±gadrian (æ) *to* '*GATHER*,' *unite* : *agree*, (refl.) *assemble*, Chr : *collect, store up*, Æ, CP : *pluck (flowers, etc.)* : *compile* : *associate (with)* : *concentrate (thoughts)*, Bo. [geador]
gadrigendlic *collective*, ÆGR 229⁴.
gǣ=geā; gǣc=gēac
gæd n. *society, fellowship*, SOL 449.
gǣd=gād I.
gǣdeling† m. *kinsman, fellow, companion in arms, comrade*, B,Da. ['*gadling*']
gæder-, gǣdr-=gader-, gadr-

gæf=geaf pret. 3 sg. of giefan.
gæfe=giefu
gæfel (MtL)=gafol
gǣfon=gēafon pret. pl. of giefan.
-gǣgan v. for-, ofer-g.
gægl-=gagol-
gæl-=geal-
gǣlan *to hinder, impede, keep in suspense*, CP : (intr.) *linger, delay* : *dupe*, KGL. [gāl]
gæleð pres. 3 sg. of galan.
gǣling f. *delay*, CP 39¹.
gǣlnes=gālnes
gǣlsa (ē) m., gǣls (OEG 611) f. *pride, wantonness, luxury*, Æ,W : *(worldly) care*, MtL 13²² : *a greedy person*, Lcd. [gāl]
gǣlslic '*luxuriosus*,' NC 291.
gǣlð pres. 3 sg. of galan.
-gǣlwan v. ā-g.
gæmnian=gamenian; gǣn-=gēan-
-gǣnan v. tō-g.; +gænge=+genge
gǣp=gēap; gær-=gear-, grǣ-
gǣr=gēar
gǣred *wedge-shaped*, BC 3·251'. [gār]
-gǣrede v. twi-, ðri-g.
gærs (grǣs) n. '*grass*,' *blade (of grass), herb, young corn, hay, plant*, An,Cp,CP,G; Æ : *pasture*, Ct. v. also grǣs, grǣs-
gærsama=gærsuma
gærsbedd n. *(grass-bed), grave*, PPs 102¹⁵.
gærscīð m. *blade of grass*, AO 38¹¹.
gærsgrēne *grass-green*, WW 199²⁴.
gærs-hoppa m., -hoppe (e¹) f. '*grasshopper*,' *locust*, MtR (grǣs-), Ps,VPs.
gærsstapa=gærstapa
gærsswȳn n. *pasturage-swine*, LL 445,2.
gærstapa m. *grasshopper, locust*, Æ,AO.
gærstūn m. *grass-enclosure, meadow*, LL. ['*garston*']
gærstūndīc m. *meadow-dike*, Ct.
gærsum mn., gærsuma f. *jewel, costly gift, treasure, riches*, Chr. ['*gersum*']
gærswyrt f. '*herba*,' *grass*, APs 36².
gærsyrð f. *pasturage in return for ploughing-labour*, LL 447,4,1c. ['*grassearth*']
gǣsne (ē, ēa) w. g. or on. *deprived of, wanting, destitute, barren, sterile*, An,Cr,Jul : *dead*. ['*geason*']
gǣst=giest
gǣst I. m.=gāst. II. pres. 2 sg. of gān.
gǣstan *to frighten*, Jul 17. ['*gast*']
gǣsð=gāst
gǣt=geat; gǣt nap. of gāt.
gǣtan=gēatan
gǣten *of or belonging to a goat*, Lcd,WW 152¹.
gǣð pres. 3 sg. of gān.
gaf=geaf pret. 3 sg. of giefan.
gafel=gafol

gafeluc m. *spear, javelin, OEG,WW*; ÆL. ['*gavelock*']

gaffetung f. *scoffing, mocking,* Æ.

gafol (æ, ea¹; e, u²) I. n. gs. **gafles** *tribute, tax, duty, due, debt, AO,Gl,MtL : interest, usury, profit, rent, Gl,Mt;* Æ (v. A 36·60, 377 and LF168). ['*gavel*'] II. f. *fork,* Æ, *LL,WW*; OET463 (v. A 36·60). ['*yelve*']

gafolbere m. *barley paid as rent,* TC 145².

gafolfisc m. *fish paid as rent,* TC 307'.

gafolfreo (e²) *tax-free,* KC 4·191,215.

gafolgerēfa (æ¹, e²) m. *taxgatherer,* MtR.

gafolgielda (i³, y³) m. *tributary, tenant, debtor,* AO.

gafolgyld n. '*fiscus,*' *revenue?* GPH 395.

gafolgyldere m. *tributary, debtor,* Æ.

gafolheord f. *taxable swarm (of bees),* LL 448,5.

gafolhwītel m. *tribute-blanket, a legal tender instead of coin for the rent of a hide of land,* LL 108,44¹.

±**gafolian** (e²) *to rent (land), Ct : confiscate, seize as tribute,* WW. ['*gavel*']

gafolland n. *leased land, land let for rent or services,* LL 126,2.

gafollic *fiscal,* OEG 6²⁰.

gafolmæd f. *meadow which was mown as part of the rent,* TC 145³.

gafolmanung (ea¹, o³) f. *place of tribute or custom,* MkR 2¹⁴.

gafolpenig m. *tribute-penny,* LL 446.

gafolræden f. *tribute, rent,* LL.

gafolrand (e²) m. *compasses,* WW.

gafolswān m. *swine-herd who paid rent in kind for permission to depasture his stock,* LL 448,6.

gafoltīning f. *fencing-wood given as part of the rent,* TC 145⁸.

gafolwydu (y³=u) m. *firewood supplied as part of the rent,* TC 145⁶.

gafolyrð f. *ploughing, etc. done by a gebūr as part of his rent,* LL 447; 3·249.

±**gafsprǣc** f. *foolish speech, scurrility,* ÆL.

gaful=gafol

gagātes, gagātstān (WW 148⁵) m. *agate, jet,* BH. ['*gagate*']

gagel m? '*gale,*' *bog-myrtle, Lcd*; Mdf.

gagelcroppan mpl. *tufts of gale,* LCD 33a.

gagelle, gagolle f.=gagel

gagol=(1) gāl; (2) gagel

gagolbærnes (gægl-) f.*wantonness,* CP,WW.

gagolisc (æ, e, ea) *light, wanton,* BH 400¹³, MHc 156¹⁸.

gāl I. n. *lust, luxury, wantonness, folly, levity.* II. adj. *gay, light, wanton, Bo,BH : proud, wicked.* ['*gole*']

±**galan**⁶ *to sing, call, cry, scream, B,Met : sing charms, practise incantation.* ['*gale*']

galder-=galdor-

galdor (ea) n. *sound, song, incantation, spell, enchantment,* Æ.

galdorcrǣft m. *occult art, incantation, magic,* BL,LL.

galdorcrǣftiga m. *wizard,* LL 38,30,VH 14.

galdorcwide m. *incantation,* RD 49⁷.

galdorgalend (e²) m. *enchanter,* WW 448²².

galdorgalere m. *wizard,* WW 346¹⁵.

galdorlēoð n. *incantation,* WW 509¹⁷.

galdorsang m. *incantation,* W 253¹⁰.

galdorword n. *magic word,* RIM 24.

galdre m. *wizard, magician,* Æ.

galdricge f. *enchantress,* GL.

galdru nap. of galdor.

galere m. *wizard, snake-charmer,* WW.

gǣlferhð *wanton, licentious,* JUD 62.

gǣlfrēols m. *revel,* '*lupercalia,*' OEG.

gālful *wanton, lustful, luxurious.* adv. -līce.

galg-=gealg-

gǣlian *to be wanton,* Sc 87¹⁰.

Galilēisc *Galilean,* G.

galla (VPs; DR)=gealla

gallac=galloc

Galleas, Gallias mp. *Gauls, Franks, French.*

galled=gealled

gǣllic *wanton, lustful, BH,Bo;* Æ. ['*golelich*'] adv. -līce, CHRD 108¹⁸.

Gallie=Galleas

Gallisc *Gaulish, French,* AO.

galloc (u²) m. *comfrey, gall-apple,* GL, LCD.

gālmōd *wanton, licentious,* JUD 256.

gālnes f. *frivolity, wantonness, lust, Sc;* Æ. ['*goleness*']

gālscipe m. *excess, luxury, lasciviousness, wantonness,* Æ : *pride.* ['*goleship*']

gālsere m. *licentious person,* W 72⁶.

gālsmǣre *frivolous, facetious, jocose,* RB 30⁸. [v. '*smere*']

galung f. *incantation,* OEG 4940. [galan]

Galwalas mp. *Gauls, Frenchmen : France,* CHR.

gambe=gombe

gamel=gamol; **gamelic**=gamenlic

gamen (o) n. *sport, joy, mirth, pastime,* '*game,*' *amusement, B,Met;* Æ,CP.

gamenian *to pun, play, joke, Æ,Sc.* ['*game*']

gamenlic *belonging to games, theatrical, Gl : ridiculous.* adv. -līce *artfully,* Æ. ['*gamely*']

gamenung f. *jesting, pastime,* BAS,LPs.

gamenwāð (o¹) f. *merry journey,* B 854.

gamenwudu (o¹)† m. *harp,* B.

gamnian=gamenian

gamol† *old, aged, hoary, ancient.* [ge-, mæl]

gamolfeax† *grey-haired.*

gamolferhð *old, aged,* GEN 2867.

gamolian (o¹, e²) *to grow old,* GNE 11.

gān pret. 3 sg. of gīnan.

±gān pret. 3 sg. ēode, anv. *to* 'GO*' ('*i-go*'), *come, move, proceed, advance, traverse, walk, Æ*; CP : *depart, go away* : *happen, turn out, take place* : (+) *get, gain, conquer, occupy, overrun*, AO : (+) *observe, practise, exercise, effect.*

gandra m. '*gander*,' *ÆGr*; Ct.

ganet=ganot

gang I. (eo, o, iong) m. *going, journey, progress, track, footprint*, B,*Lcd,LG,RB*; Æ : *flow, stream, way, passage, course, path, bed, AO,Bl,LG* : *drain, privy, Æ* : (in pl.) *steps, platform, stage*, GPH 394 : *legal process*, LL 396,2. ['*gang,' 'gong,' 'yong'*] II. imperat. and pret. sg. of gangan.

+gang n. *hap, occurrence*, WW 394⁹ : *passage (lapse) of time*, GD 179¹⁰.

±gangan⁷ (*B,Bl*) pret. geng (eo, a)=gān

gangdæg m. *one of the three processional days before Ascension day, Rogation day, Chr.* ['*gangdays*']

gangehere=ganghere

gangelwæfre=gangewifre

gangende *alive*, W : *going on foot*, Æ,AO.

gangern n. *privy*, WW 184¹⁵. [ærn]

gangewifre (eo¹, o¹; æ²; æ³) f. (*a weaver as he goes*), *spider*, LCD,Ps.

ganggeteld n. *portable tent*, WW 187³.

ganghere m. *army of foot-soldiers*, AO 154²⁴.

gang-pytt (*Scr* 21⁷) m., -setl n., -stōl m., -tūn m. (Æ) *privy*. [v. '*gong*']

gangweg m. *thoroughfare, WW*. ['*gangway*']

Gangwuce f. *Rogation week, the week of Holy Thursday, Mk.* ['*gangweek*']

gānian *to yawn, gape, open, Gl,Ps.* ['*gane*']

ganot m. '*gannet,' sea-bird, water-fowl*, B, *Chr.* ganotes bæð *the sea.*

ganra=gandra

gānung f. *yawning*, WW 162³⁷ : *gaping (in scorn)*, WW 476⁹. ['*ganing*']

-gaplan v. ofer-g.

gār† I. m. '*spear,' dart, javelin*, B,*PPs*. ['*gare*'] II. *tempest? piercing cold? sharp pain?* GEN 316. III.=gāra (Mdf).

gāra m. *corner, point of land, cape, promontory, AO*. [gār; '*gore*']

gāræcer m. *a pointed strip of land*, KC 5·153'.

gārbēam m. *spear-shaft*, Ex 246.

gārberend† m. *warrior.*

gārcēne *bold in fight*, B 1958.

gārclife f. *agrimony*, LCD.

gārcwealm m. *death by the spear*, B 2043.

gare=gearo; gāre=gār

gārfaru† f. *warlike expedition.*

gārgetrum *armed company*, CR 673.

gārgewinn† n. *fight with spears, battle.*

gārhēap m. *band of warriors*, Ex 321.

gārholt n. *shafted spear*, B 1835.

gārlēac n. '*garlic*,' *Lcd*; Æ.

gārmitting f. *battle*, †CHR 937.

gārnīð m. *conflict, war*, GNE 128.

gārræs m. *battle*, MA 32.

gārsecg m. *ocean, sea*, AO.

gārtorn m. *fighting rage*, SOL 145.

gār-ōracu f. ds. -ðræce *battle*, EL 1186.

gārōrīst *bold, daring*, EL 204.

garuwe=gearwe

gār-wiga, -wīgend m. *spearman, warrior*, B.

gārwudu m. *spear-shaft, lance*, Ex 325.

gāsrīc m. *savage animal*, OET 127.

gast=giest

gāst (æ) m. *breath, Ps,VPs* : *soul, spirit, life*, *Gen,Ex,Mt*; CP : *good or bad spirit, angel, demon, BH,Mt*; Æ : *Holy Ghost, A,Jn, VPs* : *man, human being, Gu*. ['*ghost*']

gāstan *to meditate?* AS 2²⁰ (or ? geāscian).

gāstberend (æ)† m. *living soul, man.*

gāstbona m. *soul-slayer, the Devil*, B 177.

gāstbrūcende *practising in the spirit, Æ.*

gāstcofa m. *breast*, LEAS 13.

gāstcund (æ) *spiritual*, GU 743.

gāstcwalu (æ) f. *torment, pains of hell*, GU 651.

gāstcyning m. *soul's king, God*, GEN 2883.

gāstedom (æ) *spirituality*, MFH 112⁸.

gāstgedāl† n. *death.*

gāstgehygd† n. *thought.*

gāstgemynd (æ) n. *thought*, GU 574.

gāstgenīðla (æ) m. *devil*, JUL 245.

gāstgerȳne† n. *spiritual mystery* : *thought, consideration.*

gāstgewinn (æ) n. *pains of hell*, GU 561.

gāstgifu f. *special gift of the Holy Spirit* (e.g. *gift of tongues*), WW 200⁸.

gāsthālig† *holy in spirit, holy.*

gāstlēas *lifeless, dead*, El. ['*ghostless*']

gāstlic *spiritual, holy, Æ,Bf*; CP : *clerical (not lay), BH*; Æ,CP : *ghastly, spectral, Nic.* adv. -līce *spiritually, Æ.* ['*ghostly*']

gāstlufu (æ)† f. *spiritual love*, Az.

gāstsunu† m. *spiritual son.* Godes g. *Christ.*

gat=geat

gāt f. gs. gǣte, gāte, nap. gǣt, gēt *she-'goat,' Cr,Ep,Lcd,Rd.*

gātahlerde=gāthyrde

gātahūs n. *goat-house*, WW 185⁸.

gātbucca m. *he-goat, WW.* ['*goat-buck*']

gātehǣr n. *goat's hair*, ÆT 79⁸²,⁸⁷.

gātetrēow n. *cornel tree?* LCD 32b.

gāthyrde (io) m. '*goat-herd,' LL,WW.*

gatu v. geat.

gāð pres. pl. of gān.

ge conj. *and, also, Cr,Lcd.* ge...ge *both... and, B,Chr* : *not only...but also; whether... or.* æg(hwæ)ðer ge...ge *both...and; either ...or.* ['*ye*'] ge- prefix (indicated by the sign + in this Dict.), original meaning *together*; but it has usually lost all collective or intensitive force.

gē I. (īe) pron. 2 pers. pl., dp. ēow, ap. ēow(ic) '*ye*,' *you*, B,G,Mt. II.=gēa

gēa adv. '*yea,*' *yes*, Æ,B,BH,G,WW.

geabul=gafol

gēac m. *cuckoo*, Cp, Gu. [v. '*gowk*,' '*yeke*']

gēacessūre f. *wood-sorrel*, GL.

geador† *unitedly, together*.

geadrung=gaderung

geaduling=gædeling

geaf pret. 3 sg. of giefan.

geaf-=gif-; geafl=gafol

geaflas† *jaws*, WW.

geafol=gafol

gēafon pret. pl. of giefan.

geafu=giefu

gēagl I. mn. *jaws, throat, gullet*, LCD. II.=gāl

geaglisc=gagolisc

gēaglswile m. *swelling of the jaws*, LCD.

geagn-=gegn-; gēahl=gēagl

gēahŏ=gēaŏ

geal pret. 3 sg. of giellan.

gealādl f. *gall-disease, jaundice*, LCD 40b.

gēalāgē (gēa lā gēa, AS) *yea, amen*, RHy.

geald pret. 3 sg. of gieldan.

geald-=gald-

gealg (-lh) *sad*, Æ,WW.

gealga I. (a) m. '*gallows*,' *cross*, B,Jul,WW; CP. II. m. *melancholy*, WW 445,499.

gealgian=geealgian

gealgmōd† *sad, gloomy, angry*.

gealgtrēow (a) n. '*gallows-tree*,' *gallows, cross*, B,DR.

gealh-=gealg; gēalhswile=gēaglswile

gealla (a, e) m. I. '*gall*,' *bile*, Mt,VPs,WW; Æ,CP. II. *a galled place on the skin*, Lcd. ['*gall*'] (I. and II. possibly the same word, v. NED.)

geallādl f. '*melancholia*,' v. OEG 7²²³.

geallede '*galled*' (*of horses*), Lcd.

gealp pret. 3 sg. of gielpan.

gealpettan (a) *to boast, live gluttonously?* NC 291,MFH 144.

gealpettung (æ) f. *boastfulness*, NC 291.

gēamrung (VPs)=gēomrung

gēamung=gēmung

gēan, gēana=gēn, gēna

gēan-, see also gegn-

geanbōc? f. *duplicate charter, counterpart*, Ct.

gēancyme (ē) m. *meeting*, EPs 63³,ARSHy.

gēancyrr m. (-cyrnes? f. RPs 18⁷) *meeting*, SPs 18⁷ : *return*. ['*gainchare*']

gēandele? (ē) *steep*, HGL 416.

gēandȳne *arduous*, LL (134⁶).

gēanfær n. *going again, return*, CHR 1119.

gēangang (ǣ) *return?* LL 8,84.

gēangewrit (ē) '*rescriptio*,' OEG 862.

gēanhweorfan³ *to return*, HGL.

gēanhworfennes f. *return*, HGL 470.

gēanhwurf m. *return*, OEG 559.

gēanhwyrft (ǣ) m. *turning again*, LPs 125¹.

gēannes f. *meeting*, OEG 4610.

gēanoŏ? *complaint*, OEG xiv. [Goth. gaunōŏus]

gēanryne m. *meeting*, ERLPs 58⁶.

geantalu f. *rejoinder, contradiction*, Ct (v. talu, LL 3·226).

gēanŏingian *to reply*, GEN 1009.

geanul '*obvius*,' GPH 399.

gēap I. (ǣ, ē) *open, wide, extensive, broad, spacious, lofty, steep, deep* : *bent, crooked* : *deceitful, cunning*, Æ,Shr : *intelligent, shrewd*, Lcd. ['*yepe*'] II. pret. 3 sg. of gēopan.

gēaplic *deceitful, cunning*, Æ. adv. -līce, Æ, Bf,KGl. ['*yeply*']

gēapneb adj. (*epithet of corslet*) *meshed*, WALD 2¹⁹ (?=*gēapweb *wide-meshed*).

gēapnes f. *astuteness*, WW 192¹.

gēapscipe m. *cleverness, cunning, craft, deceit, trickery, artifice*, Æ. ['*yepship*']

gēapweb v. gēapneb.

gear pret. 3 sg. of georran.

gēar (ē, ǣ) nm. '*YEAR*,' Æ,AO,CP (as to epacts v. Bf 60). tō gēare *in this year* : *yearly tribute* : *name of the rune for* g.

geara=gearwe; geara-=gearo-

gēara *of '*yore*,' formerly, in former times, once, long since*, B,BH,Met,RG,WW ; AO, CP. gēara gēo=gēogēara (gp. of gēar).

gearbōt f. *penance lasting a year*, LL (278¹¹).

±gearcian *to prepare, procure, supply*, Æ (Gen). ['*yark*']

gearcung f. *preparation*, Æ.

±gearcungdæg m. *preparation-day, day before the Sabbath*, G.

gēarcyning m. *consul*, WW 375².

geard I. m. '*yard*,' *fence, enclosure, court, residence, dwelling, land*, B,Gen,Gu; Mdf. in geardum *at home, in the world* : *hedge*, GD,MtR. II.=gierd

gēardagas† mp. *days of yore*, W : *lifetime*.

geardsteall m. *cattle-yard*, KC 3·391⁸ (v. BTs).

geardung f. *habitation*, APs 77⁶⁰.

gēare=gearwe I. and II.

geare-=gear-, gearo-; gēare=gēara

gēarfæc n. *space of a year*, W 72¹.

gearfoŏ=earfoŏ

gēargemearc n. *space of a year*, Gu 1215.

gēargemynd n. *yearly commemoration*, NC 292. ['*year's mind*']

gēargeriht n. *yearly due*, W 113⁹.

gēargerīm (ǣ) n. *numbering by years*, v. ES 39·342.

gēargetæl (æ¹, a³, e³) n. *number of years,* Lcd,LL.

gēarhwamlīce *yearly,* EC226⁶.

gēarlanges *for a year,* Æ.

gēarlēac=gārlēac

gēarlic '*yearly,*' *of the year, annual, Bas,Cp, LL;* Æ. adv. -līce, *WW*; CP.

gearlīce=gearolīce

gēarmǣlum *year by year,* Met 1⁵.

gēarmarcet n. *annual fair,* TC372¹⁵.

gearn (e) n. '*yarn,*' *spun wool, Gl.*

gearnful (NG)=geornful

gearnung=geornung

gearnwinde f. *yarn-winder, reel, Cp,WW;* LL455,15. ['*yarn-wind*']

gearo (gearu) I. (wk gearwa) gsmn. -(o)wes; asm. gearone; napn. gearu *prepared, ready, equipped, finished, An,B,Bl,Bo,Cr;* Chr. ['*yare*'] II. (e¹, a², e²)=gearwe adv. (*B, Cr,G,Met.*).

gēaro=gēara

gearobrygd m. *quick movement, deft playing (of an instrument),* Cra50.

gearofolm *with ready hand,* B2085.

gearolīce *readily, fully, clearly, El.* ['*yarely*']

gearor comp. of gearo adj. and gearwe adv.

gearo-snotor, -snottor† *very skilful.*

gearoðoncol *ready-witted,* Jud342.

gearowes gsmn. of gearo.

gearowita m. *intellect, understanding,* Bo.

gearowitol (rw-) *sagacious,* OEG56¹⁰⁸ : *austere,* LkL19²¹.

gearowitolnes (a²) f. *sagacity,* W53¹⁶.

gearowyrde *fluent of speech, BH.* [v. '*yare*']

gearowyrdig *ready of speech,* Mod51.

gēarrīm n. *number of years,* AO.

gēartorht *perennially bright,* Gen1561.

gēarðēnung f. *annual service,* LL382,38.

gearu=gearo

gearugangende *going swiftly,* Rd41¹⁷.

gēarwǣstm *yearly fruit,* EC168'.

gearwan=gierwan

gearwanlēaf=geormanlēaf

gearwe I. (gearo) adv. comp. gear(w)or; sup. gear(w)ost *well, effectually, sufficiently, thoroughly, entirely,* Æ,AO,CP : *quickly : near.* ['*yare*'] II.† f. (usu. pl.) *clothing, equipment, ornament, trappings, harness, armour.* III. (a, æ) f. '*yarrow,*' *Cp,Lcd,WW.*

±gearwian (æ, e, i, ie, y) *to equip, prepare, facilitate, do, make ready, Bo,G;* Æ,CP : *construct, erect, make : procure, supply : clothe, adorn : grant,* DR18¹¹. ['*yare*']

±gearwung f. *preparation : working : parasceve.*

gearwungdæg (eo¹) m. *parasceve,* JnR.

+gearwungnes f. *preparation,* LPs (but v. BTs).

gēasceaft v. gēosceaft.

gēasne (*Jul*)=gǣsne

geaspis *jasper,* ZDA34·239.

geat n. (æ, e) nap. gatu (geatu VPs) '*gate,*' *door, opening, Æ,BH,Bl,Ct,G,Ps;* AO,CP; Mdf.

gēat pret. 3 sg. of gēotan.

gēatan (æ, ē, ēo) *to say* '*yea,*' *consent, grant confirm, Chr.* ['*yate*']

geatolic† *adorned, magnificent, stately.*

geatwa=geatwe

geatwan *to equip,* Rd29⁶.

geatwe fp. *arms, equipments, trappings, ornaments,* Bl,Chr. [=getāwa]

geatweard m. *gate-keeper, door-keeper, porter, Jn.* ['*gateward*']

gēað† f. *foolishness, mockery.* [gēac]

gebellic (OET,Cp881)=gafollic

gēc (OET)=gēoc; gecel, gecile (Gl)=gicel

gecs-=geocs-

ged=gæd, gidd; gedd=gidd

gederian=(1) gaderian; (2) derian

gee=gēa

gef=(1) geaf pret. 3 sg. of giefan; (2) (N) gif

gef-=gief-

gēgan *to cry out,* BHt88, WW355¹³ (v. JAW17).

geglisc=gagolisc

gegn=gēn; gegn- see also gēan-.

gegncwide† m. *reply, answer, retort :* (in pl.) *conversation.*

+gegnian *to meet,* DR45¹¹. ['*yain*']

gegninga=gegnunga

gegnpǣð m. *opposing path,* Rd16²⁶.

gegnslege m. *battle,* An1358.

gegnum† adv. *away, forwards, straight on, thither.*

gegnunga adv. *immediately, directly : certainly, plainly, precisely : completely, fully.*

gegoð=geoguð; geher (NG)=ēar

Gehhol=Geohol, Gēol

gehðu† (eo, i) f. *care, anxiety, grief.*

-gelan v. tō-g.

geld=gield; geld-=gild-, gyld-

-geldan v. ā-g.

gelde *sterile,* WW226²²; 394²⁶. ['*yeld*']

gell-=geall-, giell-

gellet n? *bowl,* Lcd122a.

gelm=gilm; gelo=geolu

gelostr=geolster; gelp=gielp

gēlsa=gǣlsa; gelt (KGl)=gylt

gēm-=gīem-; gēmer-=gēomr-

gemstān (ES7·134)=gimmstān

gēmung (ēa, ī, ȳ;=īe) f. *marriage,* MtR,DR.

gēmunglan *to marry,* DR109¹⁷.

gēmunglic *nuptial,* MtR,DR.

gēn I. (īe) (A, rare in prose) adv. *yet, now, still, again : further, besides, also, moreover : hitherto.* II. adj. *direct,* AA8¹⁰. III.=gēgan, gōian

gēn-=gēan-, gegn-; gēna=gēn I.
gend=geond
gende=gengde pret. 3 sg. of gengan.
gēnde=v. gēn III.
geng I.=geong. II.=gang. III. pret. 3 sg.
of gangan.
+genga m. *fellow-traveller, companion*, W.
gengan, pret. gengde *to go*, Æ. [gong]
±genge I. *prevailing, effectual, appropriate*,
BH,Gu : *seasonable* : *agreeable*. ['genge']
II. n. *troop*, Chr; FBO,W. ['ging'] III. f.
privy, Æ,WW. ['gong']
-gengel v. æfter-, for(e)-g.
genigend=giniend pres. ptc. of ginian.
gēnlād *estuary*, KC 1·238⁶.
gēno, gēnu=gēn
gēo (īu) adv. *once, formerly, of old, before,
already, earlier,*. CP (gīo).
geoc (iu) n. *'yoke,'* Bo,CP,Gl,Mt; Æ, AO :
yoke of oxen, etc., LL,WW : *a measure of
land*, Ct,WW : *consort*, NG.
gēoc† (ēoc) f. *help, support, rescue* : *safety* :
consolation.
geocboga (iuc-) m. *yoke-bow, yoke*, WW.
gēocend† m. *preserver, Saviour*.
±gēocian (iuc-) *to 'yoke,' join together*, Æ,
WW.
gēocian (w. g. or d.) *to preserve, rescue, save*,
Æ.
geocled n. geocleta (ioc-) m. *a measure of
land*, Ct, OET (v. LL 2·527). ['yoklet']
gēocor† *harsh, terrible* : *bitter, sad.* adv.
gēocre Da 211.
geocsa (i) m. *sob*, Met : *hiccough*, G,Lcd.
[=gesca; 'yex']
geocsian (i) *to sob*, Bo. ['yex']
geocstecca m. *yoke-stick* (BTs), WW 35,459.
[sticca]
geocsung f. *sobbing*, WW 179,423. ['yex-
ing']
geoctēma (ioc-) m. *animal yoked with another*, WW 106³⁶.
geocðōa=gicða
gēodǣd (iū-)† f. *deed of old, former deed*.
gēodæg (īu) m. *day of old*, Bf,Bo.
geof=gif; geof-=gief-, gif-
geofen=geofon
geofola m. *morsel, bit of food*, WW. [=giefla]
geofon (i, y)† n. *ocean, sea, flood*.
geofonflōd m. *ocean flood*, Az 125.
geofonhūs n. *ship*, Gen 1321.
geogað=geoguð
gēo-gēara, -gēare adv. *of old*, BH.
gēog(e)lere m. *magician*, W 98⁹; HGL. [Ger.
gaukler]
geoguð (o²) f. *'youth,'* Bl,Cp,G; Æ, AO :
young people, B,CP : *junior warriors* (as
opposed to duguð) : *young of cattle*.

geoguðcnōsl n. *young offspring*, Rd 16¹⁰.
geoguðfeorh† n. *time of youth*.
geoguð-hād (Bl,Sc) m., -hādnes f. *state of
youth* : *adolescence*. ['youthhood']
geoguðlic *youthful*, BH. ['youthly']
geoguðlust m. *youthful lust*, Bl 59⁹.
geoguðmyrð f. *joy of youth* (GK), *tenderness
of youth?* (BTs),Rd 39².
Geohol, Geohhol=Gēol; Geoh(h)el-=Gēol-
geohsa=geocsa
geoht (iuht) n. *yoke, pair*, v. OEG 7¹³⁵.
gāohwīlum *of old*, Bo 8⁷.
geohðu=gehðu
Gēol n., Gēola m. *'Yule'-tide, Christmas*,
BH,KC,LL,MH. ǣrra Gēola *December*.
æftera Gēola *January*.
geolca=geoloca; geold=gield
Gēoldæg (Geoh(h)el-) m. *Yule-day, day at
Yuletide*, Ma.
geole=geolwe
gēolēan (iū-) n. *reward for past deed*, Wal 2⁷.
geoleca=geoloca; geolerēad=geolurēad
geolhstor=geolster
Gēolmōnað (Iūl-) m. *December*, Men (Chr
p 280).
geolo=geolu
geoloca, geol(e)ca m. *'yolk,'* Æ,Lcd,Met.
[geolu]
geolorand† m. *buckler covered with yellow
linden-bark*.
geol-ster, -stor mn. *matter, pus, poison,
poisonous humour, disease*, OEG.
geolstrig *secreting poison, purulent*, OEG.
geolu gmn. geolwes *'yellow,'* B,Gl,Lcd.
geolwe ādl *jaundice*.
geoluhwīt *pale yellow*, WW. [v. 'yellow']
geolurēad *reddish yellow*, WW 375¹⁸. [v.
'yellow']
geolwe *yellowish*, Lcd.
±geolwian *to become yellow*, OEG, Sc. [v.
'yellowed']
gēomann (īu)† m. *man of past times*.
gēomēowle (io)† f. *aged wife?* B.
gēomer-=gēomor-, gēomr-
gēomor (īo¹, u²) *troubled, sad, miserable*, B,
Hu. ['yomer'] adv. -more.
gēomorfrōd *very old*, Gen 2224.
gēomorgidd† n. *dirge, elegy*.
gēomorlic *sad, painful, miserable*, B; AO.
adv. -līce, Sol. ['yomerly']
gēomormōd *sorrowful*, Æ.
gēomornes f. *tribulation*, LPs 118¹⁴³.
gēomorung=gēomrung
gēomrian *to be sad, complain, lament,
bewail, mourn*, B,Bl,DHy; Æ,AO,CP.
['yomer']
gēomrung (e, ea) f. *groaning, moaning,
grief*, Æ.
geon adj. pron. *'yon,'* CP.

geon-=geond-; **gēona** (NG)=gēna, gēn
geonað pres. 3 sg. of geonian.
geond (e, i, ie, y) **I.** prep. (w. a. and, rarely,
d.) *throughout, through, over, Bo,G : up to,
as far as, during.* geond...innan *throughout.* ['*yond*'] **II.** adv. *yonder, thither, BH,
RG.*
geondan prep. (w. a.) *beyond,* CHR 1052.
geondblāwan[7] (i[1]) *to inspire, illuminate,* GL.
geondbrǣdan *to cover entirely,* B 1239 : *enlarge, extend,* VH 14.
geonddrencan (i) *to drink excessively, get
drunk,* CHRD,KGL 58[40].
geondeardian *to inhabit,* RPs 32[8].
geondfaran[7] *to traverse, pervade,* BF,GD.
geondfēolan[3] (only in pp. geondfolen) *to fill
completely,* GEN 43.
geondfēran *to traverse : surpass,* ÆL 23b[333].
geondflōwan[7] *to flow over or through,* HELL
105.
geondflōwende *ebbing and flowing,* OEG
2363.
geondfolen v. geondfēolan.
geondgangan[7] *to traverse, go round,* RB,
VPs.
geondgēotan[2] (tr. and intr.) *to pour, pour
upon, suffuse, spread, soak,* Æ.
geondhweorfan[3]† *to pass over, pass through.*
geondhyrdan *to harden thoroughly,* SOL 150[28].
geondlācan[7] *to traverse, flow over,* PH 70.
geondleccan *to water, irrigate,* LPs 103[13],
CHRD 108.
geond-leccung (gynd-) f. *moistening, watering,* Sc 27[7].
geondlīhtan (ȳ[2]) *to illuminate, enlighten,* CP.
geondlīhtend (ēo) m. *illuminator,* DHy 128[5].
geondmengan *to confuse, bewilder,* SOL 59.
geondrēcan *to fill with smoke,* LCD 124a.
geondsāwan[7] *to strew, scatter,* DA 278.
geondscēawian *to look upon,* GUTH,WA :
consider, have regard to, LPs 118[6].
geondscīnan[1] *to shine upon, illuminate,* CP.
geondscrīðan[1] *to pass through, traverse,
stride to and fro,* BF,W 250[3] : *ramble (of
the mind),* MFH 147.
geondscrīðing f. *course, passage,* OEG 263.
geond-sēcan pret. 3 sg. -sōhte *to search
thoroughly,* CP : *pervade.*
geondsēon[5] *to examine,* B 3087.
geondsmēagan *to investigate, discuss,* BH,
GL.
geondspǣtan *to squirt through,* LCD 78a.
geondsprengan *to besprinkle,* GUTH,RBL.
geondspringan[3] *to penetrate, be diffused,*
OEG 2840.
geondsprūtan[2] *to pervade,* CR 42.
gēond-strēdan, -stregdan *to scatter, suffuse,
besprinkle,* Æ.

geondstrēdnes f. *dispersion,* APs 146[2].
geondstyrian *to stir up, agitate,* MET 6[15].
geondðencan† *to reflect upon, consider.*
geondwadan[6] (i[1]) *to know thoroughly, be
versed in,* CP 9[10].
geondwlītan[1]† *to look over, contemplate,
examine, scan.*
geondyrnan[3] (=ie[2]) *to run over,* ÆGR 277[3].
geong I. (e, i, u) '*young,' youthful,* Æ,AO,
CP : *recent, new, fresh :* comp.· gingra
'*younger,'* LL,Ps : superl. gingest '*young-
est,'* AO : *last,* B,CP. **II.** (LG)=gang.
['*yong*'] **III.**=geng pret. 3 sg. of gangan.
gēong=gōung
geonga (iu-) m. *young man,* Lk,WW.
geongan (LG)=gangan. ['*yong*']
geongerdōm=geongordōm
geongewifre=gangewifre
geonglǣcan (gyng-, iung-) *to pass one's
youth, grow up,* HGL 508; OEG 4361.
geonglic *young, youthful,* Æ. ['*youngly*']
geonglicnes f. *youth,* Sc 124[3].
geongling (iu-) m. *a youth,* GD ; ÆGR 3[1].
['*youngling*']
geongordōm, geongorscipe m. *discipleship,
allegiance,* GEN. [OS. jungardōm; jun-
garskepi]
geongra (i) m. *youth : disciple, follower,
dependant, servant, vassal,* BH,Gen ; AO,
CP : *assistant, deputy,* Æ. ['*younger*']
geongre (i) f. *female attendant, assistant,*
JUD 132 : *deputy,* BH 340[17].
geonian=ginian
geonlic (MFH 103[20])=geonglic
geonofer adv. *thither.*
geonsīð m. *departure hence, death,* MFH 163.
geonung=ginung
gēopan[2] *to take in,* RD 24[9].
geormanlēaf n. *mallow,* LCD.
geormenletic *mallow,* WW 135[27]. [?=-lēaf]
georn I. (usu. w. g.) *desirous, eager, earnest,
diligent, studious,* AO,Bl,Gu; CP. ['*yern*']
II.=gearn pret. 3 sg. of +iernan.
geornan (M)=giernan
georne adv. *eagerly, zealously, earnestly,
gladly,* B,Bo,Chr ; Æ,AO,CP : *well, carefully, completely, exactly,* Æ : *quickly,* W.
['*yerne*']
geornes=geornnes
georneste (WW 499[1])=eornoste
georn-ful, -fullic *desirous, eager, zealous,
diligent,* Bo,G; AO,CP. ['*yearnfull*'] adv.
-līce, Æ.
geornfulnes f. *eagerness, zeal, diligence,* Bo,
RB; Æ,AO,CP : *desire.* ['*yearnfulness*']
geornian=giernan
geornlic adj. *desirable,* AO. adv. -līce
zealously, earnestly, diligently, carefully,
Cp BH,G ; Æ,CP. ['*yernly*']

geornnes (i, ie, y) *desire, endeavour* : *zeal, industry* : *importunity*, NG.

geornung (i, ie, y) f. *'yearning,' desire*, CP, Sc : *diligence*.

geornust-=eornost-

georowyrde (BH)=gearowyrdig

georran=gyrran; **georst**=gorst

georst-=gierst-

georstu interj. *O!* VPs. [hīeran]

gēosceaft m. *destiny, fate*, B1234.

gēosceaftgāst m. *doomed spirit*, B1266.

geostra, geostran (ie, ei, y) *'yester'(-day, -night)*, Æ,B,G,Ps.

gēot=gīet.

gēotan I. (sv²) *to pour, pour forth, shed*, Æ, BH,CP,Cr,Lcd; AO,CP : *gush, flow, flood, overwhelm*, El,Gu : (±) *found, cast*, Æ,Ps. ['*yet*'] **II.**=gēatan

gēotend m. *artery*, WW352²⁵.

geotendǣder f. *artery*, Lcd.

gēotenlic *molten, fluid*, GPH394.

gēotere m. *founder (of metal)*, AO54. ['*yeter*']

-gēoting v. in-, on-g.

gēotton pret. pl. of gēotan II.

geoðu=geohðu=gehðu; **gēow**=gīw

gēower (GPH395)=ēower

gēowian=+ēowan=+īewan

gēowine (īu) m. *departed friend*, Seaf92.

geox-=geocs-; **gēp**=gēap

ger-=gær-, gearw-, gier-; **gēr**=gēar

gerd(A)=gierd; **gerd-**=gyrd-

gerew-, gerw-=gearw-, gierw-

gernwinde=gearnwinde

gērscipe m. *jest?* Rim11.

gēs v. gōs.

gesca, gescea (eo, i) m. *hiccough, sobbing*, Gl,Lcd.

gēse (ī, ȳ) adv. *'yes,'* Æ,Bo,CP,G.

gesen *entrails, intestines*, WW231³⁹.

gēsine, gēsne=gǣsne

gest, gēst=giest, gāst; **gest-**=giest-

gēstende (OEG2499)=ȳstende; **get-**=geat

gēt I.=gǣt, nap. of gāt. **II.**=gēat pret. 3 sg. of gēotan. **III.** (VPs), gēta=gīet(a)

gētan I. *to destroy, kill*, B2940 (? for gītan or grētan). **II.**=gēatan

gētenwyrde *consenting, agreeing*, Ct (Swt). [gēatan]

gi- (NG, etc.)=ge-; **gib**=gif

giccan *to 'itch,'* Lcd.

gicce (y) *'itch,'* Ln33³.

giccig *purulent, itchy*, HGl453.

gicel(a) (y) m. *icicle, ice*, DD,WW. ['*ickle*']

gicelgebland n. *frost*, RHy7⁷⁰.

gicelig *glacial, icy*, OEG.

gicelstān (y¹) m. *hailstone*, Bl261,LRPs 147¹⁷.

gicenes (y) f. *itching, itch*, Gl.

gicer (y) n. *acre*, OET114⁹².

gicða (ie, io, y) m. *scab, itch, itching*, Æ,CP : *hiccough?* Lcd (v. BTs). ['*yekth*']

gid-=gyd-; **gīd-**=gīt-; **gidd-**=giedd-

gīe=gē; **giecða** (CP)=gicða?

giedd (e, i, y) n. *song, poem*, B : *saying, proverb, riddle* : *speech, story, tale, narrative* : *account, reckoning, reason*, VH14. ['*yed*']

±gieddian (i, y) *to speak formally, discuss* : *speak with alliteration, recite, sing*, Bo; AO. ['*yed*']

gieddung (e, i, y) f. *utterance, saying, prophecy, song, poetry, poetical recitation, metre*, LG; Æ. ['*yedding*']

gief (rare EWS)=gif; **gief-**=gif-, geof-

giefa (eo, i, y) m. *donor*, CP.

giefan⁵ (e, ea, eo, i, ia, io, y) w. d. and a. *to 'give*',' *bestow, allot, grant*, Æ; AO,CP : *commit, devote, entrust*, Da : *give in marriage*, Chr.

giefend (e) m. *giver*, DR.

giefernes (CP)=gīfernes

giefl (i, y)† n. *morsel, food* (v. also geofola).

giefnes (e) f. *grace, pardon*, DR,†Hy.

giefu (e, eo, i, y) f. *giving, gift*, B,Bo,Mt; AO,CP. tō giefe, giefes *gratis, freely* : *favour, grace*, Bl,Lk : *liberality* : *sacrifice* : *name of the rune for* g. ['*give*']

gield (eo, i) n. *service, offering, worship, sacrifice*, Jul : *money-payment, tax, tribute, compensation, substitute*, LG,LL : (±) *guild, brotherhood*, Ct : *idol, god*. ['*yield*']

gield- v. also gild-.

±gieldan³ (e, i, y) *to 'yield*',' *pay*, AO,LG : CP : *pay for*, Æ,LL : *reward, requite, render*, B,Bl,CP,Gen,Ps : *worship, serve, sacrifice to*, CP : *punish*.

-gieldere (y) v. gafol-g.

gieldra=ieldra comp. of eald.

-giella (e, i) v. stān-g.

giellan³ (e, i, y) *to 'yell,' sound, shout*, An, Fin,Rd.

giellende *'yelling,'* Ex,Lcd,Wid.

gielp (e, i, y) mn. *boasting, pride, arrogance* : *fame, glory*, Æ,B,BH,Bo; AO,CP. ['*yelp*']

gielpan³ (i, y) *to boast, exult*, B,Bo,Da,W; AO,CP : *praise*, CP. ['*yelp*']

gielpcwide† m. *boastful speech*.

gielpen (i) *boastful*, Sol207.

gielpgeorn (i, y) *eager for glory*, BH92⁴ : *arrogant*, W.

gielpgeornes (i) f. *desire for glory, pride, arrogance*, W.

gielphlǣden (i) *boastful*, B868.

gielping (y) f. *glory, boasting*, Sc144¹¹. ['*yelping*']

gielplic (i) *vainglorious, boastful* : *ostentatious, showy*. adv. -līce.

gielpna (i) m. *boaster*, CP.
gielpnes (e) f. *boastfulness*, LPs.
gielpplega (y) m. *war*, Ex 240.
gielpsceaða† (e¹, a²) m. *boastful enemy*.
gielpspræc f. *boastful speech*, B 981.
gielpword (y) n. *boast*, AO.
gielt=gylt; **giem**=gimm
gīeman (ē, ī, ȳ) (w. g. or a.) *to care for, heal,*
CP : correct, reprove : take notice of, take
heed to, regard, observe, Æ,Bl,Bo,Cr; AO,
CP : take charge of, control, Æ(Gen).
['*yeme*']
gīeme f. *care, AO,CP.* ['*yeme*']
gīemelēas (ē, ȳ) *careless, negligent, CP :*
neglected, uncared for, stray : incurable,
MtLp 20¹¹. ['*yemeles*']
gīemelēasian *to neglect, despise*, BH 362¹³.
gīemelēaslic *careless*, CP. adv. -līce, Lcd.
['*yemeslicbe*']
gīemelēasnes (ē, ȳ) f. *negligence*, BH 242²⁸.
gīeme-lēast, -līest f. *carelessness, neglect,*
CP : presumption, RB 77⁵. ['*yemelest*']
gīemen (ē, ī, ȳ) f. *care, oversight, heed,*
diligence, rule, AO,CP.
gīemend (ȳ) m. *governor*, Sc 117⁷ : *keeper :*
observer.
gīem(e)nes (ē) f. *care, anxiety*, DR,NG.
gīeming f. *care, anxiety*, CP : *custody : rule.*
gīen, gīena=gēn, gēna; **giend**=geond
gieng=geong
gierd (ea, i, y) f. '*yard,*' *rod, staff, twig, Æ,*
G,Lcd ; CP : *measure of length*, LL : g.
landes *an area of land about one-fourth of*
a hide, EC,KC,LL.
gierdweg (y) m. *road fenced on either side?*
road made with faggots? (BTs),KC.
gierdwīte (y) n. *affliction caused by*
(*Moses'*) *rod*, Ex 15.
gierede pret. 3 sg. of gierwan.
±**gierela** (e, i, y) m. *dress, apparel, adorn-*
ment, AO,CP : *banner*, WW 435¹⁵. [gear-
wian]
±**gier(e)lian** (e) *to clothe*, G,Ps.
+**gierelic** (e) adj. *of clothes*, WW 503¹⁸.
gierian=gearwian
+**giering** f. *direction*, RPs 138³.
gierman (y) *to cry, mourn, LPs* 37⁹. ['*yarm*']
±**giernan** (eo, y) (w. g.) *to* '*YEARN*' *for,*
strive, be eager, desire, entreat, seek for, beg,
demand, AO,CP. [georn]
giernendlic (y) *desirable*, Sc 111¹³, (+) EPs
18¹¹.
giernes=geornnes
gierning (CP)=geornung; **gierran**=gyrran
gierst-=giestr-
±**gierwan** (e, ea, y) *to prepare*, AO : *cook,*
CP : *deck, dress, clothe, adorn : direct*, CP.
giest (æ, e, i, y) m. '*guest*,' *B,Gen,RB :*
stranger, MtL,Rd.

giestærn (e, y) n. *guest-chamber* : *inn* :
shelter.
giesterdæg (e, io) '*yesterday,*' *JnRL* 4⁵².
giesternlic (eo, y) *of yesterday.*
giesthof (æ) n. *guest-house*, CR 821.
giesthūs (a, æ, e, y) n. '*guest-house,*' *ApT,*
Mk ; CP.
giestian (y) *to lodge, be a guest*, Sc 153'.
giestig (e) adj. *being a stranger*, MtL 25³⁸.
giesting (e) f. *exile*, GL.
giestlic (a¹) *hospitable*, GEN 209.
giestlīðe (i¹) *hospitable*, MH 168²⁴,WW 97¹⁵.
giestlīðian (æ¹) *to be hospitable*, NAR 38¹⁸n.
giestlīðnes (æ, e, i, y) f. *hospitality,*
shelter, BH.
giestmægen (i) n. *band of guests*, GEN 2494.
giestning (e) f. *hospitality, lodging*, NC 296.
giestran (e¹,o²)adv.*yesterday,Rd.* ['*yestern*']
giestranǣfen m. *yesterday evening, DD.*
adv. -ǣfene, Æ,GD. ['*yesterneve*']
giestrandæg (eo, y) m. '*yesterday,*' *Æ,G,*
PPs.
giestranniht (y) f. '*yesternight,*' *B* 1334.
giestsele (e, y) †m. *guest-hall.*
gīet I. (ē, ī, ȳ) adv. '*YET*' : *still : besides :*
hitherto : hereafter : even : even now. ðā g.
yet, still, further, also. nū g. *until now :*
hitherto, formerly : *any longer* II. pres.
3 sg. of gēotan.
gīeta=gīet
gietan (i) *to get*, RBL 56¹⁵.
gīetsere, gīetsian=gītsere, gītsian
gif I. (e, ie, y) conj. (w. ind. or subj.) '*IF,*'
Chr; CP : *whether, though, B.* II. n. *gift,*
grace, AN 575,BH 34¹⁷.
gifa, gifan=giefa, giefan
gifect (GL)=gefeoht; **gifel**=giefl
gifen I. pp. of giefan. II.=geofon
gifer m. *glutton*, SOUL 118.
±**gifere**=gīfre
gīferlīce *greedily*, BH,OEG. ['*yeverly*']
gīfernes f. *greediness, gluttony, avarice, Bo,*
Bl; Æ,CP. ['*yeverness*']
gifeðe I. *granted by fate, given.* II. n. *fate,*
lot, B 3085.
gifǣst *endowed, talented* : (w. g.) *capable of.*
gifheall f. *hall in which gifts were made*, B 838.
gifian (ea, eo) *to present, endow : glorify*, DR
78¹⁴ : (+) '*prestolari,*' DR 20⁸.
gifig *rich*, A 11·171.
gifl=giefl
gifnes† f. *grace, favour.*
gifol (e) *liberal, generous, bountiful*, CP :
gracious, WW 66¹.
gifola m. *giver*, AS 2⁸.
gīfre *useful*, RD 27²⁸ ; 50³.
gīfre *greedy, rapacious, ravenous, B,Bo;*
CP : *desirous of.* ['*yever*']

gifsceatt m. *present*, B378.

gifstōl† m. *gift-seat, throne*.

gift (y) nf. '*gift,' portion, marriage gift (by the bridegroom), dowry* : (pl.) *nuptials, marriage, Æ.* [giefan]

giftbūr m. *bride-chamber*, Bf6²⁰,EPs18⁵.

giftelic=giftlic

giftfeorm f. *marriage-feast*, NC297.

gifthūs (y) n. *house at which a wedding is being celebrated*, Mt22¹⁰.

giftian (y) *to give in marriage (of the woman)*, G.

giftlēoð n. *epithalamium*, WW165³³.

giftlic *nuptial, belonging to a wedding, Æ.*

gifu (Æ)=giefu; **giful**=gifol

gifung (y) f. *consent*, BH86²⁵.

gīg (Cp142G)=gīw

gīgant m. *giant*, B,Bl. [*L.* gigantem]

gīgantmæcg m. *son of a giant*, Gen1268.

gigoð=geoguð; **gihsa**=geocsa

gihða=gicða; **gihðu**=gehðu

gild=gield; **gild-**=gyld-

±**gilda** m. *member of a brotherhood of related persons*, v. LL2·378; 445.

gildan=(1) gieldan; (2) gyldan

gilddagas mp. *guild-days, festival-days*, WW107²².

gilde v. twi-g.

+**gilde** n. *membership of a guild*, TC.

+**gildheall** (y) f. *guild-hall*, KC4·277'

gildlic adj. *of a guild, festival*, A41·106.

+**gildrǣden** (y) f. *guild-membership*, Ct.

±**gildscipe** m. *guild, brotherhood*, Ct,LL. ['*guildship*']

gildsester (y) m. *measure of bulk belonging to a corporate body*, TC606,611.

gillan=giellan

gillister n. gillistre f. *phlegm, pus, matter*, Lcd. [=geolster]

gilm, gilma (e) m. *handful*, Lcd,OEG : *sheaf, Æ.* ['*yelm*']

gilp I. *dust, powder*, WW521¹⁸. II.=gielp

gilt=gylt

gilte (y) f. *young sow*, WW119²⁵. ['*yelt*']

gim=gimm; **gīm-**=gīem-

gimbǣre *gem-bearing, set with gems*, OEG.

gimcynn n. *precious stone, gem*, AA,Bo.

gimfæst (B1272)=ginfæst

gimm (y) m. (occl. nap. gimme) *precious stone, 'gem,' jewel, Æ,Bl,VPs*; CP : (†) *sun, star.* [*L.* gemma]

±**gimmian** *to adorn with gems*, ÆGr.

gimmisc *jewelled*, AA7⁶.

gimreced n. *bejewelled hall, palace*, Met8²⁵.

gimrodor? m. *draconite (precious stone)*, OEG (v. BTac).

gimstān m. *stone capable of being made into a gem, jewel, Æ*; AO. ['*gemstone*']

gīmung=gēmung

gimwyrhta (y) m. *jeweller*, ÆH1·64⁹.

gin I. n. *yawning deep*, Ex430. II. adj.= ginn

gīn, gīna=gēn, gēna

gīnan I. *to yawn*. II. *to drive back*, ÆL25⁶³⁶.

gind=geond

ginfæst† *ample, liberal.* [ginn]

ginfæsten n. *great fastness, stronghold?* Ex 524.

ging, gingest v. geong.

gingi-ber, -fer(e) f. '*ginger*,' Lcd.

gingra I. (Æ) v. geong. II.=geongra

gingre=geongre

ginian (eo, y) *to 'yawn,' gape, AO,CP,GD, Gl,Lcd,Ps* : *utter a sound*, WW. [gīnan]

giniend (e, eo, y) '*yawning,' AO,BH,GD.*

ginn† *spacious, wide, ample.*

ginnan=onginnan

ginnes f. *gap, interval*, Cp373i.

ginnfæst=ginfæst

ginnwīsed (y) *very wise*, Gu839? (or? ginn- wīse *of noble manners*, BTs).

ginung (e, eo, y) f. *opening of the mouth, howling, biting*, Gl. ['*yawning*']

gīo=gēo; **giofol**=gifol

giohðhād=geoguðhād; **gīow**=gīw

gīowian (RG)=giwian

gīp-=gyp-

gīr-=gearw-, geor-, gier-, gyr-

gird=gierd; **giren** (VPs)=grīn

girsandæg (VH15)=gierstandæg

girstbītung=gristbītung

girwan=gearwian

+**gīscan** *to close, bolt, bar*, Gl.

giscian *to sob*, Bo8⁸. [=geocsian]

gīse=gēse

gīsl, gīsel m. *hostage, AO.* ['*yisel*']

gīsldu (-ðu) f. *the giving of hostages*, WW 459⁷.

gīslhād m. *state of being a hostage*, Cp99o.

gīslian *to give hostages*, Chr.

gist I. m. '*yeast,' froth*, Lcd. II.=giest

gist-=giest-; **gīst**=ȳst

gistran—geostran; **gīstung**=gītsung

git *dual of pron.* 2 pers. (ðu); g. incer; d. inc; a. inc(it) *you two, B,Bl,G.* git Johannis *thou and John.* ['*yit*']

gīt, gīta=gīet, gīeta; **gitrife**=giðrife

gītsere m. *miser, Æ,CP.*

gītsian (ȳ) *to be greedy, long for, covet, B,Bo, CP,G; Æ* : (+) *obtain with greed*, CP364²². ['*yisse*']

gītsiendlic *insatiable*, RPs100⁵.

gītsiendnes f. *avarice*, W188n.

gītsung (ȳ) f. *avarice, greediness, covetous- ness, desire*, CP.

giðcorn n. *a plant, spurge-laurel?* Lcd,WW.

giðrife (y) f. *cockle*, Lcd,WW.

giðu=gehðu

gīu (Æ)=gēo; **giu-**=geo-
Giūli (Bf 24)=Iūla, Gēola
Giuling, Giūluling *July*, Cp 70 ǫ (A 20·137).
gīw (ēo) m. *griffin, vulture*, WW 258⁷.
±giwian (ī? v. A 16·98) *to ask*, NG.
giwung f. *petition*, DR,NG.
glæd pret. 3 sg. of glīdan.
glad- v. glæd.
gladian (ea) (†) *to gleam, glisten* : (±) intr.
 be glad, rejoice, JnL,Lcd : (±) tr. *gladden,
 rejoice, gratify, appease*, Æ,VPs. ['glad']
gladine=glædene
gladung f. *rejoicing*, RB : *gladdening*, W :
 appeasing, LPs. ['gladding']
glæd I. (glad- in obl. cases) (†) *bright,
 shining, brilliant, gleaming*, Gen,Ph,Sol :
 cheerful, '*glad*,' *joyous*, B,CP,Chr,Cr,G,
 Ps; Æ : *pleasant, kind, gracious*, Æ,B. **II.**
 n. *joy, gladness*, Wy 68. ['glad']
glædene (a, e) f. *iris, gladiolus*, Gl; Lcd.
 ['gladdon']
glædestede=glēdstede ·
glædine (Gl)=glædene
glædlic *bright, shining*, Wid : *kindly,
 pleasant, agreeable*, Ps. adv. -lice '*gladly*,'
 joyfully, kindly, willingly, BH,Chr.
glædman '*hilaris*,' WW 171⁴⁰ : *kind, gracious*, B 367.
glædmōd *cheerful, joyous* : *kind, gracious*.
glædmōdnes f. *kindness, bounty*, CP 391⁶.
glædnes (e¹) f. '*gladness*,' *joy*, BH ; Æ,DR
 (+) : *good-nature*, WW 74²².
glædscipe m. *gladness, joy*, JnR,Lcd.
 ['gladship']
glēdstede=glēdstede
glæm† m. *a brilliant light*, Gu : '*gleam*,'
 brilliance, brightness, splendour, beauty,
 Gen,Jul.
glæng=gleng
glæppe (a) f. *buck-bean*, Ct,Lcd.
glær m. *amber, resin*, WW.
glæren *vitreous, glassy* (Sievers 234a).
 [glæs]
glæs I. n. nap. glasu, and (once) glæsas
 (GPH 397) '*glass*,' Bo,Cr ; Æ. **II.** *a glass
 vessel*, BH,Lcd.
glæsen *of glass, glassy*, Bl. ['glassen']
glæsenēage *grey-eyed*, WW 416¹.
glæsfæt n. *glass* (*vessel*), BH 398b,o³,GD
 10¹⁶.
glæsful m. *a 'glassful*,' BH 398т³.
glæsgegot? *poured or molten glass*, WE 63⁹.
glæshlūtor† *clear, transparent.*
glæterian *to glitter*, OEG,WW.
glæterung f. *shining*, RPs 48¹⁵.
glætlic=glædlic; **glǣw**=glēaw
glappe=glæppe
glasu v. glæs; **glāw**=glēaw
glēam m? n? *revelry, joy*, Gen 12.

glēaw (ā, ǣ, ē) *penetrating, keen, prudent,
 wise, skilful*, G,Gl,VPs ; Æ,AO,CP : (†)
 good. ['glew'] adv. -e.
glēawferhð† *prudent.*
glēawhycgende (Jul), glēawhȳdig† *thoughtful, wise, prudent.*
glēawlic (ǣ, ēo) *wise, prudent, skilful, diligent*. adv. -lice.
glēawmōd *wise, sagacious*, CP.
glēawnes (ǣ) f. *wisdom, prudence, skill,
 penetration*, Æ : *diligence* : *sign, token*, Bf.
glēawscipe m. *wisdom, thoughtfulness, diligence* : *proof, indication, test*, Bf 156²⁴.
glēd (oe) f. *glowing coal, ember, fire, flame*,
 LG,Ps ; Æ. [glōwan; 'gleed']
+glēdan *to make hot, kindle*, PPs 77²³.
gleddian *to sprinkle, throw over*, Lcd 3·292¹⁴.
glēde f. *glowing coal*, LPs 17⁹.
glēdegesa m. *fiery terror*, B 2650.
gledene=glædene
glēdfæt n. *chafing-dish*, Lcd 123b : *censer*,
 WW.
gledine=glædene
glednes (KGl)=glædnes
glēdscofl (oe) f. *fire-shovel*, Cp 7 u.
glēdstede† m. *altar*, Gen.
glemm m? *blemish, spot*, W 67⁸.
glencan=glengan
glendran *to devour, swallow*, MtR.
+glendrian *to precipitate*, LkL 4²⁹.
gleng mf. (nap. gleng(e)as, glenge, glenga)
 ornament, honour, splendour, CP.
±glengan (æ) *to adorn, decorate*, ÆL : *trim
 (lamp)* : (+) *set in order, compose.*
+glengendlīce *elegantly*, OEG 1202.
glengful *decked out, adorned*, GPH 395.
glengista? (meaning doubtful) AA 1²⁰ (v.
 BTs and ac).
glenglic *magnificent, brilliant*, WW 467²⁵.
glengnes f. *adornment*, MFH 123¹⁵.
glentrian=glendran
glēo=glīw; **glēof**=glēow II.
gleomu f. *splendour*, Ruin 34?
glēow I.=glīw. **II.** pret. 3 sg. of glōwan.
glēow-=glēaw-, glīw-
glēsan *to gloss*, ÆGr 293¹³. [L. glossa]
glēsing f. *glossing, explanation*, ÆGr 293¹⁴.
glēw=glēaw
glīa (OEG 3173)=glīga gp. of glīg.
glid *slippery*, CPs 34⁶.
glida (io) m. *kite, vulture*, Æ,Cp. ['glede']
±glīdan¹ *to 'glide*,' *slip, slide*, An,B ; Æ,AO,
 CP : *glide away, vanish.*
glidder *slippery*, VHy : *lustful*. ['glidder']
gliddrian *to slip, be unstable*, OEG 4104.
glider (W 239¹⁴)=glidder
gliderung (y) f. *phantom*, WW 401⁴⁰.
glīg=glīw
glind m. *hedge, fence*, BC 1·296'.

glioda (Cp)=glida

glisian to glitter, WW. ['glise']

glisnian (y) to 'glisten,' gleam, Shr, Run.

glit pres. 3 sg. of glīdan.

glitenian to glitter, shine : be distinguished, Bf 44[6].

glitenung f. coruscation, gleam, SPs 143[8].

glitin-, glitn-=gliten-

glīw (ēo, īg, īo, īu, ēow) n. 'glee,' pleasure, mirth, play, sport, Bas,Gl,Ph : music, Gn, Ps : mockery.

glīwbeam (īg) m. musical instrument, harp, timbrel, LRSPs 149[3].

glīwbydenestre (ȳ) f. female musician, LPs 67[26].

glīwcræft m. music, minstrelsy, GD 62[13].

glīwcynn? (ȳ) a kind of music? (BTs), LPs 146[10].

glīwdrēam (ēo) m. music, mirth, B 3021.

glīwere m. buffoon, parasite, OEG.

glīwgamen (īg) n. revelry, W 46[16].

glīwgeorn (īg) fond of sport, LL.

glīwhlēoōriendlic musical, WW 446[36].

glīwian (ēo) to make merry, jest, play (music), sing, BH,LL : adorn, RD 27[13]. ['glew']

glīwiend m. performer, player, SPs 67[26].

glīwingman m. debauchee? OEG 50[9].

glīwlic mimic, jesting, GPH 396.

glīwmæden (īe) n. female musician, ERPs 67[26].

glīwman (ēo, īg) m. 'gleeman,' minstrel, player, jester, B; CP,WW : parasite, HGL.

glīwre=glīwere

glīwstæf m. melody, joy, WA 52.

glīwstōl m. seat of joy, RD 88[3].

glīwung f. boisterous laughter, mockery, OEG 1472.

glīwword (ēow) n. song, poem, MET 7[2].

glōf, glōfe f. 'glove,' pouch, B,Guth; LF 60. foxes g. foxglove.

+glōfed gloved, AS 43[4].

glōfung f. supplying with gloves, LL 450,10.

glōfwyrt f. glovewort, dog's tongue, lily of the valley, LCD.

glōm m? gloaming, twilight, CREAT 71.

glōmung f. 'gloaming,' twilight, DHy,WW.

gloria m. doxology, RB.

glōwan[7] to 'glow,' Æ,OEG.

glōwende 'glowing,' burning, Lcd 80b.

gly-=gli-

gnād pret. 3 sg. of gnīdan.

gnægen=gnagen pp. of gnagan.

gnæt m. 'gnat,' midge, AO,Lcd,Mt.

gnagan[6] to 'gnaw,' Æ,Ct,DD.

-gnāst v. fȳr-g.

gnēad-=gnēað-

gnēað niggardly, B,BH : frugal, sparing, SHR. [v. 'gnede']

gnēaðlicnes f. frugality, OEG 2437.

gnēaðnes (ē) f. frugality : scarcity, MH.

gnēðe scanty, sparing, WW. ['gnede'] adv. -līce, GD. ['gnedely']

gnēðelicnes=gnēaðlicnes

gnīdan[1] to rub, grind together, crumble, Lk; Æ,AO. ['gnide']

gnidil m. rubber, pestle, Cp 440 P.

gnīding f. rubbing, LCD 11b.

gnit pres. 3 sg. of gnīdan.

gnōgon pret. pl. of gnagan.

gnorn† I. sad, sorrowful, troubled, depressed. II. m. sadness, sorrow, trouble.

gnornan=gnornian

gnorncearig sad, troubled, JUL 529.

gnorngan=gnornian

gnornhof† n. prison, cell, AN.

gnornian to be sad, murmur, complain, mourn, lament, grieve, CP.

gnornscendende hastening away in sadness, PPs 89[10]. [scyndan]

gnornsorg† f. sadness, sorrow.

gnornung (e) f. sadness, sorrow, lamentation, discontent, Æ,AO,CP.

gnornword n. lamentation, GEN 767.

gnuddian to rub, OEG 56[33].

gnyran=gnyrran

gnyrn† f. sadness, mourning, calamity : wrong, insult, fault, blemish. [gnorn]

gnyrnwracu f. revenge, enmity, EL 359.

gnyrran to grind the teeth, W 138[29] : creak, Lcd. [v. 'gnar']

+gnysan=cnyssan; gnȳðe=gnēað

gōað 3 p. sg. pres. of gōian.

gōc=gēoc

God m. np. -as, -u a 'GOD,' image of a god, Æ; AO : God, the (Christian) Deity, Æ; CP : godlike person, Bo.

gōd I. comp. bet(e)ra, bettra, superl. bet(e)st 'GOOD' (of persons or things), virtuous : desirable, favourable, salutary, pleasant : valid, efficient, suitable : considerable, sufficiently great. II. n. good thing, advantage, benefit, gift, B,Bl,Mt; Æ, AO,CP : 'good,' goodness, welfare, CP : virtue, ability, doughtiness : goods, property, wealth, CP.

godæppel m. quince, WW 364[16]. [=coddæppel]

godbearn n. divine child, Son of God : godchild, W. ['godbairn']

godborg m? solemn pledge (given in church?), LL 18·33; 66,33 and v. 2·232,1d.

godbōt f. atonement, LL 258,51.

godcund religious, sacred, divine, spiritual, heaven-sent, Gen,Chr; Æ,CP. ['godcund']

godcundlic divine, of or from God, spiritual, celestial, Æ,CP. adv. -līce divinely, Æ : canonically.

godcundmæht n? divine majesty, MtL.

godcundnes f. *divine nature, divinity, God-head, Æ,Lcd : divine service : oblation,* LL. ['*godcundness*']

godcundspēd f. *divine nature, godhead,* VH 14.

gōddǣd f. *good work, Cr : benefit, PPs.* ['*good deed*']

goddohtor f. '*goddaughter,*' *Ct.*

gōddōnd† m. (nap. gōddēnd), *benefactor.*

goddrēam† m. *joy of heaven,* Gu.

godě-=god-

godfæder m. *God the Father :* '*godfather,*' *Ct,LL.*

godfrecnes (BH 70¹²)=godwrecnes

gōdfremmend m. *doer of good?* B 299.

godfyrht (e, i) *godfearing, An,Chr.* ['*god-fright*']

godgeld=godgield

godgesprǣce (BH)=godsprǣce

godgield (e², i², y²) n. *heathen god, idol : heathen rite,* AO.

godgildlic *of idol-worship,* WW 466¹⁶.

godgim m. *heavenly jewel?* EL 1114.

godhād m. *divine nature,* CP 261¹⁷.

±gōdian *to improve, get better, Chr,Lcd : make better : endow, enrich, KC;* Æ. ['*good*']

Goding m. *Son of God,* LkR 4¹.

gōdlār f. *good teaching,* LL 304 B.

gōdlēas *bad, evil, BH.* ['*goodless*']

godlic *godlike, divine,* WW 220,221.

gōdlic '*goodly,*' *excellent, Gen : comely, fair,* GPH 394.

gōdlīf n. *good life,* CHR 1095.

godmægen n. *divine power, divinity,* AA 37,42.

godmōdor f. '*godmother,*' *Shr.*

gōdnes f. '*goodness,*' *virtue, Bo : good-will, beneficence, kindliness, Bo,Æ : good thing.*

godsǣd n. (*God's seed*), *divine progeny?* DA 90.

gōdscipe m. *kindness, DR.* ['*goodship*']

godscyld f. *sin against God, impiety,* Jul 204.

godscyldig *impious,* Gu 834.

godsibb m. *sponsor, W.* ['*gossip*']

godsibbrǣden f. *sponsorial obligations,* W 228³.

gōdspēdig† *rich, happy.*

godspel n. '*gospel,*' *glad tidings, Mt : one of the four gospels, An;* Æ,CP : *the gospel (for the day), Mt.*

godspelbodung f. *gospel-preaching, new dis-pensation,* ÆL,ÆT.

godspellbōc f. *book containing the four gospels,* LL. ['*gospel-book*']

godspellere m. '*gospeller,*' *evangelist, Bl;* Æ,CP.

godspellian *to preach the gospel, evangelize, Ps;* Æ,CP. ['*gospel*']

godspell-ic (Æ), -isc *evangelical.*

godspelltraht m. *gospel commentary, homily,* Æ.

godsprǣce (ē) n. *oracle,* BH.

godsunu m. '*godson,*' *BH,Chr,Ma.*

godōrymm m. *divine majesty,* GD.

godōrymnes f. *divine glory,* AS 9²?

godwebb I. n. *fine cloth, purple, CP : fine clothes : curtain : flag.* II.=godwebben

godwebbcyn? (gode-) n. *purple (cloth),* Sol 152'.

godwebben *of purple,* BL 95¹⁹, LF 47¹⁵ : *of silk or cotton,* HGL.

godwebgyrla m. *cloth of purple,* W 197¹.

godwebwyrhta m. *weaver of purple,* AA 8¹⁸.

gōdwillende *well-pleased,* EHy 16⁶.

godwrǣc (e²) *wicked,* BL.

godwrǣclic *impious, sacrilegious,* GD 232¹³.

godwrece=godwrǣc

godwrecnes f. (-wyrc- Wyn 45) *wickedness, impiety,* BHB 70¹².

goffian *to be vain,* ByH 80¹¹.

gofol=gafol

gōian *to lament, groan,* BH 88(v.also gēgan).

gōl pret. 3 sg. of galan.

gold n. '*gold,*' *Æ,OET;* CP.

goldǣht f. *wealth in gold,* B 2748.

goldbeorht *bright with gold,* Ruin 34.

goldblēoh *golden-hued,* WW 140²⁴.

goldblōma m. *golden bloom?* (v. BTs), W 251¹¹; BL 105¹⁸.

goldburg† f. *city in which gold is given? rich city?* An,Gen.

golde f. '*solsequia,*' *marigold,* WW 301⁶. ['*gold*']

golde-=gold-

golden pp. of gieldan.

goldfæt† n. *golden vessel.*

goldfǣted *plated or adorned with gold,* LL 460,10 H.

goldfāg *variegated or shining with gold.*

goldfell n. *gold plate,* WW 358¹⁵.

goldfellen *of gilded leather,* ÆL 31²⁵².

goldfinc m. '*goldfinch,*' *WW.*

goldfinger m. *ring-finger,* LL.

goldfrætwe fp. *gold ornaments,* Cr,W.

goldfyld *covered with gold,* WW 518⁴.

goldfyll? *gold leaf, gold foil,* ES 8·478 (v. BTs).

goldgearwe fp. *gold ornaments,* NC 298.

goldgewefen *woven with gold,* OEG 4297.

goldgeweorc n. *golden object,* MH 222.

goldgiefa† (i, y) m. *gold-giver, prince, lord.*

goldhilted *golden hilted,* RD 56¹⁴.

goldhladen *adorned with gold,* Fin 13.

goldhoma m. *gold-adorned coat of mail,* EL 992.

goldhord nm. *treasure of gold, treasury, El, VPs;* Æ,AO. ['*goldhoard*']

goldhordhūs n. *privy*, WW 184[14].
goldhordian *to collect treasure, hoard*, Sc 173[12].
goldhroden† *ornamented with gold*. [hrēodan]
goldhwæt *greedy for gold*, B 3074?
goldlæfer f. *gold plate*, HGL 431.
goldlēaf n. *gold leaf or plate*, W 263[6]. [=læfer]
goldmæstling (e) n. *brass*, WW. [v. 'gold']
goldmāðm m. *treasure*, B 2414.
goldmestling=goldmæstling
goldōra m. *gold ore*, OEG 1810.
goldsele† m. *hall in which gold is distributed.*
goldsmið m. 'goldsmith,' Æ.
goldsmiðu f. *goldsmith's art*, WY 73.
goldspēdig *rich in gold*, JUL 39.
goldtorht *bright like gold*, CREAT 78.
goldðēof m. *stealer of gold*, LL 54,9[2].
goldðrǣd m. *gold thread*, WW 196[15].
goldweard m. *keeper of gold (dragon)*, B 3081.
goldwecg m. *a lump of gold*, OEG 451.
goldwine† m. *liberal prince, lord, king.*
goldwlanc† *brave with gold, richly adorned.*
goldwlencu f. *gold ornament*, BL 195.
goldwyrt f. *heliotrope, marigold*, OEG 26[26].
golfetung (LPs 78[4])=gaffetung
gōlon pret. pl. of galan.
golpen pp. of gielpan.
gom-=gam-
gōma m. (sg. or pl. used indifferently) *inside of mouth or throat, palate, jaws*, Lcd, Rd,VPs; Æ. ['gum']
gombe (a)† f. *tribute.*
gomor *Hebrew measure, omer*, Æ. ['gomer']
gon-=gan-; **gond-**=gand-, geond-
gōp m. *slave, servant*, RD 50[3]. [or ?=gēap]
gor n. *dung, dirt, filth*, Æ,Cp,Rd. ['gore']
gōr=gār III.
gorettan *to gaze, stare about*, OEG 5[3] : *pour forth, emit*, GPH 398.
gorettung f. *gazing*, OEG 5[3]n.
gorian *to gaze, stare about*, OEG 7[6].
gors (Cp?), gorst m. 'gorse,' furze, MH,MrR: *juniper*, Lcd : 'rhamnus,' S[2]Ps 57[10].
gorstbēam m. *furze bush*, Mk 12[26].
gōs f. nap. gēs 'goose,' LL,Rd,WW; Æ.
gōs-fugol m. nap. -fuglas *goose*, Ct.
gōshafoc (u[3]) m. 'goshawk,' WW.
gost=gorst; **gōst**=gāst
+got n. *shedding (of tears)*, BH 376[12].
Gota sg. -an pl. 'Goth,' BH.
goten pp. of gēotan.
-gotennes v. tō-g.
Got-isc (GD), -onisc (OEG) adj. *of the Goths.*
gōtwoðe f. *goatweed*, LCD. [gāt]
gōung (ēo) f. *groaning*, BH 76[15]. [gōian]
grād m. (Æ), grāde f. *step, grade, rank.* [L.]

grǣd m. *grass*, WW.
grǣda=grēada
grǣdan I. *to cry, call out*, Lcd : *crow*, CP,Rd. ['grede'] II. ds. of wk. adj. *grassy*, ÆL 18[245].
grǣde I. *grassy*, Æ. II.=grǣd
grǣde-, grǣdi-=grǣdig-
grǣdig (ē) 'greedy,' hungry, covetous, Æ,B, Bl,Sol : *eager*, CP. adv. -līce, Æ,Bas.
grǣdignes f. *greediness, avarice*, Æ.
grǣdum adv. *greedily*, GU 710.
grǣf I. (a) n. *cave, 'grave,' trench*, Seaf; Mdf. [grafan] II. n? *style for writing*, WW. [L. graphium]
grǣfa m. grǣfe f. *bush, bramble, grove, thicket*, WW; Mdf : *brush-wood (for burning), fuel*, Chr. ['greave']
grǣfen pp. of grafan.
grǣfhūs n. *grave*, SAT 708.
grǣfsex n. *graving tool*, WW. [seax]
grǣft mfn. *graven image, carved object, sculpture*, Æ.
grǣftgeweorc n. *graven image*, DEUT 5[8].
grǣfð pres. 3 sg. of grafan.
grǣg 'grey,' Æ,Ep,Gen,Met,WW.
grǣggōs f. *grey (wild) goose*, GL.
grǣghǣwe WW 402[40].
grǣghama *grey-coated*, FIN 6.
grǣgmǣl *grey-coloured*, B 2682.
grǣgōs=grǣggōs
grǣm-, grǣn-=grem-, gren-; **grǣp**=grēp
+grǣppian *to seize*, MtL 14[31].
grǣs n. (nap. grasu) 'grass,' Cp,CP. [v. also gærs]
grǣsgrēne (e[1], oe[2]) 'grass-green,' Ep.
grǣshoppa v. gærshoppa.
grǣsmolde f. *greensward*, B 1881.
grǣswang† m. *greensward*, VH 14.
grǣt I.=pres. 3 sg. of (1) grǣdan, (2) grētan. II.=grēat
grǣtan=grētan; **graf**=grǣf
grāf nm. 'grove,' KC; Mdf.
grāfa m. *grove*, KC.
grafan[6] *to dig, dig up*, Met,Rd,Rim : 'grave,' engrave, carve, chisel, PPs.
grafere m. 'sculptor,' graver, WW 164[14].
grafet n. *trench*, EC 354; 355.
gram (o) adj. *angry, cruel, fierce*, B,G; AO : *oppressive, hostile* : (as sb.) *enemy.* ['grame']
grama I. m. *rage, anger*, Æ : *trouble*, Lcd. ['grame'] II. *devil, demon*, ÆL.
gramatisccræft=grammaticcræft
grambǣre *passionate*, CP 289[5].
grame adv. *angrily, fiercely, cruelly.*
gramfǣrnes f. *wrath*, LL (226[25]). [=*grambǣrnes]
gramhegdig=gramhȳdig
gramheort† *hostile-minded*, VH 14.

gramhycgende *hostile,* PPs 68²⁵.

gramhȳdig† *hostile, malignant,* VH 14.

gramian *to anger, enrage,* W 199². grami-
gende *raging,* GPH 402.

gramlic *wrathful, fierce, cruel, severe,* Æ.
adv. -līce, *Ps.* ['gramely']

grammatic *grammatical,* ÆL 35¹⁴.

grammaticcræft m. *art of grammar,* BH
258¹⁵.

grammaticere m. *grammarian,* Bf 158¹⁷.

grammatisc=grammatic

grammōd *cruel,* Bl 223³³.

gramword n. *evil speech,* PPs 74⁵.

grand pret. 3 sg. of grindan.

grandorlēas (o) *guileless,* Jul 271.

grānian² *to 'groan,' lament; Bl,Ps.*

granu f. *moustache,* Cp 335 m (v. BTs).

grānung f. *'groaning,' lamentation,* Æ.

grāp I. f.† *grasp, grip.* [grīpan] II. pret.
3 sg. of grīpan.

±**grāpian** *to feel for, lay hold, of, seize, touch,*
Æ,B,Bl,Rd,VPs : *attain, reach,* Bf 144¹.
['grope']

grāpigendlic *tangible,* ÆH 1·230.

grāpung f. *sense of feeling, touch,* Æ.
['groping']

grāscinnen *made of grey skins or grey fur,*
Chr 1075 d. [*ON.* grāskinn]

grasian *to 'graze,'* Lcd.

grasu v. græs.

gratan (Lcd 3·292²⁴)=grotan

graðul *gradual, antiphon,* CM 1020.

grēada m. *lap, bosom,* CP,Lk. ['greade']

grēat (æ) comp. grīetra *'great,' tall, thick,*
stout, massive, A,Æ,Bo,Chr,WW : coarse,
BC,Lcd.

grēatewyrt f. *meadow saffron,* WW 298⁷.

grēatian² *to become enlarged, CP.* ['great']

grēatnes (ē) f. *'greatness,'* RB 88¹⁵.

Grēcas mpl. *Greeks* (v. AB 40·342).

Grēcisc *Greek, Grecian,* Æ.

grēd=græd; **gref-**, grēf-=græf-, græf-

grēg-=græg-; **grem-**=grim-

gremet-=grymet-

±**gremian** *to enrage, provoke, irritate, AO;*
Æ,CP : revile, Mk. ['greme']

gremman=gremian

gremung (æ) f. *provocation,* LPs 94⁹.

grēne *'green,' Ct,Gl,Lcd : young, immature,*
Lcd : raw : growing, living, LkL (oe) : as
sb., *Lcd.*

grēnhǣwen *green-coloured,* WW 379²⁴.

grēnian *to become 'green,' flourish,* Met.

grēnnes f. *greenness, BH;* CP : (in pl.) *green*
things, plants, Bf 82⁴.

grennian *to 'grin,' gnash the teeth,* Jul,Sc.

grennung (æ) f. *grinning,* Cp 174 r.

grēofa m. *pot, pan,* WW. [Ger. griebe]

grēop=grēp

grēosn (īo) *gravel, pebble,* KGl 76³. [Ger.
greiss]

grēot n. *'grit,' sand, earth, An,B,Gen; Æ.*

grēotan² *to cry, lament, B,Sol.* [v. 'greet']

grēothord n. *body,* Gu 1240.

grēow pret. 3 sg. of grōwan.

grēp, grēpe f. *ditch, furrow, drain : privy,*
ES 9·505 ; Gl. [v. 'grip']

gres-=græs-; **grēt-**=grēat-

grētan I. (±) *to 'greet,' salute, accost, speak*
to, challenge, B,Gl,Mk,Jul : (±) to seek
out, approach, visit, AO,B,Gen,LG : ill-
treat, attack, AO : touch, take hold of,
handle, deal with, ÆGr : have an effect upon,
ZDA 34·232 : *cohabit with.* hearpan grētan
play the harp, Cra. II.† (ǣ) *to weep, bemoan,*
lament, deplore, B,Cp,Cr. [v. 'greet']

grēting f. *'greeting,' BH,LkL* (oe) : *present.*

grētinghūs n. *audience chamber,* WW 184⁸.

grētingword n. *word of greeting,* ÆGr 209¹⁴.

+**grētlic** *commendatory,* RBL 103⁶.

gretta=grytta

greðe *'sodalis'?* OEG 29².

grēwð pres. 3 sg. of grōwan.

griellan=grillan

grīetra v. grēat.

grīghund m. *'greyhound,'* WW 276³.

grillan (ie, y) *to provoke, offend, CP :*
gnash the teeth, Gl. ['grill']

grim (CP)=grimm

grīma† m. *mask, helmet,* El : *ghost,* Rd.

grimena *'bruchus,' caterpillar?* EPs 104³⁴.

grimet-=grymet-

grimful *fierce, violent,* ES 39·348.

grīmhelm† m. *helmet (with visor).*

grīming *spectre,* WW 446²⁶.

grimlic *fierce, blood-thirsty, cruel, terrible,*
severe, Æ,AO,B. adv. -līce. ['grimly']

grimm *fierce, savage, B,Bl,Ma : dire, severe,*
bitter, painful, BH,Bl,Chr. ['grim']

grimman³† *to rage : hasten on,* B 306.

grimmān n. *terrible sin,* BHb 50⁸.

grimme *savagely, cruelly, severely, AO,Gen.*
['grim']

grimnes f. *ferocity, cruelty, Bl,Gu,WW :*
severity. ['grimness']

grimsian *to rage,* BH.

grimsung f. *harshness, severity,* CP 125¹⁴.

grin *'ilium,' region of the groin,* LL.

±**grīn** (ī, ȳ; also short?) nf. *snare, gin, PPs,*
VPs; Æ,CP : halter, noose, Mt. ['grin']

+**grind†** n. *impact, crash.*

±**grindan³** (y) *to rub together, grate, scrape,*
Rd : gnash, Ps : 'grind,' sharpen, Æ,Mt,
pp. *WW.*

grinde f. *shingle,* BC (v. Mdf).

grindel m. nap. grindlas *bar, bolt.* pl.
grating, hurdle, Gen 384 (v. BT).

grindere m. *grinder,* Lcd 3·178¹.

grinde-tōð, grindig- m. *grinding tooth, molar*, WW440²⁶.

grindle f. *herring*, WW356¹².

gring=cring

+**grīnian** *to ensnare*, KGl. ['*grin*']

grint pres. 3 sg. of grindan.

grinu '*avidius*' (said of some colour), WW 163¹⁹,356²⁵.

grīosn=grēosn

gripa m. *handful, sheaf*, Lcd.

±**grīpan** intr. (w: d. g. on or tō) *to seek to get hold of, assail, attack*, B,Bl,Gen; CP : tr. (w. g.) *seize, snatch, take, apprehend*, Sol,WW. ['*gripe*']

gripe m. '*grip,*' *grasp, seizure, attack*, B, WW; Æ. gūðbilla g. *shield* : *handful*, Lcd,Ps.

grīpend m. *seizer, robber*, WW516¹³.

+**gripennes** f. *seizing, snare, captivity*, EPs 34⁸.

±**grippan** (io) *to seize, obtain*, DR, LG.

gripu f. *kettle, caldron*, Sol46.

gripul '*capax,*' WW198³⁹. ['*gripple*']

-**grīsan** (ȳ) v. ā-g.

grislic '*grisly,*' *horrible*, HL15¹⁸². adv. RWH84.

grīst n. *action of grinding*, WW. ['*grist*']

gristan? *to gnash, grind*, HGL513 (cp. OEG 4605 and n).

gristbāt-=gristbit-

gristbite m. *gnashing*, W188⁵.

gristbitian *to gnash the teeth, rage*, Æ,BH, Mk,WW; Æ. ['*gristbite*']

gristbitung f. *gnashing of teeth*, Bl,Mt. ['*gristbiting*']

gristle f. '*gristle,*' Gl,WW.

gristlung (y) f. *gnashing*, Lk13²⁸.

grīstra m. *baker*, WW.

gritta=grytta

grīð n. *truce, (temporary) peace*, Ma : *protection of the person, asylum, sanctuary, guarantee of safety*, LL. ['*grith*']

grīðbryce m. *breach of* '*grið,*' LL : *penalty for such a breach*, LL. ['*grithbreach*']

±**grīðian** *to make a truce or peace*, Chr : *protect*, LL. ['*grith*']

grīðlagu f. *law of temporary or local peace*, LL470,9.

grīðlēas *unprotected*, W158⁷.

groe-=grē-

grōf pret. 3 sg. of grafan.

grom=gram; **gron-**=gran-

grond pret. 3 sg. of grindan.

gronwisc (=a) '*acus,*' Cp160A (v. AB 9·35).

grōp f. *ditch*, Ln150.

gropa m. *a liquid measure*, WW204³.

grōpian=grāpian; -**groren** v. be-g.

grorn I. m. *sorrow, sadness*, Rim89. II. adj. *sad, agitated*, OET127⁶. adv. -e.

grornhof n. *sad home, hell*, Jul324.

grornian *to mourn, complain*, Cr,Ps.

grorntorn *sadness*, Rim66?

grornung f. *complaint*, NG.

grost *cartilage*, Ln57.

grot I. n. *particle*, Bo; AO : *meal*. ['*grot*'] II. sbpl. (grotan) '*groats,*' *coarse meal*, Lcd.

grotig *earthy*, GPH396.

±**grōwan**⁷ *to* 'GROW,' *increase, flourish* : *germinate*, CP : *become ?* WW441²⁸ (v. NP15·272).

grōwende '*growing,*' Gen,KGl.

grōwnes f. *growth*, BH : *prosperity*, HL 124²⁵⁷.

grummon pret. pl. of grimman.

gruncian *to desire*, GPH396.

grund m. 'GROUND,' *bottom* : *foundation* : *abyss, hell* : *plain, country, land, earth* : *sea, water*.

grundbedd n. *ground, soil*, RD81²⁴.

grundbūend† m. *earth-dweller*.

grunddēope *depths of the sea*, APs64⁸.

grunden pp. of grindan.

grundeswelge (i³, u³, v³) f. '*groundsel,*' Gl, Lcd.

grundfūs *hastening to hell*, Mod49.

grundhyrde m. *keeper of the abyss*, B2136.

grundinga=grundlinga

grundlēas *bottomless, unfathomable*, Bo : *boundless, vast*. ['*groundless*']

grundlēaslic *boundless, vast*, CP417¹⁰.

grundling m. *groundling (fish)*, BC3·525.

grundlinga (u²) adv. *from the foundation, completely*, Æ : *to the ground, prone, prostrate*, Æ.

grundon pret. pl. of grindan.

grundscēat† m. *region*, Cr.

grundsele m. *abysmal dwelling*, B2139.

grundsopa '*cartilago,*' Gl (v. BTs).

grundstān m. *foundation-stone*, WW. ['*groundstone*']

+**grundstaðelian** *to establish firmly*, ÆL8²¹.

grundwæg m. *earth*, An582.

grundwang† m. *(ground-plain), the earth*, B : *bottom (of a lake)*.

grundweall m. *foundation*, Æ,Lk. ['*groundwall*']

+**grundweallian** *to establish, found*, EPs23².

grundwela m. *earthly riches*, Gen957.

grundwiergen (y) f. *water-wolf*, B1518.

grunian, grunnian, *to grunt* (OEG) : *chew the cud?* Sc54'.

grunnettan *to* '*grunt,*' Cp.

grun(n)ung f. *grunting, bellowing*, OEG.

grut m. *gulf, chasm, abyss* : *stone, rock*, OEG1814.

grūt f. (ds. grȳt, grūt) *groats, coarse meal,* Cp,Ct,Lcd : *grains, the spent grain after brewing,* Lcd. ['*grout*']

grutt, grutte=grut; gryllan=grillan

grym=grim(m)

grymet-(t)an, -tian (e, i) *to grunt, roar, rage,* Æ.

grymet(t)ung f. *grunting, roaring, bellowing,* Æ.

grymm=grimm

grymman I. *to mourn, wail,* LPs37⁹ (gyrm-). ['*yarm*'] II.=gremian

gryn=gyrn; grȳn=grīn

+grynd n. *plot of ground,* TC231²².

gryndan I. *to set, sink (of the sun),* WW. ['*grind*'; grund] II. (+) *to found (of a house),* MtL7²⁵ (wry-). III.=grindan

grynde n. *abyss,* Sat331.

grynel (WW291³)=cyrnel

grȳnian=grīnian

grynsmið m. *worker of ill,* An919.

grȳpe (=ī) f. *ditch, drain,* OEG. [v. '*grip*']

gryre† m. *horror, terror : fierceness, violence,* DD8 : *horrible thing.*

gryrebrōga† m. *terror, horror.*

gryrefæst *terribly firm,* El76a.

gryrefāh† adj. (used as sb.) *spotted horror,* B.

gryregæst (æ)? m. *terrible stranger,* B2560.

gryregeatwe fp. *war-gear,* B324.

gryrehwīl f. *terrible time,* An468.

gryrelēoð† n. *terrible song.*

gryrelic† *terrible, horrible,* B.

gryremiht f. *terrible power,* W195²⁰.

gryresīð m. *dangerous expedition,* B1462.

gryrran *to gnash,* DD195.

grys-, grȳs-=gris-, grīs-

grȳt I. pres. 3 sg. of grēotan. II. v. grūt.

grȳtan *to flourish,* WW240²⁹. [*grēat*]

grȳto f. *greatness,* AA127. [*grēat*]

grytt n. *dust, meal,* Gl.

grytta, gryttan f. pl. *coarse meal, bran, chaff,* Ep,Lcd,WW. ['*grit*']

grytte f. *spider,* JLVPs89⁹.

grȳttra (A4·151)=*grietra cp. of grēat. ['*greater*']

gryð-=grið-; gū=gēo

guldon pret. pl. of gieldan.

gullisc? (an attribute of silver), Sol150⁹.

gullon pret. pl. of giellan.

gulpon pret. pl. of gielpan.

guma† m. *man, lord, hero,* B. ['*gome*']

gumcynn† sn. *human race, men, nation.*

gumcyst† f. *excellence, bravery, virtue, liberality.* adv. -um *excellently.*

gumdrēam m. *enjoyment of life,* B2469.

gumdryhten m. *lord,* B1642.

gumfēða m. *troop,* B1401.

gumfrēa m. *king,* Da651.

-gumian v. ofer-g.

gummann m. *man,* B1028.

gumrīce† n. *kingdom, earth.*

gumrinc† m. *man, warrior.*

gumstōl m. *ruler's seat, throne,* B1952.

gumðegen m. *man,* Cra83.

gumðēod f. *folk, people,* Gen226.

gund m. *matter, pus,* Lcd. ['*gound*']

gundeswilge (Ep,Erf,Ln)=grundeswelge

gundig *goundy, mattery,* Erf.

gung=geong; gung-=ging-

gungon pret. pl. of gangan.

gunnon (BH) pret. pl. of ginnan.

gupan '*clunibus, renibus, coxe,*' WW205⁴¹ (v. A31·522).

gurron pret. pl. of gyrran.

guton pret. pl. of gēotan.

guttas mp. '*guts,*' *entrails,* HGl408.

gūð† f. *combat, battle, war.*

gūðbeorn m. *fighting-hero,* B314.

gūðbill† n. *battle-bill, sword.*

gūðbord† n. *war-shield,* Gen.

gūðbyrne f. *corslet, coat of mail,* B321.

gūðcearu f. *war-trouble,* B1258.

gūðcræft m. *war-craft,* B127.

gūðcwēn† f. *warrior queen,* El.

gūðcyning† m. *warrior king,* B.

gūðcyst f. *troop, warrior band?* (Kluge) : *bravery?* (BT),Ex343.

gūðdēað m. *death in battle,* B2249.

gūðfana m. *gonfanon, war-banner, ensign, standard,* Æ,AO.

gūð-flā? f., -flān? mf. *battle-arrow,* Gen 2063.

gūðfloga m. *winged fighter,* B2528.

gūðfona=gūðfana

gūðfrēa m. *warlike prince,* An1335.

gūðfrec *bold in battle* (GK), *greedy for destruction* (BTs),An1119.

gūðfreca† m. *warrior.*

gūðfremmend† m. *warrior.*

gūðfugol m. *bird of war, eagle,* Rd25⁵.

gūðgeatwe† fp. *armour,* B.

gūðgelǣca m. *warrior,* El43.

gūðgemōt† n. *battle, combat.*

gūðgetāwe=gūðgeatwe

gūðgeðingu† np. *battle, contest,* An.

gūðgewǣde† n. *war-dress, armour,* B.

gūðgeweorc† n. *warlike deed,* B.

gūðgewinn† n. *battle.*

gūðhafoc m. *war-hawk, eagle,* †Chr937a.

gūðheard *bold in battle,* El204.

gūðhelm m. *helmet,* B2487.

gūðhere m. *warlike host, army,* Gen1967.

gūðhorn m. *war-horn, trumpet,* B1432.

gūðhrēð m. *martial glory,* B819.

gūðhwæt *fierce in battle,* Ap57.

gūðlēoð n. *war-song,* B1522.

gūð-mæcga, -maga m. *warrior*, Sol 90.
gūðmōdig? *of warlike mind*, B 306.
Gūðmyrce pl. *Ethiopians*, Ex 69.
gūðplega† m. *attack, battle*.
gūðrǣs† m. *battle-rush, onslaught*, B.
gūðrēaf n. *armour*, Jul 387.
gūðrēow *fierce in battle*, B 58. [hrēow]
gūðrinc† m. *warrior, hero*.
gūðrōf† *brave in battle*.
gūðscearu f. *slaughter in battle*, B 1213.
gūðsceaða m. *ravaging invader*, B 2318.
gūðsceorp n. *armour*, Jud 329.
gūðscrūd n. *armour*, El 258.
gūðsearo† n. *armour*.
gūðsele m. *hall of warriors*, B 443.
gūðspell n. *tidings of a war*, Gen 2097.
gūðsweord n. *sword*, B 2154.
gūððracu† f. *hostile attack*, Gen.
gūððrēat m. *warlike troop*, Ex 193.
gūðweard† m. *war-lord, king*.
gūðweorc n. *warlike deed*, An 1068.
gūðwērig *wounded*, B 1586.
gūðwiga m. *warrior*, B 2112.
gūðwine† m. *battle-friend, weapon*, B.
gūðwudu m. *spear*, Fin 6.
gy-=ge-, gi-; gyc-=gic-; gyd=gid(d)
gyden (AO), gydenu f. (occl. gs. gydenan) *goddess*. [god]
gydenlic *'vestalis'* (=*dealis?* A 31·63), WW 524³³.
gydig (i) *possessed (by a spirit), insane*, OEG 5009. ['*giddy*']
gyf=gif; gyf-=geof-, gief-, gif-
gȳf-=gīf-
gyhða (Æ)=gicða; gyhðu=gehðu
gyld=gield; gyld-=gild-, gylt-
+gyld=gylden
±gyldan I. *to gild*, Ps,WW. ['*gilded*'] II. (AO)=gieldan
±gylden *golden*, B,Dan; Æ,AO,CP. ['*gilden*']
gyldenbēag (i) m. *crown*, Lev 8⁹.
gyldenbend *golden band*, LevC 8⁹.
gyldenfeax *golden-haired*, WW 348³⁵.
gyldenhilte *golden-hilted*, BC 3·74'.
gyldenhīwe *golden-hued*, OEG 43⁵.
gyldenmūða *golden-mouthed (Chrysostom)*, GD 94²⁴; ZDA 31·7.
gyldenwecg (gylding-) m. *gold mine*, WW 241¹⁷.
gylece (IM 127¹⁴)?=pylece
gylian, gyllan *to yell, shout*. gyliende '*garrulus*,' OEG 56¹³⁸.
gylm=gilm; gylp=gielp
gylt (e, i, ie) m. '*guilt*,' *sin, offence, crime, fault*, Bf,Bl,Chr,Mt,Ps; AO,CP.
±gyltan *to commit sin, be guilty*, CP,Mt,RB, VPs. ['*guilt*,' '*guilting*']
gyltend m. *sinner, debtor*, CP.

gyltig *offending, 'guilty,'* Mt.
gylting (u¹) f. *sin*, DR.
gyltlic *sinful*, Mt 26⁶⁵. adv. -līce *faultily*, Sc 35³.
gyltwīte n. (gyld-) *fine for unpaid tax*, KC 2·406 : *for a crime*, 6·240.
gylung? '*garrulitas*,' OEG 56¹⁴¹.
gym=gimm; gym-=gim-
gȳm-=gīem-; gymian=gymmian
gymm=gimm
±gymmian *to cut the flesh*, OEG 3799.
gyn-=geon-, gin-; gȳn-=gīn-
-gȳpe (=īe?) v. æ-g.
gypigend (=i) *yawning*, GPH 398.
gypung (=i) f. *gaping, open mouth*, GPH 402.
gyr I. m. *filth, mud, marsh*. II. *fir tree*, WW 269¹⁴.
gyr-=geor-, gier-; gyra=gyr I.
±gyrdan (pret. gyrde), *to 'gird' (sword)*, Gen,PPs : *encircle, surround*, JnL : (+) *invest with attributes*, PPs.
gyrdel (e) m. '*girdle*,' *belt, zone*, Lcd,Mt; Æ : *purse*.
gyrdelbred n. *writing-tablet*, WW 277¹³.
gyrdelhring n. *girdle, buckle*, WW 432.
gyrdels, gyrder=gyrdel; gyrdil-=gyrdel-
gȳren=grīn
gyrman=grymman
gyrn† mn. *sorrow, misfortune*.
gyrnstafas mp. *injury, affliction*, Jul 245.
gyrnwracu† f. *revenge for injury*.
gyrran³ [=gierran, georran] *to sound, chatter*, Æ : *grunt : to creak,grate*, An,OEG. ['*yerr*']
gyrretan *to roar (of lions)*, LPs.
gyrsandæg (MFH 97)=gierstandæg
gyrst *gnashing of teeth, anger*, HGl 513. [v. '*grist*' and OEG 4605n]
gyrstandæg (Æ)=gierstandæg
gyrtrēow n. *fir-tree*, WW 138¹¹.
gyru I. (?) *muddy*, KC 3·412. II. f.=gyr
gyrwan=gierwian
gyrwefenn n. *marsh*, ÆGr 60¹⁰.
gȳse=gēse; gȳsel=gīsl
gyst=(1) giest, (2) gist
gyst-=giest-
gysternlicdæg=gierstandæg
gyt=git pron.
gȳt I. pres. 3 sg. of gēotan. II.=giet
gȳt-=gīet-, gīt-
gyte, gytt (NG) m. *pouring forth, shedding*, Æ : *flood*, Æ. [gēotan]
gytesǣl m. (dp. gytesālum) *joy at wine-pouring, carousal*, Jud 22.
gytestrēam m. *running stream*, WW.
gytteorm f. *ploughing-feast*, LL 452,21⁴.
gyð-=gið-; gȳu=gēo

H

h is often wrongly prefixed to words, or (conversely) dropped, as in Cockney English.

hā m. *oar-thole, rowlock.* æt hā *for each oar, or each oarsman,* CHR 1040 C. [*Icel.* hār]

habban anv. ptc. pres. hæbbende; pres. 1 sg. hæbbe, 2. hæfst, 3. hæfð, pl. hæbbað, habbað; pret. 3 sg. hæfde; subj. hæbbe; imperat. hafa; pp. (±)hæf(e)d *to* 'HAVE*,' AO,CP : *possess, own, hold,* AO,CP : *keep, retain* : *entertain, cherish* : *look after, carry on* : *esteem, consider,* AO,CP : *be subject to, experience* : *get, obtain, Chr* : *assert* : used as auxiliary to indicate past tense, *have, Æ,Chr.* h. for *consider* : (+) *hold, keep from, restrain, preserve,* Æ,CP. yfle +h. *afflict, torment.*

haca m. *hook, door-fastening,* Cp 311 P (v. BTs).

-haccian v. tō-h.

hacele (æ) f. *cloak, coat, vestment, cassock,* '*pallium,*' *AO,WW*; Æ. ['*hackle*']

hacod (æ, e) m. *pike, mullet, Cp,Ep,WW.* ['*haked*']

hacole, hacule=hacele

hād m. (rare gs. hāda) *person, individual, character, individuality, Æ,BH,Mt* : *degree, rank, order, office (especially holy office), Æ,BH,CP* : *condition, state, nature, character, form, manner, B,Sol* : *sex, BH, Chr* : *race, family, tribe* : *choir.* ['*had*']

-hād masc. suffix: usu. denotes state or condition, as cildhād, mægðhād. [*Eng.* -hood]

+hada m. *brother monk,* LL.

hādārung f. *respect of persons,* LL 474,18.

hādbōt f. *compensation for injury or insult to a priest,* LL. ['*hadbot*']

hādbreca m. *injurer of one in (holy) orders,* LL.

hād-bryce, -brice m. *injury of one in (holy) orders,* LL.

hādelīce adv. *as to persons,* DHy 29⁶.

hādesmann m. *member of a particular order,* CHR 995 F.

hādgrīð n. *privilege (as regards peace) of holy orders,* LL 471,19.

±hādian *to ordain, consecrate, BH,Chr*; Æ. ['*hade*']

hādnotu f. *office of a priest,* LL 458 H.

hādor I. n. *clearness, brightness,* B 414 (or ? hador,=heaðor). II.† (æ) *bright, clear, fresh* : *distinct, loud.* [*Ger.* heiter] adv. hādre.

hādswǣpa m. *bridesman,* WW 174³⁵.

hādswǣpe (ā) f. *bridesmaid,* WW.

hādung f. *consecration, ordination, LL.* [v. '*hade*'] hādunge underfōn *to take the veil.*

hādungdæg (i²) m. *ordination day,* ÆL 33⁵⁹.

hæb, hæb- (GL)=hæf, hæf-

hæbb-=habb-, hebb-

hæbbednes f. *continence,* BF 124²⁵.

hæbbendlīc '*habilis,*' ÆGR 54⁵.

-hæbbere v. sulh-h.

hæbbung (e²) f. *constraint,* WW 372,503.

hæc-=hac-

hæc(c) I. fm. *grating,* '*hatch,*' *half-gate, Ct.* II.=hæcce I.

+hæcca *sausage,* WW 411²⁰. [haccian]

hæcce I. fn. *crozier.* II. (e) *fence,* BC 3·147'. III.=hæc

hæccelēas *without a fence? or hatch?* EC 389'.

hæcgeat (e²) n. *hatch-gate,* KC 5·376¹⁴.

hæcine (a) f. *a thin vinous drink,* '*posca,*' WW 129³ (v. A 8·451 and Ducange, s.v.).

hæcwer m. *hatch-weir, a weir in which fish were caught,* KC 3·450.

hǣdor=hādor

hǣdre† *straitly, anxiously,* SOL.

hǣdre=hādre

hǣf I.† n. (heaf-, haf- in obl. cases) *sea, ocean,* WW. II. m. *leaven,* OEG.

hǣfd=hēafod

hǣfde pret. sg. of habban.

hǣfe I. m. *leaven,* Sc. [*Ger.* hefe] II.= hefe I.

hǣfed=hēafod

-hǣfednes v. be-, for-h.

hǣfegītsung? f. *covetousness,* EPs 118³⁶.

hǣfen I. f. *the having, owning* : *property, possessions, Æ.* [*Ger.* habe] II. f. '*haven,*' *port, Chr.* III.=hefen. IV. pp. of hebban.

hǣfen-=hafen-; hǣfenblǣte=hæferblǣte

hǣfene=hæfen II.

hǣfer (e) m. *he-goat,* WW.

hǣferbīte m. *forceps,* WW 198¹⁶. [v. hæfern]

hǣferblǣte f? *bittern? snipe?* WW 116⁴¹; 361¹⁷.

hǣfergāt=hæfer

hǣfern m. *crab,* WW.

hǣfig=hefig; hǣfne=hæfen

hǣfreblēte=hæferblǣte; hǣfst v. habban.

±hǣft I. m. *bond, fetter* : *captive, slave, servant* : *bondage, imprisonment, affliction, Æ* : (±) *seizing, thing seized,* CLPs 123⁶. II. adj. *captive.* III. n. '*haft,*' *handle, Lcd, WW*; Æ. IV. pp. of hæftan.

±hǣftan *to bind, fetter* : *arrest, detain, imprison* : *condemn,* DR 197¹³. [*Ger.* heften]

hǣfte=hæft II.

hǣfteclomm m. *fetter,* †CHR 942 A.

+hǣftednes f. *captivity* : *snare,* Ps.

hǣftedōm m. *slavery, captivity,* MET 25⁶⁵.

hǣften f. *confinement,* CHR 1095.

+hǣftend m. *prisoner,* MFH 136.

hǣftenēod=hæftnīed

hæftincel (e²) n. *slave*, WW.

hæfting f. *fastening, lock*, Nic502²⁵.

hæftlic *captious*, OEG3208.

hæftling m. *prisoner, captive*, Æ.

hæftmēce m. *hilted sword*, B1457.

±hæftnes (RWH22²⁰, v. also MFH165)= hæftednes

hæftneð=hæftnoð

±hæftnian *to take prisoner : seize, detain*.

hæftnīed (ē, ȳ) f. *custody, imprisonment, bondage*. Æ,AO.

±hæftnīedan *to take captive*, GD135¹⁵.

hæftnīedling (ē², y²) m. *captive*, ÆL.

hæftnīednes (ē², ȳ²) f. *captivity*, GD346²², NC299.

hæftnoð (e²) m. *confinement, imprisonment*, Chr.

hæftnung f. *confinement, captivity*, Æ,Chr.

hæftnȳd (Æ)=hæftnīed

hæftung f. *fetter*, MFH166.

hæftworld f. *world under bondage*, Bl9⁴.

hæfð pres. 3 sg. of habban.

hæfuc=hafoc; hæg-=hago-, hagu-, hege-

+hæg n. *enclosure, meadow*, OEG; Mdf.

+hægan? *to vex, harass?* Ex169 (GK). or ?=+hnægan (BTs).

hæghāl *safe and sound*, DR.

hægsugga m. *hedge-sparrow*, ZDA33·241.

hæg-tes(se), -tis f. *fury, witch, pythoness*, Æ,Gl.

hægðorn (Æ)=haguðorn

hægweard m. *keeper of cattle in a common field*, LL452,20.

hæh-=hēah-; hæhtis=hægtes

hæl I. n. *omen*, B204,WW36². II.=hælu. III. adj.=hāl

hæl-; hæl-=hel-; hāl-, hēl-

hǣlan I. (±) *to 'heal,' cure, save*, Lcd,Mt,Ps; Æ,CP : *greet, salute*, GD36²⁷. +hæl! *Hosanna!* [hāl] II. *to castrate*, Lcd3·186²²: (+) ÆP106⁶.

+hæld=+hield

hælet† m. *man, hero*.

hæle n.=hælu

±hǣle *safe*, SPs7¹¹.

+hæled=hāl

+hǣlednes f. *healing*, GD247¹¹.

hǣlend (ē) m. *Saviour, Christ*, Æ,G. ['heal-end']

hǣlendlic *wholesome, salutary*, OEG153⁸.

hǣlet-=hālet-

hæleð† m. (nap. hæleðas, hæleð) *man, hero, fighter*, B. ['heleth']

hæleðhelm=heoloðhelm

hælf-ter, f. -tre, m. *'halter,'* WW.

hǣlgere (a²) m. *sanctifier*, DR.

hælhiht=healhiht

hǣlig *unstable, inconstant*, Bo115³.

hǣling f. *'healing,'* Nic.

hælm=healm

hǣlnes f. *salvation, safety*, CP : *sanctuary*. ['healness']

hǣlnesgrið n. *peace-privileges attaching to a sanctuary*, LL471,19.

hǣlotīd f. *prosperous time*, Chr1065d.

hǣls-=hāls-

hǣlð, hǣlðo f. *'health,'* Æ : *salvation*, Lcd; Æ : *healing*, Æ.

hǣlu f. *health*, Cr,Lcd : *prosperity*, MtL : *safety, salvation*, KC,Lk; Æ,CP : *healing, cure*. ['heal']

hǣlubearn† n. *Saviour, Christ*, Cr.

hǣlwyrt f. *'pulegium,' pennyroyal*, WW300²⁴.

hǣlynd=hǣlend

hǣmæht (MkR1²²)=hēahmiht

±hǣman *to have intercourse with, cohabit with*, Æ,CP : *marry*, MtR.

hǣmed (ē) n. (nap. hǣmedru) *cohabitation*, Æ,CP : *marriage : adultery, fornication*, WW420¹⁰.

hǣmedceorl m. *married man*, LL.

hǣmedgemāna m. *matrimony*, WW441²⁴.

hǣmedlāc n. *coition*, RD43³.

hǣmedrīm m. *'lenocinium,'* OEG5046. [=-drēam]

hǣmedru v. hǣmed.

hǣmedscipe m. *cohabitation, wedlock*, OEG.

hǣmedðing n. *coition, cohabitation*, ÆL : *marriage*.

hǣmedwīf n. *married woman*, WW450²⁴.

hǣmend m. *fornicator*, WW420¹³.

hǣmere m. *consort, bedfellow*, Æ.

hǣmet, hǣmeð=hǣmed; hæn=henn

hǣnan I. *to stone*, Jn; Æ. ['hene'] II.= hīenan

hænep (e) m. *'hemp,'* Lcd,WW.

hænfugel=hennfugol; hænn=henn

hǣnðu=hīenðo

+hæp, +hæplic (Gl) *fit, convenient*.

+hæplicnes (e) f. *convenience, opportunity*, OET122⁶.

hæppan? *to go by chance*, ÆL31⁴⁷⁷.

hæpse f. *'hasp,' fastening*, Æ.

hæpsian *to 'hasp,' fasten*, Æ.

hæpte (pret. 3 sg.) *jumped*, ÆL31⁴⁷⁷.

hǣr (ā, ē) n. *'hair,'* Lcd,Mk; Æ : *a hair*, Æ, Cp,Mk.

hǣr-=har-, hear-, her(e)-; hǣr-=hēr-

hǣre (ē) f. *sackcloth of hair*, Mt,VPs; Æ. ['haire']

+hǣre *hairy*, AA33³.

hǣren *of hair*, Bl,Lcd. ['hairen']

hǣrenfagol sb. *hedgehog*, SPs103¹⁹ (v. BTs).

hærfest (e) m. *autumn, 'harvest'-time*, Bf, Ct,WW; AO : *August*, A10·185. h. hand-ful *handful of corn (a due belonging to the husbandman on an estate)*, LL450.

hærfestlic *autumnal* : *of harvest*, Æ (108¹⁹⁸).

Hærfestmōnað m. *'harvest-month,' September*, ÆGr 43⁸.

hærfest-tīd (BH) f., -tīma (BF) m. *autumn, harvest-time*.

hærfestwǣta m. *autumn rain*, AO 102⁷.

hǣrgripa (ē) m. *seizing by the hair*, LL 611.

hǣriht *hairy*, WW 513⁸.

hǣring (ē) m. *'herring,' Gl,WW*; Æ.

hǣringtīma m. *herring season*, Ct.

hǣrloccas mp. *locks of hair*, HGl. [*'hairlock'*]

hærmberg (N)=hearmbeorg

hærn I. f. *wave, tide* : (†) *sea, ocean*. II. *brain*, CHR 1137.

hǣrnǣdl f. *curling-pin*, OEG 1200.

hærnflota m. *ship*, Gu 1307.

hærsceard n. *hare-lip*, LCD.

hǣrsyfe (ē) n. *'hair-sieve,' A* 9·264.

hǣs f. *'hest,' bidding, behest, command, Æ, Gen.* [hātan]

hæsel m. *'hazel' shrub, Gl,Lcd*; Æ; Mdf.

hæselhnutu (a¹) f. *'hazel-nut,' Gl,WW*.

hæselrǣw f. *a row of hazels*, EC 445¹⁹.

hæselwrīd m. *hazel-thicket*, KC 2·250′.

hǣsere m. *master, lord*, LkLR.

hæsl=hæsel

hæslen *of hazel*, Lcd. [*'hazelen'*]

hæsp=hæpse; **hæssuc**=hassuc

hæst† I. *violent, vehement.* adv. hæst-e, -līce. II. (ē) f. *violence, strife.*

hǣswalwe (WW 7²⁸)=sǣswealwe?

hæt m. *head-covering, 'hat,' Cp,AO*; Æ.

hǣt pres. 3 sg. of hātan.

±**hǣtan** (ā) tr. *to 'heat*,' *Lcd,Shr* : intr. *become hot*, Gl.

hǣtcole=hǣðcole

hǣte f. *heat*, Æ,AO. [hāt]

hæteru np. *garments, ÆH.* [*' hater'*]

hǣting f. *heating*, WW 281⁸.

hǣto=hǣtu; **hǣts** (ÆL 18³⁵⁰)=hǣgtes

hǣtst pres. 2 sg. of hātan.

hætt=hæt; **hǣtte**=hātte, v. hātan.

hættan=hettan

hættian I. (e) *to scalp*, LL 334,30⁵. II.= hatian

hǣtu (o², e²) f. *'heat,' warmth, Bl,Lcd,Mt, VPs*; Æ : *fervour, ardour, VHy.*

hǣð I. mn. *'heath,' untilled land, waste, Ex*; Mdf : *heather, Gl,Lcd.* II. f. (WW 317²⁴)= hǣða

hǣða m. *heat, hot weather* ÆL 14¹⁶⁸.

hǣðberie f. *whortleberry*, LCD.

hǣðcole f. *name of a plant*, WW.

hǣðen I. (ē) *'heathen,' heathenish, pagan, Æ,Bl,Ct*; AO,CP. II. m. *gentile, heathen man (especially of the Danes)*, Æ,Mk.

hǣðena m. *heathen*, LkR 21²⁵.

hǣðencyning m. *heathen king*, DA 54.

hǣðencynn n. *heathen race*, GEN 2546.

hǣðendōm m. *'heathendom,' false religion*, LL.

hǣðenfeoh n. *heathen sacrifice?* JUL 53.

hǣðenfolc n. *heathen people*, W 223¹².

hǣðengield (i³, y³) n. *idolatry*, Æ : *idol*, Æ.

hǣðengilda (y³) m. *idolater*, Æ.

hǣðenhere m. *Danish army*, CHR.

hǣðenisc *'heathenish,' pagan*, AO.

hǣðennes f. *heathenism, paganism, BH* : *heathen country*, OET 175⁷. [*' heathenesse'*]

hǣðenscipe (ē) m. *paganism, idolatry*, Æ, Chr. [*'heathenship'*]

hǣðenstyrc m. *heathen calf (the golden calf of the Israelites)*, PPs 105¹⁷.

hǣðfeld m. *heath-land*, Bo,Ct.

hǣðiht *heathy*, KC.

hǣðin-=hǣðen-

hǣðstapa† m. *heath-stalker, wolf, stag.* [stæppan]

hǣðung f. *heating, parching*, ÆH 1·286. [=hǣtung]

hǣwe *iron-coloured, bluish, grey*, GL.

hǣwen (ē) *blue, purple, azure, green*, Gl. [*' haw'*]

hǣwengrēne *cerulean*, WW 379²³.

hǣwenhydele f. *a plant*, LCD.

hafa, imperat. of habban; hafast, hafað= hæfst, hæfð pres. 2 and 3 sg. of habban.

-hafa v. wan-h ; **hafala**=hafela

hafastu=hafast ðu

hafecere=hafocere

hafela† (ea¹, o², u²) m. *head*, LCD.

hafelēst=hafenlēast

hafen pp. of hebban.

hafenian† *to hold, grasp.* [hebban]

hafenlēas *destitute, needy, poor*, Æ,WW. [*' haveless'*; hæfen]

hafenlēast f. *want, poverty*, ÆH.

hāfern=hæfern

hafetian (i²) *to clap, flap*, Æ.

hafoc (ea) m. *'hawk,' Gl,Wy.*

hafoccynn n. *hawk-tribe*, Æ.

hafocere m. *'hawker,' LL*; WW 235⁹,ÆP 140²⁴.

hafocfugel m. *hawk*, LL (162¹⁹).

hafocung f. *hawking*, BC 1·280′.

hafocwyrt f. *a plant*, LCD.

hafola=hafela; **-hafol(nes)** v. wan-h.

hafuc=hafoc

hafudland (WW 147¹⁸)=hēafodland

haga I. m. *hedge, enclosure, curtilage, WW* ; Mdf : *fortified enclosure, B* : *homestead, house, KC* 4·86′ : *game-enclosure?* GBG. [*' haw'*] II. m. *' haw,' WW* 204²⁰ : *trifle*, WW 138³⁹; 269⁵.

hagal=hagol

hagaðorn=haguðorn; **hage-**=hago-

+**hagian** (impers.) *to please, suit.* gif him (hine) tō ðǣm +hagige *if he can afford it.*

hago- v. also hæg-.

hagol (æ[1], e[1], a[2], e[2]) mn. '*hail*,' Æ,*Gen,Met, Ph,VPs* : *hail-shower, hailstorm,Bo* : *name of the rune for* h.

hagolfaru (hægl-) f. *hailstorm,* WA 105.

hagolian (a[2]) *to 'hail*,' AO 104[20].

hagolscūr (æ[1], e[2]) m. *hail-shower, An*; MEN 35. [v. '*hail*']

hagolstān m. '*hailstone*,' Æ.

hagorūn (ea) f. *spell,* NAR 50[14].

hagospind (ea) n. *cheek,* GL,LCD. [haga]

hagosteald I. (hæg-, heh-) *unmarried, independent:military* (of young men). **II.**m. *unmarried man attached to a court, bachelor, young man, young warrior, liege man.* [*Ger.* hagestolz] **III.** n. *celibacy,* RD 21[31]. **IV.** (heh-) *virgin,* LL,NG.

hagostealdhād (hægst-) m. *unmarried state,* NG.

hagostealdlic (heh-) *virgin,* DR 66[1].

hagostealdman (hægst-) m. *bachelor, warrior,* GL,RD.

hagostealdnes (heh-) f. *virginity,* Jnp 13.

hagu-=hago-

haguðorn (æ[1]) m. '*hawthorn*,' *whitethorn, Gl,Mt,Lcd.*

ha ha interj. '*ha! ha!*' ÆGr.

hal=heal; **hal-**=heal(h)-; **hāl-**=hǣl-

±**hāl** '*hale*,' '*whole*' ('*y-hole*'), *entire, uninjured, healthy, well, sound, safe, genuine, straightforward, Lcd,Mt*; Æ,CP. wes ðu h., h. westu, h. bēo ðu *hail!*

hala I. m. *after-birth,* LCD. [helan (IF 48·256)] **II.** (+) (o) m. *counsellor, confidant, supporter,* ÆL 23[290],WW 110[21].

hālbǣre *wholesome, salutary,* Sc 32[78].

halc (OET 489)=healh

hald-=heald-

hāleg, hāleg-=hālig, hālg-

±**hālettan** (ǣ) *to greet, hail, salute,* GD.

hālettend m. *middle finger* (*used in saluting*), WW.

hālettung f. *greeting, salutation,* BL.

hālfæst *pious? healthy?* RB 72[6].

hālga I. wk. form of adj. hālig. **II.** m. *saint,* Æ,Ct. ['*hallow*']

hālgawaras=hāligwaras

±**hālgian** *to '*hallow,*' sanctify,* Æ,Jn : *consecrate, dedicate, ordain, BH,Bl,Chr*; Æ : *reverence,* †Hy,Mt : *keep holy, Bl.*

+**hālgigend** m. *sanctifier,* DHy 64[2].

±**hālgung** (ǣ) f. '*hallowing,*' consecration, BH* : *sanctuary,* EPs 73[7].

hālgungbōc f. *benedictional,* NC 299.

hālgungram m. *consecrated ram,* Ex 29[22].

hāli-=hālig-

hālig '*holy*,' *consecrated, sacred, Bf,Lk* : *venerated, Æ,G,VPs* : *godly, saintly, CP, MkL* : *ecclesiastical* : *pacific, tame,* GEN 201. as sb. *what is holy, MtL.*

±**hāligan I.** *to heal up, get well,* CP : *save* : *be saved.* **II.**=hālgian

hāligdæg m. *holy day, Sabbath, MkL,LL.* ['*holiday*']

hāligdōm m. *holiness, righteousness, sanctity, Æ*; CP : *holy place, sanctuary, chapel, Æ* : *relics, holy things, LL* : *holy office,* CP 51[1] : *sacrament* : *holy doctrines,* CP 383[7]. ['*halidom*']

hāligdōmhūs m. '*sacrarium*,' CM 818.

hāligern n. *holy place,sanctuary* : *sacrament.*

hāliglīce *holily,* CHRD 117[4].

Hāligmōnað m. (*holy month*), *September,* MH.

hālignes f. '*holiness*,' *sanctity, religion, Bl, Ps*; Æ : *holy place, sanctuary, CP,W* : *holy thing, relic* : *sacred rites,* BH 136[24].

hāligportic m. *sanctuary,* CJVPs.

hālig-rift, -ryft, -reft n. *veil,* Æ.

hāligwæcca m. *vigil-keeper,* LL (224').

hāligwæter n. '*holy water*,' BH.

hālig-waras, -ware mp. *saints,* N.

hāligweorc n. *sanctuary,* APs 73[7].

halm=healm

hālnes f. '*wholeness*,' ANS.

hālor† n? *salvation,* JUL. [hǣl]

hālp=healp pret. 3 sg. of helpan.

hals-=heals-

hāls f. *salvation,* CR 587?

hālsere (ǣ) m. *soothsayer, augur,* Cp.

halsgang (WW 190[32])=healsgund

±**hālsian** (ǣ, ēa) *to adjure, Mt* : (+) *take oath, swear, Nic* : *call upon, VPs* : *convoke* : *implore, entreat, CP,OET* : *augur, WW* : *exorcise, LL.* [v. '*halse*' and healsian]

hālsi(g)end m. *exorcist, soothsayer, augur,* Æ.

halstān=healstān

hālsung f. *exorcism, LL, OET* : *augury, divination* : *entreaty,Bl,VPs.* [v.'*halsing*']

hālsunggebed n. *prayer in a church service,* RBL 39[6].

hālsungtīma m. *time of supplication,* CHRD 30[2].

hālswurðung f. *thanksgiving for safety,* Ex 581. [hāls]

halt=healt; **halð**=heald II.

hālwenda m. *Saviour, Æ* : *safety* RBL 12[13].

hālwende *healing, healthful, salutary, Æ,* CP : *sanctifying, Æ.*

hālwendlic *salutary, wholesome.* adv. -līce, Æ,CP.

hālwendnes f. *salubrity,* BH 28[30] : *salvation,* LPs.

hālwynde=hālwende
ham I. m? *under-garment* (*'subucula,'* OEG), *WW*. [*'hame'*] **II.**=hamm
hām I. m. ds. hām *village, hamlet, manor, estate, Æ,BH,Chr,LG* : *'home,' dwelling, house, BH,Ct,G,LL* : *region, country*, AO. **II.** adv. *'home,' homewards, Chr,Jn*; Æ. **III.** *'cauterium,'* A30·258; 33·390.
hama m. *covering, dress, garment* : *womb, 'puerperium,'* v. OEG : *slough of a snake*, NC299.
hāma m. *cricket*, WW.
hamacgian=āmagian? (or +m.)
hāmcūð *familiar*, MtKp11[1].
hāmcyme m. *home-coming, return*, Æ. [*'homecome'*]
hamel? *rugged*, KC.
hamela=hamola
hamele f. *rowlock* (only in phr. æt ǣlcre hamelan *for every oar*, i.e. *rower*, CHR 1039E). [ON. hamla; v. also hā]
hamelian *to hamstring, mutilate*, Chr. [*'hamble'*]
hamer=hamor; **-hamer** v. clod-h.
±hāmettan *to domicile*, Ct,LL : *bring debtors back to their home*, CHRD116[1].
hāmfærelt n. *going home*, AO146[21].
hāmfæst *resident, settled in or owning a house*, Æ.
hāmfaru f. *attack of an enemy in his house, housebreaking* : *fine for housebreaking*. [v. LL2·504]
hāmhenn f. *domestic fowl*, LCD92a.
+hāmian *to establish in a home*, JnL p188[7].
hamland (o[1]) n. *enclosed pasture*, EC208[11]. [hamm]
hāmlēas *homeless*, RD40[9].
hamm I. m. *piece of pasture-land, enclosure, dwelling, Ct*; ÆL; Mdf. [*'ham'*] **II.** f. *'ham'* (*part of leg*), *Lcd,WW*; Æ.
+hammen *patched?* (of shoes), GD37[13].
-hamod v. +fiðer-h.
hamola (o[1]) *man with cropped hair*. tō hamolan besciran *to shave the hair off* (*as insult*), LL68,35[3].
hamor (o[1], e[2]) m. *'hammer,' Jul,WW*.
hamorian (amer-) *to beat out, forge*, GPH 396.
hamorsecg m. *hammer-sedge*, LCD.
hamorwyrt f. *black hellebore, wall-pellitory*, Lcd1·374; WW300[22]. [*'hammerwort'*]
hāmscīr f. *aedileship*, GL.
-hāmscyld v. riht-h.
hāmsittende *living at home*, LL.
hāmsīð m. *return home*, HL10[273].
hāmsīðian *to return home*, WW118[18].
hāmsōcn f. *offence of attacking a man in his own house, LL* : *the franchise of holding pleas of this offence and receiving the penal-*

ties for it : *the penalty itself, Ct*. [*'hamesucken'*]
hāmsteall m. *homestead, Ct*. [*'homestall'*]
hāmstede m. *'homestead,' Ct*.
hamule (CHR1039E)=hamele
hamur=hamor
hāmweard *homewards, towards home, on the way home, Chr*; Æ,AO. [*'homeward'*]
hāmweardes adv. *'homewards,' Chr*.
hāmweorðung f. *ornament of a home*, B2998.
hāmwerd (Æ)=hāmweard
hāmwerod (eo[2], u[3]) n. *household*, BH191[22].
hāmwyrt f. *house-leek*, Lcd. [*'homewort'*]
hān I. f. (*boundary-*)*stone, BC*. [*'hone'*] **II.**?=hā
hana m. *cock*, Æ. [*Ger.* hahn]
hanasang m. *cock-crow*, MH4[16].
hancrēd (ǣ) m. *cock-crow*, Æ. [crāwan]
hancrēdtīd (o[1]) f. *time of cock-crow*, WW 413[35].
hand I. (o) f. (gds. handa) *'hand*[*]*,' Jn,VPs, WW*; Æ,AO,CP : *side* (*in defining position*), *Æ* : *power, control, possession, charge, Ps,RB* : *agency, Ps,VPs* : *person regarded as holder or receiver of something*. brād h. *palm*. on h. gān *to yield*. swīðre, winstre h. *right, left, hand*. on gehwæðere h. *on both sides*. on h. āgiefan, tō handa lǣtan *to hand over* (*to*). on handa sellan, *to give a pledge, promise, bargain*. tō handa healdan *hold* (*land*) *of another*. wel on h. *favourably*. **II.** adv. *exactly*, RBL.
handæx f. *'dextralis,'* a kind of axe, WW 221[22].
handbæftian (ea[2], a[3]) *to lament*, NG.
handbana† m. *slayer by hand*, B.
handbelle f. *'hand-bell,' Ct*.
handbōc f. *'handbook,' manual, Bf,LL,WW*.
handbona=handbana
handbred n. *palm of the hand, breadth of the hand, span*, WW158[11]; ÆL. [*'handbrede'*]
handclāð n. *towel*, Æ. [*'handcloth'*]
handcops m. *handcuff, manacle, CPs,WW*. [v. *'cops'*]
handcræft m. *manual skill, power of the hand, handicraft, Æ,LL*. [*'handcraft'*]
handcwyrn f. *hand-mill*, ANS,JUD16[21]. [cweorn]
handdǣda m. *doer with his own hand*, LL.
handele=handle
+handfæstan *to betroth*, RWH135[14].
handfæstnung (e[2]) f. *joining hands in confirmation of a pledge*, WW.
handfang-=infang-
handful nf. *'handful,' Ep,LPs*.
handgang m. *submission, surrender*, GL.
handgemaca m. *companion*, ÆL23[421].
handgemōt† n. *battle*, B

handgesceaft f. *handiwork*, GEN 455.

handgesella (o¹) m. *companion*, B 1481.

handgestealla† m. *companion*, B.

handgeswing n. *blow, stroke*, EL 115.

handgeweald n. *power, possession*, PPs 105³⁰.

handgeweorc n. '*handiwork*,' *creation*, Æ, Ps.

handgewinn n. *manual labour, work*, BH, HL : (†) *struggle, contest.*

handgewrit n. *handwriting, autograph, holograph, agreement, deed.*

handgewriðen *hand-woven*, B 1937. [wrīðan]

handgift f. *wedding present*, †Hy 10¹⁸.

handgong=handgang

handgripe m. '*hand-grip*,' B 965?

handgrið n. *security, peace, protection given by the king's hand*, LL (v. 2·494). ['*handgrith*']

handhabbend *red-handed (thief)*, LL 172,6. ['*handhabbend*']

handhæf n. *burden*, LkL 11⁴⁶.

handhamur m. '*hand-hammer*,' WW 448².

handhrægl n. *napkin, towel*, WW 127¹.

handhrine m. *touch*, AN 1022.

handhwīl f. *instant*, Æ. ['*handwhile*']

handle f. '*handle*,' Cp,WW.

handlēan† n. *requital, recompense.*

handleng(u) f. *a hand's length*, IM 124⁷⁴.

±handlian *to '*handle*,' feel*, Æ,Lcd : *deal with, discuss*, Bf 56,72.

handlīn n. *hand-cloth, napkin : maniple*, WW 124³⁴.

handlinga adv. *by hand*, ÆL 11²⁴⁷ : *hand to hand, at close quarters*, Æ. ['*handlings*']

handlocen† *joined together by hand*, B.

handlung f. '*handling*,' Æ.

handmægen† n. *bodily strength.*

handmitta=anmitta

handnægl m. *finger-nail*, LCD 125a.

handplega† m. *fight, battle.*

handprēost m. *domestic chaplain*, Æ.

handrǣs m. *onrush, attack*, B 2072.

handrōf *famed for strength*, Ex 247.

handscalu=handscolu

handscolu† f. *retinue*, B.

handscyldig *condemned to lose a hand*, LL 471,13¹.

handseald *given personally (by the king)*, LL 637,12.

handseax (e²) n. *dirk, dagger*, Æ,BH.

handselen '*mancipatio*,' WW 449²⁹.

handseten f. *signature, ratification*, Ct.

handsex=handseax; handslyht=andslyht

handsmæll m. *blow with the hand, 'alapa*,' JnLR 19³.

handspitel m. *hand-shovel, spade*, WW 241⁴⁵.

handsporu f. *claw, finger*, B 986.

handstoc n. *cuff, sleeve*, v. ES 38·352.

handswyle m. *swelling on the hand*, WW 205¹⁰.

handtam *submissive to handling*, ÆL 8⁸⁶ [v. '*hand-tame*']

handðegn m. *retainer, servant*, BH.

handðwēal n. *washing of the hands*, WW 146⁹.

handweorc n. *handiwork*, Rd,LL. ['*hand work*']

handworht *made with hands*, Mk 14⁵⁸.

handwundor n. *marvel of handiwork*, E 2768.

handwyrm (o) m. *a kind of insect*, Cp,WW. ['*handworm*']

handwyrst f. *wrist*, WW. ['*handwrist*']

-hanga v. līc-h.

+hange (o) *disposed, inclined to*, RIM 42.

hangelle f. *a hanging object, 'mentula*'? RD 45⁶.

hangen pp. of hōn.

hanglan (±) (intr.) *to '*hang*,*,' be hanged*, Æ, B,El,G; CP : *depend, rest on*, Æ : (tr.) *hang, suspend*, Æ,Chr,G,Lcd.

hangra m. '*hanger*,' *wooded slope*, KC; Mdf.

hangrǣd? (ES 39·348)=hancrēd

hangwīte? n. *penalty for miscarriage of justice*, EC. [v. '*hangwite*']

hār I. '*hoar*,' An : *hoary, grey, old*, B,Ct, Jud,Met,Wa. II.=hǣr

hara m. '*hare*,' Ep; Æ.

haranhige *hare's foot (plant)*, LCD.

haransprecel *viper's bugloss*, LCD 57b,WW 299⁶.

hāranwyrt=hārewyrt

harasteorra m. *dogstar*, WW 198³⁴.

haroð, harad m. *wood (only in placenames*, FTp 76)

hard=heard; hārehūne=hārhūne

hāre-wyrt, hāran- (LCD) f. *a plant, 'colocasia*,' WW 135⁵.

hārhūne f. *horehound*, LCD.

hārian *to become hoary or grey*, Æ,Shr. ['*hoar*']

hārnes f. *hoariness*, WW. ['*hoarness*']

hārung f. *hoariness, old age*, ÆGR 295¹⁴.

hārwelle, hārwenge (Æ) *hoary, grey-haired.*

hārwengnes f. *hoariness, old age*, WW 198³¹.

hās '*hoarse*,' ÆGr,WW.

hāsǣta m. *oarsman, rower*, CHR 1052 E. [hā]

hasewa=haswa wk. form of hasu.

hāshrīman (ȳ²) *to sound harshly*, GUTH 128¹²⁷.

hāsian *to be or become '*hoarse*,*'* ÆGr 190¹⁰.

hāslhnutu (WW)=hæselhnutu

hāsnes f. '*hoarseness*,' WW; Æ.

hassuc m. *coarse grass*, KC. ['*hassock*']

hāsswēge *sounding hoarsely*, GPH 391.

hasu† (ea) *dusky, grey, ashen.*

hasufāg grey, ashen, RD 12[1].
hasupād grey-coated, †CHR 937.
haswigfeōre grey-feathered, PH 153.
hāt I. '_hot_,' _flaming_, Gu,Lcd; Æ,AO,CP : _fervent, excited_, Bl : _intense, violent_, An, Gu,Ph : _inspiring? attractive?_ SEAF 64. II. n. _heat, fire._ III. (±) n. _promise, vow_, LkL; CP.
+**hata** m. _enemy, opponent_, WW 393[30].
±**hātan**[7] _active pret._ hē(h)t, hē(h)ton; _passive pret._ (origly. pres.) hātte (CP,Mt) _to command, direct, bid, order_, Æ,Ct : _summon_, Dan : _vow, promise_, Jul : (w. nom.=voc.) _name, call_, AO; CP : _be called_, CP,Gen,Mt; Æ. ['_hight_']
hāte adv. _hotly, fervidly_, Æ. ['_hot_']
hātheort (y²) I. n. _anger, rage._ II. (±) _wrathful, furious, passionate_, Æ,CP : _ardent, whole-hearted._ adv. -līce.
+**hātheortan**=hāthiertan
hātheorte f.=hātheort I.
hātheortnes f. _rage, mania_, Æ,CP : _zeal._
±**hāthiertan** (eo, i, y) _to be or become angry_, CP : _enrage._
hāthīge m. _anger_, PPs 89[7]. [hyge]
hāthort (KGL)=hātheort
±**hat-ian**, -igan _to ' hate,' treat as an enemy_, CP; Æ.
hātian _to be or get ' hot_,' VPs.
hatigend m. _enemy_, ÆGR 205[8].
hātigende _becoming hot_, LCD.
hatigendlic _hateful_, ÆL 3[605].
+**hātland** n. _promised land_, BH 346[8].
hātlīce _ardently_, Sc.
hātnes f. _heat_, ES 58·478.
hatol _hostile, bitter_, Æ,WW (KGl) : _odious._ ['_hatel_'; cp. hetol]
hātte v. hātan.
hattefagol sb. _hedgehog_, APs 103[8] (cp. hæren-f.).
hatung f. _hatred_, LPs; Æ. ['_hating_']
hātung f. _heating, inflammation_, LCD.
hātwende _hot, burning_, EX 74.
+**haðerian**=heaðorian
haðoliða m. _elbow_, LCD 99a (v. AB 29·253).
-**hāwe** v. earfoð-h.
hāwere m. _spectator_, CP 229[17].
±**hāwian** _to gaze on, view, look at, observe, notice_, Æ,CP.
hāwung f. _observation_, AS.
hē m., hēo f., hit n. (pers. pron.) 'HE*,' _she, it_; pl. _they_ : (reflex. pron.) _himself, herself, itself._
hēa I. np. and nsm. (wk.) of hēah adj. II.=hēah adv. III.=hīe, hī, nap. of hē.
hēa-=hēah-; **heador**=heaðor
hēador, hēadēor=hēahdēor
hēaf m. _lamentation, wailing_, AO. [=hēof]
hēafd-=hēafod-

hēafdian _to behead_, ÆL,MH.
+**hēafdod** _having a head_, WW 152[45]
hēafed=hēafod; **heafela**=hafela
hēaflan (Æ)=hēofian
hēaflic _sad, grievous_, BL 123[6].
heafo (B 2478) nap. of hæf.
heafoc=hafoc
hēafod n. gs. hēafdes '_head_,' Æ,JnR,VPs : _top_, OET : _source, origin : chief, leader_, CP, Chr : _capital (city)_, AO. hēafdes ðolian _to forfeit life._
hēafodæcer (afu) m. '_a strip of land an acre in extent, lying at the head of a field_' (BTs), KC,WW 147[19].
hēafodædre f. _cephalic vein_, LCD 95b.
hēafodbæð n. _a wash for the head_, LCD 57b.
hēafodbald (=ea³) _impudent_, WW 401[19].
hēafodbān n. _skull_, LCD.
hēafodbēag m. _crown_, Bo 112[23].
hēafodbend m. _diadem, crown : head-bond, fetter about the head_, Æ.
hēafodbeorg I. f. _helmet_, B 1030. II. m. _prominent hill?_ KC.
hēafodbeorht _with a splendid, shining head_, RD 20[2].
hēafodbiscop m. _high-priest_, ÆH 2·420[31].
hēafodbolla m. _skull_, NC 300.
hēafodbolster n. _pillow_, LCD,WW.
hēafodbotl n. _ancestral seat_, Ct.
hēafodburh f. _chief city_, Æ,AO.
hēafodclāð n. _head-cloth, head-dress_, WW; ÆL. ['_headcloth_']
hēafodcwide m. _important saying_, LL : _chapter_, DR.
hēafodcyrice f. _cathedral_, LL 282n19.
hēafodece m. '_headache_,' Lcd 7b; Æ.
hēafodfrætennes (e³) f. _hairpin, ornament for the hair_, WW.
hēafod-gemæcca, -gemaca (CP) m. _mate, companion, fellow-servant._
hēafodgerīm n. _number by heads, greatest number_, JUD 309.
hēafodgetel n. _cardinal number_, ÆGR 283[8].
hēafodgewǣde n. _face-covering, veil_, Æ,W.
hēafodgilt m. _deadly sin_, W : _capital offence_, LL 380,2.
hēafodgimm† m. _head's gem, eye_, AN.
hēafodgold n. _crown_, PPs,W.
hēafodhǣr n. _hair of the head_, WW.
hēafodhebba m. _beginning, starter_, BF 62[12] : _prime mover_, ÆL 23[365].
hēafodhrægl (u²) n. _an article of clothing or bedding_, RBL 93[3], Sc 74[2].
hēafodhrīefðo f. _scurfiness of the head_, LCD 85b.
hēafodiht (e³) _with a head or tuft_, LCD 86a.
hēafodleahter m. _capital crime, deadly sin_, Æ.
hēafodlēas '_headless_,' WW ; Æ.

hēafodlic *capital, deadly* (crime), *Bl* : *at the top*, WW : *principal*, AO. ['*headly*']

hēafodling (u²) m. *equal, fellow-servant, MtL.* ['*headling*']

hēafodloca m. *skull*, LCD.

hēafodlond n. *strip of land in a field, left for turning a plough, Ct*; WW. ['*headland*']

hēafod-mǣg†, -māga (AN) m. *near blood-relation.*

hēafodmægen n. *cardinal virtue*, ÆL 16³¹².

hēafodmann m. '*head-man*,' *captain*, WW; Æ.

hēafodmynster n. *church, cathedral*, LL.

hēafodpanne f. *skull, Mt.* ['*headpan*']

hēafodport m. *chief town*, CHR 1086.

hēafodrīce n. *empire*, AO 58³¹.

hēafodsār m. *pain in the head*, LCD.

hēafodsealf f. *head-salve*, LCD 130b.

hēafodsegn m? n? *banner*, B 2152 (v. eofor-h.).

hēafodsīen (ȳ³)† f. (*eyesight*), *eye*, GEN,WY.

hēafodslǣge (u²) m. *head of a pillar, architrave?* (BTs),WW 376¹⁵.

hēafodsmæl '*capitium*,' *part of a woman's dress*, WW 276¹⁸, 369¹⁹.

hēafodstede m. *chief place*, AO : *high place, sacred place*, LL 470,3⁵.

hēafodstocc m. *stake on which the head of a beheaded criminal was fixed*, Æ,KC.

hēafodstōl m. *capital*, AO 124,144.

hēafodstōw f. *place for the head*, BH 324³.

hēafodswīma m. *dizziness*, GEN 1568.

hēafodsȳn=hēafodsīen

hēafodsynn (ǣ¹) f. *deadly sin*, W 290²⁵.

hēafodðwēal n. *washing of the head*, WW 146⁸.

hēafodwærc m. *pain in the head*, Lcd ; WW. ['*headwark*']

hēafodweard I. f. *watch over the head, death-watch*, B 2909 : *body-guard*, LL 444,1. ['*headward*'] **II.** m. *chief protector, leader.* **III.** f. *chapter.*

hēafodweg m. *head-road* (v. BTs), Ct.

hēafodwind m. *chief wind* (*E, S, W or N wind*), LCD 3·274.

hēafodwīsa m. *chief, director*, GEN 1619.

hēafodwōð f. *voice*, RD 9³.

hēafodwund f. *wound in the head*, LL 20, 44.

hēafodwylm m. *tears*, EL 1133 : *burning pain in the head*, LCD 9b.

hēafodwyrhta m. *chief workman*, ÆH 2·530.

heafola=hafela; **hēafre**=hēahfore

hēafsang m. *dirge*, WW 430²². [hēofan]

heafu (B 1862) nap. of hæf.

heafuc (VPs)=hafoc; **hēafud**=hēafod

hēag=hēah; **heaga-**=hago-

hēage (Æ)=hēah adv.

heago-=hago-, hagu-; **hēagum** v. hēah.

hēah I. (ē) gsm. hēas, asm. hēan(n)e, gp. hēar(r)a, dp. hēagum, hēam, comp. hīerra (ē, ēah, īe, ȳ) ; sup. hīehst (ēa, ē, ȳ) 'HIGH,' *tall, lofty*, Æ : *high-class, exalted, sublime, illustrious, important, CP* : *proud, haughty* : *deep* : *right* (*hand*). **II.** adv. '*high*,' *aloft*, ÆGr.

hēahaltāre m. *high altar*, W.

hēahbeorg m. *mountain*, PPs 94⁴.

hēahbiscop m. *archbishop, pontiff, LL* : (*Jewish*) *high-priest*, HL 10⁴³⁰. [v. '*high*']

hēahbliss f. *exultation*, PPs 118¹¹¹.

hēahboda m. *archangel*, CR 295.

hēahburg f. *chief city* : (†) *town on a height.*

hēahcāsere m. *emperor*, †Hy 7⁶⁰.

hēahcleofa m. *principal chamber*, AA 6¹⁵.

hēah-clif n. nap. -cleofu *high cliff*, CR,W.

hēahcræft m. *high skill*, RD 36⁴.

hēahcræftiga m. *architect*, BH.

hēahcyning† m. *high king, B* : *God*. [v. '*high*']

hēahdēor n. *stag, deer*, CHR.

hēahdēorhund (hēador-) m. *deer-hound*, LL,TC.

hēahdēorhunta m. *stag-hunter*, Ct.

hēahdīacon m. *archdeacon*, BL,MH.

hēah-eald* superl. -yldest (CM 36) *excellent, distinguished.*

hēah-ealdor, -ealdormann m. *ruler, patrician.*

hēahengel m. *archangel*, Bf; Æ. [v. '*high*']

hēahfæder m. *God* : *patriarch, Bl* ; Æ,CP : (*church*) *father.* [v. '*high*']

hēahfæst *permanent, immutable*, WID 143.

hēahfæsten n. *fortified town, city*, DR,WW.

hēahflōd m. *deep water*, GEN : *high tide*, WW.

hēahfore f. '*heifer*,' Æ,BH,WW.

hēahfrēa† m. *high lord*, CR.

hēahfrēols m. *great festival*, LL 344,47.

hēahfrēolsdæg m. *great feast-day*, LL 252,25.

hēahfrēolstīd f. *great festival*, LL 252,22².

hēahfru (WW)=hēahfore

hēahfȳr n. *towering flame*, WH 22.

hēahgǣst m. *Holy Ghost*, CR 358.

hēahgealdor n. *charm*, PPs 57⁴.

hēahgerēfa m. *high sheriff, chief officer, proconsul, prefect*, Æ.

hēahgesamnung f. *chief synagogue*, Mk 5²².

hēahgesceaft f. *noble creature*, GEN 4.

hēahgesceap n. *fate*, B 3084.

hēahgestrēon† n. *rich treasure.*

hēahgetimbrad *high-built*, SAT 29.

hēahgetimbru† npl. *lofty edifice.*

hēahgeðōring n. *whelming flood*, RD 4²⁷.

hēahgeðungen=hēahðungen

hēahgeweorc† n. *excellent work.*

hēahgnornung f. *deep grief*, PPs 101¹⁸.

hēahgod m. *Most High, God, PPs* 56². ['*high God*']

hēahgræft *carved in bas-relief*, WW 348[9].
hēahhād m. *holy orders*, LL (334[6]).
hēahhæf? n. *deep sea*, Hu 25 (Sedgefield).
hēahhelm *loftily crested*, ZDA 33·238.
hēahheolode (ēh-) f. *elecampane*, LcD 28b.
hēahheort *proud*, Da 540.
hēahhlīð† n. *high hill*.
hēahhlūtor *very pure*, BH 348b[19].
hēahhwiolod (ē[1]) *having high wheels*, WW 140[32].
hēahhylte n. *a high-placed shrubbery*, Ct.
hēahhyrde m. *head abbot*, OEG 910.
hēahhyrne=ēaghyrne
hēahlǣce (ē[2]) m. *learned physician*, MH.
hēahland n. *mountainous country*, Ex 385.
hēahlārēow m. *head teacher*, WW.
hēahlēce=hēahlǣce
hēahleornere n. *high teacher, master*, OEG 910.
hēahlic=hēalic
hēahlufe f. *great love*, B1954.
hēahmægen n. *great force : power, virtue*, ÆL.
hēahmæsse f. *high mass*, CHR.
hēahmæssedæg m. *high mass day*, NC 300.
hēahmiht f. *high authority, great might*, PPs 150[2], VH 15 : *the Almighty*, VH 15.
hēahmōd† *high spirited, exultant : proud, haughty*.
hēahmōdnes f. *pride*, CP 301[1].
hēahmōr m. *high moor*, BHb 364[4].
hēahnama m. *most exalted name*, †Hy 7[18].
hēahnes (Æ)=hēanes; **hēahra** v. hēah.
hēahreced† n. *high building, temple*.
hēahrodor m. *high heaven*, GEN 151, ByH 124[28].
hēahrūn f. *pythoness*, WW 493[38].
hēahsācerd m. *high or chief priest*, G,HL.
hēahsǣ f. *high sea, the deep*, Met 166[3]. [v. 'sea']
hēahsǣl† f. *great happiness*, PPs.
hēahsǣðēof? m. *chief pirate*, WW.
hēahsangere m. *chief singer*, BH 314[3].
hēahsceaða m. *chief pirate*, OEG 8[228].
hēahscēawere (ē[1]) m. '*pontifex*,' DR 21[1].
hēahscīreman (ē[1]) m. '*procurator*,' DR 193[6].
hēahseld n.† *throne : rostrum*, WW.
hēahsele m. *high hall*, B647.
hēahsetl (ē) n. *exalted seat, throne, judgment-seat*, Æ,JnL. [v. 'settle']
hēahsittende *sitting on high*, A 8·368.
hēahsomnung (MkL; ē[1])=hēahgesamnung
hēahstēap *very high*, GEN 2839.
hēahstede m. *high place*, B 285.
hēahstefn† *having a high prow*.
hēahstrǣt m. *highway*, Ct. ['high street']
hēahstrengðu f. *strength*, PPs 107[7].
hēahsunne (ē[1]) adj. mp. *very sinful*, MkR 2[15].
hēahsynn f. *deadly sin, crime*, DR,LL.

hēahtīd f. *holy day*, LL. ['high tide']
hēahtimber m. *lofty building*, CRA 45.
hēahtorr m. *high mountain*, OEG 2035.
hēahtrēow f. *solemn compact*, Ex 388.
hēahðearf f. *great need*, PPs 117.
hēahðegen m. *chief officer, captain*, Æ : *apostle*, Æ : *angel*.
hēahðegnung f. *important function*, Ex 96.
hēahðēod (ē[1]) f. *great people*, GUTH.
hēahðrēa m. *great affliction*, GEN 2545.
hēah-ðrymm m., -ðrymnes† f. *great glory*.
hēahðu†=hīehðu
hēahðungen *of high rank, illustrious*, AO.
hēahweg m. *highway*, EC 130' (hēi-).
hēahwēofod n. *high altar*, WW 186[21].
hēahweorc=hēahgeweorc
hēahwita m. *high councillor*, CHR 1009.
hēahyldest v. hēaheald.
heal=(1) healh; (2)=heall
hēal (BL)=hāl; **hēal-**=hēl-
hēala m. *hydrocele*, CP 65[5].
healærn n. *hall-building*, B 78.
healc=healoc
heald I. n. *keeping, custody, guard, protection*, Chr 1036, KC : *observance, observation, watch : protector, guardian*. ['hold'; =hield] II. *sloping, inclined, bent*.
±healdan[7] (a) (tr. and intr.) *to 'hold*' ('i-hald'), *contain, hold fast, grasp, retain, possess, inhabit*, Æ,Chr; CP: *curb, restrain, compel, control, rule, reign*, Chr,CP : *keep, guard, preserve, foster, cherish, defend*, Æ, Bl,Mt,Ps; AO : *withhold, detain, lock up : maintain, uphold, support*, Æ,LL : *regard, observe, fulfil, do, practise*, Bl; Æ : *satisfy, pay : take care*, CP : *celebrate, hold (festival) : hold out* (intr.), *last : proceed, go : treat, behave to, bear oneself : keep in mind.* ongēan h. *resist*. tō handa h. *hold (land, etc.) of another.*
+**healddagas** mp. *kalends*, WW 176[27].
+**healde** *contented? careful?* v. MFH 162.
+**healden** f. *observance*, BHb 468[6].
healdend m. *protector, guardian, ruler, king, lord, God : economical person*, LcD 3·192[23].
+**healdendgeorn** (a[1]) *continent*, DR 45[10]?
+**healdfæst** *safe*, LCD.
healdiend m. *preserver*, CEPs 114[6].
healding (a) f. *keeping, observance*, VPs 118[9].
±**healdnes** f. *keeping, observance*, BH : *guard, watch*, APs 38[2] : *office of a bishop*, WW 400[9].
healdsum (hal-) *careful*, ANS 129·25.
+**healdsum** *provident, economical, frugal*, CP : *virtuous, chaste, continent*, ÆL : *safe.*
±**healdsumnes** f. *keeping, observance, devotion*, Æ : *custody, preservation : restraint, abstinence : continence, chastity.*
hēalēce (GL)=hēahlǣce

hēalede I. *suffering from hydrocele, ruptured,* CP72⁴. **II.**=hēlede

healf (a) I. adj. '*half,*' *Bf,Ct,Jud,Lcd*; Æ, AO. ŏridde h., etc.=*two and a half, etc.* [*Ger.* drittehalb] **II.** f. *half, Æ,G,Chr* : *side, Gl,Mt,Ct*; Æ,AO : *part,* CP.

healfbrocen *half-broken,* BH436⁶.

healfclǣmed *half-plastered,* HL17²⁶⁷.

healfclungen (a¹) *half-congealed,* Cp265s.

healfclypigende adj. *semi-vowel,* ÆGR.

healf-cwic, -cucu *half-dead,* AO,CP.

healfdēad *half-dead,* LCD.

healfeald (a¹) *half-grown,* LCD92a.

healffers *hemistich,* ZDA31·10.

healffēðe *lame,* GPH396.

healffrēo *half-free,* W171⁴E.

healfgemet '*diametra,*' ZDA31·10.

healfhār *somewhat hoary,* A8·449.

healfhēafod n. *front of the head,* ÆGR74⁵.

healfhrūh *half-rough,* WW152¹⁴.

healfhunding m. *cynocephalus,* AA33¹⁴, WE54¹¹.

healfhwīt *somewhat white,* WW163⁷.

healfhȳd *half a hide (of land),* LL460,7¹.

healfmann m. '*half-man,*' *ÆGr*27.

healfmarc *half a mark* (v. marc), Ct,LL.

healfnacod *half-naked,* AA15³.

healfpenigwurð n. *halfpenny-worth,* LL,W.

healfrēad *reddish,* WW149³⁵.

healfrūh *half-rough,* WW152²⁴.

healfscyldig *partially guilty,* ZDA31·23.

healfsester m. *half a* '*sester*' *(measure of bulk),* WW444⁴. [*L.* sextarius]

healfsinewealt *semicircular,* WW179²⁸.

healfslǣpende *half-asleep,* LV3; MH138¹.

healfsoden *half-cooked,* LCD,LL.

healfter=hælfter

healftryndel n. *hemisphere,* WW140⁷.

healfunga *to a certain extent, partially, imperfectly, Æ,CP.* ['*halfing*']

healfweg m. *half-way,* KC.

healfwudu m. *field-balm,* LCD44b.

healgamen m. *social enjoyment,* B1066.

healgian=halgian

healh m. (? n. at LHy6³¹) (nap. halas) *corner, nook, secret place, CP,Guth,WW : small hollow in a hill-side or slope,* Ct, (GBG). ['*hale*']

healhālgung (æa¹) f. '*ceremonia,*' WW180¹⁵.

healhihte *having many angles,* OEG121.

hēalic (ē) *high, elevated, exalted, lofty, sublime, Æ*; CP : *deep, profound, intense, Æ,* CP : *lordly, noble, great, illustrious, distinguished, notable, excellent, Æ*; CP : *proud, haughty :* *egregious, heinous,* W. adv. -līce *highly, aloft, Æ :* *in or to high position or rank, loftily, BH :* *intensely, very, Bl.* ['*highly*']

hēalicnes f. *sublimity, majesty, Æ.*

heall I. f. '*hall,*' *dwelling, house, B,Mt*; Æ, CP : *palace, temple, law-court.* **II.**=healh. **III.** *rock,* OEG4111.

heallic *palatial,* WW499²⁹.

heallrēaf n. *wall-tapestry,* TC530'.

heallreced n. *hall-building,* B68 (heal-).

heallsittend† m. *sitter-in-hall,* B (heal-).

heallðegn† m. *hall-officer,* B (heal-).

heallwāhrift n. *wall-tapestry,* TC530'.

heallwudu m. *woodwork of hall,* B (heal-).

healm I. (a, æ) m. '*haulm,*' *stalk, straw, stubble, Lcd,MtL,VPs* : '*culmen,*' *thatched roof? harvest-land?* (v. LL116,61; 3·79 and BTs). **II.**=helm

healmstrēaw n. *stubble,* SPs82¹⁴.

healoc, healc m. *cavity, sinuosity,* LCD.

healp pret. 3 sg. of helpan.

heals (a) m. *neck, Gen* : *prow of a ship.* ['*halse*']

hēals-=hāls-

healsbēag† m. *collar, necklace,* B.

healsbeorg f. *neck-armour,* OEG.

healsbōc f. *phylactery,* G. [hāls]

healsbrynige *corslet,* v. OEG2⁴¹⁸.

healsed (a¹; o²) mn. *head-cloth, NG* : *neck of a tunic,* WW514¹.

healseta m. *the neck of a tunic,* MH200¹.

healsfæst, *arrogant,* GEN2238.

healsfang n. *fine prescribed in substitution for capital and other punishments, preferential share of the* '*wergeld,*' LL (v. 2·489 and BTs). ['*halsfang*']

healsgang m. *neck-tumour,* WW190³².

healsgebedda f. *beloved bedfellow, wife,* B63.

healsgund (a¹) m. *neck-tumour,* LCD,WW.

healsian *to entreat earnestly, beseech, implore, CP*; AO. [v. also hālsian]

healsi(g)endlic (ā) *that may be intreated,* APs89¹³ : *imploring,* GD17²³. adv. -līce *importunately.*

healsleðer n. *reins,* OET522.

healsmǣgeð f. *beloved-maid,* GEN2155.

healsmyne m. *necklace, Æ* : *neck-ornament.* [mene]

healsōme f. *neck-tumour,* LCD132b.

healsrefeðer (a¹) f. *feathers of a pillow, down,* RD41⁸⁰. [cp. *OHG.* halsare '*cervical*']

heals-scod, -ed=healsed

healstān (a, e) m. *small cake,* WW.

healswærc m. *pain in the neck,* LCD113a.

healswriða m. *necklace,* RD5⁴.

healswyrt (a) f. *a plant, daffodil? Lcd,WW*; OEG. ['*halswort*']

healt (eo) '*halt,*' *limping, lame, AO.*

healt-=heald-

healtian (a) *to* '*halt,*' *limp, CP,VPs*; Æ : *hesitate,* ÆL18⁹⁸ : *fall away,* BH.

healðegn† m. *hall-officer*, B.
healwudu m. *woodwork of hall*, B 1317.
hēam v. hēah.
hēam-ol, -ul *miserly*, Cp.
hēamolscipe m. *miserliness*, NC 300.
hēan I. *lowly, despised, poor, mean, bare, abject*, B, VPs; Æ, AO. ['*hean*'] adv. hēane.
II. v. hēah. III. (±) *to raise, exalt, extol*, BH. [=*hīen, hȳn; '*high*']
hēanes f. '*highness*,' Bf (hēah-), CP : *something high, high place, height*, Mt(hēah-), VPs. *on* hēanissum *in the highest*, '*in excelsis*,' Æ : *excellence, sublimity*, CP : *high rank* : *deep place*, LkL 5[4].
hēanhād m. *difficulty*, WW 345[29], 488[4].
hēanlic *abject, poor*, AO. adv. -līce.
hēanmōd† *downcast, depressed, sad*.
hēannes I. (ē) f. *treading down*, NG. II.= hēanes
hēanspēdig *poor*, CRA 26.
hēap mf. (*of things*) '*heap*,' Cp, CP : *host, crowd, assembly, company, troop, band*, B, Bl; Æ, CP. *on* hēape *together*.
±hēapian *to* '*heap*' *up, collect, bring together, accumulate*, Lk.
hēapmǣlum adv. *by companies, in troops, flocks*, Æ, CP; AO. ['*heapmeal*']
hēapum adv. *in heaps, in troops*.
hēapung f. *heap*, BH. ['*heaping*']
hear- (N)=heor-
hēara=hēahra (v. hēah).
heard I. (a) '*hard*,' *harsh, severe, stern, cruel* (*things and persons*), B, Bl, Cr, Mt, Lcd : *strong, intense, vigorous, violent*, B, Bl : *hardy, bold*, B; AO : *resistant*, Bf 158[2]. II. n. *hard object*.
heardcwide m. *harsh speech, abuse* (or ? hearmcwide), CR 1444.
hearde adv. '*hard*,' *hardly, firmly, very severely, strictly, vehemently*, Æ : *exceedingly, greatly*, Æ : *painfully, grievously*.
heardecg I.† *sharp of edge*. II. f. *sword*, EL 758.
heard(ha)ra m. *a fish, mullet?* GL.
heardhēaw *chisel*, Cp 408 c.
heardheort *hard-hearted*, Æ : *stubborn*, Æ.
heardheortnes f. *hard-heartedness*, Æ, CP.
heardhicgende† *brave*, B.
±heardian *to be or become hard*, Lcd : *harden*, Lcd. ['*hard*']
hearding† m. *bold man, hero*.
heardlic *stern, severe, harsh, terrible* : *bold, warlike* : *excessive*. adv. -līce *harshly, resolutely, severely, sternly* : *stoutly, bravely*, Æ : *excessively* : *hardly* ('*paulatim*,' '*tractim*'), ES 42·174.
heardlicnes f. *austerity*, GUTH 70[15].
heardmōd *brave, bold, over-confident*, Æ : *obstinate*, ÆL 36[326].

heardmōdnes f. *obstinacy*, ÆH 1·252[18].
heardnebba m. *raven*, ÆH 2·144[15].
heardnes f. '*hardness*,' Ep, Mt, Lcd, RB.
heardra (OEG)=heardhara
heardrǣd *firm, constant*, GEN 2348.
heardsǣlig *unfortunate, unhappy*, Bo.
heardsǣlnes f. *calamity*, AO 104[17].
heardsǣlð f. *hard lot, calamity, unhappiness*, AO : *misconduct, wickedness*, CP.
heardung f. *hardening*, LCD.
heardwendlīce *strictly*, BH 365[15].
hearg, hearga (æ, e) m. *temple, altar, sanctuary, idol*, AO, CP : *grove*, Az 110.
heargeard (herh-) m. *dwelling in the woods*, WIF 15.
hearglic (h) *idolatrous*, WW 236[2].
heargtræf (æ[1]) n. *idol-temple*, B 175.
heargweard m. *temple-warden, priest* (herig-), AN 1126.
hearh=hearg
hearm (e) I. m. *damage*, '*harm*,' *injury, evil, affliction*, B, Chr, Gen; Æ, CP : *grief, pain*, Gen : *insult, calumny*. II. adj. *harmful, malignant, evil*.
hēarm=hrēam
hearma m. *mouse? weasel?* OET ('*mygale*,' Ep, Erf; '*netila*,' Cp). [OHG. harmo]
hearmascinnen *made of ermine*, CHR 1075 D.
hearmberg (æ) m. *mound of calamity*, FM 373, RUNE CASKET.
hearmcwalu f. *great suffering*, CR 1609.
hearmcweodelian (VPs)=hearmcwidolian
hearmcweðan[5] *to speak evil of, revile*, NG.
hearmcweðend (e[1]) m. *slanderer*, JPs 71[4].
hearmcwiddian (y[2]) *to calumniate*, Bo, LPs 118[22].
hearmcwide† m. *calumny, blasphemy* : *heavy sentence, curse*.
hearmcwidol *evil-speaking, slanderous*, Æ.
hearmcwidolian (eo[2], e[3]) *to speak evil, slander*, ARSPs 118[122].
hearmcwidolnes f. *slander*, EPs 118[134].
hearmdæg m. *day of grief*, B 3153.
hearmedwīt n. *grievous reproach*, PPs 68[21].
hearmful *hurtful, noxious*, OEG 46[13].
-hearmgeorn v. un-h.
hearmheortnes f. *complaint*, WW 511[16].
hearmian *to* '*harm*,' *injure*, Æ, Rood.
hearmlēoð† n. *elegy, lamentation*.
hearmlic *harmful, grievous*, Æ.
hearmloca† m. *prison* : *hell*.
hearmplega m. *fight, strife*, GEN 1898.
hearmscaða m. *terrible enemy*, B 766.
hearmscearu† f. *affliction, punishment, penalty*, GEN. [*sceran*]
hearmslege m. *grievous blow*, CR 1435.
hearmsprǣc f. *calumny*, WW 198[3].
hearmstæf† m. *harm, sorrow, tribulation*.
hearmtān m. *shoot of sorrow*, GEN 992.

hearpe (æ) f. 'harp,' Æ,VPs; CP.
hearpenægel m. plectrum, ApT17⁷.
hearpere (a) m. 'harper,' Bo,Ln; Æ,CP.
hearpestre f. (female) harper, WW190⁶.
hearpestreng m. 'harp-string,' ApT17⁸.
hearplan to 'harp,' Bo; Æ.
hearpnægel (WW)=hearpenægel
hearpsang m. psalm, WW129⁴⁰.
hearpslege m. plectrum (instrument for striking the harp), OEG : harp-playing.
hearpswēg m. sound of the harp, BLPs150³.
hearpung f. 'harping,' Bo.
hearra I.† (æ, e, ie, eo) m. lord, master, Chr, Gen. ['her'] II.=heorr
hēarra=hēahra (v. hēah).
hearstepanne=hierstepanne
hēarsum=hiersum
heart (NG)=heord, heorot
-hearwa v. Sigel-h.; hēas v. hēah.
heascan=hyscan; heasu=hasu
heaðo-=heaðu- (=war)
heaðor n. restraint, confinement, RD.
±heaðorian (e²) to shut in, restrain, control.
hēaðrym=hēahðrymm
heaðubyrne† f. war-corslet.
heaðudēor† bold, brave, B.
heaðufremmende fighting, EL130.
heaðufȳr† n. cruel fire, B.
heaðugeong young in war, FIN2.
heaðuglemm m. wound got in battle, RD 57³.
heaðugrim† fierce.
heaðulāc† n. battle-play, battle, B.
heaðulind f. linden-wood shield, †CHR937.
hēaðulīðende† m. seafaring warrior, B.
heaðumǣre famed in battle, B2802.
heaðurǣs† m. onrush, attack, B.
heaðurēaf n. war-gear, B401.
heaðurinc† m. warrior.
heaðuröf† famed in war, brave.
heaðusceard? dinted in war, B2830? (or ? heaðuscearp battle-sharp).
heaðusēoc wounded, B2754.
heaðusigel m. sun, RD72¹⁶.
heaðustēap† towering in battle, B.
heaðuswāt† m. blood of battle, B.
heaðusweng m. battle-stroke, B2581.
heaðutorht clear as a battle-cry, B2553.
heaðuwǣd f. armour, B39.
heaðuweorc n. battle-deed, B2892.
heaðuwērig weary from fighting, WALD2¹⁷.
heaðuwylm† (æ³, e³) m. fierce flame.
hēaum=hēagum dp. of hēah.
+hēaw n. gnashing, grinding, HL,SAT.
hēaw-=hēw- (hēawi, Cp303c=hēwen).
±hēawan⁷ to 'HEW*,' hack, strike, cleave, cut, cut down, kill : make by hewing, LL. æftan h. to slander, W160⁴.
heawen (K)=heofon

-hēawere v. hrīðer-, wudu-h.
-hebba v. hēafod-h.
±hebban⁶ (æ) pres. 3 sg. hōf, pl. hōfon, pp. hafen (hæfen) (wk. forms in LWS, pret. hefde, pp. hefod) to 'heave*,' raise, lift, lift up, exalt, Æ,B,Bl,Ps; CP : intr. rise, W100³.
hebbe=hæbbe (v. habban).
-hebbe, -hebbing v. ūp-h.
hebbendlic exalted, DR181¹⁴.
hebeld=hefeld; heben=heofon
heber=hæfer; hebuc=hafoc
hecc=hæc; heced=hacod
hēcen (y²) n. kid, BF134¹⁷,ES35·332.
hecg, hecge f. enclosure, hedge.
hecga-spind, -swind=hagospind
±hēdan I. (w. g.) to 'heed,' observe, B,LL; Æ : care for, guard, protect, take charge of, LL : obtain, receive, take, Æ. II.=hȳdan
hēddern (ȳ) n. storehouse, storeroom, BH,GL.
hēde pret. 3 sg. of hēgan.
hedeclāð m. a coarse, thick, upper garment like a chasuble, LOD1·346¹⁷.
heden m. robe, hood, chasuble, LL.
hedendlic captious, OEG3208. adv. -līce, WW199¹.
hef-=heof-
hefaldian=hefeldian
hefde I. (VPs)=hæfde pret. 3 sg. of habban.
II. v. hebban.
hefe I. (æ) m. weight, burden, Æ : 'mina, talentum,' GPH396. II.=hæfe
+hefed weighed down, WW251¹⁶.
hefeful severe, RB49¹⁸.
hefeg=hefig
hefeld n. thread (for weaving), Gl. [v. 'heald']
±hefeldian (a²) to fix the weft, begin the web, GL.
hefeldðrǣd m. thread (for weaving), Gl,Lcd. [v. 'heald']
hefelgyrd (e³) f. weaver's shuttle, GL.
hefe-lic, -līce=hefig-lic, -līce
hefen I. (æ) f. burden, RB49¹³. II.=heofon
hefetīme=hefigtime
hefeð pres. 3 sg. of hebban.
hefgian=hefigian
hefig (æ) 'heavy,' Met,Mt : important, grave, severe, serious, Bf,Bl,Mt,Chr : oppressive, grievous, Ps,LL : slow, dull. [hebban] adv. hefige, Ps.
±hefigian to make heavy, VPs : weigh down, oppress, afflict, grieve, BH,CP,Mt : aggravate, increase : become heavy, depressed, weakened, CP,Gu. ['heavy']
hefiglic heavy, weighty, serious, severe, burdensome, grievous, sad, Æ. adv. -līce, violently, intensely, CP,Lk : sorrowfully, Gen : sluggishly, Mt. ['heavily']

hefigmōd *oppressive,* ERPs54[4] : *heavy-hearted,* NC300.

hefignes (æ) f. '*heaviness,*' *weight, burden, affliction, MtL*; CP : *dulness, torpor, Bo.*

hefigtȳme (ī³) *heavy, grievous, severe, troublesome, oppressive,* Æ. [tēam]

hefigtȳmnes f. *trouble,* Æ.

hefod wk. pp., hefð pres. 3 sg. of hebban.

hefon=heofon; **heft-**=hæft-

hefug=hefigu pl. of hefig, CP285¹.

heg-=hege-; **hēg**=hīeg

±**hēgan**† *to perform, achieve* : *hold (a meeting),* An : *exalt, worship,* Da207⁷.

hegdig=hygdig

hege (ea) m. '*hedge,*' *fence,* Æ,Ct,Gl. ['*hay*']

hegeclife f. *hedge-clivers,* Lcd 20a.

hegegian=hegian

hegehymele f. *hop-plant,* WW302⁵.

hegel (VPs)=hægl, hagol

hegerǣw (e³) f. '*hedgerow,*' KC.

hegerife f. *cleavers, goose grass, Lcd.* ['*hairif*']

hegesāhl m. *hedge-stake,* GD24²⁸. [sagol]

hegessugge *hedge-sparrow,* WW131³⁴. [sucga; '*haysugge*']

hege-steall m. -stōw f. *place with a hedge,* KC.

hegewege m. *road between hedges,* KC.

hegge f. (BC,Chr)=hege

±**hegian** *to fence in, hedge, enclose, Sc.* grep h. *to cut a grip,* LL455,13. ['*hay*']

hēgnes=hēanes

hegstæf m. *bar to stop an opening in a fence* (BTs),WW205³¹.

hegstald-=hægsteald-

hēh (VPs, N), hēh-=hēah, hēah- +**hēhan** (VHy)=hēan III.

hē hē indicates laughter, ÆGr. ['*he*']

hēhst pres. 2 sg. of hōn.

hehstald=hagosteald

hēht pret. 3 sg. of hātan.

hēhðu=hīehðu; +**heige** (KGl83⁴⁰)=+hæg

hēlsta=hēhsta (v. hēah).

hēlweg=hēahweg

hel=hell, helle-

hēla (ǣ) m. '*heel,*' Gl,JnL,Lcd,OET,WW.

hēla-=hāle-

hēlade (ēa¹) *having large heels,* WW.

±**helan⁴** *to conceal, cover, hide, AO,VPs,* Æ (pp.); CP. ['*hele*']

hēlan I. (oe) *to calumniate,* MtR5⁴⁴. **II.**= hǣlan I.

held=hield

helde I. f. *tansy, Lcd,WW*; Æ. ['*helde*'] **II.**=hyldo

hele f. *subterfuge,* LL(320¹⁷). or ?=hāl (BTs). ['*hele*']

hele-=helle-, ele-

hēlend=hǣlend

helerung=heolorung; **heleð**=hæleð

helf-=healf-, hielf-

helfan *to halve,* Cp303b? (herbid).

helgod=hellgod; **helhrūne**=hellerūne

±**helian** *to conceal, cover, hide,* Æ,LL. ['*hele*']

hēlic, hēlīce=hēahlic, hēalīce

hell (y) f. *Hades,* Æ,VPs : '*hell,*' *place of torment, Gehenna, Bo,RB*; Æ,AO,CP. [helan]

hell- v. also helle-.

hellbend mf. *bond of hell,* B3072.

hellcniht m. *devil, demon,* ÆL3³⁷².

hellcræft m. *hellish power,* An1104.

hellcund *of hell,* W254¹⁵.

hellcwalu f. *pains of hell,* Cb1190.

helldor† n. *gate of hell, Gu.* [v. '*hell*']

helle m. *hell,* WW.

hellebealu n. *hell-bale,* Cr1427.

hellebrōga m. *terror of hell,* LPs,VH.

hellebryne m. *hell-fire,* Jud,W.

hellecǣgan pl. *keys of hell,* MFH128.

helleceafl m. *jaws of hell,* An1702.

hellecinn n. *hellish race,* Cr1620.

helleclamm m. *hell-bond,* Gen373.

helledēofol† mn. *devil.*

helle-dor n., -duru f. *gate of hell.*

helleflōr m. *floor of hell, courts of hell,* Sat70.

hellefȳr n. *hell-fire,* GD.

hellegāst† (ǣ³) m. *spirit of hell,* B.

hellegeat n. *gate of hell,* ÆH1·288, MP 1·610.

hellegrund† m. *abyss of hell,* VH.

hellegrut m. *pit of hell,* OEG689.

hellegryre m. *horror of hell,* Sat433.

hellehæft(a), -hæftling† m. *prisoner of hell, devil.*

hellehēaf m. *wailings or howlings of hell,* Gen38.

hellehinca m. *hell-limper, devil,* An1173. [cp. Ger. hinken]

hellehund m. *hell-hound,* KC3·350¹⁸.

hellehūs n. *hell-house,* Gu649.

hellelic=hellic

helleloc n. *hell-prison,* GD325³⁰.

hellemægen n. *troop of hell,* MFH166,VH.

hellemere m. *Stygian lake,* WW.

hellenīð m. *torments of hell,* Gen775.

hellerūne f. *pythoness, sorceress, Æ : demon,* B163.

hellescealc m. *devil,* Sat133.

hellesceaða=hellsceaða

hellesēað m. *pit of hell.*

hellestōw f. *infernal region,* GD332⁹.

hellesūsl n. *hell-torment,* Æ.

helletintreg *hell-torment,* MFH128¹⁹,VH.

helletintrega m. *hell-torment,* VH16.

helleðegn (hel-)† m. *devil.*

hellewīte n. *hell-pains, torment,* Æ,CP.

hellewītebrōga m. *horror of hell-torment,* W 151²⁴.

hellfiren f. *hellish crime,* PART 6.

hellfūs† *bound for hell.*

hellgeðwing n. *confinement in hell,* GEN 696.

hellgod n. *god of the lower world,* Bo,WW.

hellheort *terrified,* NC 301.

hellheoðo f. *vault of hell, hell,* SAT 700 (or ? two words).

hellic *of hell, hellish,* Æ. ['*hellick*']

hellsceaða m. *hell-foe, devil : grave.*

hell-træf, nap. -trafu n.· *devil's temple,* AN 1693.

helltrega m. *hell-torture,* GEN 73.

hell-waran, -ware mp., -waru fp. *dwellers in hell,* Æ. [v. '*hell*']

hellwendlic (helw-) *infernal,* WW 437³¹.

hellwerod n. *host of hell,* W 25²¹.

hellwiht (hel-) fn. *devil,* W 186².

helm I. m. *protection, defence, covering, crown,* Æ,Rd : *summit, top (of trees),* Æ, Bo,WW; CP : *helmet,* Cp,WW : (†) *protector, lord.* ['*helm*'] II. (WW 279¹⁴)=elm

helma m. '*helm,*' *rudder,* Bo,Cp,WW; Æ.

helm-bǣre, -berende *leafy,* WW. [v. '*helm*']

helmberend m.† *helmeted warrior,* B.

±**helmian** (y) *to cover, crown,* An : *provide with a helmet,* ÆGr. ['*helm*'; '*i-helmed*']

-**helmig** v. lēaf-h.

helmiht *leafy,* WW 395⁵; 493²⁸.

helmweard (holm-) m. *pilot,* AN 359.

hēlo=hǣlu; **helor**=heolor

help (y) fm. '*help,*' *succour, aid,* AO,B,Bl.

±**helpan³** (w. g. or d.) *to* '*help**,' *support, succour,* Æ,CP,Ct,G,LL,Ps : *benefit, do good to,* Lcd(intr.),LL : *cure, amend, Mk.*

helpe f.=help

helpend m. *helper, Bl.* ['*helpend*']

helpendlic adj. *to be liberated,* GPH 402.

helpendrāp m. *helping-rope,* WW 463³⁵.

helrūn=hellerune

helrūna m. *hellish monster,* B 163.

helrȳnegu f. *sorceress, witch,* WW 472¹¹.

hēlspure f. *heel,* VPs.

helt I.=hilt. II. pres. 3 sg. of heldan. III. (KGL)=hielt pres. 3 sg. of healdan.

helto-=hielto-

helðegn=helleðegn; **helur**=heolor

helustr (Ep,Erf)=heolstor

hem m. '*hem,*' *border,* WW 125¹³.

+**hēme**? *customary,* AS 33¹³n.

hemed (BC 2·522′) v. hemman.

hēmed, hēmeð=hǣmed

hemeðe n. *under-garment,* OEG 3725. [*Ger.* hemd]

hemlic (Æ)=hymlic

hemman? *to stop up, close* (GK),PPs 106⁴². [*MHG.* hemmen]

hemming (i) m. *shoe of undressed leather,* WW 468³¹. ['*hemming*']

hen=henn; **hēn**=hēan; **hēn-**=hīen- **hēnan**=hīenan

+**hendan** *to hold,* PPs 138⁸ : *seize, catch,* LPs 58¹³. [hand]

+**hende** *near, at hand,* Æ,Mk : *convenient,* AO. adv. *near, at home,* Æ : *closely, in detail,* BF 72²². ['*hend*']

-**hendig** v. list-h.

+**hendnes** f. *neighbourhood, proximity,* Æ.

henep=hænep

heng pret. 3 sg. of hōn.

hengeclif n. *overhanging cliff,* WW 180⁴.

hengen f. *hanging,* Æ : *cross,* Æ : *rack, torture,* Æ : *imprisonment.*

hengenwītnung f. *imprisonment,* LL 471,16.

hengest, hengst m. *stallion, steed, horse, gelding,* Ct,WW; Æ. ['*hengest*']

hengetrēow (enge-) n. *gallows,* GPH 395.

hengwīte n. *fine for not detaining an offender,* LL 496,4.

henn (æ) f. '*hen,*' Bf,Mt,Lcd.

henna m. *fowl,* LL (220¹³).

henneæg n. *hen's egg,* LCD.

hennebelle (æ) f. *henbane,* Lcd,WW. ['*henbell*']

hennebroð n. *chicken broth,* LCD.

hennfugol m. *hen,* Ct.

hēnnis (LG)=hīennes

hentan *to pursue, attack,* LL; Æ : (±) *appropriate, seize, Chr.* ['*hent*'; '*i-hente*']

hēo I. nasf. and nap. of pron. 3 pers. '*she,*' *they.* II.†=hīw

hēodæg adv. *to-day,* GEN 661. [*Ger.* heute]

hēof I. m. *wailing, mourning, grief,* Æ,AO. II. str. pret. 3 sg. of hēofan.

hēofan⁷? (pret. hēof, hōf, hēofon) *to lament,* CP.

heofan, heofen=heofon

hēofendlic *dismal, mournful,* WW. adv. -līce.

hēof-ian, -igian *to lament,* Æ.

heofig-=hefig-

hēofigendlic *lamenting,* A 10·146; 188.

hēofod=hēafod; **heofog** (BL)=hefig

heofon (e¹, a², e², u²) mf. (often in pl.) *sky, firmament,* Æ,Bo,Chr,Met,VPs : '*heaven,*' Æ,G : *the power of heaven,* Mt,Lk.

hēofon I. f. *lamentation?* Ex 46. II. str. pret. pl. of hēofan.

heofonbēacen n. *sign in the sky,* Ex 107.

heofonbeorht† *heavenly bright.*

heofonbig(g)ende *chaste,* DHy. [*ON.* byggja]

heofonbȳme f. *heavenly trumpet,* CR 949.

heofoncandel† f. *sun, moon, stars.*

heofoncenned *heaven-born,* DHy 108⁴.

heofoncolu npl. *heat of the sun*, Ex71.
heofoncund *celestial, heavenly*, CP.
heofoncundlic *heavenly*, W.
heofoncyning m. *king of heaven, Christ*, Bl
201. ['*heavenking*']
heofondēma m. *heavenly ruler*, Sat658.
hēofondlīce=hēofendlīce
heofondrēam† m. *joy of heaven*.
heofonduguð f. *heavenly host*, Cr1655.
heofone (Æ,W)=heofon
heofonengel m.† *angel of heaven*, Cr.
heofonflēogende *flying*, JPs103¹².
heofonflōd m. *torrent (of rain)*, BH236¹⁷.
heofonfugol† m. *fowl of the air*, Gen.
heofonfȳr n. *fire from heaven, lightning*, W
262¹⁵.
heofonhæbbend m. *possessor of heaven*,
WW385²¹.
heofonhālig *holy and heavenly*, An728.
heofonhām† m. *heavenly home*, PPs.
heofonhēah *reaching to heaven*, Da553.
['*heavenhigh*']
heofonheall f. *heavenly hall*, LL (382¹⁰). [v.
'*heaven*']
heofonhlāf m. *bread of heaven, manna*, PPs
104³⁵.
heofonhrōf m. †*vault of heaven, heaven*, Ph:
roof, ceiling. WW432⁸? [v. '*heaven*']
heofonhwealf† f. *vault of heaven*, An.
heofonhyrst f. *ornament of the heavens*,
Gen2189.
heofonisc (e²) *heavenly*, AO1⁶.
heofonlēoht n. *heavenly light*, An976.
heofonlēoma m. *heavenly light*, An840.
heofonlic '*heavenly*,' *celestial*, Bl,Lk; CP :
chaste, ÆGr66³,WW203²¹. adv. -līce,
ÆGr239⁷,WW375²².
heofonmægen† n. *heavenly force*.
heofonrīce n. *kingdom of heaven*, Bl,Cr; AO.
['*heavenric*']
heofonsetl n. *throne of heaven*, DD277.
heofonsteorra† m. *star of heaven*.
heofonstōl m. *throne of heaven*, Gen8.
heofontimber n. *heavenly structure*, Gen
146.
heofontorht† *very bright, glorious*.
heofontungol† n. *heavenly luminary*, VH
16.
heofonðrēat m. *heavenly company*, Sat222.
heofonðrymm m. *heavenly glory*, An.
heofon-ware, -waran mp., -waru fp. *inhabitants of heaven*, Æ. ['*heavenware*']
heofonwealdend (e²) *the God (ruler) of
heaven*, OEG23¹⁰.
heofonweard† m. *heaven's keeper, God*, Gen.
heofonwerod n. *heavenly host*, W.
heofonwlitig *divinely fair*, NC301.
heofonwolcen† n. *cloud of heaven*, VH16.
heofonwōma† m. *terrible noise from heaven*.

heofonwuldor n. *heavenly glory*, †Hy6¹².
hēofsīð m. *lamentable state*, Rim43? [hēof]
heofun=heofon
hēofung f. *lamentation, mourning*, Æ.
hēofungdæg m. *day of mourning*, Æ.
hēofungtīd f. *time of mourning*, Æ.
heolan=helan
heolca m. *hoar-frost*, LPs118⁸³.
heold pret. 3 sg. of healdan.
heoldan=healdan
heolfor† n. *gore, blood*, An,B.
heolfrig† *gory, bloody*, Jud.
heolor (e¹, e², u²) f. *scales, balance*, Gl.
heolorbledu (e¹, u²) f. *scale of a balance*,
WW427³⁵.
heolorian *to weigh, ponder*, Gl.
heolorung (e¹, e²) f. '*momentum*,' *the turning
of a scale*, WW450¹².
heoloðcynn n. *denizens of hell*, Cr1542.
-heoloðe v. hēah-h, hind-h.
heoloðhelm† (æ) m. *helmet which makes the
wearer invisible*.
heolp=healp; **heolr**-=heolor-
heolstor (e²) **I.** m. *darkness, concealment,
cover, hiding-place, retreat*. [helan] **II.**
adj. *dark, shadowy*, Æ.
heolstorcofa m. *dark chamber, grave*, Ph49.
heolstorhof n. *hell*, El764.
heolstorloca† m. *prison, cell*, An.
heolstor-sceado (Gen103) f., -scuwa (An
1255) m. *concealing shade, darkness*.
heolstrig *shadowy, obscure*, WW.
heolstrung ? f. *darkness*, DR182¹⁷.
heolt=healt
heom dp. of hē, hēo, hit.
heona (LkL) heonan VPs; heonane (Gen)=
heonon(e)
heono (NG)=heonu
heonon(e) (a²) *hence, from here, away*,
Mt : *from now*. h. forð *henceforth*. ['*hen*']
heononsīð m. *departure, death*, Dom86.
heononweard *transient*, Bl,Gen.
heonu (an(n)a, āne, eno, (he)ono) *if, but,
therefore, moreover, whether*, ANS91·205 :
lo! behold! NG.
heonun (Mt)=heonon
hēop (LPs67¹⁴)=hēap
hēopa m. *bramble*, LkL20³⁷.
hēopbrēmel (ȳ²) m. *dog-rose, bramble*, Lcd.
[v.'*hip*']
hēope f. '*hip*,' *seed-vessel of wild-rose*, Cp,
Lcd,WW; Æ : *bush, brier*.
heor=heorr
heora gp. of hē, hēo, hit.
hēoran=hīeran
±**heorcnian** (e, y) tr. and intr. *to* '*hearken*,'
listen, Æ,Guth.
heorcnung f. '*hearkening*,' *listening, power
of hearing*, Æ.

heord I. (e, io) f. '*herd*,' *flock*, *Æ,LL,Mt,
WW*; CP : *keeping, care, custody*, CP. **II.**
sycamore, LkR 19⁴. [heorot-?] **III.**=
hīred. **IV.** (+) (S²Ps 38²)=+heordung
heorde I. f. '*hards*' (*of flax*), *tow, Cp,WW*.
II. (VPs)=hierde. **III.**=heord
±**heordnes** f. *custody, keeping, watch*, GD,
Ps.
±**heordrǣden** (y¹) f. *custody, care, keeping,
watch, ward*, ÆL : *keeping-place*, LPs 78¹.
+**heordung** f. *guard, watch*, ERPs 38².
hēore I.† (ȳ;=īe) *pleasant, secure*, B : *gentle,
mild, pure, Gen.* ['*here*'] **II.**=hīere
heorl=eorl; **heoro**=heoru; **hēorod**=hīered
heorot (u²) m. '*hart*,' *stag, Bo* (heort), *VPs*.
heorotberge f. *buckthorn-berry*, WW.
heorotbrem(b)el m. *buckthorn*, Lcd. [v.
'*hart*']
heorotbrembellēaf n. *leaf of the buckthorn*,
Lcd 119b.
heorotbrēr f. *buckthorn*, LkR 17⁶(heart-).
heorotclǣfre f. '*hart-clover*,' *hemp agrimony*,
Lcd.
heorotcrop m. *cluster of hartwort flowers*,
Lcd.
heorotsmeoru n. *hart's grease*, Lcd 45a.
heorotsol n. *stag's wallowing-place*, KC.
heorr mf. *hinge*, B,Bo,Cp,LPs : *cardinal
point, Lcd.* ['*harre*']
heorra=(1) hearra; (2) heorr
heort I. (±) *high-minded, stout-hearted*, ÆL.
II.=heorot
heortan=hiertan
heortancnys f. '(*com*)*pulsus cordis*'? v.
ZDA 31·13n.
heortbucc m. *roebuck*, WW 119¹².
heortcoða m. *heart disease*, WW 199³⁵.
heortcoðu f. *heart disease*, Lcd 65b.
heorte f. '*heart*' (*organ*): *breast, soul, spirit*:
will, desire : *courage* : *mind, intellect* :
affections.
heortece m. '*heartache*,' *Lcd.*
heorten (y) *of a hart*, Lcd 1·216¹⁵.
heortgesida pl. *entrails*, Lev 3³.
heortgryre m. *terror of heart*, W 86¹⁵.
heorthama m. *pericardium, internal fat*, Æ.
heorthogu f. *heart-care*, W 177⁷.
heortlēas *dispirited*, DD 124,W 137²².
+**heortlīce** adv. *cheeringly*, GD 317¹⁶.
heortlufu f. *hearty love*, †Hy 9²⁹.
heortsārnes f. *grief*, GenC 6⁶.
heortscræf n. *heart*, DD 39.
heortsēoc *ill from heart disease* (Swt).
heortwærc m. *pain at the heart*, Lcd.
heorð (e) m. '*hearth*,' *fire, Gl,Az* : *house,
home*, Æ,LL.
heorð-=eorð-
heorða m. *deer-* (*or goat-?*) *skin*, WW 337³.
[hyrð]

heorðbacen *baked on the hearth*, WW. [v.
'*hearth*']
heorðcneoht m. *attendant*, CP 361¹⁸.
heorðe=heorde
heorðfæst *having a settled home*, LL 322'.
heorðgenēat† m. *retainer*, B.
heorðpening m. '*hearth-penny*,' *tax* (*for the
Church*), *Peter's penny*, LL (v. 2·506).
heorðswǣpe f. *bridesmaid*, Cp 701 P.
heorðwerod† n. *body of retainers*.
heoru† m. *sword*, B.
heorublāc *mortally wounded*, B 2488? (or
?hildeblāc).
heorucumbul n. *standard*, El 107.
heorudolg n. *deadly wound*, An 944.
heorudrēor† m. *sword-blood, gore*, B.
heorudrēorig† *blood-stained* : *deathly sick*,
Ph 217.
heorudrync m. *sword-drink, blood shed by
the sword*, B 2358.
heorufæðm m. *deadly grasp*, Ex 504.
heoruflā f. *arrow*, LPs 56⁵.
heorugīfre† *fierce, greedy for slaughter*.
heorugrǣdig† *bloodthirsty*, An.
heorugrimm† *savage, fierce*.
heoruhōciht *savagely barbed*, B 1438.
heorung=herung
heoruscearp *very sharp*, Rd 6⁸.
heorusceorp n. *war equipments*, Hell 73.
heoruserce f. *coat of mail*, B 2539.
heoruswealwe f. *falcon, hawk*, Wy 186.
heorusweng† m. *sword-stroke*.
heorut=heorot
heoruwǣpen n. *sword*, Jud 263.
heoruweallende *gushing with destruction*,
B 2781.
heoruwearg m. *bloodthirsty wolf*, B 1267.
heoruword n. *hostile speech*, FT 84.
heoruwulf m. *warrior*, Ex 181.
hēow I. pret. 3 sg. of hēawan. **II.**=hīw
hēow-=hīw-; **hēowan**=hēofan
heplic=hæplic; **her-**=hear-, hier-, here-
hēr I. adv. '*here*,' *in this place*, Æ,G,VPs :
in this world, Bl,LL : *at this point of time,
at this date, now, Chr,Ct* : *towards this place,
hither*, B. **II.**=hǣr
hēr-=hǣr-, hīer-, hȳr-
hēræfter (ȳ) adv. '*hereafter*,' *later on*, A,BH.
hērbeforan adv. *before, previously*, W 52¹¹;
FM 361²³.
hērbeufan (u², iu²) adv. *here above, previously, Ct*; CP. [v. '*here*']
hērbūende† mp. *dwellers on this earth*.
herbyrg=herebeorg; **hercnian**=heorcnian
hērcyme m. *coming here, advent*, Cr 250.
herd=heord; **herd-, hērd-**=hierd-, hīerd-
here (obl. cases usu. have herg-, herig-) m.
*predatory band, troop, army, host, multi-
tude, Chr,Mt*; AO,CP ('se h.' almost

always=*the Danish army* in CHR) : *battle, war, devastation.* ['*here*']

hĕre I. f. *dignity, importance?* MET 10⁵⁴? (Sedgef. reads 'here'). II. (VPs)=hǣre

here-bēacen, -bēacn n. *military ensign, standard* : *beacon, lighthouse.*

here-beorg, -byrg f. *lodgings, quarters,* NC 346. [*Ger.* herberge]

herebeorgian (y³) *to take up one's quarters, lodge,* CHR 1048F : RWH 137⁹. [*Ger.* herbergen]

hereblēað *cowardly,* Ex 453.

herebrōga m. *dread of war,* B 462.

herebȳme f. *trumpet, sackbut,* Ex,OEG.

herebyrgian=herebeorgian

herebyrne f. *corslet,* B 1443. [v. '*here*']

herecirm m. *war cry,* GU 872.

herecist=herecyst

herecombol n. *standard,* EL 25?

herecyst† f. *warlike band,* Ex.

+heredlic (LPs 105²)=+hierendlic

herefeld† m. *battlefield, field.*

herefeoh n. *booty,* AO 118⁵.

herefēða m. *war-troop,* CR 1013.

hereflȳma (ē, ī) m. *deserter,* BR 23.

herefolc† n. *army,* JUD.

herefong m. *osprey,* WW.

herefugol m. *bird of prey,* Ex 161.

hereg-=herg-, herig-

heregang m. *invasion,* W 312¹ : *devastation,* BH 306B⁷. [v. '*here*']

heregeatland n. *heriot-land,* EC 220. [v. '*heriot*']

here-geatu fn. gp. -geat(w)e, -geat(w)a, -geatu *war-gear, military equipment,* Bo, Ma : '*heriot,*' Ct,LL (v. 2·500).

heregild (e, eo, y) n. *war-tax, Danegeld,* Chr,Ct. ['*heregeld*']

heregrīma† m. *helmet,* B.

herehand f. *violence of war,* BH 356²².

herehlōð f. *war-host, troop,* GU 1042.

herehūð (ȳ³) f. *booty, prey, plunder,* Æ, AO.

herelāf f. *remains of a host,* Æ : *spoil,* Æ.

herelic *martial,* WW 374²⁶.

herelof mn. *fame, glory,* OEG : *trophy,* OEG.

heremæcg m. *warrior,* GEN 2483.

heremægen† n. *warlike force, multitude.*

heremann m. *soldier,* LkL 7⁸.

hĕremann=hīeremann

heremeðel n. *national assembly,* EL 550.

±herenes (æ) f. *praise,* BH,PPs.

herenett n. *corslet,* B 1553.

herenīð m. *warfare,* B 2474.

herenuma m. *prisoner,* LL (238¹¹).

herepāð† f. *corslet, coat of mail.*

her(e)-pað, -pæð m. *military road, highway,* v. CC 46 and Mdf.

hererǣs m. *hostile raid,* W 271².

hererǣswa m. *commander,* EL 995.

hererēaf f. *war spoil, plunder, booty,* Æ.

hererinc† m. *warrior.*

heresceaft m. *spear,* B 335.

heresceorp n. *war-dress,* FIN 45.

heresīð† m. *warlike expedition.*

herespēd f. *success in war,* B 64.

hĕrespel n. *glorious discourse,* CREAT 37.

herestrǣl m. *arrow,* B 1435.

herestrǣt f. *highway, main road,* CP 375⁹ and N (LL 556,10²).

heraswēg m. *martial sound,* RUIN 23.

heresyrce f. *corslet,* B 1511.

heretēam m. *plunder, devastation,* GEN : *predatory excursion,* LL.

heretēma† (ȳ³) m. *general, king, ruler.*

here-toga, -toha m. *commander, general, chieftain,* Æ,BH ; AO,CP. ['*heretoga*']

hereð m. *booty,* GD 224²⁶. [hergað]

hereðrēat m. *war-band, troop,* Ex,WW.

hereðrym m. *phalanx,* WW 411³⁴.

herewǣd f. *mail, armour,* B 1897.

herewǣpen n. *weapon,* PPs 34³.

herewæsma m. *prowess,* B 677.

herewǣða† m. *warrior,* JUD.

hereweg m. *highway,* WW 146³³.

hereweorc n. *war-work,* EL 656.

herewian=hierwan

herewīc n. *dwellings, camp,* BL.

herewīsa† m. *captain, general.*

herewōp m. *the cry of an army,* Ex 460.

hereword n. *praise, renown,* CHR 1009F.

herewōsa† m. *warrior.*

herewulf m. *warrior,* GEN 2015.

herewurd (HGL 423)=hereword

herfest=hærfest ; herg=hearg

herg-=hereg-, herig(g)-

hergað (here-, o²) m. *harrying, devastation* : *booty,* GD.

hergere m. *one who praises,* DR. ['*heryer*']

±hergian *to ravage, plunder, lay waste, 'harry,'* AO,Chr ; Æ,CP : *seize, take, capture.* ['*harrow*'; here]

hergiend m. *plunderer,* GL.

hergoð=hergað

hergung (AO), hergiung f. '*harrying,*' *ravaging, raid, invasion, attack,* BH,Chr : *plunder, booty* : '*harrowing,*' Æ.

herh=hearg

herian I. (æ) *to extol, praise, commend,* Æ,AO,BH,Bl,CP,VPs. ['*hery*'] II.= hierwan. III.=hergian. IV.=erian

herig=hearg ; v. also here.

herigend m. *flatterer,* Sc 205¹⁵.

±herigendlic *laudable, commendable,* Æ : *praising* : *excellent.* adv. -līce.

herigendsang m. *song of praise,* WW 335¹⁷.

hering=herung ; hēring=hīering

hērinne adv. '*herein*,' Æ.
herlic I. (æ) *noble*, MET. II.=herelic
hērnes=hīernes
hēroſ adv. '*hereof*,' *of this*, A.
hēron adv. *herein*, *Ct*; LL. ['*hereon*']
hērongean adv. *contrariwise*, W52⁸.
hērongemong *at this point, in this connection, meanwhile*, CP : *among others* CP.
her-pǎð, -pǒð=herepǎð
hērra=hēarra, hīerra (v. hēah).
hērrihte (æ̆) *at this point*, AS.
herst-=hierst-; hērsum=hīersum
hērtō *thus far*, OEG56⁸⁰.
hērtōēacan *besides*, W.
heřð=heořð
heřðan pl. '*testiculi*,' LL84,65.
heřðbelig m. '*scrotum*,' WW.
heřðland (NC357)=yřðland
herung (eo) f. *praise*, Æ,CP. ['*herying*']
herutbeg (OEG54²)=heorotberge
herw-=hierw-
herwǐð adv. '*herewith*,' EC236.
hes-=hys-; hēst=hǣst
hēt pret. 3 sg. of hātan.
hetan *to attack*, ÆL35²⁸⁰.
hete (ea) m. '*hate*,' *envy, malice, hostility, persecution, punishment*, B,BH,VPs; Æ, AO,CP.
hetegrim† *fierce, cruel*, AN.
hetel=hetol
hetelic *hostile, malignant, horrible, violent, excessive*, AO,B. ['*hatelich*'] adv. -līce, Æ. ['*hately*']
hetend=hettend
hetenī̌ðt m. *hostility, spite, wickedness*.
heterōſ *full of hate*, AN1422.
heterūnſ. *charm which produces hate*, RD34⁷.
hetesprǣc f. *defiant speech*, GEN263.
hetesweng m. *hostile blow*, B2225.
heteðancſ m. *hostile design*.
heteðoncol *hostile*, JUL105.
hetol *hating, hostile, evil*, Æ,WW : *savage : violent, severe*, RB67¹⁶. [v. '*hatel*']
hetolnes (e²) f. *violence, fierceness*, OEG11¹⁵².
hēton pret. pl. of hātan.
hētt (AO)=hǣt pres. 3 sg. of hātan.
hettan (æ) *to chase, persecute*, OEG8³⁸⁸.
hettend† m. *enemy, antagonist*.
hettende pres. part. of hatian.
hēðen=hǣ̌ðen; hēwen=hǣwen
hī=hēo, hīe
hice *name of a bird*, '*parruca*,' WW38².
hicemāse f. *blue titmouse*, WW132²⁴.
hicgan=hycgan
hicol m. *woodpecker*, BC1·47²⁵ (Mdf).
hī̌d I. fn. a '*hide*' *of land* (*about 120 acres, but amount varied greatly*), Chr,Ct,LL, v. ECpp457–461 and LL2·513. [hīwan]
II.=hȳd

hī̌dan=hȳdan
hider adv. '*hither*,' *to this side, on this side*, Æ,Cp,VPs. comp. hideror *nearer*. h. and ðider (Cp,CP), hidres ðidres (Bo), *hither and thither*.
hidercyme m. *advent, arrival*, BH. ['*hithercome*']
hidere *hither*, WW522³.
hidergeond adv. *thither, yonder*, Mt26³⁶.
hiderryne adj. (i¹, i³) *of our country*, OET115¹³¹.
hidertōcyme=hidercyme
hiderweard adj. and adv. '*hitherward*,' *towards this place*, Chr.
hī̌dgild I. n. *tax paid on each hide of land*, Ct. ['*hidegeld*'] II.=hȳdgild
hī̌dir-=hider-
hī̌dmǣlum adv. *by hides*, KC6·98⁴.
hī̌dres v. hider.
hīe I. nap. of hē, hēo, hit. ['HI*, hy']
II.=hēo nasf. of hē. ['HI, hy']
hīeder=hider
hīeftnīed (EPs123⁶)=hæftnīed
hīeg (ē, ī, ȳ) n. '*hay*,' *cut grass*, G,Lcd,VPs. [hēawan]
hīeghūs (ē, ī) n. *hay store*, WW. ['*hayhouse*']
hīegian (CP)=hīgian
hīegsīðe (ē) m. *hay-scythe*, GD37¹³.
hīehra, hīehst ['*highest*'] v. hēah.
hīeȟð(u) (ē, ēa, ȳ) f. (often indecl.) '*height*,' *highest point, summit*, Gen,Sc : *the heavens, heaven*, Cr,El,Gu,Sc : *glory*. [hēah]
±hīeld (æ, eo, i, y) f. (usu. +) *keeping, custody, guard, protection*, CP : *loyalty, fidelity*, Chr,LL : *observance, observation, watching : secret place : protector, guardian*. ['*held(e)*']
±hīeldan (e, y) intr. *to lean, incline, slope*, Bo : tr. *force downwards, bow or bend down*, B,Lk. ['*hield*']
hīelde (e, y) f. *slope, declivity*, KC,WW. ['*hield*']
-hīelde (y) v. earfoð-h.
+hīeldelic (y) *safe*, GD348¹⁰.
+hīeldnes (y) f. *observance*, PPs18¹⁰.
hīelfe (e, y) n. *handle*, CP,WW. ['*helve*']
hīelfling (e) m. *mite, farthing*, LkL12⁶. [healf]
hīellan *to make a noise*, EPs82³.
hīelpeð pres. 3 sg. of helpan.
hīelt pres. 3 sg. of healdan.
-hīeltan (y) v. ā-h. [healt]
hīelto (e, y) f. *lameness*, MH116¹⁰.
±hīenan (ǣ, ē, ȳ) *to fell, prostrate : overcome : weaken, crush, afflict, injure, oppress : abase, humble, insult*, B,LkL : *accuse, condemn*, CP. ['*hean*']
hīene as. of hē (CP). ['*hin*']

+hīene (ē) *ready to fall, frail*, DR189[16].

hīenend (e[1]) m. *accuser*, JnLp5[9].

hīennes (ē, ȳ) f. *crushing, destruction*, BH, LkR.

hīenðo, hīenðo (ǣ, ē, ȳ) f. *humiliation, affliction, oppression, annoyance*, CP : *loss, damage, harm* : *act of hanging*, DHy 59[7].

hīera gp. of hē, hēo, hit. ['HER*']

hīera=hīerra v. hēah.

±hīeran (ē, ēo, ī, ȳ) tr. and intr. *to* 'HEAR' ('*y-here*'), *listen* (*to*), Æ : (w. d.) *obey, follow*, Æ; CP : *accede to, grant* : *be subject to, belong to, serve*, AO : (+) *judge*.

±hīerdan (i, y) *to harden, make hard* : *strengthen, fortify, confirm, encourage*, CP. [heard]

hīerde (eo, i, y) m. (f. at ÆGR57[16]) *shepherd, herdsman*, CP,G; AO : *guardian, keeper*, B,Bl,Gen,Met,WW : *pastor*, Bl. ['*herd*']

hīerdebelig (e) m. *shepherd's bag*, Bl31[17]. [v. '*belly*']

hīerdebōc f. *pastoral book* (translation of the *Cura Pastoralis* of Pope Gregory), CP.

hīerdecnapa (y) m. *shepherd boy*, ÆL23[418].

hīerdelēas (i, y) *without a shepherd or pastor*, Æ. ['*herdless*']

hīerdelic (y) *pastoral*, CP.

hīerdeman (y) m. *shepherd*, Æ. ['*herdman*']

hīerdenn (y) f. *hardening*, SoL150'.

hīerdewyrt (i) f. *name of a plant*, LCD.

±hīerdnes (eo, i, y) f. *custody, watch, guard*.

hīerdung (y) f. *strengthening, restoring*, WW 150[34].

hīere gds. of hēo. ['HER*']

hīered=hīred

hīereman (ē, ī, ȳ) m. *retainer, servant, subject, hearer, parishioner*, Mk; CP. ['*hireman*']

+hīerend m. *hearer*, CP.

+hīerendlic (e[1], y[1]) *audible*, LPs142[8],ÆGR 152[6].

+hīering (ē) f. *hearing, hearsay*, LPs111[7].

hīeringman (ē, ȳ) m. *subject*, RWH96[5] : *hireling*, 126[35].

hīernes (ē, ȳ) f. (+) *hearing, report* : (±) *obedience, subjection, allegiance*, CP : *jurisdiction, district*.

hīerra=hearra

hīerra v. hēah, CP. ['HIGHER']

±hīerstan (e, i, y) *to fry, roast, scorch, pain*, CP. [cp. OHG. giharsten]

hīerste (e, y) f. *frying-pan* : *gridiron*, WW 214[40].

hīerstepanne (ea, y) f. *frying-pan*, CP.

hīersting (y) f. *frying, burning*, CP : *frying-pan?* ÆGR175[3].

hīerstinghlāf (e) m. *crust*, WW372[18].

±hīersum (ē, ēa, ī, ȳ) w. d. *obedient, docile*, BH,Gu. ['*hearsum*']

±hīersumian (ēa, ī, ȳ) w. d. *to obey, serve*, BH,Mt; AO : (+) *reduce, subject, conquer*, CHR. ['*hearsum*']

hīersumlic (ȳ) *willing*, GD152[1].

±hīersumnes (ī, ȳ) f. *obedience, submission*, BH; CP : *service* : *humility*. ['*hersumnesse*']

±hīertan (e, eo, y) *to cheer, encourage*, CP; Æ : *be renewed, refreshed* : *revive* : *cherish*. ['*heart*'; heort]

hīerting (y) f. *soothing*, OEG17[10].

±hīerwan (e, i, y) *to abuse, blaspheme, condemn, illtreat* : *to deride, despise*.

hīerwend (i) m. *blasphemer*, Lev24[14].

hīerwendlic *contemptible*. adv. -līce (e) *with contempt*.

hīerwing (y) f. *blasphemy*, Sc137[12].

hīerwnes (i, y) f. *contempt, reproach* : *blasphemy*, W70[12].

hīew=hīw

hīewestān m. *hewn stone*, AO212[10].

hīewet (ȳ) n. *cutting*, CP,WW. [hēawan]

hīewian=hīwian

hīewð (CP) pres. 3 sg. of hēawan.

hīf- (v. OEG3913)=hīw-

hīg=hīe I.; hīg=hīeg

hīgan=hīwan; hīge=hyge

hīgendlīce *quickly, immediately*, RWH25[13]. [hīgian]

hīgera m., higere f. *jay, magpie, jackdaw, woodpecker*. [Ger. häher]

hīggan=hycgan

hīgian *to* '*hie*,' *strive, hasten*, Bl,Bo,CP.

hīgid=hīd

hīglā '*heu!*' RPs119[5].

hīgleast=hygelēast; hīgna v. hīwan.

hīgo (N)=hīwan; hīgora, higra=higera

hīgre=higere; hīgscipe=hīwscipe

hīgð f. *exertion, effort*, ZDA. ['*hight*']

hīgung f. *effort*, GD254[34].

hīhsan=hyscan; hīht=hyht

hīhting f. *exultation, gladness*, WW233[42].

hīhðo=hīehðu; hīlc=hylc

hīlā=hīglā

hild I.† f. *war, combat*. II.=hield

hildbedd n. *deathbed*, AN1094.

hildebill† n. *sword*, B.

hildeblāc? *deadly pale, mortally wounded*, B2488 (or ?heorublāc).

hildebord† n. *buckler*, B.

hildecalla m. *war-herald*, Ex252.

hildecorðor n. *warlike band*, Ap41.

hildecyst f. *valour*, B2598.

hildedēoful n. *demon*, PPs95[5].

hildedēor *war-fierce, brave*, Æ.

hildefreca† m. *warrior*.

hildegeatwe† fp. *war-harness*, B.

hildegesa m. *terror of battle*, EL 113.

hildegicel m. *battle-icicle (blood dripping from a sword)*, B 1606.

hildegiest m. *enemy*, RD 54⁹.

hildegrāp† f. *hostile grip*, B.

hildeheard *bold in battle*, AP 21.

hildehlem† m. *crash of battle*, B.

hildelēoma† m. *Gleam of battle* (name of a sword), B.

hildelēoð n. *war-song*, JUD 211.

hildemēce m. *sword*, B 2202.

hildemecg m. *warrior*, B 799.

hildenǣdre† f. *war-snake, arrow*.

hildepīl† m. *dart, javelin*, Rd. [v. '*pile*']

hilderǣs m. *charge, attack*, B 300.

hilderand m. *shield*, B 1242.

hilderinc† m. *warrior, hero*.

hildesǣd *battle-worn*, B 2723.

hildesceorp n. *armour*, B 2155.

hildescūr m. *shower of darts*, GU 1116.

hildeserce f. *corslet*, EL 234.

hildesetl m. *saddle*, B 1039.

hildespell n. *warlike speech*, EX 573.

hildestrengo f. *vigour for battle*, B 2113.

hildeswāt m. *vapour of battle?* B 2558.

hildeswēg m. *sound of battle*, GEN 1991.

hildetorht *shining in battle*, MET 25⁹.

hildetux m. *tusk (as weapon)*, B 1511.

hildeðremma m. *warrior*, JUL 64.

hildeðrymm (AN 1034) m., hildeðrȳð (RD 20⁴) f. *warlike strength, valour*.

hildewǣpen m. *weapon of war*, B 39.

hildewīsa m. *commander*, B 1064.

hildewōma† m. *crash of battle*.

hildewrǣsn f. *fetter for captives*, SOL 292.

hildewulf m. *hero*, GEN 2051.

hildfreca=hildefreca

hildfrom *valiant in war*, AN 1204.

hildfruma† m. *battle-chief, prince, emperor*.

hildlata m. *laggard in battle, coward*, B 2846.

hildstapa m. *warrior*, AN 1260.

hildðracu f. *onset of battle*, GEN 2157.

hileð=hilð; **hilhāma**=hyllehāma

hill=hyll, hell

+hilmed (y) *helmeted*, WW 413²⁷ : *covered with foliage*, WW 405,526.

hilpestu=hilpest ðu (pres. 2 sg. of helpan and pron. 2 pers. sing.).

hilpeð, hilpð pres. 3 sg. of helpan.

hilt I.=hielt pres. 3 sg. of healdan. **II.** mn. =hilte

±hilte fn. *handle, 'hilt' (of sword)*, B,WW; (pl.=sg.) Æ,B,Sol.

hilt(e)cumbor n. *banner with a staff*, B 1022 (or ?hilde-).

hilted '*hilted,' with a hilt*, B.

hilting m. *sword*, OEG 758.

hiltlēas *having no hilt*, WW 142³⁴.

hiltsweord (y) n. *hilted sword*, BO 111¹⁶.

±hiltu np. of hilte.

hilð pres. 3 sg. of helan.

him ds. of hē, dp. of hē, hēo, hit. ['HIM']

himming (CP 1557)=hemming

hīna v. hīwan.

hinan=heonon; **hīnan**=hīenan

-hinca v. helle-h.

hind (y) f. '*hind' (female deer)*, Chr,WW.

hindan *from behind, behind, in the rear*, Æ,AO. æt h. *behind*, Æ. [Ger. hinten]

hindanweard adv. *hindwards, at the end*, PH 298.

hindberge f. *raspberry*, Cp,Ep,Lcd : *strawberry?* WW 409¹². ['*hindberry*']

hindbrēr m. *raspberry bush*, LCD 146b (hinde-).

hindcealf mn. *fawn*, WW. ['*hindcalf*']

hindema† superl. adj. *hindmost, last*.

hinder adj. *after (thought), sad, sinister (thought)?* MFH,RWH 143¹³. adv. *behind, back, after, in the farthest part, down*. on h. *backwards*, Æ.

hindergēap *wily, cunning, deceitful*, WW. ['*hinderyeap*']

hindergenga m. *one who walks backwards*, OEG 26²³ : *apostate*, OEG 5¹⁶.

hinderhōc m. *trick*, MOD 34.

hinderling I. m. *mean wretch, sneak*, LL 665'. **II.** adv. in phr. 'on hinderling' *backwards*, PPs. ['*hinderling*']

hindernes f. *wickedness, guile*, NC 301; MFH 166.

hinderscipe m. *wickedness*, DHy,OEG.

hinderðēostru np. *nether darkness*, PPs 85¹².

hinderweard *slow, sluggish*, PH 314.

hindeweard *reversed, wrong end first, from behind*, CP.

hindfalod n. *hind-fold*, KC 6·112³¹.

hind-hæleðe, -heoloð(e) f. '*ambrosia,' water agrimony*, WW. [v. '*hindheal*']

±hindrian *to 'hinder,' check, repress*, Chr, LL.

hindsīo (BL)=hinsīo

hine I. as. of hē. **II.**=heonon

hīne=hīwene

hinfūs† *ready to depart or die*.

hingang† m. *departure, death*, OET 149. [v. '*yong*']

hingrian (Bl; Æ)=hyngrian

hinn-=hin-; **hinon**=heonon

hinsīð† m. *departure, death*. [heonon]

hinsīðgryre m. *fear of death*, SAT 456.

hīo v. he; **hio-**=heo-

hionne? f. '*dura mater,'* LL 5,36.

hior=heorr; **hiored**=hīred

hioro-=heoru-

hiowesclīce=hīwisclīce; **hip-**=hyp-

hipsful (OEG 11¹⁸⁰)=hyspful

hīr=hȳr; **hir-, hīr-**=hier-, hēor-, hīer-

hira gp. of hē, hēo, hit; **hīrd-**=hīred-
hīre gds. of hēo. ['HER*']
hīred (ēo, īe, ȳ) m. *household, family, retinue, AO,Bo,Mt,WW : brotherhood, company, Æ,Ct.* ['*hird*']
hīredcniht m. *domestic, member of a household, Æ.*
hīredcūð *domestic, familiar,* So 203¹³.
hīredgerēfa m. '*ex-consul,*' WW 110⁶.
hīredlic *pertaining to a household or court, domestic, familiar.*
hīredlōf (=lēof) *friendly,* A 13·445.
hīredman m. *retainer, follower, Æ,Ma.* ['*hirdman*']
hīredprēost (ȳ) m. *chaplain,* TC 571² : *regular priest,* EC 255.
hīredwīfman m. *female member of a household,* TC 531⁶.
hīredwist f. *familiarity,* Sc 203¹².
hīru=hūru
his gs. of hē. ['HIS']
hīs (BH)=īs; **hisc-**=hysc-
hislic *suitable,* GD 183⁵.
hispan=hyspan; **hiss**=hos; **hisse**=hyse
hit v. hē. ['IT']
hittan (y) *to fall in with, meet with,* '*hit*' *upon, Chr* 1066. [*ON.* hitta]
hīð-=hȳð-; **hiðer**=hider
hiu (*NG*)=hēo
hīw I. (ēo, īe, īo, ȳ) n. *appearance, form, species, kind, Æ,Bl,Cr,G,WW : apparition,* WW 236⁸ : '*hue,*' *colour, Bf,Bl : beauty : figure of speech.* II. (io) f. *fortune,* AA 11².
hīwan mp. (gen. hīwna, hī(g)na) *members of a family, household or religious house, Chr, G; Æ.* ['*hind,*' '*hewe*']
hīwbeorht† *radiant, beautiful.*
hīwcund (hīl-) *familiar, domestic,* GL.
hīwcūð (īe) *domestic, familiar, well-known, Æ,CP.*
hīwcūðlic *domestic, familiar.* adv. -līce.
+**hīwcūðlician** *to make known or familiar to,* NC 294.
hīwcūðnes f. *familiarity,* GD 71²⁴; 140⁷.
hīwcūðrǣdnes f. *familiarity,* WW 191²⁴.
hīwen n. *household, Æ.* ['*hewen*']
+**hīwendlic** *allegorical,* WW 354⁴.
hīwere m. *dissembler, hypocrite, Æ.*
hīwfæger *comely of form,* MFH 167.
hīwfæst *comely, fair,* OEG.
hīwgedāl n. *divorce,* G.
±**hīwian** I. *to form, fashion, WW : colour : dissimulate, feign, pretend, Æ : figure, signify, Æ : (+) transform, transfigure.* ['*hue,*' '*hued*'] II. *to marry,* CP 318¹.
hīwisc n. *household, Æ : hide (of land* v. hīd). adv. -līce *familiarly.*
+**hīwlǣcan** *to form, shape, fashion,* NC 294 : *colour,* LCD 1·262¹⁴.

hīwlēas *shapeless, WW : colourless,* Lcd 11. ['*hueless*']
hīwlic I. *comely,* LCD,OEG : *figurative,* HGL. II. *matronly?* WW 442².
hīwna v. hīwan.
hīwnes f. *hue, colour, appearance,* WE 65¹⁴.
+**hīwodlīce** *in form,* ÆGR 250,251.
hīwrǣden f. *family, household, religious house, Æ.*
hīwscipe m. *family, household : hide (of land),* CC 127.
hīwð pres. 3 sg. of hēawan.
hīwung I. (ēo, ȳ) f. (±) *appearance, likeness, form, figure : portrayal,* ByH 102³³ : *pretence, hypocrisy, Æ : irony,* WW 416³². II. f. *marriage,* AO 64²⁴.
hlacerian *to deride, mock,* LPs 24⁸.
hlacerung f. *unseemly behaviour, or words, mockery,* LPs 43¹⁴.
±**hladan**⁶ (æ, ea) *to '* lade,' *draw, or take in water, Æ,JnR : heap up, lay on, build, load, burden, B,Gen,Rd; CP.*
hladung f. *drawing ('* haustus'), DHy 58⁶.
hlǣ=hlǣw
hlǣd n. *heap? burden?* CP 21¹⁶⁰. ['*lade*']
hlǣdder (*Bl*), hlǣddre=hlǣder
hlǣddisc m. *loaded dish?* WW 126³⁹.
hlǣdel m. '*ladle,*' LL,ZDA.
hlǣden I. m. *bucket,* WW 123⁵. II. pp. of hladan.
hlǣder f. '*ladder,*' *steps, Æ,Bf,LL; CP.*
hlǣderstæf f. *rung of a ladder,* ByH 80³⁰.
hlǣderwyrt f. *ladder-wort, Jacob's ladder,* LCD.
hlǣdhweogl n. *water-wheel, wheel for drawing up water,* WW 347⁷.
hlǣdrede *having steps,* BC 3·492'.
hlǣdst=hlætst pres. 2 sg. of hladan.
hlǣdtrendel m. *wheel for drawing water,* OEG 502.
hlǣfde '* sparsio panis,'* WW 277⁶.
hlǣfdige (ā, ē) f. *mistress (over servants), LL,VPs,WW : chatelaine,* '*lady,*' *queen, Chr,Ct : the Virgin Mary, Cr.* sēo ealde h. *the queen dowager,* CHR 1051 C.
hlǣfl=læfel
+**hlǣg** n. *derision, scorn,* DOM 15.
hlǣgulian (Cp 317)=hlagolian
hlǣhan (N,VPs)=hliehhan
hlǣhter=hleahtor
hlǣnan I. *to cause to lean,* JUL 63. II.= lǣnan
-**hlǣnan** v. ā-hl.
hlǣne '* lean,' Æ;* AO.
±**hlǣnian** *to become lean, CP : make lean, starve, CP.* ['*lean*']
hlǣnnes f. '*leanness,*' *Æ,OEG.*
±**hlǣnsian** *to make lean, weaken,* OEG. ['*lense*']

hlǣpewince (WW)=lēapewince
hlæst n. *burden, load, freight, B,Rd.* holmes
h. *finny tribe.* ['*last*']
+hlæstan (e) *to load, burden, BH* : *adorn*,
Jud 36. [v. '*last*' vb.]
hlæsting f. *toll on loading a ship,* TC 359,
411.
hlæstscip n. *trading-vessel,* Cp 147 h.
hlæt=læt
hlætst pres. 2 sg. of hladan.
hlǣw† (ā) mn. *mound, cairn, hill, mountain,
B* : *grave-yard, barrow, Met* : *hollow mound,
cave.* ['*low*']
hlāf m. '*loaf,*' *cake, bread, food, Bf,NG*; *Æ,
AO,CP* : *sacramental bread, ÆP* 108²³.
hlāfǣta m. ('*loaf-eater*'), *dependant, LL*
4,25.
hlāfbrytta m. *slave in charge of the bread-
store?* EC 255.
hlāfdie (VPs)=hlǣfdige
hlāfgang m. *attendance at, or participation
in, a meal,* RB : *partaking of the Eucharist,*
LL 473,27.
hlāf-gebrecu f. (PPs), -gebroc (MH) n. *bit
of bread.*
hlāfhwǣte m. *bread-wheat,* TC 144'.
hlāflēast f. *want of bread,* CAS 34²⁰.
hlāfmæsse f. '*Lammas*' (*August* 1), *AO*; *Æ.*
hlāfmæssedæg m. *Lammas-day.*
hlāfmæssetīd f. *Lammas-tide,* Lcd 6a.
hlāfofn m. *baker's oven,* WW 411⁸.
hlāford m. '*lord,*' *master, ruler, AO,B,Bf,
Chr,G*; *Æ,CP* : *husband, Ct* : *the Lord, God,
Æ.* [hlāf, weard]
hlāforddōm m. *lordship, authority, CP* :
patronage. ['*lorddom*']
hlāfordhold *loyal to a lord,* Bo 42²⁴.
hlāfordhyldo f. *loyalty, AO.*
hlāfording m. *lord, master,* W 298⁷.
hlāfordlēas *without a lord, leaderless, B.*
['*lordless*']
hlāfordlic '*lordly,*' *noble, OEG* 187¹.
hlāfordscipe m. '*lordship,*' *authority, rule,
CP* : '*dominatio*' (*title of an order of
angels*), *ÆH* 1·342'.
hlāfordsearu fn. *high treason, LL.*
hlāfordsōcn f. *act of seeking the protection of
a lord, LL.*
hlāfordswica m. *traitor, Lcd*; *Æ.* ['*lord-
swike*']
hlāfordswice m. *high treason, treachery,*
W 160.
hlāford-swicung (MFH 167; W 225²⁸), -syr-
wung (LL 16 n 5) f. *betrayal of one's lord.*
hlāfordōrimm m. *dominion, power,* NC
302.
hlāfrǣce f. *oven-rake, OEG* 53⁴³ (hlāb-).

hlāfsēnung f. *blessing of bread (on Lammas-
day),* MH 136¹.
hlāfurd=hlāford
hlāfweard m. *steward,* PPs 104¹⁷ (v. GK 884
s.v. healf-).
hlagol *inclined to laugh,* W 40⁸.
hlagolian (æ) *to sound,* Cp 317.
hlāmmæsse=hlāfmæsse
hlanc '*lank,*' *lean, thin, Jud,PPs.*
hland (o) n. *urine, Lcd.* ['*lant*']
hlaðian=laðian; hlāw=hlǣw
hleadan=hladan; hleahter=hleahtor
hleahterful *scornful,* Guth.
hleahterlic *ridiculous,* Sc 38⁷.
hleahtor (e) m. '*laughter,*' *jubilation, B,Bl,
CP,Sc* : *derision.*
hleahtorbǣre *causing laughter,* RB 18⁸.
hleahtorsmið m. *laughter-maker,* Ex 43.
hleahtrian (e) *to deride,* LPs 21⁸.
hlēapan⁷ *to* '*leap,*' *run, go, jump, dance,
spring, Æ,B,BH,Chr,CP* : (+) *leap upon,
mount* (*a horse*).
hlēapere m. *runner, courier, Chr* : *wanderer* :
horseman : '*leaper,*' *dancer, WW* : *itinerant
monk,* RB 135²⁰.
hlēapestre f. *female dancer,* WW 311³³.
hlēapettan v. *to leap up,* BH 390⁹.
hlēapewince f. '*lapwing,*' *WW.*
hlēapung f. *dancing, Æ.* ['*leaping*']
hlēat pret. 3 sg. of hlēotan.
hlec *leaky, CP,OEG.* [v. '*leak*']
hlecan⁵ *to cohere,* CP 361²⁰.
hlēda, hlēde (ȳ) m. *seat, ÆGr* 34³.
hlēf=hlǣw; -hlēfan (oe) v. ā-hl.
hlēga (*LkL* 6¹⁶)=lǣwa; hlehhan=hliehhan
hlēg(i)ende (æ¹, u²) *deep-sounding,* WW 9²⁷;
358¹⁹.
hleht-=hleaht-
hlem m. *sound,* CP 253¹⁷.
hlemman *to cause to sound, clash,* Wh 61.
hlēnan=lǣnan
+hlencan *to twist, bend?* Lcd.
hlence f. *coat of mail,* Ex 218.
hlennan=hlynnan
hlenortēar m. *hyssop,* LPs 50⁶.
hlēo† m? n? (hlēow), gs. hlēowes (no pl.)
*covering, refuge, defence, shelter, protection,
Cr,PPs* : *protector, lord.* ['*lee*']
hlēo-=hlēow-
hlēobord n. *book-cover,* Rd 27¹².
hlēoburh† f. *protecting city, B.*
hlēod=hlōd
+hleodu pl. of +hlid.
hlēohrǣscnes f. '*supplantatio*'? LPs 40¹⁰.
hlēolēas† *without shelter, comfortless.*
hleomoc m. hleomoce f. *speedwell, Lcd.*
[v. '*brooklime*']
hlēon=hlēowan; hleon-=hlin-
hlēonað m. *shelter,* Gu 222.

hlēonian *to cherish*, WW 377³².
hlēop pret. 3 sg. of hlēapan.
hlēor n. *cheek, Lcd,WW* : *face, countenance, Ep,Gu.* [*'leer'*]
hlēoran (ÆL)=lēoran
hlēorbān n. (*cheek-bone*), *temple*, LPs 131⁵.
hlēorberg? f. *cheek-guard, helmet*, B 304?
hlēorbolster m. *pillow*, B 688.
hlēordropa m. *tear*, Gu 1315.
hlēorsceamu f. *confusion of face*, PPs 68⁸.
hlēorslæge m. *a blow on the cheek*, CP 261⁶.
hlēortorht *beautiful*, Rᴅ 69⁶.
hlēosceorp n. *sheltering robe*, Rᴅ 10⁵.
hlēotan¹ *to cast lots*, Æ,AO : (±) *get by lot, obtain.*
hlēoð=(1) hlēowð; (2) pres. pl. of hlēowan.
hlēoð-=hlōð-
hlēoðor n. *noise, sound, voice, song : hearing.*
+hlēoðor *harmonious*, BH 60¹⁸.
hlēoðorcwide† m. *speaking, words, discourse, song, prophecy.*
hlēoðorcyme m. *coming with trumpet-sound*, Dᴀ 710.
hlēoðorstede m. *place of conference*, Gᴇɴ 2399.
hlēoðrere (ō) m. *rhetorician*, OET 180⁴.
hlēoðrian *to sound, speak, sing, cry aloud, resound, proclaim*, Æ.
hlēoðrung f. *sound*, MFH 130 : *harmony, hymn*, Bꜰ 198⁵ : *reproof*, SPs 37¹¹.
hleoðu v. hlið.
hlēow=hlēo
±hlēow I. (ī) *sheltered, warm, sunny*, Lcd, *Nar.* adv. hlēowe. [v. *'lew'*] II.=+hlōw
±hlēowan (ī, ȳ) *to warm, make warm, cherish*, Bl : *become warm or hot.* [*'lew'*]
hlēowdryhten m. *protector, patron*, Wɪᴅ 94.
hlēowfæst *protecting, consoling*, Cr,RB.
hlēowfeðre fp. *sheltering wings*, Gᴇɴ 2740.
hlēowlora m. *one who has lost a protector*, Gᴇɴ 1953.
hlēowmǣg† m. *kinsman who is bound to afford protection.*
hlēownes f. *warmth*, A 8·451.
hlēowon pret. pl. of hlōwan.
hlēowsian *to shelter, protect*, WW 235²⁹.
hlēowstede m. *sunny place*, WW 336³⁰.
hlēowstōl m. *shelter, asylum*, Gᴇɴ 2011.
hlēowð (ī, ȳ) f. *shelter, covering, warmth*, Æ, *Hex.* [*'lewth'*]
±hlēowung (ē, ī, ȳ) f. *shelter, protection, favour*, CM,WW.
hlestan=hlæstan, hlystan
hlet (KGL) pres. 3 sg. of hladan.
hlēt (VPs; MkR)=hliet
+hlēoða† m. *companion, denizen.* [hlōð]
hlēoðrian=hlēoðrian; hlēw=hlǣw
hlēw-=hlēow-

hlēwesa (EPs 139¹³)=lēwsa
hlēwð pres. 3 sg. of hlōwan.
hlid I. n. *'lid,' covering, door, gate, opening*, Æ. II.=hlið
+hlid† n. (nap. hlidu, hleodu) *covering, vault, roof.*
hlidan¹ *to come forth, spring up*, PPs 79¹¹?
hlidfæst *closed by a lid*, TC 516⁴.
hlidgeat n. *swing-gate, folding-door*, BC, EC; Æ; Mdf. [*'lidgate'*]
+hlidod (eo) *having a lid*, BH 320¹⁰. [*'lidded'*]
hliehhan⁶ (e, i, y) *to laugh*, Æ,CP : (±) *laugh at, deride*, Æ,MtL : *rejoice.*
hliep (ȳ) mf., hliepe f. *'leap,' bound, spring, sudden movement*, Cr,Lcd : *thing to leap from*, AO : *place to leap over?* v. CC 54 : *waterfall*, Ct.
hliepen pres. pl. of hlēapan.
hliepgeat (ȳ) n. *a low gate*, KC. [*'leapgate'*]
hliet (ē, ȳ) m. *lot, share : chance, fortune*, CP.
hlifend (hlīb-) *threatening*, Cp 223ᴍ.
hlifian *to rise high, tower, overhang*, B,GD.
hligan¹ʾ *to attribute (to)*, CP,Dᴀ.
hligsa (CP)=hlīsa
hlihan, hlihcan, hlihhan=hliehhan
hlimman³† (y) *to sound, resound, roar, rage.*
hlimme† f. *stream, torrent*, PPs.
hlin I. (=y) m. *maple-tree*, Rᴅ 56⁹. [*Ger.* lehne] II.=hlynn
hlinbedd n. *sick-bed, couch*, B 3034.
hlinc m. *ridge, bank, rising ground, hill*, EC, *Ph*; v. GBG and Mdf. [*'link'*]
hlincrǣw f. *bank forming a boundary*, EC, KC.
hlinduru† f. *latticed door.*
±hlinian (eo, y) *to 'lean,' B*; Æ : *recline, lie down, rest*, Jn,MkL; CP.
hliniend m. *one who reclines*, HGʟ 414.
hlinrǣced† n. *prison*, Aɴ,Jᴜʟ.
hlinscū(w)a† m. *darkness of confinement.*
hlinsian=hlynsian
±hlinung f. *'leaning,' Lk* : *seat, couch.*
hliosa=hlīsa
hlipð pres. 3 sg. of hlēapan.
hlira=lira
hlīsa (īo, ȳ) m. *sound* : *rumour, fame, glory*, CP.
hlīsbǣre *renowned*, OEG.
hlīsēadig *renowned, famed*, Bo.
hlīsēadignes f. *renown*, Bo 75²⁸.
hlīsful *of good repute, famous*, Æ. adv. -līce, Æ,AO.
hlīsig *renowned*, OEG 8²⁵⁰.
hlīstan=hlystan; hlīt=hlyt
hlīð I.† n. (nap. hleoðu) *cliff, precipice, slope, hill-side, hill*, Aɴ,B; Mdf. [*'lith'*] II.=hlid

hlīw=hlēow

hlīwe f. *shelter*, KC.

hloccetung f. *sighing*, HGL421[7].

hlōd pret. 3 sg. of hladan; hlodd=hlot

hlōgon pret. pl., hlōh pret. 3 sg. of hliehhan.

hlom (WW117[25]), hlond=hland

hlōse f. *pigsty*, LL454,10; NC302; Mdf.

hlosnere m. *listener*, OEG2333 : *disciple*, BF56[11].

hlosnian *to listen : wait*, Æ : *be on the look out for, spy*, Æ. hlosniende '*attonitus*,' WW.

hlōsstede m. *site of a pigsty*, KC.

hlot, hlott n. '*lot*,' *part, portion, share*, BC,LkL : (+) *selection by lot, choice, decision*, Æ,AO. hl. sendan, weorpan *to cast lots*, Bl,Mt.

hloten pp. of hleotan.

+hlotland n. *allotted land, inheritance*, Jos 24[30].

hlōð f. *troop, crowd, band*, AO : *booty, spoil : complicity with a band of robbers*, LL 94,14.

hlōðbōt f. *penalty imposed on a member of a gang of malefactors*, LL64,29.

hlōðere m. *robber*, WW506[36]. [hlōð]

hlōðgecrod n. *mass of troops*, RD4[63].

hlōðian (ēo) *to spoil, plunder*, BH.

hlōðsliht m. *murder by a member of a gang of malefactors*, LL18,29.

+hlōw n. *lowing, bellowing, bleating*, Æ.

hlōwan[7] *to* '*low,' roar, bellow*, Æ,El.

hlōwung f. *lowing, bleating, bellowing*, WW 192[7]; 195[13].

hlūd adj. comp. hlūdre, hluddre '*loud*,' *noisy, sounding, sonorous*, Bl,CP; Æ.

hlūdclipol *loud, noisy*, RBL35[11] (hlūt-).

hluddre v. hlūd.

hlūde adv. *loudly, aloud*, Bl; Æ,CP. ['*loud*']

hlūdnes f. '*loudness,' clamour*, Bf176[23].

hlūdstefne *loud-sounding*, WW416[18].

hlūdswēge adv. *loudly*, Æ.

hlummon pret. pl. of hlimman.

hlupon pret. pl. of hlēapan.

hluton pret. pl. of hlēotan.

hlūtor, hlūttor (e[2]) gsm. hlūtres *pure, clear, bright, sincere*, Æ,CP. [*Ger*. lauter] adv. -lice.

hlūtorlicnes=hlūtornes

hlūtornes f. *clearness, brightness, simplicity, purity*, Æ.

hlūtre I. adv. *clearly, brightly : untroubled*, PPs104[3]. II. ds. of hlūtor.

hlūtter, hlūttor=hlūtor

±hlūttrian *to clear, purify, make bright : to become clear*.

hlyd=hlid

±hlȳd fm. *noise, sound : tumult, disturbance, dissension*. [hlūd]

hlȳda=hlēda

Hlȳda m. *March, Lcd*. ['*Lide*'; hlūd]

hlȳdan *to make a noise, sound, clamour, vociferate*, Æ,CP. [hlūd]

hlȳde I. f. *torrent*, BC (Mdf). II. (LL455')= hlēde?

hlȳdig *garrulous*, OEG1418. [hlūd]

hlȳding f. *noise, cry*, MtL25[6] (lȳ-).

hlyhhan=hliehhan

hlymman=hlimman; hlyn=hlynn

hlynian=(1) hlynnan; (2) hlinian

±hlynn I. m. *sound, noise, din, tumult*, AO. II. f. *torrent*, JnR. ['*linn*']

hlynnan (e) *to make a noise, resound, shout, roar*.

hlynrian *to thunder*, WW519[34].

hlynsian† (i) *to resound*.

hlȳp=hliep

hlȳrian (=īe) *to blow out (the cheeks)*, LPs 80[4]. [hlēor]

hlȳsa (Æ)=hlīsa

hlȳsfullice=hlīsfullice

hlysnan *to* '*listen*,' MtL; Cp.

hlysnere m. *hearer*, DR29[4] (ly-).

±hlyst f. *sense of hearing*, Æ,Lcd : *listening*. ['*list*']

±hlystan (e, i) *to listen, hear*, CP,LL; Æ : *attend to, obey*, Lk. ['*list*']

+hlyste *audible*, CHRD22[36].

hlystend, hlystere m. *listener*, Æ.

+hlystful *attentive, gracious*, LPs89[13].

hlysting f. *act of listening*, RWH136[23].

hlyte m. *lot, portion*, WW40[13].

+hlyta m. *companion*, CPs44[9]. [hlot]

hlȳtere m. *priest*, NC302. (v. BTs)

hlytm m. *casting of lots*, B3126?

hlytman *to decide by lot*, MFH167.

hlytta m. *diviner, soothsayer*, AO184[26] : (+) *partner, fellow*, RPs44[8]. [hlot]

+hlytto (e) *fellowship, lot*, DR.

hlȳttor (HGL418)=hlūttor, hlūtor

hlȳttrian *to purify*, ÆGR222[7].

hlȳttrung f. *cleaning, refining*, WW179[36].

-hlȳðan (=īe) v. be-hl.; hlȳðre=lȳðre

hlȳw-=hlēow-; hlȳwing=hlēowung

hnacod=nacod

hnæcan *to check, destroy, kill*, Æ. [=næcan]

±hnægan I. *to bow down, bend, humble, curb, vanquish*. [hnīgan] II. *to* '*neigh*,' ÆGr. III.=nægan

hnægung f. '*neighing*,' ÆGr,Cp.

hnæpp m. *bowl*, EC,OEG,WW. ['*nap*']

hnæpp-=hnapp-

hnæppan *to strike*, Bo130[19,20].

hnæsce=hnesce

+hnæst, +hnāst† n. *collision, conflict, battle*. [hnītan]

+hnæstan (næst-) *to contend with*, RD 28[10].

hnäg, hnāh I. *bent down, abject, poor, humble, lowly* : niggardly. II. pret. 3 sg. of hnigan.

hnappian (æ, e, ea) *to doze, slumber, sleep,* CP,Mt,Sc,VPs; Æ. ['nap']

hnappung (æ, ea) f. *napping, slumbering,* VPs; CP.

hnāt pret. 3 sg. of hnītan.

hneap- (VPs)=hnap-

-hnēapan v. ā-hn.

hnēaw *mean, niggardly, stingy, miserly,* CP. [Ger. genau] adv. -līce.

hnēawnes f. *meanness,* CP.

hnecca m. '*neck,*' Æ,CP.

hnēgan=(1) nǣgan; (2) hnǣgan

hneofule f.=hnifol

hneoton pret. pl. of hnītan.

hnep (GD 186²⁷)=hnæpp

hneppian (KGL)=hnappian

hnescan=hnescian

hnesce I. (æ, i, y) *soft, tender, mild,* CP : *weak, delicate,* Æ : *slack, negligent,* CP : *effeminate, wanton,* Æ. ['NESH'] II. n. *soft object.* III. adv. *softly,* ÆL 37³⁰¹.

±hnescian *to make soft, soften,* Æ,EPs : *become soft, give way, waver,* CP,Lcd; ÆL. ['nesh']

hnesclic *soft, luxurious, effeminate,* AO. adv. -līce *softly, gently, tenderly,* CP. ['neshly']

hnescnes f. *softness, weakness, effeminacy,* CP,Lcd,MtL; Æ : *soft part of anything.* ['neshness']

hnett (MtL 4¹⁸)=nett

hnexian (Æ)=hnescian

hnifol m. *brow, forehead,* LCD,WW.

hnifol-crumb, -crump *inclined, prone,* WW.

hnīgan¹ *to bow oneself, bend, bow down* : *fall, decline, sink.* [Ger. neigen]

±hnigian *to bow down (the head),* LCD 7a, LL.

hnigian=hnygelan

hnipend *bending, lowly,* HGL 436.

hnipian *to bow down,* Met,OEG; Æ : *bow the head, look gloomy,* CP. ['nipe']

hnippan? *to bow down,* OEG 1579n.

hnisce (MkR 13²⁸)=hnesce

hnītan *to thrust, gore, butt,* Æ : *knock, come into collision with, encounter.*

hnitol *addicted to butting (of an ox),* Æ,LL.

hnitu f. *louse-egg,* '*nit,*' Ep,Lcd; Æ.

hnoc m. *wether sheep,* WW 120³⁴.

hnoll m. *top, crown of the head,* Æ,VPs. ['noll']

hnoppian *to pluck,* WW 480²⁷.

hnor? *sneezing* Ln 65. [*hnēosan]

hnossian *to strike,* RD 6⁷.

hnot *bare, bald,* '*close-cropped,*' ÆGr. ['not']

hnutbēam m. *nut tree,* Lcd; WW. [v. '*nut*']

hnutcyrnel mn. *kernel of a nut,* LCD.

hnutu f. gs. and nap. hnyte '*nut,*' Erf,Lcd, MtR; Mdf.

+hnycned *wrinkled?* LCD 97a.

hnydele=hydele

hnygelan (i) pl. *clippings,* WW.

hnȳlung f. *reclining,* WW 153²⁴.

+hnyscan *to crush,* MtR 21⁴⁴. [hnesce]

hnysce=hnesce

+hnyst *contrite,* PsC 127.

hnyte gs. and nap. of hnutu.

hō I.=hōh. II. pres. 1 sg. of hōn.

hōbanca m. *couch,* WW 280¹². [hōh]

hōc m. '*hook,*' BH,WW : *angle,* Mt,Nar.

hoc(c) m. *mallow,* Cp,Lcd. ['*hock*']

hōced *curved,* KC. ['*hooked*']

hocer=hocor; hocg=hogg

hōciht(e) *with many bends?* KC 3·365', 6·227⁹.

hōcisern n. *small sickle,* WW 235¹.

hoclēaf n. *mallow,* LCD.

hocor n. *insult, derision,* W 164¹⁷. ['*hoker*']

hocorwyrde *derisive, scornful,* W 164¹³. [v. '*hoker*']

hōd m. '*hood,*' Ep,WW.

hof n. *enclosure, court, dwelling, building, house, hall* : *temple, sanctuary.* [Ger. hof]

hōf I. m. '*hoof,*' Run,WW; Æ. II. pret. 3 sg. of hebban.

hofding m. *chief, leader,* CHR 1076. [ON. höfðingi]

hōfe f. '*hove,*' *alehoof (plant),* Lcd,WW.

hofer (o²) m. *hump,* ÆL : *swelling,* GL.

hofer-ede, -od *humpbacked,* CP,Lcd,WW. ['*hovered*']

hoferiend, +hoferod (ÆL)=hoferede

-hōfian v. be-h.

hōflic *pertaining to a court,* OEG 2996.

+hōfod *hoofed,* ÆL 25⁴⁴.

hōfon pret. pl. of hebban.

hofor=hofer

hōf-rec, -ræc n. *hoof-track, bridle-track,* LCD.

hofrede *bedridden,* WW 162⁸.

hōfring m. *print of a horse's hoof (=hr.),* OEG 18.

hofweard m. *ædile,* WW 111²⁰.

hog-=hoh-

hoga I. *careful, prudent,* DR,MtL. ['*howe*'] II. m. *fear, care* : *attempt, struggle,* OEG 8²⁸³.

hoga-=hog-, hoh-; hogade=hogode

hogascipe (o²) m. *prudence,* DR,LkL.

hogde pret. of hycgan or hogian.

hogelēas *free from care,* RWH 79³³.

hogg m. *hog,* NC 302 (v. LF 132).

±hogian (LWS for hycgan q.v.) *to care for, think about, reflect, busy oneself with,* G; Æ : *intend,* B : *strive, wish for.* ['*how,*' '*howe*']

hogu f. *care,* Æ. ['*how,*' '*howe*']

hogung f. *endeavour*, DHy8¹².
hōh m., gs. hōs, nap. hōas, hōs, dp. hōum *hough, heel*, Æ,Jn,Ps. on h. *behind* : *point of land*, Ct,Gl,Nar; Mdf. [' *ho*,' ' *hoe*'; v. also ' *hough*']
hoh-fæst, hog(a)- (NG) *cautious, wise*.
hōhfōt m. *heel*, LPs55⁷.
hohful (hoga-, N) *careful, thoughtful*, Æ : *full of care, anxious, pensive, sad*, Ct,Sc : *persistent*, ÆL31¹⁰⁸⁴. [' *howful*']
hohfulnes f. *care, trouble*, RBL, W.
hōh-hwyrfing, -hwerfing f. *heel-turning, circle?* v. OEG18n.
hōhing f. *hanging*, WNL294a¹².
hohlīce (hog-) *prudently*, LkL16⁸.
hohmōd *sad, sorrowful*, W72⁸.
hōhscanca m. *leg, shank*, LCD14a.
hōhsinu f. *sinew of the heel*, Æ,Lcd. [' *hough-sinew*']
-hōhsnian v. on-h.
hōhspor n. *heel*, WW160²⁶.
hol I. *hollow, concave*, LCD : *depressed, lying in a hollow*, CP,Ct,MH. [' *holl*'] **II.** n. *hollow place, cave, hole, den*, Ct,Lk,Met,Ps, WW; Æ,AO : *perforation, aperture;* Cp. [' *hole*,' ' *holl*']
hōl n. *calumny, slander*, ÆL,W.
-hola v. oter-h.
+hola=+hala
holc n? holca? m. *hole, cavity*, Lcd. [' *holk*']
hold I. *gracious, friendly, kind, favourable*, AO,B; Æ : *true, faithful, loyal*, Æ,LL; CP : *devout : acceptable, pleasant.* [' *hold*'] adv. holde, Ps. [' *holde*'] **II.** n. *dead body, carcase*, Mt; Æ. [' *hold*'] **III.** m. *holder of allodial land, ranking below a jarl (Danish title)*, LL : *notable, chief*, MkR6²¹. [ON. holdr]
holdāð m. *oath of allegiance*, CHR1085.
holdelīce=holdlīce
holdhlāford m. *gracious lord, liege lord*, CHR 1014E.
holdian *to cut up, disembowel*, ÆL23⁷⁸. [hold II.]
holdingstōw f. *slaughterhouse*, KC.
holdlic *faithful, friendly*, OEG50²⁹. adv. -līce *graciously*, Æ,WW : *faithfully, loyally : devoutly.* [' *holdely*']
holdrǣden f. *faithful service*, ÆH2·150³⁰.
holdscipe m. *loyalty, allegiance*, CHR.
holecerse a *plant*, LCD29b.
holegn=holen I.
holen I. m. ' *holly*,' WW; Æ; Mdf. adj. *of holly*. **II.** pp. of helan.
hōlenga=hōlinga
holenlēaf n. *holly leaf*, LCD127a.
holenrind f. *holly bark*, LCD29b.
holenstybb m. *holly-stump*, KC3·338'.
holh (CP), holg n. gs. hōles *hole*, ' *hollow*.'

holian *to hollow out, scoop out*, Æ : *to become hollow, be perforated*, Æ. [' *hole*']
hōlian *to oppress*, LPs. [' *hole*']
+holian *to obtain*, CP209¹⁹.
holing f. *hollow place*, GD113¹¹.
hōlinga (o², u²) adv. *in vain, without reason*, BH,LL.
holl=hol II.
hollēac n. *a kind of onion*, WW270²⁹. [' *holleke*']
holm m. †*wave, sea, ocean, water*, B : (in prose, esp. in place-names) *island* (esp. in a river or creek), Chr. [' *holm*']
holmærn n. *ship*, GEN1422.
holmclif† n. *sea-cliff, rocky shore*, B.
holmeg adj. *of the sea*, Ex118.
holmmægen n. *force of the waves*, RD3⁹.
holm-ōracu† f., gs. -ōræce *restless sea*.
holmweall m. *wall of sea water*, Ex467.
holmweard (AN359)=helmweard
holmweg m. *sea-path*, AN382.
holmwylm m. *billows*, B2411.
holnes f. *hollow place*, GDo99²².
holoc=holc
hōlonga=hōlinga
holpen pp. of helpan.
holrian=heolorian
holstæf m. ' *apex*,' *tittle*, MtR5¹⁸.
holt nm. *forest, wood, grove, thicket*, Æ,B; CP; Mdf : *wood, timber*, Jul. [' *holt*']
holt-hana, -ana m. *woodcock*, WW344³⁰.
hōltihte f. *calumny*, WW116²⁵,198³.
holtwudu† m. *forest, grove*, Ph : *wood (timber)*. [v. ' *holt*']
hōlunga=hōlinga; **hom**=ham
hōm=ōm; **hōman**=ōman
hōn I. (sv⁷) pret. heng, pp. hangen *to hang, suspend, crucify*, Æ : *put on (clothes)*, Bo 42¹⁵n. **II.** pl. *tendrils of a vine?* A4·143.
hon-=han-; **hona**=(1) heonu; (2) hana
hōnende *having heels*, WW161²⁶. [hōh]
+honge=+hange
hongen pp. of hōn.
hop n. *privet?* OEG36¹⁴ (but v. BTs) : *enclosed land in a marsh*, KC6·243¹⁴.
hōp m. *hoop?* NR22; v. NC303.
-hop v. fen-, mōr-h.
hopa m. ' *hope*,' Æ. [usu. tōhopa]
hōpgehnäst n. *dashing of waves*, RD4²⁷.
±hopian *to* ' *hope*,' *expect, look for*, Æ,Bf; CP : *put trust in*, Æ,Bo,Bl.
hōpig *eddying, surging*, PPs68².
+hopp n. *small bag, seed-pod*, WW405³.
hoppāda m. *upper garment, cope*, WW188¹⁴.
hoppe f. *a kind of ornament*, AO : *dog-collar*, LL194,8.
hoppestre f. *female dancer*, Æ. [' *hoppestere*']
hoppetan *to hop, leap for joy : to throb*.

hoppian to 'hop,' leap, dance, Æ : limp, ÆL21⁴¹⁷.

hopscȳte f. sheet, counterpane, Æ (9³⁰⁷).

hopsteort train of a dress, WW438¹⁶ (v. BTs).

hōr n. adultery (Swt).

hora-=horu-; horas v. horh.

hōrcwene f. whore, adulteress, LL.

hord nm. 'hoard,' treasure, B,Chr,Cr,Gen, MtR,WW.

hordærn=hordern

hordburg f. treasure-city, B,BC,GEN.

hord-cleofa, -clyfa m. treasure-chest, treasury, secret chamber, Æ.

hordcofa m. treasure-chamber, closet : (†) breast, heart, thoughts.

hordere m. treasurer, chamberlain, steward, Æ,KC. ['hoarder']

hordern n. treasury, storehouse, B,LL.

horderwȳce f. office of treasurer, CHR1137.

hordfæt n. treasure-receptacle, Æ.

hord-geat n., gs. -gates door of a treasure-chamber, RD43¹¹.

hordgestrēon† n. hoarded treasure.

hordian to 'hoard,' Æ.

hordloca m. treasure-chest, coffer : (†) secret thoughts, mind.

hordmægen n. riches, DA675.

hordmāöm† m. hoarded treasure, B.

hordweard m. guardian of treasure : king : heir, first-born.

hordwela m. hoarded wealth, B2344.

hordweorðung f. honouring by gifts, B952.

hordwynn f. delightful treasure, B2270.

hordwyrðe worth hoarding, B2245?

hōre f. whore, prostitute, OEG.

horeht=horwiht

+hor(g)ian to defile, BK : spit upon, NG.

horh (horg) mn., gs. hor(w)es, instr. horu, nap. horas phlegm, mucus, Æ,El,Ep,Lcd : dirt, defilement, uncleanness; Mdf. ['hore']

horheht=horwiht

+horian (N)=+horgian

horig foul, filthy, Æ,ApT,LL. ['hory']

hōring m. adulterer, fornicator, W309²¹.

horn m. 'HORN' (musical instrument, drinking-horn, cupping-horn), beast's horn, AO : projection, pinnacle.

hornbǣre horned, ÆGR27¹⁶.

hornblāwere m. 'horn-blower,' trumpeter, Gl.

hornboga† m. bow tipped with horn? curved like a horn?

hornbora m. horn-bearer, trumpeter, WW.

hornede having horns, AA19¹⁸.

hornfisc m. garfish, AN370.

hornfōted hoofed, WW213²².

horngēap† broad between the gables, ES 64·207.

horngestrēon n. wealth of pinnacles (on a house)? [or ?=hordgestrēon], RUIN23.

+hornian to insult, MkL12⁴. [?=+horgian]

hornlēas without horns, ES39·349.

hornpic m. pinnacle, MtL. [v. 'pike']

hornreced n. hall with gables, B704.

hornsæl n.=hornsele

hornscēað f. pinnacle, MtL4⁵.

hornscip n. beaked ship, AN274.

hornsele m. house with gables, GEN1821.

hornungsunu m. bastard, WW456¹⁰.

horo-=horu-

horpytt m. mud-hole, EC445¹⁵.

hors n. 'horse,' OET,WW,VPs; Æ,AO,CP.

horsbǣr f. horse-litter, BH; ÆL. ['horse-bier']

horsc I. sharp, active, ready, daring : quick-witted, wise, prudent. II. foul, KC3·456¹⁶.

horscamb m. 'horse-comb,' curry-comb, strigil, WW.

horschwæl (=*horshwæl) m. 'walrus,' AO 17³⁶. [v. 'horse']

horsclic squalid, foul, OEG1789. [horh]

horsclice briskly, readily, promptly : prudently, wisely, GL.

horscniht m. groom, esquire, Æ(8²⁴²).

horscræt n. 'biga,' chariot, WW194²⁶.

horselene f. elecampane, WW. ['horseheal']

horsern n. stable, WW.

horsgærstūn m. meadow in which horses are kept, KC3·414'. [v. 'horse']

horshelene=horselene

horshere m. mounted force (BTs).

horshierde (i², y²) m. ostler, groom, GL.

±horsian to provide with horses, AO,Chr. ['horse,' 'y-horsed']

horslīce=horsclīce

horsminte wild mint, LCD187b.

horspæð m. horse-track, KC5·157'.

hors-ðegn, -ðēn m. ostler, groom, equerry : muleteer.

horswǣn m. chariot, WW140⁴.

horswealh m. groom, equerry, LL22; 132.

horsweard f. care of horses, LL445,2.

horsweg m. bridle-road, KC. ['horseway']

hortan sbpl. 'whortle'-berries, v. OEG2⁴³³.

horu=horh

horusēað m. sink, pit, Bo112¹⁵.

horuweg (o²) m. dirty road? KC5·173¹⁷.

horweht=horwiht; horwes v. horh.

horwig=orweg

+horwigian=+horgian

horwiht (e²) mucose, defiled, filthy, GUTH 36⁹.

horwyll m. muddy stream, EC445¹⁹.

horxlic=horsclic

hos shoot, tendril, GL.

hōs I. f. escort, company, B924. II. v. hōh.

hosa m., hose f. 'hose,' WW.

hosebend m. *hose-band, garter*, OEG4822.

hosp m. *reproach, insult*, Æ : *blasphemy*, Æ.

hospcwide m. *insulting speech*, EL523.

hospettan *to ridicule*, Cp697s.

hosplíc *insulting*, ÆH2·232³¹.

hospspræc f. *jeer, taunt*, ÆH2·514¹¹.

hospul *despised*, RPs88³⁵.

hospword n. *abusive language, contemptuous expression*, Æ.

hoss=hos; **hosse**=hyse

hōstig (ÆL35¹⁹²)=ōstig

hosu f. *hose*, RB : *pod, husk*, Cp1867.

hotor=otor

hoðma† m. *darkness, the grave*.

hr-=r-

hrā=hræw

hraca? m. (*Lcd*)=hrace

hrāca (ǣ) m. *clearing of the throat : mucus*.

hracca (e, ea) '*occiput*,' WW463²¹.

hrace, hracu (æ) f. *throat*, Æ,*VPs* : *gorge*, KC3·440'. ['*rake*']

hrad- v. hræd-; **hrade**=hraðe

±hradian (ea, ǒ) *to be quick, hasten, come quickly : do quickly or diligently : put briefly*, BF52⁸ : *further, prosper*, ÆL20⁷⁸.

hradung (æ) f. *quickness, despatch, diligence*.

hræ-=hra-, hre-, hrea-

hrǣ-=hræw; **hrǣ-**=hrēa-, hrēo-, rǣ-

hrǣcan tr. and intr. *to 'reach,' bring up* (*blood or phlegm*), CP,Lcd; Æ.

+hrǣcan=+reccan

hrǣcea m. *clearing of the throat*, LCD9a. [=hrāca]

hrǣcetan *to eructate*, LCD84a.

hrǣcetung f. *eructation*, LCD69b.

hrǣcgebrǣc n. *sore throat*, WW.

hrǣcing=ræcing

hrǣctan=hrǣcetan

hrǣctunge f. *uvula*, LCD17a.

hrǣcung f. *clearing of the throat*, Lcd : *phlegm*, WW162³⁴. ['*reaching*']

hræd (e) (hrad- occly. in obl. cases) *quick, nimble, ready, active, alert, prompt*, Bo,CP, Gl,Mt. ['*rad*']

hrædbita m. *blackbeetle*, WW (hræð-).

hrædférnes f. *swiftness*, Bo72¹⁷.

hrædhȳdig *hasty* (Swt).

hrædhȳdignes f. *haste, precipitation*, CP.

hræding f. *haste*. on hrædinge *quickly*, Æ, W.

hrædlíc (ð) *quick, sudden, premature*, Æ, AO,CP. adv. -líce *hastily, soon, forthwith*, B,Bo,DR; Æ,CP. ['*radly*,' '*rathely*']

hrædlícnes (e) f. *suddenness*, GUTH : *earliness*, EPs118¹⁴⁷.

hrædmōd *hasty*, ÆL16³⁴².

Hrædmōnað=Hrēðmōnað

hrædnes f. (eð) *quickness, promptitude : brevity*.

hrǣdrīpe (ræd-) *ripening early*, WW.

hrǣdtǣfle *quick at throwing dice?* CRA73 (v. ES43·339).

hrǣdung=hradung

hrǣdwǣn m. *swift chariot*, MET24⁴¹.

hrǣdwilnes f. *haste, precipitation*, CP.

hrǣdwyrde *hasty of speech*, WA66.

hræfn I. hræfen (e) m. *raven*, Æ,B,G,Gl, Ma,VPs : *sign of the raven (the Danish banner)*. II.=hæfern

hræfncynn (e) n. *raven-species*, Æ.

hræfnesfōt m. *ravensfoot, cinquefoil*, Gl, Lcd.

hræfneslēac *orchid*, LCD.

-hrǣgan v. ofer-hr.

hrǣge=rǣge; **hrægel**=hrægl

hrægelgefrætwodnes f. *fine clothing*, LL (396²⁷).

hrægelðegn m. *keeper of the robes*.

hrægl n. (e) *dress, clothing, Gl,Jn*; AO : *vestment, CP : cloth, sheet : armour : sail*, BF14⁷. ['*rail*']

hræglcyst f. *clothes-box, trunk*, Ct.

hræglgewǣde n. *dress*, WW430³³.

hræglhūs f. *vestry*, RB.

hræglscēara fp. *tailors' shears*, WW241⁴⁰ (rægl-).

hrægltalu f. *clothing store*, KC,RB (v. BTs).

hræglung f. *clothing*, WW151⁵.

hræglweard m. *keeper of vestments or robes*, WW279¹⁹.

hrægnloca=brægnloca

hræmn, hræm=hræfn; **hræn**=hærn

hrǣron pret. pl. of hreran.

hrǣs v. hræw and rǣs.

hræscetung=ræscetung

-hræscian v. ā-hr.

hrætelwyrt f. *rattlewort*, WW301³.

hræð=hræd. ['*rathe*']

hrǣw I. (ā, ēa) nm. gs. hrǣs *living body : corpse, carcase, carrion*. II.=hrēaw I.

hrǣwíc (hrēa-) n. *place of corpses*, B1214.

hrāfyll m. *slaughter*, B277.

hrāgīfre *deadly*, WW408¹⁰.

hrāgra m. *heron*, GL.

hrālic=hrāwlic

hramgealla=ramgealla; **hrāmig**=hrēmig

hramma m. *cramp, spasm*, LCD,WW.

hram-sa (o) m., -se f. *onion, garlic*, Gl,Lcd, WW. ['*rams*,' '*ramson*']

hramsacrop m. *head of wild garlic*, GL.

hran (o) m. *whale*, GL.

hrān I. m. *reindeer*, AO. II. pret. 3 sg. of hrīnan.

hrand I.=rand. II. pret. 3 sg. of hrindan.

hrandsparwa (o¹) m. *sparrow*, MtL10²⁹.

hranfix (o) m. *whale*, AA33⁷,B540.

hrānhund? m. *deerhound?* v. LL2·117.

hranmere (o) m. *sea*, MET 5[10].

hranrād† f. *(whale's-road), sea*.

hratele f. *'bobonica' (plant)*, WW 296[2]. ['*rattle'*]

hratian *to rush, hasten*, OET (=hradian?).

hraðe (æ, e) I. *quick, Bo,Chr,PPs.* II. adv. comp. hraðor, superl. hraðost *hastily, quickly, promptly, readily, immediately, soon*, Æ,B,Bo,Cr,G,Ps; CP : *too soon, Bo.* swā h. swā *as soon as*, Æ. ['*rathe*,' '*rather*,' '*rathest*']

hraðer=hreðer; **hraðian**=hradian

hrāw=hrǣw

hrāwērig *weary in body*, PH 554.

hrāwlic *funereal*, WW 406[1].

hrēa I. f. *indigestion?* LCD 94b. [hrēaw I.] II.=hrēaw I. and II.

hrēac m. '*rick*,' *heap, stack*, TC,WW.

hrēaccopp m. *top of a rick*, LL 453,21[4].

hrēacmete m. *food given to the labourers on completing a rick*, LL 452'.

hrēad-=hrēod-

-hrēad v. earm-hr. [hrēoðan]

hrēaf=rēaf

hrēam m. *noise, outcry, alarm*, Æ,CP : *cry, lamentation, sorrow*, B,Cr. ['*ream*']

hrēamig=hrēmig

hrēanes=hrēohnes

hrēas pret. 3 sg. of hrēosan.

hrēat pret. 3 sg. of hrūtan.

hreaðemūs (a[2]) f. *bat*, AA,LCD.

hreaðian (VPs)=hradian

hrēaw I. '*raw*,' *uncooked*, Æ,Lcd. II.= hrǣw nm. III. pret. 3 sg. of hrēowan.

hrēaw-=hrēow-

hrēawan *to be raw*, WW 215[43] (rēaw-).

hrēawic=hrǣwic

hrēawnes I. f. *rawness*, OEG 3283. II.= hrēownes

+hrec=+rec; **hrēc-**=hrǣc-

hrecca=hracca

hred (KGL)=hræd; **-hreda** v. æfreda.

hreddan *to free from, recover, rescue, save*, Cr ; Æ : *take away*. ['*redd*']

hreddere m. *defender*, CHRD 94[4].

hreddung (æ) f. *salvation, liberation*, Æ.

Hredmōnað=Hreðmōnað

±**hrēfan** *to roof*, Æ. [hrōf]

hrefn=(1) hræfn; (2) hæfern

hrefnan=ræfnan

hrefncynn=hræfncynn

hregresi? *groin*, MLN 11·333; ZDA 33·244.

hrēh=hrēoh; **hrem**=hræfn I.

hrēman I.† *to boast*. [*Ger*. rühmen] II.= hrīeman

hrēmig (ēa)† *boasting, vaunting, exulting: clamorous, loud*.

hremm=hræfn I.

±**hremman** *to hinder, cumber*, Æ.

hremming f. *hindrance, obstacle*, GL,LCD.

hremn=hræfn I.

hrenian *to smell of, be redolent of*, Sc 106[5].

hrēo=hrēoh, hrēow; **hrēocan**=rēocan

hrēod n. '*reed*,' *rush*, Æ,BH,Gl,LG ; CP; Mdf.

hrēodan[2] *to adorn* (only in pp. ±hroden).

hrēodbedd n. '*reed-bed*,' Æ.

hrēodcynn n. *kind of reed*, NC 303.

hrēod-ig, -iht, -ihtig (e[2]) *reedy*, KC,WW.

hrēodpīpere m. *flute-player*, WW 190[7].

hrēodwæter n. *reedy marsh*, AA 30[19].

hrēof *rough, scabby, leprous*, Wh ; CP. as sb.=*leper*. ['*reof*']

-hrēoflan v. ā-hr.

hrēofl I. f. *scabbiness, leprosy*, CP. II. adj. *leprous*.

hrēofla m. *roughness of the skin, leprosy*, Æ : *leper*, Æ. [hrēof]

hrēof-lic, -lig (Æ) *leprous, suffering from skin-disease*.

hrēofnes f. *leprosy*, NUM 12[10].

hrēofol, hrēoful=hrēofl I.

hrēog=hrēoh

hrēogan *to become stormy*, AA 34[19].

hrēoh (ē) I. adj. *rough, fierce, wild, angry*, Met ; Æ,AO,CP : *disturbed, troubled, sad* (v. hrēow) : *stormy, tempestuous*, B,Bo, Chr. ['*reh*'] II. n. *stormy weather, tempest*.

hrēohful *stormy*, ES 39·349.

hrēohlic *stormy, tempestuous*, W 136[27].

hrēohmōd† *savage, ferocious* : *sad, troubled*.

hrēohnes (ēa) f. *rough weather, storm*, Æ.

hrēol sb. '*reel*,' LL,WW ; Æ.

hrēon-=rēon-

hrēones=(1) hrēohnes; (2) hrēownes

hrēop pret. 3 sg. of hrōpan.

hreopian=hrepian

hrēorig adj. *in ruins*, RUIN 3. [hrēosan]

±**hrēosan**[2] *to fall, sink, fall down, go to ruin*, Æ,B,Cr,VPs ; AO,CP : *rush* : *rush upon, attack*. ['*reose*']

hrēosendlic *perishable* : *ready to fall*, OEG.

hrēosian=hrēowsian

hrēosð (KGL) pres. 3 sg. of hrēosan.

-hrēoða (ē, ēa) v. bord-, scild-hr.

hrēoung (īu) f. *hardness of breathing*, LCD, WW.

±**hrēow** I. f. *sorrow, regret, penitence, repentance, penance*, B,Bl,CP,Cr. ['*rue*'] II. *sorrowful, repentant*, BH 352[5]. III. adj.= hrēoh? IV. *raw*, Ex 12[9]. ['*row*']

±**hrēowan**[2] (often impersonal w. d. pers.) *to affect one with regret or contrition*, Bo, CP,Gen,LL : *distress, grieve*, Cr,Gen : (intr.) *be penitent, repent*, MkL. ['*rue*,' '*i-rew*']

hrēowcearig† *troubled, sad*.

hrēowende (ǣ) *penitent*, LkL. ['*rueing*']

hrēowesung=hrēowsung

hrēowian *to repent*, MkL1¹⁵.

hrēowig *sorrowful, sad*, GEN799.

hrēowigmōd† *sad, sorrowful*.

hrēowlic (ī, ȳ) *grievous, pitiful, sad, wretched, cruel, Chr,Ps.* adv. -līce, *AO,Chr.* ['*ruly*']

hrēownes (ēa) f. *penitence, contrition, repentance, Gl,LL;* CP. ['*rueness,*' '*rewniss*']

hrēowon=rēowon pret. pl. of rōwan.

hrēowsende=hrēosende, v. hrēosan

±hrēowsian (ȳ) *to feel sorrow or penitence, AO,Mt;* CP : *do penance*, HL149¹²⁶. ['*reusie*']

hrēowsung f. *repentance, penitence, sorrow, CP,Lk;* Æ. ['*reusing*']

hrēpan *to cry out*, WW375¹⁰.

±hrepian (eo), hreppan *to touch, treat (of), Mt;* Æ : *attack*, BK6. ['*repe*']

hrepsung (ÆL)=repsung

hrepung f. *sense of touch, touch,* Æ.

±hrēran (tr.) *to move, shake, agitate.* [hrōr; *Ger.* rühren]

hrēre *lightly boiled, Lcd.* ['*rear*']

hrērednes (ȳ) f. *haste*, LPs51⁶.

hrēremus f. *bat, WW.* ['*rearmouse*'; hrēran]

hrēr(e)nes (ȳ) f. *disturbance, commotion, tempest.*

hresl=hrisil

+hresp n. *stripping, spoliation*, NC294.

+hrespan *to strip, spoil*, PPs43¹².

hrēst=hrȳst pres. 3 sg. of hrēosan.

hreð=hræd

hrēð† mn. *victory, glory.*

hrēða m. *covering of goat-skin, mantle,* GL.

hrēðan *to exult, rejoice*, Ex573.

hreðe=hraðe; hrēðe=rēðe

hrēðeadig† *glorious, victorious.*

Hrēðemōnað=Hrēðmōnað

hreðer† (a, æ) m. *breast, bosom : heart, mind, thought : womb.*

hreðerbealo n. *heart-sorrow*, B1343.

hreðercofa m. *breast*, CR1323.

hreðerglēaw *wise, prudent*, Ex13.

hreðerloca† m. *breast.*

-hrēðig v. ēad-, sige-, will-hr.

hrēðlēas *inglorious*, GU878.

Hrēðmōnað m. *month of March,* MH.

hrēðnes=rēðnes; hreðor=hreðer

hrēðsigor m. *glorious victory*, B2583.

hricg=hrycg

hrician *to cut, cut to pieces*, ÆL23⁷³.

hricsc *rick, wrench, sprain*, LCD27a.

hriddel n. '*riddle,*' *sieve*, LL455,17.

hridder(n), hrider n. *sieve* Æ,GL; GD. ['*ridder*']

hrīdrian *to sift, winnow, Lk.* ['*ridder*']

±hrīeman (ē, ī, ȳ) *to cry out : shout, rave, Æ,CP : bewail, lament, JnL.* ['*reme*']

+hrīered *destroyed*, WW496¹⁸.

hrīewð pres. 3 sg. of hrēowan.

±hrif n. *belly, womb,* Æ,AO.

hrif (AA8¹)=rif

+hrifian *to bring forth*, LPs7¹⁵.

+hrifnian (ī?) *to tear off? become rapacious?* AO142²⁶.

hrifteung f. *pain in the bowels*, WW112²³.

hrifðo f. *scurfiness*, LCD90b. [hrēof]

hrifwerc m. *pain in the bowels*, WW112²³.

hrifwund *wounded in the belly*, LL6,61.

hrig=hrycg

hrim m. '*rime,*' *hoar-frost, Cp,Ph;* Æ.

hrīman=hrīeman

-hrīman v. be-hr.

hrīmceald *icy cold*, WA4.

hrīmforst m. *hoar-frost*, LPs77⁴⁷ (rīm-).

hrīmgicel m. *icicle*, SEAF17.

hrīmig *rimy, frosty*, BL.

hrīmigheard *frozen hard*, RD88⁷.

hrimpan (rim-) pp. (h)rumpen *to twist, coil*, WW366⁴⁰.

+hrin n. *morsel*, EPs147¹⁷.

+hrīn (NG)=+rīn=+rēn

±hrīnan¹ (w. a. g. or d.) *to touch, lay hold of, reach, seize, strike, B,Ps :* *have connection with*, DR106'. ['*rine*']

hrincg=hring; hrind=rind

hrindan³ *to thrust, push*, RD55⁴.

±hrine m. *sense of touch : touch : contact*, AA41²⁷.

±hrinenes f. *touch, contact*, BH.

hring I. m. RING, *link of chain, fetter, festoon, CP : anything circular, circle, circular group, Ph :* *border, horizon, Gen :* (†) (pl.) *rings of gold (as ornaments and as money) :* (†) *corslet : circuit (of a year), cycle, course :* *orb, globe.* II.† m. (only in wōpes hr.) *sound? flood? (of tears,* v. BTs).

hringādl (?br-) f. *a disease, ringworm?* MLR19·201.

hringan *to '*ring**,' sound, clash, B,Sol :* *announce by bells, RB.*

hringbān n. *ring-shaped bone*, WW157. ['*ringbone*']

hringboga m. *coiled serpent*, B2561.

hringe f. *ring*, Æ,GL.

hringed† *made of rings*, B.

hringedstefna† m. *ring-prowed ship*, B.

hring-fāg, -fāh *ring-spotted, variegated*, GEN37³.

hringfinger m. '*ring-finger,*' *Lcd,WW.*

hringgeat n? *ring-gate*, RUIN4.

hringgewindla m. *sphere*, WW426²⁵.

hringīren n. *ring-mail*, B322.

hringloca m. *coat of ring-mail*, MA145.

hringmǣl *sword with ring-like patterns*, B.

hringmǣled *adorned with rings (of a sword)*, GEN1992.

hringmere n. *bath*, RUIN455.

hringnaca m. *ring-prowed ship*, B1863.
hringnett n. *ring-mail*, B1889.
hringpytt m. *round pit*, KC.
hringsele† m. *hall in which rings are bestowed*, B.
hringsetl n. *circus*, OEG.
hringsittend m. *spectator, onlooker*, OEG65.
hringðegu† f. *receiving of rings*.
hringweorðung f. *ring-ornament, costly ring, rings*, B3017.
hringwīsan adv. *ringwise, in rings*, AA23[14].
hringwyll m. *circular well*, KC.
hrīning f. *touch*, JnL. [v. '*rine*']
+hriorde (w)=+reorde; hrīp-=rīp-
hrīs I. n. *twig, branch*. II. *covered with brushwood?* KC.
hrisc=risc; hrīscan=hrȳscan
hrīseht *bushy, bristly*, WW513[8].
hrīsel=rysel
hrīsel, hrīs(i)l f? *shuttle : bone of the lower arm, radius*. [hrisian]
hrisian (y) (tr. and intr.) *to shake, move, be shaken, clatter*, An,B,Ps,VPs : (+) *to shake together*, WW370,485. ['*rese*']
hrīsig (rȳsig) *bushy*, OEG8[337].
hrīst pres. 3 sg. of hrēosan.
hrīstle f. *rattle*, WW391[18].
hrīstlende *noisy, creaky*, WW504[8].
hrīstung f. *quivering, rattling noise*, LCD 97a.
hrið (u) m. *fever*, LCD80a.
hrīð I. f. *snow-storm, tempest*, WA102. II.= hrīðer
hrīðādl f. *fever*, LCD80a.
hrīðer (ȳ) n. *neat cattle, ox, bull, cow, heifer*, Bl,Ct,Lcd,WW. ['*rother*']
hrīðeren *of cattle*, Lcd. ['*rotheren*']
hrīðerfrēols (ȳ) m. *sacrifice of a bull*, OEG 4719.
hrīðerhēawere (ȳ) m. *butcher*, WW129[16].
hrīðerheord (ȳ) *herd of cattle*, Æ. [v. '*rother*']
hrīðerhyrde (ȳ) m. *herdsman*, ÆH1·322'.
hrīðfald m. *cattle-pen*, WW195[34].
hrīðheorde (ie)=hrīðerhyrde
hrīðian *to shake, be feverish, have a fever*, Æ.
hrīðig (ȳ) *storm-beaten? ruined?* WA77.
hrīðing f. *fever*, LCD96b.
hrīung=hrēoung; hrīw-=hrēow-
hrīwð pres. 3 sg. of hrēowan.
hrōc m. '*rook*,' ÆL,Cp.
hrōd=rōd
hroden I. (±) *covered, adorned, ornamented* (pp. of hrēodan). II.=roden
hroder=rodor
hrōf m. '*roof*,' *ceiling*, Æ,B,Cr,G; AO,CP : *top, summit*, Bo,Cr,Mk : *heaven, sky*, Cr.
hrōffæst *with a firm roof*, MET7[6].
hrōflēas (rōf-) *roofless*, WW186[30].

hrōfsele m. *roofed hall*, B1515.
hrōfstān m. *roof stone*, ÆH1·508'.
hrōftigel f. *roofing tile*, WW.
hrōftimber n. *material for roofing*, OEG 2256.
hrōfwyrhta m. *roof-maker, builder*, WW.
hrog *mucus from the nose, phlegm*, WW 290[32]
hromsa=hramsa; hron=hran; hrop=rop
hrōp m. *clamour, lamentation*, Bl. ['*rope*']
hrōpan[7]† *to shout, proclaim : cry out, scream, howl*, Gu,Ps. ['*rope*']
-hrops v. ofer-hr.
hropwyrc=ropwærc
hrōr *stirring, busy, active : strong, brave*.
+hror n. *calamity, plague, ruin*, BH284[4]. [hrēosan]
±hroren pp. of hrēosan.
+hrorenes f. *downfall, ruin*, LPs31[4].
+hrorenlic *perishable, transitory, unstable*, NC294; MFH147.
hrōse=rōse
hrōst m. *perch*, '*roost*,' LL454,11.
hrōstbēag m. *woodwork (of a roof)*, RUIN32.
hrot m. *scum*, LCD84a.
hrōðer=hrōðor
hrōðgirela m. *crown*, RPs20[4].
hroðhund (A8·450)=roðhund
hrōðor† m. *solace, joy, pleasure : benefit*.
hrūm m. *soot*, MH,WW.
-hrūmian v. be-hr.
hrūmig *sooty*, WW362[12].
hrumpen v. hrimpan.
hrung f. *cross-bar, spoke*, Rd23[10]. ['*rung*']
hruron pret. pl. of hrēosan.
hrurul *deciduous*, BDS30·11[63].
hrūse† f. *earth, soil, ground*.
hrūt *dark-coloured?* (BTs),WW361[13].
hrūtan[5] *to make a noise, whiz, snore*, Æ,Cp. ['*rout*']
hruð=hrið; hrūðer (KC)=hrīðer
+hrūxl n. *noise, tumult*, v. ES39·344.
hrūxlian (rūx-) *to make a noise*, MtR9[23].
hryc=hrycg
hrycg (i) m. *back, spine*, Æ,CP,Lcd; AO : '*ridge*,' *elevated surface*, B,Ct,Lk,Ps; Mdf.
hrycgbān n. *back-bone, spine*, Ps. ['*ridge-bone*']
hrycgbrǣdan (hrig-) pl. *flesh on each side of the spine*, LCD3·118'.
hrycghǣr n. *hair on an animal's back*, LCD 1·360[19].
hrycghrægl (i) n. *mantle*, TC529[10].
hrycg-mearg (i, -mearð) n. *spinal marrow*, WW292[7].
hrycgme(a)rglið n. *spine*, WW265[23].
hrycgrib (i) n. *rib*, WW.
hrycg-rible, -riple *flesh on each side of the spine*, WW.

hrycgweg m. 'ridge-way,' road on a ridge, Ct.
hrycigan to plough over again, GPH 398.
hryding f. clearing, cleared land, WW 147¹².
hrȳfing f. scab, ·Lcd 32b. [hrēof]
hryg=hrycg
hrȳman=hrīeman
hrympel? wrinkle, WW 531⁴ (hryp-). [v. 'rimple']
+hryne=+ryne
hryre I. m. fall, descent, ruin, destruction, decay, Æ,B,Bo; AO,CP. ['rure'] II. perishable, Æ.
hrȳre-=hrēr-, hrēre-
hrȳsc a blow, Lcd 2b.
hrȳscan to make a noise, creak, v. ES 39·344.
hrysel=rysel; hrysian, hryssan=hrisian
hryst=hyrst
hrȳst pres. 3 sg. of hrēosan.
hrystan=hyrstan
hrȳte (y?) 'balidinus,' WW 163¹⁸ (cp. hrūt).
hrȳðer=hrīðer; hrȳðig=hrīðig
hrȳðða=ryðða; hrȳwlic=hrēowlic
hrȳwsian=hrēowsian
hrȳwð pres. 3 sg. of hrēowsian.
hū adv. 'how,' Æ,CP. hū gerādes; hū meta how. hū gēares at what time of year. hū nyta wherefore. hū ne dōð...? do not...? hū nys...? is not...? : (with comparatives) the : (±) in some way or other, Shr. hū ne nū 'nonne.'
hūcs, hūcx=hūsc
hūdenian to shake, CP 461¹⁶.
hūf=ūf I. and II.
hūfe covering for the head, Cp,WW. ['houve']
hūfian to put a covering on the head, Lev 8¹³.
+hugod minded, Gen 725.
hū-hwega, -hugu somewhere about. h. swā about.
hui! huig! interj.
huilpe=hwilpe
hulc m. I. 'hulk,' ship, LL,WW; Æ. II. hut, Æ,LL,WW.
hulfestre f. plover, WW 287¹⁴.
hūlic pron. of what sort, AO.
hulpon pret. pl. of helpan.
hulu f. husk, pod, WW. ['hull']
hūluco (AO)=hūlic; huma=uma
humele=hymele; hūmen (VHy)=ȳmen
hūmeta adv. in what way, how, Æ.
hun?=hunu
huncettan to limp, halt, RPs 17⁴⁶.
hund I. n. hundred, AO,Bf,G; Æ: (in comp.) decade. ['hund'] II. m. hound, dog, Bo, CP,Jud; Æ,AO : sea-beast (v. sæhund), OEG.
hundæhtatig (VPs)=hundeahtatig
hundællef- (-ændlæf-)=hundendlufon-

hundeahtatig num. 'eighty,' AO.
hundeahtatigoða eightieth, Gen 5²⁵.
hundeahtatigwintre eighty years old, Æ.
hunden of dogs, canine, BLRPs 77⁴⁵.
hundend-lufontig, -leftig (æ²) hundred and ten, Ct.
hund-endlufontigoða, -ælleftiogoða hundred and tenth, CP 465²³.
hundesbēo (WW 380²¹)=hundespēo
hundescwelcan pl. colocynth berries, WW 364³¹.
hundesflēoge f. dog's parasite, AO,Gl.
hundeshēafod n. snapdragon, Lcd 2·395.
hundeslūs f. dog's parasite, WW 319⁴.
hundes-micge, -tunge f. cynoglossum (plant), Lcd 3·333.
hundes-pēo (CPs), -pīe (VPs 104³¹) f. dog's parasite.
hundeswyrm m. dog's worm, parasite, WW 122²⁵.
hund-feald, -fealdlic hundred-fold, Æ. ['hundfold']
hundfrēa m. centurion, MtL 22¹⁹ mg.
hundlic of or like dogs, canine, Æ.
hundnigontēoða ninetieth, Æ.
hundnigontig ninety, Mt. [v. 'hund']
hundnigontiggēare ninety years (old), Gen 5⁹.
hundnigontigoða ninetieth, Æ,CP.
hundnigontigwintre ninety years old, Gen 17¹⁷.
hund-red, -rað n. 'hundred' (number), Bf, G,Ps,WW; Æ : hundred (political district), hundred-court, assembly of the men of a hundred, LL. hundredes ealdor, mann head of the hundred court, centurion.
hundredgemōt n. hundred-moot, LL.
hundredmann m. centurion, Æ : captain of a hundred, Ex 18²¹,Deut 1¹⁵.
hundredpenig m. contribution levied by the sheriff or lord of the hundred for the support of his office, TC 432,433.
hundredseten f. rules of the hundred, LL.
hundredsōcn f. attendance at the hundred-moot : fine for non-attendance, Ct.
hundreð (MkR)=hundred
hundseofontig num. seventy, Mt; Æ. [v. 'hund']
hundseofontigfeald seventy-fold, ÆH.
hundseofontiggēare seventy years (old), Gen 5¹².
hundseofontigoða seventieth, CP (io², io⁴).
hundseofontigseofonfeald seventy-seven-fold, Gen 4²⁴.
hundseofontigwintre seventy years old, Gen 5³¹.
hundtēontig hundred, Æ,Gen,Shr. [v. 'hund']
hundtēontig-feald, -fealdlic hundred-fold. adv. -līce, W 237⁹.

hundtēontiggēare *a hundred years old,* Æ.
hundtēontigōða *hundredth,* ÆGR,RB.
hundtēontigwintre *a hundred years old,* NC 303.
hundtwelftig *hundred and twenty,* AO.
hundtwelftigwintre *aged a hundred and twenty,* DEUTC31².
hundtwentig *hundred and twenty,* ÆT.
hundtwentigwintre *aged a hundred and twenty,* DEUT31².
hundwealh (æ²) m. *attendant on dogs,* WW 111²⁵.
hundwelle *a hundred-fold,* MtL13⁸. [= -wille]
hundwintre *aged a hundred years,* Æ (GEN).
hūne f. *horehound,* LCD.
hū ne nū *'nonne,'* RPs52⁵; Hy6⁶.
hunger=hungor
hungerbiten *starving,* CHR1096.
hungergēar mn. *famine-year,* Æ,GEN41⁵⁰.
hungerlǣwe *famishing, starving,* LHy3⁵.
hungerlic *hungry, famishing,* WW.
hungor m. *'hunger,' desire, An,Cr,VPs, WW*; CP : *famine,* Æ,Mt,Chr.
hungrig *'hungry,' famishing, Gu,MtL*; Æ, AO : *meagre,* OEG.
hungur=hungor
hunig n. *'honey,' AO,VPs*; Æ,CP.
hunigæppel m. *pastille of honey?* Ep,WW.
hunigbǣre *honeyed,* OEG.
hunigbin f. *vessel for honey,* LL455,17.
hunigcamb f. *'honey-comb,'* Sc50⁹.
hunigflōwende *flowing with honey,* GU1250.
huniggafol n. *rent paid in honey,* LL448,4⁵.
hunigsūge f. *honeysuckle? clover? privet? Cp,WW.* ['*honeysuck*']
hunigswēte *'honey-sweet,' mellifluous,* Æ.
hunigtēar m. *honey which drips from the comb,* GL,LCD.
hunigtēar-en, -lic *nectar-like,* GL.
huni-sūge, -sūce=hunigsūge
hūnsporu mf. *'dolon,' pike?* Cp356D.
hunta m. *huntsman,* Æ,AO : *a kind of spider,* Lcd54a. ['*hunt*']
huntað=huntoð
huntaðfaru f. *hunting expedition,* LL252,22.
±huntian, huntgan *to 'hunt'* (intr.), Lcd, WW; (tr.) Æ.
hunticge f. *huntress,* A6·188.
huntigspere n. *hunting-spear,* WW142¹².
huntigystre=hunticge
huntoð, huntnoð, huntnold, huntnað m. *hunting, what is caught by hunting, game, prey,* Æ,Ct,Lcd; AO. ['*hunteth*']
huntung f. *'hunting,' WW : a hunt, chase, DR : what is hunted, game,* ES37·188.
hūnðyrlu np. *holes in the upper part of a mast,* WW288¹⁵.
hunu? *a disease,* WW502³¹.

hūon=hwōn; hupbān, huppbān=hypbān
-hupian v. on-h.
hupseax=hypeseax
hurnitu=hyrnetu
hūru adv. *at least, at all events, however, nevertheless, yet, even, only, LL; Æ : about, not less than, AO : surely, truly, certainly, indeed, especially,* CP. h. swīðost *most particularly.* ['*hure*']
hūruðinga *at least, especially,* Æ.
hūs n. *'house,' B,G,RB*; Æ,AO,CP : *temple, tabernacle, G,Ps : dwelling-place, El,Ph : inn : household, JnL : family, race, Ps.*
±hūsa m. *member of a household,* G.
hūsærn n. *dwelling-house,* CHRD102¹.
hūsbonda (ō²?) m. *householder, master of a house, Mt,Chr.* ['*husband*']
hūsbonde f. *mistress of a house,* Ex3²².
hūsbryce (e², i²) m. *housebreaking, burglary, LL.* ['*housebreach*']
hūsbrycel *burglarious,* WW205²⁸.
hūsbryne m. *burning of a house,* Ct.
hūsbunda=hūsbonda
hūsc n. *mockery, derision, scorn, insult. Gen,WW.* ['*hux*']
hūscarl m. *member of the king's body-guard, Chr,KC.* ['*house carl*'; ON.]
hūsclic *shameful, ignominious, outrageous,* Æ. adv. -lice.
hūscword n. *insulting speech, An.* [v. '*hux*']
+hūsed *furnished with a house,* WW121³².
hūsel n. *'housel,' Eucharist, Æ,BH : the Host, LL : a sacrifice,* MtL12⁷.
hūselbearn (-ul) n. *communicant,* GU531.
hūselbox *housel-box,* ÆP178⁶.
hūseldisc m. *housel-dish, paten,* GL,LCD.
hūsel-fæt n. nap. -fatu *sacrificial or sacramental vessel,* BH,LL.
hūselgang m. *going to, partaking of the Eucharist,* Æ,LL.
hūselgenga m. *communicant,* v. LL2·263.
hūselhālgung f. *attendance at the Eucharist, communicating, Æ : Holy Communion,* W34⁵.
hūsellāf f. *remains of the Eucharist,* ÆP27¹⁰.
hūselportic (u²) m. *sacristy,* BH94¹⁰.
hūselðēn m. *acolyte,* LL.
hūsfæst adj. *occupying a house,* Ct.
hūshefen m. *ceiling,* WW432⁸. [heofon]
hūshlāford m. *master of the house,* Æ.
hūshlēow n. *housing, shelter,* LL(282'); W74⁴.
±hūsian *to 'house,' receive into one's house, LL.*
hūsincel n. *habitation,* DR,BJVPs.
±hūslian *to administer the sacrament, A* (pp.),*LL.* ['*housel*']
hūslung f. *administration of the sacrament,* Æ. ['*houseling*']

hūslwer (sel) m. *communicant*, Gu 768.
hūsrǣden f. *household, family*, LPs.
±hūsscipe m. *house* (e.g. *of Israel*), *race*, Ps.
hūsstede m. *site of a house*, Lcd.
hūsting n. *tribunal, court* (*esp. in London*),
 Chr. ['*husting*']
hūsul, hūsul=hūs(e)l
hūswist f. *home*, LPs 5⁸.
hūð I. f. *plunder, booty, prey*, Æ. II. f.,
 hūðe f.=hȳð
hūx=hūsc
hwā mf., hwæt n. pron. (interrog.) '*who,*'
 Æ,B,Met : '*what,*' *Æ,Bo,Ps*; AO,CP :
 (indef.) *any one, some one, anything, something*, *Æ,AO,CP* : *each*. swā hwā swā
 whosoever. swā hwæt swā *whatsoever*. tō
 hwǣm *wherefore*.
+hwā *each one, every one, any one, whoever*.
hwæcce v. hwicce.
+hwǣde *slight, scanty, small, young*, Æ.
hwǣder (CP)=hwider
+hwǣdnes f. *smallness, fewness, insignificance*.
hwǣg (ē) n? '*whey,*' *Cp,LL*.
hwæl I. (usu. hwal- in obl. cases) m. '*whale,*'
 walrus, *Æ,AO,Bf*. II. pret. 3 sg. of
 hwelan. III.=hwall. IV. (Ex 161)=wæl n?
hwælc (N)=hwilc
hwælen *like a whale*, Sol 263.
hwælhunta m. *whale-fisher, whaler*, Æ,AO.
hwælhuntað m. *whale-fishery, whaling*, AO.
hwælmere† m. *sea*, An,Rd.
hwælweg (wæl-) m. *sea*, Seaf 63.
hwæm=hwemm
hwǣm (*LkL,VPs*) ds. of hwā, hwæt.
 ['*whom*']
+hwǣmlic *each, every*, LkL 9²³.
-hwǣnan v. ā-hw.
hwæne (G)=hwone, asm. of hwā.
hwǣne=hwēne
hwænne (*G, Ps*), hwæne ('*when*')=hwonne
hwǣr=hwer
hwǣr (ā) adv. and conj. '*where,*'
 *whither, somewhere, anywhere, every-
 where*, CP. wel h. *nearly everywhere*. swā
 hw. swā *wheresoever, wherever*. elles hw.
 elsewhere. hwǣr...hwǣr *here...there*.
+hwǣr *everywhere, in all directions*, Æ : *on
 every occasion, always*, *Æ,B* : *somewhere*.
 ['*y-where*']
hwǣrf=hwearf; hwǣrfan=hwierfan
hwǣrflung=hwyrflung
hwǣr-hwega, -h(w)ugu *somewhere*.
hwæs I. *sharp, piercing*, Cr 1444. II. gs. of
 hwā, hwæt (*CP,G,WW*). ['*whose*']
hwǣst m. *blowing*, v. OEG 2452n.
hwǣstrian (ā) *to murmur, mutter*, NG.
hwǣstrung (ā) f. *murmur, whispering,
 muttering*.

hwæt I. (neut. of hwā, which see) adv. *why,
 wherefore* : *indeed, surely, truly, for*. interj.
 '*what*!' *lo!* (calls attention to a following
 statement) *ah! behold!* Æ. II. adj. (obl.
 cases have hwat-) *sharp, brisk, quick,
 active* : *bold, brave*, B,Cra; AO. ['*what*']
 III. (CP) pres. 3 sg. of hwettan.
+hwæt (*Cr*) neut. of +hwā. ['*i-hwat*']
hwǣte (ē) m. '*wheat,*' *corn*, *G,VPs*; CP.
 [hwīt]
hwǣteādig *very brave*, El 1195?
hwǣtecorn n. *corn of wheat*, Lcd 13a.
 ['*wheatcorn*']
hwǣtecroft m. *wheat-field*, BC 3·135'.
hwǣtecynn n. *wheat*, PPs 147³.
hwǣtegryttan pl. *wheaten groats*, WW 141²⁰.
hwǣtehealm m. *wheat-straw*, Lcd 49a.
hwǣteland n. '*wheat-land,*' KC 3·159²¹.
hwǣtemelu n. '*wheat-meal,*' Lcd 126a.
hwǣten '*wheaten,*' *G,Lcd,OET* ; Æ.
hwǣtesmedma m. *wheat-meal*, Lcd.
hwǣtewǣstm m. *corn, wheat*, CPs 77²⁵.
hwǣthwara=hwǣthwugu
hwæt-hwugu, -hwigu, -hugu, -hwega,
 -hwegu, -hwygu adj. sb. pron. and adv.
 somewhat, slightly, a little, something.
hwæt-hwugununges (CP), -hweganunges,
 -huguningas adv. *somewhat*.
hwǣtlīce adv. *quickly, promptly*, Ps.
 ['*whatliche*']
hwǣtmōd† *bold, courageous*.
±hwǣtnes f. *quickness, activity*, Bf,Bo.
hwǣtrēd (=rǣd) *firm, determined*, Ruin 20.
hwǣtscipe m. *activity, vigour, boldness,
 bravery*, AO,CP.
hwǣðer (e) adj. pron. conj. (with subj.)
 and adv. '*whether,*' *Æ,G* : *which of
 two*, '*whether*,*' *Æ,AO,G*. swā hw. swā
 whichever. hwæðer...ðe *whether...or* : *each
 of two, both* : *one of two, either*, CP.
+hwǣðer *both, either, each*.
hwæðere, hwæð(ð)re I. adv. *however, yet,
 nevertheless, still*, B,Lcd ; Æ,AO,CP.
 ['*whether*'] II.=hwæðer adv.
+hwæðere *nevertheless*, Run 10.
hwæðreðēah (RPs 72¹⁸)=ðēahhwæðre
hwal- v. hwæl; hwalf=hwealf I.
hwall (=æ) *forward, bold*, WW. [hwelan]
hwām (*B,Bl,G*) ds. of hwā, hwæt. ['*whom*']
hwamm (o) m. *corner, angle, prominence*,
 Æ,CP : *porch*.
hwamstān (o¹) m. *corner-stone*, MtL 21⁴².
hwan=hwon instr. of hwæt.
hwān=hwām; hwanan=hwanon
hwane (*Bl*)=hwone asm. of hwā.
hwanne (*Bl*)=hwonne
hwanon, hwanone adv. *whence*, Æ,B,Bo,
 LG,Mt. ['*when*']
+hwanon adv. *from every quarter*, Æ.

hwanonhwegu adv. *from anywhere*, Ep 1095.

hwār (*G*), hwāra (*AO*)=hwǣr

hwarne (*not*) *at all*, MtL 8³⁰.

hwāst-=hwǣst-

hwasta? m. *eunuch*, Mt,WW.

hwat- v. hwæt.

hwat-a I. m. *augur, soothsayer*, Æ. II. (æ), -an fpl. *augury, divination*, Æ,*Lev*. ['*whate*']

hwatend '*iris Illyrica*' (*plant*), WW.

hwatu f. *omen*, W.

hwatung f. *augury, divination*, LL.

hwaðer-=hweðer-

hwēal (WW 162²⁵)=ðwēal

hwealf I. *concave, hollow, arched, vaulted*. II. f. *vault, arch*. [cp. *Ger*. gewölbe]

hwealhafoc=wealhhafoc

hwealp=hwelp

hwearf I.† m. *crowd, troop, concourse, Gu*. ['*wharf*'; hweorfan] II. (a, e, eo) m. *exchange* : *what is exchanged* : (+) *vicissitude* : *error*, MtR 27⁶⁴ : *going, distance*, LkLR 24¹³. III. pret. 3 sg. of hweorfan. IV. m. '*wharf*,' *embankment*, Ct.

hwearfian=hwierfan

hwearfian (e, eo) *to turn, roll or toss about, revolve, GD*; Æ : *wave* : *change*, CP : *wander, move, pass by*, AO. ['*wharve*']

hwearflic (e³) *changing, transitory*, Bo 25¹⁰n : *quick, agile*, Fin 35? adv. -līce *in turn*.

+hwearfnes f. *conversion*, CP 447¹³.

hwearft m. *revolution, circuit, circle* : *lapse* (*of time*).

hwearftlian (y) *to revolve, turn round*, Æ : *wander, be tossed about*, OEG.

hwearfung f. *revolution* : *change, vicissitude* : *exchange*.

hwebbung=webbung; hweder=hwider

+hwēdnes (KGL)=+hwǣdnes

hwēg=hwǣg; hwega *about, somewhat*.

hwegl=hwēol

hwelan⁴ *to roar, rage*, An 495.

hwelc (AO,CP)=hwilc

±hwelian, hwellan? *to suppurate, cause' to suppurate, develop weals, come to a head*, CP,*Lcd,Sc*. ['*wheal*']

hwelp(a) (ea, y) m. '*whelp*,' *the young of an animal, cub, Lcd,LG,Sc,VPs,WW*; AO.

hwelung f. *din*, WW 423²⁰.

hwem=hwemm

hwemdragen *sloping, slanting*, Bl 207¹⁷.

hwemm (æ) m. *corner, angle*, Æ. [hwamm]

±hwemman *to bend, turn, incline*, Chr 1052.

hwēne (ǣ) adv. *somewhat, a little*, Æ,AO,CP. [instr. of hwōn]

hweogl=hwēol

hwēol, hweogol, hweohl n. '*wheel*,' *Bo,Lcd, MH,OEG* : (*as instrument of torture*) ÆL, *Bo* : *circle, Bo,DHy,MH*.

hwēolfāg *having a circular border or decoration*, WW 375³².

hwēolgodweb n. *robe with a circular border?* WW 382³⁵ (hwegl-).

hwēollāst m. *orbit*, DHy 93¹⁷.

hwēolrād f. *rut, orbit*, Cp 233o.

hwēolriōlg n. *a brook that turns a wheel*, KC 3·289,381.

hwēolweg m. *cart-road*, KC 3·386⁴.

hwēop pret. 3 sg. of hwōpan.

+hweorf I. n. *a turning*, Lcd 91a. II. *converted*, MtR 18³ (+werf) : *active?* Cra 68.

hweorfa m. *joint* : *whorl of a spindle*, Lcd. ['*wharve*']

±hweorfan³ (o, u) *to turn, Bo* : *change, CP* : *turn out, Bo* : *move, go, come* : *wander about, roam, go about, GD* : *turn back, return, turn from, depart* : *die* : *be converted*. feohtan mid hweorfendum sigum *to fight with varying success*, AO. ['*wharve*']

hweorfbān (u, y) n. *joint, kneecap*, Lcd, WW.

hweorfian=hwearfian

hwēos pret. 3 sg. of hwōsan.

hweoða=hwiða

hweowl, hweowol=hwēol

hwer (æ, y) m. *pot, bowl, kettle, caldron*, Æ.

+hwēr=+hwǣr

hwerb (WW 53¹²)=hweorfa

hwerbān=hweorfbān

hwerf=hwearf

hwerf-=hwearf-, hweorf-, hwierf-

hwergen adv. only in phr. elles hwergen *elsewhere*, B 2590.

hwerhwette f. *cucumber*, Lcd,WW.

hwēst v. hwōsan; hwēt=wǣt

hwēte (KGL)=hwǣte

hwete- (*Cp*), hwet-stān (*AO*) m. '*whet-stone*.'

±hwettan *to* '*whet*,' *sharpen, incite, encourage*, B,Bl,CP.

-hwette v. hwer-h.; hweðer=hwæðer

hweðre=hwæðere; hwī=hwȳ

hwicce f. *locker, chest, trunk*, OEG 18b¹¹. ['*whitch*']

hwicung f. *squeaking* (*of mice*), GD 185⁴ (c).

hwider (æ) adv. '*whither*,*' Æ,Bl,Bo,LG; AO,CP. swā hw. swā *wherever, whithersoever*.

+hwider *in every direction, everywhere, anywhere, whithersoever*.

hwiderhwega *somewhither*, Lcd 68a.

hwiderryne adj. *directed whither*, Ln 43³³.

hwidre *whither*, Bo 78¹.

hwīe=hwȳ

+**hwielfan** (e, y) *to arch, bend over, IM.*
[*'whelve'*]
±**hwierfan** (æ, e, ea, i, y) *to turn, revolve,
change, transfer, convert, return,* Bo,CP;
AO : *wander, move, go, depart,* AO : *exchange, barter* : (+) *overturn, destroy.*
[*'wharve'*] For comps. see hwyrf-.
-**hwierfere** v. pening-hw.
hwig=hwȳ
hwīl f. *'while,' time,* Bl,Bo,Gen,LG; Æ,CP :
a long time : hour, NG. nū hwīle *just now,
a while ago.* ealle hwīle *all the while.* ōðre
hwīle...ōðre hwīle *at one time...at another
time,* Hy. adv. hwīle *once,* Deor. ðā hwīle
(ðe) *while, whilst, meanwhile,* Bl,RB.
hwilc (e, y) interrog. pron. and adj.
WHICH*, *what,* CP : (indef.) *whosoever,
whichever : any* (one), *some* (one). swā hw.
swā *whosoever, whatever,* Chr.
+**hwilc** *each, any, every* (one), *all, some,
many, whoever, whatever.* anra +hw. *each
one.*
hwilchwega=hwilchwugu
hwilc-hwene, -hwone, -hwegno pron. *some,
some one, something,* NG.
hwilc-hwugu, -hugu (e²) (hwilc is declined)
pron. *any, some, some one,* AO,CP : *not
much, little : anything, something,* NG.
±**hwilcnes** f. *quality,* Æ.
hwīle v. hwīl.
hwīlen *passing, transitory,* WH87 : *temporal,* GD181¹². [*'whilend'*]
hwīlend-e (*Sc*; *'whilend'*), -lic (CP)=hwīl-
wend-e, -lic
hwīleð pres. 3 sg. of hwelan.
hwīlfæc n. *a space of time,* OEG1178.
hwīlhwega adv. *for some time.*
hwīlon (Æ)=hwilum
hwīlpe f. *curlew?* SEAF21. [*Du.* wilp]
hwīlsticce n. *interval, short space of time,
odd moment,* GD254²⁴,WW420²⁸.
hwīltīdum adv. *sometimes, at times,* Æ,CP.
hwīltīdum...hwīltīdum *at some times...at
others.*
hwīlðrāg f. *period of time,* GD243¹⁹.
hwīlum adv. (dp. of hwīl) *'whilom,' sometimes, once,* Met; Æ,CP. hwīlum...
hwīlum *now...now, at one time...at another,*
MH.
hwīlwende *transitory, temporary : temporal,*
Æ.
hwīlwendlic *transitory, temporary, temporal,*
G; Æ. adv. -lice, Æ. [*'whilwendlic'*]
hwimpel=wimpel
hwīnan¹ *to hiss, whizz, whistle,* Wid.
[*'whine'*]
hwinsian *to whine,* NC303.
hwinsung f. *whining,* NC303.
hwirfan=hwierfan

hwirfð pres. 3 sg. of hweorfan.
hwīrlic (HGL434)=hwearflic
hwiscettung f. *squeaking (of mice),* GD
185⁴ (o).
hwisprian *to 'whisper,' murmur,* NG.
hwisprung f. *'whispering,' murmuring,* JnR
7¹².
hwistle f. *reed, 'whistle,' pipe,* LG,WW.
hwistlere m. *'whistler,' piper,* G.
hwistlian *to 'whistle,' hiss,* Gl,Lcd.
hwistlung f. *'whistling,' hissing, piping,
music,* CP,Gu,LG,WW.
hwīt I. *'WHITE'* : *bright, radiant, glistening,
flashing, clear, fair.* II. n. *whiteness :
white food : white of egg,* Æ,Lcd.
±**hwītan** *to whiten : brighten, polish,* LPs,
WW.
hwītcorn n. *manna,* JnL6³¹mg.
hwīt-cwidu, -cudu m. *mastic,* LCD.
hwīte *white,* LCD.
hwīteclæfre f. *white clover,* LCD.
hwītegōs *white goose,* WW259,351.
hwītehlāf m. *white bread,* TC474'.
hwītel (ȳ) m. *blanket, cloak,* Æ,BH.
[*'whittle'*]
hwīteleāc n. *white leek,* WW353⁸.
hwītfōt *white-footed,* GL.
hwītian *to whiten, become white, be white,*
Æ.
hwītingmelu n. *whiting-powder,* Lcd119b.
[v. *'whiting'*]
hwītingtrēow n. *'whitten' tree,* WW139¹.
hwītleāc n. *onion,* WW353⁸.
hwītling m. *a kind of fish, whiting?* NC
303.
hwīt-loc, -loccede *fair-haired, blonde,* RD.
hwītnes f. *'whiteness,'* Bl; Æ.
hwīða m., hwiðu (eo) f? *air, breeze,* Æ,
CP.
hwol? *'ingens,'.* OEG37⁶.
hwomm=hwamm
hwon form of instr. case of hwā, only found
in adverbial phrases like 'tō hwon, *for
hwon' why,* LG : 'bi hwon' *how,* Gu.
[*'whon'*]
hwōn I. adj. *little, few.* II. n. *a little, trifle,*
Lcd,LG : *somewhat : a little while.* [*'whon'*]
III. adv. *somewhat.*
hwonan=hwanon
hwone (CP) asm. of hwā.
hwōnlic *little, small,* Æ. adv. -līce, *moderately, slightly, little,* Æ : *cursorily,* BF30¹².
hwōnlotum (=-hlot-) adv. *in small quan-
tities,* GL.
hwonne (a, æ, e) adv. *'when,' then, at some
time : at any time,* Bl,Gu,Ps; CP : *as long
as, until.* nū hw. *just now.*
hwonon=hwanon
hwōpan⁷† *to threaten,* Ex.

hworfan=hweorfan
hwōsan 3 pers. pres. hwēst; pret. hwēos
to cough, Æ,LCD 96b.
hwōsta m. *cough*, *WW*. ['*hoast?*']
hwoðerian (a¹) *to foam, surge? roar?* ÆH
2·388¹⁹. [hwiða]
hwoðrung f. *a harsh sound*, OEG 26¹⁴.
hwu (LWS)=hū; **hwugu**=hwega
hwugudǽl m. *small part*, HL 18³⁴⁶.
hwurf-=hwearf-, hweorf-, hwierf-, hwyrf-
hwurfon pret. pl. of hweorfan.
hwurful *fickle*, CP 245⁷. [hweorfan]
hwurfulnes f. *inconstancy, mutability*, CP.
hwȳ (inst. of hwæt) adv. and conj. 'WHY.'
tō hwȳ *wherefore*.
hwyder (Æ)=hwider; **hwylc**=hwilc
hwylca (=e) m. *pustule, tumour, boil*, *WW*
161¹⁷. ['*whelk*']
hwylfan=hwielfan
hwȳlon=hwīlum; **hwylp**=hwelp
hwyr=hwer; **hwyrf-**=hweorf-, hwierf-
+hwyrfe(d)nes f. *inclination*, Æ : *conversion*, BH.
hwyrfel m. *circuit, exterior, higher part?*
BL 125²¹ : (meaning doubtful), EC 328′.
hwyrfepōl m. *whirlpool, eddy*, WW 383³⁴.
hwyrflede *round*, v. OEG 23⁴².
hwyrfling m. *orb*, OEG 1992.
hwyrflung (æ) f. *change, turning, revolution*,
BF,DR : *wandering, error*, MtL 24²⁴.
hwyrfnes f. *dizziness, giddiness*, LCD.
±hwyrft m. *turning, circuit, revolution,
motion, course, orbit* : *way out, outlet.* +hw.
gēares *anniversary*.
hwyrftlian=hwearftlian
+hwyrftnes f. *return*, Ps.
hwyrftweg m. *escape*, RD 4⁶.
hwystl-=wistl-; **hwȳtel**=hwītel
hȳ=hīe; **+hȳan**=hēan III.
±hycgan (i) *to think, consider, meditate,
study* : *understand* : *resolve upon, determine, purpose* : *remember* : *hope.* h. fram
be averse to (v. also hogian).
+hycglic *considerable*, GD 328¹⁶.
hȳd I. '*hide*,' *skin*, *Chr,LL*; Æ,AO,CP.
hȳde ðolian *to undergo a flogging.* II.=hīd
+hȳd I. *furnished with a skin*, NAR 50⁵. II.
pp. of hēan. III.=+hygd
±hȳdan I. *to '*hide*'* ('*i-hede*'), *conceal, preserve*, *CP* : (refl. and intr.) *hide oneself,
CP,Ps* : *sheath* (a sword), *bury* (a corpse),
Æ. II. *to fasten with a rope of hide* (BTs),
WH 13. III.=hēdan
hȳddern=hēddern; **-hydele** v. hǽwen-h.
+hȳdelicnes=+hȳðelicnes
hȳdels m. *hiding-place, cave*, MkR,LL.
['*hidels*']
hyder=hider
hȳdesacc m. *leather sack or bag*, ANS 151·80.

hȳdgild (y²) n. *fine to save one's skin* (*i.e.
instead of flogging*), LL. ['*hidegild*']
hȳdig I. *leathern*, WW 125³⁵. II.=hygdig
+hȳdnes I. f. *comfort*, Cp 210o : *security*, CP
387. II.=+hȳðnes
hȳdscip=hȳscip
hȳf f. '*hive*,' *Cp,Lcd,WW*.
hȳg=hīeg
+hygd (i), hygd (PPs 120⁴,VH) fn. *mind,
thought* : *reflection, forethought.*
hygdig (e¹) *heedful, thoughtful,, careful* :
chaste, modest. adv. -līce *chastely.*
hygdignes f. *chastity, modesty*, DR.
hyge (i)† m. *thought, mind, heart, disposition, intention, Seaf,Da* : *courage* : *pride*,
GEN 354. ['*high*']
hygebend mf. *heart-strings*, B 1878.
hygeblind *mentally blind*, JUL 61.
hygeblīðe† *blithe of heart, glad, joyful.*
hygeclǽne *pure in heart*, PPs 104³.
hygecræft† m. *power of mind, wisdom.*
hygecræftig† *wise, prudent.*
hȳgedriht f. *band of household retainers?*
RIM 21. [hīw]
hygefæst *wise*, RD 43¹⁴.
hygefrōd *wise*, GEN 1953.
hygefrōfor† f. *consolation.*
hygegǽlsa *hesitating, slow, sluggish*, PH 314.
[gǽlan]
hygegāl *loose, wanton*, RD 13¹².
hygegār m. *wile*, MOD 34.
hygegēomor† *sad in mind.*
hygeglēaw† *prudent in mind.*
hygegrim *savage, cruel*, JUL 595.
hygelēas (e, i) *thoughtless, foolish, rash*, Æ :·
unbridled, extravagant.
hygelēaslic (i) *unbridled*, OEG 3170. adv.
-līce *thoughtlessly.*
hygelēast f. *heedlessness, folly*, Æ.
hygemǽðum (i) *reverently*, B 2909.
hygemēðe *sad. saddening*, B 2442.
hygerōf† *stout-hearted, brave*, GEN.
hygerūn f. *secret*, EL 1099.
hygesceaft f. *mind, heart*, GEN 288.
hygesnottor† *sagacious, wise.*
hygesorg† f. *heart-sorrow, anxiety.*
hygestrang (i) *brave*, MEN 42.
hygetēona† m. *injury, insult*, GEN.
hygetrēow f. *fidelity*, GEN 2367.
hygeðanc† m. *thought.*
hygeðancol† *thoughtful, wise.*
hygeðihtig (i¹) *courageous*, B 746.
hygeðrymm (i¹) m. *courage*, B 339.
hygeðrȳð (i) f. *pride, insolence*, GEN 2238.
hygewælm m. *mental agitation, anger*, GEN
980.
hygewlanc† *haughty, proud*, RD.
hyggean=hycgan; **hȳglā** (LPs)=hīglā
hyhsan=hyscan; **hȳhst** v. hēah.

hyht (e, i) mf. (±) *hope, trust, Bl,Ps; Æ,CP : joy, exultation :* (±) *desire, expectation :* (+) *comfort.* ['hight']

±hyhtan (i) *to hope, trust, Ps : rejoice, exult, be glad : soften (hardship)*, GUTH 86⁸. ['hight']

+hyhtendlic *to be hoped for*, GD 269¹³.

hyhtful (e, i) *hopeful : full of joy, mirthful, pleasant, glad.*

hyhtgiefu f. *pleasing gift*, RIM 21.

hyhtgifa m. *giver of joy*, EL 852.

hyhting (i¹) f. *exultation*, WW 233⁴².

hyhtlēas (i¹) *unbelieving*, GEN 2387.

hyhtlic† *hopeful, joyful, pleasant.* adv. -līce.

hyhtplega† m. *joyous play, sport.*

hyhtwilla m. *hoped-for joy*, SAT 159.

hyhtwynn f. *joy of hope, joy*, JUD 121.

hyhðo=hīehðu; hyl=hyll

hylc (i) m. *bend, turn*, GL : *unevenness*, WW.

+hylced *bent, curved, bandy*, GPH 398.

hyld (*Gen*)=hield

hyldan I. *to flay, skin*, Æ,WW. ['hild'; hold II.] II. (+)=ieldan

hyldāð m. *oath of allegiance*, LL 396B.

hylde=hielde

hyldemǣg† m. *near kinsman*, GEN.

hyldere m. *flayer, butcher*, GL. [hold II.]

+hyldig *patient*, SPs 7¹².

hylding (=ie) f. *curve, inclination*, WW 382². [heald]

hyldo f. *favour, grace, kindness, protection : allegiance, loyalty, reverence*, AO,CP. [=hield]

hyldrǣden (e¹) f. *fidelity*, TC 610'.

hyldu (Æ)=hyldo

hylest pres. 2 sg. of helan.

hylfe (Æ)=hielfe; -hylian v. be-h.

hyll I. mf. '*hill*,' Æ; Mdf. II.=hell

hyllehāma (i) m. '*cicada*,' *cricket, grasshopper*, GL.

hyllic (i) *hilly*, BC 3·577.

+hylman=helmian; -hylman v. for-, ofer-h.

hylp=help

hylpð pres. 3 sg. of helpan.

hylsten *baked (on the hearth)*, WW 393³¹.

hylsung (o²) f. '*tympanum*,' EPs 150⁴ ·(v. ES 53·359).

hylt=hielt pres. 3 sg. of healdan.

hylt-=hilt-

-hylte v. hēah-h.

hylto=hielto

hylu f. *a hollow*, KC 3·407.

hylwyrt f. '*hillwort*,' *pulegium*, WW.

hym=him; hymblice (GL)=hymlic

Hymbre sbpl. *Northumbrians*, OET 571.

hymele f. *hop plant*, WW; Mdf. [L.]

hymelic=hymlic; hymen=ymen

hym-lic (e) m., -līce f. '*hemlock*,' *Gl,Lcd,* WW.

hȳn=hēan; hȳnan (Æ)=hīenan

hynd=hind

-hynde v. six-, twelf-, twi-h.; of-hende.

hynden f. *community of 100 men*, LL.

hyndenmann m. *chief man in the community of 100 men*, LL 175; 178.

hyne=hine as. of hē.

±hyngran, hyngrian (i) *to be hungry, 'hunger*,' (impers.) Æ,JnL; (intr.) Cr,Lk : (trans.) *hunger for*, Mt 5⁶.

hyngrig=hungrig

hȳnnes (=īe) f. *persecution, destruction*, BH 34⁵. [hēan]

hynnilǣc (Ep)=ynnilēac

hȳnð, hȳnðu=hīenðo

hyp-=hype-

+hȳpan (Æ)=+hēapian

hype m. '*hip*' Bl,WW; Æ,CP.

hȳpe (=īe) f. *heap*, Æ.

hypebān n. *hip-bone*, WW 159²⁵.

hypebānece m. *sciatica*, LCD.

hȳpel (=īe) m. *heap, mound*, GL.

hypeseax (hup-)† n. *short sword, dagger*, GL.

+hypsan (LPs 9²⁵)=hyspan

hypwærc (i¹, e²) n. *pain in the hips*, WW 113¹⁵.

hȳr (ī) f. '*hire*,' *wages*, Æ,LL : *interest, usury*, Æ.

hyra gp. of hē, hēo, hit.

hȳra (ē) m. *follower, mercenary : servant, hireling*, CP 88¹⁵ : *dependant*, BH 104¹⁹.

hyran *to spit*, MkR 14⁶⁵. [cp. +horian]

±hȳran=(1) hīeran; (2) hȳrian

hyrcnian=heorcnian

hyrd I. f. *door*, GEN 2695 (GK). [cp. Ger. hürde] II. *parchment?* GUTH 213¹⁰.

hyrd-, heord-=hierd-

hyrdel m. '*hurdle*,' *frame*, Æ,WW.

hyre gds. of hēo; hȳre=hēore

+hȳre-=+hīere-

hȳreborg (īe) m. *interest*, WW 515¹.

hȳred=hīred; hȳrefter=hēræfter

hȳre-geoc, -geoht=hȳrgeoht

hȳregilda m. *mercenary, hireling*, WW 111¹¹.

hȳremann=hīeremann

hyrfan (TC 611⁵)=yrfan

hȳrgeoht n. *hired yoke of oxen*, LL 24,60.

hyrian *to imitate*, Bo.

hȳrian *to 'hire*' ('*i-hire*'), Æ,Mt,WW (pp.).

hȳrigmann m. *hireling.* [=hīeremann]

hyring (e¹) f. *imitation*, RB 128¹⁴.

hȳrling m. '*hireling*,' Mk 1²⁰.

hȳrmann=hȳrigmann

hyrnan *to jut out like a horn*, Ct.

hyrne f. *angle, corner, CP,Mt;* Mdf. ['hern']

±hyrned *horned, beaked, Lcd;* Æ. ['i-horned']

hyrnednebba† *horny-billed, horn-beaked*, BR,JUD. [horn]

hyrnen I. *of horn,* LRPs 97[6]. **II.** *angular,* OEG 7[20].

hȳrnes=hiernes

+**hyrnes** (VH 16)=+herenes

hyrnet, hyrenetu f. '*hornet,*' *Gl,WW* :*gadfly,* WW 121[12].

hyrnful *angular, with many angles,* OEG 121.

hyrnig *angular,* OEG 121.

hyrnstān m. *corner-stone, keystone,* ÆH 1·106.

hȳroxa m. *hired ox,* LL 116 B.

hyrra (KGL)=heorra, heorr

hȳrra I. v. hēah. **II.**=hȳra

hyrsian *to go on horseback?* BHв 194[35].

hyrst† **I.** f. (±) *ornament, decoration, jewel, treasure : accoutrements, trappings, armour.* [*Ger.* rüstung] **II.** m. *hillock, height, wood, wooded eminence, Rd,Ct.* ['*hurst*']

hyrst-=hierst-

±**hyrstan I.** *to decorate, adorn, ornament, equip.* [*Ger.* rüsten] **II.** (+) *to murmur,* LkLR 15[2]. **III.**=hierstan

hȳrsum=hiersum; **hyrtan**=hiertan

hyrten=heorten

hyrð f. *skin, hide,* ES 41·323.

hyrðil (*Cp*)=hyrdel; **hȳru**=hūru

+**hȳrung** f. *hiring,* WW 213[12].

hyrw-=hierw-

hys=his

±**hyscan** (ea, i) (tr.) *to jeer at, reproach, Ps :* (intr.) *to rail,* W. ['*heascen*']

hyscend (i) m. *reviler,* GPH 398.

hyscild (WW 170[12])=hysecild

hyse† nap. hyssas m. *son, youth, young man, warrior,* GL : *shoot, scion,* HGL 419[69].

hysebeorðor n. *the bearing of male offspring,* GL : *boy, young man,* An.

hyse-berðling, -byrding m. *the bearing of male offspring,* GL.

hyseberðre f. *woman who bears a son,* DHy 50[17].

hysecild n. *male child,* Æ,AO.

hyserinc m. *young man,* GD 338[22].

hysewīse adv. *like young men,* WW 417[35].

hysope=ysope

hyspan (e, i) pret. hyspde and hyspte *to mock, scorn, deride, revile, reproach,* AO. [hosp]

hyspend m. *calumniator,* RPs 71[4].

+**hyspendlic** *abominable,* LPs 13[1].

hyspful *contumelious,* OEG 11[180].

hysp-nes (EPs), -ung (Bo) f. *contumely.*

hysse=hyse

hyt I. f. *heat,* B 2649. [*ON.* hita; or ? read hāt] **II.**=hit pron.

hȳt pres. 3 sg. of hȳdan.

hyttan=hittan

hȳð I. f. *landing-place, harbour, creek, port, Cp,Guth,Met,Ps;* Æ,CP. ['*hithe*'] **II.**=hȳðð

hȳðan (ī) *plunder, ravage,* BH,GD. [hūð]

+**hȳðe** *appropriate, convenient,* Æ.

±**hȳðegian** *to facilitate,* GPH,Sc.

hȳðegung f. *advantage,* Sc 12[6].

±**hȳðelic** *suitable, proper, convenient, advantageous.* adv. -līce.

+**hȳðelicnes** f. '*opportunitas,*' NC 345.

hȳðgild n. *harbour festival, sacrifice or service,* OEG.

hȳðlic *belonging to a harbour,* WW.

+**hȳðlic**=+hȳðelic

+**hȳðnes** f. *advantage,* ÆL 23b[252] : *occasion,* EPs 9[22].

hȳðscip (ī) n. *a light, piratical vessel,* GL.

hȳðð, hȳððo f. *gain, advantage,* Æ.

+**hȳððo** n. *subsistence,* ÆL 23b[492].

hȳðweard m. *warden of a harbour,* B 1915.

hȳw=hīw; +**hȳwan**=+īewan

hyxan=hyscan

I

ia (Æ)=gēa; **iacessūre**=gēacessūre

iacinctus, iacintus m. *jacinth,* CP. [*L.* hyacinthus]

iagul=gēagl; **iara**=gearo

iarwan=gierwan; **īb-**=īf-

ic pron. (1st pers.) '*I,*' *Cp,Jn.* [*Ger.* ich]

ican, icean=īecan; **ice**=ȳce

icend m. '*auctor,*' ÆGR 48[12]. [īecan]

icestre f. '*auctrix,*' ÆGR 48[12].

icge only in phr. '*icge* gold,' *treasure-gold? rich gold?* B 1108 (v. Klb p 168 and BTs).

idæges adv. *on the same day,* Æ.

īdel (ȳ) **I.** (often īdl- in obl. cases) *worthless, useless, vain,* Æ,*CP,Gen,Mt,VPs* : *empty, desolate, bare, void, destitute, devoid* (*of*), Æ,B,VPs; CP : '*idle,*' *unemployed,* Mt. on ī. adv. *in vain,* Æ. **II.** n. *emptiness, frivolity, idleness, Lcd,LL,Sol* : *inattention, carelessness.*

īdelgeorn *slothful, idle,* Bo : *useless,* W.

īdelgielp (e[3], i[3]) n. *empty boasting, vainglory,* CP,DHy,WW.

īdelgild n. *vain worship, idolatry,* Æ.

īdelgildoffrung f. *offering to an idol,* Æ.

īdelhende *empty-handed, empty,* Æ,CP.

īdelinga (a[2]) '*frivola,*' GPH 389.

īdellic *vain, idle.* adv. -līce, VPs. ['*idly*']

īdelnes f. *frivolity, vanity, emptiness, falseness,* VPs; CP : '*idleness,*' *vain existence,* LL : *superstition.* in (on) īdelnisse *in vain.*

-**īdelsprǣce** v. fela-ī.

īdes *virgin :* (†) *woman, wife, lady, queen.*

īdig *busy? active?* (BT) : *greedy for? desirous of?* (GK), Pн 407?

īdl- v. īdel.

±**īdlīan** _to become empty or useless_ : _profane_, BH362¹¹.

īdol n. _idol_, LL. [_L._]

īe v. ēa.

±**īecan** (æ, ē, ī, ȳ) pret. īecte, īhte _to increase_, _enlarge_, _add to_, _augment_, _prolong_, _An,Lcd,Lk_; AO,CP : _fulfil_, _carry out_, RSL11·486. ['_eche_'; ēac]

īecinctus=īacinctus

īecessūre=gēacessūre; **īedel-**=īdel-

īeg (īg) f. _island_. [ēa]

īegbūend (ī) m. _islander_, CP.

īegclif (ēg-) n. _sea-cliff_, B2893.

īegland (ē, ī) n. '_island_,' _BH,Bo,Chr,Wh_.

īegstrēam (ē¹)† m. _current_, _river_, _sea_.

īehtan=ēhtan; **īelc-**=ilc-; **īeld**=īeldó

±**īeldan** (i, y) _to delay_, _put off_, _prolong_, _hesitate_, _tarry_, CP : _connive at_, _dissimulate_. ['_eld_'; eald]

īeldcian (CP)=elcian

īelde† (e, ea, i, y) mp. _men_.

īelden (æ) n. _delay_, BH400²⁰.

īeldendlic (e) _dilatory_, WW441².

īeldest (æ, e, y) superl. of eald '_eldest_,' _chief_, _Æ,Mt,CP_.

īeldesta (y¹) m. _chief_, Ex17⁵.

īeldful (i, y) _dilatory_, _delaying_, OEG.

īeldian (y) _to put off_, _delay_, Æ.

īelding f. _delay_, _tarrying_, CP : _dissimulation_.

īeldo (æ, e, i, y) f. _age_, _Æ,Gu,Lcd_ : _period_ : _old age_, _old people_, _Æ,Bl_; CP : _an age of the world_, _Æ,Gu_. ['_eld_'; eald]

īeldra (y) (comp. of eald) used as sbpl. _parents_, _ancestors_, _Bl,El,Ct_. ['_elder_']

īeldrafæder (æld-) m. _grandfather_, WW7³⁴.

īeldu=īeldo; **īelf**=ælf

īemung (WW277²²)=gēmung; **īerd**=gierd

īerf- v. also yrf-.

īerfa m. _heir_, OET446⁸ (erba).

īerfe (æ, e, i, y) n. _heritage_, _bequest_, _property_, CP : _cattle_. [_Ger_. erbe]

īerfian (i, y) _to inherit_, _possess_ : (+) _to stock with cattle_, TC158¹⁰.

īergan _to dishearten_, _dismay_, Jos,W. [earg]

īergō(u) f. _remissness_, _sloth_, _cowardice_, AO. [earg]

īerlic (i, y) _angry_, _vehement_, ApT.

±**īerman** _to harass_, _vex_, _afflict_, CP. [earm]

īerming (eo, e, y) m. _person of no account_, _poor wretch_, AO,CP.

īermō̃, iermõu (e, ea, eo, y) f. _misery_, _distress_, _poverty_, _B,Bo,Ps_ : _disease_ : _crime_ : _reproach_, CPs118¹³⁴. ['_ermth_'; earm]

īernan³ (æ, i, y; rinnan) pret. 3 sg. arn, orn, pl. urnon; pp. urnen (±) _to_ '_run_*,' _move rapidly_, _hasten_, _flow_, _spread_, _Æ,AO_, _CP,Lcd,VPs_ : _pursue_, _Bo,Ps_ : _cause to move rapidly_, _turn_, _grind_, _AO,BH_ : (+) _get to_, _attain_, _meet with_ : (+) _occur_ (_to one's

---

mind), GD : (+) _coagulate_, Lcd : (+) _grow up_. [v. also '_ern_']

īernes (eo, y) f. _anger_, Bl123⁸,HL.

īerning (e) f. _discharge_, _flow_, NG.

īerre I. (i, y) _wandering_, _erring_, _perverse_, _depraved_, _Ps,Sol_ : _angry_, _fierce_, _Æ,Bl,Chr_, _CP,G_; AO. **II.** n. _anger_, _Bl,CP,El,Lk_. ['_irre_']

īerremōd (y) _wrathful_, _wild_, B726.

īerrenga (eo¹, y¹, i², u²) adv. _angrily_, _fiercely_, CP.

īerreðweorh (y) _very angry_, Sat399?

īerscipe (y) m. _anger_, LPs9²⁵.

±**īersian** (i, io, y) _to be angry with_, _rage_ : _enrage_, _irritate_, CP.

īersigendlic (y) _passionate_, _emotional_, Æ.

īersung (i, y) f. _anger_, CP.

īerð-=eorð-, yrð-

īesca (Ep,Erf)=geocsa

īesend, iesende _entrails_, WW. [=gesen]

īeteð pres. 3 sg. of etan.

īeð adv. comp. (=ēað) _easily_, _An,Met_; AO, CP. ['_eath_'] For comps. v. also ēað-.

+**īeðan I.** (ē) _to alleviate_, Gu1179 : _be merciful_, GD. **II.** (æ, ē, ȳ) _to lay waste_, _ravage_, _devastate_, _destroy_, Æ.

īeðe I. _easy_, _good-natured_, _pleasant_, AO. **II.** (ē)† _barren_, _waste_, _desolate_.

īeðegean=ȳð̃gian

īeðelic _easy_, CP : _moderate sized_, GD. adv. -līce _easily_, AO,CP.

īeðnes f. _ease_, _pleasure_, CP425¹¹.

+**īeðrian** (ē) _to make or become easier_, GD, Lcd.

īeðrung? f. _amelioration_, _a making easier?_ (BTs), Soul107 (MS edring q.v.).

īeðtogen (ȳ) _easily brought about_, ÆL23³¹⁷.

±**īewan** (ēa, ēo, ȳ) _to show_, _display_, _reveal_, _disclose_, _point out_, CP. [ēage; cp. ēowan]

īfe? _a kind of plant_, WW301¹² (iue).

ifegn (Cp)=īfig

īfig n. '_ivy_,' _Gl,Lcd,Shr_.

īfigbearo _ivy-grove_, CC50.

īfig-crop, -croppa m. _cluster of ivy berries_, _Lcd,WW_. |v. '_ivy_']

īfiglēaf n. '_ivy-leaf_,' Lcd117b.

īfigrind f. _ivy-bark_, LCD121b.

īfig-tearo, -tara n. _ivy-tar_, _resin from tar_, LCD.

īfigtwig n. _ivy-twig_, LCD117a.

īfiht _ivy-covered_, KC.

ig=ic; **Ig**=īeg; **igbūend**=īegbuend

igdæges=īdæges; **igel**=īl; **igg**=īeg

iggað, iggoð, īg(e)oð m. '_ait_,' _eyot_, _small island_, _Æ,Chr_. [īeg]

igil, igl (Æ)=īl

Igland=īegland

igoð, īgð=iggað; **ih**=ic

Ihte pret. 3 sg. of īecan.

Il (igil) m. *hedgehog, porcupine, CP,Shr, WW.* ['*il*']

Iland=īegland

±**ilca** (y) pron. (usu. wk) *the same, An,Bo, Chr,Ct; CP.* ['*ilk*']

ilce adv. v. swā; **ild**-=ield-

ile (y) m. *sole of the foot, Æ* : *callosity, corn, Æ.* [cp. *Ger.* eilen]

ilfetu, ilfe(t)te (y;=ie) f. *swan,* GL; Mdf.

ill n.=ile; **illca**=ilca

illeracu f. *surfeit,* WW378[15].

+**illerocad** *surfeited,* CVPs77[65].

ilnetu (WW367[27])=ilfetu

ilugseog v. eolhseog; **imb**- v. ymb-

imberdling, imbyrdling=inbyrdling

impa? m., **impe?** f. *graft, shoot, scion,* CP 381[17]. ['*imp*']

impian *to* '*imp,*' *implant, graft,* LL454,12. (+) *busy oneself with,* CP132[25].

in I. prep. with a. and d. (instr.) (local) '*IN,*' *into, upon, on, at, to, among* : (temporal) *in, at, about, towards, during* : (purpose) *in, to, for.* II. sb. and adv.=inn

in- (v. BH xxxiii ff.)=on-, inn-

ināberan[4] (inn-) *to bring in, Æ.*

inādl f. *internal disease,* LCD.

inǣlan (VPs)=onǣlan; **ināgān**=ingān

ināgēode=inēode pret. 3 sg. of ingān.

ināsendan *to send in,* Mk2[4].

ināwritting f. *inscription,* LkL20[24].

inbærnednes (e[2]), inbærnes f. *burning, incense, frankincense.* [=onb-]

inbecweðan[5] *to inculcate,* WW429[36].

inbelǣdan *to lead in,* LHy.

inbelūcan[2] *to shut,* BL217[26].

inbend mf. *internal bond,* Gu928.

inber-=on-, in-byr-

inberan *to carry in,* LL386,1.

inbernes (VPs)=inbærnes

inbeslēan *to hack into* (any one), LL86,74.

inbestingan *to penetrate,* LL7,64[2].

inbetȳnednes f. *life of a recluse,* GD212[5].

inbewindan[3] *to enfold, enwrap,* LkL (inn-).

inbirdling=inbyrdling

inblāwan[7] *to inspire, breathe upon,* JnR : *inflate, puff up,* EC. ['*inblow*']

inboden *proclaimed.* [onbēodan]

inbolgen *exasperated,* DR. [=onb-]

inboren ptc. *indigenous, native,* SR; GPH390. ['*inborn*']

inborh m. *bail, security in cases of theft,* LL. ['*inborgh*']

inbrēdan[3] *to burst in upon,* GPH393.

in-brengan, -bringan *to bring in, present,* Mk. ['*inbring*']

inbryne (byr) m. *conflagration,* DR64[6].

inbryrd-=onbryrd-

±**inbūan** *to inhabit,* MtL23[21].

inbūend m. *inhabitant,* WW210[13].

in-burg, -burh f. *hall,* WW.

inbyrde (e[2]) *born on the estate,* TC.

inbyrdling (e[2]) m. *slave born in a master's house, Æ* : *native,* OEG.

inbyrne (DR)=inbryne

inbyrð pres. 3 sg. of inberan.

inc (*Mt,Mk*) da. of git, dual pers. pron. ['*inc*']

inca m. *question, scruple, suspicion, doubt* : *occasion,* RB : *grievance, quarrel, grudge,* BH. incan witan *to have a grudge.*

incaðēode=ingeðēode; **ince**=ynce

incēgan (=īe) *to call upon,* DR119[3].

incēgung (=īe) f. *invocation,* DR.

incempa m. *soldier of the same company,* WW207[6].

incer (y) I. gen. of git, dual pers. pron. II. adj. pron. *of or belonging to both of you,* MH,Mt. ['*inker*']

+**incfullian** *to offend, scandalize,* MtR. [inca]

incga=inca

incit acc. of git, dual personal pronoun.

incleofe (i, y) f. *chamber, closet* : *cave, den.*

incniht m. *household servant, Æ.*

incofa m. *inner chamber, Æ*L : *heart,* MET 22[18].

incoðu f. *internal disease, Æ.*

incuman[4] *to come in, go into, enter, Æ.* ['*income*']

incund *interior, internal, inward, secret, Æ*,CP. adv. -līce, Æ.

incundnes f. *inward conviction, sincerity,* W105[30] : *inward part, recess,* DHy.

incūð *strange, extraordinary.* adv. -līce, ÆT1104.

incyme m. *entrance,* LV32.

indǣlan *to infuse,* DR.

indēpan (=īe) *to dip in,* LkL16[24].

indīegelnes f. *hiding-place,* RPs17[12].

Indisc *Indian, Æ.*

indrencan *to steep, saturate* : *fill to overflowing,* VPs22[5]. [=ondrencan]

indrīfan[1] *to ejaculate, utter,* SAT80.

indrihten=indryhten

indrincan[3] *to imbibe, drink.* indruncen *plied with drink.*

indryhten *distinguished, noble, excellent,* WW.

indryhto† f. *honour, glory.*

ineardian *to dwell in, inhabit,* VPs.

inēddisc n. *household stuff, furniture,* WW 147[32]. [ȳddisc]

inelfe=innelfe; **inerfe**=innierfe

inēðung f. *inspiration, breathing,* APs17[16]. [ēðgung]

infær n. *ingress, entrance, entry, admission, Æ*,WW. ['*infare*']

infæreld n. *in-coming, entrance, admission, Æ* : *interior* : *vestibule.*

infangene-ðēof, infangen-ðēf sb. *right of judging thieves caught within the limits of one's jurisdiction, and of taking the fines for the crime*, Ct; v. LL2·523. [*'infangthief'*]

infaran⁶ I. *to enter*, Æ,*Jn.* [*'infare'*] **II.**= innefaran

infaru f. *incursion, inroad*, CHR 1048.

infeallan⁷ *to fall in*, VPs.

infeccan *to fetch in*, BL175¹.

infēran *to enter in*, Æ.

infiht n. *brawl in a house*, LL597'.

infindan³ *to find, discover*, NG.

inflǣscnes f. *incarnation*, EC161²³.

inflēde† *full of water.*

infleon² *to fly from*, RIM 44.

infōster n. *bringing up, rearing*, LL396'.

infrōd† *very aged, experienced*, B.

ing I. *name of the rune for* ng. **II.**=ging, geong. **III.**=inn

-ing suffix, as in earming, lytling (originally patronymic).

in-gān anv. pret. -ēode *to go in, enter*, BH, *Mt.* [*'ingo'*]

ingang (eo²) m. *ingress, entrance, access, beginning*, BH,Ps (inn-) : *entrance-fee.* [*'ingang'*]

ingangan⁷ *to go in, enter*, Æ.

ingebed n. *earnest prayer*, PPs87².

ingeberigan (NG)=onbyrgan

ingebringan³ *to bring in*, LL150'.

inge-cīgan, -cēgan *'invocare,'* VPs; CPs 90¹⁵.

ingedōn anv. *to put in*, BH434²⁰.

ingedrincan (GPH391)=indrincan

ingefeallan⁷ *'incidere,'* Ps.

ingefeoht n. *internal war*, BH.

ingefolc n. *native race*, Ex142.

ingehrif (-gerif) n. *womb*, LPs21⁸.

inge-hygd, -hȳd (Æ), -hīd f. *consciousness, mind, conscience, sense, understanding : meaning, intention, purpose, design.*

ingehygdnes f. *intention*, LPs48⁵.

ingelǣdan=inlǣdan

ingelaðian *to invite*, Lk14.

ingemang v. ongemang prep.

ingemynd† fn. *recollection, memory, mind.*

ingemynde *well-remembered*, EL896.

ingenga m. *visitor, intruder*, B1776.

ingeongan (LG; v. *'yong'*)=ingangan

ingēotan² *to pour in, fill*, GUTH.

ingēoting (yn-? =ymb-) f. *inpouring*, OEG.

ingerec n. *broil*, BH. [=ungerec]

ingerif=ingehrif

ingeseted *placed in, inserted*, WW427¹⁷.

ingesteald *household goods*, B1155.

ingeswel n. *internal swelling*, WW113⁵.

ingeðanc mn. *thought, mind, conscience, intention*, Æ,CP.

ingeðēod† f. *nation*, Ex,PPs.

ingeðōht *conscience*, GD72¹².

ingeweaxen *implanted*, WW427⁸.

ingewinn n. *civil war*, AO88²⁹.

ingewitnes f. *consciousness, conscience*, BH.

ingong (CP)=ingang

ingyte m. *pouring in, infusion, inspiration*, CM424. [gēotan]

inhǣtan *to inflame*, GD29⁹.

inheald *in bas-relief, embossed*, WW423²⁸.

inhebban (CR313)=onhebban

inheldan=onhieldan

inheord f. *herd kept by the lord on his lands*, LL449,7.

inhīred m. *family, household*, Æ.

in-hīwan, -hīgan sbpl. *members of a household or community, servants.*

inhold *loyal in heart*, LCD3·442'.

inhȳrnes f. *possession*, EC364'.

inlīfe=innylfe; **ininnan**=oninnan

inlād f. *right of water-passage inland*, KC 4·209⁵ : *entrance-fee*, Jn p188⁹.

inlǣdan *'inducere,' to introduce*, NG.

inlǣnd-=inlend-

±**inlagian** *to reverse sentence of outlawry*, Chr,LL. [*'inlaw'*]

inland n. *land in the lord's own occupation, domain, demesne*, EC,LL. [*'inland'*]

inlaðian *to invite*, G.

inlaðigend m. *inviter*, Sc170¹².

inlec=inlic; **inlēgan** (VPs)=onlīegan

inlēhtan=inlīhtan

inlenda m. *native*, GL.

in-lende, -lendisc (LCD) *native, indigenous.*

inlēohtan=inlīhtan

inlic *internal, interior, inward*, BH : *native.* adv. -līce *inwardly : thoroughly, sincerely, heartily*, BH,Bo. [*'inly'*]

inlīchomung f. *incarnation*, DR.

inlīgian=onlīgian

±**inlīhtan** *to illuminate, enlighten.*

inlīhtend m. *illuminator*, DR2⁶.

inlīhtian (NG)=inlihtan

inlīhtnes f. *illumination*, VPs.

inlīðewāc=unleoðuwāc

inlīxan *to become light, dawn*, LkL23⁵⁴.

inlocast superl. adv.=inlīcost

inlȳhtan=inlīhtan

inmearg n. *marrow*, GPH397.

inmēde *close to one's heart, important in one's estimation*, RB; BK15.

inn I. n. *dwelling, apartment, lodging, chamber, house*, Æ,*Mt*; AO : *quartering oneself (of soldiers)*. [*'inn'*] **II.** adv. *'in,' into, inwards, within, inside of*, Æ,AO,B, BL,G : *inwardly.* inn on *into.* inn tō is used with words of granting to indicate the grantee, CC125 (ES57·4).

inn-=in-; **inna** (LkL)=innoð

innan I. prep. (w. a. g. d.) *from within* : *within, in, into, CP.* **II.** adv. *within, inside, in, AO.* ['INNE']
innanbordes adv. *at home, CP.*
innanburhware sbpl. *residents within the walls of a town,* TC510'.
innancund *inner, inward, internal,* LCD : *thorough, hearty,* PPs118[2],[10].
innane=innan II.
innanearm m. *inner side of arm,* LCD 87b.
innantīdernes (īe,ȳ) f. *internal weakness,* LCD.
innanweard=inweard
innanwund f. *internal wound,* LCD 3b.
innað=innoð
innāwrïtting (*LkL*)=onwriting
inne adv. *in, inside, within, in-doors, A, AO,BH,Chr,Ct,Lcd.* ['*inne*']
inne-=inn-, in-
innecund adj. *inward,* CP 139.
inne-faran, -foran *bowels,* LCD.
innefeoh n. *household goods,* LL5,28; v. 3·9.
innelfe=innylfe
innemest (superl. of inne) adj. '*inmost,*' Sc : *most intimate, deep or close, CP.* adv.
innera, in(n)ra (compar. of inne) '*inner,*' *interior, GF,WW* : *mental, spiritual, BH, LL,Sc.*
inneð=innoð
inne-weard, -werd=inweard
innheardmann m. *one of the household troops,* MtL8[9]. [inhired]
innhere m. *native army,* CHR1006E.
innian *to go in, Bo* : (±) *put up, lodge, Chr* 1048 : (+) *include* : (+) *fill, restore, make good, Æ.* ['*inn*']
innierfe (e[2]) n. *household stuff, furniture, goods,* Bo31[19].
innifli (Cp1151)=innylfe
±innīwian *to renew,* DR.
innon=innan
innor (*ÆGr*) compar. of inne. ['*inner*']
innoð mf. *inside, entrails, stomach, womb, breast, heart, BH,Bo,G; Æ,CP.*
innoðmægen (e[3]) n. *strength,* EHy5[16].
innoðtȳdernes f. *weakness of the bowels,* LCD 105a.
innoðwund f. *internal wound,* LCD 88b.
innra=innera
innung f. *dwelling* : *contents, takings, revenue, Bo,KC.* ['*inning*']
innweardlīce=inweardlīce
innweorud n. *retainers, household,* WID 111.
innylfe (e, i) n. *bowels, womb,* LCD.
inorf n. *household goods, furniture,* LCD,WW.
inra (*Æ*)=innera
inrǣcan '*ingesserunt,*' WW420[18] (v. A 31·532).
inrǣsan *to rush upon,* MtL.

inrēcels n. *incense,* LkR1[9].
insæglung=inseglung
insǣte adj. *dependent,* WW185[9].
insætnes=insetnes
inscēawere m. *inspector,* DR 194.
inscēawung f. *inspection, view,* NG.
insceðende=unscæððende
in-seg(e)l (æ) n. *seal, signet, Ct,WW.* ['*inseil*'; *L.*]
±inseglian (æ) *to seal, LL;* ÆL. ['*inseil*']
inseglung (æ[2]) f. *sealing, seal, Æ.*
insendan *to send in, put in,* VPs.
inseten f. *an institution,* DR.
insetnes f. *regulation,* DR.
insettan *to institute,* BH,JnL.
insigle n. *seal, signet,* DR,TC. [insegel]
insiht f. *narrative,* JnL.
insittende *sitting within,* RD 47[7].
insmoh m. *slough,* MH162[11].
insōcn f. *brawl in a house,* LL597,80[12].
insomnian *to gather in,* BH274[1].
inspīderwiht '*spider,*' *Lcd* 167b (very doubtful, v. BTac).
inspinn n. *spindle,* WW.
instæpe I. m. *entrance,* ÆH1·84. **II.**= instæpes
instæpes (e[2]) adv. *forthwith, directly,* BL.
instæppan (Æ)=insteppan
instandan[6] (o[2]) *to be present,* DR.
instandendlic (o[2]) *required for present use,* MtR6[11].
instede (y) *immediately,* NG.
in-stepe, -stepes=instæpes
insteppan[6] (æ) *to go in, enter, Æ.*
instice m. *internal stitching pain,* LCD.
instīgan[1] *to climb in,* GD24.
instihtian *to appoint, arrange,* LkL p2[6].
insting=onsting; **instyde**=instede
inswān m. *lord's swineherd,* LL447.
inswōgan[7] *to invade,* BH278[8].
inswōgennes (ēo[2]) f. *onrush,* BH110[33].
intiga (KGL)=intinga; **intimb-**=ontimb-
intinga m. *matter, business, Æ* : *cause* : *fault.* butan intingan *in vain, emptily.*
intō prep. w. d. (instr.), a. 'INTO,' *to, against, in, Æ,Chr.*
intrahtnung f. *interpretation,* MtL p2[7].
intrepettan *to trip, dance,* Ln37[197].
inðanc (ByH132[14])=ingeðanc
inðer adv. *apart,* MtR17[1].
inðicce *crass, thick,* MtL13[15].
inðīnen f. *female servant,* GPH401.
inðing (N)=intinga; **inðwēan**=onðwēan
in-wæerc, -wræc m. *internal pain,* GD,LL.
inwǣte f. *internal humour,* LCD 97a.
inwaru f. *services due to the lord on his* '*inland,*' Ct.
inweard I. (innan-, inne-) adj. *internal, inward, inner, intrinsic, deep, sincere,*

earnest, Æ,*B,Bo,Cr.* as sbn. *inward parts,* Æ,*WW.* **II.** adv. *within* : *mentally, spiritually, LkL.* ['*inward*']

inweardlic (e, o, u) *internal, Lcd* : *inner,* RWH 136¹⁷ : *earnest, sincere,* W. adv. -*lice* '*inwardly,*' Æ : *deeply, thoroughly, heartily,* Æ,*Met.*

inwendan *to change,* VPs.

inweorc n. *indoor work,* LL454,11.

inwerd-=inweard-; **inwid**=inwit

inwidda m. *adversary, evil one,* Jud 28.

inwise f. *condiment,* Lcd 69a.

inwit **I.** n. *evil, deceit.* **II.** adj. *wicked, deceitful.*

inwitfeng m. *spiteful clutch,* B 1447.

inwitflān m. *treacherous shaft,* Mod 37.

inwitful *wicked, crafty,* Ps,WW.

inwitgæst m. *evil guest,* B 2670.

inwitgecynd n. *evil nature,* Sol 329.

inwitgyren f. *treacherous snare,* PPs 139⁵.

inwithlemm (id) m. *treacherous wound,* Rood 47.

inwithrōf m. *unfriendly roof,* B 3123.

inwitnet n. *net of malice,* B 2167.

inwitnīð† m. *cunning hostility.*

inwitrūn f. *evil, crafty counsel,* Jul 610.

inwitscear m. *murderous attack,* B 2478.

inwitsearo n. *artful intrigue,* B 1101.

inwitsorh† f. *sorrow.*

inwitspell n. *tale of woe,* Gen 2024.

inwitstæf† m. *wickedness, evil,* PPs.

inwitðanc† m. *evil thought, hostile intent.*

inwitwrāsn† f. *hostile fetter,* An.

inwræc=inwærc

inwrītere m. *writer, secretary,* ZDA31·23.

inwritting f. *inscription,* MtKp 4⁵. [=onwr-]

inwudu m. *private woodland,* BC 3·189².

inwund f. *internal wound,* Lcd 70a.

inwunenes f. *persistence,* WW 426⁵.

inwunung f. *residence in,* NC 304.

inwyrm m. *intestinal worm,* Lcd.

io-=geo-; **īo** (=īu)=gēo; **ioc**=geoc

iom=eom; **īong** (N)=geong, gang

ionna (N) adv. *within.*

ionnað=innoð

īor m. *name of a river-fish (eel?)* : *name of the rune for* io, Run 28.

iorning=ærning

iornð=iernð pres. 3 sg. of iernan.

iorsian (KGl)=iersian

Iotas mpl. *the Jutes,* Chr.

īow m.=īw; **īowan**=īewan

ippingīren=yppingīren; **īren**=īsen

irfe=ierfe; **irgian**=eargian

Iringes weg m. *Milky Way,* WW 53²².

irm-=ierm-; **irn-**=iern-, eorn-

irre=ierre; **irs-**=iers-

irsen-=īsen-; **irðling**=yrðling

is pres. 3 sg. of eom, anv.

īs n. '*ice,*' B,*BH,Met,PPs* : (pl.) *pieces of ice, BH* : *name of the rune for* i.

īsærn (Gl)=īsearn

īsceald† *icy cold, Met,Seaf.* ['*icecold*']

ise (N)=gese

īsearn (æ, e) m. *halcyon, kingfisher,* Gl.

īsen **I.** (īsern, īren) n. '*IRON,*' Æ,*CP* : *iron instrument : fetter* : (†) *iron weapon, sword* : *ordeal of red-hot iron,* LL230,6. **II.** adj. *oj iron,* '*IRON,*' Æ,*CP.* **III.** (WW)=īsearn.

īsenbend† (ir-) mf. *iron bond, fetter.*

īsenbyrne (īsern-) f. *iron corslet,* B671.

īsend=iesend; **Isenesmīð**=īsensmīð

Īsenfetor (īsern-) f. *iron fetter,* Gl.

īsengelōma (īr-) m. *iron instrument, weapon,* AA 13¹⁶.

Īsengræf m. *iron-mine,* KC 5·234'.

Īsengrǣg (grēi) '*iron-grey,*' WW.

Īsenheard (ir-) '*iron-hard,*' B 112.

īsenhearde f. ('*iron-hard*'), *black centaury, vervain, knapweed,* Lcd.

Īsenhelm (irsen-) m. *iron helmet,* WW 142².

Īsenhere (-ern) m. *iron-clad army,* Ex 348.

Īsenhyrst adj. *with iron fittings,* KC.

Īsenordāl (ȳ) n. *ordeal by iron,* LL.

Īsenōre (īsern-) f. *iron mine,* WW 237²⁰.

Īsen-panna m., -panne f. *frying-pan,* Gl.

Īsenscofl f. *iron shovel,* Gl (īsernscobl).

Īsenscūr f. *shower of arrows,* B 3116 (-ern).

Īsensmīð m. *blacksmith,* WW.

Īsenswāt? m. *dross of iron?* (v. BT s.v. swāt). Lcd 108a.

Īsentange f. *snuffers,* WW 327¹⁴.

Īsenðrēat m. *iron-clad troop,* B 330 (īr-).

Īsenwyrhta m. *blacksmith,* WW 310³³.

īsern (Lcd)=iesend

īsern (1)=īsen; (2)=īsearn

Īsgebind n. *fetters of ice,* B 1113.

Īsgeblǣd (ȳ) n. *ice-blister, chilblain?* Lcd.

Īsig '*icy,*' Met : *covered with ice,* B 33.

Īsigfeðera *with frosted wings,* Seaf 24.

īsiht *icy,* ÆL 23b⁵⁷².

Īsīðes adv. *immediately,* LL (338¹¹).

Īsmere m. *icy lake,* Met 28⁶².

±Īsnian *to cover with iron.* pp. īsnod *iron-clad,* WW 236¹⁹.

Ītest, itst pres. 2 sg., iteð, itt pres. 3 sg. of etan.

īð=īeð; **īu-,** iū=geo-, gēo; **īuc**=geoc

Īūdēas sbmp. *the Jews,* G.

Īūdēisc *Jewish,* G.

iugian=geocian; **iulh** (NG)=ēowic, ēow

Īūla (Men 221)=Gēola

Iutan=Iotas

īuwian (AS 7¹⁶ and n.}=īewan

īw (ēow) m. '*yew,*' *yew-tree, Cp,KC,Rd;* Æ; Mdf.

īwberge (ēow) f. *yew-berry,* Lcd. [v. '*yew*']

K

Words beginning with **k** will be found under **c**.

L

lā interj. *lo! behold! oh! ah!* Æ. lā lēof O Lord! O sir!: *indeed, verily*, Æ. hwæt lā *what!* wā lā wā! *alas!*

label=(*lafel), læfel; **laber** (*Lcd*)=læfer

lāc nf. *play, sport* : (†) *strife, battle* : *sacrifice, offering*, Æ,CP : *gift, present*, Mt; Æ : *booty*, B : (†) *message*. ['*lake*']

+lac† n. *tumult, commotion*. sweorda +l. *battle* : *crowd, host*, CR 896.

lācan[7] pret. 3 sg. leolc *to move up and down, leap, jump, swing, fly*, Jul : *play (instrument)* : *play upon, delude*, AO,Bo : (†) *fight, contend*, B. ['*lake*']

lācdǣd f. *munificence*, OEG 3833.

lacen? *a cloak*, WW 377[22]. [*Ger.* laken?]

lācfæsten *the offering of a fast*, BL 37[18].

lācgeofa m. *generous giver*, PPs 67[18].

+lācian *to present, bestow* : *accompany with gifts*.

lāclic *sacrificial*, ÆP D 116[8].

±lācnian (ǣ, ē) *to heal, cure, treat, look after*, Æ,BH,LkL; AO,CP : *foment, dress (a wound)*. ['*lechne*']

lācnigendlic *surgical*, HGL 478.

lācnimende only in bēon l. '*munerari*,' BHy 3[19].

lācnung (ǣ) f. *healing, cure*, Æ : *medicament, remedy*, Lcd; RB. ['*lechning*']

lācsang m. *offertory hymn*, WW 130[2].

lac-tuc(e), m. -tuca f. *lettuce*, Æ,Lcd. [*L.*]

lacu f. *stream*, EC : *pool, pond*, Chr 656 E. ['*lake*']

lād I. f. *course, journey*, An,B : (±) *way, street, water-way* : *leading, carrying*, LL : *maintenance, support*. ['*load*,' '*lode*']. II. f. *clearing from blame or accusation, purgation, exculpation*, CP.

ladan (NG)=hladan

±lādian *to exculpate oneself* : *let off, excuse*, Æ,AO,CP.

lādiendlic *excusable*, WW 233[31].

lādmann m. *leader, guide*, Æ. ['*lodeman*']

lād-rinc? -rincman m. *conductor, escort*, LL 3,7 (v. 2·441 and 3·6).

ladsar=laser

lādscipe m. *leadership*, WW 481[6].

lādtēow, lādðēow=lāttēow

lādung f. *exculpation, excuse, defence, apology*, Æ,CP.

lǣc=(1) lēac; (2) lāc; **lǣca**=lǣce

-lǣca v. āg-, ellen-l. etc.

+lǣca m. *a rival*, GPH 391.

lǣcan *to spring up, rise, flare up*, SAT 716.

+lǣcan *to emulate*, GPH 391 : *join with, make common cause with?* CPs 140[4]. [lāc]

±lǣccan *to seize, grasp, comprehend*, Æ : *capture, catch*, Chr,G,LL : *take, receive*, Æ. ['*latch*,' '*i-lecche*']

lǣccung (e) f. *reproach*, EPs 88[35].

lǣce (ē, ȳ) m. *physician, doctor*, BH,LkL; Æ,CP : '*leech*,' WW; Æ.

lǣcebōc f. *book of prescriptions*, LCD.

lǣcecræft m. '*leech-craft*,' *art of healing*, Bo,Lcd; Æ : *remedy, prescription*, Æ.

lǣcecræftig *skilled in medicine*, LCD 186b.

lǣcecynn n. *race of physicians*, RD 6[10].

lǣcecyst f. *medicine chest*, GD 344[17].

lǣcedōm (ē) m. *medicament, medicine, BH, WW* : *healing, salvation*, CP. ['*leechdom*']

lǣcedōmlic *salutary*, A 5·458.

lǣcedōmnes f. *cataplasm*, WW.

lǣcefeoh n. *doctor's fee*, LL (148[19]).

lǣcefinger m. ('*leech-finger*'), *fourth finger*, Lcd,WW.

lǣcegeatwa? (-getea) fp. *medical apparatus*, v. NC 304.

lǣcehūs n. *hostelry, hospital*, Lk 10[34].

lǣceiren n. *surgeon's knife, lancet*, GD 32.

lǣcesealf f. *medicinal ointment*, WW 514[21].

lǣceseax n. *lancet*, CP 187[9].

lǣcewyrt f. *medicinal herb, drug*, Æ : *ribwort* : *medical treatment*.

lǣcnian=lācnian

lǣdan (±) *to* '*LEAD*,' *guide, conduct, carry, lift, take, bring*, Æ,Chr; CP : (±) *produce, bring forth* : *pass, lead (life)* : *to mark or beat the bounds of land*, EC 155[8] : *do* : *place, lay*, Æ : *sprout forth, grow, spread*. wīf l. *take a wife, marry*.

lǣde (BH 400[2])=lǣwede

lǣden I. (ē, ēo) n. '*Latin*,' Bf,BH,CP,LG : *any foreign language*, Lcd. ['*leden*'] II. (ē, ȳ) adj. *Latin*.

lǣdenbōc (ē, ȳ) f. *Latin book*, Æ.

lǣdend I. m. *bringer*, CR. II. m. *excuser, apologist*, PPs 140[5]. [*lǣdan]

+lǣdendlic *ductile, malleable*, LRPs 97[5].

lǣdengereord n. *Latin language*, LCD 3·440'.

lǣdengeðēode n. *Latin language*, CP 7.

lǣdenisc *Latin*, BH.

lǣdenlār f. *knowledge of Latin*, W 124[12].

Lǣdenlic *Latin*, NC 304.

+lǣdenlic (EPs 97)=+lǣdendlic

lǣdennama m. *Latin noun*, ÆGR 292[18].

lǣdensprǣc (ē) f. *Latin language*, Æ,CP.

lǣdenstæfum (ē) adv. *in Latin*, Jn 19[20].

lǣdenware mpl. *Latin people, Romans*, CP

lǣdenword (ē) n. *Latin word*, ÆGR 122[6].

lǣdere m. *leader*, S[2]Hy 6[13].

lǣdnes f. *bringing forth*, BHo 76[15].

lǣdtēow=lāttēow

lǽf=(1) lāf; (2) lēaf

±**lǽfan** (ē) **I.** *to 'leave'* (*'yleft'*), *bequeath*, B,Jn; Æ,CP : *spare, leave behind, have left*, G : *remain*, Æ. [lāf] **II.**=līefan

lǽfel (e) m. *spoon, basin, vessel, bowl, cup*. [*Ger.* löffel; *L.* labellum]

lǽfend (WW168¹⁷)=lǽwend

lǽfer f. *rush, reed, iris, gladiolus*, Lcd,WW; Æ : *metal plate*, Æ. [*'laver'; 'levers'*]

lǽferbed n. *reed-bed*, WW138²⁹.

lǽfnes=lēafnes

lǽg pret. 3 sg. of licgan.

lǽg=(1) lēag; (2) līeg

lǽgde=legde pret. sg. of lecgan.

lǽgon pret. pl. of licgan.

lǽgt=līget

lǽht pp., læhte pret. sg. of læccan.

lǽl (ē) f., læla m. *rod, whip, switch : bruise, weal, stripe*, Ex.

lǽlan? *to be bruised*, An1445 (GK read læla m.).

lǽlian I. *to become black and blue*, WW 431³⁰. **II.** (ē) *to level, aim at*, Lcd.

lǽmen (ē) *of clay, earthen*, Æ. [lām]

lǽmian=lēmian

lǽn (ā) **I.** nf. *loan, borrowing, lease, grant, gift, present, benefit*, Æ,CP. [lēon] **II.**= lǽnland

lǽn-=lēn-

±**lǽnan** (ē) *to 'lend,'* Æ,WW; CP : *give, grant, lease*, Gen; Æ.

lǽndagas† mpl. *loan-days, transitory days, days of a man's life*, B.

lǽnde-, lǽnden-=lenden-

lǽne (ē) *lent, temporary, inconstant, transitory*, CP : *perishable, frail, poor : weak, sinful*, CP. [lǽn]

lǽnelic *passing, transitory*, Bl73⁹.

lǽnend m. *lender*, WW. [*'lenend'*]

lǽnendlic (W)=lǽnelic

lǽnere m. *'lender,'* WW189²¹.

lǽng=leng; **lǽngten-**=lencten-

lǽnian=lēanian

lǽnland n. *leased land*, v. LL2·323.

lǽnlic (LL)=lǽnelic; **-lǽnung** v. fēoh-l.

lǽpeldre f. *dish*, ÆH,WW. [lapian]

lǽpewince (e) f. *lapwing*, Gl.

lǽppa (a) m. *lappet, piece, section, lobe, portion, district*, CP,Lcd; Æ. [*'lap'*]

-lǽppede v. fif-l.

+**lǽr** *empty : empty-handed*. [*Ger.* leer]

+**lǽran** (ē) *to teach, instruct, guide*, BH,LL : *enjoin, advise, persuade, urge, preach* : (+) *convert* : (+) †*recall*, ES37·197. 1. forð *hand down* (*to others*). ±lǽred *learned* (*opposed to* lǽwed), CP. hence *clerical* (*as opposed to lay*), *spiritual* (*as opposed to temporal*), Æ,CP. [*'lere,' 'ylere(d)'*]

+**lǽre**=lǽr

+**lǽrednes** f. *learning, skill*, Æ,BH.

lǽrend m. *misleader, instigator*, HL154⁷¹.

lǽrest=lǽst

lǽrestre f. *instructress*, Æ.

lǽrgedēfe *adapted for instruction?* FT61.

lǽrig m. *border? cover?* (*of a shield*), v. A37·55 and LF171.

-lǽrigian v. ymb-l.

lǽringmǽden n. *female pupil*, ApT20¹³.

lǽringmann m. *disciple*, RB20⁶.

lǽrnes f. *emptiness*, Lcd22b. [*'leerness'*]

lǽs pret. 3 sg. of lesan.

lǽs I. (ē) adv. and sbn. *less, lest*, Æ,AO,CP. ðȳ lǽs (ðe) conj. w. subj. *lest*. **II.** f. gs. lǽswe *pasture*, JnL,WW; Æ; Mdf. [*'lease,' 'leasow'*] **III.** f. (*blood-*)*letting*, Lcd.

lǽsboren *of lower birth*, LL(246').

lǽsest (MtR)=lǽst I.; **lǽsian**=lǽswian

lǽson pret. pl. of lesan.

lǽssa (ē) adj. (comp. of lȳtel) *'less,' smaller, fewer*, Æ,Bo,Chr : *inferior*, MtL,MtR. sb. Æ,Bf. adv. BH.

lǽst f. *fault, sin*, NC305. [*ON.*]

lǽst I. superl. of lȳtel *'least,'* G,Gu,Lcd; CP, AO. ðe lǽste *lest*, CM. **II.** f. *performance, fulfilment*, Ex308. **III.**=lāst

±**lǽstan** (ē) *to follow, help, serve*, B,Bl,Met, OET; AO : *perform, do, carry out, accomplish*, B,Bo,Gen; AO : *endure, last, continue*, Cr,Met; Æ : *furnish, pay, grant*, W. [*'last,' 'ylast'*]

lǽste f. *'last'* (*for the foot*), WW.

lǽstend m. *doer, performer*, BH.

+**lǽstfullian** *to testify*, LPs80⁹.

lǽstwyrhta (eo²) m. *shoemaker*, WW.

lǽswe v. lǽs II.

±**lǽswian** tr. and intr. *to depasture, graze, feed*, Æ,LkL. [*'leasow'*]

lǽt I. (lat- in obl. cases) comp. lætra; sup. lætest, lætemest *slow*, B,Bl,CP,Lcd; Æ : *slack, lax, negligent : 'late,'* An,Lk. **II.** m. *man of the class between the slave and the ceorl*, LL (v. 2·564). [*'laet'*]

lǽt pres. 3 sg. of lǽdan.

+**lǽt**=+lǽte II.

±**lǽtan⁷** pret. 3 sg. lēt, leort *to allow to remain, leave behind, depart from, 'let' alone*, Bl,CP : *leave undone*, BH : *bequeath*, EC : *allow*, Bl,LL : *cause to do*, BH : *regard as, consider*, BH,Chr,CP : *suppose : conduct oneself : behave towards, treat : allow to escape, emit, let out, set free*, Æ,Lcd : *'let'* (*on lease*), BC : *assert, pretend*, Lk : *allot, assign*. l. from *refrain from*. l. ūt *to put to sea*. +l. nēah land *approach the shore?* (ES37·191). on bæc l. *leave behind*. l. for *to take* (*one*) *for*. on trēowe +l. *to entrust*, WW239⁷.

lǽtania=lētanīa

lætbyrd f. *slow birth*, LCD 185a.
+læte I. n. *manners, bearing*, NC 295. [*ON.* læti] II. n. *junction of roads*, Æ,CHRD.
lætemest I. adv. *lastly, finally*, NG. II. v. læt. ['*latemost*']
læthȳdig *slow-minded, dull*, CRA 10.
lætlīce adv. *slowly, Gu.* ['*lately*']
lætmest=lætemest
lætnes f. *slowness*, ÆL 23b[647] : *sloth*, GD 174[23].
lætra (*Æ,LL*) v. læt. ['*latter*']
lætrǣde *slow, deliberate, CP* 149[14]. ['*latrede*']
lætsum *backward, Chr.* ['*latesome*']
lætt f. (pl. latta) *beam, 'lath,'* WW.
læ̆ttēow=lâttēow
læ̆ttewestre f. *guide*, Æ 23b[508]. [lâttēow]
lætting=letting; -læ̆ttu v. un-l.
lǣð n. *a division of a county containing several hundreds, 'lathe,' BC* 3·162 : *landed property? (meadow) land?* LL 400,3[2].
lǣð-=lāð-
lǣðan *to abuse, revile, hate : cause to shun*, RB 11[18]. [lāð]
lǣðð, lǣððo (CP) f. *wrong, injury : hatred, malice, Bl.* ['*leth*'; lāð]
læ̆uw=lēow
læ̆w (ē) f. *injury*, W 165[9].
læ̆wa (ē) m. *betrayer, traitor, Lk; Æ.* [v. '*lewe*']
±læ̆wan *to betray*, BL,Ps. [*Goth.* lēwjan]
-læ̆we v. druncen-, hunger-l.
læ̆wede *lay, laic, unlearned.* as sb. *layman, BH; Æ,CP.* ['*lewd*']
læwel=læfel
læ̆wend m. *betrayer, traitor*, GL.
læ̆werce=lāwerce; læwil=læfel
læx=leax
lāf f. *what is left, remnant, legacy, relic, remains, rest, Bl,Chr; Æ : relict, widow*, Æ,AO. tō lāfe *alone.* tō lāfe bēon *to remain over, Bl.* wæpna, daroða l. *survivors of battle.* hamora lāfa *results of forging, swords.* ['*lave*'; līfan]
lāferce=lāwerce
±laflan *to pour water on, wash, 'lave,' bathe, B,Lcd : ladle out, Lcd.*
lafor m. *leopard*, AA 22[3].
lag-=lah-; -laga v. lund-l.
laga m. *law*, LL,WW.
lage-=lagu-
lagen pp. of lēan II.
±lagian *to ordain, W.* ['*law,' 'i-lahen*']
lago-=lagu-; -lagol v. æ-l.
lāgon=lǣgon pret. pl. of licgan.
lagu I. f. (old neut. pl. lagu; CHR 1052 D) '*law,' ordinance, rule, regulation,* Æ; *Chr, LL,RB,W : right, legal privilege,* LL : *district governed by the same laws.* II. m.

water, flood, sea, ocean, Gen,Mt : name of the rune for l. ['*lay*']
+lagu np. *extent, surface (of sea)*, SEAF 64? [*OS.* gilagu]
lagucræftig *skilled in seafaring*, B 209.
lagufæsten† n. *sea, ocean.*
lagufæðm m. *enveloping waves*, RD 61[7].
laguflōd m. *wave, stream, waters, flood, sea, ocean.*
lagulād† f. *water-way, sea.*
lagumearg m. *sea-horse, ship*, GU 1306.
lagusīð† m. *sea-journey*, GEN.
lagustræt f. *sea-path*, B 239.
lagustrēam† m. *water, sea, ocean.*
laguswimmend m. *swimming in the sea (fish)*, SOL 289.
lāh pret. 3 sg. of lēon.
lah-=lag-
lahbreca m. *law-breaker, impious man*, SC 9[10]. [lagu]
lahbrecende *impious, profane*, SC 9[9].
lahbryce m. *breach of the law*, LL.
lah-cēap, -cōp m. *money paid (by an outlaw) for restitution of legal rights*, LL.
lahlic *lawful, legal*, SC 46[2]. adv. -līce.
lahmann m. *an official declarer of the law*, LL 376. ['*lawman*']
lahriht n. *legal right*, LL.
lah-slitt fn., -slite m. *fine for breach of the (Danish) law*, LL.
lahwita m. *lawyer*, LL (308[13]).
lām n. '*loom,' clay, earth, Æ,WW;* Mdf.
lama v. (wk. adj. and sbm. *crippled, 'lame,' paralytic, weak*, Æ,BH,Cp,El,Mt,WW.
lamb (e, o) pl. lamb(e)ru, lambor (A) n. '*lamb,' Æ,G,Gl,Gu,VPs.*
lambyrd f. *imperfect birth*, LCD 185a.
lāmfæt n.† *vessel of clay (the body).*
lamp I. pret. 3 sg. of limpan. II. (KGL)= lamb
lamprede f. *lamprey*, WW 94[17]. [*L.*]
lāmpytt m. '*loampit,'* KC 3·252[24].
lāmsceall *tile*, APs 21[16].
lāmsēað m. *loampit*, EC 448[13].
lāmwyrhta m. *potter,* G.
lān=lǣn
lanan obl. cases of lanu.
land (o) n. *earth, 'land,' soil, B,BH,Gen,Sc, WW;* Mdf : *territory, realm, province, district, Cp,Chr,Bl,VPs : landed property,* Æ,Bl : *country (not town),* Æ,BH : *ridge in a ploughed field.*
+landa (o) m. *compatriot, kinsman*, WW 211[20].
landādl=hlandādl?
landælf f. *land-elf*, WW 516[27].
landägend m. *native*, BH.
landägende *owning land*, LL.
landâr f. *landed property,* Æ.

landbegenga (i²) m. *husbandman, peasant, native*, CP.
landbegengnes (o¹) f. *habitation*, BPs 119⁵.
landbigong (o¹) m. *dwelling in a country*, BPs 118⁵⁴.
landbōc f. '*land-book,' written grant of land*, *Ct,WW*.
landbrǣce m. *first ploughing (after land has lain fallow)*, WW 105¹¹.
landbūend I. mf. *inhabitant, native : husbandman*. II. f. *colony*, WE 51¹.
landbūende *dwelling on the land*, CREAT 80.
landbūnes f. *colony, settlement*, WE 51¹².
land-cēap, -cōp m. *fine paid to the lord on the alienation of land*, BC. ['*landcheap*']
landcofa m. *land, district*, LPs 59⁸.
landefn(e) n. *measure or proportion of land*, CHR 1085.
landesmann (*Æ,Chr*)=landmann
landfæsten (o¹) n. *natural fortress*, AO 80¹⁴.
landfeoh n. *recognitory rent for land*, KC.
landfolc n. '*land-folk,' natives*, *Æ*.
landfruma m. *ruler, prince*, B 31.
landfyrd f. *army*, BH,CHR.
landfyrding f. *military operations on land*, CHR 999.
landgafol n. *land-tax, tribute*, LL. ['*landgavel*']
landgehwerf (=ea³) n. *exchange of land*, TC 191⁶.
landgemaca m. *neighbour*, OEG.
landge-mǣre, -mirce n. *boundary, limit, frontier*, AO.
landgesceaft f. *earthly creature*, DA 360.
landgeweorc n. *fortified place*, B 938.
landgewyrpe n. *heap of earth?* KC.
landhæbbende *owning or ruling land*, DR, LL.
landhæfen f. *real property*, LL 22,32.
landhere m. *native force : land force (opposed to naval force)*.
landhlāford m. *lord of a country, lord of a manor, 'landlord,'* EC,LL.
landhredding f. *redemption of land*, CC 9¹¹⁸.
landlagu f. *local law*, LL. ['*landlaw*']
landlēas *not owning land*, LL. ['*landless*']
land-lēod m., nap. -lēode, -lēoda, -lēodan *inhabitant of a country, native*, AO.
landlyre m. *loss of territory*, CHR 1105.
landmann m. *inhabitant of a country, native*, Ex,LL. ['*landmann*']
landmearc m. *boundary*, Jul,KC. ['*landmark*']
landmearca m. *land, country*, LPs 59⁸.
+landod *having landed property*, LL 182,11.
landopenung f. *first ploughing of land*, WW 147⁹.
landrǣden v. ealdlandrǣden.
landrest f. *grave*, AN 782.

landrīca m. *landed proprietor*, LL.
landrīce n. *territory*, AO,WW.
landriht n. '*land-right,' right to own or occupy land or connected with its occupation, B,Ex,Gen : that which is due from land or estates*.
landscearu (a²) f. *tract of land, province, country*, CP : *boundary, landmark*. [v. CC 48]
landscipe m. *region*, GEN 376.
landscoru=landscearu
landsēta m. *settler*, WW 111¹⁵. [sǣta]
landseten f. *occupation of land*, Ct : *occupied land, estate*, LL.
landseðla m. *occupier of land*, TC 593⁶.
landsidu m. *custom of a country*, CP.
landsittende *occupying land*, CHR 1085.
landsōcn† f. *search for land to settle on*.
landspēd f. *landed property*, KC 3·349'.
landspēdig *rich in land*, ÆGR.
landsplott m. *plot of land*, KC,LPs.
landstede (o) m. *region*, WIF 16.
landstycce n. *small plot of ground*, GD,LL.
landwaru f. *inhabitants, population*, B 2321.
landweard m. *coast-warden*, B 1890.
landwela m. *earthly possessions*, PH 505.
lane=lanu
lang (o) comp. lengra, superl. lengest '*long,' tall*, ÆGr,AO,BH,G,Lcd,Ma; CP : *lasting*.
+lang (usu. w. æt or on) *dependent on, attainable from, present in, belonging to*, Æ,AO,Gu. [v. '*along*']
Langafrīgedæg m. *Good Friday*, LL.
langað=langoð
langbolster mn. *feather-bed*, WW 276³⁶.
lange (o) adv. comp. leng, lenge, superl. lengest '*long,' a long time, far*, B,BH,Bl, Bo.
langfǣre *lasting, protracted*, Æ.
langfērnes f. *length, long duration*, Sc 29¹.
langfirst m. *long space of time*, GU 920.
langgestrēon n. *old store of wealth*, B 2240.
langian I. (o) (impers. with acc. of pers.) *to 'long' for, yearn after, grieve for, be pained*, AO : *lengthen, grow longer*, Lcd : *summon*. II. *to belong*, KC 4·215⁴.
+langian *to send for, summon, call*, Æ : *apprehend, seize*, LL 202,6².
langieldo f. *advanced age* (Swt).
langlīce adv. *for a long time, long, at length*, Æ.
langlīfe *long-lived*, Æ.
langmōd *constant, patient*, Ps. adv. -lice.
langmōdig *long-suffering*, EPs 7¹².
langmōdnes f. *long-suffering*, Sc 10¹⁷.
langnes f. *length*, Æ. ['*longness*']
langoð† m. *longing, discontent*.
langsceaft *having a long shaft*, AA 23¹⁰.
langscip n. *man of war*, CHR 897 A.

langstrang 'longanimis,' LPs 102⁸.
langsum (o¹) long, lasting, tedious, protracted, B,Lcd; Æ. ['longsome']
langsumlic (o) tedious, ÆH 1·362'. adv.-líce long, AO 58¹⁷ : patiently, ÆL 23b³⁹¹.
langsumnes f. length, Ps; Æ : patience, NC 305. ['longsomeness']
langswēored (ȳ²) long-necked, HexC 253, 279.
langtwidig lasting, assured, B 1708.
langung (o) f. 'longing,' Bl : weariness, sadness, dejection, Æ : delay, CP. [langian]
langunghwīl f. time of weariness, An 125.
langweb n. warp (in weaving), WW 187¹².
langwege (o¹, oe²) 'peregre,' MkL 13³⁴.
langwyrpe oblong, NC 305³⁴⁷.
lánland=lǣnland
lann (o)† f. chain, fetter.
lanu (o) f. 'lane,' street, Bl.
lapian to 'lap' up, drink, Lcd; Æ.
lappa (GL)=læppa
lār f. 'lore,' learning, science, art of teaching, preaching, doctrine, Bl; Æ,CP : study : precept, exhortation, advice, instigation, JnL; AO : history, story : cunning, Gen 2693.
lārbōc f. book containing instruction (used of St Paul's Epistles, and Bede's works), Æ.
lārbodung f. teaching, preaching, Chrd 50¹⁰.
lārbysn f. example, WW 163⁴³.
lārcniht (e²) m. disciple, LkL p2².
lārcræft m. knowledge, Sol 3 : erudition, Chrd 66³⁶.
lārcwide† m. teaching, precept.
lārdōm m. teaching, instruction, LL 258,51.
lār-ēow, -ow, -uw(a) m. teacher, master, preacher, BH,JnL,WW; Æ,AO,CP. ['larew']
lārēowdōm m. function of teacher, instruction, CP : ecclesiastical authority, Æ,CP.
lārēowlic like a teacher, OEG,RB.
lārēowsetl n. teacher's seat, pulpit, OEG,Mt.
lārēwes=lārēowes gs. of lārēow.
lārfæsten n. prescribed fast, A 11·99.
lārhlystend m. catechumen, OEG 2881.
lārhūs n. school, HGl 405.
lārlēast (ē, ȳ) f. want of instruction, ignorance, LL,W.
lārlic of or conducive to learning, instructive, Æ : learned : doctrinal : persuasive. betwux lārlicum gefylcum amongst soldiers in training, Æ.
lārsmið† m. (nap. -smeoðas) teacher, counsellor.
lārspell n. homily, treatise, Æ. ['lorespell']
lārsum teachable, NC 305.
lārswice m. trickery, W 309¹⁴.
lār-ðēaw, -ðēow (Jn 1³⁸; 'lorthew')=lārēow

lārðegn m. teacher, NC 305.
lāruw(a) (LG)=lāreow
lārwita m. learned man, LL (308¹³).
lāser (o²) m? weed, tare, BF 30¹⁶,GL.
lāst (ǣ, ē, ēa) m. sole of foot : spoor, footprint, track, trace, B,Bl; Æ,CP : gait, step. on lāst(e) behind, after, in pursuit of. on l. lecgan to follow. lāstas lecgan to go. ['last']
±lāst (ǣ, ē) n. accomplishment, observance, RB 5⁵ : duty, due, obligation, vow.
+lāstful helpful, serviceable, LL; AO. ['lastfull']
lāstweard m. successor, heir, follower : pursuer.
lāstword n. fame after death, Seaf 73.
lasur=laser; lat- v. læt-; lāt=lād
lata m. slow person, Bl 163⁸.
late adv. comp. lator, sup. latest 'late,' Chr, Jul : slowly, Lcd : at last, AO : lately, RB. [læt]
latemest=lætemest II.; lātēow=lāttēow
±latian to be slow, indolent : linger, delay, hesitate, Æ.
lator, adv. comp., latost (æ), superl. slower, later, Bf; AO,CP. ['latter,' 'last']
latt=lætt
lattēh f. guiding rein, WW 120⁹. [lād]
lāttēow, lāttēowa (ǣ) m. leader, guide, general, Bo,VPs (lad-); AO,CP. ['lattew']
lāttēowdōm m. leadership, guidance, instruction, CP.
lātðēow, lātuw=lāttēow
latu f. delay : (+) hindrance, DR 96⁵?
latung f. delay, hindrance, OEG 7¹²⁹.
lāð I. (±) hated, hateful, hostile, malignant, evil, AO,B : loathsome, noxious, unpleasant, Chr,Ep; CP. ['loath'] II. n. pain, harm, injury, misfortune, AO : insult, annoyance, harmful thing, BH,Lcd; CP. ['loath']
lāðbite m. wound, B 1122.
lāðe adv. inimically, in detestation, BH,PPs.
lāðēow=lāttēow
lāðettan (ǣ) to hate, loathe : make hateful or repulsive, Æ.
lāðgeniðla† m. persecutor, foe.
lāðgetēona† m. enemy. B.
lāðgewinna m. enemy, Rd 16²⁹.
laðian to invite, summon, call upon, ask, Æ, CP. [Ger. laden]
lāðian to hate, be hated, AO; Æ. ['loathe']
lāðlēas inoffensive, innocent, WW. ['loathless']
lāðlic 'loathly,' hateful, horrible, repulsive, unpleasant, BH; Æ. adv. -lice, Met.
lāðscipe m. misfortune, Gen 2048.
lāðsearu n? hateful contrivance, Da 436.
lāðsīð m. painful journey, death, Ex 44.
lāðspel n. sad tidings, AO.
lāðððēow=lāttēow

±**laðung** f. *calling, invitation, CP*: *assembly, congregation, church*, Æ. ['*lathing*']
lāðwende† *hateful, hostile, bad.*
lāðwendemōd *hostile-minded*, GEN 448.
lāðwendnes f. *hostility*, LCD.
lāðweorc n. *evil deed*, PPs 105²⁶.
laur m. *laurel, bay, laver*, LCD.
laurbēam (lawer-) m. *laurel*, WE,WW.
laurberige f. *laurel-berry*, LCD.
+**laured** *laurel-flavoured*, LCD 84a.
laurice (*Cp*)=lāwerce
laurisc *of laurel*, AA 6²⁰.
laurtrēow n. *laurel-tree*, LCD.
lauwer, lawer=laur
lāwerce (ǣ) f. '*lark*,' *WW*; Mdf.
lawernbēam m. *laurel*, WE 6¹².
lēa I. (VPs)=lēo. II. gdas. of lēah.
lēac I. (ǣ, ē, ēo) n. '*leek*,' *onion, garlic, garden-herb, Lcd*; Æ. II. pret. 3 sg. of lūcan.
lēac-=lēah-
lēacblæd n. *leek leaf*, NC 305.
lēaccærse (e²) f. *cress, nasturtium, Erf*; LCD. [v. '*cress*']
lēac-trog, -troc *a bunch of berries*, GL.
lēactūn (lēah-, lēh-) m. *kitchen-garden, garden of herbs, LkL,WW*. ['*leighton*']
lēactūnweard (ē¹) m. *gardener*, WW 127¹⁴. ['*leightonward*']
lēacweard (ē¹, o²) m. *gardener*, G,WW.
lēad (ē) n. '*lead*,' *BH*; Æ,CP : *leaden vessel, cauldron*, LL.
lēaden (ē) '*leaden*,' Æ,LL.
lēadgedelf n. *lead-mine*, KC 3·401⁷.
lēadgewiht n. *lead-weight, a scale of weight*, v. CC 77.
lēadgota m. *plumber*, LL 455,16.
lēadstæf m. *loaded stick*, WW 441²⁰.
lēaf (ī) I. (±) f. '*leave*' ('*y-leave*'), *permission, privilege, BH,Chr,Sc*; Æ,CP. II. (ēo) n. '*leaf*,' *shoot*, pl. *foliage, MtL,VPs*; Æ : *sheet of paper, BH*. III. (+) *leafy*, WW 411¹².
±**lēafa** m. *belief, faith*, Æ,Bo,Mt; AO : *creed*. ['*leve*,' '*yleve*']
±**lēafe** (ǣ) f. *leave, permission, licence*, Æ.
±**lēafful** *believing, JnR* : *orthodox (Christian)* : *faithful, trustworthy, MtL*. ['*leafful*'] adv. -līce.
+**lēaffulnes** f. *faith, trust, faithfulness*, Æ.
lēafhelmig *leafy at the top*, GPH 390.
±**lēafhlystend** (e) m. *catechumen*, OEG.
+**lēaflēas** *unbelieving*, Æ.
+**lēaflēasnes** f. *unbelief*, W 294².
+**lēaf-lēast**, -lȳst f. *unbelief*, Æ.
lēaflēoht *easy to believe?* RB 5¹⁹.
+**lēaflic** *credible, faithful*, Æ : *catholic*, WW 201²⁶. adv. -līce.
lēafnes (ē, ȳ) f. *leave, permission*, BH.

+**lēafnesword** n. *password*, B 245.
lēafscead n. *leafy shade*, PH 205.
lēafsele m. *booth*, BYH 118¹⁵.
+**lēafsum** (ǣ) *believing, faithful* : *credible*.
lēafwyrm (i²) m. *caterpillar*, ASPs 77⁵¹.
lēag I. (ē) f. '*lye*,' *alkalized water, Ep,Lcd*. II.=lēah I. III. pret. 3 sg. of lēogan and lēon.
lēah I. lēage (CHR) m. *piece of ground*, '*lea*,' *meadow, BC*; v. GBG and Mdf. II.=lēag I. and III.
leahte pret. 3 sg. of leccan.
leahter=leahtor
leahtor (e¹) m. *vice, sin, offence, crime, fault*, Æ,CP : *reproach* : *disease, injury*, LCD.
leahtor-=hleahtor-
leahtorcwide m. *opprobrious speech*, JUL 199.
leahtorful (e¹, e²) *vicious, seductive*, Æ.
leahtorlēas (e²) *faultless, blameless*, EL, LL.
leahtorlic *vicious, faulty*, GUTH 101¹¹. adv. līce *foully, wickedly*, Æ.
-**leahtorwyrðe** v. un-l.
leahtras nap. of leahtor.
±**leahtrian** (e) *to accuse, revile, reprove, blame*, Æ; AO,CP : *corrupt*. ['*lehtrie*']
leahtric m. *lettuce*, LCD,WW. [*L*. lactuca]
lēahtrog=lēactrog
lēahtrung (ē) f. *derogation*, WW 150¹.
lēahtūn=lēactūn
lēan I. n. *reward, gift, loan, compensation, remuneration, retribution, B,Mt*; Æ. ['*lean*'] II. sv⁶ (pret. 3 sg. lōg, lōh) and wv. *to blame, reproach*, AO,CP.
lēangyfa m. *rewarder*, LCD 3·436'.
±**lēanian** (ǣ) *to reward, recompense, repay, requite*, Æ,CP. [*Ger*. lohnen]
lēap m. *basket, W* : *basket for catching or keeping fish, WW* : *measure* : *trunk (body)*, JUD 111. ['*leap*']
lēas I. adj. (w. g.) *without, free from, devoid of, bereft of* : (±) *false, faithless* : *untruthful, deceitful, WW*; Æ : *lax* : *vain, worthless*. II. n. *falsehood, lying, Bo*; CP : *untruth, mistake*. ['*lease*']
lēasbrēd (-bregd) I. *lying, false, deceitful*, Æ. II. m. *cheating, trickery*, LL,W.
lēasbrēda m. *trickster*, ES 43·306.
lēasbrēdende *wily, deceitful*, ÆGR 286⁶.
lēasbrēdnes (ǣ²) f. *deception, falsehood*, ÆL.
lēasbregd=lēasbrēd
lēascræft m. *false art*, BL 25¹².
lēase *falsely*, BH 122¹⁷.
lēasere m. *liar, hypocrite, MtL* : *buffoon, mime, jester, fool*. ['*leaser*']
lēasest (*MtL*)=lǣst I.
lēasettan *to pretend*, Æ,RB.
lēas-ferhð, -fyrhð *false*, NC 305.

lēasferŏnes f. *levity, folly,* CP313[10].
lēasfyrhte=lēasferhŏ
lēasgewita m. *a false witness,* ÆH1·46'.
lēasgewitnes f. *false witness,* Æ.
lēasgielp m. *vainglory,* CP367[24].
lēaslan *to lie, Ps.* ['*lease*']
lēaslic *false, deceitful, sham, empty,* Æ,CP.
adv. -līce, Æ,CP.
lēaslīccettan *to dissemble,* WW388[83].
lēaslīcettung f. *dissimulation,* GUTH12[18].
lēasmōdnes f. *instability,* CP308[6].
lēasnes f. *lying : levity,* BH322[23].
lēasōleccan *to blandish, flatter,* GD34[27].
lēasōlecung f. *empty flattery,* WW430[21].
lēassagol (u[3]) *lying, false,* Æ.
lēasscēawere m. *spy,* B253.
lēasspell n. *lie, fiction, fable,* BH,WW.
lēasspellung f. *empty or false talk,* AO.
lēassponung f. *allurement,* WW452[3].
lēast=lāst; lēast-=læst-
lēastyhtan *to cajole,* WW431[4].
lēastyhtung f. *cajolery,* WW430[21].
lēasuht (=wiht?) *enticer, seducer,* OEG4014.
lēasung f. '*leasing,*' *lying, false witness, deceit, hypocrisy, artifice, JnL : a lie, Ps : empty talk, frivolity, laxity.* II. f. *indemnity?* WW.
lēasungspell n. *idle tale,* AO40[8].
lēaswyrcend m. *deceiver,* ÆH1·102.
lēat pret. 3 sg. of lūtan.
leatian=latian; +leaŏlan=+laŏian
lēaŏor n. *soap, soda,* Lcd,WW. ['*lather*']
lēaŏorwyrt (lēoŏo-) f. *soap-wort?* LCD16a.
lēawede=lǣwede
lēawfinger (=ǣ[1]) m. *index-finger, forefinger,* PPs72[11].
leax (æ, e) m. *salmon,* Cp,Met,WW; ÆL. ['*lax*']
leb-=lef-, læf-; lec=hlec
+lec pret. 3 sg. of +lacan.
lēc I. m. *look, regard,* Æ; A11·118[50]. II.= lēac I. and II.
+lecc-=+læcc-
leccan pret. 3 sg. leahte, le(o)hte *to water, irrigate, wet, moisten, slake,* CP. [cp. *Ger.* lechzen]
leccing f. *irrigation, watering,* WW (KGl). ['*leaching*']
lēce=lǣce; lēcetere (KGL65[29])=līcettere
lecg f. *part of a weapon?* (BT) *sheath?* (WC), TC527[9].
±lecgan *to* '*lay,*' *put, place, deposit, set,* Æ, G,Gen,Lcd,Rd; CP : *dispose, arrange : attach, W : bury, Jn,Chr : put before, submit, Æ : betake oneself, go : lay* (egg), Lcd : *prostrate, cast down, lay low, kill,* Bo,Lk,LL. l. on (w. d.) *put upon, charge with,* Chr,Gu; CP. lāstas l. *go, journey,* Gen. on lāst l. *follow.* [causative of licgan]

lēciwyrt (Cp)=lǣcewyrt
lēcnian (NG)=lācnian
lectric=leahtric; lēctūn-=lēactūn-
lecŏa m. *ship's bottom or hold,* Ep,WW46[14].
+led '*catasta,*' WW (v. BTs).
lēd=lēad; lēdan=lǣdan
lēde=legde pret. 3 sg. of lecgan.
lēden=lǣden. lēaden
lēf I. (ī) *feeble, infirm, weak, injured.* II.=lēaf
lēf-=lēaf-; lēfan=(1) līefan; (2) lǣfan
+lēfed *weak, sickly, aged,* BH,W.
lefel, lefil=læfel
+lēfenscipe m. *justification,* JnL15[22].
lēfmon m. *sick person,* GNE45.
lēfung f. *paralysis,* ÆH2·486[18].
leg (=læg) pret. 3 sg. of licgan.
lēg=(1) līeg; (2) lēah; lēg-=līg-, lēog-
lēga (A)=lǣwa
legde pret. 3 sg. of lecgan.
+lege f? *lair, bed,* Mdf (or ?+legu (BTs)).
lēgelēoht n. *light (of flame),* MFH168.
legen pp. of licgan.
leger n. *lying, illness,* AO,B; Æ : '*lair,*' *couch, bed, Wif : grave, LL; Æ.* clǣne legere *consecrated grave.* on life ge on legere *in life and in death,* LL. [licgan]
lēgeræsc (RWH79,81)=līgetræsc
legerbǣre *sick, ill,* TC611[20].
legerbedd n. *bed, sick bed, Æ : grave.*
+leger-ed, -od *confined to bed, Æ.*
legerfæst *sick, ill,* RB64[7].
+legergield n. '*lupercalia,*' WW437[14].
legerstōw f. *burial place,* ÆH.
legertēam m. *cohabitation, marriage,* MH174[9].
legerwīte fm. *fine for unlawful cohabitation, LL.* ['*lairwite*']
lēges=lēages gs. of lēah.
legeŏ pres. 3 sg. of lecgan.
legie f. *legion,* AO. [L.]
+legu v. +lege.
-legu v. ealdor-l.; leh-=leah-
lēh=lēah; lēh-=lēac-; lēhnan=lȳgnian
lēht=lēoht; lēhtan (Nar)=līhtan
lehte pret. 3 sg. of leccan.
lehtor=leahtor; lēl (KGL)=lǣl
leloŏre f. *silverweed?* GL.
lemb=lamb
lēmen (KGL82[40])=lǣmen
±lemian (æ) *to subdue,* CP303[11] : *lame, disable,* B905.
lempedu f. *lamprey,* WW438[17]. ['*limpet*'; L. lampreda]
lemphealt *limping,* Gl,WW. ['*limphalt*']
lempit f. *dish, basin,* OET108'.
lēnan (KGL)=lǣnan
lencten (æ) I. m. *springtime,* Lcd,LL; Æ : *the fast of Lent, W.* II. adj. *pertaining to Lent,* Bf,RB. ['*lenten*']

lenctenādl f. *spring fever, tertian ague, dysentery*, BH,LCD.

lenctenbere m. *Lent barley*, ANS 84³²⁶.

lenctenbryce m. *breach of the Lenten fast*, LL 344,47.

lenctendæg m. *day of Lent*, CHRD,W 117¹⁵.

lenctenerðe f. *land ploughed in spring*, WW 105⁷. [eorðe]

lenctenfæsten n. *Lent*, CHRD,RB.

lenctenhǣto f. *heat of spring*, AO 102⁶.

lenctenlic *of spring, vernal*, Æ : lenten, Æ.

lenctenlifen f. *Lenten fare*, CHRD 15³.

lenctenmōnað m. *a spring month*, ExC 34¹⁸.

lenctensufel (længt-) n. *Lent food*, LL 450,9.

lenctentīd f. *spring, Lent*, Æ.

lenctentīma m. *spring*, OEG 3837 : *Lent*, Æ.

lenctenwuce f. *a week in Lent*, Jn 5⁸ (rubric).

lenctin-=lencten-

+lend I. *furnished with land (by the lord)*, LL 448′. II.=+lynd

+lenda m. *one rich in land*, OEG 3154.

lendan *to land, arrive*, Chr; Æ,AO,CP : *go* : (+) *endow with land*, Æ. ['*lend*'; land]

lende-=lenden-

lendenādl f. *disease of the loins*, LCD 87a.

lendenbān n. *loin-bone*, WW 159¹³. [v. '*lend*']

lenden-brǣde, -brēde f. *loin*, LCD,LL.

lendenece m. *pain in the loins*, LCD 24a.

lendensēoc *diseased in the loins*, LCD.

lendensīd *reaching to the loins*, NC 306.

lendenu (æ) np. *loins*, Mt,WW; Æ. ['*lend*']

lendenwyrc m. *a disease of the kidneys*, WW 113¹². [wærc]

-lendisc v. dūn-, up-, ūre-, ut-l.

lēne=lǣne

leng I. (æ) f. *length, height*, Æ. II. adv. (comp. of lange) *longer*, Æ,Lk. ['*leng*']

lengan I. (±) *to lengthen, prolong, protract, delay*, Da : *extend, reach, attain* : *belong.* on hornum gelengdum '*tubis ductilibus*,' CVPs 97⁶. ['*leng*'] II. (+) *to call for*, DHy 90³.

lengcten-=lencten-

lenge (æ) I. adj. (±) *belonging, related* : *near (of time)*, B 83. II. v. lange. III.=lengu

+lenge *belonging to, related to*, Æ : *addicted to.*

lengest (Chr,Mk) superl. of lang(e). ['*lengest*']

lengfære *more durable*, ANS 119·435.

lengian (impers. w. a.) *to long*, SOL 270.

lenglīfra comp. of langlīfe.

lengo=lengu

lengra (BH) comp. of lang. ['*lenger*']

lengten=lencten

lengtogra comp. adj. *more prolix*, Sc 161¹⁸.

lengðu f. '*length.*' on lengðe *at length, finally*, AO 144¹.

lengu f. *length*, Bo,BH : *height*, Sol. ['*lengh*']

lent f. *lentil*, GL. [L. lentem]

lenten=lencten

lēo mf. gdas. lēon, also ds. lēone, lēonan, asf. lēo, and dp. lēonum '*lion*,' *lioness, AO,Lcd,VPs,WW*; Æ. [L.]

lēoc (WW 283²¹)=lēac

lēod I. m. *man*, LL 14,25 : '*wergeld*' *for manslaughter*, LL (=lēodgeld) : (+) *fellow-countryman, compatriot* : (†) *chief, prince, king*, B. ['*lede*'] II. f. (usu. in pl. lēode) *people, nation, An,B,Bl,Lk*; Æ,AO. ['*lede*']

lēoda I.=+lēod I. II. (LWS)=lēode

lēodan²† *to spring up, grow* : *spring from.*

lēodbealu† n. *calamity to a people*, B.

lēodbisceop m. *suffragan bishop, provincial, Chr*; Æ. [v. '*lede*']

lēodburg† f. *town*, B,GEN.

lēodbygen f. *sale of one's compatriots, slave-traffic*, LL 20,11 Ld (v. 2·133).

lēodcyning m. *king, ruler*, B 54.

lēode fp. *men, people, country, B,Lk*; AO (v. lēod).

lēoden (LCD)=lǣden

lēodfruma† m. *prince, patriarch, chief.*

lēodgeard† m. *country*, GEN.

lēodgebyrga† m. *lord, protector, prince, king.*

lēodgeld n. '*wergeld*' *for manslaughter*, LL.

lēodgeðinco f. *order, rank*, LL.

lēodgewinn n. *strife*, JUL 201.

lēodgota=lēadgota

lēodgryre m. *general terror*, SOL 278.

lēodhata m. *persecutor, tyrant*, GD.

lēodhete† m. *popular hatred, hostility*, AN.

lēodhryre m. *fall of a prince (or nation?)*, B 2030,2391.

lēodhwæt *very valiant*, EL 11.

-lēodisc v. ðider-l.

lēodmǣg† m. *relative, comrade.*

lēodmægen† n. *might of the people, host.*

lēodmearc† f. *domain, country*, AN.

lēodrǣden f. *country, region*, GD 204²⁸.

lēodriht n. *law of the land*, AN,KC.

lēodrūne f. *pythoness, sorceress*, LCD 52b.

lēodscearu f. *tribe, nation*, EX 337.

lēodsceaða† m. *public enemy.*

lēodscipe m. *nation, people*, Æ : *country, region.*

lēodstefn m. *assembly*, PPs 82⁷.

lēodðēaw m. *popular usage*, AA,GEN.

lēodweard† f. *government.*

lēodweras† mp. *men, human beings.*

lēodwerod n. *host of people*, EX 77.

lēodwita m. *wise man, elder, chief*, LL 456.

lēodwynn f. *home joy*, †Hy 4⁸⁹.

lēodwyrhta=lēoðwyrhta

lēof I. (±) adj. *dear, valued, beloved, pleasant, agreeable*, Æ,B,Chr,CP,HGl,LL. ['*yleof*'] II. m. *beloved one, friend* : (in addressing

persons) *sir! sire!* Æ,EC : *impure companion,* GPH394. ['*lief*']
leofen=lifen; leofian (*Bl*)=libban
lēofæst *dear, precious,* ÆP172[13].
lēofian *to be or become dear,* Gu110.
lēoflic *dear, lovable, pleasant, beautiful, delightful, B,Cr* : *precious, valued.* adv. -līce *lovingly, kindly, gladly, willingly, BH.* ['*liefly*']
lēofspell n. *good news,* El1017.
lēof-tǣl, -tǣle *kind, lovable, loving, dear, grateful, agreeable,* CP.
lēofwende *kind, loving, gracious, acceptable, estimable, agreeable.*
lēofwendum *ardently,* Cr471.
±lēogan[2] *to '*lie,*' Bl,WW* : *deceive, belie, betray,* Æ,CP : *be in error,* ÆGr. l. on *to charge falsely.*
lēogere (e[1], o[2]) m. '*liar,*' *false witness, W, MtL; Æ* : *hypocrite,* MkL7[6].
lēoht (ē, ī) I. '*light,*' *not heavy, AO; CP* : *slight, easy, trifling, inconsiderable, CP* : *quick, agile* : *gentle.* II. n. '*light,*' *daylight, Æ* : *power of vision* : *luminary.* III. *luminous, bright, '*light,*' clear, resplendent, renowned, beautiful,BH,Lcd,VPs; AO,CP.*
lēohtan=līhtan
lēohtbǣre *brilliant, luminous,* Cra,Lcd.
lēohtbēamede *bright-shining,* ÆH1·610.
lēohtberend m. *light-bearer, Lucifer, Æ.*
lēohtberende *light-bearing, luminous, Æ* (Gen).
lēohtbora m. *light-bearer,* LV36.
lēohtbrǣdnes f. *levity, frivolity, wantonness.*
leohte=lehte pret. 3 sg. of leccan.
lēohte I. adv. *lightly, easily, comfortably, BH.* ['*light*'] II. adv. *brightly, clearly, brilliantly, Bl,Cr.* ['*light*']
lēoht-fæt n. nap. -fatu *lantern, torch, lamp, light,* Æ,CP.
lēohtfætels m. *lamp,* LPs17[29].
lēohtfruma† m. *source of light.*
lēoht-gesceot, -gescot n. *payment for providing lights in church,* LL.
lēohtian I. *to be lightened, relieved.* II. *to become light, dawn,* CM474 : *give light, illuminate.*
lēohting=līhting
lēohtīsern (ē[1]) n. *candlestick,* NG.
lēohtlēas *dark, Æ.* ['*lightless*']
lēohtlic I. *light, of little weight or importance,* Æ,CP. adv. -līce *lightly, slightly, BH, Lcd* : *inconsiderately* : *easily, quickly* : *gently, softly, slowly, CP; Æ.* ['*lightly*'] II. *bright, radiant, Rd.*
lēohtmōd *easy-going,* GnE86.
lēohtmōdnes f. *inconstancy, frivolity,* CP.
lēohtsāwend *author of light,* GPH389[2].
lēohtscēawigend *light-seeing,* WW434[20].

lēohtsceot=lēohtgesceot
lēohtwyrhta=lēoðwyrhta
leolc pret. 3 sg. of lācan.
±lēoma m. *ray of light, beam, radiance, gleam, glare, B; Æ* : *lightning.* ['*leam*']
+lēomod *having rays of light,* Lcd3·272[4]. [v. '*leam*']
leomu nap. of lim.
±lēon I. (sv[1]) *to lend, give, grant,* B,LkL. [*Ger.* leihen] II. gdas. of lēo.
lēona mf. *lion, lioness, Æ.*
lēones? *league,* WE51.
lēonesēað m. *lions' den,* GD150[9].
lēonflǣsc n. *lion's flesh,* Lcd1·364'. [v. '*lion*']
lēonfōt m. *lion's foot (plant),* Lcd,WW.
lēonhwelp m. *lion's cub,* WW434[6].
±lēoran (wv., but rare pp. loren) *to go, depart, vanish, die* (A; v. JAW44).
±lēorednes f. *departure, transmigration* : *death,* ÆL : *anniversary of a death,* MH : *vision.*
lēorende, +lēorendlic *transitory,* DR.
lēorendnes=lēorednes
lēorian=lēoran
leornan=leornian
leornere m. '*learner,*' *disciple, Æ,CP* : *scholar, BH* : *reader.*
leornes f. *learning,* BHo,ca162[20].
lēornes=lēorednes
±leornian *to* '*learn,*' *read, study, think about, Æ,Bf,BH,Bl,MkR; AO,CP.*
leorningcild n., leorningcniht (Æ,CP) m. *student, disciple.*
leorningende *teachable,* W172[22].
leorninghūs n. *school,* WW.
leornung f., ds. leornunga '*learning,*' *reading, study, meditation, CP; AO* : *discipleship,* WW223[26].
leornungcræft m. *learning,* El380.
leornungmann m. *learner, disciple* (used even of women), Æ.
leornungscōl f. *school,* GD14[6].
leort pret. 3 sg. of lǣtan.
-lēosan v. be-l., for-l.
leoð=leoðu v. lið; leoð-=lið-
lēoð n. *song, lay, poem, B,WW; Æ,AO.* ['*leoth*']
lēoðcræft m. *poetic art* : *poem, poetry, Æ.*
lēoðcræftig *skilled in song,* Deor40.
lēoðcwide m. *lay, poem,* AO120[2].
leoðe-=leoðu-
lēoðgidding f. *lay, song, poem,* An1481.
leoðlan†=liðian
lēoðlic *versified,* ÆH,Bf42[14].
leoðo-=leoðu-
lēoðorūn f. *wise counsel given in song,* El522.
lēoðowyrt=lēaðorwyrt?

lēoðr-=hlēoðr-

lēoðsang m. *song, poem, poetry*, BH.

leoðu I. f. *retinue, following?* RIM 14 (GK). II. v. lið.

leoðubend† mf. *chain, fetter, bond.*

leoðublge (i[1], e[2]) *flexible, yielding*, Æ. ['*litheby*']

leoðublgnes (i[1], o[2]) f. *flexibility of limbs*, GUTH 90[21].

leoðucǣga m. *limbs serving as a key*, CR 334.

lēoðucræft† m. *skill of hand*, B,CRA.

leoðucræftig *agile*, PH 268.

leoðufæst *able, skilful*, CRA 95.

leoðulic *appertaining to the limbs, bodily*, AN 1630.

leoðusār n. *pain in the limbs*, WW 213[8].

leoðusyrce† f. *corslet*, B.

leoðuwāc (i) *with supple limbs, flexible, pliant*, CRA 84. ['*leathwake*']

+leoðuwāclan (i) *to mitigate, soften*, Æ.

leoðuwācunga (liðe-)? '*compeditorum*,' EPs 78[11].

±leoðuwǣcan (i) *to be or become calm or pliant : appease, mitigate : revive : soften : adapt?* ÆL 31[482].

lēoðweorc n. *poetry*, WW 188[30].

lēoðwīse f. *verse, poetry*, Æ,BF.

lēoðword n. *a word in a poem*, AN 1490.

lēoðwrenc m. *trick in a poem? spurious passage?* BF 186[27].

lēoðwyrhta m. *poet*, ÆGR.

lēow (ēu) n. *ham, thigh*, KC.

-lēow (ē, ā) v. mund-l.

leowe f. *league (distance)*, WW 147[22].

lēower pl. of lēow.

lēowð (ÆGR 129 J)=hlēowð

lepewince=læpewince

leppan *to feed (hawks)*, WY 89 (v. ES 37·195).

lēran (KGL)=lǣran

lere (KGL 83[19])=lyre; lērēow-=lārēow-

+les-=+lise

lēs-=līes-

lesan[5] *to collect, pick, select, gather, glean*, Æ. ['*lease*']

lesca m. *groin*, HGL,OET.

-lesende, -lesendlic, -lesung v. ed-l.

lēst=lāst; lesu=lysu; lēsw-=lǣsw-

lēt I. pret. 3 sg. of lǣtan. II.=lǣt pres. 3 sg. of lǣdan. III.=lēat pret. of lūtan.

lētan=lǣtan

lētanīa m. '*litany*,' MH; BH,WW. [*L.* litania]

letig (KGL)=lytig

±lettan (æ) *to* '*let,*' *hinder, delay, impede, oppress*, Æ,Bo,Gu (w. g.),W; AO,CP.

lettend m. *hinderer*, ES 39·349.

letting (æ) f. '*letting,*' *hindrance, delay*, Chr, RB; CP.

lēð=lǣð; -leðer v. heals-, weald-l.

leðera=liðera

leðercodd m. *leather bag*, WW 117[3]. [v. '*leather*']

leðeren=leðren

leðerhelm m. *leathern helmet*, WW 142[1].

leðerhosu f. *leathern gaiter*, WW.

leðern=leðren

leðerwyrhta m. *tanner, currier*, GL.

leðr-=lyðr-

leðren (i) '*leathern*,' WW.

lēud=(1) lēod; (2) lǣwede

lēw f.=lǣw

+lēwed *weak, ill?* Æ (Ex 22[10], cp. limlǣweo: or ?read +lēfed).

lēwend=lǣwend; lēwer=lēower

lēwsa (=ǣ) m. *weakness*, EPs 87[9].

lex=leax; lēxnian (WW 241[21])=lācnian

lib-, libb-=lif-, lyb-

libban (y) pret. 3 sg. lif(e)de *to* '*LIVE,*' *experience, be, exist*, Æ; AO,CP.

libr-=lifer-

līc n. *body*, B,Cr : *corpse*, AO,B; Æ,CP. ['*lich*']

+līc I. adj. (w. d.) *like* : '*alike*' ('*ylike*'), *similar, equal*, B,BH,Jul,LL; Æ,CP : *suitable* : *likely*, Mt. +līcost *double, twin.* II. n. *something like another thing : similitude.*

+līca, +līce wk. forms used as sb. *an equal*, Æ,CP. adv. ±līce (usu. +; and +līc in NG) *as, like, equally, similarly*, AO,Bl. +līce *and like as if.*

līcam-=līcham-

līcbeorg f. *coffin, sarcophagus*, Cp 45s.

+līcbisnung f. *imitation*, DR 76[1].

līcburg f. *cemetery*, Cp 433c.

līccere, liccetere=liccettere

līccettan (Æ)=līcettan

līccian *to* '*lick,*' Æ,Ps : *lap, lick up*, Lcd.

līccung f. *licking*, ÆH 1·330[23].

līcema=līchama; līcendlic=līçiendlic

līcettan *to feign, dissimulate*, CP : *flatter*, BH.

līcettere (ē) m. *deceiver, hypocrite*, CP.

līcettung, līcetung f. *feigning, deceit, hypocrisy, flattery.*

līcewyrðe=līcwyrðe

līcfæt† n. *body*, GU.

±licgan[5] *to* '*LIE*,*' *be situated, be at rest, remain, be*, Æ,AO,CP : *lie down, lie low, yield, subside, fall, lie prostrate, fail, lie dead*, Æ,AO,Chr : *lead, extend to*, Æ; AO : *flow, go, run*, AO : *belong to : lie along, border?* AN 334.]. *for take the part of*, LL 152,3. 1. mid *cohabit with.* l. on cnēowum *to kneel.* wið licgendum fēo *for ready money.*

līchama m. *body, corpse*, Bo,Mt; Æ,CP : *trunk*, CR 628. ['*licham*']

+līchamian *to clothe with flesh*, RWH 136³³.
+līchamod *incarnate*, BL33¹⁵.
līchamlēas *incorporeal*, ÆT.
līchamlic (o²) *bodily, carnal, physical, material, Bo,Lk*; Æ. adv. -līce *bodily, personally, in the flesh, BH*; Æ. ['*lichamly*']
-līchamung v. in-l.; līchom-=līcham-
līchanga m. *gibbet?* KC5·321' (BTac).
līchord† n. *interior of the body*, Gu.
līchrægel n. *winding-sheet*, MH76²⁶.
līchryre m. *bodily decay, death*, GEN1099.
līchryst=līcrest; līchwamlic=līchamlic
līcian I. (±) (w. d. or impers.) *to please*, Æ, AO,Bl,Bo; CP : *be sufficient*. ['*like*,' '*ylike*'] II. (+) *to be or make like : seem likely*, AO.
līciendlic *agreeable, pleasant*, PPs. adv. -līce.
+līclǣtan⁷ *to liken, compare*, MkLR4³⁰.
līclēoð n. *dirge*, OEG.
līclic *relating to the dead, funeral*, GPH 401.
+līclic *fitting, proper*, LCD. adv. -līce *equally*.
līcmann m. *bearer, pall-bearer*, Æ.
līcnes (±) f. '*likeness*' ('*i-likeness*'), *similarity : figure, stature, image, Æ,MtL* : (+) *parable*.
līcpytt m. *grave*, ÆGR66¹⁰? (or ? dīc, pytt).
līcrest f. *sepulchre, tomb, Lcd; Æ : hearse*, ÆL26¹⁸¹ : *cemetery*, OEG4347. [v. '*lich*']
līcs-=līx-
līcsang m. *dirge*, OEG.
līcsār† n. *wound*, B,CR.
līcstōw f. *place of burial*, GD340³⁵.
līcsyrce f. *corslet*, B550.
līctūn m. *burial-ground*, LL.
līcðēnung f. *obsequies, funeral, Æ : laying out (of corpse)*, ÆL31¹⁴²⁹.
līcðōote f. *pore*, WW159¹³.
līcðrōwere m. *leper*, Æ.
līcðrūh f. *sepulchre*, GD225.
līcum-=līcham-
±līcung f. *pleasure*, CP. ['*liking*']
līcwīglung f. *necromancy*, LL(248³).
līcwund f. *wound*, Ex239.
±līcwyrðe (e, eo, o, u) *pleasing, acceptable, Bo; CP : estimable, praiseworthy : accepted, recognised, sterling*. ['*likeworth*']
līcwyrðlīce *pleasingly*, ÆL23b⁵⁷.
līcwyrðnes f. *good pleasure*, LPs88¹⁸.
līd† n. *ship, vessel*. [līðan]
līda m. *sailor*, GnE104.
Līda=Līða; līden pp. of līðan.
līdeð pres. 3 sg. of lēodan.
līdmann† m. *seafarer, sailor, pirate*.
līdrin=lēðren
līdweard m. *ship-master*, AN244.
līdwērig *weary of sea-voyages*, AN482.

±līefan I. (ē, ī, ȳ) *to allow, grant, concede, Mt,CP*. ['*leve*'; lēaf] II. (ē, ēo, ī, ȳ) tr. and intr. *to believe, trust, confide in, Bl,Bo, Met,MH*. ['*leve*,' '*yleve*'] III. (+) *to be dear to*, CR1645.
+līefed (ȳ) *believing, faithful, pious*, Æ.
+līefedlic (ȳ) *permissible*, LL(436').
+līefedlīce (ȳ) *trustfully, credulously*, AO.
+līefen (ē) *excused*, LkR14¹⁹.
+līefenscipe m. *justification*, JnLR15²².
līeffæstan=līffæstan
līeg (æ, ē, ī) mn. *fire, flame, lightning, B,Bl*; CP. ['*leye*']
līeg- v. līg-
līeget=līget
līegeð I.=legeð pres. 3 sg. of lecgan. II. pres. 3 sg. of licgan.
līeht-=lēoht-, līht-
līehð pres. 3 sg. of lēogan.
±līesan (ē, ȳ) *to loosen, release, redeem, deliver, liberate, Cr,LkR*. ['*leese*']
līesing I. (ī, ȳ) m. *freedman*, LL. II. (ē) f. *deliverance, release, LkL*. ['*leesing*']
+līesnes (ē) f. *redemption*, DR12¹⁷.
līeð-=līð-; līexan=līxan
līf I. n. '*life*,' *existence, Æ,B,Chr,JnL : lifetime, RB.* on līfe, tō līfe, līfes *alive, Æ, BH : way of life* (e.g. *monastic*), *BH,Chr, Lk,W*; CP : *place where the life is according to rule, monastery*, CHR. II.=lēf. III.= lēaf I.
līf-=līef-
līfbrycgung f. *way of life*, DR7¹⁵.
līfbysig *struggling for life*, B966.
līfcearu† f. *care about life*, GEN.
līfdæg m. nap. līfdagas (usu. in plur.) '*life-day*,' *lifetime, B,Cr*.
līfde, līfede pret. sg. of libban.
līfen (eo) f. *sustenance*, AN,GL.
līfer I. f. '*liver*,' *Bo,WW*; Æ. II. f. *a weight*, WW432²⁸. [*L. libra?*]
līferādl f. *liver complaint*, LCD,WW.
līferbȳl m. *protuberance of the liver*, LCD 76b.
līferhol n. *hollow in the liver*, LCD76b.
līferlæppa m. *lobe of the liver*, WW.
līfersēoc *ill in the liver*, LCD.
līfersēocnes f. *disease of the liver*, LCD.
līferwærc m. *pain in the liver*, LCD60a.
līferwyrt n. *liverwort*, ANS84·326.
līfesn (BH362¹⁶)=lybesn
līffadung f. *regulation of life*, LL82²² (Wilk.).
līffæc n. *lifetime, life*, LL,W.
±līffæst *living, quickened, full of life, vigorous : life-giving : settled*.
±līffæstan (īe, ȳ) *to quicken, endow with life*, Æ,CP.
+līffæstnian *to quicken*, RPs142¹¹.
līffet-=lyffet-

līffrēa† m. *Lord of life, God.*
līffruma† m. *source of life (God).*
līfgan=libban
līfgedāl n. *death,* GD.
līfgesceaft† f. *life's conditions or record,* B.
līfgetwinnan mp. *twins,* SOL 141.
līfīan (*LG,Nar*) ['*ylife*']=libban
līfīende (y) *that lives or has life, BH : when alive, BH,VPs :* as sb. *the* '*living*,' VHy.
līflād f. *course of life, conduct, RB.* ['*livelihood*']
līflǣst=līflēast
līflēas *not endowed with life,* '*lifeless*,' *inanimate, Æ : dead,* Æ.
līflēast f. *loss of life, death,* Æ.
līflic *living,* Æ : '*lively*' : *long-lived : necessary to life, vital,* DHy,Hex. adv. -līce *vitally, so as to impart life,* Æ.
līflyre m. *loss of life,* LL 466,2.
līfneru f. *food, sustenance,* AN 1091.
līfnes (BHCA 362¹⁶)=lybesn
līfre gs. of lifer I.
līfre-=līfer-
līfrig *clotted,* A 30·132.
līft=lyft
līfweard m. *guardian of life,* EL 1036.
līfweg m. *way of life, way in life,* W.
līfwela† m. *riches.*
līfwelle *living (water),* JnL 4¹⁰.
līfwraðu† f. *protection of life,* B.
līfwynn† f. *enjoyment of life.*
līg (Æ)=līeg; līg-=lyg-
līgbǣre, līgberende *flaming,* GL.
līgberend m. *flame-bearer,* WW 239²⁴.
līgbryne (ē)† m. *burning, fire.*
līgbysig (ē) *busy with fire,* RD 31¹.
līgcwalu f. *fiery torment,* EL 296.
līgdraca (ē)† m. *fiery dragon,* B.
līgegesa m. *flaming terror,* B 2780.
līgen I. (ē) *flaming, fiery,* Æ. II. pp. of lēon.
līgenword=lygeword
+līg-ere n. -ernes f. *concubinage, fornication, adultery,* AO.
līget nm., līgetu (ē) f. *lightning, flash of lightning, BH,Bl,Mt;* Æ,AO. ['*lait*'; līeg]
līgetræsc (ē) m. *lightning, flash of light, coruscation,* Lk 10¹⁸. [līget]
līgetsleht (ē¹, æ³) m. *lightning-stroke, thunderbolt,* GD,MH.
līgetung f. *lightning,* EHy 6⁴¹.
līgeð pres. 3 sg. of licgan.
līg-fǣmende, -fāmblāwende *vomiting fire,* BH 432⁷.
līgfȳr n. *fire,* Ex 77.
līgge=līege ds. of līeg; līgit=līget
līglic (ē) *fiery,* GUTH 131¹⁹⁶.
līg-locc, -locced *having flaming locks,* WW.
līgnan (=īe)† *to deny.*
līgræsc (ē¹, e²)=līgetræsc

līg-ræscetung, -ræscung (ȳ¹) f. *lightning,* LPs.
līgspīwel *vomiting flame,* GPH,W.
līgð pres. 3 sg. of licgan.
līg-ōracu† f. gds. -ōræce *fiery onset, violence of flames,* PH.
līgȳð f. *wave of fire,* B 2672.
līh imperat. sg. of lēon.
līht=lēoht
līhtan (ē, ēo, ȳ) I. (±) *to make* '*light*,' *easy, relieve, alleviate,* Lcd; CP : *dismount,* '*alight*,' BH. II. (=īe; ȳ) *to lighten, illuminate, give light, shine,* Æ,Jn : *grow light, dawn,* Da : '*light*,' *kindle.*
līhtian=līhtan
līhting I. f. *relief, alleviation, release,* LL. ['*lighting*'] II. (ēo) f. *shining, illumination, light,* Æ : *dawn : lightning.* ['*lighting*']
līhtingnes f. *lightness of taxation,* LL (306²¹).
līhtnes f. *brightness,* W 230¹². ['*lightness*']
līhð pres. 3 sg. of lēogan.
līlie f. '*lily*,' *Bl,Lcd;* Æ. [L. lilium]
lim (y) n. nap. leomu '*limb*,' *member,* Æ, B,Bl; AO,CP : *branch,* B : *agent, offspring? Bl* 33 : *bone?* CPs 6³.
līm m. *anything sticky,* '*lime*,' *mortar, cement, gluten,* Æ,Ep,WW : *bird-lime, snare,* BF 144⁶.
+līman *to cement, join, stick together,* ÆGR.
līmfīn f. *lime-heap,* BC 1·518'.
līmgelecg n. *shape,* WW.
līmgesihð f. *body,* RHy 11⁴⁰.
līmhāl *sound of limb,* GU 661.
+līmian=+līman
līming f. *smearing, plastering,* WW. ['*liming*']
limlǣw f. *injury to limbs, mutilation,* LL (278n4).
limlǣweo *maimed,* LL 132,10.
limlēas *without limbs,* Æ 2·270²².
limmǣlum adv. *limb by limb,* WW. ['*limbmeal*']
limmlama *crippled,* W 4¹².
limnacod *stark naked,* GEN 1566.
+limp n. *occurrence : misfortune, accident,* CP.
±limpan³ *to happen, occur, exist,* B,Bo,Chr, Met;* Æ,AO,CP : *belong to, suit, befit,* Ct : *concern,* CP. ['*limp*,' '*i-limp*']
±limpful *fitting, convenient,* AS 1²¹.
limplǣcan *to unite, connect,* OEG 80.
+limplic *fitting, suitable,* ÆL : *happening :* '*accidentia*,' ÆGR. adv. -līce (±).
+limplicnes f. *opportunity,* VPs 9¹⁰.
limrǣden f. *form? disposition of the limbs?* v. OEG 2530.
limsēoc† *lame, paralytic.*
limwǣde n. *clothing,* PPs 103².
limwæstm m. *stature,* SAT 130.

limwērig *weary of limb*, Rood 63.

līn n. *flax, linen, cloth, napkin, towel*, Ct,Gl, JnR,MtR; CP. ['*line*']

līnacer m. *flax-field*, EC 239¹⁰.

lind I. f. *lime-tree, linden, Ct, Gl*; Æ; Mdf : (†) *shield (of wood)*. ['*lind*'] **II.**=lynd

lindcroda m. *crash of shields, battle*, Gen 1998.

linde=lind I.

linden *made of '*linden'*-wood, GnE*.

lindgecrod n. *shield-bearing troop*, An 1222.

lindgelāc n. *battle*, Ap 76.

lindgestealla† m. *companion in war*.

lindhæbbende† m. *shield-bearer, warrior*.

lindplega† m. *shield-play, battle*.

lindrycg m. *ridge where limes grow*, EC 447²³.

lindwered n. *troop armed with shields*, El 142.

lindwīga m. *warrior*, B 2603.

lind-wīgend†, **-wīggend†** m. *shielded warrior*.

līne f. *line, cable, rope, Sol,WW : series, row : rule, direction*.

līnece (WW 286²¹)=līnete

līnen adj. '*linen*,' *made of flax, CP,Ep*; Æ.

līnenhrægl n. *linen cloth*, NG.

līnenweard *clad in linen*, ÆP 84¹⁹, RWH 66⁵.

līnete (-ece) f. *linnet*, WW 286²¹.

līnetwig(l)e f. *linnet, Cp,Erf,WW*. ['*lint-white*']

-ling suffix (1) for forming personal nouns (dēorling, ræpling). (2) for forming advbs. (hinderling).

līnhæwen *flax-coloured*, Lcd.

līnland n. *land in flax*, KC 3·19⁴.

līnlēag m. *flax ground*, EC 166².

linnan³ (w. instr. or g.) *to cease from, desist, lose, yield up (life)*, B. ['*lin*']

līnsæd (e²) n. '*linseed*,' *Lcd,LL*·

līnwǣd f. *linen cloth or garment*, NG.

līnwyrt f. *flax*, Lcd.

līo (WW 438²²)=lēo

lippa m., **lippe?** f. (LL 2·136) '*lip*,' *Lcd,RB, WW*.

līra m. *any fleshy part of the body, muscle, calf of the leg, Lcd,WW*. ['*lire*']

+līre=+ligere

līreht *fleshy*, Lcd 91a.

līs=liss; **līs-**=līes-; **līsan** (Gl)=lesan

+līse (e) nap. +leosu n. *reading, study*, BH.

+līsian *to slip, glide*, CP 437.

-lisnian, -listnian v. be-l.

liss (līðs) f. *grace, favour, love, kindness, mercy*, Æ : *joy, peace, rest, Ph,W* : *remission, forgiveness*, †Hy 10⁵⁴ : *alleviation*, Æ : *saving (of life)*. ['*liss*'; līðe]

lissan *to subdue, Sol* 294. ['*lisse*']

list mf. *art, cleverness, cunning, experience, skill, craft, Cr,Gen.* listum *cunningly, skilfully.* ['*list*']

listan=lystan

līste f. '*list*,' *fringe, border, Ep*.

listelīce adv. *carefully*, Lcd 11a.

listhendig *skilful*, Cra 95. **listum** v. list.

listwrenc m. *deception*, W 81; 128n⁹.

līsð pres. 3 sg. of lesan.

līt *colour, dye*, RWH 141¹⁰.

līt=lȳt

lītan *to bend, incline*, Met 26¹¹⁹.

līte-, lītel=lytig-, lȳtel; **lītig**=lytig

lītigere m. *dyer*, RWH 141⁹.

lītl-=lȳtl-; **lītsmann**=liðsmann

lið I. nm. nap. leoðu, liðu *limb, member, BH,Cr*; Æ,AO,CP : *joint, Lcd : tip (of finger), Lk.* ['*lith*'] **II.** n. *fleet.* [ON. lið]

līð I. n. *cider, native wine, fermented drink, CP : beaker, cup.* **II.** *mercy*, VH 16. **III.** pres. 3 sg. of licgan. **IV.**=līðe adj. **V.**=līhð

Līða m. *name of months June* (ǣrra L.) *and July* (æftera L.), Men,MH.

liðādl f. *gout*, Lcd,WW.

līðan¹ I. (±) *to go, travel, sail, B,BH* : (+) *arrive*, WW. ['*lithe*'] **II.** *to be bereft of*, GnE 26? **III.** (*CP*)=līðigian

līðe I. adj. *gentle, soft, calm, mild, ApT,B, Mt*; Æ,AO,CP : *gracious, kind, agreeable, sweet, Bo,Gen*; Æ. ['*lithe*'] **II.** adv.

līðe-=leoðu-; **līðeg**=līðig

līðelīc *gentle, soft, mild*, CP. adv. -līce, CP. ['*lithely*']

+līðen (y) *having travelled much*, CAS 26¹³. [līðan]

līðercian *to smooth down, flatter*, Gl.

līðere f., liðera m. *sling, slinging pouch, BH, Cp*; Æ. ['*lither*'; leðer]

līðeren=leðren

līðerlic *of a sling*, WW 247⁴.

līðgeat=hlidgeat

līðian (*CP*; Æ)=līðigian

±līðian (eo) *to unloose, release*, GD.

līðig *lithe, flexible, bending, yielding*, Æ,W. ['*lithy*']

līðigian (±) *to soften, calm, mitigate, assuage, appease, CP*; Æ : *be mild.* ['*lithe*']

līðincel n. *little joint*, WW.

līðlic=līðelic; **līðmann**=lidmann

līðnes f. *mildness, softness, gentleness, kindness*, Æ,CP.

līðo-=leoðu-; **līðre**=liðere

līðre=lȳðre; **līðrin**=leðren; **līðs**=liss

līðsēaw n. *synovia*, Lcd.

līðsmann m. *seafarer, pirate*, Chr.

liðu v. lið.

liðule m? *synovia*, Lcd. [lið, ele]

līðung f. *alleviation, relief*, Lcd 1·112² : '*venia*,' '*miseratio*,' OEG 8³⁹⁸.

līðwǣge n. *drinking-cup*, B1982.
līðwǣrc m. *pain in the limbs*, LCD49b.
līðwyrde *mild of speech*, NC348.
līðwyrt f. *dwarf elder*, LCD,WW.
līxan (=īe) *to shine, flash, glitter, gleam*.
līxende *splendidly*, LkL16¹⁹.
līxung f. *brilliance, brightness*, DR.
-lō pl. -lōn v. mæst-, sceaft-l.
lob (GL)=lof
lobbe f. *spider*, LPs. ['*lob*']
loc I. n. '*lock*,' *bolt, bar, Æ,BH*; AO : *enclosure, fold, prison, stronghold*, CP : *bargain, agreement, settlement, conclusion* : *clause*, OEG7¹⁹⁵. [lūcan] II.=locc I.
lōc, lōca interj. '*look*,' *see, look you*. l. hū *however* : *whatever*, Gen16⁶. l. hwænne, hwonne *whenever*. spel l. hwænne mann wille *a discourse for any occasion you please, Æ*. l. hwǣr *wherever*. l. hwǣðer *whichever*. l. hwā, l. hwæt, *whoever, whatever*. l. hwylc *whichever*. l. nu *observe, note, behold, ÆGr*.
loca I. m. *enclosure, stronghold*. II. m. *lock (of wool)*, GL.
lōca-hū v. lōc interj.
locbore f. *one who wears long hair, free woman*, LL7,73.
locc I. m. '*lock*' (*of hair*), *hair, curl, Bl,CP, Ep*; *Æ*. II.=loc I.
loccetan (MtL)?=rocettan (JAW77).
±loccian *to attract, entice, soothe*, CP
loccod *hairy, shaggy*, OEG56¹³.
locen I. pp. of lūcan. II. (SAT300?)=loc
locer=locor
locfeax n. *hair*, WW379⁴².
locgewind n. *hair*, WW199⁷.
lōc-hū, -hwænne etc. v. lōc hū, lōc hwænne, etc.
lochyrdel m. *hurdle for sheepfolds*, LL454,9.
lōcian (±) *to see, behold, look, gaze, Bl,G, Met*; AO : *observe, notice, take heed, CP*; *Æ* : *belong, pertain, Æ*. l. tō *regard with favour*, CP.
locor m. *plane (tool)*, GL.
locstān m. *stone closing an entrance*, ÆL 23³⁴⁵.
-lōcung v. ðurh-l.
loddere m. *beggar, Æ*; Mdf. [lýðre]
+lodr f. *backbone, spine*, LCD65a.
lodrung f. *rubbish, nonsense*, WW478⁸.
+lodwyrt f. *silverweed*, LCD,WW.
loerge (Ep) np. of lorg.
lof I. n. (m. *B*1536) *praise, glory, repute, Cp*; *Æ,CP* : *song of praise, hymn*. ['*lof*'] II. n. *protection, help?* AN991 (v. also lōf).
lōf '*redimicula*,' OEG5241=glōf (?), v. ES 37·186, or ?*fillet, band*, at AN991 (BTs).
lofbǣre *praising, giving praise*, VHy.
lofdǣd f. *praiseworthy deed*, B24.

lofgeorn *eager for praise*, ÆL16³⁰² : *lavish? ostentatious?* RB54⁹; 55³.
lofherung f. *praising*, LPs55¹².
lofian *to praise, exalt, Gen,PPs*; CP : (±) *appraise, value*. ['*love*']
loflāc n. *offering in honour of any one*, W 107⁶.
loflǣcan *to praise*, LPs118¹⁷⁵.
loflic *laudable*, HGL498. adv. -lice *gloriously*, BL165¹⁶.
lofmægen n. *praise*, PPs105².
lofsang m. *song of praise, canticle, hymn, psalm, BH*; *Æ* : *lauds*. ['*lofsong*']
lofsealm m. *the 148th Psalm, lauds*, RB36¹⁹.
lofsingende *singing hymns of praise*, OEG 4912.
lofsum *praiseworthy*, GEN468.
lofte (on) adv. phr. *in the air, aloft, Hex, MLN*. ['*loft*']
lofung f. *praising, laudation* : *appraising, Æ*.
lōg pret. 3 sg. of lēan.
-loga v. āð-, trēow-, wed-, word-l. [leogan]
+logendlic adj. *to be kept in order*, RBL63⁵.
lōges v. lōh; logeðer=logðer
±lōgian *to lodge, place, put by, Æ* : *put in order, arrange, collect, settle, Æ* : *discourse, Æ* : *divide, portion out*. +l. ūp *lay by, deposit*. +lōgod *interpolated*, BF70²². +lōgod sprǣc (*well*)-*ordered speech, style*.
logðer (o²) *cunning, artful*, WW.
+lōgung f. *order*, CM599.
lōh I. n., gs. lōges *place, stead* (only in phr. on his lōh), CHR779E. II. pret. 3 sg. of lēan II.
lōhsceaft m. *bolt, bar? stick with a strap to it?* (BTs), AS1².
loma=lama
±lōma m. *tool, utensil, article of furniture, BH*; GL. ['*loom*']
lomb, lomber=lamb
±lōme (1) adj. *frequent*, ÆL31¹⁰¹⁹; (2) adv. *often, frequently, Gen*. oft (and) +l. *constantly, diligently*. ['*ylome*']
+lōmed=+lēomod; lōmelic=lōmlic
±lōmlǣcan *to frequent, Æ* : *be frequent*.
+lōmlǣcende *frequent, Æ* : *frequentative* (vb), ÆGR213⁷.
+lōmlǣcing f. *frequency, frequenting*, ÆGR 213⁷.
+lōmlǣcnes f. *a numerous assembly*, Ps.
+lōmlic *repeated, frequent, numerous*, AO, CP. adv. -lice.
+lōmlician *to become frequent*, BL109².
+lōmlicnes f. *repetition*, BF174²¹ : *a numerous assembly*, CPs117²⁷.
lomp pret. 3 sg. of limpan.
+lomrǣde *frequent*, TC.
lond=land
londādl f. *strangury?* LCD108a. [hland]

lone=lane; long=lang
Longbeard-an, -as sbmpl. *Lombards*, AO.
lonn, lonu=lann, lanu
loppe f. *spider*, Bo,WW. ['*lop*']
loppestre f. '*lobster*,' WW; Æ : *locust*, MkL.
lopust, lopystre=loppestre
lor n. (in phr. tō lore, tō lose) *loss, destruction, Bl;* CP. ['*lore*']
-lora v. hlēow-l.
loren pp. (str.) of lēoran.
lorg, lorh fm. *pole, distaff, weaver's beam*, GL,Wyn 168.
los=lor ['*loss*']; losewist=loswist
losian (u) wv. (±) *to be lost, fail, perish, Bo, CP;* Æ : (±) *escape, get away* : '*lose*,' LkL 15⁴ : *destroy*, LkL 17²⁷.
losigendlic *ready to perish*, ÆH.
losing, loswist f. *loss, destruction*, NG.
lot n. *fraud, guile*, ÆL,CP.
loten pp. of lūtan.
lotwrenc m. *deception, deceit, cunning, artifice, trick*, Æ,AO,CP.
lotwrencceast f. *cunning*, Mk 12¹⁵.
loða m. *upper garment, mantle, cloak*, CP.
lox m. *lynx*, BH,WW. [*Ger.* luchs]
luba-, lube-=lufe-
lūcan² I. (±) (tr.) *to lock, close, enclose, fasten, shut up, An* : (intr.) *close up, form one mass, Ph* : *interlock, intertwine, twist, wind,* CP : *conclude.* ['*louk*'] II. *pluck out, pull up*, Met. ['*louk*'²]
-lucor v. MFB n30.
ludgæt n. *side-gate, postern gate*, GL.
ludon pret. pl. of lēodan.
lufelic=luflic
lufen f. *hope?* (BT; GK), Da 73,B 2886.
lufestice f. *lovage (plant)*, Lcd. [*L.* levisticum]
lufestre f. *female lover*, OEG.
luffendlic=lufiendlic
luffeorm f. *hospitality*, AB 34·10.
±lufian *to* '*love*,' *cherish, show love to,* Æ, Chr,JnL,VPs; CP : *fondle, caress* : *delight in, approve, practise.*
lufiend m. *lover*, Æ.
lufiende *affectionate*, ÆGr. ['*loving*']
lufi(g)endlic *lovely, beautiful*, Æ : *lovable*, Æ.
luflic *amiable, loving*, Lcd : *lovable*, Ps. adv. -līce *kindly*, CP : *willingly, gladly*, BH. ['*lovely*']
lufræden f. *love*, LPs. ['*lovered*']
lufsum *loving, lovable, pleasant*, Cr. ['*lovesome*']
lufsumlic *gracious*, BH 248¹⁷. adv. -līce.
lufsumnes f. *pleasantness, kindness*, WW 218³⁴. ['*lovesomeness*']
luftācen n. '*love-token*,' B 1863.
luf-tȳme (Æ), -tēme (RB) *pleasant, sweet, grateful, benevolent.*

luftȳmlic *pleasant*, OEG 56²⁵⁴.
lufu f. '*love*,' *strong liking, affection, favour*, Æ; AO,CP : *desire* : *kind action* : *love (of God)*, JnR : *amicable settlement*, LL 392'.
lufung f. *action of loving*, GD 73¹⁴.
lufwende *lovable, pleasant*, Bf,Lcd.
lufwendlic *friendly*, KGl 73³⁴. adv. -līce *gently*, KGl 80²¹.
lugon pret. pl. of lēogan.
luh n. *loch, pond*, NG; Mdf. [*Keltic*]
+lumpenlic *occasional*, A 10·143 : *suitable*, A 10·141. [limpan]
lumpon pret. pl. of limpan.
luncian? *to limp* LPs 17⁴⁶. [cp. *Norw.* lunke?]
lundlaga m. *kidney*, Æ,Lcd,WW.
lungen f. '*lung*,' Lcd,WW.
lungenādl f. *lung-disease*, Lcd.
lungenǣder f. *vein of the lungs*, Lcd 40b.
lungensealf f. *lung-salve*, Lcd 141a.
lungenwyrt f. '*lung-wort*,' Lcd.
-lunger v. cēas-l.
lungre† adv. *soon, forthwith, suddenly, quickly.*
lunnon pret. pl. of linnan.
lūs f. nap. lȳs '*louse*,' Æ,Cp,Hex.
lusian (GPH)=losian
lust I. m. *desire, appetite*, Æ,BH,JnL : *pleasure*, Bo,Lk (pl.) : *sensuous appetite, lust*, Jul,Lcd,WW. II. adj. *willing*, W 246¹⁰.
lustbǣre I. *desirable, pleasant, agreeable, cheerful, joyous*, Æ,AO : *desirous*, ÆL 4¹¹⁶. II. adv. *gladly, willingly.*
lustbǣrlic *pleasant*, AO. adv. -līce.
lustbǣrnes f. *enjoyment, pleasure, desire*, CP.
lustful *wishful, desirous*, AO 100²⁷ : (+) *desirable*, WW 220⁵. ['*lustful*']
±lustfullian *to rejoice, enjoy*, Æ : *desire*, Bf 4¹⁸ : *be pleasing to*, CP 70²⁴.
±lustfullīce *gladly, heartily*, Bl. ['*lustfully*']
±lustfullung f. *desire, pleasure, delight*, Æ.
±lustfulnes f. *desire, pleasure*, BH; CP. ['*lustfulness*']
lustgeornnes f. *concupiscence*, G.
lustgryn f. *snare of pleasure*, Soul 23.
+lustian *to delight in*, Sc.
lustlīce *willingly, gladly*, Bl; Æ,AO.
lustmoce f. *lady's-smock (plant)*, Lcd.
lustsumlic *pleasant*, AO. adv. -līce *willingly*.
lustum adv. *with pleasure, gladly*, Cr,PPs.
lūsðorn m. *spindle-tree*, EC 445'.
±lūtan² *to bend, stoop, decline*, Æ,AO. +loten dæg *after part of day* : *bow, make obeisance, fall down*, Bl,VPs : (+) *lay down*, MtL 8²⁰ : *entreat.* ['*lout*']

±lūtian *to lie hid, hide, lurk,* Æ,*VHy*; AO, CP. ['*lout*'²]

lūtter, lūttor=hlūttor, hlūtor

lūðer-=lȳðer-

lybb n. *drug, poison, charm,* LCD,GL.

lybban=libban

lybbestre f. *sorceress,* WW 200²⁵.

lybcorn n. *a medicinal seed, wild saffron?* GL.

lybcræft m. *skill in the use of drugs, magic, witchcraft,* BL.

lybesn (i) f. *charm, amulet, knot,* BH,GL.

lyblāc nm. *occult art, use of drugs for magic, witchcraft,* LCD,LL.

lyblǣca m. *wizard, sorcerer,* GL.

lybsin, lybsn=lybesn

lȳc-=lǣc-, līc-; **lycce**=lyge II.

lȳcð pres. 3 sg. of lūcan.

lȳden (LWS)=lǣden; **lȳt**=līf

lȳf-=lēaf-, lēf-, lief-, līf-

lyfde, lyfede pret. 3 sg. of libban.

lyfesn=lybesn

lyffetere m. *flatterer,* Æ,GL.

lyffet-tan, -tian *to flatter,* Æ.

lyffetung f. *adulation, flattery,* Æ.

lyfian=lifian, libban

lyft fmn. *air, sky, clouds, atmosphere,* B, *Lcd*; Æ,AO,CP. on lyfte *on high, aloft.* ['*lift*'; *Ger.* luft]

lyftādl f. *paralysis, palsy,* BH,LCD.

lyftedor m. *clouds,* Ex 251.

lyften *of the air, aerial,* ÆH,HEX.

lyftfæt n. *vessel in the air (moon),* RD 30³.

lyftflēogend m. *flier in the air, bird,* SOL 289.

lyftfloga m. *flier in the air, dragon,* B 2315.

lyftgelāc† n. *flight through the air,* AN.

lyftgeswenced *driven by the wind,* B 1913.

lyfthelm† m. *air, mist, cloud.*

lyftlācende† *sporting in the air, flying.*

lyftlic (u¹) *aerial,* BYH 118².

lyftsceaða m. *aerial robber (raven),* WY 39.

lyftwundor n. *aerial wonder,* Ex 90.

lyftwynn† f. *pleasure in flying.*

lyge I. (i) m. '*lie,' falsehood,* BH,Sat. II. *lying, false* (MtR 26⁶⁰; =*lygge, JAW 25). III. '*sicalia,' secale? corn? rye?* WW 301².

lygen (i) f. *lie, falsehood,* GEN,PR.

lygenian=lygnian

lygesearu† n. *lying wile, trick.*

lygespell (i) n. *falsehood,* WW 449².

lygesynnig (i) *lying, false,* EL 899.

lygetorn (i) *feigned anger or grief,* B 1943.

lygeword (i)† n. *lying word, lie.*

lygewyrhta (i) m. *liar,* LEAS.

lygnes (i) f. *falseness : false things,* WW 239⁹.

±lygnian (i) *to give one the lie, convict of falsehood,* Æ. +lygnod *perjured,* Æ.

lȳht-=līht-

lyhð pres. 3 sg. of lēan.

lȳhð pres. 3 sg. of lēogan; **lym**=lim

lȳman *to shine,* GD 171⁵.

lymp-=limp-

±lynde, lyndo (i) f. *fat, grease,* LCD.

+lyndu np. *joints of the spine,* WW 159²².

-lynian v. ā-l., tō-l.

lynibor n. *borer, gimlet,* WW 273¹³.

lynis m. '*linch'-pin, Ep,WW.*

lypenwyrhta m. *tanner,* WW.

lyre (e) m. *loss, destruction, damage, hurt,* WW; Æ. ['*lure*'; lēosan]

lyrewrenc m. *hurtful intrigue,* MFH 169.

-lyrtan v. be-l.; **lȳs** v. lūs; **lȳs-**=līes-

lysferht=leasferhð

lysnan, lysnere=hlysnan, hlysnere

lȳssa (KGL)=lǣssa; **lyssen**=lyswen

±lystan impers. w. a. (d.) of pers. and g. of thing or inf. *to please, cause pleasure or desire, provoke longing,* Æ,*Bl,Bo,Met*; AO, CP. +lysted *desirous of.* ['*list*'; lust]

lystere (OEG 4674)=? lyftere, lyffetere

+lystfullīce=lustfullīce

lysu I. *base, false, evil,* AN 1222. II. n. *evil deed,* LL.

lyswen I. *purulent, corrupt,* LCD. II. n. *pus, matter,* LCD.

lȳt adv., adj. and indecl. sb. *little, few,* B, *DD,Gen,Run*; Æ,AO. ['*lite*']

lȳtan=lūtan; **lyteg**=lytig

lȳtel I. adj. 'LITTLE,' *not large,* Æ,AO : *unimportant, mean : short (distance, time),* B : *not much, Mt,Ps.* II. adv. *little, slightly, Ps.* III. sb. *AO,Lcd,Ps.*

lȳtelhȳdig *pusillanimous,* CRA 10.

lyte-lic, -līce=lytig-lic, -līce

lȳtelmōd *pusillanimous,* CP.

lȳtelne=lȳtesne

lȳtelnes f. *smallness,* ÆGr 228¹⁴. ['*littleness*']

lȳtesnā (JUL), lȳtes(t)ne (BH) adv. *nearly, almost.*

lȳthwōn adv. and sb. (w. g.) *little, but little, very few,* Æ,CP.

lytig (e) *crafty, cunning,* AO : *prudent,* KGL.

lytigian *to feign, act crookedly,* MA 86.

lytiglic *deceitful, crafty.* adv. -līce, CP.

lytignes f. *cunning,* CP 237²².

lȳtle f. *female slave,* Æ (9⁴⁰¹).

±lȳtlian *to lessen, decrease, diminish,* Bo, *JnL*; CP : *shorten, curtail, abrogate : fall out of use,* LL 267,37 : *belittle.* ['*little*']

lȳtling m. *little one, infant, child,* Æ,CP : *unimportant person,* CHRD 2⁴.

lȳtlum adv. (d. of lȳtel) *little by little, gradually,* Æ; CP. ['*litlum*']

lȳtlung (ī) f. *diminution : (+) insufficiency, want,* Sc 57¹ (cp. EHy 5¹²).

lyttl-=lȳtl-

lyttuccas mpl. *particles, small pieces,* GPH 400.
lyð=lið; **lyða**=liða; +**lyðen**=+liðen
lyðerful *evil, vile,* W 405.
lyðerlic *bad, sordid, mean, vile,* AO. adv. -līce (ū1), *WW* 178²⁷. ['*litherly*']
lyðernes (ū1) f. *wickedness,* HL 18⁸.
lyðran (ē;=īe) *to anoint, smear, 'lather,'* *JnL,Lcd.* [lēaðor]
lyðre=liðere
lyðre I. (ē, ī) adj. *bad, wicked, base, mean, corrupt, wretched, Æ,AO,Lk,WW .* ['*lither*'] adv. SAT 62. **II.** comp. of liðe.
lyðwyrt=liðwyrt; **lyxan**=līxan

M

mā I. (ǣ) adv. [comp. of micle] *more, rather, longer, hereafter, further, Æ,CP.* ðe mā ðe *more than.* **II.** sb. (indecl.) *more, Æ.* **III.** adj. *more, Æ.* ['MO'] **IV.**=man I.
mabuldor=mapulder; **maca**=+mæcca
macalic *convenient,* MkR 6²¹.
macian *to 'make,' form, construct, do, A,Æ : prepare, arrange, cause, Æ,Gen,Mt : use, Æ : behave, fare, Æ,Bo;* CP : *compare : transform, ÆP 204¹¹.* macian ūp *to put up, Æ.*
mācræftig (=mægencr-)† *mighty.*
macung f. *making, doing,* CHR 1101.
+**mād** *silly, mad,* WW.
mādm=māðm
mādmōd n. *foolishness,* MOD 25.
mǣ (*VPs*)=mā
±**mǣc** *well-suited, companionable : similar, equal.*
mǣcan=mecgan, mengan
+**mǣcca** (a, e) mf. *mate, equal, one of a pair, comrade, companion, ÆGr,MtR :* (±) *husband, wife, Æ,Bl,Ct,Mt :* pl. *pair,* CHRD 48²⁶. ['*match*']
mǣcefisc=mēcefisc
mǣcg† m. *man, disciple : son.*
mǣcga m. *man,* Wy 52.
mǣcian=mecgan, mengan
+**mǣclic** *conjugal,* Sc.
+**mǣcnes** f. *cohabitation,* BH.
+**mǣcscipe** m. *cohabitation,* CR 199.
mǣd (ē) f. ds. (EWS) mēda; nap. mǣd(w)a, mǣdwe '*mead,'* '*meadow,'* *pasture,* BC, OEG; Æ,AO; Mdf.
+**mǣdan** *to make mad or foolish.* pp. +mǣd(ed), *Cp,Rd,WW.*
mǣddre f. '*madder,'* Lcd; Æ.
mǣden (Æ,AO,CP)=mægden
mǣdencild n. *female child, girl, AO;* Æ. ['*maiden-child*']
mǣdenhēap m. *band of virgins,* DD 289.

mǣdenlic *maidenly, virgin, Æ.*
mǣdere=mæddre
mǣderecīō m. *sprig of madder,* LCD.
+**mǣdla** m. *madness,* LCD 122b.
mǣdlacu f. *meadow-stream,* KC.
mǣdland m. *meadow-land,* KC.
mǣdmǣwect (=-wett) *mowing of a meadow,* LL 448,5².
Mǣdmōnað (e1) *July,* MEN (Hickes).
mǣdrǣden f. *mowing, tract of mown grass,* KC 6·153¹⁰.
mǣdsplott m. *plot of meadow-land,* KC 4·72⁷.
mǣdwa m., mǣdwe f.=mǣd
mǣdweland=mǣdland
mǣg I. pres. 3 sg. of magan. **II.** (Sc 4¹⁹ ; 12¹⁷)=mægen
±**mǣg** (ē) **I.** m. nap. māgas (v. LL 2·651) *male kinsman, parent, son, brother, nephew, cousin, B,Ep; Æ,AO,CP : compatriot,* A 46·76. ['*may*'] **II.**† f. *female relation, wife, woman, maiden,* Rd 10⁸. ['*may*'].
mǣgbana m. *destroyer of kinsfolk,* W 242⁵.
mǣgbōt f. *compensation paid to the relatives of a murdered man,* LL.
mǣgburg f. *family, tribe, race, people, nation : genealogy.*
mǣgcild n. *young kinsman,* Ct,LcD.
mǣgcnafa m. *youthful kinsman,* BC 2·329'.
mǣgcūð *related,* OEG.
mǣgcwalm (ē) m. *murder of a relation,* Cp 179P.
mǣgden (ǣd) n. *maiden, virgin,* LL; Æ : *girl, Mt :* *maid, servant,* Bl.
mǣgden- see also mǣden-.
mǣgdenǣw f. *marriage with a virgin,* LL (1·332').
mǣgdenhād m. '*maidenhood,' Cr;* CP.
mǣgdenmann m. '*maid,' virgin, AO,Lcd.* ['*maidenman*']
mǣge=māge
mǣgen I. (e) n. *bodily strength, might, 'main' force, power, vigour, valour, B;* Æ,CP : *virtue, efficacy, efficiency, Lcd : good deed : picked men of a nation, host, troop, army, An,Chr;* AO : *miracle.* [magan] **II.** subj. pl. of magan.
mǣgenāgende *mighty,* B 2837.
mǣgenbyrðen† f. *huge burden, B.* [v. '*main*']
mǣgencorðor n. *strong troop,* GEN 1986.
mǣgencræft† m. *main force, great strength, might.*
mǣgencyning† m. *mighty king, Cr.* [v. '*main*']
mǣgendǣd f. *mighty deed,* CRA 12.
mǣgenēaca m. *succour,* Az 138.
mǣgenēacen† *mighty, vigorous.*
mǣgenearfeðe† n. *great misery or trial.*

mægenellen n. *mighty valour*, B 659.

mægenfæst *vigorous, strong, steadfast*, Æ.

mægenfolc n. *mighty company*, Cr 877. [v. '*main*']

mægenfultum m. *mighty help*, B 1455.

mægenhēap m. *powerful band*, Ex 197.

mægenheard *very strong*, Run 5.

mægenian (gn-) *to gain strength* : (+) *establish, confirm*, BH 306¹⁸.

mægenig? (mēn-) *strong*, Ex 6¹ (BTs).

mægenlēas *powerless, feeble, helpless*, WW; Æ. ['*mainless*'] adv. -līce.

mægenlēast f. *weakness, feebleness*, Æ : *inability*, RB.

mægenrǣs m. *mighty onslaught*, B 1519. [v. '*main*']

mægenrōf† *powerful*, Ex,Rd.

mægenscype m. *might, power*, Da 20.

mægensibb f. *great love*, VH 16.

mægenspēd† f. *power, virtue*.

mægenstān m. *huge stone*, Met 5¹⁶. [v. '*main*']

mægenstrang† *of great virtue or strength*.

mægenstreng-o, -ðu f. *great might*.

mægenðegen m. *mighty minister*, Gu 1099.

mægenðīse f. *violence, force*, Rd 28¹⁰.

mægenðrēat† m. *mighty host*.

mægenðrymm m. *power, might, majesty, greatness, glory*, Mt; Æ,CP : *virtue*, Bf : *heavenly host* : (†) *Christ* : (†) *heaven*. [v. '*main*']

mægenðrymnes f. *great glory, majesty*, Æ.

mægenweorc† n. *mighty work*, PPs.

mægenwīsa m. *general*, Ex 553.

mægenwudu m. *strong spear*, B 236.

mægenwundor n. *striking wonder*, Cr 927.

mæger *meagre, lean*, Guth,Lcd.

mægerian *to macerate, make lean*, WW. [*Ger.* magern]

mægester=magister

mægeð, mægeð=mægð, mægð

mæggemōt n. *meeting of kinsmen*, AO 248¹⁸.

mæggewrit n. *genealogy, pedigree*.

mæggieldan³? *to contribute towards the fine for manslaughter by a kinsman*, LL 122,74².

mæghǣmed n. *incest*, BH 280¹.

mæghand (mēg-, mēi-) f. *natural heir, relative*, Ct.

mægister=magister

mæglagu f. *law as to relatives*, LL 266,25.

mæglēas *without relatives*, LL.

mæglēast (RWH 29⁷)=mægenlēast

mæglic *belonging to a kinsman*, ÆH.

mæglufu f. *love*, Jul 70.

mægmorðor n. *murder of a relative*, Gl.

mægmyrðra m. *murderer of a relative, parricide*, OEG,GD 239⁴.

mægn=mægen; mægnan=mengan

mægon=magon pres. pl. of magan

mægracu f. *generation, genealogy*, Æ.

mægrǣden f. *relationship*, AO.

mægrǣs m. *attack on relatives*, W 164⁴.

mægscīr [mēg-] f. *division of a people containing the kinsmen of a particular family* (BT), DR 193¹⁰.

mægsibb f. *relationship* : *affection of relatives*.

mægsibbung f. *reconciliation, peace-making*, JGPh 1·63.

mægsiblic *related*, WW 375¹⁷.

mægslaga m. *slayer of a relative, parricide, fratricide*, Æ.

mægsliht m. *murder of a relative*, W 130².

mægster=magister

mægð† f. gp. mægða, dp. mægðum, otherwise uninflected *maiden, virgin, girl, woman, wife*. [*Goth.* magaðs]

±mægð I. (ȳ) f. *family group, clan, tribe, generation, stock, race, people*, Æ,AO : *province, country*, Æ. II. *longing, ambition*, Gl,Lcd : *greed*, Bo.

mægða m. *mayweed*, Lcd,WW.

mægðblæd (geð) n. *pudendum muliebre*, GPH 400⁸.

mægðbōt f. *fine for assault on an unmarried woman?* LL 7,74.

mægðhād m. *virginity, chastity, purity*, MH; Æ,CP : *band of young persons* : *relationship*, Æ. ['*maidhood*']

mægðhādlic *maidenly*, OEG 1469

mægðlagu=mæglagu

mægðlēas *not of noble birth*, WW 219⁸.

mægðmann m. *maiden, virgin*, LL 8,82.

mægðmorðor (ē¹) nm. *murder of kin*, OEG 24¹².

mægðmyrðra m. *murderer of kin*, OEG 2³³⁵.

mægðrǣden f. *friendship, relationship*, OEG.

mægðsibb (y²) f. *kindred*, HGL 523.

mægwine† m. *friendly relative, clansman*.

mægwlite (ā, ē) m. *aspect, species, form*.

mægwlitian (ē¹) *to fashion*, MtL 17².

mægwlitlīce (ē¹) *figuratively*, MkL p 4¹⁰.

mæht=meaht, miht

mæhð (AS 38¹¹)=mægð II.

mæl I. (ā, ē) n. *mark, sign, ornament* : *cross, crucifix* : *armour, harness, sword* : *measure*, Lcd : (†) *time, point of time, occasion, season* : *time for eating, 'meal,' meals*, CP; Æ. II. f. (†) *talk, conversation* : *contest, battle*. [mæðel] III.=māl

+mǣl *stained, dyed*, An 1333.

+mǣlan *to mark, stain*, Jul 591.

±mǣlan† *to speak, talk*, Gen,Ps. ['*mele*,' '*i-mele*'; mæðlan]

mǣlcearu f. *trouble of the time*, B 189.

mæld-=meld-

mǣldæg† m. *appointed time, day*, Gen.

mældropa m. *phlegm, saliva, mucus*, WW 240⁹.

mældropiende *running with mucus*, WW 161³³.

mæle I. m. (ē) *cup, bowl, bucket, Ep,Lcd.* ['*meal*'] II. *marked*, KC.

mælgesceaft f. *fate*, B2737.

mælsceafa (æ?) m. *canker, caterpillar, WW.* ['*malshave*']

mæltan (VPs)=meltan

mæl-tang m., -tange f. *pair of compasses*, WW.

mæl-tīd f., -tīma m. *meal-time*, NC348.

mæn=menn nap. of man.

mæn-=man-, men-

±**mænan** I. (ē) *to* '*mean*,' *signify, intend, Æ, Bo,Sol*; CP : *consider.* II. *to tell : mention, relate, declare, communicate to, speak of,* B : *speak* (*a language*). III. *to complain of, lament, bewail, sorrow, grieve, Bo*; Æ,AO, CP.

mæne I. (±, usu.+) *common, public, general, universal, Mt*; AO : *owned in common,* WW : *catholic : lower* (*clergy*) : *mutual.* habban +m. *to have or hold in common.* ['*i-mene*'] II. (+) n. *fellowship, intercourse.* III. *false, mean, wicked.* [mān] IV. (+) *subdued, overpowered*, GEN,GNE. [=*+mægne, ES43·308]

±**mænelic** (usu. +) *common, ordinary : mutual : public, general, universal, Æ.* adv. -līce.

+**mænelicnes** f. *generality*, OEG.

mænibræde *relating to many things*, WW 115⁸.

mænlic=mænelic

+**mænnes** f. *community, fellowship, intercourse, union, Shr : sharing : land held in common*, BC1·597'. [v. '*i-mene*']

+**mænscipe** m. *community, fellowship : union*, W248²³ : *common ownership*, RB 103²⁰.

±**mænsumian** *to impart : partake of, participate in, have fellowship with : live with, marry : communicate : administer Eucharist, Æ.*

+**mænsumnes** f. *fellowship, participation* (*in Eucharist*), BH.

mænsumung f. *fellowship, participation, ÆH* : (+) *administration of the Eucharist*, CM,RBL.

mænu=menigu

+**mænung** f. *marriage*, HL.

mærāc f. *boundary-oak*, KC3·379'.

mēran (ā) I. (±) *to declare, proclaim, celebrate, glorify, honour.* II. (+) *to determine, fix limits*, WID42.

mærapeldre f. *apple-tree on a boundary*, KC3·390⁵.

mærbrōc m. *boundary-brook*, KC.

mærc (1)=mearc; (2)=mearg

mærcnoll m. *boundary-knoll*, EC445.

mærcumb m. *border valley*, KC.

mærdīc f. *boundary-dike*, KC.

mære=(1) mare; (2) mere I.

mære I. (ē) *famous, great, excellent, sublime, splendid, Æ,B,Ep*; AO,CP. ['*mere*'] II. *pure, sterling* (*of money*). [v. '*mere*' adj.] III. (±, usu. +) *boundary, border, Mk,VPs*; AO; Mdf : *balk of a plough-land*, GBG : *end.* IV. *declaration*, TC646,648 (v. A 46·214). ['*mere*' sb.]

mærelsrāp m. *ship's rope, cable*, WW.

mæretorht=meretorht

mærflōde *border channel*, EC370⁵.

mærford *border ford*, KC5·126'.

mærfurh *border furrow*, KC.

mærgeard *border fence*, KC3·462³.

mærgen=morgen

mærh (*Cp,Ep*), mærh-=mearg, mearh-

+**mærhaga** (ē) m. *boundary-hedge*, EC388¹⁰.

mær-hege m. *boundary-hedge*, EC447.

mærhlinc *border ridge*, KC.

mærhlīsa m. *notoriety*, WW382¹⁰.

mærian *to be distinguished*, DHy.

+**mærian**=+mærsian II.

mæringcwudu n. *mastic of sweet basil?* LCD131a.

+**mærlacu** f. *boundary-stream*, EC387'.

mærlic (ȳ) *great, splendid, glorious, famous, Æ,AO,CP.* adv. -līce, Æ.

mærnes f. *greatness, honour, fame*, LPs, WW.

mær-pōl, -pul m. *boundary-pool*, EC445⁸, KC5·198'.

mærpytt m. *pit on a boundary*, KC.

mærsc=mersc

mærsere (ē) m. *herald*, DR56¹⁷.

±**mærsian** (ē) I. *to make or become famous, proclaim, declare, announce, Æ,CP* : *celebrate : glorify, honour, exalt, praise, Æ* : *spread* (*fame*) : *enlarge.* II. *to mark out, bound, limit.*

mærsīc *border rivulet*, KC6·60¹⁷.

mærstān m. *boundary-stone*, BC3·154. ['*merestone*']

mærsung (ē) f. *fame, report, renown : celebration, festival, Æ : exalting, magnifying :* (±) *magnificence, celebrity.*

mærsungtīma m. *time of glorifying, ÆH* 2·360²⁵.

+**mærtrēow** *boundary-tree*, KC3·342'.

mærð=mearð

mærð f. *glory, fame : famous exploit, Æ, AO,CP.*

±**mær-ðorn**, -ðyrne *boundary-hawthorn*, KC.

mærðu=mærð

mæru=mearu

+mǣrung? *ending,* RHy5[10].

mǣrw-=mearu-

±mǣrweg m. *boundary-road,* Ct.

mǣrweorc m. *noble work,* PPs110[4].

+mǣrwyll m. *boundary-stream,* KC3·193[9].

mæscre (ǣ?) f. *mesh,* WW450[10].

mæsen *brazen* (Earle): *of maple* (BT), EC 250.

mæslere m. *sacristan,* GD228[15].

mæsling, mæslen (*MkL*)=mæstling

mæssanhacele=mæssehacele

mæsse (e) f. '*mass,*' *Eucharist, celebration of Eucharist, Æ,BH,Ct;* CP : *special mass-day, festival of the church.* [*L.* missa]

mæsseǣfen m. *eve of a festival,* CHR,LL.

mæsse-bōc f. nap. -bēc '*mass-book,*' *missal,* LL.

mæssecrēda m. *creed said at mass, Nicene creed,* LL. ['*mass-creed*']

mæssedæg m. '*mass-day,*' *festival, Bl.*

mæssegierela m. *mass-vestment, surplice,* CP87[19].

mæssehacele f. *mass-vestment, cope, chasuble,* LV40,WW327[22].

mæssehrægl n. *vestment, surplice,* CP.

mæsselāc n. *mass-offering, host,* WW.

mæssenlht f. *eve of a festival,* CHR,W.

mæsseprēost m. '*mass-priest,*' *clergyman, high-priest, Æ,AO;* CP. [v. also '*priest*']

mæsseprēosthād m. *office or orders of a mass-priest,* BH.

mæsseprēostscīr f. *district for which a mass-priest officiated,* LL.

mæsserbana m. *murderer of a priest,* W 165[28].

mæssere m. *priest who celebrates mass, Az.* ['*masser*']

mæsserēaf n. *mass-vestments, Æ.*

mæssesang m. *office of mass,* BH,LL.

mæssesteall m. *seat in a church choir* (Napier), *place from which the priest said mass?* (BTs), v. NC307,348.

mæssetīd f. *time of saying mass,* LL(140[20]).

mæsseðegn m. *mass-priest,* LL460,5.

mæsseðēnung f. *service of the mass, celebration of mass,* A11·8[15], ByH76[15].

mæssehta m. *hour, or service, of matins on a feast-day,* NC307.

mæssewīn (e) n. *wine used at mass,* WW.

mæssian (±) *to celebrate '*mass,*' Æ* : (+) *attend mass.*

mæssung f. *office of mass,* CHRD35[13].

mæst I. m. (*ship's*) '*mast,*' *B; Æ,AO.* **II.** m. '*mast,*' *food of swine, acorns, beech-nuts, BC.*

mǣst (ā, ē) **I.** adj. (superl. of micel), *AO, Chr,Bo,Mt.* ['*most*'] **II.** adv. *mostly, for the most part, in the greatest degree, chiefly,*

especially, very much. eal m., m. eal *almost, nearly.* m. ǣlc *nearly every one, Æ,AO,* CP. **III.** n. *most.*

±mǣstan *to feed with '*mast,*' fatten, BC;* *anoint,* RPs22[5],Æ,CP.

mǣstcyst f. *mast-socket,* WW.

mǣstelberg m. *fattened hog,* MtL6[7]. [bearg]

mǣsten n. *mast, pasture for swine,* Ct,LL.

mǣstenrǣden f. *right of feeding swine in mast-pastures,* KC3·451[10].

mǣstentrēow n. *tree yielding mast,* WW 137[23].

mǣstland f. *land yielding mast,* TC140[2].

mǣstlīcost adv. (superl.) *particularly,* CM 1169.

mǣstling I. n. *brass, WW* : *brazen vessel, Mk.* ['*maslin*'] **II.** *fatling,* OEG61[29].

mǣstlingsmlð m. *brass-worker,* WW539[6].

mǣstlōn sbpl. *pulleys at the top of a mast,* WW199[30].

mǣstrǣden=mǣstenrǣden

mǣstrāp m. *mast-rope,* Ex82.

mǣsttwist m. *rope supporting a mast,* WW.

mǣt I. pret. 3 sg. of metan. **II.**=mete m.

±mǣtan *to dream* (impers.), *Æ;* (trans.) *Lcd.* ['*mete*']

mǣte=mete

mǣte (ē) *mean, moderate, poor, inferior, small, bad.* also adv.

+mǣte *suitable, RB;* ÆL. ['*meet*']

mǣtfæst-=metfæst-

+mǣtgian (ÆL)=+metgian

mǣting f. *dream, Lcd.* ['*meting*']

mǣton pret. pl. of metan.

mǣð I. f. *measure, degree, proportion, rate, Æ;* AO : *honour, respect, reverence, LL :* *what is meet, right, fitness, ability, virtue, goodness, Æ,CP :* *lot, state, rank, Æ.* ['*methe*'] **II.** n. *cutting of grass, BC.* ['*math*']

mǣð-=mǣgð-

±mǣðegian *to honour, respect, spare, W;* ÆT. ['*methe*']

mǣðel (e) n. *council, meeting, popular assembly* : (†) *speech, interview.*

mǣðelcwide† (e) m. *discourse.*

mǣðelern n. *council-house, prætorium,* WW.

mǣðelfrlð (ðl) mn. *security* ('*frlð*') *enjoyed by public assemblies,* LL3,1 (v. 2·464 and 3·4).

mǣðel-hēgende†, -hergende *holding conclave, deliberating.*

mǣðelstede† (e) m. *place of assembly : battle-field.*

mǣðelword (e) n. *address, speech,* B236.

mǣð(e)re m. *mower,* WW235,237.

mǣðful *humane, ÆGr.* ['*metheful*']

mǣðlan=mǣðegian; mæðl=mæðel
mǣðlan (Cr)=maðelian
mǣðlēas rapacious, Æ. ['metheless']
mǣðlic moderate, proportioned, befitting, Ct, LL. adv. -līce humanely, courteously, ÆGr. ['methely']
mǣðmēd f. pay for haymaking, LL452'.
mǣðre=mǣðere
±mǣðrian to honour, LL.
mǣðung f. measuring, adjudication, CHRD 35¹⁸.
mǣw (ea, e) m. 'mew,' sea-gull, An,Cp,Shr.
mǣwpul (ā) m. sea-gulls' pool, Ct.
māfealdra comp. of manigfeald.
maffian to go astray, wax wanton, CHRD 74², 77².
mag-=mæg-
maga I. m. 'maw,' stomach, Cp,Lcd,WW; Æ,CP. II. powerful, strong : able, competent, having means.
māga I.† m. son, descendant, young man, man. II. gp. of mæg.
magan swv. pres. 1, 3 sg. mæg; 2, meaht, miht; pl. magon; pret. 3 sg. meahte to be able, Bo,G,WW : have permission or power (I 'may*,' I can), DD,G : to be strong, competent, avail, prevail, Æ,B,BH,Gl, VPs; CP. mæg wið avails against, cures, Lcd.
māgas v. mæg; magaðe=mageðe
magaðlht strong of stomach, Lcd 3·68¹⁷.
magdalatrēow n. almond-tree, WW 139¹¹. [L. amygdala]
mage f. (WW 159¹⁴)=maga
māge (ā) f. female relative, B; Æ. ['mowe']
māgeēct ptc. augmented, WW. [īecan]
mageðe (æ¹, o²) f. camomile, mayweed, Lcd, WW. ['maythe']
magian to prevail, ERPs 12⁵; NC348 : (+) recover (health), Lcd 3·184²¹? (BTac; or ?āmagian).
magister (æ) m. leader, chief, 'master,' teacher, Æ,Bo; AO,CP. [L. magister]
magisterdōm (mægster-) m. office of a master or teacher, Sc120⁹. ['masterdom']
+māglic=+mālic
mago† (magu) m. gs. maga, nap. mæcgas male kinsman, son, descendant : young man, servant : man, warrior.
magodryht f. band of warriors, B67.
magogeoguð f. youth, Cri 1429.
magorǣdend m. counsellor of men, An 1463.
magorǣswa† m. chief, prince.
magorinc† m. youth, man, warrior.
magotimber† n. child, son, Gen : increase of family, progeny, GnE.
magotūdor† n. descendant, offspring.
magoðe, magðe=mageðe

magoðegn† m. vassal, retainer, warrior, man, servant, minister.
magu=mago; māgwlite=mægwlite
±māh bad, wanton, shameless, importunate.
mahan=magon pres. pl. of magan.
+māhlic importunate : wanton, shameless : wicked. adv. -līce impudently.
+māhlicnes f. importunity, CP : wantonness, shamelessness : time of need, SPs 9²².
+māhnes f. importunity, persistence : shamelessness : boldness : contumacy, Wyn 57.
maht (VPs)=miht
Māius 'May,' Bf.
māl I. n. suit, cause, case, action, terms, agreement, covenanted pay, Chr. hē scylode ix scypa of māle he paid nine ships out of commission, Chr1049c. ['mail'] II. n. spot, mark, blemish, Æ. III.=mǣl n.
māl-=mǣl-, māhl-
malscrung f. enchantment, charm, Cp,Lcd. ['maskering']
mālswyrd (u²) n. sword with inlaid ornament, TC560'. [mǣl]
malt (Gl)=mealt; malwe (WW)=mealwe
mamme f. teat, GPH 401⁷⁷. [L. mamma]
mamor, mam(e)ra m. lethargy, heavy sleep, Gl.
mamrian to think out, design, PPs 63⁵.
man I. pron. indef. one, people, they, B,Mt; Æ. ['man'] II.=mann. III. pres. 3 sg. of munan.
mān I. n. evil deed, crime, wickedness, guilt, sin, B,Ps; Æ : false oath, ÆP 216¹⁴. II. adj. bad, criminal, false, Ps; AO. ['man']
+man (o) having a mane, WW 492²⁰.
man-=mann-
+māna m. community, company, Æ : common property : communion, companionship, intercourse, Bo,BH; CP : cohabitation, LG. tō +mānan in common, CP. ['mone,' 'ymone']
manað pres. 3 sg. of manian.
mānāð m. false oath, perjury, LL; HL. ['manath']
mānāðswaru f. perjury, LL.
mānbealu n. crime, cruelty, Da 45.
manbōt (o¹) f. fine paid to the lord of a man slain, LL (v. 2·576). ['manbote']
mānbryne m. fatal, destructive fire, Chr 962A.
mancgere=mangere
-mancian v. be-m.
man-cus, -cas, -cos, -cs m., gp. mancessa (CP) a 'mancus,' thirty silver pence, one-eighth of a pound, Æ,BC.
mancwealm m. mortality, pestilence, destruction, Chr; AO. ['manqualm']
mancwealmnes f. manslaughter, NG.

mancwyld (o) f. *mortality, pestilence*, BH 190[8].

mancynn n. *mankind*, Æ,B,Bl : *inhabitants, people, men*, CP. ['*mankin*']

mancyst f. *human virtue*, MFH169.

mand (o) f. *basket*, Cp,MtL,WW. ['*maund*']

mǽndǽd f. *sin, crime*, Ph; Æ,AO,CP. [v. '*man*']

mǽndǽda m. *evil-doer*, NC329.

mǽndǽde *evil-doing, wicked*, LL,W.

mǽndeorf *bold in evil?* ÆPd120[31].

mandrēamt m. *revelry, festivity*.

mǽndrinc m. *poison*, RD24[13].

mandryhtent m. *lord, master*, B.

+mǽne *having a mane*, WE57[16].

maneg=manig

mǽnfǣhþu f. *wickedness*, GEN1378.

manfaru f. *host, troop*, GU257.

mǽnfeld m. *field of crime*, AO108[20].

mǽnfolm f. *evil-doer*, PPs143[8].

mǽnfordǣdla m. *evil-doer*, B563.

mǽnforwyrht n. *evil deed, sin*, CR1095.

mǽnfrēat m. *lord of evil, Devil*.

mǽnfremmendet *sinning, vicious*.

mǽnful *wicked, evil, infamous, degraded*, Æ : *fearful, dire*.

mǽnfullic *infamous, evil, sinful*, Æ. adv. -līce, Æ.

mǽnfulnes f. *wickedness*, Æ.

manfultum (o[1]) m. *military force*, AO216[8].

+mang I. n. *mixture, union : troop, crowd, multitude*, Jud : *congregation, assembly : business : cohabitation*. in+m. *during*. on +m. *in the midst of*. ['*ymong*'] II. prep. (w. d. or a.) *among*, AO,G; Æ,CP. ['*ymong*']

mǽngenga m. *evil-doer*, BH36[5].

mǽngenīola m. *evil persecutor*, AN918.

+mang(en)nes f. *mingling, mixture*, OEG.

mangere m. *trader, merchant, broker*, Æ.

mǽngewyrhta m. *sinner*, PPs77[38].

±mangian *to gain by trading*, Æ,CP.

mangung f. *trade, business*, Æ.

mangunghūs n. *house of merchandise*, Jn2[16].

mǽnhūs n. *home of wickedness, hell*, Ex535.

±manian I. (o) *to remind, admonish, warn, exhort, instigate*, Æ,CP : *instruct, advise*, Æ : *claim, demand, ask*. II. (+) *to be restored to health?* GD338[30].

mǽnīdel *vain and bad (words)*, PPs143.

maniend m. *admonisher*, CP407[13] : *collector : creditor*.

manif-=manigf-

manig (æ[1], e[1], o[1], e[2]) nap. manega '*many,*' *many a, much*, Æ,AO,B,BH,Ps; CP.

manigean=manian; manigeo=menigu

manigfeald (æ, e, o[1]) '*manifold,*' *various, varied, complicated*, Æ,WW; CP : *numerous, abundant : plural*, ÆGr. adv. -fealde.

±manigfeald(l)an (æ[1], a[3], y[3]) *to multiply, abound, increase, extend*, OEG; CP : *reward*. ['*manifold*']

manigfealdlic *manifold*. adv. -līce *in various ways*, LG,VPs; CP : (gram.) *in the plural number*. ['*manifoldly*']

manigfealdnes f. *multiplicity, abundance, complexity*, LG,WW. ['*manifoldness*']

manigsīðes (mani-) adv. *often*, W144[11].

manig-tēaw (æ[1]), -tīwe, -tȳwe *skilful, dexterous*, Æ.

manigtēawnes (mænitȳw-) f. *skill, dexterity*, OEG.

manlēas (o) *uninhabited*, WW. ['*manless*']

mǽnlic *infamous, nefarious*, Æ. adv. -līce *falsely, wickedly*.

manlīca m. *effigy, image, statue*, GEN,BL.

manlīce adv. *manfully, nobly*, B. ['*manly*']

manlufu f. *love for men*, GU324.

manm-=mannm-

mann (o) m., nap. men(n) *person (male or fem.)*, Æ,Bl,Lcd,G,VHy; AO,CP : *man : mankind*, Mk,VPs : *brave man, hero : vassal, servant : name of the rune for* m. used indefinitely, like Mod. Eng. '*one,*' v. man I.

mann-, see also man-.

manna I. m. *man*, Æ. II. n. '*manna*' (*food*), Æ,CP. [L.]

mannbǽre *producing men*, ÆH1·450.

mannēaca (mon-) m. *progeny*, AO158[20].

mannhata (o[1]) m. *man-hater*, ByH38[32].

mannian *to 'man,' garrison*, Chr1087E.

mannmǽgen (o) n. *troop, force, cohort*, JnL 18[3].

mannmenigu (o) f. *multitude*, AO.

mannmyrring f. *destruction of men*, CHR1096.

mannmyrðra m. *a homicide*, LL.

mannsylen (i[2]) f. *traffic in men, sale of men unlawfully as slaves*, LL,W. [selen]

manrǣden f. *dependence, homage, service, tribute, due*, Æ. ['*manred*']

manrīmt n. *number of men*.

mǽnsceatt m. *usury*, PPs71[14].

mǽnsceaðat m. *enemy, sinner*.

mǽnscild f. *crime, fault, sin*, †Hy8[23].

manscipe m. *humanity, courtesy*, BC. ['*manship*']

mǽnscyldigt *criminal, guilty*.

mansilen=mannsylen

manslæht=manslieht

manslaga m. *man-slayer, murderer*, Æ.

mǽnslagu f. *cruel blow*, AN1218.

manslēan *to kill, murder*, RB16[18] (or ?two words).

manslege m. *manslaughter, homicide*, BL, LL.

manslieht (e[2], i[2]) m. *manslaughter, murder*, CP. ['*manslaught*']

manslot *share in ownership of land? measure of land?* v. NC307. [*ON.* mannshlutr]

-mānsumian, -mānsumung v. ā-m.

manswēs *meek,* RPs 24[9].

mānswara (o[2]) m. *perjurer, Bl.* ['*manswear*']

mānswaru f. *perjury,* LL,WW. [swerian]

mānswerian[6] *to forswear, perjure oneself,* LL. ['*manswear*']

mānswica m. *deceiver, traitor* (mann-? v. LL2·142).

mansylen (i[2]) f. *traffic in men, act of selling men as slaves.* [sellan]

manðēaw† m. *habit, custom* (? sometimes mānðēaw *sinful custom*).

manðēof m. *man-stealer,* v. L2·542.

manðrymm m. *troop of men,* MFH97[11].

manðwǣre (o) *gentle, kind, humane, mild, meek,* ÆL,CP. [*OHG.* mandwāri]

+manðwǣrian *to humanize,* CP362[21].

manðwǣrnes (o[1], y[2]) f. *gentleness, courtesy, weakness,* ÆL,CP.

manu f. '*mane,' Erf*1182; WE54[13].

manung f. *admonition,* CP : *claim : place of toll : district for purposes of tribute or taxation : residents in a taxing district.*

mānwamm (o[2]) m. *guilty stain,* CR1280.

mānweorc I. n. *crime, sin.* **II.** adj. *sinful,* EL.

manweorod (o) m. *collection of men, troop, congregation, assembly,* AO.

manweorðung f. *adoration of human beings,* LL (248[3]).

manwīse† (o) f. *manner or custom of men.*

mānword n. *wicked word,* PPs58[12].

mānwrǣce *wicked,* WW426[19].

mānwyrhta† m. *evil-doer, sinner,* PPs.

manwyrð n. *value or price of a man,* LL.

mapulder (o[2]) m. *maple tree,* Ct,LCD.

mapuldern *made of maple,* Ct,WW.

mapul-dre, -dor, -dur f., -trē(ow) m. (Mdf) = mapulder

māra m., māre fn. (compar. of micel) *greater, 'more,' stronger, mightier,* Æ,Bl, CP,LL. adv. *in addition, Mt.*

māran=mǣran

mārbēam (VPs)=mōrbēam

marc n. *a denomination of weight* (usu. half a pound), *mark* (money of account), CHR, Ct.

marcian=mearcian

mare (e) f. *nightmare, monster, Ep,Lcd.* ['*mare*']

māre v. māra; **mārels**=mǣrelsrāp

marenis=mearuwnes; **margen-**=morgen-

+mārian *to increase,* Sc40[16].

market n. *market,* TC422[20] (v.l.). [*L.* mercatum]

marma m. *marble,* LCD1·154[14]. [*L.* marmor]

marman-stān (marmel-, marm(or)-) m. *marble, piece of marble,* Æ,Bl. ['*marmstone*']

marmstāngedelf n. *quarrying of marble,* ÆH1·560[32].

-marod v. ā-m.

martir, martyr(e) m. '*martyr,' BH,Men;* Æ,AO. [*L.*]

martirlogium m. *martyrology,* IM122[45].

martr-=martyr-

martyrcynn m. *race of martyrs,* ÆL23[85].

martyrdōm m. '*martyrdom,' BH;* Æ,CP.

martyrhād m. *martyrdom,* BH,GD.

+mar-tyrian, -trian *to 'martyr,' torture, AO, BH.*

martyrracu f. *martyrology,* ÆL23[334].

martyrung f. *passion (of Christ), AO*254[24]. ['*martyring*']

mārðu=mǣrð

masc=max

māse f. *name of a small bird,* GL. [*Ger.* meise]

-masian v. ā-m.

massere m. *merchant : moneylender,* BK 10.

māst=mǣst; **matt,** matte (*CP*)=meatte

mattuc (æ[1], ea[1], e[1], eo[1], o[2]) m. '*mattock,' AO,Gl,LL;* Æ : *fork, trident.*

māð pret. 3 sg. of mīðan.

maða m. *maggot, worm, grub,* WW. ['*mathe*']

maðal-=maðel-

+maðel n. *speech, talking,* NIC507[20]. [=mæðel?]

maðelere m. *speaker, haranguer,* WW. [v. '*mathele*']

maðelian† (æ[1], e[1], a[2], o[2]) *to harangue, make a speech, speak, An,B,Cp,Cr.* ['*mell,' 'mathele*']

maðelig *talkative, noisy,* KGL75[23].

maðelung f. *loquacity,* OEG. [v. '*mathele*']

māðm=māðum

māðm- see also māððum.

māðmǣht† f. *valuable thing, treasure,* B.

māðmcleofa (mād-) m. *treasure-chamber,* Æ (9[277]).

māðmcyst f. *treasure-chest,* Mt27[6].

māðmgestrēon n. *treasure,* B,MFH.

māðmhord n. *treasure-hoard,* Ex368.

māðmhūs n. *treasure-house, treasury,* AO, CP.

māðmhyrde m. *treasurer,* Bo64[13].

maðolian=maðelian

māððum=māðum, māðm

maððum-fæt n., pl. -fatu *precious vessel,* Æ.

māððumgesteald n. *treasure,* JUL36.

māððumgifu f. *gift of treasure,* B1301.

māððumgyfa m. *giver of treasure, prince, king*, WA92.
māððumsele m. *hall of treasure*, SOL189.
māððumsigle n. *costly ornament*, B2757.
māððumsweord n. *costly sword*, B1023.
māððumwela m. *valuables*, B2750.
maðu f.=maða
māðum m., gs. māðmes *treasure, object of value, jewel, ornament, gift*, Gn,Met; CP. ['*madme*']
māðum-=māðm-, māððum-
māwan[7] *to* '*mow*,' AO,BH.
māwpul=mǣwpul
max n. *net*, WW. ['*mask*']
māxwyrt f. *mash-wort (malt soaked in boiling water)*, LCD. [v. FTP322]
me I. das. of pers. pron. ic *me*. II. (RB35[9]; 127[13])=menn
meagol (e[1]) *mighty, strong, firm, emphatic, impressive*. [magan]
meagollīce adv. *earnestly*, BL.
meagolmōd *earnest, strenuous*, A11·97[3].
meagolmōdnes f. *earnestness*, BL.
meagolnes f. *earnestness, strength of will*, BL,HL.
meaht I.=miht. II. pres. 2 sg. of magan.
meahte pret. 3 sg. of magan.
mealc pret. of melcan.
mealclīðe?=meolclīðe; mealehūs=meluhūs
mealewe=mealwe; mealm=mealmstān
-meallian v. ā-m.
mealmeht *sandy? chalky?* KC3·394[13]. [v. '*malm*']
mealmstān m. *soft stone, sandstone? limestone?* AO212[28]. [v. '*malm*']
mealt I. n. *steeped grain*, '*malt*,' Ct,Ep. [meltan] II. *sour*, LCD3·6[17]? III. pret. 3 sg. of meltan.
mealtealoð n. *malt-ale*, ANS84[325].
mealtgescot n. *payment in malt*, W171[2].
mealthūs n. '*malt-house*,' WW.
mealtwyrt (u[2]) f. '*malt-wort*,' WW.
mealu=melu
mealwe f. '*mallow*,' Lcd,WW. [*L*. malva]
mear=mearh
mearc (æ, e) f. (±) '*mark*,' *sign, line of division*, Æ,MkL,RB : *standard*, ÆGr : (±) *boundary, limit, term, border*, BC,Gen; CP; Mdf : *defined area, district, province*, AO. tō ðæs +mearces ðe *in the direction that*.
mearca m. *space marked out*, GD197[4].
mearcdīc (e) f. *boundary-ditch*, BC1·295[7].
mearcere (æ) m. *writer, notary*, OEG.
mearcford *boundary-ford*, EC382[1].
mearcgemot *court for settling boundaries of properties?* v. LL2·143.
mearcgrǣfa m. *boundary-thicket*, KC3·135'.
mearchlinc m. *boundary-ridge*, KC6·33[22].

mearchof n. *dwelling*, Ex61.
±mearcian *to* '*mark*,' *stain, brand, seal*, BC, LL,MtL,Ph; Æ : *mark a boundary, measure, define, describe, designate*, Æ, Gen : *mark out, design*, Bo : *create* : *note, observe*. +mearcod *baptized*, BF124[14].
mearc-īsern, -īsen n. *branding-iron*, GL,MH.
mearcland n. *border-land, march, moor* : (†) *province, country, district* : *sea-coast*, RD4[23].
mearcpæð[†] m. *road, path*, AN,EL.
mearcstapa[†] m. *march-haunter*, B.
mearcstede m. *border-land, desolate district*, SOL217.
mearcōrēat m. *army, troop*, Ex173.
mearcung (æ, e) f. *marking, branding* : *mark, characteristic* : (±) *description, arrangement* : *constellation* : *title, chapter*, NG.
mearcweard m. *wolf*, Ex168.
mearcweg m. *border-road*, BC,KC.
mearcwill m. *boundary-spring*, EC293'.
meard=(1) meord, mēd; (2) mearð
mēares v. mearh I.
mearg (æ, e) nm. I. '*marrow*,' *pith*, Lcd. II. *sausage*, GL. [=mærg] III.=mearh I.
mēargealla (e[1], e[2]) m. *gentian*, LCD. [mearh]
+meargian *to be rich, marrowy*, LPs65[15].
mearglic (e) *marrowy, fat*, VPs.
mearh I.[†] m. gs. mēares *horse, steed*. II.= mearg
mearhæccel n. *sausage-meat*, WW411[20].
mearhcofa m. *bone*, PPs101[3].
mearhgehæc n. *sausage-meat*, WW427[30].
mearmstān=marmanstān
mearn pret. 3 sg. of murnan.
+mearr I. n. *stumbling-block, obstruction, error*, CP : *emptiness, vanity*, RPs88[48]. II. *wicked, fraudulent*, LL140,1[5].
mearrian *to err*, Bo55[23].
mearð (æ, e) m. *marten*, Ep,AO. ['*mart*']
mearu (æ, e, y), mear(u)w- in obl. cases *tender, soft*, Lcd,MtR : *callow*, OEG : *delicate*, RB : *frail*, GD119[17]. ['*meruw*']
mearulic (merwe, mærw-) *frivolous, delicate, luxurious*, GD. adv. -līce *weakly*.
mearuwnes f. *tenderness, frailty*, CP211[18].
mēast=mǣst
meatte (a) f. '*mat*,' *mattress*, Gl. [*L*.]
mēaw=mǣw
mec as. of ic pers. pron.
+mec=+mæc
mēce m. *sword, blade*, GL. [*Goth*. mēkeis]
mēcefisc (ǣ) m. *mullet*, ÆGR308[5].
mecg=mæcg
mecgan *to mix, stir*, LCD.
mech=me
mechanisc *mechanical*, ÆL5[251]. [*L*.]
mēd I. f. '*meed*,' *reward, pay, price, compensation, bribe*, ÆL (gs. mēdes), B,BH, Bl; CP. II.=mǣd

med- in comp. principally indicates mediocrity, but often comes to have a distinct negative value; see, *e.g.*, medtrum, medwīs. [midde]

mēda v. mǣd; **-mēdan** v. on-m.

medder=mēder; **mēdder-**, mēddr-=mēdr-

meddrosna fp. *dregs of mead*, Lcd 48a.

+**mēde** I. n. *consent, good-will, pleasure*, Ct : *covenant*. II. *agreeable, pleasant : suitable*.

medel=mæðel

medema (eo[1]) m. *treadle*, WW.

medeme (eo[1]) *middling, average, mean, little : sufficient, considerable, respectable, proper, fit, worthy, trustworthy, perfect*, CP.

±**medemian** (eo[1]) *to mete out, allot, assign, place : moderate : (+) humble : respect, honour*, Æ : (+) *condescend, promote, deem worthy*, Æ : (+) *advance*, Æ.

medemlic *moderate, mediocre : intermediate : simple : worthy*. adv. **-līce** *slightly, moderately, incompletely : suitably, worthily, kindly*.

medemlicnes f. *mediocrity*, OEG.

medemmicel (Æ)=medmicel

medemnes f. *dignity, worth*, Æ,CP : *benignity, condescension*, Bl.

medemung f. *measuring, measure*, Ct,LL.

mēden=mægden

mēder ds. and LWS gs. of mōdor.

mēderce=mȳderce; **medere**=mæddre

mēderen, mēdern=mēdren

mēderwyrhta=mēterwyrhta

medewyrt=meduwyrt

mēdgilda (ǣ) m. *pensioner, hireling*, Æ.

mēdian *to reward*, GD 237[23].

mēdl-=mǣðl-; **-mēdla** v. an-, ofer-m.

medlen=midlen

medm-=medem-

medmicel I. *moderate-sized, short, small, limited, unimportant, slight, mean, poor*. II. n. *a little*.

medmicelnes f. *smallness (of mind)*, SPs 54[8].

medmicle comp. medmāre, adv. *humbly, meanly, slightly*.

medo=medu; **medom-**=medem-

+**mēdred**=+mēdren I.

mēdren I. *maternal, of a mother*. II. n. *the mother's side (by descent)*, LL 156,11.

+**mēdren** *born of the same mother*, AO 114[13].

mēdrencynn n. *mother's kindred*, CR 246.

mēdrengecynd n. *mother's nature*, W 17[7].

mēdrenmǣg m. *maternal kinsman*, LL.

mēdrenmǣgð f. *maternal kindred*, LL 392,3.

medrīce *of low rank*, WW 115[26].

mēdsceatt m. *payment, fee, reward, bribe, gift*, Æ,CP.

medsēlð (ǣ) f. *ill-fortune*, AO 164[28].

medspēdig *poor*, CRA 9.

medstrang *of middle rank*, BL 185[16].

medtrum *weak, infirm, sickly, ill*, CP : *of lower rank*. [cp. medmicel]

medtrumnes (met-; y[2]) f. *weakness, infirmity, sickness, illness, disease*, AO,CP.

medu (eo) mn. gs. med(e)wes *'mead' (drink)*, B,Rd; AO.

+**mēdu**=+mēde

meduærn (o[2]) n. *mead-hall, banqueting-house*, B 69.

medubenc† f. *bench in a mead-hall*, B.

meduburg† *mead-city, rejoicing city*.

medudrēam† m. *mead-joy, jollity*, B.

medudrenc (eo[1]) m. *mead*, W 245[4].

medudrinc (o[2]) m. *mead-drinking*, SEAF 22.

meduful† n. *mead-cup*, B,WY.

medugāl† *mead-excited, drunk*.

meduheall† f. *mead-hall*.

medum-=medem-

medurǣden (eo[1]) f. *strong drink?* (BT), *dealing out of mead?* (GK), GNE 88.

meduscenc (eo[1]) m. *mead-cup*, B 1980.

meduscerwen (ea[1]) f. *deprival of (mead-) joy, distress, mortal panic?* AN 1526.

meduseld n. *mead-hall*, B 3065.

medusetl n. (eo[1], o[2]) *mead-seat*, B 5.

medustīg f. *path to the mead-hall*, B 924.

meduwērig† *overpowered with mead, drunk*.

meduwong (eo[1], o[2]) m. *field (where the mead-hall stood)*, B 1643.

meduwyrt (eo[1], e[2]) f. *meadow-sweet*, Lcd : *'rubia,' madder*, OEG 56[40]. ['meadwort']

medwīs *dull, stupid, foolish*, CP. [cp. medmicel]

mēdwyrhta m. *a hireling*, Sc 123[12].

meg=mæg

mēg=(1) mæw; (2) mǣg

mēg-=mǣg-; **megol**=meago

meh=mec, me, as. of ic

meht=meaht, miht; **mēl**, mēig=mǣg

melge (KGL 81[32])=mǣge pres. 3 sg. subj. of magan.

melðhād (KGL 56[7])=mægðhād

mēl=mǣl n.

mela=melu

±**melcan**[3] (i) *to milk*, ÆGR,Lcd.

melcingfæt=meolcfæt

meld f. *proclamation*, DA 648.

melda m. *reporter, informer, betrayer*, Æ.

meldan (Rd)=meldian

melde f. *orache (plant)*, Lcd. ['milds']

meldfeoh n. *informer's reward*, LL 96,17.

±**meldian** *to announce, declare, tell, proclaim, reveal*, Ps; Æ : *inform against, accuse*. ['meld']

meldung f. *betrayal*, BH 240[4].

mēle=mǣle

meleðāw mn. *honey-dew, nectar*, Ph,WW (mild-). ['mildew']

melewes=melwes gs. of melu.

-**melle**, -melnes v. æ-m.
melo=melu; **melsc**=milisc
±**meltan I.** (y) (sv³) *to consume by fire,*
'*melt,*' *burn up,* B,MH,Ps,WW; Æ :
dissolve, digest. **II.**=mieltan
meltestre=myltestre
meltung f. *digestion,* Lcd.
melu (ea, eo) n., gs. mel(u)wes '*meal,*' *flour,*
Lcd; Æ.
melugescot n. *payment in meal,* W 171.
meluhūdern n. *meal-house,* LL 455,17.
meluhūs (ea¹, e²) n. *meal-house,* WW
185²⁷.
meluw (LWS)=melu
men v. mann; **mēnan**=mǣnan
mend-=mynd-; +**mēne-**=+mǣne-
mene (y) m. *necklace, collar, ornament, jewel,*
Æ. [v. KLED s.v. mähne]
menegian=myndgian; **menego**=menigu
menen=mennen
menescilling m. *moon-shaped ornament,*
coin worn as ornament, Gl.
±**mengan** (æ) tr. and intr. *to mix, combine,*
unite, Lk,Sat,WW; CP: (±) *associate with,*
consort, cohabit with, BH,Ps : *disturb,* B :
(†) *converse.* ['*meng*']
+**mengedlic** *mixed, confused,* Cp 1542. adv.
-līce] Gl.
+**mengednes**, +meng(d)nes f. *mingling,*
mixture, connection, Æ,BH : *sexual inter-*
course, CP.
mengeo, mengo, mengu=menigu
mengung f. *mixture, composition,* ZDA : *fel-*
lowship, GD : (+) *confusion.* ['*menging*']
meni (LWS)=manig; **menian**=mynian
menig (LWS)=manig; **mēnig** v. mǣgenig.
menigdu f. *band of people,* WW 448²⁷.
menigu (a¹, æ¹, eo³) f. usu. indecl. in sg. *com-*
pany, multitude, host, Æ,AO,CP. [manig]
menio, meniu (LWS)=menigu
menisc=mennisc
menn v. mann.
mennen, mennenu (æ¹, i¹) nf. *handmaiden,*
slave, GD,LL.
mennesc=mennisc
mennisc I. adj. *human, natural,* Bo,CP; Æ.
II. n. *mankind, folk, race, people,* Bl; Æ,
CP. ['*mannish*']
mennisclic *human,* Æ,CP : *humane,* Bo,
RB. adv. -līce, Æ.
mennisc-licnes (EHy 15³⁵), -nes f. *state of*
man, human nature, incarnation, BH;
Æ : *humaneness, humanity.* ['*mannish-*
ness']
menniscu f. *humanity, human state,* CP 39²⁴.
mentel (æ) m., gs. mentles *mantle, cloak,*
CP. [L. mantellum]
mentelprēon m. *mantle-pin, brooch,* TC 533'.
menung=(*mynung), mynegung

mēo mf? gs. and nap. mēon *shoe-sole, sock?*
sandal? RB,WW.
meocs=meox
+**meodnes** f. *dignity,* DR 192'. [=medem-
nes]
meodo, meodu=medu; **meodom-**=medem
meodoma=medema; **mēodren**=mēdren
meodum-=medem-
meolc I. *giving milk, milch.* **II.** (i) f
'*milk,*' BH; Æ,AO.
meolcdēond (i; -tēond) m. *suckling.* JVPs
8³.
meolcen (i¹, y¹) adj. *of milk,* Lcd
meolcfæt n. *milk-pail,* WW 123²⁸.
meolchwīt '*milk-white,*' GPH.
meolcian (i, y) *to* '*milk,*' Lcd,Shr : (±) *give*
milk, suckle, Bl.
meolclīðe (ea) *soft as milk,* CM 49.
meolcsūcend m. *suckling,* WW.
meolo (Bo)=melu; **meoloc** (CP)=meolc
meolu=melu; **meoluc**=meolc
mēon v. mēo.
mēoning m. *garter,* WW 234²² (wēon-).
meord f. *reward, pay,* BH GD. [Goth.
mizdō]
meoring f. *danger?* Ex 62?
-**meorð**=meord
mēos I. m. *moss,* BH. ['*mese*'] **II.** adj.
mossy.
mēose=mēse; **meotod**, meotud=metod
meottoc (Cp)=mattuc
+**meotu**=+metu nap. of +met.
meotud-=metod-
meoðon (BH)=miðon pret. pl. of mīðan.
mēowle† f. *maiden, virgin : woman.* [Goth.
mawilō]
meox (e, i, y) n. *filth, dirt, dung,* Æ,Bo,Lk.
['*mix*']
meoxbearwe f. *dung-barrow,* WW 336⁶.
meoxen=mixen
meoxforce (y¹) f. *dung-fork,* WW 106³⁹.
meoxscofl (e¹) f. *dung-shovel,* LL 455,17.
meoxwilie (cs) f. *dung-basket,* LPs 80⁷.
mēr-=mǣr-
mera m. *incubus,* Gl.
merc (A)=mearc; **merce**=merece
+**merce**=+mierce; **mercels**=mircels
Mercisc=Miercisc
mercong (NG)=mearcung
mere I. m. (†) *sea, ocean,* An : *lake, pond,*
pool, cistern, B,Ep,Jn; CP; Mdf. ['*mere*']
II.=mare. **III.**=miere
mēre (VPs)=mǣre I.
merebāt m. *sea-boat, vessel,* An 246.
merecandel f. *sun,* Met 13⁵⁷.
merece m. *smallage, wild celery,* Æ,Gl,Lcd.
mereciest f. *sea-chest, ark,* Gen 1317.
meredēað† m. *death at sea,* Ex.
meredēor n. *sea-animal,* B 558.

merefara m. *sailor*, B502.
merefaroð† m. *surging of the waves*.
mereflx m. *sea-fish*, B549.
mereflōd† m. *sea, body of water, deluge*.
mere-grot (Æ) n., -grota (BH) m. *pearl*. [v. '*margarite*']
meregrund† m. *lake-bottom, depths of the sea*.
merehengest† m. *sea-horse, ship*.
merehrægl n. *sail*, B1905.
merehūs† n. *sea-house, the ark*, GEN.
merehwearf m. *sea-shore*, Ex516.
mērehwīt *pure white, sterling (of silver)*. [mære II.]
merelād f. *sea-way*, HU27.
merelīðende† m. *seafaring (man), sailor*.
mere-menn(en), -menin n. *mermaid, siren*, Cp,WW. ['*mermin*']
mere-næddra m., -næddre, -nædre f. '*murena*,' *sea-adder, lamprey*, GL.
meresmylte *quiet as the sea, calm*, MET21¹².
meresteall m. *stagnant water*, MFH169.
merestrǣt† f. *sea-path*.
merestrēam† m. *sea-water*.
merestrengo f. *strength in swimming*, B523.
mereswīn n. *porpoise, dolphin*, Cp,Lcd. ['*mereswine*']
meretorht (æ)† *(rising) bright from the sea*.
meretorr m. *towering wall of the (Red) sea*, Ex484.
mereðyssa† m. *ship*, AN.
mereweard m. *sea-warden*, WH53.
merewērig *sea-weary*, SEAF12.
merewīf n. *water-witch*, B1519.
merg (Cp195M)=mearg
merg-=mearg-, meri-, morg-, myrg-
merian *to purify, cleanse*, Sol : *test*. ['*mere*']
merice (GL)=merce; **merien**=morgen
merig=(1) myrge; (2) mearg
merig-=myrg-; **merigen** (Æ,AO)=morgen
merisc=mersc
merne=mergenne ds. of mergen.
merr-=mierr-; **mērs-**=mǣrs-
mersc (æ) m. '*marsh*,' *swamp, Gl*; CP.
merschōfe m. *marsh-hove*, Lcd35b.
merschop n. *high ground in fenny country*, BC2·526.
merscland n. '*marsh-land*,' *Chr*1098.
merscmealwe f. '*marsh-mallow*,' *Lcd*.
merscmeargealla m. *gentiana pneumonanthe*, Lcd.
merscmylen f. *mill in a fen*, KC6·100¹².
merscware pl. *inhabitants of marshes*. (1) *Romney marsh*, CHR796. (2) *the fens?* CHR838.
mertze f. *merchandise*, WW32²⁵ : *trading dues*, 145²⁸. [L. mercem]
merð=mearð
merðern *made of skins of martens*, CHR 1075D.

mērðu (N)=mærð; **meru** (MtR)=mearu
meruw-, merwe-=mearu(w)-
mēs (K)=mȳs, v. mus.
mesa fpl. *dung*, Lcd37a (v. NP15·272).
mēsan *to eat*, RD41⁵². [mōs]
mēse (ēo, ī, ȳ) f. *table, Æ : what is placed on a table*, GL. [L.]
mēshrægel (ȳ¹) n. *napkin*, RBL93¹⁰.
mess-=mæss-
mēsta (KGL)=mǣsta superl. of micel.
±met (usu. +) *measure (vessel or amount), Æ : act of measuring, appointed share, quantity, Mt : space, distance, LL : boundary, limit, Bo,Met : manner, degree, way : ability, adequacy, capacity : rule, law : mood* (gram.) : *metre : moderation, MtR*. ealle +mete *in all respects*. on +m. *in vain*, RPs88⁴⁸. nānum +m. *by no means, on no account*. ['*met*,' '*i-met*']
+met† *fit, proper, apt, meet*. adv. -mēte.
+mēt=+mōt; **-mēt** v. wēa-m.
meta (Sc153)=mete; **metærn**=meteærn
±metan⁵ *to measure*, '*mete*' out ('*ymete*'), *mark off, Æ,Ex,Mt,VPs : compare, Bo*; CP : *estimate, Bl : pass over, traverse, B*.
±mētan I. *to* '*meet*,' *find, find out, fall in with, encounter, Bo,Bl; Æ,AO,CP : obtain*, CP. II. *to paint, design, ÆGr*. ['*mete*']
metbælg m. *wallet, LkR*22³⁵. [v. '*belly*']
met-cund, -cundlic *metrical*, GL.
mete (æ) m. nap. mettas '*meat*,' *food, BH, CP,Lk,Sc*; Æ,AO.
mēte=mǣte
meteærn n. *refectory*, GD,WW.
meteāflīung f. *atrophy*, WW.
meteāwel *meat-hook?* LL455¹⁷.
meteclyfa m. *food-store, pantry*, OEG56²⁷⁰.
metecorn n. *allowance of corn to dependants*, TC. ['*metecorn*']
metecū f. *cow for killing*, LL450',451.
metecweorra m. *surfeit, indigestion*, Lcd 3·60⁴.
+mētednes f. *finding, discovery*, LPs27⁴.
metefæt [met-] n. *dish*, GPH403.
metefætels m. *cupboard for food*, WW107⁵. ['*metefetill*']
meteg-=metg-
metegafol n. *payment in food*, LL448,4⁵.
metegearwa fp. *preparations of food*, Lcd 78b.
metegyrd=metgeard
metelǣst=metelīest
metelāf f. *leavings of a meal*, Æ,LL.
metelēas *without food*, Æ.
mete-līest (AO), -lē(a)st, -līst, -lȳst f. *lack of food, starvation*.
metend m. *measurer*, WW398²⁸ : *God*, GEN 1809.
+mētend '*inventor*,' GPH391.

metenéad f. *requisites in the way of food*, LL 383'? (v. 2·145).

mēter n. '*metre,' versification, Bf,BH*. [*L.*]

meterǣdere m. *reader at meal-times*, NC 309.

mētercrǣft m. *art of versifying*, BH 258[15].

mētercund *relating to metre*, WW.

mētere m. *painter*, Ct,WW.

mēterfers n. *hexameter verse*, BH.

mētergeweorc n. *verse*, BH 484[9].

mēterlic *metrical*, OEG 124.

metern=meteærn

mēterwyrhta m. *metrician, poet*, WW.

metesōcn f. *craving, appetite*, Lcd 65a.

metesticca m. *spoon*, WW 126[35].

meteswamm m. *edible mushroom*, WW.

metetīd f. *meal-time*, GD 277[24].

meteðearfende† *needing food, destitute*, An.

meteðegn m. *seneschal, steward*, Ex 131.

meteðiht *well-nourished*, Lcd 3·68[17].

meteðing n. *operation connected with cooking*, Chrd 19[19].

meteūtsiht f. *dysentery*, WW.

+metfæst *moderate, reasonable, modest, meek*.

+metfæstan (æ[1], e[2]) *to compare*, LPs 48[21].

+metfæstlic *moderate : modest, gentle.* adv. -līce *modestly, humbly, meekly.*

+metfæstnes f. *moderation, modesty, sobriety*, BH.

metfæt=metefæt

+metfæt n. *a measure (vessel)*, Æ,WW.

+metfest-=metfæst-

metgeard f. *measuring-stick, rod, pole, perch*, WW 147[20]. ·

±metgian *to moderate, control, govern*, Æ, CP : *weigh in mind, consider : assign due measure to : prepare : regulate.*

+metgiend m. *ruler, governor*, AS 11[2].

±metgung f. *moderation, temperance*, AO, CP : *reflection, meditation : rule, regulation.*

metgyrd=metgeard

metian I. *to provision*, Chr 1013. II.= metgian

mēting I. (±) f. *meeting (friendly or hostile)*, Æ,AO : *assembly, congregation*, Ps,RB : *finding, discovery : agreement*, GD. II. *painting, picture*, Æ.

+metlǣcan *to moderate*, CP 101[12].

+metlic *measurable : fitting, suitable : moderate*, CP : *mild, discreet*, CP. adv. -līce.

+metlicung f. *adjustment, regulation*, Lcd 60b,86a.

+metnes f. *moderation*, RWH 7[19].

+mētnes (MH 136[23])=+mētednes

metod† m. *fate : Creator, God, Christ*.

+metodlīce *inevitably*, ByH 40[25].

metodsceaft† f. *decree of fate, doom, death.* gewītan m. sēon, tō metodsceafte *to die*, B.

metodwang (meotud-) m. *battlefield*, An 11.

metrāp m. *measuring-rope, sounding-line*, Cp 178b.

mētsceat=mēdsceatt

metscipe m. *feeding, meal*, LL 178,8[1]. ['*meteship*']

metseax n. *meat-knife*, AO 244[18].

±metsian *to supply with food*, Æ.

metsung f. *feeding, provisioning*, Chr.

+metta m. *sharer in food, guest*, Æ. ['*mette*']

mettac=mattuc; mettas v. mete.

mette-=mete-

mētte pret. 3 sg. of mētan.

metten f. *one of the Fates*, Bo 102[22].

mettian=mētan I.; +metting=+mēting

-mētto v. wēa-m.; mettoc (*Ep*)=mattuc

mettrum=medtrum; metud (N)=metod

mēðe (†) *tired, worn out, dejected, sad : troublesome.* [*Ger.* müde]

meðel=mæðel; meðema=medema

+mēðgian *to exhaust, tire out*, Gu 950.

mēðian *to grow weary*, Lcd 57a.

mēðig *tired, weary*, AO 86,134.

meðl=mæðl, mæðel; meðl-=mæðl-, maðel-

mēðnes f. *fatigue*, OET (Bd[2]).

+mēðrian *to honour*, LL (1·384[4]).

mēw=mǣw; mexscofl=meoxscofl

micel-=micel-, micl-

micel (y) adj. comp. māra, superl. mǣst(a) *great, intense, much, many*, Æ,BC,Bo,Chr, Lcd,MH; AO,CP : (of time) *long : loud.* sb. with gen. *much*, AO,CP. adv. *greatly, much*, CP,Gen. ['*mickle*']

micelǣte (y) *greedy*, Shr 16[20].

miceldōend (i[2]) *doing great things*, DR 45[7].

micelhēafdede *big-headed*, WW 380[12].

micelian=miclian

micellic *great, splendid, magnificent.* adv. -līce *grandly : very, exceedingly.*

micelmōd *magnanimous*, PPs 144[3].

micelnes (y) f. *greatness, size*, Æ,CP : *mass : quantity : multitude, abundance : magnificence : great deed.*

micelsprecende *boasting*, LPs 11[4].

micelu (y) f. *largeness, size*, Lcd.

micg=mycg

micga, micge f. *urine*, Lcd. ['*mig*']

micgern (y) *internal fat, suet*, WW. ['*midgern*']

micgða=migoða; micl-=micel-

micle, micles, miclum adv. (obl. cases of micel) *much, very, greatly.*

±miclian (y) *to become great, increase*, An; AO : *make great, make larger, magnify, extol*, Bl. ['*mickle*']

±miclung (y) f. *the doing of great things, great deeds, greatness*, Ps.

micul=micel

mid I. prep. w. d. inst. (WS) and a. (A only) *with, in conjunction with, in company with, together with, Æ,Chr* : *into the presence of* : *through, by means of, by* : *among, in* : *at* (time) : *in the sight of, opinion of, Æ.* m. ealle, eallum *altogether, completely, entirely, Æ, Chr.* m. ðām *with that, thereupon.* m. ðām ðe *when.* m. ðām ðæt *through that, on that account, because, when.* m. ðȳ (ðe) *when, while.* **II.** adv. *at the same time, together, simultaneously, likewise, Lcd.* ['MID'] **III.**=midd **midd** superl. mid(e)mest *mid, middle, midway, BH,CP,Lcd.* tō middes adv. *in the midst.* ['mid']

middæg m. '*mid-day,' noon, Lcd* : *one of the canonical hours, sext, WW.* fram middæge oð nōn *from noon to 3 p.m., Æ.*

middæglic adj. *mid-day, meridian, BH,Ps.*

middægsang m. *mid-day service, sext, RB, LL.*

middægtīd f. *noon, WW450⁵.*

middægðēnung f. *dinner, NC309.*

middan (on) v. onmiddan.

middandæglic=middæglic

middan(g)eard m. *the globe, world, earth, B, Jn; Æ,AO,CP* : *mankind.* ['middenerd']

middan(g)earden *worldly, Sc16¹⁶.*

middangeardlic *earthly, BH118¹⁹.*

middansumer m. *midsummer* (24 *June*).

middanwinter m. *midwinter, Christmas.*

midde I. adj. *mid, middle.* **II.** f. *middle, centre* (only in phr. on middan).

middel I. n. '*middle,' centre, El,Mk,Ps, WW* : *waist, Bl.* **II.** adj. (superl. midlest) *middle, intermediate, BH,LL.*

middelǣdr f. *median vein, Lcd.*

middeldæg m. *mid-day, noon, Lcd.*

middeldǣl m. *middle, AO10⁶.*

middelfinger m. *middle finger, LL,WW.*

middel-flēra m., -flēre f. *partition, septum, WW.*

middelfōt m. *instep, WW160²⁵.*

middelgemǣru npl. *central region, Sol255.*

middelgesculdru np. *part of the body between the shoulders, WW159¹⁷.*

middelhrycg m. *middle ridge, Ct.*

middelniht† f. *midnight.*

middelrīce n. *the middle kingdom, Chr887a.*

midden-=middan-

midde-niht, -neaht, middernæht (*LkL*) f. '*midnight.'* [v. ES39·350]

middesumer=middansumer

middeweard I. adv. *in the middle of, through the midst.* **II.** adj. *middle, AO.* **III.** sb. *middle, LPs.* ['midward']

middewinter=middanwinter

middun- (N)=middan-

mideard=middangeard

midel=middel; **midemest** v. midd.

midfæsten m. *mid-Lent, Chr1047.*

mid-feorh, -feorwe (CP), -ferh(ð) mn. *youth, middle age* ('*juventus' Gl*).

midfyrhtnes f. *middle age Bl163.*

midgearwung f. *preparation, MkL p5¹⁰.*

midgeslō n. *companion,* OEG680? (v. BTs).

midhelp [mið-] f. *help, assistance, DR 29¹⁸.*

midhilte f. *middle of the hilt, WW199²¹.*

midhlȳt m. *fellowship, Tf103⁷.*

midhrif nm. '*midriff,' diaphragm, Lcd* : *bowels.*

midhriðre (y²) n. *diaphragm, Cp,WW.* ['midred']

-midian v. ā-.

mīdl n. *bit (of a bridle), Æ* : *oar-thong, WW.*

midle=middele, ds. of middel.

+midleahtrian *to reproach, Sc200⁶.*

midlen I. (e) n. *middle, centre, midst.* **II.** adj. *midmost, ÆGr14²¹.*

midlencten n. *mid-Lent, Chr.*

midlest superl. of middel.

midlhring m. *ring of a bit, WW456¹⁴.*

+midlian *to halve, divide, CPs54²⁷.*

±midlian *to bridle, curb, CP* : *muzzle, W191.*

midligend m. *mediator, BH206²⁶.*

midlung f. *middle, midst.* adv. -lunga *to a moderate extent.*

midmest v. midd; **midmycel**=medmicel

midnedæg m. *mid-day, Æ,MH.*

midnes f. *middle, midst, HL.*

midniht f. *midnight, Æ.*

midor compar. of midd, adj.

midrād f. *riding in company, LL175,4.*

midrece=mȳderce; **midrif**=midhrif

midsingend m. *one who sings with another, WW129²⁵.*

±midsīo(eg)ian *to accompany, associate with, Gl.*

midspecend m. *interlocutor, advocate, MP 1·592⁶.*

midsp(r)eca m. *advocate, ÆH* : '*liberator,' excuser, Chrd62²⁶.*

midsprecende *speaking for, Nic.*

midstrēam m. *mid-stream, KC5·380.*

midsumer (o³) m. '*midsummer,' Bf,BH.*

Midsumermōnað *June, Men* (Hickes).

midswēgan **'concinere,' EPs57³.*

midðām, midðȳ=mid ðām, mid ðȳ

midðeahtian *to consent, RHy6²⁷.*

midðolian *to sympathise, Sc.*

midðrōwung f. *compassion, Sc.*

midweg m. '*midway,' CP; GD314¹¹.*

midwinter m. '*midwinter,' Christmas, Chr, Lcd.*

Midwintermōnað *December, Men* (Hickes).

midwist f. *presence, society* : *cooperation, participation, LL378⁶.*

midwunung f. *living in company, fellowship*, Æ.

midwyrhta m. *cooperator*, CP.

midyrfenuma m. *coheir*, Sc 148⁴.

mieht=miht

±**mieltan** (i, y) (tr. and intr.) *to* '*melt*,' *El, Lcd*; Æ: *digest, CP : refine, purge : exhaust*, MH 54³.

Mierce, Miercan pl. *Mercians : Mercia*, CHR (lit. *borderers*; cp. mearc).

+**mierce** (e) n. *boundary, limit*, AA 3³ : *sign, token*, MkL 16¹⁷.

Miercisc (e) *Mercian*, LL 464,1.

miere (e, i, y) f. '*mare*,' *BH,WW.* [mearh]

mierra (e) m. *deceiver*, MtL 27⁶³.

±**mierran** (e, i, y) *to* '*mar*,' *disturb, confuse, CP : scatter, squander, waste : upset, hinder, obstruct*, Æ; AO : *err, MtL*.

mierrelse (y) f. *cause of* *offence*, JUL 338.

mierrend (y) *prodigal, wasteful*, NC 311.

mierring (e, i, y) f. *hindering : squandering, waste*, CP.

±**mīgan¹** *to make water*, LCD,ÆGR.

mīgeða=migoða; **migga** (Æ)=micga

miggung, mīging f. *making water*, WW.

migol *diuretic*, LCD.

migoða m. *urine*, LCD.

miht (a, æ, ea, e, ie, y) I. f. '*might*,' *bodily strength: power, authority, ability, BH,Bl, Lcd*; Æ : *virtue, Lcd : mighty work, miracle*, G. pl. *Gods*, OEG : *angels*, Æ. II. adj. †*mighty, powerful : possible.*

mihte pret. sg. of magan.

mihteleas=mihtleas

mihtelic, mihtlic *possible*. adv. -līce *mightily, powerfully, by might, miraculously*, Æ,BH. ['*mightily*']

mihtesetl n. *seat of power*, EETS 34·301.

mihtful *powerful*, HL 15¹³⁷.

mihtig (æ, ea) '*mighty*,' *important, BH,CP, VPs : able, effective, Lcd : possible*. adv. -līce, *Bo*. ['*mightily*']

mihtleas *powerless, weak, exhausted*, Æ.

mihtloc (ea¹) *belt of might*, CREAT 88.

mihtmōd n. *violent temper, passion*, Ex 149.

mihtu=miht ðu

mīl I. f. '*mile*,' *Bl,WW*; AO. [*L.*] II. n. *millet, WW.* ['*mile*']

milc (VPs)=meolc; **milcan**=melcan

milde I. adj.'*mild*,'*merciful, kind, generous, gentle, meek, B,Bl,Gu,LL*; AO,CP. II. adv. *mercifully, graciously*, Cr.

mildēaw=meledēaw

mildelic *propitious*. adv. *graciously, affably, kindly, AO*; Æ. ['*mildly*']

+**mildgian** *to mitigate, make mild or calm*, Ps. [mildian]

mild-heort, -heortlic *merciful, clement, compassionate, MtL* (milt-); Æ,AO. ['*mild-heart*'] adv. -līce, Æ,CP.

mildheortnes f. *loving-kindness, mercy, pity, LL*; Æ,AO. ['*mildheariness*']

mildian *to become mild*, GPH 399.

mildnes f. *mildness, mercy*, NC 309.

milds=milts

mīlgemæt m. *mile-measure, milestone?* KC 3·252²¹.

mīlgemearc n. *measure by miles*, B 1362.

mīlgetæl n. *mile*, WE 51,59.

milisc (e, y) *sweet, mild, mulled*, GL,LCD.

milite *soldiers*, NC 309.

militisc *military*, GD. [*L.* miles]

mīlpæð† m. *distance reckoned by miles? road with milestones on it?* EL,Ex,RUN.

+**milscad** *honeyed, mixed with honey*, WW.

milscapuldor f. *sweet apple tree*, GL.

milt m. (LCD 87a)=milte; **milt-**=mild-, milte-

milt-coðe, -coðu f. *disease of the spleen*, LCD.

milte mf. '*milt*,' *spleen, Gl,Lcd*; Æ.

miltesēoc *splenetic*, LCD,WW.

miltestre=myltestre

miltewærc m. *pain in the spleen*, LCD.

milts f. *mercy, compassion, benevolence, kindness, favour, B,VPs*; CP : (†) *joy*. ['*milce*']

±**miltsian** (w. d.) *to compassionate, pity, show mercy, Bo,Mt,Ps*; Æ,CP : *soften, make merciful*. ['*milce*,' '*i-milce*']

±**miltsi(g)end** m. *pitier*, Æ,Ps.

miltsigendlic *pardonable, venial*, GPH.

miltsung f. (±) *mercy, sympathy, pity, indulgence, pardon*, Æ,CP : *moderation, reduction (of punishment)*, LL 468,10.

miltwræc=miltewærc; **milz**=milts

mīma m. '*mime*,' *MH*.

+**mimor** (w. d.) *well-known*. adv. -līce *by heart*.

min†? *evil, harmful*. [v. BTs, and NED s.v. '*min*']

mīn I. pron. *my*, '*mine*,' *Æ,B,G.* mīnes ðances *by my will*. II. gs. of ic *of me*.

mind I. *diadem*, DR 92⁵ (v. LF 160). II.= mynd

mindōm? m. *state of exile*, PPs 54⁷.

mine=myne; **minet-**=mynet-

minlic *petty* (Swt).

mīnlīce adv. *in my manner*, WW 449¹⁶.

minnæn '*manipulos*,' *sheaves?* EPs 128⁷; '*magnalia*,' 105²¹.

minne I. nap. of min? II.=myne

minnen=menen

±**minsian** *to diminish*, W.

minsung f. *parsimony*, OEG 3748.

mint? (MtR), minte f. '*mint*,' *G*; CP; Mdf. [*L.*]

minthamm m. *field of mint*, KC 5·374'.

mio-=meo-
mircapuldur (Cp)=milscapuldor?
Mirce, Mircan=Mierce
mirce I. (y;=ie) adj. *murky, dark, black, uncanny, evil*, B,Ph. II. adv.? AN 1315. III. n. *murkiness, darkness*, Da 448. ['*murk*']
mircels (e, y;=ie) mf. *sign, token, seal, signet* : *mark, marked place*, ÆL : *trophy*, Gu 429. [mearc]
mire=miere; mīre=mīnre gdfs. of mīn.
mirg-, mīrig-=myrg-
mirgŏ, mirhŏ=myrgŏ; mirr-=mierr-
misbegān anv. *to disfigure*, MtL 6[16].
misbēodan[2] (w. d.) *to ill-use, injure, do wrong to*, LL,W. ['*misbede*']
misboren *abortive*, Lcd : *degenerate*. ['*misborn*']
misbrōden *drawn aside*, WW 224[21].
misbyrd f. *abortion*, GL.
misbyrdo f. *malformation*, LCD.
misbysnian *to set a bad example*, ÆH 2·50[4].
miscalfian *to cast a calf*, WW 456[12].
miscenning f. *a mistake or variation in pleading before a court : a fine exacted for this*, EC,LL (v. 2·148). ['*miskenning*']
miscian *to mix, apportion*, Bo,LCD. [L.]
miscrōcettan *to croak or shriek horribly*, GUTH 36[1]. [crācettan]
miscwēman *to displease*, ÆL 23[287].
miscweŏan[5] *to speak ill, curse*, NG : *speak incorrectly*.
miscyrran (=ie) *to pervert*, MET 2[8].
misdǣd f. '*misdeed,*' *evil deed, sin*, CP; Æ.
misdōn anv. *to do evil, transgress, do amiss, err*, JnL,LL,W. ['*misdo*']
mīse=mēse
misefesian *to cut the hair amiss*, LL (254[13]).
misendebyrdan (i[4]) *to arrange amiss*, LL 382.
misenlic, misendlic=missenlic
misfadian *to order amiss*, LL.
misfadung f. *misconduct, irregularity*, RB, WW.
misfaran[6] *to go wrong, transgress*, CP : *fare ill*, Æ,W. ['*misfare*']
misfēdan (oe) *to nourish ill*, EVPs.
misfeng m. *misdeed, sin*, NC 309.
misfēran *to do wrong, err*, Æ. ['*misfere*']
misfōn[7] *to make a mistake, be deceived : fail to get.*
misgedwield n. *error, perversion*, JUL 326.
misgehygd fn. *evil thought*, AN 772.
misgelimp n. *misfortune*, W 211[30].
misgemynd f. *evil memory*, SOL 495.
mis(ge)widere m. *bad weather, storm*, LCD, VH.
misgrētan *to greet amiss, insult*, Ct.
misgȳman *to neglect*, LL. ['*misyeme*']
mishæbbende *being ill*, MtL 8[16].

mishealdan[7] *not to keep, to neglect*, Æ (9[130]).
mishealdsumnes f. *carelessness*, LL (196[3]).
mishērnes (=ie[2]) f. *act of disobedience*, W.
mis-hweorfed, -hwyrfed, -hworfen *perverted, inverted*, Bo,GL.
mishȳran (=ie[2]) *to hear amiss, not to listen to, disobey*, RB,W. ['*mishear*']
mislǣdan *to* '*mislead,*' Æ.
mislǣran *to teach amiss, give bad advice to*, ÆL 5·119. ['*mislear*']
mislār f. *ill teaching, evil suggestion*, Sc.
mislēc-=mislīc-
mislic *unlike, various, manifold*, Bl,Bo; Æ, CP : *wandering, erratic*. ['*mislich*'] adv. -līce *in various ways, diversely, aimlessly*, Bo,Chr. ['*misliche*']
mislīcian (w. d.) *to displease, disquiet*, Æ, CP. ['*mislike*']
mislīcnes f. *variety, diversity*, Æ.
mislīcum *variously*, AS 54[4].
mislimp n. *misfortune*, VHY,WW.
mislimpan[3] impers. w. d. *to go wrong, turn out badly*, AO.
mislybban (=i[2]) *to lead a bad life*, Æ. ['*mislive*']
mismacian *to mar*, ByH 64[3].
mismicel *of varying sizes?* Ex 373.
misrǣcan *to abuse*, ÆH 2·590'.
misrǣd m. *misguidance*, Æ : *misconduct*, Æ.
misrǣdan *to advise wrongly*, RB : *read wrongly*, APT 3[11].
miss n. *absence, loss*, ÆL 23[271].
miss-=mis-
missan (w. g.) *to* '*miss*' (*a mark*), B : (w. d.) *escape the notice of a person.*
missare=missere
misscrence *distorted, shrivelled*, GUTH.
misscrȳdan *to clothe amiss*, ÆH 1·530'.
misse-=mis-
missenlic *various, manifold, different, diverse*, AO. adv. -līce, CP.
missenlicnes f. *variety, diversity* :'*qualitas*'? GD 46[9].
missere† n. *half-year, year.*
misspōwan[7] *to fare badly*, AO 82[34].
missprecan[5] *to grumble, murmur*, JnL 6[41,43].
mist m. '*mist,*' Æ,Bo,Met,WW : *dimness (of eyesight)*, Lcd.
mist-=mis-
mistǣcan *to teach amiss*, Æ. ['*misteach*']
mistel m. *mistletoe*, Cp,Ep : *basil*, Lcd. ['*missel*']
mistellām n. *birdlime*, WW 279[15].
misteltān (i[2]) m. '*mistletoe,*' WW.
mistglōm m? *misty gloom*, WH 47.
misthelm m. *covering of mist*, JUL 470.
misthlīŏ† n. *misty cliff, cloud-capped slope.*
mistian *to be or grow misty*, ÆGr. ['*mist*']
mistíd f. *evil time*, FM 360[12].

mistīdan (impers.) *to miscarry, fail,* LL 348'. [' *mistide* ']

mistig '*misty*,' B.

mistīhtan (=y²) *to lead astray, dissuade,* Æ.

mistīhtendlic *dehortative,* ÆGr 225¹².

mistil-=mistel-

mistīmian [impers. w. d.] *to happen amiss,* Bas. [' *mistime* ']

mistlic=mislic

mistran *to grow dim,* Deut 34⁷.

mistrīwan *to mistrust,* DR 39¹⁶.

mistūcian *to ill-treat,* Chr 1083,GD 15.

misðēon³ *to mis-thrive, degenerate,* Chrd,Gl.

misðyncan (impers.) *to be mistaken,* ApT 14²⁵.

misweaxan⁶ *to grow improperly,* ÆH 2·74¹².

miswendan *to pervert, abuse,* Æ : *be perverted, err,* Æ.

miswende *erring, ill-behaving,* Æ.

miswenian *to misuse, abuse,* Sc 224¹⁰ (?= miswerian, MLN 25·80).

misweorc n. *misdeed,* JnR 3¹⁹.

misweorðan³ *to turn out amiss,* W 240⁴.

miswidere=misgewidere

miswissian *to mislead,* LL 130; 381.

miswrītan¹ *to write incorrectly,* ÆGr. [' *miswrite* ']

miswurðian (=eo²) *to dishonour, ill-treat,* LL 381,25.

miswyssigan=miswissian

mīte f. '*mite*' (*small insect*), WW 122⁶ (v. BTs).

mitta m., mitte f. *a measure, bushel, Ct,* WW; Æ,CP. [' *mit* '; metan]

±mittan *to meet, meet with, find.*

mitte=mitta

±mitting f. *meeting, convention,* AO.

mittȳ=mid ðȳ; mið (*LkL*)=mid

mīðan¹ *to hide, conceal* (tr. and intr.), *keep to oneself, dissemble, BH,Bo,WW;* CP : *conceal oneself, remain concealed, Lcd* : (†) *avoid, shun, refrain from.* [' *mithe* ']

mīðgian *to conceal,* GD 122³.

mīðl=mīdl; mix=meox

mixen (y) f. *dung-heap, dung, Æ,LkL.* [' *mixen* ']

mixendynge (y¹) f. *dung,* LL 454,9.

mixenplante f. *nightshade* (*plant*), Lcd.

mixian=miscian

mōd n. (±) *heart, mind, spirit, 'mood,' temper, B,BH,Bl;* Æ,AO,CP : *courage, B;* AO : *arrogance, pride,* AO : *power, violence.*

+mōd *of one mind, harmonious, peaceful,* CP.

mōdblind† *blind, undiscerning.*

mōdblissiende *exulting,* PPs 67¹⁷.

mōdbysgung f. *anxiety,* Dom 84.

mōdcearig *sorrowful of heart,* Wa 2.

mōdcearu† f. *sorrow, grief.*

mōdcræft† m. *intelligence.*

mōdcræftig *intelligent,* Cra 62.

mōddor=mōdor

mōddren *of mothers,* ApT 4¹².

mōddri(g)e=mōdrige; mōde-=mōdig-

mōdearfoð n. *grief of mind,* †Hy 4⁸⁷.

mōdeg=mōdig; mōder=mōdor

mōdercynd=mēdrengecynd

mōderge=mōdrige

mōdful *proud, haughty,* Lcd 3·188'.

mōdgehygd† n. *thought.*

mōdgemynd† n. *mind, thought.*

mōdgēomor† *sad, dejected.*

mōdgeðanc m. *thought, understanding, mind.*

mōdgeðōht m. *thought, understanding, mind.*

mōdgeðyldig *patient,* An 983.

mōdgewinna m. *care,* Gen 2797.

mōdgian=mōdigian

mōdgidanc (N)=mōdgeðanc

mōdglæd *joyous,* Gu 1311.

mōdglēaw *wise,* Sol 180.

mōdhæp? *brave,* Ex 242 (GK).

mōdhete m. *hatred,* Gen 1756.

mōdhord n. *secret thoughts,* An 172.

mōdhwæt† *brave, bold.*

mōdig (CP), mōdi *spirited, daring, bold, brave, high-souled, magnanimous, B;* Æ : *impetuous, headstrong, Æ;* CP : *arrogant, proud, Æ,CP.* [' *moody* ']

mōdigan, mōdigian *to grow proud or overbearing, be high-minded, glory, exult, show bravery, Æ* : *take offence through pride, Æ.*

mōdiglic (mōde-) *high-souled, lofty, proud* : *brave, bold* : *splendid, magnificent.* adv. -līce, *Ma* (mōde-). [' *moodily* ']

mōdignes f. *greatness of soul* : *pride, arrogance, haughtiness, Æ.* [' *moodiness* ']

mōdilic=mōdiglic

mōdlēas *spiritless,* KGl 66⁴⁰ : *senseless,* Chrd.

mōdlēast f. *want of courage, despondency,* Æ.

mōdlēof *dear, precious,* FT 28.

mōdlufu† f. *heart's affection, love.*

mōdnes (RWH 2³⁶)=mōdignes

+mōdod *disposed,* ÆH 1·524¹⁸.

mōdor (e²) f., ds. mēder '*mother,*' WW (*of animals*), LL : AO,CP.

mōdorcild (mō-ð-) n. *a child of one's (own) mother,* PPs 68⁸.

mōdorcynn n. *maternal descent,* Chr 1067 D.

mōdorhealf f. *mother's side,* Chr 1076 D.

mōdorhrif n. *womb,* PPs.

mōdorlēas (e²) *motherless,* W 228²².

mōdorlic (e²) *maternal,* ÆGr. [' *motherly* '] adv. -līce.

mōdorlufu f. *love for a mother,* NC 309.

mōdorslaga m. *matricide,* WW 335⁶.

mōdrige, mōdrie f. *mother's sister, maternal aunt*, Æ,AO : *cousin*. [mōdor]

mōdrōf *valiant*, AN 1493.

mōdsefa† m. *heart, mind, spirit, soul : thought, imagination, purpose, character.*

mōdsēoc *sick at heart*, GEN 1235.

mōdsēocnes f. *disease of the heart*, WW 199³⁵.

mōdsnotor† *wise.*

mōdsorg† f. *heart-sorrow.*

mōdstaðol m. *principle, character*, LL (318 n1).

mōd-staðolnes, -staðolfæstnes f. *firmness of mind*, W 53¹⁰.

+**mōdsum** *accordant, in agreement*, CP 360¹³.

+**mōdsumian** *to agree*, CP.

+**mōdsumnes** f. *agreement, concord*, CP.

mōdswīð *resolute*, PsC 89.

mōd-ðracu f. gs. -ðræce *courage*, B 385.

mōdðrēa m. *anguish*, RD 4⁵⁰.

mōdðwǣre *meek*, LPs 24⁹.

mōdðwǣrnes f. *patience, meekness*, W.

mōdur=mōdor

mōdwǣg m. *proud wave*, Ex 499.

mōdwelig *gifted, talented, wise*, CP 9¹².

mōdwlanc† *stout-hearted : haughty.*

mōdwyn f. *heart's joy, property*, RD 87⁷.

moetan (Cp)=mētan

mohða, mohðe (N)=moððe

molcen n. *coagulated or curdled milk*, LCD, WW. [*Ger.* molke]

+**molcen** *milked*, LCD 34a.

molda? m. v. molde II.

moldærn (e²)† n. *grave.*

moldcorn n. *granular tuber of saxifraga granulata, and the plant itself*, LCD.

molde I. f. *sand*, '*mould*,' *dust, soil*, Cp,BH, GK; Æ : *land, country : world.* **II**? f. *top of the head*, Lcd 3·42 (or molda?). ['*mould*']

moldern=moldærn

moldgewind n. *top of the head*, NC 310.

moldgræf† n. *grave.*

moldhrērende *moving upon earth*, CREAT 27.

moldhȳpe f. *heap of dust*, ÆH 1·492'.

moldstōw f. *site, sepulchre*, GPH 391.

moldweg† m. *earth.*

moldwyrm m. *earth-worm*, SOUL 72.

molegn n. *curds*, GL.

molegnstycce n. *piece of curd*, GL.

moling=molegn

molsn n? *decay*, NC 310.

±**molsnian** *to moulder, decay*, Æ.

molten pp. of meltan.

momra=mamera, mamor; **mon**=man

mōna m. '*moon*,' *Bo,Lcd*; Æ,AO,CP.

mōnanǣfen m. *Sunday evening*, LL.

mōnandæg m. '*Monday*,' *Bf,Jn.*

mōnanniht f. *Monday eve, i.e. Sunday evening*, LL.

mōnað m. nap. mōn(e)ðas, mōnað '*month*,' BH,Bo,Lk,Lcd; AO,CP. [mōna]

mōnaðādl f. *morbus menstrualis*, BH.

mōnaðādlig *menstruous*, BH 78⁵.

mōnaðblōd n. '*menstruum*,' WW.

mōnaðbōt f. *penance for a month*, LL (278¹¹).

mōnaðfylen f. *time of full moon*, OEG.

mōnaðgecynd f. '*menstruum*,' LCD.

mōnaðlic *monthly, lunar*, GL : *as sb.*= mōnaðādl, LCD.

mōnaðsēoc I. *menstruous*, Æ. **II.**=mōnsēoc

mōnaðsēocnes (o²) f. *lunacy*, LCD 1·170⁴.

moncus=mancus; **mond**=mand

mōndæg=mōnandæg; **mōne** f.=mōna

mōnelic *lunar*, Æ,LCD.

+**mong**=+mang; **monig**=manig

mōnlic=mōnelic; **monn**=mann

mōnoð=mōnað

mōnsēoc '*moonsick*,' *lunatic, epileptic*, MtR.

mont=munt; **mōnð**=mōnað

monuc=munuc

mōr m. '*moor*,' *morass, swamp*, B; Mdf : *hill, mountain*, AO.

morað (ō?) n. *sweet boiled wine with herbs*, GL,LCD. [*L.* moratum]

mōrbēam (ā, ū) m. *mulberry tree, bramble*, VPs. [v. '*more*']

mōrberie f. *mulberry* (*fruit*), ÆL 25⁵⁷⁶.

more f. *carrot, parsnip*, Lcd,WW. ['*more*']

moreð=morað

mōrfæsten n. *moor-fastness*, CHR.

mōrflēoge f. '*cariscus*,' *a kind of fly*, NC 310.

morgen (a, e) m. ds. morgenne '*morn*,' *morning, forenoon*, B,MtL,VPs : *sunrise*, B : *morrow*, Æ,B; CP. on mor(gen)ne (1) *in the morning*, (2) *to-morrow.*

morgenceald *chill at morn*, B 3022.

morgencolla m. *morning terror*, JUD 245.

morgendæg (e¹) m. *morrow*, BL,GUTH.

morgendlic=morgenlic

morgendrenc m. *morning drink*, LCD.

morgengebedtīd f. *morning prayer*, GUTH 40²⁵.

morgengifu f. *gift by a husband to his wife the morning after the wedding*, BC,WW. ['*moryeve*']

morgenlēoht n. *dawn, morning*, B.

morgenlic *matutinal, morning : of the morrow.* morgenlica dæg *to-morrow.*

morgenlong *lasting a morning*, B 2895.

morgenmæsse f. *morning mass, first mass*, ANS 84·2.

morgenmete m. *morning meal*, SOL 192¹⁹.

morgenrēn m. *morning rain*, Az 82.

morgensēoc *sad at morn*, AN 241.

morgenspǣc f. *regular meeting of a guild on the morrow after the guild-feast*, TC. ['*mornspeech*']

morgenspell n. *news published at morn*, EL 970.

morgensteorra m. *morning star*, Bo. ['*morn-star*']

morgenswēg m. *cry at morn*, B129.

morgentīd (a¹, e¹) f. *morning*, CHR,Ps.

morgentīdlic *matutinal*, BPs129⁶.

morgentorht *bright at morn*, AN241.

morgenwacian *to rise early*, WW.

morgenwlǣtung f. *morning sickness*, LCD 169b.

mōrhǣð f. *mountain-heath*, PPs82¹⁰.

mōrheald *heathy, marshy?* Ex61.

mōrhop n. *moor-swamp*, B450.

mōrig *marshy*, GEN41².

mōrlǣs *marshy pasture*, KC3·408²².

mōrland n. '*moor-land*,' *mountain-waste*, LkL.

morne ds., mornes gs. of morgen.

morod, moroð=morað

mōrsceaða m. *robber*, NG.

mōrsecg mn. *sedge*, LCD3·140'.

mōrseohtre f. *marshy ditch*, CHRD96²⁸.

mōrslǣd n. *marshy valley*, KC.

mōrstapa m. *traverser of moors*, RUN2.

mortere m. *a mortar*, LCD,WW. [*L.* mortarium]

morð nm. *death, destruction, homicide,* '*murder*,' AO; Æ : *deadly sin.* ['*murth*']

morð-=morðor-

morðcrundel mn. *barrow raised over a dead body? deadly pool? corpse-pit?* KC3·23'.

morðdǣd f. *murder, deadly sin, crime*, Æ.

morðor nm., gs. morðres (mp. morðras) *deed of violence,* '*murder*,' *homicide, man-slaughter*, B,Bl : *mortal sin, crime* : *injury, punishment, torment, misery.*

morðorbealu† n. *violent death, murder.*

morðorbed n. *bed of death (by violence)*, B 2436.

morðorcofa m. *prison*, AN1006.

morðorcræft m. *murderous crime*, AN177.·

morðorcwalu f. *murder*, NC310.

morðorcwealm m. *murder, death*, GNE 152.

morðorhete m. *blood-feud*, B1105.

morðorhof n. *place of torment*, EL1303.

morðorhūs n. *house of torment*, CR1625.

morðorhycgende *with murderous thoughts*, WIF20.

morðorlēan n. *retribution for sin*, CR1612.

morðorscyldig *guilty*, AN1601.

morðorslaga m. *homicide, murderer*, NG.

morðorslagu f. *homicide, murder*, NG.

morðorslege m. *homicide, murder*, LL (148¹⁴).

morð(or)sliht (e²) m. *slaughter, murder.*

morð(or)wyrhta m. *murderer*, W.

morðslaga (Æ)=morðorslaga

morðsliht=morðorsliht; **morður**=morðor

morðweorc n. *deadly work, act which causes death, murder*, LL.

morðwyrhta=morðorwyrhta

moru f. *parsnip, carrot* (=more).

mōrwyrt f. *moor-wort*, LCD48b.

mōs n. I. *bog, marsh*, BC. ['*moss*'] II. n. *food, victuals*. [*Ger.* mus]

mōst, mōste v. *mōtan.

mot n. '*mote,*' *speck, atom, Mt,WW.*

mōt I. (±, usu. +) n. '*moot*' ('*gemot*'), *society, assembly, court, council, synod, Chr,MtL;* Mdf. +m. *wyrcan to take counsel : litigation*, Bo : (+) *conflict, encounter.* II. f. *toll, tribute*, MkL. [*Ger.* maut] III. pres. sg. of *mōtan.

±mōtærn (e²) n. *courthouse*, AO.

mōtan* swv. pres. 1, 3 sg. mōt, pres. 2 sg. mōst, pres. pl. mōton, pret. mōste (*may*). *to be allowed, be able to, have opportunity to, be compelled to, must*, B,Gen; AO,CP. mōste ic *would that I might!* ['*mote*']

+mōtan=mētan

mōtbell f. *bell for summoning a moot*, LL. [v. '*moot*']

±mōtbeorh m. *hill of meeting*, BC.

mōtere m. *public speaker*, WW. ['*mooter*']

mōtern=mōtærn

mōtgerēfa m. *moot-reeve, chairman of a moot*, EC342'.

±mōthūs n. *moot-hall, place of assembly*, WW; W. ['*moothouse*']

±mōtian *to speak to or about, converse with, address, harangue*, Æ : *argue, plead, discuss, dispute*, Hex. ['*moot*']

mōtlǣðu sbpl. *courts, assemblies?* TC433²² (v. BTs).

+mōtlēah m. *meadow of meeting*, BC.

+mōtmann m. *orator, counsellor*, WW164³⁵; 310²⁹.

+mōtstede m. *place of meeting*, SOUL152.

±mōtstōw f. *place of meeting, forum*, EPs, GL.

mōtung f. *conversation, discussion*, OEG. ['*mooting*']

mōtweorð (u²) *qualified to attend the moot*, EC343'.

mōðfreten *moth-eaten*, ÆL23⁴³⁷.

mōðor=mōdor

mōððe f. '*moth*,' *Lk,MtL* (mohðe).

mucgwyrt f. *artemisia,* '*mugwort*,' *Lcd, WW.*

muexle=muscelle; **mūdrica**=mȳderce

mūga m. '*mow*,' *heap of corn*, Æ.

mugan*=magan; **mugwyrt**=mucgwyrt

mūha (*Cp*)=muga

mūl m. '*mule*,' *Ps;* ÆL. [*L.* mulus]

mūlhyrde m. *mule-keeper*, ÆGR35⁵.

multon pret. pl. of meltan.

+**mun** (w. g.) *mindful, remembering*, AO 48[11].

±**munan** (usu. +) pres. 1, 3 sg. man (mon), 2 manst, pl. munon, pret. munde swv. *to think about, be mindful of, remember, mention*, *Bl,Jul,Lk*; Æ,AO,CP : *consider*. ['*i-mune*']

mund f. **I.**† *hand* :*palm (of the hand, as a measure*) : *trust, security, protection, guardianship*, Æ : *protector, guardian* : *the king's peace* : *fine for breach of the laws of protection or guardianship of the king's peace*, v. LL2·555; 641. [cp. *Ger.* vormund] **II.** m. *money paid by bridegroom to bride's father, bridegroom's gift to bride*, CR93. **III.**=mynd

mundbeorg m. *protecting hill*, PPs124².

mundberd=mundbyrd

mundbora m. *protector, preserver, guardian, advocate*, Æ : *prefect*.

mundbryce (i²) m. *breach of the laws of protection or guardianship*, LL : *fine for the breach of such laws*.

mundbyrd f. *protection, patronage, help* : *fine for a breach of the peace*, LL.

±**mundbyrdan** *to protect*, Bo,VH.

mundbyrdnes f. *protection* : *security, independence* : *protector, guardian, advocate*.

mundbyre=mundbyrde (ds. of mundbyrd).

mundcræft m. *protecting power*, LCD 1·384[13].

munde v. munan; +**munde**=+mynde

mundgripe† m. *hand-grasp*, B.

mundheals f. *protection?* CR445.

±**mundian** *to protect, watch over, act as guardian of*, Æ.

mundiend m. *protector*, TC525⁸.

mund-léow, -léu, -láu f. *wash-hand basin*, WW. [*ON.* munnlaug]

mundróf *strong with the hands*, RD84³.

mundwist f. *guardianship, protection*, NC 310.

munec=munuc

munetere=mynetere

mungung=mynegung

+**muning** f. *remembrance*, CM378.

munt m. *mountain, hill*, Æ,AO,CP. [*L.*]

muntælfen f. *mountain nymph*, WW 189⁴. [v. '*elven*']

muntclýse f. *mountain prison*, W84H.

muntland n. *hill-country*, Lk1³⁹.

munuc (e²) m. '*monk*,' *BH,RB* : (used also of women, A27·255). [*L.* monachus]

munucbehāt n. *monastic vow*, HL18⁸¹,⁹⁵.

munuccild n. *child intended for monastic life*, Æ,BF102¹⁶.

munuccnapa m. *young monk*, GD.

munucgegyrela m. *monastic garb*, BH34²⁷.

munuchād m. *monastic orders, the monastic life*, Æ,BH; CP. ['*monkhood*']

munuchéap m. *company of monks*, BF150¹⁹.

munucian (e²) *to make a monk of*, LL. ['*monk*']

munuclic *monkish, monastic*, BH; Æ. adv. -līce. ['*monkly*']

munuclīf n. *monastic life*, Æ : *cloister, monastery*, Æ,AO.

munucréaf n. *monk's garb*, GD27¹⁷.

munucregol m. *monastic rule, mode of life*, Æ : *a body of monks under a certain rule*, TC544¹².

munucscrúd n. *monk's garb*, ÆP142⁵.

munucstów f. *place of monks*, BH236²⁵.

munucðéaw m. *monastic rule*, ANS84·7.

munucwīse f. *fashion of a monk*, ÆL 6·247.

múr m. *wall*, CR1143. [*L.* murus]

múr-béam, -berie=mór-béam, -berie

murc *dismal, wretched*, PPs145⁶. [myrce]

murcian *to complain, repine, grieve*, CP.

murcnere m. *complainer*, RB21⁵.

murcnian=murcian

murcung f. *complaint, sorrow*, CP.

murge=myrge

murnan³ (and wv.) *to care, be anxious or fearful about*, *An,Bo,Wald* : *hesitate* : '*mourn,*' *sorrow, bemoan*, *Wy* : *long after*, An37.

murnung f. *complaint, grief*, Bo18¹⁹ (v.l. murcnung), LCD,VH.

murra, murre=myrra, myrre

mús f. gs. mús, múse, nap. mŷs '*mouse,*' *Bo*; Æ; Mdf : *muscle (of the arm)*, WW158⁶.

mus-celle, -cule f. *shell-fish*, '*mussel,*' *Gl.* [*L.*]

muscfléote f? *a small fly found in wine* (mustfléoge? BT), WW121²².

muscle=muscelle

músepise f. *mouse-pea, vetch*, WW148³⁵.

músfealle (a²) f. *mouse-trap*, WW.

músfealu *mouse-coloured*, WW448⁹.

múshafoc n. *mouse-hawk, buzzard*, WW.

musle=muscelle; **musscel** (GL)=muscelle

must m. '*must,*' *new wine*, *Bo*; Æ. [*L.*]

-**mútian** v. be-m.

mútung f. '*mutuum,*' *loan*, WW449³⁰.

múð m. '*mouth,*' *opening, door, gate*, Æ,BH, CP,Mt.

múða m. *mouth (of a river), estuary*, AO, CHR : (†) *entrance to a house, door*.

múðádl f. *mouth-disease*, WW.

múðberstung f. *eruption of the mouth*, WW.

múðbona m. *devourer*, B2079.

múðcoðu f. *mouth-disease*, WW.

múðettan *to blab out, let out*, Æ (6¹⁶⁰).

múðfréo *free to speak*, PPs11⁴.

múðhǽl f. *wholesome speech*, Ex552.

múðhróf m. *palate*, OEG332.

múðléas *mouthless*, RD61⁹.

mūðsàr *pain in the mouth*, LL.
mūðsealf f. *mouth-salve*, LCD 18ŀ
mūwa (*WW* 348⁶)=mūga
muxle=muscelle
myce? (ES 43·309), mycel (LWS̃=mɪcel
mycg (i) m. '*midge*,' *Cp,Lcd,WW*.
mycgern=micgern
mycgnet (i) n. *mosquito-net*, WW 183¹³.
mycl-=micl-; myd-=mid-
mydd n. *bushel*, AO 190¹². [*L.* modius]
mȳderce f. *money storing-place, chest*, ÆGR
(IF 48·267).
mygg (GL)=mycg; mȳgð=mǣgð
myhtig=mihtig
mȳhð pres. 3 sg. of mīgan.
myl n. *dust*, JAW 32; ES 41·163. [*Ger.*
mūll]
mylc=meolc
myldan=miltan; -myldan v. be-m.
myle-=mylen-
mylen mf. '*mill*,' *KC,LL,RB*; Mdf.
mylendīc f. *mill-dike*, Ct.
mylenfeld m. *mill-field*, KC 5·381'.
mylengafol n. *mill-tax, mill-rent?* NC 310.
mylengear m. *mill-yair*, Ct (v. A 46·228
and BTs).
mylenhwēol n. '*mill-wheel*,' Lcd.
mylenpull m. *mill-pool*, Ct.
mylenscearp *sharpened on a grindstone*, BR
24.
mylenstān m. *grindstone*, WW. ['*mill-
stone*']
mylen-steall, -stede m. *mill*, KC.
mylenstīg f. *path to a mill*, KC 3·389⁸.
mylentroh n. *mill-trough, mill-conduit*, WW.
mylenwaru f. *mill-weir*, KC 3·454⁷.
mylenweg *road to a mill*, KC 6·31'.
myle(n)wer m. '*mill-weir*,' *mill-dam*, *KC*
4·92'.
mylenwyrd, myleweard m. *tenant of a
(manorial) mill, miller, WW*. ['*millward*']
mylestrēam m. '*mill-stream*,' *BC* 2·377.
mylier (EC 179¹)=myle(n)wer?
mylisc, mylsc=milisc
mylma m. *retreat?* GPH 398¹⁵⁰.
myln=mylen
myltan=(1) meltan; (2) mieltan
myltenhūs n. *brothel*, ES 9·39.
myltestre (e, i) f. *prostitute*, Æ. [*L.*
meretricem]
myltestrehūs n. *brothel*, WW 186².
myltestrern? (=ærn) *brothel*, v. OEG 8²²⁵.
mymerian *to remember*, W 74¹⁵.
+mynan=+munan
±mynd (usu. +) fn. *memory, remembrance,
Æ,BH,Met : memorial, record, Æ : act of
commemoration, Bl,MH : thought, purpose,
Bl : consciousness, mind. intellect.* on
+m. niman *to recollect.* ['*mind*']

+myndblīðe (i¹) *memorial*, EP 101¹³; 134¹³.
+mynddæg f. *anniversary, BH.* [v. '*mind*']
+mynde I. *mindful*, EL 1064. II. *river-
mouth*, BH 398¹⁷ (v. JAW 31).
+mynde-=myndig-
+myndewyrðe *worth mentioning or remembering*, BH 486¹².
+myndful (e¹) *of good memory*, LCD 3·186.
±myndgian *to remember, be mindful of* :
(w. g.) *remind, W*; CP : *intend : com-
memorate, mention, PPs : exhort, impel,
warn : demand payment*, LL 206,1².
+myndgod *aforesaid.* [*ming*']
myndgiend m. *one who reminds*, B 1105.
±myndgung f. *admonition*, CP : *remembrance, memorandum*, LL 453²¹ (myng-) :
memorial, AO 98²⁵.
±myndig *mindful, recollecting, Mk : memorable : thoughtful, wise*, HELL 77. se
+myndiga *the aforesaid.* ['*mindy*']
+myn-diglic, -delic *memorable : hortatory.*
adv. -līce *by heart, Æ : thoughtfully*,
MFB 103.
+myndiglicnes f. *remembrance*, SPs 101¹³.
±myndlēas *foolish, senseless, Æ.* ['*mind-
less*']
+myndlȳst f. *madness*, ZDA 31·22.
+myndstōw f. *monument, tomb*, G,RPs.
+myndwyrðe=+myndewyrðe
myne I.† m. *memory, remembrance : feeling,
affection, love, favour : purpose, desire,
wish, B : memorial.* m. witan *to love.*
['*min*'] II. m. *minnow*, WW. III.=mene
+myne I. *mindful*, MtR 5²³. II. pres. subj.
of +munan.
mynecen, mynecenu f. *female monk, nun,
WW; Æ.* ['*minchen*'; munuc]
mynegian=myndgian
mynegiendlic *hortatory*, CM 30.
±mynegung f. *warning, admonition, exhortation, Æ : claim.* (=+myndgung)
mynelic *desirable*, WID 4.
mynescilling=menescilling
mynet n. *coin, money, Cp,Lcd,MtR.* ['*mint*';
L. moneta]
mynetcȳpa m. *money-changer*, ÆH 1·412.
mynetere m. '*minter*,' *coiner, Æ : money-
changer, Mt; Æ.*
±mynetian *to coin*, LL 158,14; BC 3·75.
mynetīsen n. *coinage? die for stamping
coin?* (BTs), ÆL 23⁴⁴⁷.
mynetslege m. *minting, coinage*, ÆL 23⁴⁷⁵.
mynetsmiððe f. *mint*, LL 158,14¹.
myng-=myneg-, myndg-
mynian (e) *to intend, be impelled : direct
oneself towards an object*, AS 1⁹.
mynig-=myneg-; mynit=mynet
mynle f. *desire*, MET 26⁶⁷.
mynnan=mynian

mynster (æ²) n. *monastery, nunnery, BH* : *mother-church, 'minster,' cathedral, LL.* [*L.* monasterium]

mynsterbōc f? *minster-book,* NC310.

mynsterclǣnsung f. *purification of a minster,* LL.

mynsterclūse f. *monastic enclosure, stall, cell, monastery,* CM22.

mynsterfæder m. *abbot,* GD293¹.

mynsterfǣmne f. *nun,* BH20¹⁹.

mynstergang m. *act of joining an order of monks,* LL(146').

mynstergēat n. *monastery gate,* GD145².

mynsterhām m. *monastery,* LL,TC.

mynsterhata m. *persecutor of monasteries,* W165²⁸.

mynsterland n. *land owned by a monastery,* KC3·60'.

mynsterlic *monastic,* Æ. adv. -līce.

mynsterlīf n. *monastic life,* Æ : *monastery.*

mynstermann m. *monk,* Æ,Bꜰ.

mynstermunuc m. *monk who lives in a monastery* (*i.e. not an anchorite*), ÆH.

mynsterprafost m. *provost of a monastery,* TC434⁴.

mynsterprēost m. *priest of a church or minster,* LL(254⁸).

mynsterscīr f. *control of a monastery,* BH 458¹¹.

mynsterstede m. *monastic buildings,* GD 182¹⁹.

mynsterstōw f. *place of a minster, town,* BH 160¹⁶.

mynstertimbrung f. *building of a monastery,* GD147¹¹.

mynsterðēaw m. *monastic custom,* BH452¹².

mynsterðegnung f. *monastic service,* RB85¹⁷.

mynsterwīse f. *monastic custom,* GF110²⁷.

+mynt n. *intention,* RWH135¹⁵.

±myntan *to intend, determine, resolve,* Æ, B,Bo : *destine* : *think, Jud* : *bring forth,* Sc215¹ : *give up to,* LL400,3. ['*mint,*' '*i-munte*']

myranhēafod n. *mare's head* (a nick-name), Cʜʀ1010ᴇ.

Myrce, Myrcan=Mierce; **myrce**=mirce

myre (Æ,AO)=miere

myrenæddra=merenæddra

myrgan *to be '*merry,' *rejoice,* PPs.

myrge adj. (e, i, u) *pleasing, agreeable,* Æ,Bo,Met : *pleasant, sweet, DHy.* ['*merry*'] adv. myrge (AS,W), myriglīce *pleasantly, melodiously,* GD286¹. ['*merry*']

myrgelēoð n. *epitaph?* BHʙ94¹².

myrgen I. f. *joy, pleasure,* Mᴇᴛ (Introd.) 5. **II.**=morgen

myrgnes f. *melody,* WW33⁸¹.

myrgð (e, i), myrhð f. '*mirth,*' *joy, pleasure, sweetness* (*of sound*), Æ,Bo.

myrig-=myrg-; **mȳrlic**=mærlic

myrr-=mierr-

myrra m., myrre f. (u) '*myrrh,*' *Æ,MtR,VPs.*

myrrelse f. *offence, scandal, stumbling-block,* Jᴜʟ338.

myrten I. n. *flesh of an animal which has died of itself, carrion,* LL. **II.** adj. *dead* (of animals which have not been killed), LL.

myrð=myrgð, v. also myrðu.

myrðra m. *homicide, murderer,* LL,W.

-myrðran, -myrðrian v. ā-, for-, of-m.

myrðrung f. *parricide, murder,* WW467²¹.

myrðu (=ie) f. *mischief, trouble,* B810.

myrw-=mearuw- (v. mearu); **mȳs** v. mūs.

±myscan *to injure, afflict,* PPs : *offend,* OEG17⁴⁷.

myscl sbpl. *flies,* PPs104²⁷.

mȳse=mēse; **mytting**=mitting

+mȳðe n. (usu. pl.) *mouth, confluence, junction of two streams,* BH,Ct.

myx=meox; **myx-**=mix-

N

nā (ō) adv. conj. *not,* '*no,*' *not at all, not even, never, by no means, Bl,Cr,Met,VPs;* Æ,AO,CP. nā ðæt ān *not only.* ...nā...nā *neither...nor,* ne nā *nor.* nā mā *no more,* ÆGr,Bl. ['*no mo*'] nā māre sb. *nothing more, Bo,Mk.* ['*no more*']

nab-=naf-

nabban anv. pres. 1 sg. næbbe, 2 næfst, 3 nafað, næfð, pl. nabbað, næbbað; pret. næfde (v. habban) *not to have, to lack, be without, Bo*(+næfd), *Jn*; AO,CP. [v. '*have*']

naca† m. *vessel, boat, ship.* [Ger. nachen]

naced=nacod; **naclan**=nacodian

nacod, nacud (æ) (+) **I.** adj. '*ɴᴀᴋᴇᴅ,*' *nude, bare, Æ,CP* : *empty* : *not fully clothed.* **II.** f. *nakedness.*

+nac(od)ian *to lay bare, strip,* BH,MkL.

næ adv.=ne

næbbað, næbbe v. nabban.

nǣbre=nǣfre

nǣcad (*Cp*499ᴇ '*exserta*')=nacod

±nǣcan (Æ)=hnǣcan

nǣced=nacod

nǣcednes f. *nakedness,* Æ.

nǣcedu f. *nakedness,* MFH169.

nǣct=niht; **nǣdder-**=nǣder-

nǣddre (CP)=nǣdre

nǣddrewinde f. *adder-wort,* WW287¹⁶.

nǣderbita m. *ichneumon,* WW.

nǣdercynn n. *snake-tribe,* Lᴄᴅ: *a kind of snake,* AA.

nǣderfāh *spotted like a snake,* HL15¹⁸³.

nǣdl (ē) f. '*needle,*' *G,Soul;* Æ.

nǣdre (ē) f. '*adder*,' *snake, serpent, viper, Mt*; AO,CP.

nǣdrewyrt (der) f. *adder-wort*, Lcd,WW.

nǣfde pret. 3 sg. of nabban.

nǣfebor *auger*, A9·263³. [nafu]

nǣfig (NG)=næftig; **nǣfne**=nefne

nǣfre (ē) adv. '*never*,' *B,Bl,Bo,Chr,G,LL*; CP. [ne, æfre]

nǣfst v. nabban.

nǣft f. *need, want, poverty*, Sc157³·⁷.

nǣftcyrrend *not returning*, CP77³⁹. [ne eft]

nǣftig *poor*, Sc190¹.

±**nǣgan** I.† (ē) (often followed by wordum) *to approach, accost, speak to* : *attack*. II.= hnǣgan

nǣgel=nægl; **nǣgen**=ne mægen

nǣgl m. 'NAIL,' *peg, AO*; Æ : *finger-nail, toe-nail, claw, Æ* : *plectrum*, Wy84 : *spear*, WW377¹⁵ : (in comp.) *handle*.

nǣgledbord† *with nailed sides.*

nǣgledcnearr m. *nail-fastened vessel*, †Chr 937.

nǣgledcræt n. *iron chariot* (Swt).

nǣgledsinc n. *studded vessel*, B2023.

±**nǣglian** '*to nail*,' *fasten with nails*, MtLR; Æ.

nǣglsex n. *knife for cutting the nails*, WW. [seax; v. '*nail*']

nǣh=nēah; **nǣhsta**=nīehsta

nǣht (NG,VPs)=niht; **nǣht**=nāht

nǣlēacan (S²Ps54²²)=nēalǣcan

nǣllǣs=nealles; **nǣm**=neom

nǣm f. *taking, receiving*, NC311.

+**nǣman** *to take away*, Guth14¹¹.

nǣmel *receptive*, NC311. ['*nimble*']

nǣming f. *bargain, contract*, WW180¹⁷.

nǣmne=nemne

+**nǣmnian** (LL455')=nemnian

nǣmniendlic=nemniendlic

nǣnig pron. *no one, none, not any, no* (used as sb. w. gen. and as adj.). nænige ðinga adv. *not at all, in no wise.* [ne, ænig]

nǣnig-wuht, -uht *in no wise, nothing*, Andr119⁶.

nǣniht (NG)=nānwiht

nǣnne v. nān.

nǣp m. *turnip, rape, Cp,Lcd.* ['*neep*']

nǣpsǣd n. *rape seed*, Lcd.

nǣpte=nefte

nǣre, nǣron (Æ,AO,CP)=ne wǣre, ne wǣron

nǣrende ptc. *not being.* [ne, wesan]

nǣrra=nēara

nǣs I. (AO,CP)=ne wæs. II. adv. *not, not at all*, CP. [=nalæs] III.=næss. IV. pret. 3 sg. of nesan.

nǣsc *fawn-skin*, Gl,Lcd.

nǣse (NG)=nese

nǣsgristle f. *nose-gristle*, Gl.

---

nǣs-hliÞ n. dp. -hleoðum *declivity, slope* (of a headland), B1428.

nǣss (e), nǣssa m. '*ness*,' *cliff, headland, cape, An,B,Chr,Ct* : (†) *earth, ground.*

nǣstan=hnǣstan

nǣster '*caucale*' (=caucalia?), *lipped vessel*, WW202¹ (v. A49·378 and IF48·266).

nǣsÞyrl n. *nostril*, Æ,Lcd.

±**nǣtan** *to annoy, afflict, press upon, subdue, injure, destroy*, CP.

nǣting f. *blaming*, CP353¹¹.

nǣðl=nǣdl

nafa I. m.=nafu. II.=ne hafa imperat. of nabban

nafað pres. 3 sg. of nabban.

nafela m. '*navel*,' AO,Gl,Lcd; Æ.

nafeða m. *nave* (of a wheel), WW106²⁷.

nafogār m. '*auger*,' Gl,WW.

nafu f. *nave* (of a wheel), Bo,WW

nafula=nafela

nafulsceaft f. *navel*, Lcd3·124'.

+**nāg** *striking, pressing?* Rim57?

nāgan* pres. 3 sg. nāh; pret. nāhte, nāhton *not to owe, not to be bound, not to be allowed, to have no right to, not to own, not to have, to lose, be unable to*, AO. nāhte *ought not*. [ne, āgan]

nāht (ǣ, āu, āw, ō) I. n. 'NAUGHT,' *nothing*, CP : *wickedness, evil-doing*, CP. instr. nāhte w. comparatives=*nothing*. II. *useless, bad, poor, Æ.* III. adv. *not, not at all, Æ, CP.* [nā, wiht]

nāhte v. nāgan.

nāhtfremmend m. *evil-doer*, PPs58².

nāhtgītsung (āu¹) f. *wicked avarice*, CP333⁵.

nāhtlic *worthless, of no avail*, Chr979e. adv. -līce (ō¹) *wickedly, badly. VPs.*36⁸·⁹. ['*noughtly*']

nāhtnes f. *worthlessness*, Chr449a.

nāhtscipe f. *worthlessness*, Chr449e.

nāh-wǣr, -wǣrn (o¹) adv. '*nowhere*,' *in no case, never, not at all, Æ,Bf,Bl,GD.*

nāhwæðer *neither, Bo,Bl*; CP. ['*nauther*']

nāhwǣr=nāhwǣr

nāhwider '*no-whither*,' *nowhere*, Bo,RB.

nāhwonan adv. *from nowhere*, Bo89².

nalǣs, nalas, nales (AO,CP), nalles (CP), nals=nealles

nalde (N,VPs)=nolde pret. of *nyllan.

nam I. pret. 3 sg. of niman. II. (N)=ne eom

nām f. (*legal*) *seizure*, LL.

nama (o) m. 'NAME,' Æ; AO,CP : *reputation* : *noun*, ÆGr.

nambōc (o) f. *register of names*, WW342¹¹.

nambred (o) n. *register of names* (on a tablet), WW499⁴⁰.

namcūÞ *well-known*, LL : *celebrated*, HL; (nome-), Æ. ['*namecouth*']

namcūðlīce adv. *by name, individually*, Æ.
namcyging (=ie²) f. *naming*, CHRD 9²⁹.
±namian *to 'name,' Gen* : *mention*, Æ : *call,
Scr* : *nominate, appoint*, Æ,LL.
nammǣlum adv. *by name*, LF 55¹⁴, OEG.
+namn adj. *of the same name*, RD 53³; 54¹³?
namnian *to address, invoke*, ÆT 683.
nāmon pret. pl. of niman.
nāmrǣden f. *learning*, WW 431⁸.
nān as. nǣnne, nānne I. pron. and adj.
'NONE,' *not one, no*. nāne ðinga *on no
account*. II. sb. w. g. *none, no one, nothing*.
[nē, ān]
nān-wiht, -(w)uht I. n. (often w. g.) *nothing,
naught*, AO,CP. II. adv. *not at all, in no
wise*.
nāp pret. 3 sg. of nīpan.
nard m. *spikenard, unguent*, LCD. [*L.
nardus*]
nart (*JnL*)=neart; naru=nearu
nas=næs=ne wæs
nāst (=ne wāst) v. nytan.
nasðyrl=næsðyrl; nasu=nosu
nāt (*Bo,Jn*)=ne wāt, v. nytan.
nāteshwōn (Æ), nāteðæshwōn adv. *not, not
at all, by no means*.
nāthwā adj. pron. *some one* (=*L*. nescio
quis).
nāthwǣr adv. *somewhere or other*, RD.
nāthwæt pron. *something or other*, RD.
nāt-hwīlc, -hwylc adj. pron. (indef.)† (*I
know not which*), *some one or other*.
nātōhwōn, nātōðæshwōn=nāteshwōn
nāðēlǣs (AO)=nāðȳlǣs
nāðer (Æ,AO,CP), nāðor (Æ)=nāhwæðer
nāðinc n. *nothing*, HL 18⁴⁸.
nāðȳlǣs (ō¹, ē²) *nevertheless*, AO.
nāuht=nāht
nāwa adv. *never*, LCD 94b. [ne, āwa]
nāwer=nāhwǣr
nāwern [=nāhwǣrn] adv. *nowhere*, WW.
nāwht, nāwiht=nāht; nāwðer=nāhwæðer
nāwuht (*CP*)=nāwiht, nāht
ne I. adv. *not, no*, Æ,CP. II. conj. *neither,
nor*, Æ,CP.
nēa-=nēah-
nēad=nīed; nēad- v. also nīed, nȳd-.
nēadclamm n. *necessity, extremity*, LPs
106²⁸.
nēadcofa m. *prison*, AN 1311.
nēadgafol n. *tax, tribute*, LL.
nēadgewuna m. *enforced custom*, WW 221⁸.
nēadgylda m. *debtor*, WW 221¹⁰.
nēadhād m. *compulsion, force*, WW 480²¹.
nēadhǣs f. *order which one must obey*, LL
12.
±nēadian I. *to compel, force, constrain, urge,
impel*, Æ. II. v. nēodian.
nēadignes f. *obligation*, OEG 2106.

nēadinga (AO), nēadlunga=nēadunga
nēadnēod f. *unavoidable necessity*, CHRD 61⁹.
nēadprin? n. *necessary equipment*, ÆP 13⁷
(or ?=nēadðing).
nēadðing n. *necessary thing*, RB 57; ÆP 13⁷?
nēadung f. *compulsion*, Æ.
nēadunga, nēadunge adv. *forcibly*, Æ.
nēadwīs *needful, fitting, due*, Æ. adv. *of
necessity*, Æ.
nēadwīsnes f. *necessity*, OEG 2396.
nēadwīte n. *inevitable punishment*, MFH
170.
nēadwraca m. *avenger by necessity*, TC 611'.
nēah I. (ē, ī) [comp. nēara, superl. nīehsta
q.v.] adj. 'NEAR' ['NAR'], 'NIGH,' *close,
AO,CP* : *late*. II. adv. 'NEAR,' 'NIGH,'
AO : *about, almost, nearly, lately, CP*. nēar
and nēar *nearer and nearer*. æt nīehstan
next, at length, finally. III. prep. w. d.
near, close to : *according to*, AO.
+nēah I.† *sufficiency, abundance*. II. (ē)
closely, seriously, BL 101³². III. pres. 3 sg.
of +nugan.
nēahbūend m. *neighbour*, RD 26².
nēahceaster f. *nearest town*, BH 52²⁷ (nēh-).
nēahcyrice f. *neighbouring church*, GD.
nēahdǣl m. *neighbourhood*, GD 71³⁰.
nēahdūn f. *neighbouring hill*, AA 20¹⁷.
nēahēa f. *neighbouring river*, AA 33⁷.
nēahēaland n. *neighbouring island*, MH 84¹⁷.
nēahfæder m. '*vicinus pater*,' GD 179⁷.
nēah-feald, -fealdlic (GD) *intimate*.
nēahfrēond (ē¹) m. *near friend, near kinsman*, GUTH 56²².
nēahgangol (w. d.) *placed near*, ÆL 23¹³¹.
nēahgebūr (ē) m. '*neighbour*,' Bf,CP,HL,
Lk.
nēahgebȳren (nēhhe-) f. *neighbour*, Lk 15⁹.
nēahgebȳrild (nēhe-) m. *neighbour*, LkL
15⁹.
nēahgehūsa (ē) m. *neighbour*, JVPs.
±neah-he, -hi(g)e (usu. +) *sufficiently* :
abundantly : *often, frequently* : *earnestly*.
nēahhebūr=nēahgebūr
+neahhelīce (nehl-) *sufficiently, frequently,
usually*, LL,GUTH.
nēahhergung f. *warring close at hand*, HL
200¹⁷⁴.
neah-hie, -hige=neahhe
+nēahian *to draw near to*, LPs 90¹⁰.
nēahlǣcan=nēalǣcan
nēahland n. *neighbourhood*, GD 69²⁸.
nēah-mǣg m. nap. -māgas *near relation*,
LL.
nēahmǣgð f. *neighbouring tribe*, BH.
nēahmann (ē¹) m. *neighbour*, BH.
nēahmunt m. *neighbouring mountain*, AA,
GD.
nēahnes (ē¹) f. *nearness, neighbourhood*, BH.

nēahnun(n)mynster *neighbouring convent,* BH254¹⁰.

nēahsibb I. adj. *related,* LL. **II.** f. *affinity, near relationship,* W.

nēahsta=nīehsta

nēahstōw f. *neighbourhood, place near,* Bo, MH.

neaht (*Met*)=niht

nēahtīd f. *approaching time,* BH290²⁹.

nēahtūn (ē) m. *neighbouring town or village,* HL199¹⁵⁷.

nēahōēod f. *neighbouring nation,* AO46,96.

nēahwæter n. *neighbouring piece of water,* AA34².

+nēahwian (ē) *to draw near, approach, cleave to,* NG.

nēahwudu m. *neighbouring wood,* GD229²⁰.

±nēalǣcan (w. d.) *to come or draw near, approach,* BH,Bl,LG; Æ,AO,CP : *be near,* GD85⁹ : *be like : cling to,* CPs136⁶. ['*nehleche*'; nēah, lǣcan]

nēalǣcung f. *approach, access,* Æ,RB. ['*nehleching*']

nēalīc (ē) *near, neighbouring.* adv. -līce *nearly, about,* Bl; CP. ['*nighly*']

nealles adv. *not, not at all, by no means,* CP.

neam=neom; **nēam-**=nēahm-

nēan adv. *from near by : close at hand, near : nearly, about.*

+nēan=+nēahwian; **neap**=hnæpp

nēar comp. of nēah, adv. *near, nearer,* AO.

+near=+ner

nēara, **nēarra** (AO), comp. of nēah, adj. *later, latter, nearer.*

neara-=nearo-; **nearo** (AO)=nearu

nearobregd f. *crafty trick,* Jul302.

nearocræft m. *skill in enclosing?* B2243.

nearofāh *intensely hostile,* B2317.

nearogrāp f. *close grasp,* Rd81⁶.

nearolīc *oppressive, straitened,* El913. adv. -līce '*narrowly,*' *closely, briefly, accurately,* Æ,CP : *strictly, stringently, oppressively : evilly.*

nearonēd f. *urgent need,* An102.

nearones f. *strait,* AO : *small space : scantiness : oppression : distress, anxiety, trouble.*

nearosearu† (u²) f. *dark cunning.*

nearosorg (u²) f. *crushing distress,* El1261.

nearoðanc (u²) m. *wickedness,* OEG.

nearoðancnes f. *wickedness,* LPs27⁴.

nearoðearf f. *dire need,* Cr69.

nearowrenc (u²) m. *evil trick,* Mod44.

neart *art not,* Bo. ['*nart*'; ne eart]

nearu I.† f? n? gs. nearu, near(o)we *strait, danger, distress, difficulty.* n. ðrōwian *to be in straits : confinement, imprisonment : prison, hiding-place.* **II.** adj. '*narrow,*' *constricted, limited, petty,* AO,B,Bo,G : *causing*

or accompanied by difficulty, hardship, oppressive, Bl,Rd : *strict, severe,* CP.

nearu-=nearo-

nearwe adv. *narrowly, closely, strictly,* B, Met : *carefully, exactly,* El; CP : *oppressively, forcibly : artfully : anxiously.* ['*narrow*']

nearwelīce=nearolīce

nearwian (±) *to force in, cramp, confine, afflict : crowd : become smaller, shrink.*

nearxnewang=neorxnawang

nēasian (VPs)=nēosian

nēat n. *animal, beast, ox,* CP,VPs; pl. *cattle,* Met,VPs. ['*neat*']

+nēat m. *companion, follower* (*esp. in war*), Chr,WW : *dependant, vassal, tenant who works for a lord,* v. LL2·427. [v. '*geneat*']

nēaten=nīeten

±nēatland n. *land of a dependant or vassal,* LL196,1¹.

+nēatmann=+nēat

+nēatriht n. *regulations as to the tenure of* '*genēatland,*' LL445,2.

+nēatscolu f. *band of comrades,* Jul684.

nēawest (AO,CP), nēawist (Æ) fm. *neighbourhood, nearness, presence : society, cohabitation.* [nēah, wesan]

nēawung f. *nearness,* MtL13²⁸.

neb(b) n. *bill, beak, beak-shaped thing,* Cp, Ph : *nose,* LL : *face, countenance, complexion,* Æ,CP. n. wið n. *face to face,* RWH138³⁸. ['*neb*']

nebb-=neb-

nebbian *to retort upon, rebuke, confront,* ÆH1·256.

nebcorn n. *pimple,* Lcd1·118'.

nebgebrǣc n. *nasal mucus,* WW.

nebsealf f. *antimony, face-powder,* OEG.

nebwlātful *barefaced, shameless,* OEG2³¹⁷.

nebwlātung f. *impudence,* OEG4306.

neb-wlite, -wlitu m. *face, countenance,* Æ.

nechebūr=nēahgebūr; **nectl-**=nihte-

ned=net(t); **nēd**=(1) nīed; (2) nēod

nēd- (A)=nēad-, nīed-, nȳd-; **nēdl**=nǣdl

nēdre (VPs), nēddre=nǣdre

nefa m. (±) *nephew,* Æ,AO : *stepson : grandson : second cousin.*

nefene f. *granddaughter : niece,* WW173³¹.

nefne=nemne; **nēfre**=nǣfre adv.

nefte f. *cat's mint,* Lcd,WW. [L. *nepeta*]

nēfugol m. *bird of prey,* Gen2158. [cp. nēobedd]

nēgan=nǣgan; **negled-**=nǣgled-

nēh=nēah; **+nehe**, +nehh(ig)e=+neahhe

nēhst, nēhsta=nīehst, nīehsta

neht=niht

neirxnawong (N)=neorxnawang

nēista=nīehsta

nele (AO,CP)=nelle (Æ) pres. 1, 3 sing., nelt=pres. 2 sg. of nellan. [v. '*will*']

nellan=*nyllan

nem-nan, -nian (±) *to name, call, Bl,Bo, Lcd,MkL*; Æ,AO,CP : *enumerate : address, speak to : nominate : invoke : mention, relate, Bo*; Æ. ['*nemn*']

nemne (A;=WS nymŏe) *conj. and prep. unless, except, save, only.*

nemnian=nemnan

nemni(g)endlic *naming, nominative*, ÆGR 22¹⁰.

nemning (æ) f. *name*, ÆL 23⁸⁶⁴.

nemŏe=nymŏe

nenā (WW 252¹)=ne nā v. nā.

nēnig (KGL)=nǣnig

nēobedd† n. *corpse-bed, bed of death*, GEN, PH. [cp. *Goth.* naus]

nēod I. f. (ē, īe, ȳ) *desire, longing : zeal, earnestness : pleasure, delight.* [FTP 299] **II.**=nīed

nēode adv. (instr. of nēod) *eagerly, zealously, diligently.*

nēodfracu f. *yearning, greed*, MET 31¹⁵ (v. ES 39·335).

nēodfrēond m. *kinsman, friend*, HL 18¹⁵⁰. [nīed]

nēodful I. *zealous, earnest*, JUL 720. **II.**= nīedful

nēodhūs (NC 312)=nīedhūs

±**nēodian** (=ēa; impers. w. g.) *to be necessary, require, be required, RB.* ['*need*']

nēodlaðu f. *wish*, B 1320.

nēodlīce adv. *eagerly, carefully, zealously, diligently*, Æ : (†) *greatly*, PPs.

nēodlof n. *zealous praise*, PPs 148¹².

nēodspearuwa m. (*restless?*) *sparrow*, PPs 123⁶.

nēodðearflic *necessary*, GD 148⁶.

nēodweorðung f. *zealous honouring*, PPs 142¹¹.

neofa=nefa; **nēol**=neowol

nēo-lǣcan (VPs), -lēcan (*MtL*)=nēalǣcan

neom=ne eom (*am not*).

neoman=niman

nēomian *to sound sweetly?* WYRD 84.

nēon=nīwan

+**nēopan²**? *to engulf, overwhelm*, Ex 475.

nēor adv.=nēar

+**neorð** *contented*, Cp 544. [from Nerthus? IF 48]

neorxnawang m. *Paradise*, Æ,CP; v. A 53·337 and IF 48·267.

neorxnawanglic adj. *of Paradise*, GD 179¹.

nēosan, nēosian (Æ) *to search out, find out, inspect : (±) visit, go to : attack, visit with affliction.*

nēoslŏ m. *death*, MOD 55.

neosu=nosu

±**nēosung** f. *access : visitation, visit*, Æ.

nēotan² (usu. w. g.) *to use, have the use of, enjoy, employ.* [*Ger.* geniessen]

nēoten=nīeten

neoð-an, -ane (i) adv. *below, down, beneath, from beneath*, Æ,Bl,Bo (-on). ['*nethen*']

neoðanweard (io) adj. *lower*, WW 26⁶.

neoðe-=niðe-; **neoðon**=neoðan

neoðor, neoðor-=niðor, niðer-

neoðoweard=niðeweard; **neoðra**=niðera

nēow-=nīw-; **neowel**=neowol

nēowērno (WW 454²⁸)=nāwērn

neowol (i) *precipitous : headlong : prone, prostrate*, Æ,Bo : *obscure, deep down, abysmal.* ['*nuel*']

neowollic (i¹, e²) *profound, deep*, ÆL 7⁶⁶.

neowolnes (i¹) f. *depth, abyss, chasm*, Æ.

nēp only in phr. forðganges n. *without power of advancing?* Ex 469.

nēpflŏd m. '*neap*'-*tide, ebb, low tide, Gl,MH.*

nepte=nefte

±**ner** (ea) n. *refuge, protection*, ÆL,AO.

nēr=nēar

+**ner-ednes** (BH), -renes (GD) f. *deliverance.*

nergend m. *saviour, preserver* (Christ, God).

nergendlic *that should be preserved?* (BTs).

±**nerian** *to save, rescue, liberate*, Æ,AO,CP : *preserve, defend, protect.* [*Ger.* nähren]

neriend, nerigend=nergend

nērra=nēar(r)a

+**nerstede** m. *refuge, sanctuary*, WW 186²³.

nerung f. *guard, protection*, OEG 5395.

nerw-=nearw-, nirew-; **nerx-**=neorx-

±**nesan⁵** (usu. +) *to escape from, survive, be saved.*

nese (æ) adv. *no*, Æ,CP. [ne, sī]

ness=næss

nest I. n. '*nest*,' *MtL,Ph*; Æ : *young bird, brood.* **II.** n. *food, provisions, victuals.*

nēst, nēsta (VPs)=nīehst, nīehsta

nestan *to spin*, NG.

nestig=nihstig

nestlian *to make a nest*, LPs 103¹⁶. ['*nestle*']

nestpohha m. *wallet*, MtL 10¹⁰.

net=nett; **net-**=nyt-

neta m. *caul*, WW 266²⁰.

netan=nytan

netel, netele f. '*nettle*,' *Lcd.*

nēten (*Bo,VPs*)=nīeten

netenes=nytennes; **nētl** (*Cp*)=nǣdl

netle (*Cp*)=netele

neton=nyton

netrāp m. *snare, gin*, WW.

nett (y) n. '*net*,' *Bo,LG,WW* : *netting, network, Ex,WW : spider's web*, PPs. [*Goth.* nati]

nette (y) f. *the net-like caul*, WW.

nettgern n. *knitting yarn*, EC377¹⁴. [gearn]
+**nettian** *to ensnare*, OEG4596.
±**nēðan** *to venture on, dare, risk*, AO. [nōð]
+**nēðedlic**=+niededlic
+**nēðerian**=+niðerian
nēðing f. *boldness, daring*, GU: *risk*, AO.
nēðl (A)=nædl
neurisn f. *aneurism*, LCD.
newesēoða (i¹) m. *pit of the stomach? bowels?*
GL,LCD.
nēwest=nēawest
nēxt (LWS)=niehst; **nī-**=nīg-, nīw-
nic, nicc adv. *not I* (=no). [ne, ic]
niccan *to say 'no,' refuse*, KC6·201⁶.
nicor (e²) m. nap. nicras *water-sprite, sea-monster, B,Bl: hippopotamus, walrus, Nar.*
['*nicker*']
nicorhūs n. *sea-monster's dwelling*, B1411.
nīd=nīed; **nīd-**=nēad-, nīed-, nȳd-
nīed I. (ē, ēa, ēo, ī, ȳ; see NED) fn. '*NEED,*' *necessity, compulsion, duty, AO*; CP : *errand, business, Æ : emergency, Æ : hardship, distress, difficulty, trouble, pain, AO : force, violence : what is necessary : inevitableness : fetter*, DEOR5 : *name of the rune for* **n. II.**=nēod
nīed- v. also nēad-, nȳd-.
nīedan (ē, ī, ȳ) *to compel, force, urge, press*, Æ,Bo,Bl,LG,VHy; AO,CP. ['*need*']
nīedbād (ē, ȳ) f. *toll, exaction, blackmail : bodily torment*, ES49·350.
nīedbādere (ē) m. *toll-collector*, TC29¹⁰.
nīedbehǣfdlic *necessary*, BH396²⁴.
nīedbehǣfednes (ē¹) f. *necessity*, Æ.
nīedbehǣfnes (ȳ¹) f. *requisite*, ÆL30⁸.
nīedbehēfe (y¹) *needful, necessary*, Æ.
nīedbe-hof (Æ), -hoflic (BH) (ȳ) *necessary*.
nīedbeðearf (y³) *necessary*, CP7⁷.
nīede, nīedes (ēa, ēo, ī, ȳ) adv. (instr. and gs. of nīed) *of need, needs, necessarily, compulsorily*, CP.
+**nīededlic** (ē) *compulsory*, BH62²³(v.l.).
nīedenga, nīedunga adv. *necessarily, by force, forcibly*, CP.
nīedfaru f. *compulsory journey, death*, OET149.
nīedful (ēo) *needful*, CM377.
nīedhǣmed (ē, ȳ) n. *rape*, LL.
nīedhīernes (ē¹, ē²) f. *slavery*, DR6⁵.
nīedhūs (ēo) *needed room*, CHRD21¹⁸.
nīedling m. *slave*, AO : *captive*, GD : *sailor*, BH.
nīedmicel (ē) *urgent*, BL233¹¹? (MS med-).
nīednǣm f. *seizure*, BH,LL.
nīedscyld f. *moral necessity*, CP57⁶.
nīedsibb (ēa) f. *relationship*, OEG,WW.
nīedðearf I. f. *need, necessity, compulsion, force*, CP : *distress : want, thing needed.*
II. adj. *necessary.*

nīedðearflic (ē, ēa, ȳ) *necessary, useful.* adv. -līce, ÆGR,GD.
nīedðearfnes (ēa, ē, ȳ) f. *need, necessity : compulsion : trouble : time of need*, EPs9²².
nīedðēow (ē, ȳ) m. *slave*, LL,W.
nīedðrafung f. *reproof*, CP297²².
nīedwǣdla m. *poor wretch*, GEN929.
nīehst (ē) **I.** adv. (superl. of nēah) *most nearly, in closest proximity : last (in time)*, Bl,Gen. **II.** adj. *latest, last, Æ : nearest*, '*NEXT*,' CP,Chr. æt nīehstan *at last, next.*
nīehsta mf. *closest friend*, CP : (±) *neighbour, MkL,VPs : next of kin, LL.* ['*next*']
nieht (CP)=niht
±**nīer-wan**, -wian (i, y) *to confine, repress : beset, rebuke, chasten.* [v. '*narrow*']
nīeten (ē, ēo, i, ȳ) n. *small animal, beast, cattle, Bo,Lcd,VPs*; AO,CP. ['*neten*'; nēat]
nīetencynn n. *kind of animal*, Æ.
nīetenlic (ē, ȳ) *animal, brutish*, Bo35²⁸. adv. -līce *like an animal*, W55¹⁶.
nīetennes (ȳ) f. *brutishness*, Æ.
nieðemest=niðemest; **nieðer**=niðer
nīewe=nīwe
nīfara (nīw-) m. *newcomer, stranger*, PPs38¹⁵.
nifol *dark, gloomy.* [=neowol]
nift f. *niece, BH,Ep,TC : granddaughter : step-daughter.* ['*nift*']
nīg-=nīw-; **nigan**=nigon; **nige-**=nigo-
nīgecyrred *newly converted*, OEG3447.
nīgefara=nifara
nīgehalgod *newly consecrated (of a king), newly crowned*, ÆL18³²⁶.
nīgehwyrfed *newly converted*, ÆL5¹²⁶.
nigend(e) (KC)=nigoða
nīghworfen *newly converted*, ÆH2·130'.
nigon (e²) '*nine*,' Bf,Bl,Chr,Ct,G; AO,CP.
nigonfeald '*nine-fold*,' ÆGr.
nigongylde *entitled to nine-fold compensation*, LL470,7.
nigonnihte *nine days old*, ANS129·22.
nigontēoða '*nineteenth*,' Chr,MH : '*ninetieth*,' OEG2521 (nigen-).
nigontīene (ȳ³) '*nineteen*,' Bf,Men.
nigontig '*ninety*,' Lk; CP.
nigontȳnlic *containing the number nineteen*, BH470²⁰.
nigonwintre *nine years old*, AO186¹⁰.
nigoða (y) '*ninth*,' Bl,KC,LG,MH : *ninth part, Bl.*
nigoðe *ninthly*, LL181,9.
nīgslȳcod ptc. *freshly smoothed, glossy, MH* 206²⁷. [v. '*slick*']
nigun=nigon; **nīh** (KGL55²⁵)=nēah
nihold (GL), nihol=neowol
nīhst, nīhsta=niehst, niehsta
nihstig *fasting*, LCD. [ne, wist]

niht (æ, e, ea, ie, y) f. (gs. also nihtes) 'NIGHT' (often used in enumerations where mod. Eng. uses days), *darkness*, AO,CP.

niht-=nyht-

nihtbealu n. *destruction by night*, B193.

nihtbutorflēoge f. *beetle or moth which flies by night*, WW121¹³; A8·450.

nihtēage *that can see at night*, WW.

nihteald *that happened yesterday*, LL.

nihtegale (a, æ, e) f. *nightingale, Cp : nightjar.* [' *nightgale*']

nihtēge=nihtēage

nihtegesa m. *nocturnal terror*, PPs90⁵.

nihtelic=nihtlic

nihterne adv. *by night : during a night*, LCD.

nihternnes f. *night season*, LCD3·288'.

nihtes (æ) adv. (g̣s. of niht) *by night*, Æ.

nihtfeormung f. *shelter at night*, GEN2433.

nihtgenga† m. *night-goer, goblin.*

nihtgenge f. *night-prowler, hyæna*, WW.

nihtgerīm† n. *number of nights.*

nihtgild n. *night sacrifice or service*, GL.

nihtglōm m? *gloom of night*, Gu916.

nihthelm† m. *shades of night.*

niht-hræfn, -hrefn, -hremn m. *night-raven, night-jar*, GL,Ps.

nihthrōc m. *night-raven*, LPs101⁷.

nihthwīl f. *space of a night*, W147⁹.

+nihtian *to become night, grow dark*, NC295.

nihtlang *lasting through the night*, Æ. adv. -langes, Æ.

nihtlic *nocturnal, of the night, at night*, Æ, CP.

nihtnihstig (ea¹, e²) *having fasted for a night*, LCD.

nihtremn=nihthræfn

nihtrest f. *couch*, GEN2863.

nihtrīm=nihtgerīm

nihtsang m. *compline : book of service for compline*, Ct.

nihtscada *night-shade (plant)*, WW135³ (v. MP24·217).

niht-scūa† m., gs. -scū(w)an *shades of night.*

nihtslǣp m. *night's sleep*, ÆL23⁴⁴².

nihtsum=nyhtsum

nihtwacu f. *night-watch*, Seaf7. [' *nightwake*']

nihtwæcce f. ' *night-watch,' vigil, Lk.*

nihtwaru f. *clothing for night*, RB90⁴.

nihtweard m. *guardian at night*, Ex116.

nihtweorc n. *deed done at night*, B827.

nihō (MP1·613) pres. 3 sg. of nēahwian.

nihwyrfed (OEG3138)=nīgehwyrfed

nīlǣred *newly initiated*, OEG3138.

nile=nyle, pres. 1 sg. of *nyllan.

±niman⁴ (eo, io, y) *to take, assume, undertake, accept, receive, get, obtain : hold, seize, catch, grasp, pluck up, carry off : occupy :*

adopt, appropriate : bear, carry, bring : betake oneself, go : contain : experience : suffer, tolerate : give : (+) *grasp, comprehend :* (+) *take to wife.* friÐ +n. *make peace.* hē hine genam *he collected himself, reflected.* sige n. *gain victory.* on n. *take effect*, LCD. se nimenda dǣl *the participle*, BF94²². ['NIM*']

-nimend, -nimendnes v. dǣl-n.

niming f. *action of taking, LkL.* [' *nimming*']

nimÐe=nymÐe; niol=neowol

nīow-=nēow-

nip? sb. *rope*, GPH399⁴⁵¹.

+nip *darkness, mist, cloud, obscurity*, Æ.

±nīpan¹† *to grow dark, obscure.*

+nipful *dark, gloomy*, ES39·347.

nirewett (nirw-) n. *narrowness : narrow place, defile, pass*, AO : *hardness of breathing.*

nirwan=nierwan

nirwÐ (=ie) f. *prison house*, WW399⁵.

nis (Æ,Bo,VPs)=ne is (*is not*). [' *nis*']

nisēoÐa=newesēoÐa

nīsoden ptc. *newly-boiled*, OEG326 (=nīw-).

nistan (VPs), nistian (SPs) *to build nests.* [' *nest*']

nistig=nihstig

nist-lan (PPs), -lian (EPs) (y) *to build nests.* [' *nestle*']

nit-=nyt-; nīten=nīeten

niton (Bo,RG)=nyton; v. nytan. [' *niten*']

niÐ n. *abyss*, SAT634?

niÐ m. *strife, enmity, attack, war : evil, hatred, spite, Bl,Cr,VPs*; AO,CP : *oppression, affliction, trouble, grief*, AO. [' *nith*']

niÐan=neoÐan

niÐan *to envy, hate*, GD117⁵.

niÐÐas=niÐÐas

niÐcwalu f. *violent death, destruction*, CR1258.

niÐcwealm m. *violent death*, PPs77⁵⁰.

niÐdraca m. *hostile dragon*, B2273.

niÐemest (Bo,Bl) v. niÐera.

niÐer (eo, io, y) adv. *below, beneath, down, downwards, B,Bo*; AO,CP. [' *nether*']

niÐera (eo, y) (comp.) adj. niÐemest, nyÐemest (superl.; positive not found) *lower, under, lowest, Bl,Bo,VPs,WW*; CP. [' *nether*']

niÐerāscūfan (ēo⁴) *to push down*, Æ.

niÐerāstīgan¹ *to descend*, Æ,CP.

niÐerbogen ptc. *bent down*, KC4·72¹.

niÐerdǣl m. *lower part*, PPs138¹³. [v. ' *nether*']

niÐere adv. *below, down, low down, Bo,Cr.* [' *nether*']

niÐerecg f. *lower edge*, KC.

niÐerflōr f. *lower story*, GD170¹⁷.

niðergán (y¹) *to descend*, Æ.

niðergang (y) m. *descent*, Lcd 3·246⁶. [v. '*nether*']

niðerheald *bent downwards*, Met 31²³.

niðerhrēosende (y) *falling down*, Æ.

niðerhryre (y¹) m. *downfall*, Sc 229¹².

±**niðerian** (e, y) *to depress, abase, bring low, oppress*, Jud,Lk,VPs; AO,CP : *accuse* : *condemn.* +nyðred *ignominious*, ÆL 23b¹⁴. ['*nither*']

+**niðerigendlic** (y) *deserving condemnation*, Sc 162¹⁸.

niðerlecgung (y) f. *deposition, entombment*, CM 421.

niðerlic *low, low-lying, inferior, lowly*, CP.

niðernes (y) f. *deepness, bottom*, BH 212²¹.

niðeronwend *downwards*, GD.

niðerra=niðera

niðerscēotende (y) *rushing downwards*, OEG.

niðerscyfe m. *rushing downwards, descent*, HGL 468.

niðersíge (y¹) m. *going down*, LPs.

niðerstígan=niðerāstīgan

niðerstíge (y¹) m. *descent*, RB. [v. '*nether*']

niðerstígende *descending*, RB. [v. '*nether*']

niðertorflan *to throw down*, GPH 390.

±**niðerung** (y) f. *humiliation, abasement, downthrow, condemnation*, BH,LG,OEG; Æ. ['*nither*']

niðerweard adj. *directed downwards.* adv. -weardes, Æ,OEG,RG. ['*netherward(s)*']

niðeweard *situated beneath, low, nethermost*, Æ,Ph. ['*netheward*']

niðful *envious, quarrelsome, ill-disposed, evil*, Æ. ['*nithfull*']

niðfullice *maliciously*, ÆH 1·46'.

niðgæst† (y²) m. *hostile alien, fell demon*.

niðgetēon n. *attack*, Gen 2068.

niðgeweorc n. *evil deed*, B 683.

niðgrama m. *anger, malice*, W 180⁹.

niðgrim† *fierce, hostile*, B,PPs.

niðgripe m. *fierce grasp*, B 976? [or ?nȳd-]

niðheard† (and EPs 27⁴) *bold, brave in battle*.

niðhell f. *hateful hell*, HL 15¹⁵⁰.

niðhete† m. *hostility, evil intent* : *affliction, torment* : *foe*, An 833?

niðhycgende† *evil-scheming*.

niðhýdig (ē²) *valorous*, B 3165.

niðig *envious, malicious*, OEG p 224n.

niðing m. *wretch, villain, coward, outlaw*, Chr,LL. ['*nithing*']

+**niðla†** m. *enemy* : *enmity, fierceness* (?+niðle).

niðlice adv. *abjectly*, OEG 744.

niðloca m. *place of torment*, Hell 64.

niðor=niðer

niðplega m. *battle, fight*, An 414.

niðr-=niðer-

niðsceaða m. *foe, persecutor*, Rd 16²⁴.

niðscipe m. *wickedness*, LPs 7¹⁰.

niðsele m. *hall of conflict*, B 1513.

niðsynn f. *grievous sin*, Sat 180.

niððas† mpl. *men*.

niðweorc n. *battle*, †Chr 973.

niðwracu† f. *severe punishment*.

niðwundor n. *dire wonder, portent*, B 1365.

níwan (ēo) adv. *newly, lately*, Æ,AO.

níwanácenned *new-born*, MH 170¹².

níwancumen (WW)=níwcumen

níwane=níwan

níwbacen (nīg-) *newly baked*, Jos 9¹².

níwcend *new-born*, BH 144²³ (nīc-).

níwcilct *newly whitewashed*, AO 286³⁰.

níwcumen (nī(g)-) *new-comer, neophyte*, RB.

níwe (ēo, íe) I. (nīg-, nī-, in compounds) adj. '*NEW*,' *fresh, recent, novel, unheard of, untried, inexperienced*, Æ,AO; CP. níwan stefne *again*. II. adv. (Bl)=níwan. ['*new*']

níwel=neowol

níwerne (ȳ) *tender*, ÆH 1·566⁵.

níwesēoða=newesēoða

níwian *to renew, restore*, Chr,El,Lcd. ['*new*']

níwiht=náht

níwlic (ȳ) *fresh.* adv. -líce *lately, recently*, Æ,AO,Ps. ['*newly*']

níwlinga (ēo) *anew*, GD 266²⁸.

níwnes (ēo, ío) f. '*newness*,' *novelty*, BH, Lcd.

níwol=neowol

níwtyrwed *newly tarred*, B 295.

níwung f. *rudiment*, OEG 914.

níwunga (eo) adv. *newly, anew*, An,NG.

nixtnig (RB 138³)=nihstig

nó (CP)=ná

noctern m? n? *nocturn* (religious service), CM 220⁵⁶¹. [L.]

+**nóg**, +**nóh** I. adj. '*enough*,' *sufficient, abundant*, An,Bo,RB; CP : *much, many.* II. adv. *sufficiently*, Bo : *fully, quite, abundantly*, Bo.

+**nógian** *to be abundant*, NC 345.

nóh-=náh-

nolde (Æ) v. *nyllan* and '*will.*'

nom pret. 3 sg. of niman.

nom-, nome-=nam-

non m. *title of senior monks*, RB.

nón fn (m. RB 73¹⁴) *the ninth hour* (=3 p.m.), B,BH,Lcd : *nones* (service held at the ninth hour), RB,WW. tō nōnes *till three o'clock.* ['*noon*'; L. nona (hora)]

nónbelle f. *noon-bell*, LL (436').

nóngereord n. *meal after nones, dinner*, RB 74⁸.

nónhring m. *ringing of the noon-bell*, Tf 114¹⁴.

nōnmete m. *afternoon meal, Sol,WW.*
['*noonmeat*']

nonne=nunne

nōnsang m. *service at* 3 *p.m., nones,* ÆP.

nōntīd f. *ninth hour, Æ,Bl.* ['*noontide*']

nōntīma m. *ninth hour,* Btk216³¹.

norð I. adj. comp. norð(er)ra, superl. norðmest *northern,* AO. II. adv. comp. norðor *northwards, Chr,Met* : *in the north,* '*north,*' *AO,B,Bl.*

norðan adv. *from the north,* AO. be...
norðan prep. (w. d.) *north of,* AO.

norðanēastan adv. *from the north-east, north-easterly,* AO.

norðanēastanwind m. *north-east wind,* WW.

Norð(an)hymbre mp. *Northumbrians, Chr* : *Northumbria.* ['*Northumber*']

norðanweard *northward,* Bl,Chr.

norðanwestan adv. *from the north-west, north-westerly,* AO.

norðanwestanwind m. *north-west wind,* WW 8¹⁰.

norðanwind m. *north wind,* Bo,WW.

norðdǣl m. *north quarter, northern part, north, Æ,AO,Chr.* ['*northdeal*']

norðduru f. *north door,* Bl203.

norðēast m. (and adv.) '*north-east,*' *BC, Chr.*

norðēastende m. *north-east end,* AO14¹⁴.

norðēasthyrne f. *north-east corner,* LV71.

norðēastlang *extending north-eastwards,* AO.

norðēastrodor m. *north-east quarter,* BH 424²⁰.

norðefes f. *northern border,* KC5·221².

norðemest=norðmest

norðende m. *northern quarter,* Chr,Met.

norðerne '*northern,*' *Northumbrian, Scandinavian, Æ,Chr,Met.*

norðerra (*BC,Chr*) comp. adj. v. norð. ['*norther*']

norðeweard adj. *northward, north,* AO.

norðfolc n. *northern folk* : *people of Norfolk.*

norðgemǣre n. *northern limit,* AO10'.

norðheald *inclined northwards,* BC2·246'.

norðhealf f. *north side, north, AO,Bl.* ['*northhalf*']

norðhere m. *army from the north,* Chr910a.

norðhylde f. *north slope,* KC3·418'.

Norðhymbre=(1) Norðanhymbre; (2) Norðhymbrisc

Norðhymbrisc *Northumbrian,* Æ (SR15⁵⁸).

norðhyrne f. *north corner,* KC3·449²⁰.

norðland n. *northern land or shore, AO,Chr.* ['*northland*']

norðlang *north-along,* KC.

norðlanu f. *north lane,* Ct.

norðlēode mp. *northern folk, Angles,* LL.

norðlic *northern,* WW361¹.

Norðmann m. *dweller in the north, Scandinavian, Æ,AO,Chr.* ['*Northman*']

norðmest (*AO,Met*) superl. of norð adj. and adv. ['*northmost*']

norðor (*AO*) v. norð. ['*norther*']

norðportic m. *north porch,* BH106².

norðra v. norð.

norðrihte (y; AO17), -rihtes (KC3·450⁵) *direct northwards, due north.*

norðrodor m. *northern sky,* Gu1253.

norðryhte=norðrihte

norðsǣ f. *northern sea, Bristol Channel, Chr* : *Baltic,* '*North Sea,*' *Æ.*

norðscēata m. *northern point, promontory,* AO28³.

norðsciphere m. *Danish fleet,* Chr980c.

norððēod f. *northern people,* BH50¹².

norððunor m. *thunder from the north,* ES 39·351.

Norð-wēalas, -wālas mp. *North Welsh* (*i.e. not Cornish*) : *Wales.*

Norðwēalcynn n. *inhabitants of* (*North*) *Wales,* Chr.

norðweard adj. and adv. *north,* '*northward,*' *Chr; AO.*

norðweardes adv. '*northwards,*' *Chr.*

norðweg m. *a way leading northwards,* Ex 68 : *Norway.*

norðwest adv. '*north-west,*' *AO,BC.*

norðwestende m. *north-west end,* AO.

norðwestgemǣre m. *north-west boundary,* AO8³¹.

norðwind m. *north wind,* WW378⁸.

nōse† f. *ness, promontory,* B.

nosgrisele (WW427)=nosugrisle

nosle (*WW*153)=nostle

nostle f. *fillet, band, CP,WW.* ['*nostel*']

nos-ðirl, -ðyr(e)l, -terl (*WW*) n. '*nostril,*' *Æ,Lcd.*

nosu f. gds. nosa, nose '*nose,*' *Æ,Chr, CP.*

nosugrisle f. *nose-gristle,* WW290³⁰

nōt m. *mark, note,* Bf182²⁴. [*L.* nota]

nōtere m. *scribe, writer,* OEG2846. [*L.*]

nōteðæshwōn=nāteshwōn

notgeorn *industrious,* W72⁹. [nēotan]

±notian I. *to enjoy* : *use, employ, Bo,RB, WW; Æ,CP* : *discharge an office.* ['*note*'] II. (+) *note,* Mt p12².

notu f. *enjoyment, use, advantage, utility, AO,RB* : *employment, office, discharge of a duty, Æ,RB; CP.* ['*note*'; nēotan]

notwierðe (u²) *useful,* ANS129·18.

notwrītere m. *one who makes notes, scribe,* WW451³⁵.

nōð† f. *daring, boldness* : *booty, plunder* (GK), Wh28?

nōðer (*CP*)=nāhwæðer. ['*nother*']

nōwend m. *shipmaster, sailor,* OEG.

nōwĕr=nāhwǣr
nōwiht (CP,VPs) (u², y²)=nāht. ['nought']
nōwðer (BC)=nāhwæðer. ['nouther']
nū I. adv. 'now,' at present, at this time, immediately, Æ,AO,Bl,VPs; CP : very recently, Bf,Bo : introducing commands, requests (Bl,Cr,Ps) and arguments (Æ,Bo, CP). nū gēn still. nū ᵹīet as yet, still. nū ðā now, already, Æ ('nowthe'). II. conj. now that, inasmuch as, because, since, when, Bl,Bo,VPs; AO,CP. III. interj. lo! behold! come! Æ. nū lā now.
+nugan* swv. impers. pres. 3 sg. +neah to suffice, not to lack.
nūhwīlum now-a-days, Bo 123⁶.
numen I. pp. of niman. II. 'vulsio,' MkL p 2¹⁷ (v. A 16·74).
numol (æ¹, e², u²) 'capax,' holding much, quick at learning, ÆGr,WW : 'mordax,' biting, CHRD 74²⁰. ['nimble']
nūna adv. now, WW 254²⁴.
nunfǣmne f. nun, GD 50,340. [v. 'nun']
nunhīred m. nunnery, TC 232⁶.
nunlīf n. life of a nun, GD 199¹⁶.
nun(nan)mynster n. convent, nunnery, Ct, GD.
nunne f. 'nun,' Æ,BH : pagan priestess, vestal, AO.
nunscrūd n. nun's dress, TC 538¹².
nuseōða=neweseōða; nūðā v. nū.
nuton (DR)=nyton (v. nytan).
nybðe (VHy)=nymðe
+nycled (GL)=+cnycled
nȳd I.=nīed. II.=nēod
nȳd-=nēad-, nīed-
nȳdbebod n. command, CREAT 72.
nȳdboda m. messenger of evil? Ex 474.
nȳdbrice (ē) m. requirement, need, ÆH 2·144'.
nȳdbysgu f. toil, trouble, RIM 44.
nȳdbysig distressed, JUL 423.
nȳdcleofa† m. prison, EL,JUL.
nȳdcosting f. affliction, GU 1126.
nȳddǣda m. one who acts under compulsion, LL 36,26.
+nȳdenlic compulsory, BH 62²³B.
nȳdfara m. fugitive, exile, Ex 208.
nȳdgedāl† n. forced dissolution, death, GU.
nȳdgenga m. wretched wanderer, DA 633.
nȳdgestealla m. comrade in need, B 882.
nȳdgewald m. tyranny, CR 1451.
nȳdgild n. exaction, tribute, W 162¹¹.
nȳdgrāp f. (RIM 73), nȳdgripe m. (B 976) coercive grip.
nȳdhǣmedre m. adulterer, OEG.
nȳdhǣmestre (ē) f. mistress? concubine? adulteress? OEG 4451.
nȳdhelp mf. help in trouble, LL (278²).
nȳdlic (ēo) necessary, Sc.

±nȳd-mǣg m., -māge f. blood-relation, cousin, LL.
nȳdmægen (ē¹) n. force, DR 117¹³.
nȳdnǣman to force, ravish, LL.
nȳdnes f. necessity, LL (158¹⁰).
nȳdnima (ē) m. one who takes by force, NG.
nȳdniman³ (ēa) to take by force, abduct, LL 360, 73, 2.
nȳdnimend (ē¹) f. rapine, MtR 23²⁵.
nȳdnimu (ē) f. rapine, forcible seizure, DR.
nȳdnimung f. rapine, abduction, WW 116²⁹.
nȳdriht n. duty, office : due, tribute, LL.
nȳdðēowetling m. bond-slave, TC 628¹³.
nȳdðēowigan to reduce to servitude, exact service from (an ecclesiastical establishment), LL 381,21.
nȳdwracu† f. violence, distress.
nȳdwrǣclīce violently, ÆL 23b⁴⁰⁴.
nȳdwyrhta m. involuntary agent, LL.
+nyhe=+neahhe
nȳhst=nīehst; nyht=niht
+nyht fn. abundance, fulness, sufficiency, CP. [+nugan]
+nyhtful abundant, plentiful, WW 40³⁴.
+nyhtlīce abundantly, WW 3².
±nyhtsum abundant, abounding : (+) satisfied, contented. adv. -līce, VPs.
+nyhtsumian to suffice, abound, Æ.
+nyhtsumnes f. abundance, plenty, VPs.
+nyhtsumung (-ihð-) f. abundance, RPs 77²⁵.
+nyhð (W 1)6²¹)=+nyht?
nyllan* anv. pret. nolde to be unwilling, Æ, CP; AO : refuse, prevent, PPs 5⁸. ['NILL*'; ne, willan]
nyman=niman; -nyme v. fore-n.
nymne=nemne
nymðe (e, i) conj. unless, except : nor, EPs 130¹.
+nyp=+nip
nypel m. trunk (of an elephant), Æ (4²⁸⁶).
nȳr=nēar=nēah adv.
nyrgend=nergend; nyrōra=norðerra
±nyrwan, nyrwian=nierwan
nyrwett=nirewett; nys=nis=ne is
nysse, nyste (Bo,Bl,VPs)=ne wisse, ne wiste v. nytan. ['nist']
nystlan=nistlan; nyt=(1) nytt; (2) nett
+nȳt pres. 3 sg. of +nīedan.
nytan (e, i) anv. pres. 1, 3 sg. nāt, 2 nāst, pl. nyton, pret. nyste, nysse not to know, to be ignorant, Æ,AO,CP. [ne, witan]
nyten ignorant, ÆH 1·62¹⁴. [ne, witan]
nȳten (Lcd)=nīeten
nytende adv. ignorantly, Æ.
nytendnes=nytennes
nytenlic ignorant, ÆH 2·134².
nytennes (e, i) f. ignorance, laziness, ignominy, Æ : unknown state, ÆL 33²⁶⁰.

nytlic *useful, profitable*, AA,LCD. [*Ger.* nützlich] adv. -līce.

nytlicnes f. *utility*, LCD 1·314[8].

nytnes f. *use, benefit, convenience*, BH,GD.

nyton v. nytan.

nytt I. f. *use, utility, advantage*, AO,CP : *duty, office, employment*, B : *supervision, care*, GD 180[28]. **II.** adj. *useful, beneficial, helpful, profitable*, AO,CP. [nēotan]

nytte=nette

±**nyttian** *to enjoy, use*, Lcd : *eat*. ['*nutte*']

nyttnes=nytnes

nytto=nytt I.

nyttol *useful*, LCD 32b.

nyttung (i) f. *profit, advantage*, WW 116[37].

nytu (*MtR* 7[16])=hnutu

nytun=nyton=ne witon

nytweorð-=nytwierð-

nyt-wierðe (CP), -wirðe, -wyrðe (Æ) *useful, profitable*.

nytwierðlic *useful, profitable*. adv. -līce, CP.

nytwierðnes (eo, y) f. *utility*, WW.

nytwurð-, nytwyrð-=nytwierð-

nyðan=neoðan

nyðe-, nyðer-=niðer-, niðr-; **nȳw-**=nīw-

nywel, nywol=neowol; **nȳxt**=nīehst

nyxtnig (LCD)=nihstig

O

o=on; **ō** (N)=ā; **ob**, ob- (K)=of, of-

obet (*Cp,Ep*)=ofet; **obst** (Cp 217 E)=ofost

oc=ac

ōc pret. 3 sg. of acan.

ōcon pret. pl. of acan.

ōcusta m. *armpit*, GL.

ōden (o?) f. *threshing-floor*, AS,Sc.

ōdencole *hollow serving as a threshing-floor*, EC 121[2].

+**ōdon**=+ēodon; **oe-**=a-, e-, ē-

oeg (N)=woeg=weg

ōeg-hwēr, -hwelc (Cp)=ǣg-hwǣr, -hwilc

oeht- (N)=ēht-; **oembeht** (Cp)=ambiht

oemseten (=ymb-) f. *shoot, slip?* (Swt), *row (of vines)?* (BT), Cp 534A.

oexen=exen v. oxa.

of I. prep. w. d. 'OF,' *from, out of*, Æ,AO, etc. : *among, concerning, about*, AO : *by*, Chr : *derived from, made of, belonging to*, Æ,AO,CP. **II.** adv. '*off*,' *away, absent*, Bl, Chr,LL,Mt.

of-=æf-

ofācēapian *to buy off*, LL 122,74.

ofāceorfan[3] *to cut or prune off*, AO,CP.

ofācsian *to find out by asking, be informed, hear of, learn*, Æ.

ofādōn anv. *to pull out, tear out*, LL 86,70[74] : *leave out, except*, LL 182,10.

ofādrincan[3] *to drain*, Æ : *quench*, AO.

ofādrygan *to dry off, wipe off*, CP 71[11]

ofæt=ofet

ofǣte? f. *food*, HEX 194.

ofāhēawan[7] *to cut off*, ÆL 29[293].

ofāniman *to take away*, GUTH 19[26].

ofāsceacan[6] *to shake off*, CM 993 : *excuse*.

ofāsciran (e, y) *to cut off*, LL 68,35[5].

ofāsēoðan[2] *to purge, purify*, BH 288[9].

ofāslēan[6] *to smite off*, CHR.

ofāsnīdan *to cut off*, LCD.

ofāteon[2] *to pull out, withdraw*, CP.

ofāweorpan *to cast aside, throw off* (or ? two words), VH 17.

ofāxian (Æ)=ofācsian

ofbēatan[7] *to beat to death, kill*, AO.

ofblindian *to blind*, JnLR 12[40].

ofcalan[6] *to chill, make or grow cold*, Æ,W.

ofclipian *to obtain by calling, call for*, Æ.

ofcuman[4] *to spring from, be derived from*, Æ.

ofcyrf m. *a section, cutting*, Æ : *amputation*, Æ.

ofdæl *inclined (downwards)*, Bo 53[14].

ofdæle (e[2]) n. *decline, declivity, descent, abyss*. CP.

ofdōn anv. *to put out, put off, take off (clothes)*.

ofdrǣdan[7] (but wk. pp. ofdrǣdd) *to fear, be afraid, terrified*, Æ,CP.

ofdrincan *to intoxicate*, LL.

ofdruncnian *to get drunk (on)*, CHRD 74[7].

ofdūne adv. *down*, AO,CP.

ofdūneheald adv. *directed downwards* (Swt).

ofdūneonwend *downwards*, GD 24[28].

ofdūnesettan *to set down*, VHy.

ofdūnestīgan[1] *to descend*, VPs.

ofdūneweard(es) adv. *downwards*, GD.

ofdūnrihte *downwards*, MFH 170.

ofe-=ufe-

ofearmian *to be pitiful*, RSPs 36[22],76[9].

ofearmung f. *compassion*, BLPs 102[4].

ofēhtan *to persecute*, RPs 43[17].

ofelēte=oflǣte

ofen m., gs. ofnes *furnace*, MH,MtLR : '*oven*,' Æ.

ofenan=ufenan

ofenbacen *baked in an oven*, Æ.

ofen-raca m., -racu f. *oven-rake*, WW.

ofer I. prep. [w. d. (rest) and a. (motion)] 'OVER,' *beyond, above, upon, in, across, past*, Æ,AO,CP. ofer bæc *backwards, back : throughout : against, in contravention of, contrary to, beyond*, AO,CHR : (*time*) *after, through, during, at the end of*, AO, Chr : *more than : in addition to, besides, beyond*. **II.** adv. *above, on high : to or on the other side*, AO : *from side to side, across*, AO : *beyond, above* (*quantity*).

ōfer (o²) m. (gs. ōfres) *border, margin, edge* : *brink, river-bank, sea-shore, Æ,B,Lcd*; AO. ['*over*'; v. Mdf]

oferæt m. *gluttony, feasting, excess, CP*; Æ : *feast.* ['*overeat*']

oferǣte *gluttonous*, RB17¹⁵.

oferāhebban=oferhebban

oferāwrit-=oferwrit-

oferbæcgetēung f. *tetanus*, WW112²⁰.

oferbebēodan² *to rule*, WW178³⁷.

oferbecuman⁴ *to supervene*, CM133,1060.

ofer-bēon anv. pres. 3 pl. -sind *to be over, command*, CM112; WW178³⁷.

oferbīdan¹ *to outlast, outlive, TC.* ['*overbide*']

oferbiternes (y³) f. *excessive bitterness, SPs.* ['*overbitterness*']

oferblica m. *surface*, OET181⁴⁴.

oferblīðe *too light-hearted*, CP.

oferbrǣdan *to spread over, suffuse, be spread over, overshadow, cover over, CP*; Æ. ['*overbrede*']

oferbrǣdels m. *outside, surface, covering* : *coverlet, veil, garment, Æ,CP* : *cerecloth*, MFH153.

oferbrāw m. *eye-brow*, Lcd3·188⁵. [brǣw]

oferbrecan⁴ *to transgress, violate*, AO.

oferbrēdan=oferbregdan

oferbrēdels (KGL)=oferbrǣdels

oferbregdan³ *to draw over, cover, overspread* : *be covered over, show a film over.*

oferbrū f. *eye-brow*, GL.

oferbrycgian (i³) *to span as by a bridge, Æ.* ['*overbridge*']

ofercǣfed *overlaid with ornament*, GPH394.

oferceald *excessively cold*, Run11. ['*overcold*']

ofercīdan *to chide sharply*, EPs,LL.

ofercīdung f. *chiding, reproof*, EPs149⁷.

ofercierr (e) m. *passing over*, MtL1¹¹.

ofercierran (e) *to cross over*, LkL16²⁶.

oferclif n. *steep place, overhanging cliff*, WW480².

oferclimban³ *to climb over*, AO134¹³. ['*overclimb*']

oferclipian *to cry out*, LkL23¹⁸.

ofercostung f. *great tribulation*, JnL16³³.

ofercræft m. *fraud*, LL(166²⁰).

ofercuman⁴ *to overcome, subdue, compel, conquer, AO,B,Lcd,WW*; CP : *obtain, attain, reach, overtake, BH,Cp,Jud,WW.* ['*overcome*']

ofercwealm *great mortality*, A3·113.

ofercyme m. *arrival*, BH436²⁸.

ofercymend (mm) m. *assailant*, LkL.

ofercȳðan *to outdo by preponderance of oaths*, v. LL2·689.

oferdōn anv. *to* '*overdo,*' *do to excess, Æ.* oferdōne ðing *excesses*, Æ.

oferdrenc (Æ)=oferdrync

oferdrencan *to make drunk*, AO,CP : *give copiously to drink*, GEN43³⁴.

oferdrīfan¹ *to overcome, defeat, dispense, Æ, DR* : *confute, Æ* : *cover (by drifting sand)*, AO40¹ : *outvote*, LL. ['*overdrive*']

oferdrinc=oferdrync

oferdrincan³ *to drink too much, get drunk, CP,LL.* ['*overdrink*']

oferdrincere m. *drunkard*, HL12⁹⁵,¹²⁴.

oferdruncen I. n. *drunkenness*, LL. **II.** ptc. *drunk.*

oferdruncennes f. *drunkenness*, Æ,CP.

oferdrync m. *over-drinking, drunkenness, CP* : *revelry, feasting.* ['*overdrink*']

oferdyre n. *lintel*, WW280¹⁶.

ofere *over, across*, v. LV8 : *from above*, RPs.

oferēaca m. *surplus, overplus, remainder, addition, increase, Æ.*

ofereald (y) *very old*, RB61¹².

oferealdormann m. *chief officer*, BH264¹ (v.l.).

ofereall *anywhere*, BF138²¹.

oferēca=oferēaca

ofereldu (HL11⁶⁰N)=oferyldu

oferēt=oferæt

ofer-etol (CP), -eotol, -ettol *gluttonous*.

oferetolnes f. *gluttony*, CP317¹⁸.

oferfær n. *passing over*, NG.

oferfæreld n. *passage, journey over or across*, Æ,AO.

oferfǣt *too fat*, WW. ['*overfat*']

oferfæðman† *to envelop, overshadow.*

oferfaran⁶ (intr.) *to pass, cross, go over, Ps* : (tr.) *traverse, go through, penetrate, Gen,W*; Æ,AO : *come across, meet with, overtake* : *pass through, withstand, overcome.* ['*overfare*']

oferfeallan⁷ *to attack*, BL203.

oferfeng I. m. *fibula, buckle, clasp*, GL. **II.** pret. 3 sg. of oferfōn.

oferfeohtan³ *to conquer*, Æ,CP.

oferfēran *to traverse, cross, pass along, over, by, or through, Æ,AO* : *come upon, meet with.*

oferferian *to carry over, transport*, OEG3680.

oferfērnes f. *fordable place*, BH58¹.

oferfēðre *overloaded*, v. ES43·312.

oferfil=oferfyll

oferflēdan *to overflow, flood*, Lcd3·252'.

oferflēde *in flood*, Lcd3·252'.

oferflēon² *to fly over, Æ* : *flee from, yield to*, B2525.

oferflēwednes=oferflōwednes

oferflītan¹ *to overcome, beat, confute*, AO.

oferflōwan *to flow over, run over,* '*overflow,*' *AO,Lk.*

ofer-flōwed(līc)nes, -flōwen(d)nes (Æ) f. *excess, superfluity.*

ofer-flōwend (*RB*), -flōwe(n)dlic *super-fluous* : *excessive*, VH 17. ['*overflowing*'] adv -līce.

oferflōwnes f. *superfluity*, CP.

oferfōn[7] *to seize, take prisoner*, AO.

oferfrēcednes f. *oppression*, V[2]Ps 31[7].

oferfroren *frozen over*, AO.

oferfull *too full*, LPs. ['*overfull*']

oferfunden *tested*, AO 296[9].

oferfundennes f. *trial, experiment*, OEG 543.

oferfylgan *to pursue, attack*, CP.

ofer-fyll, -fyllo, -fyllu f. *surfeit, gluttony, excess*, Bo,Lcd; Æ,CP : *overplus, resulting liquor*, LCD 47a. ['*overfyll*']

oferfyllan *to cram*, RB,WW.

oferfylnes f. *surfeit, excess*, GD 339[3].

oferfyrr f. *excessive distance*, AO 24[21]. [feorr]

ofergǣgan *to transgress*, Æ.

ofergǣgednes f. *transgression*, Æ.

ofergǣgend m. *transgressor*, ÆL 30[411].

ofer-gān anv., -gangan[7] *to pass over, beyond, across, traverse, cross*, Æ,Lcd,VPs; AO, CP : *transgress, overstep, Met, MtL, Ps : overrun, overcome, overspread, conquer, Chr,Ex,Lcd,Rd*; Æ : *come upon, overtake, seize, attack, Æ,An : pass off, pass away, end, AO,CP : overreach*, CHRD 110[34]. ['*overgo*', '*overgang*']

ofergaplan *to be forgetful of, neglect*, RB 112[2].

ofergēare *old*, LCD 19a.

ofergeatu f. *oblivion*, PPs 128[6].

ofergeatul=ofergitol

ofergedrync n. *excess in drinking*, BL 99[21].

ofergedyre=oferdyre

ofergemet I. n. *excess*, AS,CP. **II.** *excessive*, VH 17 (or ? two words).

ofergēmnes f. *watching for*, NG. [gīeman]

ofergenga m. *traveller*, LCD.

ofergenihtsumian *to superabound*, Sc 131[15].

ofergeong (=gang) m. *going across*, MtK p 12[13].

ofergeot-=ofergi(e)t-

ofergēotan[2] *to pour upon, suffuse, flood, overwhelm*, Æ.

ofergeotende *forgetful*, BH 114[22]. [ofergietan]

ofer-geotol, -geottol=ofergitol

ofergesāwan=ofersāwan

ofergesettan *to set over*, CP,VPs.

ofergestondan[6] (=a[4]) *to stand over*, BH.

ofergetilian *to overcome*, ÆL 23b[185].

ofergetimbran *to erect*, BL 205.

ofergetol-=ofergitol-

ofergeðyld *intolerable state*, SOL 84[24].

ofergeweorc n. *superstructure* : *sepulchre*, Æ.

ofergewrit n. *superscription, inscription*, G, WW.

ofergietan[5] *to forget, disregard, neglect*, CP.

ofergīfre *gluttonous*, CP 177,308.

ofergildan=ofergyldan

ofergīman *to neglect, disregard*, RB,SAT.

ofergitan=ofergietan

ofer-gitol, -gittol (ea, eo, y) *forgetful*, Ps.

ofergitolian (e, eo) *to forget*, JVPs.

ofergitolnes (e, eo, y) f. *forgetfulness*, BL,Ps.

oferglenged (æ[3]) *over-adorned*, ÆPD 134[11].

oferglēsan (oe) *to write glosses over*, Jn p 188[7].

oferglīdan[1] *to glide over, traverse, pass over, overshadow*, Æ.

ofergrǣdig *too covetous*, W. ['*overgreedy*']

ofergrōwan[7] *to overgrow*, CP 336[8].

ofergumian *to neglect, disregard*, RB 113[2].

ofergyld *gilt*, Æ.

ofergyldan (i) *to encase, overlay or adorn with gold*, Æ,CP.

ofergylden *overlaid with gold*, LL 460,10.

ofergȳman=ofergīman

ofergyrd ptc. *girt*, GPH 394.

ofergytan=ofergietan

ofergytnes f. *oblivion, forgetfulness*, LkR, PPs.

oferhacele f. *hood*, LL (140[22]).

oferhangen *covered*, GD 202[19].

oferhāt *over-hot*, LCD 4a.

oferhēafod adv. *in each case*, ÆH 1·30[4].

oferhēah *very tall, lofty*, Run 26. ['*overhigh*']

oferhealdan *to overcome, overtake*, VH : '*supertenere*,' LL (198[11])?

oferhealfhēafod n. *crown of the head*, WW 156[11].

oferheargian=oferhergan

oferhebban[6] *to pass over, omit, neglect*, AO, LL; CP. ['*overheave*']

oferhebbendlic *highly exalted*, DR.

oferhelian *to cover over, conceal*, Sc; CP. ['*overhele*']

oferheling f. *covering*, Sc. [v. '*overhele*']

oferhelmian *to overshadow*, B 1364.

oferheortnes f. *vehemence of feeling*, AO 166[20].

oferhergean *to overrun, ravage*, AO,CHR.

oferhīd-=oferhygd-

oferhīeran (ēo, ȳ) *to '*overhear*,' hear*, AO : *disobey, disregard, neglect*, AO.

oferhīernes (ē, ī, ȳ) f. *neglect, disobedience* : *fine for transgression of law or legal orders* (='*superauditio*'), LL.

oferhīgd=oferhygd

oferhige? m. *pride*, PPs 87[7]. [hyge]

oferhigendlīce *daringly, presumptuously*, BYH 102[16].

oferhigian *to delude, turn the head of*, B 2766.

oferhīran (AO)=oferhīeran

oferhīwian *to transfigure* : *paint over*, NG.

oferhlæstan *to overload*, AO.

oferhlēapan[7] *to jump over, surmount, overcome*, BH : *pass over*, Lcd. ['*overleap*']

oferhlēapend m. *over-leaper*, WW 190².
oferhlēoōrian *to surpass in loudness*, AA, SoL 152¹².
oferhlēoōur *failing to hear*, PPs 93⁹.
oferhlīfan¹ (OEG), oferhlīfian (Æ,CP) *to tower over, overtop, excel, exceed, surpass*.
oferhlīfung f. *loftiness, sublimity*, GL.
ofer-hlūd, -hlȳde *clamorous, noisy*, WW. ['*overloud*'] adv. -hlūde.
oferhlȳp m. *a jump, leap* (*over something*), Bf 72,112.
oferhlyttrian *to clarify, strain*, ÆGr 222⁸.
oferhoga m. *despiser, proud man*, W.
oferhogian *to despise*, Bl,Bo. ['*overhow*']
oferhogiend m. *despiser*, RB 48⁶.
oferhogodnes f. *pride, disdain*, GD 144³.
oferholt n. *phalanx of shields*, Ex 157.
oferhrǣgan (w. d.) *to tower above?* SoL 35.
oferhrēfan *to roof over, cover*, Bl,Lcd.
oferhrēred *overthrown*, WW.
oferhrops *greediness*, WW 102¹⁹.
oferhrȳfan=oferhrēfan
oferhrȳred=oferhrēred
oferhycgean *to despise*, AO,CP.
oferhȳd=oferhygd
oferhygd (i) I. fn. *pride, conceit, arrogance*, CP : *highmindedness*, AS. II. adj. *haughty, proud*.
oferhygdgian *to be proud*, CVPs 9²³.
oferhygdig I. n. *pride*, MFH,PPs. II. adj. *haughty, proud*, Æ.
ofer-hygd(ig)līce, -hīdlīce *arrogantly*, GD.
oferhygdnes f. *excessive pride, arrogance*, VH 18.
oferhygdu f.=oferhygd I.
oferhylmend m. *dissembler*, PPs 118¹¹⁹.
oferhȳran=oferhīeran
oferhȳre *heedless, neglectful*, LL (244').
oferhyrned *having horns above*, Run 2.
oferhȳrnes f. *heedlessness, neglect, disobedience*, LL.
+**oferian** *to elevate*, HGl 428 (=uferian).
oferidyllīce *vainly, emptily*, CPs 30⁷.
ofering f. *superabundance*, Bo.
oferlād f. '*translatio*,' *solemn removal of the body or relics of a saint to a shrine*, DR 62⁹.
oferlǣdan *to oppress*, Bl : *translate*. ['*overlead*']
oferlǣfan *to leave over* : *be left over, remain*, LkLR. ['*overleave*']
oferlagu f. *cloak*, GL.
oferlecgan *to place over*, CM 899 : *overburden, surfeit*, HL 11⁹⁹; 12⁷³.
oferlēof *very dear*, Run 23.
oferlēoran *to pass over, or by* : *transgress, prevaricate*.
oferlēornes f. *transgression*, CPs 100³.
oferlibban *to survive*. ÆGr,TC. ['*overlive*']
oferlīce *excessively*, W. [v. '*overly*']

oferlīfa (y³) m. *excess*, NC 348.
oferlīfian=oferhlīfian
oferlīhtan *to light upon*, ÆL 23b⁵⁵⁸ : *excel in brightness*.
oferlīōan¹ *to pass over, sail over*, Guth,MH.
oferlufu f. *too great love*, W. ['*overlove*']
oferlyfa=oferlīfa
oferlyftlic *above the air*, NC 314.
ofermǣcga m. *very illustrious being*, Gu 664.
ofermǣgen† n. *overpowering might*.
ofermǣstan *to over-fatten*, BH (Wheloc 228').
ofermǣte *excessive, immoderate*, AO,CP. ['*overmete*']
ofermǣtlic *vast*, AO 52¹⁰.
ofermǣto=ofermētto
ofermagan swv. *to prevail*, Sc 97¹⁹.
ofermāōum m. *costly treasure*, B 2993.
ofermearcung (e³) f. *superscription*, MkL p 5¹.
ofermēde I. n. *pride*, CP. II. adj. *proud, arrogant*. [mōd]
ofermēdla m. *haughtiness, pride*, LL.
ofermēdu (CP)=ofermētto
ofermete m. *gorging, gluttony*, CP.
ofermētto f. (often in pl.) *pride*, Æ,AO, CP.
ofermicel *over-much, excessive*, AO,RB. ['*overmickle*']
ofermicelnes f. *excess*, Sc 50¹³.
ofermōd I. n. *pride, insolence*, Gen,Ma. ['*overmod*'] II. adj. *proud, overbearing, insolent*, Bl; Æ,CP.
ofer-mōdgian (CP), -mōdig(i)an *to be proud, arrogant*.
ofermōdgung f. *pride*, CP 109¹¹.
ofermōdig *proud, arrogant*, Lcd; AO. adv. -līce. [v. '*overmod*']
ofermōdignes f. *pride, haughtiness, arrogance*, Mk. [v. '*overmod*']
ofermōdlic *proud, haughty, insolent*, CP. adv. -līce.
ofermōdnes=ofermōdignes
ofernēod I. (ī³) f. *extreme need*, LL,W. II. *very necessary*, CM.
oferniman⁴ (y) *to take away, carry off, seize, ravish* : *come over*, BH 410b¹².
ofernōn fn. *afternoon* (*after* 3.0 *p.m.*), WW 175⁴⁷.
oferorn=oferarn pret. 3 sg. of oferyrnan.
oferprūt I. '*over-proud*,' *presumptuous, arrogant, haughty*, Sc. II. f. *excessive pride*, W 81'.
oferrǣdan *to read over*, Æ : *consider, infer*. ['*overread*']
oferranc *too luxurious*, W 46¹. ['*overrank*']
oferreccan *to confute, convince, convict*, CP.
oferrencu f. *extravagance*, W 46².
oferrīcsian *to rule over*, CP 119¹⁹.

oferrīdan[1] *to ride across, BH*196[8]. [*'over-ride'*]

oferrōwan[7] *to row over, Æ.*

ofersǣlic *on the other side of the sea, BH*246[3].

ofersǣlig *excessively happy, DD*246.

ofersǣlō f. *excessive pleasure, MET*5[27].

ofersǣwisc *from across the sea, foreign, LCD, MH.*

ofersāwan[7] *to sow (over), Mt*13[25]. [*'over-sow'*]

ofersċēadan[7] *to scatter over, sprinkle over, LCD*67b.

ofer-sceadian (CP), -sceadewian *to over-shadow.*

ofersceatt m. *usury, interest, MtR*25[27].

ofersċēawian *to superintend, LL.*

ofersċēawigend m. *overseer, bishop, LL.*

ofersċīnan[1] *to illuminate, BF,BL : excel (in brightness), ByH*112'.

ofersċūwian *to overshadow, MtR*17[5].

ofersēam m. *bag, LkL*12[33].

ofersēcan *to overtax, B*2686.

ofersegl m. *top-sail, WW*7[4].

oferseglian *to sail across, Mt.* [*'oversail'*]

ofersēgon=ofersāwon pret. pl. of ofersēon.

ofersendan *to transmit, ÆGR*172[13].

ofersēocnes f. *great illness, LL.*

oferseolfrian (y) *to cover over with silver, AO.*

ofersēon[5] *to see over, overlook, survey, observe, see, Bo : despise, neglect, W.* [*'over-see'*]

ofersettan *to set over, VPs : overcome, GD*347[30].

ofersittan[5] *occupy, possess, Bo, VPs : forbear, desist, refrain from, Æ,B.* [*'oversit'*]

oferslæge=oferslege

oferslǣp m. *too much sleep, LCD*1·342[13].

oferslēan[6] *to subdue, overcome, RB*32[15].

oferslege n. *lintel, Æ,BF.*

oferslop n. *loose upper garment, surplice, stole, Lcd,LkL.* [*'overslop'*]

oferslype m. *over-garment, surplice, Æ.*

ofersmēaung f. *too exhaustive consideration, CP*97[17].

ofersmītan *to smear over, LCD*67b.

ofersprǣc f. *loquacity, CP.*

ofersprǣce *talkative, tale-bearing, Æ,CP.*

ofersprǣdan *to overlay, cover, RB*84[23].

oferspreca m. *one who talks too much, OEG*28[9].

ofersprecan[5] *to say too much, LPs : be abusive.*

ofersprēce=ofersprǣce

ofersprecol *talking too much, tattling, indiscreet, CP.*

ofersprecolnes f. *talkativeness, CP*308[16].

oferstǣlan *to confute, convict, convince, Æ, CP.*

oferstæppan[6] *to 'over-step,' cross, LPs : exceed, KC.*

oferstandan[6] *to stand over, BH*308[25].

ofersteall m. *opposition, ÆH*1·534[20].

oferstealla m. *survivor, MH*210[28].

oferstellan *to jump over, BH*400[22].

ofersteppan=oferstæppan

oferstīgan[1] *to climb over, mount, scale, surmount, overcome, AO; Æ,CP : surpass, excel, exceed, BH; Æ,CP.* [*'oversty'*]

oferstige m. *astonishment, ÆL*23[555].

oferstīgendlic *superlative, ÆGR*15[18].

oferstigennes[3] *passing over, OEG*405.

oferswimman[3] *to swim over or across, B* 2367. [*'overswim'*]

oferswingan[3] *'transverberare'! GD*344[33].

oferswīðan (ȳ) wv. and sv[1] *to overpower, overcome, conquer, vanquish, Æ,AO,CP : excel, surpass.*

oferswīðe adv. *over-much, excessively, Chr.* [*'overswithe'*]

oferswīðend m. *vanquisher, ÆL*30[126].

oferswīðestre f. *'victrix,' WW*224[39].

oferswīðnes f. *pressure, distress, NG.*

oferswīðrian *to prevail, conquer, LPs,RB.*

oferswīðung f. *pressure, distress, NG.*

oferswōgan[7] *to cover, choke, BL*203[9].

oferswȳðan=oferswīðan

ofersylfrian (AO)=oferseolfrian

ofersȳman (=īe) *to overload, oppress, RB.*

ofertæl n. *odd number, LCD*1·288[8].

ofertæle *superstitious, Sc*218[10].

ofertalian *to confute, convince, RWH*3[28].

oferteldan[3] *to cover over, Ex*81.

ofertēon[2] *to draw over, cover, Æ : finish, WW*209[35].

ofertogennes f. *the condition of being covered.*

ofertrahtnian *to treat of, ÆH*1·202'.

ofertredan *to tread down, GPH.* [*'over-tread'*]

ofertrūwa m. *over-confidence, LL*180,8[7]. [*'overtrow'*]

ofertrūwian *to trust too much, CP,W.*

oferðearf f. *great need, extreme distress, W.*

oferðearfa m. *one in great need, CR*153.

oferðeccan *to cover over, hide, Æ.*

oferðencan *to think over, reflect, GD.*

oferðēon[1,3] *to excel, surpass, Æ,CP.*

oferðōht *thought over, considered, GD*316[20].

oferðrēawian (ā[3]) *'increpare,' EPs*67[31].

oferðryccednes (i) f. *pressure, CPs*31[7].

oferðrymm m. *excessive power, DD*52.

oferufa *upon, above, NG.*

oferwacian *to watch over, Æ.* [*'overwake'*]

oferwadan[6] *to wade across, AO*72[33]. [*'over-wade'*]

oferwealdan[7] *to get the better of, LL*454,7.

oferwealdend m. *over-lord, ruler, EL*1236.

oferweaxan[6] *to overgrow, overspread, Æ,Bl.* [*'overwax'*]

oferweder n. *storm, tempest, CHR*794E.

oferwelig *very rich,* NC314.

oferwenian *to be proud, become insolent or presumptuous,* Sc,GL.

oferweorc n. *sarcophagus, tomb,* Æ,OEG. ['*overwork*']

oferweorpan[3] *to throw over, overthrow,* CP, Lcd : *throw down, assault,* LL56,11[1] : *cast something over another, sprinkle : stumble?* B1543. ['*overwarp*']

oferwīgan *to overcome,* SOL299.

oferwillan[7] *to boil down : boil over,* LCD. [weallan]

oferwinnan[3] *to contend with, overcome, subdue,* Æ,AO; CP. ['*overwin*']

oferwintran *to go through the winter,* WW 97[11]. ['*overwinter*']

oferwist f. *gluttony, excess,* CP,LL.

oferwistlic *supersubstantial,* MtL6[11].

oferwlencan *to be very wealthy,* AO44[12]. [wlanc]

oferwlencu f. *excessive riches,* Gu389.

oferwrecan[5] *to overwhelm,* WW35[14].

oferwrēon[1,2] *to cover over, conceal, hide, VPs : clothe, Mt.* ['*overwry*']

oferwrigels n. *covering,* GL.

oferwrit n. *epistle,* MtLp10[1] : *superscription,* LkR23[38].

oferwriten *superscription,* Mtp12[2].

oferwrīðan *to wrap round,* LCD49a.

oferwyllan=oferwillan

oferwyrcan *to cover over, overlay,* Sol; Æ, AO. ['*overwork*']

oferwyrðe *very worthy,* A11·171.

oferyld (W147[17])=oferyldu

oferyldu (=ie) f. *extreme old age,* MFH170.

oferyrnan[3] (=ie) *to go or run over, Æ,Lcd : 'overrun,' cover over, overwhelm, Æ,BH : run past, cross.*

oferyð f. *overwhelming wave,* SPs54[25].

ofesc f. *border?* KC3·393[10].

ofest=efest, ofost

ofestan (e[1]) *to hasten,* RBL.

ofetrip? n. *harvest,* ZDPh36·550.

ofet(t) (æ) n. *fruit, legume, Gen,Gl.* ['*ovet*']

ofeweard=ufeweard; offǣran=āfǣran

offaran[6] *to intercept, overtake, fall upon, attack,* Æ,AO. hindan o. *to intercept from behind, cut off retreat,* AO.

offeallan[7] *to fall upon, cut off, kill, destroy, end, Æ,Chr;* AO : *fall away from, be lost to,* LL144,6. hine offēoll *committed suicide,* CHR962A. ['*offall*']

offellan=offyllan

offēran *to overtake (an enemy),* Æ,CHR.

offerenda m. *psalm or anthem sung during the offertory,* ÆP168[15]; ANS84·5[29].

offerian *to carry off,* B1583.

offēstre f. *nurse not living in the house? foster-mother?* CC10[22].

offlēogan[3] *to fly away* (Swt).

±offrian *to 'offer,' sacrifice, bring an oblation, Æ,AO,VPs;* CP. [L. offerre]

offringclāð m. *offertory cloth,* NC314.

offringdagas mpl. *offering days,* OEG40[23].

offringdisc m. *offering-dish, paten,* Ct.

offringhlāf m. *shew-bread,* Mt12[4].

offringsang m. *hymn while an offering is made,* ÆH1·218[9]; ÆP214[23].

offringsceat m. *offering-napkin, KC.* ['*offering*']

offrung f. *presenting to God, oblation, sacrifice, Æ,Mt : thing presented, 'offering,' Æ.* [offrung- v. also offring-]

offrunghūs n. *house of sacrifice,* NC 314.

offrungspic n. *sacrificial bacon,* ÆL25[92].

offyligan *to follow up,* LkLR1[3].

offyllan (e;=ie) *to strike down, destroy, kill,* BH.

of-gān anv., pret. -ēode; -gangan[7] *to demand, require, exact, extort, Æ : attain, obtain, acquire, gain, Æ : start from, begin.* ['*ofgo*']

ofgangend-e, -lic *derivative,* ÆGR.

ofgefen (Cp)=ofgifen pp. of ofgiefan.

ofgeorn *elated,* HGL.

ofgēotan[2] *to moisten, soak, steep, Æ : quench, Æ : pour out,* JnL2[25].

ofgestignes f. *descent,* MtLp6[1].

ofgiefan[5] (i, y) *to give up, resign, leave, quit, desert,* AO. [giefan]

ofhabban *to hold back,* Ex9[2].

ofhæccan *to hack off,* LL.

ofhagian *to be inconvenient,* W275[5].

ofhealdan[7] *to withhold, retain,* Chr1035c. ['*ofhold*']

ofhearmian (impers.) *to cause grief,* JUD11[1].

ofhende *lost, absent,* MET25[34].

ofheran (RWH59[16])=ofhieran

ofhingrian (=y[2]) *to be hungry, Æ* (3[551]). ['*ofhungered*']

ofhnītan *to gore to death,* LL32,21.

ofhrēosan[2] *to overwhelm, cover over, Æ : fall down, fall headlong, Æ.*

ofhrēowan[2] *to cause or feel pity, Æ.* ['*arewe*']

ofhwylfan *to roll away,* ARHy2[12]. [v. '*whelve*']

ofhyrian *to imitate,* GD120[14].

ofirnan[3] *to overtake, Æ,Bo : tire with running, Æ.* ['*ofrun*']

oflǣtan[7] *to let go, lay aside, leave behind : let flow,* Bo66[29].

oflǣte (ā, ē) f. *oblation, offering, Ps : sacramental wafer, Æ,Lcd.* ['*oflete*'; L. oblata]

oflǣthlāf m. *bread used for the sacrament,* GD343[15].

oflangian *to long, Æ.* ['*oflonged*']

oflāte (VPs)=oflǣte

oflecgan *to lay down*, PPs 68¹.

oflēogan² *to lie, be false*, PPs 17⁴³.

oflēte=oflǣte

oflīcgan⁵ *to overlay (a child)*, LL. ['*oflie*']

oflīcian (w. d.) *to displease, be displeasing to, Æ.*

oflinnan³ *to cease, stop*, BL 247⁸ : *desist (from).*

oflongian=oflangian

oflystan *to fill with desire, please*, Æ,Bo. pp. of-lysted, -lyst *desirous of, pleased with.* ['*oflust*']

ofmanian *to exact (a fine)*, LL 201,1.

ofmunan swv. *to remember, recollect*, CP.

ofmyrðrian *to murder*, CHR 979 E.

ofn=ofen

ofnēadian *to obtain by force, extort*, TC 295²².

ofnet n? *closed vessel? (BT), small vessel?* LCD 11b. [ofn]

ofniman⁴ *to fail*, LL (170⁶).

ofor=(1) eofor; (2) ufor; (3) ofer; ōfor=ōfer

ofost f. *haste, speed, zeal, Æ.* adv. -līce. on ofoste, of(e)stum *speedily, hastily.*

ofr (GL)=hofer

ofrǣcan *to reach, obtain*, LL 333 col 2. [v. '*ofreach*']

ōfres gs. of ōfer.

ofrian, ofrung (AO)=offrian, offrung

ofrīdan¹ *to overtake by riding, overtake*, Æ, Chr. ['*ofride*']

ofsacan⁶ *to deny a charge*, LL 108B, n 5. ['*ofsake*']

ofscacan⁶ *to shudder*, OEG 4160. [v.'*shake*']

ofsceamian (a) *to put to shame*, Æ,Bo. ['*ofshame*']

ofscēotan² *to shoot down, hit, kill*, Æ,AO, CP. pp. ofscoten *elf-struck (of cattle seized with sudden disease).*

ofscleacnes (APs 43²²)=ofslegennes

ofscotian *to shoot down*, AO : *spear*, AA 23¹¹.

ofsendan *to summon*, Chr 1048. ['*ofsend*']

ofsēon⁵ *to see, behold, Æ.* ['*ofsee*']

ofsetenes f. *siege*, WW 458²⁸ : *sitting down*, EPs 138¹ (ob-).

ofsetnian *to besiege*, NC 349.

ofsettan (æ) *to beset, oppress, afflict, Hept, Lcd; Æ.* ['*ofset*']

ofsettung f. *pressure*, Sc 143⁵.

ofsittan⁵ *to press down, repress, oppress, Æ, CP : occupy, Hept,Bo; CP : hedge in, compass about, besiege.* ['*ofsit*']

ofslēan⁶ *to strike off or out, cut off, destroy : strike down, kill, AO,BH,Lcd; Æ,CP.* ['*ofslay*']

ofslegennes f. *slaughter*, JRVPs 43²².

ofslītan¹ *to bite (of a serpent)*, NUM 21⁹ (GR).

ofsmorian *to suffocate, strangle*, AO.

ofsnīðan¹ *to cut off, kill, Æ.*

ofsprǣc f. *locution, utterance*, HGL 460.

ofspring m. '*offspring,' descendants, posterity, Æ,KC.*

ofspyrian *to trace out*, LL 96,17.

ofst=ofost

ofstǣnan *to stone, kill*, APT 26²⁴.

ofstæppan⁶ *to trample upon*, Jos 10²⁴.

ofstan=ofestan

ofstandan⁶ *to remain, persist, continue, Lcd;* Æ : *restore, make restitution.* ['*ofstand*']

ofstede adv. *immediately*, Sc 193¹².

ofstende *hastening*, CM 186.

ofstician *to pierce, stab (to death), transfix*, AO.

ofstig *swift*, GPH 392.

ofstīgan *to descend*, NG : *ascend*, MtL : *depart*, MtL.

ofstingan³ *to pierce, stab (to death), AO,Chr;* Æ,CP. ['*ofsting*']

ofstint (=ofstent) pres. 3 sg. of ofstandan.

ofstlīce=ofostlīce

ofstofen, *impelled*, PPs.

ofstum v. ofost.

ofswelgan³ *to swallow up*, Bo 46¹⁵n.

ofswerian *to abjure, deny on oath*, LL.

ofswingan³ *to scourge (to death)*, AO 154⁸.

ofswȳðan (=ī) *to overcome*, LHY.

oft adv. comp. oftor, superl. oftost *often, frequently, CP,G;* Æ. oftost symle *continually.* o. and gelome *diligently.* ['*oft*']

oftacan² *to overtake*, NC 325.

oftalu f. *rejoinder, verdict against a claim*, TC 302²² (v. LL 3·226).

oftēon² *to withhold, take away, withdraw*, Æ, CP.

oftfēore *requiring many journeys to carry*, v. ES 43·312.

ofthrǣd-=oftrǣd-

oftige m. *withholding*, LL.

oftorfian *to stone to death, Æ,AO.*

oftrǣde *often or always available : frequent*, Bo 136¹⁷.

oftrǣdlic *frequent*, AO. adv. -līce, CP.

oftredan⁵ *to tread down, trample on, Æ.* ['*oftread*']

oftreddan *to tread to death*, AO 260¹⁸. ['*oftread*']

oftslō m. *frequent occasion*, AO 290²⁹. on oftsīðas *frequently*, CHR 979 C.

oftðwēal n. *frequent washing*, NC 314.

oftyrfan *to stone*, AO 172²⁸.

ofðǣnan *to be too moist*, LCD.

ofðe or, OEG 11¹⁷⁷ and n. [=oððe]

ofðecgan *to destroy*, GEN 2002.

ofðenian *to dry up?* ÆL 34¹⁴⁴.

ofðencan *to recall to mind*, CP 349¹⁰; VH 18.

ofðennan=ofðǣnan

ofðincð pres. 3 sg. of ofðyncan.

ofðīnan *to be too moist*, HL 204³¹⁹.

of-ðreccan (KGL), -ðriccan=ofðryccan

ofðringan³ to throng, press upon, ÆH,Mk.

ofðryccan (e, i) to press, squeeze, Æ: oppress, afflict, repress, destroy, Æ: occupy forcibly.

ofðryc(ced)nes f. trouble, oppression, CP.

ofðryscan to repress, subdue, CP.

ofðrysm(i)an to choke, stifle, Mk4¹⁹. [ðrosm]

ofðylman to choke, suffocate, NC314.

ofðyncan (impers.) to give offence, insult, vex, displease, weary, grieve, Æ,AO,B,Bo, CP,LL. ['ofthink']

ofðyrstan to suffer from thirst, be thirsty, thirst (for), Hept,Soul; Æ. ['athirst,' 'of-thirst']

ofðȳstrian to obscure, SPs73²¹. [ðēostrian]

ofunnan swv. to begrudge, deny, envy, Æ, CP.

ofweard (MFH170)=æfweard

ofweorpan³ to stone (to death), kill by a missile, Æ,AO.

ofworpian to kill (by stoning), LL.

ofwundrian to be astonished, Æ.

ōfȳrit (WW385³⁹)=āfȳred pp. of āfȳran.

ōga m. fear, terror, dread, Æ: terrible object, Æ. [ege]

ōgengel m. bar, bolt, WW459¹⁰.

ō-hilde (e², y²), -heald sloping, inclined, GL.

ōhsta=ōcusta

ōht I. f. persecution, enmity. ōhte grettan to profane, GD235⁶. [FTP9,558] II.=āwuht

ohtrip v. ofetrip.

ō-hwǣr, -hwæðer=ā-hwǣr, -hwæðer

ōhwanon=āhwonan; ōhylde=ōhilde

ōl pret. 3 sg. of alan.

ōlǣc-=ōlecc-

ōlǣcung f. 'conspiratio,' OEG4955 (=ān-?).

olbend=olfend

±ōleccan (æ, i) to soothe, caress, flatter : please, charm, propitiate, CP. [leccan]

ōleccere, ōlecere m. flatterer, CP,WW.

ōleccung (æ) f. soothing, flattery, persuasion, allurement, charm, CP.

ōlectend m. flatterer, Cp1519. [=ōleccend]

ōlehtung f. flattery, GD : indulgence, MFH 170 (ōlect-).

ōlfæt=ālfæt

olfend m., olfenda m., olfende f. camel, Bl, Mt; CP. ['olfend'; L. elephantem]

olfendmyre f. she-camel, GEN32¹⁵.

ōlicc-=ōlecc-

oll n. contumely, contempt, scorn, insult, Æ. on oll 'nequicquam,' OEG2000.

ollonc, ollunc, ollung (LWS; A)=andlang

ōlðwong m. strap, WW379³².

ōlyhtword n. flattering speech, BL99²⁶. [ōleccan]

m m. rust, Æ.

m-=am-

oma? m. ome? f. a liquid measure, v. NC 314. [L. (h)ama]

ōman fp. eruptions of the skin, erysipelas, LCD. [cp. healsōme]

omb-=amb-

ōmcynn n. corrupt humour, LCD31a.

omer (a¹, e¹) a bird, 'scorellus,' GL.

ōmian to become rusty, Sc196⁵.

ōmiddan=onmiddan

ōmig rusty, rust-eaten, rust-coloured : inflammatory, LCD.

ōmihte inflammatory, LCD.

ompella=ampella; ompre=ampre I.

on I. prep. (w. d., instr., and a.) (local, etc.) 'ON,' upon, on to (but ofer is more common), up to, among, AO,CP : in, into, within, Æ : (temporal) in, during, at, on, about, Æ,AO : against, towards, AO : according to, in accordance with, in respect to, Æ : for, in exchange for. II. adv. on, CP : forward, onward : continuously, Æ (forð on). on riht rightly. on ǣr adv. formerly. on ān continuously, in concert : at once, forthwith. III. pres. 3 sg. of unnan. IV. (M)=ond, and

on- I. often meaningless, and only rarely= prep. on. II.=an-. III.=un-. IV.=in-

onādōn anv. to put on, ÆL7¹⁵⁶.

onǣht f. possession, CVPs2⁸.

onǣlan to set fire to, ignite, heat, inspire, incite, inflame, burn, consume, Chr (an-), Gen,Sol; Æ,CP. ['anneal(ed)']

onǣlend m. 'incensor,' GPH399.

onǣlet n. lightning, LPs143⁶.

onǣr adv. formerly. [on, ǣr]

onǣðele (w. d.) natural to, MET13⁵¹.

onāfæstnian to make fast, bind, LPs9¹⁶.

onāhebban⁶ to lift up, exalt, CP56¹⁹.

onāl n. burning : incense, what is burnt, Ps.

onārīsan¹ to rise up (against), ERPs.

onarn pret. 3 sg. of oniernan.

onāsāwan⁷ to implant, instil, MFH170.

onāscunung=onscunung

onāsendan to send into, implant in, impart to, CM203.

onāsendednes (æ³) f. 'immissio,' LPs77⁴⁹.

onāsetednes f. a laying on (of hands), NC 349.

onāsettan to set upon, place on, impress upon, Æ,CM.

onāslagen beaten (of metal), LPs97⁶.

onāswēgan to sound forth, LPs28³.

onāwinnan³ to fight against, LPs34¹; 55².

onbæc adv. backwards, back, behind, G,Ps.

onbæcling (e) adv. backward, behind. o. gewend having one's back turned, Æ.

onbærnan to kindle, ignite, heat, excite, inspire, inflame, burn, AO,CP.

onbærn-ing (JPs65¹⁵), -nes (SPs) f. incense.

onbǣru f. *self-restraint?* Gu 1027.

onbāsnung f. *expectation*, DR 4³⁴.

onbeblāwan¹ *to blow upon*, LPs 104¹⁹

onbecling (EPs)=onbæcling

onbecuman=oncuman

onbecyme m. *approach*, Sc 211⁸.

onbēgan=onbīgan

onbēgnes (=īe) f. *bending, curvature*, WW.

onbeht=ambiht

onbelǣdan *to inflict upon*, WW 90.

onbēn f. *imprecation*, BH 104³.

onbēodan² *to command, order*, AO : *announce, proclaim*, Æ,AO.

onbeornan³ *to set fire to*, Ex : *inflame*, LCD.

onbēotend *threatening, impending*, DR 53².

onberan⁴ I. *to carry off, plunder* : *diminish, weaken*. II. *to be situated?* GD 98¹⁴.

onbergan=onbyrgan

onbescēawung f. *inspection, examination*, Sc 66¹⁰.

onbescēofan² *to thrust out*, WW 220¹⁹,²¹.

onbeslagen *inflicted*, Æ.

onbestǣlan *to convict of crime*, LL 30,15.

onbestingan=inbestingan; onbid=anbid

onbīdan¹ *to remain, wait*, B : w. g. *wait for, await, expect*, AO : *attend upon, wait on*. ['*onbide*']

onbīgan (ē;=īe) *to subdue, subjugate*, BL, Ps.

onbiht=ambiht

onbindan³ *to unbind, untie, loosen* : *release*, CP : *disclose*.

onbirgan=onbyrgan

onbītan¹ (w. g.) *to taste of, partake of, feed upon*, AA,LL.

onblǣst m. *onrush, attack*, EHy 5⁸.

onblǣstan *to break in*, WW 428¹.

onblandan³ *to mingle*, AN 675.

onblāwan⁷ *to blow on or into, inspire, breathe* : *puff up*.

onblāwing f. *breathing upon*, JnL p 8⁶(in-).

onblāwnes f. *inspiration*, BL 7²⁶.

onblinnan (MFH 118)=āblinnan

onblōtan⁴ *to sacrifice, kill a victim*, GEN 2933.

onborgian *to borrow*, CC 9¹¹⁷.

onbran=onbarn pret. 3 sg. of onbeornan.

on-bregdan, -brēdan³ tr. and intr. *to move, start up* : *burst open*.

onbring m. *instigation*, LL.

onbringelle f. *instigation*, ÆL 23b²⁹¹.

onbrosnung f. *decay, corruption*, EPs 29¹⁰.

onbryce m. *inroad*, OEG 2480.

±onbryrdan (āb-, inb-) *to excite, inspire, incite, encourage*, Æ,CP. onbryrd *excited, fired, ardent* : *contrite*. [brord]

onbryrding f. *incitement*, WW 419⁴².

onbryrdnes (e²) f. *inspiration, incitement, ardour*, Æ : *remorse, contrition*.

onbūgan²,¹ *to bend* : *bow, submit, yield to, agree with*, Bl,Mt; Æ,AO : *bend aside, deviate*. ['*onbow*']

onbūtan prep. (w. d. a.) and adv. '*about*,' *round about*, Æ : *round, around*, CP. adv. phr. west o. faran *to go west about*. [=ābūtan]

onbyhtscealc=ambihtscealc

onbyrdan=anbyrdan

onbyrgan I. (e, i) *to taste, eat*, Æ. II. *to be surety*, v. OEG 7⁹⁹.

onbyrging f. *tasting*, LCD 1·136¹².

onbyrhtan *to illuminate*, BL 105³¹.

onbyrignes f. *tasting*, BL 209¹².

oncelg- (N)=oncīg-

oncennan *to bear, bring forth*, ÆT,KGL.

oncer=ancor

oncierran (e, i, y) *to turn, alter, change, transform* : *turn off or away, avert, prevent* : *turn oneself, go*.

oncīgan (ei²;=īe) *to call upon, invoke*, DR.

oncīgnes, oncīgung (ei) f. *invocation*, DR.

onclēow=anclēow

onclifian (eo, y) *to adhere, stick to, persist in*, GD,RPs.

onclyfiende *sticking to, tenacious*, Ct.

onclypian *to call upon*, GEN 4²⁶ (GR).

on-cnāwe, -cnāwe *known, recognised*, EPs 31⁵.

oncnāwan⁷ *to understand, know, perceive, observe*, Ma; Æ,CP : *acknowledge, confess, disclose*, Æ. ['*acknow*']

oncnāwednes (RWH 92⁹)=oncnāwennes

oncnāwend m. *one who knows*, A 11·119.

on-cnāwennes (Æ),-cnāwnes (CP),-cnāwung (Sc) f. *acknowledgment, knowledge*.

oncnyssan *to cast down, afflict*, CPVPs.

oncnyttan=uncnyttan

oncor=ancor; ōncra=āncra

oncunnan swv. *to know*, GL : *reproach, blame, accuse*, CP.

oncunnes f. *accusation*, JVPs; BH 212¹⁵.

oncunning f. *accusation*, BH 212¹⁵(B).

oncwealdan *to slay*, EPs 61⁴.

oncweðan⁵ *to answer, resound, echo*, Æ : *protest*.

oncyrran=oncierran; oncyrrāp=ancorrāp

oncȳðan *to make known*, TC 117¹.

oncȳddǣd f. *hurtful deed*, AN 1181.

oncȳðig *conscious, understanding*, EL 725 : *known*, ZDA 33·73¹².

oncȳðð† f. *pain, distress of mind*, B.

ond=and

ondǣlan *to infuse*, DR,LkL.

ondǣlend m. *one who imparts, infuser*, LkL.

onde-=ande-; onder-=under-

onderslic, ondeslic (DR)=ondrysenlic

ondesn, ondesnes f. *fear*, DR.

ondgit=andgiet; ondlēan=andlēan

ondliota=ondwleota, andwlita
ondlong=andlang; ondo (NG)=anda
ondōn anv. I. to undo, open. [=un-] II. to put on (clothes), CM 390; Sc 83⁶.
ondōung f. injection, LCD 97b.
on-drǣdan⁷ (and wv.) pret. 3 sg. -drēd, -drǣd, -dreord (A), also -drǣdde, pp. -drǣd (tr.) to dread, fear, B,Chr,Mt : (refl.) be afraid, El,Lk. ['adread']
ondrǣdendlic fearful, terrible, Æ.
ondrǣding f. dread, fear, terror, AO.
ondrencan to intoxicate, GUTH 62²⁰ : fill with water, JPs 64¹¹.
ondresn=ondrysnu
ondrincan³ (w. g.) to drink, BH.
ondrislic=ondrysenlic
ondruncnian to become intoxicated, EPs 35⁹.
on-drysenlic, -drys(n)lic terrible, BH,MH. adv. -līce reverently, with fear, VH 18.
ondrysne (and-) terrible, AO : feared, venerated, venerable.
ondrysnlic=ondrysenlic
ondrysnu (and-) f. fear, CP : respect, reverence, BL : etiquette, B 1796.
ondrystlic=ondrysenlic
onds-=ands-
ondūne down, MH 214¹¹.
ondw-=andw-
one=ono
onealdian to grow old, SPs 31³.
oneardian to inhabit, CSPs (=in-).
oneardiend inhabitant, indweller, GD,PPs.
onefen, onefn=onemn
on-ēgan, -ēgnan (oe) to fear, dread. [ōga]
onēhting f. persecution, OEG 2974.
onemn I. prep. (w. d.) abreast of, alongside of, by, near, during, Æ,B,Ma; AO. ['anent'] II. adv. together, exactly, directly. o. ðǣm at the same time.
onemnōrōwigan to sympathise, ÆL 23b²⁴³.
onerian to plough up, Æ,CP.
onerning f. attack, DR 36¹. [iernan]
ōnettan to hasten, hurry forward, be quick, Æ : be busy, brisk : anticipate, Æ,CP : (+) get quickly, seize, occupy.
ōnettung f. precipitation, CP 455¹⁵.
oneðat=anda
onēðgung f. breathing on, ERPs 17¹⁶.
onfægnian to fawn on, Bo 102¹⁵.
onfǣreld n. going on, progress, journey : going in, entrance : attack, assault, Sc 212⁵.
onfǣstan to make fast, GD 224¹⁶.
onfǣstnian (e²) to pierce, Jn,SPs.
onfæōmnes f. embrace, BL 7²⁶.
onfangend m. receiver, ES 9·37.
onfangennes f. reception, acceptance, Æ.
onfealdan⁷ to unfold, GD,MH.
onfeall (e) m. swelling, Lcd. ['onfall']
onfeallende ptc. rushing on, overwhelming.

onfehtan (VPs)=onfeohtan; onfell=onfeall
onfeng I.=andfeng. II. pret. 3 sg. of onfōn.
onfeohtan³ (e) to attack, assault, fight with, CHR.
onfillende (WW 420¹⁹)=onfeallende
onfilte (WW)=anfilte
onfindan³ (but occl. wk. pret. onfunde) to find out, learn, perceive, feel, notice, observe, discover, CP : experience, suffer.
onfindend m. discoverer, GPH 391.
onflǣscnes f. incarnation, BL 81²⁹; BHy 2⁴¹.
onflyge m., onflygen n. infectious disease (BT), LCD.
onfōn⁷ to take, receive, accept, BH,Lcd,Mt; Æ : stand sponsor, Chr : harbour, favour unrighteously, LL : take hold of : undertake, (a duty) undergo (a rite), Bl : begin : conceive, Ps. onfangenum gebede after engaging in prayer, Æ. ['fang,' 'onfang']
onfōnd m. undertaker, supporter, Ps,AS 14⁶?
onfōndlic (an-) to be received, CHRD 110⁸.
onfongenes=onfangennes
onforan I. prep. before (time), at the beginning of, Chr. II. adv. before, in front of, Ps. ['afore']
onfordōn ptc. destroyed, LPs 101²¹.
onforeweard-um, -an adv. in front, in the first line, in the fore part, above all, Æ; A 5·455.
onforht=anforht
onforhtian to be afraid, fear, Æ,GL.
onforwyrd n. destruction, CSPs.
onfundelnes f. experience, LCD.
onfunden experienced, AS 14⁶.
onfundennes f. explanation : trial, experiment, experience. [onfindan]
onga=anga; ongægn, ongǣn=ongēan
ongalan⁶ to recite (a charm), LCD 3·42¹⁸, S²Ps 57⁶.
ongalend m. enchanter, BLPs 57⁶.
ongalnes f. song, BRPs 70⁶.
ongān I.=ongēan. II. anv. to approach, enter into, ES 38·20 : attack, ES 41·325.
ongang (o²) m. entrance, incursion, assault, attack : worship, BH 106¹⁴.
ongangan⁷=ongān; onge=enge
on-gēan (ā, ē) -geagn (æ, e) I. prep. towards, against, opposite to, contrary to, Æ; AO,CP : against, in exchange for. II. adv. opposite, back, Æ : 'AGAIN.' eft o. back again. o. ðæt on the other hand, on the contrary.
ongēancyme m. return, Æ.
ongēancyrrendlic relative, ÆGR 231¹⁷.
ongēanfealdan⁷ to fold or roll back, Sc 148¹¹.
ongēanfēran (agēan-) to return, CHR 1070.
ongēanflōwende ebbing and flowing, v. OEG 2363.
ongēanhworfennes f. obstacle, OEG 2713.

ongēanhwyrf (ag-) m. *return*, HGL419.
ongēanhwyrfan (ag-) *to turn again, return*.
ongēanlecgan *to lay up, store up*, Sc156⁶.
ongēansprecend m. *one who reproaches*, RSPs43¹⁷.
ongēanweard *going back or towards*, AO : *near*, BK4. adv. -weardes, Æ.
ongēanweardlic *adversative*. adv. -līce, ÆGR.
ongēanwerian *to revile in return*, RB17¹³. [wyrigan]
ongēanwinnende *resisting*, APT2⁴.
ongēanwiðerian *to oppose*, Sc33²⁰.
ongēanwyrdnes f. *opposition*, OEG3975.
ongeboren *in-born*, OEG4648,2³⁶⁰.
ongebringan *to bring upon : impose*, CM36 : *enjoin*, CM1185 : *incline, induce*,ÆL25⁵⁴⁹.
ongebyrigean (V²Ps33⁹)=onbyrgan I.
ongecīgan *to call upon, invoke*, RHy1⁴.
ongecīgung (ei³) f. *invocation*, DR99¹³.
ongecoplīce=ungecoplīce
onge-fæstnian, -festnian (Ps)=onfæstnian
ongefeht n. *attack*, DR. [feoht]
ongeflogen *attacked by disease*, LCD1·86'. [cp. onflygen]
on-gegen, -gegn=ongēan
ongehrēosan² *to rush upon, fall upon*, WW 419⁶.
ongehȳðnes f. *advantage, profit*, LL476,12.
ongel, Ongel=angel I., Angel
ongelǣdan=ingelǣdan
ongelic (NG) I. *like*. II. *likeness*. adv. -līce, AO.
ongelīcnes f. *form, pattern*, Mt p14²⁰.
ongelihtan (AS2²)=onlihtan
on-gemang, -gemong prep. (w. d.) and adv. *among, during*, CP : *meanwhile*, CM. o. ðisum, ðǣm *meanwhile*.
ongemet=ungemet
ongēn, ongend=ongēan
ongenǣman *to take away (from)*, GUTH14¹¹.
ongeotan=ongietan
ongēotan *to infuse, impregnate*, GD51¹⁴.
ongēotung f. *pouring in*, LCD88a.
on-gerwan, pp. -gered (VPs)=ongierwan
ongesēon=onsēon
ongesetenes f. *knowledge*, BH474¹⁵.
ongeslēan⁶ *to slay*, BH44¹⁷.
ongespanan¹ *to draw on, allure*, WW421²².
onget-=ongiet-
ongetǣcan *to enjoin*, CM363.
ongetimbran *to build up*, AO.
ongeðwǣre=ungeðwǣre
ongewinn n. *assault*, Sc33¹⁷.
ongewiss=ungewiss
ongewrigennes (GD139¹)=onwrigennes
ongieldan³ (i) *to atone for, be punished for, pay (the penalty) for*, AO : *pay, offer (gifts, sacrifice)*. [*Ger*. entgelten]

ongien=onginn
ongierwan (e, i, y) pret. -girede I. *to unclothe, divest, strip*, Æ (=un-). II. *to clothe*, EPs131¹⁶.
ongietan⁵ (e, eo, i, y) *to grasp, seize : understand, learn, recognise, know, distinguish, judge, consider, Mt*; AO,CP : *see, perceive : discover : hear : feel, experience : know carnally*. ['*anget*']
ongietenes f. *knowledge, understanding*, BH : *meaning*, GUTH80²².
ongifan⁵ (æ) *to give back*, Æ : *forgive*.
ongildan=ongieldan
onginn=anginn
onginnan³ *to begin, attempt, endeavour, try hard*, Æ,G; AO,CP (This vb. is often used periphrastically w. another vb. in the inf., to denote the simple action of the latter. The compound is best translated by the historical aorist of the second vb.) : *attack, assail : act*, ÆL (āg-). ['*ongin*']
onginnendlic *inchoative*, ÆGR.
onginnes f. *undertaking*, BH,WW.
on-girwan=ongierwan
ongit=andgiet; ongit-=ongiet-
Ongle (AO), Onglisc=Angle, Englisc
ongnora? ongnere=angnere
Ongol=Angel; ongong=ongang
ongrata ð? '*arridet*,' OEG33² (v. BTs).
ongris-, ongrys-=angris-
ongrynt? '*arridet*,' OEG33² (v. BTs).
ongrype m. *attack*, W187².
ongryrelic *horrible*, GUTH36²⁴.
ongseta=angseta; ongunnenes=onginnes
ongy-=ongi-
ongyrdan *to unbuckle, unfasten*, ÆL; BH 196²⁸. ['*ungird*']
ongyrnð '*inrogat*,' Sc10⁴.
ongytan=ongietan
ongyte f. *inpouring*, ÆH1·362'.
onhādian (LL66,21)=unhādian
onhǣldan (VPs)=onhieldan
onhǣle *secret, concealed, hidden*, CR896.
onhǣtan *to heat, inflame*, AO,CP.
onhagian (impers.) *to be possible or convenient, be fitting, suit, please*, Æ,CP : *be at leisure*.
onhātan¹† *to promise*, JUL.
onhātian *to become hot*, WW.
onhāwian *to behold*, ÆL3²⁶¹.
onhealdan⁷ (an-) *to keep (peace)*, MET11⁴².
onhēaw m. *trunk of tree, block of wood for hewing on*, WW.
onhebban⁶ (occl. wk. pret. onhefde) *to raise up, erect, lift up, exalt*, Bl; Æ : *leaven : begin : take away*. ['*onheave*']
onhefednes (an-) f. *exaltation*, RB23².
onheld-=onhield-
onhergian *to harass*, CP73¹⁸.

onheri-=onhyri-
onhetting f. *persecution*, OEG 2¹³⁰.
onhicgan=onhycgan
onhieldan (CP) (i²) *to bend, bend down, lean,
recline, incline* : *decline, sink* : *fall away*,
CPs 118¹⁰².
onhieldednes (e², y²) f. *declining*, CVPs 72⁴.
onhigian *to attack, despoil*, OEG.
onhindan, onhinder adv. *behind, backward*.
onhinderling adv. *back*, PPs.
onhiscan=onhyscan
onhlidan¹ *to open, reveal, unclose* : *appear*.
onhlinian *to lean on*, GL.
onhnigan¹ *to bend down, bow, worship*.
onhnigenes f. *adoration*, LF 56⁵.
onhōhsnian *to detest?* (BT), *put an end to?*
B 1944.
onhōn⁷ *to hang, crucify*, AO.
onhrēēran=onhrēran; onhrēēs=onr̯ēs
onhrēodan² *to adorn* (or? onrēodan=*redden*),
GEN 2931.
onhrēosan² *to fall upon, rush upon*, GD,Ps.
onhrēran *to move, disturb, arouse, excite*, CP.
onhrīnan¹ (w. g. or d.) *to touch, lay hold of*,
Æ,CP.
onhrine m. *touch, contact*, LCD 1·328¹.
onhrōp m. *importunity*, Æ : *reproach*, LPs
68²⁰.
onhryre *attack*, OEG 50⁷² (onri-).
onhupian *to step back, retire*, CP 441²⁸.
onhwelan⁴ *to bellow back, resound*, WW
528³⁹.
onhweorfan³ *to change, turn, reverse*, CP.
onhwerfan (y²;=ie) *to turn, change, turn
round*.
onhwerfednes (æ) f. *change*, AS 9³.
onhycgan (i²) *to consider*, DA 473.
onhyldan=onhieldan
onhyrdan† *to strengthen, encourage*. [heard]
onhyrenes f. *imitation*, CP,GD.
onhyr-gend, -iend (e, i;=ie) m. *emulator,
imitator*, GD,GL.
onhyrian (e) *to emulate, imitate*, CP.
onhyring (e) f. *imitation, zeal*, Æ,CP.
onhȳrsumian *to be busied with*, RB 71¹⁷.
onhyscan (i) *to mock at, vilify, reproach* :
detest : *deceive*. [husc]
oniernan³ (y²) (†) *to give way, open* (*of a
door*) : '*currere*,' BPs 118³² : '*incurrere*,'
LL 410,3⁵ : *pour forth*, VH 18.
oninnan prep. (w. d.) and adv. *within, into,
among*.
onlǣc (Cp 1725)=onlēac, pret. 3 sg. of
onlūcan.
onlæccan *to reproach*, EPs 105⁷.
onlǣdan=inlǣdan
onlǣnan *to lend, grant, let, lease*, CP.
onlǣpnes (BH 128²³)=ānlīpnes
onlǣtan (an-) *to relax, permit*, RB.

onlang=andlang; onlēc=anlēc
onlecgende (*salve*) *to be applied*, LCD.
onlegen f. *poultice*, LCD.
onlēoht-=onlīht-
onlēon¹† *to lend, grant, give*, WW.
onlēoðian=onlīðigan
onlēs-=onlīes-
onlic (an-) *like, resembling, similar*, Mt; CP
adv. -līce, AO,CP. ['*anlike*']
+onlician (an-; -līcan, GD 75⁴) *to compare
make like, simulate*.
onlicnes f. *resemblance, likeness, similitude,
Gen.* : *picture, image, idol*, WW; AO,CP :
parable : *stature, form*. ['*anlikeness*']
+onlicung (an-) f. *likeness*, CHRD 71¹³.
onliesan (ē, ȳ) *to loosen, set free, release*, CP.
onliesednes (ī²) f. *remission (of sins)*, AHy 9⁷⁷.
onliesend (ē, ȳ) m. *liberator*, CPs 39¹⁸ :
redeemer, GD.
onliesendlic (ȳ) *absolvable*, GD 345².
onliesnes (ē) f. *deliverance*, BL,GD.
onligan (in-) *to inflame*, JPs 104¹⁹.
onlihtan (ēo, ȳ) *to illuminate, give light to,
enlighten*, Bl,Bo; CP : *restore to sight* :
shine. ['*onlight*']
onlihtednes=onlihtnes
onlihtend m. *enlightener*, PPs 26¹.
onlihting f. *illumination, enlightenment*, Æ.
onlihtnes f. *illumination*, BH,Ps.
onliðian (eo) *to loosen, relax*, GD.
onlīðigan *to become pliant, yield*, SOL 356.
onlōcian *to look on, behold*, Æ,CP.
onlōciend m. *onlooker, spectator*, Æ.
onlong=andlang
onlūcan² (=un-) *to unlock, open, unfold,
reveal, disclose*, CP.
onlūtan² *to bow, incline, bend down*, CP.
onlūtung f. '*involucrum*,' GPH 402.
onlȳ-=onlī-; onlȳs-=onlīes-
onmǣdla=onmēdla
onmǣlan *to speak to*, DA 210.
onman v. onmunan.
onmang (Æ)=ongemang
onmearca m. *inscription*, MkL 12¹⁶ (MkR
in-).
onmearcung (e²) f. *inscription*, NG.
onmēdan *to presume, take upon oneself?*
RD 56¹⁵.
onmēdla=anmēdla
onmeltan³? *to soften*, PPs 88³⁸.
onmētan I. *to paint, cover over?* PPs 88⁴⁶.
II. *to come upon, find out*, EPs 114³.
onmiddan prep. (w. d.) *amid, in the midst,
at the middle of*, Æ.
onmitta=anmitta; onmōd=anmōd
onmunan swv. pres. 3 sg. onman, pret.
onmunde *to esteem, think worthy of, consider entitled to*, CP : refl. *care for, wish* :
remember : *remind*, B 2640.

onmyrran *to mar, disturb,* TC390′.
onn=ann, pres. 3 sg. of unnan.
onnhīgan (WW255[11])=onhnīgan
onnīman[4] *to receive, take,* PPs.
onnytt=unnytt
ono=heonu
onoeðung (VPs)=oneðung
onōrettan† *to perform with effort, accomplish.*
onorðung f. *inspiration, inbreathing,* LPs, Sc.
onoða (WW)=anda
onpennian *to open,* CP277[8].
onrād f. *riding on horseback,* Lcd 68b.
onræfniendlic=unræfniendlic
onrǣs m. *onrush, assault, attack,* Æ,CP.
onrǣsan I. *to rush* (*on*), VPs. ['onrese']
  II. nap. of wk. sb. *irruptions,* WW.
onrǣsend m. *attacker,* LPs 17[40].
onrēaflan *to strip* (*of*), A 12·505 (=un-).
onred m. *name of a plant,* Lcd.
onrēodan v. onhrēodan; **onrettan**=orrettan
onrid n. *riding horse,* CC 23[25].
onrīdan[1] *to ride* (*on a raid, etc.*), Chr 871A.
onriht *right, lawful, proper : owned by?* Ex 358. adv. *aright,* Æ. also -līce, Bl 43[16].
onrihtwīsnes=unrihtwīsnes
onrīptīd f. *harvest-time,* ES 39·352.
onrīsan (Æ)=ārīsan ['onrise']
onryne m. *course : incursion, assault,* Lcd.
onsacan[6] *to contest, dispute, strive against, resist, repel :* (†) *attack : refuse, deny, contradict, refute : exculpate, excuse oneself : renounce.*
onsæc I. *denying : denied : excused.* II. (LL 24,41 Ld)=andsæc
onsǣgan† *to prostrate,* DD,Gu.
onsǣgd-=onsǣged-
onsǣge *assailing, attacking,* B,CC,W. [sīgan]
onsǣgednes (e) f. *sacrifice, offering, Æ : oblation,* (*sacrificial*) *victim.*
onsǣgnes f. *holocaust, sacrifice,* BlPs 65[15].
onsǣgung f. *sacrifice,* WW.
onsǣlan *to untie, loosen,* B,Bl. [=unsǣlan]
onsæt I. pret. 3 sg. of onsittan. II.=onset
onsǣtnes f. *snare,* DR 121[19].
onsǣtnung f. *snare,* DR 147[7].
onsagu f. *affirmation, accusation, reproach,* Mt; Æ. ['onsaw']
onsand f. *sending against,* VPs. ['onsand']
onsang m. *incantation,* GD 73[26].
onsāwan[7] *to sow : introduce into, implant,* CM 658.
onsceacan[6] (a) *to shake, shake off, remove,* Gl.
onsceacnes f. *excuse,* EPs. [=onsacnes, Swt]
onsceamian=ofsceamian
onscendan *to confound, put to shame,* GD.

onsceon-=onscun-
onsceortian *to grow short,* MH 104[23].
onscēotan[2] (un-) *to open,* Gl.
onscillan (=y[2]) *to give back a sound, resound,* OEG 8[265].
onscōgan (an-) *to unshoe,* CP. pp. onscōd *unshod.* [=un-]
onscrȳdan *to clothe,* EPs,Sc.
onscunian (a[1], eo[2], y[2]) *to shun, avoid, fear, detest, hate, LL ; Æ,CP : put away, reject, despise : irritate.* ['ashun']
on-scuniendlic (CP), -scunigendlic (Æ), -scunodlic *hateful, detestable.*
onscunigend m. *hater,* Bl 111[29].
onscunung f. *execration, abomination : exasperation,* Ps.
onscynian=onscunian
onscyte m. *attack, assault,* Æ.
onseacan (Cp 665)=onsceacan
onsēcan *require, exact,* Jul. ['onseek']
onsecgan *to renounce, deny : offer sacrifice,* AO : *impute,* Æ : *inform,* Æ.
onsecgend m. *sacrificer,* LL.
onsēgednes=onsǣgednes
onsēn (VPs)=ansīen
onsendan *to send out, send forth, transmit, yield up,* AO,CP : *offer to,* VH.
onsēon I. (sv[5]) *to see, look on, behold, regard, take notice of,* AO. II. (A)=ansīen
on-set, -setl, n. *a sitting on, riding on,* GD 183.
onset(e)nes f. *laying on* (*of hands*), MH 84[2] : *constitution, founding.*
onsettan *to impose,* CP : *oppress, bear down.*
onsīcan[1] *to sigh, groan,* Bo.
onsīen I. (ȳ)† f. *lack, want.* II.=ansīen
onsīgan[1] *to sink, decline, descend : approach, impend,* Æ : *assail,* Æ.
onsit=onset
onsittan I. sv[5] *to seat oneself in, occupy,* Æ : *oppress.* II. sv[5] *to.fear, dread* (=ond-).
onsittend m. *rider,* CHy 41.
onslæge m. *blow,* WW. [slcgc]
onslǣpan[7] and wv. *to go to sleep, sleep,* BH.
onslāpan=onslǣpan
onslūpan[7] *to unloose,* GD 221[23]. [=un-]
onsmyrung f. *anointing,* Chrd 80[19].
onsnǣsan (LL 69,36) v. snǣsan.
onsnīðan[1] *to cut up,* Lcd (ES 43·321).
onsond=onsand
onspǣc f. *imputation, charge, claim,* LL.
onspannan[7] *to unfasten, unbind, unloose, open, disclose, release.* [=un-]
onspeca (an-) m. *accuser,* Chrd 62[26] : *claimant,* LL 138,1[3].
onspecend m. *accuser, plaintiff,* TC 169.
onspillend m. *player,* A 13·28,29.
onspornan=onspurnan
onspornend (=un-) *not stumbling,* Sc 187[8].

onsprēc f. *speech, discourse,* GD332[9] (an-).

onspreccan *to enliven,* RIM9?

onsprecend=onspecend

onspringan[3] *to spring forth, originate, rise, burst forth, burst asunder.*

onsprungennes f. *eclipse,* WW225[39].

onspurnan[3] *to strike against, stumble,* WW 420[39].

onstæl m. *order, arrangement,* GU796.

onstēlan *to impute to, accuse of,* MFH170.

onstæpe (e) m. *ingress,* ESPs67[26] (=in-).

onstæppan[6] *to walk, go,* LCD,SPs (=in-).

onstal (=ea?) m. *provision, supply,* CP4[1].

onstāl m? *charge, reproof,* OEG.

onstandende *urgent, persistent,* Sc111[14].

onstede=unstede

onstellan *to institute, create, originate, establish, give the example of, Bl*; AO,CP. ['*onstell*']

onstēpan (=īe) *to raise,* †Hy4[38].

onstīgend m. *mounted man,* VHy4[1].

onsting m. *claim, authority, jurisdiction, right of intervention,* Ct.

onstingan *to be angry (with)?* RBL115[16].

onstīðian *to harden,* JnLR12[40].

onstregdan[3] (and wk.) (i[2]) *to sprinkle,* BJVPs 50[9].

onstydfullnes f. *instability,* DR. [=uni-]

onst&ymacr;ran *to govern,* BH276[11] (v.l.).

onstyr-ednes, -enes f. *movement,* BH,Ps.

onstyrian *to move, rouse, disturb, stir, agitate, excite,* CP.

onsund=ansund

onsun-dran, -dron, -drum adv. *singly, separately, apart, Gen,Mk* : *privately* : *especially.* ['*asunder*']

onsundrian=āsyndrian

onswāpan[7] *to sweep on, blow on,* GL : *sweep away, banish.*

onswarian=andswarian

onswebban *to put to sleep, bury,* WW.

onswīfan[1] *to swing forward, turn against* : *push off, put aside, turn away.*

onswīðlic *mighty, loud,* ÆL31[281].

onswōgan=inswōgan

onswornod *confused,* NC315.

onsymbelnes f. *celebration (of mass),* BH 112[8].

ons&ymacr;n=ansīen, onsīen I.

onsyngian=unsyngian

ontalu f. *claim at law,* TC302[22] (v. LL 3·226).

ontēnan (KGL65[5])=ont&ymacr;nan

ontendan *to kindle, set fire to, inflame, Æ, Lcd,LL.* ['*tind,*' '*ontend*']

ontendnes (y) f. *burning, fire, Æ* : *inflammation, Æ* : *incitement, fuel, Æ* : *passion.*

ontēon[2] *to draw to oneself, assume, undertake,* CP : *pull, pull out* : *untie* (=un-).

ontēona m. *injury, oppression,* ERPs102[6].

ontige m. *claim, usurpation,* RB140[9].

ontiht-=ontyht-

ontimber *material, Æ* : *cause, occasion, Æ.*

ontimbernes f. *material,*MFH171: *teaching, edification.*

ontimbr-an, -ian, *to instruct,* BH.

ontre=antre

ontrēowan *to entrust, confide,* DA269?

ontrym-ian, -man '*invalescere,*' NG.

ont&ymacr;dran *to nourish, foster,* AO182[26].

ont&ymacr;dre '*sine foetu,*' *effete,* WW. [=ort&ymacr;-dre?]

ontygnes f. *accusation,* LL22,37.

ontyhtan (i) *to urge on, incite,* B3086 : *be intent on.*

ontyhting (i) f. *attention, application, aim, intention, instigation,* Sc.

ont&ymacr;nan (ē) *to open, reveal, display,* CP. [tūn]

ontyndnes=ontendnes

ont&ymacr;nnes f. *opening,* BL93[24].

onðæslic (Sc33[20])=unðæslic

onðenian *to stretch,* EPs63[3].

onðēon[1,3]† *to be useful, succeed, prosper.*

onðēowigan *to serve,* CM473.

onðicgan *to eat of, partake of,* VH18.

±onðracian (a-, an-, and-) *to fear, dread, Æ.*

onðracung (an-) f. *fear, awe,* LPs34[26].

on-ðræce, -ðræclic (an-) *formidable, dreadful, Æ.*

onðrēagung f. *reproach,* ÆL23b[672].

onðrecan[5] refl. *to fear,* GUTH132[208].

onðringan[3] *to press. on or forward,* AO : *move, be moved?* GU1300.

onðunian *to swell up? move round?* RD41[91] : *exceed bounds.*

onðwægennes f. *washing,* HL13[138, 154].

onðwēan[6] (in-) *to wash,* BH,GD.

onu=heonu

onufan prep. (w. d.) and adv. *above, upon, on, Jud*; AO : *beyond, after.* ['*anoven*']

onunder (an-) *under,* MFH171.

onuppan I. prep. (w. d.) *upon, on,* CP. II. adv. *in addition, besides.*

onūtan *out of doors,* LCD106b.

onwacan[6] *to awake,* AO : *arise, be born.*

onwaccan f. *incitement, arousing,* DR74[12].

onwacnian=onwæcnian

onwadan[6] *to penetrate into, attack, seize, occupy.*

onwæcan *to weaken, shake (a resolution), soften, mollify,* CP. [wāc]

onwæcenes f. *arousing,* GD337[33].

on-wæcnan, -wæcnian (e) *to awake, CP* : *arise, spring, be born* (=āwæcnan). ['*awaken*']

onwæld (N)=onweald

onwæmme=unwemme; **onwær-**=unwæronwæstm m. *increase*, DR 69⁹ : *branch*, PPs. [ōwæstm]

onwæterig=unwæterig

onwald, onwalh=onweald, onwealg

onwarian *to guard oneself against*, MFH 171.

onwealcan⁷ *to roll, roll round*, LCD 1·246¹⁰.

onweald (a¹, a²) I. mfn. *authority, power, rule, sway, command, AO,Lk*; CP : *jurisdiction, territory*, CP. II. adj. *mighty, powerful*. ['onwald']

onwealda (an-) m. *ruler, governor, sovereign* : *the Lord, God*.

+onwealdian (an-; æ²) *to have dominion over, get possession of*, LPs,LkLR.

onwealdig (a¹, a²) *powerful*, Bo 108¹⁸.

onwealdnes f. *power, possession*, ERPs 2⁸.

onwealg, onwealh *whole, sound, entire, uninjured, safe*, AO.

onwealglīce (an-) *wholly, completely*, CP 220²².

onwealhnes f. *soundness, wholeness, purity, modesty, chastity*.

onweard (=and-) adj. *acting against, opposed to*, Æ.

onwecnian=onwæcnian

onweg (aweg) adv. '*away*,' *forth, out, off, onward, along*, B,Chr.

onwegācyr(red)nes (=ie⁴) f. *apostasy*, BH 176 (v.l.).

onwegādrīfan¹ *to drive away*, VPs.

onwegādrīfennes f. *a driving away*, GD 185¹³.

onwegāfīrran *to remove away*, VHy.

onwegālǣdnes f. *removal*, BH 446¹⁶.

onwegāscūfan² *to push away*, VPs.

onwegāwendan *to remove*, VPs.

onwegfæreld n. *departure*, GD 119²⁶.

onweggewit n. *mental aberration*, VPs 115¹¹.

onweggewitennes f. *departure*, BH 170¹⁰.

onwegoncernes=onwegācyrrednes

onwegpullian *to pull away*, ES 43·339.

onwemme=unwemme

onwendan *to change, exchange* : *upset, end, overturn, turn aside, avert*, VPs : *change for the better, amend* : *change for the worse, pervert* : *transgress* : *deprive* : *return*.

onwendedlic *changeable*, LCD 3·164⁸.

on-wendednes, -wendnes f. *movement, change, alteration*, VPs.

onweorpan³ (in-) *cast in one's teeth, accuse* : *turn or throw aside* : *begin the web*.

onweorpnes f. *onpouring*, BH 118⁵.

onwēstan=āwēstan

onwīcan¹ *to yield, give way*, WW.

onwille *wished for, agreeable*, Gu 700.

onwindan³ *unwind, loosen* : *retreat*, AN 531.

onwinnan³ *to attack, assail*, Æ.

onwist f. *habitation*, Ex 18.

onwlite=andwlite

onworpennes f. *enticement, allurement, inspiration*, HL 200¹⁶⁴.

onwrecan=āwrecan

onwrēon¹,² *to uncover, unfold, display, explain, reveal*, Æ,CP.

on-wrig(en)nes, -wrihnes f. *revelation, exposure, exposition*, Æ. [wrēon]

onwrīting f. *inscription*, Lk 20²⁴. ['onwriting']

onwrītung=onwrīðung

onwrīðan *to unbind, unwrap* (JUD 173)= unwrīðan.

onwrīðod pp. *supported*, BF 198²³.

onwrīðung f. *ligament, bandage*, WW 439¹³ (onwrīt-).

onwunian *to inhabit, remain*, Ps.

onwunung f. *dwelling-place* : *assiduity*, OEG 75.

onwurpan=onweorpan

onwyllan *to cause to boil, inflame*, Gu 362.

onwylwan *to roll up, roll together*, EHy 2¹².

onȳðan *to pour in*, Sc 200⁷.

onȳwan (=īe) *to show, manifest* : refl. *appear*.

open '*OPEN*,' *exposed*, AO : *evident, well-known, public, manifest, plain, clear*, AO : *open to re-trial*, LL 10,9.

openærs m. *medlar*, WW 137³⁶. ['openarse']

openere m. *opener*, BF 152³.

±openian *to* '*open*,' *open up, disclose, declare, reveal, expound*, Æ,BH,Ps; CP : (+) intr. *become manifest* : (+) *be open to, exposed to*.

openlic *open, public*, WW. adv. -līce '*openly*,' *manifestly, plainly, clearly, unreservedly*, Bl,Bo,RB.

opennes f. *openness, publicity*, OEG : *manifestation*, ÆL 23b⁴².

±openung f. *opening, disclosure, manifestation*, BL,W.

oportanie=aprōtane

ōr† n. *beginning, origin* : *front*, An,B. ['ore,' cp. ord]

or prefix (lit. '*out of*'=L. ex-) is privative, as in orsorg, orwēna; or denotes origin, antiquity, as in oreald. [Ger. ur-]

ōra I. m. *border, bank, shore*, CHR; Mdf. II. m. '*ore*,' *unwrought metal*, BH,Ps,WW : *brass*, ÆGr,Cp,CP. III. *a coin of Danish origin*, LkL,LL (v. 2·601). ['ora']

orað=oroð

orblēde *bloodless*, WW 397²⁹. [blōd]

orc I. m. *pitcher, crock, cup*, B,GL. [Late L. orca; L. urceus] II. m. *demon*, GL. [L. orcus]

or-cēape, -cēapes, -cēapunga, -cēapungum
adv. *gratis, without cause.*
orc-eard, -erd (*Æ,Lcd*)=ortgeard
orcēas *inviolable, unimpugned, unassailed,*
GL.
orcēasnes f. *immunity, purity,* GL.
orcerdlēh f. *orchard,* HGL. [ortgeard, lēah]
orcerdweard m. *gardener,* WW333²⁵.
orcgeard, orcird=ortgeard
orcnǣwe (ā) *evident, well-known.*
orcnēas mp. *monsters,* B112. [*L.* Orcus]
orcðyrs m. *monster of hell, Orcus,* WW.
orcyrd=ortgeard
ord m. *point, spear-point, spear, Æ,B,CP :
source, beginning, Æ,CP : front, vanguard,
Æ : chief, prince;* in pl. *first men, the
flower.* [' *ord* ']
ordǣle *not participating, free from,* WW.
ordāl (ē) mn. ' *ordeal,' LL.* [*Ger.* urteil]
ordālīsen n. *iron used in an ordeal,* LL388,1.
ordbana m. *murderer,* GEN1097.
ordceard=ortgeard; ordēl=ordāl
ordfruma m. *fount, source, Æ : author,
creator, instigator,* AO *: (†) chief, prince.*
ordfrymm (e²) *original,* ES49·352.
ordstæpe m. *spear-stab, wound,* RD71¹⁶.
ordwyga m. *warrior,* WALD1⁶.
-ōre v. īsen-ō.
oreald *very old,* Bo102¹⁸. [*Ger.* uralt]
ōred-=ōret-
orel n. *robe, garment, mantle, veil, Æ,*GL.
[*L.* orarium]
oreldo=oryldu
orene I. *excessive,* v. SF157 *: harmful.* II. n.
excess : injury? LCD3·16⁵ (orne).
orenlīce *excessively,* MFH171.
ōret† m. *contest, battle.*
ōret-=orret(t)-
ōretfeld m. *place of contest,* OEG8⁵⁰.
ōretla m. *contumely, insult,* GD200¹⁶.
ōretlof n. *triumph,* CM497.
ōret-mæcg† (e³), -mæcga (WW) m. *champion, warrior.*
ōretstōw f. *wrestling place, place of contest,*
OEG.
ōrett-=ōret-
ōretta† m. *champion, warrior, hero.*
oreð=oroð; oreðlan=orðian
orf n. *cattle, live stock, Æ,Chr,LL.* [' *orf* ']
orfcwealm (a²) m. *cattle-plague, murrain,*
CHR,W.
orfcynn (i²) n. *cattle, Æ.*
orfeorme (y) (†) *destitute of, lacking : (†)
empty, useless : squalid, filthy.*
orfeormnes f. *squalor, filthiness,* Cp488s.
orfgebitt n. *grazing,* WW149³³.
orfiermu f. *squalor,* OET96⁹³³.
orfyrme=orfeorme
orfyrmð *refuse,* OEG609.

organ m. *canticle, song, voice,* SOL.
organa? organe? f., organ-an, -on pl.
musical instrument, Æ,ApT,Ps. [' *organ* ';
L. organum]
organdrēam (APs150⁴)=orgeldrēam
organe f. *marjoram, Lcd.* [' *organ* '; *L.*
origanum]
organian=orgnian
organystre *player on an instrument,* GEN4²¹.
orgeate=orgyte
orgel (o²) *pride, WW.* [' *orgel* ']
orgeldrēam m. *sound of a musical instrument, Bl.* [v. ' *orgle* ']
orgellic *ignominious, CP.* adv. -līce *proudly, insolently, scornfully, Æ.*
orgello (A11·98)=orgel
orgelnes f. *pride, OEG1108.* [v. ' *orgel* ']
orgelword n. *arrogant speech,* ÆH2·248¹¹.
orgete=orgyte
orgilde *not having discharged a payment (of
' wergeld '), LL.*
orglice=orgellice
orgnian *to sing to an instrumental accompaniment,* ÆGR181².
orgol=orgel
orgyte (ea, e) *well-known, manifest,* AO.
orh-=org-; orhlættre=orleahtre
orhlȳte *without lot or share in, destitute
of, Æ.*
oriege *out of sight, not visible,* ANS98·128.
orl m.=orel n.
orlæg† (e) n. *fate,* DA,DD.
orleahter m. ' *discrimen,' lack of vice or
defect,* v. ES37·179 *: danger,* CHRD2⁸.
orleahtre *blameless,* B,BL.
orleg=orlæg
orlegcēap m. *battle-booty?* GEN1994.
orlege I. n. *strife, war.* II. adj. *hostile.*
orlegfrom *keen in battle,* RD21¹⁵.
orleggifre (æ) *fond of strife,* GEN2287.
orleghwīl† f. *war-time, B.*
orlegnīð† m. *war, hostility,* GEN.
orlegsceaft f. ' *supplicium'?* SOL456? (GK).
orlegstund f. *time of adversity,* SOL374.
orlegweorc n. *battle,* GEN2020.
ormǣte I. (ā, ē) adj. *boundless, huge,
excessive, intense, Æ,Chr;* AO. II. adv.
[' *ormete* '; metan]
ormǣtlic *excessive,* CHR1117 *: tremendous,*
WYN148. adv. -līce.
ormǣtnes f. *excess, immensity, Æ.*
or-mēte, -mette=ormǣte
ormōd *despondent, despairing, hopeless,* Bo,
Hept; Æ,CP. [' *ormod* ']
ormōdnes f. *desperation, despair,* CP.
orn=arn pret. 3 sg. of iernan.
orn-=oren-
ornest n. *trial by battle,* LL.
oroð n. *breath, breathing, snorting,* B,GL.

orped *adult, active, Bf.* ['*orped*'] adv. -līce *boldly* : *clearly, definitely.*

orrest f. *battle, combat,* CHR. [*ON.* orrusta]

orretscīpe m. *infamy,* WW.

±**orrettan** *to put to confusion, disgrace.*

orsāwle *lifeless, dead,* ÆL.

orsceattinga *gratuitously,* BH 242[7].

orsorg (w. g.) *unconcerned, without care or anxiety, safe,* CP. [*OHG.* ursorg]

orsorglīc (w. g.) *secure,* CP. adv. -līce *carelessly, rashly,* Æ,CP : *without anxiety or hindrance* : *securely, safely,* CP.

orsorgnes f. *security, prosperity,* CP : *carelessness,* CHRD 50[4].

orsorh=orsorg

ortgeard (*CP*), orce(a)rd (*Æ*) m. *garden,* 'ORCHARD*.'

ortgeard-=orcerd-; **ortrēowe**=ortrīewe

ortrēownes (ȳ) f. *diffidence, mistrust,* BL, GD.

ortrīewan (y) *to despair (of)* : (+) *doubt, disbelieve.*

ortrīewe (ēo, ȳ) *despairing, hopeless, AO,W* : *treacherous, faithless.* ['*ortrow*']

±**ortrūwian** w. g. *to despair, doubt,* Æ. ['*ortrow*']

ortrūwung f. *despair,* Sc 131[3,4].

ortrȳw-=ortrīew-

ortȳdre *barren,* A 11·2[42].

orð (KGL)=oroð

orðanc I. mn. *intelligence, understanding, mind* : *cleverness, skill* : *skilful work, mechanical art,* Æ. [*OHG.* urdank] II. adj. *ingenious, skilful.*

orðancbend (o[2]) f. *cunning band,* RD 43[15].

orðances *thoughtlessly,* SOL 164.

orðanclīc *ingenious,* GD 269[13].

orðancpīl (o[2]) m. *ploughshare?* RD 22[12].

orðancscīpe m. *mechanical art,* GL.

orðancum *skilfully,* B,GL.

orðian *to breathe, gasp, Æ* : *long for, aspire to, Æ.* [oroð]

orðonc (CP)=orðanc

orðung f. *breathing, breath, Æ* : *pore.*

oruð=oroð

orwearde adv. *unguarded,* B 3127.

orweg *trackless?* A 19·110.

orwegnes f. *inaccessibility,* WW 220[34].

orwegstīg f. *out-of-the-way track,* WW.

orwēna (indecl. adj.)=orwēne

+**orwēnan** *to despair,* Æ,GD.

orwēne (w. g.) *hopeless, despairing of, Æ* : *despaired of, desperate.*

orwēnnes f. *despair,* Æ,LL.

orwīge *not fighting, unwarlike, cowardly* : *not liable to the legal consequences (of homicide),* LL 76,42[5,7].

orwīte=orwīge

orwurð n. *ignominy,* CPs 82[17].

orwyrð (VPs), orwyrðu f. *shame, dishonour* : *abuse.*

+**orwyrðan** *to disgrace,* GL.

+**orwyrðe** (-de) *traduced,* WW 51[23].

orwyrðlīc *shameful,* MH 156[21].

oryldu f. *great age.* [ieldo]

ōs m., gp. ēsa *a divinity, god* : *name of the rune for* o.

oser '*vimen*,' *osier,* OEG 10[2].

ōsle f. '*merula*,' '*ouzel*,' *blackbird, Cp,Ep, WW.* [amsel]

ōsogen (WW 501[33])=āsogen pp. of āsugan.

ōst m. *protuberance, knot, lump,* GL,MH.

osterhlāf m. *oyster-patty,* LCD 79a.

osterscyll (o[2]) f. *oyster-shell,* LCD 1·338[16].

ōstig ōstiht *knotty, rough, scaly,* GL.

ostre f. *oyster,* WW. [*L.* ostrea]

ostor-=oster-

ot I. (VPs)=æt. II.=oð

oter (*KC*)=otor

oterhola m. *otter's hole,* KC 3·23'.

otor, otr (*Ep*), ottor m. '*otter*,' *WW.*

otsperning (KGL 70[16])=ætspornung

oð I. prep. w. a. and (rarely) d. *to, up to, as far as* : *until,* Æ,AO,CP. oð ðisum *up to now,* ES 43·166. II. conj. *until.* III. as prefix. usu. denotes departure, separation, as in oðfeallan, oðwendan.

oðberan† *to bear away, carry off* : *bring.*

oðberstan[3] *to break away, escape,* KC,LL.

oð-brēdan, -bregdan[3] *to snatch away, carry off, rescue, remove, withdraw, Gu*; AO. ['*atbraid*']

oðclīfan[1] *to cleave to, stick, adhere,* CR 1267.

oðcwelan[4] *to die,* LL 112,53.

oðcyrran (=ie) *to be perverted,* JUL 338.

oðdōn anv. *to put out (eyes),* LL 32,19.

oðēawan=oðīewan

oðēcan *to add to,* VPs 68[27]. [ēac]

oðēhtian *to drive away? dispossess?* LCD 1·384[15] (A 52·118).

ōðel=ēðel; **oðēowan**=oðīewan

ōðer I. (+ at KC 6·155[9]) pron. sb. or adj. (always strong) *one of two,* Æ,AO : *second, Æ* : 'OTHER' : *something else, anything else* : *alternate, next* : *remaining, rest, AO* : *further, existing besides, Æ* : *another* : (in pl.) *the rest, the others.* ōðer...ōðer *the one...the other, Æ, CP* : *other...than, CP.* ōðer oððe...oððe *either...or.* ōðer healf *one and a half.* II. ('*aut*')=āhwæðer. comp. adv. ōðerlīcor *otherwise,* RB 87[19]. ['*otherliker*'] III. *word, speech* ('*eloquium*'), PPs 118[38]. [*ON.* ōðr]

ōðergēara adv. *next year,* LCD.

ōðerhwīle *sometimes,* BF 118[29].

ōðerlucor (RWH 77[7])=ōðerlīcor

oðēwan=oðīewan

oðfæstan† *to inflict upon*, EL,SAT : *set to (a task), entrust, commit*, CP.

oðfaran⁶ w. d. *to flee from*, Ex. ['*atfare*']

oðfeallan¹ *to fall off, decline, decay*, CP : *fall away from, be lost to, be wanting, fail* : *cease to concern*.

oðfēolan³ *to cleave, adhere*, WW416²⁴.

oðfeorrian *to take away*, LCD 1·384⁴.

oðferian *to take away, bear off* : *save (life)*.

oðflēogan² *to fly away*, PH347.

oðflēon² (w. d.) *to flee away, escape*, Æ,AO.

oðflītan¹ *to gain by legal process*, TC169'.

oðgān anv. *to go away, escape*, B2934.

oðglīdan¹ *to glide away, escape*, SOL401.

oðgrīpan¹ *to rescue*, BH408²⁷.

oðhealdan⁷ *to keep back*, CP. ['*athold*']

oðhebban⁶ *to raise, exalt, lift up*, CP.

oðhelde=oðhylde

oðhlēapan⁷ *to escape*, LL218,1¹¹.

oðhrīnan¹ *to touch*, HL16²²⁸.

oðhȳdan *to hide from*, AO94¹¹.

oðhylde (e) *contented*, LCD.

oðīan=ēðian

oðiernan³ *to run away*, LL,MET.

oðīewan (ē, ēa, ēo, ī, ȳ) tr. *to show*,Gen; CP : *show oneself, appear*, El. ['*atew*']

oðīewodnes f. *manifestation*, RWH67² (=ætēow-).

oðlǣdan *to lead away, carry off, snatch from, withdraw*, Ps. ['*atlead*']

oðlengan *to belong, pertain*, WYN49,68.

oðrān=oðhrān pret. 3 sg. of oðhrīnan.

oðrīdan¹ *to ride, proceed*, HELL40.

oðrinnan³ *to run off, escape*, Met20¹³⁸. [v. '*atrin*']

oðrōwan⁷ *to escape by rowing*, CHR897A.

oðsacan⁶ (w. g.) *to deny, abjure*, AO.

oðscacan⁶ *to escape*, LL177,6³.

oðscēotan² *to escape, slip off, turn aside*, Æ.

oðscūfan² intr. *to move off*, PH168.

oðsperning f. *stumbling-block*, KGL.

oðspurnan³ (eo) *to dash against*, BL,KGL.

oðstandan⁶ *to stand fixed, remain, cease*, AO : *stand behind*, Æ : *perplex, hinder*.

oðstillan *to stop*, LCD 1·82⁵.

oðswerian⁶ *to abjure, deny on oath*, AO,LL.

oðswīgan *to become silent*, OET631.

oðswimman³ (y) *to escape by swimming*, CHR915D.

oðtēon² *to take away*, LCD87a.

oððæt conj. *until (or two words)*.

oððe, oðða conj. *or : and*, ANS151·79. oððe...oððe *either...or*, BH ['OTHER'] : (=oð ðe) *until*.

oððēodan *to sever, dismember*, AN1423.

oððet (KGL61¹⁹)=oððæt

oððicgan⁵ *to take away*, Ex338.

oððingian *to obtain by unfair means, usurp*, LL (412⁹).

oððo (BH66²⁰), oððon (HL,LL) conj. *or*. [=oððe]

oððringan³ *to deprive of*, AO : *drive out*, GD.

oðwendan *to turn away, divert, deprive of*, Gen403. ['*atwend*']

oðwindan³ *to escape, get away*, CHR897A.

oðwītan¹ *to charge with, blame, reproach with, taunt*, AO,CP.

oðwyrcan *to harm*, LCD 1·384⁵.

oðȳwan=oðīewan

ōwæstm m. *shoot, branch, twig*, GL,PS.

ōwana (N)=āhwonan

ō-web, -wef (ā) n. *woof, weft*, CP,WW. ['*abb*']

ōwēr, ōwern (BH)=āhwǣr; ōwiht=āwiht

ōwisc f. *edge*, KC3·388²⁵.

ōwðer=āhwæðer; ōwul=āwel

oxa m. nap. oxan, œxen, exen, dp. ox(n)um '*ox*,' Ct,JnL,Rd,VPs,WW; CP.

oxancealf n. *ox-calf*, LEVC1³.

oxangang m. *an eighth of a '*plough-land*,' hide*, BC3·370. ['*oxgang*']

oxanhyrde m. *herdsman*, OEG,WW.

oxanslyppe f. '*oxlip*,' *Lcd*.

ōxn f. *arm-pit*, WW.

oxnahyrde=oxanhyrde

oxnalybb n. *ox-heal (plant)*, LCD.

ōxta=ōcusta; oxum v. oxa.

P

pād f. *covering, coat, cloak*, WW.

paddanīeg f. *toad-meadow, frog-island*, BC 2·246⁶.

padde, pade f. *toad, frog*, Chr1137; BC 2·377¹⁶. ['*pad*']

pēeca m. *deceiver*, BAS40²¹.

pēecan *to cheat, deceive*, RB,W.

pægel m. *gill, small measure, wine vessel*, WW124² (A8·450). [v. '*pail*']

pǣl m. *javelin* (v. OEG19³).

pæll (e) m. *silk robe, cloak*, ÆGr : '*pall*,' *hanging, covering*, ÆH : *purple garment, purple*, BH,WW. [L. pallium]

pællen (c) *of costly stuff, purple*, Æ. ['*pallen*']

pællerēad v. fellerēad; pǣlm=palm

pǣneg, pǣning=pening; -pǣran v. for-p.

pǣrl? '*enula*' ('*gemmula*'? Wülker), ÆGR 304⁷.

pǣtig=(prǣtig), prættig

pæð (a) mfn. nap. paðas '*path*,' *track*, Ct, Ex,Gl,Ps; Æ : *valley*, LkL.

pæððan *to traverse, travel over, pass along*, Met,Rd. ['*path*']

pāl m. '*pole*,' *stake, post*, WW334² : *spade*. [L. palus]

palendse (AO), palentse, pal(l)ente f., palent (Æ) m. *palace*. [Late L. palantium]

palentlic of a palace, palatial, WW 342⁷.
palester=palstr
pallium m. pallium, CHR 804 : splendid garment, ÆL 36¹⁶⁰. [L.]
palm (æ), palma (ea) m. 'palm'-tree, Æ, DR,JnL,VPs : palm-branch, Æ.
palm-æppel, -appel m. date, WW.
palmbearu m. palm-grove, WW 488¹³.
palm-dæg (Æ), -sunnandæg (Lk 19²⁹) m. 'Palm Sunday.'
palm-trēo, -trēow m. 'palm-tree,' Æ,JnL.
palmtwig n. palm-twig, palm-branch, Æ.
+palmtwigian† to deck with palm-branches.
palmwuce f. week of which Palm Sunday is the first day.
palstr, palster sb. prick, point, spike, GL.
palðer (AA 39¹⁵), pandher (PA 12) m. panther.
panic m. a kind of millet, LCD.
panmete m. cooked food, WW 409⁹.
panne (o) f. 'pan,' CP,WW.
pāpa m. 'pope,' BH; Æ,CP. [L. papa]
pāpanhād m. papal office, Æ. ['popehood']
pāpdōm m. papacy, CHR 592.
paper m? papyrus, WW 523⁷.
papig=popig
papolstān (o¹, e²) m. pebble, Æ,OEG. ['pebblestone'; L. papula]
pāp-seld, -setl n. papacy, BL 205²⁰.
paradis m. Paradise, HEX 512.
paralisin ds. of sb. paralysis, ÆL 25⁷²⁴.
-parian v. ā-p.
part m. 'part,' ÆGr. [L. partem]
passion f. nap. passione the part of the gospel containing the account of Christ's passion, OET 444³⁷.
pað, paðu=pæð
pāwa m. pāwe f. peacock, peahen, ÆGr,Ep, Lcd,WW. ['po'; Lat. pavo]
pēa m. peafowl, Ph 312. ['pea']
peall 'defrutum' (sc. vinum), OEG (v. ES 37·184).
peaneg=pening
pear-roc, -ruc m. 'clatrum,' fence by which a space is enclosed, Gl : enclosure, enclosed land, Bo,Chr,KC; ÆL. ['parrock']
pecg m? pig? BC 3·223²² (pygg? v. SKED).
pell, pellen=pæll, pællen
pellican m. 'pelican,' Ps 101⁵.
pen=penn
pending, pene(n)g, penig=pening
pening m. 'PENNY*,' coin, money, Æ,LL (v. 2·614) : pennyweight, Lcd.
pening-hwyrfere, -mangere m. money-changer, WW.
peningslæht (=i³) m. coining money, MtL 17²⁵.
peningwǣg f. pennyweight, LCD 47b.
peningweorð (u³) n. pennyworth, Lcd,KC; Æ.

penn m. 'pen,' fold, BC; Mdf. [L.]
pennig, penning=pening
pentecosten m. 'Pentecost,' Æ,Bf,Chr.
pēo=pīe
peonie f. 'peony,' Lcd 1·168¹⁴. [L.]
peorð n. name of the rune for p, chessman? RUN 38.
peose (piose, pyose)=pise; pere=peru
perewōs n. pear-juice, perry, WW 128²⁰.
perfince=perwince
pernex m. a supposed bird? (mistranslation of L. pernix), RD 41⁶⁶.
per-sic, -soc, -suc m. peach, LCD. [L. persicum]
Persisc Persian, Æ.
persoctrēow n. peach-tree, WW 138¹.
peru f. 'pear,' ÆGr. [L. pirum]
perwince f. 'periwinkle' (plant), WW.
petersilie f. 'parsley,' Lcd. [Ger. petersilie]
pētig=(prǣtig), prǣttig; peððan=pæððan
philosoph m. philosopher, AO.
pic n. 'pitch,' Ep,Sc; Æ. [L. picem]
pic m. point, pointed tool, pick, pickaxe, Cp,WW. ['pike']
picen pitchy, of pitch, BL,DHY.
picgbrēad? (picbred) 'glans,' mast, pig's food, WW 139³⁵. [v. 'pig']
+pician to cover with 'pitch,' Lcd 10a.
picung f. 'stigmata,' pricking, Cp 572 s. ['picking']
pie f. parasite, GL.
pierisc Pierian, A 31·535.
pigment, pihment (y) drug, LCD. [L.]
pihten part of a loom, OEG. [L. pecten]
pil m. a pointed object, spike, nail, shaft, stake, Æ,Chr : arrow, dart, javelin : pl. hairs of plants, Lcd 1·304¹. ['pile'; L. pilum]
pilce=pylece; pile=pyle
pile f. mortar, CP. [L. pila]
pilece=pylece
+piled spiked, spiky, ÆH.
pilere m. one who pounds in a mortar, WW 141¹⁹.
pilian (y¹) to peel, skin, LCD 3·114¹³.
±pilian to pound in a mortar, Ex 16¹⁴,WW 114²⁵.
pilsāpe f. 'silotrum,' soap for removing hair? WW 127³⁶,(NP 8·204).
pilstæf m. pestle, CP 267².
pil-stampe f.,-stocc m.,pilstre f. pestle, WW.
pin f. pain, anguish, torture. [L. poena]
pinbēam m. pine-tree, Æ. [v. 'pine']
pinca=pynca
pinecwalu m? n? torture, W 241¹³.
pinere m. tormentor, GPH,NG.
pinewincle=winewincle
pingan=pyngan
pin-hnutu f. ds. -hnyte fir-cone, Lcd. ['pinenut']

±pīnian *to torture, torment, AO,MtL*; Æ,CP. ['*pine*'; *L.* poena]
pinn sb. '*pin*,' *peg, Bf* : *pen*, Mt p2¹⁷.
pinnan obl. case of wk. sb. pinne? *flask, bottle*, WW97¹⁰.
pīnnes f. *pain, torture*, TC369'.
pinsian *to weigh, consider, examine, reflect*, CP. [*L.* pensare]
pintel '*penis*,' WW292¹' ['*pintle*']
pīntrēow n. '*pine-tree Lcd*; ÆL.
pīn-trēowen, -trȳwen *of or belonging to a pine-tree*, Lcd.
pīnung f. *torment, punishment*, Æ,AO.
pīnungtōl n. *instrument of torture*, Æ.
pionie (OEG56⁴¹⁸)=peonie; piose=pise
pīpdrēam m. *piping*, Lcd3·208²².
pīpe f. '*pipe*,' *tube, Lcd*; Mdf : *wind instrument, W,WW* : *channel*, KC3·380². [*L.*]
pipeneale f. *pimpernel* (Swt).
piper=pipor
pīpere m. '*piper*,' *MtR,WW*.
pīpian *to '*pipe*' (*blow an instrument*), NC* (ZDA34·234).
piplian (y) *to show eruptions, break out in pimples*, Lcd.
pīplic *musical*, OEG1644.
pipor (e²) m. '*pepper*,' *Æ,Lcd*. [*L.* piper]
piporcorn n. '*pepper-corn*,' *Lcd*.
piporcwyrn f. *pepper mill*, ANS84·325.
piporhorn (e) m. *horn for pepper*, LL455,17.
±pip(o)rian *to season with* '*pepper*,' *Lcd*.
Pirenisc *Pyrrhenian*, A31·535.
pirge (GL)=pirie
pirgrāf m. *pear-orchard*, KC5·284'.
pirie, pirige (Æ) f. ·*pear-tree*.
pīs *heavy*, NG. [*L.* pensum]
pise f. (eo, io, y) *pea, Cp,Lcd,WW*. ['*pease*·']
pisle f. *warm chamber?* WW186¹⁰. [*Low L.* pisalis]
pīslic *heavy*, NG. adv. -līce.
pistel=pistol
pistol m. *letter*, Æ : *apostolic letter*, Æ. ['*pistle*'; *L.* epistola]
pistolbōc f. *book of the epistles, LL.* [v. '*pistle*']
pistolclāð m. *vestment worn by the epistoler*, BC3·366'.
pistolrǣdere m. *epistle-reader, sub-deacon*, CM.
pistolrǣding f. *a lesson in the church service*, Æ. [v. '*pistle*']
pistolrocc (e²) m. *vestment worn by the epistoler*, TC429²².
pitt=pytt
piða wm. *inward part*, '*pith*,' *Bo*; CP.
placunis (wlacunis)=wlæcnes
plæce f. *open space, street*, DR,MtLR. ['*place*'; *L.* platea]

plæg-=pleg-; plæse, plætse=plæce
plætt m. *slap, smack*, ÆH2·248'.
plættan *to buffet, smack*, Jn19³. ['*plat*']
plagian=plegian
planēta *chasuble* (BTs). [v. '*planet*']
plante f. '*plant*,' *shoot, CP,VPs*. [*L.* planta]
±plantian *to* '*plant*,' *Æ,CP,VPs*.
plantsticca m. *dibble*, WW106¹⁷.
plantung f. '*planting*,' *WW* : *plant, Mt*.
plaster I. n. '*plaster*' (*as medicament*), DD, Lcd. [*L.* emplastrum] II.=palster
-platian v. ā-pl.
+platod *plated* (*of gold*), OEG11⁶¹.
platung f. *metal plate*, WW196²⁴. [v. '*plate*']
pleagian=plegian
plega (a, æ) m. *quick motion, movement, exercise, Chr,Cp,Cr,Gen,WW* : '*play*,' *festivity, drama, game, sport, AO,Bl*; Æ : *battle, B* : *gear for games*, ApT12¹⁷ : *applause*.
plegan, ±plegian (a, æ, eo) (pres. occly. strong) *to move rapidly, An,Gen* : *exercise, occupy or busy oneself, Bo,Bl,LL* : '*play*,' *sport with, amuse oneself, dance, CP,MtL* : *contend, fight* : *play on an instrument, Ps* : *clap the hands, applaud, El,VPs* : *make sport of, mock*, Æ : *cohabit* (*with*), Rd43².
plegemann=plegmann
plegende '*playing*,' *Shr*.
plegere m. '*player*,' WW108⁹.
plegestōw=plegstōw
plegestre f. *female athlete*, OEG4735.
plegestre f. *female athlete*, OEG4735.
pleghūs n. '*playhouse*,' *theatre*, OEG1752.
plegian=plegan
pleglic (GL) *athletic* : *scenic* : *comic*.
plegmann m. *gymnosophist, athlete*, GL.
plegol *playful, jocular*, ÆL21²⁹² : *wanton*, Chrd54²².
plegscip n. *small vessel*, WW181⁴⁰.
plegscyld (e²) m. *play-shield, small shield*, GL.
plegstede m. *playground*, KC6·244⁸.
plegstōw f. *playground, gymnasium, amphitheatre, Lcd,WW*. ['*playstow*']
plēo ds. of pleoh.
pleogan=plegan
pleoh n. gs. plēos *danger, risk, harm*, Æ,AO, CP : *responsibility*, LL70,36².
plēolic *dangerous, hurtful, hazardous*, Æ, AO.
plēon⁵ (w. g.) *to expose to danger, adventure oneself*, CP.
plett f? *fold*, NG. [*L.* plecta]
plice v. plyccan.
plicettan? *to play with*, v. NC315.
plicgan *to scrape, scratch*, GPH396.
pliht m. *peril, risk, danger, damage, VPs, WW*; Æ. tō plihte *dangerously*. [plēon; '*plight*']

plihtan *to imperil, compromise, LL.* ['*plight*']
plihtere m. *look-out man at the prow,* OEG.
plihtlic *perilous, dangerous,* LCD,WW.
ploccian=pluccian
plōg, plōh m. *what a yoke of oxen could plough in a day, a plough-land, Lcd.* ['*plough*']
plont-=plant-
plot '*plot*' *of ground,* LL400,3 (v. 3·237).
pluccian *to* '*pluck,*' *tear, Æ,Mt,WW.*
plūm f. *down?* Cp1600 (v. A47·248).
plūmblǣd f. *plum,* LCD 86a.
plūme f. '*plum,*' *Æ,Cp : plum-tree, Cp,Ep, Erf;* Mdf.
plūmfeðer f. *down,* ES9·39. [*L.* pluma]
plūmsēaw (ē²) n. *plum-juice,* LCD3·114'.
plūmslā f. *wild plum, sloe,* WW139⁴.
plūmtrēow n. '*plum-tree,*' *Lcd;* ÆGR.
plyccan only in plice 2 sg. subj. (*IM*122) and plyce (imperat.) (*IM*127) *to pluck, pull, snatch,* NC315. ['*plitch*']
plyhtlic=plihtlic
plȳme f. *plum, plum-tree,* GL. [*L.* *prunea]
pocādl f. *eruptive disease, pox,* LCD.
pocc m. '*pock,*' *blister, pustule, ulcer, Lcd.*
pocca (*LkL*)=pohha
pohha, poh(ch)a m. *pocket, bag, CP,MkL.* ['*pough*']
pohhede *baggy,* RB. ['*pough*']
pōl m. '*pool,*' *CP,JnL; Æ;* Mdf.
pōlbǣr f. *pasture-land by a pool,* KC (MLR 19·203).
polente? f. *parched corn, Æ.* ['*polenta*'; *L.*]
pollegie f. *pennyroyal,* LCD. [*L.* pulegium]
pollup m. *scourge?* (BT), LL (278').
pon-=pan-; pond=pynd
popæg (Cp)=popig
popelstān (*OEG* 1815)=papolstān
popig m? '*poppy,*' *Gl,WW.*
popul *poplar?* KC3·219⁸ (v. BT).
por, porr, porlēac n. *leek, Æ.* [*L.* porrum]
port I. mn. '*port,*' *harbour, AO : town (esp. with market rights or with a harbour), BH, Chr,LG,LL;* Mdf. [*L.* portus] II. m. *portal, door, gate, entrance, MtL,Ps;* Mdf. ['*port*'; *L.* porta]
portcwēne f. *prostitute,* NG.
porte f.=port II.
portgeat n. *city gate, Æ,WW.*
portgerēfa m. '*port-reeve,*' *mayor, Æ,Ct,LL, WW.*
portgeriht n. *town-due,* KC3·138¹⁰.
portherpað *main road to a town,* KC3·453'.
±portian *to bray (in a mortar),* CP.
portic mn. *portico, porch, vestibule, sanctuary, chapel, BH,Jn; Æ.* ['*portic*']
portmann m. *townsman, Æ,WW.* ['*portman*']
portstrǣt f. *public road,* KC.

portweall m. *city wall, Æ.*
portweg *public road,* KC6·8¹.
port-wer (DR), -weora (KC) m. *citizen* (=-wara).
±pos n. *cold in head, Lcd.* ['*pose*']
posa (NG)=pusa
poshlīwe *a kind of shelter?* KC3·82².
posl, postling m. *pellet, pill,* LCD.
post m. '*post,*' *Æ,WW.* [*L.* postis]
postol m. *apostle,* LkR. ['*postle*']
potian *to push, butt, goad, Æ,W.* ['*pote*']
pott m. '*pot,*' *Lcd*1·378' (v. late).
pottere m. '*potter,*' *BC*3·49'.
prætt m. nap. prattas *trick, craft, art, Æ,W, ZDA.* ['*prat*']
prættig (e) *tricky, sly, cunning, wily, astute, WW; Æ.* ['*pretty*']
prafost (ā¹? o¹, a², e²) m. *officer,* '*provost*' *(of a monastery), KC,MH,RB; Æ.* [*L.* propos(i)tus]
prafostfolgoð m. *order or rank of provost,* RB126⁶.
prafostscīr f. *provostship,* RB124¹⁶.
pranga v. wranga.
prass m. *noise, tumult,* ÆL.
prattas v. prætt; prēan=prēon
prēde=prȳte
prēdicere m. *preacher,* ÆGR276¹.
prēdician *to preach,* Lk8¹.
prēdicung f. *preaching,* NC315.
prēon m. '*fibula,*' *pin, brooch, TC,WW.* ['*preen*']
prēost (ēa, ē, īo) m. '*priest,*' *presbyter, BH, LL,Mt,Nic,WW; AO,CP.*
prēostgesamnung f. *community of priests,* NC315.
prēosthād m. '*priesthood,*' *BH,OEG; Æ,CP.*
prēosthēap m. *body of priests,* GD302²⁵.
prēosthīred (ȳ²) m. *body of priests,* CHRD.
prēostlagu f. *ecclesiastical law, canon law,* LL380,2³.
prēostlic '*priestly,*' *canonical, Chrd*89³⁷; CM667.
prēostlīf n. *priests' quarters, monastery,* ÆL 31⁸⁴⁶.
prēostrēaf n. *priestly garment,* CHRD64²⁷.
prēostregol m. *canonical rule,* CHRD.
prēostscȳr f. *parish, LL.* ['*priestshire*']
prēowthwīl f. *twinkling of an eye, moment, Æ.*
press f. *press (for clothes),* LL455,15.
prica m., price f. '*prick,*' *point, spot, dot, Æ, Lcd,Mt : small portion of space or time, Æ, Bf.*
-priccan v. ā-p.
pricel, pricels m. '*prickle,*' *goad, point, Lk, OEG : jot, tittle, MtL,LkL.*
±prician tr. *to pierce, Æ : prick out :* intr. '*prick,*' *sting, Sc :* (+) *point out,* BF.

pricmǣlum adv. *point by point*, Bf112³⁰.

pricðorn m. *thorn-tree*, KC3·436¹⁶.

pricung f. *'pricking,' remorse*, Æ2·88²².

prīm n? *the first hour* (6 *a.m.*) : *the service held at* 6 *a.m.*, *'prime,'* RB,WW. [*L.* prima (sc. hora)]

prīmsang m. *prime-song, service of prime*, Chrd,LL.

princ? *twinkling of an eye, moment*, v. OEG 2369.

prior m. *'prior,' Chr,TC*. [*L.*]

prīt=prȳt

-prīwan v. be-pr.

prodbor (prot-) n. *auger?* MtR.

profast=prafost

prōflan *to assume to be, take for*, LL. [*L.* probare]

profost=prafost

prūd, prūt *'proud*,' arrogant*, OEG,Sc.

prutene (ū?) f. *southern-wood, wormwood*, Lcd. [*L.* abrotanum]

prūtian *to be 'proud,' Chrd*.

prūtlic *haughty*. adv. -līce *proudly, pompously, magnificently : confidently*, Bf150¹⁴.

prūtscipe m. *arrogance, pride*, Gl,Ps.

prūtswongor *overburdened with pride*, W 257¹² (v.l.).

prūtung f. *pride, arrogance*, OEG. [v. *'proud'*]

prȳde=prȳte; prȳdecere=prēdicere

prȳt(o), prȳte f. *'pride,' haughtiness, pomp*, Æ,LL,OEG,W.

psaltere (*Lcd*)=saltere

psealm (*WW*), psalm=sealm

pūca m. *goblin*, OEG23². [*'puck'*]

pūcel m. *goblin*, GPH394²⁴². [*'puckle'*]

pucian *to poke, creep*, GPH397.

pudd n. *ditch*, GPH399.

puduc m. *wart*, GPH396.

pull mf. *pool, creek*, KC (v. GBG). [*Keltic*]

pullian *to 'pull,' draw*, AA : *pluck off* (*wool*), Lcd3·176.

pūlsper n. *reed*, MtL11⁷ (v. A39·364).

pumic m? *pumice*, Lcd38a. [*L.* pumicem]

pumicstān m. *pumice-stone*, WW148³.

pund n. *'pound'* (*in weight or in money*), *pint, Bf,Ct,G,Lcd*; Æ,AO : *weight*, Wyn 43. [*L.* pondo]

pundar, pundor=pundur

pundere m. *one who weighs*, MtLp2³.

pundern n. *pair of scales : plumb-line*, OEG.

punderngend m? *one who weighs* (BTs), KGl545.

pundfald a *'pinfold,' pound*, BC.

pundmǣte adj. *of a pound weight*, RB63¹⁶.

pundur n. *weight, plumb-line*, Cp264d. [*L.* pondere]

pundwǣg f. *pound weight, measure* (*of corn*),

pūnere m. *'pounder,' pestle*, Sc95¹⁹.

pung m. *purse, Cp*. [*'pung'*]

pungetung f. *pricking*, Lcd. [pyngan]

±pūnian *to 'pound,' beat, bruise, Lcd,Sc*.

punt *'punt,' WW*. [*L.* ponto]

pūr *bittern? sea-gull?* WW116,285. [*'purre'*]

purlamb n. *lamb without blemish*, Ex12⁵.

purpl, purple (*JnL*)=purpure

purpure f., purpur (WW152²⁰) *purple, a purple garment, AO,Mk*; CP. [*'purpur'*]

purpuren *purple*, WW151²⁴. [*'purpurine'*]

purs *'purse,' OEG*18b³⁶. [*late L.* bursa]

pusa (o) m. *bag, scrip*, NG.

puslian *to pick out*, Lcd127a.

-pūte v. æle-p.

pūtung f. *instigation*, Chrd62²⁷. [*'putting'*]

pȳcan *to 'pick,' Chr*796f?

pyff m. a *'puff' of wind*, Bo47²⁶ (Napier).

pyffan, pret. pyfte *to puff, blow*, v. OEG 1886.

pyhment=pigment; pyl-=pil-

pylce (*A*7·30)=pylece

pyle (i) m. *'pillow,' Æ,AO,CP,Lcd*. [*L.* pulvinum]

pylece f. a *warm fur garment, robe, pelisse*, A,WW. [*'pilch'*]

pylewer *pillow*, OEG56¹⁶. [*'pilliver'*]

pyll=pull

pylu (OEG29⁴), pylwe=pyle

pynca (i) m. *point*, OEG3683. [pyngan]

pynd? sb. *cistern? lake?* Rim49.

+pyndan *to impound, shut up*, CP276. [*'pind'*]

pynding f. *dam*, CP276. [v. *'pind'*]

pyngan (i) *to prick*, CP. [*'ping'*; *L.* pungere]

pypelian=piplian

pyretre f. *pellitory*, Lcd3·12¹⁹. [*L.* pyrethrum]

pyrie, pyrige=pirie, pirige

pyrtan *to strike, beat*, GPH401.

pyse (Æ)=pise

pysecynn n. *sort of pea*, Lcd71a.

pȳtan *to put out* (*eyes*), Chr796f?

pytt m. *'pit,' hole, well, grave, AO,Ct,G,LL*; CP; Mdf : *pustule*. [*L.* puteus]

pytted *'pitted,' dented, marked* (*of a sword*), EC225'.

pyttel (i) m. *hawk, kite*, WW.

Q

qu- is usually written cw-, which see.

R

rā m. nap. rān *'roe,' roebuck, BH,Gl,Lcd*; Mdf.

rabbian *to rage*, W84¹¹.

raca m. *'rake,' Bf, Gl*; GD192.

racca m. *part of the rigging of a ship*, WW.
racente f. *chain, fetter*, Bl,Bo,Sc; AO.
['*rackan*']
+**racentēaglan** *to chain*, ÆL31³⁵.
racen-tēah f. gs. -tēage *chain, fetter*, Bl; Æ.
['*rakenteie*']
racete=racente
racetēage (*Mk*)=racentēah
racian (w. d.) *to rule, govern, control* : *go
forward, move*, CP,W : *hasten*, NR28²⁵.
['*rake*']
raciend m. *speaker, orator*, GD265¹².
rācing (*JnL*)=rǣcing
racu I. f. *exposition, explanation, observation : reason, argument : account, narrative,*
Æ,CP : *rhetoric : comedy*. [reccan] II. f.
(LL455¹⁵)=raca
rād I. f. *ride, riding, expedition, journey*, BH,
Bo,Lcd : *raid*, Chr,LL : *modulation*, RUN5 :
name of the rune for r. ['*road*'; rīdan]
II. pret. 3 sg. of rīdan. III. m.=rǣd
+**rād** I. n. *reckoning, account* : *condition,
stipulation*, AO : *intention : reason, wisdom,
discernment*, Æ,AO : *accuracy*. ðus +r.
such, of this kind. hū +rādes *how*. II.
adj. *conditioned, circumstanced, disposed,
adapted*, CP : *wise, clever, skilful*, Bo;
AO : *straight*, Guth. +rāde sprǣc *prose*.
-**rād** v. brand-r.
rādcniht m. *tenant holding subject to service
on horseback*, v. LL1·73. ['*radknight*']
rade=hraðe; +**rādegian**=+rādian
rādehere, rādhere=rǣdehere
radelod *having straight branches?* BC3·44.
rādhors n. *riding-horse*, HL. ['*roadhorse*']
radian=hradian
+**rādian** (eg, ig) *to reckon with, arrange*, Bo
96¹⁵ : *call to account*.
+**rādlic** *proper, fitting*, Æ. adv. -līce, *in-
telligently, clearly*.
+**rādod** *intelligent*, LCD3·196⁷.
rador=rodor
radost=hraðost, v. hraðe.
rādpytt m. *draw-well?* RD59¹⁵.
+**rādscipe** m. *discretion*, MET22⁴⁸.
rādstefn f. *message taken by a mounted man*,
LL456,3. [cp. rādcniht]
rādumbel=rāradumbla
rādwērig *weary of travelling*, RD21¹⁴.
ræc=rec; **ræcan**, ræccan=reccan
rǣcan I. *to* '*REACH*' *out, stretch out*, Æ,CP :
offer, present, give, grant, Æ : *procure?*
(Lieb), LL447⁶ and 3·249 : *extend* (intr.).
II.=hrǣcan
+**rǣcan** '*reach*,' *attain, overtake*, Bl,Sat :
give : obtain, seize, take, get, gain, Chr;
AO : *address, speak to*, AO : *handle, deal
with : strike*.
ræcc m. *setter* (*dog*), WW276⁴. ['*rache*']

ræce f. (*Cp*)=raca; **ræced**=reced
rǣcing f. '*reaching*,' *holding out, presenting*,
JnL : *seizing, capture*, DR (hr-).
ræd=hrǣd
rǣd I. (ā, ē) m. *advice, counsel*, Æ : *resolution, deliberation, plan, way, design*, Æ,
AO : *council, conspiracy*, Æ : *decree,
ordinance*, CP : *wisdom, sense, reason,
intelligence*, Æ : *gain, profit, benefit, good
fortune, remedy*, Æ : *help : power, might*.
tō rǣde +niman *resolve*, AO. tō rǣde
ðincan *seem advisable*. ['*REDE*'] II. adj.
=rēad. III. (ē) n. *reading lesson*, NG.
±**rǣdan** (ē) pret. 3 sg. reord, rēd; also wv.
to advise, counsel, persuade, Æ : *consult,
discuss, deliberate, plot, design*, Æ, AO :
decree, decide, Æ : *rule, guide, have
control over, possess : arrange : equip,
provide for : bring, deliver* (*goods*) : *have an
idea, guess, forebode*, Æ : *read, explain*,
Æ : *learn by reading : put in order*, BH :
help. ['*READ*,' '*REDE*']
rǣdbana (ē) m. *accessory to a murder*, LL.
rǣdbora (ē) m. *adviser, counsellor*, Æ :
(*Roman*) *consul*.
rǣdda m. *robin*, WW44¹⁸. [rēad]
rǣdde wk. pret. 3 sg. of rǣdan.
rǣde (ē) I. adj. (±) *prepared, ready, ready
for riding* (*horse*), PPs : *skilled, simple.*
['*i-rede*'] II. n. (+) *trappings, armour,
accoutrements, ornaments*. III. f. *reading,
lesson*, RB18⁹. IV. (+) *design, device?*
EL1054,1108.
rǣdecempa m. *horse-soldier*, WW228³⁹.
rǣdefæsting f. *entertainment of the king's
visitors, or of his messengers when riding
on his business*, KC2·60'.
rǣdegafol n. *rent paid in one payment* (*in
money or in kind*), LL118,67.
rǣdehere m. *mounted troop, cavalry*, AO.
+**rǣdelīce**=+rǣdlīce; **rǣdelle**=rǣdelse
rǣdels mf., rǣdelse (ē) f. *enigma, '*riddle*,'
Æ : *consideration, discussion : imagination,
conjecture, interpretation*.
rǣdemann m. *horseman*, PPs32¹⁵.
rǣden (ē) f. *condition, terms, stipulation,*
Æ : *rule, government, direction : estimation,*
WW.
±**rǣdend** m. *controller, disposer, ruler :
diviner*, Sc75¹².
rǣdendlic *relating to a decree*, WW387,
494.
rǣdengewrit n. *written agreement*, TC168¹².
rǣdere m. '*reader*,' '*lector*' (*ecclesiastical
order*), Bf,RB,LL : *scholar, diviner, expounder, interpreter*, OEG.
rǣdescamol m. *couch, reading-desk?* WW.
rǣdesmann m. *counsellor, adviser : steward,*
EC. ['*redesman*']

rǣdewiga m. *horse-soldier*, WW 228³⁸.
rǣdfæst *resolute, wise*, Æ.
rǣdfæstnes f. *reasonableness*, LL(306¹⁹).
rǣdfindende *giving counsel*, WW 383⁸.
rǣdgeðeaht n. *deliberation, counsel*, EL, W.
rǣdgifa m. *counsellor, councillor*, CHR,LL : *consul*.
rǣdgift '*consulatus*,' '*senatus*,' GL.
rǣdhors n. *riding-horse*, Æ(8²³³).
rǣdhycgende *knowing, wise*, FT 26.
rǣdic (e) m. '*radish*,' Lcd,WW. [L. radicem]
rǣdin=rǣden
rǣding I. f. '*reading*,' *a reading (passage read), lesson, narrative*, Æ,CP,RB : *consideration, consultation, counselling*, Æ (100²⁷⁰); (+) WW 383²⁵. **II.**=rǣden
rǣdingboc f. *lectionary, book of the lessons*.
rǣdinggewrit (WW 115¹⁰)=rǣdengewrit
rǣdinggrād m. *steps to lectern*, NC 316.
rǣdingscam-ol (-ul) m. *ambo, rostrum, lectern, reading-desk*, OEG (=rǣdescamol).
rǣdistre f. *female reader*, GL.
rǣdlēas (ē) *ill-advised, unwise, helpless, rash, in disorder*, Chr,Da : *wretched, bad, miserable*. ['*redeless*']
rǣdlic *expedient, advisable, wise*, AO,CP. adv. -līce *wisely, prudently, skilfully, cunningly*, CP,HL : *deliberately, on purpose : fully, explicitly*, GD 102¹⁹. ['*redly*']
rǣdlīce=hrǣdlīce
rǣdmægen n. *productive force*, RIM 10? (or? rādmægen).
rǣdnes=hrǣdnes
±**rǣdnes** f. *agreement : decree : condition : definition, decision*.
rǣdo f. (RB 62¹⁵n)=rǣd III.
+**rǣdod** *harnessed, caparisoned*, Æ (cp. +rǣde).
rǣdrīpe=hrǣdrīpe
rǣdsnotter *clever, sage*, AN 473.
rǣdðeahtende† ptc. *taking counsel*, EL.
rǣdðeahtere m. *counsellor*, AO 72,256.
rǣdðeahtung f. *counsel, advice*, AO 154⁹⁷.
rǣdwǣn (AO)=hrǣdwǣn (or ? rǣd-=rād-).
rǣdwita m. *counsellor, adviser*, DD 299.
rǣdystre=rǣdistre; **rǣf**=rēaf
+**rǣf** *brought home to, convicted of*, LL 66,32.
rǣfen=hrǣfn
rǣfn-an, -ian (GD) *to perform, do : undergo*.
rǣfs-=reps-
rǣfter (e, ea) m. *rafter, beam*, BH,GL.
rǣge (ā) f. *roe*, GL,LCD. [rā]
rǣgel=hrǣgl
rǣgerēose f. *spinal muscles*, LCD.
rǣghār *grey (with lichen)*, RUIN 10. [ragu]
rǣgl=hrǣgl; **rǣgn**=rēgn
rǣgolfæst=regolfæst; **rǣgu**=ragu

rǣhte pret. 3 sg. of rǣcan.
rǣm=hrǣfn; **-rǣman** v. ā-r.
rǣnc=renco; **rǣng-**=reng-·
rǣp pret. 3 sg. of repan.
rǣpan (ȳ) (±) *to bind, fetter, capture, enslave : yoke together*, ÆL 31⁷⁸⁵.
rǣpling=rǣpling
rǣpling m. *prisoner, criminal*, Æ. [rǣpan]
rǣplingweard (ē) *warder*, WW 111¹⁰.
rǣps=reps
+**rǣptan** *to bind, fetter*, Bo 112¹.
rǣran *to '*rear*,' raise, build, create, BH,Gen : lift up, elevate, promote, Bl : establish, begin, commit, do, Cr,W*; CP : *arouse, excite, stir up, Rd*. [rīsan]
rǣs m. *rush, leap, jump, running*, Æ,Cr, LG (hr-) : *onrush, storm, attack*, Æ,B. ['*rese*']
rǣsan *to rush, hasten*, CP : *enter on rashly : rush upon, attack*, B,Bl,MH. ['*rese*']
rǣsbora† m. *counsellor, leader, guide*.
rǣsc m. *shower*, OEG 3974.
rǣscan *to vibrate, quiver*, DHy 94¹.
rǣscettan *to crackle, creak, coruscate*, DD, WW. ['*reschette*']
rǣsian=rǣswian
rǣsn n. *plank, beam, wall-plate, raising piece*, Æ,WW. ['*rasen*']
rǣst=rest
rǣswa† m. *leader, counsellor, ruler, guide : chief, prince, king*.
rǣswan, rǣswian *to think, consider, conjecture, suspect*, CP.
rǣswum dp. of *rǣs? or rǣsu? f. or *rǣswa? suggestion, deliberation, counsel*, Az 126.
rǣswung f. *reasoning, conjecture*, GL.
rǣt m. '*rat*,' WW 118⁴¹.
rǣt pres. 3 sg. of rǣdan.
rǣð-=hrǣð-; **rǣðe**=hraðe
rǣðe=rēðe
+**rǣðle**=+rǣde
rǣw I. (±) (ā, ēa) f. *row, line : succession*, LCD : *hedgerow*. [v. '*rew*' and Mdf] **II.**=hrǣw
+**rǣwed**, +rǣwe(n), +rǣwod *arranged in rows*, WW.
-**rǣflan** v. ā-r.; **rāge**=rǣge
raggig *shaggy, bristly, rough*, OEG. ['*raggy*']
ragofinc=ragufinc
ragu (æ) f. *lichen*, Æ,LCD.
ragufinc (ea¹) m. *name of a bird, kind of finch*, WW.
rāha [Cp]=rā
rāhdēor n. *roe-buck*, Æ,Lcd. ['*roedeer*']
rāhhege m. *deer-fence*, KC 3·77'.
rāhte=rǣhte pret. sg. of rǣcan.
ram=ramm; **ramesa**=hramsa
ramgealla m. *ram-gall (plant)*, LCD.

ramm (o) m. '*ram*' (*sheep*), *Æ,VPs* : (*engine of war*), *Æ,CP* : (*zodiacal sign*), *Bf.*

ran pret. 3 sg. of rinnan.

rān I. n. *open robbery, rapine.* [*ON.*] II. pret. 3 sg. of rīnan. III. nap. of rā.

ranc *froward, proud, overbearing*, *Æ* : *noble, brave, strong*, *Chr* : *ostentatious* : *full-grown, mature*, *ÆL*35²² . ['*rank*'] adv. -līce *boldly, confidently* : *ostentatiously, showily*, LL. ['*rankly*']

rancstrǣt f. *straight road? splendid road?* GEN 2112.

rand (o) m. *border, edge?* KC : (†) *boss of shield, rim of shield* : (†) *shield, buckler, B.* [v. '*rand*']

rand-bēag, -bēah m. *boss* (*of a shield*), *shield*, *Æ,*GL.

randburg f. *fortified city?* JUL 19 : *shield-wall of waves* (*in the Red Sea*), Ex 463?

randgebeorh n. *protecting shield of waves* (*in the Red Sea*), Ex 296.

randhæbbend (o¹) m. *shield-bearer, warrior*, B 861.

rand-wiga†, -wīgend†, -wīggend m. *shield-warrior, man at arms.*

rānn=rān III.

rāp I. m. '*ROPE*,' *cord, cable*, AO,CP. II. pret. 3 sg. of rīpan.

rāpgenga m. *rope-dancer*, WW 408²⁵ .

rāpincel n. (*small rope*), *cord, string*, GL.

rāplic adj. *of rope*, GPH 399.

+rār n. *roaring, howling*, MH 16²⁰ .

rāradumbla m., rāredumle f. *bittern*, GL. [*Ger.* rohrdommel]

rārian *to* '*roar*,' *bellow, cry, lament, mourn*, *Æ,MH,MtL.*

rārung f. '*roaring*,' *howling, bellowing*, WW.

rās pret. 3 sg. of rīsan.

rāsettan† *to rage* (*of fire*), CR,MET. [rǣsan]

rāsian *to explore*, B 2283.

ratian=hratian

raðe=hraðe

rāw (*Lcd* 89b)=rǣw ['*row*']

+rāwan *to arrange in line*, WW.

raxan *to stretch oneself*, Guth. ['*rax*']

rēac pret. 3 sg. of rēocan.

rēad I. '*RED*,' *Æ,CP*; (*of gold*), *Æ.* II. pret. 3 sg. of rēodan.

rēada pl. *small intestines*, WW 159³⁸ : *tonsil*, LCD. ['*read*']

rēadbasu (e²) *reddish purple*, LL.

rēade adv. *with red colour*, LCD.

rēadfāh *red of hue*, RUIN 10.

rēadgoldlǣfer f. *plating of* (*red*) *gold*, OEG 1070.

rēadian *to be or become* '*red*,' *Lcd,MtR*; *Æ.*

rēadlēaf *red-leaved*, BC; Mdf.

rēadlesc '*rubricata*' (*pellis*), v. OEG 5324.

rēadnes f. '*redness*,' *BH,Bl*; *Æ.*

rēadstalede *red-stalked*, LCD 1·378'.

rēaf (ē) n. *plunder, booty, spoil*, *LkL,Ps* : *garment, armour, vestment*, *Mt*; *Æ.* ['*reaf*,' '*reif*']

+rēafa=+rēfa

rēafere m. *robber, plunderer*, *Æ,Bo,Lk*; AO, CP. ['*reaver*']

-rēafetian v. wīn-(h)r.

rēafgend m. *robber*, KC 3·350²⁶ .

±rēafian I. *to rob, plunder, take by force, waste, ravage*, *Æ,Bo,B,G,VPs,W*; AO : *carry off, remove, transport*, CP : (+) *strip*, NG. ['*reave*'] II. *to robe*, ÆP 126¹⁰ .

rēafigende *rapacious*, *ÆL.* ['*reaving*']

rēaflāc nm. *robbery, rapine*, *ÆH* : *plunder, booty*, Bo. ['*reflac*']

rēafol *rapacious*, LCD,GL.

rēafolnes f. *rapacity*, OEG.

reafter=ræfter

rēafung f. *spoliation, plundering*, AO 84²¹ .

reagufinc (GL)=ragufinc

reahte pret. 3 sg. of reccan.

reahtigan *to dispute, discuss*, AO 130²⁶ .

rēam I. m. *cream*, Lcd 113b. ['*ream*'] II.= hrēam

rēama=rēoma

rēamwīn? n. *a kind of wine*, OEG. [cp. *Fr.* vin crémant]

rēat pret. 3 sg. of rēotan.

rēaðe=rēðe; rēaw=rǣw

rēawde=hrēawde, pret. of hrēawan.

rēc m. *smoke*, Gen,Ps. ['*reek*']

+rec I. n. *rule, government* : *decree* : *explanation.* II. n. *tumult*, MtL 27²⁴ (? for ungerec). III. *a small vessel, brigantine?* WW 30,432.

recan⁵ *to bring, convey*, WW 420¹⁸ : ·(+) *go, move, rush.*

±rēcan I. pret. 3 sg. rēhte *to fumigate, expose to smoke*, Lcd : *burn incense*, GL. [v. '*reek*'] II.=reccan II.

reccan I. *to stretch, tend, go*, CP : *extend, hold out to, give* : (±) *instruct, explain, interpret*, *Æ* : *tell, narrate*, *B,Bo,G* : *quote* : *correct, reprove*, AO : (+) *to wield* (*authority*), *give judgment, decide, direct, control*, *Æ,CP* : (+) *prove* : (+) *count, reckon*, *Æ.* ['*recche*'] II. (rēcan) *to take care of, be interested in*, *Æ,B,Bo,Cr* : *care for*, *Mk* : *care, desire* (*to do something*), Bo, *Lcd,LL,MkL,WW.* ['*reck*']

recce- (CP), recci-=rēce-

-recce v. earfoð-r.

+reccelic=+reclic

rēccelīest (e³, ea³, i³) f. *carelessness, negligence*, CP.

reccend m. *ruler, guide*, *Æ,*AO.

reccend(d)ōm m. *governance, oversight*, CP.

reccenes=+recenes

reccere m. *teacher, ruler, director,* CP : *interpreter,* MtLp2¹³.

reccing f. *narrative,* ÆL30³⁷⁵.

reced nm. *building, house, palace, hall* : '*triclinium,*' OEG.

recedlic (æ) *palatial,* WW.

±recednes f. *narrative, history,* Æ : *interpretation* : *direction, correction.* ānfeald +r. *prose.*

recedōm=reccendōm

rēcel (v. MFH171)=rēcels

rēcelēas '*reckless,*' *careless, negligent,* BH, Bo,Cp,W.

rēcelēasian *to neglect,* W. ['*reckless*']

rēcelēaslīce adv. *heedlessly, carelessly, inattentively,* CP (rēcce-), HL. ['*recklessly*']

rēcelēasnes f. '*recklessness,*' *carelessness, negligence,* LL,W ; Æ.

rēce-lēast, -līestu=rēccelīest

rēcels (ī, ȳ) m. *incense, frankincense,* MtL, Lcd,Lk; Æ. ['*rekels*'; rēc]

rēcelsbūc (ȳ) m. *censer,* WW.

rēcelsfæt (i) n. *censer,* Æ. ['*rekelsfat*']

rēcelsian *to perfume with incense,* LCD.

rēcelsrēoce f. *burning of incense,* FBO75¹⁹.

recen *ready, prompt, quick,* Wa : *rapid, violent,* Cr,Ps. ['*reken*']

recendōm=reccendōm

recene (i, y) adv. *instantly, quickly,* Æ.

+recenes f. *narrative, interpretation* : *direction, correction.*

recenian *to pay* : (+) *explain, recount, relate,* Ex525. ['*reckon*']

recenlīce (o²) adv. *immediately, forthwith,* G. ['*rekenly*']

recennes *coming together?* WW381⁷ : *going?* BHв436¹⁵.

rēcetung (VPs)=hrǣcetung

+reclic *circumstantial,* CPc193¹⁵. adv. -līce *directly, straight* : *methodically* : *smoothly.*

+recnes f. *direction, inclination,* EPs138³.

recnian=recenian

recon I. *remuneration,* GL. II.=recen

recse=risce; recyd=reced

+recu=+rec-

rēd I.=rǣd. II. pret. 3 sg. of rǣdan.

red-; rēd-=ræd-; rǣd-; rēde=rēðe

redestānm.'*synophites,*'*red ochre?* WW47¹⁵.

+redian (æ) *to reach* : *discover,* W: *effect.*

rēdon pret. pl. of rǣdan.

±rēfa (usu. +) m. *high official, '*reeve,*' steward, sheriff, count ('*comes*'), prefect, consul,* BH,Ct,Mk,MH.

+rēfærn n. *court-house,* MH124¹³.

+rēfland n. *land held by a reeve,* BC.

+rēfmǣd f. *reeve's meadow,* Ct. [v. '*reeve*']

+rēfmann m. *official, courtier,* GD308·315.

refsan=repsan

+rēfscipe m. *reeve's office, stewardship,* Æ : *consulate,* WW371,495. ['*reeveship*']

+rēfscīr f. *steward's office, prefecture,* OEG.

refter (ē?)=ræfter

regellic=regollic; regen-=regn-, rēn-

regn (rēn; Æ,MH) m. '*rain,*' VPs : *showers of rain,* Bl.

regn-=rēn-; regnan=rīnan

regnheard *very hard,* B326. (cp. regnðēof)

regnian I. *to '*rain,*' MtR5⁴⁵. II.=rēnian

regnðēoft m. *downright thief.* [FTP335]

regol (eo) m. *rule, regulation, canon, law, standard, pattern,* Æ : *monastic code of rules,* Æ : *ruler (instrument).* [L. regula]

regolbryce m. *breach of rules,* W166²².

regolfæst (æ) *rigid, strict, adhering to monastic rules,* MEN44.

regolian *to draw lines with a ruler,* NC316.

regollagu f. *monastic law,* LL266,25.

regollic *according to rules, canonical, regular.* adv. -līce.

regollīf (eo) m. *life according to ecclesiastical rules,* BH,LL.

regolsticca m. *rule, ruler (instrument),* Æ.

regolðēaw m. *discipline of (monastic) rule,* A10·144¹²⁵.

regolweard m. *regulator, director, ruler, abbot, provost,* BH.

regul=regol; reht (VPs)=riht

rehte pret. 3 sg. of reccan.

rēhte pret. 3 sg. of rēcan II.

relicgang m. *visiting of relics,* MH62,72.

reliquias. mpl. *relics of saints* (reliquium is used in sg.), MFH171.

reliquiasōcn f. *visit to a shrine,* MFH172.

rēman=rȳman

remian *to mend,* v. NC317.

Rēmisc *Roman,* JnL18¹².

remm-=hremm-; remn=hræfn

rempan *to be hasty, precipitate,* CP149¹².

rēn (AO,CP)=regn

+rēn (ī) n. *ornament,* CP : *building,* NG.

rēnboga m. '*rainbow,*' Æ.

renc, renco (æ) f. *pride, ostentation,* LL,W.

rendan *to '*rend,*' tear, cut down,* LG.

rendegn (Erf1137)=ærnðegn

+rendrian *to peel,* LCD25a.

rēndropa m. '*raindrop,*' Lcd3·278'.

rene=ryne

+rēne I. (ī) n. *ornament,* CP : *instrument* : *building,* NG. II. (±)=±ryne

renel (KGL)=rynel; reng=regn

renge (y) f. *spider, spider's web,* Ps. [L. aranea]

rengwyrm (æ) m. *intestinal worm,* LCD.

±rēnian *to prepare* : (+) *arrange, set in order, mend, set (trap)* : (+) *adorn.* +r. tō bismere *humiliate, degrade,* AO. [*regnian; Goth. raginōn]

rēniend m. *revealer*, EL880.
rēnig (*Lcd,Rd*), rēnlic (Æ) '*rainy*.'
+**rennan** *to coagulate*, EPs67¹⁶.
rēnscūr m. '*rain-shower*,' Æ.
rēnsnægl m. *snail*, OEG23²⁰.
+**rēnung** (regn-) f. *arranging*, WW371¹⁹.
rēnwæter n. '*rain-water*,' *Lcd*.
renweard m. *house-guardian*, B770. [ærn]
rēnwyrm m. *earthworm*, WW. ['*rainworm*']
rēo (1)=rēowe; (2)=hrēoh
rēoc *savage, furious*, B122.
rēocan I. sv² intr. *to emit vapour, steam or smoke*, '*reek*,' *Lcd,Ps*; Æ : *stink*. II. (WW 244³⁶)=rēcan
rēocende (ē) *smoking, steaming*, Æ,*Jud*, *MtL*. ['*reeking*']
rēod I. '*red*,' *ruddy*, Æ,*Erf,MH*. ['*reod*'] II. n. *red colour*, WW. III.=hrēod
rēodan² *to redden, stain with blood* : (†) *kill?*
reodian *to sift? search out?* (=redian? ES 51·184), EL1239.
rēodian=rēadian
rēodmūða m. '*faseacus*' (*bird*), WW234²⁵
rēodnæsc (WW38¹³)?=rēadlesc
rēofan² (only in pp. rofen) *to rend, break*, Ex463.
reogol=regol
reohhe f. '*ray*,' *thornback?* WW181⁶.
+**rēohnung**=+rēnung; **reoht**=riht
rēol=hrēol ; **reoma**=rima
rēoma (ēa) m. *membrane, ligament*, *Lcd*, WW. ['*rim*']
rēon I.=rēowon pret. pl. of rōwan. II. *lament*, HELL6.
rēone asm. of rēo(we).
±**rēonian** *to conspire, plot*, Æ.
rēonig† *mournful, sad, gloomy*, EL.
rēonigmōd† *mournful, weary*.
±**rēonung** f. *whispering, muttering, conspiracy*, ÆL,AO : *astrology*, OEG. [rūn]
reopa m. *bundle of corn, sheaf*, VPs. ['*reap*']
reopan (VPs)=repan; **reopian**=ripian
±**reord†** I. fn. *voice*, B,Cr,Ps : *language, speech*, ÆL. ['*rerde*'] II. f. *sustenance, food* : *meal, feast*. III. pret. 3 sg. of rǣdan.
reordan=reordian II.
reordberend† m. *man*, CR.
+**reorddæg** m. *feast-day*, ÆL23b⁷⁵³.
+**reordglēawnes** f. *skill in singing*, LPs32³.
reordhūs n. *eating room, refectory*, MkL14¹⁵.
reordian I. *to speak, discourse*, B,Cr,Gen : *read*. ['*rerde*'] II. (±) *to feed, refresh, entertain, feast*.
+**reordnes** f. *food, feasting, banquet* : *satiety*.
±**reordung** f. *refection, meal*, Æ.
+**reordunghūs** n. *refectory*, WW328³².
+**reordungtīd** f. *meal-time*, GD145¹³.
reosan '*pissli*,' *name of a plant?* WW300⁵.
+**rēosan**=+hrēosan; **-rēose** v. rǣge-r.

rēost *rest* (part of a plough), CP,WW. ['*reest*']
rēotan²† *to weep, mourn, wail*.
rēote v. rētu.
rēotig *mournful, sad, tearful*, RD1¹⁰.
rēow I.=hrēoh. II. pret. 3 sg. of rōwan.
rēowe f. *covering, rug, blanket, mantle*, BH, LL. [=rȳhe]
rēowlic=hrēowlic; **rēowot**=rēwet
rep-=hrep-
repan⁵ *to reap*, CHR,VPs.
repel m. *staff, rod*, GD20²⁶ (v. ES37·192).
reps m. *response* (*in a church service*), Æ, RB. [*L*. responsorium]
repsan (æ) *to reprove, blame*, GL.
repsung (æ) f. I. *a division of the night*, BF 122²¹ (hr-). II. *reproving*, GL. [=*rǣfsung]
repung=hrepung; **rēran**=rǣran
+**rerding**=+reordung; **resce**=risce
rēsele f. *answer, solution*, RD40²⁸. [=*rǣsele]
rēsian=rǣswian
+**resp** *convicted of*, LL (v.l. for +rǣf).
respons *response*, LL(140²¹).
rest (æ) f. '*REST*,' *quiet, repose, sleep*, Æ : (±) *resting-place, bed, couch* : *grave*.
±**resta** f. *bedfellow, consort, wife*, Æ.
restan (absol. and refl.) *to* '*REST*,' *repose*, Æ : (+) *give rest to, lodge* : (w. g.) *rest from, remain, lie*, Æ.
rēstan *to rejoice, exult?* PPs113⁴.
restbedd n. *bed, couch*, PPs131³.
rest-dæg (æ), reste-, resten- (Æ) m. *day of rest, Sabbath day*, CP,G. ['*restday*']
restengēar n. *year of rest from work*, LEV 25⁵.
restgemāna m. *cohabitation*, BL,LCD.
resthūs n. *chamber*, APs,BH.
restlēas '*restless*,' *without rest*, RB121¹⁴.
+**restscipe** m. *cohabitation*, BH76²⁷.
rēsung (CP)=rǣswung
±**rētan** *to delight, cheer, comfort*, CP. [rōt]
rētend m. *comforter*, W257⁴.
rētu f. (only in d. rēote) *joy*, B2457.
reðe *righteous, just*, PPs (or ?=rēðe).
rēðe (of persons) *fierce, cruel, violent, harsh, severe*, Æ,B,BH : (of things) *terrible, dreadful, Bl,Bo,CP* : *zealous*, CP. ['*rethe*']
rēðegian=rēðian
reðehygdig *right-minded*, ALM2.
rēðeman m. *usurer* (GK), PPs108¹¹. [*Goth*. raðjo?]
rēðemōd† *savage, cruel, fierce, indignant*.
rēðen *wild*, ÆL10¹⁰². (cp. AS96).
rēð-ian, -igian *to rage, be fierce*, Æ,GD.
rēðig *fierce*, WW402²³.
rēðigmōd *savage, fierce*, MET25¹⁷.
rēðlic *fierce, cruel, deadly*. adv. -līce *violently*.

rēŏnes f. *cruelty, severity, harshness, Bl,CP*; AO : *savageness, ferocity, BH,Lcd*; CP : *zeal,* CP : *storminess,* LkL8²⁴ (hr-). ['*retheness*']

±**rēŏra** m. *rower, sailor,* GL.

+**rēŏre** *constant,* CP306¹⁵.

±**rēŏru** np. *oars,* GD,HL.

rēŏscipe m. *fury, anger,* WW245¹⁷.

rēwet, rēwut n. *rowing,* Æ : *rowing-boat, vessel,* Æ. [rōwan]

rex m. inserted for 'cyning' at EL610, 1042.

riaht (K)=riht I.

rib, ribb n. '*rib,*' Æ,Cp,MH,Soul; AO.

ribbe f. *hound's-tongue, ribwort, Ep,Lcd, WW.* ['*rib*']

ribbspāca np. *rib-spokes, the brisket?* (BT), WW265²⁴.

rīca m. *influential man, ruler,* Æ.

rīcan (BDS16³⁶⁷)=rēcan (*riecan)

rīcceter, rīccetere (Æ)=rīceter

rīce I. *strong, powerful, Da*; LCD : *great, mighty, of high rank, Æ,BH,MH*; AO,CP : '*rich,*' Æ,BH,Bo,Lk. **II.** n. *rule, reign, power, might, authority, empire, Æ,Bl,Cr, MH*; AO. fōn tō rīce *to ascend the throne : kingdom, nation, diocese, B*; AO,CP : *reign (period of time).* ['*riche*']

rīcedōm n. *kingly rule,* W125⁹. ['*richdom*']

rīcels=rēcels; **rīcen-**=recen-

rīceter, rīcetere n. *force, might, power, rule, dominion, glory, greatness,* CP : *ambition,* Æ : *tyranny, oppression, violence : arrogance,* ÆL32²³³.

rīcg, ricig=hrycg

rīclic *sumptuous,* AS39⁴. adv. -līce *powerfully, Æ,CP : sumptuously, Lk.* ['*richly*']

rīcone=recene; **rīcs**=risc

rīcsere m. *ruler,* DR113³.

rīcsian *to bear rule, reign, govern, tyrannize,* Æ,AO,CP : *dominate, prevail.*

rīcsiend m. *ruler,* DR102⁸.

rīcsung f. *domination,* DR174¹⁰.

+**rid** n. *riding,* WW229².

-**rīda** v. brand-r, tot-r.

-**rīdan**¹ (±) *to '*ride*,'* AO : *move about, swing, rock, ride (at anchor) : float, sail, Gen : chafe (of fetters) :* (+) *ride over, occupy (a country), seize :* (+) *ride up to*, tō handa gerīdan *to bring into a person's power or possession.*

rīdda m. *rider, horseman, horse-soldier,* Æ.

-**rīdel** v. for(e)-r.

rīdehere m. *mounted force,* OEG2⁴⁴⁴.

rīdend m. *rider, cavalier,* B2457.

rīdere m. '*rider,*' *trooper, knight, Chr*1085L.

rīdesoht f? *fever,* NG. [hriŏ? suht?]

rīdusende *swinging,* GL.

rīdwiga m. *horse-soldier,* WW110²⁸.

rīece=rīce; **rīeht**=riht; **rīf**=hrif

rīf *violent, fierce, ravenous, noxious,* AA.

+**rīf** n. *seizing, catch (of fish) : number caught.*

+**rīf** *garment,* WW107¹¹ (v. NC295).

-**rīfe** v. hege-r.

rīfe *abundant,* Lcd3·164²¹. ['*rife*']

rīfelede *wrinkled,* OEG18b⁷⁸. ['*rivelled*']

rīfeling m. *shoe or sandal of raw hide, WW* 125. ['*rivelling*']

rīfelung f. *wrinkle,* A32·506.

+**rīfian** *to wrinkle,* ÆH1·614¹⁴.

rīft, rifte (y) n. *cloak, veil, curtain, Æ,Cp, MtL.* ['*rift*']

rīfter m. *reaping-hook, sickle, scythe,* GL.

rīftre, riftere (y) m. *reaper,* Æ,GL.

rīge=ryge; **rignan**=rīnan

rīhsian=rīcsian

±**riht** (æ, e, eo, y) **I.** n. (*what is straight*), 'RIGHT,' *equity, justice, law, canon, rule, Æ,CP : cause, legal action,* Æ : *a right, privilege, CP : correctness, truth.* on r.; mid rihte *rightly, correctly, properly : what is due, duty, obligation, CP : reckoning, account.* **II.** adj. *straight, erect, direct :* 'RIGHT,' *proper, fair, just, equitable, lawful, permissible : upright, righteous : true, correct : fitting, appropriate : real, genuine : right (as opposed to left).*

rihtæŏelcwēn f. *lawful wife,* W298¹⁸.

rihtæŏelo (y) npl. *true nobility,* Bo,MET.

rihtæw f. *lawful wedlock,* W : *lawful wife,* LL.

±**rihtan** (e, y) *to make straight : set right, amend, correct, rebuke,* Æ : *guide, govern, direct, rule : set up, assign, restore, replace, erect.* ['RIGHT']

rihtāndaga m. *proper (fixed) day,* LL.

rihtandswaru f. *retort, reproof,* PPs37¹⁴.

rihtcynecynn (y¹) n. *legitimate royal family,* AO.

rihtcyning m. *lawful king,* BH360¹⁴.

rihtcynn n. *true stock,* W13⁶.

rihtdōm *just judgment,* LL320,15b.

rihtdōnde ptc. *doing what is right,* BL.

rihte adv. 'RIGHT,' *due, straight (of direction, as in right on, due east), outright, CP : precisely, exactly, just, AO : rightly, duly, well, correctly, truly, properly, fairly, justly : directly, immediately,* Æ. ŏǣr rihte *thereupon, straightway.*

+**rihte** n. *right, due, Æ,Chr*(1074L) : *religious rite, office,* ÆL. +rihtu pl. *last offices.* on +r. *straight on.* up on +r. *upright.* ['*i-riht*']

rihtebred n. *measure, rule, square,* WW.

rihtend m. *director, ruler, leader, guide,* Bo, GD.

rihtendebyrdnes f. *right order,* NC317.

rihtere m. *director, ruler,* Bo. ['*righter*']

rihtes (e) adv. *right, straight,* KC3·392⁶.

rihtfædrencynn (e, y) n. *direct paternal descent or pedigree.*

rihtfæsten n. *duly ordained fast,* LL132,8.

rihtfæstendæg m. *duly appointed fast-day,* Æ.

rihtfæstentīd f. *duly appointed time of fasting,* Æ.

rihtfremmende (y)† *acting rightly.*

rihtful *'rightful,' honourable,* CHR1100L.

rihtgebroðru mpl. *brethren,* DR57⁴.

rihtgefēg n. *proper joint,* GD248²⁶.

rihtgefremed *catholic, orthodox,* BH456¹⁵.

rihtgegylda m. *duly appointed member of a guild,* TC606¹⁴.

rihtgehātan⁷ *to pledge oneself, swear,* RPs 14⁴.

rihtgehīwan pl. *lawfully married persons,* LL22n16.

rihtgelēafful *orthodox,* BH,LL.

rihtgelēaffulnes f. *right belief,* ÆL23b⁶⁹⁷.

rihtgelēaflīce adv. *in an orthodox manner,* CM1167.

rihtgelȳfed (ē³) ptc. *orthodox, catholic.*

rihtgelȳfende *believing rightly, faithful,* BL.

rihtgemæcca m. *lawful husband,* LL.

rihtgemǣre=rihtlandgemǣre

rihtgemet n. *proper measure,* NC317.

rihtgesamhīwan pl. *lawfully married persons,* LL22,38.

rihtgescēad n. *right understanding,* GD56².

rihtgeset *duly appointed, canonical,* CM412.

rihtgesetednes f. *right ordinance,* NC317.

rihtgesetnes f. *rightful office,* Bo12¹³.

rihtgesinscipe *lawful wedlock,* LL.

+rihtgeswinc *lawful work,* CHRD70³.

rihtgeðancod *right-minded,* LPs.

rihtgewitt (y) n. *right mind,* MH192²².

rihtgewittig *in one's right mind,* GD245²².

rihtgifu f. *irrevocable gift,* LL366,81; 385.

rihthǣmed (y¹) n. *lawful wedlock,* CP.

rihthāmscyld m. *legal means of protection to a homestead?* LL5,32 and v. ANS 115·389 (but v. BTs).

rihthāmsōcn f. *actual 'hāmsōcn' (v. hām-sōcn),* LL614,49⁵⁸.

rihthand f. *right hand,* NIC492; 508.

rihthanddǣda m. *actual perpetrator,* LL 188,1³.

rihtheort *righteous, just,* CPVPs.

rihthīwa (y¹) m. *lawful consort,* CP.

rihthlāford m. *rightful lord,* LL.

rihthlāforddōm m. *lawful authority,* CHR 918c.

rihthlāfordhyldo (e⁵) f. *loyalty,* W.

rihting f. *action of guiding aright, direction, order, rule, guidance,* Æ,RB : *correction, reproof,* Æ : *body of rights, privilege? privileged district?* CHR963E : *'regularis' (in computation),* BF30¹⁹. ['*righting*']

±rihtlǣcan *to make straight, put right, rectify, set in order,* RB,W : *direct.* ['*rightleche*']

rihtlǣce m. *duly qualified physician,* W12¹².

rihtlǣcung (y) f. *criticism, correction,* Æ,CP.

rihtlagu f. *regular legal ordinance,* W.

rihtlandgemǣre n. *lawful boundary (of land),* KC.

rihtlic (y) *right, proper, just, fit, righteous,* Æ : *adapted, fitted.* adv. -līce *justly, uprightly, virtuously,* Æ : *properly,* 'RIGHTLY,' *regularly : correctly, precisely,* CP.

rihtlīcettere m. *downright hypocrite,* W54¹⁴.

rihtlīf n. *right life, regular union (of married people),* LCD3·176'.

rihtlīflād m. *right way of life,* GD336¹.

rihtlīðlic *articulate,* WW355⁸.

rihtmēdrencynn (e¹, oe²) n. *direct mother's line,* OET651.

rihtmēterfers n. *correct hexameter verse,* BF 100⁷.

rihtmunuc m. *true monk,* RB73¹⁹.

rihtnama m. *correct name,* ÆL23⁵⁴⁷.

rihtnes (e) f. *'rightness,' rectitude, equity,* Ps : *perpendicularity, straightness,* WW : *reckoning, account,* MtL : (+) *correction.*

rihtnorðanwind (y¹) m. *north wind,* AO17¹⁷.

rihtraciend m. *expounder of righteousness (the preacher, Ecclesiastes),* GD264²⁷.

rihtracu (y) f. *correct account,* TC170⁴ : *right reason,* GD262.

+rihtreccan *to guide, show rightly,* AS26¹⁶.

rihtregol m. *right rule, canon,* LL,OEG.

rihtryne m. *right or straight course,* Bo,MET.

rihtscīr (LL252,21)=rihtscriftscīr

rihtscrīfend m. *jurisconsult, lawyer,* WW.

rihtscriftscīr f. *properly assigned district of a confessor, parish,* LL240,12¹.

rihtscylling m. *shilling of sterling money,* LL(227⁷).

rihtscytte (y) *sure of aim,* CRA51.

rihtsinscipe *lawful wedlock,* Æ(1·148).

rihtsmēaung (e¹) f. *right reasoning or argument,* MtL p9¹⁰.

rihtspell (y) n. *true discourse,* CP9¹⁰.

rihtstefn f. *ordinary voice,* GD28²⁸.

riht-tīd (BH206²⁰) f., -tima (Bo12¹³) m. *proper time.*

riht-ðēow, -ðēowa m. *lawful slave,* GD180⁶.

rihtungōrēd m. *plumb-line,* WW150⁴¹.

rihtweg m. *right way,* W.

rihtwer m. *lawful husband : legally correct 'wergild,'* LL466; 467.

rihtwestende (y¹) m. *extreme western limit,* AO8³².

rihtwīf n. *lawful wife,* LL348,54¹.

rihtwillende *wishing to do right,* Bo11¹⁷.

rihtwīs *'righteous,' just,* Bl,Bo,Chr,VPs; CP : *right, justifiable,* Bl.

rihtwīsend m. *Sadducee*, Mt3[7].

±rihtwīsian *to make 'righteous,' justify*, Lk, VPs; Æ : *direct aright, rule*.

rihtwīslīc (y[1]) *righteous*, CP. adv. -līce *rightly, reasonably*, Bo. [*'righteously'*]

rihtwīsnes f. *'righteousness,' justice*, Mt; CP : *rightness, reason : righteous acts*, Æ.

+rihtwīsung (e) f. *justification*, VPs88[32].

rihtwrītere m. *correct writer*, GL.

rihtwuldriende *orthodox*, BHB310[33].

rihtwyrðe *proper, fitting*, AS13[22].

rihtymbren n. *duly appointed Embertide*, W117.

rihtymbrendagas mp. *duly appointed Ember days*, W117.

rīm-=hrīm-

±rīm n. *number, counting, reckoning*, Chr, Cr,VPs; Æ,AO,CP. [*'rime'*]

rīma m. *'rim,' verge, border, coast*, Cp,WW.

rīman (±) *to count, number, reckon*, AO,Ps; Æ : *tell, enumerate, relate*, CP : *account, esteem as*. [*'rime'*]

rīmāð m. *oath by a number of persons*, LL 154,9.

+rīmbōc *calendar*, ÆH1·98'.

±rīmcræft m. *arithmetic, reckoning, computation : calendar*, ÆL10[1].

rīmcræftig *skilled in reckoning*, BF.

rīmcræftiga m. *one skilful at figures*, BF42[12].

-rīme v. earfoð-r.; **rīmforst**=hrīmforst

rīmge-tæl, -tel† n. *number*, GEN.

+rīmian *to calculate*, A8·307[40] (v.l.+rūnian at BF70[24]).

rīmpan v. hrimpan.

rīmre m. *reckoner, calculator*, BF70[17].

+rīmtæl (HR13[11])=rīmgetæl

rīmtalu f. *number*, EL820.

+rīn (NG)=+rēn

rīnan[1] (and wv.) impers. and intr. *to rain*, Æ,Bl,Mt : *to send down, or fall, like rain*, Lk,VPs : (+) *to wet with rain*, WW379[15]. [*'rine'*]

+rīnan=+hrīnan

rinc m. *man, warrior, hero*, B,Cr,Met. [*'rink'*]

rincgetæl n. *number of men*, Ex234.

rincsetl (HGL489)=hringsetl

rind, rinde f. *'rind,' bark, outside*, Bo,Cr, Lcd; CP : *crust*, Æ.

-rindan, -rindran v. be-r.

rindeclifer f. *wood-pecker? nut-hatch?* WW 427[29].

rinden *of bark*, GPH390.

rindlēas *hav+ng no bark*, WW190[31].

rīne=rȳne; **ring**=hring; **rīning**=hrīning

±rinnan[3] *to 'run*,*' flow*, Chr,Cr,Ps,Sat : (+) *run together, blend, coagulate*, Cp. [=iernan]

rinnelle f. *runnel, rivulet, stream*. [=rynele]

rinning (y) f. *rennet*, WW128[43] : (+) *co-agulation*, LCD1·292[8]. [*'running'*]

±rīp (ȳ) n. *harvest*, BH,Chr,Mt : *cut corn, sheaf : ripeness, maturity*, PPs118[147]. [*'ripe,' 'reap'*]

rīpan I. (±) (ēo, ȳ) *to 'reap*,*'* Æ,AO,Chr, CP,G. II. (AS10[5])=rīpian

+rīpan (hr-) *to rob*, G,W.

rīpe *'ripe,' mature*, BH,Bo.

rīpemann m. *reaper*, MtL (hr-). [*'reap-man'*]

rīpere m. *'reaper*,*'* Mt.

rīpian (ēo) *to become 'ripe,' ripen*, Æ,Bf.

rīpīsern n. *sickle*, MtLR4[29].

rīpnes f. *'ripeness,' harvest*, LPs.

rippel? *a coppice?* (BTs), Ct.

riptere=riftere

rīptīma m. *time of harvest*, Mt. [*'reaptime'*]

rīpung f. *ripening, ripeness, maturity*, Bf, RB,VPs. [*'riping'*]

+rīs n. *fury*, WW43[6].

±rīsan[1] I. (usu. +) *to 'rise,' stand up*, Ps : *rise together*, DR25[1] : *be fit, be proper*, Æ, Gu. [*'irise'*] II. *to seize, carry off*.

risc, risce (e;=y) f. *'rush,'* Cp; Mdf. [L.]

riscbedd n. *bed of rushes*, EC. [v. *'rush'*]

riscen *made of rushes*, Æ. [*'rushen'*]

rischealh (y[1]) *rushy corner? rushy slope?* BC1·183[2]. [v. *'rush'*]

risciht *rushy*, KC.

risclēac n. *rush leek, rush garlic*, WW356[36].

riscrīðig *rushy stream*, KC.

riscðȳfel m. *rush-bed*, Ct,GL.

risen-=risn-

+risen *seizure*, GUTH78[5]. [rīsan]

rīsende? *rapacious*, BL225[17].

+risenlīc *convenient, suitable, becoming, honest, honourable*, AO,CP. adv. -līce.

risiendum *'odorato'?* OEG23[4].

+rislīc *equal to, like*, BHCA450[3].

±risne I. *fit, meet, proper, convenient*. II. n. (usu. pl.) *what is fitting, dignity, honour*, AO.

+risnes f. *congruity*, WW383[16].

+risnian *to agree, accord*, WW336[37].

risoda m. *rheum*, LCD (Harl) 1b.

rīt pres. 3 sg. of rīdan.

rīð f. *favour, indulgence*, Sc224[7].

rīð fm., (±) rīðe f. *rivulet, stream*, Æ,Bo, CP; Mdf. [*'rithe'*]

rīðfald m. *cattle-pen, cow-shed*, WW195[34]. [hrīð-]

rīðig n. *streamlet*, Mdf.

rīðða=ryðða; **rix** (Æ,BH)=risc

+rixian=rīcsian; **rō**=rōw II.

rocc m. *over-garment, rochet*, LCD,WW. [Ger. rock]

roc(c)ettan *to eructate, belch forth, utter*, NG, VPs.

rocclan *to rock (a child)* RWH 137¹².

rōd I. f. *'rood,' cross, gallows, Æ,Bl,G,MH, VHy;* CP : *crucifix, Chr* : *rood (land measure),* BC : *plot of land of a square rod, BC,EC* (v. GBG and Mdf).

rōdbīgenga m. *worshipper of the cross,* WW 216¹⁶.

rōdbora m. *cross-bearer,* GPH 389.

rodd m? *'rod,' stick (to beat with),* HL 15¹¹⁹.

rōdehengen f. *hanging, crucifixion, Æ.*

roden (B1151?) pp. of rēodan.

roder=rodor

rōdetācen n. *sign of the cross, Æ.*

rōdewyrðe *deserving hanging,* HL 18³⁸⁹.

+rōdfæstnian *to crucify* (BT).

rodor (a) m., gs. rod(o)res *ether, sky, heavens, firmament, Æ,CP.*

rodorbeorht *heaven-bright,* DA 369.

rodorcyning† m. *king of heaven,* EL.

rodorlic *of the heavens, heavenly, celestial, Æ.*

rodorlīhtung (roder-) f. *dawn,* LPs.

rodorstōl (a¹) m. *heavenly throne,* GEN 749.

rodortorht *heavenly-bright,* GEN 1416.

rodortungol n. *star of heaven,* GEN 1667.

rōdwurðiend m. *cross-worshipper,* HGL 403³⁰.

roeðe (Cp,NG)=rēðe

rōf I.† *vigorous, strong, brave, noble, renowned.* II. ? *array, number,* BH (Sch) 699 n 83.

rofen pp. of rēofan; **rōflēas**=hrōflēas

rogian *to flourish,* GNE 119.

rōhte pret. 3 sg. of rēcan.

rom=ramm

Rōm (*Bl,Bo*), **Rōmeburg** (*AO*) f. *'Rome.'*

Rōmān-e, -an pl. *Romans,* AO.

rōmānisc *Roman, Æ,AO.*

romēl *sooty,* WW 10³¹ (BTs). [=hrūmig]

Rōm-feoh, -gesceot (*LL*) n., -penig (*LL, Shr,W*) m. *'Rome-penny,' 'Romescot,' Peter's pence.*

rōmian (w. g.) *to possess?* GEN 350.

romm=ramm

Rōmwalh (u¹) m. *Roman.* [wealh]

Rōm-ware (AO), -waran pl. *inhabitants of Rome, Romans.*

rond=rand

rop I.? *broth,* WW 272⁹. II.=ropp

rōp *liberal,* RD 58³.

rōpnes f. *liberality,* WW.

ropp m. *intestines,* Lcd,WW (hr-). ['*rope*']

ropwærc m. *colic,* WW 211¹².

rōrend=rōwend

rōsbedd *rose-bed,* OEG 23⁸.

+rōscian (o?FTP 353)=rōstian

rōse, rose f. *'rose,' Æ,Bf,Bl,Bo,MH.* [L. rosa]

rōsen *made of roses,* Lcd : *rose-coloured, rosy, Æ,ZDA.* ['*rosen*']

+rōsod *of roses,* OEG 3278.

rōst=rūst

+rōstian *to roast, dry,* WW.

rot=hrot

rōt *glad, cheerful, bright,* RIM : *noble, excellent, Æ.*

rōt(e)? *'root,'* NC 318.

rōtfæst ('*root-fast*'), *firmly established, Chr* 1127.

rōthwīl f. *time of refreshing,* PPs.

±rotian *to 'rot,' putrefy, Æ,Bf,CP,Lcd.*

rōtlice *gladly, cheerfully,* BH 348³.

rōtnes f. *gladness,* DR : *refuge, protection,* Pss.

+rōtsian *to comfort, gladden,* CP 417⁹.

rōtsung f. *refuge, protection, comfort,* EPs 9¹⁰.

rotung f. *corruption, ulcer,* WW 114¹⁴. [rotian]

rōðer I. m. *rower, sailor,* CP. [rōwan] II.=rōðor

rōðhund m. *mastiff,* WW. [ryðða]

rōðor n., gs. rōðres *oar, scull,* CP,WW. ['*rudder*']

rōðra=rēðra

rōw I. *quiet, calm, gentle, soft, mild,* CP. II. f. *quietness, rest,* Gu. ['*row*']

±rōwan⁷ pret. pl. rēowon, rēon *to go by water, 'row,' sail, swim,* LkL (hr-), WW; Æ.

rōwend m. *rower,* CP : *sailor, Æ.*

rōwett=rēwet

rōwing f. *'rowing,'* NG.

rōwnes f. *rowing,* BH 384²².

rudduc m. *robin,* WW. ['*ruddock*']

rūde I. m. *scabbiness, scab,* WW 161¹⁴ (=*hrūda?* A 30·253). II. f. *rue.* [L. ruta]

rudig *rubicund, 'ruddy,'* OEG 2932.

rudon pret. pl. of rēodan.

rudu f. *red colour,* ApT : *ruddy complexion,* WW : *red cosmetic, ÆL.* ['*rud*']

rues=ryges gs. of ryge; **rūg**=rūh

rugern m. *month of rye-harvest, August?* LL 12 Pro.

rūh gs. rūwes *'rough*,' Guth,Rd;* Æ : *coarse (of cloth),* DHy,WW : *hairy, shaggy, Æ : undressed, untanned,* WW.

ruhha? m. *ray (fish),* NC 324 (suhha). ['*rough*']

rūm I. adj. (±) *roomy, wide, long, spacious, ample, large, liberal,* B,Bo,Mt,VPs; Æ, CP : *unoccupied : unfettered, open, unrestricted, loose : noble, august.* II. m. (±) *space (extent or time), 'room,' Gen,Lk : scope, opportunity,* B,Met. on +rum *at large, apart.*

rūma *stumbling-block,* A 41·102²⁰.

+ruma† m. *space, place.*

rūman=rȳman

rŭme (once +) adv. *widely, spaciously, roomily, amply, liberally, extensively, abundantly, Gen,Lcd : light-heartedly : in detail,* JUL314. ['*room*']
rŭmed-=rŭmmōd-
rŭmgāl *revelling in release from confinement (Noah's dove),* GEN 1466. adv. -līce *widely,* NC318.
rŭmgifa (eo²) m. *bountiful giver,* BH 194³³.
rŭmgiful (y²) *bountiful,* Æ,CP.
rŭmgifulnes (eo², y²) f. *liberality, bounty, profusion,* Æ.
rŭmheort *large-hearted, generous,* B : *free from care,* RB. adv. -līce, VH.
rŭmheortnes f. *liberality,* LL,W.
rŭmian *to become clear of obstructions,* Lcd 1·76¹³. ['*room*']
rŭmlic *benign, liberal : plentiful,* Æ. adv. ±rŭmlīce *at large, fully, kindly, liberally, abundantly,* Æ,Bl,MtL. ['*roomly*']
rŭmmōd *liberal, lavish, kind,* CP.
rŭmmōdlic *ample, large, full, liberal, gracious.* adv. -līce.
rŭmmōdnes f. *large-heartedness, liberality, kindness,* CP.
rŭmnes f. *breadth, abundance,* Æ.
rŭmōd=rŭmmōd
rŭmor adv. comp. *still further,* GEN.
+rumpen=+hrumpen v. hrimpan.
rŭmwelle *spacious,* MtL 7¹³.
rŭn f. *mystery, secrecy, secret, El,JnL : counsel, consultation, B,KC,Wa : (secret) council : runic character, letter, BH : writing, An,Da.* ['*roun*']
+rūna m. *counsellor, confidant,* GL.
rŭncofa m. *chamber of secrets, breast, bosom,* MET 22⁵⁹.
rŭncræftig *skilled in mysteries,* DA 734.
rŭnere m. *whisperer, tale-bearer,* Æ. ['*rouner*']
rŭnian (+at BF 70²⁴) *to whisper, murmur, talk secrets, conspire,* Æ,Ps,Sol. ['*round*']
rŭniende *whispering,* WW 441. ['*rouning*']
runl *foul? running?* LCD 3·36¹⁷. [?=*hrunol]
rŭnlic *mystical,* MtL p 5¹¹.
-runn v. cȳs-gerunn.
+runnen pp. of +rinnan.
+runnenes f. *that has been cooled or congealed,* GPH 398.
rŭnstæf m. *runic letter, rune,* Æ,B. ['*runestave*']
rŭnung f. *whispering, wheedling,* Æ. ['*rouning*']
rŭnwita† m. *adviser, counsellor, wise man.*
rŭst m. '*rust,*' Cp,MtL,RB : *moral canker,* CP,HL.
rŭstig '*rusty,*' AO 251²¹.
rŭte=rŭde
rŭwa m., rŭwe f. *covering, tapestry,* W.

rŭwes v. rūh.
rūxlan (MtR 9²³)=hrūxlian
rȳan=rȳn
ryc-, rȳc-=rec-, rēc-
rȳcŏ pres. 3 sg. of rēocan.
rȳd (LL 192,2B)=rād I.
+ryddan *to clear (land),* AS 39⁵.
+rȳde *prepared, ready? easy?* RD 64¹⁵.
ryden n. *name of a plant,* LCD 122a.
rȳderian v. ā-r.
rȳe=rȳhe
rȳfe '*rife,' frequent,* Lcd 3·164²¹.
ryft (i, e) n. *covering, veil, curtain, cloak,* CP.
ryge (i) m. '*rye,*' Cp.
rygen (i) *made of rye,* Lcd. ['*ryen*']
rȳhe f. *rug, blanket,* GL. [=rēowe]
ryht-=riht; rȳm-=rīm-
±rȳman (ē) *to clear, open up, An,B,Lk,Met, W : widen, extend, prolong, enlarge,* Æ,CP : *make room, retire, yield,* Æ. ['*rime*'; rūm]
rȳmet n. *room, space, extent,* Æ : *comfort, benefit.*
rȳmetlēast f. *want of room,* ÆH 1·34²².
rȳmŏ f. *amplitude,* CM 18.
rȳn, rȳnan *to roar, rage,* Bo.
ryne (e) mn. *running, onward course,* Æ,Bf, Bo,VHy ; AO : *flux, flow (water, blood), Lk; Æ : period of time, cycle, course of life : expanse, extent : orbit.* ['*rune*']
±rȳne n. *mystery, dark saying : mystic rite : sacrament : sacramental elements,* Æ.
rynegiest m. *running spirit (=lightning)? rain-foe?* (Tupper), RD 4⁵⁸.
-rȳnegu v. hel-r.
rynel I. (e) m. *runnel, stream, Bl,GD,VPs.* ['*rindle*'] II. *runner, messenger,* Æ.
rynele f.=rynel I.
±rȳn(e)lic *secret, mystical : figurative, sacramental.* adv. -līce.
rynelīce? '*cursim,*' OEG 7⁹⁰.
rȳnemann m. *one skilled in mysteries,* RD 43¹³.
rynestrong *strong in running,* RD 20⁷.
ryneswift† *swift in running,* MET.
ryneŏrāg f. *space of time,* GU 184.
rynewǣn† m. *swift vehicle, chariot,* PPs 19⁷.
ryng-=reng-
±rȳnig *good in counsel?* CRA 51. [rūn]
ryniga? m. *liquid that runs off?* LCD.
rynning f. *rennet,* WW 128⁴³.
+rynning=+rinning
rȳnstæf (RWH 119³⁶)=rūnstæf; rȳp=rīp
+rȳnu (Æ)=+ryne
+rȳpan I. *to spoil, plunder, rob, Chr,MtL, LL,W.* ['*ripe*'] II. pl. *sheaves,* CSPs. III.=ræpan. IV.=rīpan.
rȳpere m. *robber, plunderer,* LL,W.
rȳping m. *plunder, spoliation,* OEG 3149. ['*riping*']

ryplen? *made of broom*, GPH 399 (A 31·536).
ryps=reps; **-rȳric** v. sǣ-r.; **rysc-**=risc-
rysel, rysl (Æ), rys(e)le (hl-) m. *lard, fat* :
  resin, LCD 210¹³ : *abdomen*, WW 159⁶ (cp.
  ryselwærc).
ryselwærc *pain in the stomach*, LCD 115b.
+rysen-, +rysn-=+risn-
rȳsig (OEG 8³³⁷)=hrīsig
ryt *rubbish for burning, underwood*, LL
  36,27 (v. 3·46).
rȳð I.=rīð. **II.** pres. 3 sg. of rȳn.
rȳðer=hrīðer
ryðða (i) m. *a species of dog, mastiff*, Æ,
  WW. [*Ger.* rüde]

S

sā m. *tub, bucket, Gl.* [*ON.* sār; v. '*say*']
saban m? *sheet*, WW 502³³.
sac=(1) sacu; (2) sæc
saca nap. of sacu.
±saca m. *opponent, foe*, B,BH.
sacan⁶ *to struggle, dispute, disagree, wrangle,
  fight* : *accuse, blame, bring a criminal or
  civil action against any one, lay claim to*,
  LL.
sacc (æ) m. '*sack*,' *bag*, Æ. [*L.* saccus]
sācerd mf. *priest, priestess*, Æ,CP. [*L.*]
sācerdbana m. *priest-slayer*, W.
sācerdgerīsne *befitting a priest*, BH 206¹².
sācerdhād m. *priesthood*, CP.
sācerdland n. *land allotted to priests*, GEN
  47²⁶.
sācerdlic *sacerdotal, priestly*, Æ,BH.
sācerhād=sācerdhād
sacful *quarrelsome, contentious*, Æ. ['*sak-
  ful*']
sacian *to wrangle, strive*, Æ.
saclēas *innocent*, LL : *unmolested, safe*, Chr,
  KC,MtL. ['*sackless*']
sacu f. (oblique cases often have sæc-) (±)
  *conflict, strife, war, battle, feud, sedition,
  dispute*, Æ,B,LL; AO : *reproof* : *affliction,
  persecution, trial* : *sin, fault*, B,Ph :
  prosecution, lawsuit, action. s. *and sōcn
  jurisdiction, right of holding a court for
  criminal and civil matters*, LL (v. 2·455).
  ['*sake*']
sad- v. sæd.
sāda m. *snare, cord, halter*, NG,PPs. [cp.
  Ger. saite]
sadel=sadol
±sadelian *to* '*saddle*,' Æ, KC. ['*saddled*']
sadian *to be sated, get wearied*, Bo : (+)
  satiate, fill, Ps. ['*sade*'; sæd]
sadol (e², u²) m. '*saddle*,' *B*; GD.
sadolbeorht *with ornamented saddle*, B 2175.
sadolboga (u²) m. '*saddle-bow*,' *WW*.

sadolfelg f. *pommel of a saddle*, GL.
Saducēisc *Sadducean*; as sb. m. *Sadducee.*
sadul=sadol
sǣ mf. often indecl. but also gs. sǣs, sǣwe,
  sēo; nap. sǣs, gp. sǣwa, dp. sǣwum,
  sǣ(u)m *sheet of water*, '*sea*,' *lake, pool*, Æ,
  B,Bo,G,Lcd,VPs.
sǣǣl m. *sea-eel*, WW 447³⁶.
sǣælfen f. *sea-elf, naiad*, WW.
sǣbāt† f. '*sea-boat*,' *vessel, ship, B.*
sǣbeorg m. *cliff by the sea* : *mountain of
  waves?* AN 308.
sǣbrōga m. *sea-terror*, SOL 84¹³.
sǣburg f. *seaport town*, MtL 4¹³.
sǣc I. *offensive, odious* : *guilty*. **II.** (KGL
  61²²)=sacc
sǣc-, sǣc-=sec- (and v. sacu), sēc-
sǣcc I.† f. *strife, contest.* [sacan] **II.** m.
  sackcloth, Æ. ['*sack*';=sacc]
sǣcce pres. 1 sg. of sācan.
sǣccing m. *sacking, pallet*, Mk 6⁶⁵ (v. NED).
sǣcdōm=sceacdōm
sǣceaster f. *seaport town*, MtR 4¹³.
sǣceosol m. *sea-sand, shingle*, GEN 32¹²,
  WW 147⁴¹.
sǣcerd=sacerd; **sǣcgen**=segen
sǣcir m. *sea-ebbing*, Ex 291.
sǣclian (Chr)=sīclian
sǣclif n. *cliff by the sea, Bo.* ['*seacliff*']
sǣcocc m. *cockle*, WW 94¹⁴.
sǣcol n. *jet, WW* 416². ['*seacoal*']
sǣcyning m. *sea-king*, B 2382.
sǣcysul=sǣceosol
sǣd (occ. sad- in obl. cases) w. g. *sated with,
  weary of, satiated, filled, full, Ps,Rd.* ['*sad*']
sǣd (ē) n., nap. sǣd, sǣdu '*seed*,' *Mk,VPs*;
  Æ,CP : *fruit, offspring, posterity, MkL,
  VPs* : *sowing, Met*; Æ : *growth.*
sǣdberende *seed-bearing*, Æ.
sǣdcynn n. *kind of seed*, LL,WW.
sǣde pret. 3 sg. of secgan.
sǣdēor m. *sea-monster*, LCD,MH.
sǣdere m. *sower*, Æ,MkL. ['*seeder*']
sǣdian *to sow*, MtL 13⁸ : *provide seed*, LL
  450,10.
sǣdlēap m. *sower's basket, Bf.* ['*seedlip*']
sǣdlic *belonging to seed, seminal*, DR 146⁸.
sǣdnað m. *sowing*, WW 147⁴.
sǣdnes f. *satiety*, GPH 391.
sǣdraca m. *sea-dragon*, B,GL.
sǣdtīma m. *seed-time*, HEXC 226.
sǣearm m. *arm of the sea*, AO 22⁴.
sǣelfen=sǣælfen
sǣfǣreld n. *passage of the (Red) sea*, AO
  38³³.
sǣfæsten f. *watery stronghold, ocean*, Ex 127.
sǣ-faroð, -fearoð† m. *sea-coast.*
Sǣfern f. *Severn*, CHR. [*L.* Sabrina]
sǣfisc m. '*sea-fish*,' *Cr.*

sǣflōd mn. *tide, inundation, flood, flow of the sea, flood-tide, AO* : *flow of a river,* VH : (†) *sea.* ['*seaflood*']

sǣflota m. (*sea-floater*), *ship,* An 381.

sǣfōr f. *sea-voyage,* Seaf 42.

±**sǣgan** *to cause to sink, settle* : *cause to fall, fell, destroy.* [sīgan]

sǣgd-=sǣged-

sǣgde pret. 3 sg. of secgan.

sǣgdig (N)=sǣgde ic

sǣgēap *spacious* (*ship*), B 1896 (v. ES 64·211).

±**sǣgednes** f. *sacrifice,* MkLR 12³³; APs 65¹³ : *mystery,* MtL 13¹¹ (gd-).

sǣgemǣre n. *sea-coast,* G.

±**sǣgen**=+segen

sǣgenga m. *ship,* B : *sailor,* Bf 156³¹.

sǣgeset m. *coast region,* Gl.

sǣgl=sigel; **sǣgnian**=segnian

sǣgon pret. pl. of sēon.

sǣgrund m. *sea-bottom, abyss,* Æ,CP.

sǣh=seah

sǣhealf f. *side next the sea, seaside,* Æ,Chr.

sǣhengest m. *sea-horse, ship,* An 488 : *hippopotamus,* WW.

sǣhete m. *surging of the sea,* BH 384²⁴.

sǣholm m. *ocean,* An 529.

sǣht=seht

sǣhund m. *sea-dog, sea-beast,* OEG 26⁶¹.

sǣl n. nap. salu *room, hall, castle,* B,Rd. ['*sale*']

sǣl (ē) **I.** mf. (occl. dp. sālum) *time, season, opportunity, occasion, condition, position,* Lcd; Æ,AO : *prosperity, happiness, joy,* B. on sǣlum *happy*; '*gaudete,*' GD 202⁶. tō sǣles *in due time,* NR 39. ['*sele*'] **II.**= sēl II.

sǣlāc† n. *sea-gift, sea-spoil,* B.

sǣlād† f. *sea-way, sea-voyage.*

sǣlāf f. *sea-leavings, jetsam,* Ex 584.

±**sǣlan I.** (ē) *to take place, happen,* CP : *succeed,* GD 202⁶. [sǣl I.] **II.**† *to tie, bind, fetter, fasten* : *curb, restrain, confine.* [sāl]

sǣland n. *coast, maritime district,* TC 308¹.

sǣld=seld

sǣlen I. *made of willow,* WW 518⁶. [sealh] **II.**=selen

sǣleoda=sǣlida

sǣlēoð n. *song at sea, rowers' song,* WW 379⁹.

-sǣleða v. sealt-s.

sǣlic *of the sea, marine,* Æ.

sǣlida m. *seafarer, sailor* : *pirate.* [liðan]

±**sǣlig** (+ exc. at LL 300a) *fortuitous,* OEG 4185 : *happy, prosperous, AO,Bo,Gen*; CP. ['*i-seli*']

+**sǣlige** *happily,* WW 407²³.

+**sǣliglic** (ē) *happy, blessed, fortunate.* adv. -līce, Bo,DR. ['*seelily*']

+**sǣlignes** f. *happiness,* (*good*) *fortune,* CP : *occurrence.*

sǣ-līðend, -līðende† m. *sailor.*

+**sǣllic**=+sǣliglic

sǣlmerige f. *brine,* Ægr 192¹⁸. [L. *sal-moria*; *Gk.* ἁλμυρίς]

+**sǣlnes** f. *occurrence,* Gl.

+**sǣltan** (NG)=syltan

sǣltna m. *name of a bird, bunting? robin?* WW 44¹⁷.

sǣlð f. *dwelling, house,* Gen 785.

±**sǣlð** (ȳ) f. (usu. in pl.) *hap, fortune* : *happiness, prosperity, blessing, Bo*; Æ,CP. ['*i-selth*']

sǣlwang (o²)† m. *fertile plain.*

sǣm v. sǣ; **sǣma**=sēma

+**sǣman**=+sīeman

sǣmann m. '*seaman,*' *pirate, viking,* B.

sǣmearh† m. *sea-horse, ship,* E 2.

sǣmend=sēmend

sǣmest superl. (of *sǣme?*) *worst.*

sǣmestre=sēamestre

sǣmēðe *weary from a sea-voyage,* B 325.

sǣminte f. *sea-mint,* WW.

sǣmninga=samnunga

sǣmra comp. (of *sǣme?*) *worse, inferior, weaker.*

sǣmtinges=samtinges

sǣn (ē) *maritime, marine,* OEG 6²³, 8¹²⁸.

sǣnaca m. *sea-vessel, ship,* Hu 26.

sǣnæs m. *cape, promontory,* B,Gl.

sǣncgan=sengan; **sǣndan**=sendan

sǣne (often w. g.) *slack, lazy, careless, negligent, dull, cowardly.*

sǣnet n. *net for sea-fishing,* WW 336²⁰.

sǣngan=sengan; **sǣnian**=segnian

sǣnig *maritime, marine,* A 13·32.

sǣostre f. *sea-oyster,* WE 63¹⁷.

sǣp (e) n. '*sap,*' *juice,* Cr,WW.

sǣp (ÆL 3¹⁶²)=sēap

sǣpig '*sappy,*' *juicy, succulent,* OEG 16¹.

sǣppe f. *spruce fir,* WW 269¹⁴. [L. *sappi-num; Fr.* sapin]

sǣpspōn f. *a shaving with sap in it,* Lcd 106b.

sǣre=sāre

sǣrima m. *sea-shore, coast, Chr.* ['*searim*']

sǣrinc† m. *seaman, pirate, viking.*

sǣrōf *hardy at sea,* Cra 56.

sǣrwian=searwian

sǣrȳric m. *sea-reed?* (GK); *an ait?* (BT), Wh 10.

sǣs=sess; **sǣs** v. sǣ.

sǣsceaða m. *pirate,* WW 469⁶.

sǣscell f. '*sea-shell,*' MH 18²³.

sǣsīð m. *sea-voyage,* B 1149.

sǣ-snægl, -snæl m. '*sea-snail,*' WW.

sǣsteorra m. *guiding star* (*for sailors*), HL. ['*seastar*'] sæster=sester

sǣstrand n. ' *sea-strand,*' *foreshore, ÆH.*

sǣstrēam, as mpl. *waters of the sea, An.*
[' *seastream*']

sǣswalwe (hǣ-) f. *sand-martin,* WW7[28].

sǣt pret. 3 sg. of sittan.

sǣt f. *lurking-place* : *snare, gin?* LL445,2.
[sittan]

+sǣt n. *act of sitting,* MkLp5[14].

sǣta m? *holding of land,* EC447[18].

-sǣta (ē) v. burg-s.

sǣtan=sǣtian; -sǣte v. an(d)-s.

sǣte f. *house,* KC3·79[15].

+sǣte (ē) n. *snare, ambush,* DR37[10].

Sǣterdæg=Sǣtern(es)dæg

sǣt-ere, -nere (ē) m. *waylayer, robber* : *spy* :
seditious one, seducer (the devil), CP.

Sǣtern-dæg, Sǣter(n)es- m. ' *Saturday,*'
BH,Bl,Lk. [*L.* Saturni dies]

Sǣterniht f. *Friday night,* ÆH1·216[27].

sǣtian (ē) (w. g.) *to lie in wait for, plot
against,* CP. [sittan]

sǣtil, sǣtl=setl; sǣtn-=sǣt-
+sǣtnes=+setnes

sǣton pret. pl. of sittan.

sǣtung (ē) f. *ambush, trap, plot, snare,* CP :
sedition.

sǣð (ÆL36[295])=sēað

sǣðēof v. hēahsǣðēof.

sǣðerie=saturege; sǣðnes=sēðnes

sǣðrenewudu = sūðernewudu; sǣum v. sǣ.

sǣūpwearp *jetsam,* TC421'.

sǣwǣg m. *sea-wave,* DA384.

sǣwǣter n. ' *sea-water,*' *Lcd* 10b.

sǣwan=sāwan

sǣwār n. *sea-weed,* WW135[21]. [' *seaware*']

sǣwaroð n. *sea-shore, beach,* Az,Bo.

sǣwe v. sǣ.

sǣweall† m.' *sea-wall,*' *sea-shore, beach, cliff,
B* : *wall of water (in the Red Sea).*

sǣweard m. *coast-warden,* B,LL.

sǣweg m. *path through the sea,* Ps8[8].
[' *seaway*']

sǣwērig† *weary from a sea-voyage, An.*
[' *seaweary*']

sǣwet n. *sowing,* BH. [sāwan]

sǣwīcing m. *sea-viking,* Ex333.

sǣwiht f. *marine animal,* BH26[6].

sǣwinewincle f? *periwinkle (shell-fish),*
Lcd90a.

sǣwong m. *sea-shore, beach,* B1964.

sǣwð pres. 3 sg. of sāwan.

sǣwudu m. *vessel, ship,* B226.

sǣwum v. sǣ.

sǣwylm m. *sea-surf, billow,* B393.

sǣx (Gl)=seax

sǣȳð f. *sea-wave,* Run,WW.

safene, safine f. *savine (a kind of juniper),*
Lcd. [*L.* sabina]

saftriende ptc. *rheumy,* WW161[34] (MLR
19·203).

sāg I. *a sinking,* RD79[5] (or ?sagol). II.
pret. 3 sg. of sīgan.

saga I. imperat. of secgan. II. m. *story,
narrative,* ÆL7[193]. III. m.=sagu II.

+saga n. *narrative,* LkL1[1].

sagast pres. 2 sg., sagað pres. 3 sg., sagode
pret. 3 sg. of secgan.

sāgol (e[2]) m. (sāgl- in obl. cases) *club, cudgel,
stick, staff, pole,* AO,GD,Mt; Æ,CP.
[' *sowel*']

-sagol v. lēas-, sōð-, wǣr-s.

sagu (±) I. f. ' *saw,*' *saying, report, story,
tradition, tale, Lk,WW;* Æ : *presage,
prophecy* : *witness, testimony.* [secgan]
II. f. ' *saw*' *(tool), Bf,WW.*

sāh I. pret. 3 sg. of sīgan. II. pret. 3 sg. of
sēon II.

sahl-=sealh-; sāhl=sāgol; saht=seht

sāl mf. *bond, rope, cord, rein, collar, B,Gen.*
[' *sole*'; *Ger.* seil]

sala m. *act of selling,* ' *sale,*' *WW.*

salb (*Ep*)=sealf; salch=sealh

salde=sealde pret. 3 sg. of sellan.

salf (Cp)=sealf

salfie, salfige f. *sage,* Lcd. [*L.* salvia]

salh (*Gl*), salig=sealh

salletan *to sing psalms, play on, or sing to,
the harp,* PPs104[2]. [*L.* psallere]

salm-=sealm-

sālnes f. *silence,* Bf122[22]. [cp. *Goth.* silan]

salo=salu; salor=solor

salowigpād=salwigpād

salt=sealt

saltere (ea) m. ' *psalter*,*' *collection of
psalms, service-book containing the psalms,*
Æ,BH,Ct,LL : *psaltery, Lcd* (ps-). [*L.*
psalterium]

salthaga m. *robin redbreast?* WW286[11].

salu I. (ea) *dark, dusky, Rd.* [' *sallow*']
II. nap. of sæl.

salubrūn (ea[1], o[2]) *dark brown,* Fin37.

sālum v. sǣl.

saluneb *dark-complexioned,* RD50[5].

salupād *dark-coated,* RD58[3].

saluwigpād=salwigpād

salwed ptc. *darkened, painted black (with
pitch),* Gen1481.

salwigfeðera *having dark plumage,* Gen1448.

salwigpād† *having dark plumage.*

sālwong=sǣlwang

sam conj. *whether, or.* sam...sam *whether...
or,* AO. sam ge...sam ge; sam ðe...sam
ðe *whether...or.*

sam- (=*together*) denotes union, combination, or agreement. [*ON.* sam-]

sām- (=*half*-) denotes a partial or imperfect
condition. [*L.* semi-]

sama=same v. swā.

samad-=samod-

sāmbærned *half-burnt*, OEG.

sāmboren *born out of due time*, WW356².

sāmbryce m. *partial breach (of rules, laws, etc.)*, LL468,9.

sām-cwic, -cucu (o¹) *half-dead*, Æ,AO

same only in 'swā s. (swā) *in like manner also, as*, CP.

samed=samod

samen (o¹) adv. *together*, JnR.

sāmgrēne *half-green, immature*, WW405⁴.

sāmgung *young*, CM123. [geong]

sāmhāl *unwell, weakly*, W273¹⁰.

samheort *unanimous*, PPs149¹.

±samhīwan pl. *members of the same household, married persons*, CP.

samhwylc pron. *some*, BL,LL.

sāmlǣred *half-taught, badly instructed*, Æ.

samlīce *together, at the same time*, SOL 148¹⁸.

samlinga=samnunga

sāmlocen *half-closed*, NC318.

sammǣle *agreed, accordant, united*, CHR, LL.

sāmmelt *half-digested*, LCD69b.

±samnian *to assemble, meet, collect, unite, join, gather together*, (tr.) *Da,Lcd*; (refl.) CHR : (intr.) *Ps : glean*. ['*sam*']

samninga=samnunga

±samnung (o) f. (but occl. gs. samnunges), *union, congregation, meeting, assembly, council, MkL*; Æ,CP : *collection : union in marriage*. ['*samening*']

samnunga (æ, e, o) adv. *forthwith, immediately, suddenly*. [=semninga]

samnungcwide (o¹) *collect*, DR2¹.

samod (o¹) I. adv. *simultaneously, at the same time, together*, Æ,AO : *entirely*, Æ : *also, as well, too*. II. prep. (w. d.) *together with, at (of time)*, Æ. [*Ger*. sammt]

samodcumend *flocking together*, CM282.

samodeard (o¹, u²) m. *common home*, GU 1346.

samodfæst *joined together*, CR1581.

samodgang *continuous*, GD170²³ (v. NC 318).

samodgeflit (o¹) n. *strife*, WW382³⁸.

samodgesīð m. *comrade*, GPH400.

samodherian (o¹) *to praise together*, RPs 116¹.

samodhering f. *praising*, ES40·302.

+samodlǣcan *to bring together*, RPs112⁸.

samodlīce adv. *together*, CHR1123.

samodrynelas mpl. '*concurrentes*,' BF46¹.

samodsīðian *to accompany*, MFH137¹⁸.

samodsprǣc f. *colloquy, conversation*, CM 511.

samodswēgende *consonantal*, ÆGR5¹⁷.

samodtang *continuous, successive*, v. NC 318.

samodðyrlic (o¹) adj. *concordant*, WW378⁴⁰.

samodwellung (o¹) f. *welding together*, WW 380⁴⁴. [weallan]

samodwist f. *a being one with*, GD224⁴.

samodwunung f. *common residence, living together*, LL(422').

samodwyrcende *co-operating*, WW384¹².

sāmra=sǣmra

samrād *harmonious, united*, MET11⁹⁶.

samrǣden f. *married state*, CP19¹⁸.

sāmsoden *half-cooked*, LL(166²n).

sāmstorfen *half-dead*, GPH401.

sāmswǣled *half-burnt*, OEG4388.

samswēge (u¹) adj. *sounding in unison*.

samtinges (æ¹, e¹, e²) adv. *all at once, immediately, forthwith*, Æ.

samðe conj. in phrase samðe...samðe...*as well...as...* ('*tam*'... '*quam*'...), CM,SC, etc. [sam]

sāmweaxen *half-grown*, NC319.

samwinnende ptc. *contending together*, WW 211⁷.

sāmwīs *stupid, dull, foolish*, CP. adv. -līce.

samwist† f. *living together, cohabitation*, GL.

sāmworht *unfinished*, CHR.

samwrǣdnes f. *union, combination*, Bo114⁴.

sāmwyrcan *to half do a thing*, LL350,61¹.

sanc I. pret. 3 sg. of sincan. II.=sang

sanct m. *holy person, saint*, Æ. [*L*. sanctus]

sand (o) I. f. *action of sending, embassy, mission, deputation*, Æ : *message* : (also m.) *messenger, ambassador, KC : sending, service, course of food, repast, mess, victuals, Gl*; Æ. ['*sand*'; sendan] II. n. '*sand*,' *gravel, Æ,MtR,VPs*; AO; Mdf : *sandy shore, sea-shore, beach*.

sandbeorg m. *sand-hill, sand-bank*, Bo,KC.

sandceosol m. *sand, gravel*, Æ.

sandcorn n. *grain of sand*, Æ.

sandful *sandy*, SC223¹³.

sandgeweorp (u³) n. *sand-bank, quicksand*, WW.

sandgewyrpe n. *sand-heap*, KC6·228'.

sandgrot n. *grain of sand*, HELL117.

sand-hlið n., nap. -hleoðu *sandy slope, hillock*, AN236.

sandhof n. *sand-house, barrow, grave*, GU 1169.

sandhricg m. *sand-bank*, ÆGR75⁸.

sandhyll (o¹) m. '*sand-hill*,' *Cp*.

sandig '*sandy*,' *Lcd*.

sandiht (o) *sandy, dusty*, AO.

sandland (o¹, o²) n. *sandy shore*, GU1308.

sandpytt m. *sand-pit*, ÆL35³²⁵.

sandrid n. *quicksand*, WW183⁷.

sandsēað m. *sand-pit*, KC.

sang (o) I. m. *noise, 'song,' singing, B,Bo, Cr,LkL* : *psalm, poem, lay, Bl,CP,VPs.* II. pret. 3 sg. of singan.

sangbōc f. *singing-book, service-book, KC, LL.* ['songbook']

sangcræft m. *art of singing, composing poetry, or playing an instrument,* BH,PH.

sangdrēam m. '*cantilena*,' *song, music,* CM 638.

sangere (o) m. *singer, poet, BH,Bl.* ['songer']

sangestre f. *songstress, ÆGr.* ['songster']

sangpīpe f. *pipe,* GPH 389²⁶.

-sānian v. a-s. [sǣne]

sann pret. 3 sg. of sinnan.

sǣp f? *amber, unguent,* GL.

sǣpbox m. *resin-box? soap-box?* LL455,17.

sǣpe f. '*soap*,' *salve, Lcd,WW*; Æ.

sār I. n. *bodily pain, sickness* : *wound, 'SORE,' raw place* : *suffering, sorrow, affliction, Bo,Chr.* II. adj. *sore, sad, grievous, painful, wounding, CP.*

Sar(a)cene (o², i³) pl. *Saracens,* AO,DR.

Saracenisc adj. *Saracen,* Æ.

sārbenn† f. *painful sore or wound.*

sārbōt f. *compensation for wounding,* LL 500,10¹.

Sarc-=Sarac-

sārclǣð m. *bandage,* WW.

sārcrene (ē²?) *sore, tender,* LCD 65b.

sārcwide† m. *taunt, reproach* : *lament.*

sāre (ǣ) adv. *sorely, heavily, grievously, bitterly, B,Cr,Gen,Ps* : *painfully, B.* ['sore']

sārege *grief, trouble,* RWH 88¹³.

sārettan *to grieve, lament, complain, CP.*

sārferhð *sorrowful,* GEN 2244.

sarga m. *trumpet, clarion,* GL.

sārgian (±) *to cause pain, afflict, wound, grieve* : *be pained, suffer, languish, CP.* [sārig]

sārgung f. *lamentation, grief,* Sc,W.

sārian *to become painful, CP* : *grieve, be sad, feel sorry for,* BH.

sārig '*sorry,' grieved, sorrowful, Æ,B,Bo, Cr,Ps.*

sārigcierm (e³) m. *wailing,* MFH 128⁸.

sārigferhð† *sad-hearted.*

sāriglic *sad,* GD 290⁶.

sārigmōd *dejected, mournful, B.* ['sorry-mood']

sārignes f. *sadness, grief, Æ,Chr.* ['sorriness']

sārlic *grievous, sad, doleful, painful, lamentable, bitter, Æ,B,Bo,Bl.* adv. -līce '*sorely,' grievously, mournfully, bitterly, painfully, Æ,Bl,Bo,Jul;* CP.

sārnes f. *affliction, distress, suffering, pain, grief, Æ.* ['soreness']

sārsēofung f. *complaint,* WW 488³⁶.

sārslege† m. *painful blow,* JUL.

sārspell n. *sad story, complaint,* MH 16³.

sārstæf m. *cutting word, abuse,* GU 205.

sārung=sārgung; **sarw-**=searw-

sār-wracu† f., gds. -wræce *grievous persecution, sore tribulation.*

sārwylm m. *pain, illness,* GU 1123.

saturege f. *savory (plant),* Lcd 147a,WW. ['satureie'; L.]

sāul=sāwol

±sāwan⁷ *to '*sow*,' strew seed, implant, Æ* : *disseminate, CP.*

sāwel=sāwol

+sāwelod *having a soul, G* : *endowed with life,* LL.

sāwend, sāwere (*Mt*) m. '*sower*.'

+sawenlic=+sewenlic

sāwl (CP), sāwle=sāwol

sāwlian *to expire,* Æ.

sāwlung (e²) f. *dying, Shr.* ['souling']

sā-wol (-wel, -wul, -wl) f., gs. sāwle '*soul,' life, Æ,B,Bl,Bo,Ps*; CP : *spirit, Bl,Chr* : *living being, Æ.*

sāwolberend m. *human being,* B 1004 (wl).

sāwolcund (e) *spiritual,* GU 288.

sāwoldrēor† n. *life-blood.*

sāwolgedāl† n. *death.*

sāwolgesceot=sāwolscot

sāwolhord (e², wl)† n. *life, body.*

sāwolhūs† n. *(soul-house), body,* GU.

sāwollēas *soulless, lifeless,* Æ.

sāwol-sceat (e²), -scot m. *payment to the church on the death of a person,* LL.

sāwolðearf f. *soul's need,* TC 474 (wl).

sāwon pret. pl. of sēon.

sāwul=sāwol

sca-, scā-, v. also scea-, scēa-.

scāda m. *crown of head,* PPs 67²¹. ['shode']

+scādwyrt (ēa) f. *oxeye,* LCD 103a,WW 50².

scæ-; scǣ-=scea-, sce-; scēa-

scæc (e) *fetters,* JGPh 1·329. [*Du.* schake]

scæftamund=sceaftmund

scæfð=sceafoða

scæm-=scam-

scænan I. (±) (ē, ēa) *to break, wrench open, shatter, Æ.* ['shene'] II. (+) *to render brilliant?* SOL 222 (GK).

+scæninges f. *collision,* WW 384¹⁰.

scæp=scēap; **scæptlō** (Cp)=sceaftlō

scær=scear I. and II.

scēron pret. pl. of scieran.

scēð I. (*Gen*)=scēað. II.=scegð

scafa m. *plane, Ep,LL.* ['shave']

±scafan⁶ (a, æ, ea) *to '*shave*,' scrape, polish, Cp,BH.*

scǣffōt *splay-footed,* GL.

scalde=sceolde pret. 3 sg. of sculan.

scaldhūlas pl. *reed, sedge*, WW37[15] (v. ES 43·320).

scaldȳfel=scealdȳfel

+**scaldwyrt** (WW278[25])=+scādwyrt

scamel=scamol

scamfæst '*shamefast,*' *modest, CP.*

scamful (eo) *modest, DR.* ['*shameful*']

scamian (ea, eo, o) (w. g.) *to be ashamed, blush, B,CP*: (impers., w. a. of pers. and g. of thing) *cause shame, Æ,CP.* ['*shame*']

scamlēas '*shameless,*' *impudent, immodest, CP.*

scamlēaslic *shameless, CP.* adv. -līce '*shamelessly,*' *CP.*

scamlēast (ea[1]) f. *impudence, shamelessness, immodesty,* Gl,Mk.

scamlic (æ, ea) *shameful, disgraceful, OEG*; AO : *modest.* ['*shamely*'] adv. -līce, CP.

scamlim n. *private member,* GPH390, WW 535[31]?

scamol (æ[1], e[1], ea[1], eo[1], o[1]; e[2], u[2]) m. *stool, footstool, bench, table (of money-changers), Bl,VPs.* ['*shamble*']

scamu (ea, eo, o) f. '*shame,*' *confusion, Cp, Lk : disgrace, dishonour, Cr : insult, MkR : shameful circumstance, WW : modesty, CP : private parts, Gen,WW.* s. dōn *to inflict injury.*

scamul=scamol

scamung (ea) f. *disgrace,* LRPs68[20].

scān pret. 3 sg. of scīnan.

scanca m. '*shank,*' *shin, leg, G,Ph,Gl,Sol, WW : ham? LL* (sconc).

scancbend (scang-) m. *garter,* WW152[39].

scancforad (e[3]) *broken-legged,* CP,Lcd.

scancgebeorg f. *leg-greave,* WW535[9].

scancgegirela m. *anklet, garter,* WW467[29].

scanclira m. *calf of the leg,* WW266[4].

scand I. (ea, eo, o) f. *ignominy, shame, confusion, disgrace, Chr,Cr : scandal, disgraceful thing, CP.* **II.** m. *wretch, impostor, recreant, buffoon, Æ,WW.* **III.** f. *bad woman, ÆL.* ['*shond*']

scandful *shameful, disgraceful, MH.* ['*shondfull*']

scandhūs m. *house of ill fame,* MH26[24].

scandlic (ea, o) *shameful, disgraceful, vile, unchaste, Bo; Æ,AO.* ['*shondly*'] adv. -līce *shamefully, obscenely : insultingly.*

scandlicnes (o) f. *shame, disgrace, CP : disgraceful act.*

scandlufiende *loving shamefully,* Lcd1·lxi[4].

scandword (ea) n. *abusive, blasphemous or obscene language,* W255[15].

scandwyrde *slanderous,* AB34[10].

scang-=scanc-; +**scāp-**=+scēap-

+**scapen** pp. of scieppan.

scapu-lare n., **-larie** f. *scapulary,* RB.

scar-=scear-; **scaδ-**=sceaδ-

scēab (Cp)=scēaf; **sceaba**=scafa

sceabb (æ, e) m. '*scab,*' *CP,Lcd.* ['*shab*']

sceabbede *purulent, having sores or scabs, OEG.* ['*shabbed*']

sceacan[6] (tr. and intr.) *to* '*shake,*' *move quickly to and fro, brandish* : *go, glide, hasten, flee, depart, Æ : pass from, proceed, CP.*

sceacdōm (æ) m. *flight,* Gen31[20].

sceacel (e) m. '*shackle,*' *WW : plectrum.*

scēacere m. *robber,* NG. [*Ger.* schächer]

sceacga m. *rough hair, wool, etc., WW.* ['*shag*']

sceacgede *hairy, shaggy, WW.*

sceacline (WW182[26])=sceatline

sceacnes f. '*excussio,*' EPs140[4].

sceacul=sceacel

scead (a, æ, e) n. *shadow, shade : shelter, protection : stye,* Cp1954 (ES43·326).

+**scead** (ā) **I.** n. *separation, distinction, LkL : discretion, understanding, argument, Æ; CP : reason,* ÆP142[11] : *reckoning, account, statement, Mt : accuracy : art, manner, method.* ['*shed*'] **II.** *reasonable, prudent : calculated,* Gl.

±**sceadan**[7] (ā, ē) (tr. and intr.) *to divide, separate, part, Soul; Lcd : discriminate, decide, determine, appoint : differ : scatter, '*shed,*' Lcd : expound : decree : write down.*

sceadd m. '*shad*' (*fish*), KC6·147[19].

sceaddgenge *seasonable for shad,* KC6·147[18].

scēadelīce=scēadlice

+**scēadenlīce** *severally,* WW491[36].

scēadenmǣl *damascened (sword),* B1939.

scēadesealf f. *salve or powder (for the head?),* Lcd.

sceadew-=sceadw-

sceadiht *shady,* CVHy5[3].

sceadlic *shady,* OEG2885.

+**scēadlic** *reasonable, discreet, wise, accurate, CP.* adv. -līce.

+**scēadnes** '*auctoritas,*' Chrd13[18].

sceadu (a) f., gs. scead(u)we, sceade '*shade,*' *shadow, darkness, Ex,Ps,Sol; CP : shady place, arbour, Lcd : shelter : scene,* v. OEG 2885.

sceadugeard m. *shady place,* Cp79T.

sceadugenga m. *wanderer in darkness,* B 703.

sceaduhelm (a[1]) m. *darkness,* B650.

sceadwian (a[1]) *to protect,* LPs90[4]. ['*shadow*']

sceadwig *shady,* RHy5[3].

±**scēadwīs** (ā) *sagacious, intelligent, rational, reasonable, wise, Æ.* adv. -līce, *clearly,* AO60[9].

+**scēadwīslic** (RBL14[1])=+scēadwīs

scēadwīsnes f. *sagacity, reason : discrimination, discretion : separation,* VH : *reckoning.*

sceadwung f. *overshadowing*, Lcd; Æ : *something giving shade*, OEG 438. ['*shadowing*']

scēaf I. m. '*sheaf*,' *bundle*, Æ,Lcd; CP.
II. pret. 3 sg. of scūfan.

sceaf-=scaf-

scēafmǣlum adv. *into bundles*, Mt 13³⁰.

sceaf(o)ða m. *chip, shaving, slip, scraping*, BH.

sceaft (æ, e) m. *staff, pole,* '*shaft,*' *Met,WW* : *spear-shaft, spear*, Æ; CP.

±sceaft fmn., nap. -tu, -ta, -te, tas *created being, creature*, Bo; Æ,CP : *origin, creation, construction, existence*, Bo; Æ,CP : (+) *dispensation, destiny, fate*, CP : (+) *condition, nature*. ['*shaft*']

sceaft-lō, pl. -lōn *spear-strap*, Cp (sce(a)pt-).

sceaftmund (æ) f. *span, LL.* ['*shaftment*']

sceaftriht(e) adv. *in a straight line*, CC 54.

sceafð=sceafoða

sceaga (a) m. *copse*, Ct; Mdf. ['*shaw*']

sceagod=sceacgede

sceal pres. 1 and 3 sg. of sculan.

scealc m. *servant, retainer, soldier, subject, member of a crew*, Ps : *man, youth*, B. ['*shalk*']

sceald *shallow*, BC 1·593 (v. PST 1895–8, 532 and '*shoal*').

scealde=sceolde pret. 2 sg. of sculan.

scealdȳfel (a¹) m. *thicket*, GD 100; 212.

scealfor f., scealfra (Æ) m. *diver (bird), cormorant*. [cp. OHG. scarbo]

scealga (y) m. *a fish, roach? rudd?* WW. ['*shallow*']

-scealian v. ā-s.

sceall=sceal pres. 1 and 3 sg. of sculan.

sceallan pl. '*testiculi*,' Lcd.

scealtu=scealt ðu (pres. 2 sg. of sculan, and pron. 2 pers.).

scealu (a) f. *shell, husk*, Ep : *scale (of a balance)*, Æ : *dish*, KC. ['*shale*']

scēam m. *pale grey or white horse?* RD 23⁴. [Ger. schimmel]

sceam-=scam-

scēan pret. 3 sg. of scīnan.

scēanan=scǣnan

sceanc-=scanc-

sceand=scand

+sceandnes (ÆL)=+scendnes

scēanfeld=scīnfeld

scēap (ǣ, ē, ī) n. '*sheep*,' CP,G,RB,VPs, WW.

+sceap (a) n., nap. -pu '*shape*,' *form, created being, creature*, El,Gen,WW : *creation* : *dispensation, fate* : *condition* : *sex*, DR 51⁴ : (±) '*genitalia*,' A 11·2.

-sceap v. for-s.

scēapætere (ǣ¹, ī¹; e²) m. *sheep's carcase*, LL 449,8.

sceapen pp. of scieppan.

scēapen adj. *of a sheep*, Lcd.

+sceapennes f. *creation, formation*, Æ.

scēaphām m. *sheepfold*, EC 373'.

scēapheord (y²) f. *flock of sheep*, Ex 12³².

scēapheorden n. *shed*, WW 185¹⁵.

+sceaphwīl (æ) f. *fated hour*, B 26.

scēaphyrde (i) m. '*shepherd*.' (W; Æ).

scēaplic *of a sheep*, OEG 11¹⁸⁷.

+sceaplīce *ably, fitly*, BHca 324⁴.

scēapscearu (ē) f. *sheep-shearing*, Gen 38¹².

-sceapung v. for-s.

scēapwæsce f. *place for washing sheep*, Ct.

scēapwīc n. *sheepfold*, KC 3·405⁵.

scear I. (æ, e) mn. *ploughshare*, Cp,Sc. ['*share*'] II. pret. 3 sg. of scieran.

scēara=scēarra

scearbēam m. *wood to which the ploughshare is fixed*, WW 196²⁸. [v. '*share*']

sceard I. n. *incision, cleft, gap*, Ct : *potsherd*, GPH. ['*shard*'] II. adj. *cut, mutilated, gashed, notched, hacked* : (w. g.) *bereft of*.

±scearfian *to cut off, scrape, shred*, Lcd, LkL.

. scearflian *to scrape*, Lcd 1·184'.

scearfung f. *scraping, scarifying*, Lcd.

scearian (a) *to allot*, KC.

scearn (æ, e) n. *dung, muck*, Æ,Lcd,VPs. ['*sharn*']

scearnbudda m. *dung-beetle*, ÆGr 308¹n. ['*sharnbud*']

scearn-wibba (æ, e) -wifel (-fifel, WW) m. *dung-beetle*.

scēaron=scǣron pret. pl. of scieran.

scearp (a, æ) '*sharp*,' *pointed, prickly*, Lcd, Soul,VPs : *acute, keen, active, shrewd*, Æ, Bo,Lcd : *severe, rough, harsh*, AO,Hell, Lcd : *biting, bitter, acid*, Lcd : *brave*. [scieran]

scearpe I. adv. *sharply, keenly*, Hex,Ps; Æ. ['*sharp*'] II. f. *scarification*, Lcd.

scearpecged '*sharp-edged*,' Æ.

scearpian *to score, scarify*, Lcd.

scearplic *sharp, severe, effectual*. adv. -lice '*sharply*,' *acutely, keenly*, CP : *painfully, severely*, OET,W : *effectually*, CM 192 : *attentively*, Bf : *quickly*, WW.

scearpnes f. '*sharpness*,' *acuteness, keen observation*, Bo,Cp,CP; Æ : *tartness, pungency, acidity*, Lcd,W; Æ : *effrontery*, GD : *efficacy*.

scearpnumol *effective*, Lcd.

scearpsīene *keen-sighted*, Bo 72,73.

scearpsmēawung f. *argument*, G.

scearpðanc(ful)līce adv. *efficaciously*, Sc.

scearpðancol *quick-witted, keen*, Lcd 3·440'.

scearpung f. *scarifying*, Lcd.

scēarra fpl. *shears, scissors*, CP,Gl,LL. ['*shear*']

scearseax (e, i, ie, y) n. *razor*, CP.

scearu I. (a, æ, y) f. *shearing, shaving, tonsure, Æ.* **II.** (a) f. *'share'-bone, groin,* Lcd,WW.

scearwund? *wounded in the groin,* LL6, 63.

scēat I. m. *corner, angle, edge, point, promontory,* Mdf : *quarter, district, region, surface (of the earth)* : *lap, bosom, fold,* CP : *napkin, sheet, covering, cloak, garment,* CP : *inlet, creek,* BH90²⁷. [*Ger. schoss*] **II.** pret. 3 sg. of scēotan.

scēata m. *angle, corner,* AO : *bosom, lap, lower part of a sail : napkin.* [*Ger. schote*]

scēatcod m. *wallet,* WW107⁵. [codd]

sceatlīne f. *sheet by which a sail is trimmed to the wind,* WW288²⁴.

sceatt (æ,.e) m. *property, treasure, coin, money, wealth,* LL : *payment, price, tribute, bribe, reward,* Æ : *rent, mortgage-money : money of account, denarius, twentieth part of a shilling* (Kent), v. LL2·634. ['*sceat*']

sceatwyrpan *to make the payment to the bridegroom on which the bride passes into his power from that of the father,* WW386¹ (v. ES42·170).

scēað (ǣ, ē) f. *'sheath,'* Æ,Gen,JnL (ēæ) : *spike, nail,* JnL20²⁵? [cp. hornscēað]

sceaða (a) m. *injurious person, criminal, thief, assassin,* B Mt; Æ : (†) *warrior, antagonist : fiend, devil : injury,* Gen549. ['*scathe*']

sceaðan=sceððan

sceaðe f. *injury,* VH19.

sceaðel f. *shuttle? weaver's slay?* LL455,15,1 (v. ANS115,165).

sceaðenes=sceðnes

sceaðful *hurtful,* GD209. ['*scatheful*']

±sceaðlan *to injure, spoil, steal,* Æ.

sceaðīg (æ) *injurious,* ÆGR63¹⁵.

sceaððīgnes f. *injury, harm,* WYN35.

sceaðung f. *injury, damage,* TC138¹⁸,VH.

scēawendsprǣc f. *buffoonery,* WW533⁴.

scēawendwīse f. *buffoon's song,* RD9⁹.

scēawere m. *spectator, observer, watchman, spy,* B; Æ,CP : *mirror,* NC. ['*shower*']

±scēawian *to look, gaze, see, behold, observe,* B; Æ,AO,CP : *inspect, examine, scrutinize,* Chr,Lk; Æ,AO,CP : *have respect to, look favourably on,* Æ : *look out, look for, choose,* Æ : *decree, grant, exhibit, display,* Gen. ['*show*']

scēawigend m? *spectator,* OEG,AA2¹⁴.

scēawung (ā) f. *seeing, surveying, inspection, scrutiny, examination, contemplation,* AO, CP : *respect, regard : show, spectacle, appearance,* Bl,MkL : *toll on exposure of goods.* ['*showing*']

scēawungstōw f. *place of observation,* Æ (1·210).

sceb=sceabb; **scēb**=scēaf; **scec**=scæc

scecel=sceacel; **sced**=scead

scēd pret. 3 sg. of scēadan.

scef-=sceaf-, scyf-

scegð (æ, ei) mf. *vessel, ship,* CHR,MH (v. WC137n). [ON. skeið]

scegðmann (æ) m. *sailor, pirate, viking,* Æ.

scehð=scegð; **scelð-**=scegð-

scel=(1) sceal; (2) sciell

sceld=(1) scield; (2) scyld I.

sceld-=scild-, scyld-; **scele**=scelle

scelēge (GL)=sceolhēge

scelfan³ (=ie) *to totter, shake,* LL. [ON. skialfa]

scelfor=scealfor

scell I.=sceal. **II.**=sciell

scelle (=ie) *cutting off, separation* Cp777c: *discretion* RWH145⁴ (v. FM100).

scemel=scamol; **scēnan**=scǣnan

scenc (æ) m. (±) *drink, draught,* Lcd,MtL : *cup,* CM959. ['*shench*']

±scencan (æ) *to pour out, give drink,* B,LPs, Sc; Æ,CP. ['*shench*']

scencingcuppe f. *jug,* TC536⁷.

scendan I. (±, i, ie, y) *to put to shame, confound, discomfit,* AO,VPs; CP : *blame,* CP : *corrupt, injure,* Cr,DR : *disgrace, insult.* ['*shend*'] **II.**=scyndan I.

scendle f. *reproach,* LkLR11⁸.

+scendnes (æ, e, ea, i, y) f. *shame, confusion,* Æ,Ps. ['*shendness*']

+scendð f. *confusion,* VPs108²⁹.

scendung f. *reproach, affliction,* DR,LkL.

scēne=scīene; **scēnfeld**=scīnfeld

scennum dp. of sb. *pommel of sword-hilt? plate of metal on pommel?* B1694.

+scento, +scendðo (VPs) f. *shame, confusion.*

scēo I. *cloud?* RD4⁴¹. **II.**=scēoh, scōh

sceo-; **scēo-**=sco-, scu-; **scō-, scū-**

scēoc pret. 3 sg. of sceacan.

scēod I.=scōd pret. 3 sg. of scēððan. **II.** pp. of scōgan.

scēofan=scūfan; **scēogan** (CP)=scōgan

scēoh I. '*shy*,' *timid,* Rim43. **II.**=scōh

scēohmōd *timid,* JUL672.

sceol (*sceolh) *squinting, awry,* WW. [Ger. scheel]

sceolan=sculan; **sceoldan**=scieldan

sceolh-ēge, -ē(a)gede (y) *squinting,* Æ.

sceolu=scolu; **sceom-**=scam-

scēon (±) I.† *to fall (to), occur, happen : go quickly, fly.* **II.**=scōgan

scēon-=scīen-

scēona gp. of scēoh.

sceonc-=scanc-; **sceond**=scand

scēop=scop

scēop pret. 3 sg. of scieppan.

sceoppa m. *booth,* Lk21¹. ['*shop*']

sceoppend=scieppend
sceopu nap. of scip.
sceor=scūr; sceoran=scieran
sceorf (u, y) n. '*scurf*,' BH : *a skin disease*, Lcd : (+) *irritation of the stomach*, LCD.
sceorfan³ *to scarify, gnaw*, AO : (+) *scrape, shred*.
sceorfe(n)de (u¹) *rough, scabby*, LCD 56a, 65b.
sceorian=scorian
sceorp (o) n. *ornament, clothing*, AO : *equipment, fittings (for a ship?*), LL 444,1.
±sceorpan³ *to scrape, gnaw*, LCD.
sceort=scort
scēos gs., nap. of scēoh, scōh.
sceot=scot
±scēot *ready, quick*, RB 97¹⁶.
sceota m. '*shoat*,' *trout*, WW 94.
±scēotan² *to* 'SHOOT,' *hurl missiles, cast*, Æ : *strike, hit, push, thrust, AO : run, rush, dart, press forward*, Æ : *contribute, pay : refer to, appeal to*, Æ : *allot, assign : befall, fall to, happen*, CHRD.
scēotend† m. *bowman, warrior*.
sceoton=scuton pret. pl. of scēotan.
sceoða=sceaða
scep=scyp I.; scep-=sciep-
+scep=+sceap; scēp (*VPs*)=scēap
scepen I. pp. of scieppan. II.=scipen.
III. (N)=scieppend
sceppe f. *a dry measure*, NC 319. [*ON.* skeppa].
sceptlōh, sceptōg (GL)=sceaftlō
scer=scear; scer-=scear-, scier-, scir-
scerero (OET)=scēarra
scer(n)icge (=ie) f. *actress, female jester*, A, MH,RD (sciren-).
+scert (OEG 130)=scyrt, pp. of scyrtan.
sceruru=scēarra
-scerwen v. ealu-s, medu-s.
scēt=scēat pret. 3 sg. of scēotan.
scēte=scȳte; scetel (KGL)=scyttel
scett=sceatt; scēð=(1) scēað; (2) scegð
scēðdæd (æ) f. *injurious deed, crime*, WW.
scēð-nes, -enes f. *hurt, injury*, BH.
±scēððan⁶ *and* wv. (ea, y) *to scathe, injure, hurt, crush, oppress, disturb*. [sceaða]
scēððend† m. *adversary*, DR.
+scēððendlīc *hurtful*, DR 118¹⁶.
scēððu f. *hurt, injury*, LCD 1·342'.
scēðwrǣc *hurtful, wicked*, BL 161³³.
sceu-, scēu-=scu-, scū-
scēwyrhta=sceowyrhta
scīa m. *shin, leg*, GL.
sciccels, sciccel (y) m. *coat, mantle, cloak*, Æ.
sciccing m. *mantle, cloak, cape*, GL.
scīd n. *thin slip of wood, shingle, billet*, Gl. ['*shide*']

scīdhrēac m. *rick or heap of firewood*, EC 351¹⁰.
scīdweall m. *wooden palings*, WW 146²⁸
+scīe=+scȳ
-scīelan (ȳ) v. be-s.
scield (e, i, y) m. '*shield*,' B,*VPs* : *protector*, Bl,Ph : (±) *protection, defence*, AO,CP : *part of a bird's plumage?* PH 308.
scield- v. also scild-.
±scieldan (i, eo, y) *to protect,* '*shield*' ('*i-shield*'), *guard, defend, defend oneself*, Æ,B,Bl,Bo,Lcd,VPs; AO,CP. +scieldod *furnished with shields*, Bl.
sciele (CP) pres. sg. subj. of sculan.
sciell I. f. '*shell*,' Cp,MH,OEG : *shell-fish* : *scale*, Æ,AO,CP. [scalu] II. (y) *sonorous, shrill*, Rim 27. ['*shill*']
sciellfisc (i, y) m. '*shell-fish*,' Bo.
-sciellig (y) v. stān-s.
sciellht (e) *having a shell*, LCD.
sciendan=scendan
scīene (ē, ēo, ī, ȳ) *beautiful*, B,Cr,Gen,Pa, Ph : *bright, brilliant, light*, Cr. ['*sheen*']
scīenes (ēo, ī, ȳ) f. *suggestion, instigation*, CP. [scȳan]
scienn=scinn, scīn
scīenð pres. 3 sg. of scīnan.
±scieppan⁶ (e, i, y) *to create, form,* '*shape*' ('*i-shape*'), *make*, Gen : *order, destine, arrange, adjudge, assign*, B,Wy; AO.
±Scieppend (y) m. *Creator*, B; CP. ['*sheppend*']
±scieran⁴ (æ, e, eo, i) *to cleave, hew, cut*, An, B : *cut hair*, Æ,CP : *receive tonsure, Guth* : '*shear*' *sheep*, BC. pp. scoren *abrupt*, CP 215⁸.
scierden (e) adj. *of sherds*, GPH 400. [sceard]
sciering (e) f. *shearing, shaving*, CM 610.
±scierpan (e, y) I. *to deck, clothe, equip*, ÆL. [sceorp] II. *to sharpen*, LL,*VPs* : *rouse, invigorate, strengthen*. +scierpt *acute (accent)*, BF 184¹. ['*sharp*']
+scierpla (i, y) *clothing, garments*, AN, BL.
+scierpiendlīce (y¹) *fittingly*, BHB 324⁴.
scierseax=scearseax
scīet pres. 3 sg. of scēotan.
scīete (ē, ī, ȳ) f. *cloth, towel, shroud*, Æ,BH, Cp,Mk,WW. ['*sheet*']
scīfe=scyfe
±sciftan (y) *to divide, distribute, allot, appoint*, LL : *place, order, arrange*, LL,W. ['*shift*']
scilbrung=scylfrung
scild=scield; scild-=scyld-
scildburh† (e, y) f. *shield-wall, phalanx* : *roof of shields, testudo* : *place of refuge*, SAT 309.
scilden f. *protection*, WW 52¹⁷.

±scild-end, -ere (ie, y) m. *protector, defender*, Ps.
scildfreca (y¹) m. *warrior*, B1033.
scildhete m. *foe*, AN85. [scyld]
scildhrēoða (y¹, e², ea²) m. *shield, buckler* : *testudo, phalanx*.
±scildnes (ie) f. *defence, protection*, CP.
scildtruma (y¹) m. *testudo, phalanx, company (of troops), Æ,OEG.* ['*sheltron*']
scildung (y¹) f. *protection*, Æ,DR.
scildweall (y¹) m. *wall of shields*, B3118.
scildwiga (y¹) m. *warrior*, B288.
scildwyrhta (y¹) m. *shield-maker*, Ct,LL.
scile (CP) pres. subj. of sculan.
scilfix=sciellfisc
scilfor *yellow, golden*, OEG.
scill=sciell
scilling (y) m. '*shilling*' (*consisting of a varying number of pence*), *silver coin, Æ, G,LL* (v. 2·640),*WW*.
scillingrīm n. *count of shillings*, WID92.
scīma m. *ray, light, brightness, effulgence, splendour*, CP : *twilight, gloom.* [scīnan]
scimerian (y) to '*shimmer*,' *glisten, shine*, NC319; OEG23⁵¹.
scīmian *to shine, glisten, ÆGr,LkL* : *grow dusky, dim, be dazzled, bleared, Æ.* ['*shim*']
scīn=scinn
scīnan¹ (ȳ) to '*SHINE*,' *flash, Æ,CP* : *be resplendent* : (+) *shine upon, illuminate.*
scīnbān n. '*shin-bone*,' *WW*.
scinccing (OET p. 26)=sciccing
+scincio np. *the fat about the kidneys*, LCD.
scind-=scend-
scindel m. *a shingle*, KC6·33'.
scīndlāc=scīnlāc
scīnefrian *to glitter*, WW348¹⁹.
scinelāc=scinnlāc
scīnende (ȳ) '*shining*,' *MH,WW* : *eminent, distinguished*, BH.
scīnendlic *shining*, LPs18⁹.
scīnfeld (ēa) m. *Elysian fields, Tempe*.
scinhosu f. *greave*, OEG.
scinn I. n., scinna m. *spectre, illusion, phantom, evil spirit*, CP : *magical image*, ÆL36⁴⁰⁴. II. n. *skin*, CHR1075,WW 427²⁷?
scinncræft (y) m. *sorcery, magic*, AO.
scinncræftiga m.*sorcerer*,GD27¹⁵; LL248,7.
scinnere m. *magician*, GL.
scīnnes I. f. *radiance*, MKL13²⁴. II.= scīenes
scinngedwola m. *phantom*, WW455¹¹.
scinngelāc n. *jugglery, magical practices*, AN767.
scinnhīw n. *spectre, illusion, phantasm, Æ.*
scinnlāc I. n. *sorcery, magic* : *apparition, spectre, delusion, superstition* : *frenzy, rage*, AO. II.=scinnlǣce I.

scinnlǣca (ā²) m. *wizard, magician*, AO.
scinnlǣce I. *magical, spectral*, AO. II. f. *sorceress, witch*.
scinnlic (y) *spectral*, NC320.
scinnsēoc *spectre-haunted*, LCD1·364⁴.
scinu (y) f. '*shin*,' *WW*.
scip (y) n. '*ship*,' *BH,Bo,Chr,Cp*; AO,CP.
scip=scēap
scipāc f. *oak for shipbuilding*, KC.
scipbroc n. *hardship on ship-board*, BL173⁶.
scipbrucol (y) *destructive to shipping*, GPH 401⁹.
scipbryce m. *right to claim wreckage*, KC 4·208. ['*shipbreche*']
scipbȳme (y) f. *ship's trumpet*, GPH391.
scipcræft m. *naval force*, CHR1048D.
scipdrincende *shipwrecked*, DR61¹⁶.
scipe I. m. *pay, wage*, WW; ÆL31⁵⁵ : *position, rank.* ['*shipe*'] II. (+) n. *fate*, B2570?
scipehere=sciphere
scipen (e, y) f. '*shippon*,' *stall, cattle-shed*, BH,LL.
scipere (y) m. *shipman, sailor, Chr.* ['*shipper*']
scipfǣreld n. *voyage, Æ*,GD273¹⁸.
scipfæt n. *a vessel in the form of a ship*, WW124⁸.
scipfarend (y) m. *sailor*, BH(Sch)261²
scipfērend m. *sailor*, AN250.
scipfierd f. *naval expedition, fleet*, AO.
scipflota m. *sailor, pirate*, CHR937A.
scipforðung f. *equipment of ships*, LL314'.
scipfultum m. *naval aid*, CHR1049C.
scipfylleð *private jurisdiction exercised over a group of three hundreds*, KC6·240 (v. BT).
scipfyrd=scipfierd
scipfyrdung f. *fleet, naval expedition*, CHR, LL.
scipfyrð(r)ung f. *equipment of ships*, LL.
scipgebroc n. *shipwreck*, AO,CP.
scipgefeoht (y) n. *naval battle*, GPH389.
scipgefēre m. *sailing*, BH150².
scipgetāwu f. *tackling of a ship*, WW181²⁴.
scipgyld n. *ship-tax, ship-money*, TC307²⁴.
sciphamor m. *hammer for giving a signal to rowers*, WW.
sciphere m. *naval force; fleet* (*usu. hostile*), *squadron*, AO,CHR : *crew of a warship*.
scipherelic *naval*, HGL406⁴⁰.
sciphlǣder f. *ship's ladder*, WW.
sciphlæst (y) m. *ship-load, crew*, AO,CP : *ship of burden.*
sciphlāford m. *ship-master, skipper*, WW 181²¹.
sciplan *to take* '*ship*,' *embark* : (±) *man or equip a ship, Chr.*
scipincel n. *little ship*, WW.
sciplād (y) f. *journeying by sea*, BH198²⁹.

sciplæst=sciphlæst
sciplic *naval,* GL,HL 199[127].
scipliŏ n. *naval force,* CHR 1055c.
scipliŏend m. *seaman : voyager,* ÆL 33[188].
scipliŏende ptc. *sailing,* WW.
scipmæris m. *ship's rope, cable,* WW.
scipmann (y) m. *'shipman,' sailor, rower,* BH,*Chr* : *one who goes on trading voyages.*
scipp-=sciepp-
sciprāp m. *ship's rope, cable,* AO.
sciprēŏra (y[1]) m. *rower, sailor,* GPH.
sciprōŏor n. *ship's oar or rudder,* WW 455[18].
sciprōwend m. *rower, sailor,* WW 455[14].
scipryne m. *passage for ships,* TC 341[16].
scipsetl n. *bench for rowers,* WW.
scipsōcn f. (KC 6·240′) i.q. scipfylleð.
scipsteall (y) m. *place for ships,* BC 3·316[16].
scipstēora m. *steerman, pilot,* CP.
scipsteorra m. *pole-star,* LCD 3·270′.
scip-stīera, -stȳra=scipstēora
scip-tearo, -ter, n., gs. -tearos; scip-t(e)ara, -te(o)ra m. (*ship-tar*), *bitumen, pitch,* LCD.
sciptoll n. *passage money,* ÆL 30[167].
scipwealh m. *servant whose service is connected with ships?* (BT); *one liable to serve in the fleet?* (Swt), EC 376[15].
scipweard m. *ship-master,* AN 297.
scipwered n. *crew,* WW 451[17].
scipwīsan (on) adv. *like a ship,* AA,Æ.
scipwræc *jetsam,* KC 4·146.
scipwyrhta m. *'shipwright,'* WW 112[5].
scīr I. (ȳ) f. *office, appointment, charge, authority, supremacy,* AO,*Cp*,LL (+ at DR 187[9]); *CP : district, diocese, see, province, 'shire,' parish,* AO,*Gl*,LL; Æ : *tribe.* II. adj. *bright, gleaming, shining, resplendent,* B, *Bo : clear, translucent, Cr,* WW : *pure, unmixed, B,Bo : white,* Jn 4[35]. [*'shire'*]
scīran=scieran
scīran (ȳ) *to make clear, say, tell, declare, B, CP : arrange, determine, decide, decree, act in authority,* CP, (+) LkL 16[2] : (±) *clear from, get rid of,* AO,CP.
scīrbasu *bright purple,* WW 193[12].
scīrbisceop m. *bishop of a diocese,* WW 173[30].
scīre I. adv. *brightly, An : clearly : mightily, Cr* 1142. [*'shire'*] II. *'peribolum,' enclosure, curtilage,* WW 184[22].
scīre-=scīr-
scīrecg *keen-edged,* LCD 1·390[7].
scīrenicge (RD 9[9])=scernicge
scīresmann=scīrmann
scīrfemūs (=ie) f. *shrew (mouse),* WW 477[16]. [sceorfan]
scīrgemōt n. *shire-moot,* LL,TC.
scīrgerēfa m. *'sheriff,'* KC.

scīrgesceat (ȳ) n. *property of a see,* KC 3·327[2].
scīrham *clad in bright mail,* B 1895.
±scīrian (e, y) *to ordain, appoint : allot, assign, grant :* (+) *mark off, count, reckon.*
scīriendlic (y) *derivative,* WW 222[23].
scīrigmann=scīrmann
scīrlett n. *piece or measure of land,* EC 239[9].
scīrmæled *brightly adorned,* JUD 230.
scīrmann (ȳ) m. *governor of a shire, prefect, sheriff, steward, procurator, official, KC;* Æ,CP; v. LL 2·649 : *inhabitant of a district,* Æ. [*'shireman'*]
scīrnes f. *elucidation,* WW 279[23].
scirp-=scierp-; **scīrseax**=scearseax
scīrŏegen m. *thane of a shire,* BC 1·544[8].
scīrung f. *separation, rejection,* RB 109[21].
scīr-wæter (scyr-) n. *water forming a boundary,* CHR 656 E. [scieran]
scīrwered *bright?* GU 1262.
scīrwita m. *chief man of a shire,* W.
-scītan[1] v. be-sc.
scīte=scȳte; **scītefinger**=scytefinger
scitol *purgative,* LCD 66a.
scitte f. *purging, Lcd.* [*'shit'*]
scittels (Æ)=scyttels
scl-(GL)=sl-
scmēgende (VPs)=smēagende pres. ptc. of smēagan.
scnīcend (GL)=snīcend pres. ptc. of snīcan.
scō=scōh; **sco-**=sceo-
scōas=scōs v. scōh; **scobl**=scofl
scōc pret. 3 sg. of sceacan.
scocca=scucca
scocha (=scohha) *'lenocinium,'* Ep 579.
scōcnyll m. *signal for putting on shoes,* ANS 84·10.
scōd I. pret. 3 sg. of sceðan. II. v. scōgan.
scōere m. *shoemaker, Gl.* [*'shoer'*]
scōf pret. 3 sg. of sceafan.
scofen pp. of scufan.
scofettan *to drive hither and thither,* CP 169[13].
scofl f. *'shovel,' Cp,Ep,*LL.
scōgan pp. sc(ē)od *to 'shoe,'* Æ,CP.
scōh, scō, scēo m. gs. nap. sc(ē)os, gp. sc(ē)one, dp. sc(ē)on, scōum *'shoe,' Bf,G, Mt,WW.*
scōhere=scōere
scōhnægl m. *shoe-nail,* WW.
scōhŏēn (ēo) m. *shoe-cleaner,* RBL 91[9].
scōh-ŏwang, -ŏong m. *'shoe-thong,' boot-lace,* Jn.
scōhwyrhta (ēo, ēoh) m. *shoemaker, leather-worker,* GD 322,WW 97[5].
scōlan=scōgan
scōl f. *'school,' Æ,BH,Lcd;* AO.
+scola I. m. *debtor,* WW 15[28]. [sceal] II. *companion,* OEG 2271n. [scolu]

+scōla m. *fellow-student*, OEG 2271.

scolde pret. 3 sg. of sculan.

scōlere m. '*scholar*,' *learner*, Bf,LL.

scolh (WW 241¹³)=seolh

scōliere (Bf 54²⁷)=scōlere

scōlmann m.. *scholar*, WW 314²⁹ : *client*, 163⁴⁴.

scolu I. (eo) f. *troop, host, multitude* : *shoal (of fishes)*, A 13·418. II.=scōl

scom-=scam-

scōmhylte (scomm-?) n. *brushwood, copse, thicket*, WW 411³.

scōmlic *short*, MH 98¹³.

scōn=scēon v. scēoh; scon-=scan-

scop (eo) m. *singer, poet*, B,Bo; AO. ['*scop*']

scōp pret. 3 sg. of scieppan.

scopcræft m. *poetry*, ÆGr 215⁹.

scopgereord (eo¹) n. *poetical language*, BH.

scoplēoð n. *poem*, AO.

scoplic *poetic*, OEG 119.

scora m. *hairy garment*, WW 278¹.

scoren pp. of scieran.

scorian (eo) I. *to refuse*, Æ. II. *to jut out*, GD 213⁵.

scorp=sceorp

scort (eo, y) '*short*,' *not long, not tall*, Bo, GD,Lcd : *brief*, Æ,Bf,Bl,Bo,CP.

scortian (eo) *to become* '*short*,' *shorten*, Lcd : (±) *run short, fail*.

scortlic (eo) *brief*, Sc 214¹⁶. adv. -līce '*shortly*,' *briefly, soon*, AO,LPs,ZDA; Æ.

scortnes (eo) f. '*shortness*,' *small amount* : *summary, abstract*, ÆGr : *short space of time*.

scortwyrplic (eo) *shortly coming to pass*, Lcd 3·156².

scoru a '*score*,' NC 320. [scoren; scieran]

scōs gs. of scōh.

±scot (eo) n. '*shot*,' *shooting*, OEG; AO. : *darting, rapid motion*, Men : *what is shot forth*, AO,CP : (+) *scot, payment* : *private apartment, sanctum, chancel*, Æ.

+scota m. *fellow-soldier*, WW 15,207.

scoten pp. of scēotan.

+scotfeoht n. *shooting, battle*, PPs.

scotfrēo *scot-free, free of tribute*, KC.

±scotian (eo) (tr. and intr.) *to move rapidly, shoot, hurl a javelin*, Æ.

scotlira m. *calf of the leg*, Lcd.

scotspere n. *dart, javelin*, HGl 405.

Scottas mpl. *the Scots*, BH,Chr; Æ,CP. ['*Scot*']

scotung (eo) f. *missile* : *shooting* : *darting, flashing*, Lcd 3·280'.

scōum v. scōh.

scōung f. *provision of shoes*, LL 450,10.

-scrād v. scrīðend-s.

scrādung=scrēadung

scræb m. *cormorant? ibis?* Cp 1311.

±scræf (ea, e) n. [obl. cases occly. have scraf-] *cave, cavern, hole, pit*, Æ,CP : *hovel*, Æ : *den*, MtR 21¹³.

+scrǣpe=+scrēpe

scrætte f. *adulteress, prostitute*, Gl. [L scratta]

scrǣwa=scrēawa

scrāf pret. 3 sg. of scrīfan.

scraf- v. scræf.

scrallettan† intr. *to sound loudly*.

scranc pret. 3 sg. of scrincan.

scrapian *to scrape*, IM. ['*shrape*']

scrāð pret. 3 sg. of scrīðan.

scrēad(e) f. '*shred*,' *cutting, scrap*, WW.

±scrēadian *to* '*shred*,' *peel, prune, cut off*, Æ.

scrēadung (ā) f. *shred, cutting, fragment*, MtL : *pruning, trimming*, WW. ['*shredding*']

scrēadungīsen n. *pruning-knife*, WW. [v. '*shredding*']

screaf=scræf

scrēawa m. '*shrew*' *(mouse)*, Gl.

screb=scræb; scrēc=scrīc

scref=scræf

scremman *to cause to stumble*, Lev 19¹⁴.

±screncan *to cause to stumble, ensnare, deceive*, CP,Ps : (+) *cause to shrink or shrivel*, MtL 13⁶. ['*shrench*']

+scrence *withered, dry*, LkL 6⁸.

+screncednes f. *tripping up*, CVPs 40¹⁰.

screodu v. scrid; +scrēope=+scrēpe

screopu=screpu

screpan⁵ (i,y) *to scrape, scratch*, Cp,Lcd, MkR : *prepare*, LF 47'. ['*screpe*']

scrēpan *to become dry, withered*, MkR 9¹⁸.

scrēpe (ǣ, ēo) I. n. (+) *advantage*. II. (±) *suitable, adapted, fit*. adv. -līce.

+scrēpnes (oe) f. *convenience*, Cp 568.

screpu (eo) f. *strigil, curry-comb*, Gl.

scrēwa=scrēawa; scrīban (Gl)=scrīfan

scrīc (ē, ū) *shrike, missel-thrush?* Gl.

scrid I. n. nap. screodu *vehicle, chariot, litter*. II. *quick, fleet*, An 496.

scrīdan=scrȳdan

scride m. *course, orbit*, Met 28¹¹.

scridon pret. pl. of scrīðan.

scridwǣn m. *chariot* : *curule chair*, Bo.

scridwīsa m. *charioteer*, WW 150¹⁴.

+scrif n. *judgment, edict*, WW : *ceremony*, WW.

±scrīfan¹ *prescribe, ordain, allot, assign, impose (punishment)*, LL; Æ : *hear confession*, '*shrive*,' LL : *receive absolution* : *have regard to, be troubled about, care for*, CP.

scrifen ptc? *painted?* Rim 13.

scrift m. *prescribed penalty or penance*, LL : *absolution*, LL : *confessor*, CP,Cr; Æ : *judge*. tō scrifte gān *to go to confession*, LL,W. ['*shrift*']

scriftbōc f. *book of penances, or on penance,* LL,W.

scriftscīr f. *confessor's area of jurisdiction :* diocese, LL164,26.

scriftsprǣc f. *confession,* LL.

scrimman³ *to shrink,* Lcd2b. ['*shrim*']

scrīn (ȳ) n. *chest, coffer, ark, Æ,Jn :* '*shrine,*' *Æ* : *cage (for criminals).* [*L.* scrinium]

±**scrincan³** *to* '*shrink,*' *contract, shrivel up, wither, pine away, Æ,AO,Lcd.*

scrind f. *swift course?* PPs103²⁴.

scringan=scrincan; **-scripel** (y) v. ēar-s.

scrīpen, scrīpende '*austerus,*' LkLR19²¹.

scripeð (*Cp*) pres. 3 sg. of screpan.

scritta m. *hermaphrodite,* WW161¹¹. (v. FTP473).

scrið (v. OEG2185)=scrid I.

scrīðan¹ *to go, move, glide, B,Gu.* ['*scrithe*']

scrīðe m. *course,* MET28¹¹.

-scrīðol v. wīd-s.; **scroepe,** scrōpe=scrēpe

scrofel n? *scrofula,* Lcd182a.

scrūc=scrīc

scrūd n., ds. scrȳd *clothing, dress : garment, vestment, Æ,Chr,WW.* ['*shroud*']

scrūd-=scrūt-

scrūdelshūs n. *sacristy, vestry,* ANS84¹⁵. [scrȳdan]

scrūdfeoh n.*money for buying clothes,* NC320.

scrūdfultum m. *grant towards providing clothes,* Ct.

scrūdland n. *land bequeathed as provision for clothing,* TC329¹⁹.

scrūdwaru f. *garb,* LL.

scruf [*Lcd*]=sceorf

scruncon pret. pl. of scrincan.

scrūtnere (ūd) m. *examiner,* CHRD88³³.

scrūtnian (ūd) *to examine, scrutinize, consider, Æ.*

scrūtnung (ūd) f. *search, investigation,* Lcd, ERPs.

scrybb d. *scrub, brushwood,* TC525²².

scrȳd v. scrūd.

±**scrȳdan** (ī) *to clothe, dress, Æ,Bl,Lk,Mt.* ['*shride*']

scryft=scrift

scrynce *withered,* JnL5³.

scrypan=screpan

scua m. *shadow, shade, darkness : protection.*

scucca (eo) m. *sprite, evil spirit, demon, B, Bo,Mt : the devil.* ['*shuck*']

scuccen (eo) *devilish,* NC319.

scuccgyld (eu¹) n. *idol,* PPs105²⁶.

scūdan² *to run, hurry?* Gu828.

scūfan² (ēo) *to* '*SHOVE**,' *thrust, push, Æ :* *push with violence, urge, impel,* CP : *push out, expel, deliver up* : (†) *display* : (intr.) *to move, go.*

sculan anv. pres. 1 sing. sce(a)l(l), scal, pl. sculon (eo), pret. sc(e)olde, sc(e)alde *to be obliged* ('SHALL*,' *have to, must, must needs, am bound to, ought to*), *Æ,AO,CP* : owe.

scul-dor, -dra m., nap. -dru, -dra, +scyl-dru, -dre '*shoulder,*' *Bl,Ep,Lcd,LG.*

sculdorhrægl n. *cape,* WW327²⁴.

sculdorwærc m. *pain in the shoulders,* LCD.

sculdur=sculdor

scule pres. subj. of sculan.

sculthēta (WW)=scyldlǣta

±**scunian** (y) *to* '*shun,*' *avoid,* Guth : *be afraid,* DR : (tr.) *abhor,* TC.

scunung f. *abomination,* LHy6²³ (? for on-s.).

scūr (ēo) m. (f) '*shower,*' *storm, tempest, trouble, commotion, breeze, An,LkR,Ps;* CP : †*shower of blows or missiles, El,Jud* 79.

scūra† m. *shower (of rain).*

scūrbeorg f. *roof,* RUIN5.

scūrboga m. *rainbow,* GEN1540.

±**scurf**=sceorf

scūrfāh *rainy, stormy,* A9·369; MFH172.

scūrheard† *made hard by blows (epithet of a sword).*

scūrsceadu f. *protection against storms,* GEN 813.

scutel I. m. *dish, platter,* WW280²². ['*scuttle*'] II.=scytel

scuton pret. pl. of scēotan.

scuwa=scua

+**scȳ** npl. *pair of shoes, Æ,Ps.*

scȳan? scȳn? *to suggest, persuade, prompt, incite, tempt,* BH,MtR.

scyccel, scyccels=sciccels

scydd m. *twist on a hill-side?* (Earle): *alluvial ground?* (BT),KC.

scȳde pret. 3 sg. of scēon and scȳan, scȳn.

scyfe (e, i) m. *shove, pushing, precipitation, furtherance, instigation,* CP. tō+sc. *headlong.*

scyfel(e) f. *woman's hood, head-dress,* GL.

scȳft pres. 3 sg. of scūfan.

scyftan=sciftan

+**scȳgean** *to furnish with shoes,* TC616′.

scyhhan (ES43·318)=scyn I.

scyhtan *to impel, prompt, urge,* GEN898; Gu98.

scyl=sciell

scylcen f. *female servant, slave, concubine,* ÆH2·162′. [scealc]

±**scyld** I. (e) fm. *offence, fault, crime, guilt, sin,* CP : *obligation, liability, due, debt,* CP. [sculan; *Ger.* schuld] II.=scield

scyld-=scield-, scild-

+**scyldan** *to accuse,* LL156,11.

scyldfrecu f. *wicked craving,* GEN898.

scyldful *sinful, guilty, Æ.*

scyldg-=scyldigscyld-hata, -hete† m. *enemy.*

scyldian=(1) scyldigian; (2) scyldan

scyldig (e, i) (usu. w. g.) *guilty, criminal, sinful, Æ,B*; CP : *liable, responsible, in debt to,* CP. ealdres sc. *having forfeited his life.* ['*shildy*']

scyldigian *to sin* : (+) *place in the position of a criminal, render liable to punishment.*

scyldignes f. *guilt,* DR42,103.

scyldigung f. *sum demanded as* 'wergeld,' LL156,11.

scyld-læta [-hæta? cp. sculthēta] m. *bailiff,* WW230²⁰.

scyldlēas *guiltless,* LCD.

scyldo=scyld I.

+scyldru v. sculdor; scyldu=scyld I.

scyldung=(1) scildung; (2) scyldigung

scyldwīte n. *fine for a crime of violence,* LL567,38.

scyldwreccende ptc. *avenging sin,* CR 1161.

scyldwyrcende† *evil-doing.*

scyle pres. subj. of sculan.

scylēagede=sceolhēgede

scylf m. *crag, ledge, shelf,* Mdf : *pinnacle, turret, tower, Æ.*

-scylfan v. ā-s.

scylfe m. *shelf, floor,* GEN1306.

scylfig *rocky,* OEG (scylp-).

scylfisc=sciellfisc; scylfor=scilfor.

scylfrung (i) f. *shaking, swinging?* BL99³⁴; WW516¹⁶ (-brong).

scylfð pres. 3 sg. of scelfan.

scylga=scealga

scylian (=ie) *to separate, part, divide off.* sc. of māle *to pay off, discharge,* Chr1049. ['*shill*']

scyll=sciell

scyllan (=ie) *to resound, sound loudly,* WW; OEG4890. ['*shill*']

scylling=scilling; scylp=scylf

scyltumend m. *helper,* PPs27⁸.

scylun (N)=sculon pres. pl. of sculan.

scymrian=scimerian

scȳn I. *to* '*shy,*' ÆL31⁹⁷¹. II. v. scȳan.

scȳn-=scīn-, scinn-

±scyndan I. (e) (tr., intr.) *to hurry, hasten, drive forward, impel* : *incite, exhort,* CP. II.=scendan

scyndel m. *disreputable person,* BF130²².

scyndendlīce adv. *hastily,* WW.

scyndnes f. *persuasion, prompting,* GD.

+scyndnes=+scandnes; scȳne=scīene

scȳnes, scȳnnes=scīenes

+scynian (DR32⁵)=scunian

scynn n. *skin, fur,* CHR1075D. [ON.]

scynu (WW307²⁷)=scinu

scyp I. m. *patch,* v. ES43·316. II. (Chr 1048)=scip

scypen=scipen

scyplan *to take shape,* LCD3·146¹⁵.

scypp-=sciepp-

scyr-=scear-, scier-, scir-; scȳr=scīr

±scyrdan *to harm, injure, destroy,* AN,LL. [sceard]

+scȳrdan=+scrȳdan; scyrf=sceorf

scyrft *scarifying? scraping?* Cp130s.

scyrfð pres. 3 sg. of sceorfan.

scȳrmælum adv. *stormily,* Bo47²⁵. [scūr]

scyrp-=scierp-

±scyrtan (e) tr. *to shorten,* AO : intr. *run short, decrease, fail.* [sceort]

scyrte f. *skirt,* GPH393. ['*shirt*']

scyrtest superl. of scort.

scyrting f. *shortening, abstract, epitome,* ÆH 2·460⁶.

scyrtra comp. of scort.

scȳt pres. 3 sg. of scēotan.

scyte (ē) m. *shooting, hurling,* AO : *stroke, blow,* ZDA : *dart.* ['*shute*'; scēotan]

scȳte f. (ē;=īe) '*sheet,*' *linen cloth,* BH,Cp, Mk. [scēat]

scytefinger m. *forefinger,* LL,WW.

scyte-heald, -healden *inclined, sloping, precipitous,* GL.

scytel I. (u) m. *dart, arrow,* Erf,Ps : *tongue of a balance.* ['*shuttle*'] II. (=i) m. *excrement.* [scītan]

scytelfinger=scytefinger; scytels=scyttel

scyterǣs m. *headlong rush,* WW426⁷.

scytere m. *shooter,* KC.

scytheald=scyteheald

scytta m. *shooter, archer,* Æ,AO.

scyttan (usu. for-sc.) *to bolt,* '*shut*' *to, Æ* : *discharge, pay off.*

scyttel, scyttels (e, i) m. *bolt, bar, Æ,Bl,W, ZDA.* ['*shuttle*'; scēotan]

Scyttisc I. *Scotch, Irish.* II. *Irish or Scotch language.* [Scottas]

scyððan=sceððan

sē m., sēo f., ðæt n. pers. (dem.) pron. *he, she, it, that, this* : rel. pron. *who, which* : def. art. '*THE*.' II.=sǣ. III.=swā

sēa (OET)=sēaw; sēad (NG)=sēod

sēada=sēaða; seaflan (NG)=seofian

seah pret. 3 sg. of sēon.

seaht=seht I. ; seal=sealh

sealde pret. 3 sg. of sellan.

±sealdnes (a) f. *act of giving,* WW389³⁵; *grant, gift,* KC2·5³².

sēales gs. of sealh.

sealf (a) f. '*salve,*' *ointment, unguent, medicament,* Lcd,Mk; CP.

sealfbox (e) m. *salve-box,* G,BK.

sealfcynn n. *an unguent,* WW351³⁰.

sealfe=sealf; sealfer-=seolfor-

±sealfian *to* '*salve,*' *anoint,* Erf,WW.

sealfie=salfie

sealf-læcnung, -læcung (WW 114¹⁶) f. *curing by unguents, pharmacy.* [v. '*leeching*']

sealh (a) m., gs. sēales *willow, Gl,Lcd,Ps;* Mdf. ['*sallow*']

sealhangra m. *willow-hanger,* KC6·234¹⁷.

sealhrind f. *willow-bark,* Lcd.

sealhyrst m. *willow-copse,* KC5·256'.

seallan=sellan

sealm (a, eo) m. '*psalm*,*' *song, RB,Ps;* Æ, CP.

sealma (e) m. *bed, couch,* B,Gl.

sealmcwide m. *psalm,* LPs97⁵.

sealmfæt n. only in phr. ' *on sealmfatum,*' '*in vasis psalmorum*'! PPs70²⁰.

sealmgetæl n. *number of psalms,* RB.

sealm-glīg, -glīw n. *psaltery, psalmody,* LRPs.

sealmian *to play an accompaniment on the harp, Ps* 107¹. ['*psalm*']

sealmlēoð n. *psalm,* BLPs56⁹.

sealmlof n. *psalm,* LPs.

sealmlofian *to sing psalms,* LPs104².

sealmsang m. *psalm : composition or singing of psalms, Æ : psaltery,* CPs32² : *one of the canonical hours,* GD.

sealmsangere m. *psalmist,* Chrd 112¹².

sealmsangmærsung f. *psalm-singing in the canonical hours,* ÆL23b³⁶.

sealmscop (eo²) m. *psalmist,* Æ,CP.

sealmtraht m. *exposition of psalms,* Æ (3²⁹⁷).

sealmwyrhta m. *psalmist, Æ.* ['*psalm-wright*']

sealobrūn=salubrūn

sealt I. n. '*salt,*' *Lcd,MtL;* CP. **II.** adj. *salt, briny, Cr;* AO,CP. [v. Mdf]

sealtan⁷ (a) *to* '*salt,*' *Æ,G,IM,Lcd.*

sealtbrōc (a) m. *brook running from salt-works?* KC3·206³⁰.

sealtere I. m. '*salter,*' *salt-worker, WW;* Æ. **II.** (CM362,679)=saltere

sealtern n. *salt-works, BC.* ['*saltern*']

sealtfæt n. *salt-cellar, LL,WW.* ['*saltfat*']

sealthālgung (a) f. *consecration of salt,* OET 587.

sealtherpað (a) m. *road to salt-works,* KC 3·206'.

sealthūs n. '*salt-house,*' *WW.*

sealtian (a) *to dance,* Lk7³². [*L.* saltare]

sealticge f. *dancer,* MH156¹⁴.

sealting f. *dancing,* Chrd 79¹.

sealtlēaf n. '*mozicia,*' WW (?-lēap, NP 7·215).

sealtmere m. *brackish pond,* EC449'.

sealtnes (a) f. '*saltness,*' VPs.

sealtrod *track with willows,* KC3·236'.

sealtsæleða (y¹) m. *saltness,* LPs106³⁴; RPs.

sealtsēað m. *saline spring,* BH26²².

sealtstān m. *rock-salt,* Lcd1·374¹⁴ : *pillar of salt, Gen;* Æ. ['*saltstone*']

sealtstræt f. *road to salt-works,* KC.

sealtwīc n. *a place where salt is sold,* KC.

sealtwylle (a) f. *salt spring, KC,LG.* ['*salt-well*']

sealtȳð† f. *salt wave, sea-wave.*

sēam I. (ēo) m. *burden, load, Æ,LkL,LkR : bag : harness of a beast of burden, Æ : duty of furnishing beasts of burden.* ['*seam*'] **II.** m. '*seam,*' *suture, junction, Æ,WW.*

sēamere I. m. *beast of burden, mule,* WW. [*L.* sagmarius] **II.** m. *tailor, Æ.* [sēam II.]

sēamestre f. *sempstress, (also of males) sewer, tailor, Æ,KC,WW.* ['*seamster*']

sēamhors n. *pack-horse,* WW119⁴².

sēampending m. *toll of a penny a load,* KC.

sēamsadol m. *pack-saddle,* WW119⁴¹.

sēamsticca m. *an appliance used in weaving,* LL455,15¹.

sēap pret. 3 sg. of sūpan.

sēar *dry,* '*sere,*' *barren,* GPH402⁶⁹.

seara-, seare-=searo-; **sēargian**=sārgian

sēarian *to become sere, wither, Shr.* ['*sear*']

searo (searu) n. *art, skill, cleverness, cunning : device, trick, snare, ambuscade, plot, treachery, Æ,AO,CP : work of art, cunning device, engine (of war) : armour, war-gear, trappings.*

searobend m. *artistic clasp,* B2086.

searobunden *cunningly fastened,* RD56⁴.

searocæg f. *insidious key,* Gu1118.

searocēap n. *artistic object,* RD33⁷.

searocēne *very bold,* PPs100¹⁰.

searocræft m. *artifice, treachery, wile, Æ : artistic skill, art : engine, instrument (of torture), Æ.*

searocræftig† *skilful, cunning.*

searo *fears secret path?* Rim65 (ES65·189).

searofāh *variegated, cunningly inlaid,* B 1444.

searogemme=searogimm

searogimm m. *curious gem,* B,Ps.

searogrim *fierce, formidable,* B594.

searohæbbend† m. *warrior.*

searohwīt n. *brilliant whiteness,* Rim67.

searolic *artistic, ingenious.* adv. -līce.

searomet m. *dainty, delicacy,* NC321.

searonet n. *armour-net, corslet,* B406 : *ensnaring net,* An64; 945.

searonīð† m. *treachery, strife, battle,* B.

searopīl m. *artistic javelin,* RD87².

searorūn f. *mystery,* Creat15.

searosǣled *cleverly bound,* RD24¹⁶.

searoðanc m. *sagacity, ingenuity, skill,* CP : *cunning, artifice.*

searoðancol† *shrewd, wise,* Jud.

searowrenc (y¹, a²) m. *artifice, trick,* AO.

searowundor n. *strange object,* B920.

searu=searo; **searw-** v. searo.

searwian (a, æ) *to be deceitful, dissimulate, cheat.*

searwum (dp. of searo) *skilfully.*

searwung=sierwung

seatul, seatl (NG)=setl

sēað I. (ǣ) m. *hole, pit, MkL*; CP; Mdf : *well, cistern, spring, fountain, lake,* Mdf. ['*seath*'; sēoðan] II. pret. 3 sg. of sēoðan.

sēaða m. *heartburn?* Lcd 21a.

sēaw m. *sap, juice, moisture, Gl,Lcd.* ['*sew*']

+sēaw *succulent,* Lcd 95b: *soaked,* Lcd 86[20].

seax (æ, e) n. *knife, hip-knife, short sword, dirk, dagger, Æ,B,Cp*; CP. ['*sax*']

seaxbenn (siex-) f. *dagger-wound,* B 2904.

Seaxe, Seaxan mpl. (gp. Seaxna) *Saxons,* AO.

Seaxland (e) n. *England,* Shr 16[4].

±sēcan I. *to search for,* 'seek' ('*i-seche*'), *inquire, ask for, look for,* Æ : *try, strive after, long for, wish, desire,* CP. s. on, tō *look to for, expect from,* CP : *visit, go to,* AO; Æ : *approach, attain to* : *get* : *attack, pursue, follow, Chr*; AO : *go, move, proceed, Æ.* II. (Kgl)=sȳcan

secce (B 600)=sæcce, gs. of sacu.

secful (Kgl)=sacful

secg I. m. (n) '*sedge*,' *reed, rush, flag, Gl, Lcd,WW*; Mdf. II.† f. *sword.* III.† m. *man, warrior, hero, B.* ['*segge*'] IV. m. *ocean,* OET.

secga m. *sayer, informant,* LL 396,4.

±secgan (æ) *to* 'say' ('*i-seggen*'), *speak, inform, utter, declare, tell, recite, Æ*; AO, CP : *signify, mean, Æ* : *explain, discuss* : *attribute to* : (+) *avoid?* LkL p 3[8]. s. on *accuse of, charge with, Æ.*

secge f. *speech,* Cr 190.

secgend m. *speaker, narrator,* CP,BH.

secggan=secgan

secggescēre? f. *grasshopper,* Cp 464.

secgihtig *sedgy,* WW 200[27].

secglēac n. *sedge-leek, rush-garlic,* Lcd.

secgplega m. *sword-play, battle,* An 1355.

secgrōf *brave?* (GK), *troop?* (FTp 347), Ruin 27.

secgscāra? m. *landrail, corncrake,* WW 287[11] and n.

sēcnes f. *visiting,* LkR 19[44] (oe).

sēd (VPs)=sǣd

+sēdan *to satisfy,* PPs 106[8]. [sæd]

sēde=sægde pret. 3 sg. of secgan.

sedinglīne=stedinglīne

±sedl (NG)=setl

sefa (eo) m. *mind, spirit, understanding, heart,* †CP 9[10].

sēfer-=sȳfer-; seflan=seofian

sēfre=sȳfre

sēft comp. adv. *more softly.*

±sēfte *soft, pleasant, comfortable, easy* : *gentle, mild* : *effeminate, luxurious.*

sēfteadig *prosperous,* Seaf 56.

sēftlic *luxurious,* AS 39[4].

sēftnes f. *rest, quietness, peace, Æ,AO.*

segc-=secg-; segel=segl

segen I. (æ) (±) f. *conversation, speech, statement, Æ,AO* : *premonition, prophecy,* AO : *report, story, legend.* sēo hālga +s. *Holy Writ.* II.=segn

+segenlic=+sewenlic; segg=secg

segl I. mn. '*sail,*' *AO,Bo,MH*; Æ : *veil, curtain,* Cr 1139 : *pillar of cloud,* Ex. II.=sigel

±seg-lan, -lian *to* '*sail*' : (+) *equip with a sail.*

seglbōsm m. *bellying sail,* Gl.

seglgerǣde n. *sail-tackle,* TC 549[17].

seglgyrd (e[2]) mf. *sail-yard, yard, cross-pole, Cp,WW.*

seglian=seglan

seglrād f. (*sail-road*), *sea,* B 1429.

seglrōd f. *sail-rod, sail-yard.* [v. '*rood*']

seglung f. '*sailing,*' *BH.*

segn mn. *sign, mark, token, Gen* : *ensign, banner, B,BH.* ['*senye*'; *L.* signum]

segnberend m. *warrior,* Rd 41[20].

segnbora m. *standard-bearer,* Bl,WW.

segncyning m. *king before whom a banner is borne* (BT), Ex 172.

segne f. '*seine,*' *drag-net, Ex,JnL.*

+segnes f. *expression,* ÆL 23b[73].

±segnian (ǣn) *to make the sign of the cross, cross oneself, consecrate, bless, Æ,BH.* ['*sain*']

segnung f. *blessing, consecration,* BH,GD.

sēgon=sāwon pret. pl. of sēon.

seh (VPs)=seoh imperat. of sēon.

seht I. (ea) mf. *settlement, arrangement, agreement, KC* : *friendship, peace, BH.* II. adj. *reconciled, agreed, at peace, BC.* ['*saught*']

±sehtian *to conciliate, settle, LL.* ['*saught*']

±sehtlian (a, æ) *to reconcile, to come to an agreement,* Chr.

±sehtnes f. *agreement, reconciliation, peace, Æ,Chr.* ['*saughtness*']

sēhð=sēcð pres. 3 sg. of sēcan.

±sehðe [=seh ðu] interj. *behold!*

seigl, seign=segl, segn

seim *fat, EPs 62[6].* ['*seam*'; *Late L.* sagimen]

seista=siexta; sel sn.=sæl

sēl I. adj. comp. sēlra (*Mt*), sēlla (*B*), sȳlla, superl. sēlest (*Lk*), sēlost *good, great, excellent, clever, skilful,* AO : *noble, honourable* : *fitting, fit, advisable* : *sound, healthy, happy, prosperous.* [v. '*sele*'] II. (ǣ) comp. adv. (also sēlor) superl. sēlost *better, more effectually, rather, sooner, in preference, Æ,CP.* [sǣl]

sēlan (OET,Ct)=sǣlan I. selcūð=seldcūð

seldt (æ) **I.** n. *hall, palace, residence.* **II.** n. *seat, throne, daïs, VPs.* ['*seld*']
+**selda**† *comrade, retainer.*
seldan adv., comp. seld(n)or, superl. seldost '*seldom,*' *rarely, CP; Æ.*
şeldcūð *unusual, rare, strange, novel, Bo; Æ : various, WW.* ['*selcouth*']
seldcyme m. *infrequent coming,* RD 1¹⁴.
selde f. *vestibule,* WW 183⁹⁹.
selden *few, rare,* Sc 197¹⁸.
seldguma m. *retainer?* B249.
seld-hwanne (CP), -hwænne (Æ) adv. *seldom, rarely.*
seldlic *rare, strange, wondrous, B* (syll-), *Met* (sell-) : *select, choice, excellent.* adv. -lice, *Sol; Æ.* ['*selly*']
seldnor, seldor, seldost v. seldan.
seldon=seldan
seldsīene *rare, extraordinary, unfamiliar, AO,KC?* (-sȳnde). ['*seldseen*']
seldun (*CP*), seldum (*Sol*)=seldan
sele† m. *hall, house, dwelling, prison,* KC. [*Ger.* saal]
+**sele** m. *tabernacle,* EPs 14¹.
seledrēam† m. *hall-joy, festivity.*
seleful n. *hall-goblet,* B619.
selegesceot n. '*tabernaculum,*' *tent, lodging-place, nest,* M. [*Ger.* geschoss]
selegyst m. *hall-guest,* B1545.
selen (y) f. *grant, gift : tribute,* MkL p5¹ : *munificence,* OEG. [sellan]
±**selenes** f. *tradition :* (+) *giving,* DR.
selerǣdend† m. *hall ruler or possessor.*
selerest f. *bed in hall,* B690.
selescot=selegesceot
selesecg m. *retainer,* WA34.
selest pres. 2 sg., seleð pres. 3 sg. of sellan.
sēlest v. sēl.
seleðegn m. *retainer, attendant,* B1794.
seleweard m. *hall-warden,* B667.
self I. (eo, i, y) pron. (str. and wk.) '*SELF,*' *AO,CP : own.* mid him selfum *by himself.* adj. *same, CP.* **II.**=sealf
selfǣta (y) m. *cannibal,* AN175.
selfǣte f. *a plant, wild oat?* LCD.
selfbana (o²) m. *a suicide,* GL.
selfcwala (y) *a suicide,* MFH172.
selfcwalu (y) f. *suicide,* WY56.
selfdēma, self-dēmere (RB), -dēmende (OEG58¹⁹) (y) m. '*sarabaita,*' *monk living subject only to his own rules.*
selfdōm m. *independence* (Swt).
selfe v. swā.
selflic (y) *spontaneous, voluntary,* OEG.
selflīce I. n. *self-love,* '*amour propre,*' *pride, vanity, CP : egotism,* CP25⁷. **II.** adj. *egotistic, puffed up, vain, CP.*
selfmyrðra (y) m. *one who takes his own life,* WW424²⁵.

selfmyrðrung (y) f. *suicide (action).*
selfren=seolfren
selfsceafte *not begotten,* GEN523.
selfswēgend (y) m. *vowel.*
selfwealdlīce (eo¹, e²) *arbitrarily,* GD289⁵, v.l.
selfwendlīce=selfwillendlīce
selfwill n. *own will, free-will, Bo,Met.* ['*selfwill*']
selfwille (y) *spontaneous, voluntary.* adv. -willes, *Æ,RB.* ['*selfwill*']
selfwillende *voluntary,* LPs67¹⁰.
selfwillendlīce (eo¹) *following one's own will, arbitrarily,* GD289⁵.
selian=sylian; **sēlig**=sǣlig
sēlla=sēlra, v. sēl.
±**sellan** (ea, i, ie, y) (w. d. pers. and a. thing) *to give, furnish, supply, lend, Æ,B, Mt; AO,CP : surrender, give up, betray, Æ, JnL : entrust, deliver to, appoint, allot :* lay by, hide, WW212⁴¹ : '*sell*,*' *Æ,Jn : promise.* āð s. *make oath, swear,* LL.
sellen=selen
sellend (y) m. *giver, Æ : betrayer,* MkLR 14⁴⁴.
sellendlic adj. *to be given,* CHRD102.
sellic=seldlic; **selma** (GL)=sealma
selmerige=sælmerige; **selnes**=selenes
sēlor, sēlost, sēlra v. sēl; **selt-**=sylt-
selð pres. 3 sg. of sellan; **sēlð**=sǣlð
+**sēm** n. *reconciliation,* LL10,10.
sēma (ī, ȳ) m. *arbitrator, judge,* ÆGR, GD.
±**sēman I.** *to smooth over, put right, settle, reconcile, pacify, AO,Chr,LL.* ['*seem,*' '*i-seme*'] **II.**=sīeman
sēmann (RUN45)=sǣmann
sēmend (ǣ) m. *conciliator, arbitrator,* LL.
sēmestre=sēamestre
semian=seomian; **semle**=simble
semnendlic *sudden,* GD235⁴. adv. -lice *by chance.*
semninga (M)=samnunga
semtinges=samtinges; **senap**=senep
±**sencan,** tr. *to sink, plunge (in water), submerge, drown.* [sincan]
send f. *gift,* RB87¹¹.
sendan I. (±) *to '*send*'* ('*i-send*'), *send forth, despatch, Æ,BH,Bl,CP,MtL; Æ,AO : impel, drive, MkL : throw, hurl, cast, VPs : put, place, lay : utter.* **II.** *to feast,* B600? [sand]
senderlīce (KGL74²⁷)=synderlīce
senderlīpe (HGL)=synderlīpe
sendlic adj. *about to be sent (on a journey),* RBL113⁴.
sendnes f. *sending,* WW.
+**sēne**=+sīene
senep m. *mustard,* Gl,LCD. [*L.* sinapi]

senepsǣd n. *mustard-seed*, Lcd 3·88¹⁵.

sengan (æ) *to 'singe,' burn slightly*, *LL* 449,6² : *afflict*, RPs 30¹⁰.

sēnian=segnian; **senn** (HGL519)=synn

senop=senep; **senoð** (Chr)=sinoð

senscipe=sinscipe

senst, sent=sendest, sendeð pres. 2 and 3 sg. of sendan.

senu=seonu

sēo I. f. gas. sēo(n) *pupil (of eye)*, Æ. **II.** pron. v. sē. [v. *'she'*] **III.** gs. of sǣ. **IV.** pres. 1 sg. of sēon. **V.** pres. 2 sg. subj. of bēon (wesan).

sēoc *'sick,' ill, diseased, feeble, weak*, Bl,Bo, Chr; Æ,CP : (†) *wounded : morally sick, corrupt*, Jul,RB : *sad, troubled*, FAp,Gu.

sēocan I. *to be ill, fall ill*, ANS 117·25; GD. [*'sick'*] **II.**=sēcan

sēoclian=sīclian

sēocmōd *infirm of mind*, Chrd 23⁹.

sēocnes f. *'sickness,' disease*, LL,W : a *disease*, Lcd 3·126'.

sēod (ēa) m. *scrip, purse, bag*, Æ,Gl.

seodo, seodu=sidu; **seofa**=sefa

seofafald (DR)=seofonfeald

seofan, seofen=seofon; **seofeð-**=seofoð-

seofian (e, ea, i, y) *to sigh, lament*, CP.

seofon *'seven,'* Æ,AO.

seofonfeald *'seven-fold,'* Æ,Bf,RB.

seofonfealdlīce adv. *seven times*, VPs.

seofongetel (e²) *the number seven*, OEG 1533.

seofonlēafe f. *tormentilla, setfoil (plant)*, Lcd 1·232¹.

seofonnihte adj. *seven days old*, Lcd : *lasting seven days*, Æ.

seofon-tēoða (AO), -te(o)g(e)ða *'seventeenth,'* BH.

seofontīene (y³) *'seventeen,'* BH; AO.

seofontīenenihte *seventeen days old*, Lcd 3·180.

seofontīenewintre *seventeen years old*, AO 190³⁰.

seofontīne=seofontīene

seofonwintre (y) *seven years old*, Æ,B,BH.

seofoða I. *'seventh,'* Bl,Mt; Æ,AO,CP. **II.**=sifeða

seofoðe *seventhly*, LL 158,18.

seofung f. *lamentation*, Bo,Met. [seofian]

seoh imperat. of sēon.

seohhe f. *sieve*, LL,WW. [sēon II.]

seohhian *to drain, filter*, ÆP 172²¹, (+) ES 49·353.

seohter m., seohtre (i) f. *drain, ditch*, Ct (Mdf).

seolc, seol-oc, -uc (io) m. *'silk,' silken cloth*, Bo,Lcd.

-seolcan v. ā-s.

seolcen (i) *'silken,' made of silk*, Bo,WW; Æ.

seolcwyrm m. *'silkworm,'* WW.

sēoles v. seolh; **seolf** (VPs)=self

seolfer=seolfor; **seolfern**=seolfren

seolfor (i, io, u, y) n., gs. seolfres *'SILVER,'* CP; Æ.

seolforfæt n. *silver vessel*, BH 252¹⁶.

seolforgewiht (y) m. *silver-weight*, Lcd 3·92¹⁴.

seolforhammen *plated with silver*, EC 225'.

seolfor-hilt, -hilted (TC) *'silver-hilted.'*

seolforsmið m. *'silversmith,'* WW.

seolforstycce m. *piece of silver*, A 11·8³.

seolfren (e, i, y) *made of silver, 'silvern,'* Bo,Chr,Met.

seolfring (y) m. *silver coin*, Æ.

seolh m., gs. sēoles *'seal,'* AO,Lcd,WW.

seolhbæð n. *seal's bath, sea*, Rd 11¹¹.

seolhpæð? n? *seal's path, sea, ocean*, An 1710.

seolm (WW 101¹⁶)=sealm

seoloc, seoluc=seolc; **seolofr-**=seolfr-

seoloð (io¹, e²) m. *sea*, B 2367?

seolufr-=seolfr-, seolfr-; **sēom**=sēam I.

seomian† (e) *to be tired, lie at rest, tarry, continue, stand : hang, swing, sway : lower (as a cloud) : lay wait for*, B 161.

sēomint (WW 136³¹?)=sǣminte

sēon I. (±) sv⁵ *to 'see*'* *('i-see'), look, behold*, B,G,Ps,Rd : *observe, perceive, understand, know*, Cr,Ps : *inspect, visit : experience, suffer*, B,Cr : *appear*, Bf 86⁸ : (pass) *seem* : (+) *provide*, OET 175¹³. sih ðe lo! *behold!* **II.** sv¹ (tr.) *to strain, filter*, Æ,AO : (intr.) *run, ooze, trickle, drop, drip*, Æ,AO, Lcd. [*'sye,' 'sying'*] **III.** v. sēo. **IV.**=sīen

seon-=sin-

seondon=sind pres. pl. ind. of wesan.

sēonian *to languish*, GD 284² . [OHG. siunōn]

seono (e¹, i¹; io¹, u²) f. *'sinew,'* B,Lcd; An.

seonobend f. *sinew-band?* Deor 6.

seonobenn f. *injury to a sinew*, Wy 19.

seonod=sinoð

seonodolg n. *injury to a sinew*, An 1408.

seonoð=sinoð

seonu=seono; **seonwe** gs. of seono.

seorðan³ *to lie with*, MtL 5²⁷. [ON?]

seorwum (Cp)=searwum, dp. of searo.

sēoslig *afflicted*, Gu 899. [sūsl]

sēota=sǣta; **seotl**=setl

seotol=(1) setl; (2) sweotol

seotu nap. of set.

±sēoðan² (ȳ) *'seethe,' boil*, Lcd : *be troubled in mind, brood*, B : *afflict, disturb*.

seoððan=siððan

-sēoung (ēu) v. eag-s.

sēow pret. 3 sg. of sāwan.

sēowan, sēowian (ī, īo, ȳ) *to 'sew,' knit together, link, unite*, Æ,Cp,Mk.

seox=siex; **seoxter**=sester

sep (GPH391)=sæp
sēpan† to instruct.
serc m., serce f. (y) 'sark,' shirt, B,WW : corslet, coat of mail.
serede=sierwde pret. 3 sg. of sierwan.
Sēremōnað June, MEN. [v. 'siere']
serew-, serw-=searw-, sierw-
serð=seorð, imperat. of seorðan.
sescle f. sixth part, BF192²,⁴. [L. sextula]
sess m. place for sitting, seat, bench, B,Cp.
sesslan to grow calm, AN453.
sesta=siexta
sester (eo, y) m. a certain measure of bulk, Æ : vessel, pitcher, Æ. [L. sextarius]
-sestre v. twī-s.
±set n. seat, habitation : entrenchment, camp, stall, fold : setting (of the sun). [sittan]
sēt-=sæt-
sete imperat. of settan.
+setednes=+setnes; setel (CP)=setl
seten I. f. set, shoot, slip, VPs : plantation : occupied (tilled?) land, LL118,68. II. pp. of sittan.
+setenes=+setnes
+setennes f. sitting, VPs138².
sētere=sætere; Seterndæg=Sæterndæg
setgong=setlgang
sethrægl n. covering for a seat, Ct,WW.
sētian=sætian; setln (GL)=seten
setl (æ, ea, eo, i, o) n. seat, stall, sitting, place, residence, Æ,B,BH,CP : throne, see : siege, AO. tō setle gān to set (of the sun), Æ. ['settle']
+setl n. assembly, OEG1753.
+setla (æ) m. one sitting beside, ÆL2²³⁷ : assessor, fellow-judge, OEG56²⁰.
setlan to 'settle' (cause to sit), place, put, Whale.
setlgang m. setting, sinking, Æ.
setlgangende ptc. setting, BH476¹³.
setlhrægel n. seat-cover, Ct.
setlrād f. setting, sinking, Ex109.
setlung f. sitting, setting, Æ,Ps.
sētn-=sæt(n)-
±setnes (+ exc. in N) f. foundation, creation, construction, MtL : position, size, extent : institution, law, ordinance, decree, will, Æ, BH,Mk : instruction : record, narrative : sentence, paragraph, figure of speech, composition. ['i-setness']
setol=setl
sēton=sæton pret. pl. of sittan.
setrægel (IM)=sethrægl
settan (±) to make to sit, 'SET,' lay, put, deposit, place, fix, Æ; CP : occupy, set or put down, Æ : (±) appoint, assign, institute, prepare, ordain, create, form, make, found, build, Æ,AO : sow, plant, Cp,Cr,Gen,

MtL : settle (tr. and intr.), abate, subside, sink : compose, compile, write, Æ : add : translate : (+) people, garrison : be situated : set off : lay in wait, LPs9³⁰. s. ūt issue, send forth, dismiss. s. of displace, depose. sīð s. travel, journey. ±s. wið, ongean compare. s. tō gafole let land. [sittan]
+settednes (CHRD)=+setnes
settend m. creator, ordainer, DA333.
+settendlic appointed, canonical, CM362.
sēttere=sætere
setðorn m. a kind of tree, EC291'.
+setu† np. v. +set.
±sēðan to affirm, testify, Æ : prove. [sōð]
seðel (NG)=setl
±sēðend m. asserter, affirmer, WW.
+sēðnes (æ) f. affirmation, ByH8'.
seððe=sehðe
±sēðung f. affirmation, proof, Æ.
sēw=sēow pret. 3 sg. of sāwan.
sēw-=sǣw-
sewen=sawen pp. of sēon.
+sewenlic visible, Æ,Bo. adv. -līce evidently.
sex (NG)=(1) siex; (2) seax
Sexland=Seaxland; sexta=siexta
sī 3 p. sg. pres. subj. of wesan.
sibæðeling m. related noble, B2708.
sibb (y) (v. LL2·651) f. relationship, AO,B, Chr; Æ : love, friendship : peace, happiness, BH,Chr,VPs; AO,CP. ['sib']
±sibb related, akin, B,LkL,W. as sb. kinsman, kinswoman, W,Soul. ['sib', 'i-sib']
sibb-=sib-
sibbecoss m. kiss of peace, ES33·176.
sibbegedriht=sibgedryht
±sibbian (y) to bring together, conciliate, reconcile, Æ,CP.
sibbs-=sibs-
sibcwide (y) m. pacific speech, LEAS29.
sibfæc n. degree of affinity, LL.
sibgebyrd f. blood-relationship, GEN1901.
sibgedryht† f. related band : peaceful host.
sibgemāgas mpl. blood-relations, Ex386.
sibgeornes f. pacific disposition, friendship, love, W.
sibge-sihð, -syhð f. vision of peace (lit. trans. of 'Hierosolyma'), Ps.
sibi (GL) sibian=sife, seofian
sibleger n. incest, LL,W.
siblic of peace, peaceable, Æ : related. adv. -līce.
±sibling m. relative, kinsman, Æ. ['sibling']
siblufu† f. friendship, love.
+sibnes f. affinity, relationship, WW345¹⁶.
sibrēden f. affinity, relationship, Chr1127. ['sibred']
±sibsum peace-loving, peaceable, friendly, CP. adv. -līce. [v. 'i-sibb']

+**sibsumian** *to reconcile, be reconciled*, Æ.
sibsumnes f. *peace, concord, Chr*; CP : *brotherly love.* ['sibsomeness']
+**sibsumung** f. *peace-making*, WW 172⁴¹.
sibun (Cp)=seofon
sīc n. *small stream, BC*; Mdf. ['sitch']
sīcan I. (sv¹) *to sigh, yearn for, AO,PPs*. ['siche'] II.=sȳcan
siccet-, siccett-, siccit-=sicett-
sicclian=sīclian
sice m. *sigh, Lcd* 1·388¹¹. ['siche']
sicel=sicol; **sicelian**=sīclian
sicer-=sicor-
sicerian *to trickle, penetrate, ooze, CP* 437¹⁴. ['sicker']
sicettan *to sigh, groan, mourn*, CP.
sicettung f. *sighing, sigh, sob, lamentation*, Æ.
sīcle *sick, ill*, ANS 129·21.
±**sīclian** (æ, ē, ēo, ȳ) *to sicken, become ill or weak, Lcd*; ÆL. ['sickle'; sēoc]
sicol (u²) m. *'sickle,' Bf,Mk,WW.*
sicor *sure, certain, trustworthy, A* : *secure, CP*. ['sicker']
sicorlīce (e²) *with full certainty*, NC 321 (=RWH 145¹²); FM 99. ['sickerly']
sicornes f. *certainty*, NC 321. ['sickerness']
sīd *ample, wide, broad, large, vast, An,B, Gen,LL*. ['side']
sīdādl f. *pain in the side, pleurisy*, WW 112³².
sīdan adv. wīdan and s. *far and wide, BC*. [v. 'side']
sīde I. adv. *amply, widely, extensively*, OEG. s. and wīde *far and wide, El.* ['side'] II. (±) f. 'SIDE,' Æ,CP. III. f. *silk.* [L. seta]
sīdece m. *pain in the side*, LCD 172a.
sideful (y) *decorous, modest, pure, virtuous, honest*, Æ. ['sedeful'] adv. -līce.
sidefulnes f. *virtue, modesty*, ÆL.
sidelic *sober, discreet*, GPH 389.
sidelīce adv. *fitly, suitable*, CP 153.
siden v. ælf-s.
sīden *made of silk*, OEG 3161,2.
sīdewāre f. *zedoary*, LCD 137b. [*Late L.*]
sīdfæðme, sīdfæðmed† *wide-bosomed, capacious (of a ship)*, B. [v. 'side']
sīdfeaxe, sīdfeaxode *long-haired*, Æ. [v. 'side']
sīdfolc† n. *great people or number of people.*
sīdhealf f. *a large place*, APs 17²⁰.
sīdian intr. *to extend?* RIM 65. [sīd]
+**sīdian** (y) *to arrange, set right, order.* [sidu]
sīdland† n. *extensive land*, GEN.
sīdlingweg m. *sidelong way, road that runs obliquely?* (BT), KC 3·446'.
sido=sidu
sīdrand m. *broad shield*, B 1289.

sidu (eo) m., gds. sida *custom, practice, manner, habit, rite,* CP : *manners, morality, good conduct, purity*, CP. [*Ger.* sitte]
sidung (y) f. *rule, regulation*, GPH 398.
sīdung (ȳ) f. *augmentation, growth*, BF 64²⁹.
sīdwǣrc m. *pain in the side*, GD,LCD.
sīdweg† m. *long road :* (in pl.) *distance.*
sīdwyrm (ȳ) m. *silk-worm*, WW.
sīe pres. 1 sg. subj. of wesan (bēon).
siehst pres. 2 sg., siehð pres. 3 sg. of sēon.
+**siehð**=+siht; **sielf**=self; **siellan**=sellan
siellic=seldlic
±**sīeman** (ǣ, ē, ȳ) *to load, burden*, Æ,LkL. ['seam']
siemble=simble
sīen I. (ēo, ī, ȳ) f. *power of sight, sight, vision, Jul,Lcd* : *pupil, eye.* ['sene'] II. (=sīn) pl. pres. subj. of wesan.
siendon, sient (=sindon, sind) pl. pres. of wesan.
+**sīene** (ē, ī, ȳ) *seen, visible, evident, plain*, B. ['sene'] adv. *plainly.*
+**sīenelic** (ē, ȳ) *visible*, BH 216¹⁴,VH. adv. -līce.
sierce=serce
sīere 'sere,' *dry, withered*, BC 1·515²². [sēarian]
sierian=sierwan
±**sierwan** (i, y) *to plan, devise, contrive :* *plot, lay snares for, entrap*, CP : *put on armour :* (+) *fit out, arm, equip*, MA 159. [searu]
sierwung (ea, y) f. *plotting, artifice, trap, snare, treachery*, Æ.
sieððan=siððan
siex (e, eo, i, y) 'six,' AO. For comps. v. also six-.
siexbenn=seaxbenn
siexfeald 'six-fold,' WW.
siexhund *six hundred*, AO; WID. [v. 'six']
siexta (e, i, y) 'sixth,' AO,Chr,LG,MH.
siexte (y) *sixthly*, LL 158,17.
siextig (e, i, y) 'sixty,' AO,Bl,LG.
sife (y) n. 'sieve,' Cp,Lcd,WW.
sifeða (eo, y) m. and fpl. *siftings, chaff, bran :* *tares, rubbish.*
sifian=seofian; **sifiða**=sifeða; **sīfre**=sȳfre
siftan (e, y) *to 'sift,'* Æ,Bo,Cp.
sifun=seofon
sig=sī 3 p. sing. pres. subj. of wesan (bēon).
+**sig** n. *victory*, DR 28².
sīgan¹ I. (±) *to sink, set (of the sun), B,Bo, Chr* : *decline*, CP : *descend, fall, fall down,* Æ : *move, advance, go, go to, approach*, B. *Chr.* sāh ūt *came out*, Æ. II.=sēon II.
sigbēh (NG)=sigebēah; **sigdi** (Ep)=sīðe
sige I. (y) m. *victory, success, triumph*, Æ, AO,CHR. II. m. *sinking, setting (of the sun)*, MET 13⁵⁶. [sīgan]

sige-bēacn, -bēacen n. *banner, Æ : emblem of victory, trophy, cross (of Christ)*, EL.
sigebēah m. *victor's circlet, crown*, BH.
sigebēam† m. *tree of victory, cross*.
sigebearn† n. *victor-child (Christ)*, EL.
sigebeorht *victorious*, BL 203'.'
sigebeorn m. *victorious hero*, FIN 38.
sigebrōðor m. *victorious brother*, AN 183.
sigebȳme f. *trump of victory*, Ex 565.
sigecempa m. *victorious champion*, PPs 50¹⁰.
sigecwēn† f. *victorious queen*, EL.
sigedēma† m. *victorious judge*.
sigedryhten† m. *lord of victory, God*.
sigeēadig *victorious*, B 1557.
sigefæst *victorious, triumphant*, Æ.
±sigefæstan (e³) *to triumph : crown as victor*.
sīgefæstnes f. *triumph, victory*, Ps.
sigefest=sigefæst
sigefolc† n. *victorious people*.
sigegealdor (y¹) n. *victory-bringing charm*, Lcd 1·388¹³. ['*sigalder*']
sigegefeoht n. *victory*, BH 158⁶.
sigegyrd f. *victory-bringing rod*, LCD.
sigehrēmig† (æ) *rejoicing in victory*.
sigehrēð f. *fame gained by victory? confidence or joy of victory?* B 490 (v. Klb 143).
sigehrēðig† *victorious, triumphant*.
sigehwīl f. *hour of victory*, B 2710.
sigel I.† (æ, e) m? n? *sun : name of the rune for* s. II.=sigil. III. f.=sigle I.
sigelbeorht† *sun-bright, brilliant*, MEN.
sigele=sigle
sigelēan n. *reward of victory*, EL,HGL.
sigelēas† *not victorious, defeated*.
sigelēoð† n. *song of victory*.
Sigelhearwa m. *Ethiopian*, VPs.
sigel-hweorfa m., -hwe(o)rfe f. *heliotrope*.
sigelic *victorious*, WW.
sigeltorht *radiant*, AN 1248.
Sigel-waras, -ware pl. *Ethiopians*, MH.
sigemēce m. *victorious sword*, CR 1531.
sigend m. *wave*, WW. [sīgan]
siger m. *glutton*, OET 72⁵⁶⁸.
siger-=sigor-
sigerēaf n. *triumphal robe*, WW 153¹⁵.
sigerian I. *to be gluttonous*, WW 489¹⁴. II.=sigorian
sigerīce† *victorious, triumphant*, EX.
sigerōf† *victorious, triumphant*.
sigesceorp n. *ornament of victory*, GN 136.
sigesīð (i²) m. *successful expedition*, OET.
sigespēd† f. *success*, AN,EL.
sigetācen n. *emblem of victory, sign*.
sigetīber n. *sacrifice for victory*, Ex 402.
sigetorht *brilliant in victory*, SAT 240.
sigetūdor n. *dominating race*, GU 838.
sigeðēod† f. *victorious people*, B.

sigeðrēat m. *victorious troop*, CR 844.
sigeðūf? m. *triumphal banner*, JUD 201.
sigewǣpen n. *victorious weapon*, B 804.
sigewang† m. *field of victory*.
sigewīf n. *victorious woman*, LCD 1·384'.
+sigfæstnian *to be crowned as victor*, G.
sigi-=sige-
sigil, sigl'n. *fibula, buckle, brooch, gem*. [cp. sigle]
sigirian=sigorian
siglan *to 'sail,'* AO.
sigle I. n. *necklace, collar*. II. f. *rye, black spelt*, LCD 48a. [*L*. secale]
sigor (y) m. *victory, triumph*, Æ. [sige]
sigorbēacen n. *emblem of victory*, EL 985.
sigorbeorht *triumphant*, CR 10.
sigorcynn n. *victorious race*, EL 755.
sigorēadig† *victorious*.
sigorfæst *victorious*, GD,GU.
sigorfæstnes (siger-) f. *victory*, A 11·173.
sigorian (e) *to be victorious, triumph over*, Æ.
sigorlēan† n. *reward of victory*.
sigorlic *triumphal*, GL.
sigorspēd† f. *good fortune in war*.
sigortācen n. *convincing sign*, GU 1089.
sigortīfer n. *offering for victory*, JUL 255.
sigorweorc m. *deed of victory*, Ex 316.
sigorwuldor n. *glory of victory*, GU 93.
sigrian=sigorian
sigrlend m. *victor*, DHy 38³.
sigsonte f. *a plant*, LCD 27b, 39a.
sigðe=sīðe; sih=seoh; sihsta=siexta
+siht (ie, y) f. *faculty or act of sight*, Æ,Bo, Mk; CP : *aspect : what is seen, vision, apparition*. ['*i-sight*']
-siht, -sihte v. blōd-, ūt-s.
sihte *marshy?* KC 3·430'.
+sihte=+sȳhte pret. 3 sg. of +sȳcan.
sihtre=seohtre
sihð I. f. *thing seen, vision*, JnL,MkL. ['*sight*'] II. pres. 3 sg. of sēon. III. (+)=+siht
sīhð pres. 3 sg. of sīgan.
+sihðe (BPs 53⁶)=+sehðe
+sihðnes f. *vision*, MtL p 7⁷.
silcen=seolcen; silf=self, seolf
-silfran v. be-s.
Sīlhearwa (Æ)=Sigelhearwa
sillan=sellan; silofr=seolfor
sīma I. m. *band, chain*, GEN 765. II.=sēma
simbel I. (on) adv. *always, continually*, AO. [cp. simbles] II.=simble
simbelfarende *roving, nomadic*, AO 26¹⁶.
simbelgefēra (y¹) m. *constant companion*, MET 11⁵⁰.
simble (e, y) adv. *ever, for ever, always, constantly, continually, continuously*. oftost s. *continually*.
simbles adv. *ever, always*, AN 64.

simblian (y) *to frequent*, DR15¹⁰.
simb-lunga, -linga (siml-) *continually, constantly*, DR.
simel=(1) simbel adv.; (2) symbel
simeringwyrt=symeringwyrt
siml, siml-=simbel, simbl-
sīn I. (ȳ) refl. possess. pron. *his, her, its, their.* **II.**=sīen. **III.** plur. pres. subj. of wesan.
sin- (y) prefix, *perpetual, permanent, lasting, infinite, immense.*
sinað-=seonoð-, sinoð-
sinbyrnende *ever burning*, MET8⁵².
sinc (y)† n. *treasure, riches, gold, valuables, jewel.*
sincald *perpetually cold*, Ex472.
sincaldu f. *perpetual cold*, PH17.
±**sincan³** *to* '*sink*,' *become submerged*, *MtR* : *subside*, *Gen* : *digest easily, act as aperient? Lcd*81b.
sincbrytta m. *distributor of treasure, prince*, A3·71¹⁷.
sincfæt† n. *precious vessel, precious setting.*
sincfāg† *richly adorned.*
sincgestrēon† n. *treasure, jewel.*
sincgewǣge n. *abundance of treasure*, RIM17.
sinc-giefa, -gifa† m. *giver of treasure, ruler, chief, lord, king.*
sincgifu f. *gift of treasure*, AN1511.
sincgim m. *valuable gem, jewel*, EL264.
sincgyfa=sincgiefa
sinchroden† ptc. *adorned with costly ornaments.*
sincmāððum m. *treasure*, B2193.
sincstān m. *precious stone*, MET21²¹.
sincðego† f. *receipt of treasure.* [ðicgan]
sincweorðung† f. *costly gift.*
sind plur. pres. indic. of wesan.
sinder (y) n. '*cinder*,' *dross, scoria, slag*, *Cp,WW* ; CP.
sinder-=sundor- ; **sinderlīce**=synderlīce
sinderōm m. *rust*, WW402⁴¹.
sindon plur. pres. indic. of wesan.
sindor=sinder
sindorlīpes (RB)=sundorlīpes
sindrēam† m. *everlasting joy.*
sindrig (Æ)=syndrig ; +**sīne**=+sīene
sineht *sinewy*, LCD91a. [seono]
sine-wealt, -weald (eo¹, y¹, æ²), *round, globular, concave*, Æ : *circular, cylindrical.* [sin-]
sinewealtian *to be unsteady*, WW515³¹.
sinewealtnes f. *roundness, globularity*, LCD, WW.
sinewind *artery*, WW352²⁵. [seonu]
sinfrēa m. *overlord, husband*, B1934.
sinfulle f. *house-leek*, LCD,WW.
singal *perpetual, everlasting*, Æ,CP : *continuous, constant*, Æ : *daily.*

singala, singale(s) adv. *always, continually.*
singalflōwende ptc. *ever-flowing*, WW177³⁶.
+**singalian** (y) *to continue*, ACPs88⁵¹.
singallic *incessant, continual*, CP61²¹. adv. (±) -līce.
+**singallician** *to continue*, JPs88⁵¹, 140⁶.
singalnes f. *perseverance, assiduity*, OEG.
singalrene m. *constant flow*, HGL418. [ryne]
±**singan³** (y) *to* 'SING,' *celebrate in song*, AO, CP : *crow, sing (of birds)*, Æ : *chant, intone* : *read, recite, narrate* : *(of things) sound, resound, ring, clank*, CP.
+**singe** (=+sinie?) f. *wife*, JUL54. [cp. sinig]
singendlic *that may be sung*, LVPs118⁵⁴.
sing-ere, -estre=sang-ere, -estre
singian (Æ)=syngian
singrēne (y) **I.** f. *house-leek, periwinkle*, Lcd. ['sengreen'] **II.** adj. *evergreen* : *uncooked (of vegetables).*
singrim adj. *exceeding fierce*, JUL230.
sinhere m. *huge army*, B2936.
sinhīg-=sinhīw-
±**sin-hīwan**, -hīgan npl. *wedded couple*, Æ, CP.
+**sinhīwen** (synn-) *married*, HL,W.
sinhīwscipe m. *permanent tie (marriage)*, Bo50¹.
sinhwurf-=sinhwyrf-
sinhwyrfel *round*, BL.
sinhwyrfende ptc. *round*, OEG114.
+**sinig** *marriage*, DR108⁷.
+**sinigan**, sinigian *to marry*, NG.
+**sinigscipe**=sinscipe
+**sinlīce** (y) adv. *often*, RB127⁹ : *diligently*, 97¹⁴.
sinn=synn
sinnan³† (w. g.) *to meditate upon, think of, care about* : *cease?* [Ger. sinnen]
sinnig=synnig
sinnihte† (y¹, ea²) n. *eternal night.* adv. -nihtes *in continual night, night after night.*
sinnið m. *perpetual misery*, RIM52.
sinop=senep
sinoð (e, eo, y) f. *synod, council, meeting, assembly.* [L. synodus]
sinoðbōc (e, eo, y) f. *record of the decrees of a synod, canon law*, LL46,49⁸.
sinoðdōm (eo) m. *decree of a synod*, EL552.
sinoðlic *synodical*, BH.
sinoðstōw (eo¹, a²) f. *meeting-place, place where a synod is held*, BH102⁵.
sinowalt=sinewealt
sinrǣden f. *(continuing state), marriage*, CP.
±**sinscipe** (e, y) m. *cohabitation, marriage*, Æ,CP : (+) *married couple*, CP.
+**sinsciplic** (y) *conjugal*, CHRD,LL(440⁶).
+**sinscippend** *married*, GD218⁴.

sinsnǣd f. *large piece*, B743.
sinsorg f. *perpetual grief*, Wif45.
sint=sind plur. pres. indic. of wesan.
sintre(n)dende ptc. *round, OEG*. [v. *'trend'*]
sintryndel (y¹, æ²) adj. *circular, globular*, Lcd,WW.
sinþyrstende ptc. (w. g.) *ever-thirsting*, AO 130³¹.
sinu=seono
sinuwealt, sinwealt=sinewealt
sinwrǣnnes (y) f. *constant lechery*, WW 113²².
sīo=sēo; **siodo**=sidu; **siofa**=sefa
siogor (AA)=sigor
siol-=seol-, sel-
sioloð m? *water? sea?* B2367 (v. Klb).
sion *'laber,' a marsh plant?* Lcd 1·254. [*'sion'*]
sīon=sēon II.; **sipian**=sypian
sīpian *to sink low, wane, decline*, Lcd3·151 (v. A31·538).
sīr=siger; **sirew-**, sirw-=searw-, sierw-
sisemūs f. *dormouse*, WW.
sīst=sīhst pres. 2 sg. of sēon I.
sit pres. 3 sg. of sittan.
sitl=setl
±**sittan**⁵ *to* 'SIT,' *sit down, recline, rest, Æ*; AO,CP : *remain, continue, be situated*, AO : *settle, encamp, dwell, occupy, possess*, Chr : *abide, reside*, AO : *lie in wait, besiege, invest*, Chr : *preside over, Æ*; CP : †*perch, roost* : (+) *sit out, finish*. on cnēowum s. *kneel, AO*. wið earm +s. *lean*. on s. (1) *assail, attack*; (2) *press on, weigh down, Æ*.
sīð (ȳ) **I.** m. *going, motion, journey, errand* : *departure, death* : *expedition, undertaking, enterprise* : *road, way* : *time, turn, occasion, Æ*; AO. on ānne s. *at one and the same time*. ōðre sīðe...ōðre sīðe *on one occasion ..on another* : *conduct, way of life, manner, Æ* : *fate, destiny, experience, hap, fortune, Æ*. [*'SITHE'*] **II.** adv. *late, afterwards, G.* comp. sīð, sīðor *later*. ǣr and s. *always*. ne ǣr ne s. *never*. ǣr oððe s. *ever* : a comp. adj. sīðra *late, later*, and a superl. sīð(e)mest, sīðest *latest, last* are formed from sīð. æt sīðestan *at last, finally*. [*'sithe'*] **III.** prep. and conj. *after*. s. ðam *after, afterwards*. [*Ger.* seit] **IV.** (±)=±sihð pres. 3 sg. of sēon I.
+**sīð I.** m. (rare ds. +sīðan) *comrade, companion* : (†) *follower, retainer, warrior* : *count, thane*. **II.** n. *company*, v. LL 2·427; 446.
sīðberend m. *reaper*, WW235³. [sīðe]
sīðbōc f. *itinerary*, OEG2023.
sīðboda m. *herald of departure (the pillar of cloud)*, Ex250.

sīðboren ptc. *late-born*, VPs,WW.
+**sīðcund** *fit to rank as a thane*, BH,LL.
+**sīðcundlic** *intimate*, BH120³³ (v.l.).
sīðdagas mpl. *later times*, El639.
sīðe m. *'scythe,' Æ,Gl*.
sīðemest, sīðest v. sīð II.
sīðfæt (Æ,CP), sīðfat mn. *way, journey, voyage, expedition* : *path, road, course, Æ* : *experience, conduct* : *period of time*.
sīðfrom† *ready for a journey*.
sīðgeomor *travel-weary*, Fap1.
sīðian *to go, depart, travel, wander, Æ,B*. [*'sithe'*]
+**sīðlic**=+sīðcundlic
sīðlice adv. *lately, after a time, ÆH*.
+**sīðmǣgen** n. *band of warriors*, GnE89.
+**sīðmann**=+sīð
sīðmest, sīðor, sīðra v. sīð II.
+**sīðrǣden** f. *troop*, WW206²¹.
+**sīðscipe** m. *fellowship, society*, BH.
sīðstapel *step, track*, LPs16⁵.
sīðð=sīð
sīðða adv. and conj. *afterwards*, JnL,LkL. [*'sith'*]
sīððan, sīððon (eo, y) **I.** adv. *since, afterwards, from now on, hereafter, further, then, thereupon, after, later, Æ*. **II.** conj. *as soon as, when, since, after that, inasmuch as*. sīððan...sīððan *when...then*. **III.** prep. (w. a.) (LWS) *after*. [*'SITHEN'*; sīð, ðam]
sīðweg (Gu859)=sīdweg
sīðwerod n. *travelling troop*, Gen2114.
±**sīðwīf** n. *noble lady*, GD,MH.
sīwan=sīwian
siwen pp. of sēon II.
siwen-ige, -igge, -ēge *blear-eyed*, GPH,CP 67.
±**sīwian** (ēo, ȳ) *to sew, mend, patch* : *knit together, unite*.
six=siex; **six-**; v. also siex-.
sixecge *six-sided, hexagonal*, WW.
sixfēte (y) adj. *of six (poetical) feet*, Bf 192⁸.
sixgylde *entitled to six-fold compensation*, LL3,1.
sixhynde *belonging to the class whose 'wer-geld' was 600 shillings*, LL.
sixhyndeman (e¹, y¹) m. *one of the sixhynde class*, LL30,39.
sixhyrnede (e²) *having six angles*, WW179¹³.
sixnihte *six days old*, Lcd.
sixteogoða *'sixtieth,' ÆGr,RB*.
sixtēoða (e¹, ȳ²) *'sixteenth,' MH,ÆGr*.
sixtigǣre *60-oared ship*. [ār]
sixtigfeald *'sixty-fold,' ÆGr*.
sixtigwintre *sixty years old, Æ* (Gen).
sixtȳne (y¹, e²) *'sixteen,' Bf,MH*.
sixtȳnenihte *sixteen days old*, Lcd.
sixtȳnewintre *sixteen years old*, MH190,192.

slā=slāh

slacful (=æ) *lazy*, GL,LCD.

slacian=sleacian

slād pret. 3 sg. of slīdan.

slǣ-=slea-; **slǣ**=slēa

-slǣccan v. ā-sl.

slǣd (a, e, ea) n. *valley, glade*, AO; Mdf. ['*slade*']

-slǣfan v. tō-s.

slǣg-=sleg-

slǣge m., slǣget n.=slege

slǣgen pp. of slēan.

slǣgu (ē) f. *lethargy*, GL (v. A33·387).

slǣht=slieht

slǣhtan *to strike, slay*, NG. [*Ger.* schlachten]

+slǣhte pret. 3 sg. of +sleccan.

slǣhð=sliehð pres. 3 sg. of slēan.

slǣp I. (ā, ē, ēa) m. 'SLEEP,' Æ,CP : *sleepiness, inactivity*, CP : *death.* II. m? *slippery place?* KC.

±slǣpan[7] (ē, ā) pret. 3 sg. slēp, slēap; also wk. slǣpte, slēpte, slēpde *to* 'SLEEP,' CP : *be benumbed, motionless, inactive*, Æ,CP : *lie with*, Æ : *rest in the grave, die*, Æ.

slǣpbǣre *soporific*, LCD 1·284'.

slǣpdrenc (æ²) m. *sleeping draught*, LCD 146b.

slǣpere m. *sleeper*, ÆL 1·23[1].

slǣpern (ā, ē, y²;=æ²) n. *dormitory*.

slǣping *sleeping*, APs 3[6].

slǣplēas *sleepless*, GPH 399.

slǣplēast f. *sleeplessness*, Æ.

slǣpnes f. *sleepiness*, HL 14[106].

slǣpor *drowsy, sleepy*, SOL 258[1].

slǣpwērig *weary and sleepy*, RD 5[5].

slǣpyrn=slǣpærn

slǣt=sliehð pres. 3 sg. of slēan.

slǣtan *to bait* (*a boar*), ÆL 12[72]. ['*sleat*']

slǣting f. *right of hunting*, Chr 1087. ['*sleating*']

slǣw=slāw; **-slǣwan** v. ā-s.

slǣwð (ē) f. *sloth, indolence*, Æ,Bo; CP. ['*sleuth*'; slāw]

slǣg=slāh

slaga m. *slayer, homicide*, Æ,CP : *executioner*, ÆL 12[23]?

slagen pp. of slēan.

slagu=slǣgu

slāh, slāg f. '*sloe*' (*fruit of the blackthorn*), Cp,Lcd,WW; Mdf.

slahe=slēa

slāhðorn m. *blackthorn*, Cp,Lcd; Mdf. ['*sloethorn*']

slāhðornragu f. *blackthorn, lichen*, LCD 54a.

slāhðornrind f. *blackthorn bark*, LCD.

slān I. (K,N)=slēan. II. gs. of slā (slāh).

slanc pret. 3 sg. of slincan.

slang pret. 3 sg. of slingan.

slǣp=slǣp; **slǣpel**=slāpol

slāpfulnes f. *lethargy*, WW 541[42]?

slāpian *to become sleepy*, CP.

slāpol *somnolent, lethargic*, RB,ÆGR 305[7].

slāpolnes (e²) f. *somnolence, lethargy*, Æ.

slāpornes f. *lethargy*, A11·98.

slāpul=slāpol

slar-ege, -ie f. '*clary*' (*plant*), Lcd,WW.

slāt pret. 3 sg. of slītan.

slāw 'SLOW,' *sluggish, torpid, lazy*, CP.

slāwerm (KGL 80[22])=slāwyrm

slāwian *to be slow, sluggish*, Æ.

slāwlīce adv. '*slowly,*' *sluggishly*, A,CP.

slāwyrm m. '*slow-worm,*' *snake*, Gl,Sc.

slēa f. '*slay,*' *weaver's reed*, WW. [slēan; cp. slege]

sleac (v. A39·366) 'SLACK,' *remiss, lax, sluggish, indolent, languid*, Æ,CP : *slow, gentle, easy*, Æ.

sleacian *to delay, retard, slacken, relax efforts*, Æ. ['*slake*']

sleaclic *slow, languid, idle*, HGL 472. adv. -līce.

sleacmōdnes f. *slackness, laziness*, BYH 40[27].

sleacnes (e) f. *slowness*, Æ,Bf,Lcd : *remissness, laziness*, CP. ['*slackness*']

sleacornes f. *laziness*, A11·98[40].

sleaht=slieht

slēan[6] *to strike, beat, stamp, coin* (*money*), *forge* (*weapons*), Æ : *throw, cast : sting* (*snake*) : *pitch* (*tent*), Æ : *strike across* (*country*), *dash, break, rush, come quickly*, Æ : 'SLAY*,' *kill*, Æ,AO,CP. *wæl* +s. *to slaughter : cast into chains* : (+) *strike down : play* (*harp, etc.*) : (+) *gain by fighting, win, conquer.*

slēap I. pret. 3 sg. of slǣpan. II. pret. 3 sg. of slūpan. III.=slǣp

slēaw=slāw; **slēbescōh**=slēfescōh

slec-=sleac-

+sleccan *to weaken, disable*, CR 149. [sleac]

slecg f. ('*sledge*'-)*hammer, mallet*, Nar,WW; Æ.

slecgettan *to beat, throb*, LCD 82b.

slecgwyrhta m. *metal-worker*, GENC 4[22].

sled=slæd; **slēf**=slīefe

slēfan *to slip* (*clothes*) *on*, Guth. +slēfed *furnished with sleeves.* ['*sleve*']

slēfescōh m. *slipper*, GL (slēbe-).

slēflēas=slīeflēas

slege (æ) m. *beating, blow, stroke*, Æ : *slaying, slaughter, murder*, Æ,AO,CP : *crash, impact, clap* (*of thunder*) : *destruction, defeat*, AO : (*weaver's*) '*slay*,' WW 188[5]. [slēan]

slegebȳtl m. *beetle, hammer*, LCD 122b.

slegefǣge *doomed to perish*, JUD 247.

slegel m. *plectrum*, WW 466[28].

slegen pp. of slēan.

sleghrȳðer (slægr-) n. *cattle for slaughter*, NC321.

slegnēat (æ[1], ǣ[2]) n. *cattle for slaughter*, TC 105[4].

slēgu=slǣgu

sleh=sleah imperat. of slēan.

sleht=slieht

slehð=sliehð pres. 3 sg. of slēan.

slēow=slīw

slēp I. (VPs)=slǣp. **II.** pret. 3 sg. of slǣpan.

slēp-=slǣp-

slēpan=(1) slǣpan; (2) (MET 9[55]). slȳpan

sleð (VPs)=sliehð pres. 3 sg. of slēan.

slēwð=slǣwð; **slī** (GL)=slīw

slic (ī?) n. *beater, mallet, hammer*, LL 455,15. WW 75[16].

-slicod (y) v. nīg-s.

slid (APs 34[6])=slidor I.

slīdan[1] *to 'slide*,' glide, slip, fall, fall down*, Guth : *fail, err, lapse*, Sol : *pass away, be transitory or unstable.*

sliddor=slidor

slide m. *sliding, slip, fall*, Æ,CP.

sliderian=slidrian

slidor I. *slippery*, Ps,Run. ['*slidder*'] **II.** n? *slippery place*, WW.

slidornes f. *slippery place, slipperiness*, BlPs. ['*slidderness*']

slidrian *to slip, slide*, CP,PPs. ['*sliddern*']

slīefe (ē, ī, ȳ) f. '*sleeve*,' Æ,Bl,LL,RB.

slīeflēas (ē, ȳ) '*sleeveless*,' RB,WW.

slieht (æ, ea, e, i, y) m. *stroke, slaughter, murder, death*, AO,HL : *animals for slaughter* : (+) †*battle*. ['*sleight*'; slēan]

sliehtswȳn (y[1]) n. *pig for killing*, LL.

sliehð pres. 3 sg. of slēan.

slīf, slīfe=slīefe; **-slīfan** v. tō-s.

slifer *slippery*, HGL405.

sliht (AO,Æ)=slieht

-slihtes v. eorð-s.

slihð pres. 3 sg. of slēan.

slīm n. '*slime*,' CPs,WW.

slincan[3] *to slink, creep, crawl*, AA,DD.

slincend mn. *reptile*, Æ (GEN).

slingan[3] *to worm, twist oneself, creep into.* [Ger. schlingen]

slipa=slypa

slipeg, slipig *slimy*, LCD.

slipor *slippery, filthy*, Sc : *unsteady, shifty*, Æ. ['*slipper*']

slipornes f. *filthiness*, DHy 36[8]. ['*slipperness*']

+slit n. *rending, biting, bite*, Æ : *something to be torn or rent* : *backbiting, calumny.*

±slītan[1] *to slit, tear, split, shiver, rend to pieces, divide* : *bite, sting, wound*, CP : *backbite*, CP. [v. '*slit*,' '*slite*']

slitcwealm m. *death by rending*, LL (166n).

slīte I. m. *slit, rent, tear, bite.* **II.** f? *cyclamen.*

slīten m. *schismatic, heretic*, MtL p 8[9].

slītendlic *gorging*, WW 437[5].

slītere m. *gorger, glutton*, WW : *destroyer*, W 235[24].

+slītglīw n. *raillery*, WW 372[32].

slītnes f. *desolation, destruction, tearing up*, LL,MtL.

slītol *biting, pungent*, GPH 394.

slītung f. *tearing, biting*, DEUT, LCD.

slīðan[1] *to injure, wound*, GnE 202.

slīðe†I. adj. *savage, fierce, dire, cruel, hard, hurtful, perilous.* **II.** adv. *savagely.*

slīðelic *abominable*, EPs 105[19].

slīðen *cruel, hard, evil*, B,Bo.

slīðheard† (e[2]) *cruel, severe, savage.*

slīðhende *with fell paw*, GnE 177.

slīðnes f. *abomination?* EPs 105[36].

slīw m. *a fish, tench, mullet*, GL.

slōg I. pret. 3 sg. of slēan. **II.**=slōh I.

slōh I. mfn., gs. slō(ge)s, slō; das. slō(h) '*slough*,' *mire*, BH,W. **II.** pret. 3 sg. of slēan.

-slop v. ofer-s; **slopen** pp. of slūpan.

slota m. *morsel*, Sc 153[12].

slūma m. *slumber*, DD,Gu. ['*sloom*']

slūmere m. *sleeper*, NC 322.

sluncon pret. pl. of slincan.

slūpan[2] *to slip, glide, move softly*, Ex,LL.

slȳf=slīef; **slyht**=slieht

slyhð=sliehð pres. 3 sg. of slēan.

slypa m. *slime, paste, pulp*, Lcd. ['*slip*']

slȳpan (ē;=īe) *to slip (on or off)*, A 9·32[158].

slȳpescōh m. *slipper*, WW 277[29].

slyppe f. *paste*, LCD 163a.

slypræsn n. *sliding beam?* WW 237[1]. [ræsn]

slȳpð pres. 3 sg. of slūpan.

±smacian *to coax, flatter, allure, seduce*, HGL476; OEG3005.

smæc m. '*smack*,' *taste*, WW : *scent, odour*, WW.

±smæccan *to taste*, ÆGr. ['*smatch*']

smæl I. (often smal- in obl. cases) sup. smalost, smælst '*SMALL*' : *thin, slender, narrow*, AO : *fine*, CP. **II.** v. hēafodsmæl.

smæle=smale

smæleðerm (A 13·323)=smælðearme

smæll (=ie) m. *slap, smack*, JnL. ['*small*']

smælðearmas (y[2]) mp. *small intestines*, LCD.

smælðearme n. *lower abdomen*, CP.

smǣr (smǣre?) m. *lip*, GL,LCD.

smǣre-=smeoru-

smǣte *pure, refined*, Cp,MH; Æ. ['*smeat*']

smǣtegold n. *pure gold*, WW.

smǣtegylden adj. *of pure gold*, WW.

smal- v. smæl.

smale *finely, into small pieces*, Bo : *softly (not loudly).* ['*small*']

smalian *to become thin,* Lcd 2a (Harl.).
smalum *little by little,* OEG 1553.
smalung f. *reducing (of flesh),* Lcd 98a.
smāt pret. 3 sg. of smītan.
smēac pret. 3 sg. of smēocan.
smēade pret. 3 sg. of smēagan.
smēag- v. smēah.
±**smēagan**, smēan (ē) *to think, think out, reflect, meditate on, deliberate,* Æ,CP : *examine, penetrate, scrutinize, look closely into,* Æ : *suppose : seek (opportunity).*
smēagelegen (? v. OEG 4142n) f. *syllogism.*
smēagendlic *meditative,* ÆGR 211⁶. adv. -līce *accurately,* GD 172¹⁴.
smēagung=smēaung
smēah I. adj. (smēag- in obl. cases) *sagacious, acute, subtle : penetrating.* **II.** pret. 3 sg. of smūgan.
+**smēah** n. *intrigue,* CHR 1094.
smēalic *searching, exhaustive, careful,* CP : *exquisite, choice.* adv. -līce *closely, thoroughly, accurately,* Æ,CP : *subtlely.*
smēalicnes f. *subtlety,* CHRD 98³⁵.
smēamete m. *delicacy (food),* BHCHRD.
smēan, smēang=smēagan, smēaung
smearcian (e) *to smile,* Bo; Æ. ['*smirk*']
smeart *smarting, painful,* W 295¹⁰. ['*smart*']
smeartung (e) f. *tickling,* A 8·450.
smēaþ I. f. *meditation,* SPs 118⁷⁷. **II.** pres. 3 sg. of smēagan.
smēaðanclīce adv. *in detail,* BF 78¹².
smēa-ðancol, -ðancollic *subtle.* adv. -e, -līce *exactly, thoroughly, studiously,* Æ.
smēaðancolnes f. *strictness,* ÆH 2·80'.
±**smēaung** (ē) f. *reflection, thought,* CP : *inquiry, search : intention, effort : intrigue : interpretation,* RWH 21²⁹.
smēawrenc m. *cunning device,* TC 339⁸ (smēh-).
smēawung=smēaung
smēawyrhta m. *skilled artisan,* LL 455,16.
smēawyrm m. *intestinal worm,* Lcd.
smec=smæc; **smēc**=smīc
smedma (eo) m. *fine flour, pollen meal,* Gl, Lcd; Æ. ['*smeddum*']
smedmen adj. *of fine flour,* Sc 154¹.
smēgan=smēagan
smēgawyrm=smēawyrm
smēh=smēah
smelt I. (y) m. *sardine,* '*smelt*,' Cp. **II.**= smolt
smelting (i, y) f. *amber,* ÆL.
smēocan² *to emit smoke,* Æ,Lcd WW : *fumigate,* Lcd. ['*smeek*']
smeoduma=smedma
smēoh=smēah; **smeolt**=smolt
smeortan³ *to* '*smart*,' AO 36³⁰ (or ? fȳr-smeortende=*smarting like fire*).
smeortung (e) f. *smarting,* WW 114³.

smeoru (e), smeoruw n. *ointment, fat, grease, lard, tallow, suet,* CP,VPs. ['*smear*']
smeorumangestre (e¹, e²) f. *butter-woman,* LL.
smeorusealf (e¹, a²) f. *unguent,* Lcd 55b.
smeoruðearm (æ¹, e¹) m. *entrail,* WW.
smeoruwig (e¹, e²) *rich, fat,* Lcd 79a.
smeoruwyrt f. '*smearwort*,' Cp,Lcd.
smeoðlian=smiðian
smer-=smear-, smeor-, smir-, smier-
smēr=smær; **smera**=smeoru
smere-=smeoru-
smerian *to laugh to scorn,* MtL 9²⁴.
smeringwyrt f. *name of a plant,* '*crispa, victoriola*,' WW 135¹. [cp. smeoruwyrt]
smeruwan=smierwan
smerwung=smirung; **smēte-**=smǣte-
±**smēðan** *to smooth, soften, polish,* CP : *appease, soothe,* CP.
smēðe (RB)=smiððe
smēðe *smooth, polished, soft,* Cp,JnL,Lk; Æ,AO,CP : *suave, agreeable,* CP : *not harsh (of the voice),* VHy : *lenitive.* ['*smeeth*']
±**smēðian** *to smoothen,* Lcd,OEG : *become smooth.* ['*smeeth*']
smēðnes f. *smoothness, smooth place,* Æ, WW. ['*smeethness*']
smēung=smēaung
smīc (ē, ȳ) m. *vapour, smoke,* Æ,AO,Bo, PPs,VHy. ['*smeech*'; '*smitch*']
smīcan (ē) *to smoke, fumigate,* Lcd,Ps. [smēocan]
smicer *beauteous, elegant, fair, tasteful,* Cp, Shr,TC. ['*smicker*'] adv. -ere, CP.
smicernes f. *smartness,* WW 416³¹.
+**smicerod** *well-fashioned,* WW 406²¹.
smicor=smicer; **smidema**=smedma
smīec=smīc
±**smierwan** (e, i, y) *to* '*smear*,' *anoint, salve,* Bf,Bl,G,VPs (smirian); CP. [smeoru] For comps. v. smir-.
smilte=smylte
smilting=smelting
smirels (e, y) m. *ointment, salve,* Æ,LL. ['*smerles*']
smirenes (e, y) f. *ointment, unguent,* Lcd, LG.
smirewan, smirian=smierwan
smiringele (y¹) m. *anointing oil,* Ex 29²¹.
smirung (e, y) f. *ointment, unguent,* HL, Lcd : *unction : smearing, greasing.* [smeoru]
smirwan=smierwan; **smirwung**=smirung
smītan¹ *to daub, smear, soil, pollute, defile,* Æ,Cp,Lcd. ['*smite*']
smitte f. *smudge, smut, blot,* OEG,RB : *pollution.* ['*smit*']
±**smittian** *to befoul, pollute,* WW : *infect,* OEG. ['*smit*']

smið m. *handicraftsman, ' smith,' black-smith, armourer, carpenter, Æ,B,MtL.*
smiðbelg (y²) m. *smith's bellows,* SOL 85¹³.
smiðcræft m. *manual art,* BH 442¹⁶.
smiðcræftega m. *skilled workman,* GEN 1084.
smiðian (eo) *to forge, fabricate, design, Æ, OEG.* ['*smith*']
smiðlīce adv. *dexterously,* WW.
smiððe (smeðe) f. *smithy, forge, Æ,BH,RB.* ['*smithe*']
smoc m. '*smock,' shift,* WW.
smoca m. '*smoke,' LPs,Nar* (cc).
smocen pp. of smēocan.
smocian *to emit' smoke,' Æ,LPs : fumigate,* Lcd.
-smogu v. æ-s.; **-smoh** v. in-s.
smolt I. (e, eo) *mild, peaceful, still, gentle, MtL.* ['*smolt*'] **II.** *lard, fat, CM,NC.* ['*smolt*']
smolte=smylte
smoltlīce adv. *gently,* RWH 146²⁶.
smorian *to strangle, choke, suffocate, Cp, MtR.* ['*smore*']
smōð '*smooth,' serene, calm, Sc* 6'; ES 9·40.
smucon pret. pl. of smēorcan.
smūgan² *to creep, Æ.* [*Ger.* schmiegen]
smūgendlic *creeping,* LPs 68³⁵.
smȳc=smīc
smȳcð pres. 3 sg. of smēocan.
smygel, smygels m. *retreat, burrow,* GL.
smyllan (=ie) *to crack (a whip),* GPH 388.
smylt=smelt
+smyltan *to appease,* BH 386¹² : *assuage,* LCD.
smylte I. *mild, peaceable, calm, CP : cheerful : prosperous.* **II.** adv. *softly.* [smolt]
smyltelic=smyltlic
smylting (Æ)=smelting
smyltlic *tranquil, serene,* DR,MH.
smyltnes f. *tranquillity, peace, quiet, silence, CP : gentleness, smoothness, mildness, composure, placidity, CP : evening calm.*
smyr-=smier-, smir-
smytte=smitte; **snā**=snāw
snaca m. '*snake,' serpent, Lk,W.*
snacc m. *a small vessel, war-ship, Chr.* ['*snack*']
snād=snǣd II.
-snæcce v. twī-s.
snǣd I. m. *handle of a scythe, ÆH* 2·162. ['*snead*'] **II.** (ā) m. *detached area of woodland, Ct* (Mdf). **III.** f. *piece, morsel, slice, portion of food, Æ,Lcd.* ['*snede*'; snīðan]
±snǣdan I. (ē) *to cut, slice, lop off, hew, Ln,CP,MtR.* ['*sned*'; snīðan] **II.** *to eat, take a meal,* CHR 1048.
snædel (GL)=snǣdelðearm

snǣdelðearm m. *great gut,* GL,LCD.
snǣding f. *meal, snack,* CM,RBL.
snǣdinghūs n. *cook's shop,* WW 185¹.
snǣdingscēap n. *sheep for slaughter,* PPs 43²³.
snǣdmǣlum adv. *bit by bit,* LCD 127a.
snægl (e), snægel m. '*snail,' Cp,Lcd,WW.*
snǣl=snægl; **snǣs**=snās
snǣsan (or? onsnǣsan) *to run through, pierce, spit,* LL 69,36. [snās]
snǣðfeld m. *a defined tract of pasture or woodland* (v. Mdf). [snǣd]
snās (ǣ) f. *spit, skewer,* WW 237¹⁷ and N.
snāð I. pret. 3 sg. of snīðan. **II.**(?) n? *killing* (v. OEG 3070).
snāw, snāwa (MkL 9³) m. '*snow,' Bl,Chr, Met,VPs : snow-storm, Bo.*
snāwceald *icy-cold,* MET 29⁸.
snāwgebland n. *snow-storm,* AO 186³⁴.
snāwhwīt *snow-white, Æ.*
snāwig '*snowy,' Lcd.*
snāwīt=snāwhwīt
snāwlic *snowy,* LCD,WW.
sneare, snearh f. '*snare,' OEG.*
snēdan=snǣdan; **snēl**, sneg(e)l=snægl
snell *smart, ready, rapid, keen, fresh, brisk, active, strong, bold, An,B,Cra,Ph;* AO. ['*snell*']
snellic *smart, ready, quick, rapid, bold.* adv. **-līce,** Wy. ['*snelly*']
snellscipe m. *quickness, boldness,* CHR 1057D.
snelnes f. *agility,* APT 13⁷.
snēome† adv. *quickly, speedily, swiftly : immediately, at once.*
+sneorcan³ (e) *to shrivel, dry up,* VPs 30¹³.
snēowan⁷ (ō)† *to hasten, go.*
snēr† f. *harpstring,* Ln. [cp. *Ger.* schnur]
+snerc pret. of sneorcan.
snīcan¹ *to sneak along, creep, crawl, CP,Lcd.* ['*snike*']
snid I. (±) n. *slice : cutting : slaughter.* [*Ger.* schnitt] **II.** m. *saw,* CP.
snide I. m. *incision : slaughter,* ES 13·27⁹. **II.**=snid II.
sniden pp., snidon pret. pl. of snīðan.
snidīsen n. *lancet,* LCD 78a.
snirian=snyrian
snīte f. *snipe, Cp,WW.* ['*snite*']
±snīðan¹ *to cut, lance, CP : cut off, amputate, CP : hew down, slay, kill, Æ; CP : mow, reap.* ['*snithe*']
snīðstrēo *carline thistle?* (BT), *chopped straw?* (JGPh 1·328),Cp 358s.
snīðung f. *incision, wound,* LCD : *slaughter,* WW.
snīwan *to snow, AA,BH,Cp; Æ.* ['*snew*']
snōca m. *nook? inlet?* BC 3·141' (v. Mdf).
snōd f. *hood, head-dress, fillet, Æ.*
snoffa m. '*nausea,' CM* 50.

snofl *phlegm, mucus*, Lcd 9a.
snoflig *full of phlegm*, Bf 12[18].
snofol=snofl
snoru f. *daughter-in-law*, Æ,AO. [*Ger.* schnur]
+snot n. *mucus*, Lcd 20b.
snotor, snoter *clever, prudent, intelligent, discerning, Bl,Chr,MtL*; Æ,CP. ['*snoter*']
snotorlīc (e[2]) *philosophic, wise, clever.* adv. -līce.
snotornes (e[2]) f. *wisdom, prudence,* Æ.
snotorscipe m. *ratiocination, reason, reasonableness*, OEG 3215; 2[172].
-snotorung (e[2]) v. word-s.
snotorwyrde *wise of speech, plausible*, W 107[1].
snotter, snottor, snottra (wk.)=snotor
snōwan=snēowan
snūd I. adj. *quickly approaching*, Cr 842.
II. n? *speed*, An 267.
snūde† adv. *quickly, at once*, NG.
snyflung f. *mucus from the nose*, NC 322. ['*snivelling*']
snyrian† *to hasten, hurry.*
snyring *sharp rock*, WW 371[22].
snȳtan *to blow the nose*, NC 322. ['*snite*']
-snȳtels v. candel-s.
snyteru=snyttru
snȳting f. *blowing of nose*, WW 162. ['*sniting*']
snytre *clever, wise*, Gen 2808.
snytrian *to be clever, wise*, Sol.
snytro, snytru=snyttru
±snyttru f. (often in pl.) *wisdom, cleverness, prudence, sagacity, intelligence*, AO,CP.
snyttrucræft† m. *wisdom, sagacity.*
snyttruhūs n. *house of wisdom*, PPs 77[60].
snyttrum adv. *cunningly, wisely*, B,PPs.
snyðian *to go nose or beak forwards (of a plough)*, Rd 22[6].
-snyðian, -snyððan v. be-s.
soc I. (±) n. *suck, sucking*, Æ. ['*sock*']
II. m. *soakings*, Mdf.
sōc I. pret. 3 sg. of sacan. II.=sōcn
socc m. '*sock,' light shoe, slipper*, Cp,RB. [*L.* soccus]
socian *to* '*soak,*' Lcd. [sūcan]
sōcn f. *seeking, question, inquiry, case, cause : visit, resort,* Æ,W : *attack*, B 1777 : *refuge, asylum, sanctuary,* Æ : *the exercise of judicial power, jurisdiction, right of inquisition, right of taking fines, revenue* (v. sacu), KC,LL (v. 2·454) : *district in which a* 'socn' *was exercised* (EHR 27·20). ['*soken*']
sōcnes=sēcnes
+sod n. *cooking, boiling*, Gl : *trial*, CP 267[19].
soden pp. of sēoðan.
sodomitisc *sodomitish*, A 11·101[32].

sōfte I. (=sēfte) adj. '*soft,' mild, gentle,* Æ : *quiet, calm, tranquil, undisturbed,* Æ : *luxurious : agreeable*, A 9·28. II. adv. Gen,Lcd,Met.
sōftnes f. *ease, comfort :* '*softness,' luxury,* Æ.
sogeða (o[2]) m. *hiccough, eructation*, Lcd.
sōht pp., sōhte pret. 3 sg. of sēcan.
sol I. n. *mud, wet sand, wallowing-place, slough*, CP. II. *a wooden halter or collar for beasts*, WW 462[31]. [v. '*sole*']
sōl n. *sun*, PPs 120[6].
solar=solor
sōlate f. *sunflower, heliotrope*, Lcd.
sole f. *shoe, sandal*, WW 125[25]. [*L.*]
solere=solor
solian *to soil, become defiled*, Rim 67. ['*sole*']
sōlmerca m. *sundial*, NC 350.
Solmōnað m. *February*, Men,MH.
solor m. *loft, upper room, CP,Ph :* '*palatium,' hall, dwelling*, GD 248[14] : *raised platform*, OEG 2[211]. ['*sollar*'; *L.* solarium]
solsece (æ[2]) f. *heliotrope*, Lcd,WW. [*L.* solsequia]
som=sam; sōm-=sām-
sōm f. *arbitration, agreement, reconciliation,* Æ,LL. ['*some*']
+sōm *unanimous, peaceable, friendly,* Æ.
somn-=samn-; somod=samod
somw-=samw-
sōn m. *sound, music*, CP. be sōne *aloud, loudly.* [*L.* sonus]
sōna adv. '*soon,' directly, forthwith, immediately, at once, Chr,CP.* s. swā *as soon as, when, CP.*
sonc=sanc pret. of sincan.
sōncræft m. *music*, A 13·38[306].
sond=sand
song I.=sang pret. 3 sg. of singan. II. sb. *bed*, NG. [*ON.* sæng] III. *grape*, EHy 6[32].
sonwald (NG)=sinewealt
sopa m. '*sup,' sip*, Lcd. ['*sope*']
sopcuppe f. *sop-cup*, TC.
sopp '*offula,*' '*sop,*' OEG 61[10].
soppian *to soak*, '*sop,*' Lcd 86a.
sore *mote*, MtL 7[3].
sorg f. (occl. gs. in -es) '*sorrow,' pain, grief, trouble, care, distress, anxiety*, B,Bl,Bo,Cr; CP.
sorgbyrðen f. *load of sorrow*, An 1534.
sorgcearig† *anxious, sorrowful*, B.
sorgcearu f. *sorrow, anxiety*, Gu 939.
sorgful '*sorrowful,' sad, anxious, careful,* Æ,B,CP : *distressing, doleful*, B,Ph.
sorgian (pres. ptc. sorgende) *to* '*sorrow,' care, grieve, be sorry for, be anxious about,* B,Bl,Bo; CP.
sorglēas *free from sorrow or care*, Cr,LL.
sorglēast (h) f. *security*, Lcd.

sorglēoð† (h) *dirge*, B.
sorglic *miserable*. adv. -līce, *CAS*. ['*sorrowly*']
sorglufu f. *sad love*, DEOR 16.
sorgstafas mp. *anxiety, care*, JUL 660.
sorgung f. '*sorrowing*,' W 114⁴.
sorgwīte (h) n. *grievous torment*, W 187².
sorgword (h) m. *lamentation*, GEN 789.
sorgwylm (æ²)† m. *wave of sorrow*.
sorh=sorg
sorig *sorry*, CP 227⁸.
sot=sott
sōt n. (*what settles down*), '*soot*,' *Cp,Lcd*.
sotel, sotl, sotol=setl
sotman m. *foolish man*, ÆLD 17¹⁰¹.
sotscipe m. *dulness, folly*, WW 171³³. ['*sotship*']
sott I. adj. *foolish, dull, stupid*. II. m. *dullard, fool*, Bf. open sott *downright fool*, Æ. ['*sot*']
sottian *to be foolish*, BYH 80¹¹.
sōð I. n. *truth, justice, righteousness, rectitude*, CP : *reality, certainty*. tō sōðe, tō sōðum *in truth, truly, truthfully, accurately*. tō sōðan, ðurh sōð *verily, in truth*. II. adj. *true, genuine, real*, AO,CP : *just, righteous*. ['SOOTH'] III.=*L.* pro- in compounds, in DR and NG.
sōðbora? m. *soothsayer, astrologer*, CHR 975A.
sōð-cwed, -cweden *veracious*, NG.
sōðcwide m. *true speech, truth, just saying* : *proverb*, NG.
Sōðcyning† m. *King of truth, God*.
sōðe adv. *truly, really, accurately, truthfully, rightly*, B,PPs. ['*sooth*']
sōðes adv. *verily*, Mt. [v. '*sooth*']
Sōðfæder m. *Father of truth, God*, CR 103.
sōðfæst (e²) *true, trustworthy, honest, Bl, Chr,Cr,OET,VPs* : *just, righteous, JnL, PPs*. ['*soothfast*']
±sōðfæstian *to justify*, NG.
sōðfæstlic (e) *true, sincere*, AN 876. adv. -līce *truly, honestly*, OET 452. ['*soothfastly*']
sōðfæstnes f. *truth, truthfulness, fairness, fidelity, Bf,Bl,Bo,CP,VPs* : *justice*. ['*soothfastness*']
sōðfest=sōðfæst
sōðfylgan '*prosequi*,' DR 29¹⁸.
sōðgid (ie²)† n. *true report*.
sōðhweðere conj. *nevertheless*, NG.
±sōðian *to prove true, bear witness to*, LL, NG. ['*soothe*'; '*i-sothe*']
sōðlic adj. *true, truthful, real, genuine, right*, Bo. -līce adv. *truly, indeed, really, certainly, Bl,El,G,VPs*. conj. *for, now, then, but*, CP. ['*soothly*']
sōðlufu f. *lovingkindness*, RWH 93²².
sōðsagol *truthful*, ÆGR,GD.

sōðsagu f. *truth*, W : *true story*, MtL. ['*soothsaw*']
sōðsecgan *to speak the truth*, BL.
sōðsecgendlīce *truly, genuinely*, GD 185¹⁷.
sōðsegen (æ²) f. *true statement*, ÆH.
sōðspǣce *truthful*, W 72¹⁶ E.
sōðspell n. *true story, history*, MtL p 7².
sōðsprǣc f. *true saying*, DR 171¹⁸.
sōðtācen n. *prodigy*, DR 43¹⁶.
sōðða (*JnL,LkL*)=siðða
sōðword† n. *true word*, PPs.
spāca m. '*spoke*' (*of wheel, etc.*), Bo : '*spoke-bone*' (*radius*), WW.
spade=spadu; spādl=spātl
spadu (æ) f. '*spade*,' Æ,Gl,LL. [*L.* spatha]
spæc I. pret. 3 sg. of specan. II. n. *small branch, tendril*, WW.
spǣc=sprǣc
spǣclēas '*speechless*,' GPH 398⁷².
spænð pres. 3 sg. of spanan.
spær *sparing*, Sc 52⁶.
spær-=spear-
spæren adj. *of plaster*, GL.
spærhende (y²) *sparing*, ÆGR.
spærian (N)=sparian
spærlic (e) adj. *sparing*, HGL 494. adv. -līce.
spærlīra (e, ea, eo) m. *calf of leg*, Æ. ['*sparlive*']
spærlīred *with a thick calf*, WW 161²⁷.
spærnes f. *frugality, nearness*, DR,GL.
spærstān m. *gypsum, chalk*, WW. ['*sparstone*']
spǣtan *to* '*spit*,' *spew*, G; Æ,CP. ['*spete*']
spǣtl=spātl
spǣtl(l)an *to spit*, BH : *foam at the mouth*, WW.
spǣtung f. *spitting*, LCD 65a.
spala m. *substitute*, LL 484,2¹.
spāld (*El*)=spātl. ['*spold*']
spaldur *balsam*, GL (v. ES 37·186).
span=spann
+span n. *suggestion, persuasion, allurement*, CP.
±spanan⁷ *to draw on, allure, seduce, mislead, persuade, instigate*, Æ,AO,CP.
span-e, -u, pl. -a, -an f. *teat*, LCD,WW.
spanere (o) m. *seducer, enticer*, WW.
±spang fn. *clasp, buckle*, GEN. [*Ger.* spange]
spann I. f. '*span*' (*measure*), BH,WW. II. pret. 3 sg. of spinnan.
+spann n. *fastening, band, buckle, yoke*, CP.
±spannan⁷ *to join, link, fasten, attach*, CP.
spannung f. *span*, WW.
-spanung (i²) v. for-, lēas-s.
sparcian=spearcian
±sparian *to* '*spare*,' *be indulgent or merciful to, save, BH,CP,Shr,VPs* : *use sparingly, not to use*, Æ : *forbear, abstain from*, BH, CP.

+**sparrian** *to shut, bar*, MtL6[6].

sparwa=spearwa

spātl (ǣ) n. *spittle, saliva*, CP,Lcd,NG. ['*spattle*']

spātlian *to spit out*, WW162. ['*spattle*']

spātlung f. *what is spit out, spittle*, WW162. ['*spattling*']

spāōl=spātl

spāw pret. 3 sg. of spīwan.

speaft (MkL8[23])=speoft; **speara**=spearwa

spearca (æ, e) m. '*spark*,' Bf,Bo,Cp,MH ; CP.

spearcian *to throw out sparks, sparkle*, SAT 78? (v. OEG4029).

spearewa=spearwa

spearhafoc m. *sparrow-hawk*, Cp,WW. ['*spar-hawk*']

spearlīr-=spærlīr-

spearn pret. 3 sg. of spurnan.

spearnes=spærnes

spearnlian *to spurn, kick, sprawl*, Æ,GL.

spearwa I. m. '*sparrow*,' BH,Chr,Cp,Ps. II. m. *calf (of the leg)*, GL (cp. spærlīra).

spec=spic ; **spēc**=spǣc, sprǣc

specan=sprecan

specca m. '*speck*,' *spot*, Cp,Lcd,WW.

specfāh *spotted, blotched*, Cp22.

sped '*glaucoma*,' *sticky moisture, phlegm, rheum*, Cp,OEG. ['*spade*']

spēd f. *luck, success, prosperity*, Cp,El, PPs : *riches, wealth, abundance*, Cr,Gen ; AO : *opportunity, power, faculty*, Bl,PPs : (only in dp. spēdum) '*speed*,' *quickness*, Gen. on s. *fluently, skilfully* : *offspring?* PPs103[16]. [spōwan]

±**spēdan** w. d. *to prosper, succeed*, Chr,Ma. ['*speed*']

spēddropa m. *useful drop* (ink), RD27[8].

spediende *suffering from* ‡ sped,' WW.

spēdig *lucky, prosperous, rich*, AO : *plenteous, abundant* : *powerful*.

+**spēdiglīce** adv. *prosperously*, LPs44[5].

spēdignes f. *opulence*, OEG3605.

spēdlīce adv. *effectually, effectively*, PPs.

+**spēdsumian** *to prosper*, OEG3630.

spēdum v. spēd ; **spel**=spell

spelc m? *splint*, Lcd. ['*spelk*']

spelcan *to fasten with splints*, Lcd. ['*spelk*']

speld n., nap. speld, speldru *ember, torch*, OEG,WW. ['*speld*']

+**spelia** m. *vicar, substitute, representative, deputy*.

spelian *to be substitute for, represent*, Æ,RB. ['*spele*']

speliend m. *substitute, representative*, Æ,GR.

speling f. *deputyship*, RB10[12].

spell n. *narrative, history, story, fable*, Bo : *speech, discourse, homily*, Æ,B,Bo,Da,Lcd ; AO,CP : *message, news* : *statement, observation*. ['*spell*' and v. Mdf]

spellbōc f. *book of sermons*, TC430[21].

spellboda m. *messenger, ambassador, angel speaker* : *prophet*. [beodan]

spellcwide m. *historical narrative*, AO100[12].

±**spellian** *to speak, discourse, talk*, Bo,Lcd, LkL ; Æ : *announce, relate, proclaim*, Met : *conspire*, GD106[1]. ['*spell*']

spellstōw f. *place of proclamations*, Ct.

spellung f. *speech, conversation, narrative, discourse*, Æ.

spelt I. m. '*spelt*,' *corn*, WW. [L.] II. '*planca*,' *board of a book*, WW164. ['*spelt*']

spelter (LCD3·136)=spaldur

-spendan v. ā-, for-s.

spendung f. '*spending*,' ÆH556[29].

spēnn (=spēonn) pret. 3 sg. of spannan.

spennels m. *clasp*, WW238[34].

spenst pres. 2 sg., spenð pres. 3 sg. of spanan.

speoft (MkR8[23] ; MtL27[30]) redupl. pret. of *spatan? to spit*. [v. ANS141·176]

+**speoftian** *to spit upon*, LkL18[32]. [ES 38·34]

spēon pret. 3 sg. of spanan, spannan.

Spēonisc *Spanish*, ÆL37[1].

speoru (GL) nap. of spere.

speorulīra=spærlīra

spēow pret. 3 sg. of spōwan.

spēow-=spīw-; **sper-**=spær-, spear-, spyr-

spere n., nap. spe(o)ru '*spear*,' *javelin, lance*, Æ,AO,Chr,CP,Cp,LG : *stitching pain*, LCD175a.

sperebrōga m. *terror at spears*, RD18[4].

sperehand f. *male line of descent*, BC3·340[19].

sperehealf f. *male line of descent*, TC491[20].

spereléas *without a* (spear-)*head*, WW143[7].

sperenīō n. *battle*, GEN2059.

speresceaft (æ[3]) m. '*spear-shaft*,' GD14[27].

sperewyrt (speru-) f. '*spearwort*,' *elecampane*, Lcd,WW.

speriend (WW66[20])=spyrigend

+**sperod** *armed with a spear*, ÆGR,BL.

spic n. *fat bacon*, Lcd,OET ; Æ. ['*spick*']

spīce f., spīca m. *aromatic herb, spice?* BL, LCD. [L. *species*]

spichūs n. *larder*, GL,LCD.

spīcing m. *spike, nail*, ANS125[51].

spicmāse f. *titmouse*, WW286[15].

spigettan *to spit*, Æ,Bo.

spilæg '*spilagius*' (*spalangius?*), *a venomous insect*, DR125[15].

spilc=spelc

spild m. *annihilation, ruin*, CP.

spildan *to waste, ruin, destroy*, AN,JnL.

spildsīō m. *destructive expedition*, Ex153.

spilian *to sport, play*, LL,W. ['*spile*']

±**spillan** *to destroy, mutilate, kill*, LG : *waste*, DR : '*spill*' (blood), Nic.

spillere m. *parasite, jester*, OEG679.

spilling f. *waste*, Chr 999 e.

spilð (Gl)=spild

spind sb. *fat*, WW.

spindel=sprindel

spinel f., gs. spinle '*spindle*,' *Cp,LL* : *the thread on a spindle?* OEG 17⁸⁷.

spinelhealf (nl) f. *female line of descent*, TC 491²¹.

spinge=spynge; **spinil**, spinl=spinel

-spinn v. in-s.

±**spinnan**³ *to* '*spin*,' *Æ,Cp,Lcd,MtR* : *twist, writhe, Æ.*

spir *spike, blade*, Lcd 99b.

spircan (y) *to sparkle*, Æ,Gl.

spircing (y) *sprinkling*, GPH 398.

spitel m. *small spade, dibble, LL*; GD 201²⁰. ['*spittle*']

spittan *to dig in with a spud*, LL 454,10.

±**spittan** *to* '*spit*,' *LkR,MtR,MkL.*

spittian *to spit (for cooking)* (Swt).

spitu f. '*spit*' (*cooking*), *Æ,HL.*

spiðra? m. *spider*, Lcd 53b.

spiwan¹ *to spit, spit out*, '*spew*,' *vomit, Æ, Bl,Chr,CP,Jul,MH.*

spiwdrenc (i²) m. *liquid emetic*, Lcd.

spiwe m. *vomiting*, Lcd 22b.

spiwedrenc=spiwdrenc

spiwere m. *one who spews*, WW 108⁴. ['*spewer*']

spiweða=spiwða

spiwian (io) *to spew, spit up* (w. d.), Jul 476.

spiwing (ēo) f. '*spewing*,' WW.

spiwol *emetic*, Lcd.

spiwða (eo) m. *vomiting, vomit, Æ.*

splātan? *to split*, v. ES 49·156.

splin=spinl

splott m. *spot, blot* : *patch (of land), Æ.*

+**splottod** *spotted*, TC 537'.

spōn I. m. *sliver, chip, shaving, BH,Cp,Lcd.* ['*spoon*'] **II.** pret. 3 sg. of spanan.

+**spon**, spong=+span, spang

sponge f. '*sponge*,' *Mt.*

sponn=spann

spor n. *spoor, track, trail, footprint, CP* : *trace, vestige.* [*Ger.* spur]

spor-=spur-

sporettan¹ *to kick*, CVHy 6¹⁵.

sporetung f. *kicking*, EHy 6¹⁵.

spornettan *to spurn, kick*, WW.

sporning f. *stumbling-block*, Sc 134⁵. [v. '*spurning*']

sporwrecel? m. *what is tracked after being driven off?* (BT), TC 172'.

±**spōwan**⁷ *to succeed, thrive, Æ,AO,CP* : (impers.) *profit, avail, help, Æ.*

spōwendlīce adv. *prosperously*, PPs.

spracen n. *berry-bearing alder*, Lcd,WW.

spræc I. n. *shoot, slip*, WW 44²⁹. **II.** pret. 3 sg. of sprecan.

spræc (ē) f. *language, Æ* : 'speech,' *power of speech, CP* : *statement, narrative, fable, discourse, conversation, Æ,CP* : *eloquence, Æ* : *report, rumour* : *decision, judgment* : *charge, suit, CP* : *point, question* : *place for speaking*, NG.

spræcan=sprecan

spræccyn n. *mode of speech*, BH 486¹.

spræce f. *talk, discourse*, Bo 137¹.

+**spræce** *eloquent, affable, Æ,BH.*

+**spræcelic** *incapable of being used alone (of the inseparable prepositions)*, ÆGr.

spræcful *talkative*, LPs 139¹².

spræchūs n. *senate-house, curia* : *auditorium, WW* : *guest-quarters (in a monastery)*, ÆL 31⁸⁴⁷. ['*speech-house*']

spræcon pret. pl. of sprecan.

sprædan *to spread* : (+) *stretch forth, extend.*

sprædung f. *propagation*, DR 109².

sprængan=sprengan

spranc=sprang

spranca m. *shoot, slip, branch, Gl.* ['*spronk*']

sprang pret. 3 sg. of springan.

sprangettan *to quiver*, MP 1·610; WW 473².

spréawlian *to* '*sprawl*,' *move convulsively*, GPH,OEG.

+**sprec** n. *faculty of speech* : *talk, discussion.*

sprēc=spræc

±**spreca** m. *spokesman, councillor, Æ.*

±**sprecan**¹ *to* 'speak*,' *say, utter, make a speech, Æ,AO,CP* : *converse, converse with, Æ* : *declare, tell of* : (+) *agree*, AO. sp. on *lay claim to.*

+**sprecendlic** (spec-) *that should be spoken*, Sc 123².

sprecern n. *place for speaking*, NG. [spræc, ærn]

sprecolnes (spec-) f. *loquacity*, Sc 170¹⁵.

sprecul *talkative*, SPs 139¹².

sprengan (æ) (±) *to scatter, strew, sprinkle, sow, Æ,LL* : *spring, break, burst, split.* sp. on *administer a clyster.* [causative of springan; '*sprenge*']

sprenging (i) f. *sprinkling*, CM 388.

sprēot m. *pole, pike, spear, Cp,TC,WW.* ['*sprit*']

spretting=sprytting

spreulian (OEG 50³⁴)=spréawlian

spreut (Gl)=sprēot

spricð pres. 3 sg. of sprecan.

sprincel m. *basket-snare (for catching fish)*, WW (v. ES 43·322; FM 200).

sprind *vigorous, strong*, OEG,Sol. ['*sprind*'; springan]

-sprindlad v. ā-s.

sprindlīce adv. *vigorously*, OEG 738.

spring (y) m. '*spring*,' *source, BC* : *sprinkling* : *ulcer* : *flux.*

±**springan**[3] *to jump, leap, 'spring,' burst forth, rise, B,Bo,G,Ma,MH*; Æ : *spread, be diffused, grow, Æ,Bf* : *want, lack,* VH.

springd=sprind; **springing**=sprenging

springwyrt f. *caper-plant,* LCD.

+**sprintan** *to emit, utter,* JnLp187[12].

spritting=sprytting

sprota m., sprot(t) n. *sprout. twig,* OEG, WW : *peg.* ['*sprote*']

sprott m. *sprat, ÆL,Bf,NC.* ['*sprot*']

sprungen pp., sprungon pret. pl. of springan.

-**sprūtan** v. ā-, geond-s.

sprycð pres. 3 sg. of sprecan.

spryng=spring; **sprȳtan**=spryttan

sprytle f. *chip,* BH204[56] (v.l.).

spryttan *to sprout, come forth, spring, germinate, yield fruit, BH,Lcd;* Æ : *incite.* ['*sprit*']

sprytting (e, i) f. *shoot, sprout : increase,* CM 381.

spunnen pp., spunnon pret. pl. of spinnan.

spur-=spor-

spura (o) m. *spur, Æ,Gl.*

spure f. *heel,* EPs48[5].

spurleðer n. *spur-strap,* WW97[10].

±**spurnan**[3] (o) *to strike against, kick,* PPs : '*spurn,' reject, Æ* : *stumble.*

spurnere (o) m. *fuller,* ÆGR35[2].

spurul (=*spurnul?*) *given to kicking or trampling?* OET.

spylian v. ā-s.

spynge (i), spyncge f. *sponge,* AO. [*L.* spongia]

spyrc-=spirc-

spyrd m. '*stadium,' race-course,* NG.

spyremann (e[1]) m. *tracker,* TC172'.

±**spyrian** (i) *to make a track, go, pursue, travel, journey,* CP : *follow out, ask about, investigate, BH,Bo.* ['*speer*'; spor]

spyrigend m. *investigator, inquirer,* SOL140.

spyrnan *to stumble,* RWH94[22].

spyrran (e;=ie) *to strike,* AA22[8].

spyrring f. *striking,* OEG.

spyrte (e, i) f. *wicker basket, eel-basket, Æ.* [*L.* sporta]

spyrung f. *asking, investigation,* OEG5214.

staca m. *pin, 'stake,' AO,Lcd; Æ.*

stacan (stagan) *to pierce with a stake, spit* (or ?*roast,* ES40·242), IM124[71].

stacung f. *the piercing of an effigy by a 'staca'* (*a method of injury by witchcraft*), LL.

stæde-=stede-

stæf m., nap. stafas '*staff,' stick, rod, Æ,Bo, Cp,LPs,CP* : *pastoral staff* : (often in pl.) *letter, character, writing, Æ,Bo,WW* : *document* : (in pl.) *letters, literature, learning.*

stæfad=stafod

stæfcræft m. *grammar, Æ* : (in pl.) *learning,* BH.

stæfcræftig *lettered,* OEG.

stæfcyst f. *letters, learning from books, Æ.*

stæfgefēg n. *syllable,* ÆGR : *letters,* LSPs 70[15].

+**stæflǣred** *instructed, lettered,* LCD.

stæfleahtor m. *grammatical fault,* OEG 5467.

stæfleornere m. *student,* OEG3126.

stæflic *literary* : *literal, Æ.* ['*staffly*']

stæfliðere f. *sling, 'balista,'* GL.

stæfn=stefn

stæfplega m. *literary game,* GL.

stæfrǣw f. *row of letters, line of writing,* ÆL23b[767] : *alphabet,* BH484[27].

stæfrōf *alphabet,* WW397[14].

stæfsweord n. '*dolon,' lance? javelin?* WW. ['*staffsword*']

stæfwīs (e) *lettered, learned,* LCD3·186'.

stæfwrītere=stærwrītere

stæg n. I. '*stay' (rope),* WW288[26]. II. *pool, pond.* [*L.* stagnum]

-**stǣgan** v. ā-st.

stǣgel *steep,* CR,GL. [stīgan]

stǣger I. fn? '*stair,' staircase, Æ,WW.* [stīgan] II. (BYH110[18])=stǣgel

stǣgl=stǣgel

stæl I. n. *place, spot.* on stale *in place of, instead of.* on stale bēon *stand in* (*good*) *stead, be a help to,* AO232[23] : *situation, condition.* [*Ger.* stelle] II. pret. 3 sg. of stelan.

stǣl=staðol; **stǣla**=stela

±**stǣlan** *to found, institute, carry on* : *confess, admit,* VH. synne st. *to institute sin, i.e. enter on a conflict,* MEN287 : (w. d.) *put upon, impute to; accuse of, charge with* : (†) *avenge.* [=*stæðlian*=staðolian]

stǣle=stale ds. of stalu.

stǣlg=stǣgel

stǣlgiest m. *thievish stranger,* RD48[5].

stǣlherige m. *predatory army,* CP,CHR. [stelan]

stǣlhrān m. *decoy-reindeer,* AO18[11].

stæll=steall; **stællan**=stiellan

+**stællan** *to stall, stable,* MH20[1].

stǣlon pret. pl. of stelan.

stǣltihtle f. *charge of stealing,* LL.

stǣlðing n. *theft,* CHRD19[16]. [stelan]

stǣlwierðe *serviceable, CP,Chr,Shr.* [staðol; '*stalworth*']

stǣlwyrt f. *water-starwort,* WW299[5].

+**stǣn-**=+sten-

stǣn-=stǣnen-, stān-

stǣnan (±) *to stone,* Mt; Æ,CP : *adorn with precious stones,* EL151. ['*steen*']

stǣnc=stenc

stǣne f. *pitcher, jug,* WW415[18]. ['*stean*']

stǣnen *made of stone, stony, Bl,G,MH*; Æ, AO,CP. ['*stonen*']

stǣner *stony ground*, NG.

stæng=steng

stǣnilic *stony*, Lcd 1·216'.

stǣning f. *stoning*, Æ,MH.

stæpe (a, e) m. usu. nap. stapas (stæpan, RPs139[5]) *going, gait, 'step,' pace, Ps,Rd, W*; Æ,CP : *spoor : power of locomotion : short distance, measure of length, MtR,WW : step, stair, Æ,VPs : pedestal, socket, HL* 199 : *grade, degree, Æ.* in stæpe *instantly*.

stæpegong (e) m. *stepping, going*, Rim 22.

stæpmǣlum adv. *step by step, by degrees, gradually*, CP.

±stæppan[6] (e) *to* 'STEP,' *go, advance*, Æ,CP; AO.

stæppescōh (e) m. *slipper*, WW.

stær m., nap. staras *starling, Cp,MtL.* ['*stare*']

stǣr (ē) n. *story, history, narrative*, BH. [v. A37·56 and LF161]

stærblind *stone-blind, Cp.* ['*stareblind*']

stǣrcedferhð=stercedferhð

stǣreblind (*Shr*)=stærblind

stǣrleornere? m. *student of history*, v. OEG 4145n.

stǣrlīce adv. *historically*, OEG 2[810].

stǣrling m. '*starling*,' ZDA 33·241[54].

stærn=stearn

stǣrtractere m. *commentator, historian*, WW207[1].

stǣrwrītere m. *historian*, AO.

stæð n. occl. gds. staðe, nap. staðas *shore, river-bank, AO,Chr*; Æ,CP. ['*staith*']

stæðfæst *firm, stable*, Cr981.

stæðhlȳpe I. (ē) *sloping, precipitous.* II. f. *a steep place*, GD95[16].

stæðhlȳplīce adv. *steeply*, Bl 207[20].

stæðswealwe f. *sand-martin*, Lcd,WW.

stæððan *to support*, Rd 4[74].

±stæððig *staid, serious*, Æ.

±stæððignes f. *staidness, seriousness*, Æ,CP.

stæðweall m. *barrier of the shore*, Gen 1376.

stæðwyrt f. *a plant*, Lcd 29a.

stafas nap. of stæf.

staflan *to dictate*, Æ.

stafod (æ, e) *striped*, Ep,Erf.

stāg pret. 3 sg. of stīgan.

stagan=stacan?

stagga m. *stag*, LL624,24. ['*stag*']

stāh pret. 3 sg. of stīgan.

stal=steall

+stāl n. *plaint, accusation, confession?* MFH163,VH : *contention*, GD329[15].

+stala m. *accessory in theft*, LL100,25[1].

stalað=staðol

stald=steald; stale v. stæl.

stālern n. *court of law*, WW.

staleð-=staðol-

stalgong m. *stealthy going*, Gu 1113.

stalian *to go stealthily*, AO : (±) *steal*, Æ.

±stālian *to establish, confirm, strengthen : make an accusation*, LL110b[1]. [=staðolian]

stall=steall

stalu I. (±) f. *stealing, robbery, theft, Bl, MtL; Æ : stolen article : fine for stealing.* ['*stale*'] II. *wood to which harp-strings are fixed?* WW203[36]. [v. '*stale*']

stalung f. *stealing, robbery*, AO.

stam (o) *stammering*, Gl.

stamera m. *stammerer*, EC226'.

stamerian (omr-) *to* '*stammer*,' GPH,HL.

stammetan (o) *to stammer*, WW447[30].

stamor *stammering*, Gl.

stān m. (and n. in NG) 'STONE,' *rock : gem*, CP : *calculus : milestone* (v. Mdf).

stānæx (e[2]) f. *stone-workers' axe?* WW.

stānbæð n. *vapour bath made by water poured on to heated stones* (BT),Lcd.

stānbeorg m. *rocky elevation*, B,Ct.

stānberende *stony*, WW427[36].

stānbill n. *tool for working stone*, WW447[33].

stānbogaꝉ m. *rocky arch*, B.

stānbrycg f. *stone bridge*, Ct,WW.

stānbucca m. *mountain goat*, ÆGr68[5].

stānburg f. *town or fort of stone*, Gen; Mdf.

stanc I. pret. 3 sg. of stincan. II. sb. *sprinkling*, WW.

stāncarr m. *rock*, DR19[11].

stānceastel (i[2]) m. *walled enclosure? heap of stones?* Ct (v. GBG).

stānceosel (i[2], y[2]) m. *sand*, GenC22[17],OEG.

stān-clif n., nap. -clifu, -cleofu (B) *rock, cliff, crag*, GD.

stānclūd m. *rock*, Æ,CP.

stāncnoll m. *rocky knoll*, EC248[17].

stāncræftiga m. *clever stone-worker*, MH 202[14].

stancrian *to sprinkle*, WW162[46].

stāncrop m. '*stone-crop*' (*plant*), Lcd.

stāncynn n. *kind of stone*, VH,ZDA34·233.

stāncysel=stānceosel

stāncyst(en) *chestnut-tree*, KC4·8[22]. [*L. castanea*]

stand (o) m. *delay*, MkLR6[35]. [v. '*stand*']

±standan[6] (o) *to* 'STAND*' ('*i-stand*'), *occupy a place, stand firm, Æ,AO,CP : congeal*, Lcd 35b : *remain, continue, abide*, AO, CP : *stand good, be valid, be, exist, take place, Æ,CP : oppose, resist attack : reprove : stand still, stop, Æ :* (ꝉ) *appear, flash out : arise, come :* (ꝉ) *be present to, come upon* (*of fear*). ne s. tō ahte *be of no account*, W82n. (+) *stand up, keep one's feet, Bo :* (+) *attack, assail*, ÆL : (+) *perform.* s. on *consist : depend on.*

stāndenu *stony valley*, KC3·383.
stāneht=stānihte; **stānex**=stānæx
stān-fæt n., nap. -fatu *stone vessel*, G, WAL.
stānfāh† *stone-paven.*
stānflōr m. *paving-stone, tessella*, OEG14³. [cp. flōrstān]
stang pret. 3 sg. of stingan.
stāngaderung f. *stone wall*, ERPs61³.
stāngeat n. *opening between rocks*, Ct.
stāngedelf n. *stone-quarry*, KC.
stāngefeall n. *heap of stones*, MH212²¹.
stāngefōg n. *stone-laying*, EL1021.
stāngella (i²) m. ' *staniel,' pelican*, VPs, WW.
stāngetimbre n. *masonry*, WW441⁶.
stāngeweorc n. *art of building : stone-work, masonry*, Æ.
stān-gripe m., dp. -greopum *handful of stones?* EL824.
stānhege m. *stone fence, wall*, LPs79¹³.
stānhīfet (Ct)=stānhȳwet
stānhlinc m. *stony ridge*, KC.
stān-hliō† n., nap. -hliðu, -hleoðu *rocky slope, cliff, rock.*
stānhof n. *stone building*, RUIN39.
stānhol n. *hole in a rock*, AA8,33.
stānhricg m. *rocky ridge*, OEG5465.
stānhȳpe f. *stone-heap*, KC3·431⁹.
stānhȳwet n. *stone-quarry*, WW112¹⁰.
stānig (ǣ) ' *stony,' rocky*, MtR; AO.
stāniht (ǣ) I. adj. *stony, rocky*, AO. II. n. *stony ground* (Swt).
stānincel n. *little stone*, A13·31⁸⁶.
stānlesung f. *building with loose stones*, WW 117³⁴. [lesan]
stānlīm m. *cement, mortar*, WW205⁹.
stānmerce m. *parsley*, WW.
stānrocc m. *high rock, obelisk*, GL.
stānscalu f. *shale*, EC306¹⁸.
stānscræf n. *rocky cave*, MH.
stānscylf m. *rugged rock*, HGL449.
stānscylig *shaly, stony*, Mk4⁵. [sciell]
stānsticce n. *bit of stone*, WW376¹⁸.
stānstrǣt f. *paved road*, TC525²¹.
stāntorr m. *stone tower : crag, rock*, GD 12.
stānweall m. ' *stone wall,' VPs*; Æ.
stānweg m. *paved road*, BC1·417'.
stānweorc n. ' *stone-work,' RWH43¹⁷ : stone structure*, Æ.
stānwong m. *stony plain*, RD88⁶.
stānwurma m. *mineral colour*, OEG1061.
stānwurðung f. *worship of stones*, LL.
stānwyrht? f. *stone structure*, WW341¹⁰.
stānwyrhta m. *stone-mason*, GL.
stapa m. *grasshopper, locust*, WW.
stapas v. stæpe; **stapel**=stapol
stapela m. *post, stake*, LL387,4².
stapen pp. of steppan.

stapol m., nap. stapolas, staplas *basis, trunk of a tree, post, prop, support, stay, pillar, column, An,MtL,WW : threshold? B*926 : *market and court?* (v. EC466n) : *steps up to a house door*, WW126⁸. [' *staple';* v. Mdf]
stapolweg m. *staked-out road?* KC5·281²³.
-stapplian v. under-s.; **stapul**=stapol
staras v. stær; **starc**=stearc
stareblind = stærblind
±**starian** *to ' stare,' gaze*, ÆL,B.
stað- v. stæð; **staðel**=staðol
staðol (ea¹, e², u²) m. *base, foundation, support, BH,WW*; AO,CP : *station, position, state, condition*, CP : *stability, security : firmament, heavens : underside of a turf*, Lcd : *estate, farm*, GD222. [' *staddle';* standan]
staðolǣht f. *real estate*, RIM22.
staðolfæst *fixed, firm, steadfast*, Bo,MtL. [' *stathelfast'*]
staðolfæstlic *steadfast, firm*, Æ. adv. -līce.
staðolfæstnes (ea) f. *stability*, Æ,GD.
+**staðol-fæst(n)ian**, -festian (ea¹, u²) *to make firm, establish.*
staðolfæstnung f. *foundation*, LPs136⁷.
±**staðolian** (e²) *to fix, found, establish, Bl* : *confirm, make steadfast, strengthen.* [' *stathel'*]
+**staðoliend** (e²) m. *founder*, LPs47².
±**staðolung** f. *foundation, settlement : ordinance*, RB112²⁴.
staðolwang† m. *settling place.*
staðul=staðol; **steaf-**=stæf-
+**steal** n. *structure, frame*, WA110.
stealc† *lofty, steep, precipitous*, RD.
-stealcian v. be-s.
stealcung f. *act of going stealthily*, ÆH. [' *stalking'*]
steald pret. 3 sg. of stellan.
+**steald**† n. *dwelling, habitation.*
stealdan⁷ *to possess, own*, RIM22.
steall (a) mn. *standing, place, position, state, WW* : ' *stall' (for cattle), stable, Cp*; Æ : *fishing ground.*
-**stealla** v. eaxl-, hand-, ofer-s.
steallere (a) m. *marshal, constable*, CHR, KC.
-**steallian** v. forð-s.
stēam (ē, īe) m. ' *steam,' moisture, exhalation*, Æ,Lcd,Pa : *steaming fluid, blood*, ROOD62.
stēap I. *precipitous, deep : high, lofty, B, Rd : prominent, projecting, Æ : upright?* B2566 : *bright, brilliant, Gn,Sol.* [' *steep'*] II. (ēo) m. *stoup, beaker, flagon.*
stēap-=stēop-
stēaphēah *very high*, RD26⁴.
stēapol m. *cairn?* Ct (Swt).

stearc (a) *stiff, rigid, obstinate, Æ,El : stern, severe, hard, Æ : harsh, rough, strong, violent, impetuous, WW.* [*'stark'*]

stearcferð *harsh, stern,* JUL636.

stearcheard *excessive,* DD200?

stearcheort† *stout-hearted,* B.

stearcian *to stiffen, become hard,* GPH402⁵⁶. [*'stark'*]

stearclīce adv. *stoutly, strongly, vigorously,* Chr1016D : *strictly,* CHRD54²⁶. [*'starkly'*]

stearcmōd *stubborn,* CHRD8²⁷.

stearm (NG)=storm

stearn (æ, e) m. *sea-swallow? tern?* Gl,Seaf. [*'stern'*]

stearra (DR)=steorra

steartlian *to kick, struggle,* OEG. [*'startle'*]

stea-ðel, -ðul=staðol

steb=stybb; **stebn** (GL)=stefn

stēda m. *stud-horse, stallion, Æ : entire camel.* [*'steed'*]

stede (y) m. *place, site, position, station, Æ, Bo,Ct,Lcd,RB ;* CP; Mdf : *firmness, standing, stability, steadfastness, fixity, Æ : strangury. of s. immediately.* [standan; *'stead'*]

stedefæst *'steadfast,' steady, firm,* Ma,LL; ÆL.

stedefæstnes (styd-) f. *constancy,* DR50².

stedeheard† *firm, strong,* JUD223 (or ?steðe-).

stedelēas *unsteady, unstable,* ÆL.

stedewang† m. *field, plain.*

stedewist f. *steadiness,* HGL530⁴.

+stēdhors n. *stud-horse, stallion,* BH 138CA¹.

stedig *sterile,* Æ,LPs.

+stedigian (e²) *to stand still,* ÆL31²⁴².

stedignes f. *sterility,* ERSPs34¹².

stedinglīne f. *stay (ship's rope),* WW.

stef-=stæf-, staf-; **stefen**=stefn I.

stefn (æ) **I.** f. *voice, sound,* Æ,CP. **II.** m. *message, summons, turn (of military service), time :* a *body of men who take a turn at work, the English military force?* (BT), KC5·121'. nīwan stefne *anew, again.* **III.** m. *'stem,' trunk,* Bo,Sol : *foundation, root,* Bo : *prow or stern of a vessel,* B,WW. [stæf]

stefna† (æ) m. *prow or stern of a ship,* An. [*'stem'*]

stefnan I. (±) *to institute, arrange, regulate : alternate.* **II.** (+) *to provide with a fringe,* CM288.

stefnbyrd f. *control,* CREAT45.

stefnelof n. *'vociferatio,'* LPs26⁶.

stefnettan (mn) *to stand firm,* MA122.

stefnhlōw (mn) *vocalic,* BF100¹⁶.

±stefnian (w. d.) *to summon,* CHR, MFH 163.

stefning (mn) f. *border, hem,* WW : *turn, shift,* CHR894.

stefnmǣlum (mm) *alternately,* CM280.

stela (æ, eo) m. *stalk : support,* ÆT.

±stelan⁴ *to 'steal,' rob,* Æ,Cp,LG,LL.

stēle (GL)=stȳle

stellan I. (y) *to place, put, set (example), AO,CP.* +stelled bēon mid *have an attack of,* GD. [*'stell'*] **II.**=stiellan

stelmēle m. *handled vessel,* LL455,17.

stelscofl (eo¹) f. *shovel with (long) handle?* GPH400⁴⁹⁸.

stem-=stefn-

stēm=stēam; **stēm-**=stīem-

steming=stemning

stemn (CP)=stefn

stempan *to pound,* LCD1·378'.

stempingīsern n. *stamping-iron,* WW.

+sten (æ) n. *groaning,* PPs30¹¹.

stenan *to groan,* PPs37⁹ : *rattle, clash,* EL 151.

stēnan=stǣnan

stenc m. *odour,* Æ,BH,Bl : *scent, fragrance,* CP : *'stench,' stink,* Æ,AO,BH. [stincan]

±stencan I. *to scatter : afflict?* PPs43³. **II.** *to stink,* JnL. [*'stench'*] **III.** *to pant,* HGL.

stencbǣre *stinking,* BH48¹⁷.

stencbrengende *odoriferous,* DR77'.

+stence (æ) *odoriferous,* LCD1·282'.

stencfæt n., pl. -fatu *smelling bottle,* OEG 8²⁹⁹.

±stencnes f. *odour,* DR.

stenecian *to pant,* OEG6⁵. [stenan]

steng m. *stake, pole, bar, rod, staff, cudgel,* Cp,LG,MH; CP. [*'sting'*; v. Mdf]

stent pres. 3 sg. of standan.

steol-=stel-

stēold pret. 3 sg. of stealdan.

stēop=stēap

stēopbearn n. *orphan,* Æ. [*'stepbairn'*]

stēopcild (ē, ēa) n. *orphan, unprotected one,* Bl,Jn. [*'stepchild'*]

stēopdohtor (ē) f. *'step-daughter,'* WW, RWH139¹².

stēopfæder m. *'step-father,'* AO,Ep.

stēopmōdor f. *'step-mother,'* AO,Cp.

stēopsunu m. *'step-son,'* AO,Cp,WW.

stēor I. (ȳ) f. *steering, direction, guidance,* Æ,BH : *rule, regulation,* Æ : *restraint, discipline, correction,* Æ,CP : *penalty, fine, punishment,* Æ,CP. [*'steer'*] **II.** m. *'steer,' bullock, young cow,* Gl.

stēora (īe, īo, ȳ) m. *steersman, pilot, guider, director,* CP. [*'steer'*]

stēoran=stīeran

stēorbord n. *'starboard,'* AO.

stēore f. *direction, discipline,* LL.

stēorend (ȳ) m. *corrector, director, ruler,* AN.

stēorere m. *steersman,* CP431³¹.

stēoresmann (*LL*)=stēormann ['*steers-man*']

steorfa m. *pestilence : carrion*, LL.

steorfan[3] *to die*, ÆH. ['*starve*']

steorglēaw *clever at astronomy*, OEG.

stēorlēas *not under control or rule, wild, profligate, foolish*, Bo. ['*steerless*']

stēorlēaslic *unmanageable*, GD 289[10].

stēormann m. *pilot, master of a ship*, Æ. ['*steerman*']

stēornægl m. *handle of a helm*, WW 312[4]?

steornede *having a bold forehead?* WW. [cp. *Ger.* stirn]

stēoroxa m. *steer*, WW 120[26].

steorra m. '*star*,' Chr,Lcd,VPs.

stēorrōðra m. *steersman, master of a ship*, BL.

stēor-rōðer, -rōðor n. '*rudder*,' Cp; CP.

steorscēawere m. *astronomer, astrologer*, WW.

stēorsceofol f. *rudder*, WW.

stēorsetl n. *steersman's seat, after-part of a ship*, Æ.

stēorsprēc (=æ) *reproof*, RPs 37[15].

stēorstefn m. *stern (of ship)*, WW 482[15].

steort (e) sm. *tail*, Cp,Bo : *spit of land, cape : plough-tail*. ['*start*']

stēor-weorð, -wierðe *blameworthy, reprehensible*, CP 194,195[3].

steorwigle n. *astrology*, GL.

steorwiglere m. *mathematician, astrologer*, OEG 55[8].

steorwiglung f. *astrology*, A 13·33[141].

step-=stæp-; stēp-=stēop-

stēpan† I. (±) *to erect, raise : elevate, exalt, honour, adorn, enrich :* (+) *help, support.* [stēap] II. (±) *to initiate, consecrate*, WW.

stēpel=stīpel

stēr=stǣr

stēran I. *to burn incense : fumigate*, Æ,Lcd. ['*stere*'] II.=stīeran

stercedferhð† (æ) *stout of heart, determined, bold, brave.*

stēring f. *incense*, OEG 1512.

stermelda m. *informer? complainant?* LL 9,5; v. 2·202.

stern=stearn; sterra (N)=steorra

stert=steort; sterung=styrung

stēða (WW)=stēda

steðeheard? *hardened on the anvil*, JUD 223 (v. ES 64·212).

stēup- (Ep)=stēop-

stī-=stig-; stic-=stycce-

sticādl f. *pain in the side, stitch*, WW 112[22].

sticca m. '*stick*,' Lcd : *peg, pointer : spoon*, Lcd.

sticce I. n. *sticky matter*, LCD. II.=stycce

sticcian=stician

±stice m. *sting, prick, puncture, stab*, CP, LL : '*stitch*,' *pain in the side*, Lcd.

sticel I. m. *prick, goad, thorn*, CP. II.= sticol

sticels (Æ)=sticel

sticfōdder n. *case for spoons? or made of twigs?* LL 455,17.

stician (y) (±) tr. *to '*stick*,' prick, stab, transfix, goad, gouge out*, AO,BH,MH; CP : *kill :* intr. *stick, inhere, be placed, lie, remain fixed, be hampered*, Æ,Bo; CP : *project*, KC.

sticmǣlum (Æ)=styccemǣlum

stic-ol, -ul *lofty, sharp, abrupt, steep*, Æ : *arduous, rough : scaly : biting*, GPH 417.

sticolnes (y[2]) f. *height*, OEG 4437.

stictǣnel m. *basket*, WW 403[2].

sticung f. *pricking, goading, stabbing*, AO.

sticwærc m. *stitch in the side*, WW 112[21].

sticwyrt f. *agrimony*, WW 136[21].

stīegan=stīgan

stiell m. *jump, leap, spring*, CR 720–736.

±stiellan I. (æ, e, i, y) *to leap, rush : attack*, GD. II. (y) *to make stalls for cattle? or to put them in stalls?* LL 454,11[13].

stīem=stēam

stīeman (ē, ȳ) *to emit vapour, '*steam*,' exhale (odour)*, Æ,Ph. [stēam]

stieme (ī) *a plant?* LCD 3·32[19]?

stīeming (ē) f. *fragrance*, OEG.

stiep m. *downfall?* GEN 60?

-stiepan (ē, ēa, ēo, ȳ) v. ā-s.

stīera=stēora

±stīeran (ēo, ī, ȳ) *to '*steer*,' guide, direct, govern, rule*, Æ,BH,Bo,CP : (w. d. or g.) *restrain, correct, reprove, punish*, Bl,Lcd, MkL; Æ,AO,CP. [stēor]

-stierfan (æ, e, y) v. ā-s.

stiern-=styrn-

stiernes (ȳ) f. *discipline*, Æ.

stiernlīce (CP) v. styrnlice.

stīf *rigid, '*stiff*,'* GPH 394.

stīfearh m. *little pig (kept in a sty)*, LL 449,7. [stig]

stīflan *to be or become rigid*, ÆGR.

stīfician=stȳfecian

stīfig *steep*, BC (Mdf).

stig n. *sty, pen : hall*, Ct,GL.

stīg fm. *narrow path, way, footpath, track, road, course, line*, B,G,Ps. ['*sty*']

±stīgan[1] *to move, go, reach : go up, spring up, ascend, rise, mount, scale*, Bo,VPs; AO,CP : *go down, descend*, Æ,CP. ['*sty*']

stige m. *ascent, descent*, MEN 64.

stig-el (-ol) f. '*stile*,' Ct,GD 24.

stigelhamm m. *enclosure reached by a stile*, KC 5·289[2].

stīgend I. m. *stye (on the eye)*, WW 114[10]. ['*styan*'] II. m. *sailor*, v. OEG 32n.

stigian *to shut into a '*sty*,'* Bf.

stīgnes f. *descent*, LkL 19[37].

stigrāp m. 'stirrup,' WW.

stigu=stig

stig-weard, -wita=stī-weard, -wita

stihl=stigel

+stiht n. dispensation, provision, VH20.

stihtan (±) to rule, direct, arrange, order, ordain, AO,CP : instigate. [Ger. stiften]

stihtend (y) m. disposer, JUL419 : protector, RPs58¹².

stihtere m. director, ruler, CP391²² : steward, GD221¹⁹.

stihtian (CP)=stihtan

±stihtung f. arrangement, direction, dispensation, providence, AO.

stihŏ pres. 3 sg. of stīgan.

stileŏ=stylŏ pres. 3 sg. of stelan.

±stillan (y) I. to be still, have rest, Ma : (w. d. or a.) 'still' ('i-still'), quiet, calm, appease, hush, An,BH,Gen,LL : stop, restrain, abate, relieve, Lcd. II.=stiellan

stille adj. adv. 'STILL,' quiet, calm, stable, fixed : gentle, Æ; CP : silent, Æ : secret.

stilles=stilnes

stillīce adv. silently, CM266.

stil(l)nes (AO,CP) f. 'stillness,' quiet, Æ, Bo : silence, HL : peace, AO,CP : release, relaxation, CP.

stīme=stīeme

stincan³ to emit a smell, 'stink,' exhale, ÆGr, Cp,Lcd; AO : sniff, B2289 : rise (of dust, vapour, etc.), RD30¹².

+stincan³ tr. to smell, CP : have the sense of smell, PPs. ['i-stink']

sting (y) m. 'sting,' puncture, thrust, BH, Guth.

stingan³ I. to 'sting,' stab, pierce, push through, thrust, Bo,Ma; CP. st. on lay claim to, usurp. II.=stincan

stintan=styntan; stīora=stēora

stiorc=stirc

stīpel (ē, ȳ) m. 'steeple,' tower, Æ,Mt. [stēap]

stīpere m. post, prop, WW126¹¹.

+stīr-=+stȳr; stir-=styr-

stīran=stīeran; stīrāp=stigrāp

stirc (io, y) n. calf, Æ,Gl.

stirgan=styrian; stitian=stihtan

stīŏ stiff, thick, rigid, hard, firm, strong, CP : resolute, brave, Æ : stubborn, unrelenting, austere, strict, fierce, harsh, cruel, CP; Æ. ['stith']

stīŏe I. adv. very much, strongly, well : harshly, strictly, severely, bitterly, Gen; Æ. ['stith'] II. f. name of a plant, Lcd160b.

stīŏecg stiff-edged, RD88¹⁴.

stīŏferhŏ† determined, stern.

stīŏhycgende† (-hug-) determined, resolute, brave : stern, obstinate.

stīŏhȳdig† determined, resolute.

stīŏhygd determined, resolute, JUL654.

+stīŏian to become hard : become strong, grow up, mature, Æ : make firm, CP.

stīŏlīc firm, stout, strong, hard : decided : harsh, stern, severe, Æ,CP. adv. -līce forcibly, BF94¹³.

stīŏmægen n. powerful force, DD114.

stīŏmōd† resolute, brave, firm, unflinching, stubborn, stern, severe.

stīŏnes f. hardness, rigidity, strictness, severity, rigour, Æ : firmness, constancy, Æ.

stīŏweg m. rough way, RD4³⁵.

stīweard m. 'steward,' housekeeper, guardian, WW. [stig-]

stīwita m. housekeeper? householder? GEN 2079; RD4¹⁰.

stoc n. place, house, dwelling, GD (v. ES 37·191). ['stoke']

stocc m. 'stock,' stump, stake, post, log, Æ, Bl,OET; Mdf : stocks : trumpet, MtL6². stoccen made of logs? KC3·73'.

stoclīf n. dwelling-place, city, AS.

stocweard m. citizen, OEG5272.

stocwīc n. dwelling-place, GD172⁴.

stod mf. post, WW106³³.

-stod v. wealh-s.

stōd I. f. 'stud' (of horses), KC,WW; Mdf. II. pret. 3 sg. of standan.

stōdfald m. stud-fold, paddock, Ct.

stōdhors n. stud-horse, stallion, BH138¹. [v. 'steed']

stodla m. (weaver's) slay, LL455,15¹.

stōdmyre (e²) f. brood-mare, LL58,16. ['studmare']

stōdon pret. pl. of standan.

stōdŏēof m. horse-stealer, LL54,9².

stofa, stofu, mf. bath-room, GL. [v. 'stove']

stofbæŏ (u¹) n. vapour-bath, LCD.

stofn mf. trunk, stem, branch, shoot, OEG, WW : progeny, OEG : station, position. ['stoven']

+stogen pp. of +stigan at MFB208.

stōl m. 'stool,' chair, seat, CP,Cp,G,Gen, Lcd,LL : throne : bishop's see.

stole fn. 'stole,' long outer garment, DR, NG. [L.]

stolen pp. of stelan.

stom=stam

stonc=stanc pret. 3 sg. of stincan.

stond=stand

stōp pret. 3 sg. of steppan.

stōpel m. footprint, BL127.

stoppa m. bucket, pail, GD,Gl. ['stop']

-stoppian v. for-s. ['stop']

stōr I. m. incense, frankincense, Æ. [L. storax] II. strong, great, Chr1085. ['stour']

storc m. 'stork,' Æ,Gl.

stōr-cille, -cyl(le) f. censer, Æ.

störfæt n. *censer*, IM120[14].

storm m. *tempest, 'storm,'* Lcd,LG,VPs : (†) *rush, onrush, attack, tumult, disturbance,* An,B; CP.

stormig *stormy,* OEG?,RWH66[15] (storem-).

stormsæ *stormy sea,* Bo115[22].

störsæp n. *resin,* OEG4027.

störsticca m. *rod for stirring the incense in the censer?* (BT), EC250,21.

stot m. *a kind of horse,* v. NC323. ['*stot*']

stōw f. *spot, site, station, locality, position,* B,Bo; Æ,AO,CP; Mdf : (*holy*) *place,* LL. ['*stow*']

stōwigan *to retain, restrain,* Cp1713.

stōwlic *local, limited by space,* Æ. adv. -līce *as regards place,* Æ.

strāc pret. 3 sg. of strīcan.

strācian *to 'stroke,'* CP,Lcd.

strācung f. *stroking,* WW179[9].

strād (1) pret. 3 sg. of strīdan; (2)=strēad

stræc (ǣ? e) I. *firm, strict, severe, stern, rigid, obstinate, hard,* Æ,CP : *strenuous, vehement, violent,* Æ. [streccan] II. n. *rigour : violence, force,* Æ.

stræclic *strict,* CP. adv. -līce *strictly, severely, vehemently, violently,* CP.

stræcnes (e) f. *pertinacity : rigidity, rigour,* GD.

strǣde f. *pace,* MtL5[41].

strǣdon pret. pl. of strēdan.

strægd pret. 3 sg. of stregdan.

strægdnes f. *aspersion,* BH446[15].

strægl=strǣl II.

strǣl I. fm. *arrow, dart, missile.* [*Ger.* strahl] II. f. *curtain, quilt, matting, bed,* Gl. ['*strail*']

strǣlbora m. *archer,* WW.

strǣle f.=strǣl I.

strǣlian *to shoot* (*an arrow*), RPs63[5].

strǣlwyrt f. *name of a plant,* Lcd36b.

strǣngð (VPs)=strengð

strǣt I. f. '*street,' high road,* B,Ct,G,OET; Æ,CP; Mdf. [*L.* strata (via)] II. f. *bed,* CPs. [*L.* stratum]

strǣtlanu f. *street,* NC323.

strǣtweard (ē) f. *waywarden,* LL.

strand n. '*strand,' sea-shore,* G,KC; Æ.

strang (o) comp. strengra, superl. strengest (from strenge) '*STRONG,' powerful, able, firm, bold, brave,* Æ,CP : *constant, resolute, strenuous : strict, severe,* AO; CP : *arduous : violent.*

strange adv. comp. strangor, superl. strangost *strongly, violently, furiously, severely,* BH,Met. ['*strong*']

stranghynde *strong of hand,* ÆT473.

±strangian *to strengthen, confirm,* Æ,Bl; AO,CP : *be strong, prevail,* Æ,VPs : *press* (*after*) RWH86[25]. ['*strong*']

stranglic *strong, stout, firm, solid, sound, robust,* Æ : *severe.* adv. -līce *strongly, firmly, stoutly, boldly, bravely,* Æ,CP : *fiercely, violently,* MH.

strangmōd *resolute,* RB138[28].

strangnes f. *strength, power, force,* Lk, Ps.

±strangung f. *strengthening, quickening, nourishing,* Æ : *vigour,* Æ.

strapulas mp. *breeches,* WW125[2].

strāwberige=strēawberige

strē (N), strēa=strēaw

streac=stearc

strēad pret. 3 sg. of strūdan.

streaht pp. of streccan.

strēal=strǣl

strēam m. '*stream,' flood, current, river,* Bl, Bo,G,GD,Lcd; AO,CP : (†) pl. *sea.*

strēamfaru f. *rush of water,* An1578.

strēamgewinn n. *strife of waters,* Rd4[26].

strēamlic *of water,* ÆH1·444[10].

strēamracu f. *water-course, channel,* An, WW.

strēamrād f. *course of a stream,* Gl : *sea-path,* Cra.

strēamrynes adv. *flowing like a stream,* Æ.

strēamstæð n. *shore,* Gen1434.

strēamweall m. *shore,* Gen1494.

strēamwelm m. *surging stream,* An495.

strēaw (ē, ēo) n. '*straw,' hay,* Æ,Lcd.

strēaw-berige, -beriwīse f. '*strawberry,'* Lcd,WW.

strēawian=strewian; strec (Æ)=stræc

strec-=stræc-

streccan (±) *to stretch* ('*i-stretche*'), *spread out, prostrate,* BH,G,Lcd : *reach, extend,* Æ.

streccanmōd *persistent,* ÆP80[10].

strecednes f. *bed, couch,* LPs.

streclic=stræclic

strēdan[3] (and wv; pret. 3 sg. strēdde, pp. strēded, strēd)=stregdan

strēgan *to strew,* Seaf97. ['*stray*']

stregdan[3] (and wv.) pret. strægd, strugdon (wk. stregde), pp. strogden (wk. stregd, strēdd) *to strew, sprinkle. disperse. scatter. straggle : to spread, extend.*

strēgl=strǣl II.

strehte pret. 3 sg. of streccan.

strēl=strǣl; strēn=strēowen

strēnan=strīenan

streng I. m. '*string,' cord, rope, ligature, sinew,* An,AS,B,G,Lcd. in pl. *tackle, rigging : lineage, race.* II.=strengu

+strengan *to strengthen,* LkL. +strenged *formed, made,* OEG46[9].

strenge *severe,* Gen60. [v. strang]

strengel m. *ruler, chief,* B3115. [strang]

strengest (AO,CP) v. strang.

strenglic *strong, firm,* Gen273. adv. -līce.

strengra (*Bo*; Æ,AO,CP) v. strang. ['*strenger*']

strengð, strengðu f. 'STRENGTH,' *force, vigour* : *ability, superiority* : *firmness, fortitude, Æ* : *manhood, mature years* : *violence, ApT.*

strengu f. *strength, power, vigour, ability,* B,*VPs*; CP : *firmness, fortitude,* CP : *virtue.* ['*strengh*']

strenð (KGL)=strengð

strēon I. (±) n. *gain, acquisition, property, treasure,* AO,LG,WW; Æ,CP : *traffic, usury* : *procreation, Æ.* ['*i-streon*,' v. '*strain*'] II.=strēowen

strēonan=strīenan

+strēones (ēu) f. *petty gain,* GPH389.

+strēonful *costly, valuable, precious, Æ.*

strēow=strēaw

strēowen (ē) f. *resting-place, couch, bed,* BH.

strēowian=strewian

strēownes f. *mattress, bedding,* Bl227.

strēt I. pres. 3 sg. of strēdan. II.=strǣt

strēw=strēaw; strēwen=strēowen

±strewian (ēa, ēo) *to* '*strew,*' *scatter, Bl*; CP.

strewung f. *what one lies on, bedding,* LPs 131³.

±strīc n. *plague? strife? sedition?* LCD,LL,W.

strica m. *stroke, line, mark, Æ.* ['*streak*']

±strīcan¹ *to pass lightly over the surface, stroke, rub, wipe, Lcd* : *move, go, run, Met.* ['*strike*']

stricel m. I. *fount, breast,* GL. II. *implement for smoothing corn in a measure? rope?* (ES43·325), Cp266ᴛ.

strīchrægl n. *a cloth for wiping?* CC23²¹.

+strician *to knit together, mend,* MtL4²¹.

strīdan¹ *to* '*stride,*' *Gl.* up on s. *mount* (*a horse*), GD81²⁰.

stride m. '*stride,*' *step, Cp*134ᴘ.

±strīenan (ēo, ī, ȳ) *to acquire, gain, amass,* CP : *beget, AO,Mt*; CP : *increase, augment?* CP. ['*strene*']

+strīenendlic (e, y) *begetting,* OEG : *genitive,* ÆGᴙ.

strigdeð pres. 3 sg. of stregdan.

strīman⁴ *to resist, oppose,* Cp.

strīna (=īe) m. *acquirer,* v. OEG27¹.

strīnan=strīenan

strīnend (ēo;=īe) m. *acquirer,* ES39·352.

-strīpan (y) v. be-s.

stripligan '*perfringere*'? v. OEG46²¹.

strīð m. *strife, struggle, fight, contest, dispute, contention* : *opposition, antagonism,* HᴇxC328ᴅ. [*OS.*]

stroccian *to stroke,* NC323.

+strod n. *plunder, robbery,* BH : *confiscation,* WW.

strōd n. *marshy land* (*covered with bushes or trees?*) BC(Mdf); PST95/98,537.

stroden pp. of strūdan.

strōden, strogden pp. of stregdan.

±strogdnes f. *scattering, sprinkling,* DR.

strong=strang

strop '*struppus*,' (*oar-*)*thong, strap,* WW 181⁴². ['*strop*']

strosle (GD100¹⁹)=ðrosle

-strowennes v. ā-s.

+strud (GD162³²)=+strod

±strūdan² *to ravage, spoil, plunder, carry off.*

strūdend m. *robber* : *money-lender,* WW.

strūdere m. *robber,* GL,VH.

strūdgendlīce *greedily,* CʜʀD108¹⁸.

±strūdian *to plunder,* NC296,324.

strūdung f. *spoliation, robbery,* LL,W.

strugde (NG) wk. pret. 3 sg. of stregdan.

strūta (WW)=strȳta

strūtian *to stand out stiffly, struggle,* ÆL 32²⁰⁸. ['*strut*']

strūtnian (ÆL23²⁶⁸)=scrūtnian

+strȳdan *to rob, deprive,* LL.

+strȳdd=+strēdd pp. of stregdan.

strȳdere=strȳndere

strȳn-=strīen-, strīn-

strȳnd (=īe) f. *generation, line of inheritance, race, stock, tribe,* BH,DR,LG : *gain,* WW488³⁰. ['*strind*']

strȳndan *to waste,* WW.

strȳndere m. *squanderer, prodigal,* WW.

+strynge m. *wrestler,* WW465⁴⁰.

strȳta (ū) m. *ostrich,* WW48⁸⁷. [*L.* struthio]

stubb=stybb

stūc *heap,* ES11·512.

studdian *to look after, be careful for,* RWH 136¹⁷.

studding f. *care, trouble, labour,* MFB107 and n.

studu f., gs. stude, ds. styde (also indecl. in sg.), nap. styde *column, pillar, post, buttress,* BH,WW. ['*stud*']

stufbǣð=stofbæð

stulor *stealthy, stolen, Æ.* adv. -līce, *Æ.*

+stun n. *din, crash, whirlwind,* Cʀ,WW.

stuncen pp., stuncon pret. pl. of stincan.

stund f. *short space of time, moment, period, time, An,Met* : *hard time, Rd* : *hour* : *signal.* stunde *now, at once, from time to time* (v. also stundum). ['*stound*']

+stund n. *noise,* Gᴜᴛʜ36²⁸ (=+stun).

-stundian v. ā-s.

stundmǣlum adv. *from time to time, gradually, Æ* : *time after time, alternately,* Æ,ZDA. ['*stoundmeal*']

stundum adv. *from time to time, at times, Æ* : *with effort, laboriously, eagerly, fiercely, Æ.* [dp. of stund]

stungen pp., stungon pret. pl. of stingan.

stunian *to crash, resound, roar* : *impinge, dash.*

stunra (KGL69³¹)=stuntra gp. of stunt.
stunt *dull, stupid, foolish*, Æ.
stuntlic *stupid, foolish*, Æ. adv. -líce, Æ.
stuntnes f. *stupidity, folly*, Æ.
stuntscipe m. *foolishness*, Mk7²².
stuntspræc f. *silly talk* (BT).
stuntspræce *talking foolishly*, Sc97¹⁰.
stuntwyrde *talking foolishly*, W72¹⁷.
stūpian *to 'stoop,' AO : slope*, Lcd.
sturtende (DR57¹²)=styrtende
stūt m. *gnat*, WW. ['*stout*']
stuðansceaft m. *prop*, AS1¹·¹⁰.
stuðu=studu
stybb m. *stump*, ÆGr,KC,WW; Mdf.
['*stub*']
stycce (i) n. *piece, portion, bit, fragment*, Æ :
mite (small piece of money). ymbe st. *after
a short time.* [Ger. stück]
styccemǣlum adv. *piecemeal, little by little,
by degrees, gradually : to bits, to pieces*,
AO : *here and there*, AO.
stycian=stician
styde I.=stede. II. v. studu.
styfician (i¹) *to root up, extirpate*, Lcd3·184'.
styficléah *a clearing in a wood*, BC 3·694¹⁰
(v. PST95/98·541).
styficung (e²) f. *clearing (land)?* Ct.
styhtan=stihtan
stȳlan (=íe) *to harden, attemper*, Cr679.
['*steeled*']
stȳle (ē) n. '*steel*,' B,Gl.
stȳlecg *steel-edged*, B1533.
stȳlen† *of steel, hard as steel*, Sol; VH.
['*steelen*']
styll=stiell
styllan (1)=stiellan; (2)=stillan
±styltan *to be amazed, dazed, hesitate*, NG.
stylð pres. 3 sg. of stelan.
stȳman=stíeman; styng=sting
stynt=stent pres. 3 sg. of standan.
styntan *to make dull, stupefy*, Cp89н. [stunt]
+stynðo *coercion*, NC296.
stȳpel=stípel
stȳr=stéor; styra=styria
stȳran=(1) stíeran; (2) stéran
styrc=stirc; stȳrend=stéorend
styrenes f. *power of motion, movement : disturbance, tumult :* (+) *tribulation*, DR.
styrfig adj. *belonging to an animal which
died of disease*, LL. [storfe]
styrfð pres. 3 sg. of steorfan.
styrgan=styrian
styria, styr(i)ga (i) m. *name of a fish,
sturgeon*, GL. [Ger. stör]
±styrian (i) *to 'STIR,' move* (tr. and intr.),
rouse, agitate, excite, urge, CP : *cause : tell,
rehearse*, B873.
styric=stirc
styrigendlic *moving*, Æ : *mobile*, GD149³¹.

styring=styrung
styrman *to storm, roar, rage, cry out, shout*,
B,BH,Bo. ['*sturme*']
styrne (=íe) '*stern,' grave, strict, hard,
severe, cruel*, Gen,Gl,W.
styrnenga adv. *inexorably*, Sol282.
styrnlic (íe) *hard, severe, harsh.* adv. -líce,
CP.
styrnmód *stern of mood*, Jud227.
styrtan *to 'start,' leap up.* only in pres. ptc.
sturtende (=styrtende), DR57¹².
styrung (e) f. *moving, motion*, Bf,Bo,G; CP :
disturbance, commotion, G : *exercise.*
['*stirring*']
stȳðe ds. and nap. of stuðu (studu).
sū f. *sow.* [=sugu]
suā=swā
subdiacon m. *subdeacon*, Æ,BH.
sūcan² *to 'suck,'* Æ,Lk,PPs,VHy.
sucga=sugga; sucht-, suct-=suht-
sudon pret. pl. of sēoðan.
sue-=swe-
sufel, suf(o)l n. *relish eaten with bread* (v.
LL2·754), Jn,RB. ['*sowl*']
+sufel, sufl adj. *with a relish added to it?*
(of bread), Ct,LL.
suflmete m. *delicacy, relish*, GD201²⁶.
sufon (Bf48⁹)=seofon
sūftlēre=swiftlēre
sūgan² *to suck, suck in*, CP : *have hiccough?*
Lcd.
sugga m. *a kind of bird, titlark? wagtail?* Gl.
±sugian *to be or become silent*, AO. [cp.
swīgian]
sugu f. '*sow*,' Cp,CP; Æ.
suht (y) f. *illness*, Gen472.
suhterga† m. *brother's son, nephew : uncle's
son, cousin*, WW.
suhtergefæderan, suhtorfædran† mp. *uncle
and nephew.*
suhtriga=suhterga
suindr- (NG)=syndr-
sūl (Æ), sulh (AO) sfm., gs. sūle(s), ds. sylg
(CP), syl(h), as. sūl, sulh; nap. sylh, syll
(Æ), gp. sūla, dp. sūlum *plough*, Lcd,LG :
furrow, gully : a measure of land (Mdf).
['*sullow*']
sūlerēost *rest (part of a plough)*, WW219⁶.
sulf=sufl
sulfer, sulfern (DR)=seolfor, seolfren
sulhæcer m. *a strip of land for ploughing*,
LL450,9¹.
sulhælmesse f. *ecclesiastical tax on ploughed
land*, LL.
sulhandla m. *plough tail*, WW. [v. '*sullow*']
sulhbēam m. *plough tail*, WW. [v. '*beam*']
sulhgang m. *the land which can be gone over
by one plough in a day*, W170³⁷.
sulhgesídu np. *ploughing tackle*, LL455¹⁷.

sulhgetēog n. *ploughing implements*, LCD 1·400¹⁹. [cp. *Ger.* zeug]
sulhgeweorc n. *plough-making*, GEN 1086.
sulhhæbbere m. *ploughman*, WW 495¹⁹.
sūlincel n. *small furrow*, WW 348³³.
sull, suluh=sūl
sulung n. *in Kent, the fiscal unit correspond-ing to the hide (or carucate in other counties)* (NED) *Ct,LL.* ['*suling*']
sum indef. pron. (used substantively w. g.) *a certain one, some one, something, one.* sixa s. *one of six* : (used adjectivally) *a certain,* 'SOME,' *any, Æ,AO.* sume...sume *some...others.* hit...sum...sum...*part of it...the rest...* : (used adverbially) *about.* s. hund *about a hundred.* sumes, s. on dæle *to some extent, somewhat.*
sumar, sumer=sumor
sumdǽl *somewhat, some portion. Cp.* ['*somedeal*']
sūmnes f. *delay*, MtL 25¹⁹. [cp. *Ger.* ver-sāumnis]
sumor m., gs. sumeres, ds. sumera, sumere '*summer*,' *Bo,Chr,Gn,Ph,VPs*; AO.
sumorbōc=sumorrædingbōc
sumorhāt n. *summer heat*, RIM 67.
sumorhǣte f. *summer heat*, AO,RB.
sumorhūs n. *summer-house*, ÆL 36⁹⁸.
sumorlǣcan *to draw on towards summer*, ÆH 1·614.
sumorlang† *summer-long, of the length of a summer's day.*
sumorlic *of summer*, Lcd,WW. ['*sum-merly*']
sumorlida I. m. *summer army or expedition (one which only comes for the summer)*, CHR 871. [liðan] II. (=-loda) m. *shoot, twig*, WW 450³⁰ (v. A 13·330).
sumormæsse f. *midsummer* (Swt).
sumorrǣdingbōc (e²) f. *summer lectionary*, TC 430¹⁶.
sumorselde f. *summer-house*, WW 184¹.
sumsende *swishing (of rain)*, RD 4⁴⁷.
sumswēge=samswēge
sumur=sumor
sunbēam mf. '*sunbeam*,' *Æ* : *sunshine.*
sunbearu m. *sunny grove*, PH 33.
sunbeorht *bright with sunshine*, PH 436.
sunbryne m. *sunburn*, LCD.
suncen pp., suncon pret. pl. of sincan.
sund n. *swimming, Æ,B,AO* : *capacity for swimming* : (†) *sea, ocean, water.* ['*sound*']
+sund *sound* ('*i-sound*'), *safe, whole, un-injured, healthy, prosperous, Æ,B.*
sundampre (o²) *dock (plant)*, LCD 44a.
sund-būende†, -buend mp. *sea-dwellers, man, mankind.*
sundcorn n. *saxifrage*, LCD,WW.
sundēaw *rosemary? sundew?* WW 301⁷.

+sundelic (WW 496²⁴)=+syndiglic
sunder=sundor
sunderanweald m. *monarchy*, ES 11·66.
sunderboren *reckoned apart*, OEG 26¹⁷.
sunderfolgoð m. *official teachership*, AO 286⁵.
sunder-frēodōm, -frēols m. *privilege*, Ct.
sunderlīpes *separately, specially, OEG,RBL.* ['*sunderlepes*']
sundermǣlum *separately, singly*, OEG.
sundermēd f. *private meadow*, Ct.
sunderstōw f. *special place*, Bo 80².
+sundful *sound, whole, healthy* : *pros-perous, Æ,Ps.* ['*i-sundfull*']
+sundfullian *to prosper*, Ps.
+sundfullic *sound, safe, sure.* adv. -līce *safely, prosperously, Æ.*
±sundfulnes f. *health, prosperity, Æ,Bo,CP* : *safety*, ByH 126⁸.
sundgebland n. *commingled sea, surge*, B 1450.
sundgyrd (e²) f. *sounding-rod*, WW.
sundhelm† m. *covering of water, sea*, RD.
sundhengest† m. *sea-horse, ship*, CR.
sundhwæt *good at swimming*, WHALE 57.
+sundig (y) *favourable*, BH 386¹³Ca.
+sund(ig)lic (y) *prosperous*, BH : *safe*, GD 348¹⁰ : *healthy.* adv. -līce.
sundlīne f. *sounding-line, lead*, WW.
sundmere m. *swimming-bath*, WW.
sundnytt f. *use of the power of swimming*, B 2360.
sundor adv. *asunder, apart* : *severally* : *differently.*
sundor- v. also sunder-, synder-.
sundorcræft m. *special power or capacity.*
sundorcræftiglīce *with special skill*, BHca 324³.
sundorcȳððu f. *special knowledge* LL (322³²).
sundorfeoh n. *private property*, Ct.
sundorgecynd n. *special quality*, PA 30.
sundorgenga m. *solitary (animal)*, BL 199⁵.
sundorgerēfland n. *land reserved to the juris-diction of a* 'gerēfa'? WW 421¹¹.
sundorgifu f. *special gift, privilege*, Bo,GL.
sundorhālga m. *Pharisee*, Æ.
sundorland n. *private property*, GD,WW.
sundorlic *special*, *Bo* ; CP 409¹⁰. adv. -līce *apart, Æ,Bo,LG.* ['*sunderly*']
sundorlīf n. *life in seclusion*, BH 294⁴.
sundormæsse f. *separate mass, special mass*, BK 27'; RSL 11·486.
sundornotu f. *special office*, LL 456,2.
sundornytt f. *special use, office, or service*, CP.
sundorriht n. *special right, privilege*, WW.
sundorseld (u²) n. *special seat, throne*, VPs.
sundorsetl n. *hermitage*, GUTH.

sundorspræc f. *private conversation, private conference*, Æ,AO,CP.

sundor-weorðung, -weorðmynt f. *special honour, prerogative*.

sundorwīc n. *separate dwelling*, BH 262[14].

sundorwine m. *bosom friend*, FT 29.

sundorwīs *specially wise*, EL 588.

sundorwundor n. *special wonder*, MOD 2.

sundoryrfe n. *private inheritance*, PPs 67[10].

sundplega† m. *sporting in the waves, bathing*.

sundrāp m. *sounding line, lead*, WW 358[17].

sundreced n. *sea-house, ark*, GEN 1335.

+sundrian=+syndrian. ['*sunder*']

sundrum (on) adv. *singly, separately, apart: continuously*, CM 211.

sundur=sundor

sundwudu† m. (*sea-wood*), *ship*.

suner (MtR)=sunor

sunfeld m. *Elysian fields*, SOL (K), WW.

sunfolgend '*solisequia*,' *marigold? heliotrope?* GL.

sunganges adv. *moving with the sun*, LL.

sungen pp. of (1) singan; (2) swingan.

sungīhte *solstice*, MH 104[19],[21].

sungon pret. pl. of singan.

sunhāt '*soliflua*,' OEG 56[205].

sunlic *solar, of the sun*, Æ.

sunna m. '*SUN*,' Æ.

Sunnadæg (N)=sunnandæg

Sunnanæfen m. *eve of Sunday, Saturday*. [*Ger.* Sonnabend]

sunnancorn *gromel* (*plant*), LCD 1·314[18]?

Sunnandæg m. '*Sunday**,' *Bl,G,LL*; Æ.

sunnanlēoma m. *ray of light, sunbeam*, GD 171,172.

Sunnanmergen m. *Sunday morning*, ÆL 31[1371].

Sunnanniht f. *Saturday night*, Æ : *Sunday*, LL 52,5[5].

sunnanscīma m. *sunshine*, MFH 173.

sunnansetlgong m. *sunset*, CHR 773.

Sunnanūhta m. *Sunday morning (early), early service time*, Æ,LL.

sunnb-=sunb-

sunne f. '*SUN*,' Æ,AO,CP.

sunnebēam=sunbēam

sunnelēoma (RWH 147[11])=sunnanlēoma

sunnon pret. pl. of sinnan.

sunnu=sunne

sunor (e[2]) fn. *herd of swine*, NG.

sunsceadu f. *veil*, WW 239[19].

sunscīene *radiant*, JUL 229.

sunscīn *mirror*, WW 519[4].

sunset n. *west*, NG.

sunstede m. *solstice*, BF,LCD.

sunsunu? m. *grandson*, v. LL 460,11n.

sunu m., gds. suna '*SON*,' *descendant*, Æ : *the Son* : *young of animals*.

sunucennicge f. *mother*, DR.

sunusunu=sunsunu

sunwlitig *fair with sunshine*, GNC 7.

±sūpan[2] *to swallow, sip, taste*, '*sup*,' *drink*, Æ,CP,Lcd,LG,Ps : (+) *sop up, absorb*.

sūr '*sour*,' *tart, acid*, BC,Lcd : *made sour, fermented*, Lcd,WW.

sūre f. *sorrel*, LCD,GL.

sūr-ēagede, -ēg(ed)e, -īge *blear-eyed*, Æ.

-sūrian v. ā-s.

sūr-milsc, -melsc, -melst adj. *half sour and half sweet* (*apple*).

sūrnes f. '*sourness*,' WW 347[35].

sūsel=sūsl

sūsl nf. *misery, torment, torture*, Æ,AO.

sūslbona m. *devil*, SAT 640.

sūslcwalu (-sel-) f. *painful death*, W.

sūslhof n. *place of torment*, †Hy 10[31].

sūslstede (sel-) m. *place of torment, hell*, OEG 56[184].

suster=sweostor; sutel=sweotol

sūtere m. *shoemaker*, Æ. ['*souter*'; *L.*]

-sūtian v. be-s.; sutol, sutul=sweotol

sūð* I. adj. comp. sūð(er)ra, sȳðer(r)a, superl. sūðmest '*SOUTH*,' *southern*, AO. II. adv. comp. sūðor, sȳð *southwards, south*, AO,CP.

sūðan adv. *from the south*, CP : *on or in the south*, AO. be s. (w. d.), wið s. (w. a.) *south of*.

sūðanēastan adv. *in or from the south-east: to the south-east*, AO.

sūðanēastanwind m. *south-east wind*, WW 144.

sūðanēasterne *south-eastern*, LPs.

Sūðanhymbre mp. *Mercians*, CHR.

sūðanweard=sūðeweard

sūðanwestan adv. *from the south-west*, WW.

sūðanwestan-wind, -winda m. *a south-west wind*.

sūðanwesterne *south-western*, Bo 10[13].

sūðanwind m. *south wind*, WW.

sūðdǽl m. *southern region, the south*, Æ, VPs; AO. ['*southdeal*']

sūðduru f. *south door*, BL 201[15].

sūðēast adv. '*south-east*,' AO,Chr.

sūðēastende m. *south-east end*, Bo 67[31].

sūðēasterne *south-eastern*, ÆGr 8[2].

sūðecg f. *southern edge*, KC.

sūðende m. *south end*, KC 5·86'.

Sūðengle pl. *South Anglians, people of southern England*, LL.

sūðerige '*satirion*' (*plant*), WW 137[1]. [*L.* satureia?]

sūðerne '*southern*,' *southerly*, Æ,Bo,Lcd, MtL.

sūðernewudu m. '*southernwood*,' *wormwood*, Lcd.

sūðerra v. sūð.

sūðeweard adj. *southward, south, southern*, AO.

sūðfolc n. *southern nation or people, Suffolk*, CHR,LCD.

sūðfōr f. *journey south, pilgrimage to Rome*, BC 1·446.

sūðgārsecg m. *southern ocean*, AO.

sūðgemǣre n. *southern border*, AO.

sūðheald† *inclining southwards*.

sūðhealf f. *south side*, *AO*; Æ. [' *southhalf*']

Sūðhymbre mpl. *Mercians*, CHR.

sūðland n. *southern land or shore*, Æ,Chr. [' *southland*']

sūðmǣgð f. *southern province*, BH.

sūðmann† m. *man from the south*, GEN.

sūðmest ' *southmost*,' *AO*.

Sūðmyrce (e) pl. *southern Mercians*, BH 238³⁴.

sūðor v. sūð.

sūðportic m. *south porch*, CHR 1036.

sūðra v. sūð.

sūðrihte (y) adv. *due south*, AO.

sūðrima m. *south coast*, CHR.

sūðrodor (a²) m. *southern sky*, PH.

Sūðsǣ mf. *south sea, English Channel*, Æ.

Sūð-seaxan, -seaxe pl. *South-Saxons, people of Sussex* : *Sussex*, CHR.

sūðstæð n. *south coast*, CHR 897A.

sūðwāg m. *south wall*, Æ,BL.

sūðweard adv. *towards the south, southwards*, AO,Lcd. [' *southward*']

sūðweardes adv. ' *southwards*,' *Met*.

sūðweg m. *southern country*, Ex 155.

sūðwest I. m. *the south-west*, Chr. II. adv. ' *south-west*,' *AO*.

sūðwesterne ' *south-western*,' *ApT*.

sūðwind m. *south wind*, Ex 289.

suwian (LWS)=sugian

swā (ǣ, ē) I. adv. and conj. (w. ind. or subj.) *so as, consequently, just as, so far as, in such wise, in this or that way, thus, so that, provided that*, Æ. swā swā *so as, just as, so that.* swā same (swā) *in like manner : therefore, on that account* : *as, like* : (w. comparatives) *the.* swā...swā *the...the* : *where* : *when, so soon, as soon* : *although, unless, yet* : *if; as if.* II. pron. ' *so*,*' *the same, such, that.* swā hwā swā *whosoever.* swā hwǣr swā *wherever.* bi swā hwaðerre efes swā *on whichever side.* swā ilce= swilce. swā selfe *in the same way.* ēac swā *also.* swā hwilc swā *whosoever.* swā...ne *though...not.* swā...swā *whether...or; either* ...*or.* swā ðēah *nevertheless, yet, however.*

swāc pret. 3 sg. of swīcan.

swǣ=swā

swæc (CP), swæcc (e) m. *flavour, taste* : *smell, odour, fragrance.*

+swæccan (e) *to smell* (tr.), DD 206; (intr.) ARPs 113¹⁴; ÆGR 221 т⁹.

swæcehēow ' *insania*'? RPs 39⁵ (v. ES 38·22).

swæf pret. 3 sg. of swefan.

swǣfan? *to burn*, MET 8⁴⁷.

swæfen=swefn; swæflen=sweflen

swǣg=swēg; swǣgl=swegl

±swǣlan (tr.) *to burn*, Cr,LPs. [' *sweal*']

swǣlc=swilc

swǣm m. *trifler, idler*, BF : *vain object*, CHRD.

-swǣman v. ā-s.; swǣncan=swencan

swǣp *enticement, persuasion, deceit* (v. OEG 2894n).

+swǣpa (ā, ē) pl. *sweepings, rubbish*, GL. [swāpan]

swǣpels (VPs) m? swǣpelse f. *robe, garment.*

swǣpig *fraudulent*, OEG 2894.

swǣr I. (ā, ē) *heavy, sad, Ps* : *oppressive, grievous, Cr,Gen* : *sluggish, inactive, weak, Cp,LG.* II. n. *sadness, trouble*, MFH 173. [' *sweer*']

swǣrbyrd? f. *difficult birth?* LCD 185a.

swǣre† (ā) *grievously, oppressively.*

+swǣre=swǣr

+swǣred *oppressed, weighed down*, LCD 3·120'.

swǣrlic (ā) *grievous, heavy*, Æ. adv. -līce, Æ.

swǣrmōd *indolent, sluggish*, W 257.

swǣrmōdnes (ā) f. *dulness, stupidity*, CP 149¹⁵.

swǣrnes (ā) f. *heaviness*, Æ : *sluggishness*, Bo. [' *sweerness*']

swǣrt (WW 257³)=sweart

±swǣs (ē) *intimate, special, favourite, dear, beloved* : *own* : *agreeable, gentle, benevolent* : *sweet, sugary.*

+swǣse *blandly, pleasantly*, WW 196¹².

swǣsenddagas mpl. *ides* (*in Roman calendar*), WW.

swǣsende (ē) n. (mostly used in pl. swǣsendu) *food, meal, dinner, banquet, dainties* : *blandishments*, WW 61²⁶.

swǣsing-=swǣsend-

±swǣslǣcan (ē¹) *to wheedle*, WW 61,196.

swǣslic *kind, friendly, agreeable, pleasant.* adv. -līce *kindly* : *properly* : *plausibly.*

±swǣsnes f. *wheedling*, Æ : *pleasure.*

+swǣsscipe m. *companionship*, NC 296.

swǣsung f. *lenitive, soothing application*, WW 241²⁴.

swǣswyrde *fair spoken*, WW 190³⁵.

±swǣtan *to sweat, exude*, Æ,AO,BH,Lcd, Nar : *labour, toil, CP* : *bleed*, CROSS 20 : *weld*, A 22·395 : (+) *oppress*, CPs 93⁵. [swāt]

swǣð (e) n., nap. swaðu *footprint, track*, CP : *trace, vestige*, CP. [cp. swaðu f.]

swæðel=sweðel
swæðelyne '*pinguis*,' OEG 27³².
swæðer pron. *whichever, whosoever*, CP. [swā, hwæðer]
+swæðlan *to trace out, investigate*, EPs 138³.
swæðlæcan *to search out, visit*, CHy 9⁶⁸.
swæðorian=swaðrian, sweðrian
swæðu=swaðu
swāf pret. 3 sg. of swīfan.
swāhwætswā pron. *whatsoever*.
swāhwæðer pron. *whichever*, LL.
swal(e)we=swealwe; swālīc=swilc
swaloð=sweoloð
swāmian *to become dark*, Gu 1069.
swamm (o) I. m. *fungus, mushroom*, Æ : *sponge*. [Ger. schwamm] II. pret. 3 sg. of swimman.
swan (o) m. '*swan*,' Ep,Ph,WW.
swān m. *herdsman, swineherd, peasant*, Chr, Ep : (†) *swain, youth, man, warrior*. ['*swon*']
swanc pret. 3 sg. of swincan.
swancor† *slender, trim, lithe, supple* : *languishing, weak*, PPs 118⁸¹.
swang pret. 3 sg. of swingan.
swāngerēfa m. *swineherd, reeve, officer set over the depasturing of swine in forests*, Ct.
swangettung f. *movement, agitation*, NC 324.
swangor (o) *heavy, inert*, BH,W.
swangornes (o) f. *sloth, laziness*, CP.
swanrād f. *swan's-road, sea*, B 200.
swānriht n. *law as to swineherds*, LL 449,6¹.
swānsteorra m. *evening star*, Cp 145 U.
+swāpa=+swǣpa
±swāpan⁷ *to sweep, drive, swing, rush (of wind)*, ÆGr,Bo,Ex,LPs : *sweep up, take possession of*, AO. ['*swope*']
swār=swǣr
swarc-=swearc-
-swarian (e, eo, o) v. and-s.
swarn-=sworn-; swart=sweart
swās=swǣs
swāt I. (ō) m? n? (+ at LCD 3·98¹⁷) '*sweat*,' *perspiration, exudation*, Æ,CP,Lk : (†) *blood : foam*, LkR 9³⁹ : *toil : labour*, Bl; Æ. ['*swote*'] II. (+) *sweaty, sweating*, LCD.
swatan (ā?) pl. *beer*, WW.
swātclāð m. '*sudarium*,' *napkin*, ÆP 178².
swātfāh† *blood-stained, bloody*.
swātig *sweaty*, AO : (†) *gory*. ['*swoty*']
swātighlēor *with sweaty brow*, GEN 934 (or ? two words).
swātlīn n. *napkin*, CP.
swātswaðu f. *gory track*, B 2946.
swātðyrel n. *pore of the skin*, WW 159¹³.
swāðēah adv. *however, yet, nevertheless*.
swāðēahhwæðre adv. *however*, Æ.
swaðer=swæðer

swaðian *to swathe, wrap up*, RWH 137¹³.
swaðorian, swaðrian=sweðrian
swaðu (æ, e) f. *footstep, track, pathway*, B Bo,MH : *trace, vestige*, BH : *scar*, Sh₁ ['*swath*'; cp. swæð]
swaðul m? *flame*, B 782.
swaðum (in) dp. *bandages*, WW 484¹ ['*swathe*']
swē=swā; swealewe=swealwe
swealg, swealh pret. 3 sg. of swelgan.
swealt pret. 3 sg. of sweltan.
swealwe (a, o) f. '*swallow*,' Ep,Gu,Lcd.
swearc pret. 3 sg. of sweorcan.
swearcian *to become dark*, ÆH 2·258¹⁵.
swearcmōdnes (a) f. *pusillanimity*, LPs 54⁹.
swearcung (a) f. *darkness*, RPs 17²⁹.
sweard m. *hide, rind, skin*, Gl. ['*sward*']
+swearf (LCD)=+sweorf
swearm m. '*swarm*,' *multitude*, Gl.
sweart *swarthy, black, dark*, B,Lcd; Æ : *gloomy : evil, infamous*, Æ,Jul. ['*swart*']
sweartbyrd (æ¹) *a dismal birth*, LCD 3·66'.
swearte† adv. *miserably, evilly*.
swearthæwen *dark-blue, purple, violet*, WW 376²⁴.
±sweartian *to become black*, Æ,Lcd : *make black*. ['*swart*']
sweartlāst *with black tracks*, RD 27¹¹.
sweartnęs f. *blackness, black substance*, Gl. ['*swartness*']
sweartung f. *darkness*, EPs 17²⁹.
swearð (G)=sweard ['*swarth*']
±swebban *to put to sleep, lull*, G : (†) *kill*, Æ,B. ['*sweve*']
swec (KGL)=swæc
swefan⁵ *to sleep, slumber, rest*, B,Cp : (†) *sleep in death : cease*, Ex. ['*sweve*']
swefecere m. *sleeper*, CHRD 26².
swefecung f. *sleep*, CHRD 31⁴.
swefed pp. of swebban.
swefel (æ) m. *sulphur*, Æ. [Ger. schwefel]
swefelrēc m. *sulphurous smoke*, VPs 10⁷.
swefen=swefn
swefet=sweofot
swefeð pres. 3 sg. of swebban.
+swefian *to put to sleep, lull, appease*, Æ. ['*sweve*']
swefl=swefel
sweflen *sulphurous, of brimstone*, Æ,AO.
sweflennes (eo) f. *sulphurousness*, MFH 123³.
sweflenrēc (APs)=swefelrēc
sweflsweart *sulphurous?* WW 49²⁰.
sweflðrosm m. *sulphurous smoke*, ERSPs 10⁷.
swefn n. (often pl.) *sleep*, Gen; Æ,AO : *dream, vision*, CP,Da,LG. ['*sweven*']
swefnian (w. nom. pers.) *to dream*, Lcd : (+)(w. acc. pers.) *appear in a dream*. ['*sweven*']

swefnī(g)end m. *dreamer*, GEN 37¹⁹.
swefnracu f. *interpretation of dreams*, LL (154²⁹).
swefnreccere m. *interpreter of dreams*, WW 366¹².
swefot=sweofot
swēg (ǣ) m. *sound*, Æ,AO,CP : *noise, clamour, tumult* : *melody, harmony, tone*, Æ : *voice* : *musical instrument* : '*persona*,' Sc. [swōgan]
swēgan *to make a noise, sound, roar, crash*, Æ : *import, signify*, Æ. ['*swey*']
swēgcrǣft m. *musicians' art, music*, APT 16.
swēgdynn m. *noise, crash*, CR 955.
±swēge *sonorous, harmonious*, ÆL.
swegel=swegl
swēgendlīc adj. *vocal, vowel*, ÆGR 6¹⁵.
sweger f. *mother-in-law*, Æ. [*Ger.* schwieger]
swēgesweard m. *organist* (!) JGPh 1·64.
swēghlēoðor† m. *sound, melody*.
swēging f. *sound, clang, roar*, Lk,WW.
swegl† (ǣ) I. n. *sky, heavens, ether* : *the sun* : *music*? II.=segl
sweglbefalden *ether-begirt*, SAT 588.
sweglbeorht *ether-bright, radiant*, GU 1187.
sweglbōsm m. *heaven, sky*, GEN 9 (pl.).
sweglcondel f. *heaven's candle, sun*, PH 108.
sweglcyning† m. *King of heaven*.
swegldrēam† m. *music*.
swegle† I. adj. *bright, ether-like, clear, brilliant, splendid*. II. adv. *clearly, brightly*.
sweglhorn m. *kind of musical instrument*, GL. [cp. *Goth.* swiglōn]
swēglīc *sonorous*, CM 675.
sweglrād f. *modulation, music*, RIM 29.
swegltorht† *heavenly-bright*.
sweglwered (gel-) *ether-clad*, B 606.
sweglwuldor n. *heavenly glory*, GU 1160.
sweglwundor n. *heavenly wonder*, GU 1292.
swegr=sweger
+swegra=+swigra
+swēgsumlīce? *unanimously*, HL 18¹⁶².
swehor (GL)=swēor
sweig (KGL 88⁴)=swēg
swelgð=swēgeð pres. 3 sg. of swēgan.
+swel=+swell
swelan⁴ *to burn, be burnt up* : *inflame* (*of wound*).
swelc (*Bo,LG,OET*; AO,CP)=swilc. [v. '*such*']
swelca m. *pustule*, WW 112¹⁷.
swelce=swilce
+swelg n. *abyss, whirlpool*, GL. ['*swallow*']
±swelgan³ *to* '*swallow*,' *incorporate, absorb, imbibe, devour*, Lcd,LL.
swelgend (y) fmn. (±) *whirlpool, vortex, gulf, abyss*, CP : *glutton, drunkard, debauchee*, AO.

swelgendnes f. *whirlpool*, WW 373².
swelgere m. *glutton*, WW 102¹⁵. ['*swallower*']
swelgnes f. *whirlpool*, WW 510¹⁸.
swelhð=swelgð pres. 3 sg. of swelgan.
sweliend=swelgend
+swell n. *swelling, tumour, boil*, Æ,Lcd.
±swellan³ *to* '*swell*,' B,Lcd.
swellende *burning*, OEG 377⁸.
swelling f. *swelling*, EL 245.
±sweltan³ (i, y) *to die, perish*, Æ,B,Bo; AO, CP. ['*swelt*']
sweltendlīc *about to die*, Lk,Sc.
-swemman v. be-s.
±swenc m. *trouble, tribulation, toil* : (+) *temptation*, LkL,Nar. ['*swench*']
±swencan (ǣ) *to vex, distress, trouble, afflict, torment, oppress*, B,Bl,Bo,G; Æ,CP. [causative of swincan; '*swenche*']
+swenc-ednes, -ennes, -nes (AA) f. *trouble, affliction, toil*, Æ.
sweng m. *stroke, blow, cut, thrust*, B,El. ['*sweng*']
swengan *to shake, shatter*, Gl : *swing, rush, fly out*, HL. ['*swenge*'; causative of swingan]
sweocol (CP)=swicol; sweofl-=swefl-
sweofot (e) n. *sleep*, B. ['*swevet*']
sweogian=swigian; sweolce=swilce
Swēoland n. *Sweden*, AO 19².
sweoloð (a, o) m. *burning heat, glow, fire, flame*. [swelan]
sweoloðhāt (o¹) *burning hot*, OEG 56²⁰².
sweolung? f. *inflammation*, Lcd 76b (sweop-).
Swēon pl. *Swedes*, AO,B,CHR.
swēop pret. 3 sg. of swāpan.
sweop-=swip-
sweopung v. sweolung.
swēor I. (ē, ȳ) mf. *pillar, column, prop*, CP : *bolt, bar*, ES 37·183. II. m. *father-in-law*, Æ,AO,CP : (±) *cousin*. [*Ger.* schwäher] III.=swōr pret. of swerian.
swēora (ī, īo, ū, ȳ) m. *neck, nape*, Bo,Bl,G; AO,CP. ['*swire*']
swēorbān n. *neck-bone, neck*, VHy. ['*swirebone*']
swēorbēag (u) m. *neck-band, necklace, collar, torque*, Æ.
+sweorc (o) n. *cloud, darkness, mist*, GEN, VPs.
±sweorcan³ *to grow dark, darken* (intr.), *become overcast, be obscured*, An : *be troubled, sad, become grievous, troublesome, angry*, B,Met; ÆL : *fall out* (*of mind*), JPs 30¹³. ['*swerk*']
sweorcendferhð *sombre, sad*, JUD 269.
+sweorcenes (o, cn) f. *gloom*, LL (400⁹).
swēorclāð m. *neckcloth*, WW 210³⁶.

swēorcops m. *yoke, pillory, Gl.* [v. '*cops*']
swēorcoðu f. *quinsy,* LCD.
sweord (o, u, y) n. '*sword*,' *Æ,B,Bl,Fin,G*;
AO,CP.
sweordbealo n. *sword-bale,* B1147.
sweordberende '*sword-bearing,' Gen* 1060.
sweordbīte m. *sword-wound,* JUL603.
sweordbora (u, y) m. *sword-bearer, swordsman, Æ.*
sweordfǣtels m. *sword-belt,* ÆL23¹⁷⁸.
sweordfreca m. *swordsman, warrior,* B1468.
sweordgenīðla m. *sworded foe,* EL1181.
sweordgeswing (y¹) n. *sword-brandishing,*
JUD240.
sweordgifu (y¹) f. *gift of swords,* B2884.
sweordgripe m. *sword-attack,* JUL488.
sweordhwīta (u, y) m. *sword-furbisher,* LL.
sweordlēoma (u¹) m. *flashing of swords,*
FIN35.
+sweordod (u) *provided with a sword, ÆGr,
NC.* ['*sworded*']
sweordplega m. *fighting, Wal*22. ['*sword-
play*']
sweordrǣs m. *attack,* AP59.
sweordslege m. *sword-thrust,* JUL671.
sweordtige m. *sword-drawing,* LPs9⁷.
sweordwegende (u¹) *sword-bearing,* LCD
3·204'.
sweordwīgend m. *warrior,* Ex260.
sweordwund *wounded with the sword,* WAL7.
sweordwyrhta (u¹) m. *sword-maker?* LCD
3·194¹⁰.
+sweorf (ea, y) n. *filings,* LCD.
±sweorfan³ *to file or grind away, polish,
wipe, rub, scour.*
swēorhnitu f. *nit which lives on the neck of
animals, tick,* WW.
Swēorīce n. *Sweden,* B.
swēorracentēh (ū¹) f. *neck-chain,* WW107³⁴.
swēorrōd (ū¹) f. *cross worn on the neck, EC*
250¹¹. [v. '*rood*']
swēorscacul m. *yoke, pillory,* WW116⁹.
swēortēag (ē) f. *collar,* GL.
+swēoru (ī, ȳ) np. *hills,* PPs.
swēorwærc m. *pain in the neck,* LCD.
sweostor (e, i, u, y) f. indecl. in sg., nap.
sweoster, sweostra, sweostru 'SISTER,'
*Æ,*AO : *nun.*
+sweos-tor, -tra, -tru fp. *sisters,* AO.
+sweosternu bearn *children of sisters,
cousins.*
sweostorbearn n. *sister's child, nephew,
niece,* WW452².
sweostorsunu m. *sister's son, nephew, BH,
Chr.* [v. '*sister*']
swēot† n. *troop, army, company, body,
swarm.*
sweota? sweote? '*scrotum*,' LCD, v. A
30·134.

sweotel=sweotol
sweotol (i, u, y) *distinct, clear, evident,
manifest, open, public, B,Bl,CP,OEG*;
AO. ['*sutel*']
sweotole (e, o, u) adv. *clearly, precisely,
plainly, openly, visibly,* CP.
±sweotolian (e, u, y) *to show, reveal, make
manifest, Mt; Æ : become manifest, GK :
state, explain, prove.* ['*sutele*']
sweotollic (u¹, y¹) *clear, distinct.* adv. -līce
*clearly, precisely, plainly, visibly, openly,
Æ,BH.* ['*suteliche*']
±sweotolung (i, u, y) f. *manifestation,
Epiphany : definition, explanation, exposition, declaration, Æ : written testimony,
evidence.*
±sweotolungdæg (e, u) m. *Epiphany, Æ.*
sweotul=sweotol
Swēoðēod f. *Swedes, Sweden,* B,CHR.
sweoðerian=sweðrian
sweoðol I. m? *heat, flame,* B3145. [cp.
swaðul] II.=sweðel
swēowlan=swīgian; +swēpa=+swǣpa
swēr=(1) swǣr; (2) sweger; (3) swēor
±swerian⁶ (but occl. wk. pret. swerede) *to*
'SWEAR,' *Æ;* AO,CP : *swear in (to an
office) : speak?* SOL425. [*Ger.* schwören]
swerigendlic *jurative, used in swearing (of
certain adverbs),* ÆGR227.
swertling m. *titlark? warbler?* WW131¹⁵.
swēs=swǣs; swester (N)=sweostor
±swētan *to make sweet, sweeten, Jul,Lcd*;
*Æ,*GP.
swēte I. adj. 'SWEET,' *pure, fragrant,
pleasant, agreeable,* AO,CP : *beloved, dear :
fresh (not salt).* II. n. *sweetness, sweet.*
[swōt]
swetelian (KGL)=sweotolian
swētian *to be sweet,* CP425¹⁴.
+swētlǣcan *to batten,* RPs65¹⁵.
swētlīce *sweetly, pleasantly,* BH486⁴.
swētmete m. *sweetmeat, dainty,* CP41¹⁵.
swētnes f. *sweetness, fragrance, BH,CP :
pleasantness, BH : kindliness, goodness,
Ps : something sweet, Cp*524A.
swetole=sweotole
swētswēge *agreeable (of sound),* DHy58⁸.
swētwyrde *smooth-spoken,* WW : *stuttering,*
WW.
sweð=swæð
sweðel (æ, eo) m. *swaddling band, bandage,
binding, G,Gl.* ['*sweddle*']
sweðerian=sweðrian; -sweðian v. be-.
sweðolian *to relent, be appeased,* CHR1123.
±sweðrian (a, æ, eo, i) *to retire, vanish,
melt away, abate, dwindle, decrease, subside.*
+sweðrung (æ) f. *failure,* LCD.
sweðu=swaðu

sweðung f. *poultice*, CHRD,LCD.

swic n. *illusion*, CM441 : *deceit, treachery*, AO. ['*swike*']

+**swic** n. *offence*, MtR,WW : *snare*, OEG 127² : *cessation*.

swica m. *deceiver, traitor, betrayer*, Chr,G. ['*swike*']

±**swican**¹ (†) *to wander* : (†) *depart* : (w. g.) *cease from, yield, give way*, AO,CP : (w. d.) *fail, fall short, be wanting, abandon, desert, turn traitor*, AO : *deceive*, Æ. ūt s. *go forth.* from s. *fall off, rebel.* ['SWIKE,' 'I-SWIKE']

swicc m. (BH430⁴)=swæcc

swiccræft m. *treachery*, G,LL.

swicdōm m. *fraud, deception, deceit*, AO, Chr; Æ : *betrayal, treason : scandal, offence.* ['*swikedom*']

swice I. m. (†) *escape, end* : (†) *procrastination, delay*, GU1007 : *offence, snare, treachery, deceit*, AO. ['*swike*'] II. adj. *fallacious, deceitful*. III. f. *trap, snare*, GL. ['*swike*'] IV.=swicc

+**swicednes**=+swicennes

swicend m. *deceiver*, HL18³ᵇ,⁸⁷.

+**swicennes** f. *abstention, cessation*, Æ : *repentance*.

swicful *fraudulent, deceitful*, OEG. ['*swikeful*']

swician *to wander* : *be treacherous, deceive, cheat*, Æ : *blaspheme* : *cause to offend*.

+**swicing** f. *intermission, cessation*, CM 103.

±**swicn** f. *purgation, clearance, discharge*, LL.

+**swicnan** *to clear (of a charge)*, LL.

swicol *guileful, false, deceitful*, Æ,Lcd. ['*swikel*']

swicollic *fraudulent, deceiving, deceptive, causing to stumble.* adv. -lice.

swicolnes f. *deceit*, W. ['*swikelness*']

+**swicu** f. *cessation*, RB148¹²³n.

swicung f. *deceit, fraud, deception*, A,Lcd : *stumbling-block, offence.* ['*swiking*']

swifan¹ *to revolve, sweep, wend* : *intervene*, EC164. [*Ger.* schweifen]

+**swifornes**=+swipornes

swift (y) '*swift*,' *quick*, Æ,B,Bo,CP,GD; AO. adv. -lice, Æ,LPs,W. ['*swiftly*']

swiftlēre (u, y) m. *slipper*, Æ. [*L.* subtalaris]

swiftnes f. *swiftness, speed*, Bo,Ps.

swiftu f. *swiftness*, MET28³.

swigan=swigian

swigdagas mp. *days of silence (last three days of Holy Week)*, Æ. [v. '*swie*']

swige, swigge I. f. *silence, stillness, rest*, Æ, CP. II. adj. *still, quiet, silent, taciturn*, CP.

swigen f. *silence*, ÆH2·532⁴.

swigeniht f. *night of silence*, ÆP154³ (v. swigdagas).

±**swigian** (ȳ; ī, ēo, ū) *to be or become silent, keep silence, be quiet, still*, B,BH; CP. ['*swie*']

swigendlice adv. *silently*, HL18³¹¹.

swiglice *silently*, GENC24²¹.

swiglung f. *silence*, ANS84·3. (or ? swiglunga *silently*)

swigmæsse f. *silent mass*, NC324. ['*swimesse*']

swignes f. *time of silence*, WW211⁴².

+**swigra** (e) m. *sister's son, nephew, cousin.*

swigtima (swit-) m. *silent time, eventide, early part of the night*, BF122²².

swiguht m. *dawn of the days of silence (v. swigdagas)*, ANS84·7.

±**swigung** f. *silence* : *time of silence* : *delay*, NG.

swilc (æ, e, y) pron. (used substantively) *such a one, he, the same*, Æ : (used adjectivally) '*SUCH*,' CP : (as relative) *which*, Æ. swilc...hwilc *such...as*; *so...as.* swilc...swilc *so much (many)...as*; *as much (many)...as*, Æ. ['*swilk*,' v. '*such*']

swilce (e, eo, y) adv. and conj. (w. ind.) *just as, as, in like manner, in such manner, likewise, resembling, thus* : (w. subj.) *as if, as though* : *also, moreover, too*, Bo. ['*such*']

swilchwugu *some...or other*, ÆL23b⁷⁶⁶.

swilcnes f. '*qualitas*,' *nature*, Lcd,RB. ['*suchness*']

swile=swyle

swilian, swillan *to* '*swill*,' *wash, wash out, gargle*, Cp,Lcd,Ps.

swil(l)ing f. '*swilling*,' *wash, gargle*, Lcd.

swilt=swylt

swiltan=sweltan

swilð pres. 3 sg. of swellan.

swilunge=swiglunga

swima m. *vertigo, dizziness* : *swoon*, Cr,Jud, Lcd; Æ. ['*swime*']

swimæsse=swigmæsse

±**swimman**³ (y) *to* '*swim*,' *float*, AA,Æ,B, Lcd,Rd,Wa.

swimmendlic (y) *able to swim*, ÆGR55³.

swin (ȳ) n. *wild-boar, pig, hog*, pl. '*swine*,' Bo,Cp,G,Rd; CP; Mdf : *boar-image (on a helmet)*, B.

+**swin** n. *song, melody*, PH137.

±**swinc** n. *toil, work, effort*, Æ,Ps : *hardship*, Gen : *the produce of labour*, W229⁷. ['*swing*,' '*swink*,' '*i-swinch*']

±**swincan**³ *to labour, work at, strive, struggle*, Æ,B; CP : *be in trouble* : *languish.* ['*swink*']

+**swincdagas** mp. *days of tribulation*, SEAF 2.

+**swincednes** (EPs17¹⁹)=+swencednes

±**swincful** *toilsome, painful, disastrous*, Bo; Æ. ['*swinkful*']

+**swincfulnes** f. *tribulation*, LPs 33[7] : *trouble*, Sc 60[11].

±**swincléas** (y) *without toil*, ÆH 2·364[9]. ['*swinkless*']

swinclic *laborious*, W 294[18].

+**swincnes** f. *hardship*, *trial*, CHRD,GUTH.

swind=spind

swindan[3] *to vanish*, *consume*, *pine away*, *languish*, BH,Ps. ['*swind*']

swīnen adj. *pig's*, *swine's*, LCD,Ps.

+**swing**† I. n. *surge*, *fluctuation*. II.= +swinc

swingan[3] I. *to beat*, *strike*, *smack*, *whip*, *scourge*, *flog*, *chastise*, *afflict*, Æ,B,Bl,Cp; *Lcd*; AO,CP. '*swing*' *oneself*, *fly*, B 2264. sw. on twā *to divide by a blow*. II. (Æ,Ps)= swincan

swinge (y) f. *stroke*, *blow*, *stripe* : *chastisement*, CP.

swingell f. (often swingel-, swingl- in obl. cases); swingel(l)e f. *whip*, *scourge*, *rod*, Æ : *stroke*, *stripe*, *blow* : *affliction*, CP.

swingere m. *striker*, *scourger*, RD 28[7].

swinglung f. *dizziness*, *Lcd*,WW. ['*swingling*']

swīnhaga m. *pig-pen*, KC.

swīnhyrde (ī) m. '*swineherd*,' ZDA 33·239[21].

swīnin (GL)=swīnen

swīnlic *swinish*, WW 508[29]?

swīnlīc n. *boar-image* (*on a helmet*), B 1452.

swinn m. *melody*, OEG.

swīnnes f. *pork food*, EPs 16[14].

swīnsceadu *pannage*, TC 263[7] (v. BTs).

swinsian (y) *to sound melodiously*, *make melody*, *sing*.

swinsung f. *sound*, *melody*, *harmony*, BH, GL.

swinsungcræft m. *music*, WW 442[12].

swinsweg? *melody* (v. OEG xxxiii).

swipa m., swipe f.=swipu

swipian† (eo) *to whip*, *scourge*, *beat*.

±**swipor** *cunning*, BH,SOL.

+**swipor-e**, -līce *cunningly*, Ps.

+**swipornes** (e[2]) f. *wile*, *cunning*, HL,MkR.

swippan=swipian

swipu (eo, o) f. *whip*, *stick*, *scourge*, Gl,RG, Sol : *chastisement*, *affliction*. ['*swepe*']

swir-, swīr-=sweor-, sweor-

+**swirga**, +swiria=+swigra

swirman (=ie) *to swarm*, LCD 1·384'.

swister=sweostor

swital, switel, switol=sweotol

swītīma=swigtīma

swīð (ȳ) *strong*, *mighty*, *powerful*, *active* : *severe*, *violent*. comp. swiðre *right* (*hand*, *side*, *etc.*).

±**swīðan** [wv. and sv[1]? cp. unforswiðen] *to strengthen*, *establish*, *support* : *use force against*, Æ (v. A 36·66).

swīðe (ȳ) adv. *very much*, *exceedingly*, *severely*, *violently*, *fiercely*, B,Bl,Chr,G; AO,CP. comp. swīðor *more*, *rather*. superl. swīðost *most*, *especially*, *exceedingly* : *almost*, *nearly*. for swīðe, swīðe swīðe *very much*, *very severely*, CP. ['*swith*']

swīðfæstnes f. *violence*, LL (138 n4).

swīðfeorm *rich*, *fruitful* : *violent*, RD.

swīðfeormende *becoming violent*, WW 374[11].

swīðferhð† (y) *bold*, *brave*, *rash*.

=**swīðfrom** *very strong*, *vigorous*. adv. -līce.

swīðhrēownes f. *remorse*, MFH 173.

swīðhwæt *very active*, RUN 5.

swīðhycgende (i)† *bold-minded*, B.

swīðian *to become strong* : *prevail* : *fix*, WW.

swīðlæt *very lax*, LL (318').

swīðlic *intense*, *excessive*, *severe*, *violent*, Æ : *immense*, Æ : *effective*. adv. -līce, Bo,G. ['*swithly*']

swīðlicnes f. *excess*, RBL 73[7].

swīðmihtig *very mighty*, PPs 85[13].

swīðmōd† *stout-hearted*, *brave* : *insolent*, *arrogant*.

swīðmōdnes f. *magnanimity*, A 11·173, SOL 150[4].

swīðnes f. *excess*, *violence*, CM 458.

swīðor comp. of swīðe.

swīðra comp. of swīð, Lcd,LG. ['*swither*']

swīðrian=sweðrian

swīðrian *to avail*, *become strong*, *prevail*, Æ.

swīðsnel *very quick*, *agile*, CRA 82.

swīðspecende (ȳ) *talkative*, OEG 56[140].

swīðsprecel *talkative*, LPs 11[4].

swīðstincende *strong-smelling*, WW 408[18].

swīðstrang *very strong*, BH 38[6]B.

swīðstrēme *having a strong current*, *rapid*, BH 38[6].

swīðswēge *strong-sounding*, *heroic*, OEG.

swīður=swīðor comp. of swīðe.

swiung f. *spasm*, *cramp*, WW 112[19].

swīung=swīgung

swodrian *to be fast asleep*, SPs 3[5]. ['*swother*']

swoeg=swēg; **swoesendu**=swæsendu

swoetnes (GL,VPs)=swētnes

swōg (VPs)=swēg

swōgan[7] *to sound*, *roar*, *howl*, *rustle*, *whistle*, *rattle*, Cr,Gen. ['*sough*']

+**swogen** *in a swoon*, *silenced*, *dead*, Æ,Lcd. ['*swow(n)*']

+**swogennes** v. in-s.

+**swōgung** f. *swooning*, Lcd. ['*swowing*']

swol n. *heat*, *burning*, *flame*, *glow*. [swelan; Ger. schwül]

swoleð=sweoloð

swolgen pp. of swelgan.

swolgettan *to gargle*, *wash the throat*, LCD.

swolig f. *burning*, LCD,WW.
swollen (*Ep*) pp. of swellan.
swoloð, swoloða (OEG 23⁵⁵)=sweoloð
swolten pp. of sweltan.
swoluð (Æ)=sweoloð; swolwe=swealwe
swom=swamm I. and II.; swon=swan
swoncor=swancor
swong=swang pret. 3 sg. of swingan.
swongor=swangor; swonrād=swanrād
+swōpe *sweepings, refuse*, Ln 111¹⁵.
swopu (NG)=swipu
swor (Ex 239)=spor
swōr I. pret. 3 sg. of swerian. II.=sār.
    III.=swēor
swōra=swēora; swore=sweorc
sworcen pp. of sweorcan.
sword=sweord
sworen pp. of swerian.
swōretendlic *short-winded*, WW 355⁹.
swōrettan *to breathe hard, pant, yawn, sigh*,
    Æ.
swōret-ung, -tung f. *hard breathing, panting,
    sobbing, sighing, moaning*, Æ.
sworfen pp. of sweorfan.
swornian (a) *to coagulate*, GL.
swōron pret. pl. of swerian.
swostor=sweostor
swōt I. *sweet*, *JnL,Nar,OEG*. adv. swōte
    ÆGr. [' *soot*'] II.=swāt
swōtlic *savoury, sweet*, CP 311⁸. adv.
    -līce.
swōtmete m. *sweetmeat, dainty*, Bo 33²³.
swōtnes f. *sweetness*, *DR,Shr.* [' *sootness*']
swotol=sweotol
swōt-stence (WW 341⁵), -stencende (DR)
    sweet-smelling.
swoðung=sweðung
+swōwung=+swōgung
swūgian (CP)=swīgian; swulc=swilc
swulgon pret. pl. of swelgan.
swulton pret. pl. of sweltan.
swulung=sulung
swuncon pret. pl. of swincan.
-swundennes v. ā-s.
swur-, swūr-=sweor-, swēor-
swust-er, -or, -ur (Æ)=sweostor
swut-el-, -ol-, -ul-=sweotol-
swūwian=swīgian; swyc-=swic-
swyft=swift; swȳg-=swīg-
swȳge=swīge; swyl-=swil-
swyle (i) m. *tumour, swelling*. [swellan]
swyliend=swelgend
swylt† (i) m. *death*. [sweltan]
swylt-=swelt-
swyltcwalu† f. *agony of death*, AN.
swyltdæg† m. *death-day*.
swyltdēað m. *death*, PPs 55¹¹.
swylthwīl† f. *hour of death*, PH.
swym-=swim-; swȳn=swīn

swyn-=swin-; swyp- (N)=swip-
swȳr=swēor; swyrd=sweord
+swyrf=+sweorf
swyrfð pres. 3 sg. of sweorfan.
+swȳsnes=+swǣsnes; swyster=sweostor
swytel, swytol=sweotol; swȳð=swīð
swȳwian=sūgian, swīgian
sȳ=sīe pres. subj. of bēon.
syb, sybb=sibb
±sȳcan (ē, ī) *to suckle* : *wean*, ASPs 130².
    [sūcan]
syce (i, ī?) *sucking*, OEG 57⁸.
sȳclian=sīclian
sycomer m. *sycamore*, BK 4.
sȳcð pres. 3 sg. of sūcan; sȳcan.
+syd n. *wallowing-place*, WW 146¹⁵. [sēo-
    ðan]
sȳd=sīd; +sydian=+sidian
syde m. *a decoction*, LCD 1·280³. [sēoðan]
syfan=seofon; syfe=sife
sȳferǣte *abstemious*, RB 119²⁵.
sȳferlic (ē) *neat, cleanly, pure, sober,
    moderate.* adv. -līce.
sȳferlicnes f. *purity*, VH 20.
sȳferne asm. of sȳfre.
sȳfernes f. *cleanliness, purity, sobriety,
    moderation*, Æ.
syfeða=seofoða; syfian=seofian
+syfian *to provide with relishes, flavour*, TC,
    W. [sufl]
syflige (RBL), syfling (Æ) f. *food, pap,
    broth, soup* : *seasoning, relish*.
syfol=sufel; syfon=seofon
sȳfre (ē, ī) *clean, pure, chaste, sober,
    abstinent, temperate*, Æ. [*Ger.* sauber]
syftan=siftan
syge I. m. *sight, aspect*, FT 64? II.=sige I.
sygel=sigel; sygor=sigor
syh=seoh imperat. of sēon; syht=suht
syhð pres. 3 sg. of sēon I. and II.
+syhð=+sihð
+syhðe (BPs 120⁴)=+sehðe; syl=syle
sȳl I. f. *column, pillar, support*, AO. [*Ger.*
    säule] II. ds. of sūl, sulh.
sȳla m. *ploughman*, OEG 2357. [sulh]
sȳlæx f. *a kind of axe*, WW 379³³ (v. ES
    43·327).
syle, sylen *miry place, wallowing-place*,
    OEG. [sol]
sylen=selen
syleð pres. 3 sg. of syllan; sylf=self
sylfer, sylfor, sylfur (M)=seolfor
sylfren (Æ)=seolfren
sylfwill- (Æ)=selfwill-
sylg ds., sylh ds. and nap. of sūl, sulh.
Sȳlhearwa=Sigelhearwa
±sylhð(e) n. *team of oxen*. [sulh]
sylian (e) *to sully, soil, pollute*, CP,Met.
    [' *sule*']

syll I. f. *'sill,' threshold, foundation, base, basis,* Æ,B,*CP*. **II.** nap. of sulh.

sylla m. *giver,* RBL25⁶. [sellan]

sȳlla (DEOR6)=sēlla (sēlra) v. sēl I.

syllan (Æ)=sellan; **sylle**=syll I.

syllend (Æ)=sellend; **syllic**=seldlic

sylofr, sylofren=seolfor, seolfren

sȳlra=sēlra v. sēl I.

±**syltan** (æ, e;=ie) *to salt, season,* Æ. [sealt]

sylu f. *bog, miry place,* Ct.

sȳma=sēma; **sȳman**=sīeman

symbel I. n. *feast-day, festivity, revel, feast,* AO : (†) *festival, holy day : solemn office.* **II.**=simbel

symbelcalic (i) m. *chalice,* TC515¹⁸.

symbelcennes f. *feast of a nativity,* DR.

symbeldæg m. *feast-day, festival, holiday,* Æ.

symbele=simbel

symbelgāl *wanton with feasting, drunk,* DD 79.

symbelgereord n. *feasting, carousal,* SOL 407.

symbelgifa m. *giver of feasts,* AN1419.

symbelhūs n. *guest-chamber,* LkLR22¹².

symbelian=symblian

symbellic *festive : solemn.* adv. -līce *solemnly,* DR,RBL.

symbelmōnaðlic adj. *of a festival month?* WW375³⁸.

symbelnes f. *festival, feasting, festivity,* Æ : *festal character,* BF84² : *solemn assembly, solemn office.*

symbeltīd f. *festival-time,* DR.

symbelwērig *weary with feasting,* GEN 2640.

symbelwlonc *elated with feasting,* MOD 40.

symbelwynn f. *joy of feasting,* B1782.

symblan *to feast, banquet,* CP.

symble (Æ)=simble adv.

symblian (i) *to feast, carouse,* CP.

symel=symbel

symeringwyrt f. *violet,* WW322⁹.

syml=symbel I.; **syml-**=simbl-'symnenlic**=semnendlic; **syn**=synn

sȳn I.=sīen f. **II.**=sīn, sīen pres. pl. subj. of wesan (bēon). **III.**=sīn I.

syn- v. also sin-, synn-.

syna=suna gs. of sunu.

synbend m. *bond of sin,* NIC504²³.

synbōt f. *penance,* LL(316').

synbryne m? *burning ardour of sin,* MFH 143¹⁸.

synbyrðen f. *burden of sin,* BL,CR.

synbysig *guilt-haunted,* B2227.

syncræft m. *evil art?* BYH102³⁰.

synd=sind pres. pl. ind. of wesan (bēon).

+**synd-**=+sund-

syndǣd f. *sinful deed,* PPs,W.

syndan=sendan

synder-=sundor-

synderǣ (u²) f. *special law,* DR190¹⁰.

synderlic (e¹, i¹) *singular, separate, special, peculiar, private,* Bo,*CP* : *remote.* adv. -līce Æ, BH, Bo, MkL. *['sunderly']*

synderlicnes f. *separateness, separation seclusion,* OEG : *singularity, special excellence,* GD286¹¹.

synder-līpe, -lȳpe, -lȳpig *peculiar, special.* adv. -līpes (ȳ), OEG,RB. *['sunderlepes']*

+**syndgian** *to make to prosper,* BH320¹².

syndig *skilled in swimming,* CRA58.

+**syndig** *favourable,* BH386¹³.

+**syndiglic** (del-) *prosperous,* BH388¹⁸.

syndir-=synder-

+**syndlǣcan** (synt-) *to cause to prosper,* RPs117²⁵.

syndolh n. *deadly wound,* B817 (or=sin-?).

syndon=sindon pres. pl. ind. of wesan (bēon).

Syndonisc *Indian,* MFH173, NIC592. [*L. Gk.*]

syndra? m., **syndre?** f.=sinder

±**syndrian** (u) *to 'sunder,' separate, divide,* KC,LG,Sc.

syndrig (i) *separate, single, PPs : 'sundry,' various, distinct,* Æ,BH : *special, private, peculiar, exceptional, particular,* Æ; AO, CP : *characteristic :* (distributive) *one each.* [sundor]

syndrige adv. *separately, specially, apart, alone,* LG. *['sundry']*

syndrigendlic *discretive,* ÆGR229⁷.

syndriglic *special, peculiar,* BH. adv. -līce *specially : separately,* BH. *['sundrily']*

syndrung v. ā-s.

syndurǣ=synderǣ

synew-=sinew-; and v. seonu.

synfāh *sin-stained,* CR1083.

±**syngian** *to sin, transgress, err,* Æ,CP.

syngrigendlic=syndrigendlio

syngrin (y²) f. *snare of sin, harm,* W.

syngung f. *transgression,* HL12¹³⁷. *['sinning']*

synleahter m. *stain of sin,* W134²⁴.

synlēas *'sinless,' guiltless, innocent,* CP,Jn, W.

synlēaw *injury caused by sin,* W165²⁵.

synlic *sinful, foul, wicked.* adv. -līce.

+**synlīce**=+sinlīce

synn (e, i) f. (†) *injury, mischief, enmity, feud : 'sin,' guilt, crime,* Bl,Bo,Chr,G,Sc, VPs; CP.

synn- see also syn-.

synnadæg (N)=sunnandæg

synnecge f. *female sinner,* MH126⁴.

synneðōht *sinful thought,* BYH136¹³.

synnful '*sinful*,' *guilty, wicked, corrupt, Bl, LG,VPs*; CP.

synngiend m. *sinner*, EPs 111[10].

+**synnian** *to commit adultery*, NG.

synnig *guilty, punishable, criminal* : *sinful*, CP.

synnlust m. *desire to sin*, Æ.

synoð=seonoð

synræs m. *temptation*, LL (284[9]).

synrūst m. *canker of sin*, CR 1321.

syn-sceaða, -scaða† m. *sin-stained wretch, sinful outrager*, VH 20.

synscyldig *wicked*, DD 168.

synt=sind pres. pl. ind. of wesan (bēon).

+**synt-**=+**synd-**

±**synto** f. *soundness, health : prosperity, welfare, salvation.* [gesund]

synwracu† f. *punishment for sin.*

synwund f. *wound of sin*, CR,LL.

synwyrcende† *sinning.*

sypan=sypian

sype m. *wetting, act of soaking through*, Bo. ['*sipe*']

sypian (i) *to absorb, drink in*, Lcd 94b. ['*sipe*']

sȳpian=sīpian ; **sypo**, syppo=swipu

syrc m., syrce f.=serc, serce

syre=searwe, v. searo; **sȳre**=sīere

syredon=sier(w)edon pret. pl. of sierwan.

syretung f. *lurking place*, WW 440[6]. [searu]

syrewrenc=searowrenc

syrewung=searwung

syrfe f. *service-tree*, EC 373[11]. [*L.* sorbus]

syrftrēow n. *service-tree*, KC 3·379'.

syric, syrice=serc, serce

sȳring f. *sour milk, buttermilk*, LL,WW. [sūr]

Syrisc *Syrian*, ÆL 18[402].

syrode=sierwde pret. 3 sg. of sierwan.

syru=searo

syrwa=searwa gp. of searo.

syr-wan, -wian (Æ)=sierwan

Syrware mpl. *Syrians*, PH 166.

syrwung=sierwung

syrwwrenc=searowrenc; **syster**=sester

syt-=sit-

sȳð I.=sīð. **II.** v. sūð adv. **III.** pres. 3 sg. of sēoðan.

sȳð-=sīð-; **sȳðan**=siððan

sȳðerra (BC,Lcd) v. sūð. ['*souther*']

sȳðst pres. 2 sg. of sēoðan.

syððan=siððan; **sȳwian**=sēowian

syx, syx-=siex, siex-, six-

T

tā I. f. '*toe*,' Cp,LL,WW. **II.** f. (Æ)=tān m.

tabele, tablu, tabul, f., tabula m.=tabule

tabule f. '*table*,' BH : *a wooden hammer, or piece of wood struck as a signal for assemb-* *ling monks*, CM : *writing tablet*, Bf : *gaming table*, Gl : *table of the law.* [L.]

tacan[6] *to* '*take*,' *seize*, Chr 1072,1076. t. on *to touch.*

+**taccian** *to tame, subdue*, GPH 402 (= +ðaccian).

tācen, tācn n., nap. tācen, tācnu '*TOKEN*,' *symbol, sign, signal, mark, indication, suggestion, Æ,CP : portent, marvel, wonder, miracle : evidence, proof : standard, banner.*

tācen-=tācn-

tācencircol m. *indiction*, TC 126[3].

tācnan (Cp)=tǣcnan

tācnberend m. *standard-bearer*, ÆGR 27[15].

tācnbora m. *standard-bearer : guide*, APT.

±**tācnian** *to mark, indicate : betoken, denote, signify, represent, Bl,Bo; AO,CP : symbolise, ÆH,Bl : portend : demonstrate, express.* ['*token*']

+**tācni(g)endlic** *typical, emblematic*, ÆH 2·278[14]; ÆP 122[17].

±**tācnung** f. *sign, presage, token, signal, Bo : manifestation, signification, type, Bo,BH : indication, symptom, proof : dispensation, AO 60[1] : phase (of moon), zodiacal sign,* ANS 145·256. ['*tokening*']

tācon, tācun=tācen

tācor, tācur m. *brother-in-law*, Æ.

tāde, tādi(g)e f. '*toad*,' WW.

tæbere *a weaving tool? tenterhook?* WW 294[17].

tæcan, pret. tǣhte *to transfer, translate*, Æ. [ON. taka]

±**tǣcan** *to show, declare, demonstrate, Æ, AO : TEACH*' ('*i-tæche*'), *instruct, train, Æ; CP : assign, prescribe, direct, Æ,CP : warn : persuade*, MtR 28[14]. +t. fram *dismiss*, LL 162,22.

tǣcing f. *teaching, instruction, Æ : doctrine : direction, injunction, command, rule.*

tǣcnan *to mark by a token, denote, designate, mark out.* [Ger. zeichnen]

-**tǣcne** v. earfoð-t.

tǣcnend m. *index-finger*, A 13·329, WW 426[38].

tǣcnian=tācnian

tǣcning f. *demonstration, proof*, Bo 90[1].

tæfl, tæfel (e[2]) fn. *cube, die, game with dice or tables*, Gl,Wy. [L. tabula; v. '*tavel*']

tæfl-an, -ian *to gamble*, Gl. ['*tavel*']

tæfle adj. *given to dice-playing*, GnE 185.

tæflere m. *gambler*, WW. [v. '*tavel*']

tæflstān m. *gambling-stone, die*, Gl. [v. '*tavel*']

tæflung f. *gaming, playing at dice*, NC 325.

tǣg (A)=tēag

tægel, tægl (e) m. '*tail*,' LL,WW; Æ.

tæglhǣr n. *hair of the tail*, LCD 1·360'.

tægðian (M)=teogoðian

tæherian (*NG*)=tēarian

tæhher (NG)=tēar

tæhte pret. 3 sg. of tǣcan.

tæl (a, e) n. *number, Æ.*

tǣl (ā) f. *blame, reproach, calumny, abuse,* *CP,WW* : *blasphemy* : *disgrace.* [*'tele'*]

+tæl I. (e, ea) n., nap. +talu *number, series,* *Æ,LG* : *numeral, ÆGR* : *number of* *people, tribe* : *catalogue,* WW418³⁶ : *reckoning, estimation, opinion.* [*'tel,'* *'i-tel'*] **II.** adj. np. +tale *swift, ready,* PPs56⁵ : *competent,* WW505³. [v. *'tall'*]

tæla=tela

±tǣlan (ē) *to blame, censure, scold, reprove,* *reproach, accuse,* Æ,AO,CP : *speak ill of,* *slander, insult, deride,* Bo,*LRG,LL,WW* : *despise, maltreat: dispute.* [*'tele'*]

tælberend=telgberend

+tælcircul m. *cycle, series,* WW204⁴².

+tælcræft (e) m. *arithmetic,* OEG3117.

+tæld=+teld; **-tǣle** v. lēof-, un-t.

tǣlend m. *slanderer, backbiter* : *mocker,* *scoffer* : *reprover.*

tǣlende *censorious, slanderous,* BL,LL.

tǣlere (ē) m. *derider, scoffer,* KGL75¹⁶.

+tælfæst *measurable,* LPs38⁶.

tælfers (e¹) n. *'versus catalecticus,'* OEG127.

+tælful *numerous,* Sc231¹⁰.

tǣlful (ā) *blameworthy,* CHRD67³⁶.

tælg=telg

tǣlhlehter m. *derision,* WW172⁴. [hleahtor]

tælian=talian

tæling f. *reproof,* CP : *derogation* : *slander,* *derision.*

tælla (GPH394)=telga; **tællan**=tellan

tǣllēas *blameless,* CP. adv. -līce, CP.

tǣllic (ā) *blameworthy* : *slanderous, blas-* *phemous.* adv. -līce *reprehensibly* : *shame-* *lessly?* CHRD70⁵.

tælmearc f. *date, period,* GU849. [talu]

tælmet n. *measure, portion,* AN113. [talu]

tǣlnes (ē) f. *blame, reproof,* CP : *derogation* : *slander, calumny, insult.*

+tælrīm n. *order, succession,* SOL38.

±tælsum *in numbers, rhythmic,* OEG.

tǣlweorð-=tǣlwierð-

tǣl-wierðe, -wierðlic *reprehensible, blame-* *worthy,* CP. · adv. -līce.

tǣlwierðlicnes (eo²) f. *blameableness,* CP 52¹⁵.

+tælwīs (e) *skilled in arithmetic,* BF112⁹, WW207⁴⁰.

tǣlwyrd-, tǣlwyrð-=tǣlwierð-

tǣman=tīeman

tæmespīle f. *sieve-frame, sieve-stand?* *sieve-* *stake?* LL455,17 and 3·255. [v. *'temse'*]

tæmian (GD11⁹)=temian

tænel (ē¹, ī²) m. *wicker basket,* Æ,Gl. [*'teanel'*; tān]

tǣnen *made of twigs,* OEG. [tān]

tæng-=teng-; **tǣnil**=tǣnel

tæppa m. *'tap,' spigot, IM.*

tæppe f? *strip of stuff or cloth, 'tape,'* WW 107³³.

tæpp-ed, -et n. *figured cloth, tapestry, carpet,* *TC,WW.* [*'tapet'*]

tæppelbred n. *footstool,* NG.

tæppere m. *tapster, tavern-keeper,* Sc,*WW.* [*'tapper'*]

tæppestre f. *tapstress, female tavern-keeper,* *ÆGr.* [*'tapster'*]

tæppet=tæpped

tæppian *to open* (*a cask*)? *furnish it with a* *tap or spout?* IM125. [*'tap'*]

tæppilbred=tæppelbred

tær pret. 3 sg. of teran; **tǣr**=tēar

tǣsan (±) *to pull, tear, comb, card,* Lcd : (†) *wound, injure, assault*: (+) *influence,* CP 297¹⁸. [*'tease'*]

±tǣse I. *pleasant, Met* : *convenient, suitable,* *B.* [*'i-tase'*] **II.** (+) n. *advantage, con-* *venience,* CP387 : *useful thing, implement.*

tǣsel f. *'teasel' (plant),* Lcd1·282¹⁵.

+tǣslic *convenient.* adv. -līce *conveniently* : *gently, softly, smoothly,* CP.

tæslīce (NG)=ðæslīce

+tǣsnes f. *advantage, convenience,* WW.

tæso=tēosu

+tǣsu=+tǣse II.

tǣtan *to gladden, cheer,* WY4.

tætteca m? *rag, tatter, shred?* Æ,KC (v. BT).

tǣð=tēð, v. tōð.

-tǣwe (ēo) v. æl-t.

tāh pret. 3 sg. of tēon II.

+tāh n. *teaching,* RIM2 (ES65·188).

tāhe (GL)=tā

tāhspura m. *spur, tip of toe?* WW197¹⁴.

tāhte=tǣhte pret. 3 sg. of tǣcan.

tal (N)=talu; **tāl**=tǣl; **tala**=tela

tald=teald pp. of tellan.

+tale v. tæl.

talente f. *'talent' (money of account),* AO. [L.]

±talian (æ) *to count, calculate, reckon,* *account, consider, think, esteem, value,* BH,*CP,LG,W* : *argue,* CP : *tell, relate,* LG; Æ : *impute, assign,* Æ,BH. (=tellan.) [*'tale'*]

+talscipe m. *multitude,* NG.

talt-=tealt-

talu f. *'tale,' series, calculation* : *list,* WW : *statement, deposition, relation, communica-* *tion, narrative,* Æ,KC : *fable, tale, story* : *accusation, action at law* (v. LL3·226).

+talu v. +tæl.

tālwyrð-=tǣlwierð-

tam *'tame,'* Æ,Bo,WW : *tractable, gentle,* *mild,* Bo,Gn.

tama m. *tameness*, Bo,Met.

tamcian *to tame, soothe*, Chrd 96[18].

-tamcol v. un-t.

tān I. m. *twig, rod, switch, branch* : *rod of divination.* **II.** *shooting? spreading?* Gen 2360. **III.** pl. of tā.

tānede *diseased in the toes?* WW 161[28].

±tang, tange (o) f. (sg. and pl.) *pincers, 'tongs,' forceps, Æ,BH,Bf,Gl*; Æ.

+tang (w. d.) *in contact with* (=pret. 3 sg. of +tingan). adv. +tange (o), Rim 42?

+tanglīce *together*, RB 47[15].

tānhlyta m. *soothsayer, augur, diviner*, WW 189[3]. [tān, hlot]

tānhlytere m. *soothsayer, diviner*, WW 183[32].

+tanned *tanned*, WW 118[7]. ['tanned']

tannere m. '*tanner,' KC* 2·411'.

taper (*Lcd,WW*)=tapor

taperæx f. *small axe*, Chr 1031a, CC 28[16]. [ON. taparöx]

tapor (ea[1]; e[2], u[2]) m. *lamp-wick, 'taper,' candle, CP* : *a feeble light*, Ph 114. [*Keltic?*]

taporberend m. *acolyte*, Gl.

taran v. teoru.

targa? m., **targe?** f. *small shield, buckler, KC.* [v. '*targe*']

+targed *furnished with a shield*, OEG 2259.

taru? f. *tear, rent*, WW 416[27]. [teran]

tasol, tasul (Gl)=teosel; **-tāwere** v. flæsc-t.

±tāwian *to prepare, make ready, make* : *till, cultivate, BH* : *harass, afflict, insult, Æ, AO.* t. tō bysmore *outrage, profane, Æ,W.* ['taw']

+tāw-u, -a np.' *apparatus, implements* : *genitalia*, Lcd 26a.

te-=tō-; **tēa** (NG)=tīen

+tēad (ē) pp. of +tēon and +tēagan.

tēafor I. n. *red, red lead, vermilion, purple, WW.* [v. '*tiver*'] **II.** meaning doubtful, or ? tēaforgēap (v. GK), Ruin 31.

tēag (æ, ē) **I.** f. *cord, band, thong, fetter, Cr, WW.* ['*tie*'] **II.** *case, chest, Æ,WW* : *enclosure, BC.* ['*tye*']

+tēagan (ē) pret. +tēde, pp. +tēad *to make, prepare, dress, till.*

teagor (*Gu*)=tēar

tēah I. pret. 3 sg. of tēon I. and II. **II.**= tēag

teal-=tal-, tæl-, tel-

tēal-=tǣl-; +teald=+teld

tealde pret. 3 sg. of tellan; **tealgor**=telgor

tealt *unstable, precarious*, Run,W. ['tealt']

tealt(r)ian (a) *to totter, shake, stumble, waver* : *be untrustworthy* : *amble.* [cp. Ger. zelter]

tēam (ē) m. *descendant, family, race, line, Æ,Mk,TC* : *child-bearing, Æ* : *brood, Æ* : *company, band, Æ* : '*team*' (*of horses, oxen,*

etc.), *WW* : *vouching to warranty, right of jurisdiction in matters of warranty, EC,LL.*

+tēama (ȳ) m. *warrantor, surety*, LL.

tēaman=tīeman

tēamful *fruitful, LPs,WW.* [v. '*teemful*']

tēamian=tīeman

tēampōl m. *breeding pool*, EC 322'.

tēan- (A)=tēon-; **teaper** (K)=tapor

tēapor (*Lcd*)=tēafor

tēar m. *drop, Cr,Lcd* : '*tear*,' B,Bl*; CP : *what is distilled from anything in drops, 'nectar,' WW*; CM.

tearflian *to turn, roll, wallow*, Mk 9[20].

tēargēotende *tear-shedding, tearful*, Nic 508[15].

tēarian (tæherian, ē[1]) *to weep*, JnL. ['*tear*']

tēarig *tearful*, HGL : *watery*, Lcd 125a.

tēarighlēor *with tearful cheeks*, Gen 2274.

tearn (WW 286[7])=stearn; **tearos** v. teoru.

teart *sharp, rough, severe, Æ,OEG.* ['*tart*'; tær pret. of teran]

teartlic *sharp, rough, Æ.* adv. -līce, OEG. ['*tartly*']

teartnes f. *sharpness, roughness, hardness, OEG;* Æ. ['*tartness*']

teartnumol *biting, effectual*, Lcd 1·152[3].

teaslīce (NG)=ðæslīce

tēað=tēoð pres. pl. of tēon I. and II.

tebl, tebl-, tebil-=tæfl, tæfl-

tēc-=tǣc-; **tēd-**=tīed-; **+tēd**=+tēad

tēde pret. of tēagan.

tēder=tȳder; **tēdr-**=tīed(e)r-, tȳdr-

tefel, tefil=tæfl

tēfrung (=īe) f. *picture*, AS 21[4].

tēg=tēag; **tēgan**=(1) tiegan; (2) tēagan

tēge=tīge; **tegl**=tægl; **tēgð-**=tēoð-

tēh=tēah pret. 3 sg. of tēon.

teherian (A)=tēarian

tehher, teher (*NG*)=tēar

tēhton=tǣhton pret. pl. of tæcan.

teissu (LkL)=teosu; +tel=+tæl; **tēl-**=tǣl-

tela (i, ea, eo) **I.** adv. *well, fitly, properly, rightly, very, good*, CP : *prosperously, beneficially.* **II.** interj. *well! good!*

±teld n. *tent, pavilion, tabernacle, Æ,BH, TC.* ['*teld*']

+teldgehlīwung f. *tabernacle*, Bf 74[14].

teldian *to spread* (*net*), *set* (*trap*), *Cp,PPs* : *entrap.* ['*teld*']

teldsticca m. *tent-peg*, Jud 4[21,22].

+teldung f. *tabernacle*, EPs 18[5]; 77[60].

+teldwurðung f. *feast of tabernacles*, WW 107[17].

teldwyrhta m. *tent-maker*, ÆH 1·392'.

telede=tealde pret. 3 sg. of tellan.

+telfers (OEG)=tælfers

telg (æ) m. *dye, colour, tincture*, BH,Gl.

telga m. *twig, branch, bough, shoot*, CP : *pole, stock*, EC 95'.

+**telg-an**, -ian *to dye*, WW.

telgberend *yielding a dye*, WW462¹⁹.

telge f.=telga

telgestre (æ¹) m. *dyer*, GD342³.

telgian I. *to put forth branches*, RIM34. II.=talian. III.=telgan

telgor mf., telgra m., telgre f. *twig, branch, shoot*, Æ,Gl,Lcd. [v. '*tiller*']

telgung f. *dye, purple dye*, WW.

telian=tilian

±**tellan** (æ, ea) *to* 'TELL' ('*i-telle*'), *reckon, count, number, compute, calculate*, Æ : *account, estimate, consider, think, esteem, believe*, CP : *charge against, impute to* : *assign*: *state, recount, enumerate, announce, relate*, Æ. t. gelīc *compare*. [talu]

-**tellendlic** v. un-t.

teltrē, teltrēo n. *weaving-tool? tenterhook? tent-peg?* WW.

+**telwīs** *skilled in reckoning*, BF112⁹.

tēm=tēam; **tema**=tama

tēman=tīeman

tēmbyrst m. *failure to secure a voucher*, EC 202¹. [tēam]

Temes, Temese f. *river Thames*, AO. [*L.* Tamisia]

±**temesian** (i²) *to sift*, MkL. ['*temse*']

±**temian** *to tame, subdue*, Æ,CP,Lcd,LG : (+) *suffer, permit*, ÆL23⁸¹⁰. ['*teme*']

tempel, templ n. '*temple*,' Æ,Bl,CP,G,VPs. [*L.* templum]

tempel-=templ-

tempelgeat n. *temple-door*, W49²⁵.

tempelhūs n. *temple*, ByH118²⁴.

templgeweorc n. *structure of the temple*, W277²⁵.

templhālgung f. *dedication of the temple*, OEG40³⁶.

templic adj. *of a temple*, OEG.

±**temprian** v. *to* '*temper*,' *moderate*, Æ,Gl, Sc : *cure, heal*, Æ : *control, curb*, Æ (refl.), Lcd. [*Lat.*]

temprung f. *tempering, moderation*, Sc.

tēn (VPs)=tīen; **tēnan**=tȳnan

-**tendan** (y) v. ā-, for-, on-t.

tender=tynder

tend-ing, -ling f. *burning, stinging*, NC,GD. [v. '*tind*']

tēne=tīen; **tēnel** (*Ep*)=tænel

±**tengan** (æ) *to press towards, hasten*, Æ. āweg t. *get away, get off*. +t. on *assail*, AO.

+**tenge** *near to, resting on* : *oppressing, burdensome*, AO.

tēnil=tænel

tennan *to lure, coax?* WY4?

tēo pres. 1 sg. of tēon I. and II.

teochian=teohhian

tēode pret. of tēon III., tēogan, teohhian.

teofenian† *to join, put together*, CREAT.

tēofor=tēafor

tēofrian *to appoint?* PPs117²¹.

tēogan=teohhian

teogeða, teogoða=tēoða

teogoðlan *to* '*tithe*,' *grant or pay tithes*, Æ, CP,G : *divide by ten*, Æ.

teoh fm., gds. teohhe *race* : *band, troop, company, society*. [*Ger.* zeche]

tēoh imperat. of tēon.

+**tēoh** n. *matter, material, universe?* RIM2.

teohhe v. teoh.

±**teohhian** (i, io) *to determine, intend, propose*, Æ,CP : *consider, think, judge, estimate*. [*OHG.* gizehōn]

+**teohhung** f. *arrangement, ordering*, HL 13⁶⁹.

teohian=teohhian; **teol-**=tel-, til-

teolðyrl n. '*foramen*,' '*fenestra*,' OEG.

teom (MtR21⁵)=tam

tēon I. (±) sv² *to pull, tug, draw, drag, row (boat)*, CP : *draw together* : *withdraw, take*, LL356,70 : *entice, allure, induce, lead, bring*, CP : *bring up, educate*, Æ : *bring to, attract*, AO : *arrogate*, CP : *bring forth, produce*, Æ : *restrain*, LL : *betake oneself to, go, roam* : (+) *dispute*, NG : (+) *string up, play (instrument)*. +togen *lengthened, long (of vowels)*, ÆGR49¹⁴. ['*TEE**,' '*i-teon*'; *teohan] II. sv¹ (but forms belonging to tēon I. often found) *accuse, censure*, Æ,LL; AO : *proceed against successfully*, ANS144·253. ['*tee*'; *tīhan] III. wv. (±) *to prepare, furnish forth, arrange, adorn, deck* : *produce, work, do, create, make*, Æ : *settle, fix, establish, constitute, ordain*. [=teohhian] IV. num.= tīen. V. n.=tēona. VI.=dēon (v. JAW19).

tēona m. *injury, hurt, wrong*, Bl,Mt; AO : *accusation, reproach, insult, contumely*, Æ, AO,CP : *anger, grief* : *malice*, Æ : *enmity, hostility*. ['*teen*']

tēoncwide† m. *hurtful speech* : *blasphemy*.

tēoncwidian *to slander, calumniate*, GL.

tēond I. m. *accuser*, LL. II. *drawer*, BH 288¹⁴.

tēone f.=tēona

tēonere m. *slanderer*, LPs71⁴.

tēonful *slanderous, evil, rebellious, painful*, SPs,W; Æ. ['*teenful*']

tēonhete† m. *malicious hate*.

tēonian (ȳ) *to injure, irritate*, LPs : *slander*. ['*teen*']

tēonlēas *free from suffering*, MFH174.

tēonlēg† m. *destroying flame*.

tēonlic *destructive, shameful, hurtful*. adv. -līce.

tēonrǣden (e²) f. *abuse, wrong, injury, humiliation*, Æ.

tēonsmlð m. *evil-doer*, Gu 176.
tēontig=hundtēontig
tēonword n. *reproach, abuse, calumny*, Æ, Lcd.
±tēorian *to fail, cease, become weary, be tired, exhausted, Gl,Lcd,LL,PPs* : '*tire*,' *weary, exhaust, PPs*. [teran]
±tēorigendlic *failing, defective*, Sc 181⁴, ByH 56¹⁵.
teoro=teoru
+tēorodnes f. *debility, weariness*, Gl.
teors m. '*calamus*,' '*veretrum*,' *Lcd,WW*. ['*tarse*']
teoru (e) n., occl. gs. tearos and wk. a. taran '*tar*,' *bitumen, distillation from a tree, resin, gum, balsam, Gl,Lcd* : *wax from the ear*.
±tēorung f. *exhaustion, weariness*, Æ.
teosel (a, e) m. *die* ('*tessera*'). [L.]
teosu (æ, e) f. *harm, injury, ruin, wrong*.
teosuspræc f. *harmful speech*, PPs 139¹¹.
teosuword (teso-) n. *calumny, harmful speech*, NC.
teoswian (e) *to injure, harm*, Sol 94.
tēoð pres. pl. of tēon I. and II.
tēoða (ē) '*TENTH*,' *Æ,AO,Chr*. tēoðan dæl *tenth part*. [teogeða]
tēoðe *tenthly*, LL 181,10.
±tēoðlan *to divide by ten, tithe, Æ* : *take a tenth* : *give tithes, Æ,BC,CP,G*.
tēoðing=tēoðung
tēoðingdæg m. *tithing day, tenth day*, Æ.
tēoðingealdor m. *ruler over ten, dean, captain of ten*, RB.
tēoðingmann m. '*tithing-man*,' *headborough, LL* : *captain of ten, Æ*.
tēoðung f. *division into ten, decimation, tenth part, tithe*, '*tithing*,' *Æ,Lk,LL* : *band of ten men*, LL.
tēoðungcēap m. *tithe*, Bl 39¹¹.
tēoðunggeorn *diligent in paying tithes*, A 12·518²⁶.
tēoðungland n. *land set apart for tithes*, LL 2·750.
tēoðungsceatt m. *tithing-money, tithes*, Bl, LL.
tēowllc=tōwlic
teped (*KGl*), tepet=tæpped; tēr (*Lcd*)=tēar
+ter n. *tearing, laceration* : *thing torn* : *tumult, discord*.
±teran⁴ (ea, eo) *to* '*TEAR*,' *lacerate*.
terdnes (A 13·34)=teartnes
tergan=tirgan
termen (i²) m. *term, end*, Bf,Lcd. [L.]
tero, teru (*Ep,WW*)=teoru
tes-=teos-; +tēse=+tǣse
teter m. '*tetter*,' *skin eruption, eczema, ringworm, CP,Gl,Lcd,Sc*.
teting=tyhting; tēð v. tōð.
tēða=tēoða; -tewestre v. wull-t.

+tēðed *toothed*, AA 31⁷.
Tī=Tīw; tīan (N)=tēon III.
tīber† n. *offering, sacrifice, victim*, Gen.
tībernes f. *sacrificing, destruction*, AO 50¹⁸.
ticcen (y) n. *kid, Æ,MtL*. ['*ticchen*']
ticgen (NG)=ticcen
ticgende *proudly adorned*, OEG.
ticia m. '*tick*' (*insect*), Gl.
tictator m. *dictator*, AO 70³. [L.]
tīd f. *time, period, season, while* : *hour* : *feast-day, festal-tide* : *canonical hour or service*. on tīde *at the proper time*. ['*TIDE*']
tīdan (±) *to betide, happen, Bo,LL* : *fall to* (*one's lot*), BC. ['*tide*,' '*i-tide*']
tīdanðēnung=tīdðēnung
tidd-=tīd-, tȳd-
tiddæg† m. *lifetime*.
tīdelīce=tīdlīce
tīdembwlātend=tīdymbwlātend
tīder=tīedre
tīdfara m. *one who travels at his own convenience?* Cr 1674 (or ? two words).
tīdgenge *having a monthly course, periodical*, GPH 392.
tīdlic *timely, seasonable, opportune*, AO : *temporal* : *temporary*. adv. -līce.
tīdlicnes f. *opportunity, fit time*, NG.
tīdran=tȳdran
tīdre=tīedre
tīdrēn m. *timely rain*, Deut 28¹².
±tīdrian (ȳ) *to become feeble, weak* : *decay*.
tīdsang mn. *canonical hours, lauds*, Æ.
tīdscēawere m. *astrologer*, WW 176⁴.
tīdscriptor m. *chronographer, chronicler*, WW 204¹⁷ (hybrid word).
tīdðēnung f. *service at one of the canonical hours*, FBO.
tīdum adv. *at times, occasionally*.
tīdung f. (usu. pl.) *event, tidings, news*, Chr. ['*tiding*']
tīdwrītere m. *chronicler*, Gl.
tīdwurdung f. *service at one of the canonical hours*, HL 11⁶⁷.
tīdymbwlātend (e²) m. *astrologer*, Lcd.
tīeder=tīedre
tīederlic (ē, ī, ȳ) *weak*, CP.
tīedernes (ē, ī, ȳ) *frailty* (*of body or soul*), CP.
tīedran=tȳdran
tīedre (ē, ī, ȳ) *weak, frail, infirm*, CP : *faint-hearted* : *fleeting*.
±tīegan (ē, ī, ȳ) *to* '*tie*,' *bind, Æ*; CP : *join, connect, ÆGr*. [tēag]
tīegle=tigle; tīeht-=tyht-
tīehð pres. 3 sg. of tēon I. and II.
tiel-=til-; tīema=tīma
tīeman (ǣ, ē, ī, ȳ) *to bring forth, engender, beget, propagate, Æ,W* : *make answerable for another person, call as witness, Æ,Bas* : (±) *vouch to warranty*, LL. ['*teem*'; tēam]

+**tīeme** I. (ē, ȳ) *suitable*. II. (ȳ) *team, yoke,* Æ.

tīen (ē, ī, ȳ) num. 'TEN,' *CP*.

tīenambre (ȳ) *holding ten ambers,* Lcd 32b.

tīenbebod (ē) n. *decalogue,* OEG 11¹⁰⁸

tīenfeald (ȳ) *ten-fold,* Æ.

tīengewintred (ȳ) *ten years old,* LL 19,27 H.

tīennihte (ȳ) *ten days old,* Bf 162¹³.

tīenstrenge (ē, ī) *ten-stringed,* VPs.

tīenwintre (ȳ) *ten years old,* Æ : *ten years long,* AO.

tīer *heap?* (GK), *drop?* (Sedgef.), Met 20⁸¹.

tīfe f. *bitch,* Lcd 64a.

tīfer=tīber

-**tīg** (ē, ȳ) v. fore-, forð-t.; **Tīg**=Tīw

tīgan=tīegan; **tīge**=tyge

tigel, tigele (o²) f. *earthen vessel, crock, pot, potsherd* : 'tile,' *brick, AO*; Mdf : *slabs for roofing, Cp,Lcd,VPs*.

tigelærne f. *tile kiln? house of brick?* KC 3·130′.

tigelen *made of pot, earthenware,* SPs 2⁹.

tigelfāg *tile-adorned,* An 842.

tigelgetel n. *tale of bricks,* Ex 5¹⁸.

tigelgeweorc n. *brick-making,* Æ.

tigellēah m *brick-field,* KC 5·267²¹.

tigelstān m. *tile,* ES 11·66. ['*tilestone*']

tigelwyrhta (y) m. *brick-maker, potter.*

tigen pp. of tēon II.

tiger pl. tigras '*tiger,*' Æ,Nar.

tīging f. *tie, connection.* ÆGr 14¹⁴. [tīgan]

tīgl=(1) tigel; (2) tygel

tigle f. '*muraenula,*' *sea-mullet?* WW 180³⁰.

tigle, tigol(e)=tigel, tigele

tigon pret. pl. of tēon II.

tīgrisc *of a tiger,* A 4·161.

tigðian (*AO*)=tīðian

-**tigu** v. egeðgetigu [egðe]; **tigule**=tigele

tihian=teohhian

tiht (y) m. *charge, crime,* LL,WW. [tēon II.]

tihtan I. (y) *to accuse,* LL. [tēon II.] II.= tyhtan

tihtbysig *involved in accusations, of bad reputation,* v. LL 2·305 and ANS 144·253.

tihtle (y) f. *accusation, suit, charge,* AO.

tihtlian *to accuse, charge,* LL.

tīhð pres. 3 sg. of tēon II.

til I. *good, apt, suitable, useful, profitable* : *excellent* : *brave* : *abounding.* II.† n. *goodness, fitness.* III. n.=till. IV. prep. *to, MtL,OET.* ['*till*']

tila=tela

tilen (eo) f. *endeavour,* GD 194¹².

tilfremmende *well-doing,* Rd 60⁷.

tilgan=tilian; **till** (OET)=twilic

tilia, tilig(e)a (y) m. *tiller, workman, hind, labourer, farmer, husbandman, Mt*; Æ. ['*tilie*']

tilian (eo, y) *to aim at, aspire to, strive after, try, endeavour,* Æ; CP : (±) *procure, obtain, gain, provide,* Æ : *exert oneself, work, make, generate,* Æ,CP : *tend, cherish, cultivate,* 'TILL,' *plough, CP* : *trade, traffic,* Æ : (±) *treat, cure.*

tiligea=tilia

tiling=tilung

tilt† n. *station, standing-place.*

till-=til-, tyll-

+**tillan** *to touch, attain,* Æ.

tillic† adj. *fit, good,* Rd. adv. -līce.

tilmōdig† *well-disposed, kind, good.*

±**tilð**, tilðe (y) f. '*tilth,*' *labour, husbandry, LL,W* : *crop, harvest, LL* : *gain, profit,* OEG.

tilung (eo, ie, io, y) f. *acquisition, procuring* : *care, solicitude* : *occupation, work, performance,* CP : *tending, culture, husbandry,* Æ : *produce, gain, income,* Æ.

tīma m. 'TIME,' *period, space of time,* Æ, AO : *lifetime,* Æ : *fixed time,* Æ,AO,CP : *favourable time, opportunity, CP* : *a metrical unit, Bf.*

tīman=tīeman

±**timber** n. '*timber,*' *building material, LL* : *act of building* : *building, structure, BH, Lcd,MtL,VPs* : *trees, woods, AO.* [v. Mdf]

timbergeweorc n. *cutting timber,* BC 1·344⁹.

+**timberhālgung** f. *feast of tabernacles,* OEG 56²⁸⁷.

timberhrycg m. *wooded ridge?* KC.

timberland (y¹, o³) n. *land given for repairing and maintaining buildings* : *land on which to grow timber* (BTs), KC 5·236¹².

+**timbernes** f. *building up, edification,* MFH 124.

timbor I. *a revolving borer, auger?* WW. 273⁸. II. =timber

±**timbran**, timbrian *to build, construct, erect,* BH,CP,G,Gen,LL : *effect, do, AO,CP*; Æ : *edify, instruct* : *cut* '*timber.*'

+**tim-bre** n., -bru f. *building, structure,* Æ, AO.

timbr(i)end mf. *builder,* BH,GD.

±**timbrung** f. *act of building,* Æ : *structure* : *edification.*

+**tīmian** (ȳ) *to happen, fall out,* Æ,Bf.

tīmlīce *quickly, soon,* ÆT 12.

timpana m. *timbrel,* Æ,CP,VPs. ['*tympan*']

timpestre f. *female timbrel-player,* LPs 67²⁶.

timple f. *a weaver's instrument,* LL 455,15¹ (cp. ātimplian).

tin I. n. '*tin,*' *CP.* II. f. *beam, rafter,* Gl. III.=tinen

tin num.=tīen

tinclian *to tickle,* Sc 52,88.

+**tinclic**=+tyngelic

tind m. *spike, beak, prong, tooth of a fork,* *Cp,Ep,Sol.* ['*tine*']

tindig *spiked,* WW 116¹².

tindiht *forked, jagged, beaked,* Gl,MH.

tindre=tyndre

tinen *made of tin,* ÆGr. ['*tinnen*']

+**ting,** tinge=+tyng, tynge

+**tingan³** *to press against,* An 138.

+**tingcræft** m. '*mechanica,*' *rhetoric,* HGl 479.

-**tining** v. gafol-t.

tinn *beam,* A 19·491.

tinnan *to stretch,* Gl : *desire, long for? burn?* Rim 54.

tinnen=tinen

tinstrenge=tienstrenge

tinterg=tintreg

tinterðegn=tintregðegn

tintreg (*AO*; Æ) n., tintrega m. *torture,* *torment, punishment,* AO,Lk,W. ['*tin-tregh*']

tintreganlic=tintreglic

tintregend (terg) m. *torturer,* WW 341¹⁹.

±**tintregian** *to torment, torture, punish,* Æ, AO.

tintreglic *full of torment, infernal,* BH 346¹².

tintregstōw f. *place of torment,* Guth 38⁴.

tintregðegn m. *torturer, executioner,* MtR, WW.

tintregung f. *torture, punishment,* Æ,WW.

tintrian (AO)=tintregian

tio-=teo-; **tiol-**=tel-, til-

tīr (ȳ) m. (†) *fame, glory, honour, ornament :* *name of the rune for* t : *name of a planet and a god* (*Mars*), Run 17.

tīreadig† *glorious, famous.*

tīrfæst† *glorious, famous.*

tīrfruma m. *prince of glory,* Cr 206.

tirgan (e, y;=ie) *to worry, exasperate, pain, provoke, excite,* Gl,Gu. ['*tar*']

tirging (y) f. '*zelus,*' *provocation,* BLPs.

tīrlēas *inglorious, infamous,* B 843.

tīrmeahtig† *of glorious might.*

tirð pres. 3 sg. of teran.

tīrwine m. (*famous*) *follower, retainer,* Met 25²¹.

tit, tite=titt

±**tītelian** *to indicate by a written mark, entitle, ascribe,* Æ : *appoint,* LL. [*L.*]

tītelung f. '*recapitulatio,*' *a giving of titles or headings,* OEG 1153.

titolose '*tidulosa*' (*plant*), OEG 56⁴²⁵.

titt m. '*teat,*' *nipple, breast,* Lcd,LkLR.

tittstrycel m. *teat,* WW 158⁴⁴.

tītul m. '*title,*' *superscription,* MkL 15²⁶. [*L.*]

tīð I. f. *assent, permission : giving, grant, boon, favour, concession,* Æ,BH (tigð). tiðe fremian *to grant.* ['*tithe*'] II. pres. 3 sg. of tēon I. and II.

tīða m., tīðe f. (only in phr. t. bēon, weor-ðan) *sharer in, receiver, grantee,* BH,Mt. ['*tithe*']

±**tīðian** (often w. g. thing and d. pers.) *to give, bestow, grant, permit,* Æ,AO. ['TITHE']

tīðing=tēoðung

tīðrian (ȳ) *to be favourable (to),* RWH 66¹³.

+**tīung** f. *preparation, arrangement,* Cp 684a.

tīurung=tēorung

Tīw *Tiw* (*northern god of war*), *Mars,* Gl, MH : *name of the rune for* t.

Tīwesdæg m. '*Tuesday,*' Bf; RB.

Tīwesniht f. *Monday night,* Lcd.

tō I. prep. α (w. d.) (motion) 'TO,' *into,* Æ,AO,CP. tō emnes *abreast of* : (rest) *at* : (figurative direction, object of verb) *conducing to, to.* fōn tō rīce *to ascend the throne* : (definition, destination) *for, as a.* wyrcan tō wīte *to contrive as a punishment* : *in accordance with, according to* : (time) *at.* tō midre niht *at midnight.* tō dæg *to-day.* tō langum fyrste *for a long time* : (with gerunds) *to express purpose, etc.* β (w. g.) (of time) *at.* II. adv. *besides, also, Bo* : '*too,*' *excessively, Bl,Cr* : *thereto* : *towards, in the direction of* : *in addition, besides.* adverbial phrases;—tō ðām (ðǣm), tō ðæs (1) *so* (adeo), *to such an extent.* (2) *to that end.* (3) *moreover, however.* tō hwæs *whither.* tō ðām ðæt, tō ðȳ ðæt *in order that.* tō ðon ðæt *until.* tō ðæs ðe *when, where.* tō hwon, tō hwȳ *for what, wherefore.* tō sōðum *truly.* tō ðearfe *according to what is needed.* ðǣr tō ēacan *in addition thereto.* ne tō wuhte *by no means.* tō him *next or nearest to him.*

tō- prefix I. with accent (stress) it has the meaning of adv. tō (as in tōcweðan, tō-bringan, tōcuman). [*Ger.* zu-] II. without accent=*asunder* (as in tōbrecan). [*Ger.* zer-]

tōætȳcan (ē³) *to increase,* BH 112¹. [ēac]

tōætȳcnes f. *increase,* BH 226 ca³¹.

tōāmearcian *to mark out, assign,* Sc 29⁵.

tōbǣdan *to elevate, exalt,* Bf 144²,LPs 36³⁵.

tōbēatan⁷ *to beat severely, destroy by beating,* AO,Chr. ['*tobeat*']

tōbefealdan⁷ *to fold together,* WW 343¹⁰.

tōbeflōwan⁷ *to flow up to,* LPs 61¹¹.

tōbegietan⁵ *to acquire, purchase,* EHy 4¹⁶.

tōbelimpan³ (impers.) *it belongs, behoves,* Bl 49¹.

tōberan⁴ *to carry, remove, carry off, purloin,* Bl : *scatter, dissipate, distract, destroy* : *swell,* CP : *separate.* ['*tobear*']

tōberennes f. *difference,* WW 390²⁷.

tōberstan[3] (intr.) *to burst apart, go to pieces,* Æ,AO : (tr.) *cause to burst apart, shatter,* Æ. ['*toburst*']

tōberstung f. *bursting,* LCD 74a.

tōbīgend *bowing down, tottering,* WW 386[30].

tōblǣdan *to inflate, puff up,* Sc 82[10] : *dilate, enlarge,* LHy 3[1].

tōblāwan[7] *to blow to pieces, blast, scatter,* Æ : *puff up, inflate, distend,* Lcd. ['*toblow*']

tōblāwennes f. *inflation,* ÆH 1·86[13].

tōborstennes f. *abscess,* LCD 1·322'.

tōbrǣdan *to spread abroad, disperse, scatter,* AO,CP : *spread out, extend,* Bo,Mt; Æ : *open, dilate* : *multiply.* ['*tobrede*']

tōbrǣd(ed)nes f. *broadness, breadth,* Ps.

tōbrecan[4] *to break in pieces, break up, shatter, destroy, ruin, wreck, overthrow, annul,* Æ, Bo,Lcd; AO,CP : *diffuse* : *break through, violate, force,* KC; Æ,AO : *interrupt.* ['*tobreak*']

tōbrēdan I.=tōbregdan. II.=tōbrǣdan

tōbregdan[3] *tear in pieces, wrench apart, rend, lacerate,* AO,MtR : *distract* : *cast off, shake off* : *turn to, turn about.* slǣpe tōb. *awake, wake up.* ['*tobraid*']

tōbrengnes f. *oblation, offering,* EPs 39[7].

tōbrittian=tōbrȳtan

tōbrocenlic *brittle, fragile,* W 263[13].

tōbrȳs-an, -ian *to bruise, shatter, crush, break to pieces,* Mt; Æ. ['*tobruise*']

tōbrȳtan *to break in pieces, destroy,* Æ : *be repentant.* ['*tobryt*']

tōbrȳtednes f. *contrition, sorrow,* LPs.

tōbrȳtendlic *brittle, fragile,* WW 242[12].

tōbrytling f. *crushing, contrition,* Sc 82[12].

tōbryttian=tōbrȳtan

tōc pret. 3 sg. of tacan.

tōceorfan[3] *to cut, cut to pieces, cut off, cut away,* Æ,MkL. ['*tocarve*']

tōcēowan[2] *to bite to pieces, chew, eat,* Æ. ['*tochew*']

tōch=tōh

tōcīme=tōcyme

tōcīnan[1] *to split open, cleave asunder, splinter, crack,* Cp,Lcd; Æ. ['*tochine*']

tōcirhūs n. *lodging-house, inn,* WW 147[25].

tōclǣfan *to split, cleave,* OEG 18b[38].

tōclēofan[2] *to cleave asunder, split, divide,* Æ,Bo. ['*tocleave*']

tōcleoflan=toclifian

tōclifian *to cleave to, adhere, stick to,* BPs.

tōclifrian *to be torn in pieces, scratched about,* Æ.

tōclip-=tōclyp-

tōclypigendlic *vocative, used in calling,* ÆGR 241[15].

tōclypung f. *calling upon, invocation,* Æ.

tōcnāwan[7] *to know, acknowledge, recognise, distinguish, discern,* Æ,CP.

tōcnāw(en)nes f. *understanding, discernment,* ÆH 2·362'; GD 311[11].

tōcnyssan *to shake,* RB 121[6].

tōcuman[4] *to come, arrive,* CP.

tōcwæs-cednes (RPs 105[30]), -tednes (SPs) f. *trembling, shaking, shattering.*

tōcweðan[5] *to forbid, interdict, prohibit,* Æ.

tōcwīsan=tōcwȳsan

tōcwylman *to torment,* HL 12[56].

tōcwȳsan *to crush utterly, grind to pieces, bruise, destroy* : *be crushed,* Æ.

tōcwȳsednes f. *crushed condition,* Æ : *contrition,* GD 125[11].

tōcyme m. *coming, advent, arrival,* Æ,Bl, CP. ['*tocome*']

tōcyrcanwerd *towards church,* ÆL 31[902].

tōcyrran (intr.) *to part, separate,* CHR.

tōdæg, tōdæge adv. '*to-day,*' Æ,CP; AO.

tōdǣl=tōdāl

tōdǣlan (ē) tr. and intr. *to divide, separate, scatter, disperse,* Æ,AO,Bo,Chr,W : *dismember, cut off, destroy* : *distribute,* Æ : *discriminate, distinguish* : *be divided* : *express, utter,* CPs. ['*todeal*']

tōdǣledlīce adv. *separately, distinctly, diversely,* ÆGR.

tōdǣlednes f. *division* : *severance, separation* : *difference, intermission, respite, cessation,* Æ.

tōdǣlendlic *separable, distinct.* adv. -līce.

tōdǣlnes f. *division, separation,* CP.

tōdāl n. *partition, division, separation,* Æ : *difference, distinction, discretion,* Æ : *dispersion* : '*comma,*' *dividing point, clause, section, period.*

tōdēlan (KGL)=tōdǣlan

tōdēman *to decide, judge, sentence, determine.*

tōdihtnian *to dispose, arrange,* BLPs 82[6].

tōdōn anv. *to apply, put to, add,* LCD : *divide, separate, distinguish,* Hex,LL : *undo, open, unbind,* PPs. ['*todo*']

tōdrǣfan *to scatter, disperse, separate, drive out or apart,* BH,Mt; Æ. ['*todreve*']

tō-drǣfednes (Æ), -drǣfnes (JnL) f. *dispersion, scattering.*

tōdrēosan[2] *to be destroyed, perish, decay,* MH. ['*todrese*']

tōdrīfan[1] *to scatter, disperse, drive away,* B, JnL; Æ : *destroy, repel.* ['*todrive*']

tōdwǣscan† *to put out, extinguish.*

tōēacan prep. and adv. *besides, moreover, also,* Æ,AO,CP.

tōēcan=tōēacan; tōēcnes=tōīecnes

tōefenes, tōemnes (AO) prep. (d.) *alongside.*

tōendebyrdnes f. *order, series,* BH 216[20].

toeð (VPs)=tēð

tōēðlan *to inspire,* GD 270[13].

tōfǣng=tōfeng

tōfǣr n. *departure, decease,* LkL 9[31].

tōfaran[6] intr. *to be scattered, disperse, separate, disappear, Gen,Lcd*; AO. ['*tofare*']

tōfealdan[7] *to come to land* (trans. of *L.* 'applicare'), ÆGR 138[9].

tōfeallan[7] *to fall down, collapse, AO* : *fall apart, fall off, Æ.* ['*tofall*']

tōfeng I. (?) m. *grip, seizure,* LPs 123[6]. II. pret. 3 sg. of tōfōn.

tōfēran *to go in different directions, separate, disperse, Æ* : *deal out, distribute, Æ.*

tōferian *to scatter, disperse, get rid of* : *put off* : *digest,* RB 32[14].

tōfēsian *to drive away, rout,* W 132,133.

tōflēam m. *refuge,* RPs 93[22].

tō-flēon, -flēogan[2] *to be dispersed, fly apart, burst, Lcd.* ['*tofly*']

tōflēotan[2] *to carry away by a flood, Chr* 1097. ['*tofleet*']

tōflōwan[7] *to flow down or apart, be split, melt, Æ,CP* : *flow away, ebb* : *flow to, pour in* : *distract,* CP.

tōflōw-(ed)nes, -en(d)nes f. *flowing, flux, Æ* : *diffusion,* GD 94[21].

tō-foran (e[3], o[3]) prep. (w. d.) (time and place) *before, BH,Chr,G* : (superiority) *above, over, beyond, Æ,Bo* : *besides, ÆH* 2·584'. ['*tofore*']

tōforlǣtan[7] *to dismiss,* OEG 605.

tōforlǣtennes f. *intermission,* ÆH,RBL.

toft m. *homestead, site of a house, Ct,Lcd*; LL 400. ['*toft*']

tōfyllan *to smite in pieces,* PPs 67[21].

+tog n. *tugging, contraction, spasm, cramp,* Lcd : pl. *traces* (*of a horse*), ÆL 31[973].

tōgædereweard adv. *towards one another,* AO.

tō-gædre, -gædere, -gadere adv. '*together,' An,BC,Mt.* tōg. gān, fōn, cuman *to engage in battle,* CHR. [gaderian]

tōgægnes=tōgegnes, tōgēanes

tōgǣlan *to profane, defile,* LPs 88[32].

tōgǣnan *to say, affirm,* LPs 93[4].

tōgān anv. pret. 3 sg. tōēode *to go to or into* : (impers. w. g.) *come to pass, happen* : *separate, part, depart, Æ,HR.* ['*togo*']

tōgang m. *approach, access, attack,* CM,Lcd.

tōgangan[7] *to go away, pass away, BH,Rd.* ['*togang*']

tōgēan prep. w. d. *towards, MkL* (-eægn). ['*togains*']

tōgēanes prep. w. d. and a.; adv. *in opposition to, against, B,Chr,SPs* : *towards, to, Æ,Bl,MkL* : *before,* CP : *in return, in reply.* him tōg. *to meet him, Chr,MtL.* ['*togains*']

tōgēare adv. *in this year,* BF 156[17].

tōgeclīfian (eo, y)=tōclīfian

tōgecorennes f. *adoption,* DR 29[14].

tōgeēcan=tōgeīecan

tōgeefnan? *to associate with, join oneself to?* AS 39[6]. [MS tōgeenan]

tōgegnes=tōgēanes

tōgehlytto f. *fellowship, union,* DR 109[15].

tōgeīecan *to add to, increase,* BF,GD.

tōgeīecendlic (ī[3]) *added to, adjectival, adjective,* ÆGR.

tōgeīht pp. of tōgeīecan.

tōgeīhtnes f. *addition, increment,* BF 46[33].

tōgeladung f. *assembly,* MFH 174.

tōgelǣstan (e[8]) *to accompany,* WW 365[41].

tōgelan[4] *to diffuse,* GD 192[18].

tōgelaðung f. *concourse,* MFH 173.

tōgelēstan=tōgelǣstan

tōgelicgende *belonging,* KC 3·350[1].

togen pp. of tēon I. (and occly. II.).

tōgenēalǣcan=tōnealǣcan

tōgēnes=tōgēanes

tōgengan *to separate,* GEN 841.

-tōgennes v. ofer-t., ðurh-t.

tōgeotan[2] *to pour away, spill* : *spread* : *exhaust.*

tōgescēadan[7] *to expound, interpret,* LkR 24[27].

tōgescofen (CP) pp. of tōscūfan.

tōgesettan *to put to,* RPs 9[39].

tōgetēon[2,1] *to draw towards, attract,* BPs.

togettan impers. *to twitch, be spasmodic,* Lcd 81a. [togian]

tōgeðēodan (īe, ȳ) *to adhere, cling to* : *adjoin,* BH 56[30].

tōgewegen *applied,* BH.

tōgewunod *accustomed,* AS 23[19].

tōgeȳcan=tōgeīecan

togian *to draw, drag,* HL 15[308]. ['*tow*']

tōgife, tōgifes adv. *freely, gratis.*

toginan[1] *to be opened, split, gape, yawn.* [cp. *Ger.* gähnen]

tōglīdan[1] *to glide away, split, slip, fall asunder, vanish, B,Met.* ['*toglide*']

tōgolen pret. of tōgelan.

tōgotennes f. *pouring out, effusion, shedding, spreading,* Lcd.

+togu np. *traces* (*of a horse*), ÆL 31[973].

togung f. *tugging, twitch, spasm,* Lcd.

tōh '*tough,' Cp,Ep* : *tenacious, sticky, Lcd.*

tōhaccian *to hack to pieces, Æ* (3[186]). ['*tohack*']

tōhǣlan *to emasculate, weaken,* MFH 174.

tōheald (a[2], y[2]) adj. and adv. *inclined, forward, in advance.*

tōhēawan[7] *to hew in pieces, Æ,Chr.* ['*tohew*']

tōhīgung f. *result, effect,* DR.

tōhīht=tōhyht

tohl=tōl

tōhladan[6] *to scatter, disperse, destroy* (or ? *tōhlacan), GEN 1693.

tōhlēotan[2] *to divide by lot*, BL,PPs.

tōhlic *tough, tenacious*. adv. -līce, GL.

tōhlīdan[1] *to split, open, spring apart, burst, gape, break*, AO.

tohlīne f. *tow-line*, WW. [togian]

tōhlocen=tōlocen pp. of tōlūcan.

tōhlystend m. *listener*, CP96.

tōhnescan *to soften*, LCD94a.

tōhopa m. *hope, Bo,PPs*; CP. ['*tohope*']

tōhopung f. *faith, trust*, ÆL23[155].

tōhrēosan[2] *to fall to pieces, decay, BH,W*; ÆL. ['*toreose*']

tōhrēran *to break, shake to pieces, destroy*, GL.

tōhricod ptc. *cut off, dispersed*, GPH398, 399.

tōhrȳran *to shake in pieces*, v. OEG2261.

+toht n. *battle array, battle*, MA104.

tohte† f. *fight, conflict, battle, campaign*.

tōhuntian *to hunt*, WE65[7].

tōhwega adv. and sb. *somewhat, some, a little*.

tōhweorfan[3] *to go away, separate, scatter, disperse*, CHR.

tōhwon adv. *wherefore, why : to which (point), to what extent, how far, how long : to which end, for what purpose or reason.*

tōhwyrfan (=ie[2]) *to overturn*, LPs117[13].

tōhyht m. *hope, refuge, consolation*, RUN.

tōhyld=tōheald

tōīecan (ē[2], ȳ[2]) *to increase*, BH112[1]B.

tōīecnes (ē[2]) f. *increase*, BH226[31].

tōīernan[3] *to run to, run together : flow away, be dispersed : run hither and thither, wander about.*

tōīrnan=tōīernan; tol=toll

tōl n. '*tool,' instrument, implement*, Æ,Bo, LL : *weapon*, ZDA9·424.

tōlǣgon pret. pl. of tōlicgan.

tōlǣtan[7] *to disperse, relax, release*, CP.

tōlǣtennes f. *despondency*, LCD1·262[3].

tolcendlīce adv. *wantonly*, GPH401.

tolcettende '*indruticans*,' v. OEG1218.

tolcetung f. *wanton excitement*, OEG.

tōleoðian=tōliðian; tōlēs=tōlȳs-

tolfrēo '*toll-free*,' KC4·209[19].

tolgetung=tolcetung; tōlic=tōhlic

tōlicgan[5] *to lie or extend in different directions, separate, part, divide*, AO,BC. ['*tolie*']

tōliðian (eo) *to dismember, separate*, Æ : *relax, cancel*, GD349[28].

toll mn. *impost, 'toll,' tribute*, Chr,EC,G, Gl : *passage-money*, Æ : *rent*, Æ : *act or right of taking toll*, Æ.

tollere m. *tax-gatherer, publican*, Æ,WW. ['*toller*']

tollsceam-ol, -ul m. *seat of custom, treasury*,

tollscīr f. *taxing district*, ÆH2·468'.

toln f. *toll, custom, duty*, TC. ['*tolne*']

tolnere m. *tax-gatherer*, WW. ['*tolner*']

tōlōcian *to belong to*, CC22[7].

tolsetl n. *place of toll or custom*, Æ.

tōlūcan[2] *to pull apart, dislocate, destroy, BH.* ['*tolouk*']

tōlȳsan (ē;=īe) *to dissolve, loosen, relax*, Æ : *unhinge, separate, break open.*

tōlȳs(ed)nes (ē) f. *loosing, dissolution, dispersion, destruction, release, dismissal : desolation*, GD : *death.*

tōlȳsend m. *destroyer*, WW220[13].

tōlȳsendlic *destructive*, LPs119[4].

tōlȳsing (ē) f. *loosing, release, redemption : destruction*, LCD3·206[20].

tom=tam

tōm adj. w. g. *free from*, Cr1211. ['*toom*']

tōmǣldan *to hinder by speech*, DD26. [meldian]

tōmearcian *to distinguish, describe, note down, enrol*, G,SPs.

tōmearcodnes f. *enumeration, census, enrolment*, Lk2[2].

tō-mergen, -merigen (Æ)=tōmorgen

tōmetan[5] *to mete out*, LPs107[8].

tōmiddes prep. (w. d.) *amidst, among, in the midst of*, Æ,Jn; AO,CP. adv. *into the midst*, B,Lcd. ['*tomids*']

tōmorgen adv. *to-morrow*, Bf,CP. ['*to-morn*']

tōn dsmn. of tōh.

tōnama m. *surname*, MkL; Æ. ['*toname*']

+tōnamian *to name besides, surname*, LKL6[14] (tor-).

tōnēalǣcan *to approach*, Pss.

tōnemnan *to distinguish by name, name*, AO.

tōnēolīcan=tōnēalǣcan

tong, tonge=tang, tange

tonian *to thunder*, ÆGr138[3].

tonice=tunece

tōniman[4] *separate, take apart : take away.*

tōnom-=tōnam-

top I. m. '*top*' (*highest part*), WW143[25] : *tassel, tuft.* II.'*top*'(*plaything*)? *ball? ApT* 13[13].

toppa m. *thread, tuft?* OEG23[45].

tor=torr

tōrǣcan (pret. 3 sg. tōrǣhte) *to join, put together*, OEG4489.

tōrǣndan=tōrendan; toranēage=torenīge

tōrbegete (o?) *hard to get*, LCD43b.

torcht, torct-=torht, torht-

torcul n. *wine-press*, MtR21[33]. [*L.*]

torcyrre *hard to convert*, MH110[15].

tord n. *piece of excrement, dung, filth*, LCD.

tordwifel m. *dung-beetle*, LCD.

toren pp. of teran.

tōrendan (æ) to rend apart, tear in pieces, MkL,PPs. ['torend']

toren-ēage, -īg(g)e, -īege blear-eyed, CP.

tōrēosan=tōhrēosan

±**torfian** to throw, cast missiles, shoot, stone, Mk; Æ : be tossed, NC326. ['torve']

torfung f. throwing, casting (of stones), AO.

torht I. n. clearness, brightness. II. adj. bright, radiant, beautiful, splendid, noble, illustrious, Ph. ['torht'] adv. -e brightly, clearly : beautifully, splendidly.

torhtian to show, Cp2161.

torhtlic† bright, clear, radiant, glorious. adv. -līce.

torhtmōd† glorious, noble.

torhtnes f. radiance, splendour, GL,LCD.

tōrinnan (CP)=tōiernan

torn I. n. anger, indignation : grief, misery, suffering, pain. [Ger. zorn] II. adj. bitter, cruel, grievous.

+**tornamian**=+tōnamian

torncwide† m. offensive speech.

torne† adv. indignantly, insultingly, bitterly, grievously.

torngemōt n. battle, B1140.

torngeniōla† m. angry opponent.

tornīge=torenīge

tornlic sorrowful, grievous, PPs125⁵.

tornmōd angry, Gu621.

tornsorg f. sorrow, care, FT76.

tornword n. offensive expression, CR172.

tornwracu f. revenge, Gu272.

tornwyrdan to be incensed? AO54².

toroc grub, weevil? WW224³⁸ (ES41·164).

tōroren=tōhroren pp. of tōhrēosan.

torr m. 'tower,' watch-tower, CP,MtL; AO : rock, crag, Mdf. [L. turris; v. ES41·102]

torrian to tower, ByH130¹³.

tōryne m. running together, concourse, ES 39·353.

tōrȳpan to scratch, EC164¹⁸.

tōsǣlan (impers., w. d. pers. and g. thing) to be unsuccessful, fail : lack, want.

tōsamne=tōsomne

tōsāwan⁷ to strew, scatter, spread, Æ.

tosca m. frog, toad, DR,PPs.

tōscacan=tōsceacan

tōscād-=tōscēad-

tōscǣgde v. tōscecgan.

tōscǣnan to break in pieces, break, Æ,JnL, MkLR. ['toshene']

tōscarian=tōscearian

tōsceacan⁶ (a) to shake in pieces, WW : drive asunder, drive away, shake off, Æ. ['to-shake']

tōscēacerian to scatter, ÆL23²⁴.

tōscēad n. distinction, difference, Æ,CP.

tōscēadan⁷ (ā) to part, separate, scatter, divide : set at variance, CP : discern, discriminate, distinguish, decide, Æ,Bo; CP : differ : express, LPs. ['toshed']

tōscēadednes f. separation, MFH101.

tōscēadend m. divider, separator, WW223³⁰.

tōscēadenes (ā) f. separation, distinction, HL158¹⁶².

tōscearian (a²) to scatter, APs67².

tōscecgan (æ) to be separate, differ, BH 160²⁵n.

tōscellan=tōscylian

tōscendan to destroy, GD121²⁴.

tōscēotan² intr. to spring apart, disperse, Æ. ['toshoot']

tōscerian (KGL)=tōscirian

tōscirian (e, y) to divide, distribute, MFH : detach, separate, GL : distinguish, CHRD.

tōscrīðan² to flow apart, disperse, MET20⁹³.

tōscūfan² to push apart, scatter : impel, incite, CP : do away, remove.

tōscyftan (=i) to divide, distribute, Chr. ['toshift']

tōscyl-ian, -ian (e) tr. and intr. to separate, divide, NC351.

tōscyrian=tōscirian

tōsendan (tr.) to send to : send apart, send out, disperse.

tōsēoðan² to boil thoroughly, LCD.

tōsetednes f. disposition, EPs72⁷.

tōsettan to dispose, Pss,BL.

tōsēðan? to test, prove, AS7¹¹.

tōsigan¹ to wear out, be threadbare, Æ.

tōsittan⁵ to be separated, AO14¹⁸.

tōslacian to slacken, relax, WW73¹⁰.

tōslǣfan to cut up, NR32².

tōslēan⁶ to strike in pieces, destroy, Æ,AO. Gl : drive away, RB18³,⁴. ['toslay']

tōslīfan¹ to split, WW.

tōslītan¹ to tear asunder, rend, wound, break open, open, Æ,CP : interrupt : separate, scatter, destroy, CP : distract : be different, NG.

tōslitnes (y²) f. laceration, BH : division, NG.

tōslūpan² to slip away, be relaxed, fall to pieces, open, dissolve, Æ,CP : melt (with fear) : be paralysed. tōslopen relaxed, loose, dissolute.

tōslūping f. dissolving, dissolution, Sc68⁸.

tōsmēagan to inquire into, consider, Bo148⁵.

tōsnǣdan to cut up, NR28⁵.

tōsnīðan¹ to cut asunder, cut up : cut off amputate.

tōsōcn f. visiting, CHRD67³⁶.

tōsōcnes f. pursuit, DR28¹⁸.

tōsōcnung f. pursuit, DR81⁷.

tōsomne adv. together, Æ,AO,Bl; CP. t. cuman to engage in battle. ['tosame']

tōsomnian *to collect together, bring together,* BH 230[7].

tōsōðan adv. *in sooth, in truth* (or ? two words).

tōspræ**c** f. *speaking to* (*another*), *conversation,* Æ,CP.

tōspræ**dan** *to spread out, IM;* Æ. ['*tospread*']

tōspringan[3] *to spring apart, fly asunder, crack,* Æ. ['*tospring*']

tōsprytting f. *inciting,* CHR 1101.

tosta=tosca

tōstæ**ncan**=tōstencan

tōstandan[6] *to be put off, not to occur : stand apart, differ from, be discordant,* Æ.

tōstencan (æ) *to scatter, disperse, drive apart, drag along,* Æ,CP : *nullify, destroy : perish,* SPs 82[9].

tō-stencednes (Æ), -stenc(en)nes, f. *dispersion, dissolution, destruction.*

tōstencend m. *prodigal,* LCD.

tōsteng-=tōstenc-

tōstician *to pierce,* AO 128[14].

tōstihtan *to order, arrange,* CPs 111[5].

tōstincan[3] *to distinguish by smell,* ÆH 2·372'.

tōstingan[3] *to thrust in, pierce,* LCD.

tō-stregdan, -strēdan[3] (and wv.) *to scatter, dissipate, disperse,* CP : *distract : destroy.*

tōstrēt (CP) pres. 3 sg. of tōstregdan.

tōsundrian *to separate,* LHy 7[8].

tōswā**pan**[7]† *to disperse.*

tōswellan[3] *to swell out,* Æ. ['*toswell*']

tōswengan *to drive asunder, destroy.* [swingan]

tōsweorcan[3] *to obscure,* OEG 1737.

tōswīfan[1] intr. *to separate,* MET 11[36].

tōsyndrian *to sunder, separate, divide : discriminate.*

+**tot** n. *pomp, parade, vainglory,* ÆH.

tōtalu f. *reputation,* DR 102[3].

tōtellan *to distinguish,* MET 16[15].

tōtēon[2,1] *to draw asunder, pull apart, rend, destroy,* AO : *take to oneself, claim for oneself,* LL (or ? tō prep.).

tōteran[4] *to tear in pieces, bite, lacerate, cut out,* Æ,AO,CP : *destroy : harass* (*mind*).

tōtian *to peep out, stick out, CP* 105[5]. ['*toot*']

tōtihting f. *instigation,* CHR 1094.

tōtorfian *to cast about, toss,* Mt 14[24].

tōtræ**glian** *to pull to pieces, strip,* GPH 396[267].

tōtredan[5] *to tread to pieces?* GL.

totrida m. *swing?* GL,WW 276[27].

tōtwæ**man** (ē, ēa, ȳ) *to separate, divide, dissever, AO : distinguish : break up, break in pieces, dissolve : scatter : defer, postpone,* LL 298,17[2] : *divorce,* CHR 958 D. ['*totweme*']

tōtwæ**mednes** f. *separation, distinction,* W 194[22].

tō-twē(a)man, -twȳman=tōtwæman

tōð m., ds. and nap. tēð, occl. ds. tōðe and nap. tōð(as) '*tooth*,*'* *Cp,Guth,Lcd,LL, MtR,VPs;* AO : *tusk,* WW 397[27]. tōðum ontȳnan *to utter.*

tōðece (æ[2]) m. *toothache,* AS 41[4].

tōðenednes f. *stretching, distension,* OEG 5452.

tōðēnian *to attend upon, serve,* Sc 102[9].

tōðening f. *distension,* OEG 2[476].

tōðēnung f. *administration,* CM 1185.

tōðerscan[3] *to dash in pieces,* CHR 1009.

tōðgār m. *tooth-pick,* LCD 13b.

tōðindan[3] *to swell up, inflate, puff up,* Æ : *be arrogant.*

tōðlēas *toothless,* GPH 394.

tōðmæ**gen** n. *strength of tusks,* GNC 20.

tōðræ**stan** *to crush, destroy,* CPs 106[16].

tōðreoma=tōðrima; **tōðrescan**=tōðerscan

tōðrima (eo[2]) m. *enclosure of teeth, gum,* LCD.

tōðringan *to drive asunder,* RD 4[27].

tōðsealf f. *tooth-salve,* LCD.

tōðsticca m. *tooth-pick,* WW 219[3].

tōðunden pp. of tōðindan.

tōðundenes f. *the state of being puffed up, arrogance,* Æ.

tōðundenlic *arrogant.* adv. -līce, RB.

tōðunian *to astonish,* WW 346[22].

tōðwæ**rc** m. *toothache,* LCD.

tōðwīnan[1] *to disappear,* HL 15[200]. [dwīnan]

tōðwyrm m. *a worm in the teeth,* LCD 19a.

tōwæ**lede** pret. sg. of *tōwieltan to roll to,* MkL 15[46].

tō-ward, -wardes=tō-weard, -weardes

towcræ**ft** m. *spinning,* HL 10[339].

tōweard I. adj. *facing, approaching, impending, BH,Bl,Lcd : future,* Æ,Bl,Bo, Mk. **II.** prep. (w. d., g.) *towards, AO,CP.* **III.** adv. *towards, forwards.* ['*toward,' 'towards*']

tōweardes=tōweard II., III.

tōweardlic *in the future,* Æ. adv. -līce, BH 368[21].

tōweardnes f. *future, time to come,* BH,Bl.

tōweaxan[7] *to grow apart,* NR 22.

tōweccan *to arouse, excite,* B 2948.

tōwegan[5] *disperse, scatter,* PH 184.

tōwendan *to overthrow, subvert, destroy,* Æ, AO. ['*towend*']

tōweorpan[3] (e, u, y) *to cast down, break in pieces, dissipate, blot out, destroy,* Æ,Bo, Mt; AO,CP : *throw out,* CP. ['*towarp*']

tōwerd=tōweard; **tōwerpan**=tōweorpan

tō-wesnes (CP), -wesenes, -westnes (BH) f. *dissolution : separation, discord, dissension.*

towettan *to associate with,* LL (322').

towhūs n. *tow-house, spinning-house or chamber*, WW 186²⁹. [FTP 166]

tōwieltan v. tōwælede

tōwītan *to depart, pass away*, ByH 90².

tō-wiðere, -wiðre prep. (w. d., a.) *against*, Ex : *in answer to*, CR.

towlic *belonging to thread.* t. weorc *material for spinning*, WW.

towmȳderce f. *tow-chest? work-box?* TC 538²¹.

tōword (VPs)=tōweard

tōworpednes=tōworpennes

tōworp(en)nes f. *subversion, destruction, desolation*, Æ,CP : *dispersion : expulsion.*

tōwrecan † *to drive asunder, scatter, dissipate.*

tōwrītan⁵ *to describe*, OEG 1065.

tōwritennes f. *writing down, description*, Æ.

tōwrīðan¹ *to twist apart, distort*, ÆGR 155¹⁵.

towtōl n. *spinning implement*, LL 455,15¹.

tōwunderlic *'admirabilis*,' SPs 41⁴.

tōwurpan (Æ)=tōweorpan

tōwyrd I. f. *opportunity*, BH 52²¹. II.= tōweard

tōwyrpan=tōweorpan

tōwyrpendlic *destructible*, GPH 394.

tōwyrpnes=tōworpennes

toxa (OEG 1858)=tosca

tōȳcan=tōīecan; **tōyrnan**=tōiernan

tracter *funnel*, NC 351. [*L.* trajectorium]

træd pret. 3 sg., trædon pret. pl. of tredan.

træf n., nap. tr(e)afu *tent, pavilion : dwelling, building*, An 844.

træglian *to pluck, pull*, GPH 398.

trændel=trendel; **træppe**=treppe

trafu v. træf.

trāg I.† adj. *evil, mean, bad.* II. f. *evil, affliction*, EL 668.

trāge adv. *evilly, cruelly*, PPs 108²⁰.

-trāglīce v. un-t.

traht m. *text, passage : exposition, treatise, commentary*, Æ. [*L.* tractus]

trahtað m. *commentary*, WW. [*L.*]

trahtbōc f. *(religious) treatise, commentary*, Æ. [trahtian]

traht-ere, -nere (Æ) m. *expounder, commentator, expositor.*

±traht-ian, -nian (Æ) *to treat, comment on, expound, consider : interpret, translate*, NG. [*L.*]

trahtnung, trahtung f. *explanation, exposition, commentary*, Æ.

trālsc *tragic*, BH 154³.

tramet m. *page (of a book)*, ÆGR.

trandende (o¹) *precipitous, steep*, Cp 805 P.

trappe=treppe; **tratung**=trahtung

trē (NG), trēa (VPs)=trēow I.

treafīlce *grievously*, PPs 102⁶.

treafu v. træf.

±trēagian *to sew together, mend*, OEG.

treaht-=traht-; **trēawa**=trēowa

+tred n. *crowd*, WW 209¹⁰.

±tredan⁵ (eo) tr. and intr. *to 'tread*,' *step on, trample*, B,CP,G,PPs; Æ,AO : *traverse, pass over, enter upon, roam through*, B.

treddan *to tread on, trample*, WW : *investigate*, PPs.

tredde f. *press (for wine, etc.)*, GD.

treddian† *to tread, step, walk*, B.

trede *fit to tread on, firm*, CR 1166.

tredel m. *step*, WW 117⁶ : *sole of foot*, LL 438,21. ['*treadle*']

tredend m. *treader*, WW 197⁹.

trefet '*trivet*,' *tripod*, BC 3·367'.

trēg (WW 281³⁵)=trīg

trega m. *misfortune, misery, trouble, grief, pain*, Gen,Met,RB. ['*tray*']

tregian *to trouble, harass, vex*, EPs,W.

+tregian *to feel repugnance at*, A 2·358.

treht-=traht-; **trem**=trym

tremegan=trymian, trymman

tremes=trymes; **tremm-**=trymm-

-tremman v. wið-t.

trendan *to turn round, revolve, roll*, A 1·285. ['*trend*']

trendel (æ, y) n. *sphere, circle, ring, orb*, Æ,Bf,Chr,Lcd : *circus*. ['*trendle*']

trendeled (y¹, y²) *made round*, WW 152⁵. [v. '*trindle*']

trendelnes f. *circuit, surrounding space*, RPs 11⁹ (u¹).

-trendlian v. ā-t.; **trēo**=trēow

treodan (VPs)=tredan; **trēoð**=trēowð

trēow I. n. (nap. trēowu, trēow) '*tree*,' Æ, BH,CP,VPs; Mdf : *wood, timber*, BH : *beam, log, stake, stick*, AO,Bl; CP : *wood, grove : tree of the cross, cross*, Rood. II. f. (ū, ȳ) *truth, fidelity, faith, trust, belief : pledge, promise, agreement, treaty : favour, grace, kindness.* [*Ger.* treue] III.=trēowe

trēowa (AO,CP)=trūwa

trēowan=trīewan

trēowan (ē, ī, īe, ȳ) trans. w. d. *to believe, trust in, hope, be confident, rely (on)*, B,Bo, Gen : intr. *trust*, PPs : refl. *exculpate oneself*, LL : (+) *persuade, suggest*, AO : *make true or credible : be faithful (to) : confederate (with)*, GL. ['*trow*']

trēowcynn n. *species of tree*, Æ.

trēowe I. (ē, ī, īe, ū, ȳ) '*true*' ('*i-treowe*'), *faithful, honest, trustworthy*, B,Chr,Gen, Gu,LL,WW; AO : *genuine*. II.=trēow II.

trēowen (ī, ȳ) *of a tree, of wood, wooden*, Lcd,WW 125²⁸; Æ. ['*treen*']

±trēowfæst *true, faithful*, MtL,PPs; Æ. ['*truefast*']

+trēowfæstnian *to be trusty*, MtL p 4¹².

trēowfēging f. *joining together (of boards)*, WW 206³⁴.

trēowfugol m. *forest bird*, Gu 707.

±**trēowful** *faithful, trusty, true.* adv. -līce.

+**trēowfulnes** f. *'Israel'!* RPs 21²⁵; Hy 7⁸³.

trēowgeðofta† m. *faithful comrade*, AA 45⁴.

trēowgeweorc n. *wood-work, a structure of timber*, BH 272⁵.

trēowgewrid n. *thicket of trees*, GUTH 20⁷.

trēowian = trēowan

±**trēowlēas** *faithless, treacherous, false*, CP : *unbelieving.*

trēowlēasnes f. *treachery, faithlessness*, BH : *unbelief, heresy*, GD.

trēowlic *true, faithful, trusty* : *safe.* adv. -līce, *PPs* : *confidently*, GL. ['truly']

trēowloga m. *pledge-breaker*, B 2847.

trēowlufu f. *'true love,'* Cr 538.

±**trēownes** (ē) f. *object of trust*, Bo 149²⁵,VH. ['trueness']

trēowrǣden f. *state of fidelity*, GEN 2305.

±**trēowsian** (ȳ) *to plight one's faith*, Chr, LL : *exculpate oneself.* ['treouse']

trēowsteall n. *grove, plantation*, EC,KC.

trēowstede m. *grove*, WW 149¹⁷.

trēowteru (trēot-) n. *tree-tar, resin*, WW.

±**trēowð** (ie, ȳ) f. *'truth,' veracity*, AO : *troth, faith, fidelity*, Æ,AO : *pledge, covenant*, Æ.

trēowðrāg f. *time for faithfulness, fidelity*, RIM 57.

trēowufæst = trēowfæst

trēowwæstm m. *produce of trees*, CHR.

trēowweorðung f. *tree-worshipping*, LL.

trēowwyrhta (ȳ) m. *wood-worker, carpenter.*

trēowwyrm m. *cankerworm, caterpillar*, CJVPs 77⁴⁶.

treppan I. *to 'trap,'* KGl 211. II. *to tread*, KGl 144.

treppe (a, æ) f. *'trap,' snare*, WW.

tret (KGL) pres. 3 sg. of tredan.

trēu = trēo, trēow

trēw = trēow

tribulian = trifulian

+**tricce** *contented*, RB 109⁷.

trideð, triedeð = tredeð, tritt pres. 3 sg. of tredan.

trīew- = trēow-

trifelung f. *grinding, pounding, stamping*, WW 423²⁵.

trifet (KGL), trifot (GL) sb. *tribute.* [L. tributum]

±**trifulian** *to break, bruise, stamp.* [L. tribulare]

trīg (ē) n. *wooden board, 'tray,'* Lcd.

trilidi = ðrilīðe; **trim-** = trym-

trimilchi = ðrimeolce

trinda? m., trinde? f. *round lump, ball*, LCD 139b.

trindhyrst m. *circular copse?* (Swt), KC 2·411' (? place-name).

tringan³ *press*, APs 103³³ (?*twingan, BT).

trīo- = trēo-, trēow-

trit, tritt pres. 3 sg. of tredan.

trīw = trēow

trochscip = trogscip

trod n., trodu f. *track, trace, B,LL.* ['trod'; tredan]

trog m. *hollow vessel, 'trough,' tray, BC,Gl, JnL,Lcd* : *canoe, boat*, AO.

trōg (NG) = drōg pret. 3 sg. of dragan.

troghrycg *ridge where there is a water-trough?* EC 447²⁰.

trogscip n. *a kind of boat*, WW.

troh (LWS) = trog; **trōh** = ðrōh

trondende *precipitous, steep*, Cp 805P.

tropere m. *a book containing verses sung at certain festivals before the Introit*, IM,TC. [*Late L.* troparium]

trūa = trūwa, trēowa

±**trucian** *to fail, run short*, Æ : *deceive, disappoint.* ['troke']

trūg- = trūw-

trūgon (NG) = drōgon pret. pl. of dragan.

trūht (u?) *trout*, Æ. [L. tructa]

trum *firm, fixed, secure, strong, sound, vigorous, active*, Æ,CP : *trustworthy*, BF 172²⁰.

+**trum†** n. *legion, army, host*, WW.

truma m. (±) *legion, troop*, AO ; Æ : *regular order, array*, AO. ['trume']

±**trumian** *to grow strong, recover health, amend*, BH : *make strong.*

truming = trymming

trumlic *firm, durable, substantial, sound*, CP : *confirming, exhorting.* adv. -līce, *considerably*, BF 80².

trumnað m. *confirmation*, Gu 729.

trumnes f. *soundness, health*, CP : *firmness, strength, stability*, Æ : *sureness, reliability* : *the firmament, heavens* : *confirmation, support.*

trundulnes = trendelnes

trūs (u?) m. *brushwood (for fuel)*, KC. ['trouse']

trūð m. *trumpeter, buffoon, actor*, Æ.

trūðhorn m. *trumpet, clarion*, GL.

trūw = trēow

±**trūwa** (ēo, ȳ) m. *fidelity, faith, confidence, trust, belief* : *pledge, promise, agreement, covenant* : *protection.*

+**trūwe** = +trēowe

±**trūwian** (ȳ) occl. pret. trūwde *to trust*, Æ,CP : *inspire with trust*, WW 243⁶ : *persuade*, AO : *exculpate oneself*, LL. ['TROW']

+**trūwung** f. *prop, stay, confidence*, CPs 88[19].
+**tryccan** *to confide, trust*, JnL 16[33].
tryddian=treddian
trydeð=tredeð, tritt pres. 3 sg. of tredan.
trym† (e) n. *small piece, short length*. fōtes t. *a foot's length*.
trym-=trum-, trymm-
+**trym** n. *firmament*, PPs 71[16].
+**trymednes** (LPs 104[16])=+trymnes
try-mes (*Mt*) mf., -messe f., -messa m. *a drachm weight : an English coin* (v. LL 2·683) : *a Roman coin* ('*tremissis*'=3 *denarii*), LG. ['*thrimsa*']
trymian, trymman (e) *to strengthen, fortify, confirm, comfort, exhort, incite,* CP,Chr : *set in order, arrange, prepare, array, arm,* AO : *become strong* : *be arrayed* : *give* (*hostages*) : *testify, attest.* ['TRIM']
-**trymig**, -trymmig v. un-t.
trymmend m. *supporter*, PPs : *one who makes an agreement*, GL.
trymmendlic *hortatory, encouraging*, BH,GL.
±**trymming** f. *confirmation, strengthening, encouragement,* Æ : *support, prop* : *edification,* Æ : *ordinance* : (+) *fortress*, KGL 67[4].
±**trymnes** f. *firmness, solidity* : *firmament, prop, support* : *confirmation, strengthening, encouragement* : *exhortation, instruction* : *arrangement, setting in order*. [trumnes]
tryms=trymes
trymð (i) f. *strength, support, staff, prop,* AS,LPs.
tryndel=trendel
trȳw=trēow; **trȳw-**=trēow-
tu=ðu; **Tū**=Tīw; **tū**=twā
tua=tuwa; **tuā**=twā
tube f. *trumpet*, GPH 391. [*L.* tuba]
±**tūcian** *to disturb, ill-treat, torment, punish,* Æ,Bo,Met : (+) *bedeck*, PPs 44[11] (? a mistake for +tunecian, IF 48·262). ['*tuck*']
tud? mn., tudu f? *shield*, OEG 5025 (cp. 747n).
tūdder, tūddor=tūdor
tūddorfōster m. *nourishment of offspring*, WW 219[17].
tūddorful *prolific, fruitful*, GL.
tūddorspēd f. *fertility*, GEN 2752.
tūddortēonde† *begetting issue*.
tūddres gs. of tūddor.
tūdor, tūder n. *offspring, descendant, issue,* Æ,CP,Lcd,WW : *fruit*. ['*tudder*']
tūdorfæst *fertile*, WW 400[85].
tūdornes f. *offspring*, OEG 3849 (tydder-).
tugon pret. pl. of tēon.
tui-=twi-
tulge comp. tylg, superl. tylgest *strongly, firmly, well*.
tumbere m. *tumbler, dancer, player*, ÆGR 35[6].

tumbian *to tumble, leap, dance,* G. ['*tumb*']
tumbing f. *dancing*, CHRD 79[1].
tūn m. *enclosure, garden, field, yard, Chr, Gl,G,Lcd* : *farm, manor, BC,LL* : *homestead, dwelling, house, mansion, BH,MH;* AO,CP : *group of houses, village,* '*town*,' Æ,Gl,JnL,KC,MH, v. LL 2·352. on tūn gān *to appear to men*, BF,MEN. [v. Mdf]
tūn-cerse (æ[2]) f., -cressa m. *garden-cress, nasturtium, Cp,Ep,Lcd.* ['*towncress*']
tūncirce f. *church in a* 'tūn,' TC.
tunder=tynder
tunece f. *under-garment, tunic, coat, toga,* Æ,AO. [*L.* tunica]
+**tunecod** *clothed in a toga*, GPH 393 (v. also IF 48·262).
tūnesman (*LL*)=tūnmann. ['*townsman*']
tunge f. (m) '*tongue*,' Æ,BH,CP,Lcd : *speech, language, CP,Mk,RB.*
tūngebūr m. *inhabitant, resident*, GL.
tungel=tungol
tungele? *talkative*, OEG 56[139].
tūngerēfa m. *town-reeve, bailiff,* Æ : *prætor.*
tungeðrum *tongue-ligament,* Lcd. [v. '*thrum*']
tungful *talkative*, Sc 81[9].
tungilsinwyrt=tunsingwyrt
tungle ds. of tungol.
tunglen *starry*, DHy. [tungol]
tunglere m. *astrologer*, GL.
tungol (e[2], u[2]) nm., nap. tunglu, tungol and (late) tunglan *luminary, star, planet, constellation,* Æ,AO.
tungolæ (e[2]) f. *astronomy*, OEG.
tungolbære (e[2]) *covered with stars*, OEG.
tungolcræft (e[2]) m. *star-craft, astronomy,* Æ.
tungolcræft(i)ga (e[2], u[2]) m. *magician, astrologer.*
tungolcræftwīse (e[2]) f. *astronomy*, WW 346[2].
tungolgescēad (e[2]) n. *astrology*, GL.
tungolgim m. (*bright*) *star*, CR 1151.
tungolspræc f. *astrology*, HGL.
tungolwitega m. *star prophet, astrologer,* Æ.
tungul=tungol
tungwōd *sharp-tongued*, Sc 223[13].
tūnhōfe f. *ground ivy*, Lcd 123a. ['*tunhoof*']
tunice=tunece
tūnincel n. *small property, small farm*, GL.
tuningwyrt=tunsingwyrt
tūnland n. *land forming a* 'tūn' *or manor*, EC 445[6].
tūnlic *rustic*, WW 127[15].
tūnmann m. *villager, rustic, villein,* Æ,WW. ['*townman*']
tūnmelde f. *orach* (*plant*), WW 215[33].
tunne f. '*tun*,' *cask, barrel, BC,Cp;* Æ.
tunnebotm m. *bottom of a cask, drum?* WW 123[10].
tūnprēost m. *village priest*, CHR 870 F.

tūnræd m. *town council*, ÆL30²⁹⁷.

tūnscipe m. '*township*,' *population of a village*, BH,LL.

tūnscīr f. *administration of an estate, stewardship*, Lk16.

tunsingwyrt f. *white hellebore*, LCD.

tūnsōcn f. '*villarum jura regalia*,' *legal jurisdiction over a village*, TC308⁷ (v. LL 2·455)

tūnsteall m. *farm-stead, farm-yard?* KC.

tūnstede m. *farm-stead?* WW144²⁶.

tunuce=tunece

tūnweg m. '*privata via*,' *by-road*, KC, WW.

tūnyncel=tūnincel

tūr m. '*tower*,' *fortress*, Chr1097.

turf f., gds. tyrf '*turf*,' *sod, soil*, Chr,Cp, Guth,Lcd : *greensward*, BH,WW.

turfhaga m. *grassy plot* (or ?=tyrfhaga A 35·141), EL830.

turfhlēow n. *covering of turf*, KC3·15'.

turflan=torfian

turl *ladle*, Cp290T. [*L*. trulla]

turnian *to turn, revolve*, Æ,LCD.

turnigendlic *revolving*, A6·12n.

turning f. *rotation*, W253¹⁴.

turtla m., turtle f. '*turtle'-dove*, G,Ps; Æ. [*L*. turtur]

turtur m. *turtle-dove*, Bl,LG,VPs. ['*turtur*']

tūsc m. *grinder, canine tooth*, Guth,Lcd,LL. ['*tusk*']

tuu=tū, twā; Tuu=Tīw

tuwa (Æ,AO,CP), tuwwa (=twiwa) adv. *twice*.

tūx=tūsc

tūxel, tūxl m. *tusk, canine or molar tooth*, Lcd. ['*tuscle*']

twā I. (tū, v. twēgen), Æ,AO. ['*two*'] II. adv. *twice*. tū swā lang(e) *twice as long*.

twa-=twi-

twaddung? twædding f. *adulation*, CHRD.

twǣde num. *two parts out of three, two-thirds*, LCD. [twā]

+twǣfan w. g. *to separate from, deprive of* : *hinder* : w. a. *put an end to*.

twǣgen (M)=twēgen

twǣlf (M)=twelf

twǣm v. twēgen.

±twǣman (ē) *to divide into two, separate*, Bf,W : *cause to cease, adjust, settle* : *defer, postpone*, LL242¹⁹. ['*tweme*']

twǣmendlīce adv. *alternately, separately*, OEG1368.

twǣming f. *parting, division, separation*, Æ : *distinction*, Æ.

twǣonung=twēonung; twām v. twēgen.

+twanc n. *collusion, deception*, OEG1517.

twānihte *two days old*, LCD.

twe-=twi-

twēgen num. nom. m.; nom. f. twā; nom. n. tū, twā; gen. mfn. twēg(e)a, twēgra; dat. twǣm, twām *two*, Æ; AO,CP. tū swā lang *twice as long*. t. and t., twām and twām *in parties of two each*. ['*TWAIN*']

twēgentig (oe; NG)=twēntig

twelf '*TWELVE*,' CP.

twelffeald *twelve-fold*, ÆH.

twelfgylde *twelve-fold*, LL3,1.

twelfhund *twelve hundred*, LL.

twelfhynde adj. *belonging to the class whose* '*wergild*' *was 1200 shillings*, LL.

twelfnihte *twelve days old*, LCD3·178'.

twelfta I. '*twelfth*,' An,Lcd,MH; AO. II.= Twelftadæg

Twelftadæg m. *Twelfth day*, LL296,17.

Twelftamæsseǣfen *Eve of the Epiphany*, CHR1066.

twelfte, *twelfthly, in the twelfth place*, LL 182,12.

twelftig=hundtwelftig

twelfwintre *twelve years old*, CP.

twēman=twǣman

twengan *to pinch*, IM. ['*twinge*']

twēntig '*TWENTY*,' Æ,AO.

twēntigfeald *twenty-fold*, ÆGR.

twēntiggēare *twenty years old*, ÆL32³⁷.

twēntigoða (io³, o³, u³) '*twentieth*,' Lcd,MH; Æ,AO.

twēntigwintre *twenty years old*, W3¹.

±twēo m. *doubt, ambiguity*, Æ,AO,CP.

tweo-=twi-, twy-; twēogan=twēon

twēogende *doubting*, BH.

twēogendlic *doubtful, uncertain*, AO. adv. -līce.

tweolf=twelf

twēolic (ī, ȳ) *doubtful, ambiguous, equivocal*. adv. -līce, AO,CP.

±twēon I. pret. sg. twēode *to doubt, hesitate*, AO,CP : (impers. w. a. of pers.) *seem doubtful*. II. (ī, ȳ) m. *doubt*, Bo.

twēona m. *doubt*, VH21.

twēonelēoht n. *twilight*, WW175²⁴.

±twēonian (ȳ) (pers. and impersonal) *to doubt, be uncertain, hesitate*, CP.

twēonigend, twēoniendlic (ī, ȳ) *doubtful, expressing doubt*, Æ. adv. -līce *perhaps*.

twēonol (ȳ) *doubtful*, Sc,WW.

twēontig=twēntig

twēonullēoht (WW175³⁹)=twēonelēoht

twēonum in phr. '*be* (sǣm, etc.) twēonum,' *between* (*the seas, etc.*).

twēonung (ī, ȳ) f. *doubt, scruple*, Æ.

+tweosa=+twisa; twēoung=twēonung

tweowa=tuwa; twi, twia=tuwa

twī=twig n.

twi- prefix with meaning *two, double*. [*Ger*. zwie-]

twibēte adj. *subject to double compensation*, LL.

twibill n. (*two-edged*) *axe*, *Guth*,*WW*; Æ. ['*twibill*']

twibille *double-edged*, WW 141²⁷.

twibleoh *twice-dyed, double-dyed*, CP : *bi-form*, CHRD 78⁶.

twibōte (adj. and adv.)=twibēte

twibrowen (y) *twice-brewed*, LCD 45b.

-twicce (æ) v. angel-t.

twiccen=twicen

twiccere m. *one who divided up the food in a monastery*, WW 127³³.

twiccian *to pluck, gather* : *catch hold of*, Lcd, *Shr*,*WW*. ['*twick*']

twi-cen, -cene, -cyne (y¹) f. *junction of roads*.

twicere=twiccere

twidæglic (a², y²) *lasting two days*, BH 350³².

twidǣl m. *two-thirds*, LCD.

twidǣlan *to divide into two* : *differ*, Sc.

twidēagod *twice-dyed*, OEG 1060.

-twidig v. lang-t.; twie-=twi-

twi-ecge, -ecgede *two-edged*, BH,Ps.

twiendlīce *doubtingly*, GUTH 70. [twēon]

±twi-feald (Æ), -fald (CP) *two-fold, double, ambiguous*, BH,CP. ['*twifold*']

±twifeald-an, -ian (y¹, y²) *to double*, Æ.

twifealdlic (a) adj. *two-fold, double*. adv. -līce, Æ,*Mt*. ['*twifoldly*']

twifealdnes (ie) f. *duplicity*, CP : *irresolution*, CP 307³ : *duplication*, BF 174¹⁶.

twifēre *accessible by two ways*, WW 194³⁰.

twiferlǣcan (y) *to dissociate*, Sc,6⁸.

twifēte (eo, y) *two-footed*, ÆGR.

twifeðerede *as if with two wings, forked*, ÆGR 288¹¹.

twifingre (y) *two fingers thick*, LL 110, 49³.

twifyldan=twifealdan

twifyrclian (y¹, e²) *to branch off, deviate from*, ÆGR 288¹⁰ : *split into two*.

twifyrede *two-furrowed*, ÆGR 288¹¹.

twig n. '*twig*,' *branch, shoot, small tree*, LG; Æ,CP.

twig-=twi-; twiga=(1) twig; (2) tuwa

twigǣrede (y) *cloven*, ÆGR 288¹¹.

twigan=twēogan, twēon

twigea=tuwa; twigedēagod=twidēagod

twigilde (adj. adv. and ? sb.) *paying double, liable to a double fine*, LL.

twih num. (acc.) only in phrase '*mid unc twih*' *between us two*, GEN 2253. [cp. *Goth.* tweihnai]

twihēafdede (y) *double-headed*, ÆGR.

twiheolor f. *balance*, Cp 140B.

twihinde=twihynde

twihīw(ed)e (ēo) *of two colours or shapes*.

twihīwian *to dissimulate*, Sc 44⁸.

twihlidede *having two openings*, ÆGR 288⁶ (y).

twihwēole *two-wheeled*, LCD.

twihwyrft m. *double period*, OEG 2513.

twihynde I. *having* '*wergild*' *of* 200 *shillings*. II. *a* '*wergild*' *of* 200 *shillings*, LL.

twihyndeman m. *man of the* '*twihynde*' *class*, LL 601,87⁴.

twiicce=twiecge

twilæpped *with two lappets*, WW 153¹⁷.

twilafte *two-edged*, WW 194³⁵.

twilībrocen *woven of threads of two colours?* TC 537²³ (v. WC 113⁷). [twilic]

twilic *double, woven of double thread*, Gl. ['*twilly*']

twilic=twēolic

twimylte *twice-melted*, OEG 4462.

twīn I. n. *double thread, twist*, '*twine*,' *linen-thread, linen*, (*byssus*), CP,Gl,Lk. II.= twēon II.

twinclian *to* '*twinkle*,' *wink*, Bo,CP.

twinebbe (y) *having two faces*, GPH 397⁴⁴⁸.

twīnen *of linen*, OEG.

twing? sb. *cluster*, HGL 496.

twingan v. tringan.

twīnigend-=twēonigend-

twinihte (y) *two days old*, LCD 27b.

twinn '*twin*,' *two-fold, double, two by two*, Gl.

+twinn m. *twin*. pl. '*twins*,' *triplets*, MH, SHR.

+twinnes (y) f. *junction*, BF 176⁴.

twīnung=twēonung

twīnwyrm, m. '*buprestis*,' *small insect*, WW 122²⁷.

twio=tweo

twirǣde (io, y) *uncertain* : *disagreeing*, Bo, *Mt*. ['*twirede*']

twirǣdnes (y¹, e²) f. *disagreement, discord, sedition*, Æ.

+twis *having the same parents*, GL.

+twisa m. *twin*, Æ.

twisceatte adv. *to the extent of a double payment*, LL 84,66¹.

twiscyldig *liable to a double penalty*, LL 90 H.

twiseht (y) *disunited, discordant*, Sc 192¹³.

twisehtan (y) *to disagree*, LCD 3·204', ANS 125·56²⁹⁵.

twisehtnes f. *dissension, disagreement*, Sc 6¹².

twiseltōð *with forked teeth?* WW 108¹⁵.

twisestre *containing two sesters*, JnL 2⁶(mg).

twisla m. *confluence, junction*, BC; KC 5·198'. ['*twisel*']

twislian *to fork, divide into two*, KC. ['*twisel*,' '*twisled*']

twisliht *forked, branched*, KC.

twislung f. *division, partition*, Lcd 3·436³ : *difference*, CHRD. ['*twisling*']

twisnæcce *double-pointed, cloven*, ÆGR 288¹¹.

twisnēse *double-pointed, cloven,* GPH 393⁷³.
twisprǣc f. *double speech, deceit, detraction.*
twisprǣce *double-tongued, deceitful, detracting,* Æ.
twisprǣcnes (y) f. *double speech, detraction.*
twisprecan *to murmur,* NG.
twispunnen *twice-spun,* CP 83²³.
-twist v. candel-, mæst-t.
twistrenge *two-stringed,* ÆGR 288¹⁰.
twitælged *double-dyed,* GL,VPs.
twi-ŏrāwen, -ŏrǣwen *twice thrown or twisted, twice woven,* CP.
twiwa=tuwa
twiwǣg f. *pair of scales,* WW 194²⁸.
twiweg m. *junction of two roads,* WW 177¹³.
twi-wintre, -winter adj. *two years old,* Æ.
twiwyrdig *ambiguous,* AO.
twoelf=twelf
twōgon=ŏwōgon pret. pl. of ŏwēan.
twuga, twuwa, twuwu=tuwa
twux=tusc; twy-=twi-
twȳ=twēo
twȳgean=twēogan, twēon I.
twȳlic (Æ)=twēolic; twȳn=twēon
twynihte=twinihte
twyspēcnes=twisprǣcnes
tȳ pres. 1 sg. of tȳn.
tyccen=ticcen; tycht-, tyct-=tyht-
tȳd (1)=tīd; (2) pp. of tȳn.
tȳd-=tīd-
+tȳd, tydd *skilled, learned.*
tydd-=tīd-, tūd-, tȳd-
tȳdde I. pret. 3 sg. of tȳn. II.=tīŏde pret. 3 sg. of tīŏian.
tȳde pret. sg. of tȳn.
tȳdernes (ydd) f. *branch,* OEG 3849.
+tȳdnes f. *edification,* CHRD 58³.
±tȳdran *to bring forth, produce, beget, propagate : be prolific.* [tūdor]
tȳdred *provided with offspring,* PPs 143¹⁷.
tȳdrian=(1) tīdrian; (2) tȳdran
tȳdriend m. *propagator,* WW 238²².
tȳdrung f. *propagation, production : branch,* ÆGR 216¹⁵. [tūdor]
tyg-=tig-
tȳg=tēag
tyge (i) m. *drawing together, pulling, tug, pull* Æ : *leading* (water) : *draught* (of water) : *inference, statement,* Æ. [tēag, tīegan]
tygehōc (i¹) m. *hook for pulling,* LL 455,15.
tygehorn (i) m. *cupping-horn,* LCD 46a.
tygel m. *pulling-rope, rein,* Æ,WW. ['*tial*']
tygele f. '*murenula,' lamprey?* WW.
tygŏian=tiŏian; tyhhian=teohhian
tȳhst pres. 2 sg. of tēon.
tyht I. (i) m. *instruction, training, habit,* Bo : *going, course, motion, progress,* El : *region,* GU 1255. ['*tight*'; tēon] II.=tiht

tyht-=tiht-
±tyhtan I. (i) (+) *to stretch, draw, pull, CM* : *invite, incite, instigate, provoke, talk over, persuade, attract, lead astray, seduce,* Æ : (+) *teach, train,* PPs. ['*tight*'; tēon· I.] II.=tihtan
tyhten f. *incitement, excitement,* GL. [tēon I.]
tyhtend m. *inciter, instigator,* GL.
tyhtendlic (i) *persuading, hortatory,* Æ.
tyhtere (i) m. *inciter, enticer,* WW.
tyhting (i) f. *incitement, impulse, instigation, exhortation, suggestion, instruction, advice,* Æ : *enticement, allurement,* Æ. ['*tighting*']
tyhtnes (i) f. *inward impulse, instinct, conviction,* WW.
tȳhŏ pres. 3 sg. of tēon.
tyl=til
tyldsyle f. *tent,* WW 187⁴. [teld]
tylg, tylgest v. tulge; -tyllan v. for-t.
tȳm=tēam; tȳm-=tēam-, tīm-; tyma= tama
tȳman (Æ)=tīeman
tymb-=timb-
±tȳn I. *to instruct, teach,* Æ,AO. II. (Æ)=tīen
tȳn-=tīen-
±tȳnan I. *to hedge in, fence, enclose, shut,* A,BH,LG,LL. ['*tine*'] II. (=īe) *to irritate, vex, trouble,* Bas,Bl,LL : *insult, revile,* Æ. ['*teen*']
tyncen n. *bladder?* AO 72⁸⁰.
tynder (e, i, u) f. '*tinder,' fuel,* Bo,Gl,Sc; Æ : *cautery.* [tyndan]
tyndercynn n. *combustible,* WW.
tyndig=tindig; tyndre, tyndren=tynder
+tȳne n. *entrance, court,* PPs 115⁸.
±tynge I. adj. *fluent, eloquent : skilful.* II. adv. (also -lice) *courteously,* OEG 2853.
+tyng(e)lic *polished, elegant, rhetorical.* adv. -lice.
+tyngnes (i) f. *fluency, eloquence,* Æ,CP : *skill,* BF 14²².
-tȳning v. æcer-t.; gafol-t.
tyntreg=tintreg
tyr-, tȳr- v. also tir-, tīr-.
-tyran (=ic) v. be-t.
tȳran (=īe) *to shed tears,* Æ : *run with water* (eyes), LCD. [tēar]
tyrdelu, tyrdlu npl. *droppings, small pieces of excrement,* LCD. ['*treddle*']
tȳrende *having watery eyes,* LCD. ['*tear*']
tyrewa=tyrwa; tyrf v. turf.
+tyrfan *to strike, afflict,* GD 29⁹. [torfian]
tyrfhaga f. *hoe, mattock,* LN 17².
tȳrgan=tēorian
tȳriāca m. (*treacle*), *sovereign remedy,* LCD, WW. [L. theriacum; Gk. θηριακός]
tȳrian=tēorian
tyrnan *to turn, move round, revolve,* Æ. [L. tornare]

tyrngeat n. *turnstile*, KC3·405⁴.
tyrning (u) f. *turning round, rotation*, OEG : *rotundity, roundness*, OEG : *crookedness, deceit*, OEG56⁸⁶.
tyro=teoru
tyrð pres. 3 sg. of teran.
tyrwa m., tyrwe f. '*tar*,' *resin*, Æ. [=teoru]
tyr-wan, -wian I. (e, i;=ie) *to harass, vex*, LPs. ['*tar*'] II. *to* '*tar*,' *B* 295 : *to make like tar*, LCD 140a.
tysca m. *buzzard*, WW259¹².
tyslian *to put on*, CM 260,ES 8·62⁵.
tyslung f. *dressing*, ES 8·62⁶.
tysse f. *coarse cloth*, JGPh 1·63. [*OHG.* zussa]
tȳtan *to sparkle, shine*, DD45.
tytt=titt; **tȳð**=tīð; **tȳw-**=tīw-

Ð

ðā I. adv. and conj. *then, at that time*, Æ, *AO,CP* : *after that time, thereupon, AO, Jul* : *when, at the time that, whilst, during, AO,B,Bl,Ps* : *there, where*, CHR : *seeing that, inasmuch as, if, when, since, as, because*. ðā ðā *when*. ðā…ðā *then…when*. ðā hwīle ðe *while, whilst, so long as*. ðā gīet v. ðāgīet. ['*tho*'] II. asf. and nap. of sē. ðā ðe *which*.
ðaca I. (±) m. *roof, covering*. II. gp. of ðæc.
±ðaccian *to clap, pat, stroke, touch gently*, *CP,Shr* : *smack, beat*, GD : *tame?* GPH 402. ['*thack*']
ðacele=ðæcele
ðacian *to thatch*, LL454,10. ['*thack*']
ðacum dp. of ðæc.
ðadder (*JnL* 7³⁵)=ðider
ðæc I. (ea) n. *covering, roof of a building*, *Chr,MtR,PPs* : *thatch*, Æ,BH. ['*thack*'] II.=ðec pron. (das. of ðu).
ðæccille (N)=ðæcele; **ðæce** f.=ðæc I.
ðæcele (e) f. *torch, lamp, light*, AA,NG. [=fæcele]
ðæccen=ðecen; **ðæcile**=ðæcele
ðæctigile f. *roof-tile*, Cp 571.
ðæder, ðædres=ðider
ðæderlendisc (MH 178²⁵n)=ðiderlēodisc
+ðæf w. g. *agreeing to, consenting to, admitting* : *contented*.
ðæf (*JnR*)=ðēof; **ðæfet-**=ðafet-
ðæge mnp. pron. *they, those, them*, Lk,Jn, Sol. ['*thaie*']
ðægen, ðægn=ðegen, ðegn
ðægon pret. pl. of ðicgan.
ðæh (N)=ðēah I. and II.
ðæht (N)=ðeaht
ðæm (ā, ē) dsmn. and dp. of sē pron. be ðæm, on ðæm *thereon, therein*. ēac ðæm *in addition to this, besides this, also, moreover*. ǣr ðæm ðe *before*. æfter ðæm *after*,

later, next, after that (fashion). for ðǣm (ðe) *therefore, on that account, for that reason, because*. on ðǣm ðe *in this, in that*.
ðǣn=ðegn
ðǣnan *to moisten*, GD,LCD.
ðæncan=ðencan; **ðæncung**=ðancung
ðæne=ðone asm. of sē.
ðǣnian=ðānian
ðǣnnan=ðennan; **ðænne**=ðonne
ðǣr (ē) adv. and conj. 'THERE*,' *thither, yonder* : *where, whither* : *then* : *when* : *though, if, so far as, whilst, provided that* : *in that respect*. ðǣr ðǣr *where, wherever*. ðǣr…of *therefrom*. ðǣr wið *in regard to that*.
ðǣra gp. of sē, sēo, ðæt.
ðǣrābūtan *about that place*, ÆL. ['*thereabout*']
ðǣræfter adv. '*thereafter*,' *CP,Lcd,Mt*.
ðǣræt '*thereat*,' *BH* 282⁶.
ðæran *to dry*, HL 13¹⁰³.
ðǣr-big, -bie adv. '*thereby*,' *thus*, *CP* 42,43¹⁴.
ðǣrbinnan (o³) adv. *therein*, Æ,AO.
ðǣrbufan *besides that*, CP52¹⁰.
ðǣre gdf. of sē.
ðærf=(1) ðearf; (2) ðeorf; **ðærf-**=ðearf-
ðǣrforan conj. *before that*, Æ.
ðærh=ðurh
ðǣrin '*therein*,' *wherein*, Met.
ðǣrinne (ē) *therein*, CP. ['*thereinne*']
ðærle=ðearle
ðǣrmid adv. *therewith*, Æ,Bo. ['*theremid*']
ðǣrnēhst *next to that*, LL 280,2¹.
ðǣrnian *to lose?* CHR 1119 (v. MFH 174).
ðǣrof adv. '*thereof*,' *of that*, Lcd.
ðǣrofer *over or above that*, CP,G. ['*thereover*']
ðǣron adv. *therein*, Æ,CP : '*thereon*,' Bl : *thereinto, thereof*.
ðǣronbūtan (*Chr*)=ðǣreābūtan
ðǣronemn *alongside*, ÆP164¹⁸.
ðǣrongēn adv. *on the contrary*, W 248²¹. ['*thereagain*']
ðǣronuppan adv. *thereupon*, Æ.
ðǣrrihte, ðærrihtes (ā, ē) adv *thereupon, forthwith, instantly, immediately, straightway*, Æ,Bl,DHy. ['*thereright(s)*']
ðærsc pret. 3 sg. of ðerscan.
ðǣrscan (NG)=ðerscan
ðærsc-wald, -wold=ðerscold
ðærst (SPs 74⁸)=ðærst
ðǣrtō adv. '*thereto*,' *to it, to that place*, Æ : *besides*, Æ,BH : *for that purpose*, Æ : *belonging to*, Æ.
ðǣrtōēacan adv. *besides, in addition to that*, ÆH 2·84⁸. ['*thereteken*']
ðǣrtōgēanes adv. *on the contrary, in opposition thereto*, Æ : *in exchange for*, TC 436¹⁷. ['*theretoyens*']

ðǣrðǣr adv. *wherever*, Æ.

ðǣrunder adv. *beneath*, CP. ['*thereunder*']

ðǣruppan *thereon*, ÆL30²⁰⁰. ['*thereup*']

ðǣrūt, ðǣrūte adv. *outside, without*, AO, CP,Mk. ['*thereout*']

ðǣrwið adv. *against, in exchange for*, Æ : '*therewith*,' Bo.

ðǣrymbe adv. *thereabout, on that point*, W 273¹.

ðǣrymbūtan *thereabouts*, BH,Bo.

ðæs I. adv. (gs. of ðæt) *afterwards*, AO,Chr : *thence* : *accordingly, according as*, Æ : *therefore, because*, CP : *therefore, wherefore, because, that* : *as, according as; provided*; (to express proportion) *the* (*more, etc.*), CP. tō ðæs *to that point, to that degree*. ðæs ðe *since, after, afterwards, the more*, CP,Mt. ['THES'] II. gs. of sē and ðæt.

±ðæslǣcan *to agree with, be suitable*, GL.

ðæslīc I. adj. *suitable, congruous*, Æ : *harmonious* : *fair, elegant*. II.=ðyllic

ðæslīce adv. *opportunely, suitably, aptly, after this manner, similarly, thus*, Æ,AO.

ðæslicnes f. *fitness, convenience*, ÆH 1·326'.

ðǣsma m. *leaven, yeast*, RB10¹⁸.

ðǣsternes=ðēostornes

ðæsðe=ðæs ðe v. ðæs.

ðæt I. conj. and adv. 'THAT,' *so that, in order that, after that, then, thence*. ðæt ðe *that*. II. nas. of sē, ðæt. ['THAT*']

ðætte I. pron. *which, that which*. II. conj. *that, so that, in order that*. tō ðon ðætte *so that*. [ðæt ðe]

+ðafa I. m. *favourer, supporter, helper*, CP. II. adj. (cpve +ðafera) *agreeing, consenting, acquiescing*.

ðafetere, ðafettere m. *one who acquiesces in, or condones, what is wrong*, CP.

+ðafettan (æ, ea) *to consent*, EHy6²⁷.

±ðafian (ea) *to allow, suffer, endure, permit, tolerate*, BH,Bo,Ct,G,LL,W; CP : *approve, consent to, submit to*, AO,CP. [' (*i*)-*thave*']

ðaforlīc=ðaroflic, ðearflic

+ðafsum *consenting, agreeing*, MtL5²⁵.

+ðafsumnes f. *consent, agreement*, Mt pref. 14¹⁴.

±ðafung f. *permission, consent*, Æ.

ðāg, ðāh pret. 3 sg. of ðicgan, ðēon.

ðage=ðæge

ðāgēn=ðe āgēn *who again*, Bl167⁶.

ðāgīet, ðāgȳt adv. *still : yet*.

ðāgon pret. pl. of ðicgan.

ðāh=ðēah; ðām=ðǣm

ðamettan *to clap* (*the hands*)? APs97⁸.

ðan=ðon adv.

ðān I. adj. *moist, irrigated*, WW. II. n. *irrigated land*. [ðīnan] III. (LWS)=ðǣm

ðanan=ðanon

±ðanc (o) m. *thought, reflection, sentiment, idea*, Æ : *mind, will, purpose* : *grace, mercy, favour, pardon* : *thanks, gratitude*, CP; AO, CP : *pleasure, satisfaction*, CP : *reward, recompense*, Gu442. Gode ð. *thanks* (*be*) *to God*. Godes ðances *through the mercy of God*. Drihtnes ðances *according to the will of the Lord*. mīnes ðances *by my favour, of my own will*. on ð. *willingly, gladly*. an ðance *acceptable, pleasant*, AO. dēofla ðonces *in honour of devils*, AO. tōðance *for the sake of* ['THANK']

+ðanc mn. *thought, mind*, Lk. ['*i-thank*']

ðances adv. *thankfully, gladly* : *voluntarily, gratis*, BC,Bo,Chr. [v. '*thank*']

ðancful adj. (+) *thoughtful, ingenious, clever* : '*thankful*,' Bl : *contented, satisfied*, BH,WW : *pleasing, agreeable*, CM : *energetic, spirited*. adv. -līce '*thankfully*,' ÆL30¹⁴⁴.

ðanchycgende *thoughtful*, B2235.

±ðancian (o) (w. g. thing and d. pers.) *to thank, give thanks*, Æ; CP : *recompense, reward* : (w. i.) *rejoice*. ['THANK']

+ðancmetian *to think over, deliberate*, Gen 1917. [metgian]

ðanc-metung (o¹, eo²), -metegung f. *deliberation, thought*, BH88⁴ (v.l.).

±ðancol *thoughtful, mindful* : *prudent, wise* : (+) *desirous* : (+) *suppliant*.

ðancolmōd† *thoughtful, considerate, prudent, wise, attentive*.

ðanc-snot(t)or† *wise, prudent, ingenious*.

ðancung f. '*thanking*,' *thanksgiving*, Æ,AO, JnL.

ðanc-weorð, -weorðlic (u², y²) *thankworthy, acceptable* : *thankful, grateful* : *memorable*. adv. -līce *gladly, willingly*, CP.

ðancword n. *thanks*, Wid137.

ðanc-wurð, -wyrð(e)=ðancweorð

ðand pret. 3 sg. of ðindan.

ðane (KGl)=ðone

ðanēcan ðe (o¹) adv. *whenever, as often as*, Bo.

+ðang n. *growth*, Sol180¹² (or ?=+ðanc, BTac).

ðānian (ǣ) *to be or become moist, moisten*, WW.

ðanne=ðonne

ðanon (CP), ðanone (o¹, a²) adv. *from that time or place, thence, away* : *whence, from which, of which*, CP. ðanon...ðanon *thence...whence* : *then, thereupon, henceforth* : *by which, through that*. ['THENNE']

ðanonforð (o¹, a²) adv. *after that, then, thenceforward*, OET,W.

ðanonweard adv. *departing thence*, Bo103⁷.

ðanun=ðanon

ðar-=ðear-, ðer-; ðār=ðǣr

ðāra I.=ðǣr. II. gp. of sē, sēo, ðæt.

ðas=ðæs gsmn. of sē.

ðās I. afs. and nap. of ðēs. ['those'] II. nap. of ðāw=ðēow

ðassum (N)=ðissum, dmns. of ðēs.

ðat=ðæt; ðāðā v. ðā.

ðāw I.=ðēaw I. II.=ðēow

+ðāwenian=+ðwǣnan

ðāwian to 'thaw,' Lcd 3·274'.

ðe I. rel. pron. (when govd. by a prep. the prep. follows) who, which, that. ðe is often associated by attraction with pers. pronouns. ðe ic I. ðe we we. ðe...his whose. sē ðe his he whose. II. conj. when : or : (=ðā) then : (=ðǣr) where, EL 717 : (with comparatives) than. hwæðer ðe...ðe whether...or. ðe...ðe the...or, either...or. III. art. the (indecl.), CHR 963 E and late. IV. particle added to ðēah, for ðǣm, ðæs, etc., without affecting their meaning. V. das. of ðu. ['THEE']

ðē=ðȳ; ðēa (NG)=ðēow

ðeac=ðæc; ðeaca=ðaca

ðēada (VPs)=ðēoda gp. of ðēod I.

ðēadōm (DR)=ðēowdōm

ðēaf (NG)=ðēof; ðeaflan=ðafian

ðeah pret. 3 sg. of ðicgan.

ðēah I. (ē) conj. and adv. 'though*,' although, even if, that, however, nevertheless, yet, still, Bl,Bo : whether, Bo. ð. ðe although. swā ð. nevertheless, yet. ð....ð. although, still, yet. II. pret. 3 sg. of ðēon.

ðēah-hwæðere, -hweðre adv. yet, moreover, however, nevertheless, but, Bl,CP. swā ð. yet, nevertheless. ['thoughwhether']

ðeaht n. counsel, advice, design, Æ. [ðencan]

+ðeaht fn. thought, consideration, counsel, advice, direction : design, contrivance, scheme, Æ,CP : council, assembly, Æ.

+ðeahta m. adviser, counsellor, WW 99⁵.

ðeahte pret. 3 sg. of ðeccan.

+ðeahtend m. counsellor, WW.

+ðeahtendlic deliberative, LL 12.

±ðeahtere m. counsellor, BH.

±ðeahtian to ponder, consider, deliberate upon, take counsel, Æ,CP : agree, MtL 18¹⁹.

±ðeahtung (æ) f. counsel, consultation, GD, NG.

ðeahðe=ðeah ðe

ðēana adv. nevertheless, yet. swā ð. however, ever.

ðēara=ðāra, gmfp. of ðæt.

ðearf I. (a, e, y) f. need, necessity, want, behoof, B,Lcd; CP. tō ðearfe as is needed, according to what is needed : benefit, profit, advantage, utility, Æ : trouble, hardship, privation, distress, danger : duty, employment. ['tharf'] II. needful, necessary. III.=ðeorf. IV. pres. 3 sg. of ðurfan.

ðearfa (æ, eo) I. m. poor man, pauper, beggar, Æ,CP. II. destitute, poor, needy, Æ.

+ðearfan to be in want, SOL 268⁷³.

ðearfednes f. poverty, BH.

ðearf-end, -igend (o) m. poor man, BK.

ðearfende needy, in want, poor, CP.

ðearfendlic needy, poor, miserable, APT, GD.

ðearfendnes=ðearfednes

ðearfian to starve, be in need, want, PPs 71¹³. [Ger. darben]

+ðearfian to impose necessity, B 1103.

ðearflēas adj. without cause or need, Æ. adv. -lēase.

ðearflic profitable, useful, convenient, necessary, Æ. adv. -lice.

ðearflicnes f. want, poverty, GL,Sc.

ðearl adj. vigorous, strong, severe, strict, harsh, violent, heavy, excessive. adv. ðearle. swīðe ðearle with all their might.

ðearlic severe, cruel, harsh, violent, grievous. adv. -lice, CP.

ðearlmōd† stern, severe, violent, strong, mighty, JUD.

ðearlwīs strict, severe, relentless, CP.

ðearlwīslic severe, GD. adv. -lice, CP.

ðearlwīsnes f. severity, strictness, BH,GD.

ðearlwȳs-=ðearlwīs-

ðearm (a, e) m. gut, entrail, Æ,Gl. ['tharm']

ðearm(ge)wind n. windpipe (=windðearm), OET 509 (v. ES 43·332).

ðearmgyrd m. girdle, belt, WW 220¹.

ðearsc=ðærsc pret. 3 sg. of ðerscan.

ðearsm (BH 426²⁴)=ðrosm

ðēat pret. 3 sg. of ðēotan.

ðēatan=ðēotan

ðēater m? theatre, AO 154².

ðēatscipe (N)=ðēodscipe

ðēaw I. m. usage, custom, habit, conduct, disposition, AO,B,JnL; CP : (in pl.) virtues, (good) manners, morals, morality, Æ,AO,Bo,Bl; CP. ['thew'] II.=ðēow

+ðeawe customary, usual, GD 142³³.

ðēawfæst decorous, moral, virtuous, honourable, LL : gentle, CRA.

ðēawfæstlice correctly, ÆL 5²²².

ðēawfæstnes f. obedience, discipline, Æ.

ðēawful moral, virtuous, W 250⁴.

ðēawian I.=ðēowian. II. (+) to bring up well, Æ.

ðēawlēas ill-mannered, ÆH 2·380¹¹.

ðēawlic customary, Æ : decent, moral, Æ : figurative. adv. -lice.

+ðeawod well-mannered, moral, Æ.

ðēb- (GL)=ðēof-

ðec das. of ðu. ['thee']

ðeccan (±) to cover, cover over, conceal, B, Gen,Lcd,PPs : (†) swallow up? ['thatch']

ðeccbryce m. tile, HGL 459⁴².

ðeccend m. *protector, defender*, PPs70.
ðecele=ðæcele
ðecen f. *thatch, tile, covering, roof* : (fig.)
house, Æ. [ðeccan]
ðecest pres. 2 sg. of ðeccan.
ðecgan I. *to consume*, Lcd. II. obl. case of
sb? *receptacle?* (BT) or=ðeccan? (Lieb.),
LL454,10.
+ðēd=+ðēod
ðēde pret. of ðēon (ðȳwan).
ðēf=ðēof
ðēfanðorn, ðefonðorn (APs57¹⁰), ðēfeðorn
=ðȳfeðorn
ðefel *mulled wine?* OEG104.
ðēfel=ðȳfel
ðeflan *to pant, heave, palpitate*, HGl.
ðeften (*HGl*461⁵⁶)=ðyften; ðēfð=ðīefð
ðegan *to serve*, Gu140.
ðegen I.=ðegn. II. pp. of ðicgan.
ðegen-=ðegn-, ðēn-
ðegeð 3 p. sg. pres. of ðecgan.
ðegh (Gl)=ðēoh; ðegin=ðegn
ðegn (æ) [v. LL456; 2·680] m. *servant,
minister, retainer, vassal, follower, disciple,*
AO,CP : *freeman, master (as opposed to
slave)* : *courtier, noble (official, as distinguished from hereditary), Æ :* (†) *military
attendant, warrior, hero, AO.* ['THANE']
ðegn- v. also ðēn-.
ðegnboren (ðegen-) *well-born*, LL.
ðegngylde n. *legal money value of a thane,*
W162¹⁰.
ðegnhyse m. *attendant, retainer*, WW.
±ðegnian (æ, ēn) (w. d.) *to serve, minister,
wait on*, B,BH,Bl,G; CP : *supply another
with anything* : *perform (an office).*
['theine']
ðegnlagu f. *rights, duties or privileges of a
thane*, LL,W.
ðegnlic *noble, brave, loyal, Æ.* adv. -lice.
ðegnrǣden f. *thaneship, service*, Bl,Gl.
ðegnriht n. *rights or privileges of a thane,*
LL.
ðegnscipe m. *service, duty* : *ability, AO* :
manliness, valour, AO : *body of retainers.*
ðegnscolu f. *band of vassals*, WW371⁷.
ðegnsorh f. *sorrow for loss of thanes*, B131.
ðegnung=ðēn-ung, -ing
ðegnweorud n. *band of followers*, CR751.
ðegnwer m. *thane's* 'wergild,' LL.
ðego=ðegu
ðegon=ðǣgon pret. pl. of ðicgan
-ðegu v. bēah-, wīn-ð.; ðeh (A)=ðec
ðēh I.=ðēoh I. II. (A,K)=ðēah
ðeht=ðeaht
ðel, ðell n. *board, plank, (metal) plate*, AA,
W. [*Ger.* diele]
ðelbrycg f. *bridge of planks*, Ct.
ðelcræft=ðȳlcræft

ðellfæsten n. *fastness made of planks, ship,
ark*, Gen1482.
ðellian=ðilian
ðelma m. *noose, snare*, HGl429¹⁷.
-ðelu v. buruh-, benc-ð. ['theal']
ðēm=ðǣm; ðēn=ðegn
±ðencan I. *to* 'THINK*' ('*i-thenche*'),
*imagine, think of, meditate, reason, con-
sider, Æ;* AO,CP : *remember, recollect, CP* :
intend, purpose, attempt, devise, AO :
learn : *wish, desire, long for.* [ðanc] II.
=ðyncan
ðencendlic *thoughtful*, MFH174.
ðende=ðenden; ðēnde=ðēonde
ðenden conj. and adv. *meanwhile, while, as
long as, until.*
ðene=ðone
ðēnest f. *service, entertainment*, CHR1054D.
[*Ger.* dienst]
ðēnestmann (ēo¹) m. *serving-man, retainer,*
CHR656E.
ðēnestre f. *servant, handmaiden*, OEG1358.
ðeng=ðegn
ðengelǂ m. *prince, king, lord, ruler.*
ðenian=ðennan
ðēnian (Æ,CP)=ðegnian
ðēnigmann=ðēningmann
ðēningfæt n. *serving-vessel*, RB59.
ðēninggǣst m. *ministering spirit, ÆH
1·510¹⁵.*
ðēninghūs n. *workshop*, GPH394.
ðēningmann m. *serving-man*, Æ,CP.
ðēnisc (*religious*) *service*, EC265'?
±ðennan (æ) *to stretch out, extend*, Lcd,
PPs : *prostrate* : *exert oneself* : *spread the
fame of, magnify*, OEG. ['thin']
ðenning f. *stretching, extension*, A11·172.
+ðēnsum *obedient, helpful, useful, Æ.*
[ðegen]
ðēnung (ðegn-) *service, ministry*, BH,Bl,
Bo; CP : (pl.) *attendants, retinue* : *use* :
church service, mass-book : *meal-time,
meal, Æ.* ['theining']
ðēnungbōc f. *book for divine service, mass-
book*, ÆH1·98' : *Leviticus*, ÆT286².
ðēnungwerod n. *body of serving-men*, MH
218¹².
ðēo I.=ðēow m. II. ds. of ðēoh. III.=
sēo II. IV. pres. 1 sg. of ðēon.
ðēod I. f. *people, nation, tribe*, Chr,Hy,Lk;
AO,CP; Mdf : *region, country, province,
Bo* : *men, war-troop, retainers* : (in pl.)
Gentiles, Æ,MtR : *language.* ['thede']
II. *fellowship*, RB.
+ðēod pp. of +ðēon, ðȳwan.
±ðēodan (ī, īe, ȳ) *to join, associate (with),
attach or subject oneself to, Æ,CP: come to,
be near* : (+) *engage in* : (+) *translate. ð.
fram separate.*

ðēodbealu† n. *public calamity.*
ðēodbūende† mp. *earth-dwellers, mortals.*
ðēodcwēn f. *queen, empress,* EL 1156.
ðēodcyning m. *monarch* : (†) *God.*
ðēode pret. 3 sg. of ðēon.
+ðēode n. *speech, language,* AO,CP : *nation* : *translation, Æ* : *meaning.*
ðēodegsa m. *general terror,* CR 834.
ðēoden m. *chief of a tribe, ruler, prince, king* : *God, Christ.* [ðēod]
ðēodend m. *translator,* OEG 15⁶.
+ðēodendlīc *copulative,* ÆGR 259¹.
ðēodengedāl n. *separation from one's lord (through his death),* GU 1324.
ðēodenhold† *faithful to one's lord.*
ðēodenlēas *without a ruler or chief, lordless,* B 1103.
ðēoden-māðm (-mādm) m. *treasure given by a prince,* GEN 409.
ðēodenstōl† m. *throne.*
ðēodeorðe f. *inhabited earth,* W 240¹⁵.
ðēodfēond m. *public enemy,* W.
ðēodfruma m. *prince, ruler,* MET 29⁹⁴.
ðēodgestrēon n. *people's treasure, great possession,* B 44; 1218.
ðēodguma† m. *man, warrior, retainer,* JUD.
ðēodhere m. *national army, host,* GEN 2160.
-ðēodig, -ðēodig-lic, -nes v. el-ð.
ðēodisc I.† n. *speech, language,* MET. II. adj. *Gentile,* OEG 8³⁵⁰. [*Ger.* deutsch]
+ðēodlǣcan *to adhere, cleave to,* LPs 24²¹.
ðēodland n. *inhabited land, district, country, empire* : *the continent.*
ðēodlīc *national,* ÆGR 65⁶.
+ðēodlīc *social, intimate,* WW 212⁶.
ðēodlīcetere m. *public deceiver, arch-hypocrite,* W 54¹⁸.
ðēodloga m. *arch-liar,* W.
ðēodmægen n. *troop, host,* EX 342.
±ðēodnes f. (+) *joining, suture* : *conjunction, association, society* : (+) *conjugation,* ÆGR : (+) *translation.*
±ðēodrǣden f. *intercourse, fellowship, Æ.*
ðēodsceaða† m. *public pest, criminal,* W.
ðēodscipe (+ in VH) m. I. *nation, people, community, population.* II. *connection, association* : *discipline, training, teaching, instruction, testimony* : *learning, erudition,* CP : *administration, law, authority* : *conduct.*
ðēodstefn m. *tribe, nation,* PPs 83¹⁰.
+ðēodsumnes f. *agreement,* LkL p 8¹.
ðēodðrēa f? m? *general distress,* B 178.
ðēodwiga m. *great warrior,* PA 38.
ðēodwita m. *learned man* : *senator, Æ.*
ðēodwundor n. *great wonder,* CR 1155.
ðēof I. (ǣ, ēa) m., *criminal,* '*thief,*' *robber,* G,LL,OET. II. f. *theft,* RBL 19¹².

ðēofdenn n. *robber's cave,* KC 3·15'.
ðēofend (only found in pl. ?) f. *thieving, theft.*
ðēofet = ðiefð
ðēofeðorn = ðȳfeðorn
ðēoffeng m. *seizure of thieves by an owner on his own land* : *right to fines payable on conviction for theft?* TC (v. BT).
ðēofgild n. *payment for theft,* LL.
±ðēoflian *to 'thieve,' steal,* LL,TC.
ðēofmann m. *robber, brigand,* AO,ÆP.
ðēofsceaða m. *robber,* v. ANS 129·24 n 6.
ðēofsceolu = ðēofscolu
ðēofscip (ðeb-) n. *pirate-ship,* EP. [v. '*thief*']
ðēofscolu f. *band of robbers,* BO 33¹⁰.
ðēofscyldig f. *guilty of theft,* LL 226'.
ðēofslege m. *slaying of a thief,* LL 97.
ðēofslīht m. *slaying of a thief,* LL 104B.
ðēofstolen ptc. *stolen,* LL.
ðēofð = ðiefð
ðēofung f. *thieving,* NC 327.
ðēofunt (NG) = ðēofend
ðēofwracu f. *punishment for theft,* LL 174.
ðēoging f. *increase, profit* : *advance, progress.*
ðēoh I. (ē, ī) n. (gs. ðēos, ds. ðēo; gp. ðēona) '*thigh,*' *hip,* AO,Gl,Lcd,MH. II. imperat. of ðēon.
ðēohece m. *pain in the thigh,* LCD.
ðēohgelǣte n. *thigh-joint,* LCD.
ðēohgeweald np. '*genitalia,*' LCD.
ðēohhweorfa m. *knee-cap,* LCD.
ðēohscanca m. *thigh-bone,* LCD,WW.
ðēohseax (æ²) n. *hip-sword, short sword, dirk,* WW.
ðēohwrǣc m. *pain in the thigh,* LCD 1·354'.
±ðēon I. (sv¹,³) *to thrive, prosper, flourish, grow, increase, ripen, Æ,B,Bl,Bo,Lk,Sc* : *be profitable, to become or be great, succeed, excel,* CP : *lengthen (of days).* +ðogen *adult.* ['*thee,*' '*i-thee*'] II. (wv.) = ðȳwan. III. (wv.)† *to perform, do.* IV. (+) *to receive, take.*
ðēona v. ðēoh; ðeonan = ðanon
ðēonde pres. ptc. of ðēon I.
ðēonen = ðanon; ðēonest = ðēnest
ðēonyð = ðēownȳd
ðēor m? *inflammation?* LCD.
ðēorādl f. *inflammation? blistering heat?* LCD.
ðēorcung = deorcung
ðēordrenc m. *a drink used for inflammation,* LCD.
ðēorf (æ, e, o) I. adj. *unleavened, Æ,G,WW* : *fresh? skim? (milk),* LCD. II. n. *unleavened bread, Æ.* ['*tharf*']
ðēorfa = ðearfa
ðēorfdagas mp. *days of unleavened bread,* BF 168³³.

ðeorfhlãf m. *loaf of unleavened bread*, Æ.
ðeorfling m. *unleavened bread*, WW 348²⁸.
['*tharfling*']
ðeorfnes f. *freedom from leaven, purity*,
Æ.
ðeorfsymbel n. *feast of unleavened bread*,
Ex 23¹⁴.
ðeorgerid n. *inflammation?* LCD 187a.
ðeorscwold=ðerscold
ðeorwærc m. *inflammatory disease?* LCD
45b.
ðeorwenn f. *inflammatory tumour or blister,
carbuncle*, LCD 123a.
ðeorwyrm m. *inflammatory (parasitic)
worm*, LCD 45a.
ðeorwyrt f. *fleabane*, LCD.
ðēos I. dem. pron., nom. fem. *this*. v. ðēs.
II. gs. of ðēoh. III. gs. of (ðēo=)ðēow.
ðeossa, ðeossum=ðissa, ðisum
ðēoster=ðēostor
ðēostor, ðēostre (īe, ī, ȳ) *dark, gloomy*, B,
BH,PPs : *sad, mournful*. ['*thester*']
ðēostorcofa† m. *dark chamber*.
ðēostorful (ȳ) *dark, dusky*, Æ,Mt. [v.
'*thester*']
ðēostorfulnes (ē, ȳ) f. *darkness*, OEG.
ðēostorlic (e²) *obscure, dark*, Æ. ['*thesterly*']
ðēostorloca m. *tomb*, EL 485.
ðēostornes (æ, ī, ·ȳ) f. *darkness*, AO,Bo.
['*thesterness*']
ðēostre=ðēostor, ðēostru
±ðēostrian (ȳ) *to grow dark, become dim, be
eclipsed*, Æ,BH : *darken, obscure*, Bo,MkL.
['*thester*']
ðēostrig (ȳ) *dark, obscure, blinded*, GD,Mk.
['*thestri*']
ðēostru f. (ī, īe, ȳ), ðēostre n. (often in pl.)
darkness, gloom, B,BH,CP,Mt; Æ. ['*thester*']
ðēostrung (ȳ) f. *twilight, gloom*, GUTH 36¹⁴.
ðeosum=ðisum
+ðēot I. n. *howling*, GUTH 48⁴. II. pres.
3 sg. of +ðēodan.
ðēotan². (ēa, ū) *to roar, howl*, Æ,Bo,Met :
sound forth, resound, murmur, WW.
['*theoten*']
ðēote f. *torrent, fountain, cataract, waterfall* :
conduit, pipe, Æ. [ðēotan]
ðēow I. fm. *servant, slave*, AO,CP,DR,G.
II. adj. *servile*, Æ,AO,Bo,W. ['*theow*']
ðēowa m. (Æ,CP)=ðēow I.
+ðēowa m. *enslaved person*, v. MFH 104.
ðēowæt=ðēowot
ðēowan I. (ē, ī, ȳ) *to press, impress, force*,
Æ : *thrust, pierce, stab* : *crush, push,
oppress, check* : *threaten*. II.=ðēowian
ðēowatdōm=ðēowotdōm
ðēow-boren, -berde *not free-born, born in
servitude*.

ðēowcnapa m. *bondservant*, ÆH 2·510'.
ðēowdōm (ēa) m. *slavery, servitude, service,
vassalage, subjection*, Æ,AO,DR; CP :
divine service. ['*theowdom*']
ðēowdōmhãd m. *service*, BH 480¹⁰.
ðēowe f. *female slave, handmaiden*, BH,
MtL (ī). ['*theow*']
ðēowen, ðēowene=ðēowe
ðēowet (Æ)=ðēowot, ðēowt-
ðēowhãd m. *servitude, service*, BH.
ðēowian I. (±) (ē, ēa) (w. d.) occl. pret.
ðēowde *to serve, minister to, be subject to*,
Bo,Lk,Mt; AO,CP : *enslave, give over into
slavery*, Æ. ['*theow*'] II.=ðȳn. III. (+)
V²Ps 140⁴=+ðēodan
ðēowin=ðēowe
ðēowincel (īo) n. *little servant*, CVHy 3³.
ðēowing (ȳ) f. *threat, reproof*, GD 238¹⁷.
ðēowlic *servile*, ÆGR 55¹n.
ðēowmann m. *servant*, ByH 134²⁰.
ðēowne as. of ðēowen.
ðēownȳd (ē²)† f. *serfdom, slavery*, DA.
ðēowot n. *service, ministry, servitude, bondage*, Æ,AO,CP.
ðēowotdōm m. *service*, CP 2¹⁰.
+ðēowtian *to bring into captivity*, RWH
141¹⁶.
ðēowraclan *to threaten, menace*, SPs 102⁹.
ðēowracu (Æ)=ðēowwracu
+ðēowrǣden (RB)=ðēodrǣden
ðēowtlic *of a slave, servile*, Æ.
ðēowtling (wet) m. *servant, slave*, Æ.
ðēowtscipe m. *service*, ÆL 23b²⁶.
ðēowð=ðīofð, ðīefð
ðēowu=ðēowe; ðēowut=ðēowot
ðēowwracu f. *commination, threat, threatening*, Æ.
ðeox *hunting-spear*, HGL 423.
ðēr=ðǣr
ðeran *to rush*, Cp 150J.
ðerc-, ðercs-=ðersc-
ðerc(c)an (WW)=ðerscan
ðerexwold=ðerscold; ðerf=ðeort
ðerflicnes (KGL)=ðearflicnes
ðerh (NG)=ðurh
ðērinne=ðǣrinne; ðērrihte=ðǣrrihte
+ðersc n. *thrashing, beating*, GD.
±ðerscan³ (a, æ, ea, i, y) *to thresh*, '*THRASH*,
beat, strike*, CP.
ðerscel (y) f. *flail*, WW. ['*threshel*']
ðerscelflōr f. *threshing-floor*, Mt 3¹².
ðerscing f. *thrashing*, DR 40¹⁵.
ðersc-old, -wald, -wold, ðerx(w)old (æ, eo,
i, y) m. '*threshold,*' *border, limit*, Æ,BH,
Bl,Bo,Lcd,WW.
ðes=ðæs
ðēs (e?) m., ðēos f., ðis n. dem. pron.
'*THIS*.' beforan ðissum, ǣr ðissum *before
this, formerly*.

ðester-=ðeostor-; ðestrian=ðeostrian
ðet, ðette=ðæt, ðætte
ðēw-=ðēow-; ðī=ðȳ
ðīada (VPs 134¹⁵)=ðēoda gp. of ðēod.
+ðian=+ðēon IV.
ðicce I. adj. 'THICK,' viscous, solid, AO : dense, stiff, CP : numerous, abundant, AO : hazy, gloomy, Æ : deep, AO. II. adv. thickly, closely, Bo,Lcd,WW : often, frequently, Gen 684. III. (VPs 28⁹)=ðiccet.
ðiccet n. thick bushes, 'thicket,' SPs. [ðicce]
ðiccian tr., intr. to thicken, Æ,WW : crowd together, Shr. ['thick']
ðiccnes=ðicnes
ðiccol, ðiccul fat, corpulent, WW.
ðicfeald dense, OEG 278.
+ðicfyldan to make dense, GL.
±ðicgan⁵ (and wv. in WS) (a, æ, e, ea) to take, receive, accept, Chr,Lcd : partake of, consume, taste, eat, drink, Mk; AO,CP. ['thig']
ðiclīce thickly, often, continually, frequently, in large numbers, AO.
ðicnes f. 'thickness,' density, viscosity, hardness, GD,Lcd, SPs : depth : anything thick or heavy (as clouds or rain), LPs,ZDA : darkness : thicket.
ðīd-=ðēod-; ðīdan=ðyddan
ðider (æ, y) adv. on that side, 'THITHER*,' whither, Æ; AO,CP. hider and ð. or. hidres ðidres (ðædres) hither and thither, CP : where, wherever.
ðidercyme m. a coming hither, NC 327.
ðidergeond thither, Æ.
ðiderinn (y¹, y²) adv. therein, into that place.
ðiderlēodisc to that people, native, MH 178²⁵.
ðiderweard, ðiderweardes adv. 'thitherwards,' thither, Æ,AO,Bo.
ðīdres=ðider; ðīed-=ðēod-
ðieder (CP)=ðider; ðief-=ðēof-
ðiefefeoh n. stolen goods, LL 100,25¹.
ðiefð (ē, ēo, ȳ) f. 'theft,' Lcd,LL : stolen goods, LL (ðēoft). [ðēof]
+ðiegen=+ðegen; ðīen=ðȳn
ðiende=ðēonde; ðienen=ðīnen
ðienga=ðinga gp. of ðing.
ðiestr-=ðēostr-; ðīf-=ðīef-, ðȳf-
ðigde, ðigede pret. 1, 3 sg. of ðicgan.
ðigen I. f. receiving, taking (of food or drink), eating, Æ : food or drink, Æ. [ðicgan] II. pp. of ðēon I. and ðicgan.
ðigeð pres. 3 sg. of ðicgan.
ðignen=ðīnen
ðīgon pret. pl. of ðēon I.
ðīh=ðēoh
ðīhsl=ðīsl
-ðīht v. maga-ð., mete-ð. and 'thight.'
ðihtig=ðyhtig
ðīhð pres. 3 sg. of ðēon I.

ðill-=ðyl-
ðillian (e, y) to lay with planks, board over, Æ. [Ger. dielen]
ðillic=ðyllic
ðilling f. boarding, floor : table, GD 97⁴.
ðille n. thin board, plank, flooring, GL. [Ger. diele]
ðillian=ðilian; ðillic=ðyllic
ðimiama m. incense, Æ. [L. thymiama]
ðīn I. gs. of ðu. II. adj. pron. 'THINE,' thy. III.=ðigen I.
ðīnan to grow moist, Lcd 13b.
ðinc=ðing
ðincan=(1) ðyncan; (2) ðencan
+ðincðo=+ðyncðo
+ðind n. swelling, Lcd,WW.
ðindan³ to swell, swell up, Æ : (wrongly, through confusion betw. 'tabescere' and 'tumescere') melt, pass away, PPs 111⁹, 118¹⁵⁸ : be angry.
ðīnen f. maid-servant, handmaid, Æ : midwife, Æ. [ðegn]
ðing n. 'THING,' creature, Æ : object, property, Æ : cause, motive, reason, Æ : lawsuit : event, affair, act, deed, enterprise, Æ, CP : condition, circumstances, Æ : contest, discussion, meeting, council, assembly : court of justice, v. LL 2·449 : point, respect. mid nānum ðingum adv. not at all. for his ðingum for his sake. for ðisum ðingum for this reason. be fullum ðingum abundantly. ænige ðinga anyhow, in any way, somehow. raðost ðinga at the earliest. ælces ðinges entirely, in every respect.
ðingan to invite, address? GL.
+ðingan I. sv³ to thrive. II.=ðingian
+ðinge n. meeting, council : arrangement, agreement, covenant : intercession : fate.
±ðingere m. advocate, intercessor, mediator, priest, GL,CP.
ðingestre f. female advocate, mediatrix, HL 10⁶⁹⁸.
ðinggemearc n.† reckoning of time, allotted time.
ðingian (w. d.) to beg, pray, ask, intercede for, LL,Sat; CP : covenant, conciliate, compound with, settle : prescribe : (refl.) reconcile oneself (with) : determine, purpose, design, arrange : talk, harangue. ['thing']
ðinglēas free (from sin or crime), LL 412.
ðingrǣden f. intercession, pleading, mediation, intervention, Æ.
+ðingsceat m. ransom, CP 339¹⁰.
ðingstede† m. place of assembly.
ðingstōw f. meeting-place, place of council : place where ways meet, village : market.
+ðingð f. intercession, agreement : court where claims are settled? (BTs), LL 228,1¹.
+ðingðo=+ðyncðo

ðingum adv. (instr. pl. of ðing) *purposely.*

±ðingung f. *advocacy, intercession, mediation,* Æ,CP.

ðinn-=ðynn-

ðīnne asm. of ðīn II.

ðinnen=ðīnen

ðinra=ðynra comp. of ðynne.

ðīnra gp. of ðīn II.

ðint pres. 3 sg. of ðindan.

ðīo, ðio-=ðēo, ðeo-

ðīr f. *a female servant,* JnLR18[17]. [*ON.* ðir]

ðird- (*NG*)=ðrid-

ðīre=ðīnre gdsf. of ðīn II.

ðirel=ðyrel; ðirl-=ðyrl-

ðirnet=ðyrniht

ðirsceflōr, ðirscelflōr=ðerscelflōr

ðirsceð pres. 3 sg. of ðerscan.

ðirscwald=ðerscold; ðirst=ðurst

ðīs v. ðes; ðisa=ðissa gp. of ðes.

ðisan=ðisum dsmn. of ðes.

ðises gsmn. of ðes.

ðīsl f., ðīsle f. *waggon-pole, pole, shaft.* [*Ger.* deichsel]

ðislic=ðyllic; ðism=dism

ðisne as. of ðes.

ðison=ðisum dsmn. of ðes.

ðissa gp., ðisse, ðissere gdsf.; ðisson, ðissum dsmn. and dp. of ðes.

ðistel (y[1]) m. '*thistle,*' *Gl,WW*; Mdf.

ðistelgeblǣd n. *blister caused by thistle,* Lcd 162b.

ðistellēag m. *thistle-covered meadow?* KC 5·265[22].

ðisteltwige f. *a kind of bird, goldfinch? linnet?* Gl.

ðīsternes (CP)=ðēostornes

ðīstr-=ðēostr-

ðīstra m. *trace, article of harness?* WW.

ðīsum dsmn. and dp. of ðes.

ðīðer=ðider

ðiustra '*ambulas*' (*amplas?*) Cp535A.

ðīw-=ðȳw-, ðēow-; ðīxl (Gl)=ðīsl

ðō f. *clay, loam,* Gl. [*Ger.* ton]

ðocerian, ðocrian *to run up and down,* WW.

ðoddettan *to strike, push,* W.

ðoden (ō?) n. *whirlwind, high wind, whirlpool,* Æ,Cp,CP,Chr. ['*thode*']

ðōdor=ðōðor

ðoft, ðofte f. *bench for rowers,* WW. ['*thoft*']

+ðofta m. *comrade, mate,* Æ,AO : *follower, client.*

+ðoftian *to join, unite, associate* (wið), AO.

±ðoftrǣden f. *fellowship,* Æ.

±ðoftscipe m. *companionship,* W : *alliance* CP : *intimacy,* Chrd 67[34].

+ðogen *adult* : *virtuous, excellent.* [pp. of ðēon]

ðōh (Gl)=tōh

ðōhe f. *clay,* Gl (=ðō).

±ðōht (+exc. N) mn. *process of thinking* '*thought*' : *mind* : *a thought, idea, purpose* : *decree* : *compassion,* '*viscera,*' LkLl 1[78]. [ðencan]

+ðohta=+ðofta

ðōhte pret. 3 sg. of ðencan.

+ðōhtung f. *counsel,* ZDA21·189.

ðōiht *clayey,* WW348[11].

ðol m. '*thole,*' *oar-pin, Cp,WW.*

ðolebyrde *patient, Sc.* ['*tholeburde*']

ðolebyrdnes f. *endurance,* Sc3[8](i[2]). ['*thole burdness*']

ðolemōd=ðolmōd

±ðolian *to suffer, endure, undergo. B,CP, Gen,MkL*; AO : *allow, KC* : *persevere, hold out* (intr.), *remain, survive* : (w. g.) *to lose, lack, forfeit, dispense with, Æ.* ['*thole*']

ðoll=ðol

ðolle f. *saucepan,* OEG4115.

ðolmōd I. *forbearing, patient, Æ,HL,Sc, OEG.* II. m. *patience? ÆL* 16[334] D. ['*tholemode*']

ðolmōdnes f. *forbearance, patience, Æ.* ['*tholemodeness*']

ðolo-=ðol(e)-

ðolung f. *passion, Sc.*

ðon I. instr. sing. of sē. II. adv. *then, now* : *thence* : (in negative clauses, with comparatives) *in comparison with* : *inasmuch as, when.* æfter ðon *after that.* ær ðon *before that* (antequam). nō ðon lange... *not long until....* tō ðon *to that extent, so that, after that.* III. (VPs)=ðonne

ðōn=ðǣm; ðonan=ðanon; ðonc=ðanc

ðone asm. of sē *the, that.*

ðonēcan=ðanēcan; ðonen=ðanon

ðong=ðanc

ðonne (a, æ) adv. and conj. THEN*, AO; CP : *therefore, wherefore* : *yet* : *while, when* : *thereafter, henceforth* : *rather than, Ps* : *since* : *although* : (with comparatives) '*than,*' *Æ,CP.* ðonne...ðonne *when...then.* ð. hwæðere *yet, nevertheless.* ð. gȳt *as yet, even.* ð. ðe *since.*

ðonon=ðanon

Ðor m. *Thor, W*; Lcd.

ðorf (NG)=ðeorf

ðorfæst *useful,* DR,LkR. [ðearf]

ðorfend=ðearfend

ðorfnian v. ðornian.

ðorfte pret. 3 sg. of ðurfan.

ðorh (VPs)=ðurh; ðorhnïht=ðorniht

ðorlēas *useless,* NG. [ðearf]

ðorn m. '*thorn,*' *thorn-bush, Æ,Bo,Cr,G,Gl*; CP; Mdf : *name of the rune for* ð, *Run.*

ðorngeblǣd n. *blister caused by a thorn,* Lcd 162b.

ðornian *to lose,* v. MFH174. [for ðorfnian?]

ðornig 'thorny,' Æ,W.
ðorn-iht, -eht(e) thorny, GL,KC.
ðorning m. thorny place, BC 1·480⁸ (Mdf).
ðornrind f. thorn-bark, LCD 19a.
ðorof (MtL)=ðeorf
ðorp (ðrop) m. farm : village, Chr,Gl. ['thorp']
ðorscen pp. of ðerscan.
ðost m. dung, Lcd. ['thost']
+ðōt=+ðēot
ðoterian (o²) to cry, howl, lament, Æ.
ðoterung f. groaning, wailing, Æ.
ðotor-, ðotr-=ðoter-
ðōð (CHR 1135)=ðēah I.
ðōðor, ðōðer m. ball, AS,GL.
ðox=dox; ðrā=ðrēa
+ðracen hardy, WW 108²⁵.
ðracian to fear, dread, shun, RHy 9⁵⁰.
ðracu† f., gs. ðræce pressure, fury, storm, violence : onrush, attack.
±ðræc (usu. +) n. throng : pressure, force, violence : equipment, OEG.
ðræcful? (e) strong, RPs 58⁴.
ðræcheard brave in battle, EL 123.
ðræchwīl f. time of misery, JUL 554.
ðræcian=ðracian
ðræcrōf keen in fight, GEN 2030.
ðræcswald=ðerscold
ðræcwīg m. violent combat, Ex 182.
ðræcwudu (e¹) m. spear, B 1246.
ðrǣd (ē) m. 'thread,' Bo,Cp,Lcd; Æ.
+ðræf n. pressure, CHRD 12⁶. (or +ðrafu)
+ðrǣf (on) unanimously (Swt).
ðræft n. contentiousness, MOD 42.
ðrǣgan† to run, EL.
ðrǣging=ðrēagung
ðrǣl (ēa) m. serf, 'thrall,' LL,NG.
ðrǣlriht n. serf's right, W 158¹⁵.
ðrǣs (ē) fringe, hem, GL.
ðrǣscan=ðrǣstan; ðræsce (Cp)=ðrysce
ðrǣst=dærst
±ðrǣstan to writhe, twist, press, force, BH : crush, oppress, torment, constrain, bind, GL : destroy. [v. 'threst,' 'i-thrast']
+ðrǣstednes f. contrition, GD : crushing, WW.
ðrǣstnes f. trouble, pain, grief : (+) contrition.
ðrǣstung f. affliction, torment, CP 317⁷.
ðrǣwen=ðrāwen pp. of ðrāwan.
ðrǣwung=ðrēagung; ðræxwold=ðerscold
ðrafian to restrain, reprove, CP : urge, push, press, Æ : demand, CHRD 12¹⁰.
+ðraful? f. compulsion, CHRD 12⁶.
ðrafung f. reproof, correction, CP.
ðrāg f. space of time, time, while, period, season, Gen,Jul : occasion, B,Bl,Bo : evil times : paroxysm. ðrāge for a time, some time, long time. ðrāgum at times, some-

times. ealle ðrāge all the time, continually. ['throw']
ðrāgbysig long busy? RD 5¹.
ðrāglic (ðrah-) long-continued, MFH 175.
ðrāgmǣlum† at times, sometimes.
ðrāh=ðrāg; ðrāll=ðrēal, ðrǣl
ðrang pret. 3 sg. of ðringan.
+ðrang n. throng, crowd, tumult, MA 299.
±ðrāwan⁷ to turn, twist, curl, Æ,Gl; CP : rack. ['throw']
ðrāwere m. perverse person, APs 17²⁷.
ðrāwingspinl f. crisping-pin, OEG.
ðrāwu (GL)=ðrēa; ðrē=ðrēo
ðrēa I. mfn. threat, menace, abuse, CP : rebuke, castigation : oppression, attack : calamity, throe. [ðrēowan] II. imperat. of ðrēagan.
ðreacs=ðreax
ðrēade pret. 1, 3 sg. of ðrēagan.
±ðrēagan, ðrēawian (ē) to rebuke, chastise, correct, punish, CP,Mt; Æ : threaten, menace : attack, oppress, torture, afflict, vex, harass. ['threa']
ðrēagend m. reprover, OEG 5380.
ðrēagung (ǣ, ēaw-) f. threatening, reproof, correction, Æ,CP.
ðreahs=ðreax
ðrēal I. f. discipline, correction, punishment, Æ : reproof : threat. II.=ðrǣl
ðrēalic† severe, terrible, calamitous, GEN.
ðrēan (Æ)=ðrēagan; ðrēanēd=ðrēanīed
ðrēang=ðrēagung
ðrēanīed (ē², y²)† f. affliction, misery, distress, calamity.
ðrēanīedla (ē², ȳ²)† m. affliction, misfortune.
ðrēanīedlic calamitous, JUL 128.
ðrēanȳd=ðrēanied
ðrēap m. troop, band, DD,DHy,OEG.
ðrēapian to reprove, correct, CP 165¹⁷. ['threap']
ðrēapung f. reproof, CP 167¹⁴. ['threaping']
ðrēaswinge f. chastisement, APs 37¹⁸.
ðrēat I. (ēo) m. press, crowd, throng, host, troop, B,El,Mk : oppression, coercion, calamity, Bl,Jul : threatening? Æ. ['threat'] II. pret. 3 sg. of ðrēotan.
ðrēatend m. violent person, MtL.
ðrēatian to urge, press, force, attack, harass, Æ,Cp,MH,MtL : threaten, PPs : reprove, rebuke, check, PPs; Æ,CP. ['threat']
ðrēatmǣlum (ē) adv. in swarms, WW 31²⁷.
ðrēatnes f. affliction, tribulation, MFH 117.
ðrēatnian (Æ)=ðrēatian ['threaten']
ðrēatung f. threatening, compulsion, ill-usage, AO : correction, reproof, CP.
ðrēaung=ðrēagung
ðrēaw pret. 3 sg. of ðrēowan.
ðrēawend=ðrōwend
ðrēaweorc n. misery, GEN 737. [OS.]

ðrēawian, ðrēawung=ðrēag-ian, -ung

ðreax (e) *rottenness, rubbish, refuse,* Bas 48²⁰; ÆL35¹⁵⁰. [*ON.* ðrekkr; v. ES43·332]

ðrec=ðræc

ðrece m. *force, violence,* W : *weariness,* LPs. [ðracu]

ðrecswald=ðerscold; ðrēd (*Cp*)=ðræd

ðrefe *a measure of corn or fodder, BC* 3·367. ['*thrave*']

+ðrēgan=+ðrēan; ðrēgian=ðrǣgan

ðrehtig=ðrohtig; ðremm=ðrymm

ðrēo v. ðrīe; ðreo-=ðri-

ðreodian (y) *to think over, deliberate* : *meditate* : (+) *resolve,* GD.

ðreodung (i) f. *deliberation, consideration,* BH : *scruple, hesitation,* W.

ðreohtig=ðrohtig

ðrēohund n. *three hundred,* Æ.

ðrēohundwintre *of the age of three hundred years,* Gen 5¹³.

ðreom v. ðrīe.

ðrēonīht f. *period of three days,* Pa 38.

ðrēora v. ðrīe

ðrēostru=ðēostru; ðrēot=ðrēat

ðrēotan² *to vex, weary,* AS47².

ðrēotēoða (ȳ) '*thirteenth,*' Æ,MH (-tegða), *Mt*; AO.

ðrēotīne (ē², ȳ²) '*thirteen,*' BH,*Men.*

ðrēotīnegeare *thirteen years old,* MH216¹⁶.

ðrēott-=ðrēot-

ðrēow I. pret. 3 sg. of ðrāwan. II.=ðrīe

ðrēowian=ðrōwian; ðreoxwold=ðerscold

ðrep? '*fornix,*' Ln34⁵⁹ (drep).

ðrepel=ðrypel; ðrerēðre=ðrirēðre

ðrēs=ðræs; ðrescan=ðerscan

ðrescold, ðrescwald=ðerscold

ðrēst-=ðrǣst-; ðrēt=(1) ðrēat; (2) ðræd

ðrēung=ðrēaung; ðrex=ðreax

ðrex-=ðersc-; ðrī=ðrīe; ðria=ðriwa

ðribeddod (y) *three-bedded, having three couches,* WW184²⁴.

ðriccan=ðryccan

ðridæglic (eo, y) *lasting three days,* BH 350³².

ðridǣled (co, y) *tripartite,* OEG.

ðridda (y) num. adj. '*third**,' *Bl,Cr,Lcd, LG*; AO,CP. ðridde healf *two and a half.*

ðriddandǣl m. *third part,* LL.

ðridung=ðreodung

ðrīe (ī, ȳ) num. nam.; nafn. ðrēo; gmfn. ðrēora; dmfn. ðrim (ðreom) 'THREE*.'

ðrie-=ðri-; ðrīeste=ðrīste adv.

ðrietan *to weary* : *force,* Bo.

ðrifeald '*three-fold,*' Æ,RB.

ðrifealdlic *three-fold, triple.* adv. -līce *in three ways,* LL. ['*threefoldly*']

ðrifeoðor=ðrifeðor

ðrifēte '*three-footed,*' ÆGr.

ðrifeðor *triangular,* GL.

ðrifingre (y) *three fingers broad or thick,* LL 110,49³.

ðriflēre (y) *three-storied,* ÆH 2·70¹⁷.

ðri-fotede, -fotad (y) '*three-footed,*' WW.

ðrifyldan (=ie) *to triplicate,* ÆGr287⁴.

ðrifyrede *three-furrowed,* ÆGr288¹²n.

ðrig=ðrīe; ðriga=ðriwa

ðrigǣrede (eo¹) *three-pronged,* ÆGr288¹⁰.

ðrigēare *three years old* : *space of three years.*

ðrigylde I. adj. *subject to three-fold payment, or compensation,* LL. II. adv. LL.

ðrihēafdede (y) '*three-headed,*' ÆGr67¹¹.

ðrihing=ðriðing

ðrihīwede (y) *having three forms,* ÆGr 287¹⁰.

ðrihlidede (y) *having three openings,* ÆGr 288⁶.

ðri-hyrne, -hyrnede (eo) *three-cornered,* Æ, Lcd.

ðrilēfe (y) *three-leaved.* as sb.=*trefoil? wood-sorrel?* WW133²². ['*threeleaf*']

ðrilen (WW151³⁴, y), ðrilig, ðrili adj. *woven with three threads,* Gl; LV. ['*thrile*']

ðrilic (y) *triple, three-fold,* VHy.

ðrilīðe n. *year with an extra month* (*a third, named* liða), v. BT.

ðrim I.=ðrymm. II. v. ðrīe.

ðrim-=ðrym-

ðrimen (y) *a third part,* Lcd 47a.

Þri-meolce, -milce n. *May,* MH.

Þrimilcemōnað (y¹, y²) m. *May,* Men (v. Chr p276).

ðrims, ðrimse=trymes; ðrindan=ðrintan

ðrinen (y) *three-fold,* CM.

Þrines f. *Trinity,* Æ,BH,Bl,Cr,DR. ['*three-ness,*' '*thrinness*']

+ðring (y) n. *crowd, pressure, commotion, An*; ÆL. ['*thring*']

±ðringan³ *to press, squeeze, crowd upon, throng, press forward, rush on, hasten, advance,* AO : *oppress* : (+) *pinch* (*with cold*) : *gain* (*by force*). ['THRING*']

ðrinihte *three days old,* Lcd.

ðrinlic *three-fold,* NC327.

ðrinna *three-fold, three times,* LL. ['*thrin*']

Þrinnes (Æ)=Þrines

ðrintan³ *to swell,* Mod 24.

ðrīo=ðrēo, v. ðrīe.

ðrīostr- (KGL)=ðēostr-

ðrirēðre *with three rows of oars.* as sb. *trireme,* AO (īe).

ðrisce=ðrysce; ðriscelflōr=ðerscelflōr

ðriscȳte (y¹) *triangular,* AO. [sćēat]

ðrislite (ie) *tripod, three-forked,* A4·151.

ðrisnæcce (y¹, e²) *three-forked,* ÆGr288¹²

ðrisnes=ðristnes

ðrist, ðrīste I. adj. *daring, rash, bold* : *audacious, shameless,* CP,W. II. adv. *boldly, daringly.* ['*thriste*'; *Ger.* dreist]

ðrīstelic=ðrīstiglic
ðrīstful *presumptuous*, CM369.
ðrīsthycgende† *brave-minded*.
ðrīsthȳdig† *bold, valorous*, B.
+ðrīstian *to dare, presume*, BH,LL.
ðrīstiglic *rash, bold, daring*. adv. -līce.
±ðrīstlǣcan *to presume, dare*, CP.
ðrīstlǣcnes f. *boldness*, GD.
+ðrīstlǣcung f. *presumption*, MFH164.
ðrīstlēasnes f. *want of boldness?* A11·101.
ðrīstlic *bold*, MFH. adv. -līce.
ðrīstling m. *bold person?* (BT), *thrush* (Mdf),
EC450¹⁵.
ðrīstlong *very long?* (or=ðristling?) BC
3·618.
ðrīstnes f. *rashness, boldness*, CM,Sc.
ðrīstra=ðīstra
ðrīstrenge (eo, y) *three-stringed*, ÆGr288¹⁰.
ðrīt (Æ) pres. 3 sg. of ðrīetan.
ðrītig 'THIRTY,' Æ; AO,CP.
ðrītigfeald '*thirty-fold*,' Mt.
ðrītigoða (ēo, ȳ, tt) '*thirtieth*,' ÆGr,BH,Mt.
ðrītigwintre *thirty years old*, Æ.
ðrittēoða=ðrēotēoða
ðrittig=ðrītig; ðrīð=ðrȳð
ðrīðing *third part of a county, 'riding*,'
LL.
ðrīðinggerēfa m. *governor or sheriff of a*
'*ðrīðing*,' LL.
ðriwa adv. *thrice*, Mk,RB; AO. ['*thrie*']
ðriwin-tre, -tra, -ter *three years old*, WW.
[v. '*thrinter*']
ðroc n. *table*, Mk11¹⁵ : *piece of wood on*
which the ploughshare is fixed, WW219⁶.
['*throck*']
ðroehtig=ðrohtig
ðrōh I. '*rancor*,' GL. II. '*rancidus*,' OEG.
ðroht† I. m. *exertion, labour, endurance, toil*,
trouble, suffering. II. adj. *dire, trouble-*
some, tormenting.
ðrohtheard† *strong in enduring*, AN,EL :
hard to endure, EL.
ðrohtig (e? eo) *enduring, persistent, per-*
severing, laborious.
ðrong=ðrang pret. 3 sg. of ðringan.
ðrop=ðorp; ðrosle=ðrostle
ðrosm m. *smoke, vapour*, Æ.
ðrosmig *vaporous, smoky*, W138²⁶.
ðrostle (ō?) f. '*throstle*,' *thrush*, BC,Cp,GD.
ðrota (WW306¹³)=ðrote
ðrotbolla m. *gullet, windpipe, larynx*, Æ,
Gl,LL. ['*throatboll*']
ðrote, ðrotu f. '*throat*,' Æ,Bo,WW.
ðroten pp. of ðrēotan.
ðrotu (Æ)=ðrote; ðrōung=ðrōwung
ðrōwend m. *serpent, scorpion, basilisk*, Æ.
ðrōwend-=ðrōwiend-
ðrōwere m. *sufferer, martyr*, DR,LCD.
ðrōwerhād, ðrōwethād m. *martyrdom*, GD.

±ðrōwian (o?) *to endure, suffer, die*, Æ,B,
Bl,Bo; AO,CP : *pay for, atone for : sym-*
pathise. ['*throw*']
ðrōwiendhād (e²) m. *martyrdom*, GD231⁸c.
ðrōw-lendlic, -igendlic *suffering, enduring*,
passive, Æ. ð. dēað *apoplexy*.
ðrōwung f. *suffering : passion, martyrdom*,
Æ,CP : *painful symptom : anniversary of*
martyrdom. ['*throwing*']
ðrōwungrǣding f. *reading about martyrs*,
martyrology, CM286.
ðrōwung-tīd f., -tīma n. *time of suffering*, Æ.
+ðrūen pp. of ðweran.
ðrūh fmn. *pipe, trough*, Gl,MH : *chest :*
tomb, coffin, Æ,BH ['*through*']
ðrum=ðrim v. ðrīe.
-ðrum v. tunge-ð. ['*thrum*']
ðrungen pp., ðrungon pret. pl. of ðringan.
ðrustfell n. *leprosy*, Cp103B.
-ðrūt v. fisc-ð.
ðrūtigende *strutting, bouncing*, Æ : *threaten-*
ing, ÆL10²⁷³.
ðruton pret. pl. of ðrēotan.
ðrūtung *anger, pride : threatening*, ÆL7⁷⁶.
ðrūðhorn=truðhorn; ðrȳ=ðrīe, ðrī
ðryan=ðrȳn
±ðryccan pret., ðrycte, ðryhte (tr.) *to*
trample on, crush, oppress, afflict, repress,
Bo; CP : (intr.) *press, push*, Gu. ['*thrutch*']
±ðryccednes f. *distress, trouble*, RWH67³².
ðrycnes f. *tribulation, affliction*, MtR.
ðryd-=ðrid-, ðreod-; ðrȳd-=ðrȳð-
+ðrȳde pret. 3 sg. of +ðrȳn.
ðrȳh=ðrūh
ðryhte pret. 3 sg. of ðryccan.
ðryl=ðyrl, ðyrel
+ðrȳl n. *crowd, multitude*, ÆL23⁹². [ðrȳn]
ðrym=ðrymm
ðrymcyme m. *glorious coming*, Gu1230.
ðrymcyning† m. *glorious king, king of glory*,
God.
ðrymdōm m. *glory*, W254¹⁴D.
ðrymen=ðrimen
ðrymfæst† *glorious, illustrious, noble*,
mighty.
ðrymful† *glorious, majestic, peerless*.
ðrymilce=ðrimeolce
ðrymlic *glorious, magnificent*, AO : *powerful*,
mighty. adv. -līce.
ðrymm m. *multitude, host, troop*, ÆL,Cr :
torrent : force, power, might, ability : glory,
majesty, splendour, Bl. ['*;hrum*']
ðrymma m. *brave man, hero*, AN1141.
ðrymme, ðrymmum adv. *powerfully, vio-*
lently.
ðrymrīce n. *realm of glory, heaven*, BL105¹¹.
ðrymsa=trymes
ðrym-seld n., -setl (Æ) n. *seat of honour*,
throne.

ðrymsittende† ptc. *sitting in glory, dwelling in heaven*, AN.

ðrymwealdend I. adj. *all-ruling, Æ.* II. m. *lord of glory.*

+ðrȳn *to press, bind*, v. NC328 : *repress* : *express.*

ðrync (AO76³⁴)=drinc imperat. of drincan.

ðrynen=ðrinen; Ðrynes=Ðrines

ðryng sb. *conduit, channel?* (=ðring?) WW 198¹⁴.

Ðrynnes (Æ)=Ðrines; ðryosm=ðrosm

ðrȳpel (ē) m. *instrument of torture, cross?* WW225⁴¹. [ðrēapian].

ðrȳpelūf '*eculeus*,' '*catasta*,' WW180¹³.

+ðryscan-*to weigh down, afflict, oppress*, CP. [ðerscan]

ðrysce (æ, i) '*thrush*,' WW.

ðryscel-=ðerscel-

±ðrysman, +ðrysmian *to press, oppress, stifle*, AO. [ðrosm]

ðryssce=ðrysce; ðrȳst=ðrīst

ðrȳst-=ðēost-

ðrȳt pres. 3 sg. of ðrēotan.

ðrȳð† f. (often in pl.) *might, power, force, strength : majesty, glory, splendour : multitude, troop, host.*

ðrȳðærn n. *noble house, palace*, B657.

ðrȳðbearn n. *strong youth*, AN494.

ðrȳðbord n. *strong shield*, EL151.

ðrȳðcyning m. *king of glory, God*, AN436.

+ðrȳðed *mighty*, PH486.

ðrȳðful (†) *strong, brave : splendid, glorious*, VH.

ðrȳðfullian (ðrȳd-) *to fill up*, RPs130¹.

ðrȳðgesteald n.*noble dwelling,palace*,CR354.

ðrȳðig *mighty, strong*, GEN1986?

ðrȳðlic *strong, valiant*, B. adv. -līce (?), B.

ðrȳðo=ðrȳð

ðrȳðswȳð† n. *mighty, powerful*, B.

ðrȳðu=ðrȳð

ðrȳðum† *very, violently.*

ðrȳðweorc n. *mighty work*, AN774.

ðrȳðword n. *lofty discourse*, B643.

ðu (ū) pron. 2 pers., gs. ðīn, das. ðe, ðec; dual n. git, gīt, g. incer, d. inc, a. incit, inc; np. gē, gīe. gp. ēower, dp. ēow, ap. ēowic, ēow 'THOU*.'

ðūf m. *tuft : banner, standard, crest.* [L. tufa]

+ðūf *thriving, luxuriant*, WW.

ðūfbǣre *leafy*, OEG2222.

ðūfeðistel=ðūðistel

ðūflan *to shoot forth, grow luxuriantly*, WW 408².

ðūfig *leafy*, WW408³.

ðūft m. *thicket*, WW408¹⁴.

ðugon pret. pl. of ðēon.

+ðūhsian *to make misty, dark*, W137⁹.

ðūhte pret. 3 sg. of ðyncan.

+ðūhtsum *abundant*, MH138¹⁵.

ðullic=ðyllic

ðūma m. '*thumb*,' Ep,Lcd,LL.

ðumle sbpl. *entrails*, Cp210U.

+ðun n. *loud noise*, PPs,WW.

ðunar=ðunor

ðunden pp. of ðindan.

ðunelic=ðunorlic

ðuner, ðuner-=ðunor, ðun(o)r-

ðung m. *a poisonous plant, wolf's-bane, aconite, nightshade?* GL.

+ðungen *full grown, thriven : competent, excellent, distinguished, virtuous*, ÆL. as sb. *notable, king's thane.* [pp. of ðēon]

+ðungenlīce adv. *virtuously, soberly*, WW.

±ðungennes f. *growth, maturity : goodness, excellence, virtue, perfection.*

ðunian *to stand out, be prominent : be proud : roar, thunder, crash, groan.*

ðunnung=ðunung; ðunnur=ðunor

ðunor (e², u²) m., gs. ðun(o)res '*thunder*,' AO,Cp,Jn,Rd : *thunder-clap*, Lcd : *the god Thunder, Thor : Jupiter.*

ðunor-=ðunr-

ðunorbodu f. *sea-bream?* WW180³⁴.

ðunorclǣfre f. *bugle (plant)*, LCD.

ðunorlic (e²) *thundery*, OEG.

ðunorrād f. *thunder, thundering, Æ.*

ðunorrādlic *thundering*, HGL451⁴⁶.

ðunorrādstefn f. *voice of thunder*, PPs76¹⁴.

ðunorwyrt f. *thunder-wort, houseleek*, LCD.

Ðunresdæg m. '*Thursday*,' LL.

ðunreslege m. *thunder-clap*, RWH83,85.

Ðunresniht f. *Thursday eve, Wednesday night.*

±ðunrian *to '*thunder*,'* Bo,Jn (impers.) ; PPs (pers.).

ðunring f. *thundering*, CHR1085.

ðunung f. *creaking, noise, din*, WW.

ðunur, ðunur-=ðunor, ðun(o)r-

ðun-wang (e, o), -wange (æ, e) f. (n?) *temple (of the head), Æ,WW.* ['*thunwang*']

Ður-=Ðor

ðuren=ðworen pp. of ðweran.

Ðuresdæg=Ðunresdæg

ðurfan swv. pres. 1, 3 sg. ðearf, pl. ðurfon; pret. sg. ðorfte; subj. pres. ðurfe, ðyrfe *to need, be required : must, have occasion to, CP : want, be needy : be under an obligation, owe.* ['THARF*'; ðearf]

ðurg=ðurh prep.

ðurh (e, o) I. prep. (w. d. a. g.) (space) 'THROUGH' ('*thorough*'), G : (time) *through, during*, PPs : (causal : agent, means, instrument) *through, by, by means of, in consequence of, because of.* ðurh ealle *entirely* : (manner) *in, with, by, in conformity with : for the sake of, in the name of :* (end, aim) *with a view to, on behalf of.* II. adv. *through, throughout.*

ðūrh=ðrūh

ðurharn pret. 3 sg. of ðurhiernan.

ðurhbeorht *very bright, transparent, radiant, clear*, Æ.

ðurhbiter *very bitter, sour, perverse*, CERPs 77⁸.

ðurhblāwan⁷ *to inspire, animate*, CM370.

ðurhborian *to bore through*, AA29¹⁷.

ðurhbrecan⁴ *to break through*, Æ,B.

ðurhbregdan³ *to draw through, transport.*

ðurhbrengan *to bring through*, LPs77¹³.

ðurhbrūcan² *to enjoy fully*, WW98¹.

ðurhburnen *thoroughly burnt*, Lcd165b.

ðurhclǣnsian *to cleanse thoroughly*, MtR3¹².

ðurhcrēopan² *to creep or pass through*, Bo93⁵.

ðurhdelfan³ *to dig through, pierce*, Æ.

ðurhdrencan (æ²) *to saturate*, RWH138¹⁷.

ðurhdrēogan² *to work through, accomplish, pass (time)*, CM.

ðurhdrīfan¹ *to drive or push through, strike : pierce, perforate : penetrate, imbue.*

ðurhdūfan² *to dive through*, B1619.

ðurhendian (e¹) *to accomplish, perfect*, LL 411,2².

ðurhetan⁵† *to eat through, consume*, WW.

ðurhfær n. *secret place*, Sc39².

ðurhfæreld '*transitus*,' V²Ps143¹⁴.

ðurhfæstnian *to transfix*, JnLR19³⁷.

ðurhfaran⁶ *to pass through, traverse, penetrate, pierce*, CP.

ðurhfarennes f. *inner chamber*, ASPs104²⁸.

ðurhfēran *to pass through, traverse, penetrate*, BH. ['*thoroughfare*']

ðurhfēre I. *penetrable*. II. n. *secret chamber*, MkL24³⁶.

ðurhflēon² *to fly through*, BH136¹.

ðurhfōn⁷ *to penetrate*, B1504.

ðurh-gān anv., pret. -ēode *to go through, pass through, penetrate*, Æ. ['*throughgo*']

ðurhgangan⁷=ðurhgān

ðurhgefeht (o¹) n. *war*, Cp205P.

ðurhgēotan² *to fill entirely, imbue, saturate, impregnate*, BH,W.

ðurhglēdan *to heat through*, Da244.

ðurhhǣlan *to heal thoroughly*, Lcd.

ðurhhālig *most holy*, Chrd,Gl.

ðurhhefig *very heavy*, GD104²⁶.

ðurhholod *bored through*, OEG4035.

ðurhhwīt *quite white*, WW163⁶.

ðurhhiernan³ *to run through, pierce*, Æ,WW.

ðurhlǣran *to persuade*, Sc38¹².

ðurhlǣred *very learned, skilled*, WW118²³.

ðurhlāð *very hateful*, WW130²⁸.

ðurhlēor-an, -ian *to penetrate*, GD : *pass through*, JVPs.

ðurhleornian *to learn thoroughly*, GD136⁴.

ðurhlōcung f. *preface, introduction*, WW 172³⁸.

ðurhrǣsan *to rush through*, RD4³⁶.

ðurhscēotan² *to shoot through, pierce*, Æ,AO.

ðurhscīnan (ȳ) *to shine through, be transparent*, WW148⁷. ['*throughshine*']

ðurhscīnendlic *illustrious, splendid*, LPs 15⁶.

ðurhscrīðan¹ *to go through, traverse*, Bf4³⁰ : *examine, consider : pry into*, Bf142¹¹.

ðurhscyldig *very guilty*, ÆL11³²¹.

ðurhscȳne *transparent*, WW148⁷.

ðurhsēcan *to search through, inquire thoroughly into*, Sc209³. ['*thoroughseek*']

ðurhsēon⁵ *to look through, examine : penetrate*, Bo. ['*thoroughsee*']

ðurhslēan⁶ *to strike or pierce through*, Æ : *attack, afflict, kill.*

ðurhsmēagan *to search thoroughly, investigate, think out*, Chr,MH.

ðurhsmūgan² *to pierce, bore through, eat through : go through carefully or slowly.*

ðurhsmyrian *to smear, anoint*, W229³.

ðurhspēdig *very rich*, ÆH1·502⁸.

ðurhstandan *to continue*, GD200⁸.

ðurhsticcian (o¹) *to transfix*, JnL19³⁷.

ðurhstingan³ *to pierce through, thrust through, prick*, Æ; CP. ['*throughsting*']

ðurhstrang *very strong*, OEG50²⁵.

ðurhswimman³ *to swim through*, WW52¹.

ðurhswīðan *to prevail*, LPs51⁹.

ðurhswōgan *to penetrate*, BH430⁵ (v.l.).

ðurhsȳne (=īe) *limpid, transparent*, OEG 23³⁵.

ðurhtēon² *to carry or put through : finish, fulfil, carry out, effect*, Æ,AO,CP : *draw, drag : continue : afford : undergo.*

ðurhtogennes f. *a religious reading at monastic meal-times*, RBL118⁷.

ðurhtrymman (e¹) *to confirm*, JnLR10²⁵.

ðurhðrāwan *to twist through*, Lcd.

ðurh-ðyddan, -ðȳn *to pierce, thrust through*, Æ.

ðurhðyrel (i²) *pierced through, perforated*, LL.

ðurh-ðyrelian (CP), -ðyrlian *to pierce, penetrate.*

ðurhunrot *very sad*, ZDA33·238¹¹.

ðurhūt prep. (w. a. Chr) adv. *right through*, Æ. ['*throughout*']

ðurhwacian *to keep vigil*, Bl227⁷.

ðurhwacol (e³, u³) *wide-awake, sleepless*, Æ.

ðurhwadan⁶ *to penetrate, go through, bore, pierce.*

ðurhwæccan *to keep vigil*, LkL6¹².

ðurhwæcendlic *very vigilant*, ÆL23b⁴³.

ðurhwǣt *thoroughly wet*, ÆP172¹⁸.

ðurhwerod *quite sweet, very sweet*, Gl.

ðurhwlītan¹† *to look through, see*, Cr.

ðurhwrecan⁵ *to thrust through*, HL,WW.

ðurhwundian *to pierce through, wound badly,* LL82,61¹.

ðurhwunenes f. *perseverance,* MFH176.

ðurhwunian *to abide continuously, remain, continue, settle down,* Æ,AO,CP : *persevere, hold out, be steadfast,* CP.

ðurhwunigendlic *constant, continued.* adv. -līce.

ðurhwunol *perpetual,* CHRD92¹⁷.

ðurhwunung f. *perseverance, persistency,* RB,Sc : *continued residence,* RB.

Ðurresdæg=Ðunresdæg

ðurruc m. *small ship? hold of a ship?* WW181³⁵. [v. '*thurrock*']

ðurscon pret. pl. of ðerscan.

Ðursdæg (*Jn*)=Ðunresdæg

ðurst (y) m. '*thirst,*' Bf,Lcd; Æ,AO,VPs.

ðurstig (y) '*thirsty,*' PPs,Mt; Æ : *thirsting after, greedy,* Bo.

ðuru=duru; ðuruh=ðurh

ðus adv. '*THUS,*' *in this way* : *as follows* : *to this extent* (qualifying adjs.), Æ.

ðūsend num. (sbn., always followed by gen.) '*thousand,*' Æ,AO,Chr; CP.

ðūsend-ealdor, -ealdorman m. *captain of a thousand men,* v. OEG4747.

ðūsendfeald '*thousand-fold,*' Æ,W.

ðūsendgerīm n. *computation by thousands,* SOL290.

ðūsendgetel n. *a thousand,* ÆGR284⁴.

ðūsendhīwe *multiform,* WW101¹.

ðūsendlic adj. *of a thousand,* BL,WW.

ðūsendmǣle? adj. *a thousand each, a thousand,* PPs,WW.

ðūsendmǣlum† adv. *in thousands,* SAT.

ðūsendmann m. *captain of a thousand,* Æ.

ðūsendrīca m. *chief of a thousand,* WW110¹¹.

ðūsent-=ðūsend-; ðuslic=ðyllic

ðuss=ðus; ðūtan=ðēotan

ðūðistel m. *sow-thistle,* Gl. ['*thowthistle*']

+ðūxsian (DOM105)=+ðūhsian

ðwā (NG)=ðwēa pres. 1 sg. of ðwēan.

ðwǣgen pp. of ðwēan.

ðwǣl=ðwēal

ðwǣle? (ē) f. *fillet? towel?* v. OEG53²⁶.

±ðwǣnan *to soften, moisten,* BH,CP,LCD.

ðwǣng=ðwang; ðwǣr-=ðwēr-

±ðwǣre (usu. +) *united, concordant, harmonious,* Æ : *compliant, obedient* : *agreeable, pleasant, gentle* : *peaceful* : *prosperous.* adv. -līce.

±ðwǣr-ian, -lǣcan¹ (ē) *to agree, consent to* : *reconcile* : *suit, fit.*

+ðwǣrlic *agreeing, harmonious* : *symmetrical,* BF180¹. adv. -līce *gently.*

±ðwǣrnes f. *concord, peace,* CP : *gentleness.*

+ðwǣrung f. *consent,* Sc228¹².

ðwagen rare pp. of ðwēan.

ðwāh (A)=ðwēah imperat. of ðwēan.

ðwang (æ, e) mf. '*thong,*' *band, strap, cord,* Æ,G,WW : *phylactery,* MtL,R.

ðwār-=ðwǣr-; ðwarm=ðwearm

ðwastrian *to whisper,* HL18³⁸¹.

ðwāt pret. 3 sg. of ðwītan.

ðwēa pres. 1 sg. of ðwēan.

ðwēal (ǣ, ē) n. *washing, bath, laver,* CP,JnL12³ : *soap,* ES43·334 : *ointment.* [Goth. ðwahl]

±ðwēan⁶ *to wash, cleanse,* Æ,CP : *anoint,* MtL6¹⁷.

ðwearm m? *cutting tool,* GL.

ðwēhl=ðwēal; ðwēle=ðwǣle

ðwēnan=ðwǣnan; ðweng (NG)=ðwang

ðwēor, ðweorg=ðweorh

+ðwēor v. buter-geð.

ðwēora m. *depravity* : *perversity,* CP222⁸.

ðwēores adv. (gen. of ðweorh) *athwart, transversely, obliquely,* AO : *perversely.*

ðweorh adj., gmn. ðwēores *cross, transverse, bent, crooked* : *adverse* : *angry* : *perverse, depraved,* CP.

ðweorh-fero, -furu, -fyri *cross-furrow,* GL.

ðweorhtēme=ðwēortīeme

ðweorian=ðweran

±ðwēorian *to oppose, thwart, be opposed to or far from.*

ðwēorlic *perverse, contrary, adverse,* Æ : *reversed, out of order.* adv. -līce *insolently,* GD.

±ðwēornes (ȳ)· f. *perversity, frowardness, obstinacy, depravity,* Æ.

ðwēorscipe m. *perversity,* CP269⁶.

ðwēortīeme (ē², ī², ȳ²) *contentious, perverse, wicked,* CP.

ðweoton (BH204³²)=ðwiton pret. pl. of ðwītan.

ðwēr, ðwerh=ðweorh

±ðweran⁴ *to stir, churn* : (†) *beat, forge, render malleable, soften.*

ðwēre (ǣ) *pestle,* OET102,103.

ðwihð (ie) pres. 3 sg. of ðwēan.

ðwīnan *to decrease, lessen,* LCD.

+ðwinglod *fastened up?* (BT), HL18²¹⁸.

ðwīr=ðweorh

ðwiril m. *handle of a churn, whisk,* WW280³¹. [ðweran]

+ðwit n. *cuttings,* BH204³² (v.l.). [ðwītan]

ðwītan¹ *to cut, whittle, cut off, cut out,* BH, Lcd. ['*thwite*']

ðwōg, ðwōh pret. 3 sg., ðwogen pp. of ðwēan.

ðwong=ðwang

ðworen pp. of ðweran.

+ðwōrnes=+ðwēornes; ðwurh=ðweorh

ðwyhð pres. 3 sg. of ðwēan.

ðwȳr (Æ), ðwȳr-=ðweorh, ðweorðwȳrs=ðwēores

ðȳ I. pron. (instr. sing. of sē, ðæt). æfter ðȳ after (that), later. II. conj. and adv. because, since, on that account : therefore, CP, Lcd : then : (with comparatives) the. ðȳ... ðȳ the...the. mid ðȳ while, when. tō ðȳ ðæt for the purpose that, in order that. for ðȳ ðe because. ðȳ læs (ðe) lest. ['thy']

ðȳan=ðȳn; ðȳc-=ðic-

ðȳdan=ðēodan

ðȳddan to strike, stab, Æ,CP : thrust, press, Æ. ['thud']

+ðȳde (ie) good, virtuous, CRA 68.

ðȳder=ðider; ðȳf=ðēof

ðȳfel m. shrub, bush, copse, thicket, Æ,Lcd, LPs,WW. ['thyvel'; ðūf]

ðȳfeðorn y? (ē, ēo, ī) m. hawthorn? bramble? Gl,Lcd. ['thevethorn']

ðȳflen? (or ? ryplen) bushy, GPH 399⁴⁵⁷.

ðȳften f. handmaid, OEG. ['thuften']

ðȳfð=ðiefð; ðȳgan=ðȳn

+ðȳht pleasing, RIM 18.

ðȳhtig (i) strong, B 1558.

ðȳhð pres. 3 sg. of ðēon.

ðȳlæs conj. lest. ðȳ læs ðe lest.

ðȳlc=ðȳllic

ðȳlcræft (e) m. elocution, rhetoric, OEG.

±ðȳld (usu. +) nf. patience, LkLR. ['thild']

±ðȳldelic patient. adv. -līce patiently, quietly.

+ðȳld-ian, -(i)gian to be patient, bear, endure, CP : give in, agree, OEG 3237 : wait for, Ps.

±ðȳldig (usu. +) adj. patient, DR; Æ,CP. [v. 'thild'] adv. -līce.

+ðȳldmōd patient, W 72⁷.

+ðȳldmōdnes f. patience, NC 297.

+ðȳldo (u²)=+ðȳld

+ðȳldum patiently, steadfastly, B 1705.

ðȳle m. speaker, orator : jester, WW 385³.

ðȳlian (Æ)=ðilian; ðȳling=ðiling

+ðȳll n. air, breeze, DR 121¹⁸.

ðȳllan to calm, assuage, BH.

ðȳllic pron. such, such a, Æ,AO,CP. ['thellich']

+ðȳllic 'densus,' OEG 5⁴ (?=+ðiclic; or +ðȳllic, from ðȳn).

+ðȳlmed brought down, abashed, LPs 19⁹.

ðȳmel m. thumbstall, 'thimble,' Lcd.

ðȳmele adj. of the thickness of a thumb, LL 110,49³.

ðȳn (1)=ðīn; (2) (±)=ðȳwan, ðēowan

±ðȳncan (i) (impers. w. d.) pret. 3 sg. ðūhte to appear, seem, CP; AO. mē ðyncð methinks. him ðūhte it seemed good to him. ['THINK*']

±ðȳneðo (i) f. dignity, rank, office, Æ,CP : meeting, assembly, court of justice, LL : private arrangement (to defeat justice), LL 112,52.

ðȳnden=ðenden

+ðȳnge=+ðinge

±ðȳngo progress, promotion, N.

ðȳnhlǣne wasted, shrunk, WW 446²⁴.

ðȳnne (i) 'thin,' BH,Lcd,RB : lean, Lcd, WW : not dense, Æ,BC : fluid, tenuous, BH,Lcd,Met : weak, poor, BH,Lcd.

ðȳnnes (i) f. lack of density, tenuity, fluidity, Lcd 73b : poverty, feebleness (of sight), Lcd 1·134. ['thinness']

±ðȳnnian (i) to 'thin,' make thin, lessen, dilute, Æ,Gl,Lcd : become thin, ÆL.

ðȳnnol (u²) lean, thin, WW 172¹⁶.

ðȳnnung, ðynung f. 'thinning,' act of making thin, Lcd 98a.

ðȳnwefen thin woven, WW 439³⁴.

ðȳrel (ȳ?) I. n. hole, opening, aperture, perforation, BH,MtL,Sc,WW. II. adj. pierced, perforated, full of holes, CP. ['thirl']

ðȳrelhūs n. turner's workshop, WW 185³¹ (ðryl-).

ðȳrelian=ðyrlian

ðȳrelung f. piercing, CP 153²⁵.

ðȳrelwamb with pierced belly, RD 79¹¹.

ðȳrf=ðearf

ðȳrfe subj. pres. sing. of ðurfan.

ðȳrl=ðȳrel

ðȳrlian (i) to perforate, pierce, excavate, Æ, WW. ['thirl']

-ðȳrlic v. samod-ð.; ðȳrn=ðorn

ðȳrne f. thorn-bush, bramble, Æ; Mdf.

ðȳrnen thorny, of thorns, Æ,CP. ['thornen']

ðȳrnet n. thorn, bramble, thorn-thicket, OEG.

ðȳrniht, ðȳrnihte thorny, LCD.

ðȳrran to dry, render dry, RD 29⁴.

ðȳrre withered : dry, Lcd. [Ger. dürr]

ðȳrs m. giant, demon, wizard, B,Cp; Mdf. ['thurse']

ðȳrscel=ðerscel

ðȳrscð pres. 3 sg. of ðerscan.

ðȳrscwold=ðerscold

ðȳrst=ðurst

+ðȳrst thirsty, MH 170⁶.

ðȳrstan (pers. and impers.) to 'thirst,' thirst after, AO,CP,G,Lcd,Sc. [ðurst]

+ðȳrstgian=+ðrīstian

ðȳs instr. smn. of ðes.

ðȳs-=ðis-; ðȳslic=ðȳllic

ðȳsma=disma

-ðȳssa v. brim-ð.

ðȳster=ðēostor; ðȳstr-=ðēostr-

ðȳt, ðȳtt pres. 3 sg. of ðēotan.

-ðȳtan v. ā-ð. [OHG. dōzōn]

ðȳðel (LPs 79¹¹)=ðȳfel

ðȳðer=ðider; ðȳw-=ðēow-

±ðȳwan to press, impress, Æ : stab, pierce : crush, push, oppress, check : threaten.

+ðȳwe=+ðēawe

ðȳwð=ðiefð

U

uce, ucu=wuce, wucu
üder n. 'udder,' WW61[16].
udu (N)=wudu
üf I. m. owl, GL : vulture, ÆGR48[17]n. II.
m. uvula, WW.
ufa=ufan
ufan (o) adv. from above, Æ,AO,CP : over,
above, on high, CP. on u.; u. on ðæt
besides. on u. hærfest in late autumn. on u.
midne winter after Christmas. [Ger. oben]
ufancumende coming from above, GD285[6].
ufancund from above, supreme, divine, CP.
ufane=ufan
ufanweard adj. (often used w. d. as a prep.)
highest, topmost, Æ. ufanweardum above,
at the top.
ufemest (superl. of uferra, ufor) highest,
uppermost, topmost, Æ. ['ovemest']
ufen=ufan
ufenan, ufenon I. adv. from above, Chr,Jn,
W. II. prep. over and above, DD. on
ufenan upon the top of. ['ovenon']
ufera=uferra
±uferian (of-) to delay, put off, Æ : (+)
raise up, elevate, Bk8 : extol, honour, Æ.
[ufor]
uferor (u[3]) higher, OEG5058.
uferra comp. adj. above, higher, upper, BH ;
CP : outer, Lcd,WW : after (of time), later,
future, AO,Lcd ; CP. ['over,' 'uver']
uferung f. delay, GD245[8].
ufeweard I. adj. upward, ascending, upper,
higher up, Æ,CP : later. II. sb. upper part,
outside, Æ.
ufewerd=ufeweard ; uffrian=uferian
ufon=ufan
ufor adv. higher, further away, further up,
Æ,CP : later, posterior, subsequent.
ufora=uferra ; ufur=ufor
uf-weard, -werd=ufeweard
uht=wuht=wiht fn.
üht m., ühte f. twilight, dusk, early morning,
dawn, Lcd : nocturns. on ühtan at day-
break, B,Bl. tō ühtes towards dawn.
['ughten']
ühtantīd=ühttīd
ühtantīma m. time of nocturns, Btk194[14].
ühtcearu f. sorrow at dawn, Wif7.
ühtentīd=ühttīd
ühtfloga m. twilight-flier, dragon, B2760.
ühtgebed n. morning prayer, matins, Guth,
WW.
ühthlem m. crash at dawn, B2007.
ühtlic I. morning, matutinal, of matins, BH.
II.=ütlic
ühtsang m. morning song, matins, BH,RB :
nocturns. ['uhtsong']

ühtsanglic nocturnal, used at nocturns, CM
1014.
ühtsceaða m. twilight foe, B2271.
ühttīd f. twilight, early morning, dawn, BH.
[v. 'ughten']
ühtðegnung f. matins, WW129[33].
ühtwæcca f. night watch, vigils, RB40[10].
üle f. 'owl,' Æ,Cp.
ulf (JnL10[12])=wulf
ulmtrēow n. elm tree, WW138[12]. ['ulm-
tree'; L.]
ultur m. vulture, Bo102[33].
üma m. a weaver's beam, WW.
umb, umbe=ymb, ymbe
umbor n. infant, GnE31.
umborwesende† being a child, B.
un- I negative or pejorative prefix. II.
occasionally=on- (prefix expressing reversal of a previous action) as in unbindan.
unābeden neg. ptc. unbidden, Æ.
unābēgendlic=unābȳgendlic
unāberendlic unbearable, Æ,CP. adv. -līce.
unāberiende unbearable, Lcd3·260[23]n.
unābēt=ungebēt
unābindendlic indissoluble, Bo.
unāblinn n. irrepressible state, unceasing
presence, Guth46[10].
unāblinnend-e, -lic unceasing, perpetual.
adv. -līce, Æ,AO,CP.
unāboht=ungeboht
unābrecendlic inextricable, WW419[2].
unābȳgendlic (ē) inflexible, WW421[30].
unācenned unbegotten, ÆH1·464'.
unācnycendlic that cannot be untied or
loosened, DR108[10]. [cnyccan]
un-ācumendlic (Æ), -ācumenlic unbearable,
unattainable, impossible.
unācumenlicnes f. unbearableness, RBL
114[9].
unācwencedlic unquenchable, G.
unādrūgod undried, not dried, not hardened,
CP383[32].
unādrysn-ende, -en(d)lic unquenchable, NG.
un-ādwæsced, -ādwæscendlic, -ādwēscedlic
inextinguishable, unquenchable, Æ.
unēaðe=unēaðe
unǣfastlīce=unæwfæstlīce
unǣm(et)ta m. want of leisure, work, occupation, hindrance, Chrd,LL.
unǣmtigian to deprive of leisure, AS36[19].
unǣrh=unearg
unǣsecgenlic (EPs100[6])=unāsēðendlic?
unǣt f. gluttony, Deut21[20].
unǣtspornen not hindered, GD60[26].
unǣðelboren not of noble birth, low-born, Æ.
unǣðele of low birth, ignoble, base, CP.
unǣðellan (an-) to degrade, debase, Bo,Met.
unǣðelīce adv. ignobly, basely, BH442[11].

unæðelnes f. *ignobility*, GD 151²⁴.
unǣwīæstlīce adv. *irreverently* : *unlawfully*.
unǣwisc (ē) '*pudicus*,' WW 291²⁵.
unāfandod *untried*, AS 32¹⁹.
unāfe(o)htendlic (æ³) *what cannot be contended against, inevitable*, DR,WW.
unāfīled *undefiled*, LPs 17³¹.
unāfūliende=unfūliende
unāfunden *undiscovered*, Æ : *untried*.
unā-fylledlic, -fyllendlic *that cannot be filled, insatiable*, Æ. adv. -līce.
unāga m. *one who owns nothing*, PPs 112⁶.
unāgǣledlīce *unremittingly*, BL 121⁵.
unāgān adj. *not lapsed, in force*, KC.
unāgelȳfed=unālȳfed
unāgen *not one's own or under one's control, precarious*, CP.
unāgifen *unpaid*, TC 201'.
unāgunnen *without a beginning*, ÆH.
unāhefendlic *unbearable*, MFH 176.
un-ālīef-, -lē(a)f-=unālȳf-
unālogen *not false, true*, NC 328.
un-ālȳfed (CP), -lȳfe(n)dlic (īe) *not allowed, unlawful, illicit.* adv. -līce *unlawfully, without permission*, Sc.
unālȳfednes (ē³;=īe) f. *what is forbidden, licentiousness*, BH.
unālȳsendlic *without remission*, ÆH 1·500'.
unāmǣlt *unmelted*, GL.
unāmānsumod *not excommunicated, in church fellowship*, Æ.
un-āmeten, -metenlic, -metgod *unmeasured, unbounded, immeasurable, immense*, Æ, RPs.
unan-=unon-
unandcȳðignes (o²) f. *ignorance*, JVPs 24⁷.
unandergilde *irreplaceable, invaluable*, Bo 27²⁰.
unandett *unconfessed*, W 71⁷.
unand-gittol, -gytful *unintelligent, incapable, ignorant, foolish*.
unandhēfe (-hoife) *insupportable*, MtR 23⁴.
unandweard *not present, absent*, ÆH 1·128¹⁷.
unandwendlic=unāwende(n)dlic
unandwīs *unskilful*, WW.
unānrǣdnes f. *inconstancy*, BL 31³⁴.
unāpīnedlīce adv. *with impunity*, DR 113¹⁵.
unār f. *dishonour*, AO.
un-āræf(n)ed, -āræfne(n)dlic *not permissible, impracticable*, Æ : *intolerable.* adv. -līce.
unāreccendlic *unexplainable, wonderful*, Sc 26¹⁵.
unārefnendlic (VPs)=unāræfnendlic
unāreht *unexplained*, Bo 77¹⁶.
+unārian *to dishonour*, AO,CP.
unārīmed adj. *unnumbered, countless, innumerable*, AO.

unārīme(n)dlic *innumerable, immeasurable*, AO. adv. -līce, AO.
unārlic *dishonourable, dishonest, disgraceful* : *contrary to what is fitting, unnatural (of a will)*, WW. adv. -līce *dishonourably* : *unmercifully*.
unarodscipe f. *remissness, cowardice*, CP 149¹⁵.
unārwurðian (eo) *to dishonour*, ÆH 1·442'.
unārwurðlic *dishonourable*, CHRD 63²⁴.
unārwyrðnes f. *irreverence, indignity*, Sc 224¹.
unārȳmed=unārīmed
unāsǣcgendlic=unāsecgendlic
unāsǣdd=unāsedd
unāscended *unhurt*, DR.
unāscruncen *not withered, undecayed*, DR 24¹⁶.
unāscyrigendlic *inseparable*, ÆH 1·326²⁷.
unāscyrod *not separated*, WW 253³.
unāsecgende *unspeakable, ineffable*, BH 264³⁰.
unāsecgendlic *indescribable, unspeakable, ineffable*, Æ. adv. -līce.
unāsedd *unsatisfied, unsatiated*, GL.
unāsēðenlic (KGL), -āsēðendlic *insatiable*.
unāsīwod (ēo) *unsewed, without seam*, Jn 19²³.
unāsmēagendlic *inconceivable, inscrutable, unsearchable*, Æ.
unāsolcenlīce *diligently*, RB 20¹⁹.
unāspring-ende, -endlic (GD) *unfailing*.
un-āspyriendlic (e³, o³) *unsearchable*, GD, WW.
unāstīðod *not hardened, not firm*, CP 383³².
unāstyr-ed, -od *unmoved*, GD.
un-āstyriende, -āstyri(g)endlic adj. *immovable, firm* : *motionless*, Æ.
unāsundrodlic *inseparable*, DR.
unāswundenlīce adv. *diligently*, BH.
unātaladlic (N)=unātellendlic
unāteald (Scr 28³²)=unteald
unātellendlic (ea) *innumerable*, CHR.
unātemed *barbarous*, BH.
unātemedlic *untameable, wild, fierce*, BH 162²⁸.
unātēoriende *indefatigable*, OEG.
unātēorigendlic *lasting, permanent, unceasing*, Æ : *indefatigable, unwearied.* adv. -līce.
unātēorod *unwearied*, OEG 2373.
un-ātēriend-, -toriend-=unātēorigend-
unātwēogendlīce=untwēogendlīce
unāðrēotend *unwearied, assiduous, persistent*, CR 388.
unāðroten *unwearied, indefatigable, vigorous*, CP 171⁹. adv. -līce, CP.
unāwǣgendlic *unshaken*, TC 319⁹.
unā-wæscen, -waxen *unwashed*, WW 190, 439.

unāwemmed (ALRSPs), -lic (DR) *un-stained, spotless.*
unāwemmednes f. *incorruption*, BF168²¹.
unā-wend, -wended(lic) *unchangeable, unchanged, inviolate* : *unmoved.*
unāwendend-e (MET), -lic (Æ) *unchangeable, unceasing.* adv. -līce.
unāwerded (oe;=ie) *unhurt*, N.
unāwīdlod *undefiled*, DR24¹⁶.
unāwriten *unwritten*, Æ.
un-bældo, -bældu=unbieldo
unbærende=unberende; **unbald**=unbeald
unbealaful *guiltless, innocent*, W.
unbeald (a) *cowardly, timid, weak, irresolute, distrustful, CP,Jul.* ['unbold']
unbealu n. *innocence*, PPs100².
unbeboht *unsold*, AO18¹⁰.
unbebyriged *unburied*, GD,W.
unbecēas *incontestable*, LL112,53¹.
unbecrafod *unquestioned, not subject to claims*, LL358,72.
unbecweden *unbequeathed*, TC.
unbeden '*unbidden*,' LL (386).
unbe-fangenlic, -feonglic (BHCA224¹⁹) *unintelligible, incomprehensible*, Æ.
unbefliten *undisputed*, EC69'.
unbefohten *unopposed, unattacked*, MA57.
unbefōndlic *incomprehensible*, BHo224¹⁹.
unbegān *untilled*, LCD: *unadorned*, HGL435.
unbegrīpendlic *incomprehensible*, BL.
unbegunnen *without a beginning*, Æ. ['un-begun']
unbehēafdod *not beheaded*, ÆL23¹⁸⁵.
unbehēfe *not suitable, inconvenient*, WW 508³⁴.
unbehelendlīce adv. *without concealment*, W138³.
unbehelod *uncovered, naked*, GENC9²¹.
unbehrēowsigende *unrepenting*,ÆH1·500¹⁵.
unbelimp=ungelimp
unbeorhte (y) *not brightly*, Bo.
unbereafigendlic *never to be taken away*, ÆL23b²⁴³.
unberende *unbearable* : *unfruitful, barren*, Æ,LG,VPs. ['unbearing']
unberendlic *unbearable*, LCD3·260²³.
unberendnes (eo²) f. *barrenness*, DR,VPs.
unbermed *unleavened, unfermented*. [beorma]
unbesacen (æ²) *undisputed*, LL.
unbesænged=unbesenged
unbescēawod *improvident, inconsiderate*, GL,Sc. adv. -līce.
unbescoren *unshorn*, RB135²⁹.
unbesenged *not singed, unburnt*, W25¹⁹.
unbesēondlic (BH224¹⁹)=unbefōndlic?
unbesmiten *undefiled, pure, spotless*, Æ.
unbesorh *unconcerned, not interested*, ÆH 2·486⁹.

unbēted *uncompensated, unexpiated, unatoned*, CR1312.
unbeōōhte adv. *unthinkingly*, CP434².
unbeweddod *unbetrothed, unmarried*, Æ.
unbewelled *not boiled away*, LCD93b. [weallan]
unbiddende *not praying*, ÆH1·156⁴.
unbieldo (æ) f. *want of boldness, diffidence, timidity*, CP.
unbilewit (y²) *harsh*, OEG56²³².
unbindan³ *to 'unbind,' loosen*, LG; Æ : *pay* (NG; trans. of '*solvere*'). [=onbindan]
unbiscopod *not confirmed by a bishop*, LL, W. ['unbishoped']
unblōyrfe† *useless, idle, vain.*
unblēoh *clean, bright*, DD, PPs.
unbletsung f. *curse*, LL(310').
unblinnendlīce *incessantly*, BH34⁶.
unbliss f. *sorrow, affliction*, Æ.
+unblissian *to make unhappy*, NC297.
unblīōe *joyless, sad, sorrowful*, CP : *unfriendly.*
unblīōemēde *sad of heart*, MtL26³⁷.
unblōdig *bloodless*, GPH395¹⁶.
unblonden *unmixed*, DR68¹⁵.
unboht '*unbought*,' *free*, NG.
unboren '*unborn*,' Æ,CP.
unbrād *narrow*, Ct,LCD.
unbrǣce† *unbreakable, indestructible.*
un-brece, -brice=unbryce; **unbrīece**=unbryce.
unbrocheard *delicate, tender*, Bo,WW.
unbrosn-igendlic (Æ), -endlic (GD) *indestructible, incorruptible.*
unbrosnodlīce *incorruptibly*, GD348²³.
unbrosnung f. *incorruptibility*, Æ.
unbryce† *unbreakable* : *indestructible, everlasting.* [brecan]
unbryce (īe) *useless*, GL,PPs. [brūcan]
unbrӯde *honestly*, LL400,2.
unbunden (*LL, Rd*) pp. of unbindan.
unbӯed *uninhabited desert*, NG.
unbӯergo np. *uninhabited places*, DR1⁹ (? for unbӯencg, MLR18·273).
unbyrged '*unburied*,' MH28²¹.
unbyrhte=unbeorhte
unbyrnende *without burning*, B2548.
unc pers. pron. (d. a. dual) *us two.*
uncænned=unācenned
uncāfscipe m. *sloth, neglect*, CHR47.
uncamprōf *unwarlike*, GPH399.
uncapitulod *without headings* (*to chapters*), LL(204¹).
uncēap(ed) *gratuitous, gratis*, MtL10⁸.
uncēapunga *gratuitously*, DA746.
uncēas(t) n? *oath of reconciliation*, LL104,35.
uncenned=unācenned
uncer I. g. dual of pers. pron. *of us two.*
II. poss. pron. *belonging to us two.*

uncet=unc

unclǣmod *unsmeared*, GPH 398.

unclǣne '*unclean*,' *BH,Bl,Cr,LG,WW*.

unclǣnlic *unclean, impure, DR.* adv. -līce, *ÆH.* ['*uncleanly*']

unclǣnnes f. *uncleanness, impurity*, AO, *CP,DR,Mt,OEG.*

unclǣno f. *uncleanness*, NG.

±unclǣnsian *to soil, pollute*, AO,CP.

unclǣnsod *unpurified, CP.* ['*uncleansed*']

unclēn-=unclǣn-

uncnyttan *to unbind, untie, loosen, Lk;* Æ. ['*unknit*']

uncoren *evil, reprobate*, VH 21.

un-coða m., -coðu f. *disease,* Æ : *plague*, CHRD 70[7].

uncræft m. *evil practice*, LL,W.

uncræftig *helpless*, DD 239.

uncrafod (LL 232,14)=unbecrafod

uncre gdf. of uncer II.

uncristen *infidel*, BHo 306[23]. ['*unchristian*']

uncumlīðe *inhospitable*, W 257[14].

uncūð *unknown, strange, unusual,* Æ,AO : *uncertain,* Æ,CP : *unfriendly, unkind, rough.* ['*uncouth*']

uncūða m. *stranger,* Jn 10[5].

uncūðlic *unknown.* adv. -līce *in an unfriendly manner, unkindly, LL.* ['*uncouthly*']

uncūðnes f. *strangeness*, GD 278[15].

uncwaciende *firmly*, CP 41[7].

uncweden (*unsaid*), *revoked*, WW 114[45].

uncwēme *not pleasing,* MFH 176. ['*unqueme*']

uncweðende *speechless, dumb,* Bo,SolK.

uncwisse *dumb*, BH 290[12].

uncwyd(d) *uncontested, undisputed*, LL.

uncȳme *unseemly, mean, paltry, poor,* BH, Bl.

uncynde *unnatural,* Bo 91[21]B.

un-cynn, -cynlic (Bo) *unsuitable, improper.*

uncȳpe *gratuitous,* WW 514[31].

uncȳped=uncēaped

un-cyst, -cyste f. *mistake, error* : *vice, wickedness, crime,* Æ,CP : *stinginess, parsimony,* Æ : *disease,* LCD. [*cēosan*]

uncystig *mean, stingy, niggardly,* Æ, CP.

uncȳð=uncūð

uncȳðig *ignorant, unacquainted with* : *devoid of,* Gu 1199.

un-cȳðð, -cȳððu f. *ignorance,* Æ,CP : *foreign country.*

undǣd f. *wicked deed, crime,* W.

undǣftelīce=ungedǣftlīce

un-dǣled, -dǣld *undivided,* Bo.

undēaded *not deadened,* LCD 3a.

undēadlic *immortal, for all eternity,* Æ,DR. adv. -līce. ['*undeadly*']

undēadlicnes f. *immortality,* Æ. ['*undeadliness*']

undēagollīce=undēogollīce

undearnunga adv. *openly,* LL.

undēað-=undēad-

undēaw *without dew,* LCD 35a.

undeclīnigendlic *indeclinable,* ÆGR.

undēd=undǣd

undēogollīce (ēa, ī) adv. *plainly, clearly,* CP.

undēop *shallow, low,* CP.

undēopðancol *shallow, silly,* ÆH 1·286'.

undēor=undēore I.

undēore I. adj. *cheap, CP,WW.* ['*undear*'] II. adv. *cheaply.*

undeornunga=undearnunga

under I. prep. w. d. and a. '*UNDER*,' *beneath,* Æ : *among,* AO : *before, in the presence of* : *under the shelter of,* CHR : *in the service of, in subjection to, under the rule of,* Æ,AO,Chr : *during,* AO,Chr : *by means of, by.* swerian u. God *to swear by God.* u. bæc=underbæc. II. adv. *beneath, below, underneath,* Æ,B,Chr,MH.

underāgendlic adj. '*subnixus*,' DR 182[16].

underandfōnd (o[3], oe[4]) '*susceptor*,' DR 193[6].

under-bæc, -bæcling adv. *backwards, back, behind,* Æ,CP.

underbēgan *to subject,* DR. [bīegan]

underbeginnan[3] *to undertake, purpose,* ÆT 76[7].

underberan[4] *to support, endure,* DR,Sc. ['*underbear*']

under-brǣdan, -bregdan *to spread under,* WE.

underbūgan[2] *to submit (to),* Æ.

underburg f. *suburb,* DEUT 32[32].

underburhware mp. *dwellers in a suburb* (BT).

undercerran *to overturn, subvert,* LkLR 23[2]. [cierran]

undercing=undercyning

undercrammian *to stuff between, fill out underneath,* ÆH 1·430[4].

undercrēopan[2] *to be secretly grasped, seized by something,* Æ : *penetrate, undermine,* GD.

undercuman[4] *to assist,* DR.

undercyn(in)g m. *under-king, viceroy,* Æ.

underdelf n. *undermining,* ASPs 79[17].

underdelfan[3] *to dig under, undermine, break through,* Æ,Lk. ['*underdelve*']

underdīacon m. *subdeacon,* LL.

underdōn anv. *to put under,* Lev 1[12].

underdrencan *to choke by drowning,* MkL 5[13].

underdrifennes f. *subjection,* LkLp 6[16].

underēade (N)=underēode, pret. 3 sg. of undergān.

undereoton (Ruin 6)=undereten pp. of undoretan.

underetan⁵ *to eat underneath, undermine, subvert,* Bo 27².

underfang '*susceptor,*' SPs.

underfangelnes=underfangenes

underfangen (pp. of underfōn) *neophyte,* ÆL 31⁷³⁰.

underfang-enes, -elnes f. *undertaking, assumption : recéption, hospitality,* GD 76²².

underfealdan '*subdere,*' EHy 6³⁰.

underfeng I. m. *undertaking, taking in hand,* CP 23²². **II.** pret. 3 sg. of underfōn.

underflōwan⁷ *to flow under,* Rd 11².

underfolgoð m. *subordinate office,* AO 286⁵ c.

underfōn *to receive, obtain, take, accept,* Æ, AO,CP : *take in, entertain : take up, undertake, assume, adopt,* Æ,AO,CP : *submit to, undergo,* Æ : *steal.* ['UNDERFO']

underfōnd m. *one who takes anything in charge,* LPs.

underfōnlic *to be received,* RBL 97⁸.

underfyligan '*subsequi,*' LkL 23⁵⁵.

undergān anv. *to* '*undergo*' : *undermine, ruin,* Lcd.

undergangan⁷=undergān

undergend-=under(i)gend-

undergeoc *under the yoke, tame,* MkL 21⁵.

undergerēfa m. '*proconsul,*' *deputy-governor,* Æ.

undergereord=underngereord

undergesett *placed under,* GD 307¹².

undergestandan⁶ *to stand under,* LL 108,44.

undergeðēoded *subject,* LL 88'.

undergeðēodnes=underðēodnes

undergietan⁵ (i, y) *to note, mark, understand, perceive,* Æ,AO,Chr,Mt. ['underyete']

underginnan³ *to begin, undertake,* ÆT 76⁷n.

undergitan (Æ)=undergietan

undergynnan=underginnan

undergytan (Æ)=undergietan

underhebban⁶ *to bear, support, lift,* NG.

underhlystan '*subaudire,*' *to supply an omitted word,* ÆGr 151.

underhlystung f. *the act of supplying an omitted word,* ÆGr 151.

underhnīgan¹ *to submit to, undergo,* Æ,CP : *succumb to, sink under.*

underholung f. '*suffossum,*' LV²Ps 79¹⁷.

underhwītel m. *under-garment,* WW 187²¹.

underhwrǣdel=underwrǣdel

underi-ende, -gende, -gendlic *inoffensive, harmless,* AO.

underiernan³ *to run under* : '*succurrere,*' DR 43⁸.

underlāttēow m. *consul,* AO 68² c.

underlecgan *to* '*underlay,*' *prop, support,* Æ,CP.

underlicgan⁵ *to* '*underlie,*' *to be subject to, give way to,* Æ,CP,RB.

underlihtan *to alleviate,* DR.

underling m. *underling, inferior,* HL,KC.

underlūtan² *to bow or bend under* : *support, sustain,* CP.

undermete=undernmete

undern m. *morning (from* 9.0 *a.m. to* 12.0 *noon) : the third hour* (=9.0 *a.m.*; *later,* 11.0 *a.m.*), Lcd; Æ : *service at the third hour,* RB. ['undern']

underne=undierne

underneoðan (y³) adv. *underneath,* AO.

underngereord m. *morning meal, breakfast,* AO.

underngeweorc n. *breakfast,* GD 66¹².

underngi(e)fl n. *repast, breakfast,* CP 322¹⁹.

underniman⁴ *to take in, receive, comprehend, understand,* Æ : *blame, be indignant at* : *take upon oneself,* Æ : *steal,* Lcd. ['undernim']

undernīðemest *lowest of all,* Met 20³⁵.

undernmǣl n. *morning-time,* Æ,B. ['undernmeal']

undernmete m. *morning meal, breakfast,* AO.

undernrest f. *morning rest,* MH 42⁶.

undernsang m. *tierce (religious service about* 9.0 *a.m.*), RB,LL.

undernswǣsendu np. *early meal,* BH 164³⁰.

underntīd f. *the third hour* (=9.0 *a.m.*), *noon, morning-time,* BH,Mt; Æ : *tierce.* ['underntide']

undernyðan (Æ)=underneoðan

underondfōnd=underandfōnd

underplantian '*supplantare,*' Sc,SPs.

undersang=undernsang

underscēotan² *to prop up, sustain, support,* CP : *intercept, pass under.*

underscyte m. *passage underneath, transit,* Æ : *brake, drag-chain,* OEG 50¹⁵.

undersēcan *to examine, investigate, scrutinize,* CP. ['underseek']

undersettan '*supponere,*' LPs 36²⁴?

undersingan³ '*succinere,*' ÆGr 181².

undersittan⁵ '*subsidere,*' ÆGr 157⁵.

undersmūgan² *to creep under, surprise,* RB.

understandan⁶ (o³) *to* 'UNDERSTAND,' *perceive,* Æ; CP : *observe, notice, take for granted,* ÆL 23b¹⁸⁶ : '*subsistere,*' DR.

understandennes (o³) f. '*substantia,*' DR 31²⁰.

understanding f. '*understanding,*' Sc 221¹³.

understapplian '*supplantare,*' LPs 16¹³.

understaðolfæst=unstaðolfæst

understingan³ *to prop up, support,* CP 113¹¹.

understond-=understand-

understrēdan *to strew under,* MH 18²¹.

understrēowed *underlaid,* ÆL 37²⁰¹.

undersyrc m. *undershirt*, WW379³⁰. [serce]
undertíd (*Chrd*)=underntíd
undertõdal n. *secondary division*, ÆGR291⁵.
undertunge f. '*sublingua*,' *part under or behind the tongue, tongue-ligament*, WW 264¹⁷ (or ? two words, Cp,LPs9²⁸; 65¹⁷).
undertungeõrum *tongue-ligament*, Lcd. [v. '*thrum*']
underõencan (æ³) *to consider*, CP49²³ : (refl.) *change one's mind, repent*, LL438,22.
underõēnian *to serve under*, Sc5⁶.
underõēod *subjected, subject* : *assistant, suffragan.*
underõēodan (īe, ȳ) *to subjoin, add* : *subjugate, subject, subdue, reduce, degrade*, Æ, CP : *support*, OEG4339.
under-õēodendlic, -õēodenlic *subjunctive*, ÆGR.
underõēodnes (ī³) f. *subjection, submission, obedience*, Æ : '*supplantatio*,' EPs40¹⁰.
underõēow m. *subject, slave*, AO.
underõīedan (AO,CP)=underõēodan
underõīednes (ī³)=underõēodnes
underõȳdan=underõēodan
underweaxan⁶ '*succrescere*,' Sc104⁸.
underwedd n. *deposit, pledge*, Æ.
underwendan '*subvertere*,' Sc196⁶.
underweorpan '*subjicere*,' EPs143².
underwrǣdel m? *waistband*, WW153¹.
underwreõian (eo, i, y) *to support, sustain, uphold, strengthen, establish*, Æ,CP.
underwreõung f. *propping up, support, sustentation*, Sc,WW.
underwrítan *to write at the foot of, subscribe*, BH312³⁰.
under-wríõian, -wrýõian=underwreõian
underwyrtwalian '*supplantare*,' EPs17⁴⁰.
underȳcan (īe) *to add*, CM385²⁹².
underyrnan=underiernan
undierne (e, i, y) I. *open, manifest, clearly known* : *public, nuncupatory.* II. adv.
undígollíce=undēogollíce
undílegod *unerased*, CP423²³.
undolfen *untilled*, GD204⁴.
undõm m. *unjust judgment, injustice*, W.
undõmlíce *indiscreetly*, Sc202¹⁵.
undõn anv. *to* '*UNDO*,' *open, loosen, separate*, Æ,AO : *cancel, discharge, abrogate, destroy*, LG.
undrēfed *untroubled, undisturbed, undefiled*, CP31³.
undrifen *not driven or tossed*, LL222,2.
undruncen *sober*, CP295⁸.
undrysnende *inextinguishable*, MtL3¹².
undȳre=undēore
undyrne=undierne
unēacen (ē) *barren*, OEG27³¹.
unēacniendlic *unfruitful, sterile*, OEG1030.
unearfoõlíce adv. *without difficulty*, OEG.

un-earg, -earh (Æ), -earhlic (Æ) *not cowardly, dauntless, bold, brave.*
unēaõe (y) I. adj. *not easy, difficult, hard, disagreeable, grievous*, Æ,An,WW. II. adv. *not easily, hardly*, Bo,Chr,LG, WW : *unwillingly*, Æ,BH : *scarcely, only just*, Æ. ['*uneath*']
unēaõelic *difficult, hard, impossible* : *troublesome*, Nic611'. adv. -líce.
unēaõelicnes (ā², ǣ², ē², ȳ²) f. *difficulty*, BH 296²¹.
unēaõ-lǣ(c)ne, -lācne *not easily cured*, Lcd.
unēaõmylte *indigestible*, Lcd82b.
unēaõnes (ē, īe) f. *difficulty, inconvenience, trouble, worry*, Æ : *severity, harshness.*
unēawfæstlíce=unǣwfæstlíce
un-efn, -efen(lic) *unequal, unlike*, Cr : *anomalous, irregular*, ÆGR. adv. -efne, Ps. ['*uneven*']
un-ēmetta, -ēmota=unǣmta
unemn=unefn
unendebyrdlíce *in a disorderly manner*, CP.
unered *unploughed, uncultivated*, WW147³.
unēstful *ungracious*, WW191¹⁷.
unēõ-=unēaõ-, uníeõ-
unēwisc=unǣwisc
unfǣcne (ā) *without malice, sincere, honest, faithful*, B,LL.
unfæderlíce adv. *in an unfatherly manner*, W106⁶.
unfǣge† *not fated to die*, B.
unfæger *not beautiful, unlovable, deformed, ugly, hideous*, B,Bo,Bl. ['*unfair*']
unfægernes (e) *ugliness, disfigurement*, GD 279¹⁵ : *abomination*, MtL24¹⁵.
unfæglic *not fatal*, Bo107²⁹.
unfægre (ǣ) adv. *unfairly, foully*, Gen. ['*unfair*']
unfǣhõ f. *peace* (*dropping of a feud*), LL 100,28.
unfǣle *wicked, unlovely, unholy, evil*, Gen, Mk,WW. ['*unfele*']
unfæst *not fixed, not firm, loose, unsteady, tottering*, Bo,CP. ['*unfast*']
unfæstende *not fasting*, LL(252¹).
unfæstlíce adv. *not firmly, vaguely, indistinctly*, CP156¹³.
+unfæstnian *to unfasten*, MFH165.
unfæstrǣd *unstable, inconstant*, CP.
unfæstrǣdnes f. *inconstancy*, CP.
unfæsõ-=unfæst-
unfāh *exempt from hostility, not under a ban*, LL186,1¹.
unfealdan⁷ *to unfold, open*, G,GD : *explain*, Sc.
unfeax *without hair, bald* (Swt).
unfēcne=unfǣcne
unfēferig *not feverish*, Lcd1·164'.
unfeger-=unfæger-

unfēlende 'unfeeling,' insensible, Lcd 99a.
unfenge not acceptable, MFH 176.
un-feor, -feorr adv. not far from, near.
unfeormigende (on-) inexpiable, ÆL 23b⁴²⁶.
unfēre disabled, invalided, CHR 1055.
unfērnes f. impotence, infirmity, RWH 137¹²
unflitme? unreservedly? B 1097.
un-flycge, -fligge unfledged, OEG 28¹³.
unforbærned unburnt, Æ,AO.
unforboden unforbidden, lawful, Æ.
unforbūgendlīc unavoidable. adv. -līce without turning away, ÆL 23b⁴³¹.
unforburnen unburnt, ÆH 2·480⁷.
unforcūð reputable, good, honourable, noble, brave, CP. adv. -līce. [fracoð]
unfordytt unobstructed, OEG 3613.
unforebyrdig impatient, Sc 8¹³.
unfored (od) unbroken, Æ.
unforedlic (o³) indissoluble, OEG.
unforescēawod hasty, unconsidered, HEXC 387.
unforescēawodlic hasty, precipitate, WW 426⁸. adv. (v. unforsc-).
unforfeored unbroken? WW 231³³.
unforgifen unforgiven, CP : not given in marriage.
unforgifende (y³) unforgiving, GD 320¹.
unforgitende unforgetting, mindful, GUTH 76²².
unforgolden unpaid, LEV 19¹³.
unforhæfednes (fd) f. incontinence, CP.
unforhladen unexhausted, WW 255³⁹.
unforht adj. fearless, bold. adv. -e, -līce.
unforhtigende fearless, ÆH 2·140'.
unforhtlēasnes? fear, timidity, VH 21.
unforhtmōd fearless, ÆH.
unforlǣten (ē) not left, NG.
unformolsnod neg. ptc. uncorrupted, undecayed, Æ.
unformolten unconsumed, ÆH 1·488⁷.
unforod = unfored
unforrot-edlic (HGL), -iendig (ÆP 14⁷), -iendlic (OEG) incorruptible.
unforscēawodlīce unawares, WW 92¹⁰ : inconsiderately, hastily, ÆH.
unfor-spornen, -spurned not hindered, GD 60²⁸.
unforswǣled unburnt, ÆH 2·20¹⁵.
unforswīgod not passed over in silence, ÆL 23b³⁵.
unforswȳðed unconquered, AA 3¹¹.
unfortredde sb. the plant which cannot be killed by treading, polygonum aviculare, knot-grass.
unfortreden not destroyed by treading, LCD 3·299'.
unforwandigendlīce adv. unhesitatingly, boldly, APT 21⁹.

unforwandodlic adj. unhesitating, fearless, CP. adv. -līce recklessly, CP : unswervingly.
unforwealwod unwithered, BL 73²⁵.
unforwordenlic (u³) undecayed, OEG 60.
unforworht I. innocent. II. unrestricted, free, KC.
unforwyrded undecayed, NC 351.
un-fracodlīce, -fracoðlīce honourably, becomingly, fitly, Bo.
unfratewod unadorned, unpolished, GPH 396. [frætwian]
unfremful unprofitable, Æ,GL.
unfremu f. damage, hurt, GEN.
unfrēondlīce unkindly, GEN 2689. ['unfriendly']
unfriogende unquestioning, GEN 2649.
unfrið m. breach of peace, enmity, war, AO : state of being outside the king's peace.
unfriðflota m. hostile fleet, CHR 1000 E.
unfriðhere m. hostile army, CHR.
unfriðland n. hostile land, LL 222,3¹.
unfriðmann m. alien enemy, LL 222,3³.
unfriðscip n. hostile ship, CHR,LL.
unfrōd young, inexperienced, B 2821.
unfröforlīce uncontestably, OEG 56¹⁸⁷?
unfrom† inert, B,PPs.
unfūl 'insulsum' MkLR 9⁵⁰.
unfulfremed imperfect, Æ.
unfulfremednes f. imperfection, CP.
unfulfremming f. imperfection, LPs 138¹⁶.
un-fūliende (HGL), -fūliendlic (OEG) incorruptible.
unfullod unbaptized, LL.
unfulworht imperfect, unfinished, RB 20³.
unfyrn adv. not long ago, BL : soon, GD.
ungænge useless, vain, MtR 15⁶.
ungan = ongan pret. 3 sg. of onginnan.
ungeǣndod = ungeendod
ungeǣsce unheard of, GD 284²⁰.
un-geǣwed (-iǣwed) unmarried, OEG 5248.
ungeandett without confession, W 135³².
ungeaplīce carelessly, unskilfully, CHRD 123⁹.
ungēara adv. not long ago, lately, recently : soon, shortly.
ungearo = ungearu
ungearu, gsm. ungear(o)wes unready, disinclined, unprepared, untilled, AO,CP. on ungearwe unawares, AO.
ungearuwitolnes f. dulness of mind, GD 331¹⁵.
ungearwyrd not respected, WW 421³².
ungeāðe = uneāðe
ungeāxod unasked, ÆH 1·428⁶.
ungebarde = ungebierde
ungebēaten unbeaten, unwrought, Ln 23⁵.
ungebēgendlic = ungebīgendlic
ungebeorhlīce rashly? intemperately? ÆH 2·322²⁶.
unge-bēt(ed), -bett unatoned for, CP : unacquitted, EC 217¹⁰.

ungebierde (a, y) *beardless*, GL.
ungebíged *unbent*, OEG 2977.
ungebígendlic *inflexible, rigid* : *indeclinable*, ÆGR.
ungebleoh *of different colours, unlike*, ÆGR.
ungeblētsod *unblessed*, JUL 492.
ungeblȳged *intrepid*, GU 913. [blēoh]
ungeboden *without being summoned*, TC.
ungeboht *unbought, unbribed*, LL 398,8.
ungeboren *yet unborn*, LL 126 Pro.
ungebrocen *unbroken*, WW 398³².
ungebrocod *uninjured*, ÆH 1·464⁶.
ungebrosnendlic *undecaying*, BH,GD.
ungebrosnod *uncorrupted, undecayed*, Æ.
ungebrosnung f. *incorruption*, Sc 71².
ungebunden *unbound*, ÆGR 14¹³; GD 214¹⁶.
ungebyrde I. *uncongenial*, Bo 92²². II.=ungebierde
ungebyrded *inviolate*, GD 199⁴.
ungebyredlic *incongruous*, DR 179¹⁷.
ungecindelic=ungecyndelic
ungeclǣnsod *unclean, impure*, Æ.
ungecnāwen *unknown*, APT 17¹³.
ungecnyrdnes f. *negligence, indifference, idleness*, ÆH 2·552ʹ.
ungecoplic *unsuitable, unbefitting, troublesome*. adv. -līce, Sc 80¹⁴.
ungecoren *reprobate*. u. āð *oath taken by a body of persons generally* (*opposed to* cyreāð), LL.
ungecost *reprobate*, BH 480⁴.
ungecwēme *unpleasing, disagreeable*, Sc 38¹⁵.
ungecyd *unsaid, not declared*, LL 212,9.
ungecynde *unnatural*, Bo : *alien*, CHR.
unge-cyndelic, -cyndlic, -cynelic *unnatural, monstrous, terrible*. adv. -līce.
ungecyrred *unconverted*, LCD 3·442¹.
ungedæftelīce=ungedæftlīce
ungedæftenlic=ungedafenlic
ungedæftlīce adv. *unseasonably*, CP 97¹⁶.
ungedæftnes f. *untimely intervention or interruption*, CP 97¹⁹.
ungedafenlic *improper, unseemly*, Æ : *unseasonable, troublesome*, CP (v. A 33·272). adv. -līce *improperly, unduly, unreasonably, unjustly, unsuitably*.
ungedafenlicnes f. *unfitness, inconvenience*, CPs 9²².
ungedafniendlic (HGL 492)=ungedafenlic
ungedallic *infinite, without end*, GD 337¹¹.
ungedēfe *improper, not fitting, disagreeable*. adv. -līce.
unge-dēfelic, -dēflic=ungedafenlic
unge-dered, -derod (Æ) *unhurt, uninjured, unmolested*.
ungederstig=ungedyrstig
ungedrehtlīce adv. *indefatigably*, WW 428³.

ungedrȳme *inharmonious, discordant*, CHRD 57¹². [drēam]
ungedwimorlīce *clearly, without any delusion*, NC 328.
ungedyrstig *timid*, CP 209¹⁰.
ungeeahtendlic (a³, æ³) *estimable*, BH,GD.
ungeended=ungeendod
ungeendigendlic *infinitive*, ÆGR : *infinite*.
unge-endod (CP), -endodlic *unending, endless, infinite, boundless*.
ungefæd (a) *indiscretion*, CHRD 13¹⁴.
ungefæglic=unfæglic; ungefær-=ungefēr-
ungefandod *untried, having no experience*, CP 407,409.
ungefaren *impassable, without a road*, BLPs.
ungefēa m. *unhappiness*, NC 328.
ungefēalīce *miserably*, CHR 755.
ungefēge *unfit, improper*, WW 191²².
unge-fēle, -fēled *without feeling*, LCD.
ungefēre I. *impassable* : *impenetrable, inaccessible*, CP. II. adv. *impassably*.
ungefēred *inaccessible*, AA 30⁷.
ungefērenlic *difficult, trackless*, AA 25⁹.
ungefērlic *unsocial, internecine*. adv. -līce *in civil war*.
ungefērne *impassable*, VPs (oe).
ungefeðered *not feathered*, WW 427¹⁶.
unge-fōg, -fōh I. *immoderate, excessive*, Æ : *overbearing, presumptuous, unbending*, Æ. II. n. *excess*, CHRD 70¹⁶. adv. -fōge *excessively*, AO.
unge-fōglic (AO), -fōhlic *fierce, strong* : *immense*. adv. -līce.
unge-fræg-e, -elic *unheard of, unusual, inconceivable*. adv. -līce.
ungefrætwod *unadorned*, WW 419¹¹.
ungefrēdelīce adv. *callously*, CP 265¹⁶.
ungefrēglīce=ungefræglīce
ungefremed *unfinished*, LL,WW.
ungefremmung (on-) f. *imperfection*, RPs 138¹⁶.
ungefullod I. *unfulfilled*, RD 60¹⁴. [fullian] II.=ungefulwod
ungefulwod *unbaptized*, Æ,BL.
unge-fyld (Bo), -fylle(n)d(lic) *insatiable*.
ungefynde *worthless, barren?* CP 411¹⁹.
ungefyrn adv. *not long hence, not long ago, not long after*, Æ.
ungegearwe=ungearwe v. ungearu.
unge-gearwod (DR), -gerad (MtR) *not clothed*.
ungeglenged *unadorned*, OEG 1210.
ungegrēt *ungreeted*, GUTH 22²⁰.
ungehādod *not ordained, not belonging to an order* (*used of men and women*), IM 127¹⁸.
un-gehǣlendlic, -gehǣledlic *incurable*, VHy.
ungehǣmed *unmarried*, OEG 1174.
ungehǣplic *unsuitable, unfit*, A 8·452.
ungehālgod *unhallowed, unconsecrated*, Æ.

ungehāten *unpromised, unbidden*, Bl 189²⁷.
ungehēafdod *not having come to a head*, Lcd 1·92'.
ungehealdsum *unchaste*, Æ. adv. -līce.
ungehealdsumnes f. *incontinence, unchastity*, KC,LL.
ungehealtsum=ungehealdsum
ungehefegod *not pregnant*, OEG 27³¹.
ungehende (æ³) *remote*, HL 12⁸.
ungehendnes f. *remoteness, distance*, ÆGr 14¹⁹.
ungeheort *disheartened*, ÆL 23⁶².
ungehēred=ungehȳred
unge-hīersum (CP), -hīrsum (Æ) *disobedient, rebellious*.
ungehīrsumnes (ȳ) f. *disobedience*, Æ,VH.
ungehīrsumod (ȳ) *disobedient*, RBL 12⁸.
unge-hīwod, -hīwodlic *unformed, not fashioned, unshapen : unfeigned, genuine*.
ungehlēoðor *inharmonious*, WW 224⁷.
ungehrepod *untouched*, Æ.
ungehrinen *untouched*, BH,GD.
ungehwǣde *much*, Lcd 53b.
ungehwǣrnes=ungeðwǣrnes
ungehȳr-=unge-hīer-, -hīr-
ungehȳred (ē³) *unheard of, untold*, BH 40³³.
ungehȳrnes f. *hardness of hearing, deafness*, Lcd.
ungehyrt *disheartened, fearful*, W 192²⁴.
ungel m. *fat, tallow, suet*, Æ.
ungelācnod *unhealed*, Guth 66¹⁶.
ungelādod *not acquitted*, EC 217¹⁰.
ungelæccendlic *unreprovable*, Sc 119¹¹.
ungelǣred *untaught, illiterate, unlearned, ignorant, rude*, Æ,CP. adv. -līce.
ungelǣredlic *unteachable*, GD 110²¹.
ungelǣrednes f. *unskilfulness, ignorance*, CP.
ungelaðod *uninvited*, ÆH 1·128¹⁸.
ungelēaf *unbelieving*, PPs 67¹⁹.
ungelēafa m. *unbelief*, Bl,Chr.
ungelēafful *unbelieving*, CP : *incredible*, ÒEG.
ungelēaffullic *unbelieving : incredible*. adv. -līce.
ungelēaffulnes f. *unbelief*, Bl,G.
ungelēaflic *incredible*, Æ.
ungelēafsum *unbelieving*, BH.
ungelēafsumnes f. *unbelief, infidelity, heathenism*, BH 70²⁵.
ungelēf-=ungelīf-; ungelēofa=ungelēafa
ungelīc *unlike, different, dissimilar, diverse*, Æ,Bo,Bl,OEG; CP. adv. -līce. ['*uniliche,*' '*unilike*']
ungelīca m. *one unlike others*, ÆL 7²⁸.
ungelīcian *to displease*, Æ (94⁶⁶).
ungelīclic *improper*, Guth 12¹⁷. adv. -līce, Lcd 59a.
ungelīcnes f. *unlikeness, difference*, CP.

ungelīef-=ungelīf-
ungelīfed (ȳ) I. *unbelieving*, Æ. II. *illicit*, BH 2·229.
ungelīf-edlic, -endlic (īe, ȳ) *incredible, extraordinary*. adv. -līce.
unge-līfen, -līfende (e³, y³) *unbelieving*, NG.
ungelīfend (ē) m. *unbeliever*, NG.
ungelīfnes (ē) f. *unbelief*, NG.
ungeligen=ungelygen
ungelimp nm. *mishap, misfortune*, Æ.
ungelimplic *inconvenient, unfortunate, disastrous*, Æ : *abnormal, unreasonable*. adv. -līce.
ungelȳf-=ungelīf-
ungelygen *not lying, true*, LL.
ungēm-=ungȳm-
ungemaca m. '*impar,*' *not a match*, ÆGr.
ungemǣc *unlike*, GD 91¹⁵; WW 223³⁵.
ungemǣt=ungemet
ungemǣte I. *immense, extraordinary*, Chr 1115. ['*unimete*'] II. adv. *immensely*.
ungemǣtlic *excessive*, AO 28²⁷.
ungemēde *unbearable, unpleasant*, Mod 25.
ungemēdnes f. *adversity*, DR 63¹³.
ungemeltnes f. *indigestion*, Lcd 68b.
ungemenged *unmixed, pure*, Bo 100⁸¹.
ungemet n. *excess, superfluity : immensity : want of moderation*, Bo,Lcd. ['*unimete*']
ungemēt *not met with, unknown*, OEG 2488.
ungemete I. adj. *huge*, GD 12⁹. II. adv. *excessively, immeasurably, immoderately, extremely*, B,Ps. ['*unimete*']
ungemetegod (Æ)=ungemetgod
ungemetelice=ungemetlice
ungemetes=ungemete II.
ungemetfæst *not moderate, intemperate, excessive : very firm*, Met 7³³.
ungemetfæstnes f. *excess, intemperance*, Bo 109⁹.
ungemetgod *out of due proportion, excessive*, CP : *unbridled, intemperate*.
ungemetgung f. *excess*, Æ,CP.
ungemetigende *intemperate, unrestrained*, VH 22.
ungemetlic *immeasurable, immense*, AO : *excessive, immoderate, violent*. adv. -līce, AO,CP.
ungemetnes f. *extravagance*, OET 180³.
ungemetum adv.=ungemete
ungemīdlod *unrestrained, unbridled*, Æ, Chrd.
ungemiht *without strength, weak*, Bo 108⁵n.
ungemihtig=unmihtig
ungemindig=ungemyndig
ungemōd *discordant, dissentient, quarrelsome*, CP.
ungemōdignes f. *contentiousness*, W 8¹⁵n.
ungemōdnes f. *strife*, CP 344⁹.
ungemolsnod *undecayed*, MH 78¹.

ungemunecod *not made a monk,* LL (142⁴).
ungemylt *undigested,* LCD 2a (Harl).
ungemynd f. *madness,* LCD.
ungemyndig (w. g.) *unmindful, forgetful, heedless (of),* Æ.
ungenæmnendlic *unknown?* GD 341¹³.
ungenīdd (ē, īe) *uncompelled,* AO,CP.
ungeocian *to 'unyoke,'* ÆGr 277³.
ungeonbyrded=ungebyrded
ungeorne *negligently* : *unwillingly,* AO.
ungeornful *indifferent, remiss, slothful,* CP.
ungerād I. (w. g.) *ignorant, foolish, unskilled, unfit,* Æ,CP : (w. d.) *at variance, wrong, discordant, dissentient,* Æ,AO : *ill-conditioned, rude,* Æ. II. n. *discord,* CP : *folly,* Æ.
ungerādnes (ǣ) *disagreement,* LCD.
ungerǣd=ungerād
ungerǣde *foolish,* MFH 176.
ungerǣdlic *unteachable, ignorant, rough,* GD 110¹¹. adv. -līce *sharply, roughly, violently.*
ungerǣdnes f. *disagreement, sedition,* AO.
ungerǣdod *without harness,* KC.
ungerec n. *tumult,* BH,MtR 27²⁴.
ungereccan *to clear oneself of an accusation,* LL 168,1².
ungereclic *unruly, unrestrained,* BL 19⁶. adv. -līce *confusedly, recklessly.*
ungerēdelīce=ungerǣdlīce
ungerēnod *not ornamented,* TC 515'. [regn-]
ungereord *uninstructed, barbarous,* WW 193³.
ungereord(ed)lic *insatiable,* CVPs 100⁵.
ungereordod *unfed, empty,* ÆL 19⁹¹.
ungerepod=ungehrepod
ungerian=ungierwan ; **ungeriht**=unriht
ungeriht *uncorrected, unreformed,* CHRD.
ungerīm I. n. *countless number, host,* Æ. II. *countless, untold,* Æ.
unge-rīmlic, -rīmed(lic) *countless, untold.*
ungerinen=ungehrinen
ungerinselīce=ungerisenlīce
ungerīped *immature, too early,* Æ.
ungerisedlīce=ungerisenlīce
ungerīsende *indecent,* OEG 3673.
ungerisene I. *unseemly, improper* : *incongruous, inconvenient.* II.=ungerisnu
ungerisenlic *unbecoming, improper,* CP. adv. -līce, CP.
ungerīsnes (uni-) f. *impropriety,* HGL 507.
ungerisnu n. (often pl.) *inconvenience* : *impropriety, indignity, disgrace,* AO.
ungerōtsian=unrōtsian
ungerwan=ungierwan
ungerȳde I. *rough, boisterous,* W 137⁷. II. n. *rough place,* Lk 3⁵.
ungerȳdelic *rough, violent,* GD 265²; LV 47. adv. -līce *suddenly, impetuously,* Æ.

ungerȳdnes f. *noise, tumult,* Sc 82².
ungesadelod=unsadelod
ungesǣlig *unhappy, unfortunate,* Æ,AO, CP. adv. -līce *unhappily* : *wickedly.*
ungesǣlignes f. *unhappiness, misfortune,* BH,BL.
ungesǣllīce=ungesǣliglīce
ungesǣlð f. *trouble, misfortune, unhappiness, sorrow,* CP.
ungesawen=ungesewen
ungescaðignes=ungesceððignes
ungescēad I. n. *want of intelligence, senselessness.* II. adj. *unreasonable,* LCD : *excessive,* VH. III. adv. *exceedingly,* DA 243.
ungescēadlic *unreasonable, indiscreet.* adv. -līce *unreasonably, absurdly.*
ungescēadwīs(lic) *unintelligent, irrational, imprudent, foolish,* Æ,CP. adv. -līce.
ungescēadwīsnes f. *want of intelligence, indiscretion, folly, ignorance,* CP.
ungesce(a)pen *uncreated, unformed,* Æ.
ungescended *unhurt,* DR 146¹¹.
ungesceððed *unhurt,* BH 218²⁵.
ungesceððignes (a, æ) f. *innocence,* ÆH.
ungescrēpe (ǣ) I. n. *an inconvenience,* BH 382⁹. II. *inconvenient, useless,* BH,WW.
ungescrēpnes (ǣ) f. *discomfort,* BH 322³⁰.
ungescrōp n. *an inconvenience* BHc 382⁹.
ungesegenlic=ungesewenlic
ungeseht adj. *at variance,* FM 358²⁸.
ungesēl-=ungesǣl-; **ungesēne**=ungesȳne
ungesēnod *not signed with the cross,* SOL 148¹⁰. [segn]
ungeseonde *blind,* LCD 1·368'.
ungeseowenlic=ungesewenlic
unge-sewen, -sewen(d)lic *unseen, invisible,* Æ,CP. adv. -līce.
ungesibb *not related,* RD,SOL : *unfriendly, hostile,* BL,BH.
ungesibsum *quarrelsome, contentious,* CP.
ungesibsumnes f. *quarrelsomeness, discord,* CP 351¹.
ungesilt=unsealt
ungesoden *unsodden, unboiled,* LCD.
ungesom *at variance,* ÆH 1·478'.
ungespēdig=unspēdig
ungestæððe-=ungestæððig-
ungestæððig *unsteady, inconstant, unstable, fickle,* CP. adv. -līce.
ungestæððignes f. *inconstancy, frivolity,* CP.
ungestrēon n. *ill-gotten treasure,* W 183⁹.
ungestroden *not subject to confiscation,* LL 12,4¹.
ungesund *unsound, faulty,* RWH 105².
ungesundlīce *excessively, exceedingly,* GD 15².
ungeswēge *inharmonious, dissonant, discordant, out of tune, harsh,* GL.
ungeswenced *unceasing,* NC 329.

ungeswencedlic *unwearying*, BH436[16].
ungeswīcende *unceasing*, A2·357.
ungeswīcendlīce *incessantly*, Sc.
ungeswuncen *not laboured over, not well done*, WW430[11].
ungesylt=unsealt
ungesȳne (ē) *unseen, invisible*, WW17[46].
ungesȳnelic *invisible*, BL,W.
ungetǣse I. n. *trouble, hardship, severity*, CP. II. adj. *troublesome, inconvenient.*
ungetǣslīce adv. *inconveniently*, AS30[10].
ungetǣsnes f. *unsuitableness, inconvenience*, WW419[38].
ungetel *innumerable* (BT).
ungetemed=unātemed
ungetemprung f. *inclemency*, CM461.
ungetēori(g)endlic *inexhaustible*. adv. -līce *incessantly*, LL.
ungetēorod *unfailing*, Æ: *unwearied*, CHRD.
ungetēse=ungetǣse II.
unge-tīmu f? -tīme n? *evil time, adversity, mishap*, AO,GD.
ungetinge (Æ), ungetingful (GPH) *not eloquent.* [tunge]
ungetogen *uneducated*, Æ. ['*untowen*']
ungetrēowe (ī, īe, ū, ȳ) *untrue, faithless*, Æ.
ungetrēownes f. *unbelief*, CP447[6] : *faithlessness*, GD160[5].
ungetrēowsian=untrēowsian
ungetrēowð f. *unfaithfulness, treachery*, W 160[6].
ungetrum *weak, infirm*, Bo132[32].
unge-trūw-, -trȳw-=un(ge)trēow-
ungetwǣre (WW248[17])=ungeðwǣre
ungetwēogendlīce (GD231[21]) = untwēogendlīce.
unge-tȳd, -tȳdd *ignorant, untaught, unskilful*, CP.
ungetȳred=ungetēorod
ungeðæslic *unfit, improper, unseemly*, WW 191[23].
ungeðanc mn. *evil thought*, W.
ungeðancful *unthankful, ungrateful*, W241[4].
ungeðeaht n. *evil counsel*, RB118[10].
ungeðeahtendlīce *hastily*, BH124[13].
ungeðēawe adv. *not customary*, GUTH72[17].
ungeðeawfæst *ill-regulated*, RBL14[16].
ungeðēod *disunited, separate*, GEN1698.
ungeðinged *unexpected*, CP317[13],VH.
ungeðungen *base*, NAR42[12].
ungeðwǣre I. *disagreeing, quarrelsome, troublesome, stubborn, vexatious, undutiful, irreverent*, Æ,CP. II. n. *disturbance*, MtR 26[5].
ungeðwǣrian *to be discordant, disagree, be at variance with*, Æ.
ungeðwǣrlic *inharmonious, discordant*, RB 19[2] : *hostile*, GD349. adv. -līce *peevishly.*

ungeðwǣrnes f. *disturbance, quarrel, discord*, AO : *violence*, BH44[27].
ungeðwēre=ungeðwǣre
ungeðyld fn. *impatience*, CP. [ðolian; *Ger.* ungeduld]
ungeðyldelīce adv. *impatiently*, Bo.
ungeðyldig *impatient*, Æ,CP.
ungeðylō=ungeðyld
ungeðyre '*discensor*'? Cp283D.
ungewæder=ungewider
ungewæm-=ungewem-
ungewǣpnod *without weapons, unarmed*, Æ.
ungewealden *disordered (of the stomach)*, LCD : *involuntary, unwilling*, VH.
un-gewealdes, -gewaldes adv. *involuntarily, by chance*, CP.
ungeweaxen *immature*, WW352[27].
ungeweder=ungewider
un-gewemmed (Æ), -gewemmedlic *unspotted, unblemished, undefiled, uninjured.* adv. -līce *uncorruptly*, BH276[20].
ungewem(med)nes f. *freedom (from stain).*
ungewende(n)dlic *immovable*, GD,LCD.
ungewendnes f. *unchangeableness* (Swt).
ungewēned *unexpected*, LCD.
ungewēnedlic *unhoped for*, GD347[14].
ungewēnendlic *incalculable*, GD284[20].
un-gewērged, -gewērigod *unwearied, untiring.*
un-gewidere n., gs. -gewidres *bad weather, storm.*
ungewiderung f. *bad weather*, CHR1086.
ungewild (y) *unsubdued*, OEG.
ungewilde (y) *not subject to, independent of*, AO : *untamed, unbridled.* [geweald]
ungewildelic (y) *unyielding*, ÆH2·92[2].
ungewill *displeasing*, CHR.
ungewilles *undesignedly*, LL31,21[13].
ungewintred *immature, young*, LL18,26.
ungewirhtum=ungewyrhtum
ungewis=ungewiss
ungewislic *unaccustomed*, Bo15[22]n.
ungewīsnes f. *uncertainty, ignorance*, BH.
ungewiss I. n. *uncertainty, ignorance*, Æ, AO : *unconsciousness : ignominy, shame*, SPs82[15]. II. adj. *uncertain*, Æ,CP : *unwise, ignorant, inexperienced : doubtful*, Æ : *causing shame, shameful*, KGL75[10].
ungewisses *unconsciously, involuntarily*, CP.
ungewītendlic *permanent, imperishable*, ÆL 34[298]. adv. -līce *permanently, perpetually*, CP441[21].
ungewitfæstnes f. *madness*, LCD82b.
ungewitful *unwise, senseless, mad*, CP.
ungewitfulnes f. *madness*, CP185[1].
ungewitlic *stupid, foolish*, LCD65a.
ungewitnes f. *folly*, GD95[23] (v. BTs).

ungewītnigendlīce *freely, with impunity*, ÆGR233⁶n.
ungewītnod *unpunished*, Æ,CP.
ungewitt n. *folly, madness*, Æ.
ungewittig *irrational, foolish, mad*, Æ.
ungewittiglīce (-witte-) *unwisely, foolishly, madly*, GD2; 104.
ungewittignes f. *folly, madness*, GD163; 247.
ungewlitig *not bright, dull*, AS31¹⁹.
±ungewlitigian *to disfigure*, AS.
ungeworht *unformed, unfinished*, Æ.
ungewriten *unwritten*, WW.
ungewuna I. m. *evil habit, vice*, CP169⁹. II. *unusual*, Æ : *uninhabited*, Æ.
ungewunelic *unusual, strange*, Æ. [*Ger.* ungewöhnlich] adv. -līce, Æ.
ungewuniendlic *uninhabitable*, LCD.
ungewyder=ungewider
ungewyld-=ungewild-
ungewylles=unwilles
ungewynelic=ungewunelic
ungewyrded *uninjured*, PH181.
ungewyrhtum (be) adv. phr. *without a cause*, CVPs.
ungier-wan, -ian (e, i, y) *to unclothe, divest of*.
ungifre *pernicious*, GEN2470.
ungifu f. *evil gift*, W52,58.
unginne *not great or broad*, GNE206.
ungl=ungel; unglad=unglæd
unglæd (a) *cheerless, dull*, Bo14¹⁴. ['*unglad*']
unglædlic *implacable*, GPH392 : *cheerless*, VH22.
unglædnes f. '*imperitia*,' WW423²⁹. [mistake for ungléawnes?]
ungléaw=ungléaw
ungléaw *ignorant, foolish, unwise*, Æ. adv. -līce, CP.
ungléawnes f. *want of discernment, folly, ignorance*, PA70.
ungléawscipe m. *folly*, Sc83¹⁶.
unglenged=ungeglenged
ungnȳðe (ē) *not niggardly, not sparing, liberal*. adv. -līce, GD.
ungōd I. adj. *not good*, Lcd. ['*ungood*'] II. n. *evil*.
ungor=hungor
ungrædiglīce *abundantly*, GD175¹.
ungrāpigende *not grasping*, ÆH1·366'.
ungrēne *not green, bare of grass*, GEN 117.
ungrīpendlic *irreprehensible*, EPs18⁸.
ungrund *vast*, Ex508.
ungrynde *bottomless*, RIM49.
ungyfeðe *unaccorded*, B2921.
un-gyld, -gylde n. *excessive tax*, CHR. [gieldan]

ungylda m. *one who is not a member of a guild*, TC606¹⁶.
ungylde adv. *not entitled to compensation*, LL.
ungyltig *innocent*, AO184⁹.
un-gȳmen, -gȳming f. *carelessness*, BH.
ungȳmende (ē) *careless*, BH434⁵.
ungyrdan=ongyrdan
ungyrian=ungierwan
ungystlīðe (=ie) *inhospitable*, NC329.
unhādian (on-) *to unfrock, divest of holy orders*, LL.
unhādod=ungehādod
unhādung f. '*exordinatio*,' RBL110⁸.
unhǣl=unhāl, unhǣlu
+unhǣlan *to weaken, debilitate*, Sc51¹⁰.
unhǣlð f. *ill-health, weakness, infirmity*.
unhǣlu f. *sickness, unsoundness*, AO,Chrd, LL,MtL : *mischief, evil*, B,BF. ['*unheal*']
unhǣmed *unmarried*, WW530¹⁹.
unhǣr=unhār
unhāl *sick, ill, weak*, Æ,Bo; CP. ['*unwhole*']
unhālgod *unhallowed, unconsecrated*, Æ.
unhālian *to pine away*, BPs118¹³⁹.
unhālig (ǣ) '*unholy*,' *profane*, ELPs42¹.
un-hālwende (RHy), -hālwendlic (Æ) *incurable, deadly* : *unprofitable*.
unhandworht *not made with hands*, Mk14⁵⁸.
unhār (=an-) *hoary, grizzled*, B357.
unhéah (ē) *not high, low*, Æ.
unhéanlīce *valiantly*, CHR755 : *not inadequately*, GD43²⁵.
unhearmgeorn *inoffensive*, ÆH2·44²⁰.
unhéarsumnes=unhīersumnes
un-hēg, -hēh=unhéah
unhelde (CHR1095)=unhyldo
unhelian *to uncover, reveal*, Lk12². ['*unhele*']
un-héor-, -hér-=unhīer-
unhered *unpraised, not celebrated*, Bo68²⁴.
unherigendlic *not praiseworthy*, ÆH2·406¹⁷.
unhetol *peaceable*, NC329.
unhiere (ē, ēo, ȳ) I. *horrible, monstrous, fierce, wild, tempestuous*. II. adv. *horribly*.
unhīerlic *wild, fierce, savage, gloomy*. adv. -līce (GD161¹⁰).
unhīersum (ȳ) *disobedient*, GUTH12¹⁴. adv. -līce.
unhīersumnes (ȳ) f. *disobedience*, CP.
unhierwan (y²) *to calumniate*, WC70¹⁵.
unhīredwist f. *unfamiliarity*, Sc203¹³.
unhīwe *formless*, GPH399²⁵⁹.
unhīwed *not feigned*, OEG.
unhléowe *unfriendly, chill*, Ex494.
unhlīdan (Æ)=onhlīdan
unhlīs(e) *infamous, disreputable*, KGL68⁴².
unhlīsa m. *ill-fame, discredit, dishonour*, Æ.
unhlīsbǣre *disreputable*, WW354¹⁷.

unhlíséadig *infamous*, WW420[15].
unhlísful *infamous*, GL.
unhlísig *infamous*, KGL56[5].
unhlítme *very unhappily*, B1129 (or ?= unflitme).
unhlúd *not loud*, GD85[5].
unhlýs-=unhlís-
unhnéawt *generous, liberal*.
unhoga *foolish*, MkL7[18].
unhold *disloyal, unfriendly, hostile*, Æ,BH. ['*unhold*']
unholda m. *monster, devil*, CR762.
unhrædspræce *slow of speech*, Ex6[30].
unhréoflig *not leprous*, ÆH1·124'.
unhrór *without motion*, Bo146[26].
unhúfed *bareheaded*, OEG4466.
unhwearfiende *unchangeable, fixed*, Bo20[29].
unhwílent *eternal*.
unhýdig *ignorant, foolish*, AN,Bo.
unhýhst=unhéhst superl. of unhéah.
unhyldo (e) f. *displeasure, disfavour, unfriendliness*, CP. [*Ger.* unhuld]
unhyr-=onhyr-
unhýr-=unhíer-
unhýðigt *unhappy*, AN, GU.
uni-=unge-
uníeð adv. (comp.) *with greater difficulty, more hardly*, CP. [éað]
uníeð-=unéáð-
unin-seglian, -sæglian (Æ) *to unseal*.
uníðe=uníeðe; uniucian=ungeocian
unláb=unláf
unlácnigendlíc *incurable*, LCD1·262[1].
unlácnod *unhealed*, CP61[4].
unlǽce m. *bad physician*, LCD60b.
un-lǽd, -lǽde *poor, miserable, wretched, unhappy, unfortunate : accursed, wicked : straying?* (*of cattle*).
unlǽdlíc *miserable*, NC329. adv. -líce.
unlǽgne=unlíegne
unlǽne *permanent*, W264[18].
unlǽred *unlearned, untaught, ignorant*, CP.
unlǽrednes=ungelǽredneȝ
unlæt *unwearied, indefatigable*, WW.
unlǽttu f. *sin*, GD289. [unlǽd]
unláf f. *posthumous child*, WW.
unlagu f. *abuse of law, bad law, oppression, injustice*, LL. æt unlagum *unlawfully*. ['*unlaw*']
unland m. *desert, waste : counterfeit, supposed land*, WH13.
unlandágende m. *not owning land*, LL112.
unlár f. *bad teaching*, LL,W.
unlaðod (BYH26[23])=ungelaðod
unléafful=ungeléafful
unleahtorwyrðe *not culpable*, PPs18[7].
unléanod *unpaid*, EC148[4].
unléas *not false, true : truthful*. adv. -líce.
unléoð=unlýcð pres. 3 sg. of unlúcan.

unléfedlíc=unlýfendlíc; unlégne=unlíegne
unléoft *not dear, hated*.
unleoðuwác (e[3]) *inflexible, rigid, stubborn*.
unleoðuwácnes f. *inflexibility*, WW.
unlésan=unlíesan; unlib-=unlyb-
unlíc=ungelic
unlíchamlíc *incorporeal*, Æ,GD.
unlícð (Æ)=unlýcð pres. 3 sg. of unlúcan.
unlícwyrðe *displeasing*, ÆL23b[374].
unlíefed=unálýfed
unlíegne (ǽ, é) *not to be questioned*, LL.
unlíesan (é, ý) *to unloose*, Æ : *set free, put on a free footing*.
unlíf n. *death*, MFH176.
unlífes *dead*, ÆL18[203].
unlifi(g)ende (y) *lifeless, dead*. [libban]
unliss? (hl-) *disfavour*, OET464 (v. ANS 142·254).
unlítel=unlýtel
unlíðe *ungentle, harsh, severe*, Æ.
unlíðowác=unleoðuwác
unlofod *unpraised*, PR62.
unlond=unland
unlúcan[2] *to unlock, open*, CHRD; Æ. ['*unlouk*']
unlust m. *evil desire, lust, sensuality*, Æ : *disinclination, weariness, laziness*, Æ,Sol : *nausea*, LCD. [*Ger.* unlust]
+unlustian *to loathe*, BL59[8].
unlyb-ba m., -be f. *poisonous drug, poison*, Æ : *witchcraft*, Æ. [lybb]
unlybbende (MH164[21])=unlifigende
unlybwyrhta m. *worker with spells or poisons, wizard*, Æ.
unlýfednes=unálíefednes
unlýfendlíc *illicit, unlawful*, ZDA31[8].
unlýfigende=unlifigende
unlyft f. *bad air*, LCD6a.
unlygen *unlying, truthful*, LL156,12.
unlýsan (Æ)=unlíesan
unlýt n. *a great deal*, PPs61[9].
unlýtel *not small, much, great, very large*.
unmǽdlíce=unmǽðlíce
unmǽg? m. *evil kinsman? alien?* WALD2[23].
unmǽge *not akin*, PPs68[8].
unmægel=unmeagol
unmægnes f. *weariness*, WW224[14].
unmǽgðlíce=unmǽðlíce
unmǽht- (N)=unmiht-
unmǽle *unspotted, immaculate, pure, virgin*.
unmǽne *not criminal, honest, innocent, truthful : free (from)*.
un-mǽre, -mǽrlíc *inglorious*, Bo.
unmǽte *excessive, immense, great, vast, BH*; Æ : *countless, innumerable*. ['*unmeet*']
unmǽtlíc (é) *enormous*, AA6[3],22[4].
unmǽtnes f. *vastness, excessive greatness*, BH.
unmǽð f. *transgression, sin*, HL13·234.

unmǣðful *immoderate, excessive,* NC329.
unmǣðlic *excessive,* Æ. adv. -līce *excessively,* Æ : *unmercifully, cruelly,* Æ.
un-maga m., -magu f. *needy person, dependant, orphan,* LL.
unmanig *not many, few,* GUTH,BH.
unmann m. *monster, wicked man,* Æ : *hero,* GUTH 12²⁷.
un-meagol, -meahl *insipid,* WW.
unmeaht=unmiht
unmedome (e³, u³) *incompetent, unfit, unworthy,* Æ,CP.
unmedomlīce adv. *negligently, carelessly,* LL.
unmeht=unmiht
unmeltung f. *indigestion,* LCD 95a.
unmendlinga=unmyndlinga
unmēne=unmǣne
unmenged *unmixed,* WW.
unmenn nap. of unmann.
unmennisclic *inhuman,* Bo 70²⁶.
unmēt-=unmǣt-
unmicel (y²) *little, small,* GD.
unmīdlod *unrestrained, unbridled,* CP.
unmidome=unmedome
unmiht (ie) **I.** f. *weakness,* CP. ['*unmiht*'] **II.** (æ) *impossible,* MtL.
+**unmihtan** *to deprive of strength,* ÆL 25⁷⁷¹.
un-mihtelic, -mihtlic *impossible,* G.
unmihtig (æ, e) *weak, powerless,* Æ,Bo : *impossible,* NG. ['*unmighty*']
unmihtiglic (æ) *weak,* LCD : *impossible,* LkLR.
unmihtignes f. *weakness,* LCD.
unmilde *not meek, harsh,* BH 100²⁹. ['*unmild*']
unmildheort *merciless,* Æ.
unmilts f. *severity, anger,* Ct.
unmiltsigendlic *unpardonable,* ÆT 78⁶³. [milts]
unmiltsung f. *hardness of heart,* AO 64¹⁶.
unmirigð=unmyrhð
unmōd n. *depression,* LCD 65a.
unmōdig *humble,* CP : *timid.*
unmolsniendlic *uncorrupted,* OEG 60.
un-monig, -moneg=unmanig
unmurn *untroubled,* PPs 75⁴.
unmurnlīce† adv. *unpityingly, without sorrowing.*
unmycel=unmicel
unmyhtig=unmihtig; **unmylts-**=unmilts-
unmyndgian=unmynegian
unmynd-linga, -lenga, -lunga adv. *unawares, unexpectedly,* Æ,AO : *undesignedly.*
unmynegian *to overlook, not to demand,* LL 382,43.
unmyrge *unpleasant? sad?* WW 211¹⁶.
unmyrhð f. *sadness,* W 148⁹,VH.
unna m.=unne

±**unnan** pres. 1 sing. an(n), on(n), pl. unnon; pret. sg. ūðe, pp. ±unnen swv. w. d. pers. and g. *thing to grant, allow, bestow, give,* B,Bo,CP,Chr,G,Ps; AO,Æ : *be glad to see, wish, desire,* AO,Ps. *unnendre handa voluntarily.* [' (*i*)-*unne*']
unne f. *favour, approval, permission, consent* : *grant* : *liberality.*
unnēah adj. adv. *not near, far, away from.*
un-nēde, -nēdig=unnīedig
unnēdelīce (GD 346⁹; JAW 55,56)=ungnȳðelīce
unnēg, unnēh=unnēah
unnend m. *one who grants,* DR 5⁵.
unnet=unnyt
unnīed-ig, -enga adv. *without compulsion or restraint, willingly,* CP. [nēad]
unnit=unnyt II.
unnīðing m. *honest man (not an outlaw),* CHR 1087; v. ANS 117·22.
un-nyt, -nytt **I.** adj. *useless, unprofitable,* Æ,CP. **II.** m. *unprofitableness, emptiness, vanity, folly* : *useless thing.*
unnytenes=unnytnes
unnytlic *useless, unprofitable, foolish,* CP. adv. -līce.
unnytlicnes f. *uselessness,* LCD.
unnytnes f. *unprofitableness, frivolity, emptiness,* LL,W.
unnytwyrðe *unprofitable, useless,* Æ,CP. adv. -wurðlīce, Æ.
unnȳðnes? f. *peace, freedom from hate,* VH 23.
unofercumen *unsubdued,* GL.
unoferfēre (oe⁴) *impassable,* GL.
unoferhrēfed *not roofed in,* BL 125²¹.
unoferswīð-ed, -edlic, -ende, -endlic *unconquerable, invincible.*
unoferwin-nene (WW), -nendlic (AO) *invincible.*
unoferwrigen *not covered,* ÆL 23b²⁰⁹.
unoferwunnen *unconquered,* AO 156²⁸.
unoferwunnendlic=unoferwinnendlic
unoflinnedlīce *unceasingly,* NC329.
unofslegen *not killed,* ÆH 2·544'.
unondcȳðignes f. *ignorance,* JVPs 24⁷.
unondgetful=unandgittol
unongunnen *without a beginning,* ByH 80²³.
unonlȳsendlic *unpardonable,* GD 348⁴.
unonstyred *unmoved,* GD 270⁹n.
unonstyrigendlic *motionless,* GD 225⁴.
unonwend-endlic, -edlic *unchangeable, constant, immovable.* adv. -līce.
unorne *old, worn out, decrepit,* Ma 256. ['*unorn*']
unornlic *old, worn,* Jos 9⁵.
unplēolic *not dangerous, safe,* Æ. adv. -līce.
unrǣd m. *folly, foolish plan* : *crime, mischief, injury, plot, treachery,* Æ,AO.

unrǣden f. *ill-considered act*, GEN 982.
unrǣdfæst *unreliable, incompetent*, ÆP 212¹⁵.
unrǣdfæstlīce *unwisely, rashly*, ÆL 18⁴⁵⁶.
unrǣdlic *thoughtless*, BL 99²¹. adv. -līce, Æ.
unrǣdsīð m. *foolish enterprise*, RD 12⁴.
unræfniendlic *intolerable*, SPs 123⁴ (on-).
unreht=unriht
unrehthǣmdere=unrihthǣmere
unreordlic v. ungereordlic
±unrētan *to make sad*, AO. [rōt]
unrētu f. *sadness, disquiet, anxiety*, AA 46⁹.
unrēðe *not cruel, gentle*, ÆH 2·44'.
unrīce *poor*, LL,RB.
unriht (e, y) I. n. *wrong, sin, vice, wickedness, evil*, Æ,B,Bo,Chr : *injustice, oppression*, Bo,LL; Æ : *wrong act*, Bo. II. adj. *wrong, unrighteous, wicked, false* : *unlawful*, Bo,Ps. ['*unright*']
unrihtcræfing f. *unjust claim*, TC.
unrihtcyst f. *vice*, LL (262').
unrihtdǣd f. *evil doing*, BH,W.
unrihtdǣde *iniquitous*, LPs 9²⁴.
unrihtdēma m. *unjust judge*, W.
unrihtdōm m. *iniquity*, DA 183.
unrihtdōnd m. *evildoer*, BL 63¹⁵.
unrihte *unjustly, wrongly*, B,Ps. ['*unright*']
unrihtfēoung f. *unrighteous hate*, MET 27¹.
unrihtful *unrighteous, wicked*, NC 329.
unrihtgestrēon n. *unrighteous gain*, BL 63⁸.
unrihtgestrod n. *ill-gotten booty*, NC 330.
unrihtgewill n. *evil desire*, Bo 9²³.
unrihtgewilnung (y)=unrihtwillnung
unrihtgilp m. *vainglory*, LL (262').
unrihtgītsung f. *wrongful greed*, BL,Bo.
unrihthǣman *to fornicate, commit adultery*.
unrihthǣmdere (VPs 49¹⁸)=unrihthǣmere
unrihthǣmed I. n. *fornication, adultery*. II. adj. *adulterous*.
unrihthǣmedfremmere m. *adulterer*, NC 330.
unrihthǣmend m. *adulterer*, BL 63.
unrihthǣmere m. *fornicator, adulterer*, Æ.
unrihthǣmeð=unrihthǣmed I.
unrihthēmere (KGL)=unrihthǣmere
unrihtlic (e, y) *unrighteous, wrongful, wicked*, Æ. adv. -līce, MH,RB. ['*unrightly*']
unrihtlust m. *unlawful desire*, Bo 19²⁰,VH.
unrihtlyblāc nm. *unlawful magic*, W 253¹¹.
unrihtnes (e²) f. *wrong, wickedness*, BL.
unrihttīd f. *improper occasion*, MFH 177.
unrihtweorc n. *secular work done on Sunday*, LL (130²⁵).
unrihtwīf n. *unlawful consort, mistress*, TC 373'.
unrihtwīfung f. *unlawful wedlock*, BH 116³.
unrihtwillend (y²) m. *evil-disposed person*, CP 89²².

unrihtwillnung f. *unlawful desire, lust, ambition*, CP.
unrihtwīs '*unrighteous,' wrong, unjust*, Bl, Bo,G,VPs; Æ,CP. adv. -līce, CP. ['*unrighteously*']
unrihtwīsnes (e, y) f. *injustice, 'unrighteousness,' iniquity*, Bf,VPs; Æ,CP.
unrihtwīsu f. *unrighteousness*, BL,Ps.
unrihtwrīgels n. *covering of error*, BL 105³⁰.
unrihtwyrcend m. *evildoer*, BL.
unrihtwyrhta (y) m. *evildoer*, CP.
unrīm I. n. *countless number, huge host, large quantity, mass.* II.=unrīme
unrīme *countless, innumerable*, BH.
unrīmfolc n. *countless number (of people)*, CP 51¹².
unrīmgōd? n. *incalculable good*, BH 94¹⁹.
unrīpe *immature, 'unripe,'* WW.
unrōt *sad, dejected*, Æ,CP : *displeased, angry*.
unrōtian *to become sad* : (±) *make sad.*
unrōtlic *sad, gloomy*, MtL. adv. -līce, MtR 16³.
unrōtmōd *sad-hearted*, BL 113¹².
unrōtnes f. *sadness, contrition, disquietude*, Æ,CP.
±unrōtsian *to be or become sad, be grieved*, Æ : *make sad.*
unrūh *smooth, without seams*, JnLR 19²³.
unryht (AO,CP)=unriht
unrȳne m. *diarrhœa*, LCD 1·172¹².
unsac *not accused, innocent*, LCD 3·288⁶.
unsadelod *not saddled*, LL.
unsǣd *unsated, insatiable*, PPs 100⁵.
unsǣd I. n. *evil seed*, W 40²³. II. *not said*, ÆH. ['*unsaid*']
unsǣht=unseht
unsǣl m. *unhappiness*, W 236²⁶. ['*unsele*']
unsǣlan *to untie, unfasten*, WW.
unsǣle *wicked*, WW 421²³. ['*unsele*']
unsǣlig *unfortunate, unhappy, wretched*, Jul,W : *mischievous, pernicious*, Gen 637 : *wicked*, An. ['*unseely*']
unsǣlð f. *unhappiness, misfortune, adversity, misery*, Bo,Ps; CP. ['*unselth*']
unsǣpig *sapless*, ÆH 1·102⁴.
unsalt=unsealt
unsamwrǣde *contrary, incongruous*, Bo 106⁶.
unsār *painless*, AO,CP.
unsāwen *unsown*, LL 450,10.
unscǣðed=ungesceððed
unscǣðful (e, ea) *innocent*. adv. -līce, CP.
unscǣðfulnes (ea, e) f. *innocence*, CP.
unscǣðð-ednes, -ignes (e) f. *harmlessness, innocence*, Æ.
unscǣðð-ende (e²), -ig *innocent, harmless*, Æ,BH.

unscamfæst *impudent, shameless,* GL.
unscamfulnes (eo²) f. *shamelessness, immodesty,* MkL7²⁰.
unscamig *unashamed,* Jul552.
unscamlic *shameless, immodest,* Æ. adv. -līce.
unscað-=unscæð(ð)-
un-scēad(e)līce *unreasonably,* RB54¹³.
unscēadwīslic *unreasonable,* ÆH2·210′.
unsceaft f. *monster?* Rᴅ88³².
unsceam-=unscam-
unsceapen *uncreated, unformed,* Bʏʜ72²⁰, RHy54¹³.
unscearp *not sharp (of wine),* Lᴄᴅ.
unscearpnes f. *dulness,* BH402²⁹.
unscearpsȳne *not sharp-sighted,* Lᴄᴅ11b.
unsceað-=unscæð-
unscelleht (=ie) *not having a shell,* Lᴄᴅ33b.
unscellīce *without discrimination, recklessly?* RWH141³ (v. scelle).
unscende (y)† *blameless, glorious.*
un-scende, scendende *uninjured, uncorrupted.*
unscennan *to unharness,* WW91¹³.
unscēod=unscōd pp. of unscōgan.
unscēogan=unscōgan
unsceom- (NG)=unscam-
unscēotan (WW190³⁰)=onscēotan
unsceð-=unscæð-; unscildig=unscyldig
unscirped *unclothed,* MtL22¹¹.
unscōgan (ēo) *to unshoe.* pp. unscōd '*unshod,*' Æ,CP.
unscom-=unscam-
unscoren *unshorn,* CM,WW.
unscortende *not failing,* LkLR12³³.
unscrȳdan (ē², ī²) *to put off (clothes), undress, uncover, strip, deprive of,* Æ. unscrȳdd pp. *naked.* [scrūd]
unscyld f. *innocency,* SPs40¹³.
unscyldgung f. *innocence,* ERPs17²⁵.
unscyldig (ī) *guiltless, innocent,* Æ,CP : *not responsible.*
unscyldiglīc *excusable,* Bʟ189³². adv. -līce *innocently,* Bᴋ12.
unscyldignes f. *innocence,* Ps.
unscynde=unscende
unscȳrdan=unscrȳdan
unscyttan *to undo, unbolt,* ÆL31⁸⁶³.
unscyðende=unscæððende
unseald *ungiven,* HL10⁴⁹⁵.
unsealt (a, y) *unsalted, insipid,* G,WW.
unsēfernes=unsȳfernes
unsefful *senseless,* RHy6³¹. [sefa]
unsegenlic (Bʏʜ6, 8)=unsewenlic
unseglian *to unseal,* RWH78³³.
unseht I. mfn. *discord, disagreement, quarrel.*
II. adj. *not agreed, hostile, Chr.* ['*unsaught*']
unsehtnes f. *discord, quarrel,* NC330. ['*unsaughtness*']

un-seldan, -seldon (Æ) *not seldom, repeatedly, frequently,* LL. ['*unselde*']
unsēofene *not sighing,* MFH177.
unsewenlic *invisible,* Bo138².
unsibb f. *dissension, contention, war, strife,* AO.
unsibbian *to disagree,* WW.
unsibsumnes f. *anxiety,* JnL·p6¹.
unsideful *immodest, unchaste,* WW.
unsidefullnes f. *immodesty,* OEH300′.
unsidelīce *immodestly, indecorously,* Cʜʀᴅ 60³⁴.
unsidu m. *bad custom, vice, impurity, unseemliness.* [*Ger.* unsitte]
unsīf-=unsȳf-
unsigefæst *not victorious,* ÆL18⁴⁴.
unsingian=unsyngian
unsīð m. *unfortunate journey or expedition, misfortune, mishap,* Æ.
unslǣpig *sleepless,* WW427¹⁵.
unslāw (ǣ, ēa) *not slow, active, Æ,W.* ['*unslow*'] adv. -līce, CP381¹.
unsleac *not remiss, active, diligent,* WW. adv. -līce, RB20¹⁸.
unslēaw=unslāw
unslid? unslit (Cp33s) n. *fat, grease, tallow.* [*Ger.* unschlitt; or ?=unsylt]
unslitten *untorn,* JnL19²³.
unslȳped *open, loosed,* W83⁹.
unsmǣðe=unsmēðe
unsmeoruwig *notgreasy,* Lᴄᴅ106b (smerig).
unsmēðe *not smooth, uneven, rough, scabby.*
unsmēðnes f. *roughness,* WW.
unsmōð=unsmēðe
unsnotor (e³) *unwise,* ÆGʀ. adv. -līce.
unsnotornes (y², e³) f. *folly : wickedness,* LPs.
unsnott-=unsnot-
unsnyttru† f. *folly, ignorance.*
unsnyttrum† adv. *foolishly.*
unsoden *uncooked,* Lcd. ['*unsodden*']
unsōfte *harshly, bitterly, severely, violently,* Gu,Lcd; Æ : *with difficulty, hardly, scarcely : uncomfortably.* ['*unsoft*']
unsōftlīce *harshly,* ÆH1·434⁷.
unsōm f. *disagreement,* LL.
unsorh *free from care,* Bʟ217²⁹.
unsōð I. adj. *untrue, false.* II. n. *falsehood.*
unsōðfæst *untruthful : unjust, unrighteous.*
unsōðfæstnes f. *injustice, unrighteousness.*
+unsōðian *to falsify, disprove,* LL202,320.
unsōðsag-ol, -ul *untruthful,* Æ.
unspannan⁷ *to unfasten,* WW231³⁵.
unspecende=unsprecende
unspēd f. *want, poverty,* LG,Ps. ['*unspeed*']
unspēdig *poor,* Æ,AO : *not fertile,* Gᴇɴ 962.

unspiwol *that stops vomiting?* LCD.

unspornend=onspornend

unsprecende *not able to speak*, Æ.

unstæfwīs *illiterate*, GPH393.

unstæðōīg *unstable, irregular, weak, frīₜol ous, wanton*, Æ.

unstæðōīgnes f. *instability, inconstancy, wantonness*, Æ.

unstaðolfæst *unstable, unenduring, weak, fickle*, Æ.

unstaðolfæstnes f. *instability, weakness, fickleness*, Æ.

unstenc m. *stench, stink*, DD,W.

+**unstill-an**, -ian *to disturb, agitate*, RB.

unstille *moving, changeable, restless, inquiet, uneasy*, CP.

unstil(l)nes f. *agitation, restlessness, disturbance, disquiet, trouble, disorder, tumult*, Æ,AO.

unstrang *weak, infirm, feeble*, MH,RB; Æ. ['*unstrong*']

unstrenge *weak*, ÆH 2·390'.

unstydful *inconstant, apostate*, DR121[10]. [=unstede-]

unstydfullnes (on-) f. *instability*, DR.

unstyrendlic *immovable, hard to carry*, MtL 23[4].

unstyriende *immovable, stationary*, Bo.

unswǣs *unpleasant, disagreeable, uncongenial*. adv. -swǣse.

unswǣslic *ungentle, cruel*, JUD65. [swǣs]

unswefn n. *bad dream*, LCD 3·288'.

unsweotol *imperceptible, indistinct*, Bo, MET.

unswēte *not sweet : foul*, GD,Lcd. ['*unsweet*']

unswicen *unbetrayed, unharmed, safe*, CHR 1048.

un-swicende, -swiciende *true, faithful*, CHR.

unswicol *trustworthy, true*, GL,W.

unswīð *not strong*, LCD. adv. -swīðe *sluggishly*, OEG56[83].

unsydeful=unsideful

unsȳferlic *impure*, BL43[17].

unsȳfernes f. *impurity, foulness*, BH.

unsȳfre (ī) I. adj. *impure, unclean, filthy*. II. adv. *filthily*, CR1484?

unsylt=unsealt

unsyngian *to exculpate*, LL98,21[1].

unsynnig *guiltless, innocent*, Æ : *undeserved*.

unsynnum adv. *guiltlessly*, B1072.

untǣle *blameless, faultless*, Æ.

untǣled *unblamed*, CP351[20].

untǣllic (ā) *blameless, immaculate, undefiled, praiseworthy*. adv. -līce, Æ,CP.

untǣl-wierðe (y[3]) *blameless*, CP. adv. -wierðlīce.

untǣslic=unðæslic; **untǣl-**=untǣl-

untala (NG)=untela

untamcul *untameable*, GPH397.

unteala=untela

unteald *uncounted*, LCD 3·264[11].

untealt *stable, steady*, CHR897D.

untela adv. *not well, amiss, badly, ill, improperly, wrongly*, CP.

untellendlic *indescribable* (Swt).

untemed *untamed*, CPs,WW. ['*untemed*']

untēmende=untȳmende

untēnan (KGL)=ontȳnan

untēogoðad *untithed*, CP439[29].

unteola=untela

untēorig *untiring, unceasing*, MET28[17].

untīdǣt *untimely eating*, NC330.

untīdful f. *untimely eating or drinking*, W46[14].

untīdgewidere n. *unseasonable weather*, CHR1095.

untīdlic *unseasonable*, AO. adv. -līce.

untīdspǣc f. *untimely speech*, LL(322[9]).

untīdweorc n. *work at an improper time (e.g. on Sunday)*, W.

untīena (AO)=ontēona

untīgan *to 'untie,' loosen, unchain*, G; Æ. [tēag]

untilad *destitute*, Bo16[12].

untīma m. *unseasonableness, wrong time*, Æ,CP : *bad time, misfortune*, W297[7]. ['*untime*']

untimber *worthless material?* (BTs), MFH 176 (or ?=on-t.).

untīme *ill-timed, unfortunate*, Æ. ['*untime*']

untīmnes f. *evil times*, W207[18].

untīnan=ontȳnan

untōbrocen *unbroken*, Æ.

untōclofen *uncloven*, ÆL25[45].

untōdǣled *undivided, individual, indivisible, inseparable*, BF,Bo.

untōdǣl(ed)lic *inseparable, indivisible*, Æ. adv. -līce.

untōdǣl(ed)nes f. *undividedness*, BF118[1].

untō-dǣl(end)-, -dāl-, -dēlen-=untōdǣled-

untogen *untied, loose*, GD222[3].

untōlǣtendlīce *incessantly*, GD117[23].

untō-lēsende, -lȳsende *that cannot be loosed, inextricable*, WW.

untōlȳsendlic *unforgivable*, GD342[26].

untōsceacen *unshaken*, TC.

untōslegen *unshattered*, AS22[23].

untōsliten *untorn, uninjured*, CP.

untōsprecendlic *ineffable*, TC.

untōtwǣmed *undivided*, ÆH.

untōworpenlic (e[2], a[4]) *inviolable*, OEG11[153].

untrāglīce *frankly*, EL410.

untrēow=untrēowð

untrēowe (ī, ȳ) '*untrue,' unfaithful*, LL.

untrēowfǣst (ī, ȳ) *unfaithful, unreliable*, GPH,NIC475[28].

untrēowlīce *faithlessly, AO.* [*'untruly'*]
untrēownes f. *unfaithfulness,* GD160[5].
untrēowsian *to defraud, deceive,* CP : *offend,*
G.
untrēowð f. *unfaithfulness, treachery,* AO.
untrum *infirm, weakly, sick, ill, BH,Bl,*
VPs; Æ,CP. [*'untrum'*]
untrumhād m. *infirm state,* BH78[28].
untrumian *to be or become sick or infirm :*
make weak, Æ.
untrumlic *infirm, weak,* NUM13[20].
untrumnes f. *weakness, sickliness, infirmity,*
illness, Chr,CP,Mt; Æ,AO.
untrymed *unconfirmed (by a bishop),* LL
(140[19]).
un-trymig, -trymmig *sick, infirm,* NG.
untrymigan *to become weak,* JnL6[2].
untrymmigo f. *illness,* MtL10[1].
untrymnes=untrumnes
untrymð f. *weakness, illness,* LL,PPs.
untrȳw-=untrēow-
untwēgendlīce=untwēogendlīce
untwēo m. *certainty,* CR961.
untwēod *undoubting,* AN1244.
untweofeald=untwiefeald
untwēogende *unhesitating, not doubting,*
CP.
untwēogendlic *indubitable, certain.* adv.
-līce *indubitably, unhesitatingly, undoubt-*
ingly, AO,CP.
untwēolic (ī) *undoubted,* OEG. adv. -līce
certainly, with certainty, Æ.
untwēonde=untwēogende
untwēon(d)līce=untwēogendlīce
untwēonigend (ȳ) *undoubting,* A9·115[45].
untwī-, untwȳ-=untwēo-, untwie-
untwie-feald, -feld *not double,* CP : *not*
double-minded, without duplicity, sincere,
CP.
untȳd *unskilful, inexperienced,* CP.
untyddre=untȳdre; untȳdlic=untīdlic
untȳdre I. *firm, unbending,* AN1254. II. m.
monster, B111.
untȳdrende *barren,* LCD33b.
untȳgian=untigan
untygða *unsuccessful (in getting one's wish),*
CP257[18].
untȳmende *barren, unfruitful,* Æ. [*tīeman*]
untȳnan=ontȳnan
untȳned *unfenced,* LL106,40.
unðærfe *in phr.* 'unðærfe ðing' *'nequa-*
quam,' MtL2[6]. [unðearf]
unðæslic *inappropriate, unseemly, unbe-*
coming, absurd, Æ. adv. -līce, Æ.
unðæslicnes f. *impropriety,* ÆH2·316[8].
unðæslicu f. *incongruity,* RB124[13].
unðanc m. *ingratitude, disinclination, dis-*
pleasure, AO,Sol; Æ,CP : *evil intention,*
an ill turn, ApT,Chr,CP; Æ. unðances

unwillingly, compulsorily, AO, Chr,LL.
[*'unthank'*]
unðancful *unthankful,* CP,GD.
unðanc-ol, -ul *ungrateful,* NC330.
unðanc-wurðe, -wyrðe *ungrateful :* not
acceptable, disagreeable, Æ.
unðancwyrðlīce *ungratefully,* NC330.
unðearf f. *damage, hurt, detriment, ruin,*
Æ.
unðearfes *without a cause,* PPs13[6].
unðēaw m. *vice, sin, fault, CP;* Æ. [*'un-*
thew']
unðēawfæst *disorderly, ill-mannered, dis-*
solute, Æ. adv. -līce.
unðēawful *uncontrolled, disorderly,* WW.
unðinged *unexpected, sudden,* CP.
unðingod *unatoned for,* CP423[35].
unðolemōdnes f. *impatience, A.* [*'unthole-*
moodness']
unðoligendlic *intolerable,* Sc208[14].
unðorfæst *unprofitable,* DR179[17].
un-ðrīste, -ðrīeste *diffident,* CP.
unðrōwendlicnes f. *impassibility,* ZDA
31·14.
unðrōwigendlic *unsuffering,* Æ.
unðurhscēotendlic *impenetrable,* LCD.
unðurhtogen *unperformed,* CP329[14].
unðwægen=unðwogen
unðwǣre=ungeðwǣre
+unðwǣrian *to disagree,* Æ,CP.
unðwǣrnes f. (ē) *discord, division,* CHR.
un-ðwean, -ðwagen, -ðwægen, -ðwegen,
-ðwēn=unðwogen
unðwērnes=unðwǣrnes
unðwogen *unwashed,* G.
unðyhtig *weak,* OET107.
unðyldig=ungeðyldig
unðyldicnes f. *difficulty,* BH2·340.
unwāclic† *steadfast, strong, noble, splendid.*
adv. -līce.
unwǣded (ē) *not clothed,* MtL22[11].
unwǣder=unweder
unwǣlgrim *gentle, merciful,* GD133[6].
unwǣm-=unwem-
unwǣr (-war- *in obl. cases) incautious, care-*
less, unthinking, foolish, Æ,Bl,CP :
unaware, unexpected. on un-wǣr, -waran,
-warum *unawares, unexpectedly, Chr.*
[*'unware'*]
unwǣres (o[1], a[2]) *unawares, suddenly, Chr.*
[*'unwares'*]
unwǣrlic *unwary, heedless,* CP. adv. -līce,
AO,Bl,Chr; CP. [*'unwarely'*]
unwǣrnes f. *heedlessness,* W299[7].
unwǣrscipe m. *folly,* ÆH1·68[4].
unwæscen *'unwashen,'* Lcd41b.
unwæstm mfn. *barrenness,* W : *tare, weed,*
NG.
unwæstmbǣre *unfruitful, barren,* Æ,CP.

unwæstm-bærnes (Æ,AO), -berendnes (Æ) f. *unfruitfulness, barrenness, sterility.*
unwæstmberendlic *sterile,* WE 54⁹.
unwæstmfæst *barren,* BL 163⁶.
unwæstmfæstnes f. *barrenness,* BL 163¹⁷.
unwæterig *dry, desert, Lk.* ['*unwatery*']
unwandiende *unhesitating,* CP 381²⁵.
unwar- v. unwær.
unwarnod '*unwarned,*' LL 382³³.
unwealden *involuntary,* VH 23.
unwealt *steady, stable,* CHR 897.
unwearnum† adv. *irresistibly : suddenly, in a moment.*
unwearð=unweorð
unweaxen† *not grown up, young.*
unwēded=unwǣded
unweder n. *unfavourable season, bad weather, storm, Chrd, LG;* Æ. ['*unweather*']
unwederlice adv. *tempestuously,* Mt 16³.
unweg=onweg
unwegen *not weighed,* LCD 1·376⁷.
unwemlic *unsullied, pure,* WW 522³⁵.
un-wemme(d) *unblemished, unstained, uninjured,* Æ,DR,Ps : *inviolate.* ['*unwemmed*']
unwemmend m. *innocent man,* REPS 36¹⁸ (on-).
unwemming f. *incorruptibility, incorruption,* Sc 41¹⁰.
unwemmu (æ²) f. *spotlessness,* RWH 136³⁵.
unwemnes f. *purity,* HL 18⁴²².
unwended=unāwended
+unwendnes=onwendnes
unwēne *unexpected : hopeless,* Æ.
unwēned *unexpected, unhoped for,* AA,Sc.
unwēnlic adj. *unpromising, hopeless, desperate,* AO,CP. adv. -līce *unexpectedly, by chance,* GD 88¹⁷.
unwēnunga *unexpectedly,* Bo 140¹⁰.
unwēod n. *ill weed,* W 92¹⁹.
unweoder=unweder
unweorcheard *delicate, weakly, infirm,* RB 75⁸.
unweorclic (o) *unsuitable for work,* BF 122²⁴.
un-weorð (u, y), -wierðe (u) adj. adv. *unworthy,* Æ : *poor, mean, of low estate,* AO, *Chrd,RB : worthless : contemptible, ignoble, Bo.* ['*unworth*']
±unweorðian (o, u) *to slight, treat with contempt, dishonour,* Æ,LG; CP : *become worthless, vile, dishonour oneself.* ['*unworth*']
unweorðlic (u) *unworthy, dishonourable,* AO : *unimportant, humble,* CP. adv. -līce *unworthily, dishonourably, ignominiously,* AO,CP : *indignantly.*
unweorðnes f. *slight, contempt, disgrace,* AO,CP.

unweorðscipe m. *dishonour, disgrace, Bo : indignation,* CP 222⁹. ['*unworship*']
unweorðung (u) f. *disgrace : indignation,* CP 222¹² : *dishonouring,* CHRD 40.
unweotod=unwitod
unwer (KGL)=unwær
unwered *unprotected,* GEN 812.
unwērig *unwearying, indefatigable, persistent, AO, Lcd;* Æ. ['*unweary*']
unwerlice=unwærlice
unwerod *not sweet,* CP 447¹⁹.
unwestm=unwæstm; unweðer=unweder
unwīd *not wide,* NC 330.
unwidere n. *bad weather,* W.
unwidlod *unpolluted,* DR 90¹⁷.
unwierðe=unweorð
unwīese=unwīse, unwīslice
unwilla m. *repugnance, displeasure,* Æ,AO, *LL,Sol,WW.* ['*unwill*']
unwillan=unwillum
unwillende '*unwilling,' involuntary,* CP : *averse (to), HL.*
unwilles adv. *unwillingly, involuntarily, reluctantly,* Æ.
unwillum adv. *unwillingly, reluctantly.* his unwillum *against his will,* AO : *involuntarily, unintentionally.*
unwilsumlice adv. *involuntarily, against one's will,* BH 442²³.
unwindan³ (=on-) *to unwind, uncover,* Æ.
unwine m. *foe, enemy,* CHR,Ct.
unwinsum=unwynsum
unwīs '*unwise,' foolish, ignorant, uninformed, Bl,VPs;* CP : *insane,* GD.
unwīsdōm m. '*unwisdom,' imprudence, folly, ignorance, CP,VPs.*
unwīse=unwīslice
unwīslic *foolish.* adv. -līce, *CP,Lcd;* Æ. ['*unwisely*']
unwīsnes f. *ignorance : wickedness,* DR.
unwita m. *witless person, ignoramus,* LL.
unwitende '*unwitting,' ignorant,* AO.
unwītnigendlice *without punishment, with impunity,* ÆGR 233⁶.
unwītnod *unpunished,* CP.
unwītnung f. *impunity,* Sc 235⁵.
unwitod (io, u) *uncertain,* DR,GNE.
unwittig *unconscious, ignorant, stupid,* Æ. ['*unwitty*']
unwittignes f. *folly,* GD 163³⁴.
unwittol *ignorant,* Sc 80¹².
unwitweorc n. *evil work,* BL 111². [?inwit-]
unwiðerweard *friendly,* CP 361²⁰.
unwiðerweardlic *not discordant,* NC 330.
unwiðmetenes f. *incomparability,* OEG 587.
unwiðmetenlic *not comparable, incomparable,* Æ. adv. -līce.
unwlite m. *dishonour,* WW.
unwliteg=unwlitig

±**unwlitegian** _to become disfigured_, CP : _dis-figure, transform_, CP.
unwlitegung f. _disfigurement_, WW391[5].
unwlitig _unsightly, deformed, disfigured, ill-favoured_, Æ.
unwlitignes f. _disfigurement_, BH384[4].
unworclic=unweorclic
unword n. _abuse, slander_, AB34·10.
unworht v. ungeworht.
unworðian=unweorðian
unwrænc=unwrenc
unwrǣne _not lustful_, LCD.
unwrǣst(e) (ē) _feeble, weakly, evil_, AO, _Chr_ : _unsteady, untrustworthy, Chr._ ['un-wrast']
unwrǣstlīce adv. _incongruously, inac-curately_, BF186[25]. ['unwrastly']
unwrecen _unpunished, unavenged_, B,Bo.
unwrenc (æ) m. _vice, evil design_, CP,W. ['unwrench']
unwrēon[1,2] _to uncover, reveal_, Æ,Bf,G,VPs. ['unwry']
unwrēst=unwrǣst
unwrig-ednes, -ennes f. _uncovering, revela-tion_, RBL42[16].
unwrigen _open, unconcealed_, MFH101[7] (pp. of unwrēon).
unwriten _unwritten_, Bo.
unwrītere m. _incorrect copyist_, ÆGR3[24](= ÆT80[120]).
unwrīðan _to untwist, unbind_, CP.
unwunden I. _not wound_, WW187[30]. II. pp. of unwindan.
unwundod '_unwounded_,' Gen183.
unwuniendlic _uninhabitable_, LCD3·262[2].
unwurð=unweorð; **unwuted**=unwitod
unwynsum _unpleasant_, Æ.
unwynsumnes f. _unpleasantness_, Æ.
unwyrcan _to undo, destroy_, A11·113.
unwyrd f. _misfortune, trouble_, Bo,LCD.
unwyrht f. _ill-doing_, Bo123[32].
unwyrtrumian _to root out_, MtL13[29].
unwyrð=unweorð-; **unwyrðe**=unwierðe
unymb-fangen, -fangenlic _incomprehensible_, GD.
unymbwendedlic _unalterable_, DR164[16].
unymbwriten _not circumscribed_, GD268[24].
unȳð-=uneað-
unȳðgian _to trouble_, EPs34[15].
ūp adv. 'UP,' Æ,CP : _up stream, up country (inland)_, AO,Chr : _upwards._ lǣtan ūp _to put ashore._ ūp forlǣtan _divide._
ūpāblāwan[7] _to blow up, be in eruption (of a volcano)_, ÆL8[222].
ūpābrecan[4] _to break out or through, boil up_, Æ.
ūp-ābregdan, -ābrēdan[3] _to lift up, raise up, exalt_, Æ,CP : _expand_, BF70[11].
ūpāfangnes f. _reception, assumption_, A5·464.

ūpāhæf-=ūpāhaf-
ūpāhafenlīce (æ) adv. _arrogantly_, OEG667.
ūpāhafennes f. _exultation, presumption, arrogance, pride_, CP : _uplifting, elevation_, Æ.
ūpāhafu _lifting up_, CHRD30[21].
ūpāhebban[6] _to lift up, raise up, exalt_, Æ,CP : _rise in the air, fly._
ūpāhefednes (Æ), -āhefennes=ūpāhafen-nes
ūpāhōn[7] _to hang up_, Æ.
ūpāmȳlan? _to come to light, appear_, HGL 463 (v. OEG4784).
ūpārǣran _to raise up, lift up, exalt_, AO,CP : _excite : introduce_, BF122[16].
ūpāreccan _to erect, raise, build_, VPs.
ūpārīsan[1] _to rise up_, CP.
ūpārisnes f. _resurrection_, EHy14[6].
ūpāspringan[3] _to spring up, arise_, BF84[11].
ūpāspringnes (u[3]) f. _uprising_, BF,LPs102[12].
ūpāspryttan _to sprout forth, germinate_, BF 58[1].
ūpāstīgan[1] _to rise, ascend_, Æ,CP.
ūpā-stigen(nes), -stīgnes f. _ascent, ascen-sion, means of going up._
Ūpāstīgnestīd f. _Ascension-tide_, VH23.
ūpāstreccan _to uplift_, CM38.
ūpātēon[2,1] _to draw up, bring up, rear : draw out, pull out, pluck up : lift up, place in an upright position_, Æ.
ūpāðenian _to elevate, lift up_, CP.
ūp-āweallan, -āwallan[7] _to well up, steam up, boil up_, Æ.
ūpāwegan[5] _to lift up, support_, Æ.
ūpāwendan _to turn upwards, raise_, Æ. pp. ūpāwend _supine_, ÆGR.
ūpbrēdan[3] _to reproach with, upbraid_, W248[9].
ūpcuman[4] _to come up, arise._
ūpcund _from above, heavenly_, CP.
ūpcyme m. _rising, origin, source_, DA,VPs.
ūpeard m. _land above, heaven_, GU1051.
ūpende m. _upper end_, Bo,KC.
ūpengel† m. _heavenly angel._
ūpēode pret. 3 sg. of ūpgān.
ūpfæreld n? _ascension_, ÆH1·444[1].
ūpfeax _bald in front_, WW276[32].
ūpfēgan _to erect_, CP.
ūpfēran _to go forth, spring forth_, GPH401.
ūpferian _to carry up, to raise_, Sc130[7].
ūp-flēogan (Æ), -flēon[2] _to fly up._
ūpflēring f. _upper floor (of house)_, Æ.
ūpflōr fm., ūpflōre f. _upper chamber or story, garret_, Æ.
ūpflugon pret. pl. of ūpflēogan.
ūpgān anv. _to go up : make to go up, raise : rise (of sun)_, GUTH148[41].
ūpgang m. _rising, sunrise_, Æ : _going up approach, ascent : landing, going inland._

ūpganga m. *landing*, MA 87.
ūpgebrēdan (W 249³)=ūpbrēdan
ūpgemynd n. *contemplation of things above*, AN 1066.
ūpgēotan² *to well up*, GUTH 131¹⁹⁹.
ūpgodu np. *the gods above, heathen gods*, WW 497²⁵.
ūpgong=ūpgang
ūphafenes=ūpāhafennes
ūphēafod n. *upper end*, KC 6·79¹⁰.
ūphēah *uplifted, tall, high, elevated : sublime, noble, upright*.
ūpheald n. *support*, KC 4·232⁵. ['*uphold*']
ūphebban (JRsVPs)=ūpāhebban
ūphebbe f. *water-hen, coot*, PPs 103¹⁷.
ūphebbing f. *uprising*, LkL 8⁸.
ūp-hefenes (VPs), -hefnes=ūpāhafennes
ūpheofon m. *heaven above, sky*, BH,W.
ūphladan⁶ *to draw up*, HGL 418.
ūphūs n. *upper room*, WW 384³.
ūpland n. *country (as opposed to town)*, CHR 1087.
ūplang (o²) *upright, erect : tall*, AA 33⁴.
ūplegen f. *hair-pin*, WW 223¹⁶.
ūplendisc *from the uplands, rural, rustic, from beyond the town*, Æ. [ūpland]
ūplic *upper, supreme, lofty, sublime, heavenly, celestial*, Æ,CP.
ūplyft fnm. *upper air, ether, sky*, BTK 196,198.
ūpnes f. *height*, LPs 103³.
ūpniman⁴ *to raise up*, EHy 3⁸.
upon=uppan; **upp**=ūp
uppan (o²) prep. (w. d. and a.) *on, upon, up to, against*, Æ,Chr,G,RB : (time) *on, after*, Chr,G : *in addition to*. wið u. *above*. on u. *against*.
+**uppan**=+yppan
uppe I. adv. *above, aloft, up, inland*, CP. u. on *upon*. II.=yppe
uppe-=ūp-
uppian *to rise up, swell*, CP 277⁷.
uppl-=ūpl-
uppon=uppan
ūprador=ūprodor
ūprǣcan *to reach up*, BL 223¹⁰.
ūpriht *upright, erect*, Æ : *face upwards*, OEG 2157. adv. -rihte *straight up*, KC.
ūprine=ūpryne
ūprocettan *to belch up*, EPs 118¹⁷¹.
ūp-roder, -rodor† m. *upper heavens, ether, firmament*, EX.
ūpryne m. *ascent, rising (of sun)*, BH,Bo.
ūpsittan⁵ '*residere*,' ÆGR.
ūpspring (u²) m. *rising up, origin, birth*, Æ : *what springs up*.
ūpsprungennes f. *eclipse*, BH 240²⁰B.
ūpstandende '*upstanding*,' *erect*, Lcd,WW 154.

ūpstīgan¹ *to move up, rise, ascend*, Cr,Jn 1⁵¹. ['*upsty*']
upstīge m. *ascent, ascension*, Æ : *staircase*, GD 170²⁴.
ūpstīgend m. *one who mounts up, rider*, DR; CHy 4¹.
ūptēon² *to draw up*, AA 24¹³.
ūpðyddan *to swell up*, GUTH 131¹⁹⁷.
ūpwǣg=ūpweg
ūpwǣstm m. *stature*, STC 68¹⁸.
ūpware mp. *inhabitants of heaven*, WW 355²⁹.
ūpweallan⁷ *to boil up*, AO.
ūpweard, ūpweardes adv. *up*, '*upward(s)*,' Æ : *towards heaven : backwards (in time)*, Bf 156¹⁶.
ūpweg† m. *ascent, ascension*.
ūpyrnan³ (eo;=ie) *to run up, grow, increase : rise*.
ūpyrne=ūpryne
ūr m. *bison, aurochs : name of the rune for* u. [*Ger.* auer]
ūre I. possess. pron. 'OUR,' *ours*, Æ,AO, CP. II. gp. of ic.
ūrelendisc *of our country*, ÆGR 93¹⁷.
ūrigfeðere† *dewy-winged*.
ūriglāst *leaving a damp track*, WY 29.
ūrne asm. of ūre I.
urnen pp., urnon pret. pl. of iernan.
ūron=ūrum dsmn. and dp. of ūre I.
ūs dap. of pers. pron. ic '*us*.'
ūser I. poss. pron. gen. ūsses *our*. II. gp. of ic.
ūsic, ūsig, ūsih=ūs; **ūsse**=ūre; **ūsser**= ūser
ūsses v. ūser; **ūssic**=ūsic, ūs
ūsspīung f. *expectoration*, WW 113⁹. [ūt, spīwung]
ūssum dsn. of ūser.
ūt adv. '*out*,' AO,BH,Bo,G,Lcd : *without, outside*.
ūta- (N)=ūtan-
ūtāberstan³ *to burst out, burst forth*, CP.
ūtābrecan⁴ *to break out*, Æ.
ūtācnyssan *to drive out*, ERPs 35¹³.
ūtacumen=ūtancumen
ūtacund *extraneous, external, foreign*, NG.
ūtacunda m. *stranger*, LkL 17¹⁸.
ūtacymen=ūtancymen
ūtādelfan³ *to dig out*, ÆGR.
ūtādōn anv. *to do out, put out*, Æ.
ūtādrǣfan *to drive out, expel, destroy*, Æ.
ūtādrīfan¹ *to drive out, disperse, dispel*, LL.
ūtǣðmian (ē) *to breathe out*, MFH 122⁸.
ūtāfaran⁶ *to come forth, go out, depart*, CP.
ūtāflōwan=ūtflōwan
ūtālǣdan *to lead out*, LL,VPs : *produce : release*, VH.
ūtālēoran *to cause to depart, flee away*, CVPs 51⁷.

ūtāmǣr-an, -ian *to drive out, expel, depopulate,* BH.

utan=wuton

ūtan adv. *from outside, An,Chr* : *on the outside, without, Bo,Gen.* ūtan landes *abroad, PPs* 64[8]. ['*outen*']

ūtanbordes adv. *from abroad,* CP 3[11].

ūtan-cumen, -cymen I. *foreign, strange, AO, W*; Æ : *belonging to another.* ['*outcome*'] II. m. *stranger, foreigner.*

ūtane adv. *from without, outwards, outside, externally,* CP : *abroad,* AO 164[14].

ūtanlandes v. ūtan.

ūtanweard *external, outside, WW.* ['*outward*']

ūtānȳdan *to drive out, expel,* RPs 43[3].

ūtanymbstandnes (o[4]) f. *surrounding,* JPs 140[3].

ūtascēotan[2] *to sprout forth, burst forth,* CP : *to pierce out,* AO.

ūtāsellan *to grant outright,* KC 6·154'.

ūtāslēan[6] *to strike outwards, break out,* CP.

ūtāslīdan[1] *to slip forwards, fall (into),* GPH 388.

ūtāspīwan[4] *to spew forth,* CP 447[17],[19].

ūtātēon[2],[1] *to draw out,* Æ.

ūtātȳnan *to exclude,* VPs.

ūtāðȳdan *to thrust out, cast out,* Æ.

ūtaweard (NG)=ūtanweard

ūtāwindan[3] *to slip forwards, fall (into),* GPH 388.

ūtberstan=ūtāberstan

ūtcumen=ūtancumen

ūtcwealm (a, æ) m. *utter destruction, extirpation,* Cp 461i.

ūtcȳðan *to promulgate, announce,* A 4·166.

ūtdrǣf f. *decree of expulsion,* ÆL 21[85].

ūtdrǣfere m. *driver out,* WW 172[46].

ūtdragan[6] *to remove,* LL 454,9.

ūtdrīfan[1] *to drive out or away, expel, scatter, disperse.*

ūte adv. *out, without, outside, abroad,* BH, Chr,LL,Mt; Æ : *out.* ['*oute*']

ūtemest=ȳtemest

ūten, ūtene=ūtan, ūtane

ūtera, ūterra adj. (ȳ) (comp.) *outer, exterior, external,* BH,LL,Ps,Sc; AO,CP. superl. ȳtemest *uttermost, utmost, extreme, last.*

ūterlic (o[2]) *external,* MFB 102: *material,* 125.

ūtermere m. *outer sea, open sea,* CHR 897A.

ūteweard adj. *external, 'outward,' outside, extreme, last, Chr.* as sb. *outward part, exterior, LG.* on ūteweardan *on the outside, outwardly.*

ūteweardum *outwards, Chr* 893. ['*outward*']

ūtfær n. *going out, exit, departure,* Æ.

ūtfæreld n. *exodus, going out,* Æ,AO.

ūtfangeneðēof *right of judging thieves caught outside one's jurisdiction, and of taking fines for the crime, Ct.* [v. '*outfangthief*']

ūtfaru f. *going out,* Æ,RB. ['*outfare*']

ūtflōwan[7] *to flow out,* Æ,CP : *scatter, be dispersed,* EHy 5[6].

ūtfōr f. *evacuation (from body),* LCD 6a.

ūtforlǣtan *to cast out,* Æ,AO,CP.

ūtfūs *ready to start,* B 33.

ūtgān anv. *to go out,* CP.

ūt-gānde, -gangende *outgoing,* CD.

ūtgang (eo, o) m. *going out, departure, exit, exodus* : *latter part,Guth,MtL,VPs* : *privy* : *dejecta, excrement,* LCD : '*anus.*' ['*outgang*']

ūtgangan[7]=ūtgān

ūtgārsecg m. *remotest sea,* CREAT 70.

ūtgefeoht n. *external war,* BH 47[2] (Schipper).

ūtgegān=ūtgān; ūtgelǣdan=ūtlǣdan

ūtgemǣre n. *extreme or remotest limit,* PPs.

ūtgenga m. *exit,* MtR 22[9].

ūtgēð (KGL) pres. 3 sg. of ūtgān.

ūtgong=ūtgang

ūthealf f. *outer side,* WW 153[45].

ūthere m. *foreign army,* CHR.

ūthlēap n. *fine for a man escaping from his lord,* TC.

±ūtian *to put out, expel,* LL : *alienate (property).* ['*out*']

ūtirning (io) f. *flux,* MkL 5[25].

ūtlād f. *right of passage outwards by water,* EC 344 : *assembling (of material)?* AS 2[7].

ūtlǣdan *to lead out, bring out,* LL 54,8[1].

ūtlǣdnes (ē) f. '*abductio,*' EHy 6[36].

ūtlænda=ūtlenda; ūtlændisc=ūtlendisc

ūtlǣs f. *out-pastures,* KC 6·214.

ūtlaga m. '*outlaw,*' Æ,W.

±ūtlagian *to 'outlaw,' banish, Chr.*

ūtlagu? f. *outlawry,* LL. [ON. útlagi]

ūtlah *outlawed,* CHR,LL.

ūtland n. *foreign land, PPs* : *outlying land (granted to tenants), TC* 502. ['*outland*']

ūtlec=ūtlic

ūtlednes=ūtlǣdnes

ūtlenda m. *foreigner, stranger, alien,* GL.

ūtlende=ūtlendisc

ūtlendisc (æ) I. *strange, foreign,* Æ,Chr. II. m. *foreigner, stranger.* ['*outlandish*']

ūtlēoran *to go out, pass,* GD.

ūtlic *foreign,* BH : *remote,* CHRD 61.

ūtmǣran *to proclaim, announce,* AA 49[10].

ūt-mǣst, -mest=ȳtemest

uton=wuton; ūton=ūtan

ūtone=ūtane

ūtor (comp. of ūte) adv. *beyond, outside.*

ūtrǣsan *to rush out,* CHR.

ūtre=ūterre f. and n. of ūterra.

ūtrīdan[1] *to ride or go away,* LL 210,8.

ūtrine=ūtryne

ūt-roccettan, -roccian *to belch out*, EJPs.
ūtryne m. *running away, issue, exit, outlet*, Ps,Sc : *what runs out*, LCD.
ūtsang=ūhtsang
ūtscēotan[2] *to abut on*, EC121[8] : *suffer to escape, aid the escape of*, LL194,6[1].
ūtscūfan[2] *to push out, shut out, exclude*, Æ.
ūtscyte m. *outfall, outlet, exit*, Æ.
ūtscytling m. *stranger, foreigner*, Sc200[4].
ūt-siht, -sihte f. *flux, diarrhœa*, Æ,AO.
ūtsihtādl f. *diarrhœa, dysentery*, LCD.
ūtsīon[1] *to issue out*, AO38[7].
ūtsīð m. *going out, departure* : *death*, Gu.
ūtspīwung v. ūsspīung.
utter, uttor=ūtor; **uttermæst**=ȳtemest
utun=wuton
ūtwǣpnedmann m. *stranger*, BH354[25].
ūtwærc m. *dysentery?* LCD.
ūtwald m. *outlying wood*, EC289[17].
ūtwaru f. *foreign defence*, LL.
ūtweallan[7] *to well out, flow forth*, AA41[17].
ūtweard adj. *outside of, going away, striving to get out*, B. ['*outward*']
ūtweardes adv. '*outwards*,' CP.
ūtweorc=ūtwærc
ūtwīcing m. *sea-rover*, CHR1098.
ūtyrnende *diuretic, purgative, diarrhœic*, LCD.
ūtyrning (io[2]) f. *flux*, MkL5[25].
ūð- intensive prefix.
ūðe pret. sg. of unnan.
ūðgende=ūðgenge
ūðgenge *fugitive, alien, fleeting, vanishing, departing*, B,BH.
ūðmǣte *huge*, MH76[1]n.
ūðon pret. pl. of unnan.
ūðuta=ūðwita; **ūðweot-**=ūðwit-
ūðwita (eo[2], u[2]) m. *scholar, sage, philosopher, scribe, Pharisee*, Æ.
ūðwitegung f. *philosophy*, Æ.
ūðwitelīc=ūðwitlīc
ūðwitian *to study philosophy*, ÆGR146[2].
ūðwitlīc *philosophical, academical*, WW.
ūðwuta (NG)=ūðwita; **ūðwyt-**=ūðwit-

V

vīpere f. *viper*, MtR23[33].

W

wā I. (see also wēa) m. '*WOE*,' *affliction, misery, evil*, AO,CP; Æ. **II.** interj. (occly. governs d.) *woe! alas!* CP. wā lā, wā lā wā, wei lā wei *ah! oh! alas!* Æ,Bo,LPs. ['*wellaway*,' '*wellawo*']

wāc I. adj. *weak, soft, feeble, effeminate, cowardly, timid, pliant*, Æ,CP,Wa : *slender, frail* : *insignificant, mean, poor*, TC; Æ : *bad, vile*. ['*woke*'] **II.** n. *weakness*, LL. **III.** pret. 3 sg. of wīcan.
wac-=wæc-
wacan[6]† *to awake, arise, be born, originate.* [v. '*wake*']
waccor=wacor
wāce *weakly, slowly, negligently*, LL.
wacel=wacol
wacen (æ[1], ea[1], a[2], o[2], u[2]) f. *wakefulness* : *watching, vigil* : *division of the night*, NG : *incentive*, DR63[15].
wacian (æ, e) *to be awake or active, keep awake, watch*, Æ,CP. ['WAKE']
wācian *to become weak, languish* : (±) *waver, be cowardly, flinch*, Chr,Ma. ['*woke*']
waciende *watching, vigilant.*
wāclic *weakly, mean, vile, insignificant, trifling*, Æ. adv. -līce, Æ,Met. ['*wokely*']
wācmōd n. *faint-hearted, cowardly*, CP : *weak-minded, irresolute*, Æ.
wācmōdnes f. *weakness (of mind or body), cowardice*, CP.
wācnes f. *weakness, insignificance*, Æ, OEG. ['*wokeness*']
wacnian=wæcnan
wacol *awake, vigilant, watchful, attentive*, Æ. adv. -līce, Æ.
wacon=wacen
wacor *watchful, vigilant*, LL; CP. ['*waker*'] adv. -līce, CP.
wacsan=wascan
wācscipe m. *weakness, slackness*, LL208,1[5].
-wacu v. niht-w.; **wacul**=wacol
wǣcung f. *vigilance*, GD.
wād I. n. '*woad*,' ÆGr,Gl,Lcd; Mdf. **II.** (?) *drag-net*, OEG61[15] (v. A31·528).
wad- v. wæd.
wadan[6] *to go, move, stride, advance*, An,B : '*wade*,' *Ma*; AO : (+) *traverse, pervade, Ma.*
wadom=waðum
wādsǣd n. *woad-seed*, LL454,12.
wādspitl m. *woad-dibble*, LL455,15. [v. '*spittle*']
wadu? v. wād II.
wadung f. *travelling, going*, Æ.
wǣ (N,VPs)=wā; **wǣarhrōd**=weargrōd
wæb, wæbb=webb; **wǣc-**=wāc-
±**wǣcan** *to weaken, oppress, trouble*, BH. [wāc]
wæccan (±) *to '*watch*,' wake*, DR. [=wacian]
wæcc(e) f. '*watch*,' *vigil, wakefulness*, Æ,Bo, Bl,Lcd,Lk; CP.
wæccen=wacen
wæccende *watchful, awake*, B,Bl,Chrd,LL. ['*watch(ing)*']

wæccendlíce *watchfully*, GD 242¹⁴.
wæccer=wacor
+**wæcednes** f. *weakness*, ÆH 2·552'.
wæcen=wacen; **wæcg** (GL)=wecg
wæcian=wacian
wæcnan, wæcnian [v. also wacan] *to come into being, awake, come forth, spring from, arise, be born*, B. ['waken']
±**wæd** n. [usu. pl.; wad- in obl. cases] *ford, water, sea, ocean.*
wǣd f. *robe, dress, apparel, clothing, garment, covering*, Æ,Bo,Da : *sail*, ES 40·326. ['weed']
wǣd-=wēd-
wǣdbrēc (ā) fp. *breeches*, GEN 3⁷.
wǣdd=wedd; ±**wǣde** n.=wǣd f.
wǣdelnes (ē) f. *poverty*, CP.
wǣden=waden pp. of wadan
wǣden *of woad, bluish, purple*, OEG. [wād]
wǣder=weder
wǣderāp m. *stay, halyard*; pl. *rigging*, WW 515¹⁵.
+**wǣdian** *to clothe, dress, equip, furnish*, G.
wǣdl (ē, ēð) f. *poverty*, Bo; CP : *barrenness*, AO. ['waedle']
wǣdla (ē) *poor, destitute*, VPs. as sb.= *beggar, poor man*, VPs; Æ,CP. ['waedle']
wǣdle=wǣdl
wǣdlian *to be poor, destitute, beg*, Æ.
wǣd-lig (Æ), -ligend (GD) *poor.*
wǣdling m. *poor person*, JPs 87¹⁶.
wǣdlnes=wǣdelnes
wǣdlung f. *poverty, want*, Æ : *begging*, Æ.
wǣdo=wād
wæf pret. 3 sg. of wefan.
+**wæf**=+wef
wǣfan *to clothe*, W 119⁶.
wǣfels (ē) mn. *covering, mantle, cloak, dress, clothing, garment*, Æ.
wǣfergange f. *spider*, CPs 89⁹. [wefan]
wǣfergeornnes f. *eagerness for sightseeing*, LL (wǣfereorn-).
wǣferhús n. *amphitheatre*, ÆL 24⁴⁹.
wǣferlic *of a theatre, theatrical*, OEG 62.
wǣfernes f. *show, pomp, pageant*, OEG 4465.
wǣfer-sēn, -sēon=wǣfersўn
wǣfersolor m. '*pulpitum*,' *stage*, OEG 3458.
wǣferstōw (ēa) f. *theatre*, LCD.
wǣfersўn (ē³, ēo³, ī³, īe³) f. *spectacle, sight, show, display*, Æ. [wāfian]
wæflian *to speak foolishly*, v. NC 333.
wǣfon pret. pl. of wefan.
wǣfre *unstable, unsteady, wavering, wandering, restless : flickering, expiring.*
wæfs=wæps
wæfð, wæft f. *show, spectacle*, Bo,MET.
wǣfung (GL)=wāfung
wæg I. m.=weg. II. pret. 3 sg. of wegan.

wǣg (ā, ē) I. m. *motion : water : wave, billow, flood, sea*. [wegan] II. (±)=wǣge. III.=wāg. IV.=hwǣg
wǣgan=wegan
±**wǣgan** (ē) *to trouble, afflict*, CP : *deceive, falsify*, Æ : (+) *frustrate*, DOM 115.
wǣgbora m. *child of the waves?* B 1440.
wǣgbord n. *ship, vessel*, GEN 1340.
wǣgdēor n. *sea-animal*, CR 988.
wǣgdropa m. *water-drop, tear*, GU 1030.
wǣge I. f. *weight, scales, balance*, Æ,Sc, VPs,WW ['weigh'] : 'wey' (*of cheese, wool*, etc.), BC,LL : '*pensum*,' *burden*. II.† (ē) n. *cup, chalice.*
+**wǣge** n. *weight, measure*, LCD.
wǣgel (WW 124²)=pægel?
wǣgen=wægn; **wǣgenðīxl**=wægneðīxl
wǣgescalu=wǣgscalu
wǣgetunge f. *tongue of a balance*, WW 148¹⁹.
wǣgfær n. *sea-voyage*, AN 925.
wǣgfæt n. *water-vessel, clouds*, RD 4³⁷.
wǣgfaru f. *track in the sea*, EX 298.
wǣgflota† m. (*wave-floater*), *ship.*
wǣghengest† m. *ship.*
wǣgholm m. *sea, ocean*, B 217.
wǣglǣst=weglēast
wǣglīðend† m. *sea-farer, sailor.*
wǣglīðende† *seafaring.*
wægn (wægen, wǣn) m. *carriage, 'wain,' waggon, chariot, cart, vehicle*, B,Cp. Carles wǣn; wǣnes ðīxl *the constellation of the Great Bear*, Bo. [wegan]
-**wǣgnan** v. be-w.
wǣgnere (ǣn) m. *waggoner*, WW.
wǣgnere m. *enticer*, WW 436¹². [wǣgnian]
wægnest=wegnest
wægnfaru f. *chariot-journey*, WW.
wægngehrado (ǣn) *waggon-plank*, WW 267³³.
wægngerefa (ǣn) m. '*carpentarius*,' *waggonmaster?* WW.
wægngewǣde (ǣn) n. *waggon-cover*, LL 455,17.
+**wǣgnian** *to deceive : condemn*, CHRD 97.
wægnscilling m. *tax on waggons*, TC 138¹².
wægntrēow (ǣn) n. *log given to the carter of a load of wood*, LL 453,21⁴.
wægnðōol (ǣn) *cart-pin?* WW 343³⁹.
wægnweg (ǣn) m. *cart-road*, KC.
wægnwyrhta (ǣn) m. '*carpentarius*,' *cartwright*, WW. ['wainwright']
wǣgon pret. pl. of wegan.
wǣgpundern n. *weighing-machine*, LL.
wǣgrāp? m. *wave-rope, wave-bond* (*ice*), B 1611. [or? wælrāp]
wǣgryft=wāgrift
wǣgscalu f. *scale of a balance*, WW 437¹⁹. [scealu; *Ger.* wagschale]

wǣgstæð n. *sea-shore*, RD 23².
wǣgstrēam m. *current*, Ex 311.
wǣgsweord n. *sword with wavy pattern*, B 1489.
wǣgðel† n. *ship, vessel*.
wǣgōrēa f. *peril of the sea*, GEN 1490.
wǣgōrēat m. *deluge*, GEN 1352.
+wǣht pp. of +wǣcan and +wǣgan.
wæl I. n. [nap. walu] *slaughter, carnage*, BH; AO. w. +slēan *to slaughter : field of battle* : (usu. in pl.) *dead bodies*, AO. ['*wal*'] II. m.=wiell. III.=wel
wǣl mn. *whirlpool, eddy, pool*, Æ,CP : *ocean, sea, river, flood*. ['*weel*']
wæl-=wel-; wǣl-=wēal-
wæla=wela
±wǣlan *to afflict, vex, torment*, GU,MtR.
wælbedd† n. *slaughter-bed*.
wælbend f. *band of destruction*, B 1936.
wælbenn f. *deadly wound*, Ex 491.
wælblēat *deadly-pale?* B 2725.
wælceald *deadly-cold*, SOL 468.
wælcēasega m. *carrion-picker (raven)*, Ex 164.
wælclomm m. *deadly fetter*, GEN 2128.
wælcræft m. *deadly power*, RD 87¹¹.
wælcwealm m. *violent death*, RD 2⁸.
wæl-cyrige, -cyrie f. *(chooser of the slain), witch, sorceress*, Gl,Nar. ['*walkyrie*']
+wǣldan (MkLR)=+wieldan
wǣldēað m. *death in battle, violent death*, B 695.
wǣldrēor† n. *blood of battle, battle-gore*, GEN.
wælegian=weligian; wæler=weler
wælfǣhð f. *deadly feud*, B 2028.
wælfæðm m. *deadly embrace*, Ex 480.
wælfāg *blood-stained*, B 1128.
wælfeall=wælfill
wælfel *greedy for corpses, ghoulish*, EL 53.
wælfeld m. *battlefield*, CHR 937.
wælfill m. *slaughter, death, destruction*, GEN.
wælfūs *awaiting death*, B 2420.
wælfyll=wælfill
wælfyllo f. *fill of slaughter*, B 125.
wælfyr† n. *deadly fire : funeral pyre*, B.
wælgǣst† m. *murderous sprite*, B.
wælgār† m. *deadly spear*.
wælgenga m. *sea-monster?* OEG 5⁴¹; 8³⁰⁵.
wælgīfre† *bloodthirsty, murderous*.
wælgimm m. *death-bringing gem?* RD 21⁴.
wælgrǣdig *flesh-eating, cannibal*, AN 135.
wælgrim *fierce, violent, bloody, cruel : fateful, dire*. adv. -līce, AO.
wælgrimnes f. *cruelty, torture*, GD.
wælgryre m. *deadly horror*, Ex 137.
wælhere m. *slaughtering army*, GEN 1983.
wælhlem m. *death-stroke*, B 2969.
wælhlence† f. *coat of mail*.

wælhrēow (ēa²) *cruel, fierce, savage, blood-thirsty*, CP.
wælhrēowlic *cruel*, VH. adv. -līce.
wælhrēownes f. *cruelty, ferocity, atrocity, slaughter*, Æ,CP.
wælhwelp m. *destroying hound*, RD 16²³.
wælig=welig; wǣlisc=wīelisc
wæll=weall; wæll-=wæl-
wælla=willa II.; wællan (N)=willan
wælle (VPs)=wille; wælm=wielm
wælmist† m. *mist of death*.
wælnett n. *death-net*, Ex 202.
wælnīð† m. *deadly hostility, war*.
wælnot m. *baleful inscription*, SOL 161.
wælpīl m. *deadly arrow, dart*, GU 1127.
wælræst† m. *deadly onslaught*, B.
wælræst=wælrest; wælrǣw=wælhrēow
wǣlrāp? m. *flood-fetter (ice)*, B 1610?
wælrēaf n. *spoil from the slain : act of spoiling the slain*, LL.
wælrēc m. *deadly reek*, B 2661.
wælregn (ll) m. *deluge*, GEN 1350.
wælrēow=wælhrēow
wælrest (æ²)† f. *bed of slaughter, grave*.
wælrūn f. *murderous song?* EL 28.
wǣlsc=wīelisc
wælsceaft m. *deadly spear*, B 398.
wælscel n? *carnage*, JUD 313.
wælseax n. *dagger*, B 2703.
wælsliht (ea, i, y) m. *slaughter, carnage*, Chr : (†) *combat*. [v. '*wal*']
wælslihta m. *murderer, slayer*, GD 254²².
wælslītende *corpse-biting*, W 187¹⁴ : *deadly-biting*, W 241¹².
wælspere n. *deadly spear*, MA 322; LCD 175b. [v. '*wal*']
wælsteng m. *spear-shaft*, B 1638.
wælstōw f. *place of slaughter, battlefield*, AO. āgan wælstōwe geweald *to obtain possession of the battlefield, conquer*.
wælstrǣl mf. *deadly shaft*, GU 1260.
wælstrēam m. *deadly flood*, GEN 1301.
wælsweng m. *deadly thrust*, GEN 987.
wælt *part of thigh, sinew*, LL 7,68. [weald]
wæltan=wyltan
wælwang m. *field of the slain*, AN 1227.
wælweg (SEAF 63)=hwælweg
wælwulf† m. *warrior*, MA : *cannibal*, AN.
wælwyrt=wēalwyrt (or ? wæl- v. '*wallwort*').
wæm=(1) wamm; (2) hwamm
wæm-=wem-
wæmbede *big-bellied*, WW 161²². [wamb]
wæmman=wemman
wǣmn (LWS)=wǣpen
wǣmnian=wǣpnian; wæmst-=wæstm-
wæn=wenn; wæn-=wen-
wǣn=wægn; wǣnan=wēnan
wǣnes=(1) wācnes; (2) wōhnes

wæng, wænge=wang, wange

wænunga=wēnunga; **wǣpan**=wēpan

wǣpen n. (nap. wǣp(e)n, wǣp(e)nu) 'weapon,' sword, B,Chr; pl. arms, Bo, Gu,VPs; Æ,AO,CP : membrum virile, WW.

wǣpenbora m. weapon-bearer, warrior, knight, Æ.

wǣpend, wǣpened=wǣpned

wǣpen(ge)tæc n. wapentake' (subdivision of a riding), LL.

wǣpengeðræc n. clash of spears? DR 168³.

wǣpengewrixl(e) n. hostile encounter, CHR, W.

wǣpenhād=wǣpnedhād

wǣpenhete m. armed hate, AP 80.

wǣpenhūs n. armoury, WW 348¹³.

wǣpenlēas unarmed, Æ,OEG. ['weapon-less']

wǣpenlic male, WW.

wǣpenstrǣl fm. arrow, PPs 56⁵.

wǣpentæc=wǣpengetæc

wǣpenðracu† f. storm of weapons.

wǣpenðrǣge weapon, equipment? CRA 61?

wǣpenwīfestre=wǣpnedwifestre

wǣpenwiga m. armed warrior, RD 15¹.

wǣpmann (Æ, 'wapman')=wǣpnedmann

wǣpn=wǣpen; **wǣpnahūs**=wǣpenhūs

wǣpned I. adj. male, AO. **II.** m. male person.

wǣpnedbearn n. male child, BH 76⁸.

wǣpnedcild n. male child, Æ,LCD.

wǣpnedcynn n. male sex, Æ.

wǣpnedhād m. male sex, Æ : sexual power, GD 26³⁰.

wǣpnedhand f. male line, TC 491'.

wǣpnedhealf f. male line, TC 491¹⁶.

wǣpnedmann m. male, man, AO.

wǣpnedwīfestre f. hermaphrodite, WW.

±**wǣpnian** (mn) to arm, Æ,Chr; CP. ['weapon']

wǣpnmann=wǣpnedmann

+**wǣpnu** np. arms, LPs 45¹⁰.

±**wǣpnung** f. armour, Æ : army.

wæps m. 'wasp,' Gl; Æ. [L. vespa]

wǣr I. (napm. ware) wary, cautious, prudent, Æ,CP : (w. g.) aware of, Æ,Chr : ready, prepared, attentive. ['ware'] **II.**† n. sea, ocean. [ON. verr] **III.**=wer. **IV.**=wearr

wǣr I. adj. true, correct, GEN 681. **II.** f. faith, fidelity : keeping, protection : agreement, treaty, compact, pledge, covenant : bond (of friendship).

+**wǣr** wg. 'aware' (of), watchful, on one's guard, Chr 1095.

wǣr-=war-, wear-, wer-, wier-, wyr-

wǣran=werian

wǣrc (wræc) m. pain, suffering, anguish, BH,Lcd (A; often confused with WS. weorc. v. JAW 52). ['wark']

wǣrcan to be in pain, Lcd. ['wark']

wǣrcsār (e) n. pain, MkR 13⁸.

wǣre=wer II.

wǣre I.=wǣr II. **II.** pret. 2 sg. of wesan.

wǣrfæst† (e²) honourable, faithful, trusty.

wǣrg=wērig

wǣr-genga, -ganga (ē¹)† wm. one seeking protection, stranger (or ?=wer-).

wǣrigian=wērgian

+**wǣrlǣcan** to warn, Æ.

±**wǣrlan** to go, pass by, DR,NG.

wǣrlēas† faithless, perfidious.

wǣrlic I. careful, wary, circumspect, El,LL, WW. ['warely'] adv. -līce, Æ,CP. **II.**= werlic

wǣrlīce adv. truly, GEN 652?

wǣrlicnes f. wariness, HL 13²⁶³. ['wareliness']

wǣrloga† m. troth-breaker, traitor, liar, devil. ['WARLOCK'; lēogan]

wǣrlot n. craftiness, deceit, WW 354³¹.

wǣrna=wrenna

wǣrnes I. f. wariness, caution, Bl. ['wareness'] **II.**=weargnes

wǣron pret. pl. of wesan.

wǣrnung=wiernung

wǣrsagol cautious in speech, W 72¹⁷.

wǣrscipe m. cunning, caution, prudence, Bo; AO,CP. ['warship']

wǣrstlic=wrǣstlic

wǣrword n. word of warning, WW.

wǣrwyrde cautious in speech, FT 57.

wæs pret. 1, 3 sg. of wesan.

wæsc f. ablution, washing, CM 441. [v. 'wash']

+**wæsc** n. only in wætera +w. 'alluvium,' WW 179³⁵,187⁸. [v. 'wash']

-**wæsce** v. scēap-w.

wæscen=wascen pp. of wascan.

wæscern n. washing-place, WW 185².

wæscestre f. washer, house-keeper, 'presbytera,' GD 276. m. at GD 191²³ ('fullo'). ['washester']

wæschūs n. 'wash-house,' bath-house, ZDA 31·13³²³.

wæscing m. washing, ablution, Ct.

wǣsend=wāsend; -**wæsma** v. here-w.

wæsp=wæps; **wæst**=west

wæst-=wēst-; **wæstem-**=wæstm-

wæstling m. sheet, blanket, GL.

wæstm (e) mn. (nap. wæst-mas, -me) growth, increase : plant, produce, offspring, fruit, Bo,Bl,G; Æ,CP : result, benefit, product : interest, usury : abundance : stature, form, figure, B,G. ['wastum']

wæstmaseten f. planting, Mt 15¹³.

wæstmbǣre *fruitful*, Æ,CP.

+wæstmbǣrian *to be or make fruitful*, WW.

wæstmbǣrnes (io) f. *fruitfulness*, Æ.

wæstmbǣro f. *fruitfulness*, AO58²⁰.

wæstmberende *fertile*, AO.

wæstmberednes f. *fertility*, BH74³⁰ʙ.

wæstme f.=wæstm

wæstmfæst *fruitful*, ANS122²⁴⁷.

wæstmian *to grow, increase, bear fruit*, Bʟ, LG.

wæstmlēas *unfruitful*, RG; Æ. ['*wastum-less*']

wæstmlic *fruitful*, DR18¹³.

wæstmsceatt m. *interest, usury*, Ps,WW.

wæsŏm=wæstm

wǣt (ā, ē) I. adj. '*wet*,' *moist, rainy*, Æ; AO. II. n. *moisture*, Bo : *liquid, drink*, RB; Æ. ǣt and w. *food and drink*, Æ.

wǣta m. *wetness, moisture, humours, fluid, water*, CP,Bl,G; Æ : *drink*, Æ : *sap* : *urine*. ['*wete*']

±wǣtan *to* '*wet*,' *moisten, water*, Gu,Lcd, Rd : *become wet* : *bedew*, VPs.

wǣte f.=wǣta m.

wǣter (e) n. (gs. wætres, wæteres) '*WATER*,' Æ,CP; Mdf : *sea*.

wǣterādl f. *dropsy*, Lcd.

wæter-ǣdre, -ǣddre f. *spring of water, source*, Æ.

wǣterælfādl f. *a disease*, Lcd.

wǣterælfen f. *water-elf*, WW457⁸.

wǣter-berend (OEG871), -berere (WW) m. *water-bearer, sutler, camp-follower*.

wǣterbōh m. *succulent shoot, sprig*, WW 149²⁵.

wǣterbolla m. *dropsy*, Lcd.

wǣterbrōga† m. *frightful flood*, An.

wǣterbūc m. *water-pot, pitcher*, Æ.

wǣterbucca m. *water-spider*, WW122⁴.

wǣterburne f. *water-stream*, DD3.

wǣterbyden f. *bucket, cask*, WW503¹⁴.

wǣterclāŏ m. *towel*, RB59⁷.

wǣtercrōg m. *water-pot*, WW484²⁸.

wǣtercrūce f. *water-pot*, Cp283ᴜ.

wǣtercynn n. *water, form or kind of water*, VH23.

wǣterdrinc m. *a drink of water*, NC331. [v. '*water*']

wæter-egsa, -egesa† m. *water-terror*.

wǣterelfen=wæterælfen

wǣterfæsten n. *water-fastness, place protected by water*, CHR894ᴀ.

wǣter-fæt n., nap. -fatu *water-pot, flagon*, Jn; Æ. [v. '*water*']

wǣterflaxe f. *water-pitcher*, Mk14¹³. [v. '*flask*']

wǣterflōd m. '*water-flood*,' *inundation, deluge*, AO; Æ.

wǣterfrocga m. *water-frog*, CHRD96²⁷. [v. '*water*']

wǣterful *dropsical*, WW.

wǣterfyrhtnes f. *hydrophobia*, WW112²⁴.

wǣtergāt f. *water-spider*, WW122⁴.

wǣtergeblǣd n. *watery pustule?* LCD162b.

wǣtergefeall n. '*waterfall*,' CC116.

wǣtergelād n. *conduit*, WW339⁴.

wǣtergelǣt n. *aqueduct*, WW211¹³.

wǣtergesceaft f. *nature of water*, GD220¹⁷.

wǣtergewæsc n. '*alluvium*,' WW187¹.

wǣtergrund m. *sea-bottom, depth*, PPs106²³.

wǣtergyte m. '*Aquarius*' (*sign of the Zodiac*), LCD3·246⁴.

wǣterhæfern m. *crab*, LCD16b.

wǣterhālgung f. *consecration of water*, DR 117¹.

wǣterhelm m. *covering of ice*, GnE74?

±wǣterian *to* '*water*,' *moisten, irrigate, supply water* (*to*), Æ,Ps,CP : *lead* (*cattle*) *to water*, Æ (Gen).

wǣterig '*watery*,' *watered*, Æ,Lcd,WW.

wǣterlēas '*waterless*,' Æ (Gen),LG.

wǣterlēast f. *want of water*, Æ (9¹⁷⁷).

wǣterlic *aquatic*, GPH394.

wǣtermēle (ǣ³) m. *bowl, basin*, ÆGr.

wǣternǣdre f. *water-snake*, WW.

wǣterordāl n. *water-ordeal*, LL388,2.

wǣterpund n. '*norma, libella aquatica*,' WW150³⁷.

wǣterpytt m. '*water-pit*,' *well*, Æ.

wǣterrīŏe? f. *conduit* (v. OEG1714n).

wǣterscēat m. *napkin, towel*, WW127³.

wǣter-scipe (Æ,CP), -scype m. *sheet of water, waters* : *conduit*.

wǣterscȳte f. *towel, napkin*, Æ.

wǣtersēaŏ m. *cistern* : *pool, lake*, GD112¹⁷.

wǣtersēoc *dropsical*, G; Æ. ['*watersick*']

wǣtersēocnes f. *dropsy*, Æ,Lcd.

wǣterslæd n. *watery glade*, KC.

wǣterspryng m. *water-spring*, Dᴀ386.

wǣtersteall m. *standing water, pond*, Gᴜᴛʜ 205.

wǣterstefn f. *voice of waters*, PPs92⁴.

wǣterstoppa m. *bucket*, GD11²².

wǣterstrēam m. *river*, OEG,Ps. ['*water-stream*']

wǣtertīge m. *canal, aqueduct*, HGL418⁵⁰.

wǣterŏēote f. *conduit, flood-gate, torrent, cataract*, Æ.

wǣter-ŏīsa, -ŏissa m. *whale*, Wʜ50 : *ship*, Gᴜ1303.

wǣterŏrūh f. *water-pipe, conduit*, Gʟ.

wǣterŏrȳŏ f. *rush of waters*, PPs106²².

wǣterung f. '*watering*,' *providing with water, carriage of water*, Æ.

wǣterwǣdlnes f. *dearth of water*, ÆL23b⁶³⁸.

wǣterweg m. *watercourse*, KC,WW. ['*waterway*']

wæterwrīte f. '*clepsydra*,' *water-clock*, WW 378[39].

wæterwyll m. *spring, fountain*, LL312,5[1].

wæterwyrt f. *water star-wort*, LCD. ['*water-wort*']

wæterȳð f. *billow*, B2242.

wǣtian *to be wet*, WW447[1].

wætig (GPH389)=pætig

wætla m. *swathe, bandage*, LCD78a.

wǣtnes (ē) f. *moisture*, LkL8[6]. ['*wetness*']

wætrian=wæterian; wætter (N)=wæter

wǣtung f. *wetting, moisture*, LCD.

wæð n. *ford*, CHR1073D. [*ON*. vað]

-wǣða v. here-w.

wǣðan *to wander, roam about* : *hunt*. [wāð]

wǣðeburne f. *fishing stream?* BC (Mdf).

wǣðelnes=wǣdelnes; wǣðl=wǣdl

wǣwǣrðlic *serious?* BF192[30]. adv. (e[2], y[2]) -līce *confidently? plausibly?* BF6[18],W169[1].

wæx (N)=weax

wǣx=wēox pret. 3 sg. of weaxan.

wæxð pres. 3 sg. of wascan.

waflan *to* '*wave*,' *Æ,Lcd*.

wāflan *to be agitated, astonished, amazed, gaze at, wonder at, admire*, Æ : *hesitate*.

wāflende '*theatralis*,' '*visibilis*,' OEG233.

wāforlic=wǣferlic

wāfung (ǣ, ē) f. *spectacle, display, pageantry, sight*, Æ : *astonishment*, Æ. [wāfian]

wāfungstede m. *place for shows, theatre*, WW.

wāfungstōw f. *place for shows, theatre*, LCD 3·206[16].

wāg I. (ǣ) m. *wall*, *Æ,AO,B,Bl*; CP. ['*wough*'] II.=wǣg I.

wāghrægel n. *tapestry, vail*, NG.

wagian *to move, shake, swing, totter*, *Æ,Bo, Cp,Rd*. ['*waw*']

wagn=wægn

wāgon=wǣgon pret. pl. of wegan.

wāgrift (e, y) n. *tapestry, vail, curtain*, Æ.

wāgðeorl *doorway?* LPs61[4]. [ðyrel]

wāgðyling (wāh-) f. *wainscoting*, WW147[31]. [wāg, ðille]

wagung f. *moving, shaking*, LCD.

wāh I. *fine*, LCD101b (IF48·264). II. (*Æ,Bo*)=wāg

wāh-=wāg-

wahsan=wascan; wal=wæl I.

wal-=wæl-, weal-; wala (N)=wela I.

wālā! wālāwā! interj. (w. g.) v. wā.

walan v. walu I.; Wālas=Wēalas

walc-=wealc-

wal-crigge, -cyrge=wælcyrige

walcspinl (o[1]) f. *curling-iron, crisping-pin*, WW198[1]; OEG26[70].

wald (*BC,Jud*) ['*wold*']=weald

wald-=weald-

walde (CP443[11])=wolde

waldenīge *blue or grey-eyed, wall-eyed*, Erf 1166.

waldmora=wēalhmora

Wāle (=ēa) f. *Welshwoman, female slave*, RD.

waled *striped*, WW416[23]. ['*waled*']

waler (DR)=weler; walh=wealh

wālic *woful, lamentable*, SAT100.

wall (VPs)=weall

wallað (DR)=pres. pl. of wællan, willan.

walm (N)=wielm

walu I. f. *ridge, bank, KC* : *rib, comb (of helmet)*, B1031? : *weal, mark of a blow*, OEG. ['*wale*'] II. v. wæl I.

wālwyrt=wēalwyrt; wam=wamm

wamb (o) f. *belly, stomach, LG,Ps,Rd,WW*; Æ,CP : *bowels, Lcd* : *heart, VHy* : '*womb*,' *LG,VPs* : *hollow, BC,Rd*.

wambādl f. *stomach-ache*, LCD81a.

wambhord n. *contents of the belly*, RD18[10].

wambscyldig? *gluttonous?* v. NC331.

wambsēoc *having pain in the stomach*, LCD.

wamcwide (o)[†] *shameful speech, curse, blasphemy*.

wamdǣd (o)[†] f. *deed of shame, crime*.

wamfreht (o) n. *sinful divination*, WW.

wamful[†] *impure, shameful, sinful, bad*.

wamlust (o) m. *allurement, enticement*, A 13·28; OEG7[37].

wamm (o) I. mn. *stain, spot, scar, B,KGl* : *disgrace, defect, defilement, sin, evil, crime* : *injury, loss, hurt, misfortune*. ['*wam*'] II. adj. *shameful, bad*.

wamsceaða (o)[†] m. *sin-stained foe, devil*.

wamscyldig (o) *sinful, criminal*, GEN949.

wamwlite (o) m. *wound in the face*, LL.

wamwyrcende (o) *worker of sin*, CR1093.

wan I. (o) (usu. undecl. and used predicatively) *wanting, deficient, lacking, absent, BH,Bl,Cr,VPs*; CP. ānes wan ðe ðritig *or* ānes wana ðrittigum *twenty-nine*. ['*wane*'] II. pret. 3 sg. of winnan. III.= wann

wan- expresses *privation or negation*.

wana I. m. *lack, want, deficiency, Bo,Gl*; Æ. w. bēon *to lack, fail*, Æ. ['*wane*'] II.= wan I.

+wana *lacking, wanting*, MtL19[20]. ['*wane*']

wanǣht (o) f. *want, poverty*, †Hy4[103].

wananbēam m. *spindle-tree*, GL.

wancol (e) *unstable, unsteady, tottering, vacillating, weak, Bo*. ['*wankle*']

wand I. pret. 3 sg. of windan. II. f? *mole (animal), Gl*. ['*want*']

+wand n. *fear*, RB68[8] : *hesitation, scruple*. būtan gewande '*incunctanter*,' CHRD52[25]. [windan]

wandeweorpe (u[3]) f. *mole (animal)*, Æ.

wandian (o) *to hesitate, flinch, desist from, omit, neglect,* Æ,Bl,CP : *fear, stand in awe,* Æ : *have regard to, care for.* ['wonde']

wandlung f. *changeableness,* Bo 15²⁷.

-wandodlīce v. unfor-w.

wandrian *to 'wander,' roam, fly round, hover,* Bo,CP,Fin,LL : *change : stray, err.*

wandung f. I. *feeling of respect,* CHRD 61³⁴. II. *turning aside,* CHRD 99¹⁹.

wand-wurp, -wyrp=wandeweorpe

wanfāh (o) *dark-hued,* RD 53⁶.

wanfeax (o) *dark-haired,* RD 13⁸.

wanfōta m. *pelican,* WW 287¹⁰.

wanfȳr (o) n. *lurid flame,* CR 966.

wang I. (o) m. *plain, mead, field, place,* B, Bl,Ph : *world.* ['wong'] II. m.=wange

wangbeard m. *whisker,* LCD 73a.

wange (e, o) n. *jaw, cheek,* Æ,Lcd,RG. ['wang']

wangere m. *pillow, bolster,* BH,WW. ['wanger']

wangstede† m. *place, locality,* RWH 67¹².

wangtōð m. *molar, grinder,* LL,WW. ['wangtooth']

wangturf f. *meadow-turf,* LCD 1·400⁷.

wanhæf-=wanhaf-

+wanhǣlan *to weaken,* Æ.

wanhǣlð f. *weakness, sickness,* Sc 54¹⁹.

wanhǣw (o) *bluish,* WW 376²³.

wanhafa m. *poor man,* SPs 85¹.

wanhafol *needy,* ÆL.

wan-hafolnes, -haf(e)nes (æ²) f. *want, hunger.*

wanhāl *unsound, weak, ill, maimed,* Æ, CP.

+wanhālian *to make weak,* HL 12⁵¹.

wanhālnes f. *weakness, ill-health,* RB,Sc.

wanhlȳte *having no share in, free from,* WW 398³³.

wanhoga m. *thoughtless one, fool,* SOL.

wan-hygd, -hȳd† f. *carelessness, reckless-ness, daring.*

wanhygdig (hȳdig)† *careless, rash.*

±wanian *to diminish* (tr.), *lessen, curtail, injure, impair, take from,* Ct,Rd; Æ,AO : *infringe, annul : diminish* (intr.), *dwindle, decline, fade, decay,* B,Chr,Chrd,Jn; Æ, CP : 'wane' (moon), Bl.

wānian *to complain, bewail, lament, bemoan,* B,Cr,Jul; AO. ['wone']

wan-iendlic, -gendlic *diminutive,* ÆGR.

wann I. (o) *dark, dusky, lurid,* B,Gl,Met. ['wan'] II. pret. 3 sg. of winnan.

wannhāl=wanhāl

wannian *to become dark-coloured, turn black,* NC 332 : *become discoloured?* ÆP 178¹¹ ['wan']

wanniht *wan, pale, livid,* WW 431²¹.

wansǣlig (o¹)† *unhappy.*

wansceaft (o¹)† f. *misery, misfortune.*

wansceaf-ta m. (or -te f.) *a disease,* LCD.

wanscrȳd *poorly clad,* ÆH 2·500¹⁷.

wansēoc 'commitialis'? v. OEG 4937.

wansian *to diminish,* Chr 656E. ['wanze']

wanspēd f. *poverty, want,* AO,Sc. ['wan-speed']

wanspēdig *poor, indigent,* Æ. ['wanspeedy']

wanung (o) f. *waning, decrease, deprivation, diminution, loss, injury, weakening,* Æ, BH,Lcd.

wānung f. *howling, lamentation,* Æ,LG. ['wonung']

wanwegende *waning* (moon), LCD.

wāpe (a²?) *napkin, towel?* IM 122²³.

wapelian, wapolian *to bubble, froth, exhale, emit, pour forth,* GL.

wapul m? *bubble, froth,* WW.

war=wearr

wār I. n. *sea-weed,* Gl : *sand.* ['ware'] II.=wǣr

wara, gs. of waru.

-waran v. burg-, ceaster-, eorð-w.

waras (N)=weras nap. of wer I.

-waras v. burg-, eorð-w.

warað=waroð

ward=(1) weard; (2) wearð (weorðan)

-ware v. burg-, eorð-, ceaster-w.

waren-=warn-; **warht**=worht

warian I. *to be wary, beware,* Gen,KGl,LL : (±) *guard, protect, defend : warn,* Gl; CP : (†) *hold, possess, attend :* (†) *inhabit.* ['ware'] II. *to make a treaty* (with), BH.

wārig *weedy, dirty,* GnE 99.

wāriht *full of sea-weed,* GL.

waritrēo=weargtrēow

warnian (ea, are) (±) *to 'warn,' caution,* Æ, Chr,Lcd,W : (±) *take warning, take heed, guard oneself against,* Æ,Lk; CP : *deny* (oneself, *etc.*). [wearn]

warnung (ea) f. 'warning' : *foresight, caution,* Æ,Cr,Sol.

waroð (a¹, ea¹, e¹, a², e², u²) n. *shore, strand, beach,* B,Met,Ps. ['warth']

wāroð n. *alga, sea-weed,* RD 41⁴⁹.

waroðfaruð m. *surf,* AN 197.

waroðgewinn (u²) n. *surf,* AN 439.

warp=wearp I.; **warr**=wearr

warpenig v. weardpening

warscipe=wærscipe

warð I. (N)=waroð. II. (N)=wearð pret. 3 sg. of weorðan.

waru I. f. 'ware,' *article of merchandise,* Æ, WW. II. f. *shelter, protection, care, custody, guard, defence, vindication,* AO,Gu; Æ. ['ware']

-waru v. burg-, ciric-, eorð-w.

waruð, wāruð=waroð, wāroð

was=wæs; -wāsa v. wudu-w.
wascan[6] (æ; acs, a(c)x) to 'wash,' cleanse, Æ,BH,G,TC : bathe, lave.
wāse (v. OEG 1818) f. mire, marsh, Gl. ['ooze']
wāsend (ǣ) m. 'weasand,' windpipe, gullet, Gl,Lcd.
wāsescīte f. cuttlefish, WW 181[7]. [wāse, scēotan]
wāst pres. 2 sg. of witan.
wāt I. pres. 3 sg. of witan. II. pret. 3 sg. of wītan. III.=wǣt
watel (o[2], u[2]) m. 'wattle,' hurdle, covering : (pl.) thatching, BH,Gl,LkL.
water=wæter; watol=watel
watr-=wætr-, wæter-
watul=watel
wāð† f. wandering, journey : pursuit, hunt, hunting, chase, MET 27[13].
wāðan? to wander, flee, GUTH 113n.
waðema=waðuma
wāðol wandering? or m. full moon? FIN 8?
wað-um, -uma† m. wave, flood, stream, sea.
wāwa ['wowe'; ÆGr,Gen]=wēa
wāwan[7] to blow (of wind), RD 41[81].
waxan=(1) wascan; (2) weaxan
waxgeorn=weaxgeorn
we (ē) pron. (1st pers. plur.) g. ūser, d. ūs, acc. ūs(ic) 'WE.'
wēa m. misfortune, evil, harm, trouble : grief, woe, misery : sin, wickedness.
weacen=wacen
wēacwānian to lament, SAT 320.
wēadǣd† f. evil deed.
wēadhōc (Ep 887)=wēodhōc
weadu (K)=wudu
wēafod=wēofod; weag=weg
wēagesīō m. companion in trouble, W.
weagian=wagian
weahte pret. 3 sg. of weccan.
weahxan=weaxan
weal=(1) weall; (2) wæl
wēal=wealh; weal-=weall-, wel-
wēalāf† f. wretched remnant.
wēaland=wēalland
Wēalas (pl. of wealh) the 'Welsh,' Chr,LL : Wales. West Wē(a)las West-Welsh, Cornish.
+wealc n. rolling, tossing motion : attack, CHR 1100.
wealca (a) m. †billow, rolling wave : light floating garment.
wealcan[7] (±) to move round, revolve, roll, toss, Gl; CP : fluctuate : revolve in one's mind, discuss, scheme, reflect, Æ,CP : roll together : (+) go, traverse, Gl. ['walk']
wealcere m. fuller, WW 407[29]. ['walker']
±wealcian (a) to curl, OEG 26[69] : roll up, HGL 489[56].

wealcol mobile, not firmly fixed, GPH 399[441].
wealcspinl (a, o) f. crisping-pin, OEG,WW.
Wēalcynn n. the Welsh kin, EC 146'.
weald I. (a) m. weald, forest, wood, grove, BC,Chr,Jud; AO : bushes, foliage, GEN 846. ['wold'] II. m. power, dominion, mastery, AO (usu. +) : groin, LCD 1·12[9]. III. powerful, RB 117[5]. IV. conj. in case. w. ðeah perhaps, possibly, ÆH. ['wald']
+weald (a) n. might, power, possession, A, B,Rood : control, command, dominion, AO, Bl : bridle : protection : subjection : groin : pudenda : muscles of the neck? LL 88,77. (his) gewealdes of his own accord, intentionally, LL. ['wield']
±wealdan[7] (a) w. g. d. (instr.) and a. to rule, control, determine, direct, command, govern, possess, AO,CP : 'WIELD*' (a weapon), exercise : cause, bring about, CP.
wealdbǣr f. place affording mast for swine, EC 60[23].
+wealden I. adj. subject (to), easily controlled : inconsiderable, small, AO,CP. II. adv. moderately.
wealdend (a) I. m. leader, controller, ruler, lord, king (often of God), B,Bo. ['waldend'] II. f. female ruler.
±wealdende ruling, powerful, Æ,Cr. ['wielding']
Wealdendgod m. Lord God, PPs.
+wealdendlīce powerfully, PPs 135[16].
wealdendras late nap. of wealdend.
+wealdenmōd self-controlled, CRA 70.
wealdes (usu. +) of one's own accord, voluntarily, CP 198[22].
wealdgenga m. robber, thief, ÆT 1089.
±wealdleðer n. rein, bridle, Æ.
wealdmoru=wēalhmoru
wealdnes (a) f. rule, VPs 144[13].
wealdswaðu (a[1]) f. forest-track, B 1403.
weale=wale; wēales v. wealh.
wealfæsten=weallfæsten
wealg nauseous? CP 447[18]. ['wallow']
wealgat=weallgeat
wealh (a) m. (gs. weales) foreigner, stranger, slave : Briton, Welshman : shameless person, HGL 527[22].
wealhāt boiling hot, red-hot, Lcd 96a. ['wallhot']
wealhbaso f. foreign red, vermilion, GL.
Wealhcynn n. men of Wales, Britons, CHR.
wealhen=wīelen
wealhfæreld (a) n. a force which patrolled the Welsh border? KC 2·60'.
wealh-gefēra, -gerēfa m. commander of the 'wealhfæreld,' CHR 897A.
wealhhāfoc m. foreign hawk, falcon, AA, GL.
wealhhnutu (a) f. 'walnut,' WW 452[34].

wealhisc=wīelisc

wealh-moru, -more (a[1]) f., -mora m. *carrot, parsnip*, LCD,WW.

wealhstod m. *interpreter, translator*, Æ,CP : *mediator*, CP.

Wealhðēod f. *Welsh nation*, LL.

wealhwyrt [v. 'wallwort']=wēalwyrt

weallan *to be defiant*, ÆL12[48].

wēalic *woeful, sorrowful*, WY12.

weall I. (a, æ) m. 'WALL,' *dike, earthwork, rampart, dam*, Æ; AO,CP; Mdf : (†) *rocky shore, cliff.* II. f. *fervour*, HGL465. III.= wæl. IV.=wiell

weallan[7] (±) *to be agitated, rage, toss, well, bubble, seethe, foam, be hot, boil*, AO,B, Lcd; CP : *swarm*, Æ,WW : *flow*, Æ. ūp w. *to rise (of a river)*, AO. ['wall']

wēalland n. *foreign country*, GEN2706 (weal-) : *Normandy*, CHR1040E. [wealh]

Wēallas=Wēalas

weallclif n. *sea-cliff*, B3132.

wealldīc f. *a walled ditch?* KC5·346[19].

wealldor n. *door in a wall*, CR328.

+**wealled**=+weallod

weallende *boiling, raging*, Æ,B : *fervid, ardent, energetic, fiery* : *swarming (with vermin)*, Æ,WW. [v. 'wall,' 'walling']

weallfæsten n. *walled place, rampart, fortification, fortress.*

weallgeat† n. *rampart-gate, postern.*

weallgebrec n. *wall-breaking, act of making a breach*, AO134[30].

weallgeweorc n. *building of a wall*, Æ : *destruction of walls*, ÆGR12[5].

weallian *to go abroad, travel, wander* : *go as pilgrim*, LL. ['wall']

weallīm m. *cement, mortar*, GEN11[3].

wēallisc=wīelisc

+**weallod** *walled*, Num. [v. 'wall']

weallstān† m. *stone used in building*, Cr, Ruin. ['wallstone']

weallstaðol (e[3]) m. *interpreter, translator*, RWH41[33] (wealh-?).

weallsteall m. *wall-place, foundation?* WA88.

weallstēap† *steep as a wall*, GEN.

weallstilling (y) m. *repair of walls* (v. BT).

weallstōw=wælstōw

weallōrǣd (a[1]) m. *plumb-line*, WW522[27].

weallung (a, y) f. *agitation, fervour, zeal.*

weallwala† m. *part of a house-wall? foundation?* RUIN21.

weallweg (a[1]) m. *walled road?* Ct.

weallwyrhta m. *mason*, GL.

weallwyrt=wealhwyrt

wēal-mora, -more=wealhmoru

wealnes (CPs)=wealdnes

wealowian=wealwian

wealsāda m. *cord (for binding captives)?* PPs139[5]. [wealh]

wealstilling (y[2])=weallstilling

wealstod=wealhstod

wealt=wielt pres. 3 sg. of wealdan.

wealte f. *a ring*, Erf1105.

wealweorc n. *masonry*, Æ.

wealwian I. (a, y) *to roll* (intr.), Bo,BH, CP : *roll* (tr.). ['wallow'] II. *to dry up, shrivel, wither, decay*, Bo. ['wallow']

wealword n. *defiant word*, A11·98[37]. [wealh]

wealwyrt (a, æ) f. *dwarf elder*, Cp,Lcd. ['wallwort']

wēamēt, wēamētto f. *passion, anger*, Æ.

wēamōd *ill-humoured, angry*, CP. ['wemod']

wēamōdnes f. *anger, impatience*, Æ,CP.

weaps=wæps

wear=(1) wearr; (2) hwer

wear-=wær-

wearas=weras npl. of wer.

wearc=wærc

weard I. fm. *watching*, 'ward,' *protection, guardianship*, Æ,B; AO,CP : *advance post*, AO : *waiting for, lurking, ambuscade.* II. m. *keeper, watchman, guard, guardian, protector*, B,Bl; AO : (†) *lord, king* : (†) *possessor.* III. adv. *towards, to.* wið... weard *towards.* IV.=wearð. V. 'sandix,' v. A30·249.

weardian *to watch, guard, keep, protect, preserve*, LL,Ps : *hold, possess, occupy, inhabit* : *rule, govern*, Da665. lāst w. *keep the track of, follow closely.* swaðe w. *remain behind.* leger w. *keep one's bed.* ['ward']

weardmann m. *watchman, guard, patrol*, Æ.

weardpening? (warp-) m. *rent paid in lieu of military service*, Ct1087? ['wardpenny']

weardseld, weardsetl (Æ) n. *guardhouse, watch-tower.*

weardsteall m. *watch-tower*, WW.

weardwīte n. *penalty for not keeping guard*, TC411[31]. ['wardwite']

wearf I. (EC202[15])=wearp pret. 3 sg. of weorpan. II.=hwearf

wearg (e) I. m. (wolf), *accursed one, outlaw, felon, criminal, Rood*,WW; Æ. ['wary'] II. (-erig, -yrig) adj. *wicked, cursed, wretched.* [ON. vargr]

weargberende *villainous*, WW407[27].

weargbrǣde (-geb-) f. *a warty eruption, impetigo, stye in the eye, tetter, ringworm, mole, freckle*, Lcd,WW. ['waribreed']

wearglic (ere-, eri-) *wretched.* adv. -līce (y[1]).

weargnes (æ, e, y) f. *evil*, MtL,PPs.

weargrōd f. *scaffold, gallows*, GL.

weargtreafu (rht) np. *hell*, EL927.

weargtrēow (ari-) n. *gallows*, KC. ['warytree']

weargung (e) f. *misery*, EPs 87¹⁹.
wearh I.=wearg. **II.**=wearr
wēariht=wearriht
wearm '*warm*,' *Bo,Met,Rd*; Æ,CP. adv. -e, *Lcd*.
wearmelle=wurmille
±**wearmian** *to become or make* '*warm*,' *Æ*, *BH,G,HL,Ph,Rd*; CP.
wearmlic *warm*, DA 350.
wearmnes f. *warmth*, ÆL 11¹⁶⁰. ['*warmness*']
wearn I. f. *reluctance, repugnance, refusal, denial*, CP : *resistance* : *reproaches, abuse*. [waru] **II.**=worn
wearn-=warn-, wearrn-
wearnmǣlum (ē) adv. *in troops*, WW 25¹. [worn]
wearnwīslīce adv. *obstinately*, WW.
wearod, wearoð=waroð
wearp I. (a) m. '*warp*,' *threads stretched lengthwise in a loom*, *Cp,Rd* : *twig, osier*. **II.** pret. 3 sg. of weorpan.
wearpfæt n. *basket*, WW. ['*warpfat*']
wearr (a, æ, eo) m. *callosity*, *Cp,Lcd*. ['*warre*']
wearrig (Æ), wearriht *warty, knotty*.
wearrihtnes f. *roughness* (*of skin*), GL.
wearrnes (wearn-) f. *knottiness* (Swt).
wearscipe (AS 69¹⁵)=wærscipe?
weart, wearte (a, e) f. '*wart*,' *Cp,Lcd*.
weartere (æ) m. *occupier, dweller*, CHR 565. [weard]
wearð I. n.=weorð. **II.** pret. 3 sg. of weorðan. **III.**=waroð
wearð-=weorð-
wēas adv. *by chance, accidentally*, CP. mid w. *by chance*.
weasc-=wæsc-
wēasgelimp n. *chance occurrence*, WW 410¹⁰.
wēaspell n. *evil tidings*, B 1315.
weastern (CHR 1015)=western
weastm=wæstm
wēatācen† n. *sign of grief*.
wēaðearf f. *woeful need*, WIF 10.
weax (e) n. '*wax*,' *BC,Bl,Ps*; AO.
weaxæppel m. *ball of wax*, SOL 150³³.
±**weaxan** (e) **I.** sv⁷ *to* '*WAX*,' *grow, be fruitful, increase, become powerful, flourish*, Æ, CP; AO. **II.**=wascan
weaxberende m. *candle-bearer, acolyte*, DR 195⁸ (io²).
weaxbred (e) n. *writing-tablet*, Æ,RB : *diagram, table*, BF 180³⁰. ['*waxbred*']
weaxcandel (e¹, o²) f. '*wax candle*,' *Cp,WW*.
weaxen (e¹) **I.** *waxen, made of wax?* LCD. **II.** pp. of weaxan.
weaxgeorn (a) *very greedy*, WW 102¹³.
weaxgesceot n. *payment in wax*, W 171¹.

weaxhlāf m. *wax tablet*, LCD.
weaxhlāfsealf f. *wax salve*, LCD 92b.
±**weaxnes** f. *increase, growth : interest, usury*.
weaxscot=weaxgesceot
weaxsealf (e) f. *wax salve*, LCD,WW.
weaxung f. *growth, increase*, Bf 138¹⁹. ['*waxing*']
web, webb n. '*web*,' *weft* : *woven work, tapestry*, *B,Cp,Sc*; Æ. [wefan]
webba m. *weaver*, WW. ['*webbe*']
webbēam m. *weaver's beam*, WW : *treadle of a loom*, WW. ['*webbeam*']
webbestre f. *female weaver*, WW 188¹¹. ['*webster*']
webbgeweorc n. *weaving*, HL,MH.
webbian *to contrive, devise*, AN,BL,EL.
webbung (hw) f. *plotting, conspiracy*, OEG 2975 : '*scena*' (=wāfung? v. OEG 2920).
webgerēoru np. *weaver's tool*, WW 294¹⁶.
webgerod n. *weaver's implement*, Cp 1988.
webhōc m. *weaver's comb, reed?* WW.
weblic *pertaining to a weaver*, GL.
websceaft m. *weaver's beam*, WW 293³⁹.
webtāwa m. *thread, line*, WW 433⁸.
web-tēag (æ¹, ǣ²) f. *weaving-thread*, OET 615.
wēbung (Cp 180s)=wāfung
webwyrhta m. *fuller*, MH.
wecca=wēoca
weccan (±) *to awaken, arouse*, B,BH,CP, Cr : *call up, bring forth, produce* : *recall* : *exhort, encourage* : *move, set in motion* : *kindle*. ['*wecche*']
weccend m. *instigator*, GPH 393.
wēce=wāc I.
wecedrenc m. *emetic*, LCD.
wecg m. '*wedge*,' *Cp,Sc* : *mass of metal, lump*, Æ : *piece of money*, Æ,BH,WW.
wecgan *to move, agitate, drive hither and thither*, *Met,Ps* : *be moved*. ['*weigh*']
wecian (VPs)=wacian
wecnian=wæcnian
wed=wedd
wēd=wǣd
+**wēd I.** n. *fury, rage, foolishness, madness*. [wōd] **II.** (ZDA 31·9¹⁶⁸) pp. of wēn.
±**wēdan** (ǣ) *to be or become mad, rage*, Æ, BH,G; AO,CP. ['*wede*']
wēd-beorge, -berge=wēdeberge
wedbrice=wedbryce
wedbrōðor m. *pledged brother* (*in a brotherhood of compact, not of blood*), CHR. [wedd]
wedbryce m. *treachery*, W. [? v. '*wed*']
wedd n. *pledge, agreement, covenant, security*, B,Bl,Chr; Æ,AO,CP : *dowry*, WW. ['*wed*']
+**weddian** *engage, pledge oneself, covenant, promise, vow*, Lk,LL : *give to wife, betroth* : '*wed*,' *marry*, Chrd,LL.

weddung f. *pledging, betrothal, Nic*474³³. ['*wedding*']

wēde I. *raging, mad,* LCD,LkL. [wōd] II. (A)=wǣde

+wēde n. *fury, rage, madness, Æ.* [wōd]

wēdeberge f. *hellebore,* LCD,GL.

wēdehund m. *mad dog,* LCD,MET.

wēdelnes (VPs)=wǣdelnes

wēden (MFH178)=wǣden

wēdend *raving, Bo,Cp.* [v. '*wede*']

wēden(d)sēoc *mad,* GD135n; 223.

wēdenheort I. *mad, insane,* WW. II. n. *madness.*

wēdenheortnes f. *madness, frenzy,* CP.

weder I. n. 'WEATHER,' *air, AO : sky, firmament : breeze, storm, tempest.* II.=weðer

+weder=+wider

wederblāc *bleached by the weather,* A8·449.

wederburg f. *exposed town,* AN1699.

wedercandel f. *sun,* PH187.

wederdæg m. *day of fine weather,* Az96.

wederfest *weather-bound,* CHR1046E.

wederian *to exhibit a change of weather,* LCD.

wedertācen n. *sun,* GU1267.

+wederu=+wideru

wederung (æ) f. *(bad) weather, Chr*1085. ['*weathering*']

wederwolcen n. *cloud,* EX75.

wedewe=wuduwe

+wedfæstan (wet-) *to pledge,* Cp635s.

wēding f. *madness,* GD164²⁷; WW409³⁸.

wēdl-=wǣdl-

wedlāc n. *pledge, plighted troth,* '*wedlock,*' GL.

wedloga m. *violator of agreement, traitor.*

+wef n. *woof, web,* WW490³⁸ : *text, context?* BF172¹¹.

wēf-=wāf-, wǣf-, wēof-

wefan⁵ (eo) (±) *to* '*weave,*' *BH,LPs, WW; Æ : devise, contrive, arrange.*

wefl I. f. *woof, warp,* GL : *an implement for weaving, shuttle?* LL455,15 and 3·254. II.=wifel

weft, wefta m. '*weft,*' *A*9·263.

weg I. (æ) m. 'WAY,' *direction, AO; Æ : path, road, highway,* Mdf : *journey, Æ : course of action,* CP. ealne w. (ealneg) adv. *always.* on w. (āweg) adv. *away.* be...wege *on the way (to).* II.=wæg II.

wēg=(1) wǣge; (2) wīg

weg-=onweg-; wēg-=wǣg-

wegan⁵ (±) *to carry, B,Nar : support, sustain, bear, bring,* CP : *move : wear, BH, CP : (±)* '*weigh,*' *measure, ÆGr,Lcd,W.*

+wegan *to fight,* B2400.

weg-brāde, -brǣde (Æ) f. '*way-bread,*' *plantain, dock, Gl,Lcd.*

wegfarende (ǣ, ē) '*wayfaring,*' *ÆL.*

wegfērend m. *wayfarer, traveller,* Bo,GD.

wegfērende *wayfaring, ÆH,GD.* ['*wayfering*']

wegfōr f. *travel, journey,* WW423³³.

wegg=wecg

weggedāl n. *road-dividing, cross-way,* GL.

weggelǣte fn. *junction of roads, Gl.* ['*wayleet*']

weggē-slō? -sīða? (v. OEG861) *travelling companion.*

weggewit n. *aberration (of mind),* CPs115¹ⁿ.

weg-lā interj. '*euge!*' PPs69⁴. [=wā lā]

weglēas *out of the way, erroneous : without a road,* WW. ['*wayless*']

weglēast (ī²) f. *trackless place, wilderness,* ARSPs106⁴⁰.

wegnest (æ¹) n. *food for a journey,* HL : *viaticum,* BH.

wegrēaf n. *highway robbery,* LL.

wegtwiflung f. *branching of roads,* WW 179¹⁶. [=-twislung]

wegu f. *vehicle,* GD314²⁵.

wegur (WW143¹³)=wīgār

wehsan=weaxan

wehte pret. 3 sg. of weccan.

wei v. wā; weig=weg

wel I. adv. (comp. bet) 'WELL,' *abundantly, Æ,CP : very, very easily, very much : fully, quite, Æ :* nearly : *pleonastic (as in ēac* w.=*also), sometimes=indeed, to be sure.* tō w. *too well.* w. nēah *nearly, almost.* w. hwǣr, w. gehwǣr *for the most part, nearly everywhere.* wella *alas!* (cp. wā lā). II.=wæl. III.=wiell. IV.=wiel

wel-=hwel-, wæl-, weal-, wiel-

wela (a, ea, eo) m. '*weal,*' *prosperity, happiness, riches* (often in pl.), *BH,Bo,Bl,G, Gen; AO,CP.*

Wēland m. *the Smith-God, Northern Vulcan.*

welbescēawod *discreet, considerate,* RB, WW.

welboren '*well-born,*' *noble, Æ,LG.*

welcn=wolcen

weldǣd (ē²) f. *good deed, benefit, kindness, Ph.* ['*weldede*']

weldōn anv. *to do well,* CP : *benefit, satisfy, please,* MtL15¹⁵.

weldōnd (ōe) m. *benefactor,* GL,DR.

weldōnnes f. *well-doing, kindness,* DR13¹⁷.

weleg=welig

welena gp. of wela.

weler (eo) mf. *lip, Æ,*CP.

weleðig *rich,* ANS128·299.

welfremming f. *good deed, benefit,* DR187¹⁷.

welfremnes f. *benefit,* DR.

welg=welig

welga=weliga wm. of welig adj.

welgā interj. *hail!* WW25²³.

welgeboren=welboren

welgecwēme *well-pleasing,* SPs,VH.

welgecwēmedlic *well-pleasing*, SPs.
welgecwēmnes f. *favour*, DR.
welgedōn *well-done, good, beneficent*, CP.
welgehwǣr=welhwǣr
welgelīcian *to please well* : *be well pleased*, AO,CVPs.
welgelīcwirðe *well pleased, acceptable*, VPs 118¹⁰⁸.
welgelīcwirðnes f. *good pleasure*, VPs 140⁷.
welgespring=wyllspring
welgestemned *having a good voice*, ANS 84·6.
welgetȳd *well-instructed*, ES 39·354.
welgewende *thriving*, MFH 178.
welgian=weligian
welhǣwen *beautifully coloured*, CP 411²⁸.
welhrēowlīce=wælhrēowlīce
welhwā †pron. *each, every.*
±welhwǣr adv. (*nearly*) *everywhere*, CP.
±welhwilc† (e, y) pron. *each, any, nearly every.*
welig I. *well-to-do, rich, prosperous*, AO,B, WW; CP. ['*wealy*'] II. m. '*willow*,' LCD, LG.
±weligian *to be prosperous, abound* : *enrich*, Æ. [v. '*awelgien*']
weligstedende (woegl-) *making rich*, DR 98⁹.
well=(1) will; (2) wel; wella=wiella
wellā=wā lā; welle=wille
wellende (VPs)=willende pres. ptc. of willan.
wellere *bosom, fold, hollow*, WW.
wellibbende (y²) *living well, well conducted, reputable*, CP.
wellīcian *to please well*, MFH 178.
wellīcung f. *agreeableness*, EPs 68¹⁴.
wellīcwyrðe (u³) *well-pleasing*, BCPs 146¹⁰.
wellyrge (GL)=wælcyrige
welm(a)=wielm(a)
-welm v. fōt-w.; Wēlond=Wēland
welor=weler; welp=hwelp
welrēab (Ep, Erf 642)=wælrēaf
welrūmlīce adv. *graciously*, DR.
welrūmmōd *gracious*, DR 12²⁰.
wel-spring, -sprynge (CP)=wyll(ge)spring
welstincende *fragrant*, CP 439³³.
welswēgende *melodious*, SPs 150⁵.
welt, welð=wielt, wielð pres. 3 sg. of wealdan, weallan.
welðungen† *honoured, in high repute.*
weluc=weoloc
welung f. *revolution* (*of a wheel*), OEG 28³⁰. [wielwan]
welweorðe *of high esteem*, LCD 3·432'.
welwilled-=welwillend-
welwillende *well-wishing, benevolent, kindly, good*, Æ,Chrd; CP. ['*well-willing*']
welwillendlīce *benevolently, lovingly, kindly.*

wel-wille(n)dnes, -wilnes f. *benevolence, good-will, kindness*, Æ. ['*wellwillingness*']
wel-wyll-, -wylle(n)d-=welwillend-
welwyrcend m. *well-doer*, BL 137¹⁴.
welwyrcende *well-doing*, AS.
wem=wamm
wēman *to sound, be heard*, AN 740 : *announce*, AN 1480 : (±) *persuade, convince, lead astray.*
wēmend m. *herald, declarer*, EL 880.
wēmere m. *procurer*, WW 171²⁸.
±wemman (æ) *to defile, besmirch, profane, injure, ill-treat, destroy*, BH,Lk,LL,Ps; Æ, CP : *abuse, revile.* [v. '*wem*,' '*awem*']
+wemmedlic *corruptible*, ÆL 2·348⁸. adv. -līce, WW.
+wemmednes f. *defilement*, Æ.
±wemmend m. *adulterer, fornicator*, OEG.
+wemmendlic *seducing, corrupting*, OEG 2912.
±wemming m. *defilement, blemishing, spoiling*, OEG : (+) *profanation.* ['*wemming*']
+wemmodlīce (æ) adv. *corruptly*, WW 89².
wemnes=wemmednes
wen=(1) wynn; (2) wenn
wēn I. fm. (n?) *belief, hope, opinion, expectation, supposition*, Bo : *probability*, B : *estimation.* w. is ðæt *perhaps*, Bl,CP : *name of the rune for* w. ['*ween*'] II.= wǣgn
+wēn *to bend, twist*, NC 297 (A 14·139).
wēna m. *hope, opinion, expectation, idea, fancy*, CP.
±wēnan (w. g. or a.) *to* '*WEEN*,' *fancy, imagine, believe, think*, Æ; CP : *expect, hope*, Æ,AO,CP : *fear* (*for*), *despair* (*of*) : *esteem* : *wonder*, ES 37·191.
wenbȳl m. *boil, carbuncle*, LCD.
wencel I. (i) n. *child*, Bas,GD. ['*wenchel*'] II.=wancol
wend m. *what turns up, an event*, Bo,TC.
+wend=+wind
±wendan *to turn, direct*, Æ,CP : '*WEND*' *one's way, go*, Æ,AO : *return* : *change, alter, vary, restore*, Æ : *happen* : *convert* : *translate*, CP. w. on *to turn against.* [windan]
wēnde pret. 3 sg. of wēnan.
Wendelsǣ mf. *Mediterranean Sea*, AO.
-wenden v. ed-w.
wendend m. *that which turns round*, WW 489¹².
wendende *movable, revolving*, Sc 97⁴.
wendere m. *translator, interpreter*, OEG 5259.
Wendle† mp. *Vandals.*
wendung f. *change, turning, rotation*, CP, Sc. ['*wending*']
+wēne *perhaps*, MkR 14² (oe).

wēnendlic *to be hoped for,* GD 269[14].

wēnere=wægnere

wēnestu=wēnstu; weng=wang

±wenian *to accustom, habituate, inure, train,* Æ,CP : *entertain, treat* : (+) *tame : break off,* '*wean' from, RB.* w. mid wynnum *treat kindly.* w. tō wiste *feast, entertain.*

wēninga=wēnunga

wēnlic *comely,* Æ : '*conveniens,*' MkL. adv. -līce *handsomely,* BF 44[8].

wenn I. mf. '*wen,*' *tumour, Lcd,WW.* II. (K)=wynn

wennan=wenian

wenncīcen n. *little wen,* ZDA 31·46.

wennsealf (wen-) f. *wen-salve, ointment for a tumour,* LCD.

wenspryng m. '*nævus,*' *mole,* WW 451[19].

wēnstu=wēnst ðu, pres. 2 sing. of wēnan.

wensum=wynsum

went pres. 3 sg. of wendan.

Wentas, Wente, Went-Sæte, -Sætas mp. *people of Gwent* (roughly=Monmouth-shire).

wēnð pres. 3 sing. of wēnan.

wēnung f. *expectation, hope, BH*; AO 112[12] : *doubt.* ['*weening*']

wēn-unga, -unge (ǣ) adv. *possibly, perhaps, by chance,* Æ.

wenwyrt f. *crowfoot? lesser celandine? darnel?* LCD.

wēo (RD 57[5])=wōh? or wēa?

wēobed, wēobud=wēofod

wēoce f. *lamp or candle-'wick,' IM.*

wēocs=wēox pret. 3 sg. of weaxan.

wēocson pret. pl. of wacsan (=wascan).

wēocsteall (ES 11·64)=wēohsteall

weocu=wucu

wēod n. *herb, grass, G*; CP : '*weed,' Bo.*

weodewe=wuduwe

wēodhōc m. '*weed-hook,' hoe, Cp*; LL 455,15.

wēodian *to 'weed,' LL* 454,9.

wēodmōnað m. *August,* MEN,MH.

weodo, weodu=wudu

weoduma=weotoma

wēodung f. '*weeding,' WW* 105[3].

weofan (VPs)=wefan

wēofod (e[2]) nm. *altar, CP,Mt,RB.* ['*weved*']

wēofodbōt f. *fine for injuring a priest, which was applied in support of the altar,* v. LL 2·276.

wēofodheorð (wībed-) m. *altar-hearth,* GD.

wēofodhrægl (wīgbed-) n. *altar-cover,* BH 90[2].

wēofod-scēat (Æ), -scēata m. *altar-cloth.*

wēofodsteall m. *place of the altar,* LL (254n).

wēofod-ðegn, -ðēn m. *altar-attendant, priest.*

wēofodðēnung f. *altar-service,* LL 380,2.

wēofodwiglere (wīgbed-) m. *soothsayer,* WW 108[10].

+weofu pl. of +wef.

wēofud=wēofod

weofung f. *weaving,* WW 490[38].

wēog=wīg

weogas=wegas nap. of weg.

wēoh=wīg

wēohse=wēox pret. 3 sg. of weaxan.

wēohsteall m. *place of the altar, sanctuary, choir,* LL.

weol=weoll; weol- (A)=wel-

weolc I. pret. 3 sg. of wealcan. II.=weoloc

weolcn=wolcen

weolc-rēad, weolcen-=weolocrēad

weold pret. 3 sg. of wealdan.

weoll pret. 3 sg. of weallan.

weolm=wielm

weolme (=ea) f. *choice, pick of one's fellow-creatures,* CR 445.

weoloc (e, i, y) m. '*whelk,' cockle, murex, BH,Gl* : (*purple*) *dye from the murex.*

weolocbasu *purple,* GL.

weolocrēad *shell-fish red, scarlet, purple,* BH,GL.

weolocscyll (e[3]) f. *whelk, cockle, shell-fish,* BH.

weoloctælg m. *purple dye,* WW. [telg]

weolt pret. 3 sg. of wealtan.

weoning (WW 234[22])=meoning

wēop pret. 3 sg. of wēpan.

wēop-=wēp-; weor=wer I.

weorad=werod

weorc (e, o) n. 'WORK,' *labour, action, deed,* Æ,CP : *exercise* : (†) *affliction, suffering pain, trouble, distress* (v. JAW 52) : *forti-fication.* weorcum *with difficulty.*

+weorc n. *work, workmanship, labour, con-struction : structure, edifice,* Æ : *military work, fortification.*

weorc- v. also wyrc-.

weorccræft m. *mechanics,* OEG 55[6].

weorcdǣd (oe[1], ē[2]) f. *action, operation,* DR 125[18].

weorcdæg m. *work-day,* CM,RB.

weorce I.† adj. *painful, bitter, difficult, hard.* II. adv. *hardly, with difficulty,* JUL.

weorcful *active,* Sc 169[1] : *industrious,* OEG 55[6].

weorcgerēfa m. *foreman, overseer,* Æ.

-weorcheard, -weorclic v. un-w.

weorchūs (e) n. *workshop,* WW.

+weorclic *pertaining to work,* OEG 1042.

weorcmann (e) m. '*workman,' Bo,LG.*

weorcnȳten n. *working cattle,* LL 26n.

weorcrǣden f. *corvée-work,* EC 377[1].

weorcsige m. *success in work,* LCD 1·388'.

weorcstān m. *hewn stone*, Æ.

weorcsum *painful*, GEN 594.

weorcōēow† mf. *servant, slave*, GEN.

weorcuhta m. *hour of matins on a non-festival day*, NC332 (cp. mæsseuhta).

weorcum v. weorc.

weorcwyrðe *fit for work, able-bodied*, MFH 178.

weord=wyrd

weordungdæg (WW 206³²)=weorðungdæg

weored=werod I.; **weoreld**=woruld

weoren pp. of weosan.

weorf n. *beast of burden* (v. CC129), *cattle*.

weorf-=hweorf-

weorfemeoluc? f. *milk from wild cattle?* LCD 102a (MS ðeorfe-).

weorftord (-oruf-) m. *dung of cattle*, PPs 112⁶.

weorht=worht pp. of wyrcean.

+**weorht**=+wyrht; **weorian**=werian

weorld (BL)=woruld; **weorm**=wyrm

weormian=wearmian; **weorn**=worn

weornan=wiernan

±**weornian** (u) *to pine away, become weak, fade, wither, destroy*, Æ.

weorod=werod I. and II.

weorold=woruld

+**weorp** n. *throwing, dashing, tossing*, AN 306 : *what is thrown up*.

±**weorpan** (o, u, y) **I.** sv³ *to throw, cast, cast down, cast away*, Bo,G; Æ,AO,CP : *throw off, out, expel* : *throw upon* : *open*, ÆL : *drive away*, Jn : *sprinkle*, B,Lcd : *hit*, Bo : (+) *reach by throwing*, CP. w. tō handa *to hand over.* w. handa on *lay hands on (a person)* : (w. d. pers.) *charge with, accuse of.* ['*warp*'] **II.**=wierpan

weorpere m. *thrower, caster*, Rd 28⁷. ['*warper*']

weorpian *to pine away*, ERPs 38¹².

weorras (Cp 161c)=wearras, nap. of wearr.

weort=wyrt; **weorteard**=ortgeard

weorð I. (e, ea, i, o, u, y) n. '*worth,*' *value, amount, price, purchase-money, ransom*, AO,G,VPs; CP. **II.** (ie, o, u, y) adj. *worth*, LL : *worthy, honoured, noble, honourable, of high rank*, Æ,BC,Bo; CP : *valued, dear, precious*, AO,CP : *fit, capable.* **III.**=worð I.

±**weorðan³** (u, y) *to become, get, be* (passive auxiliary), *be done, be made*, CP : *happen, come to pass, arise, take place, settle* : (+) impers. *get on with, please, agree*, AO,Chr : *think of, occur to.* ['WORTH,' '*i-worth*']

weorðe=weorð, wierðe

weorðere m. *worshipper*, JnL.

weorðful (u¹) *worthy, honourable, honoured, glorious, good*, B,G,Chr,Lcd. ['*worthful*']

weorðfullic (u) *worthy, honoured, honourable, distinguished*, CP. adv. -līce, AO.

weorðfulnes f. *dignity, honour*, AO.

weorðgeorn *desirous of honour, high-souled.*

±**weorðian** (o, u, y) *to esteem, honour, worship, distinguish, celebrate, exalt, praise*, AO,CP : *adorn, deck* : *enrich, reward.* ['WORTH,' '*i-wurthi*']

-**weorðiend** v. rōd-w.

weorðig=worðig

weorðlēas (u) *worthless*, WW130²⁰.

weorðlic (u, y) *important, valuable, splendid*, Æ 'O,Chr,Jul : *worthy, estimable, honourable, distinguished, exalted*, Bo,Chr : *fit, becoming.* adv. -līce. ['*worthly*']

weorðlicnes f. *worthiness, honour, estimation.*

weorðmetednes (u¹) '*adinventio,*' SPs 76¹².

weorð-mynd, -mynt (u) fmn. *honour, dignity, glory*, AO,CP : *mark of distinction.*

weorðnes (e, ie, o, u, y) f. *worth, estimation* : *splendour, rank, honour* : *integrity.*

weorðscipe (o, u) m. *worth, respect, honour, dignity, glory*, Æ; AO,CP : *advantage, good* : *distinction (in behaviour)*, LL. ['*worship*']

weorððearfa (u¹, y¹) *poor man*, BK 12.

weorðung f. *honouring, distinction, honour, glory*, CP,LG : *celebration, worship*, Æ : *excellence* : *ornament.* ['*worthing*']

weorðungdæg m. *day for bestowal of honours or offices, festival*, BK 23.

weorðungstōw f. *place of worship, the Tabernacle*, Æ.

weoruc=weorc; **weorud**=werod

weoruf=weorf; **weoruld**=woruld

wēos gs. and nap. of wēoh.

weos-=wes-

weosnian=wisnian

weot-=wit-; **weotod**=witod

wēoðel=wēðel, wædl

weoðerweard=wiðerweard

weoðo-, wēoðo-=wiðo-, wiðo-

wēox pret. 3 sg. of weaxan.

weoxian *to cleanse?* A 9·261,262.

±**wēpan**⁷ *to* '*weep,*' *complain, bewail, mourn over, deplore*, Æ,BH,CP,G,MH.

wēpen=wǣp(e)n

wēpende adj. '*weeping,*' Æ,BH,Ps.

wēpendlic *deplorable, mournful*, CHR. adv. -līce.

wēpman=wǣpnedmann

wēpn, wēpned=wǣpen, wǣpned

wēpnian=wǣpnian

wer I. m. *male being* : *man* : *husband*, Æ, AO : (†) *hero.* ['WERE'] **II.** m. *the legal money-equivalent of a person's life, a man's legal value* (=wergild), LL. **III.** m. '*weir,*' *dam, fish-trap*, CP,Ct; Mdf : *catch, draught.* [werian] **IV.** (or were?) *troop, band*, WW, ÆL 30¹⁹⁵.

wĕr=wǣr II.; **weran**=werian
werbēam m. *warrior*, Ex 486.
wer-borg, -borh m. *pledge for the payment of* '*wergild*,' LL.
werc (GL,VPs)=weorc
wercan=wyrcan
wercyn n. *human race, tribe*, RIM 61.
werdan=wierdan; **were**=wer
wĕre (M)=wǣre II.
wered=werod; **wĕreg**=wĕrig
weregan (KGL)=wiergan
werfǣhð f. *feud by which* '*wer*' *is incurred, breach of the peace*, LL.
werfan=hwierfan
werg=(1) wearg; (2) wyr(i)g
wergan (A)=(1) wiergan; (2) werian I.
wĕrgan wk. ds. of wĕrig.
wergeld=wergild; **wergend**=weriend
wĕrgenga=wǣrgenga; **wergian**=wiergan
±**wĕrgian** *to* '*weary*,' *exhaust, be or become tired*, BH,GD; Æ,AO,CP.
wergild (æ[1], e[2], i[2], y[2]) n. *compensation, value of a man's life* (v. LL 2·731). ['*wergeld*']
wergildðēof m. *thief who might be redeemed by payment of his* '*wergild*,' BC,LL. ['*wergeldthief*']
wergnes=weargnes
wergulu f. *crab-apple*, LCD 3·34[14] (v. BTs and MP 24·220).
wĕrgum dsmn. of wĕrig.
wergyld=wergild
werhād m. *male sex, virility, manhood*, Æ.
werhbrǣde=weargbrǣde
werhta=wyrhta
wĕrl=wĕrig
±**werian** (æ) **I.** *to guard, keep, defend*, AO : *ward off, hinder, prevent, forbid* : *restrain* : *occupy, inhabit*, GU 322 : *dam up*, CP 469[2]. ['WERE'] **II.** *to clothe, cover over* : *put on*, '*wear*,' *use*, AO,Chr,LL : *stock* (*land*). **III.** (+) *to make an alliance*, BH 52[19].
wĕrian=wĕrgian
weriend m. *defender*, Æ,W.
werig=wearg, wyrig
wĕrig '*WEARY*,' *tired, exhausted, miserable, sad*, AO,CP : *unfortunate*. [wōr]
werigcweðan=wyrgcweðan
werigen=werian
werigend=weriend
wĕrigferhð† adj. *weary, cast down*.
wĕrigian=wĕrgian
wĕrigmōd† *weary, cast down*.
werignes=wyrignes
wĕrignes f. '*weariness*,' BH.
werilic=werlic; **wĕrines**=wĕrignes
wering f. *weir, dam*, CP 277[8].
werlād f. *clearing by the oaths of a number of men according to a man's* '*wer*,' LL.
werlēas *without a husband*, LL.

werlic *male, masculine*, ÆGR : *manly* : *marital*. adv. -līce, Æ.
wĕrloga=wǣrloga; **werm**-=wearm-
wermǣgð† f. *tribe, nation*, GEN.
wermet n. *man's measure, stature*, WW.
wermōd m. *wormwood, absinthe*, Æ.
wern-=wearn-, wiern-
werna (Cp)=wrenna
wernǣg(e)l m. (*man's nail?*), *wart, tumour*, Æ. ['*warnel*']
werod (eo[1], e[2]) **I.** n. [nap. werodu, werod] *throng, company, band, multitude*, BL,Cp, G; Æ : *host, army, troop, legion*, Æ,AO. ['*wered*'] **II.** *sweet*, Æ. **III.†** n. *sweet drink, mead*.
werodian *to grow sweet*, BO 51[4].
+**werodlǣcan** (e[2]) *to make sweet or pleasant*, SC 196[5].
werodlēst f. *lack of fighters*, EL 63.
werodlīce adv. *sweetly*, CM 887.
werodnes f. *sweetness, pleasantness*, Æ.
werold=woruld
wĕron (M)=wǣron pret. pl. of wesan.
weroð=waroð
werp f. *recovery* (*from sickness*), CP 457[16]. [=wyrpe]
werpan=weorpan
werrēaf n. *civil clothing*, CHRD.
werrest (BL)=wierrest
werscipe=wǣrscipe
werse, **werst**=wierse, wierrest
werstede m. *place of a weir*, EC 246[10].
wert (KGL)=wyrt; **werte**=wearte
wer-tihtle, -tyhtle f. *charge involving the penalty of* '*wer*,' *homicide*, LL.
werð=wierð pres. 3 sg. of weorðan.
werðēod† f. *folk, people, nation*.
werōnes (K)=weorōnes; **werud**=werod
weruld=woruld; **wĕrun** (NG)=wǣron
werwulf (-rew-) m. '*werewolf*,' *fiend*, LL.
wes (VPs)=wæs pret. 3 sg. of wesan.
wēsa m. *drunkard*, WW 84[5]. [wōs]
wesan anv. pres. 1 sg. eom, bēo, 2 eart, bist, 3 is, bið; pl. sind(on); bēoð; pret. wæs, wǣron; subj. pres. sīe, sȳ, bēo; sīn, bēon; pret. wǣre, wǣren *to* '*BE*'* : *happen*. v. also bēon.
+**wesan** *to strive, contend*, SOL 181. [cp. +wosa]
±**wēsan** *to soak, macerate* : *ooze*, LCD : *dye*, OEG 5196. ['*weese*']
wesand=wesend; **wesc**=wæsc
wēse *moist, macerated*, LCD 3·292[6]. [wōs]
wesend (eo) m. *bison*, GL.
wesendhorn m. *bison's horn*, TC 536[1].
wesendlīce *essentially*, GD 336; 337.
wesing f. '*confectio*,' '*debilitatio*.' v. OEG 1857.

wesle, weosule (Gl) f. 'weasel,' Æ,LL.
+wesnes f. dissension, BH274⁵.
wesp=wæps
west adv. westwards, 'west,' in a westerly direction, Bo,Chr,Ct,Ma; AO.
westan, westane adv. from the west, Gen, Lcd; AO. be westan (prep. w. d.) west of. ['westan']
±wēstan to lay waste, ravage, AO,PPs. ['weste']
westanhealf=westhealf
westannorðan north-west (wind), OEG.
westansūðan south-west, AO.
westansūðanwind m. south-west wind, CVPs 77²⁶.
westanweard westward, AA38¹⁶.
westanwind m. west wind, AO17¹⁵.
West-Centingas mp. people of West Kent, CHR999.
westdǣl m. west quarter, western part, Bl, VPs; AO. ['westdeal']
West-Dene mp. West Danes, B.
wēste waste, barren, desolate, deserted, uninhabited, empty, B,BH,G,VPs. wēste land waste land, desert, EHR1912. ['weste']
westem (VPs)=wæstm
westema v. westerne
wēsten I. nmf. waste, wilderness, desert, Æ, AO,CP. II. adj. waste, desolate, Æ.
westende m. 'west end,' AO,Chr.
wēstengryre m. terror of the desert, Ex117.
wēstensetla m. hermit, anchorite, MH,RB.
wēstenstaðol m. waste place, RUIN28.
westenwind=westanwind
wēstern (LG; 'western')=wēsten
westerne 'western,' westerly, BH,Chr,Gl. wester(r)a more westerly; westema, westmest (AO) most westerly.
westeweard=westweard
westhealf f. west side, AO,Chr. ['westhalf']
wēstig (oe) waste, deserted, desert, NG,RG. ['westy']
westlang adv. extending westwards, KC.
westm (VPs)=wæstm
westmearc f. western boundary, OET484.
westmest (AO,BC,KC; 'westmost') v. westerne.
wēstnes f. desolation : desert place, EPs77¹⁹.
westnorðlang adv. extending north-west-wards, AO22¹⁷.
westnorðwind m. north-west wind, WW.
westra (BC; 'wester')=westerra; v. westerne.
westrīce n. western kingdom, AO,CHR.
westrihtes (y²) adv. due west, westwards, AO.
westrodor† m. western (=evening) sky.
westsǣ f. western sea, AO,BH.

West-Seaxe, -Seaxan mp. West Saxons : Wessex.
westsūðende m. south-west extremity, AO8²³.
westsūðwind m. south-west wind, WW.
westu=wes ðu, 2 pers. imperat. of wesan.
West-Wēalas mp. Cornishmen, CHR.
westwe(a)rd I. adv. westwards, Chr,Lcd. ['westward'] II. adj. westerly, AO,Ct.
westweg m. western way, PPs74⁶.
westwind m. 'west wind,' BH458¹⁷.
wesule=wesle
wēt I. pres. 3 sg. of wēdan. II. adj.=wæt
wet-, wēt-=wæt-, wæt-
weterēdre=wæterædre
+wetfæstan=+wedfæstan
wetma=wituma
wēðan to assuage, make calm, PPs106²⁸.
wēðe sweet, mild, pleasant, BH,CR.
weðel swathe, bandage, WW22¹⁴.
wēðel=wēðl, wædl; wēðelnes=wædelnes
weðer I. m. 'wether' sheep, ram, Æ,GD. ᶜ II.=weder I.
weðerwynde=wiðewinde; wēðl=wædl
±wēðnes f. suavity, mildness, DR,PPs.
wex (VPs)=weax; wexe=weax
wēxon=wēoxon pret. pl. of weaxan.
wh-=hw-
wī I.=wīg. II. (K)=weg
wiaht (K)=wiht
wiarald, wiaruld (K)=woruld
wibba m. crawling thing, beetle, WW121²⁵.
wībed (VPs)=wēofod
wiber=wifer; wibil (GL)=wifel
wībora=wīgbora
wīc nf. dwelling-place, lodging, habitation, house, mansion, B,BH,Gen; CP : village, town, Bl,Mk : in pl. entrenchments, camp, castle, fortress : street, lane : bay, creek. ['wick'; v. Mdf]
wīc-=wuc-
±wīcan¹ to yield, give way, fall down, B,Ex.
wīcbora=wīgbora
wicca m. I. wizard, magician, soothsayer, astrologer, LL,WW. ['witch'] II.=wicga
wicce (y) f. 'witch,' Æ,OEG.
wiccecræft m. 'witchcraft,' magic, OEG,LL.
wiccedōm m. witchcraft, BK20; HL11¹²³. ['witchdom']
wiccian to use witchcraft, LL. ['witch']
wiccræft (CRA70)=wiccecræft? or wicg-cræft (skill with horses)? (BT).
wiccung f. enchantment, LL. ['witching']
wiccungdōm m. witchcraft, DA121.
wicdæg=wucdæg
wice I. mf. 'wych'-elm, Gl,Lcd. II. (Chr, BH)=wuce. III.=weoce
wīce f. office, function, Æ : officer, CHR1120. ['wike']
wīceard m. dwelling-place, GU907.

wīceng=wīcing
wīcfreoðu f. *protection of a dwelling*, GNE129.
wīcg (y) n. *horse*, B (v. rare in prose).
['widge']
wīcga m. *insect, beetle*, LCD,WW.
wīcgefēra (CHR897A)=wīcgerēfa
wīcgerēfa m. *bailiff, reeve of a 'wīc' or vill*,
CHR897BCD : '*publicanus*,' *tax-gatherer*,
WW.
wicgung=wiccung
wīcherpað m. *a public road to a 'wīc'* (BT),
KC3·418²⁶.
±wīcian *to dwell, lodge, rest in*, WW; Æ,
AO : *encamp, bivouac*, CP : *harbour,
anchor*, AO. ['wick']
wīcing m. *pirate, viking*, AO.
wīcingsceaðe f. *piracy*, GL.
wīcnera, wīcnere (Æ) m. *steward, bailiff, A,
ZDA.* ['wickner']
wīcnian *to attend upon*, Æ,RB127³.
wīcscēawere m. *provider of a home*, BL163¹².
wīcsteall m. *camping-place*, EX92.
wīcstede† m. *dwelling*, B.
wīcstōw f. *dwelling-place, residence : camp,
encampment*, Æ,AO.
wīctūn m. *vestibule, court*, PPs.
wicðēn=wucðegn; wicu=wucu; wid=wið
wīd 'WIDE,' *vast, broad, long*, Æ; AO,CP.
w. and sīd *far and wide*. tō wīdan ealdre,
tō wīdan fēore, wīdan fyrhð *for ever*.
wīdan adv. *from far* (v. also wīd), KC.
['widen']
wīdbrād *wide-spreading*, GEN643.
wīdcūð adj. *widely known, celebrated*, Æ.
wīde (once+) adv. *widely, afar, far and
'wide*,' Æ,AO,CP. sīde and w. *far and
wide.* ['WIDE']
wīdefeorh†=wīdeferð
wīdefeorlic (wīder-) *eternal*, WW117²¹.
wīde-ferhð†, -fyrhð I. mn. (*long life*), *long
duration, long time.* II. adv. *always.*
wider-=wiðer-
+wi-dere pl. -d(e)ru n. *weather (good or bad),
storm, tempest*, AO. [weder]
+widerian (impers.) *to be fine weather*, LL
454,12.
widewe=wuduwe
wīdfǣðme† *ample, extensive*, AN.
wīdfarend m. *wanderer*, CP315⁴.
wīdfeorh=wīdeferhð
wīdfērende† *coming from afar.*
wīdferhð=wīdeferhð
wīdfloga† m. *wide-flier (of a dragon)*, B.
wīdfolc n. *great nation*, GEN1638?
wīdgal=wīdgil
wīdgangol *wandering, roving*, CP.
wīdgenge *wandering (monk)*, OEG58¹⁰.
wīd-gil, -gill (e, ie) *wide-spread, broad, extensive*, Æ,CP : *wandering*, GD.

wīdgilnes f. *amplitude, spaciousness*, Æ.
wīdgongel=wīdgangol; wīdgyl=wīdgil
wīdhergan *to extol*, CP439³⁴.
wīdian *to become wider*, GD315.
wīdl mn? *impurity, filth, defilement*, GD,
WW.
wīdland† n. *extensive country*, GEN.
wīdlāst† I. *far-wandering.* II. m. *long
wandering, long way or road*, RD.
±wīdlian *to defile, pollute, profane*, LL,
NG.
±wīdmǣran=±wīdmǣrsian
wīdmǣre *celebrated, well-known*, AO,CP.
±wīdmǣrsian (tr., intr.) *to spread abroad,
divulge*, Æ : *celebrate.*
wīdmǣrsung f. *proclamation*, SC96¹¹.
wīdmērsian=wīdmǣrsian
wīdnes f. *width*, WE60¹⁸.
wīdoban=wiðoban
wīdor=weder; wīdor-=wider-
wīdor comp. of wīd.
wīdrynig *far-flowing*, AN1509.
wīdsǣ mf. *open sea, ocean*, Æ,AO.
wīdsceop adj. *widely distributed*, PA6.
wīdscofen *scattered far and wide*, B936.
wīdscrīðol *erratic, wandering*, CHRD,LL.
wīdsīð† m. *long journey : far-traveller.*
wīdðīl (DR98¹²)=wīdl; widu=wudu
widuw-, widw-=wuduw-
widwegas† mp. *distant regions.*
wiebed=wēofod; wiebel=wifel
wiece=wuce; Wieht=Wiht
wiel (e) m. *slave, servant*, Æ.
wiel- v. also wil-, wyl-.
+wield (i, eo) *power, control*, AO. ['wield']
±wieldan (æ,i,y) *to have power over, control,
CP : tame, subdue, conquer, seize*, CHR,CP :
(+) *compel*, LL265,15 : (+) *temper.* [v.
'WIELD*']
wielde I. (±) (y) *powerful, victorious*, Æ,AO,
GD. II. *in the power of, under the control
of*, Æ.
+wieldend (y) *subduer*, GPH391.
wielding (y) f. *domination, rule*, LPs.
wielede pret. 3 sg. of wielwan.
wielen (i, y) f. *foreign woman, female slave*,
AO.
wielincel n. *little servant, slave*, GPH401.
wielisc (æ, e, ea, i, y) *foreign : British (not
Anglo-Saxon), BC,Chr,LL : 'Welsh' : not
free, servile.* [wealh]
wiell, wiella m., wielle (AO) f. (e, i, y)
'WELL,' *fountain, spring*, CP; Mdf.
[weallan] For comps. v. wyll-.
wielle=wille pres. 3 sg. of willan.
wielm (a, æ, e, eo, i, y) m. *boiling, swelling,
sur , billow, current, stream*, AN,B,BH,CP,
*Jul : burning, flame, inflammation : fervour
ardour, zeal*, CP. ['walm'; weallan]

wielma (e) m. *inflammation*, LCD 31a (v. A 46·227).

wielmfȳr (æ) n. *blazing fire*, CR 932.

wielmhāt (y) *burning hot*, Gen 2584. [v. '*walm*']

wieln-=wiln-

wielt I. pres. 3 sg. of wealdan. II.=wielð

wielð pres. 3 sg. of weallan.

wien-=win-

wieoldon=weoldon pret. pl. of wealdan.

±**wierdan**, +wierdlian (e, i, y) *to spoil, injure, destroy, violate, obstruct*, Bo,Cp, LG,Ps. ['*werde*']

wierding (oe, y) f. *bodily injury*, DR, LL 410,3⁵ : *blemish*, OEG 649.

wierdnes (oe) f. *injury, vice*, DR.

wiergan (æ, e, i, iri, yri, y) *to abuse, outlaw, condemn, curse, proscribe*, Æ,CP,G,Gl : *blaspheme*, Æ : *do evil*. [For compounds v. wyrg-, wyrig-] ['*wary*']

wiergen v. grund-w.

wiernan (e, i, y) (w. g. of thing and d. of pers.) *to withhold, be sparing of, deny, refuse, reject, decline*, AO,CP : *forbid, prevent from*. ['WARN']

wiernung (æ) f. *refusal*, LL 152,3. ['*warning*']

wierp m. *cast, throw, shot, blow*, AO.

±**wierpan** (æ, y) *to recover from illness, get better*, CP.

wierpð pres. 3 sg. of weorpan.

wierrest (superl. of yfel) '*worst*,' Æ,Bl,Bo, CP,G,Ps.

wiers (y) adv. 'WORSE,' CP.

wiersa m., wierse fn. (comp. of yfel 'WORSE,' CP. [For comps. v. wyrs-]

wierst=wierrest

wierð pres. 3 sg. of weorðan.

wierðe (Bl,CP,G; '*wurthe*')=weorð

wiese=wīse pl. of wīs.

wieste=wiste, v. witan.

wiet-, wiet-=wit-, wīt-

wiexð pres. 3 sg. of weaxan.

wīf n. *woman, female, lady*, BH,Bl,Cp,LG; Æ,AO,CP : '*wife*,' Bo,Mt; Æ,AO,CP.

+**wīf** I. n. *fate, fortune*. [wefan] II. n. *a disease of the eye*, LCD 3·292².

wīfcild n. *female child*, BH 76⁹.

wīfcynn n. *womankind, female sex*, BH,Bl. ['*wifkin*']

wīfcȳððu f. *company of a woman? intercourse with a woman?* CHR 755A.

+**wīfe**=+wīf

wīfel I. m. '*weevil*,' *beetle*, Cp,Rd. II. (HGl; '*wifle*')=wifer

wīfer *missile, arrow, dart*, v. OEG 1103.

wīfērend (KGL)=wegfērend

wīffæst *bound to a wife, married*, LL 348,54.

wīffex n. *woman's hair*, WW. [feax]

wīffrēond m. *female friend*, LkLR 15⁹.

wīfgāl *licentious, unchaste*, CP 453³⁰.

wīfgemǣdla m. *woman's fury*, LCD 122b.

wīfgemāna m. *intercourse with a woman*, LCD 1·336.

wīfgeornes f. *adultery*, MtL 15¹⁹.

wīfgifta fp. *dowry, outfit? marriage?* JUL 38.

wīfhād m. *womanhood*, Æ : *female sex*, Æ.

wīfhand f. *female inheritor, female side*, Ct.

wīfhealf f. *woman's* (*i.e. mother's*) *side*, CHR p 3'.

wīfhearpe f. *timbrel*, CPs 150⁴.

wīfhīred n. *nunnery*, GD 27⁸.

wīfhrægel n. *woman's clothing*, GD 212¹⁰.

±**wīfian** *to take a wife, marry* (*of the man*), Æ,Bo,LL. ['*wive*'; '*i-wive*']

wīflāc n. *cohabitation, fornication*, LL.

wīflēas *unmarried*, LL (190⁸). ['*wifeless*']

wīflēast f. *lack of women*, ÆL 10²¹⁶.

wīflic *womanly, feminine, female*, AO,BH, Gl. adv. -lice. ['*wifely*']

wīflufu† f. *love for a woman*.

wīfmann (o²) m. '*woman*,' Æ,AO,BH,LG; CP : *female servant*.

wīfmyne m. *love for a woman*, GEN 1861.

-wifre v. gange-w.

+**wīfsǣlig** *fortunate*, WW 496⁸.

wīfscrūd n. *woman's clothing*, ÆP 142; TC 530.

wift=weft

wīfðegn m. *procurer*, WW.

wīfðing n. *marriage, cohabitation*, LCD,LL. ['*wifthing*']

±**wīfung** f. *marrying* (*of the man*), *wedlock*, Æ.

wig (KGL)=weg.

wig I. n. *strife, contest, war, battle*, Æ,AO, CP : *valour* : *military force, army*, Æ. II. (wīh, wēoh)† n. *idol, image*.

wiga m. *fighter*, An,Men : *man*. ['*wye*']

wīgan¹ *to fight, make war*, Æ,B.

wīgār m. *spear, lance*, WW 143¹². [wīg, gār]

wīgbǣre *warlike*, WW 193¹⁸.

wīgbealu n. *war-bale*, B 2046.

wīgbed=wēofod

wīgbill n. *sword*, B 1607.

wīgblāc *bravely caparisoned*, Ex 204.

wīgblēd? m. *luck in war*, RIM 26 (wilbec).

wīgbora m. *fighter*, ÆGR 27¹⁶.

wīgbord† n. *shield*, B,Ex.

wīgcræft m. *war-power, art of war*, AO.

wīgcræftig *strong in battle*, B 1811.

wīgcyng=wīcing

wīgcyrm m. *noise of battle*, GEN 1990.

wīgelung=wīglung

wīgend† m. *warrior, fighter*.

wīgende *fighting*, Æ.

wīgfreca† m. *warrior*.

wīgfruma† m. *war-chief*.

wigg=(1) wīg I.; (2) wicg; **wigga**=wicga
wīggebed=wēofod; **wīggend**=wīgend
wīggetāwe fp. *war-gear*, B368. [wīg, geatwe]
wīggild (wīh-) n. *idol*, DAN,NC.
wīggryre m. *war-terror*, B1284.
wīghaga† m. *war-hedge, phalanx.*
wīgheafola m. *helmet*, B2661.
wīghēap m. *troop of warriors*, B477.
wīgheard *brave in battle*, MA,OEG.
wīghete m. *hostility*, B2121.
wīghryre m. *slaughter, defeat*, B1619.
wīghūs n. *battlement, tower*, AO,CP : *turret (on an elephant's back)*, ÆL25[560].
wīghyrst f. *war-gear, accoutrements*, RUIN 35.
wīgian *to fight*, LL132,6[5].
wīgle n. *divination*, A,OEG. ['wiel']
wīglēoð n. *war-cry, battle-signal*, Ex221.
wīglere m. *soothsayer, wizard*, Æ. ['wielare']
wīglian *to take auspices, divine*, Æ,LCD.
wīglic *warlike*, Ex,Gl. adv. -līce.
±**wīglung** f. *soothsaying, augury, witchcraft, sorcery*, Æ,WW (wī-). [v. 'wiel']
wīgmann m. *warrior*, LL,W.
wīgnoð m. *warfare, war*, WW442[1]?
wigol *divining, foreboding*, WW133[2].
wīgplega† m. *war-play, battle.*
wīgrād (ō) f. *war-path*, GEN2084.
wīgrǣden f. *state of war, battle*, WALD1[22].
wīgsigor† m. *victory in a battle.*
wīgsīð m. *military expedition*, GEN2094.
wīgsmið I. m. *maker of idols*, PPs113[12]. II.† m. *warrior.*
wīgspēd† f. *success in war.*
wīgspere n. *war-spear, dart*, WW143[14].
wīgsteall n. *rampart, entrenchment*, LV,GL.
wīgstrang *mighty in war*, WW360[36].
wīgtrod n. *path of an army*, Ex491 (or ? wigrod *battle-pole*, Sedgefield).
wīgðracu† f. *onslaught in battle, attack.*
wīgðrīst *bold in battle*, JUL432.
wīgwǣgn m. *war chariot*, AO38.
wīgwǣpen n. *weapon of war*, W170[8].
wīgweorðung† (ēoh[1]) f. *idol-worship.*
wīh=wīg; **wīhaga**=wīghaga
wīhian=wōhhian
wihst pres. 2 sg. of weaxan.
wiht I. (u, y) fn. 'WIGHT,' *person, creature, being : whit, thing, something, anything.* II. adv. *at all.* ne w., nǣnig w. *not at all.* nān w. *no whit.* III. (+) f. *weighing, 'weight,'* LCD,LL.
Wiht f. *Isle of Wight*, CHR. [*L.* Vectis]
wihte adv. (d. instr. of wiht) *at all.*
±**wihte** n. 'weight,' LCD.
wihtga=wītega
Wihtland n. *Isle of Wight*, BH,CHR.

wihtmearc f. *plumb-line*, OEG3005.
Wiht-sǣtan, -sǣte mp. *inhabitants of the Isle of Wight*, BH52[4].
Wihtware mp. *inhabitants of the Isle of Wight*, CHR.
wīhūs=wīghūs; **wil**=wiell
wīl n. 'wile,' *trick*, CHR1128.
wil-=wiel-, wigl-, will-, wyll-
wila (y) '*catenarum*,' v. OEG3560n and 7[257].
wīlāwei=wā lā wā
wīlbec m. *stream of tears*, RIM26. [or? winbrec (*war's alarms*) ES65·189]
+**wilbod** n. *commandment*, WW191[22].
wilboda m. *messenger of joy, angel*, GU1220.
+**wilcð** n. *rolling, tossing*, JPs88[10]. [weal-can]
wilcuma I. m. 'welcome' *guest*, B,DHy,Sat. II.=wilcume
wilcume interj. '*welcome!*' GD,LG,WW.
±**wilcumian** *to* '*welcome,*' *greet*, Æ,Mt.
wild? *wild*, OEG4706n.
wild-=wield-
wildæg m. *day of joy*, CR459.
wilddēor n. (occl. dp. wildrum) *wild beast*, Bo,Bl,VPs; AO : *deer, reindeer.* ['wild-deer']
wilddēorcyn n. *species of wild beasts*, RWH57[15].
wilddēoren *like wild beasts, fierce*, Sc99[7].
wilddēorlic *savage*, CP. adv. -līce.
wilde I. 'WILD,' *untamed, uncontrolled*, A, AO : *uncultivated, desert*, AO. II. adv.
+**wilde**=+wielde
wildēar (N), wil(de)dēor, wilder, wildor= wilddēor
wildefȳr n. *lightning*, CHR : *erysipelas*, WW.
wildeswīn m. *wild boar*, ANS129·44.
wildgōs f. *wild goose*, WW364[1].
-wildian v. ā-w.
wildrum v. wilddēor.
wile pres. 3 sg. of willan.
+**wile**=+will
wileg(e)=wilige
wilewīse=wiligwīse
wilfægen *fain, glad*, Æ.
wilfullīce adv. *willingly*, Gl. ['wilfully']
wilgæst (e[2]) m. *welcome guest*, MOD7.
wilgedryht† f. *willing band.*
wilgehlēða m. *intimate companion*, RD15[b]. [hlōð]
wilgeofa=wilgiefa
wilgesīð† m. *willing companion.*
wilgest=wilgæst
wilgestealla=willgestealla
wilgiefa† (eo, i) m. *gracious giver, king.*
wilhrēmig *rejoicing in satisfied desire*, WW 376[26].
wilhrēðig *exultant*, EL1117.
wilia=wiliga; **wilian** (Æ)=wylwan

±**wilian** (y) *to connect, bind*, Sc11⁸; W.
wilie=(1) wilige; (2) wielle
wiliga m., wilige (y) f. *basket*, Æ,*Mk*,*WW*. ['*willy*']
wiligwīse (wile-) *basket-wise*, Bl125²¹.
wiliht (y) *full of willows*, Ct.
wīlisc=wielisc
will (1) n.=willa m.; (2)=wiell
+**will** n. *will, wish, desire, Bo*; AO,CP. ['*i-will*']
will-=wiell-, wyll-
willa m. I. *mind*, '*WILL*,' *determination, purpose*, Æ,CP. sylfes willum *of one's own accord : desire, wish, request : joy, delight, pleasure : desirable thing, valuable.* II. (æ, e, y) *fountain, spring.*
willan (y) anv. pres. 1, 3 sg. ind. and subj. wile, wille, wielle, pret. wolde *to* '*WILL*,' *be willing, wish, desire*, Æ,AO,CP : (denoting habit, repetition) *to be used to*, Æ : *to be about to* : (sign of the future tense) *shall, will*, Æ,CP.
willcuma=wilcuma
willen I. *willing, desirous*, AS63²⁴. II.= wyllen
-**willen** v. dol-w.
wīllendlic (BH)=hwīlwendlic
wīllendlīce adv. '*willingly*,' *WW*; VH.
willes adv. *willingly, voluntarily*, Æ.
willfægen=wilfægen
willgebrōðor mp. *brothers*, Gen971.
willgesīð=wilgesīð
willge-steald, -steall n. *riches, wealth*, Gen 2146? (or ? willgestealla m. *willing companion*).
willgesweostor fp. *sisters*, Gen2607.
willgeðofta m. *pleasant companion*, Gen 2026.
±**willian** *to wish, desire*, Bo,Ps.
willic (y) *from a fountain*, WW. [wiell]
willīce (y) adv. *willingly, voluntarily*, CM. ['*willy*']
willnung=wilnung
willsele m. *pleasant dwelling*, Ph213.
willsīð=wilsīð
willspell† n. *good tidings*, El.
willsum=wilsum
willung f. *desire*, BH. ['*willing*']
willwong m. *pleasant plain*, Ph89.
willwyrdan *to be complaisant*, AB34·10.
wilm=wielm
wiln (Æ)=wielen
+**wilnes** f. *desire, wish*, LPs20³.
±**wilnian** (w. g. or a.) *to wish, long for, desire, will*, *An*,B,*Bo*,*Chr*,CP,*G*; AO : *beg for, supplicate, entreat, petition for : tend towards*, CP. ['*wilne*']
±**wilniendlic** *desirable : capable of desire*, ÆL1⁹⁷ : (+) *unbridled*, ÆH2·398'.

±**wilnung** f. *desire, longing (good or bad)*, AO,CP. ['*wilning*']
wiloc=weoloc
Wil-sǣte, -sǣtan mp. *people o Wilts : Wiltshire*, Chr.
wilsc=wielisc .
wilsīð m. *desired journey*, An,BH.
wilsum(lic) *desirable, delightful : ready, willing, voluntary, spontaneous : devoted.* adv. -līce.
±**wilsumnes** f. *willingness, devotion*, BH : *free-will offering*, LRPs : *vow.*
wilt I. pres. 2 sg. of willan. II. pres. 3 sg. of wealdan.
wiltīðe *having obtained one's wish, glad*, OEG2219³⁵⁸⁹.
wilð pres. 3 sg. of weallan.
wilðegu f. *agreeable food*, An153.
wiluc-=weoloc-
wiluncel (GPH401)=wielincel
wilwendlic=hwilwendlic
wimman, wīman=wīfmann
wimpel (win-) m. '*wimple*,' *covering for the neck, cloak*, Gl.
win=winn
wīn n. '*wine*,' B,Bl,OET,WW; CP. [*L.*]
wīnærn n. *tavern, cellar*, Gl : *drinking hall, wine hall*, B655.
wīnbælg=wīnbelg
wīnbēam m. *vine*, WW.
wīnbeger n. *grape*, NG.
wīnbelg (æ) m. (*leather*) *bottle for wine*, Mt. [v. '*belly*']
wīn-berge, -beri(g)e f. *whortle-berry*, OEG : '*wine-berry*' ('*whimberry*'), *grape*, G,WW.
wīnbōh m. *vine-shoot, vine*, Æ.
wīnbrytta m. *wine-seller, inn-keeper*, WW.
wīnburg† f. *festive city : walled vineyard, castle.*
wīnbyrele m. *inn-keeper*, WW377⁴.
wincan=wincian
wince f. '*winch*,' *pulley*, WW416⁶.
wincel I. m. *corner*, Ct. [*Ger.* winkel] II.=wencel
wincettan *to wink*, PPs34¹⁹.
wincian *to close one's eyes, blink*, Æ,CP. ['*wink*']
winclo=wenclu, nap. of wencel.
wīnclyster n. *cluster of grapes*, OEG18b³.
wīncole *wine vat*, WW439³⁰.
wīncynn n. *wine*, NC333.
wind m. '*WIND*,' *CP*; Æ,AO.
+**wind** n. *winding thing, winding path*, WW : *woven thing.*
windǣddre f. *windpipe*, WW.
±**windæg†** m. *day of strife or toil.*
±**windan³** (tr.) *to* '*WIND*,' *plait, curl, twist : unwind : whirl, brandish, swing : (intr.) turn, fly, leap, start, roll, slip, go*, Æ,CP;

AO : *busy oneself with,* Bo 18¹⁸ : *delay, hesitate,* Gu 265 : *roll up* : *repair,* AS (v. NED).

windbǣre (ē²) *windy,* OEG 43¹⁰.

windbland (o²) n. *blast of wind,* B 3146.

+**winde** *blowing,* BH 202⁷.

-**winde** v. ed-, næddre-, wudu-w.

windecræft=wyndecræft

windel m. *basket,* Æ,*CP.* ['*windle*']

windelocc m. *curly lock,* WW.

windelstān m. *tower with a winding staircase,* (BT),WW 145¹⁷.

windelstrēaw n. '*windle-straw,*' *Lcd,WW.*

windeltrēow n. *oleaster, willow,* WW.

wind-fona, -gefonna m. *winnowing fan,* LkLR.

windfylled *blown down,* LL 452,19.

windgeard m. *home of the winds, sea,* B 1224?

windgereste f. *resting-place of the winds,* B 2456?

windhladen (æ²) *windy,* ANS 120·297.

windig '*windy,*' *breezy, Æ,B,Lcd,Lk.*

windiht (GPH)=wundiht; **windil**=windel

windiuscoful=windscofl

windles gs. of windel.

windong=windung

windrǣs m. *storm of wind,* MkL 4³⁷.

wīndrinc (e, y) m. *wine-drink, wine,* PPs; Æ. [v. '*wine*']

wīndruncen *elate, intoxicated with wine,* Da, RBL.

windscofl f. *fan,* WW 478²⁵.

windsele m.† (*windy hall*), *hell,* Sat.

windswingel f. (*wind-whip*), *fan,* WW 154¹⁰.

windumǣr (wudu-?) f. *echo,* WW 474⁸.

windung I. f. *winnowing, chaff, tares, straw,* NG. II. f. *something woven, hurdle,* WW. ['*winding*']

windwian wv. *to fan,* '*winnow,*' *MH,VPs.*

windwig=windig

windwigceaf n. *chaff,* OEG 2439.

windwigsyfe n. *winnowing-sieve, fan,* WW 141¹¹.

wine† m. [occl. gp. winig(e)a] *friend, protector, lord,* B : *retainer, B,Chr.* ['*wine*']

wīneard=wīngeard

wine-dryhten (i³)† m., gen. -dryhtnes *friendly lord, lord and friend.*

wīnegeard=wīngeard

winegēomor *mourning for friends,* B 2239.

winelēas† *friendless.*

winemǣg† m. *dear kinsman.*

wīnern=wīnærn

winescipe m. *friendship,* Gu,WW.

winestre=winstre

winetrēow f. *conjugal fidelity,* Hu 50.

wineðearfende† *friendless.*

winewincle f. *periwinkle* (*shell-fish*), Lcd, WW.

wīnfæt n. *wine-vessel, wine-vat,* WW.

+**win-ful,** -fullic *laborious, tedious, hard,* BH,GD. adv. -līce.

wīngāl† *flushed or intoxicated with wine.*

wīngeard m. *vineyard, Bl,Bo,Chr* : *vine?* WW. ['*winyard*']

wīngeardbōg m. *vine-tendril,* WW 118³.

wīngeardhōc m. *vine-tendril,* WW 201³¹.

wīngeardhring m. *cluster of fruit,* WW 213¹⁷.

wīngeardseax n. *vine pruning-knife,* WW 234⁴⁴.

wīngeardwealh (wīneard-) m. *worker in a vineyard,* Chrd 68².

wīngedrinc n.(†) *wine-drinking, drinking bout* : *wine,* WW.

wīngerd=wīngeard

wīngetredde=wīntredde

wīngyrd=wīngeard

wīnhāte f. *invitation to wine,* Jud 8.

wīn(h)rēafetian *to gather grapes,* LPs 79¹³.

wīnhūs n. *wine-house, tavern,* Gl,LL.

winiga, winigea v. wine.

wining (eo, y) m. *leg-band, garter,* IM,WW.

wīnland n. *wine-growing country,* Chrd 15²¹. ['*wineland*']

wīnlēaf n. *vine-leaf,* OEG 18B⁷³.

wīnlic *vinous, like wine,* Æ.

wīnmere m. *wine-vat,* WW 439³⁰.

±**winn** n. *toil, labour, trouble, hardship,* BH, Lk : *profit, gain,* PPs : *conflict, strife, war,* Bo,Gen; AO. ['*win,*' '*i-win*']

±**winna** m. *enemy, adversary,* Æ,CP.

winnan³ (y) *to labour, toil, trouble oneself* : *resist, oppose, contradict,* Bo : *fight, strive, struggle, rage,* B,Bl. on w. *attack* : (+) *conquer, obtain, gain, Chr,Met,Nar* : *endure, bear, suffer* : *be ill.* ['*win*'; '*i-win*']

winnend m. *fighter* Gl.

+**winnesful**=+winful

±**winnstow** f. *wrestling place,* WW.

winnung=windung; **winpel**=wimpel

wīnreced† n. *wine hall.*

wīnreopan⁵ (=e²) *to gather in the vintage,* VPs 79¹³.

wīnsǣd *satiated with* '*wine,*' Jud 71.

wīnsæl n. *wine-hall,* Wa 78.

wīnsele† n. *wine-hall.*

wīnsester m. *wine-vessel,* WW 122³¹. [*L.*]

winstōw=winnstōw

winstre I. adj. *left,* Æ,CP. II. f. *left hand.*

winsum=wynsum

wint pres. 3 sg. of windan.

wīntæppere m. *wine-tapster, tavern-keeper,* OEG 2652. [v. '*wine*']

winter mn. [ds. wintra; nap. wintru, winter] '*WINTER,*' Æ,AO,*CP* : pl. (in computing time) *years,* Æ,AO,*CP.*

winterbiter† *bitterly cold.*

winterburna m. *winter-torrent, BC,LG.* ['*winterbourne*']

winterceald† *wintry-cold.*

wintercearig *winter-sad, sad with years?* WA 24.

winterdæg m. '*winter day,*' Bo.

winterdūn f. *hill on which sheep were kept in winter?* LL 453,1.

winterfeorm f. *Christmas feast,* LL 452,21[4].

Winterfylleð *October,* MEN,MH.

wintergegong m. *fate,* WW 406[6].

wintergerīm† n. *number of years.*

wintergetel n. *number of years,* CHR 973A.

wintergewǣde n. *garment of winter, snow,* PH. [v. '*winter*']

wintergew(e)orp n. *snow-storm,* PH 57.

winterhūs n. '*winter-house,*' ÆL 36[98].

winterig=wintrig

winterlǣcan *to grow wintry,* CHR,LCD.

winterlic *wintry, winter,* Æ. ['*winterly*']

winterrǣdingbōc f. *lectionary for the winter,* TC 430[16].

winterrīm=wintergerīm

wintersæt=wintersetl

winterscūr m. *winter-shower,* Ph 18. [v. '*winter*']

winterseld=wintersetl

wintersetl n. *winter-quarters, AO;* CHR. [v. '*winter*']

wintersteal m. *stallion a year old,* LL 378,7.

winterstund f. *winter-hour, short time, year?* GEN 370.

wintersufel n. *food for winter,* LL 450,9. [v. '*winter*']

wintertīd f. *winter-time, Æ,BH.* ['*wintertide*']

wīntīber n. *wine-offering, libation,* WW 130[13] (-tīfer).

+wintīd f. *time of affliction,* GD 210[15].

wintra v. winter.

-wintre v. ān-, twi-w., etc.

+wintred *grown up, adult, CP* : *aged, AO, LL.* ['*wintered*']

wīntredde f. *winepress,* OEG 2647.

wintreg=wintrig

wīntrēow n. *vine, LG;* Æ. ['*winetree*']

wīntrēowig adj. *of the vine,* GPH 390.

wintrig '*wintry,*' AO,Bo.

wīntrog m. *wine-vessel,* MtL 21[33]. [v. '*wine*']

wīntunne f. *wine-cask* (or ? wīntūn *winehouse*), ÆP 19[1]. [v. '*wine*']

wīntwig n. *vine-twig,* WW.

winð pres. 3 sg. of winnan.

wīnðegu† f. *banquet of wine.*

wīnwircend m. *vine-dresser,* Mt pref. 19[3].

+winworuld f. *world of care,* GU 829.

winwringe f. *winepress,* Mt,GL.

wio-=weo-, wi-, wu-; wiohbed=wēofod

wīpian *to* '*wipe,*' *cleanse, Æ,Lcd,RB.*

wīr I.† m. '*wire,*' *metal thread, wire-ornament, B,Rd.* II. (ȳ) m. *myrtle,* GL; Mdf.

wir-=wear-, wier-, wyr-

wīrboga m. *twisted wire?* RD 15[3].

wirc-=weorc-, wyrc-

wird-=wierd-

+wīred *made of wire,* TC 537′.

wirg- (Æ)=wierg-, wyr(i)g-

wīrgrǣfe? f. *myrtle-grove,* WW.

wirian=wiergan

wirig-=wierg-, wyr(i)g-

wirman (WW 399[16])=wyrman

wirpð pres. 3 sg. of weorpan.

wīrtrēow n. *myrtle,* LCD,WW.

wīrtrēowen (y[1], ȳ[2]) adj. *myrtle,* LCD 1·236[1].

wirtruma=wyrtruma

wirð I.=weorð I. II.=wierð pres. 3 sg. of weorðan.

wirðe=worð I.

wīs I. adj. '*WISE,*' *learned, Æ,AO,CP* : *sagacious, cunning* : *sane* : *prudent, discreet, experienced, Æ,AO,CP.* as sb. *wise man, CP.* II.=wīse I.

+wīs=+wiss

wīsa† m. *leader, director.*

wīsan=wesan; wīsan (DAN 35)=wīsian

wīsbōc f. *instructive book?* PPs 138[14].

wīsc- (Æ)=wȳsc-

wīsce n. *meadow liable to floods, BC,KC;* PST 95/98,542. ['*wish*']

wīschere m. *diviner?* ÆL 21[466].

wīsdōm m. '*wisdom,*' *knowledge, learning* : *experience, B,Bo,G,LL;* Æ,CP.

wīse I. f. '*WISE,*' *way, fashion, custom, habit, manner, Æ,CP* : *testamentary disposition* : *business, affair, thing, matter, Æ,CP* : *condition, state, circumstance, AO,CP* : *reason, cause, Æ* : *direction* : *melody,* MEN 70 : *idiom.* II. adv. *wisely.* III. (ȳ) f. *sprout, stalk, Lcd,Rd,WW.* ['*wise*']

wīs-fæst, -fæstlic (PPs) *wise, sagacious, discreet, learned, intelligent.*

+wīsfullīce *knowingly,* GD 95[31].

wīshycgende *wise, sagacious,* B 2716.

wīshȳdig† *wise, discreet, sagacious,* GEN.

±wīsian (w. d. or a.) *to direct, instruct, guide, lead, B;* Æ,CP : *point out, show,* GEN. ['*i-wisse*']

wīslic *certain, sure, true,* PPs. ['*wisly*'] adv. (±) -līce *certainly, truly, Lcd,Lk,PPs* : *moreover.* ['*iwisliche,*' '*wisely*']

wīslic *wise, sagacious, prudent,* BH,W; Æ. AO. adv. -līce, *Bo,CP,Gen,LL,Met.* ['*wisely*']

wisligan=hwistlian

wīsnes f. *teaching,* LCD 3·82[2].

wisnian to dry up, wither, waste away, BL. [weornian]

+**wiss** I. n. what is certain, certainty, surety, Æ. II. adj. certain, sure, trustworthy, BH, Bo,Guth,Nic : knowing. tō (ge)wissan (Æ, OEG), gewissum; mid gewisse especially, certainly, RB,HL. ['wis,' 'i-wis']

wiss-=wis-

wisse=wiste pret. 3 sg. of witan.

wissefa m. wise-souled man, SOL 438?

wissian (Æ,W; 'wis')=wīsian

±**wissian** to direct, instruct, guide, Æ,Gen : point out, show, Æ. ['i-wisse']

wiss-iend, -igend m. governor, director : driver (of chariot), Æ.

+**wisslīce**=+wislīce

wisste=wiste pret. 3 sg. of witan.

wissum (tō) adv. altogether, completely, OEG.

±**wissung** f. showing, instruction, guidance, Æ,LL : certainty : rule, regulation, government, Æ. ['wissing,' 'iwisse']

wist f. being, existence : well-being, abundance, plenty : provision, nourishment, subsistence, food, meal, feast, delicacy, Æ,CP. [wesan]

wiste pret. 3 sg. of witan.

wīstfæstlic=wīsfæstlic

wistful productive, CHR 1112.

±**wistfulgend** m. banqueter, EPs 41⁵.

±**wistfullian** to feast, Æ.

wistfullīce adv. luxuriously, WW 513⁶.

wistfulnes f. good cheer, BAS 50²⁵.

±**wistfullung** f. feasting, OEG.

wistfyllo f. fill of food, B 734.

wistgifende fertile, WW 457²⁵.

+**wistian** to feast, G.

wistl-=hwistl-

+**wistlǣcan** to feast, banquet, G.

wist-mete m., nap. -mettas, sustenance, ÆL 23b⁵⁸².

wiston pret. pl. of witan.

wisōlung=hwistlung

wīswylle wise in purpose, PPs 118⁴⁰.

wīswyrdan to be wise in speech, A 13·38.

wīswyrde prudent in speech, W 72¹⁸.

wit I. pron. 1 pers. (nom. dual), gs. uncer, d. unc, acc. unc(it) we two, B,Mt; CP. wit Æthered Æthered and I. ['wit'] II. (±)=witt

±**wita** (eo, ie, u) m. sage, philosopher, wise man, adviser, councillor, elder, senator (v. LL 2·737), Æ,BH,LG; AO : witness, BH, LG; Æ,CP : accomplice. ['wite'; witan]

±**witan** (eo, y) swv. pres. 1, 3 sg. wāt, 2 wāst, pl. witon, subj. pres. sg. wite, pl. wit-en, -on; pret. sg. wiste, pp. witen to be aware of or conscious of, know, understand, AO,CP : observe, perceive : (+)

ascertain, learn. andan w. dislike. incan w. (tō) to have a grudge (against). ege w. to fear. dōn tō witanne to cause to know, inform. ['WIT*'; 'i-wite']

±**wītan**¹ I. to guard, keep : look after, Lcd, LL. ['wite²'] II. to impute or ascribe to, accuse, reproach, blame, AO,B,Bo. ['wite¹'] III. to depart, go, go out, AO, Met : leave off : pass away, die (often forðgew.), Æ,CP. ['wite³']

wīte n. punishment, torture, plague, injury, Bo,Gen,VPs; CP : penalty, fine, LL : contribution, in money or food, to sustenance of king or his officers, LL 356,69² : woe, misery, distress. ['wite']

wītebend† mf. bonds of torture or punishment, AN.

wītebrōga m. tormenting dread, W.

wītedlīce=witodlīce

wītedōm (BH)=wītegdōm.

wītedōmlic prophetic, GUTH.

wītefæst penally enslaved, TC.

wīt-ega, -(i)ga m. wise man : lawyer, NG : prophet, soothsayer, CP,LG : prophecy. [wītan; 'witie']

wītegeard? m. amphitheatre, v. OEG 3333.

wītegdōm (i²) m. prophecy, prediction : divination, DA.

wītegestre f. prophetess, ÆT 715,Lk 2³⁶.

±**wītegian** to prophesy, predict, Æ,LG; AO. ['witie']

wītegung f. prophecy, divination, Æ,LG. ['witieng']

wītegungbōc f. book of prophecy, ÆL.

wītehrægl n. penitential garb, sackcloth, PPs 68¹¹.

wītehūs n. torture-house, prison, hell : amphitheatre (as place of torture and martyrdom), OEG.

wītel=hwītel

wītelāc† n. punishment.

wītelēas without punishment or fine, LL 360,73⁴. adv. -līce with impunity, TF 109²⁶.

wītelēast f. freedom from punishment or fine, Swt.

wītelic toilsome, carking, MFH 178 : penal, GD 330; 332.

wītelīce (GD 102²⁴)=witodlīce

witenagemōt n. meeting of the wise men, national council, Æ,Chr. ['witenagemot'; wita]

+**wītende** transitory, MFH 165.

wītendlic=wītigendlic

+**wītendlic** transitory, perishable, Æ,CP.

witendlīce=witodlīce

+**wit-endnes** (G), -ennes f. departure, death, BH,MH.

wīterǣden f. punishment, fine, BC,LL. ['witereden']

+**witerian** *to inform*, RWH 135¹⁸. [witter]

witern n. *prison*, WW199³¹. [ærn]

witescræf n. *pit of torment, hell*, SAT691.

wit(e)steng m. *pole used for torture*, OEG.

witestōw f. *place of torment or execution*, BH.

witeswinge f. *scourging, punishment*, GEN 1864.

witeðēow adj. and sbm. *man reduced to slavery by the law*, Ct,LL.

witewyrðe *punishable*, GD 208⁵.

+**witfæst** *of sound mind*, GUTH 66¹⁷.

witg-=witeg-

-**witian** v. be-w., uð-w.

witiendlic=witigendlic; **witig**=wittig

witig-=witeg-

witigende (ByH102²⁶)=+witende

wit-igendlic, -t(i)endlic *prophetic*, OEG.

witiglic *punitive, of punishment*, GD.

witingstōw=witnungstōw

±**witlēas** *foolish, mad*, Lcd,Met. ['witless']

witlēasnes f. *want of intelligence, folly*, OEG 47³. ['witlessness']

±**witlēast** f. *folly, madness*, Æ. [witt]

+**witloca** m. *mind*, MET,CP469².

witmæreswyrt f. *spoonwort?* LCD 12a.

witnere m. *tormentor, torturer*, Æ.

±**witnes** f. *knowledge, 'witness,' testimony*, Bl,Bo,DR,G : *a witness*, CP. nīwa gew. *the New Testament.* ['i-witness']

+**witnian** *to confess*, ÆH 2·124²² (or ? +witnian).

±**witnian** *to punish, chastise, torture, afflict*, Æ,AO,CP.

witnigend m. *punisher*, EPs 78¹¹.

witnung f. *torment, torture, punishment, purgatory*, Æ.

witnungstōw f. *place of punishment, purgatory*, ÆH.

witod=witodlice

witodlic *certain, sure*, LkR 20⁶ (wutud-); adv. and conj. -lice *truly, for, verily, certainly, undoubtedly, indeed, thus, but, and, therefore, wherefore*, Æ,AO,CP. [witan]

-**witol** v. fore-w.

witolnes f. *wisdom*, GD 331¹⁵. [witan]

witon I. pres. pl. of witan. **II.**=wuton

witrod=wigtrod

+**witscipe** m. *evidence, knowledge*, BH. ['witship']

±**witsēoc** *possessed, insane*, Æ.

±**witt** n. *understanding, intellect, sense*, Æ, B,Bo,Lk,Met : *knowledge, consciousness : conscience*, CP. ['wit,' 'i-wit']

+**witt-**=+wit-

witter *wise, prudent*, CHR 1067 D. [ON. vitr]

±**wittig**† *wise*, B,Cra,Ex,LL : *sagacious, reasonable : skilful*, Cra,OEG : *conscious, in one's right mind*, Æ. adv. -lice. ['witty']

wittignes f. *intelligence*, OEG 78 (wytti-).

wittol=witol

witu nap. of wite.

witud=witod

wituma (e, eo, y) m. *dowry* (v. LL 2·739).

witumbora m. *bridesman, paranymph*, OEG 1774.

witungstōw=witnungstōw

witword n. *written evidence, will, covenant*, LL,TC. ['witword']

wið I. prep. (w. a.) WITH, *by, near, against, beside, at, through* : (w. d.) *from (separation), with (opposition), for, in return for, on condition of, beside, near, opposite* : (w. g.) *towards, to, at, against.* w. ēastan (1) adv. *to the east;* (2) prep. *east of.* w. ūp *upwards, above.* w. ðan ðe *because, in consideration of, provided that.* wið...weard prep. (w. a.) *towards.* **II.** conj. *until.*

wiðæftan I. adv. *from behind, behind, after*, AO. **II.** prep. *behind, at*, Æ.

wiðblāwan⁷ *to blow away*, CP439²⁴.

wið-bregdan³, -brēdan³ *to withhold, restrain, withstand, oppose*, Æ,CP : *take away*, GD 203⁵.

wiðcēosan² *to reject*, Ps. pp. wiðcoren *rejected, reprobate, outcast*, BH,MH.

wiðcostian 'reprobare,' EPs 32¹⁰.

wiðcwædenes=wiðcwedennes

wiðcwedennes f. *contradiction*, CHR,Ps.

wiðcwedolnes=wiðercwedolnes

wiðcweðan⁵ *to speak against, contradict, gainsay, oppose, resist*, Æ : *forbid, refuse, deny : reject, renounce*, CP.

wiðcweðenes=wiðcwedennes

wiðdrīfan¹ *to repel, drive off*, PPs.

wiðe-=wiðig-

wiðēadon (N)=wiðēodon pret. pl. of wiðgān.

wiðēastan *eastward, eastwards*, AO.

wiðeftan=wiðæftan

wiðer I. prep. and adv. *against.* **II.** adj. *hostile*, GPH 394. ['wither']

wiðerbersta m. *adversary*, SOL 86⁵.

wiðerbreca (a³, eo³, o³, u³) m. *adversary* : *the devil, Satan.*

wiðerbrocian *to oppose*, CVPs.

wiðerbrōga m. *adversary, the devil*, CR 564.

wiðerbruca=wiðerbreca

wiðercerran *to turn against, prance* (Swt). [cp. wiðercyr]

wiðercora m. *adversary, rebel, apostate, sinner*, Æ.

wiðercoren *rejected, reprobate, wicked*, Æ.

wiðercorennes f. *reprobation*, ÆH 2·290¹⁹.

wiðercwednes (CP143²⁰)=wiðercwidennes

wiðercwedol *opposing, contradicting*, Ps.

wiðercwedolnes f. *contradiction*, GL.

wiðercwedung f. *contradiction*, SPs51⁴.

wiðercweð-=wiðercwed-

wiðercweðan⁵ *to withstand*, LPs.

wiðercwida (y) m. *contradicter*, OEG1893 : *opposer, rebel*, WW110²³.

wiðercwiddian (y³) *to murmur*, LPs40⁸.

wiðercwide m. *contradiction*, PPs : *opposition, resistance*, LL.

wiðercwidel-=wiðercwedol-

wiðercwidennes (e³, y³) *contradiction*, LPs.

wiðercwyd-=wiðer-cwed-, -cwid-

wiðercyr m. *rearing (of a horse)*, EL926.

wiðerdūne (ē³, y³) *narrow? uphill? steep?* (BTs), Mt7¹⁴.

-wiðere v. tō-w.

wiðerfeoht-=wiðfeoht-

wiðerflita m. *opponent, adversary*, AO,CP.

wiðerhabban *to resist*, PPs72²⁰.

wiðerhlinian *to lean against*, GL.

wiðer-hycgende, -hȳdig *refractory, perverse, antagonistic, hostile.* as sb. *rival, adversary.*

wiðerian *to resist, oppose, struggle against*, Æ : *irritate, provoke : be provoked.* ['*wither*']

wiðerlæcan (y¹, ē³) *to deprive*, EPs83¹³.

wiðerlēan† n. *requital : compensation.*

wiðerling m. *opponent, adversary*, EHy4⁷. ['*witherling*']

wiðermāl n. *counter-plea, defence*, CHR1052.

wiðermēde *perverse, antagonistic.*

wiðermēdnes (oe) f. *perversity*, DR : *adversity*, DR.

wiðermēdo f. *antagonism*, GEN : *perversity*, PPs : *adversity*, DR.

wiðermetan⁵ *to compare*, WW.

wiðermōd *unwilling, contrary*, CP212⁷.

wiðermōdnes f. *adversity*, CP83¹⁹.

wiðermoednes (DR)=wiðermēdnes

wiðerrǣde *contrary, opposed, adverse, perverse, rebellious*, Æ : *disadvantageous : disagreeable, unpleasant.*

wiðerrǣdlic *contrary, adverse*, ÆGR264¹.

wiðerrǣdnes f. *opposition, discord, variance, disadvantage, adversity*, Æ.

wiðerræhtes (=rihtes) adv. *opposite*, B 3039.

wiðerriht n. *recompense*, WW118¹².

wiðersaca m. *adversary, enemy*, Mt,RB; Æ : *betrayer : apostate*, Æ. ['*withersake*']

wiðersacian *to renounce, become apostate*, OEG : *blaspheme.*

wiðersacung f. *apostasy*, GL : *blasphemy*, Sc.

wiðersæc I. n. *contradiction, hostility, opposition*, Æ : *apostasy.* [sacan] II. *unfavourable*, LCD97a.

wiðersprecend m. *a contradicter*, CHRD41²⁹.

wiðerstæger *steep*, WW.

wiðerstandan⁶ *to resist*, EPs16⁸.

wiðersteall (a³) m. *resistance, opposition*, Æ.

wiðersȳnes adv. *backwards*, BL93¹⁹.

wiðertalu f. *defence*, ÆH1·530⁶ (v. LL 3·226).

wiðertihtle f. *counter-charge*, LL.

wiðertrod† n. *return, retreat.*

wiðertȳme *troublesome, grievous*, LPs34¹³ : *contrary*, BF174¹.

wiðerweard *contrary, perverse, adverse*, Bo, G : *rebellious, hostile*, Bl; AO,CP : *inconsistent : unfavourable, noxious, bad.* ['*witherward*']

wiðerwearda m. *adversary*, BL,LPs17²⁷.

wiðerweardian (o³) *to oppose*, SPs.

wiðerweardlic *contrary, inimical, perverse*, Æ. adv. -līce.

wiðerweardnes f. *opposition, perversity, arrogance, enmity*, CP; Æ : *adversity, calamity, trouble*, CP. ['*witherwardness*']

wiðerwengel m. *adversary*, ARHy4⁷, RPs 73¹⁰.

wiðerwenning f. *controversy*, Sc146¹⁵. [winnan]

wiðer-werd-, -wi(e)rd-=wiðerweard-

wiðerwinn n. *contest*, OEG2³.

wiðerwinna m. *opponent, rival, adversary, enemy*, Æ,CP; AO. ['*witherwin*']

wiðerwinnan³ *to revolt*, GPH389.

+wiðerwordian=+wiðerweardian

wiðerwyrd=wiðerweard

wiðewinde=wiðowinde

wiðfaran⁶ *to come off, escape*, Ex573.

wiðfeohtan³ *to fight against, rebel*, BH, WW.

wiðfeohtend m. *adversary*, BH,CP.

wiðfēolan³ *to apply oneself to*, BH.

wiðferian† *to rescue, redeem*, PPs.

wiðflita=wiðerflita

wiðfōn⁷ (w. d.) *to grasp at, clutch*, B760.

wiðforan I. prep. *before, in the presence of.* II. adv. *before, previously.*

wið-gān *anv.*, -gangan⁷ *to go against, oppose : pass away, vanish, disappear.*

wiðgehæftan=wiðhæftan

wiðgemetnes f. *comparison*, BH430²⁰.

wiðgeondan prep. *beyond*, Mt3⁵.

wiðgrīpan¹ *to grapple with*, B2521.

wiðgȳnan *to reject*, ÆL23⁵⁴¹.

wiðhabban (æ²) (w. d.) *to oppose, resist, restrain, hold out*, AO.

wiðhæftan *to restrain*, A7·12.

wiðheardian *to harden*, ARSPs94⁸.

wiðhindan adv. *behind*, Æ.

wið-hogian (w. g.) *to disregard, reject*, GEN 2864.

wiðhycgan† *to reject, despise, scorn.*

wiðl-=wiðig-

wiðig, wiði(g)e m. *withe, 'withy,' willow*, BC; Æ (Mdf) : *band, fetter, fillet, garland.*

wiðigrǣw f. *hedgerow*, KC. [v. '*rew*']

wiðigrind f. *willow bark*, Lcd 37a.
wiðing-=wiðig-
wiðinnan I. adv. *'within,' from within*, Æ,
Ps. II. prep. (w. d. a.) *within*.
wið-inne, -innen, -innon=wiðinnan I.
wiðir- (N)=wiðer-; wiðl (GD)=widl
wiðlædan *to lead away, remove, rescue*, Ps.
wiðlædnes f. *abduction*, Ps (BT).
wiðlan (N)=widlian
wiðlicgan[5] *to oppose, resist*, Chr, Chrd.
wiðmetan[5] *to compare with, liken to*, Æ.
wiðmetednes f. *invention, device*, SPs.
wiðmeten(d)lic *comparative (in grammar)*,
ÆGr.
wiðmetennes f. *comparison*, Æ.
wiðmeting f. *comparison*, Sc.
wið-neoðan (Æ), -niðan, -nyðan adv. *below, underneath, beneath*.
wiðobān (wido-) n. *collar-bone*, Lcd,LL.
wiðobend (eo[1]) *woodbine*, Lcd 113b. ['*with-
bind*']
wiðone (Bl)=wið ðone
wiðor-=wiðer-
wiðowinde f. *convolvulus, woodbine*, Gl,Lcd.
['*withwind*']
wiðræde=wiðerræde
wiðret n. *resistance, opposition*, B. ['*wither*']
wiðrēotan[2] *to abhor? resist?* El 369 (GK).
wiðrian=wiðerian
wiðsacan[6] *to forsake, abandon, renounce,
refuse, deny*, Bl,G; Æ,AO,CP : *oppose,
strive against*, AO.
wiðsacendlic *used in negations*, ÆGr 226[3].
wiðsacung f. *denial, renunciation*, Sc 60[14].
wiðsceorian (o[2]) *to refuse*, CP 59[12].
wiðscriðel=widscriðol
wiðscūfan[2] *to thrust back, refute, repel*, BH.
wiðsecgan *to renounce*, DR. ['*withsay*']
wiðsēon[5] *to rebel, rise against*, AO.
wiðsetnes f. *opposition*, Gl.
wiðsettan *to withstand, resist*, HL,LPs :
condemn, RWH 137[21]. ['*withset*']
wiðslēan[6] *to oppose, bring to naught*, Æ,
CP.
wiðsprecan[5] *to contradict, gainsay* : *converse*, AS : *revile* : *speak with*, GD 345[8].
wiðspurnan[3] *to hit against*, MtL 4[6].
wiðstæppan[6] *to step or go out of*, Ps.
wiðstandan[6] (w. d.) *to 'withstand,' resist,
oppose*, Æ,Bl,Bo,Lcd,LG,Wa; AO,CP : *be
lacking*, LL 102,31.
wiðsteall=wiðersteall
wiðsteppan=wiðstæppan
wiðstond-=wiðstand-
wiðstunian *to dash against*, Lcd 160b.
wiðstyllan *to retreat*, WW 17[26].
wiðstyltan *to hesitate, doubt*, MtL 21[21].
wiðtēon[2] *to take away* : *restrain*, CP.
wiðtremman *to step back*, CP 441[27].

wiððe f. *cord, band, thong, fetter*, Æ,WW.
['*withe*'; v. also wiðig]
wiðer-=wiðer-
wiððingian *to be reconciled to*, MFH 178.
wiððir (DR 168[2])=wiðer
wiððyddan *to blunt*, v. OEG 4235.
wiðufan I. prep. (w. d.) *above*. II. adv.
before, previously.
wið-uppon, -uppan adv. *above*.
wiðūtan I. prep. (w. d.) *outside of*, AO,LL,
Mt : *except*, Lcd : '*without*.' II. adv. *from
outside, outside*, HL.
wiðweorpan[3]t *to reject, repudiate*.
wiðwestan *to the west of*, AO 8[12].
wiðwinde=wiðowinde
wiðwinnan[3] *to fight against, oppose*, AO,
CP.
wiðwiðerian *to resist, withstand*, GD 117[19].
wixlan (N)=wrixlan
wixð=wiexð pres. 3 sg. of weaxan.
±wlacian *to become lukewarm, be tepid*, Æ,
CP.
wlaco, wlacu, wlæc *tepid, lukewarm, cool*,
CP. ['*wlak*']
wlacunes=wlæcnes; wlæc v. wlaco.
wlæce n. *tepidity*, GPH 397.
wlæclic *lukewarm*. adv. -līce.
wlæclīce (PPs 148[5])=wræclīce
wlæcnes f. *lukewarmness*, CP.
wlæffetere m. *stammerer*, GPH 403.
wlæffian (ea) *to stammer, speak indistinctly*,
Chrd 74[11]. ['*wlaffe*']
wlænc=wlanc, wlenc
wlænco=wlenco
wlæta=wlætta
+wlætan *to defile, debase*, Bo 114[23].
wlætlīce=wlæclīce
wlætta m. *loathing, nausea, eructation, heartburn*, Lcd,RB; Æ : *an object of loathing* :
disfigurement, OEG 4461. ['*wlat*']
wlætung (ā, ē) f. *nausea*, Cp,Lcd : *disfigurement*, OEG 4461. ['*wlating*']
wlanc (æ, o) *stately, splendid, lofty, magnificent, rich*, B,Ph : *boastful, arrogant, proud*,
B. ['*wlonk*']
wlancian *to become proud or boastful, exult*,
Gl.
wlanclic adj. *proud, arrogant*. adv. -līce,
Gl.
wlāt pret. 3 sg. of wlītan.
wlātere m. *spectator*, Chrd 96[24].
-wlātful v. neb-w.
wlātian I.t *to gaze, look upon, behold*.
[wlītan] II. (impers.) *to loathe*, Æ,Lcd.
['*wlate*']
wlātung I. f. *sight, spectacle*, Chrd 79[4].
II.=wlæt(t)ung
wleaffian=wlæffian
±wleccan *to make tepid*, CP. [wlæc]

wlenc, wlenco (AO,CP), wlencu f. *pride, arrogance, haughtiness* : *glory, pomp, splendour*, AO,CP : (†) *bravado* : *prosperity, riches, wealth.* [wlanc]

+wlencan *to enrich, exalt*, EL,TC,VH.

wlēttung=wlǣtung

wlisp, wlips (Æ) *lisping.*

-wlispian v. ā-wl.

wlita m. *countenance*, GL.

wlītan[1]† *to gaze, look, observe.*

wlite m. *brightness* : *appearance, form, aspect, look, countenance*, LG : *beauty, splendour*, Bl,VPs; Æ : *adornment*, CP. ['wlite']

wliteandet? n. *confession of splendour*, PPs 103[2].

wlitebeorht† *beauteous.*

wliteful *beautiful*, Sc 21[8].

wliteg-=wlitig-

wlitelēas *ugly*, AN 1171.

wlitelīce *handsomely*, BL 205[6].

wlitescīne (ē[3], ȳ[3]) †*lovely, beautiful*, LPs 80[4].

wlitesēon f. *sight, spectacle*, B 1650.

wlitetorht† *brilliant, lovely.*

wlitewamm (o[3]) m. *disfigurement of the face.*

wliteweorð n. *legal value of a man's life, ransom*, GD 179[21].

wlitig *radiant, beautiful, fair, comely*, Æ; CP. adv. -ige, -iglīce. ['wliti']

wlitigfæst *of enduring beauty*, PH 125.

±wlitigian *to beautify, adorn* : *become beautiful*, SEAF 49 : *form, fashion*, PSS.

wlitignes f. *beauty, splendour*, BL.

wlitu=wlite; wlō=wlōh

wlōh f., dp. wlō(u)m *fringe, ornament, tuft* : *bit*, GU 1127.

+wlōh *adorned*, GEN 1789.

wlonc=wlanc

wlott *spot, blemish*, OEG 648?

wlōum v. wlōh.

wlyt-=wlit-; wō=wōh

wōc pret. of wacan (v. 'wake').

wōcer=wōcor

wōcie, wōcige *noose*, OEG 962; 3560.

wōclic=wōhlic

wōcor† f. (gs. wōcre) *increase, growth* : *offspring, progeny, posterity, race* : *usury*

wocorlīce=wacorlīce

wōcs=wōsc pret. 3 sg. of wascan.

wōd I. adj. *senseless, mad, raging*, AS,Chr, Cp,G,Lcd; AO : *blasphemous.* ['wood'] II. pret. 3 sg. of wadan.

wōda I. m. *madman*, Æ. II. m. *storm, flood? danger?* TC 341[8].

wodawistle=wodewistle

woddor n. *throat, gullet?* SOL 95.

wōddrēam m. 'dæmonium,' RPs 95[5] (v. ES 38[25]).

wōdelic=wōdlic

Wōden m. *Woden* : *Mercury*, WW.

wōdendrēam m. *madness*, WW 245[10]. ['widdendream']

Wōdenesdæg=Wōdnesdæg

wōdewistle f. *hemlock*, GL.

wōd-frec, -frǣc *madly ravenous*, LL,W.

wōdheortnes f. *madness*, MFH 178.

wōdian=wēdan

wōdlic *foolish, mad, furious*, Æ. adv. -līce *madly, furiously*, Æ,Bas,HL : *blasphemously.* ['woodly']

wōdnes f. *madness, frenzy, folly*, Æ.

Wōdnes gs. of Wōden.

Wōdnesdæg m. *Woden's day*, 'Wednesday,' G.

Wōdnesniht f. *Tuesday night*, LL,W. [v. 'Wednesday']

wōdōm=wōhdōm

wōdon pret. pl. of wadan.

wōdscinn n. *madness, folly*, W 80[3].

wōdscipe m. *insanity*, WW 245[12].

wōdsēoc *mad*, GD 135[1].

wōdðrāg f. *paroxysm, madness, fury*, CP.

woecan (N)=wæccan

woerc- (N)=weorc-; woerd-=wird-

woffian *to shout, rave, blaspheme*, Æ.

woffung f. *madness, raving*, GD : *blasphemy*, Lk 24[11].

wōg=wōh

wōgere m. 'wooer,' *suitor, sweetheart*, Æ, Chrd.

wōgerlic *amorous*, CHRD 78[34].

wōgian *to* 'woo,' *court, marry*, Æ,Sc,TC.

wōgung f. 'wooing,' ÆL 7[301].

wōh I. n. *bending, crookedness* : *error, mistake*, Æ : *perversity, wrong, iniquity, depravity.* on w. *wrongly, wickedly.* ['WOUGH'] II. adj. *bent, awry, twisted, crooked* : *uneven, rough* : *wrong, perverse, evil, depraved, bad, unjust*, CP : *false (weight)*, W 70[3]. on wōn *wrongfully, in error.* ['wough']

wōhbogen† *bent, crooked.*

wōhcēapung f. *fine for illegal trafficking*, KC 5·143[22].

wōhdǣd f. *wrong deed, crime*, BL,GD.

wōhdōm m. *unjust judgment*, BF 242[6] (ōd).

wōhfōted *having deformed feet*, WW 161[30].

wōhfremmend m. *evildoer*, MET 9[36].

wōhful *wicked*, NG.

wōhfulnes f. *wickedness*, NG.

wōhgeorn *inclined to evil*, W 183[8].

wōhgestrēon n. *ill-gotten property*, W.

wōhgod n. *false god, idol*, PPs 78[58].

wōhhǣmed n. *fornication, adultery*, CP.

wōhhǣmend m. *fornicator, adulterer*, CP.

wōhhǣmere m. *fornicator, adulterer*, CP 401[30].

wõhhandede *maimed (of the hands)*, WW 161[29].

wõhhian? *to speak wildly, rave?* GD314[7].

wõhlic *perverse, wrong, unjust, evil.* adv. -līce, Æ.

wõhnes f. *crookedness, crooked place*, Æ : *wrong, error* : *wickedness*, Æ.

wõhs, wõhson=wõsc, wõscon pret. 3 sg. and pret. pl. of wascan.

wõhsum *evil*, DR27[9] (wõg-).

wõl mfn. *pestilence, mortality, disease*, AO, CP.

wõlbærnes f. *calamity, pest*, AO 62[34].

wõlberende *pestilential, pernicious*, CP.

wõlberendlic *pestilential*, CHR1086.

wõlbryne m. *pestilence*, AO86[24].

wolc (WW175[20])=wolcen

wolc-=walc-, wolcen-

wolcen nm. (nap. wolcnu) *'convolutio,' ball, lump*, PPs147[5] : *cloud*, B,Bl,Chr,CP,G, VPs : *sky, heavens*. ['*welkin*']

wolcenfaru† f. *scudding of clouds*.

wolcengehnäst n. *meeting of clouds (in a storm)*, RD4[60].

wolcenrēad=weolocrēad

wolcenwyrcende? ptc. *cloud-making (Centaurs)*, WW456[24].

wolcn=wolcen; **wolcrēad**=weolocrēad

wolcspinl=walcspinl

wol-cyrge, -cyrige=wælcyrige

wold=weald

wõldæg m. *day of pestilence*, RUIN26.

wõldberendlic=wõlberendlic

wol-de, -don pret. 3 sg. and pret. pl. of willan.

wõlgewinn n. *calamitous war*, AO64[15].

wõlic=wõhlic

wollentēare *streaming with tears*, B3032.

-wolma v. fõt-w.; **wom**=wam(m)

wõm I.=wõgum dp. of wõh, adj. II.= wõma

wõma m. *noise, howling, tumult* : *terror, alarm.* swefnes w. *dream-tumult, vision* : *eloquence?* OEG8b[10].

woman *to infringe*, EC151[16] : (+) w. d. pers. and g. thing *deprive of*, EC151[17]. [wamm]

won I.=wan, wann. II. pret. 3 sg. of winnan.

wõn I. wk. gdsn. and dpmn. of wõh. II.= hwõn

won-=wan-

wõna gp. of wõh II.

wondor=wundor

wõnes=wõhnes; **wong**=wang

wõp I. m. *cry, shrieking, weeping, lamentation*, B,G; Æ,CP. ['*wop*'] II.=wēop pret. 3 sg. of wēpan.

wõpdropa m. *tear*, SOL283.

wõpen pp. of wēpan.

wõperian *to weep*, HL18[32].

wõpig *sad, lamenting*, ÆL.

wõplēoð n. *dirge, elegy*, OEG3504.

wõplic *tearful, sad*, Æ. adv. -līce.

wõpstõw f. *place of mourning*, Æ.

wõr=wõs, wāse

wõra gp. of wõh.

worc=weorc

word I. n. '*WORD*,' *speech, sentence, statement*, Æ : *command, order* : *subject of talk, story, news, report*, Æ,AO : *fame*, Æ : *promise* : *verb*, Æ : *(incarnate) Word*. II. *rod*, CPs : *(gooseberry) bush?* LkL6[44] (v. ES38·340; 40·152). III.=werod

word-bēot† n., -bēotung (HU14) f. *promise*.

wordcærse (WW416[8])=worðigcærse?

wordcennend m. *the begetter of the Word*, GPH389.

wordcræft† m. *poetic art, eloquence*, El. [v. '*word*']

word-cwide (e, y), -cwyðe m. *words, speech, language, utterance*.

worden pp. of weorðan.

wordes adv. *with words, verbally, orally*.

wordfæst *true to one's word, true*, OEH 301[13].

wordful *talkative, verbose, fluent*, Sc.

wordgebēot=wordbēot

word-gecwide (æ[3]) n., -gecweodu np. *verbal agreement*, LL,TC.

wordgemearc n. *definition or limitation by words*, GEN2355.

wordgerȳne† n. *dark saying*.

wordglēaw *skilful in words*, DA418.

wordgydd m. *lay, dirge*, B3173.

wordhlēoðor† n. *voice, speech*.

wordhord† n. *treasury of words*.

wordig '*wordy*,' *verbose*, OEG1416.

wordlāc n. *speech*, LPs18[4].

wordlār f. *teaching*, CHRD53[22].

wordlatu f. *delay in speech?* AN1519.

wordlaðu† f. *conversation, speech*.

wordlēan n. *reward for song*, RD78[9].

wordlian (u[1]) *to talk, commune*, BF : *conspire*, GD106[1].

wordliend m. *speaker*, OEG2321.

wordloc n. *art of logic*, WW388[11].

wordloca m. *(word-hoard), speech*, AN470.

wordloga m. *deceiver, liar*, W40[10].

wordlung n. *talk, discourse* : *empty talk*.

wordmittung f. '*collatio*,' WW178[35].

wordpredicung f. *preaching*, CHRD66[23].

wordrian=wordlian

wordriht n. *suitable word*, B2631 : *spoken law*, Ex3.

wordsāwere m. *rhetorician*, CP97[4].

wordsige m. *success in speech*, LCD1·188'.

wordsnoter (o[3]) *eloquent, wise in words*.

wordsnoterlic *philosophical, learned,* OEG 2270.

wordsnoterung f. *sophism,* OEG 2268.

wordsomnere m. *enumeration, catalogue,* WW 212²⁷.

wordsomnung f. *'collatio,'* WW 178³⁵.

wordsprecende *able to speak,* VH 24.

wordwīsa m. *sophist,* WW 493³⁰.

wordwrītere=wyrdwrītere

wordwynsum *affable,* WW 191²¹.

wōre dsf. of wōh.

worf=weorf; **worflan**=woffian

wōrhana m. *moor-cock, cock-pheasant,* GL.

wōrhenn f. *hen pheasant,* WW.

wōrhona=wōrhana

worht pp. *(Bl;* '*ywrought*'), worhte pret. 3 sg. of wyrcan.

wōrht-=wrōht-

wōrigan *to roam, wander,* Æ : *move round, totter, crumble to pieces.* [wōr, wērig]

world=woruld; **worm**=wyrm

wormōd=wermōd

worms (u, rsm) nm. *matter, pus, virus, Ep, Lcd;* AO,CP. ['*worsum*']

worn (ea, eo) m. *large amount, number* : *troop, company, multitude, crowd* : *progeny.*

worngehāt n. *promise of numerous offspring,* GEN 2364?

wornlust=wamlust

worod=werod; **woroht**=wrōht

worold (AO,CP)=woruld

worpan=weorpan

worpen pp. of weorpan.

worpian *to cast, throw, pelt,* CP,EL.

worsm=worms; **wort**=wyrt

worð I. (eo, u) nm. *court, courtyard, curtilage, farm,* Mdf : *street.* **II.**=waroð

worð-=weorð-

worðig (eo, u, y) m. *enclosed homestead, curtilage, farm,* Æ,CP; Mdf : *street.*

worðigcærse f. *name of a plant,* LCD 3·303.

worðignetele f. *nettle,* LCD 44a.

worðscipe=weorðscipe; **worud**=werod I.

woruftord=weorftord

woruld (e¹, eo¹, ia¹; o²) f. '*WORLD*,' *age, AO, CP* : *men, humanity* : *way of life, life* : *long period of time, cycle, eternity.* tō worulde, ā on worulda world, in woruld worulde *world without end, for ever.*

woruldǣht f. *worldly possessions,* BH, LL.

woruldafol (-el) n. *secular or worldly power,* LL,W (ES 45·161).

woruldār f. *worldly honour,* CP : *secular property.*

woruldbearn n. *man,* RD 81²⁷.

woruldbebod n. *universal command, edict,* VH 24.

woruldbisgu f. *worldly occupation,* LL.

woruldbisgung (eo¹, y²) f. *worldly business* : *worldly misery, trouble.*

woruldbismer (o²) nm. *worldly reproach,* CP 61¹⁰.

woruldbliss f. *worldly bliss,* GU 135.

woruldbōt f. *compensation prescribed by the secular power,* LL 128,2.

woruld-broc n., -bryce (o²) m. *worldly trouble,* CP 259² : *use for secular purposes,* MH 136⁹.

woruldbüend† m. *world-dweller.*

woruldcamp m. *secular warfare,* ÆP 140⁴.

woruldcandel f. *sun,* B 1965.

woruldcearu (a³) f. *worldly care,* Æ.

woruldcempa m. *earthly soldier,* ÆL.

woruldcræft m. *secular art,* Æ. in pl. *world's hosts,* DA 362 (MP 26·434).

woruldcræftig *skilled in secular arts,* ÆP 128²⁵.

woruldcræft(ig)a m. *secular artificer,* ÆP 128¹⁰.

woruldcund *worldly, secular,* CP. adv. -līce, CP.

woruldcyning† m. *earthly king,* Æ.

worulddǣd f. *worldly business,* LL (414').

worulddēad *dead,* PPs 142⁴.

worulddēma m. *secular judge,* LL.

worulddōm m. *secular judgment,* Æ.

worulddrēam† m. *earthly joy.*

worulddrihten m. *world's lord, God,* MET 29¹.

woruldduguð† f. *worldly riches,* GEN.

woruldearfoð† n. *earthly misery,* MET.

woruldege m. *earthly fear,* LL (310¹⁹).

woruldende m. *end of the world,* B 3083.

woruldfægernes f. *earthly beauty,* MH 34⁶.

woruldfeoh n. *earthly goods, wealth,* GEN 2142.

woruldfolgað m. *worldly occupation,* BL.

woruldfrætwung (world-) f. *worldly ornament,* BL 125³⁶.

woruldfrēond (ȳ³) m. *friend in this world,* W.

woruldfrið m. *worldly peace,* LL 220,1.

woruldfruma m. *primeval man, patriarch,* GUTH 12²⁸.

woruldgālnes f. *lust of pleasure,* W 219¹⁴.

woruldgebyrd n. *worldly origin,* BH.

woruldgedāl n. *death,* EL 581.

woruldgefeoht (o²) n. *earthly fight,* MH 36²⁶.

woruldgeflit n. *dispute, lawsuit?* LCD 3·174'.

woruldgerǣ**dnes** (eo¹) f. *secular ordinance,* LL.

woruldgeriht n. *worldly justice, secular right or due,* LL 210,2¹.

woruldgerȳsnu np. *secular customs,* LL.

woruldgesǣlig *prosperous,* MA 219.

woruldgesǣlða (o²) fp. *worldly fortune,* AO.

woruldgesceaft† f. *creature of this world* : *world.*

woruldgestrēon† n. *worldly riches.*

woruldgeswinc (o²) n. *earthly toil, misery,* CP.

woruldgeðincð f. *worldly honour, dignity,* GD,W.

woruldgeððht (world-) mn. *worldly thought,* BL 15¹⁴.

woruldgewinn n. *earthly war,* ÆL 25⁸³².

woruldgewritu np. *secular writings,* BH.

woruldgewuna m. *customary law,* LL 206,1a.

woruldgielp (i³, y³) mn. *pride of this world, glory,* CP.

woruldgifu f. *worldly gift,* BH,CHR.

woruldgītsere m. *coveter of worldly things,* MET 14¹.

woruldgītsung f. *covetousness,* BO,MET.

woruldglenge m. *worldly pomp,* BL,LL.

woruldgōd n. *worldly good,* BO,BH.

woruldgylp (Æ)=woruldgielp

woruldgyrla (o²) m. *secular garment,* CHRD 96¹¹.

woruldhād m. *secular state,* BH,GD.

woruldhlāford m. *secular lord,* CP.

woruldhlīsa m. *worldly fame,* ÆH 2·566⁶.

woruldhremming (o²) f. *worldly hindrance,* CHRD 75³⁵,101⁴.

woruldhyht m. *earthly joy,* AZ 136.

woruldlǣce m. *earthly physician,* ÆH 1·472¹³.

worulc-lagu f., -laga m. *civil law,* LL,W.

woruldlēan n. *earthly reward,* LL (422¹²).

woruldlic *earthly,* Æ,BO : '*worldly,*' *secular,* MH ; Æ. adv. -līce *temporally.*

woruldlīf n. *life in this world* : *secular life,* BH.

woruldlufu f. *love of this world,* Æ.

woruldlust m. *worldly pleasure,* BO.

woruldmǣg m. *earthly kinsman,* GEN 2178.

woruldman m. *human being, man of the world, layman,* CR,MET ; Æ,CP. ['*worldman*']

woruldmēd f. *earthly reward,* LL (422¹⁴).

woruldnēod f. *temporal need,* LL 267,32.

woruldnytt f. *worldly use or profit,* GEN, LCD.

woruldprȳdo f. *worldly pride,* LCD 3·428', BYH 124³. [v. '*pride*']

woruldrǣden f. *way of the world,* B 1143 (v. MLN 25·113).

woruldrīca m. *great man,* Æ.

woruldrīce I. n. *earthly kingdom, CP* : *world-realm, world.* ['*worldriche*'] II. adj. *having worldly power or riches.*

woruldrīcetere (o²) n. *worldly power,* CHRD 68³⁴.

woruldriht (y³) n. *secular or civil law* : *God's law for the world.*

woruldsacu f. *worldly strife,* W 170⁹.

woruldsǣlða fp. *earthly blessings,* BO.

woruldscamu (ea³) f. *public disgrace,* LL,W.

woruldsceaft† f. *earthly creature,* AZ.

woruldscēat m. *part of the world, region.*

woruldscēawung f. *worldly sight,* CHRD 76³⁰.

woruldscipe m. *worldly matter, CP.* ['*worldship*']

woruldscīr (world-) f. *life in the world* (*i.e. not monastic*), *worldly affairs* GD 3⁷.

woruldscrift (eo¹, y³) m. *confessor,* BYH 132¹.

woruldsnotor *world-wise* : *scientific,* MH 44²⁵.

woruldsorg f. *earthly care,* CP,BO.

woruldspēd f. *worldly wealth, success in the world, CP.*

woruldspēdig *rich in this world,* CP 333².

woruldsprǣc f. *worldly talk,* LL.

woruldstēor f. *secular penalty,* LL 258,51.

woruldstrang *having worldly power,* NC 334.

woruldstrengu f. *physical strength,* RD 27².

woruldstrūdere m. *spoliator, robber,* LL,W.

woruldstund *sojourn upon earth,* EL 363.

woruldðearf f. *this world's needs,* BH.

woruldðearfa m. *poor man,* PPs 69⁶.

woruldðearfende *poor in worldly goods,* CR 1351.

woruldðēaw m. *worldly affair,* BO 7¹³.

woruld-ðegen, -ðegn, -ðēn m. *earthly or secular servant,* LL.

woruldðēnung (o²) f. *secular office,* NC 334.

woruldðēowdōm m. *secular service,* CHR 963.

woruldðing (o²) n. *worldly affair, thing,* Æ, AO,CP : *earthly riches.*

woruldðrymm m. *worldly glory,* BYH 124⁵ (world-).

woruldwǣpn (o²) n. *earthly weapon,* BL 213⁴.

woruldwæter n. *ocean, sea,* SOL 186'.

woruldwela m. *worldly wealth, CP.*

woruldwelig *rich in worldly goods,* NC 335.

woruldweorc n. *secular work,* LL : *mechanics.*

woruldweorðscipe m. *worldly honour,* LL.

woruldwīdl n. *world-filth,* CR 1007.

woruldwig n. *worldly contest,* LL.

woruldwilla m. *earthly good,* BO 24².

woruldwilnung f. *earthly desire,* CP.

woruldwīs (o²) *worldly-wise,* CP : *learned,* CP.

woruldwīsdōm m. *worldly wisdom, science,* Æ.

woruldwīse f. *custom of the world,* MH 68⁹B.

woruldwita m. *learned layman, sage,* LL.

woruldwīte n. *punishment, fine,* CR,LL.

woruldwlenco f. *magnificence, ostentation,* CP.

woruldwrenc (o²) m. *worldly cunning,* CP.

woruldwuldor n. *worldly glory,* CHRD 66²⁰.

woruldwuniende (o²) *dwelling,* MET 13¹⁷.

woruldyrmðu f. *earthly wretchedness,* AO.

wōrung f. *wandering, roving,* Æ,MFH 179.

wōs I. n. *sap, juice*, Lcd. ['*ooze*'] II. gs. of wōh.

+wosa m. *conversation, intercourse*, DR.

wōsan (NG)=wēsan

wōsc pret. 3 sg., wōscon pret. pl. of wascan.

wōse=wāse

wōsig *juicy, moist*, Lcd.

-wost v. fore-w.

wōð† f. *sound, noise : voice, song, poetry : eloquence.*

wōðbora† m. *orator, speaker, seer, prophet, poet, singer.*

wōðcræft† m. *art of speech or song.*

-woðe v. got-w.

wōðgiefu f. *gift of song*, RD 32[8].

wōðsong m. *song*, CR 46.

wōum dp. of wōh, adj.

wōx I. pret. 3 sg. of weaxan. II.=wōsc

wracian I. *to be in exile, wander, travel.* II. *to carry on, prosecute*, AO 50[21].

wraclīce=wræclīce

wracnian (æ) *to be a wanderer, traveller, pilgrim*, Æ.

wraco=wracu

wracu (e) f. (g. often wræce) *revenge, vengeance, persecution, enmity*, B,BH,G, LL,VPs,W; AO,CP : *punishment, penalty*, AO,CP : *cruelty, misery, distress, torture, pain, Ph*; AO. on ðā wrace *in retaliation.* ['*wrake*']

wræc I. (e) n(f?) *misery*, CP : *vengeance, persecution, BH,Bl : exile.* ['*wrack*'] II. *what is driven*, OET 37[62]. III. pret. 3 sg. of wrecan. IV.=wærc (A; v. JAW 52)

wræca=wræcca; wræcan=wrecan

wræcca (e) m. '*wretch,*' Jul; CP : *fugitive, outcast, exile, B,Bo,Chr*; AO : *adventurer, stranger : sojourner.*

wræccan=wrecan; wræce v. wracu.

wræcend=wrecend

wræcfæc n. *time of exile, banishment, misery*, RIM 64.

wræcful *wretched, miserable*, ÆH.

wræchwīl f. *time of exile or distress*, PH 527.

wræclāst† (e) m. *path of exile.*

wræclāstian *to banish*, WW.

wræclic adj. *foreign : strange, unfamiliar, extraordinary : wretched, exiled.* adv. -līce.

wræclic=wrætlic

wræc-mæcg†, -mæcga (JUL 260) m. *exile, outcast, miserable man.*

wræcmon m. *fugitive*, Ex 137.

wræcnes=wrecnes

wræcnian=wracnian

wræcon pret. pl. of wrecan.

wræcscipe (e) m. *exile*, BL,EPs 119[5].

wræcsetl n. *place of exile*, Gu 267.

wræcsīð m. *journey of exile or peril, pilgrimage*, Æ : *exile, persecution*, Æ,AO : *misery.*

wræcsīðian *to wander, travel abroad, be in exile*, Æ.

wræcstōw f. *place of exile or punishment*, Bo, GEN.

wræcwīte n. *punishment*, BL 5.

wræcworuld f. *miserable world*, W 1[2],VH.

wrǣd f. *band, bandage, wreath*, CP : *bundle : band, flock.* [wrīðan]

wrǣdmǣlum adv. *in companies*, WW 411[42].

wrǣg-=wrēg-

wrǣne (ē) *unbridled, loose, lustful*, AO.

wrǣnna (Æ)=wrenna

wrǣnnes f. *luxury, lust, wantonness*, AO, CP.

wrǣnsa m. *wantonness*, OEG 2347.

wrǣnscipe (ē) m. *wantonness*, OEG 5290.

wrǣnsian *to be wanton*, NC 335.

wrǣsnan *to alter, change, modulate*, RD 25[1].

wrǣst (ā) *firm, able, strong, excellent : delicate.* adv. -e.

wrǣstan I. (±) *to* '*wrest,*' *bend, twist, twang*, Sol,Wy. II. *to be or make elegant?* WW.

wrǣstlere m. '*wrestler,*' WW 431[26].

wrǣstlic I. *pertaining to wrestling*, WW. II. (ā) *delicate, elegant*, WW.

wrǣstliend *wrestler*, WW 431[25]. [wrǣstan]

wrǣstlung f. '*wrestling,*' *struggling*, GD, OEG.

wræt=wrætt; wrǣt=wrǣtt

wrǣtbaso (e[1]) *red*, GL. [wrǣtte]

wrǣtereād *red*, Lcd 111b.

wrǣtlic *artistic, ornamental : curious, wondrous, rare.* adv. -līce. [wrǣtt]

wrætt m., wrætte f. *rubea tinctoria? crosswort? hellebore?* Lcd,WW (A 30·248).

wrætt† f. *ornament, work of art, jewel.*

wrǣð I.=wrǣd. II.=wrǣððo

±wrǣðan (ē) *to anger*, ByH 112[12] : *get angry, be angry*, DR : *resist violently*, Lcd 3·212[4].

wrǣðian=wreðian; wrǣðo=wrǣððo

wrǣð-studu, -stuðu (e) f. *column, pillar, support*, BH,W.

wrǣððo, wrǣð(ð)u (ā) f. '*wrath,*' *anger, indignation*, DR,Leofric Missal,NG.

wrǣxlian=wraxlian

wrāh pret. 3 sg. of wrēon.

wrang (o) I. n. '*wrong,*' *injustice*, LL,W. II. *rough, uneven*, KC. III. pret. 3 sg. of wringan.

wranga (pr-) *hold of a ship*, WW. ['*wrong*']

wrangwīs *rough, uneven*, OEG 1770.

wrāsen (ǣ) f. *band, tie, chain*, WW 34[24].

wrāst=wrǣst

wrāt pret. 3 sg. of wrītan.

wráð I. adj. 'WROTH,' *furious, angry, hostile, AO* : *terrible, horrible* : *grievous. harsh, bitter, malignant, evil, cruel.* adv. -e, *Bo, G,Gu,Ps.* ['*wrothe*'] **II.** f. *cruelty* : *hardship.* [wríðan] **III.**=wrǽd. **IV.** pret. 3 sg. of wríðan.

+wráðian (refl.) *to be angry, Chr* 1070,*RG.* ['*wroth,*' '*iwrathe*']

wráðlíc† *grievous, severe, bitter.* adv. -líce, *B.* ['*wrothly*']

wráðmōd† *angry,* GEN.

wráðscræf n. *pit of misery, hell.* RD 41[41].

wráððo=wrǽððo

wraðu† f. *prop, help, support, maintenance,* BH.

+wraxl? *wrestling-place, gymnasium,* OEG 18b[68]?

wraxlere m. *wrestler,* OEG.

wraxlian *to wrestle, Æ.* ['*wraxle*']

wraxliende *wrestling, contending, striving,Æ.*

wraxlung f. '*wrestling,*' WW 150[8]. ['*wraxling*']

wrēah pret. 3 sg. of wrēon; **wrec**=wræc

wrecan[5] (eo) *to drive, impel, push* : *press forward, advance* : *fulfil, accomplish* : *utter, deliver, pronounce* : *expel, banish, persecute,* CP : (±) 'WREAK,' *revenge, avenge, punish, CP*;AO.

wreccan I. *to awake, arouse, Æ,CP.* ['*wrecche*'] **II.**=wrecan

-wrecel v. spor-w.

wrecend m. *avenger,* B,LL.

wrecnes (æ) f. *vengeance,* NG : *wickedness,* BHCA 70[12].

wrecscip (æ?) '*actuaria*'? ES 43·336.

wrecu (VPs)=wracu

±wrecan I.† *to excite, stir up.* **II.** *to accuse, impeach, Æ,Chr,Cp,MH.* ['*wray*']

+wrēgednes f. *accusation,* ES 62·114[2].

wrēgend m. *accuser,* BH,GL.

±wrēgendlíc *accusative,* ÆGR 22[20].

wrēgere m. *accuser, informer, Æ.* ['*wrayer*']

wrēgistre (ǣ) f. *female accuser,* ÆL 2[208].

wrēgung f. *accusation, ÆGr.* ['*wraying*']

wrēhte pret. 3 sg. of wrēgan.

wrehtend m. *instigator,* WW 420[29].

wrehtend m. *accuser,* KGL 73[23].

wrēn-=wrǣn-

wrenc m. *wile, stratagem, trick, deceit, Bo, Sc* ; AO : (†) *modulation, melody, song.* ['*wrench*']

wrencan *to twist, IM* : *spin intrigues, devise plots,* MOD 33. ['*wrench*']

wrenna (æ) m., **wrenne** f. '*wren,*' *Cp,WW.*

wreocan=wrecan

wreogan (M)=wrigon pret. pl. of wrēon.

±wrēon[1,2] *to cover, clothe, envelop, conceal, hide, Gen,Lcd,LG,LL* : *protect, defend, Gen, Rd.* ['*wry*']

wrēotan=rēotan; **wreotian**=writian

wreotu nap. of writ.

wrēoð=(1) wrǽd; (2) wrǣððo

wreoðenhilt *with twisted hilt,* B 1699. [=*wriðenhilt*]

wreoðian=wreðian; **wrēoðian**=wrīdian

wretbasu=wrǣtbaso

±wreðian *to support, sustain, uphold, Bo, GD* ; CP. ['*wrethe*']

wreðstudu=wrǣðstudu

wrīanne (N)=wrēonne gerund of wrēon I.

wricð, wriceð pres. 3 sg. of wrecan.

wrid m. *shoot, plant, bush, BC,Gl,Lcd* ; Mdf. ['*wride*']

+wrid I. n. *thicket?* GUTH. **II.** *husk,* WW 412[3].

wrīdan[1] *to grow, thrive, flourish,* GEN,LCD.

wriden pp. of (1) wrīdan; (2) wríðan.

wrīdian† *grow, flourish, spring up,* AA.

wriecð=wricð pres. 3 sg. of wrecan.

wriexl=wrixl

wrigelnes f. *covering,* JPs 60[5].

wrigels mn. *covering, cloak, veil, HL,VPs.* ['*wriels*']

wrigen pp., wrigon pret. pl. of wrēon.

wrigennes (gn-) f. *a covering,* EPs 60[5].

wrigian *to go, turn, twist, bend, Bo,Rd* : *strive, struggle, press forward, endeavour, venture, Bo.* ['*wry*']

wrīhst pres. 2 sg., wrīhð pres. 3 sg. of wrēon.

+wrinclian *to wind about,* KC 4·34[9]. +wrinclod *serrated,* GPH 39[8].

+wring n. *liquor, drink,* WW 128[17].

wringan[3] *to* '*wring,*' *twist* : (±) *squeeze, press out, Æ,Bo,GD,Lcd.*

wringe f. (*oil-*)*press,* GD 250[15]. ['*wring*']

wringhwǣg n? *strained whey,* LL 451,16.

+wrisc=+wrixl; **wrislan**=wrixlan

wrist f. '*wrist,*' *LL* 386,2.

±writ n. *letter, book, treatise, Ph* : *scripture, writing, DR,LG* : '*writ*' ('*i-writ*'), *charter, document, deed, AO,Bl* : '*stilus,*' GPH 402.

±wrītan[1] (ȳ) *to incise, engrave,* 'WRITE,' *draw, Æ,Chr,CP* ; AO : *bestow by writing.*

writbred n. *writing tablet,* MH,WW.

-wríte v. wæter-w.; **-writennes** v. tō-w.

±wrītere m. '*writer,*' *scribe, author, portrayer, painter, Æ,Bf,Bo,CP,Mt* : *secretary, CP,GD.*

writeȳren (MH 146[12])=writīren

writian I. (eo) *to chirp, chatter,* v. OEG 37[3]. **II.** *to cut? draw a figure?* ES 8·478.

wrīting f. *writing,* SPs 44[2].

wrītingfeðer f. *pen,* EPs 44[2].

wrītingīsen n. *style, pen,* MH 146[12]c.

writīren (ȳ[2]) n. *writing instrument, style,* MH 146[12].

+writrǣden f. *written agreement,* WW 217[7].

writseax n. *style, pen*, MtLp2[18].

writt-=wrīt-

+wrīð n. *strap, thong*, WW143[13]? (v. A
8·451).

wrīða m. *band, thong, bridle*, Æ,Sc : *collar,
ring*, Æ,Rd. ['*wreath*']

±wrīðan[1] (ȳ) I. *to twist*, ÆGr : *wrap, bind
up, bind, tie, fasten, fetter, check*, BC,LL :
vex, torture, Æ. ['*withe*'] II.=wrīdan

+wrīðelian *to bind?* OEG23[7]?

wrīðels m. *band, fillet, bandage*, WW411[17].

+wrīðennes f. *binding*, LCD.

wrīðlan=wrīdian

+wrīðing f. *binding*, Sc202[13].

wrix(i)endlic *mutual*, GD2[7]. adv. -līce *turn
about, one by one, by turns, in turn*, CP.

wrixl f., wrixla m. *change, exchange, barter*,
CP.

+wrixl, +wrixle n. *turn, change : exchange,
purchase, intercourse : requital : office.*

wrixlan (±) *to change, barter, exchange,
reciprocate, lend*, AO. wordum w. *converse* : (+) *recompense, requite* : (+) *obtain*,
CP.

+wrixle *alternate : vicarious*, GL.

wrixlian=wrixlan

+wrixlic *alternating*, OEG2[135].

±wrixlung f. *change*, BF120[20] : *loan*, WW
115,449.

wroegan=wrēgan

wrogen pp. of wrēon.

wroht=worht pp. of wyrcan.

wrōht I. f. *blame, reproach, accusation,
slander : fault, crime, sin, injustice*, Æ :
strife, enmity, anger, contention, dispute,
AO,CP : *hurt, injury, calamity, misery.*
[wrēgan] II. m. *tale-bearer*, ÆGR217[2].

wrōhtberend m. *accuser*, APs,WW.

wrōhtbora m. *accuser, monster*, WW : *the
devil*, CR.

wrōhtdropa m. *criminal bloodshed*, GNE196.

wrōhtgeorn *contentious*, CP357.

wrōhtgetēme n. *series of crimes?* (BT),GEN
45.

wrōhtian *to do harm?* HL15[105].

wrōhtlāc n. *calumny*, W160[5]n.

wrōhtsāwere m. *sower of strife*, CP359.

wrōhtscipe m. *crime*, GEN1672.

wrōhtsmið† m. *worker of evil, evildoer.*

wrōhtspitel *slanderous*, EGL. [spittan]

wrōhtstæf m. *accusation*, EL926 : *injury*,
RD72[12,14].

wrong (WW201[35])=wrang II.

wrōt m. *snout, elephant's trunk*, Cp,WW.
['*wroot*']

wrōtan[7] *to root up*, Cp,Ps,Rd. ['*wroot*']

wrugon pret. pl. of wrēon.

wrungen pp. of wringan.

wrycð pres. 3 sg. of wrecan.

wryhta=wyrhta

wrȳhð=wrīhð pret. 3 sg. of wrēon.

+wryndan (MtL7[25])=+gryndan

wrȳt-=wrīt-

wrȳte (CM56[83])=prȳte

wrȳðan=wrīðan

wucaðēn=wucðegn

wuc-dæg, wuce-, wicu- m. '*week-day*,' BH
Æ.

wuce=wucu

wucðegn (i[1]) m. *monk or priest appointed for
a week's duty, weekly servant*, CM,RB.

wucðēnung f. *service for a week*, RB59,60.

wucu (i, ie, io) f. '*week*,' Bf,Lcd,RB; AO,CP.

wucubōt f. *penance lasting a week*, LL
(278[12]).

wucweorc (i[1]) n. (*compulsory*) *work for a
week, by a tenant*, KC,LL. ['*weekwork*']

wude=wudu

wudere m. *wood-man, wood-carrier*, WW
371[5]. ['*wooder*']

wudewe=wuduwe

wudian *to cut wood*, Æ,W.

wudig *wooded, having trees*, Az120.

wudigere, wudiere (WW; '*woodyer*')=
wudere

wudiht *thick (with trees), forest-like*, GPH
402.

wudo-=wudu-

wudu (i, io) m., gs. wuda, wudes; nap.
wudas, wuda '*wood*,' *forest, grove*, BC,CP,
LL,VPs; Æ,AO; Mdf : *tree*, B,Cp,Ph : *the
Cross, Rood* : *wood, timber*, Bo,CP,Gn :
(†) *ship*, B : *spear-shaft*, B398.

wuduælfen (e[3]) f. *wood-elf, dryad*, WW.

wuduæppel f. *wild apple, crab*, LCD71a.

wudubǣr f. *woodland pasture*, KC.

wudubǣre *wood-bearing*, OEG1806.

wudubærnett n. *burning of wood*, LL16,12;
24n[2].

wudubāt n. *wooden boat*, AN907.

wudubēam† m. *forest tree.*

wudubearo m. *forest, grove*, AA,W.

wudu-bend, -bind m.=wudubinde

wudubill n. *hatchet*, Cp; GD. ['*woodbill*']

wudubinde I. (-bindle) f. '*woodbine*,' *convolvulus*, Gl,Lcd,LG. II. f. *bundle of sticks*,
OET35[18].

wudubiðr (=bora?) m. *wood-carrier*, HGL
427.

wudublǣd† (-blēd) f. *forest blossom.*

wudubucca m. *wild buck, wild goat*, LCD.

wudubyrðra m. *wood-carrier, camp-follower*,
OEG869.

wuducerfille f. *wood-chervil, cow-parsley*,
GL.

wuducocc m. '*woodcock*,' Gl.

wuducroft m. *a croft with trees on it?* (BT)
KC3·376[6].

wuduculfre m. *wood-pigeon,* WW.
wuducūnelle f. *wild thyme,* LCD.
wuducynn n. *an aromatic (?) wood,* JnL 12³.
wududocce f. *wild dock, sorrel,* LCD.
wuduelfen=wuduælfen
wudufæsten n. *place protected by woods, woodfastness : ship.*
wudufald *a fold in a wood,* KC.
wudufeld m. *wooded plain,* PPs 131⁶.
wudufeoh n. *forest-tax,* LCD.
wudufille=wuducerfille
wudufīn f. *pile of wood,* ÆGR.
wudufugol m. *forest bird, wild fowl,* Bo, MET.
wudugāt f. *wild goat,* LCD.
wudugehæg n. *woodland pasture* (BTs), KC 3·176¹.
wuduhēawere m. *wood-cutter, Æ.* [v. 'wood']
wuduherpaδ m. *public path through a wood,* KC 3·213².
wuduhīewet n. *illegal cutting of wood,* LL 567,37.
wuduholt n. *forest, wood, grove,* PH.
wuduhona m. *woodcock,* WW 38⁸.
wuduhrofe=wudurofe
wuduhunig n. *wild honey, Mk; Æ.* [v. 'wood']
wudulād f. *carting wood,* LL 452,21⁴.
wudu-læs f., gs. -læswe *wood-pasture, run (for cattle) in a wood,* Ct.
wuduland n. *'woodland,'* BC.
wudu-leahtric, -lectric m. *wood-lettuce, wild sleepwort,* LCD.
wudulēswe=wudulæswe
wudulic adj. *woody, wooded, wild,* Æ,WW.
wudumǣr (ē³) f. *wood-nymph, echo,* GL.
wudumann m. *woodman,* KC 3·275⁹.
wudumerce m. *wild parsley, wood-mint,* LCD. [v. 'wood']
wudung f. *getting of wood, Æ : right of estovers,* KC. ['wooding']
wudurǣden f. *wood-regulation, right of estovers,* LL.
wudurēc m. *smoke from a funeral pyre,* B 3144.
wudurima m. *border of a wood,* KC 3·34¹⁵.
wudurofe f. *'woodruff,'* Lcd,WW.
wudurose f. *wild rose,* LCD 34b?
wudusnīte f. *wood-snipe,* WW.
wudusūræppel f. *crab-apple?* LCD 160a.
wudutelga m. *branch of a tree,* SOL 421.
wudutrēow n. *forest tree,* LL,W.
wuduδistle m. *wood-thistle,* LCD.
wuduwa (wyde-) m. *widower,* LL. ['widow']
wuduwald m. *forest,* WW 426³⁵.
wuduwanhād m. *state of a woman who has not a husband, chastity, 'widowhood,'* CP, HL.

wuduwāsa m. *faun, satyr,* WW. ['wood-wose']
wuduwe (i, eo, y¹; e²) f. *'widow,' Chr,G,Ps.*
wuduweard m. *forester,* LL 452,19. ['wood-ward']
wudu-weax n., -weaxe f. *wood-waxen. genista tinctoria, Lcd.* ['woodwax']
wuduwēsten mn. *wild forest,* CHR p5n.
wuduwinde f. *woodbine,* GL.
wuduwyrt f. *plant which grows in woods,* BL 59³.
wudwe=wuduwe
wuhhung f. *rage, fury, madness :* (pl.) *the Furies.*
wuht AO,CP=wiht; wuhung=wuhhung
wul=wull; wulder=wuldor
wuldor n. *glory, splendour, honour, Bo,VPs; Æ,CP : praise, thanks : heaven,* EL. ['wulder']
wuldor-bēag, -bēah m. *crown of glory, Æ.*
±wuldorbēagian *to crown,* ÆH.
wuldorblǣd m. *glorious success,* JUD 156.
wuldorcyning m.† *King of Glory, God.*
wuldordrēam m. *heavenly rapture,* MFH.
Wuldorfæder† m. *Glorious Father.*
wuldorfæst *glorious.* adv. -fæste, -fæstlīce.
wuldorfæstlicnes f. *glory, Æ.*
wuldorful *glorious, Æ : vainglorious,* SC.
±wuldorfullian *to glorify, Æ.*
wuldorfullīce adv. *gloriously,* ÆH.
wuldorgāst m. *angel,* GEN 2912.
wuldorgeflogena m. *one who has fled from glory, devil,* LCD 3·36¹⁵.
wuldorgestealdf† np. *glorious possessions, realms of glory.*
wuldorgeweorc n. *wondrous work,* ES 43·167.
wuldorgifuf† (eo) f. *glorious gift, grace.*
wuldorgim m. *glorious jewel, sun,* RD 81²⁰.
Wuldorgod m. *Glorious God,* BHB 344⁸.
wuldorhamaf† (o³) m. *garb of glory.*
wuldorhēap m? *glorious troop,* NC 335.
wuldorhelm m. *crown of glory,* BL.
wuldorlēan† n. *glorious reward.*
wuldorlicf† *glorious,* BL,Ps. adv. -līce.
wuldormāga m. *heir of heaven,* GU 1067.
wuldormago m. *heir of heaven,* GU 1267.
wuldormicel *gloriously great,* †Hy 7⁹⁴.
wuldornytting f. *glorious service,* RD 81¹⁹.
wuldorsang m. *glorious song,* MFH 114¹⁰.
wuldorspēd f. *glorious wealth,* GEN 87.
wuldorspēdig *glorious,* AN 428.
wuldortān m. *plant with medicinal virtues?* (BT), LCD 3·34'.
wuldortorhtf† *gloriously bright, clear, brilliant, illustrious.*
wuldorδrymm m. *heavenly glory,* AN,BL.
wuldorweorud n. *heavenly host,* CR 285.
wuldorword n. *glorious word,* †Hy 7⁴⁶.

wuldrian (±) *to glorify, praise, extol,* Æ : *boast, brag,* Æ : *live in glory,* Æ.

wuldrig *glorious,* DR.

wuldrung f. *glorying, boasting,* Sc,DR.

wuldur=wuldor

wulf m. *(he-)* '*wolf,*' *Cp,LG,Wy*; Æ,AO, CP; Mdf : *wolfish person, devil,* Cr, MH.

wulfescamb m. *wild teasel,* Lcd,WW.

wulfeshēafod n. *head of a wolf,* Lcd : *outlaw,* LL (v. NED). ['*wolfshead*']

wulfestǣsel f. *(wolf's) teasel,* Lcd.

wulfhaga m. *shelter from wolves?* CC53.

wulfhēafodtrēo m. *cross, gallows?* Rd56¹².

wulfheort† *wolf-hearted, cruel,* Da.

wulf-hlið n., nap. -hleoðu *hillside inhabited by wolves,* B1358.

wulfhol n. *wolf's hole,* WW.

wulflȳs n. *fleece of wool,* WW198²⁶.

wulfmod=wullmod

wulfpytt m. *wolf's hole?* BC,KC.

wulfsēað m. *wolf's hole,* KC3·264⁵.

wulfslǣd n. *valley of wolves,* KC3·456⁶.

wull f. '*wool,*' *Gl,Lcd,VPs*; Æ.

wullcamb m. *comb for wool,* LL454,15¹. ['*woolcomb*']

wullcnoppa (?hn-) m. *tuft of wool,* WW.

wulle=wull

wullen (*KC*; '*woollen*')=wyllen

wullian *to wipe with wool,* Lcd1·356'.

wullmod m? *distaff,* Gl.

wulltewestre f. *wool-carder,* Lcd.

wulluc *cover, wrapper,* A31·65.

wullwǣga f. *scales for wool,* WW148²¹.

+wun=+wuna

±wuna I. m. (usu. +) *habit, custom, practice, rite,* Bo; Æ. on gew. habban *to be accustomed to,* CP. ['*i-wune*'] **II.** (+) *wonted, customary, usual,* Chr,LG. ['*wone*']

wund I. f. '*wound,*' *sore, ulcer,* B,BH,Cr, Lcd,RB; CP : *wounding, injury,* Æ. **II.** adj. *wounded, sore,* AO.

wundel f. *wound,* LL,RB.

wundelīce=wundorlīce

wunden (*B*; '*wounden*') pp. of windan.

wundenfeax *with twisted mane,* B1400.

wundenhals *with twisted prow,* B298.

wundenlocc† *with braided locks.*

wundenmǣl *etched, damascened (of a sword),* B1531.

wundenstefna m. *ship with curved or wreathed prow,* B220.

wunder=wundor

±wundian *to* '*wound,*' Æ,CP,Chr,LL,Ps; AO.

wundiend '*vulnerator,*' ERHy6⁴².

wundiht, wundig *ulcerous, full of sores,* GPH.

wundle=wundel

wundlic *wounding, wound-inflicting,* GPH 402⁵¹.

wundon pret. pl. of windan.

wundor (often confused with wuldor) n. (gs. wundres) '*WONDER,*' *miracle, marvel, portent, horror,* Æ; AO,CP : *wondrous thing, monster.*

wundorāgrǣfen *wondrously graven,* An712.

wundorbēacen n. *strange sign,* PPs73⁵.

wundorbebod n. *strange order,* B1747.

wundorblēo n. *wondrous hue,* Cr1140.

wundorclam n. *strange bond,* Cr310.

wundorcrǣft† m. *miraculous power.*

wundorcrǣftiglīce *with wondrous skill,* BH 324³o.

wundordǣd f. *wondrous deed,* Bl.

wundordēað m. *wondrous death,* B3037.

wundoreardung f. *wondrous dwelling.* VH24.

wundorfæt (e²) n. *wondrous vessel,* B1162.

wundorful (e²) '*wonderful,*' OEG; Æ. adv. -līce.

wundorgehwyrft (e⁴) *wondrous turn,* GPH 390.

wundorgeweorc=wundorweorc

wundorgiefu f. *wondrous endowment,* Wy72.

wundorhǣlo (u²) f. *wondrous healing,* BH 446¹².

wundorhūs? n. '*solarium,*' *upper room,* GD 119²⁶.

+wundorlǣcan *to make wonderful, magnify,* SPs16⁸.

wundorlic *wonderful, remarkable, strange,* AO,Bl; Æ,CP. adv. -līce, Æ,CP,Lcd. ['*wonderly*']

wundormāðm m. *wonderful treasure,* B2173.

wundorsēon f. *wonderful sight,* B995.

wundorsmið m. *skilled smith,* B1681.

wundortācen n. *miracle,* PPs104²³.

wundorweorc n. '*wonder-work,*' *miracle,* An,Bl.

wundorworuld f. *wonderful world,* Rd40¹⁷.

wundorwyrd f. *wonderful event,* El1071.

wundres v. wundor.

±wundrian (w. g.) *to* '*wonder,*' *be astonished* (*at*), *Bl,Bo,G,Ph*; Æ,AO,CP : *admire* : *make wonderful, magnify.*

wundrigendlic *expressing wonder,* ÆGr 241¹⁶.

wundrum adv. (d. of wundor) *wonderfully, strangely, terribly.*

wundrung f. *wonder, astonishment, admiration,* Æ,Cr : *spectacle,* OEG4370. ['*wondering*']

wundspring m. *ulcerous wound,* Lcd1·356'.

wundswaðu (e) f. *scar,* VPs37⁶.

wundur=wundor

wundwīte n. *compensation for wounding,* LL76H.

+**wunelic** *usual, customary*, Æ,CP : *accustomed (to), adapted (to)*. adv. -līce, BH. ['*i-wuneliche*']

wunenes, wununes f. *dwelling, habitation* : *perseverance*, DR. [wunian]

wungynde=wuniende pres. ptc. of wunian.

wunian (±) *to inhabit, dwell, abide, exist*, B, Bl,Cp,G; AO,CP : (+) *remain, continue, stand*, Æ,B,Bl; AO,CP : (±) *be used to, be wont to*, ÆGr : (+) *habituate oneself to*, CP73¹⁴. ['*wone*']

wuniendlic *perpetually*, GD264⁷.

wunigend m. *inhabitant*, RBL5¹¹.

+**wunlic**=+wunelic; **wunn**=wynn

wunnen pp., wunnon pret. pl. of winnan.

+**wunod** *domiciled*, GUTH9²³.

wunones=wunenes; **wunsum**=wynsum

wununes=wunenes

wunung f. *act of dwelling, living*, Bl,RB : *dwelling, habitation*, Æ,HL. ['*wonning*']

wunungstōw f. *abiding-place*, GD31¹⁹.

wuraðo (N)=wræððo; **wurcan**=wyrcan

wurd=(1) wyrd; (2) word

wurdon pret. pl. of weorðan.

wurht, wurhton=worhte pret. sg., worhton pret. pl. of wyrcan.

wurm=wyrm

wurma m., wurme f. *murex, purple-fish* : *any dye, woad, purple* : *a plant used for dyeing*.

wur-mille, -mele (ea¹) f. *wild marjoram*, GL.

wurms=worms; **wurnian**=weornian

wurpan=weorpan

wurpul *that which throws down*, GL.

wursm=worms; **wurst**=wierrest

wurt=wyrt; **wurð**=weorð

wurðe=weorð(e), wierðe; **wurðig**=worðig

wūscbearn n. *(dear) little child*, JnL13³³. [wȳscan]

wūso (JnR13³³)=wūscbearn

wussung=wissung; **wuta**=wita

wutan=wuton

wutedlīce, wutodlīce (NG)=witodlīce

wuton 1 pers. pl. subj. of wītan *to go*. used to introduce an imperative or hortatory clause *let us...! come!* CP.

wutu (M), wutum, wutun (N)=wuton

wutudlīce=witodlīce

wūðwuta (DR)=ūðwita; **wȳc**=wīc

wyc-=wic-; **wȳd**=wīd; **wyd-**=wud-

wyder-=wiðer-; **wȳf-**=wīf-

wyglere=wiglere; **wyht**=wiht

wyl-=weal-, wel-, wi(e)l-; **wȳl-**=wīel-

wylcð pres. 3 sg. of wealcan.

wylf f. *she-wolf*, OET.

wylfen I. adj. *wolfish*, DEOR,OEG. II. f. *she-wolf, fury*, Lcd; GL. ['*wolfen*']

wylian=wylwan

wȳliscmoru=wēalmoru

wyll I. f. *wool*, LL(166n⁴). II.=wiell

wyllan (æ, e;=ie) *to boil*, Lcd. ['*well*']

wylleburne †f. *spring*.

wyllecærse (i) *watercress*, Lcd,WW. ['*wellcress*']

wyllen (i) *made of wool, woollen*.

wyllestrēam m. *running water*, Ph. ['*wellstream*']

wyllewæter n. *spring water*, Lcd. ['*wellwater*']

wylleweg *road to a well or spring*, KC 5·150¹². .

wyllflōd (i) *flood, deluge*, GEN1412.

wyllgespring n. *spring*, BH,PH.

wyllspring(e) (e¹, i¹) m. *spring*, Æ,CP, WW. ['*wellspring*']

wyloc=weoloc; **wyn**=wynn

±**wyltan** (æ, e;=ie) *to roll*.

wylw-an, -ian (e, i;=ie) *to roll, roll together* : *compound*, join.

wyn-=win-, winn-; **wȳn-**=wīn-

wynbēam m. *tree of gladness, holy cross*, EL844.

wynburh f. *delightful town*, PPs127².

wyncondel f. *pleasant light, sun*, Gu1186.

wyndæg† m. *day of gladness*.

+**wynde** n. *weaving*, GL.

wyndecræft m. *art of embroidery*, GL.

wyndle f. *wound*, LL381,23.

wyndrēam m. *jubilation, joyful sound*, Ps.

wyndrēamnes f. *jubilation*, LPs150⁵.

wyndrian=wundrian; **wyne**=wine

wynele m. *gladdening oil*, PPs108¹⁸.

wynfæst (e) *joyful*, PsC50¹⁹.

wyngesīð m. *pleasant companion*, PPs100³.

wyngrāf mn. *delightful grove*, PPs94¹³.

wynigað=wunigað pres. pl. of wunian.

wynland† (o²) n. *land of delight*.

wynlēas† *joyless*.

wynlic *pleasant, beautiful, joyful*, HL,Ph. adv. -līce, Ps. ['*winly*']

wynlust m. *sensual pleasure*, Æ.

wynmæg f. *winsome maiden*, Gu1319.

wynn f. (occl. late as. wyn) *joy, rapture, pleasure, delight, gladness*, B; AO. ['*win*']

wynn- v. also wyn-, win(n)-.

wynnum† *joyfully, beautifully*. [wynn]

wynpsalterium n. *psalm of joy*, PPs56¹⁰.

wynrōd f. *blessed cross*, SOL235.

wynsang m. *joyful song*, W265³¹.

wynstaðol m. *joyous foundation*, RD92³.

wynsum (e, i; once +wuns-) '*winsome*,' *pleasant, delightful, joyful, merry*, B,MH, Ph; CP : *kindly*, BH.

+**wynsumian** *to rejoice, exult*, DR : *make glad, make pleasing*.

±**wynsumlic** adj. *pleasant, delightful* adv. -līce *pleasantly, happily* Æ

wynsumnes (i) f. *loveliness, pleasantness, rejoicing,* Æ.

wynwerod n. '*chorus,' joyous band,* GL.

wynwyrt f. *pleasant plant,* DD5.

wynyng=wining

wyorðmynd (BL)=weorðmynd

wȳr=wīr; **wyrc**=weorc

±**wyrcan** (e, eo, i) *to prepare, perform, do, make, 'WORK*,' construct, produce, effect,* Æ; AO,CP : *use (tools) : dispose, constitute : amount to :* (w. g.) *strive after : deserve, gain, win, acquire.* Ēastron w. *to keep Easter, eat the passover.*

+**wyrce** n. *work : proceeds of work, perquisite,* LL449,7 (v. BTs).

wyrcend m. *worker, doer,* ÆH.

wyrcnes f. *work, operation,* BH.

wyrcta (Ep,MtL)=wyrhta

wyrcung f. *working, work,* DR.

±**wyrd** I. fn. *fate, chance, fortune, destiny,* B,Bo,Cp,Seaf; Æ,AO : *Fate, the Fates, Providence,* CP : *event, phenomenon, transaction, fact,* Bl,Cr : *deed :* (+) *condition : pleasure,* AO126³³. ['*weird*'; weorðan] II. f. *verbosity,* OEG1419.

wyrdan=wierdan

+**wyrde** I. n. *speech, conversation : ordinance.* II. *acknowledging, agreeing with,* CHR1055. III.=+wyrðe

+**wyrdelic** *historical, authentic,* Æ : *fortuitous,* OEG. adv. -līce *eloquently : accurately, verbatim : wisely,* OEG208.

+**wyrdelicnes** f. *eloquence,* A13·38³²¹.

wyrdgesceapum *by chance,* WW400²⁵.

+**wyrdignes** f. *eloquence,* OEG5488.

+**wyrdlian**=+wierdan

wyrdnes f. *condition, state,* Bo128n.

wyrdstæf m. *decree of fate,* Gu1325.

±**wyrdwrītere** m. *historian, chronicler,* Æ.

wyred=werod

wyregung=wyrgung

wyrest=wierrest; **wyrfan**=hwierfan

wyrg=wearg

wyrgan I. *to strangle,* Cp; Æ. ['*worry*'] II.=wiergan

wyrgcwedol (e;=ie) *ill-tongued, given to cursing.*

wyrgcwedolian (e) *to curse,* VPs.

wyrgcwedolnes (e¹, i²) f. *cursing,* Ps.

wyrged (æ) *the devil,* NG.

-**wyrgednes** v. ā-w.

wyrgels=wrigels; **wyrgelnes**=wyrgnes

wyrgend (e) m. *reviler, evildoer,* ÆL.

wyrgende *given to cursing,* W70¹⁸.

wyrgnes f. *abuse, cursing,* Æ,BH.

wyrgðu† (æ, e) f. *curse, condemnation, punishment : evil, wickedness.*

wyrgung (e) f. *curse, cursing, condemnation, banishment,* Æ.

+**wyrht** (eo) fn. *work, deed, service : desert, merit,* AO,CP : *transgression.* mid gewyrhtum *deservedly.*

wyrhta m. '*wright,' artist, labourer, worker, maker, creator,* Æ,Bl,Bo,G,LL; CP : (+) *fellow-worker :* (+) *accomplice.*

wyri-=wearg-; **wyrian**=wiergan

wyricean=wyrcan; **wyrig**=werig

wyrig-=wearg-, wyrg-

wyrld=woruld

wyrm (eo, o, u) I. m. *reptile, serpent, snake, dragon,* Æ,AO : '*WORM,' insect, mite : poor creature,* VPs. [wurma] II.=wearm

wyrma=wurma; **wyrmǣt**=wyrmǣte (I.)

wyrmǣte I. f. *attack of worms, worm-eaten state,* A,LCD. II. adj. *worm-eaten,* LCD. ['*wormete*']

±**wyrman** (æ, e, i;=ie) *to warm, make warm.*

wyrmbaso *red, scarlet,* OET113⁶⁷.

wyrmcynn n. *serpent-kind, sort of serpent,* AO,B,G. ['*wormkin*']

wyrmella=wurmille

wyrmfāh *adorned with figures of snakes, damascened?* B1698.

wyrmgal(d)ere (u) m. *snake-charmer,* Æ.

wyrmgealdor n. *charm against snakes,* LCD 148a.

wyrmgeard m. *abode of serpents,* SOL469.

wyrmgeblǣd n. *swelling from snake-bite? (or insect-bite?)* LCD162b.

wyrmhǣlsere m. *diviner by serpents,* WW 441³⁵.

wyrmhīw n. *likeness of a serpent,* ÆL10¹⁰⁴.

wyrmhord n. *dragon's hoard,* B2222.

wyrming (æ, e;=ie) f. *warming,* BHB196²⁷. [wearm]

wyrmlīc n. *form of a serpent,* WA.

wyrmmelu n. *worm-meal, 'pulvis e vermibus confectus,'* LCD.

wyrmrēad (u¹) *purple, scarlet,* Æ.

wyrms nm. *virus, corrupt matter,* Æ.

±**wyrmsan** *to fester,* CP.

+**wyrms(ed)** *purulent,* LCD,WW.

wyrmsele m. *hall of serpents, hell,* JUD119.

wyrmshrǣcing f. *spitting up of matter,* WW 113⁸?

±**wyrmsig** (u) *purulent,* WW.

wyrmslite m. *snake-bite,* W188¹.

wyrmsūtspīung f. *spitting up of matter,* WW 113⁸?

wyrmwyrt f. *worm-wort,* LCD.

wyrn=wearn; **wyrnan**=wiernan

wyrp m. *a throw, cast,* Lk22⁴¹. ['*wurp*']

wyrpan=wierpan

wyrpe (e;=ie) f. *revolution, change, recovery, relief, improvement.* [weorpan]

+**wyrpe** n. *heap,* KC5·78'; Mdf.

wyrpel m. *jess (in falconry),* WY87 (v. ES 37·195).

-wyrplic v. scort-w.
wyrpst, wyrpð pres. 2 and 3 sg. of weorpan
and wyrpan.
wyrrest=wierrest; wyrs=wiers
wyrshrǣcung=wyrmshrǣcing
wyrsian (=ie) to get 'worse,' Æ,VPs,W.
wyrslic (=ie) bad, vile, mean, RD,W.
wyrsm-=wyrms-
wyrst=(1) wrist; (2) wierrest
wyrt (e, i) f. I. herb, vegetable, plant, spice,
CP,Lcd,LG,VPs; AO : crop : root. ['wort']
II. 'wort' (brewing), Lcd.
wyrtbedd m. bed of herbs, LCD.
+wyrtbox f. fragrant herb or perfume box,
OEG 8²⁹⁹.
wyrtbrǣð m. fragrance, Æ.
wyrtcynn n. species of plant, JnL,WW.
wyrtcynren n. the vegetable world, LPs 146⁸.
wyrtdrenc m. herbal drink, medicine, Cp.
[v. 'drench']
wyrteceddrenc m. herbal acid drink, LCD
63b.
wyrtfæt n. scent-bottle, OEG.
wyrtforbor n. restraint from action by the
operation of herbs (BT), LCD 111b.
wyrtgælstre f. witch who works with herbs,
LCD 3·186¹¹.
wyrtgeard m. (kitchen) garden, CPs 143¹³.
wyrt-gemang (Æ) n., -gemangnes (e³) f.
mixture of herbs, spices, perfume.
wyrtgyrd=wyrtgeard
±wyrtian to season, spice, perfume, LCD,
WW.
wyrtig garden-like? full of herbs? ÆL 30³¹².
wyrtmete m. dish of herbs, pottage, WW.
wyrt-rum, wyrt-(t)ruma m., -rume f. root,
root-stock, CP : origin, beginning, stock.
[v. CC 68]
±wyr(t)truman to take root : establish : root
out, DR.
wyrttūn, ±wyrtūn (Æ) m. garden.
wyrttūnhege f. garden enclosure, GD 67¹⁸.
wyrtung f. a preparation of herbs, LCD
1·342'.
wyrtwala (i, eo, u¹; æ, e²) m. root, stock,
LCD : base, lower part, KC.
wyrtwalian (æ²) to set, plant, root : root up,
ÆGR.
wyrtwalu f.=wyrtwala
wyrtweard m. gardener, GD 23; Jn 20¹⁵.
wyrtwela=wyrtwala
wyrð=weorð
wyrðan to irrigate with manure, A 36·77.
+wyrðan I. (=ie) to value, appraise. II.=
+weorðan
wyrðe=weorð
+wyrðe (=ie) n. bulk, contents, amount,
LCD.
wyrðeland=yrðland

wyrðig I. fitting, deserved, AO 256¹¹. II.=
worðig
wyrðing m. fallow land? cultivated land?
WW 495²⁰.
wyruld-=woruld-; wys-=wis(s)-
±wyscan (ī) (w. d. pers. and g. thing) to
'wish,' Æ,CP; AO : (+) adopt, ÆH.
+wyscednes f. adoption, RBL 11¹⁴.
+wyscendlic desirable, CM 109 : optative
(mood), ÆGR : adoptive. adv. -līce.
+wyscing (ī) f. adoption, RB 10².
wysdōm (Æ)=wīsdōm; wyt=wit pron.
wyt-, wȳt-=wit-, wīt-; wytt=wit pron.
wytuma m. paranymph, A 13·30⁸². [=
witumbora? (BT)]
wyð-=wið-
wyxð pres. 3 sg. of weaxan.

Y

yb (AA)=ymb
ybilberende (OEG 53¹⁶)=yfelberende
ȳcan, ȳcean=īecan
yce (WW 468²²)=hice
ȳce (ī) fm. toad, frog, LCD,WW.
ȳcte pret. 3 sg. of ȳcan.
ȳdæges=īdæges
ȳddisc n? household stuff, furniture, possessions, Æ. [ēad]
ȳde=ēode; ȳdel=īdel; ydes=ides
ȳdisc=ȳddisc; ȳdl-=īdl-; yel-=iel-
yfæsdrype=yfesdrype
yfel I. adj. gsm. yfel(e)s bad, ill, Bl,Lcd,Mt :
'evil,' wicked, wretched, Bl,CP,Mt. comp.
wiersa, wyrsa worse. superl. wierrest(a),
wiersta, weorsta, wyr(re)sta worst, Æ,AO.
II. n. 'evil,' ill, wickedness, misery, B,Bl,
CP,OET,RB,Ps.
yfeladl f. 'cachexia,' consumption, WW
113¹³.
yfelberende (ybil-) bringer of evil tidings,
OEG 53¹⁶ (v. ANS 85·310).
yfelcund evil, malignant, LPs.
yfelcwedolian (ð) to speak evil, ERPs 36²².
yfel-cweðende, -cweðelgiende (EPs) evil-
speaking, SPs 36²³.
yfeldǣd f. ill deed, injury, Æ.
yfeldǣda m. evildoer, ÆL.
yfeldǣde evil-doing, Æ,LCD,GL.
yfeldēma m. wicked judge, NC 335.
yfeldönd m. evildoer, JnL 18³⁰.
yfeldönde evil-doing, LL (424²⁰).
yfeldysig 'stultomalus,' WW 165¹⁸.
yfele=yfle
yfelful malicious, wicked, A 11·116¹³.
yfelgiornes f. malice, wickedness, DR.
±yfelian to inflict evil, hurt, wrong, injure,
Ps : become bad, grow worse, suffer, W.
['evil']

yfelic, yfellic *evil, bad* : *poor, mean* : *foul, ugly.* adv. -līce.

yfellǣrrende *persuading to evil*, GPH390.

yfellibbende *evil-living*, RBL118¹⁰.

yfelnes f. *wickedness, depravity*, Æ; CP. ['*evilness*']

yfelsacend (eo¹, u²) m. *blasphemer*, GD289²⁷.

±**yfelsacian** *to blaspheme*, BL189; GD289²⁷.

yfelsacung f. *calumny, blasphemy*, Æ,BL.

yfelsǣc (eo¹, u²) n? *blasphemy*, EL524.

±**yfelsian** (ebol-) *to blaspheme*, NG,WW.

yfel-sprǣce, -sprecende *evil-speaking*, Ps.

yfelsung (ebol-, eoful-) f. *blasphemy*, LL.

yfeltihtend m. *inciter to evil*, ÆH.

yfeltihtende *inciting to evil*, ÆH.

yfelwille *malevolent*, Sc196¹⁸.

yfelwillende *vicious*, Æ,CP.

yfelwillendnes f. *malice*, LPs.

yfelwilnian *to desire evil*, LPs.

yfelwoerc n. *evil deed*, DR103¹.

yfelwyrcende *evil-doing*, ÆL.

yfelwyrde *evil-speaking*, ES39·354.

yfemest superl. adj. *highest, uppermost*, CP. [ufan]

ȳfer v. ȳfre.

yfera=yferra; **yferdrype**=yfesdrype

+**yferian** *to exalt*, LPs.

yferra comp. adj. *after, subsequent* : *higher.* [ufan]

yfes f.=efes

yfesdrype (æ²) m. '*eaves-drop*,' EC141¹⁶.

ȳfig=īfig

yfle adv. (comp. wirs) *evilly, badly, ill, wrongly, miserably, hurtfully*, Bl,G,Gen, Ps,Rd. ['*evil*']

±**yflian**=yfelian

yflung f. *injury*, GD197¹².

yfmest=yfemest

ȳfre? ȳfer? *escarpment*, BC,KC (v. GBG).

ȳgett=iggað

ȳgland=īegland; **ȳgðelīce**=īeðelīce

ȳhte=īhte; **ȳl**=īl; **ylca** (Æ)=ilca

ylcian=elcian; **yld**=ield; **yle**=ile

ylf, ylfe=ælf

ylfet, ylfetu, ylfette (Æ)=ilfetu

ylfig *raving, mad*, WW. [v. '*giddy*']

ylful (HGL529)=ieldful

ylp m. *elephant*, WW; Æ. ['*elp*']

ylpen=elpen(d)-; **ylpesbān**=elpendbān

yltsta=ieldesta wk. masc. superl. of eald.

yltwist f? *catching of birds*, WW351⁶.

ym-=ymb(e)-; **ymb**=ymbe

ymb-=imb-

ymbærnan *to travel round*, BH288⁸.

ymbbegang=ymbgang

ymbberan⁴ *to surround*, JUL,MkLR.

ymbbīgnes (bebīg-) f. *bending round, bend, circuit, sweep (of a river)*, BH424¹⁰. [bīegan]

ymbbindan³ *to bind round*, MkL9⁴².

ymbcǣfian *to embroider round, bedeck*, RPs 44¹⁵.

ymbceorfan³ *to circumcise*, NG.

ymbceorfnes f. *circumcision*, JnR7²³ (-cernes).

ymbcerr (=ie) m. *turning about, going, migration*, NG : *tergiversation, trickery*, DR.

ymbcerran=ymbcyrran

ymbclyccan *to enclose*, RPs16¹⁰ (ES38·25).

ymbclyppan (i) *to embrace, clasp*, ÆGR.

ymbclypping f. *embracing*, OEG4529 (emc-).

ymbcyme m. *assembly, convention*, LL12 (ymc-).

ymbcyrran (e²; =ie) *to turn round, go round, make the circuit of* : *overturn, change*, NG.

ymbdringend=ymbhringend

ymbe (e¹, u¹) I. prep. w. a. d. and adv. (of place) *around, about, at, upon, near, along* : (of time) *about, at, after, before.* ymb utan *about, by, around* : (causal, etc.) *about, in regard to, concerning, on account of, owing to.* ðæs y. lītel *soon after.* y. bēon *to set about a thing.* ['EMBE,' 'UMBE'] II. (=i) n. *swarm of bees*, LCD1·384'; Mdf.

ymbe-=ymb-

ymbeaht mp. '*collatio*,' WW; OEG53²² (v. ES11·492).

ymbeardian *to dwell round*, VPs30¹⁴.

ymbebǣtan *to curb, restrain*, MET24³⁷.

ymbebēgnes=ymbbīgnes

ymbeornan=ymbiernan

ymbesprǣc f. *talk, remark, criticism*, Æ.

ymbe-ðanc, -ðonc, -ðanca m. *thought, reflection*, CP.

ymbeðencan=ymbðencan

ymbeðridian *to think about*, NC335.

ymb-fær (embef-) n., -færeld (Æ) nm. *journey round, circuit.*

ymbfæstnes f. *enclosure*, DR174⁹.

ymbfæstnung f. *monument, tomb*, JnL19⁴¹.

ymbfæðmian *to embrace*, SOL150'.

ymbfaran⁶ *to surround*, AO80²⁰ : *travel round*, GD490³.

ymbfaru (emf-) n. *circuit*, HGL422¹⁴.

ymbfeng I. m. *envelope, cover*, OEG468. II. pres. 3 sg. of ymbfōn.

ymbfēran *to go about, journey round*, AA 30¹⁰; GPH396.

ymbfōn⁷ *to surround, encompass, embrace, grasp, seize*, AO.

ymbfrætewian *to decorate, deck round*, LPs, W.

ymb-gān anv., -gangan⁷ *to go round, surround.*

ymbgang (eo²) m. *going about, circuit, circumference, surrounding belt*, AO.

ymbgearwian *to clothe, dress*, NG.
ymbgedelf n. *digging round*, ÆH 2·408[11].
ymb-gefrætwian, -gefretwian (VPs)=ymb-
frætewian
ymbgeong (N)=ymbgang
ymbgerēnian *to deck round*, BLPs 143[15].
ymb-gesett, -geseten *neighbouring*, BH
2·362.
ymbgesettan=ymbsettan
ymbgirdan=ymbgyrdan
ymbgong=ymbgang
ymbgyrdan (i) *to gird about, encircle,
surround*, Æ.
ymbhabban *to surround*, AO : *include, contain* : *detain*.
ymbhaga (=i[1]) m. *enclosure for bees*, LCD
1·395[4]. [ymbe II.]
ymbhaldan=ymbhealdan
ymbhammen *surrounded, covered*, WW
340[14].
ymbhangen pp. of ymbhōn.
ymbhealdan[7] *to encompass*, SAT 7.
ymbhēapian *to crowd about*, WW.
ymbhēdig=ymbhȳdig
ymbhegian *to hedge round*, ÆGR.
ymbhēpan=ymbhȳpan
ymbhīwan (WW 381[2])=ymbhȳpan
ymbhlennan (emb-) *to surround*, OEG 24.
ymbhoga m. *care, anxiety, solicitude, consideration*, Mt; CP. [v. '*embe*']
ymbhogian *to be anxious about*, LPs.
ymbhōn[7] *to surround, deck, clothe*, HL,W.
ymb-hringan *to surround, fence round*, CP :
wind round, WW.
ymbhringend m. *attendant member of a
retinue*, GL.
ymbhūung=ymbhȳwung
ymbhwearft=ymbhwyrft
ymbhweorfan[3] (e[2], u[2]) *to turn round, revolve : go round, encompass : tend, cultivate*,
CP.
ymbhweorfnes f. *change, revolution*, DR 37[18].
ymbhweorft (e[2])=ymbhwyrft
ymbhwerf- (u[2], y[2])=ymbhweorf-
ymbhwyrft (e, ea, eo, i) m. *rotation, revolution, turn : circle, extent, environment,
circuit, orbit*, Æ,CP : *circle of the earth, orb,
globe, world*, Æ,AO : *region, district :
cultivation*, Æ.
ymb-hȳde, -hȳdi-=ymbhȳdig-
ymbhȳdig *anxious, solicitous, careful, sus-
picious : to be observed, needing attention*,
Æ. adv. -līce.
ymbhȳdiglic *anxious, careful, solicitous.*
adv. -līce.
ymbhȳdignes f. *anxiety, solicitude*, ÆH.
ymbhygd f. *anxiety*, BL,GD.
ymbhygdig=ymbhȳdig
ymbhȳpan *to press round, assail*, BH,WW.

ymbhȳwung (-hūung) f. *circumcision*, JnL
7[22].
ymbiernan[3] (io, y) *to run round : surround*,
MH.
ymblǣdan *to lead round*, OET (VHy 7[18]).
ymblǣrgian (emb-) *to provide with a rim,
surround*, OEG 8[377]. [lǣrig]
ymblicgan[5] *to surround, enclose*, AO.
ymblīðan *to sail round*, BH 408[25].
ymblōcian *to look round*, NG.
ymblofian *to praise*, LPs 116[1].
ymblyt m. *circle, circuit, circumference*,
SAT 7?
Ymbren n. '*Ember-'tide, Ember-day*, Lk,LL.
[ymbryne]
Ymbrendæg m. *Ember-day*, BF,W.
ymbrene=ymbryne
Ymbrenfæsten n. *periodical fast (at Embertide)*, LL; Æ. [v. '*ember*']
Ymbrenwuce (i[3]) f. *Ember-week*, LL 78,43.
[v. '*ember*']
Ymbrigdæg=Ymbrendæg
ymbrine=ymbryne
ymbryne (e[2], i[2]) m. *revolution, circuit, course,
anniversary*, Æ : *lapse of time*, Æ.
ymbscēawian *to look round*, NG.
ymbscēawiendlīce adv. *circumspectly*, BH
450[21].
ymbscēawung f. *looking round*, DR.
ymbscīnan[1] *to shine round*, ÆH.
ymbscrīðan[1] *to revolve about*, MET 20[208].
ymbscrȳdan *to clothe*, Æ. [scrūd]
ymbscūwan *to screen, defend* ('*obumbrare*'),
EPs 139[8].
ymbscȳnan=ymbscīnan
ymbsēan (N)=ymbsēon II.
ymbsellan *to surround, enclose, beset*, Æ :
endue, clothe, VH 24.
ymbsēon I. sv[5] *to look round.* II. f. *behold-
ing, regard.*
ymb-set, -setl n. *siege*, BH.
ymbsetennes f. *siege*, Ps.
ymbsetnung f. *sedition*, LkL : *siege*, GL.
ymbsett *neighbouring*, BH 362.
ymbsettan *to set round, surround, beset, encompass*, Æ : *plant.*
ymbsewen *circumspect*, GD 107[11].
ymb-sierwan, -sirwan pres. 3 sg. -sireð *to
design, plot*, CP : *lay in wait for.*
ymbsittan[5] *to set round, surround, invest,
besiege*, Æ,AO,CP : *sit over, reflect upon.*
ymbsittend† m. *one living near, neighbour.*
ymbsmēagung (embe-) f. *consideration*,
WW 165[28].
ymbsnāð, ymbsniden, pret. 3 sg. and pp. of
ymbsnīðan.
ymbsnidennes f. *circumcision*, Æ.
ymbsnīðan[1] (em-) *to circumcise*, Lk; Æ.
[v. '*embe*']

ymbspænning f. *allurement*, CHRD 66³³.
ymbspannan⁷ *to span or clasp round, embrace*, BH 392⁶.
ymbspræc f. *conversation, comment, criticism*, Æ.
ymbspræce *spoken about, well known*, MET 10⁵⁹.
ymbsprecan³ *to speak about*, Lk 19⁷.
ymbstandan⁶ *to stand around, surround*, BO, BH.
ymbstandend m. *bystander*, Æ (emb-).
ymbstand(en)nes f. '*circumstantia*,' Pss.
ymbstocc (=i¹) m. *stump containing a swarm of bees*, KC 5·234.
ymbstrícan *to smooth round*, LCD 36b.
ymbstyrian *to stir about, overturn*, LkL 15⁸.
ymbswæpe f. *digression*, WW 5²⁸.
ymbswāpan⁷ *to sweep round, environ : envelop, clothe.*
ymbswāpe=ymbswæpe
ymbswīfan¹ *to revolve round*, NC 352.
ymbsyllan=ymbsellan
ymbsyrwan=ymbsierwan
ymb-trymian, -trymman (Æ,CP) *to surround : fortify, protect.*
ymbtrymming m. *fortification*, Æ.
ymbtȳnan *to hedge round, surround*, MtR 21³³, W 146²⁷. [tūn]
ymbtyrnan *to turn round*, LCD : *surround*, WW.
ymbðeahtian *to consider, reflect*, CP.
ymbðencan *to think about, consider*, CP.
ymbðonc=ymbeðanc
ymbðreodian (embðryd-) *to deliberate*, GL.
ymbðreodung (i, y) f. *deliberation, consideration*, GL.
ymbðringan³ *to press round, throng about*, Ps,WW.
ymbðringend=ymbhringend
ymbðrydung=ymbðreodung
ymbūtan (e¹) prep. (w. a.) and adv. *around, about, outside, beyond*, Mk; AO,CP. [v. '*embe*']
ymbwæfan *to clothe*, LPs 44¹⁵.
ymbwærlan *to turn (oneself) about, turn towards*, NG.
ymbweaxan⁶ *to grow round, surround*, AO.
ymbwendan *to turn round : turn away, avert.*
ymbwendung f. *reviving : behaviour*, DR.
ymbweorpan³ *to surround*, AN 1555.
ymbwícigan *to surround, beleaguer*, Ex 65.
ymbwindan³ *to clasp round, hold : wind round.*
ymbwlātian *to contemplate*, Æ 145¹².
ymbwlātung f. *contemplation*, ÆGR.
ymbwrītan¹ *to score round*, LCD 124a.
ymbwyrcan *to hedge in*, CP : *weave*, MtL 27²⁹.

ymbyrnan=ymbiernan
ymcyme=ymbcyme
ymel (æ, e) m. *weevil, mite, beetle, caterpillar*, ÆGR; GD.
ymele, ymle f. *scroll*, ÆL,WW.
ymen m. '*hymn*,' *sacred song*, Bl,Ps. [L. hymnus]
ymenbōc f. '*hymn-book*,' BH 484²³.
ymener (BC 3·660')=ymnere
ymensang m. *hymn*, GD,AJPs.
ymesēne *blind*, ÆH 1·418'.
ymest=yfemest; **ymle** (Æ)=ymele
ymmon, ymn=ymen
ymnere m. *hymn-book*, BC,KC 4·275'. ['*hymner*'; L. hymnarium]
ymnyttan=emnettan; **ȳmon**=ȳmen
ymryne=ymbryne; **yn-**=in-
ynce m. '*inch*,' LL,Sol. [L. uncia]
yndse f. *ounce*, AO : *piece of money, shekel.* [L. uncia]
yngrian=hyngrian; **ynn-**=inn-
ynnelēac (ene-, yne-, ynni-) n. *onion*, GL.
ynse, yntse (Æ)=yndse
yplen (WW)=ypplen
±**yppan** *to bring out, open, manifest, disclose, display, reveal, betray*, BH,CP,WW : *come forth, be disclosed* : (+) *utter.* ['*uppe*']
yppe I. (u) f. *upper room : raised place, high seat, tribune : stage, platform*, WW 150⁹. II. *evident, known, open, manifest.*
ypping f. *manifestation : accumulation, extent, expanse?* Ex 498.
yppingíren (ip-) n. *crowbar?* LL 455,15 (or ? cippingíren ANS 115·164).
ypplen n. *top, height*, OEG 2862.
ypte pret. 3 sg. of yppan.
ȳr I.† m. *name of the rune for* y : *bow?* : *gold? horn?* RUN 27. II. n? *back of axe*, CHR,LCD.
yrcðu=iergðu; **yrd**=eard; **yrd-**=yrð-
ȳre I. m. *a coin of Danish origin*, BC 3·371². II.=ȳr
ȳren=íren
yreðweorh (JUL 90?)=ierreðweorh
yrf- v. also ierf-.
yrfan *to inherit : leave (by will) : honour with a funeral feast* (BTac), TC 611⁵.
yrfcwealm (a²) m. *murrain*, CHR 986 CE. [orf]
yrfebēc fp. *will, testament*, WW.
yrfecwealm=yrfcwealm
yrfeflit n. *dispute about an inheritance*, EC 145¹⁶.
yrfefyrst m. *legal formality or delay before entering on an inheritance*, WW 115³.
yrfegedāl n. *division of an inheritance*, Æ.
yrfegewrit (e¹) n. *will, testament, charter*, EC 145.
yrfehand (e¹) f. *natural successor*, EC 111¹⁴.
yrfelāf f. *bequest, inheritance : heir*, Ex 403.

yrfeland (ie) n. *inherited land*, CP.
yrfelēas (ie) *unprovided with cattle*, TC162'.
yrfe-numa, -nama (RWH53²⁰) mf. *heir, successor, Æ.*
yrfestōl† m. *hereditary seat, home.*
yrfeweard (ie) m. *heir, son*, AO,CP.
±**yrfeweardian** *to inherit*, CLSPs.
yrfeweardnes (ie) f. *heritage*, CP.
yrfeweardwrītere, yrfewrītend m. *will writer, testator, Æ.*
yrfweard-=yrfeweard-; +**yrgan**=eargian
yrgð, yrgðo, yrhðu=iergðu
yrm-=eorm-, ierm-; **yrnan**=iernan
yrre=ierre; **yrs-**=iers-
yrsebin f. *iron box*, LL455,17 (?=īsern, BT).
yrð (ea;=ie) f. *ploughing, tilling, LL* : *standing corn, crop, produce*, BH. ['*earth*']
yrðland (æ, ie) n. *arable land*, KC,WW; Æ. ['*earthland*']
yrðling (æ, e, eo, i) m. *husbandman, farmer, ploughman, WW*; Æ : *wagtail?* ANS 119·434. ['*earthling*']
yrðmearc f. *boundary of ploughed land*, KC.
yrðtilia=eorðtilia; **ys**=is, v. wesan.
ȳs=īs; **ysel**=esol; **ysele**=ysle
ȳsen, ȳsern=īsen, īsern
ysl, ysle f. *spark, ember, Æ.* ['*isel*']
yslende *glowing*, WW235²⁸.
ysope f., ysopo (indecl.) '*hyssop*,' *Æ,Lcd, VPs.*
ȳst f. *storm, tempest, hurricane*, AO,CP.
ȳstan *to storm, rage*, OEG.
ȳstas=ēstas np. of ēst.
ȳstig *stormy, of the storm*, Lcd,PPs.
yt=itt pres. 3 sg. of etan.
ȳtan I. *to drive out, banish*, CHR1058D : *squander, dissipate*, RB55⁴. [ūt] II.= ūtan
Ytas=Iotas

ȳtemest superl. adj. *uttermost, extreme, last*, Bo,DR,LG,VPs; AO,CP. on ȳtemestum sīðe '*in extremis.*' ['*utmost*']
ȳtend m. *devastator*, WW232³⁷.
yteren *made of otter-skin*, AO18²¹. [otor]
ȳterra=ūterra
yteð=iteð pres. 3 sg. of etan.
ȳting f. *outing, journey, Æ*,RB.
ȳt-mest, -mæst=ȳtemest
ytst, ytt=itst pres. 2 sg., itt pres. 3 sg. of etan.
ȳttera, ȳttra=ūter(r)a
ȳð I. f. *wave, billow, flood, An,B*; Æ,CP : (†) *sea* : *liquid, water.* ['*ythe*'] II.=ieð
ȳð-=ēað-, ieð-
ȳðan=(1) ieðan; (2) ȳðgian
ȳðbord n. *ship? ship's side?* CRA57.
ȳðeg=ȳðig; **ȳðegan**=ȳðgian
ȳðfaru† f. *wave-course, flood.*
ȳðgebland† n. *wave-mixture, surge*, B.
ȳðgewinn† n. *wave-strife, life in the waves*, B.
ȳðgian *to fluctuate, flow, surge*, CP : *roar, rage.*
ȳðgung=ȳðung
ȳðhengest m. (*wave-horse*), *ship*, CHR1003E.
ȳðhof† n. *water-dwelling, ship.*
ȳðian (Æ)=ȳðgian
ȳðig *billowy, stormy*, ÆL16⁷⁰.
ȳðlād f. *sea-voyage*, B228.
ȳðlāf† f. *sand, shore, beach.*
ȳðlid† n. *ship, vessel*, AN.
ȳðlida m. *wave-traverser, ship*, B198.
ȳðmearh† m. *sea-horse, ship.*
ȳðmere m. *ocean of waves*, PH94.
ȳðung f. *agitation, commotion, Æ* : *inundation, Æ.*
ȳðwōrigende *wandering on the waves*, WW 243³.
ȳwan, ȳwian=iewan

SUPPLEMENT

ADDITIONAL SIGN AND ABBREVIATIONS

:   After an entry the colon indicates that the word is already in the main part of the dictionary and that a meaning given after the colon is believed to take precedence over the one given in the main part.

AHD Die althochdeutschen Glossen, ed. E. Sievers and E. Steinmeyer, Bd. 1–4, Berlin, 1879–98.

AJP American Journal of Philology.

ASPR The Anglo-Saxon Poetic Records, 6 vols., ed. G. Krapp and E. Dobbie, New York, 1931–53.

BHW The Homilies of Wulfstan, ed. D. Bethurum, Oxford, 1957.

BPG The Old English Prudentius Glosses at Boulogne-sur-Mer, ed. H. Meritt, Stanford, 1959 (Stanford Studies in Language and Literature, 16).

CGL Corpus Glossariorum Latinorum, 7 vols., ed. G. Goetz, Leipzig, 1888–1923.

CPC The Peterborough Chronicle, ed. C. Clark, Oxford, 1958.

EGS English and Germanic Studies.

EI The Old English Exodus, ed. E. Irving, New Haven, 1953.

FF Der Flussname Themse und seine Sippe, by Max Förster, Sitzungsberichte der Bayerischen Akademie der Wissenschaften, phil.-hist. Abt., Bd. 1, München, 1941.

FGR Zur Geschichte des Reliquienkultus in Altengland, by Max Förster, Sitzungsberichte der Bayerischen Akademie der Wissenschaften, phil-hist. Abt., Hft. 8, München, 1943.

FL Fact and Lore about Old English Words, by H. Meritt, Stanford, 1954.

GAT The Old English Apollonius of Tyre, ed. P. Goolden, Oxford, 1958.

GLL Lehnbildungen und Lehnbedeutungen im Altenglischen, by H. Gneuss, Berlin, 1955.

HAW Anglo-Saxon Writs, by F. Harmer, Manchester, 1952.

HBK Kommentar zum Beowulf, by J. Hoops, Heidelberg, 1932.

HBS Beowulfstudien, by J. Hoops, Anglistische Forschungen 74, Heidelberg, 1932.

HEW Altenglisches Etymologisches Wörterbuch, by F. Holthausen, Heidelberg, 1934.

HSC Studien zum altenglischen Computus, H. Henel, Beiträge zur Englischen Philologie 36, Leipzig, 1934.

JEGP- Old English Glosses, Mostly Dry Point, by H. Meritt, to appear in JEGP.

JM The Jespersen Miscellany, London, 1930.

JW Wulfstanstudien, by K. Jost, Schweizer Anglistische Arbeiten, Bd. 23.

KCM Catalogue of Manuscripts Containing Anglo-Saxon, by N. Ker, Oxford, 1957.

KF One leaf of a Latin-Old English Glossary, now at the University of Kansas (see KCM 240).

KN Untersuchungen einiger altenglischen Krankheitsnamen, by J. Geldner, Braunschweig, 1906.

KW Die Wunder des Ostens, ed. F. Knappe, Berlin, 1906.

LCG The Corpus Glossary, ed W. Lindsay, Cambridge, 1921.

MÆ Medium Ævum.

MAG The Battle of Maldon, ed. E. Gordon, London, 1937.

MNG Notes on Some Old English Glosses in Aldhelm's De Laudibus Virginitatis, by T. Mustanoja. Bulletin de la Société Néophilologique de Helsinki, 51, 49–61 (1950).

SUPPLEMENTARY ABBREVIATIONS

MPS The Poetical Dialogues of Solomon and Saturn, ed. R. Menner, New York, 1941 (MLA Monograph 13).

OEGC Old English Glosses, A Collection, ed. H. Meritt, New York, 1945 (MLA General Series 16).

PM Medicine in Anglo-Saxon Times, by J. Payne, Oxford, 1904.

RAC Anglo-Saxon Charters, ed. A. Robertson, Cambridge, 1956.

RES Review of English Studies.

SFF Seasons for Fasting, ed. in ASPR 6, 98–104.

SHS The Hymns in SPS.

SK Lexicographical notes kindly sent to me by Sherman Kuhn.

SN Studia Neophilologica.

SPS The Salisbury Psalter, ed. C. and K. Sisam, EETS 242 (London, 1959).

TLG The Later Genesis, ed. B. Timmer, Oxford, 1948.

VHF Die Vercelli Homilien, 1 Hälfte, ed. Max Förster, Bibliothek d. ags. Prosa, Bd. 12 (Hamburg, 1932).

VLC The Life of Saint Chad, ed. R. Vleeskruyer, Amsterdam, 1953.

VM The Vercelli Manuscript (photostat reproduction), Rome, 1913.

WB Beowulf, ed. C. Wrenn, revised ed. London, 1958.

YWES The Year's Work in English Studies.

ADDITIONS TO DICTIONARY

abal *strength*, TLG 32, 499; v. afol
ābetēon *to accuse*, OEGC 4, 368
āblāwung: add *swelling*, LCD 18a
āblegned: add LCD 3, 42, 25
ācæglod: *locked with a key*, FL 2, A 1
accent m. *accent*, A 8, 333, 23
ācdrenc: lemma cirta = tiriaca, to which the part ac belongs?
āchangra m. *oak wood on a slope* (BTs)
ācholt m. *an oak wood* (BTs)
ācursian *to malign*, SPS 36, 8
ādihtian *to compose*, ASPR 6, 202, nn. 3–4
ādlberende *disease-bearing*, OEGC 8, 19
ādloma: = āðloga, FL 2, A 2
ādwollan *to degenerate*, OEGC 28, 234
æbbung: delete *gulf, bay*, FL 3, H 40
æcersplott m. *an acre* (BTs)
æcerweg m. *a field-road* (BTs)
āecgan? *to set on edge*, OEGC 30, 99, n.
ǣcin *a kind of law?*; lemma tabetum for tabletum? *a tablet of the law*, WW 279, 1 (printed wrongly cecin)
ǣfrelīce *in perpetuity*, ANS 111, 276
æfterfylgung: add *sect*, FL 2, B 20
æftergancnes,
 -gegencednes = æftergengnes, ÆL, 10, 219, v.l.
æfteronfōnd *one about to receive*, FL 3, A 1
ǣgmore: = angnere?
ǣgnian: = ængian, *to oppress?* (EI 265, n.)
± ǣlan: add [āl]

ælepe: delete, FL 2, B 2
ælere *fleabane?* FL 2, B 2
ælfisc? *elfish*, ES 38, 300; AHD 2, 162, 8
ælfsogoða: add *jaundice?*, KN 14
ælifn: *alum*, CGL 5, 343, 3 (Ep. Gl.); v. HEW s.v. ælefne
ǣmetla m. *one at leisure*, ASPR 3, 308, 183
ǣmynd: v. ANS 171, 22; HEW enters ǣmynde, *forgetfulness*
ǣmyrce: literally *not murky*, FL 3, D 1
ǣnetlīf n. *solitary life*, OEGC 9, 4; 10, 2
ǣrādl *early illness*, ASPR 3, 305, 31
ǣrǣt: *overeating*, HBS 20; for defence of *too early eating*, v. A 66, 17, n. 1
ǣreldo: delete, FL 3, A 2
ǣrglæd: *very kind?*, HBS 23
ǣrgōd: *very good*, HBS 20
ǣristhyht *hope of resurrection*, BH 220, 28
ǣrlēof: delete, FL 2, B 3
ǣrlyft: delete, FL 2, B 4
ǣrnignweg = ærneweg, BH B 398, 30
ǣsmæl: *contraction of the pupil*, LCD 2, 338, 1
æstel: *bookmark*, FGR 11, n. 3
æthȳd: delete, FL 3, I 1
ætrihte II: add ætrihtes, VHF 2, n. 3a
ætstandan: add *to blight (crops)*, CPC 1086, 20
āettan: delete, FL 2, B 59
ætwenian: add OEGC 28, 44 n.
ǣwiscberend: *middle finger* (lemma impudicus from Isid. *Etym.* 11, 1, 71)

ǣwul: delete, FL2, A11

æxfaru:=æscfaru, *military expedition*, FL 4, B1

Afrlcanlsc *African*, WW445, 39

āgan: add+ (BTs)

āgānian *to gape*, GD216, 17

agen *ear of grain*, ANS117, 21

āgenland *land held in absolute possession?*, RAC p. 415

āgnian: delete *to enslave*; v. āgnian=āengian

āgnīden: delete first entry; the word is a ptc.; v. LCG, D78

āheordan? *to set free (from captivity)*, WB2930 n.

āhīðend *a ravager*, WW412, 19

āhwettan *to drive away with a curse*, TLG31, 406

āhwīlc: delete, FL2, A3

ahwlīc *terrible*, FL2, A3

alb: read albe

aldgeddung *an old saying*, FL4, B2

alefne *alum*, WW134, 38; 146, 21; ms. efne to which should be added the al of lemma alumen; v. ælifn

ālendan *to lease*, RAC142, 24

Alexandrinesc *Alexandrian*, Mt p. 8, 13

allefne adj. or adv. *quite equal* or *universally*, RES8, 162

Alleluia m. *the Alleluia*, HSC40, n. 9

ālȳfednes? *granting*, FL3, H10

āmānsumung: add *Hermon*, KCM319a

amerian: delete, BPG580 note

āmerian: add BPG580

anbesettan *to inflict*, BPG608

anbeweorpan *to cast into*, BPG1000

anburge *sureties*, RAC p. 344

āncor: read ancor, HEW

andbīcnian: add context of lemma concerns dogs harassing a cat

andēages: delete, HBK

andfenge: add *receptacle*, OEG105

andfylstan *to aid*, SPS43, 26

andlang: add B2695, *by his side?* (ASPR4, 255) *related?* (HBK)

andrecefæt: delete, FL3, H4

āndrencefæt *a cup emptied at one swallow*, FL3, H4

andwliteful: *with grim look*, BPG382

ānhealfrūh *having one side rough*, FL3, H24

ānrǣde=ānrǣd, BTs

anspel: delete, FL3, A3

anstīg: v. FL3, I2

anstōr *incense*, GLL68

āntīd: v. HBK

anung:=andung? (FL2, A4)

ānwald *monarchy*, WW440, 25 (GLL40)

ānwalda? *lone ruler*, VHF112, n. 26

Arabisc *Arabian*, ÆGR65, 12

ārǣfsan *to intercept*, KF

ārfæst(i)an *to show mercy*, SPS102, 3

Arrianisc *Arian*, GD240, 8

arscamu: delete, ASPR5, 212

āscrīfan *to describe*, OEGC4, 255

āscyled *made manifest*, OEGC2, 212

āsēcendlic *to be sought*, LPs110, 2

āslīding: *a slip of the tongue*, BPG51

assedun *dun-coloured like an ass*, WW163, 16

Assirisc *Assyrian*, OEG26, 20

āstrīcan *to strike severely*, VHF4, 38

āstrogdnis *sprinkling*, GLL69; or āstregdnes, q.v.

āstrowenes: *spread?*, FL3, A4

āsyngian *to sin*, GLL73

ātendnes *incentive*, A65, 230

Athēnisc *Athenian* (BTs)

ātordrinca: delete; the part drincan is a verb at MH94, 20

ātorgeblǣd: add *abscess*, BTs

ātwiccian *to excerpt*, OEGC4, 222

āðȳtan: delete entry II; aðytið=aytið; v. OEG4080

āwǣgnian *to fail to perform, annul*, HAW458, 9

āwārnian: for ās-warnian read ā-swārnian

āwesnis *essence*, OEGC72, 1

āwilnian *to wish for*, VM67a, 15

āyttan: delete (FL2, B59)

bǣdan: add a query; v. FL5, A1

+**bǣlcan**: delete, FL6, A2

+**bēran**: for meaning exultare v. JEGP49, 238

bǣrfōt: add W181, 1

bancoða: read bāncoða, *bone disease*, LCD2, 102, 16

bānloca: *muscle*, HBK p. 94

Barda m. *the Apennines*, AO186, 33; v. FL4, C1

bēag: add *treasured things*, B2635 (HBS p. 75); *a treasured thing (sword)*, B2041 (WB)

bēaghyrne: delete, FL3, H5

bēagian: only+, not±, GLL222

bealuhycgende: v. OEGC61, 52

bēansǣd: add RAC252, 15

bebbisc=hehbiscop?, FL2, A6

bebyrwan: delete, FL2, A7

becierran: add *to change*, VHF151, n. 11

bedbǣr: v. OEGC51, 5 n.

+**bedgiht**: *time for going to prayer*, FL4, D13

begēn *to affirm*, CR1307 (ANS166, 82)

begietend: add VHF57, 47

begroren:=begnornende? (ASPR1, 232)

behleonian *to lean (something) against*, VHF42, n. 197

bellringestre f. *bellringer*, A76, 502

bemīðan: add WW218, 21 (FL2, B6)

bēn: add *favour*, B428 (ASPR4, 138)

bēogang: *flight of bees*, FL2, A8

bēolǣs *pasture with flowers for bees?* (BTs s.v. lǣs)

bēotung: add+, WW408, 35

+berbed:= +byrded, *bordered*, FL2, A26

berigeblæ *an instrument for forking barley?*, WW411, 25

besceadwung f. *overshadowing*, *Selmo*, LPs67, 15

bescēawodnes: add, interprets *Sion*

bescīrung glosses exordinatio, JEGP- v. unhādung

besparrian: add OEGC48, 1

beswīcfalle: two words, not a cpd., JEGP46, 415

besylcan *to exhaust*, EL697

betellan: add *to prove one's claim to*, HAW481, 31

betweohceorfan glosses intercidere, GLL 209

beðrāwan: add (*in making candles*); v. BPG242

bīd: read bid and add on bid wrecen, *brought to bay*, B2962

bīegan: add+, BTs

+bīgnes:= begegnes, FL2, A27

bigstandan *to stand by, help*, VHF35, n. 156

+bind: add *constipation*, WW232, 33

bisceopēðel *episcopal see*, BHB262, 11

bisceophādðēnung f. *episcopal service*, BHB232, 16

bisceophālgung f. *consecration of a bishop*, BHB72, 16

bisceopwyrtil: add *betony*, A41, 139

biscopstæf *bishop's staff*, FGR76, 162

biterlic *sad, bitter*, ÆL23, 250

bitrum adv. *bitterly*, EL1244n. (ed. Gradon)

bizant m. *a coin*, BPG548

+blǣcan: add *to make pale*, FL6, A2

blǣce: add *psoriasis*, PM48, 134

blǣcern: *lantern*

bledu: v. heolorbledu

+blīðian: add±, SPS91, 5 •

blōdiorn *bloody flux*, MkL p. 3, 7

blōdorc *sacrificial vessel*, BPG673

blōdspīwung *spitting of blood*, OEGC73b, 24

blōdwracu f. *revenge for bloodshed*, VHF28, n. 123

bōccynn n. *a kind of book*, SolK192, 8

bōcholt *a beechwood* (BTs)

bogefōdder: *case for the bow*, FL3, H6

bōhtimber: v. HEW

bōl *necklace*, LCG, M302 (HEW)

bordstæð: *the rigging of a ship*, ASPR2, 110, 442

borgwedd: prob. not a cpd.

brādian: add *to become broad*, W262, 7d

brādsweord *broadsword*, Jud. 317 (ASPR4, 289)

brǣcdrenc: add+, and read WW351, 28

brǣdīsen: delete, FL3, D2

brand: add brand Healfdenes, *Hrothgar*, B1020 (WB)

breahtmung: *flickering* (*of the eyelids*), FL3, A5

brēdīsern: delete

bredīsern *tablet knife, writing instrument*, FL3, D2

+bregd: add *fabric*, BPG852

+bregdstafas: *cunning skill in letters*, MPS

brēmelōyfel m. *a bramble-thicket* (BTs)

brēmelwudu *a bramble-wood* (BTs)

breneð: 3 sg. of brȳnan, *to make brown?* (ASPR6, 157, 43)

brēosa: a ghostword that came to life; v. MLN51, 331

brēostgyrd: delete?; v. prēostgyrd

brīdelgym *a bridle ornament*, OEGC28, 456

brimsa?: v. MLN51, 331

broht:= broð, FL2, A10

broðhund:= roðhund, FL4, A2

brūmiddel *intercilium*, KF

brūneða: read bruneða, HEW

brȳdan= bregdan, ÆGR176, 3d

+bryddan: v. MPS16 n.

bryrdnes: add+, *compunction*, GLL50

brȳtofta: delete; fol. 18r of Additional MS. 32, 246 reads brytgifta

brȳðen: add WC p. 54, 10

bucheort *a tragelaph*, FL2, B29

buclic *like a goat* (gloss to tragicus) OEGC 28, 55

buf the interjection *buff*, FL4, E1 n.

būl: delete I after būla

būla: add DR4, 3; OEG8, 319

Bulgarisc *Bulgarian*, GD300, 21

burgende? *city boundary*, EL31 (ed. Gradon)

buterstoppa: add *churn?*

bȳl: delete the queries; add Mod. Eng. *bile* (HEW)

bylda: *builder* at CRA75

+byrd: to *fate* add MPS376 n.

byrdicge: prob. from same original gloss as byrding

byrdling: *offspring*, FL3, A7

byre: delete *storm*, BPG873

+byrgen: *grave*, WW277, 7 (FL2, A28)

byrst: add *a crash*, WW215, 27

byrstende: ptc. of berstan (BTs)

byrðincel n. *a little burden*, OEGC2, 193

cærswill m. *a spring where cress grows* (BTs)

caflwyrt: delete, FL2, A54

Caldisc *Chaldean*, OEGC28, 118

camp *a fetter*, PPs149, 8

căn: delete, ASPR5, 216, 79

Cananisc *of Canaan*, MkR3, 18

Cappadonisc *Cappadocian*, OEG2302

Carles wæn *Charles' Wain*, LCD3, 270, 11

casebill: delete; v. cēasbill

cēacbora: *jugbearer?*; v. LCG A659 n.

cēacfull *a jugful*, LCD70b

cealccrundel *a chalk ravine* (BTs)

cealfwyrt: delete, FL2, A54

cēaptoln f. *toll on buying and selling*, HAW p. 78

cēasbill *a club associated with philosophical dispute*, BPG438 n.

ceasterwyrhta *city builder* (a mistaken glossing of polimitarium) WW469, 21

cecil:=cēcel; v. LCG S698 n.

cecin: delete; ms. æcin; v. æcin

cellod: cf. scutum cælatum?

cenep: add BPG947 n.; and to meaning *bit* add (*bristling with points*)

cenningstān: delete, FL4, A3

ceorcing: delete, BPG745 n.; v. ceorung

ceorung: add BPG745

ceoselstān: add *stone* (*disease*), WW113, 18; the lemma comes from Isid. *Etym.* 4, 7, 32

cicropisc: *Cecropean*; v. Isid. *Etym.* 9, 3, 16

+cīd: read ±cīd (v. gecīd in BTs)

cildild f. *childhood*, BF12, 7

Cillinesc *Cyllenian*, WW379, 4

cine I: read cīne (HEW)

cintōð: delete *front tooth* and add WW85, 10

circwyrhta m. *church-builder*, HAW p. 510

cist: delete *horn*, FL4, D5

clangettung *clangour*, MLN67, 554

clēot *a cleat*, LCG P411 (v. HEW)

clericmann m. *a clerk* (BTs)

clifhlēp: delete the query, FL4, A5

±clifian: add BPG982 n.

clifwyrt: *burdock?* (it is a glossary variant of clate)

clynian: delete entry I, BPG982

cnēorift: delete *kneehose*, FL4, D2

cnēosār *pain in the knee*, OEGC73c, 12

cocer: delete *spear*, NP1, 209

+cōcnian: add WW372, 12 (misprinted gerecanade)

cocrōd f. *a clearing for netting woodcocks* (BTs)

Cōferflōd *the river Chebar*, MPS20 n.

coltemære *boiled wine*, MNG54

cōlcwyld: delete, FL3, J3

+collenferhtan: *to enhearten*, FL6, A3

corcīð: delete; v. corncīð

+corded: delete the query, FL3, H18

corncīð *growth of grain*, FL2, A12; note also corwurm=cornwurm, OEG1064

cornwurma: add OEGC51, 7

corporale *a cloth for covering the Host*, FGR90

corōr *a whisk?*, LCG V93 (v. HEW)

costere: delete *spade, shovel*, FL2, B10; v. fostere

+cow: v. VHF97, n. 148

cræftbōc f. *commentary*, OEGC30, 88

crammingpohha: *a bag crammed with ill-gotten gains?*, FL4, A6

cranc *chronicle*, RAC250, 16

credic?:=cremdisc?, *a cream dish*, FL3, C1

crinc: read cinc? *derision*, FL4, D3

crismclāð *chrism-cloth, headband*, FGR90

crismsmyrels *anointment with holy oil*, FGR90

crīst: read crist, Förster, *Alteng. Lesebuch* 45

crompeht: add OEGC19, 1

+crōwed= +crōged, OEGC27, 21

cursian: delete *to plait*, FL2, A14; JEGP-

cūself: delete, BPG280 n.

cūter *chewing gum*, FL4, B4

cwecesand: read cwece sund, *lively strait of water?*, FL2, A15

cwedelian=wyrgcwedolian, GLL122

cwelderæde: v. OEGC36, 10 n.

cwiccliende: for twincliende?, FL4, D4

Cwicelmingas *descendants of Cwicelm*, ÆGR15, 3

cynehelm: on the meaning *royal power* v. HAW477, n. to l. 24; add *garland*, GAT 26, 8 n.

cynesetl: add WW71, 6

cynestræt: for 71, 6 read 467, 7

cynewāðen: delete, WC14, 16n.

cyninge f. *a queen*, BL13, 1

cyningstān *an instrument used in casting dice*, WW150, 24 (FL4, A3)

cyningwīc *stately dwelling*, GnE107 (ASPR 3, 307, n. to 108)

cynling *clan*, ANS111, 276

+cyrtan: *to lop off*, BPG919

cyst: for meaning *picked host, company*, add EI229 n.; v. ciest in HEW

cytwer: *a basket-weir*; v. cietwer in HEW

dæg: add ær dæge ond æfter dæge, *in perpetuity*, HAW479, l. 10

dægmælscep: Additional MS. 32, 246, fol. 7r dægmeles-; add dægmæles pīl and dægmæles pinn, ÆGR321, 6

dægword? *Chronicles*, Ex519 (ASPR1, 216, 519 n.)

dælnymendlic *participial*, ÆGR134, 20

+ **dafenes** glosses oportuno at SPS 144, 15
+ **dāl**: add ± (BTs)
dalc: add Jos 7, 21
dalisc: lemma dedalei taken as de dalei, FL 3, K 1
dalmatice: omit the query
daroðæsc? *spear*, EL 140 (ASPR 2, 134, n. to 140)
dað: delete, FL 2, A 16
dēagwyrmede: for assoc. with *gout* v. FL 4, D 6
dēawdrīas: delete, ASPR 1, 224, 276
dēawwyrm: add *itch-mite, foot-worm*, PM 44
delfīn: delete, FL 2, B 12
dengan: add CP 461, 16 (FL 3, F 2)
dennian: v. ASPR 6, 147, 12
dēog: v. WB 850 n.
dēopðancenlīce = dēopðancollīce, RWH 42, 3
+ **deorflēas**: for GL read BPG 1017 n.
dēð: delete entry II, FL 6, A 1
dīcsticce *stick supporting a dike*, FF 772, n. 1
dīerlingðegn *favourite follower*, A 73, 19
docga: add (*referring to cruel persons*), FL 3, J 4
dolhsmeltas: = dolhsweðlas?, FL 2, A 17
dōmesdæg = dōmdæg, VM 3 b 15; 114 a 18
doxian: v. VHF 100, n. 165
dracu f. *affliction*, W 91, 7 e
dragan: add *to suffer*, MLR 27, 452
droht: *a pull at the oars*, WW 486, 27; context of lemma remorum tractibus
dropa: delete the query (HEW)
+ **dropa**: for assoc. with drop v. FL 3, A 13
dryhtdōm: delete; part dryht repeated from preceding dryhten, SK
dryncelēan: *entertainment given by the lord of the manor*, ANS 127, 196
dryslic: read ondryslic, FL 2, B 41
dūstswerm: add *atoms*, FL 4, A 7
+ **dwildæfterfolgung**: delete, FL 2, B 20
dwoligendlic *heretical*, GD 239, 21, o
+ **dyhtedum** adv. *splendidly*, OEGC 62, 17
dȳst, dȳð = dēst, dēð, ÆGR 3, 24 d; 210, 1 d; 212, 5 d

ēabrycg f. *bridge over a river*, ÆL 27, 53
ēad-: for eað- read ēað-
ēaganbyrhtm m. *a flash of the eye, moment*, VHF 78, n. 41
ēaghyll: *the hairless prominence between and above the inner corners of the eyes*; lemma glebenus from glaber
ēaland: *maritime land* also at OEGC 4, 199
ēalandcyning m. *island king*, BHB 308, 8
ealdgeðungen *old and distinguished*, W 99, 15

ealdhryðerflǣsc *meat that has been stored away*, WW 127, 33; v. succidia at Isid. Etym. 20, 2, 24
ealdorlēas: *lacking a leader*, B 15
ealdorlēas: *lifeless*, B 1587
ealdwerig: read ealdorwērig? *fatally weary*, EI 50 n.
ēalic *of a river*, OEGC 28, 216
ealleðern *wholly of leather*, Additional MS. 32,246, fol. 12r; scetra: ealleþern scyldas; v. Isid. Etym. 18, 12, 5
eallhālgung: *all worship*, FL 3, H 25
ealuscerwen: *serving of bitter ale*, EGS 4, 67 ff.; v. also WB
eardere *a dweller*, SHS 4, 15
eardlufu: delete the query (HBK)
eardrīce: delete; ms. eardwica
ēarede: add (*of a pitcher having* duas ansas, Isid. Etym. 20, 5, 3); cf. ansa: auris, CGL 6, 73
earhwinnende *cowardly conquering* (*of a poisoned arrow*), VM 133 b, 23
earmheortnes *pity*, FL 2, A 38
earngēap: add *falcon?* (HEW)
earningland: *land for which service was rendered?*, WC p. 178, 21
ēarðyrel: in support of *ear-passage* v. FL 3, J 5
ēastān *a river-stone?*, LCD 2, 218, 23
ēaðbelg m. *irritability*, VHF 103, n. 176 a
Ebrēisclīce adv. *in Hebrew*, JnL 19, 13
eceddrinca: delete; v. VM 8 a, 9 where the part drincan is a verb
ecgclif n. *steep shore*, B 2893 (HBK)
edginnan *to begin again*, OEGC 27, 35
edspellung f. *recapitulation*, OEGC 20, 3
efengemetgian *to temper equally*, FL 5, A 5
efenhemman: delete, FL 5, A 5
Eflcisc *of Ephesus*, FL 3, H 8
efne: delete *alum*; v. alefne
eftgān *to go*, GLL 215
eftgewæxen *grown again*, LCD 1, 378, 15
egnwirht: delete, FL 5, A 2
eiðe = egðe; printed ciþe at WW 105, 2
eleberende *containing oil*, OEGC 8, 17
elegrēofa: *tinder from residue of pressed olives*, FL 3, A 9
elleahtor *misuse of the letter l*, FL 2, A 20
elleoht: delete; v. elleahtor
ellheort *disheartened*; v. hellheort
ellhygd = elhygd, GD 108, 4
emleahtor *misuse of the letter m*, FL 2, A 20
emleoht: delete; v. emleahtor
eoforhēafodsegn: read eoforhēafdod segn? *banner with a boar's head*; cf. geheafdod hring, *ring with a head*, WW 152, 45; mycelheafdod, 161, 19; and Latin aper, *military banner*
eolene: = eolha, *elk?* BPG 417 n.

eorle the Eruli?, WB6 n.
eorðgestrēon n. earthly treasure, W263, 24d
eorðryne earthquake, A73, 19 (ms. eorð-renas)
eotonweard: watch against the monster
ēowigendlic demonstrative, ÆGR231, 5, o
ern grain, harvest, ANS171, 19; v. rugern
esne: add scholar, FL3,H8
ēst: add history? origin?, B2157 (HBK)
ēstnes bliss, NP28, 49
ēt: for æt read æt

fācennes deceitfulness, JEGP-
fǣcnung suspicion, A65, 230
fædernama m. surname, RWH53, 21
fæderrīce n. heaven, VM70b, 22
fǣrbifongen: add a query; not wholly legible
fǣrcumen sudden, OEGC9, 100
fǣrfrīge with freedom to go, JEGP33, 346
fǣrnes suddenness, JEGP-
fǣsting: for LL58, 7 read 58, 17
fæðel: delete, FL4,B5
fāg: add tessellated, WB725 n.
fāgwyrm: v. FL4,A8
faldwyrðe entitled to have his own fold, HAW p. 476
falðing: something that falls; glossaries assoc. lemma moles with ruina
farendlic pervious, JEGP-
faul: an expression used as a charm
+feallan: add on lufe, to fall in love, GAT2, 10; 26, 22
fearhhama: womb of a pig, FL3,H12
fēawnes: add+, GLL188
feaxclāð: band for the hair
feaxēacan: delete, FL4,D7
feaxscēara: hair shears, FL3,H13
feht: add shaggy pelt, FL3, J6
felafricgende well informed, B2105 (HBS p. 119)
felarīce very rich, ÆH1, 582, 14
felasprecol=felaspecol, LCD3, 192, 22
felcyrf: add JEGP-
feltüngrēp: add privy, VHF146, n. 48
fenfugol: add (ms. fenfixas)
feohhord treasury, JEGP-
feohlufu f. love of money, BH(Sch)160, 13 (an elliptical compound)
fēolheard: hard as a file, MAG108 n.
fēondulf: on the authenticity of this word v. BPG617 n.
feorhcynn: kinds of living creatures, B2266 (ASPR4, 235)
feorhlegu: life at B2800 (HBK)
feorhnest n. provisions, JEGP-
feorm: add disposal, WB451 n.
fēowergǣrede four-pointed, ÆGR288, 11
fēowerstrenge four-stringed, ÆGR288, 11 (bifidus taken as from fides)

fēowertȳnenihte fourteen nights old, BH206, 28
+fēra: for fera read fēra
ferhweard guard of life, B305 (EGS4, 67)
+fērlǣcan: add+, ÆGR191, 17, j
ferð crowd, WA54 (EGS4, 84)
fetelhilt: v. NP28, 43
feðerberende adj. feathered, OEGC28, 481
fiah=feoh, OET446, 9
fīfmægen: quintuple powers, MPS136 n.; delete fīfel
fingerdocca: foxglove? OEGC70, 22 n.
firenðēof: delete, FL2,B16
fiscfell:=fiscwell, FL2,A21
fiscflōdu: not a cpd.? (ASPR6, 204)
flǣre: one of the spreading sides at the end of the nose, FL3,H15
flǣsccostnung f. carnal desire, KCM p. 120, 3
flǣsclīce adv. carnally, CP207, 16
flǣsctāwere: butcher
flǣðecomb: two separate words? (FL2, A22)
+flenod: read +flerod, flared? (FL4,D14)
fleoðomum glosses flactris, WW239, 38; d. pl. of flēotham? watery place; note wætersteall to flactiris and cf. flōdham, wæterham
flind=flint, WW415, 10 (FL3,A11)
flocgian: v. BPG846 n.
flōdgrǣg flood-grey, GNC31 (ASPR6, 175)
flōdweard: guardian of the flood?, EI494 n.
flogoða: venom, BPG997
flustrian: to flatter, JEGP-
fnæs: delete ref. to WW425, 27, where fnasum is error for snasum; add LkL8, 44
fōdder: delete hatchet, FL5,B1
fōdderbill an instrument for cutting fodder, FL5,B1
fōgclāð a patch, FL2,A24
foldgrǣg: delete; v. flōdgrǣg
foldwylm earth-stream, PH64; usually, but unnecessarily, emended (SK)
fonfȳr firefang, JEGP-
foraldung old age, OEGC28, 312
forbēn: on this nonce word cf. FL2,A23
forbīgels: delete, FL2,B18
forboren restrained from the effect of herb, bewitched?, LCD2, 114, 9; v. 2, 306, 12; KN19
forcinnan? to destroy, MPS107 n.
forcompian? to fight for, BPG31 n.
ford: add waterway, B568 (HBS p. 99)
fordēad: as if dead, FL3,D3
fordēmednes: add GD345, 3
foreādihtian: delete; v. ādihtian
forebīcnung f. prophecy, ÆH1, 540, 26
foreblǣsting: delete, FL4,D8
forecennednes progeny, SHS8, 50

foredēman *to prejudge*, RBL105, 6
forefæger: read forfæger
forefengnes *a protective skirting (of woods)*, OEGC4, 28
forefrēfrend *proconsul*, DR190, 9*b*
foregesellan *to advance (money)*, BHB330, 6
foreglelpan: delete (BTs)
forehālig: delete; v. NP28, 46
forelāttēow *leader*, LkL22, 26
foresettendlic *prepositive*, ÆGR267, 6
foretimbrigende *enclosing, impeding* BH (Sch)552, 63
+**forewrit** *prologue*, KCM280, 4
forgebind n. *stricture?*, LCD1, 338, 3
forgiefednes *forgiveness*, GLL39
forgīeman: insert ī before ȳ
forgifung: *the nuptial gift before the morning gift*, FL3, H16
forgrindet: 3rd sing. pr. of forgrindan (LCGC776)
forhrædlīce adv. *too soon*, CP445, 1
forhtlēasnes f. *fearlessness*, VHF4, n. 13*a* (context calls for un-)
forhto *fear*, SPS88, 41
forlǣtu: v. VHF138, n. 6
forlētere *a forsaker*, LkL p. 9, 17
formǣlan *to negotiate*, ANS111, 280
forrǣpe *assart*, SN16, 33
forrēcelēasian *to neglect*, BTs
forscēotan: add *to advance money*, NP28, 45
forscired: based on same doc. as forscyrian
forsittan: add *to give out, fail*, B1767 (v. FL3, A5 n. 2)
forsuncen *faded out (of the written page)*, KF
forsweflan: *to kill, perish*, FL5, A3
fortīn n. *a portent*, FL4, B6
fortog: read innanfortog, LCD109b
fortogen: *griped*
forðāgān *to pass away*, Mt14, 15
forðāloten *prone*, A65, 230
forðātȳdred *propagated*, OEGC4, 91
forðegide *consumed*, SFF214 (v. Sisam, *Studies*, p. 57)
forðgelǣdan *to bring forth, cause to grow*, GLL232
forðhebban *to further*, GLL220
forðmid *at the same time*, FGR68
forðrǣsted *contrite*, GLL52
forðringan: preferably *drive out* at B1084 (HBK)
forðsecgan *to announce, proclaim*, GLL90
forðsendan *to send forth*, ÆL23b, 204
forðswebung *a killing?*, FL5, A3
forðtihtan *to persuade*, KCM p. 52, 8
forðtilian *to go on striving*, VM72b, 11

forðwegan *to further*, GLL220
forðyldegung *tolerance*, A65, 230
forðysmed:=forðrysmed
foryldu: context calls for *weariness* at BPG1030
fostere *a spade*, FL2, B10
fōtclāð: delete; v. fōgclāð
fōtgemet: delete *foot-fetter*, FL5, A5; add *a foot in measure*, HSC60
fōtgeswell n. *swelling of the foot*, LCD3, 70, 27
fōtlǣstlēas *soleless*, FL3, H32
fōtrāp: *rope by which the foot of a sail is tied*, JEGP46, 416
fōðorn: delete; ms. slit mid ðe foðorne= mid ðefeðorne; v. ðefeðorn at LCD3, 56, 27, and on the use of a thorn as a scalpel v. LCD2, 106, 5
framādrȳfan: add VHF69, 165
framāscūfan *to drive away*, VHF69, 163
frēahbeorhtian: add+, GLL103
frēawrāsn: *splendid band*, AJP62, 338, n. 30
frēcenful *dangerous*, OEG628
fregen II: add ANS135, 399
fregensyllic: delete, ES36, 325; ANS135, 399
fregnðearle: delete; noun fregn and adverb ðearle; not a cpd.
frēols:add *charter of freedom*, HAW447, n. 5
Fresilc: read Fresisc
Frīandæg *Friday*, RBL43, 13
frigedōm m. *deliberation*, RBL97, 8
frihtere: WE61, 14 (ms. frif-)
frīs: *Frisian*, ASPR3, 306, 95
friðowang: *place of refuge* (WB)
fromācnȳsian *to degenerate*, OEGC30, 105
frumcenning m. *first-born*, SPS77, 51
frummeoluc: *beestings*, JEGP52, 372
frumtēam *first team (of animals harnessed in line)*, WW427, 31
frysca: quite possibly a form of fersc, *fresh, youthful*; v. buteonem at CGL6, 158 and butio glossed frysca, WW10, 8
fugeldoppe: two words?, A41, 111 n. 7
fulhealden: *sufficient, ample*; cf. German vollhaltig
fullhealden: delete; v. ful-
fullnes: read 111, 13 and v. SPS p. 37
fultumgestre f. *a helper*, A65, 230
fyrclian: *to fork into many rays*, EGS5, 84; CPC p. 81
fyrdhama: read fyrdhom (ASPR4, 196)
fyrdtīber: delete the query (FL3, H14)
fȳrencylle f. *lamp*, BHB476, 15
fyrgenhēafod? *mountain headland*, Charms 4, 27 (ASPR6, 213)
fȳrrace: a dubious word, doc. as ferrece; note Latin ferrea in glosses to lemma vatilla at CGL7, 395

fyrsrǣw f. *a row of furze* (BTs)
+**fyxan** *to trick*, FF792, n. 8; v. also JEGP33, 345, n. 25

gadinca: read gādinca, *maimed animal?*, FL4, B7
gæstliðend *hospitable*, WE66, 12
gafolgyld: delete the query, BPG548 n.
galend *enchanter*, GLL97
gangtūn m. *latrine*, ÆL18, 379
gār: on the meaning at GEN316 v. FL4, B8 and NP39, 204
gāra: add *strip of cloth, saddle cloth*, WW332, 10
gāstglfu: read WW200, 18
gātaloc n. *goat-house*, WW275, 31
gealga: delete entry II; galgan at WW445, 35 and 499, 14=geallan; v. OEG2950
geallādl: add *jaundice*, KN7
gealpettan: delete *to live gluttonously?*, VHF76, n. 22
gēancyrrendlic *relative*, ÆGR231, 17j
gēansprecan *to contradict*, GLL124
gearofang *grappling hook?*, FL4, D12
Gēatisc? *of the Geats*, WB3150 n.
gefestre f. *a giver*, A76, 502
gēgan: v. FL3, A14
gēnde: delete=; add=gīnde, gȳnde at ÆL 25, 636c
gēoabbod m. *former abbot*, GDh41, 27
gēomagister m. *former teacher*, BHc410, 13
gēomēowle: only B2931
gēotend:=gēotendǣder, FL2, B51
gēotenlic: for gegotenlic? BPG437 n.
gētan: delete grētan; v. HBK
gielphlǣden: *laden with glorious words*, ASPR4, 159
gilddagas: delete *guild-days*; lemma ceremonia from Isid. *Etym.* 6, 19, 36
gildet *gelded*, WW120, 38; v. ðrysumer
gildfrēo *free of tax*, ANS111, 276
gildlic: delete *of a guild*; v. FL3, H25 n.
gildsetl n. *meeting-place of a guild*, FF792, n. 9
gilp: for doubt about meaning *dust, powder*, v. JEGP46, 419; add=grip, *furrow?*
gilte: add *barren pig*, LCD2, 88, 24
gimrodor:=gimhrōðor, *gem-splendour*, FL 3, A17
ginfæsten: delete, EI567 n.
+**gīscan:**=giscian?, *to yex*, FL3, A15
+**gite** *conscious*, OEGC28, 409
glǣs: delete glǣsas, BPG678
glēd: add *an instrument of torture*, FL4, D22
glemm: read W67, 18
glīwcynn: possibly for onclēow; v. JEGP 43, 438

glīwingman: *mocker*, FL4, A10
glōf: delete *pouch* (HBS p. 118)
gluto *glutton*, Ælfric's Colloquy, ed. Garmonsway, 297 n.
glyrende *looking askance*, FL3, J15; BPG 440
glȳs-=glēs-, ÆGR293, 13d
godcundlicnes=godcundnes, ÆL23b, 230g
godē-: read gode-
godgesprǣcen=godsprǣce; v. godgesprǣce in BTs
godwebben: v. VHF23, n. 103
goldhordhūs: *treasury*, not *privy*, FL4, D23; JEGP-
goldhwǣt: v. WB3074n.
goldwreken *inlaid with gold*, WC p. 74, 7
gorettan: delete *pour forth, emit*, FL3, J16
gōseflǣsc n. *gooseflesh*, Klaeber, *Studies* (1929), p. 272
grammaticancrǣft=grammaticcrǣft, ÆL 35, 14
grēðe: *a companion?*, FL3, C2
griffus *griffon*, MPS256
grimena: ms. grimena ðus rendering bruchus cuius=grime maðu ðæs?; v. grame ceaferas at corres. passage in PPs104, 30
grimhȳdig=gramhȳdig, VHF77, n. 38
grimman: v. WB306 n.
+**grindswile** *a swelling caused by friction*, intertrigo, KF
grinu: not necessarily a colour; v. FL2, A33
grīstra: *miller*; glosses cerealis pistor, WW 141, 4; 202, 29
grōwan: delete *become*, FL3, A18
grundwiergen: *accursed monster of the deep*, HBK
grunian: *to desire*, not *chew the cud*, FL3, E1; v. gruncian, BPG597
grytte: delete *spider*;=grytt, *dust*; aranea taken as arena (SK)
gullisc: *gilded*, MLN59, 111
gūðfrēa: delete, FL2, B25
gūðgeorn *tempting, looking for a quarrel*, OEGC60, 12
gūðmōd *of warlike mind* (Klb.); *warlike mind* (WB), B306
gūðmōdig: delete
Gūðmyrce: *warlike border-dwellers?* EI59 n.
gydenlic: *of a goddess*; add (from the same context) OEG3193; 7, 233; 8, 170
gyrdelbred: add (*carried in the purse?*) FL2, A34
gyrlgyden f. *goddess of dress*, BPG670

hādswǣpa:=hādswǣpe, *bridesmaid*
hæcce: *frontal*, rather than *crozier*, EGS5, 72, n. 22

hæcine: add, from Latin acinum, FL4, D24

hæfegītsung: delete, FL2,A35

hæferbīte: delete, FL4,D25

hæfergāt: delete; two words separated by point in Harley 3376

± hæftnīedan: only +

hǣlestre f. *saviour*, A65, 230

hǣmedrīm: *number of dallyings*, FL3,A20

+ hǣrede *hairy*, ANS117, 24

hǣðenfeoh: delete, FL2, B26

hǣðenwēoh *idol*, JUL53 (emended to -feoh in Woolf's ed.)

hǣwmænged *mixed purple*, OEGC4, 12

hafenian: *to lift up*, MaG42 n.; B1573

hālettend: *forefinger*, FL2,A36

hālewǣge *a holy cup*, ANS171, 29

hālgungbōc: *book containing coronation liturgy*, ASPR6, LXXXIX

hālswurðung: read halswurðung, *neck ornament*, EI549 n.

hamorian: delete, BPG580

hand: add ymb hand, *at once*, BPG52; bām handum twām, *zealously*, ANS162, 230

handæx: add *hatchet*

handwyrm: add *itch-mite*, PM44

harasteorra: read hāra-, FL4,A11

hāredagas *dog days*, OEGC63, 17

hāreminte *white mint?*, A41, 140 n.

hārewyrt: delete WW135, 5 and v. A41, 140 n.

hāsgrumel *sounding hoarsely*, OEGC15, 2

hātlīce: add *vehemently*, BHт352, 21

hattefagol: add a query; v. BTs under hæreanfagol

hāwung: *ability to see*, VHF99, n. 155

+ hēafdod: add *(referring to a ring)*

hēafodbeorg: *protection for the head* at B1030

hēafodbryce *breaking of the skull*, LCD1, 150, 22

hēafodclāð: add *the cloth used for covering the head of a dead person*, ÆL31, 1425 (v. B445)

hēafodsegn: read eoforhēafdod segn?

hēafodslæge: *a head-stroke, beheading*, FL3,A21

hēafodsmæl: *part of a tunic* (BTs)

hēahdēma m. *high judge*, W254, 8d

hēahfexede a slavish gloss to alticomum (iubar), OEGC9, 35; v. hēahhelm in BTs and feaxede of a comet

hēahgræft: *prominent sculpture*, FL3,D6

+ healddagas: v. FL3,H20

healdend: add + at LCD3, 192, 23

healfes hēafdes ece *migraine*, LCD2, 20, 21

healfgewriten *half-written* LkL, 16, 6 (FL3, D16)

healfhrūh: v. ānhealfrūh

healfhundisc *semi-canine*, WNL191x

healfrūh: delete

healhālgung: delete, FL3,H25

hēalic = ēalic, FL2,A37

heallðegn: = healðegn

healðegn: *occupier of the hall* at B142 (WB)

hēanhād: delete; two words—context for the glosses is ardui formam propositi; v. BTsII, 2b under hēah

hēap: add forloren hēap, *ruined troop*, ÆH1, 342, 25

heardhīðende *ravaging*, RD33, 7 (ASPR3, 340)

hearma: add netila = nitella, *dormouse*

hearmdæg: delete; v. Klb., 2nd supplement, p. 470

hearmheortnes: delete, FL2,A38

hearplic *of a harp*, OEGC7, 21; 8, 15

hebbendlic: delete; ms. oferhebbendlic

hegessugge: read hegesugge

hellegāst: delete†; add GD189, 26

hellemūð *mouth of hell*, RWH118, 4

hellepīn *hell-torment*, RWH75, 28

hellerūne: delete B163; v. helrūna

hellfenlic *like a fen of hell*, FL2,B27

hellheort: prob. for ellheort, *disheartened*; cf. ellhygd

hellwendlic: delete, FL2,B27

helpendrāp: influenced by opiferra = opisphora

helrūna: add *one knowing the mysteries of hell*

helung *covering*, SPS35, 8

hemman: delete, FL2,B28

hēofon: read heofon, *heaven*, EI46n.

heofonarīce = heofonrīce, VHF46, 32

heofonhæbbend: read WW355, 21

heofonhlytta = efenhlytta, GLL60

heofonhūs *ceiling*, WW29, 22; v. hūshefen (FL4,A15)

heortbucc: delete, FL2,B29

heorða: delete the query, FL4,C3

heoruwearg: *accursed foe*, Klb.

herehorn m. *trumpet*, ÆGR40, 7 n.

herescipe *troop*, SFF18

hergere? *plunderer*, OEGC28, 341n.

herian: add *to help*, B1833 (HBS)

hīa = hīe, NG

hice(māse): read hīce(māse), HEW

hiellan: delete, FL5,A4

hierdung: delete *restoring*, FL3,H29

higesynnig? *sinful*, SFF168; or hige, synnig man (Sisam, *Studies*, p. 51)

hig, hig *o, o*, WW91, 7

hildefrōfor *battle-comfort*, WAlII, 12 (ASPR 6, 140)

hildelēoma: *battle-flame (sword)* B1143; *destructive flame (of the dragon)* B2583 (HBK) hiltlēas: v. FL3, H26

hīredcniht: v. WC p. 127

hīredgerēfa: v. FL3, H27

hīwian: add hīwian on, *to change to*, VHF101, n. 169

hīwiend *one who forms*, OEG365n.

hīwlic: *of marriage*, not *matronly*, JEGP46, 420

hīwsprǣc *artfully formed speech*, SPS39, 5 (ms. hwispræce); v. spǣcehēow

hlæddisc: *dish laden with varied viands*, v. Isid. *Etym.* 20, 2, 8

hlǣfde: = læfðe

hlǣpewince: delete

hlāfhūs *Bethlehem (domus panis)*, ÆH1, 34, 15

hleg(i)ende: read hleg(l)ende

hlēohrǣscnes: v. hlēorhrǣscnes

hlēonian: delete, FL3, A22

hlēorhrǣscnes *a striking in the face*, FL6, A6

hlēoðrian: add *to bark*, WW378, 3

hlēowfæst: add *protected*, VHF143, 67

hlīdan: = liðian?, FL4, B12

hlīf m. *moon-shaped ornament*, OEGC55, 5

hlīpcumb *a valley with steep sides* (BTs)

hlōse: add *lewze*, FL4, D37

hnoc: delete, FL4, D28

hnot: add *hornless*, WW444, 19

hnȳlung: prob. = hlinung

hoferede: add *strumous*, ÆGR322, 1

hofrede: = hoferede, *hump-backed*, FL2, A41

hōh: add *headland*, WB3157 n.

hohfullīce *carefully*, RBL89, 6

hōl: *malice?, envy?*, BHW269, 57 n.

± holen *prince, protector*, MÆ12, 65

holstæf: delete, FL4, A12

hōn: delete *tendrils of a vine*, BTs

hōnende: read hōnede

+ hopp: delete *small bag*, FL3, D4

hoppetan: read hoppettan, LCD2, 352, 1; GD118, 25

hopscȳte: add WC p. 62, 22

hopsteort: read hōpsteort, FL4, D30

hordestre *stewardess*, A76, 502

horines *filth*, SHS6, 5

hornādl *a disease (connected with venery)*, LCD60b

hornungbrōðor *bastard brother*, OEGC8, 13

hospan *to reproach*, SPS41, 11; 118, 42

hracca: delete, JEGP52, 373

+ hradod *quick*, A67, 126, n. 4

hræfnsweart *black as a raven*, VHF101, n. 168

hrægltalu: *supply of clothing*, RAC48, 26

hræglōēnestre f. *keeper of the robes*, A76, 502

hrandsparwa: delete?, FL2, A42

hrēodgyrd f. *reed used as fishing rod*, BPG 145

hrēðmann? *glorious warrior*, WB445 n.

hrēðsecg? *glorious warrior*, WB490 n.

hrīcian: add BPG722

hrimpan: *to wrinkle, contract*, FL3, D5

+ hrin: delete, FL6, A4

hrinde *frost-covered*, B1363 (HBK)

hring: on wopes hring cf. EGS2, 68ff.

hringgewindla: *the coil of a serpent*, FL3, A23

hrīstle: = hrīsel; v. LCG E10

hrōflēas: add *with no houses*, RAC p. 460

hrohian *to cough*, MÆ1, 208

hrohung *spitting*, MÆ11, 90

hrycigan: = hrīcian, BPG722

hrympel: delete the query; ms. hrympellum

hrȳmðe *noise*, A73, 23 n. 50

hūdenian: delete, FL3, F2

+ hūfud *with pontifical headband*, BPG674

hund: delete *sea-beast*, FL4, A13

hundesberie *nightshade?*; glosses uua canina, OEGC73a, 8

hunigæppel: *round cake made with honey*, FL4, A14

hunigsmæc m. *the taste of honey*, ASPR2, 60, 28

hunigtēaren: for GL read BPG123

hūnsporu: *part of the rigging of a ship?*; gloss to dolon, q.v. at Isid. *Etym.* 19, 3, 3; v. hūnðyrlu

hunu?: v. FL2, B30

hwelpian *to bring forth offspring*, OEGC61, 7

hwilpe: *yarwhilp*, YWES14, 77

hwītian: add *to make white*, VHF145, 86

hwītlēadtēafor *salve of white lead*, AB34, 115

hwītstōw *Lebanon* (BT)

hwol: = wolma, FL5, D1

hwȳorf *cattle*, FL2, B31

+ hȳdan: delete *to fasten with a rope?*, JM46

hȳdscip: *a ship made with hides*, FL3, H30

hȳge *the top of the gullet*, WW264, 16; 405, 10 (HEW)

± hyhtlīce *suitably*, VHF62 n. 61

+ hylced: *bent apart*, BPG764 n.

hylsung: = hwistlung, FL4, D32

hypsār *sciatica*, OEGC73c, 11

hȳreborg: prob. two words, each acc.

hyrsian: prob. = hȳrsumian, FL2, A43

hȳðscip: = hȳdscip

īdelbliss f. *vain joy*, ANS132, 330, 26

īdellust *vain desire*, KCM p. 120, 3

idig: ms. idge = igde, ecgede, *edged?*, FL3, D7

īegclif: delete; v. ecgclif
īerfa: read 446, 4
+ īht *yoked together*, ÆGR 289, 2
inbrecan *to break into*, BPG 330 n.
inbrēdan: delete; v. inbrecan
incūð: add *wicked*, SN 14, 216
indēpan: add +, BPG 162
in(for)lǣtan *to let in*, VHF 8 n. 26
ingebed: delete, FL 2, A 44
ingerǣcan *to give (something) in (to some-body)*, BPG 235
inlād: for first entry subst. *toll on goods carried into market*, HAW 477
inlendiscnes *habitation*, JEGP-
inmearg: delete, BPG 665
innanfortog *gripe*, LCD 2, 300, 27
innangund = innancund, LCD 1, 196, 17
innanonfeal *internal swelling*, LCD 2, 10, 11
innanwyrm *intestinal worm*, LCD 1, 82, 22
insǣte: *of ambush*, FL 3, H 31
insceaft f. *internal generation*, MPS 447 n.
inscūfan *to shove in*, VM 135 b, 18
± intimbrian *to edify*, VHF 67, n. 85
inðer: delete, FL 2, B 32
inðicce: delete; ms. inðicce but *in* dotted for deletion
inwegan gloss to inlabi, GLL 230
inweorpan *to begin (the weft)*, OEGC 55, 9
inwrecg = inwærc, BPG 1077 n.
inylma pl. of innylfe, BPG 725
Īringes weg v. FL 4, C 4
Ispanisc *Spanish*, GD 237, 21
istoria *history*, MPS 4 n.

lāclic: delete; JW 130, n. 3
lācnystre f. *physician*, A 76, 502
lǣ *hair of the head*, WW 263, 21; 368, 14 (FL 3, H 55)
+ lǣdendlic: add ±, SPS 97, 6
lǣfel: delete ref. to löffel
lǣfðe *a sprinkling*, FL 4, D 27
lǣlan?: add, v. ASPR 2, 120
lætcumen *late*, OEGC 27, 29
lahgewrit n. *rule*, KCM 414, 12
lāmen = lǣmen, RWH 76, 17
landefne: *the resources of the land*, CPC 1085, 12 n.
landgemirce: add *shore*, B 209
langlīfe: read langlīf(e), ÆGR 320, 1
langmōdlīce *patiently*, GLL 113
lārfæsten: v. A 66, 29 n. 4
latimer m. *interpreter*, EHy 16, 5
lēad: add *an instrument of torture*, BPG 344
lēafsele: *place for shade*, FL 4, D 34
lēasbrēden f. *falsehood*, ÆL 17, 107 v.l.
lēasgespeca *a falsifier*, A 65, 230
lēasōlæccere *false flatterer*, ÆGR 303, 8
lēawfinger: v. FL 4, D 33
+ led: = glēd

+ legergield: v. FL 4, D 15
lengian: delete, MPS 262 n.
lengtogra: positive langtog at OEGC 27, 31
lent: delete?; v. BPG 152 n.
lēoht: add *world*, TLG 34, 310
leornestre f. *a student*, A 76, 502
lēoðucræft: read leoðu-
leoðuwācunga: read liðewācung, *mitigation*, FL 5, A 5
lēpene *a basket*, RAC 200, 9
lēwsa: add *misery*, WW 202, 31 (FL 4, D 35)
Libanisc *of Lebanon*, OEGC 28, 364
+ līcbisen *an imitation*, DR 50, 4; *an imitator*, 12, 11
līgfȳr: add VPs 28, 7 (SK)
līgrægel *a garment of varied hues*, WW 126, 1 (FL 4, D 36)
limgesīhð: read limgesīð, FL 4, B 13
līnsētcorn *a grain of linseed*, ASPR 6, 128, 11
līð: add *point*, OEGC 4, 111 n.
līðelēaf *camomile*, OEGC 73 c, 9 (lemma aviane = apiana)
līðerlic: v. FL 3, J 21
lodrung: read loðrung, *delusion*, A 36, 71
lōf: *band*, MLN 40, 411
lōhsceaft: v. HEW
lōse = hlōse, LCG F 342
lufe wk. f. *loved home*, B 1728 (WB)
lufen: *beloved home* (HBS 111)
Lundonisc *of London*, VLC 162, 11
lungencoðu f. *lung disease*, LCD 1, 388, 1
lyftedor: v. EI 251 n.
lyftwynn: *joyous air*, B 3043 (HBK)
lyge: delete section III (FL 2, A 45)
lȳpenwyrhta: *basket maker*, AB 29, 253
lȳtel: add lȳtlan ond lȳtlan, *little by little*, OEGC 9, 69
lytwist? *deception*, FL 2, A 61

mādmōd: delete; v. vngemedemad
mǣdæcer m. *a meadow* (BTs)
mǣddīc f. *a dike in a meadow* (BTs)
mǣdmann *mower*, FGR 80, 4
mǣgdeneorðe f. *virgin soil*, NP 28, 49
mǣgmann m. *clansman*, BH(Sch) 115, 213
mǣgðblæd: read mǣgðblǣd, *glory of virginity*, BPG 920 n.
mǣgðegesa? *viking*, GNE 106 (ASPR 3, 306)
mǣl: add 730 *meals* in a year, HSC 67
mǣnibrǣde: v. FL 3, H 33
mǣnihīwe *multiform*, AJP 59, 213
mǣrehwīt *pure white*, ANS 132, 399
mǣr-hege: read mǣrhege
mǣrhlisa: delete? (FL 3, A 24)
mǣssandæg = mǣssedæg, ÆL 25, 203 c
mǣssecapitel m. *chapter of the mass*, CM 536
māgatoga? *pedagogue*, OEGC 4, 117, n.

māhling *parent, kinsman*, ANS117, 21
Mailrosisc *of Melrose*, OEGC9, 22
+man: delete WW492, 20; add WE57, 15
mānfolm: *hand* (FL5, C1)
market: add *market rights*, HAW476, 16
masc *mash*, RAC198, 31
mealmstān: *sandstone* (HEW)
meduscerwen: v. EGS4, 74
meduwyrhta *brewer*, HAW508, 12; or=
  mēdwyrhta?
Memfitisc *of Memphis*, OEGC28, 415
menescilling: add LCG L277
mēoning: delete, FL2, B35
meoring: *hindrance?*, EI63 n.
Merewīoing *the Merovingian*, B2921
metenīōing *food-niggard*, ANS117, 23
+metfæstlīce: add±, ÆGR294, 1, *j*
+methāt? *temperate*, A47, 51
mēōlg: add SFF228
micelnes: add+, GLL45
middangeardtōdǣlend *cosmographer* (BTs)
middelflēre: *the part of the nose between the
  flaring sides at the end*, FL3, H15
middelsǣ *middle sea*, RAC160, 1
midfeorh adj. *middle-aged*, BH440, 31
midgetellan *to count, include*, A65, 230
midhilte: two words? lemma capulus at
  Isid. *Etym.* 18, 6, 2 follows ensis glossed
  hiltlēas sweord
milescian *to become mellow*, WW441, 28
min: add JEGP43, 441 ff.
mindōm: *pusillanimity* (FL4, D38)
mīnlic adj. *in my manner*, GD231, 17, 0
minnæn: delete, FL6, A7
misbēodan: add *to announce wrongly*,
  ANS111, 280
misbregdan *to change*, JEGP-
misfēdan: v. GLL208
mīðgihlytto *fellowship*, DR93, 13
mōdhǣp: read mōdhēap, *bold host*, EI242 n.
mōdsēocnes: *fright, sadness*; v. cardiacus at
  Isid. *Etym.* 4, 6, 4
mōdðrȳðo? *arrogance*, WB1931 n.
molsn: add OEGC28, 453
monighēowlic *multifarious*, OEGC4, 405
morgensēoc: for AN241 read ASPR3, 218,
  96
mōrhop: *a hollow in the moor*; v. fenhop
  and ASPR4, 140, 450
morðcwalu = morðorcwalu, VHF103, n.179
muntgīu *the Alps*, W152, 9
muscflēote: read mustflēoge; lemma bibi-
  ones from Isid. *Etym.* 12, 8, 16 and
  among words glossed fleoge
mūsere m. *mouse-hawk*, OEGC36, 14
mūsðēof *a thieving mouse*, WW408, 4
  (FL3, A25)
mȳgð = mǣgð, KGL876
mylenoxa *a mill-ox*, RAC254, 7

mylma: delete, BPG725
+myndblīōe: delete, FL2, A30
mynetīsen: for 447 read 477
mynna m. *intention*, ANS111, 276
mynsterōing n. *property of a monastery*,
  RB56, 11n.
myrðu: or myrðe?, *murderous*, WB
+mȳtan = +mētan II, HGL525, 3

nacudwräxler *gymnosophist*, KCM382; v.
  Isid. *Etym.* 8, 6, 17
nægl: delete *spear*, FL3, A26
nǣnigðinga *not at all*, VHF148, 117
nǣrende: v. MPS330 n.
næsc: WW337, 3; LCD2, 104, 13
nāhwanan *not at all*, VHF11 n. 45
nāmrǣden: read namrǣden, *naming*, FL3,
  A27
Nazarenisc *Nazarene*, Mk10, 47
nēahmynster = nēahnunmynster, BHB254,
  10
nearoðanc: add *evil thought*, VHF51, 99
nēobedd: *bed of spirits*, in GEN (TLG36,
  343)
nēodlaðu: *urgent summons*, WB
nēodspearuwa: delete *restless*, FL5, C2
+neorð: delete, FL4, D17
netwerōlicnes *utility*, OEGC30, 20
Nicēnisc *Nicene* (BTs)
nīgecyrred: read OEG3477
nīgende = hnīgende?, RD8, 8 (ASPR3, 326)
nihtbutorflēoge: v. FL3, H35
nihtēage: *a disease of the eye*, WW114, 6;
  456, 34 (v. FL3, H36)
nihterne adj. *nightly*, ANS132, 331
nip: delete, BPG838
niðer(ā)settan *to set down*, GLL238
niðerlǣtan *to lose heart*, ANS117, 22
niðerlang *stretching downward* (BTs)
nīōing: v. metenīōing, unnīōing
norōgārsecg m. *northern ocean*, BHB308,
  35
Norōmandisc *Norman* (BTs)
norōweall m. *north wall*, RAC36, 8
nōð: read nōw?, *ship*, at WH28 (FL2, A47)
nūhwænne *straightway*, VHF14, n. 57
nūna: prob. scribal error for nū ðā occurring shortly before; infl. by following
  naviculam
nūten = nīeten, VLC182, 218
nȳdgefēra *inevitable companion*, EL1260 n.
  (ed. Gradon)
nȳdgylta *debtor*, GLL145
nȳfellan = nīwfyllan, *to fill anew*, SOLK85,
  12
nytðearflic *useful*, HAW340, 14; 358, 8
nyðan = neðan, GD18, 10
nyðerāworpen *one who has been cast down*,
  KCM169, 26

ōdencole: read ōdencolc, FL2, B63
oemseten: delete *shoot, slip*, FL4,D61
ofācennan *to generate*, KW63, 6
ofāstīgan *to descend*, GLL211
ofdūneāstīgan *to descend*, GLL211
ofer: add *without*, B685
oferberan *to carry over*, VHF31 n. 130
oferblisslan glosses supergaudeant, SPS34, 19; 24
oferbrū: add LCD3, 186, 25
oferbrūwa m. *eyebrow*, ÆGR298, 3; WW263, 25
oferbrycg(i)an: add MPS297 n.
ofercliī: delete, FL3,D10
oferdæg m. *remaining day (in computation)*, HSC55
oferfæst *transfixed*, LkL p. 11, 13
oferfeallan: add *to fall upon*, A73, 26
oferflēdnes *fluctuation, vacillation*, GLL138
ofergemet: v. VHF66 n. 81
ofergeswincfull *excessively troublesome*, CHR1097 (p. 234, 2)
oferhīgian: *overpower* (HBK)
oferhrǣgan: delete, MPS297 n.
oferhrēosan *to fall*, SPS57, 9
oferhyrned: *having great horns?*, RUN 4 (ASPR6, 153, n. to 4)
ofermǣnan *to confute*, FL3,A28
ofermistian *to obscure*, OEGC4, 371
oferrǣdlīce *frequently*, RBL93, 4
ofersēam: *a special bag*, FL3,D11
ofersewenness *contempt* (BTs)
ofersiwenlic *contemptible*, CP208, 11 (v.l., p. 507, where read 208 for 206)
oferspyrian *to traverse*, OEGC28, 232
ofertælod p. ptc. of ofertalian, RWH70, 17
ofertredan: for GPH substitute ZDA20, 37
oferweorpan: delete the query after *stumble*
oferwēsnes *over-indulgence*, OEGC4, 259
oferwyrðe: delete, FL2,B37
oferȳð: *wavering, vacillation* (GLL138)
ofetrip: delete, NP5, 352
offrettan *to devour*, MkL12, 40
ofgeorn: delete, FL2,B38
ofheran: read ofhēran,=ofhīeran, *to hear, overhear*, RWH59, 16
ofnet: ms. ofnete=on fæte, *in a jug?*
ofsittan: add *to sit upon*, B1545
ofspræc: delete, FL2,B39
oftrahtung *a pulling out*, LkL, p. 8, 10
ofðȳstrian: add Pembroke College MS. 312 (binding fragment)
ofwyrtrumian *to eradicate*, LkL17, 6
ōgengel:=ongegnel?, *opposite*, FL4,D42
ohtrip: read ōhtrīp, *forced work at harvest*, NP5, 352
ōlðwong: part ol may be from note indicating corrigia=colligia
onācenned *inborn?*, OEGC9, 68

onǣht: two words?, v. II under ǣht in BTs
onǣlend: prob. for p.ptc. of onǣlan, BPG 801
onāgēotan *to infuse*, GLL228
onāhōn *to hang on*, VHF31, n. 130a
onālihtan *to illuminate*, GLL33
onāslīdan *to fall away, fail*, GLL230
onbebringan *to bring upon*, VM107b, 21
onbefeallan *to fall upon*, BPG18
onberan: delete *to be situated*, MLR42, 358
onbesendan *to send to*, FGR65, n. 2
onbesmītan *to defile*, A66, 27
onbrosnung: delete, FL2,B40
ondegslic *terrible*, FL2,B41
ondlēanian *to grant*, FL3,A22
ongeador *together*, B1595
ongēanclyppan *to call back*, A65,230
ongēanryne *a course*, GLL216
ongēanstandan *to stand toward*, W252, 18
ongefealdan *to wrap*, OEGC61, 54
ongelīcnes: for 14, 20 read 17, 7; add *parable*, LkR4, 23
ongeniman *to take away*, WW397, 23
ongesendan *to send to*, FGR65, n. 2
onhiscend m. *a mocker*, OEGC2, 175
onīdlian *to empty*, SPS74, 9
onlūtung: *a lurking place*, BPG1011
onmeltan: delete, FL2,B42
onmētan: *to paint*, PPs88, 39
onnīed f. *oppression?*, EI139 n.
onopenian *to open*, SPS77, 23
onorðian *to inspire*, BPG200
onsǣlan: for B read B489?
onscǣgan *to deride*, MÆ1, 137
onsēcan: add B1942
onslīdan *to fall away, fail*, GLL230
onspǣtan *to spit on*, JEGP-; *to spew into*, WW526, 1 (onspec=onspet)
ontōblāwen *blown on*, BPG263
onweggewit: read onweggewite m. *departure* (SK)
orcðyrs: delete, HBS p. 19
orfgebitt: *food for cattle where there is no pasturage*, FL3,H38
orgel: for WW read W148, 32
orrest: *trial by battle*, EGS5, 85, n. 63; CPC p. 77
ōðer: delete *word, speech*, FL5,C3
oðhylde: delete, FL2,B43

pardus *a leopard*, AA123, 12
pēcung *deception*, OEGC24, 32
picgbrēad: v. FL4,A18
pīlstre: delete, FL2,B44
pīpe: add *tube for drinking sacramental wine from chalice*, RAC226, 25 n.
plegian: add p. mid hondum, *to clap hands*, EL805 n. (ed. Gradon)

plicettan: delete, BPG682 n.
plicgan:=plyccan?, BPG598 n.
plōgesland *ploughland*, RAC164, 25
plyccan: add *to pluck with desire*, BPG682
pocādl: add *smallpox*, PM43, 130
prass: add *pomp*, W148, 32; *proud array*, MA68
preg m. *a pointed stick*; *pray*, OEGC38, 3
prēostgyrd? *staff carried by member of clergy?*, FL2,A9
prodbor:=wrōhtbora?, FL2,A50
prologa *prologue*, MPS89
pucian: delete, BPG664 n.
pudd: *a sore, wound*, BPG793 n.
puduc: *a little sore*, BPG793 n.
purlamb: *a male lamb, a pur* (HEW)
pyfian *to blow*, BPG664
pyrtan:=pȳtan?, BPG934

+rādod: delete, A67, 126 n. 4
+rǣcan: add *to wound*, FL3,J12
rǣdescamol: delete *couch* and add= rǣdingscamol, FL3,D12
rēada: delete *small intestines*; v. tolia at Isid. *Etym.* 11, 1, 57
+rec: delete entry III?; v. FL2,A31
+recenes: add *proof*, WW381, 7 (context of lemma is testimoniorum congerie); add also BHB436, 15 (lemma vocatio assoc. in glossaries with demonstrare)
recennes: delete; v. +recenes
recon: delete, FL2,B46
recondlic glosses numerosus, SPS77 heading
redestān: read rēde-; delete the query and also read *sinopis*
regulares *regular days in computation*, HSC53
reliquias: add r. rǣran, *to carry relics in procession*, FGR7
+rēne: for *instrument, building* subst. *edification*, FL6,A4
rēniend: delete; ms. wemend
rēnlic *rainy*, BPG964
rēodmūða: *parrot*, FL4,D43
rēstan: delete, FL4,D44
rīcehéaldend *guardian of the kingdom*, A67, 117 n. 12
+rid *food*, GD323, 3; v. bedgerid
rīfnes *fierceness*, OEGC4, 329
rihtgewittelic *rational*, SHS15, 32; 37
±rīm: add *a calendar, numeral*, RAC250, 13
rīpð *harvest*, OEGC24, 23
risiendum: ptc. of hrisian, FL4,B14
rið: delete, FL2,B48
rōdetācen: add *crucifix*, VM108a, 11
rōmian: *to try to obtain*, TLG28, 360
+rōstian: read +roscian, JEGP52, 373

rudian *to be ruddy* ES8, 478, 60
rūma: delete, FL2,B49
+runnenes: delete, BPG721
ryplen: delete the query, BPG843

sadolfæt *harness?*, WC80, 22 n.
sadolgāra *saddle cloth*, WC p. 74, 11 (there taken as *harness*); v. gāra
sǣdsworn *a coalescing of seed*, FL4,D45
sǣebbung *ebbing of the sea*, FL3,H40
sǣhund: v. FL4,A13
sǣlwāg? *hall*, AN1493 (ASPR2, 121)
sǣmearh: for E2 read EL228
sǣsteorra: add *title of Virgin Mary* (BTs)
±samhīwan: add *members of a guild?*, FF792, n. 4
samodherigendlic glosses conlaudabilis, GLL57
samodwellung: add (*of substance in the birth of a bee*) FL3,A30
sārcrene: v. cren in HEW
scægan *to jeer*, MÆ1, 137
scamlim: read WW532, 31 and delete the query; ms. scamescan lim=scame, scamlim
sceadugeard: v. FL4,A19
scēatcod: read sceattcod, *bag for provisions*, FL4,D46
sceaðe: read sceaðu, VHF143, n. 33
scēawungstōw: add *Sion* (BTs)
scenc: add *cupful*, GD127, 11
scencen *pig's shank*, FL4,A20; also scencel
scencingcuppe: v. WC p. 112
scennum: v. EGS2, 75
scer *clear, undisputed* (*in legal terminology*) HAW62, 10 n.
scilfor: *glittering*, OEG532 (v. FL3,A31)
scinncrǣftig *magical* (referring to Satan), A65, 230
scinngedwola: delete, FL3,A32
scipberende *carrying ships*, OEGC28, 321
scipgefeoht: v. BPG89 n.
scipgefēre: read scipgefær (BTs)
scipwealh: *Welsh sailor*, RAC204, 22 n.
scipwered: v. FL4,B15
scīrgesceat: delete; note the reading reported by Neil Ker at FF784
scitte: add *diarrhoea* (BTs)
+scola: for *debtor* substitute *fellow-debtor*, MNG55
+scōla: delete, MNG56
scōm-: read scom; v. scamm in HEW
scoplic: for 119 read 199
scora: v. FL4,D47
scortwyrplic: *soon effecting an improvement?*, ES60, 82
scrǣb: add OEGC36, 17
scriccettan *to screech*, OEGC15, 4

scrifttæcer *land whose yield served as payment for a priest?*, RAC240, 4 n.

scrīpen: read scirpen?, *sharp*, FL4, C5

scufrægl *pullable curtains*, RAC194, 20 n.

scūrheard: for relation to regnheard v. WB p. 81

scylfrung: *glittering*, FL3, A31

scypgesceot *ship-scot*, HAW63, 2 n.

scȳr *a hut*, OEGC55, 1

scyte: delete *stroke, blow?*, v. FL3, A33

Scyððisc Scythian, ÆL7, 345

sealmbōc *psalter*, ÆH1, 604, 24

sealmfæt: v. FL5, C4

sealtlēaf: read sealtlēap, *salt basket*, FL4, A23

sēamtoln *toll on the packhorse load*, HAW 117, 4

sēftēadig: ms. eft eadig

selfæte: *groundsel*; (senecio is glossed selbeza in OHG, gundswelga in OE)

± sellan: delete *lay by, hide*, FL5, B2

sendan: for *to feast* subst. *to put to death*, ASPR4, 147

sendnes: *Mass*, WW445, 34; 498, 39 (context missarum sacramentis)

seofonhīwe *septiform*, A65, 230

sēoðan: add *to seethe (wrath)*, BPG478 n.

sepulcer *grave*, FGR70, n. 1

+ sēðedlic *probable*, OEGC28, 20

sīa = sēo, OET446; 447

sibgeleger = sibleger, W164, 5 c

sicera m. *an intoxicating drink*, CHRD74, 6

sīcing f. *sighing*, OEGC30, 59

sidung: *arrangement (of the dining table)?*, BPG750 n.

sigehrēð: v. hrēðsecg

Sigelhearwa: = Sigelearpa, *sun-darkened?*, FL2, A40

siger: add *groundsel*, WW301, 24 (syr = siger; v. WW30, 39)

sigerīce: *realm of victory*, EI27; 530

sinderhǣwe? *cinder-grey*, OEGC51, 4 n.

sinewind: delete, FL2, B51

Sionbeorg *Sion*, SN20, 202

sīðboren: the word misinterprets depost fetantes: v. GLL200

+ sīðscipe: add ±, BH246, 18 n.

sinulīra *muscle*, FL2, A51

sixecge: add sixecgede, ÆGR289, 5

slǣpfulnes: delete; slapel at WW541, 42 incomplete for slapfulnis at 162, 19; but fol. 4r of Antwerp MS. 47 reads slapulnis

slidor: II, *slides for launching and pulling up ships*, WW182, 18

slitol: delete, BPG420 n.

slypton wk. pret. of slūpan?, VPs75, 6 (SK)

smēa *titbit?*, RAC74, 20 n.

smeringwyrt: = symeringwyrt, WW135, 1

smyllan: *to smack*, BPG4

snǣdan: add, a strongly urged (HBK) emendation for sendan at B600

snāð: delete entry II, MNG58

snyring: possibly for styrung, JEGP46, 424

snyttruhūs: add *Silo*, FL6, B4

sōcnman *sokeman*, HAW85, 13 n.

socða *broth, gruel*, FL4, D48

sol *dark, dirty*, FL4, D50

solcennes f. *laziness*, ANS117, 22

sore: delete, FL2, B52

sorgbyrðen: read sorgbryðen, *brew of sorrow*, ES67, 340

sōðlufu: two words? VHF54 n. 1 a

sōðwundor n. *true wonder*, EI24; EL1121

spǣcehēow v. swæcehēow

spēd: delete *offspring*, FL6, A8

spircing: *sparkling*, BPG755

stæf: add *Sunday letter (in computation)* HSC47, n. 20

stæfplega: glosses ludus litterarius, LCG L289; WW433, 14 (context Ludi litterarii disciplina, Orosius 1, 18, 1)

stæfsweord: *swordstick*, FL3, H43

stæfwrītere: *grammarian*, WW372, 34; 414, 11; 487, 14

stǣna *stone jug*, MtL26, 7

+ stāl: add ±, VHF83, 113 n.

stānbryce *a piece of stone*, FL2, A53

stānbrycg: delete WW

stānfæt: add *jewelled sheath?* WAL II, 3 (ASPR6, 139)

Stānhenge *Stonehenge*, FF326, n. 2

stānwalu f. *a bank of stones* (BTs)

stānwyrht: delete WW341, 10 and add WW150, 32 (FL4, D51)

stānwyrhta: add WW341, 10 (FL4, D51)

± staðolfæstan = ± staðolfæstnian   ÆGR 192, 2

staðolnes *firmament*, GLL174

stelscofl: = stēorsceofl, BPG875 n.

stencan: delete *to afflict*, FL3, D14

stēordalc *steering pin, helm*, JEGP-

steornede: = steorrede

steorrede *starred (of a white mark on horse's forehead)* FL4, D52

stēða: delete; fol. 6r of Additional MS. 32246 reads steda

± stīgan: add hēanne bēam gestīgan, *to climb the high oak (to beat down acorns)* AJP66, 1–12

stīgend: add *rider*, GLL239

stincan: delete? *sniff*, B2289 (HBK)

stincan *to move rapidly?*, B2288 (HBK); RD29, 12 (ASPR4, 236, n. to B2288)

stondnis *substance*, OEGC72, 2

stōrsticca: *incense spoon*, RAC226, 32 n.

strecednes: *spreading*, FL4, B16

+strēones: delete, BPG93
±strīc: *plague* at BHW269, 57 n.
strīcel, I: *teat*, FL3,A35; BPG155 n.
strīpligan:=plyccan?, BPG598 n.
strȳnd: delete *gain*; gestreonde at WW488, 30=gestreone; v. WW190, 3
+strynge: = +styrung?, v. FL3,A16
stuntsprǣc: ms. stuntspæc
stȳcing f. *a clearing (of land)*, FF771 n. 8
styntan: add+, *to repress*, BPG278
+stynðo: v. VHF97, n. 144
sum: add *an important one*, WB glossary
sunboga *arc of the sun*, JEGP-
sunderboren: *born of disparate parents*, FL4,D53
sūðēasthealf f. *the south-east*, OEGC4, 384
sūðerne: add *of southern make*, MAG134 n.
swæcehēow: read spæcehēow, *form of speech*, FL6,A9; note also hīwlice spǣce in BTs
swǣfan: read swǣlan?
swǣrbyrd?: for LCD185a subst. LCD3, 66, 22; ms. swærtbyrde
swǣsenddagas: v. FL4,A25
swǣslic: add+ (BTs)
swǣðelyne: delete, FL3,B1
sweartbyrd: v. swǣrbyrd; for possible ref. to *blue baby* v. ANS171, 33
swēgesweard: delete; ms. suge sweard (LCG U222) *sow's hide*; v. vistilia at CGL7, 423
sweglwered: *clothed with radiance* (HBK)
swelling: *swelling sail*, EL245 n. (ed. Gradon); but a case can be made for ms. spellingum
swētwyrde: delete *stuttering*; add *lisping*, FL4,A26
swīnhege m. *a fence to keep swine from straying* (BTs)
swīnlic: delete the query; ms. swinlice
swiung: delete, JEGP-
swŏr:=swol?, EI239 n.
swōrettan: add *to sigh (about something)*, VHF85, n. 75
sworian? *to sigh*, VHF101, n. 168
swūrplætt m. *a stroke on the neck*, FL2,B53
swȳrige? *troublesome*, JM49
syllestre f. *a giver*, A76, 495 n.
sylting *seasoning*, KCM94, ix
symbelbrēad *bread for a feast (of water and a loaf in the desert)* SFF122
symbelmōnaðlic: delete the query, FL4, D54
symeringwyrt: *mallow?*, A41, 139

+taccian: delete, BPG1022 n.
+tācnigendlīce *figuratively*, ÆH2, 114, 25
tæg tæg *te-hee*, FL4,E1

±tæl: delete *competent*, WW505, 3; add *having mastery of*, WW502, 3 (lemma competem=compotem)
tæmespīle: *sieve-stake*, FF463, n. 2
tala=talu, WW204, 3 (FL3,H47)
tamcian: add+, BPG1022 n.
tēafor: add *pigment, salve*, AB34, 101
teltrē:=teldtrēow, *tent-peg*; v. claus · lignum tentorii, WW205, 20
tēofrian: add: v. CP153, 23
teolðyrl: *an opening in a beehive, service entrance*, FL3,A37
+tēwian *adorn*, W262, 22d
tīdfara: *one who goes at his allotted time?*, BPG286 n.
tīmlic *suitable, of proper age*, BPG922
Tirisc *of Tyre*, OEGC8, 14
tōætēacnes f. *increase*, BH295, 12 (Sch)
tōætēacnian *to increase*, BH295n. (Sch)
tōātēon *to draw in*, GLL243
tōāwrītan glosses conscribere, GLL98
tōbesettan *to put to*, GLL245
tōbringan *to bring to*, BPG49
tōforlǣtan: add *to leave to*, VM69b, 7
tōgecīgan *to call to*, GLL92
tōgegearwian *to prepare*, A65, 230
tōgelǣdan glosses adducere, GLL234
tōgelaðian *to invite along*, OEGC60, 17
togeteohhian glosses apponere, GLL245
tōgetēon *to draw in*, GLL243
tōhāwiend *spectator*, JEGP56, 65
tōhelpan *to help*, MkR9, 24
tolcettende: *talking vainly?*, BPG931 n.
tōlīhtan *to illuminate*, GLL33
tōlūtan *to incline to*, VHF24, n. 106
tōlynnan *to take away* (BTs)
top: on the meaning *plaything*, v. GAT p. 52
tōrǣcan: *proffer*, VHF37, n. 171; *to apply (fire in torture)*, OEG4489
toroc: the word is Celtic, like guohioc in same glossary
torr: with meaning *tower* this is a different word from torr, *rock*; v. HEW
tōsettan *to put to*, GLL245; *to clamp*, BPG302
tōspillan *to destroy*, SPS82, 5
tōtræglian: v. BPG602 n.
totrida: delete the query, FL4,E2
træglian: *tear apart, destroy*, BPG602 n.
trēowlēasnes: add+ (BT)
+trēownes: add *faithfulness*, VHF99, 309
treppan: delete *to trap*, FL2,B54
treumbicin? glosses (mel) silvestre Mt 3, 4 (KCM p. 476, 6)
+trīowed *shafted*, WW143, 5 (FL3,H21)
trogscip: *boat made from a hollowed log*, FL3,H49
trym: add ænge trym, *step by step*, FL4,D1

tube: delete, BPG 257 n.

tud: delete; v. tudenard

tudenard *a shield*, MNG 59

tunge: add on halre tungan, *unequivocally?*, *viva voce?*, RAC p. 284, n. 11

tungele: delete; v. tunggelælle

tunggelælle adj. *verbose*, FL 2, B 55

tūnstede: add, based on loca inter agros, Isid. *Etym.* 15, 2, 14

turfgret *turfpit*, WC 86, 19 n.

twelfmōnð *twelvemonth*, VM 108 a, 1

twentigesnihte *twenty nights old*, BHc 206, 30

twifingre: add (*of fat on swine*)

twihǣmed *one who marries twice*, KCM p. 93 c

twilafte: read twilāste (FL 2, B 56)

twiman renders homo dubius, WE 55, 2

twing: delete, FL 2, B 57

twīnwyrm: read twinwyrm, FL 4, A 27

twiseltōð: *with two protruding front teeth*, FL 3, H 50

twisnēse: v. BPG 328 n.

tȳdrung *weakness, sterility*, OEG 1031

tyncen: *little tub*, FL 2, A 55

tȳriāca: delete WW

± **ðaccian:** delete *to tame*, BPG 1022 n.

ðǣrgemang *thereamong*, BPG 54

ðamettan: very likely scribal error for ðafettan

ðearfendlīce *poorly*, VHF 128, n. 121

ðearflic: add *poor*, RBL 100, 4

ðearmgyrd: read WW 120, 1

ðeccbryce: delete?; v. OEG 2256 n.

ðelneðung *some kind of plant*, OEGC 73, 1

ðencan: add ± ðencan mid, *to remember someone with* (*a gift*), VHF 99, 314

ðeodfēond: *archfiend*, BHW 137, 52 n.

ðeodlāreow *great teacher*, SFF 96

+ **ðicfyldan:** *to make dense* (*the material for a fire*), *to pile up*, BPG 974

ðīstra: delete the query, A 76, 411–21

ðiustra: = ðēoster, FL 4, D 55

ðolle: *instrument on which a martyr was burned*, FL 3, A 38

ðornðȳfel m. *thorn bush*, FGR 69, n. 3

+ **ðracen:** *stout of frame*, FL 4, C 2

+ **ðrǣsted** *contrite*, GLL 53

ðrāg: add sume ðrāge, *at times*, OEGC 4, 381

ðrāgmǣl n. *unhappy time*, JUL 344 (ed. Woolf)

ðreclic *terrible*, SPS 95, 4

ðrepel *a torture instrument of three stakes*, FL 2, B 60

ðrifingre: add (*referring to the fat of swine*)

ðrihǣmed *one who marries thrice*, KCM p. 93 c

ðristlēasnes: delete, A 66, 31 n.

ðrosm: add BPG 760 n.

ðrōwungdæg m. *day of martyrdom*, Luick Festgabe (1925), p. 192

ðrūh: delete *chest*, BPG 867 n.

ðrydægðȳrn *period of three days*, OEGC 7, 13

ðrymdōm: *glorious judgement*

ðrȳpel: delete; v. ðrepel

ðrȳpelūf: delete, FL 2, B 60

ðrysumer? *three years old*, WW 120, 38 (ms. triennis · þrywinter ł sumer gildeto(x))

ðunorbodu: v. FL 3, H 51

ðunorsliht m. *thunderstroke*, A 73, 25

ðurh: add, with inst. case, VHF 116, n. 43

ðurhlǣdan glosses perducere, SPS 77, 52

ðurhlonge? adv. *continuously*, GEN 307; v. TLG p. 38

ðurhrǣdan *to read through*, OEGC 28, 23

ðurhūtlīce adv. *thoroughly*, NP 28, 49

ðurhwunigendlic: add A 65, 230

ðurhwunungnes *perseverance*, SPS p. 37

ðweorhtimber *resolutely made*, JUL 550 n. (ed. Woolf)

ðwērian = ðwēorian, VHF 148, 117

ðȳflen: delete, BPG 843

ðȳfilg *brambly*, OEGC 30, 32

ðȳmele: add (*referring to the fat of swine*)

ðȳrncin *kind of thorn*, FL 4, A 28

unǣtnes *affliction*, RAC p. 60, 8; unǣtnessa gebīdan, *to die*

unāhladen *unexhausted*, JEGP-

unāmyrred *uninjured*, ÆL 35, 285

unbecweden: add *uncontested*, RAC p. 92, 14

unbesprecen *uncontested*, RAC p. 60, 29

unbeðōht *unexpected*, JEGP-

unbȳrgo: delete; ms. unbyengo, DR ed. Lindelöf, p. 206, n. 1

underbeðēodan *to subject*, JEGP-

underburhware: add SHS 6, 32

undergrīpan *to seize*, RWH 122, 23

underslīcende *slipping under*, JEGP 56, 65

underðēodan: add *to instruct*, VLC 172, 120 n.

+ **unfæstnian:** delete; see foll. word

± **unfæstnod** *not fixed in the mark* (*referring to an arrow*), VHF 104, n. 182

unforhtlēasnes?: v. forhtlēasnes

unforðōht *unexpected*, JEGP-

unfrōforlīce: no *un* in ms.

unfūl: read unful, *empty*, FL 4, D 56

ungearwyrd: delete, JEGP 52, 376

ungebierde: add WW 395, 16; OEG 7, 247

ungedōn *not done*, OEGC 28, 486

ungeearned *undeserved*, A 65, 230

ungefynde: *undeveloped*, FL 4, E 3

ungemēde: substitute ungemedemad, *unmeasured*, ASPR 3, 299, 25

ungemetlicnes *intemperance*, KF

ungenīwiendlic *unrenewable*, OEGC 28, 188

ungeorwyrd *unsullied,* JEGP52, 377
ungescæðfulnes *innocence,* GLL134
ungeðyre:=ungeðwǣre; lemma discensor
=dissensor, a glossary equivalent of
discordator, q.v. at WW223, 10
ungewyldendlic *impatient,* OEGC30, 18
ungléaw: add *very sharp?*, WB2564 n.
unhǣlwendlic: add *not salutary,* ANS122,
257, 7
unhlitme: *without casting lots?* ASPR4,
177, 1128
unlǣdu *misery,* VHF29, n. 124
unlagu: delete *bad law,* BHW356, 16
unmiht: add *faintness?*, WW199, 36
unmihtiglic: add *faint?*, LCD2, 60, 8
unmihtiglīcnes *inability,* LCD1, 56, 15
unmōdnes *pride,* A66, 32, n. 4
unmyrge: delete the queries; v. colludium
at CGL6, 231, where dolus might be taken
to equal dolor
unnīðing: add *liberal man,* ANS117, 23
unorne: *simple,* MAG256 n.
unrād f. *cruel raid,* CPC1111, 6 n.
unrēone? *very sad,* VHF92, n. 116a
unrihthǣd *improper manner,* VHF76, 44 n.
unrihthǣming f. *fornication,* ANS111, 280
unrihttīd: *time of evil,* VHF94, n. 128
unrihtwilla *bad intention,* A66, 28
unrīmgōd: *unnumbered good works,* ÆL33,
241
unsǣle: delete; ms. unfæle
unscæððīg *innocent,* ÆH1, 512, 12
unsceandlīce *shamelessly,* ÆL23b, 372
unsceððiglīce *innocently,* FGR80, 3
unsēofene: read unseofiende
unsettan *to take down,* MkL15, 36
unslid:=unsilt, *unsalted;* v. LCG P400 and
LCD3, 18, 5
untamcul: *invincible,* BPG680 n.
untellendlic: add CPC1137, 20
untīdlic: add *timeless,* BPG452
untōdǣled: add *unshared,* VHF33, n. 146
untōslopen *undissolved,* JEGP-
untrum: add +, ÆL21, 187
unðurhfǣre *impenetrable,* OEGC27, 25
ūpāhafen *exalted,* VHF75, 34
ūpālūcan *to eradicate,* GLL251
ūpfeax: *with bristling hair,* FL4, D57
ūpgelǣded *led up,* VM135a, 24
ūpgodu: delete *heathen gods,* FL3, A40
ūphebbe: delete, FL2, A57
ūprǣran *to raise up,* GLL249
ūpreccan *to erect,* GLL250
ūpscīnan *to rise shiningly,* OEGC62, 5
ūpsettan *to exalt,* SHS8, 52
ūpspringan *to rise up,* Lk1, 78
ūsspīung: delete; fol. 4v of Additional
MS. 32, 246 reads wyrmsspiung
ūtāblegned *ulcerated,* LCD2, 10, 5; 2, 98, 25

ūtālūcan *to pluck forth,* GLL251
ūtāslīdan: *to slip out,* BPG50 n.
ūtāwindan: *to slip out,* BPG50 n.
ūtāwyrtrumian *to root out,* VM75a, 5
ūtfaran *to go out,* SPS145, 4
ūtfēolan *to get out,* VHF95, 255, n. 130
ūtforlǣtan: add *to let out,* VHF133, 57
ūtlād: for *right of passage* substitute *toll on
goods carried out of market,* HAW477, 16
ūtofgān *to go out of,* VHF39, n. 182
ūtyrnan *to have diarrhoea,* LCD63b

wād: add cpds. with beorh, denu, lond
(BT)
wǣgbora: add *wave-bearer?* (HBK)
wǣgel: delete the query
wǣgngerefa:=wǣgngefēra,   *wagon-com-
panion;* v. carpentarius, collegiatus at
CGL6, 230
wǣgnðol: delete; v. wǣhðoll
wǣhðoll *battering ram,* FL3, A41
±**wǣlan**: add MPS143 n.
wǣlblēat: *deadly* (HBK)
wǣlgenga: read wælgenga and delete the
query, FL4, A29
wǣlkyrging renders gorgoneus, WE55, 6
wǣpenbǣre *weapon-bearing,* OEGC27, 11
wǣterbucca: v. FL4, D58
wǣtergāt: v. FL4, D58
wǣterlēod *fish,* OEGC28, 386
wǣtersol *pool,* Jn5, 2
wāgðeorl: *a break in a wall;* v. ðyrelung
ðæs wages, CP153, 25
waled: *ridged,* FL3, D17
walu:*metal ridge on top of helmet, like that on
Sutton Hoo helmet* at B1031; v. WB, p. 319
wambecoðu f. *stomach trouble,* LCD87b
wambegicða m. *itching of the stomach,*
LCD90a
wambewyrm *intestinal worm,* LCD90a
wambscyldig: read wamscyldig, *sinful,*
VHF93, n. 120
wancian *to waver,* RD87, 7 (ASPR3, 377)
wanfōta: v. Canopos at Isid. *Etym.*12, 7, 26
wansēoc: *melancholic,* FL4, D59
wassen *vassal,* ANS111, 277 (Celtic); v.
HAW p. 532
wēagesīð: *companion in crime,* ASPR4,
282, 16
+**wealc**: add *military expedition,* ES72, 10
wealcol: *rolling in the waves,* BPG831
wealdweaxe *sinew,* OEGC52, 12 n.
wealhwyrt: *elecampane,* A41, 133 n. 6
weallstaðol: delete the query, FF157, n. 1
weallwala: *wall panelling?*, AJP62, 336
wealte: add *a snare,* BPG138
wealword: v. A66, 34 n.
weardstōw *watchtower,* OEGC6, 1
wederāwendednes *variation of weather,* KF

wegend? *a bearer*, OEGC28, 294
wegtwiflung: fol. 19v of Additional MS. 32, 246 reads wegtwislung
wellere: WW278, 19, prob. equivalent to wellyrgae, *walkyrie?*, LCG S379 n.
wellwill *a spring*, KC5, 344, 29
wenncīcen: v. ANS171, 21
weolocbasu: add OEGC51, 6
weoning:=wining, FL2,B35
weorcland *land subject to labour services*, RAC166, 7 n.
+**weorclic**: delete, FL2,A32
weorf:=hwȳorf
weorððearfa: delete, ES62, 129
werbǣr f. *pasture land near a weir* (BTs)
werbēam: read wǣrbeam? *protecting pillar*, EI486 n.
±**werian**: add *discharge obligations on (land)*, HAW p. 450, n. 3
werping *loss?* (gloss to iactura), ANS117,23
wēstenlic *eremitic*, OEGC4, 140
westrihte *westward*, OEGC4, 112 n.
weðel: delete, FL2,B62
wicðēnestre f. *weekly servant*, A76, 502
wīcung *lodging*, WW147, 26
wīdefeorlic: delete wīder; fol. 5v of Additional MS. 32, 246 reads wide-
wīdl: add JEGP56, 66
wīdnes: add ÆH2, 578, 10
wīdu f. *width*, KW55, 13 (=WE60, 18c)
wielincel: delete, BPG925
wīfcȳððu: v. OEGC4, 79 n.
wifrian *to shake (a weapon)*, OEGC25, 3
wiga *the Holy Spirit?*, EL937 n. (ed. Gradon)
wiglian: add+, GLL97
wīgnett? *gladiator's net*, FL2, A58
wīgnoð: delete the query, FL4,C8
willodlīce *willingly*, SPS53, 8
willung: add+, GLL109
wilnincel *a little female servant*, BPG925
wiluncel: delete; v. wilnincel
wilweg n. *desired way*, W252, 17
winclian? *to wink*, FL4,D4
wīncole: read wīncolc, FL2,B63
windiht: delete
wīngeard: delete the query after *vine* and add WW136, 36 (lemma brionia=vitem albam at Isid. *Etym.* 17, 9, 90)
wīngeardhring: *vine tendrils*, FL3,H56
wīnian *to pluck (grapes)*, LkL6, 44
winnendlic *fighting*, MNG61
wiorðegend *worshipper*, EPs108, 11 (fenerator taken as venerator)
+**wīred**: add *ornamented*, KCM p. 163c; v. also WC14, 12 n.
wīsbōc: *book of wisdom*, GLL99
wīsnes: *wisdom*, VHF59, n. 35; +, *understanding*, LCD3, 82, 2

wītecyll *sack in which parricides were put to death*, FL4,D31
wītewyrðe: read wītewyrðe
witnesman *witness*, ANS111, 277
witod:=witodlīce, BHW139, 87
witodlīce: add+, W113, 13 n.; 119, 17 n.
wiðerstede *substitution*, JEGP-
wiðersȳnes: add *withershins*
wiðerung *obstinacy*, KCM p. 319a
wiðgehæftan *to fight against*, BPG822 n.
wiðig: cpds. with bed, brōc, ford, grāf, lēah, mǣd, mere, mōr, pōl, pytt, slǣd, ðȳfel (BT)
wiððingian: *to talk against, contradict*, VM65b, 6
+**wixlan** *to change*, MLR27, 453
wlǣce:=wlǣc?, BPG652 n.
wlǣtlic *foul*, OEGC28, 431
+**wlencan**: add±, VHF93, n. 118
wlita: delete, FL2,B64
wlīteandet: delete the query, FL5, C4
wlītescēawung *Sion*, BH212, 11
wlitiglīce: add VHF39, 331b
wōdscinn: *mad trickery?*, BHW118, 34 n.
wordbebod *command*, VHF113, 52
wordcennend: v. BPG115 n.
wordclipinde *able to speak*, VHF88, n. 93a
wordriht: *statement of what is right according to law or custom*, WB2631 n.
woruldbebod: *secular edict*, VHF113, n. 30
woruldgefiit: delete the query (ANS134, 288)
woruldgeðingu *worldly things*, VM69b, 10
woruldhogu f. *worldly care*, BHW204, 82
wrætbaso: add OEGC51, 8
wraðo=wraðu?, FL2,A60
+**wrinclod**: *wrinkled?*, BPG750 n.
±**writ**: delete *stilus*, BPG1018 n.
wrōhtbora: delete *monster*
wuduclāte *a plant*, aristolochia OEGC73b, 9
wuducynn: *a kind of tree*, FL4,A31
wuduhætt *leafy top*, OEGC8, 16
wuldorbēacn *sign of glory*, A73, 18, n. 12
wuldorbēag: add *iris of the eye*, FL3, H58
wulfsēað: *pit in which wolves were trapped*, RAC4, 12 n.
wyrmsūtspīung: delete; ms. wyrmsspiung
wyrpendlic *suitable for throwing*, OEGC9, 12

yfelmynan *to consider wickedly*, SPS82, 4
yfelonbecweðende *persuading to evil*, BPG 179
yltwist: v. lytwist
ymbeardung *dwelling around*, GLL214
yrsebin: read yrfebin, *fodder basket for cattle*, FGR55n.
ȳðwōrigende: *wave-wandering (fish)*, FL3, K2

MEDIEVAL ACADEMY REPRINTS FOR TEACHING